UNIVERSITY CASEBOOK SERIES

EDITORIAL BOARD

DAVID L. SHAPIRO
DIRECTING EDITOR
Professor of Law, Harvard University

ROBERT C. CLARK
Dean of the School of Law, Harvard University

DANIEL A. FARBER
Professor of Law, University of Minnesota

OWEN M. FISS
Professor of Law, Yale Law School

GERALD GUNTHER
Professor of Law, Stanford University

THOMAS H. JACKSON
President, University of Rochester

HERMA HILL KAY
Dean of the School of Law, University of California, Berkeley

HAROLD HONGJU KOH
Professor of Law, Yale Law School

ROBERT L. RABIN
Professor of Law, Stanford University

CAROL M. ROSE
Professor of Law, Yale Law School

Photo Courtesy of Judge Albert B. Maris

THE COURTHOUSE ON THE ISLAND OF TOBAGO*

"Can the island of Tobago pass a law to bind the rights of the whole world?" per Lord Ellenborough in Buchanan v. Rucker, page 35, infra.

* This is the courthouse referred to by Lord Ellenborough. It has been replaced by a modern building.

CASES AND MATERIALS

Conflict of Laws

TENTH EDITION

by

MAURICE ROSENBERG
Late Harold R. Medina Professor of Procedural Jurisprudence
Columbia University

PETER HAY
L.Q.C. Lamar Professor of Law
Emory University
and
University Professor
Technische Universität Dresden

RUSSELL J. WEINTRAUB
John B. Connally Chair in Civil Jurisprudence
University of Texas

WESTBURY, NEW YORK
THE FOUNDATION PRESS, INC.
1996

COPYRIGHT © 1936, 1941, 1951, 1957, 1964, 1971, 1978, 1984, 1990 THE FOUNDATION PRESS, INC.
COPYRIGHT © 1996 By THE FOUNDATION PRESS, INC.
                        615 Merrick Ave.
                        Westbury, N.Y. 11590–6607
                        (516) 832–6950

All rights reserved
Printed in the United States of America

Library of Congress Cataloging-in-Publication Data

Rosenberg, Maurice, 1919–
    Cases and materials on conflict of laws / by Maurice Rosenberg,
Peter Hay, and Russell J. Weintraub. — 10th ed.
       p.   cm. — (University casebook series)
    Rev. ed. of: Cases and materials on conflict of laws / by Willis
L. M. Reese, Maurice Rosenberg, and Peter Hay. 9th ed. 1990.
    Includes bibliographical references and index.
    ISBN 1–56662–333–2
    1. Conflict of laws—United States—Cases.   I. Hay, Peter, 1935–
.   II. Weintraub, Russell J.   III. Reese, Willis L. M.   Cases and
materials on conflict of laws.   IV. Title.   V. Series.
KF410.R44   1996
340.9'0973—dc20   96–577

TEXT IS PRINTED ON 10% POST CONSUMER RECYCLED PAPER   Printed with Printwise Environmentally Advanced Water Washable Ink   ∞

To the memory of

WILLIS L.M. REESE
(1913–1990)

and

MAURICE ROSENBERG
(1919–1995)

*

PREFACE

The most important features of this edition are greatly increased emphasis on comparative coverage and a thorough reorganization and re-analysis of choice of law. In addition, in order to provide useful background information and to guide analysis, there are even more extensive notes and comments.

In our experience, the order of presentation is an important aid in mastering the materials. Choice-of-law issues take on added meaning after the student understands when and why a court may proceed against a defendant who has perhaps only tenuous connection to the forum state; appreciates that a court the plaintiff has chosen may decline to proceed against the defendant even though it could assert jurisdiction; and is aware of the nearly unchallengeable effects of the full-faith-and-credit principle in the context of the interstate recognition of judgments.

The treatment of domicile, the "chosen point of entry" in Anglo-American conflicts law, has received substantial revision to aid in an early understanding of its many faces (chapter 2). Similarly, we have made extensive changes in the presentation of jurisdictional matters in chapters 3 and 4.

We continue to deal at an early point in the choice-of-law materials (chapter 7) with major aspects of the substance-procedure dichotomy despite blurring or disappearance of the bright line once thought to separate these categories. This prepares the student for the complexities that result when interest analysis is applied to issues previously deemed procedural. We have discontinued, however, the separation into two chapters, in the predecessor editions, of the choice-of-law materials now presented in unified form in chapter 8. The new chapter is designed to show, in systematic progression, the development of choice-of-law theory and its application, thereby to enable the student to deal with modern approaches and to appreciate future developments as they are certain to occur. We continue to give particular attention to the pressing and emerging issues of the day, such as choice of law in mass tort cases.

The previous edition began to focus on comparative aspects of conflicts law. We believed that foreign developments with respect to jurisdiction and choice of law are not only of growing importance in an era of increased international dealings but may also hold important lessons for us as we consider and reconsider our own law. Eighteen European countries—the members of the European Union and the three members of the European Free Trade Association—now share uniform rules on jurisdiction and the recognition of judgments, several members of the European Union have adopted uniform rules of choice of law in contract (while the national law of others is similar), and the United States has made a long-range proposal for a worldwide judgments convention. We have taken account of these developments. This edition therefore includes substantial comparative notes throughout the materials.

The search continues, both in this country and abroad, for accommodation in litigational matters and for satisfactory policy-centered approaches to choice of law. As we concluded the Preface to the previous edition: "All this bodes well for the importance of conflicts for courts and lawyers in the 21st century."

It is fitting that we dedicate this edition to **Willis L.M. Reese,** Reporter for the Restatement (Second) of Conflict of Laws and an editor of this book from the fourth through the ninth editions, and to **Maurice Rosenberg,** who became an editor beginning with the fifth edition. Their passing has taken from us colleagues whom we held in high esteem and whose numerous and rich contributions to our field are indeed lasting.

PETER HAY
RUSSELL J. WEINTRAUB

SUMMARY OF CONTENTS

Preface	v
Table of Cases	xxiii
Table of Books and Articles	xxxvii

CHAPTER	1	Introduction	1
CHAPTER	2	Domicile: The Chosen Point of Entry	7
CHAPTER	3	Jurisdiction of Courts	34

Sec.
1. Introduction and General Considerations — 34
2. Bases of Judicial Jurisdiction Over Natural and Legal Persons — 41
   - A. The Historic Bases: Jurisdiction Theory Before *International Shoe* — 41
   - B. In Search of New Jurisdictional Standards: The Era of *International Shoe,* "Minimum Contacts", and "Fairness" — 47
   - C. Continuance of Jurisdiction — 122
3. Jurisdiction Over "Things" — 123
   - A. Land — 125
   - B. Chattels — 128
   - C. Intangibles — 130
4. Competence of Court and Notice — 156

CHAPTER 4 Limitations on the Exercise of Jurisdiction — 168
1. Limitations Imposed by Contract — 168
2. Fraud, Force and Privilege — 179
3. Forum Non Conveniens — 181
4. Other Limitations Imposed by the Forum — 198
5. Limitations Imposed by the State of the Transaction — 206
6. Effect of Interstate Commerce — 215

CHAPTER 5 Foreign Judgments — 218
1. Policies Underlying the Recognition and Enforcement of Foreign Judgments — 218
2. Recognition and Enforcement in General — 227
   - A. In Personam Judgments — 228
   - B. Judgments Based on Jurisdiction Over Things or Over Status — 235
3. Particular Effects — 238
   - A. Persons Affected — 238
   - B. Issues Affected — 251
   - C. Limitations on Full Faith and Credit — 254
4. Defenses — 279
   - A. Nature of the Original Proceedings — 279
   - B. Nature of Original Cause of Action — 297
   - C. Lack of a Competent Court — 310
   - D. Foreign Country Judgments — 311
   - E. Matters Subsequent to F–1 Judgment — 314

ix

Summary of Contents

CHAPTER 6	The Impact of the Constitution	317

Sec.
1.	The Obligation to Provide or to Refuse a Forum	318
2.	Choice of Law	325
3.	Unreasonable Discrimination	368
4.	Privileges and Immunities	368
5.	Government Seizure; Interstate Commerce	371

CHAPTER 7	Threshold Problems of the Forum in Choice of Law	375
1.	Admitting or Rejecting the Action or Defense	375
2.	Notice and Proof of Foreign Law	392
3.	Use of The Forum's "Procedural" Rules	402
	A. Introduction	402
	B. Presumptions and Burden of Proof	408
	C. Rules of Evidence: Privilege	411
	D. Time Limitation	417
4.	Reference to the Choice-of-Law Rules of Another Jurisdiction	441

CHAPTER 8	The Problem of Choosing the Rule of Decision	448
1.	The Received System and Tradition	448
	A. Territoriality and the Jurisdiction–Selecting Process	448
	B. Examples of the System in Operation	451
2.	Escape Devices	493
	A. Characterization	493
	B. Renvoi	500
	C. Public Policy	503
	D. Property: Equitable Conversion and the Contract–Conveyance Distinction	505
3.	Transition: The Search for New Approaches	506
	A. Early Gropings	506
	B. Scholarly Camps	511
4.	The New Era	520
	A. Adopting New Choice-of-Law Rules	520
	B. The Courts at Work	554
	C. Problems Emerged and Emerging	583
	D. Additional Problems	631

CHAPTER 9	Conflicts Problems in Federal and International Settings	663
1.	Special Problems in Federal Courts	663
	A. The Constraints and Tolerances of the Erie Principle	663
	B. The Erie Doctrine and Conflict of Laws in Diversity Cases	687
	C. Federal Questions in Relation to State Law	711
2.	Conflicts Problems in International Settings	726
	A. International Conflicts Cases and the Federal Control of Foreign Affairs	727
	B. Treaties	744
	C. International Conflicts Cases in the Absence of Federal Limitations or Preemption	746

CHAPTER 10 Property		757

Sec.
1.	Land		757
	A.	Succession on Death	759
	B.	Security Transactions	767
	C.	Conveyances and Contracts	769
2.	Movables, in General		778
	A.	Succession on Death	778
	B.	Inter Vivos Transactions	781
	C.	Security Transactions	786
	D.	Future Interests and Trusts	799
3.	Intangibles		814
4.	Interpretation and Construction of Documents		816

CHAPTER 11 Family Law			820
1.	Marriage		821
2.	Divorce		836
	A.	Conditions for Decreeing Divorce	836
	B.	Extraterritorial Recognition	846
	C.	Extraterritorial Recognition: Limits on Attack for Jurisdictional Defects	856
	D.	Extraterritorial Recognition: Divisible Divorce	866
3.	Annulment		878
4.	Judicial Separation		881
5.	Legitimation		883
6.	Adoption		884
7.	Custody of Children		887
8.	Support		901
	A.	Enforcement of Support Claims Without Regard to Reciprocal Support Legislation	901
	B.	Reciprocal Support Legislation	910
9.	Marital Property		915

CHAPTER 12 Administration of Estates			934
1.	Decedents' Estates		934
2.	Debtors' Estates		955

CHAPTER 13 Agency, Partnerships and Corporations			972
1.	Agency		972
2.	Partnerships and Other Associations		976
3.	Corporations		982
	A.	Corporate Personality; Basic Principles	982
	B.	Corporate Activity	987
	C.	The Law Governing Corporate Activities	996
4.	Dissolution and Winding–Up		1012

INDEX	1013

TABLE OF CONTENTS

Preface	v
Table of Cases	xxiii
Table of Books and Articles	xxxvii

CHAPTER 1 Introduction — 1

1. The Subject Matter — 1
2. The Functions of Conflicts as a Body of Law — 2
3. History — 3
4. The Conflict of Laws Today — 4
5. The Future of Conflicts — 5

CHAPTER 2 Domicile: The Chosen Point of Entry — 7

Introductory Note — 7
1. Intestate Succession to Movables — 7
   In Re Estate of Jones — 7
2. Validity of a Will — 17
   In Re Estate of Clark — 17
3. Diversity Jurisdiction — 20
   Rodriguez–Diaz v. Sierra–Martinez — 20
4. Judicial Jurisdiction — 26
   Alvord & Alvord v. Patenotre — 26
5. Special Situations — 28

CHAPTER 3 Jurisdiction of Courts — 34

Sec.
1. **Introduction and General Considerations** — 34
   Buchanan v. Rucker — 34
2. **Bases of Judicial Jurisdiction Over Natural and Legal Persons** — 41
   A. The Historic Bases: Jurisdiction Theory Before *International Shoe* — 41
   B. In Search of New Jurisdictional Standards: The Era of *International Shoe*, "Minimum Contacts", and "Fairness" — 47
   International Shoe Co. v. State of Washington — 47
   McGee v. International Life Insurance Co. — 53
   Hanson v. Denckla — 56
   World–Wide Volkswagen Corp. v. Woodson, District Judge of Creek County, Oklahoma — 66
   Asahi Metal Industry Co., Ltd. v. Superior Court of California, Solano County — 78
   Helicopteros Nacionales de Colombia, S.A. v. Hall — 94
   Volkswagenwerk Aktiengesellschaft v. Schlunk — 105

Sec.
2. Bases of Judicial Jurisdiction Over Natural and Legal Persons—Continued

   Burnham v. Superior Court of California 112
  C. Continuance of Jurisdiction 122
   Michigan Trust Co. v. Ferry 122

3. Jurisdiction Over "Things" 123
 Introductory Note 124
  A. Land 125
   Combs v. Combs 126
  B. Chattels 128
   Martin v. Better Taste Popcorn Co. 128
  C. Intangibles 130
   Harris v. Balk 131
   New York Life Insurance Co. v. Dunlevy 133
   Shaffer v. Heitner 136
   Rush v. Savchuk 148

4. Competence of Court and Notice 156
 Thompson v. Whitman 156
 Mullane v. Central Hanover Bank & Trust Co. 160

CHAPTER 4 Limitations on the Exercise of Jurisdiction 168

Introductory Note 168

1. Limitations Imposed by Contract 168
 M/S Bremen v. Zapata Off-Shore Co. 169
 Carnival Cruise Lines, Inc. v. Shute 172

2. Fraud, Force and Privilege 179
 Terlizzi v. Brodie 179

3. Forum Non Conveniens 181
 Gulf Oil Corp. v. Gilbert 182
 In re Union Carbide Corporation Gas Plant Disaster at Bhopal, India in December, 1984 185
 In Re Union Carbide Corporation Gas Plant Disaster at Bhopal, India in December, 1984 186

4. Other Limitations Imposed by the Forum 198
 United States v. First National City Bank 198
 Slater v. Mexican National R. Co. 201

5. Limitations Imposed by the State of the Transaction 206
 Buttron v. El Paso Northeastern Ry. Co. 206
 Tennessee Coal, Iron & Railroad Co. v. George 208
 James v. Grand Trunk Western Railroad Co. 211

6. Effect of Interstate Commerce 215

CHAPTER 5 Foreign Judgments 218

1. Policies Underlying the Recognition and Enforcement of Foreign Judgments 218
 Hilton v. Guyot 219

2. Recognition and Enforcement in General 227
  A. In Personam Judgments 228

Sec.
2. **Recognition and Enforcement in General**—Continued
  Lynde v. Lynde 229
  Emery v. Hovey 230
  Uniform Enforcement of Foreign Judgments Act (Revised 1964 Act) 233
 B. Judgments Based on Jurisdiction Over Things or Over Status 235
  Combs v. Combs 235
  Harnischfeger Sales Corp. v. Sternberg Dredging Co. 235

3. **Particular Effects** 238
 A. Persons Affected 238
  Sovereign Camp v. Bolin 238
  Riley v. New York Trust Co. 242
  Kremer v. Chemical Construction Corp. 246
  Marrese v. American Academy of Ortho. Surgeons 248
 B. Issues Affected 251
 C. Limitations on Full Faith and Credit 254
  Fall v. Eastin 254
  Yarborough v. Yarborough 259
  Magnolia Petroleum Co. v. Hunt 266
  Industrial Commission of Wisconsin v. McCartin 271
  Thomas v. Washington Gas Light Co. 273

4. **Defenses** 279
 A. Nature of the Original Proceedings 279
  Adam v. Saenger 281
  Thompson v. Whitman 283
  Treinies v. Sunshine Mining Co. 286
  Lynde v. Lynde 290
  Barber v. Barber 290
  Worthley v. Worthley 293
  Levin v. Gladstein 296
 B. Nature of Original Cause of Action 297
  Huntington v. Attrill 297
  Fauntleroy v. Lum 302
  Watkins v. Conway 307
 C. Lack of a Competent Court 310
  Kenney v. Supreme Lodge of the World, Loyal Order of Moose ... 310
 D. Foreign Country Judgments 311
 E. Matters Subsequent to F–1 Judgment 314
  (a) *Payment or Other Discharge* 314
  (b) *Successive Judgments* 315
  (c) *Reversal of Earlier Judgment* 316

CHAPTER 6 The Impact of the Constitution 317

Introductory Note 317
1. **The Obligation to Provide or to Refuse a Forum** 318
 Hughes v. Fetter 318
 Wells v. Simonds Abrasive Co. 321

Sec.
2. **Choice of Law** ... 325
   Home Insurance Co. v. Dick ... 325
   Order of United Commercial Travelers v. Wolfe ... 333
   Pacific Employers Insurance Co. v. Industrial Accident Commission ... 336
   Carroll v. Lanza ... 339
   Watson v. Employers Liability Assurance Corp., Limited ... 343
   Clay v. Sun Insurance Office, Limited ... 346
   Allstate Insurance Co. v. Hague ... 349
   Phillips Petroleum Co. v. Shutts ... 362
3. **Unreasonable Discrimination** ... 368
4. **Privileges and Immunities** ... 368
   Supreme Court of New Hampshire v. Piper ... 368
5. **Government Seizure; Interstate Commerce** ... 371

CHAPTER 7 Threshold Problems of the Forum in Choice of Law ... 375

Introductory Note ... 375
1. **Admitting or Rejecting the Action or Defense** ... 375
   Loucks v. Standard Oil Co. of New York ... 375
   Mertz v. Mertz ... 379
   Intercontinental Hotels Corp. (Puerto Rico) v. Golden ... 382
   Wong v. Tenneco ... 387
   Holzer v. Deutsche Reichsbahn–Gesellschaft ... 390
2. **Notice and Proof of Foreign Law** ... 392
   Walton v. Arabian American Oil Co. ... 393
   Leary v. Gledhill ... 396
   James v. Powell ... 399
3. **Use of The Forum's "Procedural" Rules** ... 402
   A. Introduction ... 402
      Noe v. United States Fidelity & Guaranty Co. ... 403
   B. Presumptions and Burden of Proof ... 408
      Levy v. Steiger ... 408
   C. Rules of Evidence: Privilege ... 411
      Samuelson v. Susen ... 412
   D. Time Limitation ... 417
      Bournias v. Atlantic Maritime Co., Limited ... 419
      Heavner v. Uniroyal, Inc. ... 422
      Cropp v. Interstate Distributor Co. ... 426
      Trzecki v. Gruenewald ... 430
      Sun Oil Company v. Wortman ... 434
4. **Reference to the Choice-of-Law Rules of Another Jurisdiction** ... 441
   In Re Annesley ... 441

CHAPTER 8 The Problem of Choosing the Rule of Decision ... 448

1. **The Received System and Tradition** ... 448
   A. Territoriality and the Jurisdiction–Selecting Process ... 448

Sec.
1. **The Received System and Tradition**—Continued
   B. Examples of the System in Operation 451
      1. The Forum Applies Its Own Rule of Decision 451
         Introductory Note 451
         People v. Olah 452
      2. Traditional Rules 453
         (a) Tort 453
             Alabama Great Southern Railroad Co. v. Carroll 453
             Victor v. Sperry 456
             Gordon v. Parker 460
         (b) Contract 463
             Milliken v. Pratt 464
             Louis–Dreyfus v. Paterson Steamships, Limited 468
             Pritchard v. Norton 470
             Seeman v. Philadelphia Warehouse Co. 472
             Kinney Loan & Finance Co. v. Sumner 475
             Siegelman v. Cunard White Star, Limited 478
         (c) Real Property 485
             Sinclair v. Sinclair 485
             Toledo Society for Crippled Children v. Hickok 487

2. **Escape Devices** 493
   A. Characterization 493
      1. Substance vs. Procedure 493
         Grant v. McAuliffe 493
      2. Nature of the Action 495
         Haumschild v. Continental Casualty Co. 495
         Garza v. Greyhound Lines, Inc. 497
   B. Renvoi 500
      American Motorists Insurance Co. v. ARTRA Group, Inc. 500
   C. Public Policy 503
      Kilberg v. Northeast Airlines, Inc. 503
   D. Property: Equitable Conversion and the Contract–Conveyance Distinction 505

3. **Transition: The Search for New Approaches** 506
   A. Early Gropings 506
      Schmidt v. Driscoll Hotel, Inc. 506
      Auten v. Auten 508
   B. Scholarly Camps 511

4. **The New Era** 520
   A. Adopting New Choice-of-Law Rules 520
      Babcock v. Jackson 520
      Neumeier v. Kuehner 525
      Duncan v. Cessna Aircraft Company 536
      Rudow v. Fogel 549
   B. The Courts at Work 554
      Schultz v. Boy Scouts of America, Inc. 554
      Cooney v. Osgood Machinery, Inc. 561
      Trailways, Inc. v. Clark 566
      Bernkrant v. Fowler 568

Sec.

4. The New Era 520
    Peugeot Motors of America, Inc. v. Eastern Auto Distributors, Inc. 573
    Bledsoe v. Crowley 577
  C. Problems Emerged and Emerging 583
    1. Predictability 583
      Dym v. Gordon 583
      DeSantis v. Wackenhut Corporation 587
    2. Resolving Policy Clashes 594
      Lilienthal v. Kaufman 594
      Casey v. Manson Construction And Engineering Co. 598
      Bernhard v. Harrah's Club 600
    3. Changes in Circumstances 606
      Reich v. Purcell 606
      Miller v. Miller 610
    4. Fairness 613
      Rosenthal v. Warren 613
    5. "No Interest" Cases 621
      Reyno v. Piper Aircraft Co. 621
    6. Complex Litigation 624
  D. Additional Problems 631
    1. Multistate Defamation 631
      Dale System, Inc. v. Time, Inc. 631
    2. Dépeçage 635
      Lillegraven v. Tengs 636
      Marie v. Garrison 638
    3. No Fault 639
      Uniform Motor Vehicle Accident Reparations Act (1972) ... 641
    4. Workers' Compensation 644
      Wilson v. Faull 645
    5. Admiralty 648
      Lauritzen v. Larsen 648
    6. Assignment of Contractual Rights 652
    7. Arbitration 654
      Parsons & Whittemore Overseas Co., Inc. v. Societe Generale de L'Industrie Du Papier (RAKTA) 656
    8. Negotiable Instruments 660
      Introductory Note 660
      Koechlin Et CIE. v. Kestenbaum Brothers 661

CHAPTER 9 Conflicts Problems in Federal and International Settings 663

1. Special Problems in Federal Courts 663
  A. The Constraints and Tolerances of the Erie Principle 663
    Introductory Note 663
    Erie Railroad Co. v. Tompkins 665
    Guaranty Trust Co. v. York 670
    Byrd v. Blue Ridge Rural Electric Cooperative, Inc. 674
    Hanna v. Plumer 678

Sec.
1. **Special Problems in Federal Courts**—Continued
   B. The Erie Doctrine and Conflict of Laws in Diversity Cases 687
      Klaxon Co. v. Stentor Electric Manufacturing Co. 688
      Ferens v. John Deere Company 693
      Samuelson v. Susen 700
      Doggrell v. Southern Box Co. 702
      Angel v. Bullington 705
   C. Federal Questions in Relation to State Law 711
      Introductory Note 711
      D'Oench, Duhme & Co. v. Federal Deposit Insurance Corp. ... 713
      United States v. Kimbell Foods, Inc. 717
      Bank of America National Trust & Savings Association v. Parnell 723
2. **Conflicts Problems in International Settings** 726
   A. International Conflicts Cases and the Federal Control of Foreign Affairs 727
      Zschernig v. Miller 727
      Dougherty v. Equitable Life Assurance Society 730
      Johansen v. Confederation Life Association 733
      Banco Nacional de Cuba v. Sabbatino 740
   B. Treaties 744
   C. International Conflicts Cases in the Absence of Federal Limitations or Preemption 746
      Hartford Fire Insurance Co. v. California 749

CHAPTER 10 Property 757

Introductory Note 757
1. **Land** 757
   Note 757
   A. Succession on Death 759
      In Re Estate of Barrie 759
      In re Schneider's Estate 765
   B. Security Transactions 767
      Swank v. Hufnagle 767
   C. Conveyances and Contracts 769
      Polson v. Stewart 770
      Irving Trust Co. v. Maryland Casualty Co. 776
2. **Movables, in General** 778
   A. Succession on Death 778
   B. Inter Vivos Transactions 781
      Youssoupoff v. Widener 781
      Cammell v. Sewell 784
   C. Security Transactions 786
      Green v. Van Buskirk 786
      John J. Shanahan v. George B. Landers Construction Co. 790
      Gordon v. Clifford Metal Sales Co. 796
   D. Future Interests and Trusts 799
      Hutchison v. Ross 799
      Shannon v. Irving Trust Co. 801

Sec.

2. **Movables, in General** —Continued
    Wilmington Trust Co. v. Wilmington Trust Co. 804
    In Re Bauer's Trust 806
    Farmers and Merchants Bank v. Woolf 808
    Mullane v. Central Hanover Bank & Trust Co. 813
3. **Intangibles** 814
    Morson v. Second National Bank of Boston 814
4. **Interpretation and Construction of Documents** 816

CHAPTER 11 Family Law 820

Introductory Note 820
1. **Marriage** 821
    In Re May's Estate 821
    Wilkins v. Zelichowski 825
    In Re Ommang's Estate 829
    In re Estate of Lenherr 832
2. **Divorce** 836
    A. Conditions for Decreeing Divorce 836
        Alton v. Alton 836
    B. Extraterritorial Recognition 846
        Williams v. North Carolina 847
        Williams v. North Carolina 851
    C. Extraterritorial Recognition: Limits on Attack for Jurisdictional Defects 856
        Sherrer v. Sherrer 856
        Johnson v. Muelberger 860
        Cook v. Cook 862
        Krause v. Krause 864
    D. Extraterritorial Recognition: Divisible Divorce 866
        Estin v. Estin 866
        Simons v. Miami Beach First National Bank 871
3. **Annulment** 878
    Whealton v. Whealton 878
    Wilkins v. Zelichowski 880
4. **Judicial Separation** 881
5. **Legitimation** 883
    Introductory Note 883
6. **Adoption** 884
    Note 884
7. **Custody of Children** 887
    May v. Anderson 887
    Quenzer v. Quenzer 891
8. **Support** 901
    A. Enforcement of Support Claims Without Regard to Reciprocal Support Legislation 901
        Introductory Note 901
        Kulko v. California Superior Court 902
        Lynde v. Lynde 907
        Yarborough v. Yarborough 907

Sec.
8. **Support**—Continued
    Barber v. Barber — 907
    Worthley v. Worthley — 907
    Estin v. Estin — 907
    State of California v. Copus — 908
  B. Reciprocal Support Legislation — 910
9. **Marital Property** — 915
  Introductory Note — 915
  Rozan v. Rozan — 916
  Wyatt v. Fulrath — 921
  Estate of O'Connor — 926
  Addison v. Addison — 928

CHAPTER 12 Administration of Estates — 934

1. **Decedents' Estates** — 934
  Introductory Note — 934
  Milmoe v. Toomey — 935
  In Re Fischer's Estate — 938
  Riley v. New York Trust Co. — 939
  Wilkins v. Ellett, Adm'r — 941
  Estate of Hanreddy — 944
  Lenn v. Riche — 946
  Ghilain v. Couture — 947
  Eubank Heights Apartments, Limited v. Lebow — 950
2. **Debtors' Estates** — 955
  Introductory Note — 955
  Blake v. McClung — 955
  Morris v. Jones — 958
  Converse v. Hamilton — 966
  Broderick v. Rosner — 968

CHAPTER 13 Agency, Partnerships and Corporations — 972

1. **Agency** — 972
  Introductory Note — 972
  Mercier v. John Hancock Mutual Life Insurance Co. — 973
2. **Partnerships and Other Associations** — 976
  First National Bank of Waverly v. Hall — 977
  Barrows v. Downs & Co. — 978
  Greenspun v. Lindley — 980
3. **Corporations** — 982
  A. Corporate Personality; Basic Principles — 982
    Introductory Note — 982
  B. Corporate Activity — 987
    Eli Lilly & Co. v. Sav-on-Drugs, Inc. — 989
    Sioux Remedy Co. v. Cope — 993
    Union Brokerage Co. v. Jensen — 993
  C. The Law Governing Corporate Activities — 996
    German–American Coffee Co. v. Diehl — 1000
    Western Air Lines, Inc. v. Sobieski — 1001

Sec.
3. **Corporations**—Continued
   Edgar v. MITE Corp. 1005
   CTS Corp. v. Dynamics Corp. of America 1008
4. **Dissolution and Winding–Up** 1012

INDEX 1013

TABLE OF CASES

Principal cases are in bold type. Non-principal cases are in roman type. References are Pages.

Abbott v. Owens–Corning Fiberglas Corp., 66
Ackermann v. Levine, 110, 313
Adam v. Saenger, 43, **281**
Addison v. Addison, 919, **928**
A. E. Staley Mfg. Co. v. Swift & Co., 192, 214
Agent Orange Product Liability Litigation, In re, 635 F.2d 987, p. 720
Agent Orange Product Liability Litigation, In re, 580 F.Supp. 690, p. 721
A.I. Credit Corp. v. Liebman, 279
Air Crash at Detroit Metropolitan Airport, Detroit, Mich. on Aug. 16, 1987, In re, 700
Air Crash Disaster at Boston, Massachusetts on July 31, 1973, In re, 197
Air Crash Disaster Near Bombay, India on Jan. 1, 1978, In re, 190
Air Crash Disaster Near Chicago, Illinois on May 25, 1979, In re, 624
Air Crash Disaster Near New Orleans, La. on July 9, 1982, In re, 687
Air Products & Chemicals, Inc. v. Fairbanks Morse, Inc., 426
Alabama G.S.R. Co. v. Carroll, 453, 711
Alaska Packers Ass'n v. Industrial Acc. Com'n, 335, 336
Albany Ins. Co. v. Anh Thi Kieu, 651
Alcoa Steamship Co., Inc. v. M/V Nordic Regent, 189
Aldrich v. Aldrich, 159
Alfaro v. Alfaro, 876
Allain v. Allain, 911
Allen v. McCurry, 248
Allen v. Nessler, 495
Allenberg Cotton Co., Inc. v. Pittman, 991
Allied Bank Intern. v. Banco Credito Agricola de Cartago, 744
Allstate Ins. Co. v. Hague, 349, 360, 361, 362, 515, 699, 726
Alton v. Alton, 346, **836,** 843
Aluminal Industries, Inc. v. Newtown Commercial Associates, 41
Alvord & Alvord v. Patenotre, 26, 27
Ambatielos v. Foundation Co., 289
Amchem Products Inc. v. Worker's Comp. Bd., 190, 191
Americana of Puerto Rico, Inc. v. Kaplus, 387
American Banana Co. v. United Fruit Co., 755

American Cyanamid Co. v. Picaso–Anstalt, 193
American Dredging Co. v. Miller, 90, 184, 195, 687
American Home Assur. Co. v. Insurance Corp. of Ireland Ltd., 189, 193
American Motorists Ins. Co. v. ARTRA Group, Inc., 500
American Surety Co. v. Baldwin, 285
Amtorg Trading Corporation v. Camden Fibre Mills, Inc., 654
Amusement Equipment, Inc. v. Mordelt, 41
Anderson v. Sonat Exploration Co., 63
Andre v. Morrow, 258
Angel v. Bullington, 382, 685, **705**
Anglo–American Provision Co. v. Davis Provision Co., 311
Annesley, In re, 14, **441,** 445, 727, 780
Anton Piller KG v. Manufacturing Process Ltd., 147
Application of (see name of party)
Arguello v. Industrial Woodworking Mach. Co., 86
Armour Intern. Co. v. Worldwide Cosmetics, Inc., 415
Armstrong v. Manzo, 886
Armstrong v. Pomerance, 148
Arndt v. Griggs, 125
Arrowsmith v. United Press Intern., 66
Asahi Metal Industry Co., Ltd. v. Superior Court of California, Solano County, 53, **78,** 86, 89
Asbury Hospital v. Cass County, N. D., 985
Associated Business Telephone Systems Corp. v. Greater Capital Corp., 232
Atchison, T. & S. F. R. Co. v. Sowers, 207
Atchison, T. & S. F. R. Co. v. Wells, 216, 217
Atherton v. Atherton, 846
Atlas Credit Corp. v. Ezrine, 279
Attorney General v. Eichmann, 180
Auten v. Auten, 508
Avery's Estate, Matter of, 885
Avitzur v. Avitzur, 877

Babanaft International Co. SA v. Bassatne, 147

...cock v. Jackson, 379, 386, 396, 460, ...20, 587, 615, 619, 727
...charach v. Spriggs, 944
...achchan v. India Abroad Publications Inc., 314
Bader by Bader v. Purdom, 532
Bailey v. Grand Trunk Lines New England, 987
Baldwin v. Iowa State Traveling Men's Ass'n, 217, 218, 281, 284
Baltimore & O. R. Co. v. Kepner, 217
Balts v. Balts, 497
Banco Ambrosiano, S.P.A. v. Artoc Bank & Trust Ltd., 66
Banco Nacional de Cuba v. Farr, 743
Banco Nacional de Cuba v. Sabbatino, 227, 392, **740,** 743
Bank of America Nat. Trust & Sav. Ass'n v. Parnell, 723
Bank of Augusta v. Earle, 983
Banque Libanaise Pour Le Commerce v. Khreich, 227
Barber v. Barber, 290, 907
Barrack v. Van Dusen, 196, 694, 700
Barrie's Estate, In re, 730, 759
Barrios v. Dade County of State of Fla., 408
Barrows v. Downs & Co., 978
Barry E. (Anonymous) v. Ingraham, 886
Bassi's Estate, In re, 884
Bates v. Cook, Inc., 432
Battell, Matter of, 818
Bauer's Trust, In re, 806
Baxter v. Sturm, Ruger and Co., Inc., 418
Beauchamp v. Bertig, 505, 775
Bechtel, State ex rel. Weede v., 1003
Belanger v. Keydril Co., 398
Bell, State v., 835
Bendix Autolite Corp. v. Midwesco Enterprises, Inc., 374, 432
Benjamin, State ex rel. California v., 913
Berghammer v. Smith, 613
Bergner & Engel Brewing Co. v. Dreyfus, 986
Berkovitz v. Grinberg, 877
Bernhard v. Harrah's Club, 600
Bernhardt v. Polygraphic Co. of America, 655, 673
Bernkrant v. Fowler, 495, 568, 571
Betcher v. Hay-Roe, 45
Bezold v. Bezold, 31
Biscoe v. Arlington County, 578
Blackmer v. United States, 42
Blais v. Deyo, 531, 640
Blake v. McClung, 368, 946, **955,** 985
Blanco v. Pan-American Life Ins. Co., 740
Blanco's Estate, In re, 884
BLC Ins. Co. v. Westin, Inc., 507
Bledsoe v. Crowley, 577
Blumle v. Kramer, 123
Boatland, Inc. v. Brunswick Corp., 576
Boit v. Gar-Tec Products, Inc., 86
Bonwich v. Bonwich, 886
Borax' Estate v. C.I.R., 834
Boston Safe Deposit & Trust Co. v. Alfred University, 813
Boudreaux v. Welch, 860

Bournias v. Atlantic Maritime Co., 419, 433
Boxer v. Boxer, 860
Brack's Estate, Matter of, 825
Bradford Electric Light Co. v. Clapper, 339, 342, 343
Braniff Airways, Inc. v. Curtiss-Wright Corp., 638
Broderick v. Rosner, 321, 334, **968**
Brooke v. Willis, 901
Brown v. Merlo, 453
Bryant v. Finnish Nat. Airline, 101, 102
Bubar v. Dizdar, 180
Buchanan v. Rucker, 34, 36
Burge v. State, 417
Burger King Corp. v. Continental Ins. Co., 348
Burger King Corp. v. Rudzewicz, 64, 76, 92, 101
Burlington Northern R. Co. v. Woods, 685
Burnham v. Superior Court of California, County of Marin, 42, 112, 119, 120, 121
Burr v. Beckler, 768, 772
Buscema v. Buscema, 28
Bushkin Associates, Inc. v. Raytheon Co., 571
Bustamante v. Bustamante, 28
Buttron v. El Paso Northeastern Ry. Co., 206
Byrd v. Blue Ridge Rural Elec. Co-op., Inc., 674
Byrd, United States v., 415
Byrne v. Cooper, 395
Byrnes v. Kirby, 684

C. v. C., 901
C. A. B. v. Deutsche Lufthansa Aktiengesellschaft, 200
Cabalceta v. Standard Fruit Co., 687
Cable v. Sahara Tahoe Corp., 604
Cabral v. State Bd. of Control, 28
Calder v. Jones, 76
Caldwell v. Caldwell, 876
California, State ex rel. v. Benjamin, 913
California v. Superior Court of California, San Bernardino County, 899
California v. Texas, 102 S.Ct. 2335, p. 15
California v. Texas, 98 S.Ct. 3107, p. 15.
California, State of v. Copus, 908
Calzavara v. Biehl & Co., 176
Cameron v. Cameron, 933
Cameron v. Hardisty, 426
Cammell v. Sewell, 130, **784,** 786
Canadian Northern Ry. Co. v. Eggen, 368, 432
Canadian Overseas Ores Ltd. v. Compania de Acero Del Pacifico S.A., 190
Cannon Mfg. Co. v. Cudahy Packing Co., 104
Canty v. Canty, 914
Carbulon v. Carbulon, 866
Carefree Vacations, Inc. v. Brunner, 176
Carnegie v. First National Bank of Brunswick, 818

TABLE OF CASES   XXV

Carnival Cruise Lines, Inc. v. Shute, 102, **172,** 175, 177, 178
Carnival Cruise Lines, Inc. v. Superior Court (Williams), 174
Carolina Power & Light Co. v. Uranex, 146
Carr v. Carr, 874
Carrington v. Rash, 29
Carroll v. Lanza, 339, 343, 367, 647
Case C–129/92, p. 194
Casey v. Manson Const. & Engineering Co., 598
Castree v. E.R. Squibb & Sons Ltd., 87
Catalano v. Catalano, 828
Cavell v. Cavell, 871
Cavic v. Grand Bahama Development Co., Ltd., 398
Celanese Corp. v. Duplan Corp., 181
Cepeda, Application of, 415
Certisimo v. Heidelberg Co., 86
Chambers v. Dakotah Charter, Inc., 525
Chaplin v. Boys, 533
Chapman v. Aetna Finance Co., 251
Chappell v. United Kingdom, 147
Chappell's Estate, In re, 810
Chase Manhattan Bank, Application of, 200
Chemical Nat. Bank of New York v. Kellogg, 467
Chicot County Drainage Dist. v. Baxter State Bank, 286
Chila v. Owens, 532
Christoff's Estate, In re, 886
Cipolla v. Shaposka, 531
City of (see name of city)
Clark, In re Estate of, 17, 780
Clark v. Allen, 728, 729
Clark v. Clark, 515
Clark v. Graham, 976
Clark v. Jeter, 884
Clark v. Williard, 966
Clarkson Co., Ltd. v. Shaheen, 314
Clay v. Sun Ins. Office, Limited, 329, 333, 335, **346,** 643
Clearfield Trust Co. v. United States, 712, 719, 725
Clements v. Macauley, 191
Coakes v. Arabian American Oil Co., 190
Coan v. Cessna Aircraft, 432
Coe v. Coe, 286, 859, 860, 866
Cohen v. Beneficial Indus. Loan Corp., 673
Cohen v. Hathaway, 688
Colby v. Colby, 289
Coleman v. Coleman, 870
Collett, Ex parte, 195
Colorado River Water Conservation Dist. v. United States, 686
Colpitt v. Cheatham, 884
Combs v. Combs, 126, 235, 237
Compagnie Tunisienne de Navigation S.A. v. Compagnie d'Armement Maritime S.A., 484
Competex, S.A. v. Labow, 748
Conklin v. Horner, 515
Conlon by Conlon v. Heckler, 843
Connecticut v. Doehr, 130
Connolly v. Bell, 302

Connolly v. Foudree, 685
Considine v. Rawl, 876
Consolidated Gold Fields PLC v. Minorco, S.A., 756
Converse v. Hamilton, 966
Cook v. Cook, 860, **862,** 866
Cooney v. Osgood Machinery, Inc., 561
Corbett v. Stergios, 886
Cordis Corp. v. Siemens–Pacesetter, Inc., 195
Cort v. Ash, 720
Cortes v. Ryder Truck Rental, Inc., 500
Cory v. White, 15
Cotten, United States v., 180
Cousins v. Instrument Flyers, Inc., 531
Cowans v. Ticonderoga Pulp & Paper Co., 226, 227, 312
Craig v. Craig, 763
Crichton v. Succession of Crichton, 926
Crichton's Estate, In re, 924
Crider v. Zurich Ins. Co., 211, 644
Croft v. National Car Rental, 531
Cropp v. Interstate Distributor Co., 426
Cross v. United States Trust Co. of New York, 810
CTS Corp. v. Dynamics Corp. of America, 1000, **1008,** 1010, 1011
Cuevas v. Cuevas, 258
Cummings v. Dresher, 252
Curry v. McCanless, 15
Curtis v. Campbell, 382
Custody of a Minor (No. 3), 900

Dahl v. United Technologies Corp., 189
Dale System, Inc. v. Time, Inc., 631
Dalip Singh Bir's Estate, In re, 834
Dallas v. Whitney, 456
Dane v. Board of Registrars of Voters of Concord, 31
Davenport v. Webb, 505
Davidson v. Garden Properties, Inc., 408
Davis v. Davis, 219, 286, 856
Davis v. Farmers' Co-op. Equity Co., 215, 985
Davis v. Furlong, 382, 407
Davis v. United States Steel Supply, Div. of U. S. Steel Corp., 248
Davison v. Sinai Hospital of Baltimore, Inc., 580
Dawson v. Dawson, 460
Day v. Wiswall, 258
Day & Zimmermann, Inc. v. Challoner, 690, 692
Deemer v. Silk City Textile Machinery Co., 622
DeGroot, Kalliel, Traint & Conklin, P. C. v. Camarota, 251
Dehmlow v. Austin Fireworks, 86
DeJames v. Magnificence Carriers, Inc., 87
De Lano's Estate, In re, 943
de Lara v. Confederation Life Ass'n, 740
Del Valle, Matter of Estate of, 884
de Melo v. Lederle Laboratories, Div. of American Cyanamid Corp., 190
Demjanjuk, Matter of, 180
Demjanjuk v. Petrovsky, 180

DeNicols v. Curlier, 2 Ch. 410, p. 916
DeNicols v. Curlier, A.C. 21, p. 916
Denilauler v. SNC Couchet Freres, 280
Depas v. Mayo, 919
Derby & Co., Ltd. v. Weldon, 147
de Reyes v. Marine Management and Consulting, Ltd., 102
DeSantis v. Wackenhut Corp., 587
DES Cases, In re, 103
Deschenes v. Tallman, 126, 257
Desert Palace Inc. v. State of Japan, 387
De Sylva v. Ballentine, 712
Detroit, City of v. Gould, 389
D. H. Overmyer Co. Inc., of Ohio v. Frick Co., 44, 178
Dick v. New York Life Ins. Co., 678
Diehl v. Ogorewac, 532
Director, Office of Workers' Compensation Programs, United States Dept. of Labor v. National Van Lines, Inc., 279
District Court of Ninth Judicial Dist., Curry County, State ex rel. Truitt v., 128
Dobkin v. Chapman, 167
Doe and Dowling v. Armour Pharmaceutical Co., 191
D'Oench, Duhme & Co. v. Federal Deposit Ins. Corporation, 713
Doetsch v. Doetsch, 813
Doggrell v. Southern Box Co. of Mississippi, 378, 379, 702
Doherty & Co. v. Goodman, 985
Donnell v. Howell, 860
Dority v. Dority, 126, 553
Dorrance's Estate, In re, 14
Doster v. Schenk, 746
Dougherty v. Equitable Life Assur. Soc. of United States, 730
Douglas v. New York, N. H. & H. R. Co., 321, 368
Doulgeris v. Bambacus, 886
Downs v. American Mut. Liability Ins. Co., 652
Dreer's Estate, In re, 885
Drexel Burnham Lambert Inc. v. Ruebsamen, 147
Drudge v. Overland Plazas Co., 433
Dubin v. City of Philadelphia, 45
Duckwall v. Lease, 764
Duffield, State ex rel. Sivnksty v., 179
Duggan v. Bay State St. Ry. Co., 409
Duncan v. Cessna Aircraft Co., 536, 568
Duncan v. Smith, 911, 914
Durfee v. Duke, 285, 286
Dym v. Gordon, 525, **583**

Eastern Townships Bank v. H.S. Beebe & Co., 228, 315
Eckard v. Eckard, 257
Eddie v. Eddie, 884
Edgar v. MITE Corp., 1000, **1005,** 1011
Edinburgh Assur. Co. v. R.L. Burns Corp., 652
Educational Studios v. Consolidated Film Industries, 130
Edwardsville Nat. Bank and Trust Co. v. Marion Laboratories, Inc., 619
Eisenberg v. Commercial Union Assur. Co., 987
Eli Lilly & Co. v. Sav–On–Drugs, Inc., 985, **989**
Elkind v. Byck, 264, 265, 910
Elkins v. Moreno, 28
Ellis v. Garwood, 273
Ellis v. McGovern, 316
Elman v. Belson, 65
Elston v. Industrial Lift Truck Co., 648
Embry v. Palmer, 219
Emery v. Burbank, 572
Emery v. Emery, 496
Emery v. Hovey, 230
EMI Film Distributors, Ltd. v. L. D. S. Film Co., 195
EMI Records, Ltd. v. Modern Music GmbH, 280
Engelhardt's Estate, In re, 884
Engelson v. Mallea, 913
Enis v. State, 825
Equifax Services, Inc. v. Hitz, 685
Erie R. Co. v. Tompkins, 177, 197, 379, 583, **665,** 673
Erlanger Mills, Inc. v. Cohoes Fibre Mills, Inc., 90
Erwin v. Thomas, 622
Estate of (see name of party)
Estin v. Estin, 866, 871, 874, **907**
Etheredge v. Genie Industries, Inc., 418
Eubank Heights Apartments, Ltd. v. Lebow, 950
Evans Transp. Co. v. Scullin Steel Co., 214
Ex parte (see name of party)
Ezell v. Hayes Oilfield Const. Co., Inc., 549
Ezeonu, People v., 835

Factors Etc., Inc. v. Pro Arts, Inc., 701 F.2d 11, p. 686
Factors Etc., Inc. v. Pro Arts, Inc., 541 F.Supp. 231, p. 702
Fairchild, Arabatzis & Smith, Inc. v. Prometco (Produce & Metals) Co., Ltd., 314
Fall v. Eastin, 254, 257, 258, 492, 919
Farmers and Merchants Bank v. Woolf, 808
Farrell v. Piedmont Aviation, Inc., 156
Farris v. Sambo's Restaurants, Inc., 995
Fauntleroy v. Lum, 302, 314
Feder v. Evans–Feder, 901
Feder v. Turkish Airlines, 146
Fehr v. McHugh, 290
Feigenbaum v. Feigenbaum, 881
Fells v. Bowman, 637
Ferens v. John Deere Co., 195, 197, 418, **693,** 698
Fernandez v. Fernandez, 181
Financial Bancorp, Inc. v. Pingree and Dahle, Inc., 549
First Commerce Realty Investors v. K–F Land Co., 778
First Nat. Bank in Fort Collins v. Rostek, 532

First Nat. Bank of Boston v. Maine, 15
First Nat. Bank of Chicago v. United Air Lines, 321
First Nat. Bank of Waverly v. Hall, 977
First Nat. City Bank v. Banco Nacional de Cuba, 743
First Nat. City Bank, United States v., 85 S.Ct. 528, p. 146
First Nat. City Bank, United States v., 396 F.2d 897, pp. **198,** 200
First National City Bank, United States v., 146
Fischl v. Chubb, 456
Fischer's Estate, In re, 938
Fisher v. Fielding, 41
Fisher v. Fisher, 825
Fisher Governor Co. v. Superior Court of City and County of San Francisco, 94
Fitch v. Whaples, 214
Fitzpatrick v. International Ry. Co., 410
Fitzsimmons v. Johnson, 123
Flexner v. Farson, 986
Foote v. Newell, 280
Ford Motor Co. v. Leggat, 416
Foreman v. George Foreman Associates, Ltd., 576
Foster v. Leggett, 531
Frankel v. Allied Mills, 976
Fraser v. Fraser, 914
Freeman v. Alderson, 128
Fricke v. Isbrandtsen Co., 485
Frisbie v. Collins, 180
Fritzshall v. Board of Police Com'rs, 13, 14
Frummer v. Hilton Hotels Intern., Inc., 395, 411, 515
Fuentes v. Shevin, 133

Gallagher v. Mazda Motor of America, Inc., 105
Galva Foundry Co. v. Heiden, 26
Garfein v. McInnis, 126
Gargiul v. Tompkins, 250
Garrett v. Moore–McCormack Co., 673
Garza v. Greyhound Lines, Inc., 497, 568
Gasper v. Wales, 17
Gelineau v. New York University Hospital, 91
Gellerstedt v. United Missouri Bank of Kansas City, N.A., 954
Gengler, United States v., 180
Gentry v. Jett, 648
German–American Coffee Co. v. Diehl, 1000
Ghilain v. Couture, 947
Gianni v. Fort Wayne Air Service, Inc., 426
Gilbert v. Gulf Oil Corp., 687
Gilman Paint & Varnish Co. v. Legum, 979
Gluckin & Co. v. International Playtex Corp., 192
Godard v. Gray, 218, 280
Goldey v. Morning News of New Haven, 111
Golding v. Golding, 877
Gonzalez v. Naviera Neptuno A.A., 189
Gordon v. Clifford Metal Sales Co., Inc., 796

Gordon v. Gordon, 497
Gordon v. Parker, 460
Gordon v. Shea, 937
Gosschalk v. Gosschalk, 28
Gould v. P.T. Krakatau Steel, 86
Grace v. MacArthur, 41, 119
Graham, People v., 417
Grand v. Livingston, 472
Grand Jury Proceedings, In re, 694 F.2d 1256, p. 200
Grand Jury Proceedings, In re, 691 F.2d 1384, p. 200
Grand Jury Proceedings, In re, 532 F.2d 404, p. 200
Grant v. McAuliffe, 493
Granville–Smith v. Granville–Smith, 841
Gray v. American Radiator & Standard Sanitary Corp., 65
Gray v. Gray, 460
Great River Shipping Inc. v. Sunnyface Marine Ltd., 191
Green v. Van Buskirk, 130, **786**
Greenberg v. Panama Transport Co., 722
Greene v. Lindsey, 167
Greenlaw v. Smith, 899
Greenspun v. Lindley, 980, 986
Greschler v. Greschler, 875
Griffin v. McCoach, 691
Griffith v. United Air Lines, Inc., 396, 524
Gross v. Owen, 195
Grubel v. Nassauer, 42
Guaranty Trust Co., United States v., 662
Guaranty Trust Co. of New York v. York, 670, 673, 674
Guardian Royal Exchange Assur., Ltd. v. English China Clays, P.L.C., 65
Gulf Oil Corporation v. Gilbert, 182, 186
Gutierrez v. Collins, 204, 568

Haag v. Barnes, 511
Haberman v. Washington Public Power Supply System, 1011
Haddock v. Haddock, 846
Hall v. Zambelli, 86
Hamilton National Bank of Chattanooga v. Hutcheson, 818
Hammerstein v. Hammerstein, 31
Hammond's Estate, In re, 373
Hanau, Estate of v. Hanau, 730 S.W.2d 663, p. 933
Hanau, Estate of v. Hanau, 721 S.W.2d 515, p. 933
Hancock Nat. Bank v. Farnum, 219
Hanna v. Plumer, 166, 673, **678,** 684
Hannan, In re Estate of, 763
Hanreddy's Estate, In re, 944
Hansberry v. Lee, 240
Hanson v. Denckla, 53, **56,** 63, 64, 76, 77, 78, 943
Harden, United States v., 309
Hardy v. Betz, 910
Harnischfeger Sale Corporation v. Sternberg Co., 236

Table of Cases

Harnischfeger Sales Corporation v. Sternberg Dredging Co., 195 So. 322, p. 237
Harnischfeger Sales Corporation v. Sternberg Dredging Co., 191 So. 94, pp. 156, **235**
Harral v. Harral, 916
Harris v. Balk, 131, 156
Harrison v. Wyeth Laboratories Division of American Home Products Corp., 623
Harris Trust and Sav. Bank v. SLT Warehouse Co., Inc., 195
Harrods (Buenos Aires) Ltd., In re, 191
Hart, In re Estate of, 886
Hart v. American Airlines, Inc., 251
Hartford v. Superior Court In and For Los Angeles County, 843
Hartford Accident & Indemnity Co. v. Delta & Pine Land Co., 332
Hartford Fire Ins. Co. v. California, 749
Hartmann v. Time, Inc., 635
Hassain v. Hussain, 835
Hatas v. Partin, 950
Hataway v. McKinley, 5, 525
Haughton v. Haughton, 432
Haumschild v. Continental Cas. Co., 495, 497
Hausman v. Buckley, 999
Havoco of America, Ltd. v. Freeman, Atkins & Coleman, Ltd., 685
Haynie v. Hanson, 497, 500
Headen v. Pope & Talbot, Inc., 825
Headrick v. Atchison, T. & S.F. Ry. Co., 195
Heavner v. Uniroyal, Inc., 422
Heinle v. Fourth Judicial Dist. Court In and For County of Missoula, 906
Helicopteros Nacionales de Colombia, S.A. v. Hall, 38, 53, **94,** 101, 102, 103, 119, 175
Hellenic Lines Ltd.v.Rhoditis, 651
Hemphill v. Orloff, 981
Herczog v. Herczog, 915
Her Majesty the Queen In Right of Province of British Columbia v. Gilbertson, 309
Hershkoff v. Board of Registrars of Voters of Worcester, 30
Hess v. Pawloski, 44, 45, 985
Hewett v. Zegarzewski, 866
Higginbotham v. Higginbotham, 258
Hilton v. Guyot, 218, **219,** 224, 227, 312, 727
Hirsch v. Blue Cross, Blue Shield of Kansas City, 56
Hobbs v. Firestone Tire & Rubber Co., 433
Hodge v. Hodge, 286
Hoes of America, Inc. v. Hoes, 549
Hoffman v. Blaski, 195
Holemar, Matter of Marriage of, 825
Holiday Airlines Corp., In re, 690
Holman v. Johnson, 389
Holzer v. Deutsche Reichsbahn–Gesellschaft, 390, 727, 743
Home Ins. Co. v. Dick, 50 S.Ct. 338, pp. 325, 329, 392, 727, 740
Home Insurance Company v. C.J. Dick, 33 S.W.2d 428, pp. 389, 851

Hong Kong & Shanghai Banking Corp. v. Sherman, 191
Hoopeston Canning Co. v. Cullen, 346
Hope v. Brewer, 810
Hot Oil Service, Inc. v. Hall, 711
House v. Lefebvre, 502
House of Spring Gardens Ltd. v. Waite, 147
Howard v. Reynolds, 13
Huddy v. Fruehauf Corp., 613
Hudson, In re Marriage of, 890
Hudson v. Hermann Pfauter GmbH & Co., 745
Hudson v. Hudson, 870
Hughes v. Fetter, 210, **318,** 321, 367
Hughes v. Winkleman, 485
Hunt v. BP Exploration Co. (Libya) Ltd., 225, 313
Hunter v. Derby Foods, 456
Huntington v. Attrill, 297, 378, 705
Huntington Nat. Bank v. Sproul, 920
Huron Holding Corporation v. Lincoln Mine Operating Co., 219
Hurtado v. Superior Court of Sacramento County, 623
Hutchison v. Ross, 799

Illinois v. City of Milwaukee, Wis., 726
Indussa Corp. v. S. S. Ranborg, 177
Industrial Commission of Wis. v. McCartin, 271, 274
Industrial Indem. Co. v. Chapman and Cutler, 425
Indyka v. Indyka, 842
Ingersoll v. Coram, 952
Inland Revenue Commission v. Bullock, 16
In re (see name of party)
Insurance Corp. of Ireland, Ltd. v. Compagnie des Bauxites de Guinee, 77, 78, 119
In–Tech Marketing Inc. v. Hasbro, Inc., 314
Intercontinental Hotels Corp. (Puerto Rico) v. Golden, 382, 388
Intercontinental Planning, Limited v. Daystrom, Inc., 571
Intermeat, Inc. v. American Poultry Inc., 145
International Mill. Co. v. Columbia Transp. Co., 216, 217
International Paper Co. v. Ouellette, 726
International Shoe Co. v. State of Wash., Office of Unemployment Compensation and Placement, 66 S.Ct. 154, pp. 4, **47,** 53, 64, 68, 102, 119, 147
International Shoe Company v. State of Washington, 65 S.Ct. 1579, pp. 851, 984, 985, 988
Irving v. Owens–Corning Fiberglas Corp., 86
Irving Trust Co. v. Maryland Casualty Co., 776
Irvin L. Young Foundation, Inc. v. Damrell, 293
Islamic Republic of Iran v. Pahlavi, 190
Istim, Inc. v. Chemical Bank, 797

TABLE OF CASES   **xxix**

Jackson v. Johns–Manville Sales Corp., 721
Jaffrey v. McGough, 916
James v. Grand Trunk Western R. Co., 192, **211**
James v. Powell, 393, **399,** 400
James' Will, In re, 315
Janney's Estate, In re, 553
Jepson v. General Cas. Co. of Wisconsin, 361
Jerguson v. Blue Dot Inv., Inc., 987
Johansen v. Confederation Life Ass'n, 733
John Hancock Mut. Life Ins. Co. v. Yates, 330, 348
Johnson v. Allen, 976
Johnson v. Helicopter & Airplane Services Corp., 985
Johnson v. Hugo's Skateway, 685
Johnson v. Muelberger, 860, 866
Johnson v. Pischke, 426
Johnson Bros. Wholesale Liquor Co. v. Clemmons, 306
Johnston v. Compagnie Generale Transatlantique, 226
Jones, Matter of Estate of, 943
Jones' Estate, In re, 7
Jones, Estate of, 780
Jonnet v. Dollar Sav. Bank of City of New York, 148

Kalb v. Feuerstein, 286
Kamen v. Kemper Financial Services, Inc., 678
Keeton v. Hustler Magazine, Inc., 104 S.Ct. 1473, pp. 75, 76, 78, 101
Keeton v. Hustler Magazine, Inc., 815 F.2d 857, pp. 88, 293
Keeton v. Hustler Magazine, Inc., 549 A.2d 1187, p. 441
Kenney v. Supreme Lodge of the World, L O M, 310, 313
Kentucky Finance Corp. v. Paramount Auto Exch. Corp., 368, 957, 995
Kilberg v. Northeast Airlines, Inc., 396, **503,** 615, 619, 637
Kimbell Foods, Inc., United States v., 717
King v. Sarria, 979
King–Porter Co., In re, 720
Kinney Loan & Finance Co. v. Sumner, 475
Kirkbride v. Hickok, 492
Klaiber v. Frank, 179
Klaxon Co. v. Stentor Electric Mfg. Co., 197, 396, 669, **688,** 690, 699, 726
Klippel v. U–Haul Co. of Northeastern Michigan, 685
Koechlin Et CIE. v. Kestenbaum Brothers, 661
Kohr v. Allegheny Airlines, Inc., 720
Kolendo v. Jerell, Inc., 176
Koon v. Boulder County, Dept. of Social Services, 914
Koplik v. C. P. Trucking Corp., 496
Kopp v. Rechtzigel, 460
Korean Air Lines Disaster of Sept. 1, 1983, In re, 197

Krause v. Krause, 864
Kreindler v. Marx, 995
Kremer v. Chemical Const. Corp., 219, **246,** 248
Kryger v. Wilson, 330, 774
Kubon v. Kubon, 265
Kulko v. Superior Court of California In and For City and County of San Francisco, 63, 64, 69, **902**
Kumar v. Santa Clara County Superior Court, 890

Labree v. Major, 532, 623
Lafayette Ins. Co. v. French, 44
Lake v. Richardson–Merrell, Inc., 190
Laker Airways Ltd. v. Sabena, Belgian World Airlines, 193
Lakeside Bridge & Steel Co. v. Mountain State Construction Co., Inc., 92
Lalli v. Lalli, 884
Lams v. F. H. Smith Co., 572
Landers v. Landers, 460
La Plante v. American Honda Motor Co., Inc., 619
Lauritzen v. Larsen, 648, 651
LaVay Corp. v. Dominion Federal Sav. & Loan Ass'n, 197, 698
Lawrence v. Lawrence, 855
Leary v. Gledhill, 396, 398
Ledesma v. Jack Stewart Produce, Inc., 433
Lee v. Walworth Valve Co., 102
LeForest v. Tolman, 456
Leman v. Krentler–Arnold Hinge Last Co., 232
Lenherr's Estate, In re, 832, 834
Lenn v. Riche, 946
Leo Feist, Inc. v. Debmar Pub. Co., 314
Leszinske v. Poole, 828
Levin v. Gladstein, 296
Levy v. Daniels' U–Drive Auto Renting Co., 499, 500
Levy v. Mutual Life Ins. Co. of N.Y., 416
Levy v. Pyramid Co. of Ithaca, 699
Levy v. Steiger, 408
Liaw Su Teng v. Skaarup Shipping Corp., 190
Lien Ho Hsing Steel Enterprise Co., Ltd. v. Weihtag, 652
Light v. Light, 295
Lilienthal v. Kaufman, 594
Lillegraven v. Tengs, 636
Lindgren's Estate, In re, 866
Linn v. Employers Reinsurance Corp., 467
Lira, United States v., 180
Lisle Mills v. Arkay Infants Wear, 995
Littell v. Nakai, 711
Little Lake Misere Land Co., Inc., United States v., 726
Liverpool & London Life & Fire Ins. Co. v. State of Massachusetts, 986
Locke v. McPherson, 916
Loeb v. Loeb, 870
Loebig v. Larucci, 398
London Finance Co. v. Shattuck, 476
Long v. Pan Am. World Airways, Inc., 615

Louart Corp. v. Arden-Mayfair, Inc., 1005
Loucks v. Standard Oil Co. of New York, 375, 382, 388, 835
Louis–Dreyfus v. Paterson Steamships, 468
Lowe v. Plainfield Trust Co. of Plainfield N.J., 492
Lowell v. Zurich Ins. Co., 685
Lulling v. Barnaby's Family Inns, Inc., 176
Lund's Estate, In re, 884
Lurie, In re Marriage of, 913
Lynde v. Lynde, 21 S.Ct. 555, pp. **229,** 290, **907**
Lynde v. Lynde, 35 A. 641, p. 229
Lynde v. Lynde, 56 N.E. 979, p. 229
Lynn v. Lynn, 870

M., Re, 901
Ma v. Continental Bank N.A., 314
Macey v. Rozbicki, 525
Mack, Matter of Estate of, 258
Macmillan Inc. v. Bishopsgate Investment Trust PLC, 798
Macrete v. Guardian Royal Exchange Plc., 191
Magnolia Petroleum Co. v. Hunt, 219, 251, **266,** 279
Mahaffey v. Bechtel Associates Professional Corp., D.C., 214
Mallory Associates, Inc. v. Barving Realty Co., Inc., 773
Malone By and Through Alexander v. Jackson, 433
Maner v. Maner, 290
Manetti–Farrow, Inc. v. Gucci America, Inc., 177
Manley v. Engram, 197
Mansfield Hardwood Lumber Co. v. Johnson, 999
Marathon Enterprises, Inc. v. Feinberg, 712
Marchlik v. Coronet Ins. Co., 407
Marcus v. Marcus, 31
Marek v. Flemming, 829
Mareva Cia Naviera SA v. International Bulk Carriers SA, 147
Marie v. Garrison, 638
Marina Associates v. Barton, 386
Marrese v. American Academy of Orthopaedic Surgeons, 105 S.Ct. 1327, p. **248**
Marrese v. American Academy of Orthopaedic Surgeons, 628 F.Supp. 918, p. 250
Marriage of (see name of party)
Marris v. Sockey, 878
Marshall v. Murgatroyd, 12
Martin v. Better Taste Popcorn Co., 128
Martyne v. American Union Fire Ins. Co. of Philadelphia, 963
Maryland Cas. Co. v. Jacek, 637
Marzano, United States v., 180
Mason v. Homer, 916
Maspons Y Hermano v. Mildred, 975
Massie v. Watts, 125
Mastrobuono v. Shearson Lehman Hutton, Inc., 576

Matanuska Val. Lines, Inc. v. Molitor, 232
Matter of (see name of party)
Matusevitch v. Telnikoff, 314
Maxwell Shapiro Woolen Co. v. Amerotron Corp., 654
May v. Anderson, 887
Mayfield, State ex rel. Southern Ry. Co. v., 205
May's Estate, In re, 821, 824, 828, 834
McCabe v. Great Pacific Century Corp., 485
McCarty v. McCarty, 921
McCluney v. Joseph Schlitz Brewing Co., 362
McCord v. Jet Spray Intern. Corp., 227
McCornick & Co. v. Tolmie Bros., 661
McDermott Inc. v. Lewis, 999
McDonald v. Mabee, 41
McDougal's Will, In re, 764
McElmoyle, for Use of Bailey v. Cohen, 307, 314
McGee v. International Life Ins. Co., 53, 55
McGee v. Riekhof, 91
McGowan v. University of Scranton, 685
McKnett v. St. Louis & S.F. Ry. Co., 205, 321
McNeal v. State Farm Mut. Auto. Ins. Co., 407
McSwain v. McSwain, 497
Meekins v. Meekins, 883
Meisenhelder v. Chicago & N. W. Ry. Co., 711, 832
Mellk v. Sarahson, 524
Mendez v. Bowie, 228
Mendoza, United States v., 252
Mennonite Bd. of Missions v. Adams, 167
Mercier v. John Hancock Mut. Life Ins. Co., 973
Merritt Dredging Co., Inc., In re, 543
Mertz v. Mertz, 254, **379,** 382, 388, 407
Metcalf v. City of Watertown, 219
MGM Desert Inn, Inc. v. Holz, 387
Michigan Trust Co. v. Ferry, 122
Mieyr v. Federal Surety Co. of Davenport, Iowa, 966
Migra v. Warren City School Dist. Bd. of Educ., 250
Milanovich v. Costa Crociere, S.p.A., 576
Miller v. Miller, 441 N.Y.S.2d 339, p. 126
Miller v. Miller, 290 N.Y.S.2d 734, pp. **610,** 615, 619
Miller v. United States Fidelity & Guaranty Co., 17
Milliken v. Meyer, 42, 43, 280
Milliken v. Pratt, 464, 984
Milmoe v. Toomey, 935
Milwaukee, City of v. Illinois and Michigan, 726
Milwaukee County v. M.E. White Co., 308, 389, 705
Miner v. Gillette Co., 624
Minichiello v. Rosenberg, 156
Minton v. McManus, 900
Miree v. DeKalb County, Ga., 725, 726
Missouri ex rel. Southern Ry. Co., State of v. Mayfield, 205, 321
Mitchell v. Craft, 515

Mitchell v. W. T. Grant Co., 133
Mitsubishi Motors Corp. v. Soler Chrysler–Plymouth, Inc., 172, 659
Moatly v. Zagha, 877
Mondou v. New York, N.H. & H.R. Co., 204, 321
Moore v. Livingston, 764
Moore v. Moore, 914
Morgan v. Bisorni, 640
Morris v. Jones, 958, 962
Morson v. Second Nat. Bank of Boston, 814
Moses H. Cone Memorial Hosp. v. Mercury Const. Corp., 686
Mott v. Duncan Petroleum Trans., 825
Moyer v. Citicorp Homeowners, Inc., 576
Moyer v. Van–Dye–Way Corp., 654
M/S Bremen v. Zapata Off–Shore Co., 169, 172, 549
Mullane v. Central Hanover Bank & Trust Co., 47, 125, **160,** 166, 280, **813,** 843
Munley v. Second Judicial Dist. Court of State In and For County of Washoe, 175
Munzer v. Dame Munzer-Jacooby, 224
Musgrave v. HCA Mideast, Ltd., 549
Mutual Life Ins. Co. of New York v. Liebing, 332, 335
Muzingo v. Vaught, 432
My Bread Baking Co. v. Cumberland Farms, Inc., 104

Naphtali v. Lafazan, 460
Nash v. Benari, 953
NASL Marketing, Inc. v. de Vries, 181
National Equipment Rental, Limited v. Szukhent, 44
National Shawmut Bank of Boston v. Cumming, 803
Nedlloyd Lines B.V. v. Superior Court of San Mateo County (Seawinds Ltd.), 549
Nelson v. Eckert, 422, 453, 495
Nelson v. Miller, 65
Nelson by Carson v. Park Industries, Inc., 87
Neporany v. Kir, 313
Netherlands Shipmortgage Corp., Ltd. v. Madias, 989
Neumeier v. Kuehner, 525, 531, 532, 615, 619, 623
Nevada v. Hall, 211, 348
Nevarez v. Bailon, 835
Newcomb's Estate, In re, 15
New England Mut. Life Ins. Co. v. Spence, 653
New York, City of v. Exxon Corp., 192
New York, City of v. Shapiro, 279, 309
New York Life Ins. Co. v. Dodge, 330
New York Life Ins. Co. v. Dunlevy, 123, **133**
New York Times Co. v. Sullivan, 749
New York Trust Co., Matter of, 813
Nicol v. Tanner, 225
Nieves v. American Airlines, 195

Noe v. United States Fidelity & Guaranty Co., 403
Nordberg Division of Rex Chainbelt Inc. v. Hudson Engineering Corp., 92
Norkan Lodge Co. Ltd. v. Gillum, 225, 313
North Carolina Land & Lumber Co. v. Boyer, 130
Northern Aircraft, Inc. v. Reed, 65
North Georgia Finishing, Inc. v. Di–Chem, Inc., 133
Norwood v. Kirkpatrick, 194
Nowell v. Nowell, 290

O'Connor v. Lee–Hy Paving Corp., 648
O'Connor v. O'Connor, 640
O'Connor's Estate, In re, 926
Offshore Rental Co., Inc. v. Continental Oil Co., 605
Ohio, Dept. of Taxation, State of v. Kleitch Bros., Inc., 309
Ohlquist v. Nordstrom, 123
Oil Shipping (Bunkering) B.V. v. Sonmez Denizcilik Ve Ticaret A.S., 797
Oil Spill by Amoco Cadiz off Coast of France on March 16, 1978, In re, 104
Okl. Tax Commission, State ex rel. v. Rodgers, 389
Olah, People v., 452, 453, 513
Olberding v. Illinois Cent. R. Co., 45
Oltarsh v. Aetna Ins. Co., 407
Olympic Corp. v. Societe Generale, 189
O'Melveny & Myers v. F.D.I.C., 716, 726
Ommang's Estate, In re, 829
Omni Aircraft Sales, Inc. v. Actividades Aereas Aragonesas, 146
Omni Capital Intern. v. Rudolf Wolff & Co., Ltd., 88, 89
Opperman v. Sullivan, 914
Order of United Commercial Travelers of America v. Wolfe, 333, 335, 362
Oregon, United States v., 373
Owen v. Owen, 881

Pacific Employers Ins. Co. v. Industrial Accident Commission of State of California, 336, 340
Pacific Employers Ins. Co. v. M/V Capt. W.D. Cargill, 190
Padula v. Lilarn Properties Corp., 524
Pahmer v. Hertz Corp., 453
Pain v. United Technologies Corp., 189
Palmer v. Ford Motor Co., 678
Palmer v. Hoffman, 673
Palmisano v. News Syndicate Co., 635
Panama Processes, S. A. v. Cities Service Co., 189
Pan–American Life Ins. Co. v. Recio, 740
Paris Air Crash of March 3, 1974, In re, 197, 624
Parklane Hosiery Co., Inc. v. Shore, 252
Parsons Steel, Inc. v. First Alabama Bank, 250

Parsons & Whittemore Overseas Co., Inc. v. Societe Generale De L'Industrie Du Papier (RAKTA), 656
Pate v. Stout, 890
Paul v. Virginia, 983
Paulo v. Bepex Corp., 604
Paulson v. Forest City Community School Dist. in Winnebago, 30
Pazzi v. Taylor, 885
Peabody v. Hamilton, 41
Pearson v. Northeast Airlines, Inc., 210, 211, 505
Pelle v. Pelle, 860
Pemberton v. Hughes, 159
Pendleton v. Russell, 962
Penn v. Lord Baltimore, 125
Pennoyer v. Neff, 41, 45, 47, 77, 78, 280
Pensacola Tel. Co. v. Western Union Tel. Co., 985
People v. _____ (see opposing party)
People of State of N.Y. ex rel. Halvey v. Halvey, 890
Perkins v. Benguet Consol. Min. Co., 53, 93, 103, 121
Petersen v. Petersen, 910
Pettus v. American Airlines, Inc., 278, 279
Peugeot Motors of America, Inc. v. Eastern Auto Distributors, Inc., 573
Pfaff v. Chrysler Corp., 193
Pfau v. Trent Aluminum Co., 446
Philadelphia, City of v. Austin, 302
Philip Carey Mfg. Co. v. Taylor, 195
Phillips v. Phillips, 257
Phillips Petroleum Co. v. Shutts, 241, 362, 673, 699, 726
Phrantzes v. Argenti, 204
Pine v. Eli Lilly & Co., 425
Pink v. A.A.A. Highway Exp., 334, 968
Piper Aircraft Co. v. Reyno, 104, 184, 185, 186, 190, 622, 686
Planters Mfg. Co. v. Protection Mut. Ins. Co., 678
Poitra v. Demarrias, 711
Pollard, Ex parte, 772
Polson v. Stewart, 505, 770, 774
Porisini v. Petricca, 313
Porter v. Groat, 698
Presley's Estate, In re, 884
Pritchard v. Norton, 470
Proctor v. Frost, 768, 769
Purcell v. Kapelski, 497

Quarty v. Insurance Co. of North America, 348
Quenzer v. Quenzer, 891
Quill Corp. v. North Dakota By and Through Heitkamp, 367
Quilloin v. Walcott, 886

Ragan v. Merchants Transfer & Warehouse Co., 673
Ramey v. Rockefeller, 29
Randall v. Randall, 824, 829
Red Fox, Matter of Marriage of, 835
Red Sea Insurance Co. v. Bouygues SA, 533
Redwing Carriers, Inc. v. Foster, 176
Reed v. Allen, 316
Reed v. General Motors Corp., 678
Reich v. Purcell, 459, 606, 612
Reiersen v. Commissioner of Revenue, 32
Relfe v. Rundle, 966
Remington Products Corp. v. American Aerovap, Inc., 192
Renard's Estate, Matter of, 19
Republic of Haiti v. Duvalier, 147
Rescildo by Rescildo v. R.H. Macy's, 433
Resolution Trust Corp. v. Northpark Joint Venture, 769
Reyno v. Piper Aircraft Co., 621
Reynoldsville Casket Co. v. Hyde, 374, 432
Rhode Island Hospital Trust Co. v. Hopkins, 884
Rice v. Dow Chemical Co., 620
Rice v. Rice, 855
Richards v. United States, 446, 711
Richardson v. Mellish, 386
Riederer, State v., 205
Riggle's Estate, In re, 937
Riley v. New York Trust Co., 242, 251, 939
Rindal v. Seckler Co. Inc., 177
Ritchie v. McMullen, 224
Riverside & Dan River Cotton Mills v. Menefee, 111
Robbins v. Chamberlain, 29
Robertson v. Collings, 914
Roboz v. Kennedy, 28
Roche v. McDonald, 305
Rodgers, State ex rel. Okl. Tax Commission v., 389
Rodriguez De Quijas v. Shearson/American Exp., Inc., 172
Rodriguez-Diaz v. Sierra-Martinez, 20
Roecker v. United States, 712
Rogers v. U-Haul Co., 531
Rolls Royce (Canada), Ltd. v. Cayman Airways, Ltd., 189
Romero v. International Terminal Operating Co., 651
Romero v. State Farm Mut. Auto. Ins. Co., 407
Rong Yao Zhou v. Jennifer Mall Restaurant, Inc., 604
Rosenberg Bros. & Co. v. Curtis Brown Co., 101, 102
Rosenstiel v. Rosenstiel, 875
Rosenthal v. Warren, 475 F.2d 438, pp. **613,** 619
Rosenthal v. Warren, 374 F.Supp. 522, p. 619
Ross v. Colorado Outward Bound School, Inc., 198, 699
Ross v. Ostrander, 313
Ross v. Ross, 914
Rossano v. Manufacturers' Life Assurance Co., 740
Royal Bank of Canada v. Trentham Corp., 225

TABLE OF CASES   **xxxiii**

Royal Bed and Spring Co., Inc. v. Famossul Industria e Comercio de Moveis Ltda., 687
Rozan v. Rozan, 129 N.W.2d 694, p. 919
Rozan v. Rozan, 317 P.2d 11, p. **916**
Rubin v. Irving Trust Co., 570
Rubinfeld v. Bahama Cruise Line, Inc., 987
Rudow v. Fogel, 549
Rush v. Savchuk, 148, 156, 330, 345, 870
R.V. Secretary of State for the Home Dep't. ex parte Raham, 835
Rydder v. Rydder, 901
Rzeszotarski v. Rzeszotarski, 28

Sable Corp. v. Dual Office Suppliers, Inc., 995
Sadler v. NCR Corp., 1011
Saiken, People v., 417
Salve Regina College v. Russell, 686
Sampson v. Channell, 687
Samuelson v. Susen, 412, 700
Sanders v. Armour Fertilizer Works, 135
San Juan Dupont Plaza Hotel Fire Litigation, In re, 699
Sanson v. Sanson, 915
Santovenia v. Confederation Life Ass'n, 740
Sasse v. Sasse, 31
Satchwill v. Vollrath Co., 515
Saul v. His Creditors, 916
Sawyer v. Slack, 881
Scanapico v. Richmond, F. & P. R. Co., 217
Scheer v. Rockne Motors Corporation, 973
Scheiner v. Wallace, 314
Scherk v. Alberto–Culver Co., 172
Schibsby v. Westenholz, 35, 36, 280, 312
Schlobohm v. Schapiro, 181
Schmidt v. Driscoll Hotel, Inc., 506, 604
Schneider v. Nichols, 515
Schneider, Gilbert, Matter of, v. Burnstine, 727
Schneider's Estate, In re, 446, **765**
Schreiber v. Kellogg, 232
Schroeder v. City of New York, 167
Schultz v. Boy Scouts of America, Inc., 554
Sea–Gate Tire & Rubber Co. v. Moseley, 130
Seattle Case, 746
Second Bank-State Street Trust Co. v. Weston, 818
Seeman v. Philadelphia Warehouse Co., 472
Seetransport Wiking Trader Schiffartgesellschaft, MBH & Co. v. Navimpex Centrala Navala, 314
Seider v. Roth, 937
Selover, Bates & Co. v. Walsh, 773
Semler v. Psychiatric Institute of Washington, D. C., Inc., 273
Seren v. Douglas, 28
Severnoe Securities Corporation v. London & Lancashire Ins. Co., 131
Sewart, In re, 818
Shaffer v. Heitner, 36, 120, 133, **136,** 145, 146, 147, 148, 216, 238, 330, 851, 890
Shanahan v. George B. Landers Const. Co., 790, 793

Shannon v. Irving Trust Co., 801
Shapiro v. Shapiro, 877
Shapiro & Son Curtain Corp. v. Glass, 181
Sharp v. Johnson, 460
Shasta Livestock Auction Yard, Inc. v. Bill Evans Cattle Management Corp., 975
Shell UK v. Andrew Innes, 191
Shelley's Case, 817
Sherrer v. Sherrer, 286, **856,** 860, 866, 876
Shevill v. Presse Alliance S.A., 65, 75, 441
Shingleton v. Bussey, 407
Shippy, In re Estate of, 824
Shoup v. Bell & Howell Co., 254
Shun T. Takahashi's Estate, In re, 835
Shute v. Carnival Cruise Lines, 175
Sibaja v. Dow Chemical Co., 190, 687
Siegelman v. Cunard White Star Limited, 478
Siegmann v. Meyer, 456
Silliman, United States v., 251
Silver v. Garcia, 346
Simler v. Conner, 678
Simmons v. City of Philadelphia, 685
Simons v. Miami Beach First Nat. Bank, 870, **871**
Sinclair v. Sinclair, 485
Sioux Remedy Co. v. Cope, 215, 985, **993**
Sivnksty, State ex rel. v. Duffield, 179
Skiriotes v. Florida, 42, 374
Slade v. Slade, 31
Slater v. Mexican Nat. R. Co., 201, 449, 498, 568, 727
Slattery v. Hartford–Connecticut Trust Co., 885
Smith v. Ingram, 769
Smith v. ODECO (UK), Inc., 430
Smith v. Smith, 647 P.2d 722, p. 913
Smith v. Smith, 270 P.2d 613, p. 914
Sniadach v. Family Finance Corp. of Bay View, 133
Societe Nationale Industrielle Aerospatiale v. United States Dist. Court for Southern Dist. of Iowa, 200, 744
Somportex Limited v. Philadelphia Chewing Gum Corp., 225, 227
Sorenson v. De vennootshap ... Aramco Overseas Co., 546
Sorenson v. Sorenson, 279
Sosna v. Iowa, 843
Southern Milk Sales, Inc. v. Martin, 685
Southern Ry. Co., State ex rel. v. Mayfield, 205
Southland Corp. v. Keating, 655
Sovereign Camp, W.O.W. v. Bolin, 238, 334
Spatz v. Nascone, 177
Spiegel, Inc. v. F.T.C., 55
Spiliada Maritime Corp. v. Cansulex Ltd. (The Spiliada), 191
Staedler v. Staedler, 860
Stambaugh v. Stambaugh, 870
Standard Oil Co. of Cal., United States v., 720
Stanford v. Utley, 232
Starkowski v. Attorney General, 825

Table of Cases

State v. ———— (see opposing party)
State by Furman v. Amsted Industries, 373
State ex rel. v. ———— (see opposing party and relator)
State of (see name of state)
State Tax Commission of Utah v. Aldrich, 15
Steele v. Bulova Watch Co., 374
Stentor Elec Mfg Co v. Klaxon Co, 690
Stephanie M., In re, 900
Stewart Organization, Inc. v. Ricoh Corp., 176, 177, 190, 195
Stifel v. Hopkins, 31
Stiller v. Hardman, 232
St. Joseph's Hosp. and Medical Center v. Maricopa County, 28
Stoll v. Gottlieb, 219
Stone v. Gibson Refrigerator Sales Corp., 985
Stone v. Southern Illinois & Missouri Bridge Co., 996
Stoner v. New York Life Ins. Co., 678
Stout v. Pate, 890
Stovall v. Price Waterhouse Co., 253
Sugg v. Thornton, 112
Sumitomo Shoji America, Inc. v. Avagliano, 987
Sun Oil Co. v. Guidry, 776
Sun Oil Co. v. Wortman, 434, 620, 672, 673, 694
Supreme Council of the Royal Arcanum v. Green, 334
Supreme Court of New Hampshire v. Piper, 368
Sutton v. Leib, 289, 881
Swank v. Hufnagle, 767, 769
Swarb v. Lennox, 44, 178
Swift v. Tyson, 663
Syndicate 420 at Lloyd's London v. Early American Ins. Co., 189
Szantay v. Beech Aircraft Corp., 710

Tal v. Tal, 877
Tallmadge, In re, 445
Tarango v. Pastrana, 91
Tardiff v. Bank Line, Ltd., 45
Tatro v. Manor Care, Inc., 175
Taylor v. Barron, 279
Teas v. Kimball, 977
Tel–Phonic Services, Inc. v. TBS Intern., Inc., 699
Tennessee Coal, Iron & R. Co. v. George, 207, **208,** 210, 407
Terlizzi v. Brodie, 179
Terral v. Burke Const. Co., 985
Testa v. Katt, 205, 321
Tex., State of v. Pankey, 726
Texas, State of v. Florida, 15
Texas, State of v. New Jersey, 12, 372
The Abidin Daver, 190
Theye Y Ajuria v. Pan Am. Life Ins. Co., 740
Thomas v. Hanmer, 640
Thomas v. Washington Gas Light Co., 273
Thompson v. Thompson, 108 S.Ct. 513, p. 899

Thompson v. Thompson, 645 S.W.2d 79, p. 265
Thompson v. Whitman, 156, 283
Thomson v. Kyle, 505, 768, 769, 772
Thornton v. Cessna Aircraft Co., 418
Thornton's Estate, In re, 932
Tice v. E. I. Du Pont De Nemours & Co., 495
Tiernan v. Westext Transport, Inc., 515
Tischendorf v. Tischendorf, 901
Titus v. Wallick, 310
Tjepkema v. Kenney, 620
Toledo Soc. for Crippled Children v. Hickok, 487, 505
Toler v. Oakwood Smokeless Coal Corporation, 834
Toll v. Moreno, 102 S.Ct. 2977, p. 28
Toll v. Moreno, 397 A.2d 1009, p. 29
Tomlin v. Boeing Co., 426
Tooker v. Lopez, 525, 615, 644
Torlonia v. Torlonia, 33, 451
Toronto–Dominion Bank v. Hall, 227
Toscanino, United States v., 500 F.2d 267, p. 180
Toscanino, United States v., 398 F.Supp. 916, p. 180
Towley v. King Arthur Rings, Inc., 531
Trailways, Inc. v. Clark, 2, 566
Travelers Indem. Co. v. Lake, 5
Travelers Ins. Co. v. Fields, 654, 815
Treinies v. Sunshine Mining Co., 281, 283, **286,** 289, 316
Trimble v. Gordon, 12, 884
Trionics Research Sales Corp. v. Nautec Corp., 231
Truitt, State ex rel. v. District Court of Ninth Judicial Dist., Curry County, 128
Trzecki v. Gruenewald, 430
Tube Turns Division of Chemetron Corp. v. Patterson Co., Inc., 92
Tulsa Professional Collection Services, Inc. v. Pope, 167
Turner Entertainment Co. v. Degeto Film GmbH, 193
Twohy v. First Nat. Bank of Chicago, 549
Tyler v. Judges of the Court of Registration, 125

Udny v. Udny, 11
Union Brokerage Co. v. Jensen, 215, 985, **993**
Union Carbide Corp. v. Union of India, 189
Union Carbide Corp. Gas Plant Disaster at Bhopal, India in Dec., 1984., In re, 809 F.2d 195, p. **186**
Union Carbide Corp. Gas Plant Disaster at Bhopal, India in December, 1984, In re, 634 F.Supp. 842, p. **185**
Union Nat. Bank of Chicago v. Chapman, 467
Union Nat. Bank of Wichita, Kan. v. Lamb, 306
United Air Lines, Inc., United States v., 252
United Elec., Radio and Mach. Workers of America v. 163 Pleasant Street Corp., 110

TABLE OF CASES xxxv

United Mine Workers of America Employee Ben. Plans Litigation, In re, 700
United Rope Distributors, Inc. v. Kimberly Line, 102
United Royalty Co., State v., 986
United States v. ——— (see opposing party)
United States Brewers Ass'n, Inc. v. Healy, 373
United States ex rel. v. ——— (see opposing party and relator)
United States Financial Securities Litigation, In re, 624
United States for Use and Benefit of Hi-Way Elec. Co. v. Home Indem. Co., 232
University of Chicago v. Dater, 502

Vacu-Maid, Inc. v. Covington, 92
VanBibber v. Hartford Acc. & Indem. Ins. Co., 408
Vancouver case, 746
Vanderbilt v. Vanderbilt, 870
Van Dusen v. Barrack, 196, 621
VanDyck v. VanDyck, 191
Vanston Bondholders Protective Committee v. Green, 720
Vargas v. M/V Mini Lama, 189
Varkonyi v. S. A. Empresa De Viacao Airea Rio Grandense (Varig), 190
Varone v. Varone, 258
Vause v. Vause, 900
Vaz Borralho v. Keydril Co., 189
Vencedor Mfg. Co., Inc. v. Gougler Industries, Inc., 92
Vermeulen v. Renault, U.S.A., Inc., 985 F.2d 1534, p. 110
Vermeulen v. Renault, U.S.A., Inc., 975 F.2d 746, p. 110
Vermeulen v. Renault U.S.A., Inc., 965 F.2d 1014, p. 110
Vervaeke v. Smith, 876
Victor v. Sperry, 456
Viking Penguin, Inc. v. Janklow, 181
Vimar Seguros y Reaseguros, S.A. v. M/V Sky Reefer, 177
Vincenza v. Vincenza, 914
Volkswagenwerk Aktiengesellschaft v. Schlunk, 104, 105, 110, 744
Volt Information Sciences, Inc. v. Board of Trustees of Leland Stanford Junior University, 576
Voth v. Milandra Flour Mills, 191

Waitus, State v., 180
Walker v. Armco Steel Corp., 673, 683, 684
Walker v. City of Hutchinson, Kan., 167
Walton v. Arabian American Oil Company, 393, 727
Warner v. Buffalo Drydock Co., 253, 254, 382
Warner's Estate, In re, 919
Warren v. Foster, 885
Wartell v. Formusa, 497

Washington ex rel. Gibson, State of v. Gibson, 913
Waterside Ocean Nav. Co., Inc. v. International Nav. Ltd., 748
Watkins v. Conway, 307
Watson v. Employers Liability Assur. Corp., 156, **343,** 345
Watson v. Merrell Dow Pharmaceuticals, Inc., 190
Watts, Estate of, 884
Watts v. Swiss Bank Corp., 398
Webb v. Rodgers Machinery Mfg. Co., 1012
Webb v. Zurich Ins. Co., 407
Weber v. Superior Court of Los Angeles County, 871
Weber v. Weber, 864
Weede, State ex rel. v. Bechtel, 1003
Weesner v. Weesner, 201, 258
Weidman v. Weidman, 311
Weiss v. Routh, 687
Weissman v. Banque De Bruxelles, 662
Wells v. Simonds Abrasive Co., 320, 321, 335
Wenche Siemer v. Learjet Acquisition Corp., 121
Wendelken v. Superior Court In and For Pima County, 553
Wernwag v. Pawling, 279
West American Ins. Co. v. Westin, Inc., 507
Western Air Lines, Inc. v. Sobieski, 1001, 1003
Westinghouse Elec. Corp. Uranium Contracts Litigation, In re, 200
Weston Banking Corp. v. Turkiye Garanti Bankasi, A.S., 743
Whealton v. Whealton, 878
Wheat v. Wheat, 842
Wheeling Steel Corp. v. Glander, 985
Whirlpool Corp. v. Ritter, 692
White v. Tennant, 11, 13, 780
White v. United States, 818
White v. White, 524
WHYY, Inc. v. Borough of Glassboro, 985
Wiener v. Specific Pharmaceuticals, 950
Wierbinski v. State Farm Mut. Auto. Ins. Co., 641
Wilburn Boat Co. v. Fireman's Fund Ins. Co., 651
Wilkins v. Ellett, 941
Wilkins v. Zelichowski, 825, 880
Wilkinson v. Manpower, Inc., 382
Williams v. Curtiss-Wright Corp., 744
Williams v. State of North Carolina, 65 S.Ct. 1092, p. 842
Williams v. State of North Carolina, 63 S.Ct. 207, pp. **847, 851,** 863
Williams v. Williams, 328 F.Supp. 1380, p. 28
Williams v. Williams, 390 A.2d 4, p. 553
Wilmington Trust Co. v. Wilmington Trust Co., 804
Wilson v. Faull, 645, 648
Wilson v. Humphreys (Cayman) Ltd., 175
Wilson v. Louisiana-Pacific Resources, Inc., 1003
Wilson v. Nooter Corp., 678

Wilton v. Seven Falls Co., 686
Winkworth v. Christie, Manson and Woods, Ltd., 786
Wisemantle v. Hull Enterprises, Inc., 954
Wong v. Tenneco, Inc., 387
Wood v. Mid–Valley Inc., 690
Wood v. Wood, 2 All E.R. 14, p. 871
Wood v. Wood, 262 N.Y.S.2d 86, p. 875
Woods v. Interstate Realty Co., 673, 995
Woods–Tucker Leasing Corp. of Georgia v. Hutcheson–Ingram Development Co., 719
Woolery v. Metropolitan Life Ins. Co., 825
World–Wide Volkswagen Corp. v. Woodson, 66, 75, 78, 101, 102, 119, 507
Worthley v. Worthley, 293, 295, 907, **907,** 911
Wratchford v. S. J. Groves & Sons Co., 678
Wright, Matter of Estate of, 446
Wright v. Armwood, 977
Wright v. Yackley, 90
W. U. Tel. Co. v. Com. of Pa., by Gottlieb, 371

Wyatt v. Fulrath, 921

Yarborough v. Yarborough, 259, 748, **907**
Yohannon v. Keene Corp., 690
Young v. Fulton Iron Works Co., 1012
Young v. Masci, 972, 973
Youngstown Sheet & Tube Co. v. Westcott, 661
Youpe v. Strasser, 181
Youssoupoff v. Widener, 781

Z. v. Z., 877
Zacharakis v. Bunker Hill Mut. Ins. Co., 55
Zandman v. Joseph, 624
Zelinger v. State Sand & Gravel Co., 497
Zietz' Estate, In re, 446
Zschernig v. Miller, 727
Zuck v. Interstate Pub. Corp., 634
Zurich Ins. Co. v. Shearson Lehman Hutton, Inc., 386
Zurzola v. General Motors Corp., 497

TABLE OF BOOKS AND ARTICLES

References are to Pages

Adams, The 1972 Official Text of the Uniform Commercial Code: Analysis of Conflict of Laws Provision, 45 Miss.L.J. 281 (1974), 795

Adams and Adams, Ethical Problems in Advising Migratory Divorce, 16 Hastings L.J. 60 (1964), 855

Aksen, American Arbitration Accession Arrives in the Age of Aquarius, 3 Sw. U.L.Rev. 1 (1971), 656

Alexander, The Application and Avoidance of Foreign Law in the Law of Conflicts, 70 Nw.L.Rev. 602 (1975), 396

Andersen, OECD Mutual Assistance Convention to Amplify Members' Tax Treaties, 1 J. Int'l Tax'n 252 (1990), 390

Anderson, Transnational Litigation Involving Mexican Parties, 25 St. Mary's L.J. 1059 (1994), 2

Annotation, 8 A.L.R.2d 1185 (1949), 1003

Annotation, 28 A.L.R.Fed. 685 (1976), 180

Annotation, 100 A.L.R.3d 792, pp. 227, 234, 312

Annotation, Court–Authorized Permanent or Temporary Removal of Child by Parent to Foreign Country, 30 A.L.R.4th 548 (1984), 901

Annotation, Power of Divorce Court to Deal with Real Property Located in Another State, 34 A.L.R.3d 962 (1970), 126

Annotation, Questions as to Convenience and Justice of Transfer under Forum Non Conveniens Provision of 28 U.S.C.A. § 1404(a), 1 A.L.R. Fed. 15 (1969), 195

Baade, article by, Symposium, 1 Hofstra L.Rev. 104 (1973), 532

Baade, Interstate and Foreign Adoptions in North Carolina, 40 N.C.L.Rev. 691 (1962), 886

Baade, Marriage and Divorce in American Conflicts of Law, 72 Colum.L.Rev. 329 (1972), 822

Bailey, Conflict of Laws in the Law of Bank Checks, 80 Banking L.J. 404 (1963), 661

Baron, Federal Preemption in the Resolution of Child Custody Jurisdiction Disputes, 45 Ark.L.Rev. 885 (1993), 899

Basedow, Conflicts of Economic Regulation, 42 Am.J.Comp.L. 423 (1994), 1000

Batiffol & Lagarde, Traité de droit international privé, vol. 2, 593 (7th ed. 1983), 224

Baxter, Choice of Law and The Federal System, 16 Stan.L.Rev. 1 (1963), 690, 692

Beale, A Treatise on the Conflict of Laws 1929 (1935), 450

Beale, Conflict of Laws, sec. 102.1 (1935), 130

Berger and Lipstadt, Women in Judaism from the Perspective of Human Rights, in: Witte and Van der Vyver (eds.), Religious Human Rights in Global Perspective 295 (1995), 877

Bianca & Bonnell, eds., Commentary on the International Sales Law (1987), 547

Bisignaro, Intercountry Adoption Today and the Implications of the 1993 Hague Convention on Tomorrow, 13 Dick.J.Int'l L. 123 (1994), 886

Blumberg, The Corporate Personality in American Law, 38 Am.J.Comp.L. 49 (Supp. 1990), 104

Bodenheimer, Interstate Custody: Initial Jurisdiction and Continuing Jurisdiction Under the UCCJA, 14 Fam.L.Q. 203 (1981), 900

Bodenheimer, Progress Under the Uniform Child Custody Jurisdiction Act and Remaining Problems: Punitive Decrees, Joint Custody, and Excessive Modifications, 65 Calif.L.Rev. 978 (1977), 900

Bodenheimer, The Rights of Children and The Crisis in Custody Litigation, 46 Colo. L.Rev. 495 (1975), 900

Bodenheimer, The Uniform Child Custody Jurisdiction Act: A Legislative Remedy for Children Caught in the Conflict of Laws, 22 Vand.L.Rev. 1207 (1969), 900

Booth, Recognition of Foreign Bankruptcies: An analysis and Critique of the Inconsistent Approaches of United States Courts, 66 Am.Bank.L.J. 135 (1992), 958

Borchers, contribution by, Symposium, Fifty Years of *International Shoe:* The Past and Future of Personal Jurisdiction, 28 U.C.Davis L.Rev. 513 (1995), 53

Borchers, Forum Selection Agreements in the Federal Courts After *Carnival Cruise:* A

Proposal for Congressional Reform, 67 Wash.L.Rev. 55 (1992), 177

Borchers, The Death of Constitutional Law of Personal Jurisdiction: From *Pennoyer* to *Burnham* and Back Again, 24 U.C.Davis L.Rev. 19 (1990), 47

Borchers, The Return of Territorialism to New York's Conflict Law: Padula v. Lilarn Properties Corp., 58 Albany L.Rev. 775 (1995), 524

Borm–Reid, Recognition and Enforcement of Foreign Judgments, 3 Int'l & Comp.L.Q. 49 (1954), 228

Born, A Reappraisal of the Extraterritorial Reach of U.S. Law, 24 Law & Policy in Int'l Business 1 (1992), 755

Boyd, Constitutional, Treaty, and Statutory Requirement of Probate Notice to Consuls and Aliens, 47 Iowa L.Rev. 29 (1961), 937

Boyd, Consular Functions in Connection with Decedents' Estates, 47 Iowa L.Rev. 823 (1962), 937

Boyd, The Administration in the United States of Alien Connected Decedents' Estates, 2 Int.Law 601 (1968), 938

Brand, Enforcement of Foreign Money–Judgments in the United States: In Search of Uniformity and International Acceptance, 67 Notre Dame L.Rev. 253 (1991), 227, 234, 312

Brand, Enforcement of Judgments in the United States and Europe, 13 Journal of Law and Commerce 193 (1994), 227, 234, 312

Bright, Permitting a Non–Resident to Choose a Place of Probate, 95 Trusts and Estates 865 (1956), 780

Brilmayer, Conflict of Laws: Foundations and Future Directions 107 (1991), 620

Brilmayer, contribution by, Symposium: The Future of Personal Jurisdiction, 22 Rutgers L.J. 559 (1991), 121

Brilmayer, How Contacts Count: Due Process Limitations on State Court Jurisdiction, 1980 Supreme Court Review 77, pp. 89, 103, 155

Brilmayer, Interest Analysis and the Myth of Legislative Intent, 78 Mich.L.Rev. 392 (1980), 514

Brilmayer, Related Contacts and Personal Jurisdiction, 101 Harv.L.Rev. 1444 (1988), 89, 103

Brilmayer and Underhill, Congressional Obligation to Provide a Forum for Constitutional Claims: Discriminatory Jurisdictional Rules and the Conflict of Laws, 39 Va.L.Rev. 819 (1983), 205

Brockelbank, Interstate Enforcement of Family Support (The Runaway Pappy Act) (2d ed. Infausto 1971), 912, 913

Brockelbank, Is the Uniform Reciprocal Enforcement of Support Act Constitutional?, 17 Mo.L.Rev. 1 (1952), 914

Brockelbank, The Problem of Family Support: A New Uniform Act Offers a Solution, 37 A.B.A.J. 93 (1951), 912

Broyde, The New York State Jewish Divorce Law, 30 Tradition: A Journal of Jewish Thought ___ (1995), 877

Bruch, contribution by, Symposium, Fifty Years of *International Shoe:* The Past and Future of Personal Jurisdiction, 28 U.C.Davis L.Rev. 513 (1995), 53

Bruch, Interstate Child Custody Law and Eicke, 16 Fam.L.Q. 277 (1982), 899

Buchschacher, Rights of a Surviving Spouse in Texas in Marital Property Acquired While Domiciled Elsewhere, 45 Tex.L.Rev. 321 (1966), 933

Burbank, Interjurisdictional Preclusion, Full Faith and Credit and Federal Common Law: A General Approach, 71 Cornell L.Rev. 733 (1986), 250

Caballero, A Reexamination of Mexican "Quickie" Divorces, 4 Int.Lawyer 871 (1970), 875

Cameron/Johnson, contribution by, Symposium, Fifty Years of *International Shoe:* The Past and Future of Personal Jurisdiction, 28 U.C.Davis L.Rev. 513 (1995), 53

Carbonneau, The Exuberant Pathway to Quixotic Internationalism: Assessing the Folly of Mitsubishi, 19 Vand.J.Transnat'l Law 265 (1986), 659

Carey and MacChesney, Divorces by the Consent of the Parties and Divisible Divorce Decrees, 43 U.Ill.L.Rev. 608 (1948), 860, 869

Carrington, Collateral Estoppel and Foreign Judgments, 24 Ohio St.L.J. 381 (1963), 253

Carter, Domicil: The Case for Radical Reform in the United Kingdom, 36 Int'l & Comp.L.Q. 713 (1987), 16

Carter, Rejection of Foreign Law: Some Private International Law Inhibitions, 55 Brit.Ybk. Int'l L. 1984 (1985), 310

Cary, Federalism and Corporate Law: Reflections upon Delaware, 83 Yale L.J. 663 (1974), 1005

Casner, Estate Planning ch. 16 (4th ed. 1980), 954

Cavers, A Critique of the Choice-of-Law Problem, 47 Harv.L.Rev. 173 (1933), 450, 516

Cavers, Change in Choice-of-Law Thinking and Its Bearing on the Klaxon Problem, in the American Law Institute's Study of the Division of Jurisdiction Between State and Federal Courts (Official Draft 1969), 690

Cavers, comment by, Symposium: Choice of Law Theory After Allstate Insurance Co. v. Hague, 10 Hofstra L.Rev. 1 (1981), 360

Cavers, "Habitual Residence": A Useful Concept? 21 Am.U.L.Rev. 475 (1972), 17, 20

Cavers, International Enforcement of Family Support, 81 Colum.L.Rev. 994 (1981), 914, 915

Cavers, *Principles of Preference,* 516

Cavers, Re–Restating the Conflict of Laws: The Chapter on Contracts, XXth Century Comparative and Conflict Laws 349 (1961), 472

Cavers, The Choice–of–Law Process (1965), 449, 637

Cavers, The Conditional Seller's Remedies and the Choice-of-Law Process, 35 N.Y.U.L.Rev. 1126 (1960), 784, 793

Cavers, The Two "Local Law" Theories, 63 Harv.L.Rev. 822 (1950), 973

Cavers, Trusts Inter Vivos and the Conflict of Laws, 44 Harv.L.Rev. 161 (1930), 806

Chafee, Broadening the Second Stage of Interpleader, 56 Harv.L.Rev. 541 (1943), 135

Chafee, Federal Interpleader Since the Act of 1936, 49 Yale L.J. 377 (1940), 135

Chafee, Interpleader in the United States Courts, 41 Yale L.J. 1134 (1932), 135

Chafee, Interstate Interpleader, 33 Yale L.J. 685 (1924), 135

Chafee, Modernizing Interpleader, 30 Yale L.J. 814 (1921), 135

Chafee, The Federal Interpleader Act of 1936, 45 Yale L.J. 963 (1936), 135

Chappell, A Uniform Resolution to the Problem a Migrating Spouse Encounters at Divorce and Death, 28 Idaho L.Rev. 993 (1991/1992), 933

Chayes, The Bead Game, 87 Harv.L.Rev. 741 (1974), 684

Cheatham, Book Review, 45 A.B.A.J. 1190 (1959), 746

Cheatham, Federal Control of Conflict of Laws, 6 Vand.L.Rev. 581 (1953), 690

Cheatham, The Statutory Successor, the Receiver and the Executor in Conflict of Laws, 44 Colum.L.Rev. 549 (1944), 943, 971

Cheatham and Maier, Private International Law and Its Sources, 22 Vand.L.Rev. 27 (1968), 743

Cheatham and Reese, "Choice of the Applicable Law," 52 Colum.L.Rev. 959 (1952), 511

Chemerinsky, contribution by, Symposium, Fifty Years of *International Shoe:* The Past and Future of Personal Jurisdiction, 28 U.C.Davis L.Rev. 513 (1995), 53

Cheshire and North, Private International Law (12th ed. 1992) by North and Fawcett, 191, 234

Clark, State Law in the Federal Courts: The Brooding Omnipresence of Erie v. Tompkins, 55 Yale L.J. 267 (1946), 669

Clausnitzen, Property Rights of Surviving Spouse and the Conflict of Laws, 18 J.Fam.L. 471 (1980), 926

Collins, Anton Piller Orders and Fundamental Rights, 106 L.Q.Rev. 173 (1990), 147

Collins, Dicey and Morris' Conflict of Laws (11th ed. 1993), 16

Collins, Dicey and Morris' Conflict of Laws (12th ed. 1993, and 1995 Supp.), 64, 121, 147, 178, 225, 228, 234, 485, 843, 877, 986, 1012

Collins, The Territorial Reach of Mareva Injunctions, 105 L.Q.Rev. 262 (1989), 147

Comment, 12 Houston L.Rev. 924 (1975), 333

Comment, Application of the Uniform Commercial Code to Federal Government Contracts: Doing Business on Business Terms, 16 Wm. & Mary L.Rev. 395 (1974), 719

Comment, Choice of Law: The Validity of Trusts of Movables—Intention and Validation, 64 Nw.L.Rev. 388 (1969), 806

Comment, Limited Liability of Shareholders in Real Estate Investment Trusts and the Conflict of Laws, 50 Calif.L.Rev. 696 (1962), 982

Comment, Pendent Personal Jurisdiction and Nationwide Service of Process, 64 N.Y.U.L.Rev. 113 (1989), 699

Comment, Taking Away the Pawns: International Parental Abduction and the Hague Convention, 20 N.C.J.Int'l L. & Com.Reg. 137 (1994), 901

Comment, United States Recognition of Foreign, Nonjudicial Divorces, 53 Minn. L.Rev. 612 (1969), 877

Conference on Jurisdiction, Justice, and Choice of Law for the Twenty–First Century: Case Three—Personal Jurisdiction, 29 New England L.Rev. 627 (1995), 63

Cook, The Jurisdiction of Sovereign States and The Conflict of Laws, 31 Colum.L.Rev. 368 (1931), 757

Cook, The Logical and Legal Bases of the Conflict of Laws 452 (1942), 825

Cook, The Powers of Congress under the Full Faith and Credit Clause, 28 Yale L.J. 421 (1919), 234

Coombs, Custody Conflicts in the Courts, 16 Fam.L.Q. 251 (1982), 899

Coombs, Interstate Child Custody: Jurisdiction, Recognition, and Enforcement, 66 Minn.L.Rev. 711 (1982), 899

Cooper, article by, Symposium on the Complex Litigation Project, 54 La.L.Rev. (March 1994), 628

Corcoran, The Trading with the Enemy Act and the Controlled Canadian Corporation, 14 McGill L.J. 174 (1968), 987

Cowen, English and Foreign Adoptions, 12 Int'l & Comp.L.Q. 168 (1963), 886

Cowen and Da Costa, The Unity of Domicile, 78 L.Q.Rev. 92 (1962), 32

Cox, Case Three: Personal Jurisdiction, 29 New England L.Rev. 627 (1995), 120

Cox, Case Three: Personal Jurisdiction, Conference on Jurisdiction, Justice, and Choice of Law for the Twenty–First Century, 29 New England L.Rev. 642 (1995), 38

Currie, Change of Venue and the Conflict of Laws, 22 U.Chi.L.Rev. 405 (1955), 197

Currie, Change of Venue and the Conflict of Laws: A Retraction, 27 U.Chi.L.Rev. 341 (1960), 197

Currie, Conflict, Crisis and Confusion in New York, 1963 Duke L.J. 1, p. 511

Currie, Full Faith and Credit, Chiefly to Judgments: A Role for Congress, 1964 Sup.Ct.Rev. 89, p. 286

Currie, Full Faith and Credit to Foreign Land Decrees, 21 U.Chi.L.Rev. 620 (1964), 258

Currie, Notes on Methods and Objectives in the Conflict of Laws, 1959 Duke L.J. 171, pp. 513, 514

Currie, On the Displacement of the Law of the Forum, 58 Colum.L.Rev. 964 (1958), 395

Currie, Selected Essays on the Conflict of Laws (1963), 197, 320, 324, 330, 368, 395–396, 511, 513, 524, 622

Currie, Suitcase Divorce in the Conflict of Laws, 34 U.Chi.L.Rev. 26 (1967), 834, 855, 874, 875

Currie, The Constitution and Choice of Law, 26 U.Chi.L.Rev. 9 (1958), 330

Currie, The Constitution and the "Transitory" Cause of Action, 73 Harv.L.Rev. 36 (1959), 320, 324

Currie, The Multiple Personality of the Dead: Executors, Administrators and the Conflict of Laws, 33 U.Chi.L.Rev. 429, (1966), 943, 947, 952, 954

Currie and Schreter, Unconstitutional Discrimination in the Conflict of Laws: Equal Protection, 28 U.Chi.L.Rev. 1 (1960), 368

Currie and Schreter, Unconstitutional Discrimination in the Conflict of Laws: Privileges and Immunities, 69 Yale L.J. 1323 (1960), 368

D'Oliveira, "Characteristic Obligation" in the Draft EEC Obligation Convention, 25 Am. J.Comp.L. 303 (1977), 546

Da Costa, The Canadian Divorce Law of 1968 and its Provisions on Conflicts, 17 Am. J.Comp.L. 214 (1969), 32

Da Costa, The Formalities of Marriage in the Conflict of Laws, 7 Int'l & Comp.L.Q. 217 (1958), 825

Davies, comment by, Symposium: Choice of Law Theory After Allstate Insurance Co. v. Hague, 10 Hofstra L.Rev. 1 (1981), 360

DeBoer, Beyond Lex Loci Delicti (1987), 532

Degnan, Federalized Res Judicata, 85 Yale L.J. 741 (1976), 252

Dehart, Comity, Conventions and the Constitution: State and Federal Initiatives in International Support Enforcement. 28 Fam.L.Q. 89 (1994), 914

DeMott, Perspectives on Choice of Law for Corporate Affairs, 48 Law and Contemporary Problems 161 (1985), 996

Dicey and Morris, Conflict of Laws (11th ed. 1993 by Collins), 16

Dicey and Morris, Conflict of Laws (12th ed. 1993 by Collins, and 1995 Supp.), 64, 121, 147, 178, 225, 228, 234, 485, 843, 877, 986, 1012

Dobbs, The Validity of Void Judgments: The Bootstrap Principle, 53 Va.L.Rev. 1003 (1967), 286

Dockray & Laddie, Piller Problems, 106 L.Q.Rev. 601 (1990), 147

Domke, The Law and Practice of Commercial Arbitration, 256 (1968), 654

Dougherty, Validity of Contractual Provision Limiting Place or Court in which Action may be brought, 31 A.L.R.4th 404 (1984), 176

Downes, 35 Int'l & Comp.L.Q. 170 (1986), 855

Drinker, Legal Ethics (1953), 855

Drinker, Problems of Professional Ethics in Matrimonial Litigation, 66 Harv.L.Rev. 443 (1953), 855

Drobnig, Rabel's The Conflict of Laws: A Comparative Study (2d ed.), 3, 430

Ebke and Parker, Foreign Country Money-Judgments and Arbitral Awards and the Restatement (Third) of the Foreign Relations Law of the United States: A Conventional Approach, 24 International Lawyer 21 (1990), 227

Ehrenzweig, Conflict of Laws 180–182 (1962). In Wren, Problems in Probating Foreign Wills and Using Foreign Personal Representatives, 17 Sw.L.J. 55 (1963), 947

Ehrenzweig, Contracts and the Conflict of Laws, 59 Colum.L.Rev. 973, 1171 (1959), 472

Ehrenzweig, The "Bastard" in the Conflict of Laws—A National Disgrace, 29 U.Chi. L.Rev. 498 (1962), 511

Ehrenzweig, The Statute of Frauds in the Conflict of Laws, 59 Colum.L.Rev. 874 (1959), 571

Ely, Choice of Law and the State's Interest in Protecting Its Own, 23 Wm. & Mary L.Rev. 173 (1981), 620

Ely, The Irrepressible Myth of Erie, 87 Harv. L.Rev. 693 (1974), 684

Engdahl, Proposal for a Benign Revolution in Marriage Law and Marriage Conflicts Law, 55 Iowa L.Rev. 56 (1969), 834

Epstein, 33 A.L.R. Fed. 344 (1977), 180

Ester and Scoles, Estate Planning and Conflict of Laws, 24 Ohio S.L.J. 270 (1963), 780, 806, 954

Farange, Multiple Domiciles and Multiple Inheritance Taxes—A Possible Solution, 9 Geo.Wash.L.Rev. 375 (1941), 16

Fentiman, The Validity of Marriage and the Proper Law, 44 Camb.L.J. 256 (1985), 835

Field, Sources of Law: The Scope of Federal Common Law, 99 Harv.L.Rev. 881 (1986), 726

Fine, Choice of Law for Putative Spouses, 32 Int'l & Comp.L.Q. 708 (1983), 836

Fine, The Application of Issue–Analysis to Choice of Law Involving Family Law Matters in the United States, 26 Loyola L.Rev. 31 (1980), 822, 834

Foster, Child Custody Jurisdiction: UCCJA and PKPA, 27 N.Y.L.Sch.L.Rev. 297 (1981), 899

Freund, Chief Justice Stone and the Conflict of Laws, 59 Harv.L.Rev. 1210 (1946), 692

Freund, Rice v. Rice—A Comment, 23 Conn. Bar J. 182 (1949), 855

Friendly, In Praise of Erie—and of the New Federal Common Law, 19 Record of N.Y.C.B.A. 64 (1964) 725

Friendly, In Praise of Erie—and of the New Federal Common Law, 39 N.Y.U.L.Rev. 383 (1964), 669, 725

Fusco, Effect, on Application of 28 U.S.C.S. § 1404(a) or Forum Non Conveniens in Diversity Case, of Contractual Provision Fixing Forum for Enforcement or Laws Governing Interpretation—Post–Bremen Cases, 123 A.L.R.Fed. 323 (1995), 176

Gaillard and Trautman, Trusts in Non–Trust Countries: Conflict of Laws and the Hague Convention on Trusts, 35 Am. J.Comp.L. 307 (1987), 746, 811

Gilbert, Choice of Forum Clauses in International and Interstate Contracts, 65 Ky.L.J. 1 (1977), 177

Gilmore, Security Interests in Personal Property (1965), 794

Ginsburg, Judgments in Search of Full Faith and Credit: The Last-in-Time Rule for Conflicting Judgments, 82 Harv.L.Rev. 798 (1969), 289

Goldman, My Way and the Highway: The Law and Economics of Choice of Forum Clauses in Consumer Form Contracts, 86 Nw.L.Rev. 700 (1992), 177

Goldstein, contribution by, Symposium, Fifty Years of *International Shoe:* The Past and Future of Personal Jurisdiction, 28 U.C.Davis L.Rev. 513 (1995), 53

Gottlieb, The Incidental Question Revisited, 26 Int'l & Comp.L.Q. 734 (1977), 821

Graveson, Conflict of Laws 235 (7th ed. 1974), 234

Greenberg, Extrastate Enforcement of Tax Claims and Administrative Tax Determinations Under the Full Faith and Credit Clause, 43 Bklyn.L.Rev. 630 (1977), 390

Greenspan, Crider v. Zurich Insurance Co.: Decline of Conceptualism in Conflict of Laws, 27 U.Pitt.L.Rev. 49 (1965), 211

Gruson, Forum–Selection Clauses in International and Interstate Commercial Agreements, 1982 U.Ill.L.Rev. 133, p. 177

Gruson, Governing Law Clauses in Commercial Agreements—New York's Approach, 18 Colum.J.Transnat'l L. 323 (1980), 478

Guilford, Guam Divorces: Fast, Easy, and Dangerous, M.A.R. Army Law (1990), 876

Hale, Unconstitutional Conditions and Constitutional Rights, 35 Colum.L.Rev. 321 (1935), 986

Halloran and Hammer, Section 2115 of the New California General Corporation Law, 23 U.C.L.A.L.Rev. 1282 (1976), 1005

Hancock, Conceptual Devices for Avoiding the Land Taboo in Conflict of Laws: The Disadvantages of Disingenuousness, 20 Stan.L.Rev. 1 (1967), 492, 778

Hancock, Equitable Conversion and the Land Taboo in Conflict of Laws, 17 Stan.L.Rev. 1095 (1965), 778

Hancock, Full Faith and Credit to Foreign Laws and Judgments in Real Property Litigation, 18 Stan.L.Rev. 1299 (1966), 778

Hancock, "In the Parish of St. Mary le Bow, in the Ward of Cheap," 16 Stan.L.Rev. 561 (1964), 553, 778

Harding, Matrimonial Domicil and Marital Rights in Movables, 30 Mich.L.Rev. 859 (1932), 915

Hart, The Relations Between State and Federal Law, 54 Colum.L.Rev. 489 (1954), 692

Hart and Wechsler, The Federal Courts and The Federal System (1953), 692

Hartley, Civil Jurisdiction and Judgments (1984), 225

Haworth, The Mirror Image Conflicts Case, 1974 Wash.U.L.Q. 1, p. 532

Hay, Flexibility versus Predictability and Uniformity in Choice of Law, 226 Academy of International Law Recueil des cours (Collection of Courses) (1991–I), 6, 120, 534, 545

Hay, Fremdwährungsanprüche und -urteile nach dem US-amerikanischen Uniform Act, [1995] Recht der Internationalen Wirtschaft 113, p. 748

Hay, Full Faith and Credit and Federalism in Choice of Law, 34 Mercer L.Rev. 709 (1983), 78, 325, 335, 361

Hay, Informationsbeschaffung über schriftliche Unterlagen und Augenscheinsobjekte in Zivilprozess, ___ Veröffentlichungen der Wissenschaftlichen Vereinigung für Prozessrecht ___ (1996), 201

Hay, Judicial Jurisdiction and Choice of Law: Constitutional Limitations, 59 Col.L.Rev. 9 (1988), 346

Hay, The Interrelations of Jurisdiction and Choice-of-Law in U.S. Conflicts Law, 28 Int'l and Comp.L.Q. 161 (1979), 148

Hay, The Recognition and Enforcement of American Money-Judgments in Germany, 40 Am.J.Comp.L. 1001 (1992), 224

Hay, The Situs Rule in European and American Conflicts Law—Comparative Notes, in Hay & Hoeflich, eds., Property Law & Legal Education (1988), 126, 258, 758

Hay, Transient Jurisdiction, Especially Over International Defendants: Critical Comments on *Burnham v. Superior Court*, 1990 U.Ill.L.Rev. 593, p. 121

Hay and Ellis, Bridging the Gap Between Rules and Approaches in Tort Choice of Law in the United States: A Survey of Current Case Law, 27 International Lawyer 369 (1993), 561

Hay and Müller-Freienfels, Agency in the Conflict of Laws and the 1978 Hague Convention, 27 Am.J.Comp.L. 1 (1979), 975

Hay and Walker, The Proposed Recognition-of-Judgments Convention between the United States and the United Kingdom, 11 Texas Int.L.J. 421 (1976), 225

Hazard, A General Theory of State-Court Jurisdiction, 1965 Supreme Court Review 241 (Kurland ed.), 66

Heiser, Forum Selection Clauses in Federal Courts: Limitations on Enforcement after *Stewart* and Carnival Cruise, 45 Fla. L.Rev. 553 (1993), 176

Henderson, Marital Agreements and the Rights of Creditors, 11 Comm.Prop.J. 105 (1984), 915

Henkin, The Foreign Affairs Power of the Federal Courts: *Sabbatino*, 64 Colum.L.Rev. 805 (1964), 743

Henn, Law of Corporations (3d ed. 1983), 986, 988

Herzog, Brussels and Lugano, Should You Race to the Courthouse or Race for a Judgment, 43 Am.J.Comp.L 379 (1995), 194

Hill, Choice of Law and Jurisdiction in the Supreme Court, 81 Colum.L.Rev. 960 (1981), 361

Hill, Governmental Interest and the Conflict of Laws—a Reply to Professor Currie, 27 U.Chi.L.Rev. 463 (1960), 514

Hill, The Erie Doctrine and The Constitution, 53 Nw.U.L.Rev. 427 (1958), 692

Hofstetter, Parent Responsibility for Subsidiary Corporations: Evaluating European Trends, 39 Int'l & Comp.L.Q. 576 (1990), 110

Hogue, Law in a Parallel Universe: Erie's Betrayal, Diversity Jurisdiction, Georgia Conflict of Laws Questions in Contracts Cases in the Eleventh Circuit, and Certification Reform, 11 Ga.State U.L.Rev. 531 (1995), 685

Homburger, Recognition and Enforcement of Foreign Judgments, 18 Am.J.Comp.L. 367 (1970), 234, 312

Hopkins, Conflict of Laws in Administration of Decedents' Intangibles, 28 Iowa L.Rev. 422 (1943), 943

Horowitz, Toward a Federal Common Law of Choice of Law, 14 U.C.L.A.L.Rev. 1191 (1967), 693

Hovermill, A Conflict of Laws and Morals: The Choice of Law Implications of Hawaii's Recognition of Same-Sex Marriages, 53 Md.L.Rev. 450 (1994), 834

James, Hazard and Leubsdorf, Civil Procedure (4th ed. 1992), 228

Jay, Origins of Federal Common Law, 133 U.Pa.L.Rev. 1003 (1983), 726

Jhong, Application of Common-law Doctrine of Forum Non Conveniens in Federal Courts after Enactment of 28 U.S.C.A. § 1404(a) Authorizing Transfer to Another District, 10 A.L.R.Fed. 352 (1972), 182

Jhong, Construction and Application of Change of Venue or Transfer Provision of 28 U.S.C.A. § 1404(a), Apart from Questions of Convenience and Justice of Transfer, 7 A.L.R. Fed. 9 (1971), 195

Johnson and Parachini, Forged Indorsements and Conflict of Laws, 82 Banking L.J. 95 (1965), 661

Johnston, Party Autonomy in Contracts Specifying Foreign Law, 7 Wm. & Mary L.Rev. 37 (1966), 478

Jones, An Interest Analysis Approach to Extraterritorial Application of Rule 10b-5, 52 Tex.L.Rev. 983 (1974), 333

Juenger, A *Shoe* Unfit for Globetrotting, 28 U.C.Davis L.Rev. 1027 (1995), 38

Juenger, American Jurisdiction: A Story of Comparative Neglect, 65 Colo.L.Rev. 1 (1993), 176

Juenger, article by, Symposium on the Complex Litigation Project, 54 La.L.Rev. (March 1994), 628

Juenger, Choice of Law and Multistate Justice (1993), 518

Juenger, Choice of Law in Interstate Torts, 118 U.Pa.L.Rev. 202 (1969), 519

Juenger, Conflict of Law: A Critique of Interest Analysis, 32 Am.J.Comp.L. 1 (1984), 514

Juenger, contribution by, Symposium, Fifty Years of *International Shoe:* The Past and Future of Personal Jurisdiction, 28 U.C.Davis L.Rev. 513 (1995), 53

Juenger, Forum Shopping, Domestic and International, 63 Tulane L.Rev. 553 (1989), 38

Juenger, Lessons Comparison Might Teach, 23 Am.J.Comp.L. 742 (1975), 631

Juenger, Marital Property and the Conflict of Laws: A Tale of Two Countries, 81 Colum.L.Rev. 1061 (1981), 926

Juenger, Recognition of Foreign Divorces, 20 Am.J.Comp.L. 1 (1972), 874

Juenger, The Inter-American Convention on the Law Applicable to International Contracts: Some Highlights and Comparisons, 42 Am.J.Comp.L. 381 (1994), 548

Juenger, What's Wrong with Forum Shopping?, 18 Sydney L.Rev. 5 (1994), 194

Juenger, What's Wrong with Forum Shopping? [a rejoinder], 18 Sydney L.Rev. 28 (1994), 194

Kalis, article by, Symposium on the Complex Litigation Project, 54 La.L.Rev. (March 1994), 628

Kanowitz, Comparative Impairment and Better Law: Grand Illusions in the Conflict of Laws, 30 Hastings L.J. 255 (1979), 604, 606

Kaplan, Foreign Corporations and Local Corporate Policy, 21 Vand.L.Rev. 433 (1968), 1005

Katz, A Modest Proposal? The Convention on Protection of Children and Cooperation in Respect of Intercountry Adoption, 9 Emory Int'l L.Rev. 293 (1995), 886

Katz, Child Snatching (1981), 899

Katzenbach, Conflicts on an Unruly Horse: Reciprocal Claims and Tolerances in Interstate and International Law, 65 Yale L.J. 1087 (1956), 386

Keeton and O'Connell, Basic Protection for the Traffic Victim (1965), 640

Kegel, Exequatur sur exequatur ne vaut, Festschrift für Müller-Freienfels 377 (1986), 306

Kegel, Internationales Privatrecht (6th ed. 1987), 549, 999

Kegel, The Crisis of Conflict of Laws, Hague Academy of International Law, 112 Collected Courses 91 (1964-II), 3

Kelner, 'Adrift on an Uncharted Sea': A Survey of Section 1404(a) Transfer in the Federal System, 67 N.Y.U.L.Rev. 612 (1992), 195

Kennedy, Adoption in the Conflict of Laws, 34 Can.B.Rev. 507 (1956), 886

Kim, International Insolvencies: an English-American Comparison with an Analysis of Proposed Solutions, 26 GW J.Int'l L. & Econ. 1 (1992), 958

King, article by, Symposium, 1 Hofstra L.Rev. 104 (1973), 532

Kirgis, The Rules of Due Process and Full Faith and Credit in Choice of Law, 62 Corn.L.Rev. 94 (1976), 335

Kogan, contribution by, Symposium: The Future of Personal Jurisdiction, 22 Rutgers L.J. 559 (1991), 121

Korn, The Choice-of-Law Revolution: A Critique, 83 Colum.L.Rev. 772 (1983), 532

Kozyris, An Interim Update, 1973 Duke L.J. 1009, p. 644

Kozyris, article by, Symposium on the Complex Litigation Project, 54 La.L.Rev. (March 1994), 628

Kozyris, Corporate Wars and Choice of Law, 1985 Duke L.J. 1, p. 996

Kozyris, No-Fault Automobile Insurance and the Conflict of Laws—Cutting the Gordian Knot Home-Style, 1972 Duke L.J. 331, p. 643

Kozyris, Reflections on Allstate—The Lessening of Due Process in Choice of Law, 14 U.C.D.L.Rev. 889 (1981), 361

Kramer, Interest Analysis and the Presumption of Forum Law, 56 U.Chi.L.Rev. 1301 (1989), 396

Kramer, Rethinking Choice of Law, 90 Colum.L.Rev. 277 (1990), 343, 576

Kramer, Return of the Renvoi, 66 N.Y.U.L.Rev. 979 (1991), 446

Kramer, The Myth of the "Unprovided-For" Case, 75 Va.L.Rev. 1045 (1989), 622

Krause, Child Support in America (1981), 912

Krauskopf, Divisible Divorce and Rights to Support, Property and Custody, 24 Ohio St.L.J. 346 (1963), 869

Kreindler, Luncheon Address, American Association of Law Schools Workshop on Conflict of Laws, Program 8032R Tape 10, July 9, 1988, p. 396

Kropholler, Europäisches Zivilprozessrecht anno. 19 preceding Art. 2 (3d ed. 1991), 191

Kulzer, Recognition of Foreign Country Judgments in New York: The Uniform Foreign Money-Judgments Recognition Act, 18 Buff.L.Rev. 1 (1969), 227, 312

LaFave, Search and Seizure § 1.9(a) (2d ed. 1987), 180

Lake, Escheat, Federalism and State Boundaries, 24 Ohio St.L.J. 322 (1963), 373

Latty, Pseudo-Foreign Corporations, 65 Yale L.J. 137 (1955), 999, 1003

Lay, Community Property in Common Law States, 41 Temp.L.Q. 1 (1967), 919

Lay, Marital Property Rights of the Non-Native in a Community Proterty State, 18 Hast.L.J. 295 (1967), 933

Lay, Migrants from Community Property States—Filling the Legislative Gap, 53 Corn.L.Rev. 832 (1968), 933

Lay, The Role of the Matrimonial Domicile in Marital Property Rights, 4 Fam.L.Q. 61 (1970), 933

Laycock, Equal Citizens of Equal and Territorial States: The Constitutional Foundations of Choice of Law, 92 Colum.L.Rev. 249 (1992), 330, 620

Leary, Horse and Buggy Lien Law and Migratory Automobiles, 96 U. of Pa.L.Rev. 455 (1948), 794

Leflar, *Choice-Influencing Considerations*, 515

Leflar, Choice of Law in Criminal Cases, 25 Case Wes.L.Rev. 44 (1974), 417

Leflar, comment by, Symposium: Choice of Law Theory After Allstate Insurance Co. v. Hague, 10 Hofstra L.Rev. 1 (1981), 360

Leflar, Conflict of Laws and Family Law, 14 Ark.L.R. 47, 49 (1960), 31

Leflar, From Community to Common Law State; Estate Problems of Citizens Moving from One to Other, 99 Trusts & Estates 882 (1960), 919

Leflar, Review, 34 Am.J.Comp.L. 387 (1986), 554

Leflar, The New Uniform Foreign Judgments Act, 24 N.Y.U.L.Q. 336 (1949), 232

Leflar, McDougal and Felix, American Conflicts Law (4th ed. 1986), 219, 297, 346, 515, 746

Lewis, Mutuality in Conflict—Flexibility and Full Faith and Credit, 23 Drake L.Rev. 364 (1974), 253

Lipstein, Recognition of Divorces, Capacity to Marry, Preliminary Questions and Dépeçage, 35 Int'l & Comp.L.Q. 178 (1986), 821, 855

Lorenzen, Territoriality, Public Policy and the Conflict of Laws, 33 Yale L.J. 736 (1924), 386

Lowenfeld, In Search of the Intangible: A Comment on Shaffer v. Heitner, 53 N.Y.U.L.Rev. 102 (1978), 145, 148

Lowenfeld, International Litigation and Arbitration 276 (1993), 104

Lowenfeld, International Litigation and the Quest for Reasonableness—General Course on Private International Law, Hague Academy, 245 Collected Courses (1994–I), 66, 104, 120, 121

Lowenfeld, Mass Torts and the Conflict of Laws: The Airline Disaster, 1989 U.Ill. L.Rev. 157 (1989), 720

Lowenfeld, Public Law in the International Arena: Conflict of Laws, International Law, and Some Suggestions for Their Interaction, 163 Collected Courses [Recueil des cours] Academy of International Law 311 (1979), 755

Lowenfeld, "Tempora Mutantur"—Wills and Trusts and the Conflicts Restatement, 72 Colum.L.Rev. 382 (1972), 781

Maltz, Choice of Forum and Choice of Law in the Federal Courts: A Reconsideration of Erie Principles, 79 Ky.L.J. 231 (1991), 698

Maltz, contribution by, Symposium: The Future of Personal Jurisdiction, 22 Rutgers L.J. 559 (1991), 121

Mann, The Legal Aspect of Money (5th ed. 1992), 748

Marcus, Conflicts Among Circuits and Transfers Within the Federal Judicial System, 93 Yale L.J. 677 (1984), 197, 700

Marsh, Marital Property in Conflict of Laws (1952), 920, 933

Martin, comment by, Symposium: Choice of Law Theory After Allstate Insurance Co. v. Hague, 10 Hofstra L.Rev. 1 (1981), 360

Martin, Constitutional Limitations on Choice of Law, 61 Corn.L.Rev. 185 (1976), 335

Martiny, Maintenance Obligations in the Conflict of Laws, Hague Academy, 247 Collected Courses 131 (1994–III), 64

McClanahan, Community Property Law in the United States (1982, 1984 Supp.), 933

McDowell, Foreign Personal Representatives (1957), 943

McLachlan, The New Hague Sales Convention and the Limits of the Choice of Law Process, 102 L.Q.Rev. 591 (1986), 547

Meador, State Law and the Federal Judicial Power, 49 Va.L.Rev. 1082 (1963), 673, 690

Merrill, The Common Law Powers of Federal Courts, 52 U.Chi.L.Rev. 1 (1985), 726

Miller, Federal Rule 44.1 and the "Fact" Approach to Determining Foreign Law: Death Knell for a Die–Hard Doctrine, 65 Mich.L.Rev. 613 (1967), 396, 402

Miller and Crump, Jurisdiction and Choice of Law in Multistate Class Actions After Phillips Petroleum Co. v. Shutts, 96 Yale L.J. 1 (1986), 241, 367

Mishkin, The Variousness of "Federal Law": Competence and Discretion in the Choice of National and State Rules for Decision, 105 U.Pa.L.Rev. 797 (1957), 725

Moore & Bendix, Congress, Evidence and Rulemaking, 84 Yale L.J. 9 (1974), 678

Morse, contribution by, Symposium, Fifty Years of *International Shoe:* The Past and Future of Personal Jurisdiction, 28 U.C.Davis L.Rev. 513 (1995), 53

Mullenix, Another Choice of Forum, Another Choice of Law: Consensual Adjudicatory Procedure in Federal Court, 57 Fordham L.Rev. 291 (1988), 176

Mullenix, article by, Symposium on the Complex Litigation Project, 54 La.L.Rev. (March 1994), 628

Mullenix, contribution by, Symposium, Fifty Years of *International Shoe:* The Past and Future of Personal Jurisdiction, 28 U.C.Davis L.Rev. 513 (1995), 53

Müller, Die Gerichtspflichtigkeit wegen "doing business" (1992), 103

Müller–Freienfels, Conflicts of Law and Constitutional Law, 45 U.Chi.L.Rev. 598 (1978), 362

Nadelmann, Bankruptcy in Canada: Assets in New York, 11 Am.J.Comp.L. 628 (1962), 958

Nadelmann, Bankruptcy Jurisdiction: News from the Common Market and a Reflection for Home Consumption, 56 Am.Bank. L.J. 65 (1982), 958

Nadelmann, French Courts Recognize Foreign Money–Judgments: One Down and

More to Go, 13 Am.J.Comp.L. 1 (1964), 224

Nadelmann, Full Faith and Credit to Judgments and Public Acts, 56 Mich.L.Rev. 33 (1957), 40, 324

Nafziger, article by, Symposium on the Complex Litigation Project, 54 La.L.Rev. (March 1994), 628

Neuman, Legal Advice Toward Illegal Ends, 28 U.Rich.L.Rev. 287 (1994), 855

North and Fawcett, Cheshire and North's Private International Law (12th ed. 1992), 112, 177, 191, 234

North, Draft U.K./U.S. Judgments Convention: A British Viewpoint, 1 N.W.J.Int.L. & Bus. 219 (1979), 225

North, Reform, not Revolution, Hague Academy of International Law, 220 Collected Courses 9 (1990–I), 549

Norwood, Double Forum Shopping and the Extension of Ferens to Federal Claims that Borrow State Limitations Periods, 44 Emory L.J. 501 (1995), 700

Note, 52 B.U.L.Rev. 64 (1972), 979

Note, 35 Baylor L.Rev. 168 (1983), 933

Note, 66 Colum.L.Rev. 377 (1966), 711

Note, 52 Corn.L.Q. 157 (1966), 982

Note, 77 Harv.L.Rev. 559 (1964), 66

Note, 77 Harv.L.Rev. 1463 (1964), 635

Note, 102 Harv.L.Rev. 1403 (1989), 181

Note, 14 St. Mary's L.J. 789 (1983), 933

Note, 16 Sw.L.J. 660 (1962), 373

Note, 55 Tex.L.Rev. 127 (1976), 289

Note, 114 U.Pa.L.Rev. 771 (1966), 876

Note, 47 Wash.L.Rev. 441 (1972), 656

Note, A Comparative Study of U.S. and British Approaches to Discovery Conflicts: Achieving a Uniform System of Extraterritorial Discovery, 18 Fordham Int'l L.J. 1340 (1995), 201

Note, A Comparison of Iowans' Dispositive Preferences with Select Provisions of the Iowa and Uniform Probate Codes, 63 Iowa L.Rev. 1041 (1978), 12

Note, Anti-suit and Anti–Anti-suit Injunctions: a Proposed Texas Approach, 45 Baylor L.Rev. 499 (1993), 194

Note, Collateral Estoppel Effects of Administrative Agency Determinations: Where Should Federal Courts Draw the Line?, 73 Cornell L.Rev. 817 (1988), 253

Note, Collateral Estoppel in Multistate Litigation, 68 Colum.L.Rev. 1590 (1968), 253

Note, Collateral Estoppel: The Changing Role of the Mutuality Rule, 41 Mo.L.Rev. 521 (1976), 253

Note, Community Property and the Problem of Migration, 66 Wash.U.L.Q. 773 (1988), 933

Note, Conflict of Laws, 65 Calif.L.Rev. 290 (1977), 604

Note, Constitutionality of a Uniform Reciprocal Registration of Judgments Statute, 36 N.Y.U.L.Rev. 488 (1961), 234

Note, Developments in the Law—International Environmental Law, 104 Harv. L.Rev. 1484 (1991), 104

Note, Diversity Jurisdiction and Alien Corporations: The Application of Section 1332(c), 59 Ind.L.J. 659 (1984), 987

Note, "Doing Business:" Defining State Control of Foreign Corporations, 32 Vand. L.Rev. 1105 (1979), 986

Note, Effectiveness of Choice-of-Law Clauses in Contract Conflicts of Law: Party Autonomy or Objective Determination?, 82 Colum.L.Rev. 1659 (1982), 542

Note, Equitable Interest in Enhanced Earning Capacity: The Treatment of a Professional Degree at Dissolution, 60 Wash. L.Rev. 431 (1985), 920

Note, Extraterritorial Discovery: An Analysis Based on Good Faith, 83 Colum.L.Rev. 1320 (1983), 200

Note, Foreign Attachment after *Sniadach* and *Fuentes,* 73 Colum.L.Rev. 342 (1973), 133

Note, Formulating a Federal Rule of Decision in Commercial Transactions after Kimbell, 66 Iowa L.Rev. 391 (1981), 719

Note, Forum Selection Clauses in Light of the Erie Doctrine and Federal Common Law: Stewart Organization v. Ricoh Corporation, 72 Minn.L.Rev. 1090 (1988), 176

Note, Forum Selection Clauses: Substantive or Procedural for Erie Purposes, 89 Colum.L.Rev. 1068 (1989), 176

Note, Judicial Wandering Through a Legislative Maze: Application of the Uniform Child Custody Jurisdiction Act and the Parental Kidnapping Prevention Act to Child Custody Determinations, 58 Mo. L.Rev. 427 (1993), 900

Note, *Interest Analysis Applied to Corporations: The Unprincipled Use of A Choice of Law Method,* 98 Yale L.J. 597 (1989), 700

Note, Interstate Child Custody and the Parental Kidnapping Prevention Act: The Continuing Search for a National Standard, 45 Hastings L.J. 1329 (1994), 900

Note, Interstate Enforcement of Support Obligations Through Long–Arm Statutes and URESA, 18 J.Fam.L. 537 (1980), 913

Note, Legislative Jurisdiction, State Policies and Post–Occurrence Contacts in Allstate Insurance Co. v. Hague, 81 Colum.L.Rev. 1134 (1981), 361

Note, Limited Liability of Shareholders in Real Estate and Investment Trusts, and the Conflict of Laws, 50 Calif.L.Rev. 696 (1962), 986

Note, Marital Property and the Conflict of Laws, 54 Calif.L.Rev. 252 (1966), 933

Note, Marital Property Rights of the Non–Native in a Community Property State, 18 Hast.L.J. 295 (1967), 933

Note, Modernizing the Situs Rule for Real Property Conflicts, 65 Tex.L.Rev. 585 (1987), 258, 758

Note, Post Transaction or Occurrence Events in Conflict of Laws, 69 Colum.L.Rev. 843 (1969), 612

Note, Pseudo–Foreign Corporations and the Internal Affairs Doctrine, 1960 Duke L.J. 477, p. 999

Note, Quasi in Rem Jurisdiction and Due Process Requirements, 82 Yale L.J. 1023 (1973), 133

Note, Revival Judgments under the Full Faith and Credit Clause, 17 U.Chi.L.Rev. 520 (1950), 306

Note, Sanctions for Failure to Comply with Corporate Qualification Statutes: An Evaluation, 63 Colum.L.Rev. 117 (1963), 989

Note, State Remedies for Federally–Created Rights, 47 Minn.L.Rev. 815 (1963), 205

Note, 'Til Death Do Us Part: Granting Full Faith and Credit to Marital Status, 68 S.Cal.L.Rev. 397 (1995), 834

Note, The Case for a Federal Common Law of Aircraft Disaster Litigation, 51 N.Y.U.L.Rev. 232 (1976), 720

Note, The Effect of the Parental Kidnapping Prevention Act of 1980 on Child Snatching, 17 N.Eng.L.Rev. 499 (1982), 899

Note, The Hague Convention on the Civil Aspects of International Child Abduction: Are the Convention's Goals Being Achieved? 2 Ind.J.Global Legal Stud. 553 (1995), 901

Note, The Law Applied in Diversity Cases: The Rules of Decision and the *Erie* Doctrine, 85 Yale L.J. 678 (1976), 678

Note, The Nonrecognition of Foreign Tax Judgments, International Tax Evasion, U.Ill.L.Rev. 241 (1981), 310

Note, The Parental Kidnapping Prevention Act, 27 N.Y.L.Rev. 553 (1982), 899

Note, The Uniform Interstate Family Support Act: The New URESA, 20 U.Dayton L.Rev. 425 (1994), 913

Note, Unconstitutional Discrimination in Choice of Law, 77 Colum.L.Rev. 272 (1977), 368

Note, Viva Zapata! : Toward a Rational System of Forum–Selection Clause Enforcement in Diversity Cases, 66 N.Y.U.L.Rev. 422 (1991), 176

Nowak and Rotunda, Constitutional Law (4th ed. 1991), 986

Oakley, contribution by, Symposium, Fifty Years of *International Shoe:* The Past and Future of Personal Jurisdiction, 28 U.C.Davis L.Rev. 513 (1995), 53

Oakley, The PiWalls of "Hit and Run" History: A Critique of Professor Borchers' "Limited View" of Pennoyer v. Neff, 28 U.C. Davis L.Rev. 591 (1995), 47

Okilski, Foreign Corporations: What Constitutes "Doing Business" under New York's Qualification Statute?, 44 Ford.L.Rev. 1042 (1976), 989

Oldham, Conflict of Laws and Marital Property Rights, 39 Baylor L.Rev. 1255 (1987), 920, 933

Oldham, Regulating the Regulators: Limitations upon a State's Ability to Regulate Corporations with Multi–State Contacts, 57 Denver L.Rev. 345 (1980), 1005

Opeskin, The Price of Forum Shopping—A Reply to Professor Juenger, 18 Sydney L.Rev. 14 (1994), 194

Overton, The Restatement of Judgments, Collateral Estoppel and the Conflict of Laws, 44 Tenn.L.Rev. 927 (1977), 253

Paul, The Act of State Doctrine: Revived but Suspended, 113 U.Pa.L.Rev. 691 (1965), 743

Paulsen, Migratory Divorce: Chapters III and IV, 24 Ind.L.J. 25 (1948), 860

Paulsen, Support Rights and an Out-of-State Divorce, 38 Minn.L.Rev. 709 (1954), 870

Paulsen and Sovern, "Public Policy" in the Conflict of Laws, 56 Colum.L.Rev. 969 (1956), 254

Perschbacher, contribution by, Symposium, Fifty Years of *International Shoe:* The Past and Future of Personal Jurisdiction, 28 U.C.Davis L.Rev. 513 (1995), 53

Peterson, Jurisdiction and Choice of Law Revisited, 59 Col.L.Rev. 37–66 (1988), 346

Pierce, Institutional Aspects of Tort Reform, 73 Calif.L.Rev. 917 (1985), 640

Pilkington, Illegal Residence and the Acquisition of a Domicile of Choice, 33 Int'l & Comp.L.Q. 885 (1984), 24

Pilkington, Transnational Divorces Under the Family Law Act of 1986, 37 Int'l & Comp.L.Q. 131 (1988), 877

Polacheck, The "Un–Worth-y" Decision: The Characterization of a Copyright as Community Property, 17 Hastings Comm./ Ent.L.J. 601 (1995), 921

Pollack, Proof of Foreign Law, 26 Am. J.Comp.L. 470 (1978), 396

Posnak, Choice of Law: A Very Well–Curried Leflar Approach, 34 Mercer L.Rev. 731 (1983), 343

Posner, The Problems of Jurisprudence (1990), 5

Pound, The Progress of the Law—Equity, 33 Harv.L.Rev. 420 (1920) 214

Powers, Formalism and Nonformalism in Choice of Law Methodology, 52 Wash. L.Rev. 27 (1976), 532

Prebble, Choice of Law to Determine the Validity and Effect of Contracts: A Comparison of English and American Approaches to the Conflict of Laws, 58 Cornell L.Rev. 433 (1973), 478

Prosser, Interstate Publication, 51 Mich. L.Rev. 959 (1953), 635

Pryles, Impeachment of Sister State Judgments for Fraud, 25 Sw.L.J. 697 (1971), 297

Quigley, Convention on Foreign Arbitral Awards, 58 A.B.A.J. 821 (1972), 656

Rabel, Conflict of Laws (2d ed. 1958), 886, 999

Rabel, The Conflict of Laws: A Comparative Study (2d ed. by Drobnig 1958), 3, 430

Ragazzo, Transfer and Choice of Federal Law: The Appellate Model, 93 Mich. L.Rev. 703 (1995), 700

Ratner and Schwartz, The Impact of Shaffer v. Heitner on the Substantive Law of Corporations, 45 Brooklyn L.Rev. 641 (1979), 1005

Redish, contribution by, Symposium: The Future of Personal Jurisdiction, 22 Rutgers L.J. 559 (1991), 121

Redish, Due Process, Federalism, and Personal Jurisdiction: A Theoretical Evaluation, 75 Nw.U.L.Rev. 1112 (1981), 78

Redish and Phillips, *Erie* and the Rules of Decision Act: In Search of the Appropriate Dilemma, 91 Harv.L.Rev. 356 (1977), 685

Redish/Beste, contribution by, Symposium, Fifty Years of *International Shoe:* The Past and Future of Personal Jurisdiction, 28 U.C.Davis L.Rev. 513 (1995), 53

Rees, American Wills Statutes: II, 46 Va. L.Rev. 856 (1960), 763

Reese, Chief Judge Fuld and Choice of Law, 71 Colum.L.Rev. 548 (1971), 532

Reese, Choice of Law: Rules or Approach, 57 Corn.L.Q. 315 (1972), 532

Reese, comment by, Symposium: Choice of Law Theory After Allstate Insurance Co. v. Hague, 10 Hofstra L.Rev. 1 (1981), 360

Reese, Conflict of Laws and the Restatement Second, 28 Law & Contemp.Prob. 679 (1963), 520

Reese, Dépeçage: A Common Phenomenon in Choice of Law, 73 Colum.L.Rev. 58 (1973), 637, 821

Reese, Full Faith and Credit to Statutes: The Defense of Public Policy, 19 U.Chi.L.Rev. 339 (1952), 320

Reese, Legislative Jurisdiction, 78 Colum.L.Rev. 1587 (1978), 330, 362

Reese, Marriage in American Conflict of Laws, 26 Int'l & Comp.L.Q. 952 (1977), 822, 834

Reese, Power of Parties to Choose Law Governing Their Contract, 1960 Proc.Am.Soc. Int'l Law 49, p. 542

Reese, Review of M. Hancock, Studies in Modern Choice of Law, 9 Dalhousie L.J. 181 (1984), 553–554

Reese, The Law Governing Airplane Accidents, 39 Wash. & Lee L.Rev. 1303 (1982), 624

Reese and Flesch, Agency and Vicarious Liability in Conflict of Laws, 60 Colum.L.Rev. 764 (1960), 975

Reese and Green, That Elusive Word, "Residence," 6 Vand.L.Rev. 561 (1953), 16

Reese and Johnson, The Scope of Full Faith and Credit to Judgments, 49 Colum.L.Rev. 153 (1949), 265, 274

Reese and Kaufman, The Law Governing Corporate Affairs: Choice of Law and the Impact of Full Faith and Credit, 58 Colum.L.Rev. 1118 (1958), 996, 1002

Reese and Leiwant, Testimonial Privileges and Conflict of Laws, 41 Law & Contemp.Prob. 85 (1977), 416

Reichert, Problems with Parallel and Duplicate Proceedings: the Litispendence Principle and International Arbitration, 8 Arbitration International 237 (1992), 194

Reppy, Conflict of Laws Problems in the Division of Marital Property, 1 Valuation and Distribution of Marital Property § 10.03 (1985), 921

Restatement, First, Conflict of Laws § 7, p. 445

Restatement, First, Conflict of Laws § 8, p. 445

Restatement, Restitution § 74, p. 316

Restatement, Restitution § 74, p. 316

Restatement, Second, Conflict of Laws § 6, pp. 518, 519

Restatement, Second, Conflict of Laws § 6(2)(b), p. 445

Restatement, Second, Conflict of Laws § 6(2)(c), p. 445

Restatement, Second, Conflict of Laws § 8, Comment k, p. 446

Restatement, Second, Conflict of Laws § 8(2), p. 445

Restatement, Second, Conflict of Laws § 8(3), p. 446

Restatement, Second, Conflict of Laws § 9, p. 361

Restatement, Second, Conflict of Laws § 11, pp. 32, 986

Restatement, Second, Conflict of Laws § 13, p. 33

Restatement, Second, Conflict of Laws § 18, p. 15

Restatement, Second, Conflict of Laws § 22, p. 14

Restatement, Second, Conflict of Laws § 24, p. 36

Restatement, Second, Conflict of Laws § 26, p. 122

Restatement, Second, Conflict of Laws § 29, p. 27

Restatement, Second, Conflict of Laws § 31, p. 42

Restatement, Second, Conflict of Laws § 32, p. 43
Restatement, Second, Conflict of Laws § 33, p. 43
Restatement, Second, Conflict of Laws §§ 42–52, p. 66
Restatement, Second, Conflict of Laws § 43, p. 259
Restatement, Second, Conflict of Laws § 47, p. 44
Restatement, Second, Conflict of Laws § 53, pp. 198, 200
Restatement, Second, Conflict of Laws § 60, p. 128
Restatement, Second, Conflict of Laws §§ 70–74, p. 836
Restatement, Second, Conflict of Laws § 72, Comment b, p. 842
Restatement, Second, Conflict of Laws § 75, p. 881
Restatement, Second, Conflict of Laws § 76, p. 881
Restatement, Second, Conflict of Laws § 78, p. 884
Restatement, Second, Conflict of Laws § 80, p. 168
Restatement, Second, Conflict of Laws § 81, p. 43
Restatement, Second, Conflict of Laws §§ 82–83, p. 179
Restatement, Second, Conflict of Laws § 82, Comments e-f, p. 179
Restatement, Second, Conflict of Laws § 83, Comment b, p. 181
Restatement, Second, Conflict of Laws § 84, Comment i, p. 215
Restatement, Second, Conflict of Laws § 86, p. 214
Restatement, Second, Conflict of Laws § 91, p. 206
Restatement, Second, Conflict of Laws § 94, p. 245
Restatement, Second, Conflict of Laws § 95, p. 251
Restatement, Second, Conflict of Laws § 95, Comment (c)(1), p. 228
Restatement, Second, Conflict of Laws § 98, pp. 312, 747
Restatement, Second, Conflict of Laws § 102, Comment b, p. 258
Restatement, Second, Conflict of Laws § 103, pp. 264, 265
Restatement, Second, Conflict of Laws § 105, p. 156
Restatement, Second, Conflict of Laws § 110, Comment b, p. 254
Restatement, Second, Conflict of Laws § 112, p. 290
Restatement, Second, Conflict of Laws § 114, pp. 289, 316
Restatement, Second, Conflict of Laws § 116, p. 314
Restatement, Second, Conflict of Laws § 132, p. 401
Restatement, Second, Conflict of Laws § 136, p. 401
Restatement, Second, Conflict of Laws § 139, pp. 415, 416
Restatement, Second, Conflict of Laws § 139(1), p. 416
Restatement, Second, Conflict of Laws § 139(2), p. 416
Restatement, Second, Conflict of Laws § 142, pp. 426, 432
Restatement, Second, Conflict of Laws § 142(1), p. 426
Restatement, Second, Conflict of Laws § 142(2), p. 426
Restatement, Second, Conflict of Laws § 144, Comment g, p. 748
Restatement, Second, Conflict of Laws § 145, pp. 518, 519
Restatement, Second, Conflict of Laws § 146, p. 629
Restatement, Second, Conflict of Laws § 149, p. 634
Restatement, Second, Conflict of Laws § 150, p. 634
Restatement, Second, Conflict of Laws § 166, Comment b, p. 920
Restatement, Second, Conflict of Laws § 181, p. 645
Restatement, Second, Conflict of Laws § 182, p. 644
Restatement, Second, Conflict of Laws § 187, pp. 463, 541, 542, 548, 576, 590, 973
Restatement, Second, Conflict of Laws §§ 187–188, p. 973
Restatement, Second, Conflict of Laws § 187, Comment e, p. 543
Restatement, Second, Conflict of Laws § 187, Comment g, p. 594
Restatement, Second, Conflict of Laws § 187, Comment i, p. 543
Restatement, Second, Conflict of Laws § 187(1), p. 590
Restatement, Second, Conflict of Laws § 187(2), p. 590
Restatement, Second, Conflict of Laws § 188, pp. 475, 544, 546, 652
Restatement, Second, Conflict of Laws § 188(1), p. 547
Restatement, Second, Conflict of Laws § 188(2), p. 547
Restatement, Second, Conflict of Laws § 188(3), p. 546
Restatement, Second, Conflict of Laws §§ 189–190, p. 545
Restatement, Second, Conflict of Laws §§ 189–199, p. 546
Restatement, Second, Conflict of Laws § 192, p. 740
Restatement, Second, Conflict of Laws §§ 192–193, p. 546
Restatement, Second, Conflict of Laws § 193, pp. 501, 652
Restatement, Second, Conflict of Laws § 196, p. 546

Restatement, Second, Conflict of Laws § 197, p. 545
Restatement, Second, Conflict of Laws § 197, Comment (b), p. 545
Restatement, Second, Conflict of Laws § 199, p. 571
Restatement, Second, Conflict of Laws § 203, pp. 475, 546
Restatement, Second, Conflict of Laws § 203(2), p. 629
Restatement, Second, Conflict of Laws § 204, p. 819
Restatement, Second, Conflict of Laws § 206, p. 470
Restatement, Second, Conflict of Laws § 208, p. 653
Restatement, Second, Conflict of Laws § 209, p. 653
Restatement, Second, Conflict of Laws § 209, Comment a, p. 653
Restatement, Second, Conflict of Laws § 210, p. 653
Restatement, Second, Conflict of Laws § 211, p. 653
Restatement, Second, Conflict of Laws § 212, p. 484
Restatement, Second, Conflict of Laws § 214, p. 660
Restatement, Second, Conflict of Laws § 215, p. 662
Restatement, Second, Conflict of Laws § 216, p. 662
Restatement, Second, Conflict of Laws §§ 216–217, p. 661
Restatement, Second, Conflict of Laws § 217, pp. 628, 662
Restatement, Second, Conflict of Laws § 219, p. 654
Restatement, Second, Conflict of Laws § 220, p. 654
Restatement, Second, Conflict of Laws § 223, pp. 757, 770
Restatement, Second, Conflict of Laws §§ 223–243, p. 757
Restatement, Second, Conflict of Laws § 223, Comment a, p. 750
Restatement, Second, Conflict of Laws § 223(2), p. 757
Restatement, Second, Conflict of Laws § 224, pp. 817, 818
Restatement, Second, Conflict of Laws § 224, Comment e, p. 817
Restatement, Second, Conflict of Laws § 224(1), p. 757
Restatement, Second, Conflict of Laws §§ 233–234, p. 915
Restatement, Second, Conflict of Laws § 240, pp. 817, 818
Restatement, Second, Conflict of Laws § 240(1), p. 757
Restatement, Second, Conflict of Laws § 244, p. 781
Restatement, Second, Conflict of Laws §§ 244–266, p. 778
Restatement, Second, Conflict of Laws § 245, p. 781
Restatement, Second, Conflict of Laws § 251, p. 797
Restatement, Second, Conflict of Laws §§ 252–253, p. 794
Restatement, Second, Conflict of Laws § 257, p. 916
Restatement, Second, Conflict of Laws §§ 257–259, p. 915
Restatement, Second, Conflict of Laws § 258, Comment c, p. 920
Restatement, Second, Conflict of Laws § 260, p. 779
Restatement, Second, Conflict of Laws § 260, Comment b, p. 780
Restatement, Second, Conflict of Laws § 263, p. 779
Restatement, Second, Conflict of Laws § 263, Comment i, p. 780
Restatement, Second, Conflict of Laws § 264, p. 818
Restatement, Second, Conflict of Laws § 267, p. 814
Restatement, Second, Conflict of Laws §§ 267–282, p. 799
Restatement, Second, Conflict of Laws § 268, p. 818
Restatement, Second, Conflict of Laws § 270, p. 803
Restatement, Second, Conflict of Laws § 270, Comment a, p. 803
Restatement, Second, Conflict of Laws § 270, Comment e, p. 804
Restatement, Second, Conflict of Laws § 271, p. 811
Restatement, Second, Conflict of Laws §§ 271–272, p. 813
Restatement, Second, Conflict of Laws § 271, Comment a, p. 811
Restatement, Second, Conflict of Laws § 271, Comment c, p. 812
Restatement, Second, Conflict of Laws § 271, Comment h, p. 812
Restatement, Second, Conflict of Laws § 272, p. 812
Restatement, Second, Conflict of Laws § 283, p. 828
Restatement, Second, Conflict of Laws §§ 283–284, p. 821
Restatement, Second, Conflict of Laws § 283, Comments f-h, p. 824
Restatement, Second, Conflict of Laws § 283, Comment i, p. 824
Restatement, Second, Conflict of Laws § 284, p. 835
Restatement, Second, Conflict of Laws § 285, p. 843
Restatement, Second, Conflict of Laws § 287, p. 883
Restatement, Second, Conflict of Laws § 288, pp. 883, 884
Restatement, Second, Conflict of Laws §§ 289–290, p. 884

Restatement, Second, Conflict of Laws § 291, p. 973
Restatement, Second, Conflict of Laws §§ 291–292, p. 975
Restatement, Second, Conflict of Laws § 291, Comment f, p. 973
Restatement, Second, Conflict of Laws § 292, p. 975
Restatement, Second, Conflict of Laws § 293, p. 976
Restatement, Second, Conflict of Laws § 294, p. 976
Restatement, Second, Conflict of Laws § 295, p. 977
Restatement, Second, Conflict of Laws § 299, p. 962
Restatement, Second, Conflict of Laws § 301, pp. 996, 1000
Restatement, Second, Conflict of Laws §§ 301–303, p. 996
Restatement, Second, Conflict of Laws § 302, pp. 996, 1000
Restatement, Second, Conflict of Laws § 302, Comment e, p. 1001
Restatement, Second, Conflict of Laws § 311, p. 988
Restatement, Second, Conflict of Laws § 313, p. 999
Restatement, Second, Conflict of Laws §§ 314–315, p. 937
Restatement, Second, Conflict of Laws §§ 314–366, p. 934
Restatement, Second, Conflict of Laws § 317, p. 940
Restatement, Second, Conflict of Laws § 345, p. 946
Restatement, Second, Conflict of Laws § 354, p. 950
Restatement, Second, Conflict of Laws §§ 357–358, p. 660
Restatement, Second, Conflict of Laws § 358, p. 952
Restatement, Second, Conflict of Laws §§ 367–423, p. 955
Restatement, Second, Conflict of Laws § 378, p. 628
Restatement, Second, Judgments c. 4, p. 246
Restatement, Second, Judgments § 8, Comment g, p. 238
Restatement, Second, Judgments § 17, p. 228
Restatement, Second, Judgments §§ 19–20, p. 254
Restatement, Second, Judgments §§ 24–26, p. 228
Restatement, Second, Judgments § 24, Comment a, p. 229
Restatement, Second, Judgments § 30, p. 128
Restatement, Second, Judgments § 32, p. 128
Restatement, Second, Judgments § 70, p. 297
Restatement, Second, Judgments § 87, p. 253
Restatement, Second, Torts § 577A, p. 634
Restatement, Second, Torts §§ 766–774, p. 723
Restatement, Third, Foreign Relations Law of the United States (1987), pp. 36, 180

Restatement, Third, Foreign Relations Law of the United States § 403, pp. 201, 775
Restatement, Third, Foreign Relations Law of the United States § 403(2), p. 755
Restatement, Third, Foreign Relations Law of the United States § 403(2)(a), p. 755
Restatement, Third, Foreign Relations Law of the United States § 421(2)(a), p. 120
Restatement, Third, Foreign Relations Law of the United States § 443, p. 744
Restatement, Third, Foreign Relations Law of the United States §§ 481–486, p. 312
Restatement, Third, Foreign Relations Law of the United States § 823, p. 747
Restatement, Third, Foreign Relations Law of the United States § 823, Comment c, p. 748
Reynolds, The Iron Law of Full Faith and Credit, 53 Maryland L.Rev. 412 (1994), 194, 286
Reynolds, The Proper Forum for a Suit: Transnational Forum Non Conveniens and Counter–Suit Injunctions in the Federal Courts, 70 Tex.L.Rev. 1663 (1992), 194
Rheinstein, Domicile as Jurisdictional Basis of Divorce Decrees, 23 Conn.Bar J. 280 (1949), 855
Rheinstein, Review of Falconbridge, Essays on the Conflict of Laws (1947), 15 U.Chi. L.Rev. 478 (1948), 477
Rheinstein, The Constitutional Bases of Jurisdiction, 22 U.Chi.L.Rev. 775 (1955), 842
Riesenfeld, Shaffer v. Heitner: Holding, Implications, Forebodings, 30 Hast.L.J. 1183 (1979), 148
Robertson, Forum Non Conveniens in America and England: "A Rather Fantastic Fiction," 103 L.Q.R. 398 (1987), 189
Robertson, The Federal Doctrine of Forum Non Conveniens, 29 Tex.Int'l L.J. 353 (1994), 189
Rodgers and Rodgers, The Disparity between Due Process and Full Faith and Credit: The Problem of the Somewhere Wife, 67 Colum.L.Rev. 1363 (1967), 289
Rosenberg, Collateral Estoppel in New York, 44 St. John's L.Rev. 165 (1969), 228–229, 253
Rosenberg, Comments on *Reich v. Purcell*, 15 U.C.L.A.L.Rev. 551, p. 630
Rosenberg, The Comeback of Choice-of-Law Rules, 81 Colum.L.Rev. 946 (1981), 514

Santell, Escheat, Unclaimed Property and the Supreme Court, 17 West.Res.L.Rev. 50 (1965), 373
Schack, Perspektiven eines weltweiten Anerkennungs–Und Vollstreckungsabkommen, 1 Zeitschrift für Europäisches Privatrecht (1993), 225
Scharf, Case 2, Conference on Jurisdiction, Justice and Choice of Law for the 21st

Century, 29 New Eng.L.Rev. 618 (May 1995), 756

Schilling, Some European Decisions on Non-Possessory Security Rights in Private International Law, 34 Int'l & Comp.L.Q. 87 (1985), 816

Schlesinger, Baade, Damaska and Herzog, Comparative Law (5th ed. 1988), 402, 747

Schlesinger, A Recurrent Problem in Transnational Litigation: The Effect of a Failure to Invoke or Prove the Applicable Foreign Law, 59 Corn.L.Rev. 1 (1973), 395

Schnitzer, Handbuch des internationalen Privatrechts I, 52 and II, 639 (4th ed. 1957–58), 545

Schreter, "Quasi–Community Property" in Conflict of Laws, 50 Calif.L.Rev. 206 (1962), 933

Scoles, Apportionment of Federal Estate Taxes and Conflict of Laws, 55 Colum.L.Rev. 261 (1955), 813

Scoles, Conflict of Laws and Creditors' Rights in Decedents' Estates, 42 Iowa L.Rev. 341 (1957), 946

Scoles, Interstate and International Distinctions in Conflict of Laws in the United States, 54 Calif.L.Rev. 1599 (1966), 228, 389

Scoles and Hay, Conflict of Laws (2d ed. 1992 & 1995 Supp. with Borchers), 16, 31, 33, 66, 86, 190, 219, 227, 228, 257, 258, 297, 362, 656, 746, 747, 803, 819, 822, 829, 835, 853–872, 875, 877, 884, 914, 943, 946, 953, 954

Scoles and Rheinstein, Conflict Avoidance in Succession Planning, 21 Law and Contemp.Prob. 427 (1956), 954

Scott, Criminal Jurisdiction of a State over a Defendant Based upon Presence Secured by Force or Fraud, 37 Minn.L.Rev. 91 (1953), 180

Scott, Spendthrift Trusts and the Conflict of Laws, 77 Harv.L.Rev. 845 (1964), 806

Scott, What Law Governs Trusts? 99 Trusts and Estates, 186 (1960), 806

Scott and Fratcher, The Law of Trusts (4th ed. 1989), 803, 819

Sedler, article by, Symposium, 59 Brooklyn L.Rev. 1323 (1994), 566

Sedler, article by, Symposium, 1 Hofstra L.Rev. 104 (1973), 532

Sedler, article by, Symposium on the Complex Litigation Project, 54 La.L.Rev. (March 1994), 628

Sedler, comment by, Symposium: Choice of Law Theory After Allstate Insurance Co. v. Hague, 10 Hofstra L.Rev. 1 (1981), 360

Sedler, The Erie Outcome Test as a Guide to Substance and Procedure in the Conflict of Laws, 37 N.Y.U.L.Rev. 813 (1962), 409, 417

Segerdahl, article by, Symposium on the Complex Litigation Project, 54 La.L.Rev. (March 1994), 628

Seidelson, article by, Symposium on the Complex Litigation Project, 54 La.L.Rev. (March 1994), 628

Seidelson, Interest Analysis: The Quest for Perfection and the Frailties of Man, 19 Duq.L.Rev. 207 (1981), 517

Seidelson, Recasting *World–Wide Volkswagen* as a Source of Longer Jurisdictional Reach, 19 Tulsa L.J. 1 (1983), 175

Shapira, article by, Symposium, 1 Hofstra L.Rev. 104 (1973), 532

Shreve, article by, Symposium on the Complex Litigation Project, 54 La.L.Rev. (March 1994), 628

Shreve, Preclusion and Federal Choice of Law, 64 Tex.L.Rev. 1209 (1986), 250

Siegel, The U.C.C. and Choice of Law: Forum Choice or Forum Law, 21 Am. U.L.Rev. 494 (1972), 543

Silberman, article by, Symposium, 59 Brooklyn L.Rev. 1323 (1994), 566

Silberman, comment by, Symposium: Choice of Law Theory After Allstate Insurance Co. v. Hague, 10 Hofstra L.Rev. 1 (1981), 360

Silberman, contribution by, Symposium, Fifty Years of *International Shoe*: The Past and Future of Personal Jurisdiction, 28 U.C.Davis L.Rev. 513 (1995), 53

Silberman, contribution by, Symposium: The Future of Personal Jurisdiction, 22 Rutgers L.J. 559 (1991), 121

Silberman, Shaffer v. Heitner, The End of an Era, 53 N.Y.U.L.Rev. 33 (1978), 145, 148

Singer, A Pragmatic Guide to Conflicts, 70 B.U.L.Rev. 731 (1990), 622

Slomanson, Real Property Unrelated to Claim: Due Process for Quasi in Rem Jurisdiction?, 83 Dickinson L.Rev. 51 (1978), 148

Smit, Report of the Adm. Board of the N.Y.Jud.Conf. (1967), 402

Smit, The Uniform Interstate and International Procedure Act Approved by the National Conference of Commissioners on Uniform State Laws: A New Era Commences, 11 Am.J.Comp.L. 415 (1962), 401

Smith, Blue Ridge and Beyond: A Byrd's-Eye View of Federalism in Diversity Litigation, 36 Tul.L.Rev. 443 (1962), 678

Stein, contribution by, Symposium: The Future of Personal Jurisdiction, 22 Rutgers L.J. 559 (1991), 121

Sterk, Full Faith and Credit, More or Less, to Judgments: Doubts About Washington Gas Light Co. v. Thomas, 69 Geo.L.J. 1329 (1981), 279

Sterk, Testimonial Privileges: An Analysis of Horizontal Choice of Law Problems, 61 Minn.L.Rev. 461 (1977), 416

Stewart, A New Litany of Personal Jurisdiction, 60 U.Colo.L.Rev. 5 (1989), 63

Stone, The Recognition in England of Talaq Divorces, 14 Anglo–American L.Rev. 363 (1985), 877

Storke, Annulment in the Conflict of Laws, 43 Minn.L.Rev. 849 (1959), 881
Story, Conflict of Laws (8th ed. 1883), 449
Stumberg, Conflict of Laws (3d ed. 1963), 12
Sullivan, Unconstitutional Conditions, 102 Harv.L.Rev. 1413 (1989), 986
Swisher, Foreign Migratory Divorces—A Reappraisal, 21 J.Fam.Law 9 (1982/83), 875
Symeonides, article by, Symposium on the Complex Litigation Project, 54 La.L.Rev. (March 1994), 628
Symeonides, Choice of Law in the American Courts in 1993 (and in the Six Previous Years), 42 Am.J.Comp.L. 599 (1994), 5
Symeonides, Exception Clauses in American Conflicts Law, 42 Am.J.Comp.L. 813 (1994), 531
Symeonides, Louisiana Conflicts Law: Two "Surprises," 54 La.L.Rev. 497 (1994), 430
Symeonides, Louisiana's New Law of Choice of Law for Tort Conflicts: An Exegesis, 66 Tul.L.Rev. 677 (1992), 524
Symposium, 59 Brooklyn L.Rev. 1323 (1994), with articles by Sedler, Silberman and Twerski, 566
Symposium, 59 Col.L.Rev. 1 (1988), 346
Symposium, 1 Hofstra L.Rev. 104 (1973), with articles by Twerski, Sedler, Baade, Shapira and King, 532
Symposium, 63 Iowa L.Rev. 991, p. 148
Symposium, 61 Ky.L.J. 368 (1973), 531
Symposium, 22 Rutgers L.J. 559 (1991), 42
Symposium, 1978 Wash.U.L.Q. 273, p. 148
Symposium: Choice of Law Theory After Allstate Insurance Co. v. Hague, 10 Hofstra L.Rev. 1 (1981), with comments by Cavers, Davies, Leflar, Martin, Reese, Sedler, Silberman, Trautman, Twerski, von Mehren and Weintraub, 360
Symposium, Comments on Babcock v. Jackson, 63 Colum.L.Rev. 1212 (1963), 524
Symposium, Conference on Jurisdiction, Justice, and Choice of Law for the Twenty-First Century, Case Four: Choice of Law Theory, 29 New England L.Rev. 669 (1995), 566
Symposium: Conflict of Laws and Complex Litigation Issues in Mass Tort Litigation, 1989 U.Ill.L.Rev. 35, pp. 628, 721
Symposium, Fifty Years of *International Shoe*: The Past and Future of Personal Jurisdiction, 28 U.C.Davis L.Rev. 513 (1995), with contributions by Perschbacher, Weintraub, Borchers, Oakley, Silberman, Cameron/Johnson, Chemerinsky, Mullenix, Redish/Beste, Goldstein, Morse, Juenger and Bruch, 53, 63
Symposium on No–Fault Automobile Insurance, 71 Colum.L.Rev. 189 (1971), 640
Symposium on the Complex Litigation Project, 54 La.L.Rev. (March 1994), with articles by Cooper, Juenger, Kalis, Kozyris, Mullenix, Nafziger, Sedler, Segerdahl, Seidelson, Shreve, Symeonides, Trautman, Waldron and Wilkins, 628

Symposium: The Future of Personal Jurisdiction, 22 Rutgers L.J. 559 (1991), with contributions by Brilmayer, Silberman, Stein, Weintraub, Kogan, Twitchell, Redish and Maltz, 121

Taintor, Foreign Judgments in Rem: Full Faith and Credit v. Res Judicata *in Personam,* 8 U.Pitt.L.Rev. 223 (1942), 237
Taintor, Marriage to a Paramour after Divorce: The Conflict of Laws, 43 Minn. L.Rev. 889 (1959), 828
The American Law Institute Proceedings (1925), 32
The Validity of Forum Selecting Clauses, 13 Am.J.Comp.L. 157 (1964), 177
Thomas, 89 A.L.R.Fed. 238 (1988), 189
Trautman, article by, Symposium on the Complex Litigation Project, 54 La.L.Rev. (March 1994), 628
Trautman, comment by, Symposium: Choice of Law Theory After Allstate Insurance Co. v. Hague, 10 Hofstra L.Rev. 1 (1981), 360
Trautman, Some Notes on the Theory of Choice of Law Clauses, 35 Mercer L.Rev. 535 (1984), 478
Traynor, Is This Conflict Really Necessary?, 37 Texas L.Rev. 657 (1959), 495
Traynor, Professor Currie's Restrained and Enlightened Forum, 49 Calif.L.Rev. 845 (1961), 514–515
Traynor, War and Peace in the Conflict of Laws, 25 Int'l and Comp.L.Q. 121 (1976), 514
Twerski and Mayer, Toward a Pragmatic Solution of Choice-of-Law Problems—at the Interface of Substance and Procedure, 74 N.W.U.L.Rev. 781 (1979), 631
Twerski, article by, Symposium, 59 Brooklyn L.Rev. 1323 (1994), 566
Twerski, article by, Symposium, 1 Hofstra L.Rev. 104 (1973), 532
Twerski, comment by, Symposium: Choice of Law Theory After Allstate Insurance Co. v. Hague, 10 Hofstra L.Rev. 1 (1981), 360
Twitchell, A Rejoinder to Professor Brilmayer, 101 Harv.L.Rev. 1465 (1988), 89, 103
Twitchell, contribution by, Symposium: The Future of Personal Jurisdiction, 22 Rutgers L.J. 559 (1991), 121
Twitchell, The Myth of General Jurisdiction, 101 Harv.L.Rev. 610 (1988), 89, 103

Vaznaugh, Extraterritorial Jurisdiction—Environmental Muscle for the North American Trade Agreement, 17 Hastings Int'l & Comp.L.Rev. 207 (1993), 104
Vernon, Labyrinthine Ways: Jurisdiction to Annul, 10 J.Pub.L. 47 (1961), 881

Vernon, Recorded Chattel Security Interests in the Conflicts of Laws, 47 Iowa L.Rev. 346 (1962), 794

Vernon, State–Court Jurisdiction: A Preliminary Inquiry Into the Impact of Shaffer v. Heitner, 63 Iowa L.Rev. 997 (1978), 870

Vestal, A Comprehensive Uniform Limited Partnership Act? The Time Has Come, 28 U.C.Davis L.Rev. 1195 (1995), 979

Vestal, Expanding the Jurisdictional Reach of the Federal Courts: The 1973 Change in Federal Rule 4, 38 N.Y.U.L.Rev. 1053 (1963), 699

Vestal, Preclusion/Res Judicata Variables: Parties, 50 Iowa L.Rev. 27 (1964), 685

Vestal, Res Judicata/Preclusion by Judgment: The Law Applied in Federal Courts, 66 Mich.L.Rev. 1723 (1968), 685

Vestal, Res Judicata Preclusion: Expansion, 47 So.Cal.L.Rev. 357 (1974), 685

von Mehren, Choice of Law and the Problem of Justice, 41 Law and Contemp.Prob. 27 (1977), 631

von Mehren, comment by, Symposium: Choice of Law Theory After Allstate Insurance Co. v. Hague, 10 Hofstra L.Rev. 1 (1981), 360

von Mehren, Special Substantive Rules for Multi–State Problems: Their Role and Significance in Contemporary Choice of Law Methodology, 88 Harv.L.Rev. 347 (1974), 629

von Mehren and Trautman, Jurisdiction to Adjudicate: A Suggested Analysis, 79 Harv.L.Rev. 1121 (1966), 66, 90

von Mehren and Trautman: *The Functional Analysis,* 515

Voxman, Jurisdiction over a Parent Corporation in Its Subsidiary's State of Incorporation, 141 U.Pa.L.Rev. 327 (1992), 110

Wade, Domicile: A Re–Examination, 32 Int'l & Comp.L.Q. 1 (1983), 16

Waldron, article by, Symposium on the Complex Litigation Project, 54 La.L.Rev. (March 1994), 628

Warner, Multistate Publication in Radio and Television, 23 Law & Contemp.Prob. 14 (1958), 635

Weber, Purposeful Availment, 39 S.C.L.Rev. 815 (1988), 63

Weinberg, Against Comity, 80 Georgetown L.J. 53 (1991), 320

Weinberg, Choice of Law and Minimal Scrutiny, 49 U.Chi.L.Rev. 440 (1982), 361

Weinberg, Choosing Law: The Limitations Debates, 1991 U.Ill.L.Rev. 683, p. 433

Weinberg, Federal Common Law, 83 Nw. U.L.Rev. 805 (1989), 669, 726

Weinberg, Mass Torts and the Neutral Forum: A Critical Analysis of the ALI's Proposed Choice Rule, 56 Alb.L.Rev. 807 (1993), 628

Weinberg, The Federal–State Conflict of Laws: "Actual" Conflicts, 70 Tex.L.Rev. 1743 (1992), 250

Weinberg, The Place of Trial and the Law Applied: Overhauling Constitutional Theory, 59 Col.L.Rev. 67 (1988), 346

Weinberger, Party Autonomy and Choice-of-Law: The Restatement (Second), Interest Analysis, and the Search for a Methodological Synthesis, 4 Hofstra L.Rev. 605 (1976), 542

Weinstein, Recognition in the United States of the Privileges of Another Jurisdiction, 56 Colum.L.Rev. 535 (1956), 417

Weintraub, A Map Out of the Personal Jurisdiction Labyrinth, 28 U.C.Davis L.Rev. 531 (1995), 64, 102, 120, 121

Weintraub, Affecting the Parent–Child Relationship Without Jurisdiction Over Both Parents, 36 Sw.L.J. 1167 (1983), 890

Weintraub, An Objective Basis for Rejecting Transient Jurisdiction, 22 Rutgers L.J. 611 (1991), 120

Weintraub, Beyond Dépeçage: A "New Rule" Approach to Choice of Law in Consumer Credit Transactions and a Critique of the Territorial Application of the Uniform Consumer Credit Code, 25 Case Western Res.L.Rev. 16 (1974), 639

Weintraub, Case Three: Personal Jurisdiction, 29 New England L.Rev. 664 (1995), 86

Weintraub, Choosing Law with an Eye on the Prize, 15 Mich.J. Int'l L. 705 (1994), 386, 518

Weintraub, Commentary on the Conflict of Laws (3d ed. 1986) and (Supp. 1991), 5, 66, 86, 258, 329, 543, 690, 758, 778, 795, 890, 899

Weintraub, comment by, Symposium: Choice of Law Theory After Allstate Insurance Co. v. Hague, 10 Hofstra L.Rev. 1 (1981), 360

Weintraub, contribution by, Symposium, Fifty Years of *International Shoe:* The Past and Future of Personal Jurisdiction, 28 U.C.Davis L.Rev. 513 (1995), 53

Weintraub, contribution by, Symposium: The Future of Personal Jurisdiction, 22 Rutgers L.J. 559 (1991), 121

Weintraub, Due Process Limitations on the Personal Jurisdiction of State Courts: Time for Change, 63 Or.L.Rev. 485 (1984), 120

Weintraub, In Inquiry into the Utility of "Situs" As a Concept in Conflicts Analysis, 52 Cornell L.Q. 1 (1966), 553

Weintraub, International Litigation and Forum Non Conveniens, 29 Texas Int'l L.J. 321, (1994), 38, 623

Weintraub, The Contributions of Symeonides and Kozyris in Making Choice of Law Predictable and Just: An Appreciation and Critique, 38 Am.J.Comp.L. 511 (1990), 524

Weintraub, The Extraterritorial Application of Antitrust and Security Laws: An Inquiry into the Utility of a "Choice-of-Law" Approach, 70 Texas L.Rev. 1799 (1992), 756

Weintraub, The Future of Choice of Law for Torts: What Principles Should be Preferred? 41 L. & Contemp.Prob. 146 (1977), 517

Weintraub, Who's Afraid of Constitutional Limitations on Choice of Law?, 10 Hofstra L.Rev. 17 (1981), 320

Wellborn, The Federal Rules of Evidence and The Application of State Law in The Federal Courts, 55 Tex.L.Rev. 371 (1977), 685

Westerheim, The Uniform Foreign–Money Claims Act: No Solution to an Old Problem, 69 Texas L.Rev. (1991), 312

Wilde, Dépeçage in the Choice of Tort Law, 41 S.Calif.L.Rev. 329 (1968), 639

Wilkins, article by, Symposium on the Complex Litigation Project, 54 La.L.Rev. (March 1994), 628

Wright, Law of Federal Courts (5th Ed.1994), 669, 678

Wurfel: Jet Age Domicil: The Semi–Demise of Durational Residence Requirements, 11 Wake Forest L.Rev. 349 (1975), 30

Wurfel, Recognition of Foreign Judgments, 50 N.Car.L.Rev. 21 (1971), 227

Yntema, The Objectives of Private International Law, 35 Can.Bar.Rev. 721 (1957), 3

CONFLICT OF LAWS

*

CHAPTER 1

INTRODUCTION

1. THE SUBJECT MATTER

The conflict of laws is the study of how the answer to a legal problem is affected by the fact that the elements of the problem have contacts with more than one jurisdiction. In a world in which interstate and international transactions take place with increasing frequency, no lawyer can ignore the subject. A knowledge of the conflict of laws is necessary not only for litigators, but also for all lawyers who give advice or draft documents relating to interstate and international activities.

In interstate and international transactions, there are three major topics that must be addressed either in the planning or dispute resolution stage. (1) Where can any dispute arising out of the transaction be resolved by suit or other means, such as arbitration? (2) What law will be applied to resolve the dispute? (3) What will be the effect of any judgment or award? An example may be helpful.

A group of Texas residents contracts for a vacation bus tour of Mexico. In their home city of Corpus Christi, they board a Texas Lines bus to Brownsville, a Texas city on the border with Mexico. Texas Lines is a Texas company. In Brownsville, they board a bus owned by a Mexican bus company. While traveling in Mexico, this bus plunges off a cliff and all of the occupants are fatally injured. Some die immediately, some a few days later. Now let us consider the three major conflict-of-laws issues in the context of this case.

Where can suit be brought? The dependents and representatives of the decedents wish to bring wrongful death and survival suits against Texas Lines and, because liability of Texas Lines is doubtful, especially against the Mexican bus company. If plaintiffs sue in Mexico, there is no doubt that there is personal jurisdiction over the Mexican defendant, but is there jurisdiction over Texas Lines? If plaintiffs sue in Texas, can they obtain personal jurisdiction over the Mexican company? If plaintiffs can obtain jurisdiction over the Mexican defendant in a Texas state court, will that defendant be able to remove to a federal court? Will a Texas state court dismiss suit under the doctrine of forum non conveniens? Will a federal court sitting in Texas apply Texas doctrines of jurisdiction and forum non conveniens?

What law will be applied? Under Mexican law, there are low statutory caps on some elements of recovery, such as lost wages, and there is no compensation for other harm, such as pain and suffering. As a result, the average recovery per passenger would be about $25,000. Under Texas law, there are no statutory caps on damages and there is recovery for several kinds of non-economic injury, including pain and suffering. Not including punitive damages, which may be available on these facts under Texas law, but are not available under Mexican law, the average recovery per passenger under Texas law would be about $1,000,000. If plaintiffs sue in Mexico, a Mexican court will apply Mexican law because the fatal injuries occurred in Mexico.[1] If plaintiffs sue in Texas, will a Texas state court apply Texas law?[2] If suit is brought in or removed to a federal court sitting in Texas, will the federal court apply the same law as would be applied by a Texas state court?

What will be the effect of any judgment? Because of the difference in damages obtainable under Mexican and Texas law, it would be advantageous for the plaintiffs to sue in Texas and have Texas law applied. If a large judgment is obtained against the Mexican bus company in a Texas court, does that defendant have sufficient assets in Texas or other states of the United States for satisfaction of the judgment? If not, will a Mexican court recognize and enforce the Texas judgment?

These are the questions that all parties in the litigation arising out of the bus crash must carefully research. Moreover, they must do the research before taking any action. For example, whether or not a Mexican court will recognize and enforce a Texas judgment depends, in part, on the method used to serve process on the Mexican defendant.[3]

This illustration concerned an unintentional tort. Parties to commercial transactions should ask and research the same basic questions before any contract is signed. In commercial agreements, the parties can, by properly drafted provisions, exercise substantial control over the place and method of dispute resolution, and the law that will be applied.

2. THE FUNCTIONS OF CONFLICTS AS A BODY OF LAW

For the first and third of the basic topics of conflict of laws, jurisdiction and judgments, it is obvious that a coherent body of rules is necessary. Within a federal nation, such as ours, these rules control the jurisdictional reach of state and federal courts and determine the respect that must be accorded to their judgments in other state and federal courts. Internationally there are or should be standards to determine what bases for jurisdiction are legitimate and under what circumstances judgments will be respected. No country that believes a foreign court has improperly exercised jurisdiction, will recognize that court's judgment. Lord Ellenborough's comment on the Island of Tobago, quoted in the caption of the frontispiece photograph, is an eloquent expression of this concept.

---

1. Mexican Civil Code for the Federal District and Territories, Art. 12 (as amended by decree published in the Diario Official, January 7, 1988).

2. In Trailways, Inc. v. Clark, 794 S.W.2d 479 (Tex.App.—Corpus Christi 1990, writ denied), infra page 566, a case similar to the illustration, Texas law was applied to the Mexican bus company.

3. See Anderson, Transnational Litigation Involving Mexican Parties, 25 St. Mary's L.J. 1059, 1111 (1994).

But what of choice of law? Do we really need rules here? Why should not every court simply apply the law of its own jurisdiction? This would certainly be simpler than entertaining complex arguments concerning what law applies and then, if the decision is that local law is displaced, attempting to apply without distortion the law of another state or country.

Ernst Rabel, a great scholar of comparative conflict of laws, wrote that "it has been customary to regard the attainment of uniform solutions as the chief purpose of" choice-of-law rules.[4] But surely there must be other more cogent reasons for rules concerning choice of law than an attempt to insulate the result from the selection of the forum.[5] Rabel himself quickly translated the need for "uniform solutions" into protection of "the legitimate expectations of the parties."[6] In recent decades, there has been increased recognition that one purpose for choosing law is to give effect to the policies underlying the diverse domestic rules of the jurisdictions that have contacts with the parties or the transaction. There are also relevant universal policies, such as facilitating interstate and international transactions.

3. HISTORY

Our debt to England is here not as large as in other fields, for conflict of laws had an arrested development in English jurisprudence. The early centralization of power in the king and the establishment of a common law for the whole realm put an end to the conflicting laws inside the kingdom and eliminated the intra-national conflict of laws which elsewhere stimulated the development of the subject. International conflict of laws cases were kept out of the common law courts by a principle of venue; for, since the trial was to be by a jury of the vicinage, the courts felt themselves unable to try cases arising in other countries. International cases had to go into special courts—the merchants courts and the court of admiralty. In time the difficulty of venue was surmounted in the common law courts by a fiction: the facts were treated as having occurred in England. But the idea persisted that a case must be determined under the ordinary law of the court in which it was tried and not any other. Not until the nineteenth and twentieth centuries did England develop a coherent body of doctrines of conflict of laws and by that time developments on this side of the ocean had taken their own course.

---

4. E. Rabel, 1 The Conflict of Laws: A Comparative Study 94 (2d ed. by Drobnig 1958).

5. The "primitive idea that jurisdiction implies the applicable law, or in other words that a court can apply only the rules prescribed by its hierarchic superior, universally prevailed in ancient times, until about 1200 the general equitable conception was introduced that the more convenient and useful law should furnish the rule of decision conformably to the nature of the case." Yntema, The Objectives of Private International Law, 35 Can.Bar.Rev. 721–22 (1957).

6. Rabel, supra note 4, id. See also Kegel, The Crisis of Conflict of Laws, Hague Academy of International Law, 112 Collected Courses 91, 188 (1964–II): "since every state has to insure the achievement of justice on its own, these interests [in international uniformity of result] are, despite widespread opinion to the contrary, rather sharply delimited."

On the continent of Europe, the need for principles of conflict of laws had become apparent very early, at first in Italy and later in France. The development of the principles of conflict of laws began in the Italian universities in the 1200's and 1300's during the revival of the study of Roman law. The conditions demanded it. Northern Italy was divided into a number of city states. While they were a part of the Holy Roman Empire and regarded Roman law as a common law applicable to all of them, each had its local laws governing many matters. Trade was brisk between them and conflicts between their local laws arose with some frequency. A Bologna-Padua case or a Florence-Perugia case was apt to involve conflicting laws; in time, principles were developed to settle these conflicts. The local laws of the city states were called "statuta." The basic method or theory of the emerging system concerning the choice of the law to be applied to a case came to be called the statuta or statute theory. It is discussed in some American cases.

Afterwards, France and then the Netherlands developed conflicts theories that were in a sense intra-national, reflecting the diversity of legal systems among their constituent provinces. The writings of a Dutch jurist, Huber, proved highly influential in America, for his conception of territorial sovereignty made a deep impact on a great, early theorist in American conflicts law, Justice Joseph Story. In 1834 Story published his Commentaries on the Conflict of Laws, the first comprehensive treatment in English on the subject. For his general views he relied on continental theorists, particularly Huber, and Huber's dedication to the idea of territorial sovereignty as the foundation of thinking about the subject.

The course of growth in the next century was heavily influenced by the Story-Huber approach. This was embraced in its main parts by Professor Joseph H. Beale, who had an enormous influence through his teachings, commentaries, and, ultimately, his work as Reporter for the American Law Institute's first Restatement of Conflict of Laws, published in 1934.

4. THE CONFLICT OF LAWS TODAY

Judicial Jurisdiction. The due process clauses of the Fourteenth and Fifth Amendments limit the jurisdiction of state and federal courts. Theoretically, this should free our courts to exercise jurisdiction within broad boundaries of civilized reasonableness. When International Shoe Co. v. State of Washington,[7] displaced a power theory of jurisdiction with the requirement that the defendant "have certain minimum contacts with [the forum] such that maintenance of the suit does not offend 'traditional notions of fair play and substantial justice,'" the day of this jurisdictional freedom seemed to have dawned. Instead, in its attempt to give more concrete meaning to the general standard of International Shoe, the Supreme Court of the United States has added layer upon layer of complexity to the task of determining when the exercise of jurisdiction is constitutionally permissible. Approximately five hundred reported cases a year

---

7. 326 U.S. 310, 66 S.Ct. 154, 90 L.Ed. 95 (1945).

now focus on personal jurisdiction, and these are a small fraction of the unreported cases in which the issue is briefed and argued. One reason for this amount of litigation concerning jurisdiction is that prediction of the result is difficult. It is commonplace that the determination of jurisdiction is fact driven; minor changes in circumstances can affect the result. The task is, however, even more formidable than this would suggest, because in many instances, our courts cannot agree on what facts are relevant.

Choice of law. Here there has been revolutionary change. In 1960, every United States court would have chosen Mexican law as applicable to the bus accident discussed previously. This was because Mexico was the place of injury. As of January 1, 1995, thirty-seven states plus the District of Columbia and Puerto Rico,[8] would choose law by a rule or method that took into account the content and purposes of the Mexican and Texas laws. Similar changes in conflicts theory have also occurred in other countries. The abandonment of rigid territorial conflicts rules has ameliorated some problems, but has generated new difficulties. Richard Posner has listed the change in choice-of-law method among the "legal reforms [that] have miscarried [resulting in] the destruction of certainty in the field of conflict of laws as a result of the replacement of the mechanical common law rules by 'interest analysis.' "[9] The choice-of-law materials in this book focus on the issues of whether this criticism is justified and on whether there is a desirable via media between territorial rules that select law without regard to its content, and methods that result in ad hoc chaos.

Judgments. Within the United States, docket pressures have greatly increased the ability of non-parties to utilize a judgment to preclude relitigation of issues decided. Internationally, the United States is not a signatory of any bilateral or multinational treaty for the recognition of judgments. Almost all of our states grant broad comity to foreign judgments and American judgments have usually been respected abroad except to the extent that they include punitive or multiple damages.

5. THE FUTURE OF CONFLICTS

Jurisdiction. Domestically, the challenge is to stem the flood of cases that contest this threshold issue and to improve predictability. Perhaps comparative study of how others, such as the European Union, have formulated jurisdictional rules, would facilitate the task. Internationally, we must respond to the charge that some of our bases for jurisdiction over foreigners are exorbitant.

---

8. Thirty-five states plus the District of Columbia and Puerto Rico are listed with citation of cases in R. Weintraub, Commentary on the Conflict of Laws (3d ed. 1986) and (Supp.1991). Two subsequent additions are Delaware: Travelers Indem. Co. v. Lake, 594 A.2d 38 (Del.1991) and Tennessee: Hataway v. Mckinley, 830 S.W.2d 53 (Tenn.1992).

The same jurisdictions are listed without citation of cases in Symeonides, Choice of Law in the American Courts in 1993 (and in the Six Previous Years), 42 Am.J.Comp.L. 599, 606–08 (1994).

9. R. Posner, The Problems of Jurisprudence, 429–30 (1990).

Choice of Law and Judgments. Courts and legislatures will continue their attempts to fashion rules that avoid mechanical approaches yet provide reasonable predictability.[10] The recent Louisiana codification[11] is an attempt to do this. One method of eliminating conflicts between state rules is to substitute federal law. In the past, attempts to do this for issues such as products liability and airplane accidents have failed, but the efforts are likely to continue. Some scholars have argued that we cannot trust the states to decide when their law applies and that either Congress or federal courts should impose rules under the aegis of such clauses of the United States Constitution as due process, full faith and credit, commerce, and equal protection. As the materials in this book indicate, for a time in the early decades of this century, the United States Supreme Court did appear to raise some territorial choice-of-law rules to constitutional status. More recently, the Court has allowed the states to do pretty much what they will with choice of law.

Internationally, there are many treaties in force affecting choice of law. One that the United States was instrumental in drafting and has ratified is The United Nations Convention on Contracts for the International Sale of Goods. Instead of choice-of-law rules, the Convention sets out uniform law to cover certain aspects of international sales. The United Nations, The Hague Conference on Private International Law, The International Bank for Reconstruction and Development, and regional organizations such as the European Union and the Organization of American States, have sponsored the drafting of and opened for signature multinational conventions covering the major topics of the conflict of laws and facilitating international dispute resolution. Frequent reference will be made to these conventions as part of the comparative coverage that is found throughout this book. The future will see many more such international collaborative efforts. The United States is urging the Hague Conference on Private International Law to sponsor the drafting of a judgments recognition convention.

Prediction is always hazardous. One certainty is that resolution of problems in the conflict of laws is vital to a peaceful and prosperous future.

---

10. For a survey of contemporary approaches, see Hay, Flexibility Versus Predictability and Uniformity in Choice of Law, Hague Academy of International Law, 226 Collected Courses 281–412 (1991–I).

11. La.Civ.C.Ann. arts. 3515–49 (effective January 1, 1992).

CHAPTER 2

Domicile: The Chosen Point of Entry

INTRODUCTORY NOTE

Domicile is a concept that is used in a number of traditional choice-of-law rules and for other purposes related to the subject matter of the Conflict of Laws. This chapter is then an introduction to traditional thinking in Conflict of Laws and, at least as important in view of widespread changes in doctrine, an introduction to the rebuttals and questioning that this traditional system invited.

1. INTESTATE SUCCESSION TO MOVABLES

In Re Estate of Jones
Supreme Court of Iowa, 1921.
192 Iowa 78, 182 N.W. 227, 16 A.L.R. 1286.

Plaintiff claims that she is the illegitimate child of the decedent, Evan Jones, and as such is his sole heir and entitled to his entire estate. The administrator of the estate is made a party and also the brothers and sisters of the said decedent, who claim that the estate of the decedent descends to them. The court denied the plaintiff the relief sought, and she prosecutes this appeal. Reversed.

■ FAVILLE, J. The decedent, Evan Jones, was a native of Wales. When he was about 33 years of age, he came to America as an immigrant. This was in 1883. He came over on the same ship with the wife and children of one David P. Jones. At that time, David P. Jones was living in Oskaloosa, Iowa, to which place the decedent went. After the death of David P. Jones, the decedent married his widow, who subsequently died in January, 1914. The decedent, Evan Jones, was a coal miner, an industrious, hard-working, thrifty Welshman, who accumulated a considerable amount of property. In 1896, he was naturalized in the district court of Wapello county, Iowa, and thereafter voted at elections. The reason for his leaving Wales at the time he did was because of bastardy proceedings which had been instituted against him by the mother of the appellant. In 1915, the decedent disposed of his property, which then consisted of two farms and some city real estate. He was advised by his banker to leave the greater part of his money in a bank at Ottumwa until he got to Wales, and did so deposit it. He purchased a draft for about $2,000 and left some $20,000 on deposit in the bank, and also a note and mortgage for collection, and left with the banker the address of a sister in Wales, stating that he intended to live with said sister. He sailed from New York on May 1, 1915, on the ill-fated Lusitania, and was drowned when the boat was sunk by a German submarine on May 7, 1915. The Lusitania was a vessel of the Cunard line, flying the British flag....

I. The question for our determination in this case is whether or not, under the facts stated, the domicile of the decedent at the time of his death was in Wapello county, Iowa, or in Wales. If his domicile at the time that the Lusitania sank was legally in Wales, then it is conceded by all the parties that, under the laws of the British Empire, the appellant, as his illegitimate child, would have no interest in his estate. On the other hand, if the decedent at said time legally had his domicile in Wapello county, Iowa, then the property passed to the appellant as his sole heir under the laws of this state.

For the purposes of the present discussion, it may be conceded that the evidence is sufficient to justify a finding that the appellant was the child of the decedent and had been so recognized and declared to such an extent as to satisfy the requirements of Code, § 3385.

It may also be conceded, for present purposes, that it is established by the evidence in the case that the decedent had by acts and declarations evidenced a purpose to leave his home in Iowa permanently and to return to his native country, Wales, for the purpose of living there the remainder of his life....

It is well settled that every person, under all circumstances and conditions, must have a domicile somewhere.

There are different kinds of domiciles recognized by the law. It is generally held that the subject may be divided into three general classes:

(1) Domicile of origin.

(2) Domicile of choice.

(3) Domicile by operation of law.

The "domicile of origin" of every person is the domicile of his parents at the time of his birth. In Prentiss v. Barton, 19 Fed.Cas. 1276, No. 11384, Circuit Justice Marshall said: "By the general laws of the civilized world, the domicile of the parents at the time of birth, or what is termed 'the domicile of origin', constitutes the domicile of an infant, and continues, until abandoned, or until the acquisition of a new domicile, in a different place."

The "domicile of choice" is the place which a person has elected and chosen for himself to displace his previous domicile.

"Domicile by operation of law" is that domicile which the law attributes to a person independent of his own intention or action of residence. This results generally from the domestic relations of husband and wife, or parent and child.

In the instant case, we have to deal only with the first two kinds of domicile; that is, domicile of origin and domicile of choice. Applying these general definitions to the facts of this case, the domicile of origin of Evan Jones was in Wales, where he was born, and the domicile of choice was Wapello county, Iowa. The question that concerns us is: Where was his domicile for the purpose of descent of personal property on the 7th day of May, 1915, when the Lusitania was sunk off the coast of the British Isles?

The matter of the determination of any person's domicile arises in different ways and is construed by the courts for a variety of different purposes. Apparent inconsistencies occur in the authorities because of the failure to clearly preserve the distinctions to be made by reason of the purpose for which the determination of one's domicile is being legally ascertained. The question frequently arises where it becomes important to determine the domicile for the purpose of taxation, or for the purpose of attachment, or for the levy of execution, or for the exercising of the privilege of voting, or in determining the statute of limitations, or in ascertaining liability for the support of paupers, and perhaps other purposes. Definitions given in regard to the method of ascertaining the domicile for one purpose are not always applicable in ascertaining the domicile for another purpose....

In the instant case, we are concerned only in the matter of the domicile of the decedent, Evan Jones, as it affects the question of the descent of his personal estate.... [D]ecedent's intention was to abandon his domicile of choice and return to his domicile of origin. He died in itinere. It is needless for us to cite the vast number of cases announcing the general rule that the acquisition of a new domicile must have been completely perfected, and hence there must have been a concurrence both of the fact of removal and the intent to remain in the new locality before the former domicile can be considered lost....

At the outset, it is obvious that under the circumstances of the instant case the domicile of the decedent at the time of his death must in any event be determined by the assumption of a fiction. All will agree that the decedent did not have a domicile on the Lusitania. In order to determine his domicile, then, one of two fictions must be assumed, either that he retained the Iowa domicile until one was acquired in Wales, or that he acquired a domicile in Wales the instant he abandoned the Iowa domicile and started for Wales, with the intent and purpose of residing there. Which one of these fictions shall we assume for the purpose of determining the disposition of his personal property? This question first came before the courts at an early day, long before our present easy and extensive methods of transportation, and at a time before the present ready movement from one country to another. At that time men left Europe for the Western Continent or elsewhere largely for purposes of adventure or in search of an opportunity for the promotion of commerce. It was at a time before the invention of the steamboat and before the era of the oceanic cable. Men left their native land knowing that they would be gone for long periods of time, and that means of communication with their home land were infrequent, difficult, and slow. The traditions of their native country were strong with these men. In the event of death, while absent, they desired that their property should descend in accordance with the laws of the land of their birth....

These reasons, which were, to an extent at least, historical and patriotic, found early expression in the decisions of the courts on the question of domicile. The general rule was declared to be that a domicile is retained until a new domicile has been actually acquired. At an early time, however, an exception was ingrafted upon this rule to the effect that, *for the purposes of succession,* a party abandoning a domicile of *choice,* with the intent to return to his domicile of *origin,* regains the latter the instant that the former domicile is abandoned....

The leading and most frequently cited English case is that of Udny v. Udny, L.R. 1 H.L. (Sc.) 441. In this case the question arose as to the domicile of one Udny, who was born in Scotland and who afterward resided in England and in France. The Lord Chancellor declared: "But the domicile of origin is a matter wholly irrespective of any animus on the part of its subject. He acquires a certain status civilis, which subjects him and his property to the municipal jurisdiction of a country which he may never even have seen and in which he may never reside during the whole course of his life, his domicile being simply determined by that of his father."

It is further said: "It seems reasonable to say that if the choice of a new abode and actual settlement there constitute a change of the original domicile, then the exact converse of such a procedure, viz., the intention to abandon the new domicile, and an actual abandonment of it, ought to be equally effective to destroy the new domicile.... Why should not the domicile of origin cast on him by no choice of his own, and changed for a time, be the state to which he naturally falls back when his first choice has been abandoned animo et facto, and whilst he is deliberating before he makes a second choice." ...

It is true that the question of domicile is not to be determined by the question of citizenship, but when we are assuming the fiction that the domicile of origin reverts immediately upon the abandonment of a domicile of choice and assume that fiction, because of native allegiance, to the land of one's birth, then the basis for the fiction and assumption is destroyed when it appears that the party has renounced his native allegiance and has secured citizenship in the land of his domicile of choice. The reason for the rule having failed, the rule fails also....

One reason that is persuasive why such a rule should not be adopted is that a person who in these days abandons his domicile of origin and acquires a legal domicile in another jurisdiction, presumably, at least, is familiar with the laws, of the jurisdiction of the latter domicile, and there is to say the least, as strong a presumption that he desires his estate to be administered according to the laws of that jurisdiction as of the jurisdiction of the domicile of origin. While there may have been a good reason for the establishment of the English rule at the time and under the conditions under which it was announced, we do not believe that any good reason exists for the recognition of such a rule under the circumstances disclosed in this case. The general rule that a domicile once legally acquired is retained until a new domicile is secured, and that, in the acquisition of such new domicile, both the fact and the intention must concur, it seems to us is a rule of universal and general application and that there is neither good logic nor substantial reason for the application of an exception to that rule in the case where the party is in itinere toward the domicile of origin. In other words, going back to the original proposition, the fiction is assumed generally that any domicile, either of choice or of origin, is retained until a new domicile has been legally acquired. We see no good reason for changing that rule in the one instance where the descent of property is involved and the party is in itinere to the domicile of origin....

[Judgment of the trial court reversed and the estate ordered distributed under Iowa law to the decedent's child as his sole heir.]

WHITE V. TENNANT, 31 W.Va. 790, 8 S.E. 596 (1888). Michael White, until a month before he death, had been a life-long domiciliary of West Virginia, where his wife and brothers and sisters were also domiciled. His mother, brothers, and sisters lived in the mansion-house of the family farm, which was on the West Virginia–Pennsylvania border and extended into both states. Michael White and his wife occupied a separate farm fifteen miles away in West Virginia. He sold that farm and made an agreement with his mother and siblings to occupy a house on part of the family farm that was in Pennsylvania. The day he left his farm intending not to return, he stopped off at the Pennsylvania house to unload household goods and turn live-stock loose. His wife was not feeling well and on the invitation of his family, Michael and his wife stayed that night at the mansion house in West Virginia. His wife was found to have typhoid fever. She recovered, but Michael also contracted the fever and died intestate before ever living in the Pennsylvania house. Under West Virginia intestacy law, Michael's entire estate would go to his widow, but under Pennsylvania law, half went to his siblings and half to his widow. The court decided that Michael died domiciled in Pennsylvania and that therefore the distribution of his estate was governed by Pennsylvania law. The court reasoned that he had the intention of making the Pennsylvania house "his residence for an indefinite time [and] when he and his wife arrived at his new home, it become eo instanti his domicile...."

NOTES

1. As the passages from Udny v. Udny, L.R. 1 H.L. 441 (1869) quoted in Estate of Jones suggest, the Iowa court misinterpreted the English rule on revival of the domicile of origin. The rule was applicable not only when a domicile of choice was abandoned to return to the domicile of origin, but also whenever a domicile of choice was abandoned until a new domicile of choice was established. Id. at 448, 454, 460–61. A reason for the rule, in addition to notions of patriotism, was that one fictitious domicile was sufficient. When a person left a domicile of choice intending never to return and it seemed unrealistic to say that the person retained a domicile there, the domicile of origin, originally acquired by operation of law, would renew again by operation of law, until a new domicile of choice had been acquired. Is it likely that a correct understanding of the doctrine of reverter would have changed the result in Estate of Jones?

The doctrine of reverter has been abolished in Australia and New Zealand. Aust. Acts of Parliament, Domicile Act of 1982 § 7; New Zealand Domicile Act § 11. The English and Scottish Law Commissions have proposed similar legislation (The Law of Domicile, Law.Com. No. 168 ¶ 5.25), but there is as yet no implementing legislation.

2. The court states "[a]ll will agree that the decedent did not have a domicile on the Lusitania." The issue was whether Jones had acquired a domicile in Wales. The Restatement takes the position that if domicile of choice in a state is the issue, the physical presence part of the requirement is met by "presence anywhere in the state." Restatement (Second) Conflict of Laws § 16, comment a (1969). Wales and England share the same legal system. Marshall v. Murgatroyd, 6 Q.B. 31 (1870), involving application of a bastardy statute limited in its operation to England and Wales, declared: "It is part of the common law and of the law of nations, that a ship on the high seas is a part of the territory of that state to which she belongs; and therefore an English ship is deemed to be part of England. The child having been born on board an English ship, the statute applies." Id. at 33–34. Should the siblings of Evan Jones have made an argument that the Lusitania was part of the jurisdiction in which he had a present intention to acquire a domicile?

3. In order for the brothers and sister to succeed in the argument suggested at the end of note 2, they probably must present it to the court as a way of selecting the law the court thought it made most sense to apply to the issue of intestate succession. Shaping such an argument requires a focus on the reasons why the law of the domicile at death is traditionally utilized in Anglo–American law for intestate distribution of personal property ("movables" in Conflicts jargon). The reason sometimes advanced for the domicile rule is to insure that all movables in the estate, wherever situated, are distributed in the same manner. G. Stumberg, Conflict of Laws 374 (3d ed. 1963). But any choice-of-law rule, uniformly interpreted and applied, will provide this assurance. Is uniformity likely to result from use of a rule that has as the contact word at its heart so slippery a concept as "domicile"? Texas v. New Jersey, 379 U.S. 674 (1965) rejected "last domicile of the creditor" as the test of which state has jurisdiction to take title to abandoned intangible property. The Court states: "And by using a standard of last know address, rather than technical legal concepts of residence and domicile, administration and application of escheat laws should be simplified." Id. at 681.

The Iowa court suggests that selecting the law of domicile at death for intestate succession is likely to accord with the intention of the decedent who "presumably, at least, is familiar with" its laws. Is this presumption realistic? A survey of Iowa citizens indicated that in certain hypothetical situations, a majority of them would want their property distributed in a manner different from that provided by Iowa intestacy law. Note, A Comparison of Iowans' Dispositive Preferences with Select Provisions of the Iowa and Uniform Probate Codes, 63 Iowa L.Rev. 1041, 1077, 1091, 1146 (1978). See also Trimble v. Gordon, 430 U.S. 762, 775 n. 16 (1977): "With respect to any individual, the argument of knowledge and approval of the state law [on intestate succession] is sheer fiction."

Is the domicile at death the state that will usually bear the social consequences of the method of intestate distribution? Was that true in Estate of Jones? The record reveals that all of the contestants, the illegitimate daughter and the brothers and sisters of the decedent, were residents of Great Britain and, with the exception of one sister who had sojourned in the United States, had been so all their lives. Appellant's Abstract of Record, pp. 2, 11, 114–15, 128–30. Howard v. Reynolds, 283 N.E.2d 629 (Ohio 1972) applied Vermont law as that of the domicile at death of the intestate even though all of the property was in Ohio, most of the claimants were in Ohio, none lived in Vermont, and the intestate's assets were under guardianship in Ohio during the entire time that the intestate, a "mentally ill person," resided in Vermont. The court reversed the opinion of the Ohio Court of Appeals which had applied Ohio law on the ground that there were "most persuasive reasons" for departing from the rule of domicile at death, including the reason that "the state of Ohio has all the governmental interests in how the intestate property is to be distributed." Id. at 630 n. 1.

Were there "persuasive reasons" for applying West Virginia rather than Pennsylvania intestacy law in White v. Tennant? If so, there were two ways to accomplish this result: (1) find that Michael had not yet acquired a new domicile of choice in Pennsylvania; (2) hold that the domicile rule for intestate succession is only a presumption that is rebutted on the facts of the case, because West Virginia has a more significant relationship to the issue. If you were representing Michael's widow, which course would you pursue?

4. *Domicile of wives and children.* The court states that domicile by operation of law "results generally from the domestic relations of husband and wife, or parent and child." The common law rule was that a married woman was incapable of determining her own domicile and had the same domicile as her husband. In the United States, the rule concerning domicile of a wife gradually evolved from (1) she may acquire a separate domicile if she has justifiably left her husband, to (2) she may acquire a separate domicile if in fact she is separated from her husband, to (3) the domicile of either spouse is determined by their individual intentions and actions.

The modern view is expressed in Fritzshall v. Board of Police Commissioners, 886 S.W.2d 20 (Mo.App.1994). Kansas City, Missouri required its police officers to be "residents" of the city. "Residents" was interpreted as "domiciliaries." For many years, this policy was not enforced and Fritzshall purchased a house in a suburb where he lived with his wife and children while listing his uncle's address in Kansas City as Fritzshall's "paper" address. The police department then began to enforce its residence policy. Fritzshall took several actions in response, including spending duty days at his uncle's house, voting and paying taxes in Kansas City, and having his vehicles registered in the city. Nevertheless, a lengthy dispute between Fritzshall and police department officials resulted in Fritzshall's dismissal. At one point in the dispute, Fritzshall obtained an order from a local United States District Court judge that in determining the domicile of a police officer, the department must focus on "factors that relate to that officer's residence, not based on his or her spouse's residence or where the officer plans to retire." The Missouri Court of Appeals affirmed Fritzshall's discharge, which was based on factors unrelated to his wife's residence, but commented as follows on the federal court's order:

> If the District Court assumes that the residences of marital partners are not interrelated as a general rule, we would suggest that such an assumption would appear to be contrary to Missouri law and to the law of other states. It would also appear to be fundamentally at odds with the nature of marriage. While people who are legally married may have separate, fixed, permanent

homes, such a state is not the norm for marriage. In most cases, such a permanent arrangement would be called separation. Our view of the District Court's order is that, in order to protect Fritzshall from the Board relying *dispositively* on the spouse's residence, the court determined it was best as a remedial matter to prohibit consideration of her residence altogether in this particular case. We conclude, however, that the court did not decide that consideration of a spouse's residence is always and necessarily immaterial, which would be an absurd proposition.

The United Kingdom, Australia, and New Zealand, have abolished the rule that a wife must have her husband's domicile. U.K. Domicile & Matrimonial Proceedings Act § 1 (1973); Aust. Family Law Act 1975 § 4(3); N.Z. Domicile Act § 5(1) (1976). Previously, English courts had held that even though the marital domicile had been in England, if the husband deserted the wife and moved abroad, the wife could not obtain a divorce in England although she continued to reside there, because she was no longer "domiciled" there. Herd v. Herd [1936] P. 205.

Until emancipated, a legitimate child's domicile is that of the parents and, if the parent's are separated, that of the parent with whom the child is living. Restatement (Second) Conflict of Laws § 22 discusses rules to determine the domicile of an illegitimate child or one who does not live with a parent.

(5) *Declarations of intention.* In Fritzshall v. Board of Police Commissioners, discussed in note (4) supra, Fritzshall declared on many occasions that he resided in Kansas City. The court said: "While a declaration of residence is entitled to some deference, it may be overcome by evidence of strong circumstances to the contrary. Behavior may speak louder than words."

In In Re Annesley, infra p. 441, the court said: "The intention required is not an intention specifically directed to a change of domicil, but an intention of residing in a country for an unlimited time." This insight into the nature of domiciliary intention was perhaps overlooked by the lawyer who advised John T. Dorrance that maintaining his domicile in New Jersey "was largely a matter of intention." Dr. Dorrance planned to purchase a mansion in Pennsylvania and move there with his family, but to avoid Pennsylvania taxes during his life and for various estate planning reasons, he wished to maintain his domicile in New Jersey. After moving to Pennsylvania, he and his family spent a few weeks each year at their former New Jersey residence, he made many formal and informal declarations that he was domiciled in New Jersey, and he kept many contacts with New Jersey such as church membership and car registration. Nevertheless, the Pennsylvania Supreme Court found that he had acquired a domicile in Pennsylvania. This finding subjected stocks and bonds in his estate to Pennsylvania estate and personal property taxes. The court dismissed his declarations and his New Jersey contacts as "things which he did to avoid the appearance of identifying himself with the community in which he resided with his family." New Jersey courts, however, determined that Dorrance never intended to change his New Jersey domicile. Thus New Jersey also levied an estate tax on the stocks and bonds. In Re Estate of Dorrance, 170 A. 601, 172 A. 503 (N.J.Prerogative Ct., 1934), aff'd, 176 A. 902, (N.J.App.1935), 184 A. 743 (N.J.1936), cert. denied, 298 U.S. 678 (1936).

On the other hand, Mrs. Newcomb was successful in having a New York probate court give effect to her formal declarations that she elected to make New Orleans, Louisiana her "place of domicile and permanent home." She had been domiciled in New York and spent time at homes in both New York and Louisiana. She wished to change her domicile to Louisiana so that probate jurisdiction over her estate would be there and her relatives would have more difficulty contesting her will, which left substantially all her property to Tulane University in New Orleans. In affirming dismissal of probate proceedings, the Court of Appeals of New York said: "While acts speak louder than words, the words are to be heard for what they are worth." In Re Newcomb's Estate, 84 N.E. 950 (N.Y.1908).

The "Reporter's Note" to Restatement (Second) Conflict of Laws § 18 suggests that statements of domiciliary desire should be accorded more weight "in areas where normally the desires of the person concerned are supreme, such as in matters relating to the distribution of property upon death," but the Note states that there is "little evidence that such distinctions have been drawn by the courts."

6. *Estate tax on intangible property.* At the time of the Dorrance litigation, discussed in the previous note, only the domicile at death had the constitutional power to levy an estate tax on intangible property, such as stocks and bonds. Unless the taxing authorities of the two or more states claiming the power to tax could be brought into the same court, there was danger of multiple taxation, as in Dorrance. In Texas v. Florida, 306 U.S. 398 (1939), the situation for the estate was so bad that it was good. In that case the Court accepted original jurisdiction of a dispute among four states as to where Edward Green, son of the legendary wall street investor, Hetty Green, died domiciled. The combined state and federal estate taxes would have exceeded the value of the estate. The Court confirmed a master's finding that Green had died domiciled in Massachusetts.

Soon after Texas v. Florida, the Supreme Court abrogated the doctrine that only the domicile at death could tax intangibles. Curry v. McCanless, 307 U.S. 357 (1939), decided that Alabama and Tennessee may each impose death taxes upon intangibles held in trust by an Alabama trustee but passing under the will of a beneficiary decedent domiciled in Tennessee. State Tax Comm'n of Utah v. Aldrich, 316 U.S. 174 (1942), held that Utah may impose an estate tax on stock in a Utah corporation, even though the stock was owned by a person who died domiciled in New York. In rejecting domicile at death as the sole constitutional nexus for death taxes on intangibles, the Court said: "Another State which has extended benefits or protection, or which can demonstrate 'the practical fact of its power' or sovereignty as respects the shares may likewise constitutionally make its exaction."

Despite this change in doctrine, California v. Texas, 457 U.S. 164 (1982), again granted leave to file a complaint under the Court's original jurisdiction when federal and state death taxes threatened to exceed the value of the Howard Hughes estate. In a previous proceeding in the matter, the Court had denied the complaint. California v. Texas, 437 U.S. 601 (1978). Justice Stewart, concurring in this denial, suggested that the estate bring an interpleader action in federal district court against the tax officials of each state. Under the Federal Interpleader Act, 28 U.S.C.A. §§ 1335, 1397, 2361, federal district courts have nationwide jurisdiction in interpleader proceedings. Justice Stewart premised this interpleader suggestion on the rule that "intangible personal property may, at least theoretically, be taxed only at the place of the owner's domicile. First National Bank v. Maine, 284 U.S. 312 (1932)." First National Bank v. Maine was expressly overruled on this point by State Tax Comm'n v. Aldrich, supra this note, which Justice Stewart did not cite. The Hughes estate administrator did file an interpleader, but it was held in another matter that the 11th Amendment barred such an action. Cory v. White, 457 U.S. 85 (1982). The second and successful invocation of the Court's original jurisdiction then followed. A special master was appointed to hear the case, but the matter was settled before the master ruled.

In view of the fact that both California and Texas probably had sufficient nexus with the Hughes estate to levy a tax on its intangible property, was original jurisdiction prudently granted? Were California and Texas free to construe their residence-based estate statutes as encompassing any contacts that were constitutionally sufficient to tax intangibles?

Under the Uniform Interstate Compromise of Death Taxes Act, 8A U.L.A., adopted in 17 states as of January 1, 1995, the taxing authorities of the states involved and the estate representative are authorized to make a written compromise of tax claims. Under the Uniform Interstate Arbitration of Death Taxes Act, 8A U.L.A., adopted in 15 states as of January 1, 1995, binding arbitration is authorized to "determine the domicile of the decedent at the time of his death." Farange, Multiple Domiciles and Multiple Inheritance Taxes—A Possible Solution, 9 Geo.Wash.L.Rev. 375, 379, 383 (1941), suggests that although the due process clause permits more than one state to levy an estate tax on intangibles, it may compel each state to tax only a fair share of the intangibles.

7. The English presumption against a change of domicile is stronger when the change is from the domicile of origin. See 1 Dicey and Morris, Conflict of Laws 125 (11th ed. 1993 by Collins). The rigidity of the English rules has not escaped criticism from English writers. See Wade, The English Concept of Domicile, 21 Netherlands Int.L.Rev. 265 (1974). See, also, Wade, Domicile: A Re-Examination, 32 Int'l & Comp.L.Q. 1 (1983); Carter, Domicil: The Case for Radical Reform in the United Kingdom, 36 Int'l. & Comp.L.Q. 713 (1987). In 1987, the Law Commission of England and Scotland (Law Com. No. 168; Scot. Law Com. No. 107) proposed that the distinction between domicile of origin and domicile of choice be abolished and that no higher or different quality of intention need be shown when a change of domicile is from a domicile of origin. This recommendation has not been enacted into law.

8. Under English law, the necessary attitude of mind for the acquisition of a domicile of choice in a place is the intention to reside there permanently. How strictly this rule is applied is evidenced by Inland Revenue Commission v. Bullock (1976) 1 W.L.R. 1178 (Court of Appeal) where a man, whose domicile of origin was Canada but who had lived in England for purposes of income taxation, since 1932, was held not to have acquired a domicile of choice in England since it had always been his intention to return to Canada to live if his English wife predeceased him.

9. *"Nationality" as a connecting factor.* In many continental countries, nationality rather than domicile is used as the basis, or "connecting factor," for determining the governing law for certain personal rights. For a consideration of the relative advantages and disadvantages of nationality and domicile for this purpose, see Scoles and Hay, Conflict of Laws §§ 4.11–4.12 (2d ed. 1992).

10. *Residence.* Residence, rather than domicile, is the connecting factor usually found in statutes. In most contexts, "residence" is used as a synonym for "domicile" but at times the words convey different meanings; for example, "residence" has been held to differ from "domicile" in depending basically upon physical presence. Given the many differing contexts in which it appears, the word "residence" must be examined very carefully when it appears in a legal context, and given a meaning which fits the particular situation where it is encountered. For a thorough discussion, see Reese and Green, That Elusive Word, "Residence," 6 Vand.L.Rev. 561 (1953). See also Scoles and Hay, Conflict of Laws §§ 4.13–4.14 (2d ed. 1992); Restatement, Second, Conflict of Laws § 11, Comment *k*.

Following the divorce of his parents, a child spent weekends with his father and the rest of the time with his mother. He was held to be a resident of the "household" of each parent and hence covered by each parent's "homeowner policy." Accordingly, each insurer was held liable for the damage caused by a fire that had been set by the child. The court declared that "[w]hile a person may have only one true domicile, he may have more than one residence." Miller v. United States Fidelity and Guaranty Co., 127 N.J.Super. 37, 316 A.2d 51 (1974).

Habitual residence. The Hague Conference on Private International Law normally uses "habitual residence" rather than "domicile" in its conventions. This is partly because domicile bears different meanings in English and American law. For a discussion of "habitual residence" and whether it might have a useful role to play in American law, see Cavers, "Habitual Residence": A Useful Concept? 21 Am.U.L.Rev. 475 (1972).

11. The impropriety of a person's motive in coming to a place does not prevent his acquisition there of a domicile of choice. In Gasper v. Wales, 223 App.Div. 89, 227 N.Y.S. 421 (1st Dep't 1928), the court had the problem of a man with two places of abode. The family home was in Connecticut. Relations with his wife were exceedingly strained. The court concluded that his real home was in New York where he had lived with another woman for many years. Proskauer, J., said: "While the furtiveness of this New York home is one of the facts to be considered in deciding whether he intended it to be his legal domicil, it is not controlling.... The [trial judge] seems to have assumed that Beach could not have a legal residence for an illegal purpose. Legal residence, however, does not depend upon the legality of the object of the residence; it rests upon physical presence in a dwelling coupled with an intent to make that dwelling one's home."

2. VALIDITY OF A WILL

In Re Estate of Clark

Court of Appeals of New York, 1968.
21 N.Y.2d 478, 288 N.Y.S.2d 993, 236 N.E.2d 152.

■ FULD, CHIEF JUDGE.

This appeal poses an interesting and important question concerning a widow's right of election to take against her husband's will. More particularly, may her husband, domiciled in a foreign state, by selecting New York law to regulate his testamentary dispositions, cut off or otherwise affect the more favorable right given his widow to elect by the law of their domicile?

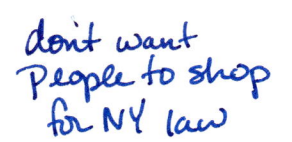

In the case before us, Robert V. Clark, Jr., died in October of 1964, domiciled in Virginia, and there his widow continues to reside. His estate, consisting of property in Virginia and in New York, had an aggregate value of more than $23,000,000—the bulk of which consisted of securities on deposit with a New York bank. His will, made in 1962, contained a provision that "this Will and the testamentary dispositions in it and the trusts set up shall be construed, regulated and determined by the laws of the State of New York." It devised the Clark residence in Virginia, together with its contents, to the widow and created for her benefit a preresiduary marital deduction trust—under which she would receive the income for life, with a general testamentary power of appointment over the principal of the trust. The residue of the estate, after payment of estate taxes, was placed in trust for the testator's mother. There has been a bistate administration of the estate. The New York executors who are administering the major portion of the estate—consisting, as noted, of securities held in New York during Mr. Clark's lifetime—and the Virginia executors are administering the balance, including the real and tangible personal property located in Virginia.

The testamentary trust for the widow's benefit would satisfy the requirements of section 18 of our Decedent Estate Law, Consol.Laws, c. 13 [and defeat her right to elect against the will]. However, it is conceded that, under the statutes of Virginia, the widow has an absolute and unconditional right to renounce her husband's will and take her intestate share (in the absence of issue, one half) of his estate outright (Virginia Code, § 64–16). Timely notice of the widow's election having been given, the New York executors initiated this special proceeding in the Surrogate's Court.... The executors contend that, by declaring that his testamentary dispositions should be construed by the laws of New York, the testator meant to bar his widow from exercising her Virginia right of election and that section 47 of the Decedent Estate Law requires that we give effect to his purpose. That section—replaced, since the testator's death, by a very similar provision (EPTL 3–5.1, subd. (h))—provided, in essence, that, when a nondomiciliary testator recites in his will that he elects that his *"testamentary dispositions"* [of property in New York] shall be construed and regulated by the laws of New York, "the validity and effect of *such dispositions* shall be determined by such laws."

The Surrogate upheld the executor's position. On appeal, the Appellate Division reversed, deciding that the widow's right to take in opposition to the will must be determined by the law of the domicile of the parties. Section 47—which relates solely to the decedent's "testamentary dispositions" and their validity and effect—was inapplicable, the court concluded, because "the right of a widow to inherit despite the will is not a 'testamentary disposition' in any sense" but is, on the contrary, "a restriction on the right to make a testamentary disposition." (28 A.D.2d 55, 57, 281 N.Y.S.2d 180, 183.)

We thoroughly agree with the Appellate Division's construction of the statute and with the conclusion it reached....

A moment's reflection is all that is necessary to establish the difference between statutes which have to do with restrictions placed on the decedent's testamentary power—for instance, to disinherit his spouse or other members of his family—and those which bear on discerning and carrying out the testator's wishes and desires. Section 47 is an example of the latter sort of legislation. Its earliest version (Code Civ.Proc., § 2694 (L.1880, ch. 178)) simply reflected the traditional choice of law rules, referring dispositions of personal property to the law of the decedent's domicile. It provided that the "validity and effect * * * of a testamentary disposition" of real property were to be regulated by the law of the situs and those of personalty by the law of the domicile; no exception was made for a case in which the testator might express a contrary intent....

Moreover, consideration of general principles of choice of law serve to confirm the conclusion, at which we have arrived, that it is the law of Virginia as to the widow's right of election, not that of New York, which here controls. As between two states, the law of that one which has the predominant, if not the sole, interest in the protection and regulation of the rights of the person or persons involved should, of course, be invoked....

While Virginia, as well as New York, has demonstrated concern for surviving spouses, the two states have done so in substantially different ways. A right to the income of a trust, sufficient under our law, is by no means the equivalent of taking the principal outright as would be the widow's right upon her election under Virginia law. Whether the widow in the case before us would be adequately provided for under the will or on our own law is irrelevant, for the same principles must apply to an estate of $23,000 as to one of $23,000,000, and we reject the notion that New York ought to impose upon its sister states its own views as to the adequacy of a surviving spouse's share....

■ BURKE, SCILEPPI, BERGAN, BREITEL and JASEN, JJ., concur.

KEATING, J., taking no part.

Order affirmed.

NOTES

1. The "very similar provision" mentioned in the opinion, EPTL 3–5.1(h), which replaced § 47 of the Decedent Estate Law, refers to "disposition of property situated in this state" and the "validity ... of any such disposition," rather than, as did § 47, to "testamentary dispositions." This change proved decisive in In Re Estate of Renard, 439 N.E.2d 341 (N.Y.1982), which construed the successor provision as choosing New York law to prevent a son's election under French law against his mother's will. The son, although a citizen of both France and the United States, was domiciled in the United States. His mother died domiciled in France.

2. Estate of Clark refers to "traditional choice of law rules," which apply the law of the testator's domicile at death to the validity of testamentary dispositions of personal property and the law of the situs to dispositions of realty. The Convention on the Law Applicable to Succession to the Estates of Deceased Persons, promulgated under the auspices of the Hague Conference on Private International Law on October 20, 1988, departs from both of these rules. For testate and intestate succession of either personalty or realty, the Convention refers to the country in which the decedent was "habitually resident" at death, with alternative references under some circumstances to the law of the decedent's nationality. A survey of countries that are members of the Conference revealed two major differences in the law applicable to estates. One difference was that some countries applied the same law to both personal and real property (unity principle) and some applied the law of the situs to realty and some other law to personalty (scission principle). The other difference was the law applied to all property in the "unity principle" countries, and the law applied to personalty in the "scission principle" countries. Here the division was between countries that applied the law of the domicile at death and those that applied the law of the decedent's nationality. The scission principle and reference to domicile rather than nationality, prevailed primarily, but not exclusive-

ly, in common law countries. Droz, Commentary on the Questionnaire on Succession in Private International Law, and Van Loon, Update of the Commentary, in Proceedings of the Sixteenth Session of the Hague Conference on Private International Law.

For discussion of habitual residence as a substitute for domicile, see Cavers, "Habitual Residence": A Useful Concept? 21 Am.U.L.Rev. 475 (1972).

3. DIVERSITY JURISDICTION

Rodriguez–Diaz v. Sierra–Martinez
United States Court of Appeals, First Circuit, 1988.
853 F.2d 1027.

■ Before CAMPBELL, CHIEF JUDGE, and TORRUELLA and SELYA, CIRCUIT JUDGES.

■ LEVIN H. CAMPBELL, CHIEF JUDGE.

Plaintiff Wilfredo Rodriguez Diaz (Rodriguez Diaz) appeals from an order of the United States District Court for the District of Puerto Rico dismissing his complaint for negligence and medical malpractice for lack of diversity jurisdiction. Rodriguez Diaz brought this action in the district court following a motor vehicle accident in Puerto Rico when he was 17 years of age. All the defendants reside in Puerto Rico. However, between the time of the accident and the commencement of this action, Rodriguez Diaz moved from his family's home in Puerto Rico to New York, and attained his 18th birthday. He then sued in the United States District Court for the District of Puerto Rico, on his own behalf and through his parents as next friends, alleging that he is a citizen of New York and that there is diversity of citizenship under 28 U.S.C. § 1332 (1982).

I

The facts relevant to the jurisdictional issue are these: On November 21, 1984, Rodriguez Diaz, while operating a motorcycle in Caguas, Puerto Rico, was in a collision with an automobile driven by Marcelo Sierra Martinez. Rodriguez Diaz suffered bodily injuries. He was immediately taken to the Hospital Regional de Caguas, from where he was transferred to the Centro Medico for emergency treatment. Rodriguez Diaz alleges in the present complaint that the treatment he received at the Centro Medico caused him to suffer a massive bone infection and aggravation of a leg injury. From Centro Medico he was transferred to Hospital General San Carlos where he alleges he also received improper treatment. Sometime later, Rodriguez Diaz was transferred to a hospital in New York City. He alleges he was living in New York at the time he brought this action in the United States District Court for the District of Puerto Rico. He further alleges in his complaint that he intends to remain in New York and make it his permanent home, and that he is now domiciled there. Rodriguez Diaz had turned 18 [the age of majority in New York] by the time he brought this action. His parents were and still are residents and domiciliaries of Puerto Rico, where the age of majority is 21.

The defendants in the action brought by Rodriguez Diaz were the driver of the automobile, Sierra Martinez, and two Puerto Rico hospitals, all of whom are residents and domiciliaries of Puerto Rico. The defendants moved in the United States District Court for the District of Puerto Rico where the action was brought to dismiss the complaint for lack of diversity jurisdiction. The district court concluded that, under Puerto Rico law, Rodriguez Diaz is a minor, and, therefore, his domicile is that of his parents. 665 F.Supp. 96 (D.P.R.1987). Ruling that as a matter of law Rodriguez Diaz's domicile at the time of the filing of this action was Puerto Rico, the court dismissed the complaint for lack of diversity. This appeal followed.

In its decision, the district court observed that, for purposes of diversity jurisdiction under 28 U.S.C. § 1332(a)(1), state citizenship and domicile are equivalents. The court also noted that in a diversity case the capacity of a person to sue or be sued is determined by the law of the state of the litigant's domicile. Fed.R.Civ.P. 17(b). The court then made certain observations crucial to its analysis. These were that the citizenship of a minor was the citizenship of his parents, and that the latter's domicile determined whether the minor had become emancipated so that he could establish a domicile of choice elsewhere. 665 F.Supp. at 98–99. On the basis of the foregoing, the district court concluded that the law of Puerto Rico—the home of Rodriguez Diaz's parents—controlled the issue of Rodriguez Diaz's present domicile. As under Puerto Rico law plaintiff was still a minor, being under 21 at the time of suit, and as he was unemancipated under Puerto Rico law, he could not establish a domicile of choice outside Puerto Rico. It followed that he was still a domiciliary of Puerto Rico, and that, therefore, there was no diversity of citizenship. Id.

II

While the case is close, we disagree with the district court's conclusion that the domicile of Rodriguez Diaz's parents—Puerto Rico—is the jurisdiction whose law must necessarily determine his capacity to acquire a domicile of choice.

We begin with certain generally accepted principles: As the lower court correctly noted, state citizenship for diversity purposes is ordinarily equated with domicile.... It is the domicile at the time suit is filed which controls, and the fact that the plaintiff has changed his domicile with the purpose of bringing a diversity action in federal court is irrelevant. Thus, except for the possible effect of his being a minor under Puerto Rico law, plaintiff's settling in New York with the requisite domiciliary intent would make him a citizen of New York and entitle him to pursue this action....

We shall assume for purposes of resolving the legal issue raised in this appeal that New York is plaintiff's "true, fixed home." The question before us is whether this is enough for plaintiff to have acquired a New York domicile for diversity jurisdiction purposes.

The parties and the district court have framed the issue as one of choice of law: which law is applicable, Puerto Rico law or New York law.

It is a general principle of common law, recognized also in Puerto Rico, that the domicile of an unemancipated minor is ordinarily that of his parents.... Depending on which law is applied, the argument goes, Rodriguez Diaz will be treated as an adult or as a minor, with the capacity or lack of capacity to establish his own independent domicile. Plaintiff argues that we have to apply New York law, because that was his "domicile" at the time the action was filed. Not surprisingly, defendants argued, and the district court agreed, that whether Rodriguez Diaz was an adult with capacity to establish his domicile of choice is governed by Puerto Rico law.

As we see it, resolution of the issue before us does not and should not turn solely upon a conflicts of laws analysis. Although federal courts have to apply the choice of law rules of the forum to determine the substantive law in diversity cases, the "determination of litigant's state citizenship for purposes of section 1332(a)(1) is controlled by federal common law, not by the law of any state." Kantor v. Wellesley Galleries, Ltd., 704 F.2d 1088, 1090 (9th Cir.1983).... That does not mean that state law and state conflicts rules regarding domicile should be ignored. At very least, they are "useful in providing basic working definitions." Stifel v. Hopkins, 477 F.2d 1116, 1120 (6th Cir.1973). However, as the Sixth Circuit pointed out in Stifel, the considerations undergirding state choice-of-law rules have often been "developed in such diverse contexts as probate jurisdiction, taxation of incomes or intangibles, or divorce laws." Id. Choice-of-law formulae, therefore, cannot be the sole guideposts when determining, for federal diversity purposes, whether a party is domiciled in one or another state. Id. at 1126. The ultimate decision must be such as will best serve the aims of the federal diversity statute and the perspectives of a nationwide judicial system.

III

In the case at bar, the district court noted that in a suit brought by the next friend, the minor's domicile was controlling for diversity purposes. The court went on to state: "Under the common law, the citizenship of a minor is the citizenship of his parents, and to determine whether the minor has become emancipated so that he may establish a domicile of choice, we look to the law of the state of the citizenship of the parents." ...

The difficulty with this rationale, as we see it, lies in the court's basic premise that the law of Puerto Rico controls. If Rodriguez Diaz were clearly a minor (under, say, both New York and Puerto Rico law), the court's analysis would be hard to fault....

The problem here, however, is that the question is not whether, as a minor, plaintiff was emancipated, but whether he is a minor. That, in turn, depends upon a determination of where he is domiciled, the ultimate question. We do not, therefore, find the district court's analysis persuasive....

The fact is, there is no purely logical way out of the dilemma. We cannot decide whether plaintiff is a minor under Puerto Rico law or an adult pursuant to New York law, without first determining where he is domiciled. On the other hand, we cannot make a determination whether he has the capacity to establish his own domicile without first knowing if he has reached the age of majority. We have, therefore, come full circle. To know if he has the legal capacity to establish his domicile of choice we need to know if he is an adult. But to determine whether he is an adult or a minor we first have to know where he is domiciled. There is, to be sure, a possible way out of this circle under formal conflict of laws principles. We could apply forum law to determine Rodriguez Diaz's legal capacity. Restatement of the Law, Conflicts of Law (Second), §§ 13 and 15(a) (1971).[5] This might be a proper resolution had the question of plaintiff's domicile arisen in a Commonwealth of Puerto Rico court, where the question of domicile is likely to implicate local matters over which Puerto Rico has the final say. But we do not think the lex forum provides a satisfactory resolution where the overriding and ultimate question is plaintiff's citizenship for purposes of federal diversity jurisdiction. Federal district courts sit throughout the nation. While it is unlikely a tort action like this, based on an accident in Puerto Rico, with all defendants residing there, could be pursued elsewhere than in the District of Puerto Rico, plaintiff could be involved in other federal diversity cases in other federal district courts, including the district courts located in New York. Were we to apply the rule of lex forum, Rodriguez Diaz could be viewed at one and the same time, and within the same judicial system, as both a citizen of New York and a citizen of Puerto Rico. That this is even theoretically possible suggests the unsatisfactoriness of determining state citizenship here, for federal diversity purposes, on the basis of lex forum. Rodriguez Diaz, we think, must be a "citizen" of one or the other state—not of both simultaneously.

We do not, moreover, see any compelling reasons of policy for adopting the law of the forum here. As pointed out already, while Puerto Rico doubtless has legitimate reasons for regulating persons such as plaintiff in respect to the making of contracts, property dispositions, support, and the like in Puerto Rico, it has little if any interest, based simply on the continuing presence of his parents in Puerto Rico, in denying to Rodriguez Diaz, while physically residing in New York, the right to sue under the diversity jurisdiction in a federal district court whether in Puerto Rico or elsewhere. While not crucial to our result, we also note that even plaintiff's parents have joined him in bringing this action: thus the parents' separate interests provide no reason to deny him the right to sue in a federal court....

IV

Since neither pure logic nor conflict rules provide a meaningful solution, we feel free to make the choice we think fits best with the aims of the

---

5. "[A] person cannot acquire a domicile of choice unless he has legal capacity to do so. Whether such legal capacity exists will be determined by the law of the forum." Restatement of the Law, Conflicts of Law (Second) § 13, comment d.

diversity statute and the national character of the federal judicial system. We hold that Rodriguez Diaz is a domiciliary of the State of New York—or, rather, that, if he can satisfy the district court that he meets the requisite factors of physical presence and intent, he is entitled to be a New York domiciliary for diversity purposes notwithstanding his minority status under Puerto Rico law. In reaching this result, we focus upon the physical and mental aspects of plaintiff's own situation, rather than imposing upon him a disability foreign to the law of the state where he now resides and having little meaning in this situation even to the place—Puerto Rico—whose law calls for it. To hold that one who meets all the domiciliary requirements (including capacity) of the state where he currently resides is a citizen of that state, seems clearly the most reasonable result here....

In the present case, there are perhaps no urgent reasons of federal diversity policy.... Since Rodriguez Diaz is recently from Puerto Rico, and his parents reside there, it is unlikely he would encounter prejudice were he forced to sue in Puerto Rico's own courts. The more realistic comparison, however, may be between the relative unfairness of denying a federal forum to Rodriguez Diaz while granting it to another young Puerto Rican of similar age whose parents moved to New York with him. Federal diversity jurisdiction exists as a matter of right for those who meet the statutory criteria, whether or not the plaintiff would actually encounter prejudice in the courts of another state. Federal courts should not, therefore, deny the right on the basis of pointless technicalities. In this case, if Rodriguez Diaz, being physically present in New York, qualifies under regular domiciliary rules as a domiciliary of New York, we do not think the difference in law between his former domicile, Puerto Rico, and New York concerning the age of majority should deny him the right to sue as a citizen of New York in federal court....

Vacated and remanded for further proceedings not inconsistent herewith.

■ TORRUELLA, CIRCUIT JUDGE (dissenting)....

Since there is no case in which a change in domicile has taken place without, at the very least, a physical departure from the place of original domicile, and it is legally impossible to acquire a new domicile without first losing the old one, we must determine the legal significance of such action in that jurisdiction; i.e., Puerto Rico. The issue thus is what, if any, is the legal significance, for change of domicile purposes, of an 18 year old resident of Puerto Rico leaving that jurisdiction.

The answer under Puerto Rican law is clear: none....

That a state has a paramount interest in protecting, regulating and controlling its minor citizens is beyond cavil....

Because this is, as it should be, an area highly reflective of local attitudes, values and mores, it is particularly unsuited to federalized tinkering. Thus, the majority is mistaken in placing emphasis on the "right of access to a federal court" as the central issue raised by this appeal....

Diversity jurisdiction, particularly in this day and age, is not in need of unnatural expansion, and especially not at the expense of important, non-selective local interests....

The majority also implicitly rejects without explanation the only precedent directly on point, cited by the district court. In Spurgeon v. Mission State Bank, 151 F.2d 702 (8th Cir.1945), the court determined whether an eighteen-year-old minor who moved to Kansas from his parents' home in Missouri was "capable of acquiring a domicile of his choice" for purposes of diversity jurisdiction. The court determined that the appellant had acquired a domicile in Kansas by first ruling that "[w]hether the appellant was an emancipated minor at the time of his departure from the home of his parents is a question controlled by Missouri law." Id. at 703. That is, for purposes of determining whether an eighteen-year-old had the capacity to acquire a domicile of choice, the court looked to the law of the jurisdiction from which the youth had departed.

Admittedly, the above cited authority can be read to support an alternative rule of law, a rule implicitly applied by at least one court but also rejected by my brothers. In Appelt v. Whitty, 286 F.2d 135 (7th Cir.1961), the court denied diversity jurisdiction after it used Illinois law to determine that the minor plaintiff, who had moved from Michigan to Illinois, was emancipated. Although the court gave no reason why it applied Illinois rather than Michigan law (nor did it suggest that the outcome would have been different), it appears to have used the principle of lex loci, since the case came on appeal from the District Court of the Northern District of Illinois. The lex loci approach to capacity is also the suggested approach of the Restatement (Second) Conflict of Laws (1971), as stated in comment d to its section 13, for determining capacity to acquire a domicile of choice.[11]

Appellant is not looking to federal court for protection from bias and parochialism but rather is forum shopping by filing in the federal jurisdiction in Puerto Rico where he is entitled to a civil jury trial....

Assuming there is a federal policy to make federal courts more widely available to litigants and to not "deny the right [to federal court] on the basis of pointless technicalities," the majority's approach does not satisfy even this goal. For example, if any individual in appellant's situation now wanted to file a diversity suit against a New York citizen in New York (a forum much more likely to be unfriendly), he would be barred from access to federal court due to lack of diversity. Thus, the majority's approach provides neither greater access nor eliminates "pointless technicalities" as a barrier to federal court....

11. A preference for the lex loci approach is also suggested by rule 17(b) of the Federal Rules of Civil Procedure which, while stating that the "capacity of an individual ... shall be determined by the law of his domicile," also states that "[i]n all other cases [not concerning a corporation or an entity whose capacity is determined by federal law] capacity ... shall be determined by the law of the state in which the district court is held...." The rules, therefore, suggest that when domicile is not determinative, capacity should be determined according to the law of the forum.

GALVA FOUNDRY CO. v. HEIDEN, 924 F.2d 729 (7th Cir.1991). An Illinois company sued its former president for fraud. The plaintiff attempted to invoke diversity jurisdiction on the ground that the defendant had acquired a domicile in Florida. Defendant had a vacation home in Florida and took several steps to indicate his change of domicile to Florida, including registering to vote, acquiring a driver's license, and listing the Florida address on his federal tax return. The defendant had sold his stock in the plaintiff and if he were domiciled in Florida, he would avoid Illinois taxes on the profit from this sale. The district court dismissed the case for lack of diversity, and the Seventh Circuit affirmed:

> Unfortunately, in this age of second homes and speedy transportation, picking out a single state to be an individual's domicile can be a difficult, even a rather arbitrary, undertaking. Domicile is not a thing, like a rabbit or a carrot, but a legal conclusion, though treated as a factual determination for purposes of demarcating the scope of appellate review. And in drawing legal conclusions it is always helpful to have in mind the purpose for which the conclusion is being drawn. The purpose here is to determine whether a suit can be maintained under the diversity jurisdiction, a jurisdiction whose main contemporary rationale is to protect nonresidents from the possible prejudice that they might encounter in local courts. This argues for finding the defendant, Mr. Heiden, to be a domiciliary of the same state as the plaintiff, Galva—that is, Illinois. Heiden is a long-time resident of Illinois and unlikely therefore to encounter hostility in its state courts. And anyway he does not want to be in federal court. It is Galva that wants to be in federal court. Yet Galva is indisputably a citizen of Illinois....
>
> Heiden intended no change in the manner or style of his life, the center of gravity of which was and remains in Peoria, but only a change in his tax rate. The aura of fraud that surrounds his maneuverings in 1988 [to acquire indicia of Florida citizenship] would help Galva if citizenship for diversity purposes could be acquired by estoppel—which Galva does not argue, and rightly so, for such an argument would be inconsistent with the rule that diversity is a jurisdictional requirement, which a defendant cannot, therefore, waive. But since citizenship cannot be acquired by estoppel, the aura of fraud hurts Galva. It shows that Heiden did not want to change his domicile. He just wanted to fool the taxing authorities in Florida and particularly Illinois (for it was Illinois taxes that he was trying to escape) into thinking he did. This is shady business but it cannot convert a suit between two residents of Illinois into a suit against a Floridian.

4. JUDICIAL JURISDICTION

Alvord & Alvord v. Patenotre

Supreme Court of New York, Special Term, New York County, 1949.
196 Misc. 524, 92 N.Y.S.2d 514.

Action by Alvord & Alvord against Raymond Patenotre and Eleanor Patenotre, wherein defendants moved to vacate order for substituted service and the service made pursuant thereto.

■ MILLER, J. . . .

The order for substituted service was obtained on October 5, 1949 and service pursuant thereto was made by affixing to the door of the moving defendant's apartment a copy of the summons, complaint and order on the same day and by depositing a copy of the papers in the mails at 1:05 A.M. on the next day, October 6th.

Concededly the moving defendant did not arrive in France until October 5th. The affidavit of his attorney submitted in support of the present motion states that the movant "departed from this country for the purpose of establishing his domicile in Switzerland and with the intent and purpose to change his domicile in this country which had existed in or about the years 1946 and 1947". No claim is made that at the time service was effected pursuant to the order for substituted service the movant had already arrived in Switzerland. It is thus clear that his presence in France was merely a temporary stopover en route to Switzerland. In view of the admission of movant's attorney that the movant's domicile had been in this country up to the time he left, it is clear that the domicile was still in this country at the time service was made, for the movant had not yet arrived in Switzerland, his allegedly intended new domicile. "The existing domicile, whether of origin or selection, continues until a new one is acquired." Rawstorne v. Maguire, 265 N.Y. 204, 208, 192 N.E. 294, 295. . . .

In the court's opinion the moving defendant, concededly domiciled here at the time of the service, may not obtain vacatur of the order for substituted service and the service made pursuant thereto merely because he had just left this state for the purpose of avoiding service. . . .

[Motion denied.]

NOTE

Why is it usually reasonable to exercise general jurisdiction over a domiciliary? ("General jurisdiction" means that the defendant can be sued at the domicile on any cause of action, even one not arising out of or related to anything occurring in the forum, see infra p. 38.) Is that reason present in *Alvord*? Restatement (Second) Conflict of Laws § 29, originally read: "A state has power to exercise judicial jurisdiction over an individual who is domiciled in the state." In 1988, § 29 was revised to read: "A state has power to exercise judicial jurisdiction over an individual who is domiciled in the state, except in the highly unusual case where the individual's relationship to the state is so attenuated as to make the exercise of such jurisdiction unreasonable."

Convention on Jurisdiction and Enforcement of Judgments in Civil and Commercial Matters ("Brussels Convention"), in force in the European Union, Art. 2: "Subject to the provisions of this Convention, persons domiciled in a Contracting State shall, whatever their nationality, be sued in the courts of that State." For further discussion of this Article, see p. 43.

If a New York court could not exercise jurisdiction over the defendant in *Alvord* based on his technical retention of domicile, does that mean that the defendant could not be sued in New York or anyplace else until he had acquired a new domicile? What of jurisdiction arising from or related to the defendant's conduct?

5. SPECIAL SITUATIONS

Refugees. The domicile of refugees is likely to raise peculiar problems. An example is Roboz v. Kennedy, 219 F.Supp. 892 (D.D.C.1963) which involved a suit for the return of property vested in the Attorney General under the International Claims Settlement Act (22 U.S.C.A. § 1631). By the terms of the Act, the vesting of plaintiffs' property would have been proper if the plaintiffs had been "domiciled" in Hungary after March 13, 1941. The plaintiffs were mother and son. They and the father were nationals of Hungary and, so far as appears, had lived in that country all of their lives up to the crucial date. At that time, they were all in Hungary, the father in a Nazi prison and the mother engaged in seeking his release. "In view of the increasing Nazi orientation of the Hungarian Government," the plaintiffs and the father had planned to leave Hungary since 1939. In 1940, the plaintiffs obtained United States visas. They did not leave at that time because of the imprisonment of the father and only reached the United States in 1947 "resolved never to return to Hungary under any circumstances." Held for the plaintiffs. "The facts ... demonstrate conclusively that plaintiffs had a firm and continuing intent to leave Hungary forever before March 13, 1941 ... Clearly, they were involuntarily in Hungary. They therefore cannot be considered ... domiciled in ... Hungary" within the meaning of the statute. "Congress could not have intended so inequitable a result...."

NOTES

1. At times a person has been found to have a domicile in the United States although here on a temporary basis or after the person's visa had expired. Rzeszotarski v. Rzeszotarski, 296 A.2d 431 (D.C.App.1972) (expired temporary visa—divorce); Seren v. Douglas, 30 Colo.App. 110, 489 P.2d 601 (1971) (expired student visa—in-state tuition benefits); Williams v. Williams, 328 F.Supp. 1380 (D.V.I.1971) (temporary worker visa—divorce and adoption); Bustamante v. Bustamante, 645 P.2d 40 (Utah 1982) (tourist visa—divorce). Contra: Gosschalk v. Gosschalk, 48 N.J.Super. 566, 138 A.2d 774 (1958), affirmed 28 N.J. 73, 145 A.2d 327 (1958) (alien on temporary visa held incapable of acquiring domicile for divorce).

2. *Illegal entrants.* In Cabral v. State Board of Control, 112 Cal.App.3d 1012, 169 Cal.Rptr. 604 (1980), aliens who had entered the United States illegally were held capable of acquiring a domicile in California for purposes of recovering under that state's Victims of Violent Crimes Act. However, in Buscema v. Buscema, 20 N.J.Super. 114, 89 A.2d 279 (1952), an alien who was released on his own recognizance while awaiting a deportation hearing for having illegally entered the United States was held incapable of acquiring a domicile for divorce purposes. See, also, St. Joseph's Hosp. v. Maricopa County, 142 Ariz. 94, 688 P.2d 986 (1984). Illegal aliens were held to be domiciled in the county where they were receiving emergency medical care for purposes of the statutes determining eligibility for such care. See also Pilkington, Illegal Residence and the Acquisition of a Domicile of Choice, 33 Int'l & Comp.L.Q. 885 (1984).

3. The Constitution has been held to require a state to apply its ordinary rules of domicile in determining whether an alien is eligible for state entitlements. Elkins

v. Moreno, 435 U.S. 647 (1978); Toll v. Moreno, 458 U.S. 1 (1982) (eligibility for reduced tuition at state university). The conditions imposed on an alien's entry into the United States may, however, cast light upon whether the alien bears the proper attitude of mind towards the place where he claims domicile. Toll v. Moreno, 284 Md. 425, 397 A.2d 1009 (1979).

Students. A student will usually be held not to have acquired a domicile of choice in the place where the school or college is located. The tendency of most students to continue to regard their parents' dwelling as "home" and the relative shortness of the intended stay at the school or college work against regarding the school's situs as home.

The situation is different if the student has abandoned the parental home and has struck out to make an independent life, particularly if the student has married. It then becomes far more likely that the court will accept the claim that the location of the institution of learning is the student's "home" and constitutes a domicile of choice. See Robbins v. Chamberlain, 297 N.Y. 108, 75 N.E.2d 617 (1947).

NOTES

1. The United States Constitution has been held to limit the power of a state to impose rules that make it difficult for certain classes of persons, such as servicemen and students, to acquire a local domicile for purposes of voting. In Carrington v. Rash, 380 U.S. 89 (1965), the Supreme Court struck down a Texas constitutional provision which precluded servicemen stationed in the state from acquiring a domicile there for voting purposes. Speaking of students, Judge Friendly said in Ramey v. Rockefeller, 348 F.Supp. 780 (E.D.N.Y.1972) that, although a state may insist that all applicants for the vote fulfill the requirements of bona fide residence,

"The only constitutionally permissible test is one which focuses on the individual's present intention and does not require him to pledge allegiance for an indefinite future. The objective is to determine the place which is the center of the individual's life now, the locus of his primary concern. The determination must be based on *all* relevant factors; it is not enough that a student, or any other former nondomiciliary, would find that the place of his presence is more convenient for voting or would enable him to take a more active part in political life. The state may insist on other indicia, including the important one of abandonment of a former home.

We think therefore that, in determining bona fide residence for a person physically present, the state cannot constitutionally go further than the test set out in the Restatement (Second) of the Conflict of Laws § 18 (1971), namely, that he 'must intend to make that place his home for the time at least.'"

In Newburger v. Peterson, 344 F.Supp. 559 (D.N.H.1972), the plaintiff, a Dartmouth student, complained of a New Hampshire statute which disqualified a person from voting in a town if he had a firm intention of leaving that town at a fixed time in the future. The statute was held unconstitutional. The court said:

"In this day of widespread planning for change of scene and occupation we cannot see that a requirement of permanent or indefinite intention to stay in one place is relevant to responsible citizenship...

We are sensitive to the compelling need 'to preserve the basic conception of a political community'.... But the challenged New Hampshire law forces persons who are in every meaningful sense members of New Hampshire political communities to vote in communities elsewhere which they have long departed and with whose affairs they are no longer concerned, if indeed the former community still recognizes the right...."

2. Any minor over eighteen years of age has the capacity to acquire a domicile of choice for voting purposes, and his capacity is not impaired by living in a college dormitory and receiving parental support. Hershkoff v. Board of Registrars of Voters of Worcester, 366 Mass. 570, 321 N.E.2d 656 (1974). See also Paulson v. Forest City Community School District, 238 N.W.2d 344 (Iowa 1976).

3. Wurfel: Jet Age Domicil: The Semi-Demise of Durational Residence Requirements, 11 Wake Forest L.Rev. 349 (1975) discusses decisions, including those of the Supreme Court, on the use of domicile for voting, tuition, welfare, occupational qualification, and divorce purposes. The author concludes that although durational residence requirements are constitutionally suspect, domicile "continue[s] to be the legal test of individual rights and duties."

RESTATEMENT, SECOND, CONFLICT OF LAWS (1988 REVISIONS) *:

§ 17. Presence Under Compulsion

A person does not usually acquire a domicil of choice by his presence in a place under physical or legal compulsion.

b. Inmates of prisons. Under the rule of this Section, it is difficult for a person to acquire a domicil of choice in the prison in which he is incarcerated. To enter prison, one must first be legally committed and thereby lose all power of choice over the place of one's abode. Under such circumstances it is highly unlikely that a person will form the attitude of mind toward the place of his incarceration that is requisite for the acquisition of a domicil of choice. If he were to form such an attitude of mind, however, he would there acquire a domicil.

c. Members of armed services. A member of the armed services who is ordered to a station to which he must go and live in quarters assigned to him will usually not acquire a domicil there though he lives in the assigned quarters with his family. He must obey orders and cannot choose to go elsewhere. On the other hand, if he is allowed to live with his family where he pleases provided it is near enough to his post to enable him to perform his duties, he retains some power of choice over the place of his abode and may acquire a domicil. To do so, however, he must regard the place where he lives as his home. Such an attitude on his part may be difficult to establish in view of the nomadic character of military life and

---

* Quoted with the permission of the copyright owner, The American Law Institute.

particularly if he intends, upon the termination of his service, to move to some other place.

NOTES

1. In Stifel v. Hopkins, 477 F.2d 1116 (6th Cir. 1973), a person sent to a Pennsylvania prison under life sentence was held capable of claiming to be a Pennsylvania citizen for the purpose of bringing a diversity action. He had refused a transfer to an Indiana prison and said in an affidavit that he considered Pennsylvania his home and intended to remain there indefinitely.

In Dane v. Board of Registrars, 374 Mass. 152, 371 N.E.2d 1358 (1978), the court held that persons incarcerated in Massachusetts jails had the capacity "to form the requisite intent to make ... the place of their incarceration their domicile for voting purposes." It said that "We think that prisoners, like servicemen or students, should be able to 'rebut' the presumption that by reason of their involuntary presence at the place of incarceration, they have retained their former domicile."

Would the result in these two cases have been the same if the issue had involved either succession or taxation?

2. Where the serviceman lives off the base and shows a clear intention to make his home where he lives, he may acquire a domicile there. See Sasse v. Sasse, 41 Wn.2d 363, 249 P.2d 380 (1952). A serviceman was found to be domiciled in the state in Slade v. Slade, 122 N.W.2d 160 (N.D.1963), even without such evidence. For a typical case refusing to find a soldier domiciled for purposes of divorce jurisdiction in the place where he was stationed, although he had testified that he intended to make that place his home following his discharge from the Army, see Hammerstein v. Hammerstein, 269 S.W.2d 591 (Tex.Civ.App.1954). A few courts have held that service personnel living on base have acquired a domicile in the state for divorce purposes. See Bezold v. Bezold, 95 Idaho 131, 504 P.2d 404 (1972); Marcus v. Marcus, 3 Wn.App. 370, 475 P.2d 571 (1970).

3. More than a dozen states have statutes providing that a serviceman living in the state for a specified period shall be deemed a resident for purposes of divorce suits. See generally Leflar, Conflict of Laws and Family Law, 14 Ark.L.R. 47, 49 (1960); see also Scoles and Hay, Conflict of Laws § 4.26 and § 15.5 (2d ed. 1992).

Is Domicile a Unitary Concept?

Domicile is used in three broad areas of conflict of laws: judicial jurisdiction; choice of law, particularly in matters where continuity of the application of the same law is important, such as family law and decedents' estates; and governmental benefits and burdens. A question is whether domicile has a constant meaning throughout or whether its meaning may vary somewhat from context to context. Stated in another way, the question is whether at the same time a person may have a domicile in one place for one purpose and another domicile in a second place for some other purpose.

Do the cases you have read up to now provide an answer to this question? Do you think it likely that a clear answer would be found in the cases? A famous debate on this question took place between Professors Walter Wheeler Cook and Austin Wakeman Scott at an early American Law

Institute meeting. 3 The American Law Institute Proceedings 226–231 (1925). In the course of this debate, Professor Cook said:

> There is no doubt that what you might call the core of the concept is the same in all these situations; but as you get out towards what I like to call the twilight zone of the subject, I don't believe the scope remains exactly the same for all purposes....
>
> The court has a concrete problem to solve. It is trying to decide whether the courts of the state should grant a divorce on constructive service; whether the man is sufficiently connected with the state to make that a reasonable thing to do. It may be reasonable to do that, but not reasonable to apply the same concept in the case involving the validity of the provisions of a will. The court has a will to consider, or a divorce, or the administration of an estate, or whatever it may be, and the exact point at which it draws the line is undoubtedly drawn with the concrete problem that they have before them in mind....
>
> I do not believe we can make up our minds as to the exact scope [domicile] ought to have for a particular purpose without having that purpose in mind, and we ought to address ourselves to the question of whether it ought to have the same exact scope for all purposes. I do not believe it should. I am not talking about a theoretical thing, but what the courts actually do. What I think the courts should do and are actually doing is, that while they use the same word as if they had a single concept, actually you will find they have not....

The Restatement (Second) Conflict of Laws § 11 comment o, states that "in close cases, decision of a question of domicile may sometimes depend upon the purpose for which the domicile concept is used in the particular case."

NOTES

1. See Reese, Does Domicile Bear a Single Meaning, 55 Colum.L.Rev. 589 (1955). Professor Cook's last word is found in Cook, Logical and Legal Bases of the Conflict of Laws 194–210 (1942). Expressly according a person different domiciles for different purposes is Reiersen v. Commissioner of Revenue, 26 Mass.App.Ct. 124, 524 N.E.2d 857 (1988).

2. Section 5 of the Canadian Divorce Act of 1968 (Stat.Can.1968, c. 24) provides that a provincial court shall be competent to grant a divorce if the petitioner is domiciled in Canada and if either the petitioner or the respondent has been "ordinarily resident" in the province for one year prior to the filing of the petition. As a result, a person can be domiciled in Canada for divorce purposes and domiciled in a province for another purpose. Da Costa, The Canadian Divorce Law of 1968 and its Provisions on Conflicts, 17 Am.J.Comp.L. 214 (1969). A somewhat similar situation prevails in Australia. Cowen and Da Costa, The Unity of Domicile, 78 L.Q.Rev. 92 (1962).

By what law is the meaning of domicile determined? The word "domicile" appears in many rules of law of many states. When the states involved in a conflicts case determine domicile by different rules, should the forum's rule always prevail or should the court look at times to the rule of the other state? A case in point is Torlonia v. Torlonia, 108 Conn. 292, 142 A. 843 (1928) where a wife sought a divorce in Connecticut from her Italian husband, claiming that she was domiciled in Connecticut and that accordingly that state had divorce jurisdiction. The husband argued that the action should be dismissed, since "as a matter of law, the plaintiff cannot have a domicile ... other than that of her husband," because "under the law of Italy the husband is entitled to the control of the wife to the extent that she must follow him wherever he chooses to establish his residence, except as such control may be modified or affected by a decree of an Italian court of competent jurisdiction." The trial court granted the divorce and on appeal its action was affirmed. The appellate court said:

> We hold, then, that a wife separated from her husband, ... is not precluded from establishing an independent domicil in this State; indeed, we are convinced that this right has long been tacitly recognized and frequently given effect in divorce actions in our trial courts, although its existence has not, heretofore, been challenged on appeal.
>
> Since domicil, as well as the other questions upon which the granting of a divorce depends, is governed by the laws of the forum in which the action is pending, the Italian law, above stated, pertaining to control of the wife by the husband, does not preclude the plaintiff from acquiring an independent domicil in Connecticut.

NOTE

See Restatement, Second, Conflict of Laws § 13; Scoles and Hay, Conflict of Laws, §§ 4.8–4.10 (2d ed. 1992).

CHAPTER 3

JURISDICTION OF COURTS

SECTION 1. INTRODUCTION AND GENERAL CONSIDERATIONS

Buchanan v. Rucker
Court of King's Bench, 1808.
9 East 192.

The plaintiff declared in assumpsit for 2000*l*. on a foreign judgment of the Island Court in Tobago; and at the trial before Lord Ellenborough, C.J., at Guildhall, produced a copy of the proceedings and judgment, certified under the hand-writing of the Chief Justice, and the seal of the island, which were proved; which, after containing an entry of the declaration, set out a summons to the defendant, therein described as "formerly of the city of Dunkirk, and now of the city of London, merchant," to appear at the ensuing court to answer the plaintiff's action; which summons was returned, "served, etc. by nailing up a copy of the declaration at the courthouse door," etc. on which judgment was afterwards given by default. Whereupon it was objected, that the judgment was obtained against the defendant, who never appeared to have been within the limits of the island, nor to have had any attorney there; nor to have been in any other way subject to the jurisdiction of the Court at the time; and was therefore a nullity. And of this opinion was Lord Ellenborough; though it was alleged, (of which however there was no other than parol proof,) that this mode of summoning absentees was warranted by a law of the island, and was commonly practised there: and the plaintiff was thereupon nonsuited. And now

Taddy moved to set aside the nonsuit, and for a new trial, on an affidavit verifying the island law upon this subject; which stated "That every defendant against whom any action shall be entered, shall be served with a summons and an office copy of the declaration, with a copy of the account annexed, if any, at the same time by the Provost Marshal, etc. six days before the sitting of the next Court, etc.; and the Provost Marshal is required to serve the same on each defendant in person. But if such defendant cannot be found, and is not absent from the island, then it shall be deemed good service by leaving the summons, etc. at his most usual place of abode. And if the defendant be absent from the island, and hath a power of attorney recorded in the secretary's or registrar's office of Tobago, and the attorney be resident in the island, or any manager or overseer on his plantation in the island, the service shall be either upon such attorney personally, or by leaving it at his last place of abode, or upon such overseer or manager personally, or by leaving it at the house upon the defendant's plantation where the overseer or manager usually resides. But if no such attorney, overseer or manager; then the nailing up of a copy of the declaration and summons at the entrance of the court-house shall be held good service."

■ LORD ELLENBOROUGH, C.J. There is no foundation for this motion even upon the terms of the law disclosed in the affidavit. By persons absent from the island must necessarily be understood persons who have been present and within the jurisdiction, so as to have been subject to the process of the Court; but it can never be applied to a person who for aught appears never was present within or subject to the jurisdiction. Supposing however that the act had said in terms, that though a person sued in the island had never been present within the jurisdiction, yet that it should bind him upon proof of nailing up the summons at the court door: how could that be obligatory upon the subjects of other countries? Can the island of Tobago pass a law to bind the rights of the whole world? Would the world submit to such an assumed jurisdiction? The law itself, however, fairly construed, does not warrant such an inference: for "absent from the island" must be taken only to apply to persons who had been present there, and were subject to the jurisdiction of the Court out of which the process issued: and as nothing of that sort was in proof here to shew that the defendant was subject to the jurisdiction at the time of commencing the suit, there is no foundation for raising an assumpsit in law upon the judgment so obtained.

PER CURIAM, Rule refused.

SCHIBSBY v. WESTENHOLZ, L.R. 6 Q.B. 155 (Court of Queen's Bench, 1870): The plaintiff sought the recognition and enforcement of a French judgment in England. The French court had based jurisdiction on the plaintiff's French residence; the defendants were neither French nationals nor residents and had no property in France. It appeared that English statutory law likewise permitted the exercise of jurisdiction over foreigners under certain circumstances. Blackburn, J., however, drew the following distinction: "Should a foreigner be sued under the provisions of the statute referred to, and then come to the courts of this country and desire to be discharged, the only question which our courts could entertain would be whether the Acts of the British legislature, rightly construed, gave us jurisdiction over this foreigner, for we must obey them. But if, judgment being given against him in our courts, an action were brought upon it in the courts of the United States (where the law as to the enforcing foreign judgments is the same as our own), a further question would be open, viz., not only whether the British legislature had given the English courts jurisdiction over the defendant, but whether he was under any obligation which the American courts could recognize to submit to the jurisdiction thus created. This is precisely the question which we have now to determine with regard to a jurisdiction assumed by the French jurisprudence over foreigners." He concluded that, since the defendants were not French subjects or residents and had not otherwise submitted to French jurisdiction, "there existed nothing in the present case imposing on [them] any duty to obey the judgment of a French tribunal."

NOTE

"Jurisdiction" is a concept which appears in many legal contexts and bears diverse meanings depending upon the nature or purpose of the inquiry at hand. The meaning of the word jurisdiction that is in widest use and that has been employed in compiling this book is: the power of a state to create or affect legal interests that will be recognized as valid in other states. See Restatement, Second, Conflict of Laws § 24. Analogously, the Restatement, Third, Foreign Relations Law of the United States (1987) defines "jurisdiction" (in § 401) to encompass "jurisdiction to prescribe . . .; to adjudicate . . .; [and] to enforce. . . ."

In the broad sense of those definitions, a state may exercise jurisdiction through its executive, legislative or judicial arms of government. The concern in this chapter is with the last type—the power of a state through its judicial tribunals to affect legal interests, and specifically with whether a particular judgment will be recognized as valid in other states.

The assertion of lack of jurisdiction may seek to convey either of the following ideas:

1. The state where the judgment was rendered did not have a proper basis upon which to go ahead to a decision. (The state, so it is said, "lacked jurisdiction over the person of the defendant" or "over the res" or "the thing in suit," tangible or intangible.)

2. The law of the state where the judgment was rendered did not authorize the court to exercise the state's judicial power in that type of litigation or upon the jurisdictional basis that existed and was relied upon in that particular action. (The court which rendered the judgment, it is variously said, "lacked competence" or "lacked jurisdiction over the subject matter.")

The first of these propositions refers to the "proper basis" for the exercise of jurisdiction. Who decides what is a proper basis? In conferring jurisdiction on its courts, a state will ordinarily not be concerned with extraterritorial effects: will other states approve of this exercise of jurisdiction and recognize a judgment based on it. Jurisdictional bases are defined by *national* law, and they express *national* concerns. Such a national concern may be, for instance, to provide a citizen with a national forum in which to sue a foreign defendant (see Arts. 14, 15, French Civil Code) or to let a local plaintiff proceed on the sole basis that the defendant has assets in the forum state (see *Shaffer,* infra at p. 136). Other states may not approve and consequently might refuse to recognize such a judgment. In this sense, it is the recognizing court that decides what, as far as it is concerned, is a "proper basis" for jurisdiction. The test, to use the European terminology, is not whether the rendering state had jurisdiction by its own standards, but whether it had "jurisdiction *in the international sense*". Consider in this light the decisions in the *Buchanan* and *Schibsby* cases, supra.

Acceptable bases of jurisdiction ("jurisdiction in the international sense") may be established by agreement among states, as they are by the "Brussels Convention" among the member states of the European Union and the "Lugano (Parallel) Convention" between them and the remaining states of the European Free Trade Association.[1] The Brussels Convention not only establishes the acceptable bases of jurisdiction but also lists, with reference to each member state, the bases of jurisdiction which may *not* be invoked in litigation with respect to parties or causes to which the Convention applies. Such excluded bases of jurisdiction—generally any basis of jurisdiction which will not be accepted for purposes of granting recognition to an ensuing judgment—are known as "*exorbitant* bases of jurisdiction." In the European Union, these include, among others, transient jurisdiction under English and Irish law, the plaintiff's forum nationality under Belgian and French law, and the presence of assets unrelated to the action.

In the absence of agreement on acceptable bases of jurisdiction, each state defines "jurisdiction in the international sense" for itself. As a rule, it will use its own standards. "Jurisdiction in the international sense" then may become the mirror image of its domestic practice.

Among the states in the United States the subject of jurisdiction takes on a constitutional character, for even though there is no constitutional provision that in terms refers to the judicial jurisdiction of the states,* the Supreme Court has ruled that the issue is covered by the due process guarantee. Due process requires that the defendant have an appropriate nexus to the forum before its courts are authorized to adjudicate the dispute. A separate due process requirement insures that a party otherwise subject to a court's jurisdiction has an adequate opportunity to be heard: it requires *notice*.

The old ideology drew a clear line between in personam and in rem actions and caused important consequences to turn upon the distinction. Now the line has been blurred to the point where, for example, it will no longer do to say that a state can validly seize a nonresident's property simply because it is within the state, even though the state could not validly reach the nonresident; and that notice by publication will suffice in an action *because* it is "in rem" instead of "in personam."

---

1. Convention on Jurisdiction and the Recognition of Judgments in Civil and Commercial Matters, 33 Official J.E.C. No. 189, July 28, 1990, pp. 1–34; reprinted 29 I.L.M. 1413. Accession to membership in the European Union requires the new member to accede to the Jurisdiction and Judgments Convention as well. Since adjustments will be required, the Convention must be amended and then carries the name of the place where the last version was signed. The current version is that of San Sebastian. It is not yet in force among all member states, i.e. different versions may apply as between or among different members depending on the state of ratifications. For convenience, we refer to the Convention by its original name—the "Brussels Convention." With the accession of Austria, Finland, and Sweden to the European Union in 1995, yet another revision of the Convention will be required. When it becomes effective, the Lugano Convention will remain in force only with respect to Iceland, Norway and Switzerland.

* In specialized areas of federal authority, such as patent and copyright cases, Congress has given "exclusive" jurisdiction to the federal courts and thereby limited the jurisdiction of state courts.

The nexus to the forum required by the due process guarantee (or by the concept of "jurisdiction in the international sense") generally serves to connect the cause of action or the defendant to the forum in some meaningful manner: is title to forum real property involved, did a product manufactured and sold by the defendant into the forum cause injury there, is the defendant domiciled in the forum? The first of these represents the classic *in rem* jurisdiction, the latter two are cases of personal (*in personam*) jurisdiction. Of these, the products case shows a relation between the forum contacts (injury caused by a defective product) and the cause of action (tort claim). In the domicile example, it is the *defendant* who has a particular connection with the forum, while the facts giving rise to the plaintiff's claim may be quite unrelated. The difference is that between *"specific"* and *"general"* jurisdiction.[2] Obviously, the wider a legal system's definition of "general jurisdiction" (i.e., not requiring claim-relatedness), the greater are the plaintiff's opportunities to draw in a distant defendant.

For many reasons and perceived advantages of American substantive or procedural law (e.g., availability of jury trial, of damages for intangible harm, of punitive damages, and of discovery procedures)[3] plaintiffs—including foreign plaintiffs—like to litigate in the United States. This country has become a magnet forum. When the defendant is foreign and perhaps the underlying facts also occurred mainly abroad, it is a frequent source of international tension and irritation that the defendant should be subject to jurisdiction in the United States (and its local assets put at risk) because it engages in general (but unrelated) business activity here. Exorbitant rules of jurisdiction of foreign countries in turn are an irritant to U.S. parties, although their impact is not so great in practice. A proposal now pending before the Hague Conference on Private International Law and initiated by the United States calls for work on a convention—to be open for acceptance by all countries—with some basic common rules on jurisdiction and on the recognition of judgments. The Brussels Convention of the European Union, mentioned earlier, is an obvious model. Work on such a proposed convention is expected to take several years, with the aim to have it completed in time for the quadrennial session of the Conference in the year 2000. For brief discussion of the project and of the difficulties involved, see Juenger, A *Shoe* Unfit for Globetrotting, 28 U.C.Davis L.Rev. 1027, 1041–45 (1995), with further references.

2. Recognition and acceptance of this distinction has been relatively recent in the United States. *See* the *Helicopteros* decision, infra at 94. It has been standard European procedure law to add to one or two bases of general jurisdiction a limited number of special situations that justify the exercise of jurisdiction. In the United States, the suggestion has been made that "a person should not be counted present before a court in abstract or in plenary fashion, but only as the particular suit gives the forum state legitimacy to intrude on that person's life." Cox, Case Three: Personal Jurisdiction, Conference on Jurisdiction, Justice, and Choice of Law for the Twenty–First Century, 29 New England L.Rev. 642, 648 (1995).

3. See also Weintraub, International Litigation and Forum Non Conveniens, 29 Texas Int'l L.J. 321 (1994); Juenger, Forum Shopping, Domestic and International, 63 Tulane L.Rev. 553 (1989).

CONSTITUTION OF THE UNITED STATES

Full Faith and Credit Clause—Article IV, Section 1:

Full Faith and Credit shall be given in each State to the public Acts, Records, and judicial Proceedings of every other State. And the Congress may by general Laws prescribe the Manner in which such Acts, Records and Proceedings shall be proved, and the Effect thereof.

Privileges and Immunities Clause—Article IV, Section 2:

The Citizens of each State shall be entitled to all Privileges and Immunities of Citizens in the several States.

Supremacy Clause—Article VI:

. . .

This Constitution, and the Laws of the United States which shall be made in Pursuance thereof; and all Treaties made, or which shall be made, under the Authority of the United States, shall be the supreme Law of the Land; and the Judges in every State shall be bound thereby, any Thing in the Constitution or Laws of any State to the Contrary notwithstanding. . . .

Fifth Amendment:

No person shall . . . be deprived of life, liberty, or property, without due process of law; . . . .

Fourteenth Amendment:

Section 1. All persons born or naturalized in the United States, and subject to the jurisdiction thereof, are citizens of the United States and of the State wherein they reside. No State shall make or enforce any law which shall abridge the privileges or immunities of citizens of the United States; nor shall any State deprive any person of life, liberty, or property, without due process of law; nor deny to any person within its jurisdiction the equal protection of the laws.

. . .

Section 5. The Congress shall have power to enforce, by appropriate legislation, the provisions of this article.

STATUTORY PROVISIONS

TITLE 28, UNITED STATES CODE ANNOTATED, § 1738 (approved June 25, 1948):

The Acts of the legislature of any State, Territory, or Possession of the United States, or copies thereof, shall be authenticated by affixing the seal of such State, Territory or Possession thereto.

The records and judicial proceedings of any court of any such State, Territory or Possession, or copies thereof, shall be proved or admitted in other courts within the United States and its Territories and Possessions by the attestation of the clerk and seal of the court annexed, if a seal exists, together with a certificate of a judge of the court that the said attestation is in proper form.

Such Acts, records and judicial proceedings or copies thereof, so authenticated, shall have the same full faith and credit in every court within the United States and its Territories and Possessions as they have by law or usage in the courts of such State, Territory or Possession from which they are taken.

NOTE

What is now § 1738 was previously found in section 905 of the Revised Statutes, and was then included in Title 28, § 687, of the original United States Code Ann. Prior to the revision in 1948, the last paragraph began: "And the said records and judicial proceedings", with no reference to "Acts". The only comment of the revisers was: "This follows the language of Article IV, section 1 of the Constitution." Does the change extend the effectiveness of the statutory provision to "Acts", which had not previously been covered by the statute? The process followed in making the revision is described in Nadelmann, Full Faith and Credit to Judgments and Public Acts, 56 Mich.L.Rev. 33, 81–86 (1957).

In 1980 Congress added Section 1738(A) to the Code, one part of which calls for full faith and credit to child custody decrees in defined circumstances. Section 1738(A) is quoted below at pp. 893–894. The Full Faith and Credit for Child Support Orders Act of 1994 (PL 103–383, 108 Stat. 4063, to be codified as 28 USCA § 1738B) is discussed infra at p. 913.

Jurisdiction of the district courts of the United States is prescribed in considerable detail in Title 28, United States Code Ann., secs. 1331–1359. Section 1332, the diversity statute, was amended in 1988 to raise the required minimum amount in controversy from $10,000 to $50,000 where federal district court jurisdiction is based on the parties' diversity of citizenship. Provisions governing venue appear in Title 28, United States Code Ann., §§ 1391–1412.

Service of process is governed by Rule 4 of the Federal Rules of Civil Procedure for the United States District Courts, promulgated by the Supreme Court under the authority of Title 28, United States Code Ann., § 2072.

Prior to 1993, federal district courts could exercise nationwide service upon special statutory authorization, such as in interpleader and certain situations under the bankruptcy act and the antitrust laws. In most other cases, the reach of district court service and jurisdiction was coextensive with that of the courts of the state in which they sat. The 1993 amendments to the Federal Rules now provide for nationwide service, subject to Constitutional limits, "with respect to claims arising under federal law" if the defendant is "not subject to the jurisdiction of the courts of general jurisdiction of any state." FRCP 4(k)(2). See further infra at p. 89.

Service may also be effected in a foreign country "(1) by any internationally agreed means ..., such as the Hague Convention on the Service Abroad of Judicial and Extrajudicial Documents; or (2) ... (A) in the manner prescribed by the law of the foreign country ...; or (3) by other means not prohibited by international agreement ...". Rule 4(f). See also infra at p. 110.

SECTION 2. BASES OF JUDICIAL JURISDICTION OVER NATURAL AND LEGAL PERSONS

A. THE HISTORIC BASES: JURISDICTION THEORY BEFORE *INTERNATIONAL SHOE*

NOTE

1. *Territoriality and the "Power" Theory of Jurisdiction.* For many years the basic decision on judicial jurisdiction was Pennoyer v. Neff, 95 U.S. 714 (1878). It focussed on the forum state's sovereign power over people and things within its borders (a summary of the decision concludes this subsection). Justice Holmes put it this way over a generation later: "The foundation of jurisdiction is physical power. ..." McDonald v. Mabee, 243 U.S. 90, 91 (1917). Despite frequent attacks by some conflicts scholars the power theory continues to be accepted and to serve as the foundation for presence in the state as a basis for jurisdiction. The Restatement, Second, Conflict of Laws, states in section 28: "A state has power to exercise judicial jurisdiction over an individual who is present within its territory, whether permanently or temporarily." This rule has found application to defendants sojourning only transiently in a state. In one well-known old case the defendant was en route by British steamer bound from Nova Scotia to New York when the vessel made for Boston harbor and was about to be moored when he was served with process. Peabody v. Hamilton, 106 Mass. 217 (1870). A Connecticut court upheld an English judgment based on jurisdiction obtained while the defendant was on a transient stop in a hotel, notwithstanding that the purpose of serving the defendant in England was to prevent the defendant from making his defense unless he prolonged his stay abroad indefinitely. Fisher v. Fielding, 67 Conn. 91, 34 A. 714 (1895).

In Grace v. MacArthur, 170 F.Supp. 442 (E.D.Ark.1959), jurisdiction was upheld over a defendant who had been served with process while flying over Arkansas in a plane. Modern decisions include: Amusement Equipment, Inc. v. Mordelt, 779 F.2d 264 (5th Cir.1985) (service on West German defendant while attending a trade show in the forum state); Aluminal Industries, Inc. v. Newton Commercial Associates, 89 F.R.D. 326 (S.D.N.Y.1980) (service at an airport).

Presence, or more accurately, personal service on a person present within the state, is not a wholly satisfactory basis of jurisdiction. On the one hand, it is too narrow and has to be supplemented by other bases. The explosive expansion of those bases is explored in the remainder of this section. On the other hand, many critics of presence as a basis for personal jurisdiction considered it unfair to compel a person to defend a civil action in whatever state the person can be served with process, merely by reason of transient physical presence. However, in Burnham v. Superior Court, 495 U.S. 604 (1990), the United States Supreme Court unanimously, albeit for reasons on which the Justices differed, upheld the continued constitutional validity of "transient jurisdiction." *Burnham* is the subject of an extensive symposium in 22 Rutgers L.J. 559 (1991). The decision is set out below, following decisions of the United States Supreme Court that consider other jurisdictional bases.

In Continental countries jurisdiction may not be based on service on the defendant during a brief sojourn. Upon their accession to the Brussels Convention, supra p. 37, Ireland and the United Kingdom therefore had to give up this "exorbitant" basis of jurisdiction in relation to defendants domiciled or with their corporate seat in the European Union. Art. 3 Brussels Convention. The same provision appears in the Lugano Convention.

2. *Domicile, Residence and Nationality.* The sovereign's power also reaches the subject or citizen while temporarily outside the state's territory. In Blackmer v. United States, 284 U.S. 421 (1932), a citizen of the United States, domiciled in France, was required to appear as a witness at a criminal trial in the United States under a statute authorizing the service of a subpoena for that purpose. Such service was effected by a United States consul in France. When Blackmer failed to appear, he was fined for contempt. The Supreme Court rejected his objection that the trial court lacked jurisdiction. As a citizen, he was "bound to take notice of the laws that are applicable to him and to obey them." The decision is accepted as establishing the principle of jurisdiction on the basis of citizenship, even though it arose in the context of a subpoena in a criminal trial. Restatement, Second, Conflict of Laws § 31 now also so provides. But see Grubel v. Nassauer, 210 N.Y. 149, 103 N.E. 1113 (1913): New York did not have to recognize German jurisdiction over a German citizen and therefore could refuse to recognize a judgment based on such a jurisdictional basis. The case is distinguishable in that the defendant had emigrated to the United States and filed for naturalization here.

From a practical perspective, it is far more important to ask whether *state court* jurisdiction (or a federal court's jurisdiction in a diversity case) may be based on the defendant's affiliation with the forum state. In Milliken v. Meyer, 311 U.S. 457 (1940), the Supreme Court gave an affirmative answer. "As in case of the authority of the United States over its absent citizen [citing to *Blackmer*], the authority of a state over one of its citizens is not terminated by the mere fact of his absence from the state. The state which accords him privileges and affords protection to him and his property by virtue of his domicile may also exact reciprocal duties.... The responsibilities of [state] citizenship arise out of the relationship to the state which domicile creates." See also Skiriotes v. Florida, 313 U.S. 69 (1941), affirming a Florida state court conviction for illegal sponge taking outside Florida's three-mile limit: "if the United States may control the conduct of its citizens upon the high seas, we see no reason why the State of Florida may not likewise govern the conduct of its citizens" outside the state with respect to matters in which it has a legitimate interest. The notion of a *state* citizenship appears in the Federal Constitution: persons are citizens of the United States and of the state "wherein they reside." U.S. Const.Amend. XIV, § 1. The Restatement, Second, Conflict of Laws acknowledges jurisdiction on the basis of "nationality and citizenship" (§ 31), but also states: A state has power to exercise judicial jurisdiction over an individual who is a resident of the state unless the individual's relationship to the state is so attenuated as to make the exercise of such jurisdiction unreasonable." The *Milliken* decision was based on *domicile*. Does mere *residence* make for state citizenship in the Constitutional sense? Would mere residence of a presently absent defendant support jurisdiction in any event? The Brussels Convention (Art. 2) refers to "domicile", but European law ordinarily defines this as something less than domicile in the Anglo–American sense, but as more than casual residence. See the discussion of domicile and "habitual residence", supra p. 17, and the Notes following the *Burnham* decision, infra p. 119. At the same time, "residence" in the European sense falls short of "domicile" in the Anglo–American sense. In order to accommodate the Brussels Convention, sec. 41(2), (3) of the English Civil Jurisdiction and Judgments Act 1982 now provides that, for purposes of Art. 2 of the Convention, an individual is domiciled in the United Kingdom if he is resident in, "and the nature and circumstances of his residence indicate that he has a substantial connection with the United Kingdom...." See Dicey & Morris, Conflict of Laws 290–94 (12th ed. by Collins, 1993). Three months' residence raise a presumption of a "substantial connection." Id. at 294. Contrary to the usual common-law rule, the English provision now makes it possible for a person to have more than domicile (for jurisdictional purposes). Id. at 292.

3. *Appearance and Consent in Advance.* The Restatement, Second, Conflict of Laws summarizes the case law as follows for cases in which the defendant either appears in an action or consented to jurisdiction in advance:

RESTATEMENT, SECOND, CONFLICT OF LAWS: *

§ 32. Consent

A state has power to exercise judicial jurisdiction over an individual who has consented to the exercise of such jurisdiction.

§ 33. Appearance as Defendant

A state has power to exercise judicial jurisdiction in an action over an individual who enters an appearance as defendant in that action.

§ 81. Special Appearance

A state will not exercise judicial jurisdiction over an individual who appears in the action for the sole purpose of objecting that there is no jurisdiction over him.

Does a nonresident who starts an action in a forum that previously lacked any jurisdictional basis over him thereby become amenable to jurisdiction for counterclaim purposes? In Adam v. Saenger, 303 U.S. 59, 67–68 (1938), p. 281, infra, the Supreme Court said: "The plaintiff having, by his voluntary act in demanding justice from the defendant, submitted himself to the jurisdiction of the court, there is nothing arbitrary or unreasonable in treating him as being there for all purposes for which justice to the defendant requires his presence. It is the price which the state may exact as the condition of opening its courts to the plaintiff."

The Model Choice of Forum Act (since withdrawn by the Conference of Commissioners on Uniform State Laws) provided in its § 2(a) that a state has jurisdiction when the parties had so stipulated in advance in writing, provided that:

---

* Quoted with the permission of the copyright owner, The American Law Institute.

(1) the court has power under the law of this state to entertain the action;

(2) this state is a reasonably convenient place for the trial of the action;

(3) the agreement as to the place of the action was not obtained by misrepresentation, duress, the abuse of economic power, or other unconscionable means; and

(4) the defendant, if within the state, was served as required by law of this state in the case of persons within the state or, if without the state, was served either personally or by registered [or certified] mail directed to his last known address.

Of these, No. 1 is self-evident: parties cannot confer subject matter jurisdiction on a court. No. 4 goes to the separate due process requirement of notice (see supra p. 160, No. 3 tests the agreement by standards of ordinary contract law. However, a special concern relates to so-called *cognovit* (confession-of-judgment) notes or clauses. They authorize the *creditor,* through counsel, to enter an appearance on behalf of the *debtor* and to confess judgment against the latter. The potential for abuse in consumer transactions is obvious. The U.S. Supreme Court has sanctioned them in principle, subject to review. See National Equipment Rental, Limited v. Szukhent, 375 U.S. 311 (1964); D.H. Overmeyer Co., Inc. of Ohio v. Frick Co., 405 U.S. 174 (1972); Swarb v. Lennox, 405 U.S. 191 (1972). The latter two decisions are treated briefly infra at p. 178. Substantive (consumer protection law) may place restrictions on the use of cognovit clauses. See, e.g., § 1.201(8)(b–e) of the Uniform Consumer Credit Code (resident consumer's agreement to jurisdiction, venue, amenability to out-of-state service invalid in credit transaction). The Brussels Convention identifies two categories of parties in need of protection against potential overreaching by their economically stronger contracting parties. These specially protected groups are consumers and insureds. See Arts. 14, 15 and 8 *et seq.,* respectively. The European Union Convention on the Applicable Law to Contractual Obligations (The Rome Convention), infra p. 547, similarly protects these groups against one-sided and potentially unfavorable stipulations of the law applicable to the principal transaction. European Communities: Convention on the Law Applicable to Contractual Obligations, 19 I.L.M. 1942, (1980).

No. 2 of § 2(a) of the Model Act may go to the heart of the problem: to what extent may the parties really bind themselves firmly to have future disputes litigated in one or more preselected courts, with the flip side of this question being whether other courts, with good jurisdiction on other grounds, should honor the agreement and decline to entertain a case brought in them in violation of the stipulation. These aspects are explored infra at p. 168.

4. *Local Actions or Local Effects.* Jurisdiction that emphasizes territoriality, sovereign power based on allegiance, or—absent these—the defendant's consent will prove inadequate for the needs of a society that is at once highly mobile and in which people interact in a variety of ways across state lines. Very early out-of-state corporations ("foreign corporations") were required to appoint resident agents or to consent to service on a governmental officer of the host state. When an agent was appointed, consent to service might be implied. See Lafayette Insurance Co. v. French, 59 U.S. (18 How.) 404 (1856). In due course, the "implied consent" rationale was abandoned, and courts recognized that a state may exercise jurisdiction over a corporation that does business in the state, at least with respect to that business. Restatement, Second, Conflict of Laws § 47.

The states similarly desired to exercise jurisdiction over foreign individuals and partnerships. Again, "implied consent" served as an early justification. The U.S. Supreme Court's influential decision in Hess v. Pawloski, 274 U.S. 352 (1927) upheld the constitutionality of a Massachusetts statute providing for the exercise of judicial jurisdiction over nonresident motorists with respect to claims arising from car accidents in the state. By operating a motor vehicle in the state, the nonresident was deemed to have appointed a specified state official to be his agent for the service of process. The Supreme Court noted that "the difference between the formal and implied appointment is not substantial, as far as concerns the application of the due process clause of the Fourteenth Amendment. *Hess* supported not only nonresident motorist statutes, but was extended to statutes dealing with travel by air and sea. See, e.g., Tardiff v. Bank Line, Ltd., 127 F.Supp. 945 (E.D.La.1954), sustaining the nonresident vessel owner statute. See also Dubin v. City of Philadelphia, 34 Pa.D. & C. 61 (1938) (nonresident owner of real property subject to jurisdiction for actions arising out of injuries sustained on such property); Betcher v. Hay-Roe, 429 Pa. 371, 240 A.2d 501 (1968) (jurisdiction over nonresident lessor for injuries occasioned by the breaking of a chair in a rented house). However, in 1953 the U.S. Supreme Court explained in the context of a nonresident motorist statute that "jurisdiction in these cases does not rest on consent at all. The defendant may protest to high heaven his unwillingness to be sued and it avails him not. The liability rests on the inroad which the automobile has made on the decision of Pennoyer v. Neff . . . , as it has on so many aspects of our social scene. The potentialities of damage by wayfaring motorists, in a population as mobile as ours, are such that those whom he injures must have opportunities of redress against the absentee motorist provided only that he is afforded an opportunity to defend himself." Olberding v. Illinois Central R. Co., 346 U.S. 338 (1953).

Olberding stresses the needs of modern society. The due process claim of the defendant who has acted in the state becomes one of receiving a fair opportunity to be heard and to defend against the suit. However, the focus on territoriality in *Pennoyer v. Neff* served not only to define the *defendant's* due process rights. The emphasis on sovereignty also addressed the *relationship of the states* to each other. This is a notion derived from public international law; in *Pennoyer,* it is used to describe the circumstance of the *federal structure* of the United States. The various aspects of *Pennoyer*—state power and due process, interstate federalism—should be themes that you keep in mind as you consider the modern case law. A brief summary of *Pennoyer* sets the stage, together with the early inroads discussed above.

PENNOYER V. NEFF, 95 U.S. (5 Otto) 714 (1878). Neff owed Mitchell for services. When he failed to pay, Mitchell sued in Oregon state court, serving Neff, who had moved to California and whose address was unknown, by publication in an Oregon state court. Neff did not appear, and a default judgment was entered. Mitchell, the judgment creditor, had a tract of land belonging to Neff seized and sold at a sheriff's sale. He bid on the property, acquired it and sold it at a profit to Pennoyer. Neff sued Pennoyer in Oregon federal court claiming title under his original deed. He argued that the sheriff's deed, through which Pennoyer claimed title, was invalid because it was based on a judgment by court that lacked personal jurisdiction over him. The U.S. Supreme Court agreed.

> "[There are] two well established principles of public law respecting the jurisdiction of an independent State over persons and property. . . . One of these principles is, that every State possesses exclusive jurisdiction and sovereignty over persons and property within its territory. . . . The

other principle of public law referred to follows from the one mentioned; that is, that no State can exercise direct jurisdiction and authority over persons or property without its territory. ... The several States are of equal dignity and authority, and the independence of one implies the exclusion of power from all others. And so it is laid down by jurists, as an elementary principle, that the laws of one State have no operation outside of its territory, except so far as is allowed by comity; and that no tribunal established by it can extend its process beyond that territory so as to subject either persons or property to its decisions. ..."

The Court blended the issue of whether Oregon had a valid basis for in personam jurisdiction with the question of how the nonresident had been notified of the Oregon state court suit declaring:

"Substituted service by publication, or in any other authorized form, may be sufficient to inform parties of the object of proceedings taken where property is once brought under the control of the court by seizure or some equivalent act. The law assumes that property is always in the possession of its owner, in person or by agent; and it proceeds upon the theory that its seizure will inform him, not only that it is taken into the custody of the court, but that he must look to any proceedings authorized by law upon such seizure for its condemnation and sale. Such service may also be sufficient in cases where the object of the action is to reach and dispose of property in the State, or of some interest therein, by enforcing a contract or a lien respecting the same, or to partition it among different owners, or, when the public is a party, to condemn and appropriate it for a public purpose. In other words, such service may answer in all actions which are substantially proceedings in rem. But where the entire object of the action is to determine the personal rights and obligations of the defendants, that is, where the suit is merely in personam, constructive service in this form upon a non-resident is ineffectual for any purpose. Process from the tribunals of one State cannot run into another State, and summon parties there domiciled to leave its territory and respond to proceedings against them. Publication of process or notice within the State where the tribunal sits cannot create any greater obligation upon the non-resident to appear. Process sent to him out of the State, and process published within it, are equally unavailing in proceedings to establish his personal liability. ..."

"Except in cases affecting the personal status of the plaintiff, and cases in which that mode of service may be considered to have been assented to in advance, ... the substituted service of process by publication, allowed by the law of Oregon and by similar laws in other States, where actions are brought against non-residents, is effectual only where, in connection with process against the person for commencing the action, property in the State is brought under the control of the court, and subjected to its disposition by process adapted to that purpose, or where the judgment is sought as a means of reaching such property or affecting some interest therein; in other words, where the action is in the nature of a proceeding in rem. ..."

NOTES

1. The opinion blends the questions of notice and opportunity to be heard with the question of valid personal jurisdiction over the defendant. Both are due process

requirements and both are often thought of together when the reference is to "service of process." But they are distinct requirements. Consider, for instance, whether the result would have been different if Neff had in fact received notice in California (by mail or other means). See Mullane v. Central Hanover Bank, 339 U.S. 306 (1950), infra p. 167.

2. The Oregon state court judgment had been entered prior to the adoption of the Fourteenth Amendment, but the Court said that due process required adherence to the principles announced in the decision.

3. *Pennoyer* continues to be debated with great passion in the literature. Compare Borchers, The Death of Constitutional Law of Personal Jurisdiction: From *Pennoyer* to *Burnham* and Back Again, 24 U.C. Davis L.Rev. 19 (1990) (arguing that *Pennoyer* has been misconstrued and that the Due Process Clause has no function of allocating jurisdiction among the states) with Oakley, The Pitfalls of "Hit and Run" History: A Critique of Professor Borchers' "Limited View" of Pennoyer v. Neff, 28 U.C. Davis L.Rev. 591 (1995).

B. IN SEARCH OF NEW JURISDICTIONAL STANDARDS: THE ERA OF *INTERNATIONAL SHOE*, "MINIMUM CONTACTS", AND "FAIRNESS".

International Shoe Co. v. State of Washington

Supreme Court of the United States, 1945.
326 U.S. 310, 66 S.Ct. 154, 90 L.Ed. 95, 161 A.L.R. 1057.

Appeal from the Supreme Court of Washington.

■ CHIEF JUSTICE STONE delivered the opinion of the Court.

The questions for decision are (1) whether, within the limitations of the due process clause of the Fourteenth Amendment, appellant, a Delaware corporation, has by its activities in the State of Washington rendered itself amenable to proceedings in the courts of that state to recover unpaid contributions to the state unemployment compensation fund exacted by state statutes, Washington Unemployment Compensation Act, Washington Revised Statutes, § 9998—103a through § 9998—123a, 1941 Supp., and (2) whether the state can exact those contributions consistently with the due process clause of the Fourteenth Amendment.

The statutes in question set up a comprehensive scheme of unemployment compensation, the costs of which are defrayed by contributions required to be made by employers to a state unemployment compensation fund. The contributions are a specified percentage of the wages payable annually by each employer for his employees' services in the state....

In this case notice of assessment for the years in question was personally served upon a sales solicitor employed by appellant in the State of Washington, and a copy of the notice was mailed by registered mail to appellant at its address in St. Louis, Missouri. Appellant appeared specially before the office of unemployment and moved to set aside the order and notice of assessment on the ground that the service upon appellant's salesman was not proper service upon appellant; that appellant was not a corporation of the State of Washington and was not doing business within the state; that it had no agent within the state upon whom service could be made; and that appellant is not an employer and does not furnish employment within the meaning of the statute.

The motion was heard on evidence and a stipulation of facts by the appeal tribunal which denied the motion and ruled that respondent Commissioner was entitled to recover the unpaid contributions. That action was affirmed by the Commissioner; both the Superior Court and the Supreme Court affirmed. 22 Wash.2d 146, 154 P.2d 801. Appellant in each of these courts assailed the statute as applied, as a violation of the due process clause of the Fourteenth Amendment, and as imposing a constitutionally prohibited burden on interstate commerce. The cause comes here on appeal under § 237(a) of the Judicial Code, 28 U.S.C. § 344(a), appellant assigning as error that the challenged statutes as applied infringe the due process clause of the Fourteenth Amendment and the commerce clause.

The facts as found by the appeal tribunal and accepted by the state Superior Court and Supreme Court, are not in dispute. Appellant is a Delaware corporation, having its principal place of business in St. Louis, Missouri, and is engaged in the manufacture and sale of shoes and other footwear. It maintains places of business in several states, other than Washington, at which its manufacturing is carried on and from which its merchandise is distributed interstate through several sales units or branches located outside the State of Washington.

Appellant has no office in Washington and makes no contracts either for sale or purchase of merchandise there. It maintains no stock of merchandise in that state and makes there no deliveries of goods in intrastate commerce. During the years from 1937 to 1940, now in question, appellant employed eleven to thirteen salesmen under direct supervision and control of sales managers located in St. Louis. These salesmen resided in Washington; their principal activities were confined to that state; and they were compensated by commissions based upon the amount of their sales. The commissions for each year totaled more than $31,000. Appellant supplies its salesmen with a line of samples, each consisting of one shoe of a pair, which they display to prospective purchasers. On occasion they rent permanent sample rooms, for exhibiting samples, in business buildings, or rent rooms in hotels or business buildings temporarily for that purpose. The cost of such rentals is reimbursed by appellant.

The authority of the salesmen is limited to exhibiting their samples and soliciting orders from prospective buyers, at prices and on terms fixed by appellant. The salesmen transmit the orders to appellant's office in St. Louis for acceptance or rejection, and when accepted the merchandise for filling the orders is shipped f.o.b. from points outside Washington to the purchasers within the state. All the merchandise shipped into Washington is invoiced at the place of shipment from which collections are made. No salesman has authority to enter into contracts or to make collections.

[Here the opinion of the State court is summarized and the contention of appellant that the statute imposes an unconstitutional burden on interstate commerce rejected.]

Appellant also insists that its activities within the state were not sufficient to manifest its "presence" there and that in its absence the state courts were without jurisdiction, that consequently it was a denial of due process for the state to subject appellant to suit. It refers to those cases in which it was said that the mere solicitation of orders for the purchase of goods within a state, to be accepted without the state and filled by shipment of the purchased goods interstate, does not render the corporation seller amenable to suit within the state.... And appellant further argues that since it was not present within the state, it is a denial of due process to subject it to taxation or other money exaction. It thus denies the power of the state to lay the tax or to subject appellant to a suit for its collection.

Historically the jurisdiction of courts to render judgment in personam is grounded on their de facto power over the defendant's person. Hence his presence within the territorial jurisdiction of a court was prerequisite to its rendition of a judgment personally binding him. Pennoyer v. Neff, 95 U.S. 714, 733. But now that the capias ad respondendum has given way to personal service of summons or other form of notice, due process requires only that in order to subject a defendant to a judgment in personam, if he be not present within the territory of the forum, he have certain minimum contacts with it such that the maintenance of the suit does not offend "traditional notions of fair play and substantial justice." Milliken v. Meyer, 311 U.S. 457, 463. See Holmes, J., in McDonald v. Mabee, 243 U.S. 90, 91. Compare Hoopeston Canning Co. v. Cullen, 318 U.S. 313, 316, 319. See Blackmer v. United States, 284 U.S. 421; Hess v. Pawloski, 274 U.S. 352; Young v. Masci, 289 U.S. 253.

Since the corporate personality is a fiction, although a fiction intended to be acted upon as though it were a fact, Klein v. Board of Tax Supervisors, 282 U.S. 19, 24, it is clear that unlike an individual its "presence" without, as well as within, the state of its origin can be manifested only by activities carried on in its behalf by those who are authorized to act for it. To say that the corporation is so far "present" there as to satisfy due process requirements, for purposes of taxation or the maintenance of suits against it in the courts of the state, is to beg the question to be decided. For the terms "present" or "presence" are used merely to symbolize those activities of the corporation's agent within the state which courts will deem to be sufficient to satisfy the demands of due process. L. Hand, J., in Hutchinson v. Chase & Gilbert, 45 F.2d 139, 141. Those demands may be met by such contacts of the corporation with the state of the forum as make it reasonable, in the context of our federal system of government, to require the corporation to defend the particular suit which is brought there. An "estimate of the inconveniences" which would result to the corporation from a trial away from its "home" or principal place of business is relevant in this connection. Hutchinson v. Chase & Gilbert, supra, 141.

"Presence" in the state in this sense has never been doubted when the activities of the corporation there have not only been continuous and systematic, but also give rise to the liabilities sued on, even though no consent to be sued or authorization to an agent to accept service of process has been given.... Conversely it has been generally recognized that the casual presence of the corporate agent or even his conduct of single or isolated items of activities in a state in the corporation's behalf are not enough to subject it to suit on causes of action unconnected with the activities there.... To require the corporation in such circumstances to defend the suit away from its home or other jurisdiction where it carries on more substantial activities has been thought to lay too great and unreasonable a burden on the corporation to comport with due process.

While it has been held in cases on which appellant relies that continuous activity of some sort within a state is not enough to support the demand that the corporation be amenable to suits unrelated to that activity, Old Wayne Mut. Life Ass'n v. McDonough [204 U.S. 8]; Green v. Chicago, Burlington & Quincy R. Co. [205 U.S. 530]; Simon v. Southern R. Co., 236 U.S. 115; People's Tobacco Co. v. American Tobacco Co. [246 U.S. 79]; cf. Davis v. Farmers' Co-operative Equity Co., 262 U.S. 312, 317, there have been instances in which the continuous corporate operations within a state were thought so substantial and of such a nature as to justify suit against it on causes of action arising from dealings entirely distinct from those activities. See Missouri, K. & T.R. Co. v. Reynolds, 255 U.S. 565; Tauza v. Susquehanna Coal Co., 220 N.Y. 259, 115 N.E. 915; cf. St. Louis S.W.R. Co. v. Alexander [227 U.S. 218].

Finally, although the commission of some single or occasional acts of the corporate agent in a state sufficient to impose an obligation or liability on the corporation has not been thought to confer upon the state authority to enforce it, Rosenberg Bros. & Co. v. Curtis Brown Co., 260 U.S. 516, other such acts, because of their nature and quality and the circumstances of their commission, may be deemed sufficient to render the corporation liable to suit. Cf. Kane v. New Jersey, 242 U.S. 160; Hess v. Pawloski, supra; Young v. Masci, supra. True, some of the decisions holding the corporation amenable to suit have been supported by resort to the legal fiction that it has given its consent to service and suit, consent being implied from its presence in the state through the acts of its authorized agents.... But more realistically it may be said that those authorized acts were of such a nature as to justify the fiction. Smolik v. Philadelphia & R.C. & I. Co., D.C., 222 F. 148, 151. Henderson, The Position of Foreign Corporations in American Constitutional Law, 94–95.

It is evident that the criteria by which we mark the boundary line between those activities which justify the subjection of a corporation to suit, and those which do not, cannot be simply mechanical or quantitative. The test is not merely, as has sometimes been suggested, whether the activity, which the corporation has seen fit to procure through its agents in another state, is a little more or a little less. St. Louis S.W.R. Co. v. Alexander [227 U.S. 228]; International Harvester Co. v. Kentucky [234 U.S. 587]. Whether due process is satisfied must depend rather upon the quality and nature of the activity in relation to the fair and orderly administration of the laws which it was the purpose of the due process clause to insure. That clause does not contemplate that a state may make binding a judgment in personam against an individual or corporate defendant with which the state has no contacts, ties, or relations. Cf. Pennoyer v. Neff, supra; Minnesota Commercial Men's Ass'n v. Benn, 261 U.S. 140.

But to the extent that a corporation exercises the privilege of conducting activities within a state, it enjoys the benefits and protection of the laws of that state. The exercise of that privilege may give rise to obligations; and, so far as those obligations arise out of or are connected with the activities within the state, a procedure which requires the corporation to respond to a suit brought to enforce them can, in most instances, hardly be said to be undue....

Applying these standards, the activities carried on in behalf of appellant in the State of Washington were neither irregular nor casual. They were systematic and continuous throughout the years in question. They resulted in a large volume of interstate business, in the course of which appellant received the benefits and protection of the laws of the state, including the right to resort to the courts for the enforcement of its rights. The obligation which is here sued upon arose out of those very activities. It is evident that these operations establish sufficient contacts or ties with the state of the forum to make it reasonable and just according to our traditional conception of fair play and substantial justice to permit the state to enforce the obligations which appellant has incurred there. Hence we cannot say that the maintenance of the present suit in the State of Washington involves an unreasonable or undue procedure.

We are likewise unable to conclude that the service of the process within the state upon an agent whose activities establish appellant's "presence" there was not sufficient notice of the suit, or that the suit was so unrelated to those activities as to make the agent an inappropriate vehicle for communicating the notice. It is enough that appellant has established such contacts with the state that the particular form of substituted service adopted there gives reasonable assurance that the notice will be actual.... Nor can we say that the mailing of the notice of suit to appellant by registered mail at its home office was not reasonably calculated to apprise appellant of the suit....

Only a word need be said of appellant's liability for the demanded contributions of the state unemployment fund. The Supreme Court of Washington, construing and applying the statute, has held that it imposes a tax on the privilege of employing appellant's salesmen within the state measured by a percentage of the wages, here the commissions payable to the salesmen. This construction we accept for purposes of determining the constitutional validity of the statute. The right to employ labor has been deemed an appropriate subject of taxation in this country and England, both before and since the adoption of the Constitution. Steward Machine Co. v. Davis, 301 U.S. 548, 579 et seq. And such a tax imposed upon the employer for unemployment benefits is within the constitutional power of the states. Carmichael v. Southern Coal & Coke Co., 301 U.S. 495, 508 et seq.

Appellant having rendered itself amenable to suit upon obligations arising out of the activities of its salesmen in Washington, the state may maintain the present suit in personam to collect the tax laid upon the exercise of the privilege of employing appellant's salesmen within the state. For Washington has made one of those activities, which taken together establish appellant's "presence" there for purposes of suit, the taxable event by which the state brings appellant within the reach of its taxing power. The state thus has constitutional power to lay the tax and to subject appellant to a suit to recover it. The activities which establish its "presence" subject it alike to taxation by the state and to suit to recover the tax....

Affirmed.

■ JUSTICE BLACK delivered the following opinion....

I believe that the Federal Constitution leaves to each State, without any "ifs" or "buts", a power to tax and to open the doors of its courts for its citizens to sue corporations whose agents do business in those States. Believing that the Constitution gave the States that power, I think it a judicial deprivation to condition its exercise upon this Court's notion of "fair play", however appealing that term may be. Nor can I stretch the meaning of due process so far as to authorize this Court to deprive a State of the right to afford judicial protection to its citizens on the ground that it would be more "convenient" for the corporation to be sued somewhere else.

There is a strong emotional appeal in the words "fair play", "justice", and "reasonableness." But they were not chosen by those who wrote the original Constitution or the Fourteenth Amendment as a measuring rod for this Court to use in invalidating State or Federal laws passed by elected legislative representatives.... Superimposing the natural justice concept on the Constitution's specific prohibitions could operate as a drastic abridgment of democratic safeguards they embody, such as freedom of speech, press and religion, and the right to counsel. This has already happened. Betts v. Brady, 316 U.S. 455. Compare Feldman v. United States, 322 U.S. 487, 494–503. For application of this natural law concept, whether under the terms "reasonableness", "justice", or "fair play", makes judges the supreme arbiters of the country's laws and practices.... This result, I believe, alters the form of government our Constitution provides. I cannot agree....

NOTES

1. The International Shoe case is a landmark in the law of judicial jurisdiction. What test or tests of jurisdiction does it announce? What factors does it identify as determinative of whether a state's courts have jurisdiction in a given case? Should the existence of "minimum contacts" guarantee "fairness" or is "fairness" a separate standard that must be satisfied even when the defendant has minimum

contacts with the forum state? See Asahi Metal Industry Co., Ltd. v. Superior Court of California, 480 U.S. 102 (1987), p. 78, infra.

2. We referred earlier to the distinction between "general" and "specific" (i.e., claim-related) jurisdiction. Supra p. 38. Note that the Court in *International Shoe* points to the company's "systematic and continuous" business activity in Washington. Does this mean that Washington courts could have exercised (general) jurisdiction over an *unrelated* claim, say, a tort committed by a corporate officer, acting on behalf of the company, at its Missouri head office? See Perkins v. Benguet, infra p. 93. Or was it important that the claim in issue arose out of the Washington activities? If so, why is it important that the activities were systematic and continuous? See *McGee,* immediately following. For recognition and application of the difference between general and specific jurisdiction, see the *Helicopteros* decision, infra p. 74.

3. The Court here declares that the State's power to impose tax obligations on the International Shoe Company was established by the same factors that subjected the company to suit in Washington. Of course, that does not mean that the factors that suffice to subject a nonresident to judicial jurisdiction are always co-extensive with those that make it amenable to the State's law-making authority. See Hanson v. Denckla, p. 56, infra, and Phillips Petroleum v. Shutts, p. 362, infra.

4. For an extensive modern reassessment of the *International Shoe* decision, see Symposium, Fifty Years of *International Shoe:* The Past and Future of Personal Jurisdiction, 28 U.C. Davis L.Rev. 513–1058 (1995) (with contributions by Perschbacher, Weintraub, Borchers, Oakley, Silberman, Cameron/Johnson, Chemerinsky, Mullenix, Redish/Beste, Goldstein, Morse, Juenger, and Bruch).

McGee v. International Life Insurance Co.
Supreme Court of the United States, 1957.
355 U.S. 220, 78 S.Ct. 199, 2 L.Ed.2d 223.

■ Opinion of the Court by JUSTICE BLACK, announced by JUSTICE DOUGLAS.

Petitioner, Lulu B. McGee, recovered a judgment in a California state court against respondent, International Life Insurance Company, on a contract of insurance. Respondent was not served with process in California but by registered mail at its principal place of business in Texas. The California court based its jurisdiction on a state statute which subjects foreign corporations to suit in California on insurance contracts with residents of that State even though such corporations cannot be served with process within its borders.

Unable to collect the judgment in California petitioner went to Texas where she filed suit on the judgment in a Texas court. But the Texas courts refused to enforce her judgment holding it was void under the Fourteenth Amendment because service of process outside California could not give the courts of that State jurisdiction over respondent. 288 S.W.2d 579. It is not controverted that if the California court properly exercised jurisdiction over respondent the Texas courts erred in refusing to give its judgment full faith and credit. 28 U.S.C. § 1738, 28 U.S.C.A. § 1738.

The material facts are relatively simple. In 1944, Lowell Franklin, a resident of California, purchased a life insurance policy from the Empire

Mutual Insurance Company, an Arizona corporation. In 1948 the respondent agreed with Empire Mutual to assume its insurance obligations. Respondent then mailed a reinsurance certificate to Franklin in California offering to insure him in accordance with the terms of the policy he held with Empire Mutual. He accepted this offer and from that time until his death in 1950 paid premiums by mail from his California home to respondent's Texas office. Petitioner, Franklin's mother, was the beneficiary under the policy. She sent proofs of his death to the respondent but it refused to pay claiming that he had committed suicide. It appears that neither Empire Mutual nor respondent has ever had any office or agent in California. And so far as the record before us shows, respondent has never solicited or done any insurance business in California apart from the policy involved here.

Since Pennoyer v. Neff, 95 U.S. 714, this Court has held that the Due Process Clause of the Fourteenth Amendment places some limit on the power of state courts to enter binding judgments against persons not served with process within their boundaries. But just where this line of limitation falls has been the subject of prolific controversy, particularly with respect to foreign corporations. In a continuing process of evolution this Court accepted and then abandoned "consent," "doing business," and "presence" as the standard for measuring the extent of state judicial power over such corporations. See Henderson, The Position of Foreign Corporations in American Constitutional Law, c. V. More recently in International Shoe Co. v. State of Washington, 326 U.S. 310, the Court decided that "due process requires only that in order to subject a defendant to a judgment *in personam,* if he be not present within the territory of the forum, he have certain minimum contacts with it such that the maintenance of the suit does not offend 'traditional notions of fair play and substantial justice.'" Id., 326 U.S. at page 316.

Looking back over this long history of litigation a trend is clearly discernible toward expanding the permissible scope of state jurisdiction over foreign corporations and other nonresidents. In part this is attributable to the fundamental transformation of our national economy over the years. Today many commercial transactions touch two or more States and may involve parties separated by the full continent. With this increasing nationalization of commerce has come a great increase in the amount of business conducted by mail across state lines. At the same time modern transportation and communication have made it much less burdensome for a party sued to defend himself in a State where he engages in economic activity.

Turning to this case we think it apparent that the Due Process Clause did not preclude the California court from entering a judgment binding on respondent. It is sufficient for purposes of due process that the suit was based on a contract which had substantial connection with that State. Cf. Hess v. Pawloski, 274 U.S. 352; Henry L. Doherty & Co. v. Goodman, 294 U.S. 623; Pennoyer v. Neff, 95 U.S. 714, 735. The contract was delivered in California, the premiums were mailed from there and the insured was a resident of that State when he died. It cannot be denied that California has a manifest interest in providing effective means of redress for its residents when their insurers refuse to pay claims. These residents would be at a severe disadvantage if they were forced to follow the insurance company to a distant State in order to hold it legally accountable. When claims were small or moderate individual claimants frequently could not afford the cost of bringing an action in a foreign forum—thus in effect making the company judgment proof. Often the crucial witnesses—as here on the company's defense of suicide—will be found in the insured's locality. Of course there may be inconvenience to the insurer if it is held amenable to suit in California where it had this contract but certainly nothing which amounts to a denial of due process. Cf. Travelers Health Ass'n v. Commonwealth of Virginia ex rel. State Corporation Comm., 339 U.S. 643. There is no contention that respondent did not have adequate notice of the suit or sufficient time to prepare its defenses and appear.

The California statute became law in 1949, after respondent had entered into the agreement with Franklin to assume Empire Mutual's obligation to him. Respondent contends that application of the statute to this existing contract improperly impairs the obligation of the contract. We believe that contention is devoid of merit. The statute was remedial, in the purest sense of that term, and neither enlarged nor impaired respondent's substantive rights or obligations under the contract. It did nothing more than to provide petitioner with a California forum to enforce whatever substantive rights she might have against respondent. At the same time respondent was given a reasonable time to appear and defend on the merits after being notified of the suit. Under such circumstances it had no vested right not to be sued in California....

Judgment reversed and cause remanded with directions.

NOTES

1. On the facts of the McGee case, would Texas have had judicial jurisdiction to entertain an action brought by the insurance company against the insured for a declaratory determination that it was not liable under the policy? In Spiegel, Inc. v. The Federal Trade Commission, 540 F.2d 287 (7th Cir.1976), the court upheld an FTC order restraining the defendant mail order house from suing customers in states other than their domiciles or where the mail order contract was made. Without deciding whether Illinois long-arm jurisdiction could constitutionally reach out-of-state customers, the court upheld the FTC order as a reasonable exercise of its authority to police unfair trade practices.

2. A Pennsylvania insurance company mailed to a resident of New York a policy insuring hotel property in New Hampshire and received a premium payment by mail from New York. Judicial jurisdiction in New York over the insurance company was upheld on the basis of that single transaction under a statute that made "delivery of contracts of insurance to residents" of New York an act "in this state" even though delivery was by mail. Zacharakis v. Bunker Hill Mut. Ins. Co., 281 App.Div. 487, 120 N.Y.S.2d 418 (1st Dep't 1953).

3. Many observers regard the McGee decision as the high water mark in the Supreme Court's progressive expansion of the permissible bases of a state's personal jurisdiction over nonresident defendants. Is its holding confined to insurance claims? Would it support the result in Hirsch v. Blue Cross, Blue Shield of Kansas City, 800 F.2d 1474 (9th Cir.1986)? A Kansas employer had contracted for group health insurance, in Kansas, for its Kansas employees, with a Kansas insurance carrier. The parties subsequently added three California employees to the coverage. The carrier issued membership cards to the California employees whose premiums were paid through Kansas payroll deductions. When the carrier subsequently failed to pay a Californian's claim, the insured employee sued in California. The defendant had no office, property, or employees in California, and did not solicit business there. Held: there was limited jurisdiction over the defendant with respect to this plaintiff's claim.

Hanson v. Denckla
Supreme Court of the United States, 1958.
357 U.S. 235, 78 S.Ct. 1228, 2 L.Ed.2d 1283.

[This case, involving due process and full faith and credit, is a contest between the appointees under an inter vivos power of appointment who won in the courts of Delaware, and residuary legatees who won in the courts of Florida.

In 1935, Mrs. Donner, domiciled in Pennsylvania, executed a deed of trust of corporate securities to a Delaware trust company as trustee and delivered the securities to it. She reserved for herself the income for life, a power of appointment of the corpus by deed or will, the power to amend or revoke the trust agreement in whole or in part and to change the trustee, and indirect control over the investments by the trustee.

In 1944, the settlor became domiciled in Florida and remained so until her death in 1952. In 1949, she executed an instrument of appointment with only one witness, under which she made small gifts to several individual beneficiaries and appointed $400,000 all told to two trusts set up by one of her daughters with another Delaware trust company as trustee for the benefit of the issue of that daughter. The same day she executed her will under which she gave the residue of her property to her executrix in trust for two other daughters.

The will was probated in Florida. In Florida the two daughters who were the beneficiaries under the residuary clause of the will filed a petition for a declaratory judgment on what property passed under that clause. Personal service was made upon the executrix, upon some but not all of the beneficiaries under the 1949 appointment, but upon neither of the Delaware trust companies who were named in the 1935 deed and the 1949 appointment.

Before the Florida court rendered a decree the executrix began a declaratory judgment action in Delaware to determine who was entitled to the trust assets in that state. All of the trust companies, beneficiaries, and legatees appeared and participated except one of the two daughters taking under the residuary clause of the will. The executrix was enjoined by the

Florida court from further participation in the Delaware case, but the other parties continued to press their claims.

The decree of the Florida Chancellor came down first. He ruled that he lacked jurisdiction over the parties on whom there had been no personal service and over the trust corpus because it was outside the state. But as to the parties before the court he ruled the power of appointment was testamentary and the exercise void under the applicable Florida law, and the $400,000 in question passed under the residuary clause of the will.

The Florida decree was presented in the Delaware proceeding as res judicata. The Delaware Chancellor decided to the contrary, that the power of appointment and the inter vivos exercise were governed by Delaware law and were valid, and that the assets under the 1949 exercise were rightly paid over by one Delaware trust company to the other.

The executrix then made a motion in the Supreme Court of Florida, where the Florida case was pending on appeal, and asked that court to remand the case to the trial court with instructions to dismiss as she was bound by the Delaware decree. Denying the motion, the Supreme Court of Florida agreed with its state Chancellor that the inter vivos power of appointment and its exercise were governed by Florida law and were invalid. On the matter of jurisdiction, it went beyond the Chancellor, and its ruling, as stated by the Supreme Court of the United States, was:

"The court ruled that jurisdiction to construe the will carried with it 'substantive' jurisdiction 'over the persons of the absent defendants' even though the trust assets were not 'physically in the state.' Whether this meant jurisdiction over the person of the defendants or jurisdiction over the trust assets is open to doubt."

The Supreme Court of Delaware refused to give effect to the Florida decree.

The two cases, from Florida and Delaware, were carried to the Supreme Court of the United States.]

■ CHIEF JUSTICE WARREN delivered the opinion of the Court....

The issues for our decision, are, *first,* whether Florida erred in holding that it had jurisdiction over the nonresident defendants, and *second,* whether Delaware erred in refusing full faith and credit to the Florida decree. We need not determine whether Florida was bound to give full faith and credit to the decree of the Delaware Chancellor since the question was not seasonably presented to the Florida court.

Appellants charge that this [Florida] judgment is offensive to the Due Process Clause of the Fourteenth Amendment because the Florida court was without jurisdiction. There is no suggestion that the court failed to employ a means of notice reasonably calculated to inform nonresident defendants of the pending proceedings or denied them an opportunity to be heard in defense of their interests. The alleged defect is the absence of those "affiliating circumstances" without which the courts of a State may not enter a judgment imposing obligations on persons (jurisdiction *in personam*) or affecting interests in property (jurisdiction *in rem* or *quasi in rem*). While the *in rem* and *in personam* classifications do not exhaust all the situations that give rise to jurisdiction, they are adequate to describe the affiliating circumstances suggested here, and accordingly serve as a useful means of approach to this case.

In rem jurisdiction. Founded on physical power, McDonald v. Mabee, 243 U.S. 90, 91, the *in rem* jurisdiction of a state court is limited by the extent of its power and by the coordinate authority of sister States. The basis of the jurisdiction is the presence of the subject property within the territorial jurisdiction of the forum State.... Tangible property poses no problem for the application of this rule, but the situs of intangibles is often a matter of controversy. In considering restrictions on the power to tax, this Court has concluded that "jurisdiction" over intangible property is not limited to a single State. State Tax Commission of Utah v. Aldrich, 316 U.S. 174; Curry v. McCanless, 307 U.S. 357. Whether the type of "jurisdiction" with which this opinion deals may be exercised by more than one State we need not decide. The parties seem to assume that the trust assets that form the subject matter of this action were located in Delaware and not in Florida. We can see nothing in the record contrary to that assumption, or sufficient to establish a situs in Florida.

The Florida court held that the presence of the subject property was not essential to its jurisdiction. Authority over the probate and construction of its domiciliary's will, under which the assets might pass, was thought sufficient to confer the requisite jurisdiction. But jurisdiction cannot be predicated upon the contingent role of this Florida will. Whatever the efficacy of a so-called *"in rem"* jurisdiction over assets admittedly passing under a local will, a State acquires no *in rem* jurisdiction to adjudicate the validity of *inter vivos* dispositions simply because its decision might augment an estate passing under a will probated in its courts. If such a basis of jurisdiction were sustained, probate courts would enjoy nationwide service of process to adjudicate interests in property with which neither the State nor the decedent could claim any affiliation. The settlor-decedent's Florida domicile is equally unavailing as a basis for jurisdiction over the trust assets. For the purpose of jurisdiction *in rem* the maxim that personalty has its situs at the domicile of its owner is a fiction of limited utility. Green v. Van Buskirk, 7 Wall. 139, 150, 19 L.Ed. 109. The maxim is no less suspect when the domicile is that of a decedent. In analogous cases, this Court has rejected the suggestion that the probate decree of the State where decedent was domiciled has an *in rem* effect on personalty outside the forum State that could render it conclusive on the interests of nonresidents over whom there was no personal jurisdiction. Riley v. New York Trust Co., 315 U.S. 343, 353; Baker v. Baker, Eccles & Co., 242 U.S. 394; Overby v. Gordon, 177 U.S. 214. The fact that the owner is or was domiciled within the forum State is not a sufficient affiliation with the property upon which to base jurisdiction *in rem*. Having concluded that Florida had no *in rem* jurisdiction, we proceed to consider whether a judgment purporting to rest on that basis is invalid in Florida and must therefore be reversed.

Prior to the Fourteenth Amendment an exercise of jurisdiction over persons or property outside the forum State was thought to be an absolute nullity, but the matter remained a question of state law over which this Court exercised no authority. With the adoption of that Amendment, any judgment purporting to bind the person of a defendant over whom the court had not acquired *in personam* jurisdiction was void within the State as well as without. Pennoyer v. Neff, 95 U.S. 714. Nearly a century has passed without this Court being called upon to apply that principle to an *in rem* judgment dealing with property outside the forum State. The invalidity of such a judgment within the forum State seems to have been assumed—and with good reason. Since a State is forbidden to enter a judgment attempting to bind a person over whom it has no jurisdiction, it has even less right to enter a judgment purporting to extinguish the interest of such a person in property over which the court has no jurisdiction.[23] Therefore, so far as it purports to rest upon jurisdiction over the trust assets, the judgment of the Florida court cannot be sustained. Sadler v. Industrial Trust Co., 327 Mass. 10, 97 N.E.2d 169.

In personam jurisdiction. Appellees' stronger argument is for *in personam* jurisdiction over the Delaware trustee. They urge that the circumstances of this case amount to sufficient affiliation with the State of Florida to empower its courts to exercise personal jurisdiction over this nonresident defendant. Principal reliance is placed upon McGee v. International Life Ins. Co., 355 U.S. 220. In *McGee* the Court noted the trend of expanding personal jurisdiction over nonresidents. . . . [T]he requirements for personal jurisdiction over nonresidents have evolved from the rigid rule of Pennoyer v. Neff, 95 U.S. 714 to the flexible standard of International Shoe Co. v. Washington, 326 U.S. 310. But it is a mistake to assume that this trend heralds the eventual demise of all restrictions on the personal jurisdiction of state courts. See Vanderbilt v. Vanderbilt, 354 U.S. 416, 418. Those restrictions are more than a guarantee of immunity from inconvenient or distant litigation. They are a consequence of territorial limitations on the power of the respective States. However minimal the burden of defending in a foreign tribunal, a defendant may not be called upon to do so unless he has had the "minimal contacts" with that State that are a prerequisite to its exercise of power over him. See International Shoe Co. v. Washington, 326 U.S. 310, 319.

We fail to find such contacts in the circumstances of this case. The defendant trust company has no office in Florida, and transacts no business there. None of the trust assets has ever been held or administered in Florida, and the record discloses no solicitation of business in that State either in person or by mail.

---

23. This holding was forecast in Pennoyer v. Neff, supra. When considering the effect of the Fourteenth Amendment, this Court declared that in actions against nonresidents substituted service was permissible only where "*property in the State* is brought under the control of the court, and subjected to its disposition by process adapted to that purpose. . . ." (Emphasis supplied.) 95 U.S. at page 733. [Footnote by the Court.]

The cause of action in this case is not one that arises out of an act done or transaction consummated in the forum State. In that respect, it differs from McGee v. International Life Ins. Co., 355 U.S. 220 (1957) and the cases there cited. In *McGee,* the nonresident defendant solicited a reinsurance agreement with a resident of California. The offer was accepted in that State, and the insurance premiums were mailed from there until the insured's death. Noting the interest California has in providing effective redress for its residents when nonresident insurers refuse to pay claims on insurance they have solicited in that State, the Court upheld jurisdiction because the suit "was based on a contract which had substantial connection with that State." In contrast, this action involves the validity of an agreement that was entered without any connection with the forum State. The agreement was executed in Delaware by a trust company incorporated in that State and a settlor domiciled in Pennsylvania. The first relationship Florida had to the agreement was years later when the settlor became domiciled there, and the trustee remitted the trust income to her in that State. From Florida Mrs. Donner carried on several bits of trust administration that may be compared to the mailing of premiums in *McGee.* But the record discloses no instance in which the *trustee* performed any acts in Florida that bear the same relationship to the agreement as the solicitation in McGee. Consequently, this suit cannot be said to be one to enforce an obligation that arose from a privilege the defendant exercised in Florida. Cf. International Shoe Co. v. Washington, 326 U.S. 310, 319. This case is also different from McGee in that there the State had enacted special legislation (Unauthorized Insurers Process Act) to exercise what *McGee* called its "manifest interest" in providing effective redress for citizens who had been injured by nonresidents engaged in an activity that the State treats as exceptional and subjects to special regulation. Cf. Travelers Health Assn. v. Virginia, 339 U.S. 643, 647–649; Doherty & Co. v. Goodman, 294 U.S. 623, 627; Hess v. Pawloski, 274 U.S. 352.

The execution in Florida of the powers of appointment under which the beneficiaries and appointees claim does not give Florida a substantial connection with the contract on which this suit is based. It is the validity of the trust agreement, not the appointment, that is at issue here. For the purpose of applying its rule that the validity of a trust is determined by the law of the State of its creation, Florida ruled that the appointment amounted to a "republication" of the original trust instrument in Florida. For choice-of-law purposes such a ruling may be justified, but we think it an insubstantial connection with the trust agreement for purposes of determining the question of personal jurisdiction over a nonresident defendant. The unilateral activity of those who claim some relationship with a nonresident defendant cannot satisfy the requirement of contact with the forum State. The application of that rule will vary with the quality and nature of the defendant's activity, but it is essential in each case that there be some act by which the defendant purposefully avails itself of the privilege of conducting activities within the forum State, thus invoking the benefits and protections of its laws.... The settlor's execution in Florida of her power of appointment cannot remedy the absence of such an act in this case.

It is urged that because the settlor and most of the appointees and beneficiaries were domiciled in Florida the courts of that State should be able to exercise personal jurisdiction over the nonresident trustees. This is a non sequitur. With personal jurisdiction over the executor, legatees, and appointees, there is nothing in federal law to prevent Florida from adjudicating concerning the respective rights and liabilities of those parties. But Florida has not chosen to do so.

As we understand its law, the trustee is an indispensable party over whom the court must acquire jurisdiction before it is empowered to enter judgment in a proceeding affecting the validity of a trust. It does not acquire that jurisdiction by being the "center of gravity" of the controversy, or the most convenient location for litigation. The issue is personal jurisdiction, not choice of law. It is resolved in this case by considering the acts of the trustee. As we have indicated, they are insufficient to sustain the jurisdiction.[27]

Because it sustained jurisdiction over the nonresident trustees, the Florida Supreme Court found it unnecessary to determine whether Florida law made those defendants indispensable parties in the circumstances of this case. Our conclusion that Florida was without jurisdiction over the Delaware trustee, or over the trust corpus held in that State, requires that we make that determination in the first instance. As we have noted earlier, the Florida Supreme Court has repeatedly held that a trustee is an indispensable party without whom a Florida court has no power to adjudicate controversies affecting the validity of a trust. For that reason the Florida judgment must be reversed not only as to the nonresident trustees but also as to appellants, over whom the Florida court admittedly had jurisdiction.

No. 117, The Delaware Certiorari. The same reasons that compel reversal of the Florida judgment require affirmance of the Delaware one. Delaware is under no obligation to give full faith and credit to a Florida judgment invalid in Florida because offensive to the Due Process Clause of the Fourteenth Amendment.... Since Delaware was entitled to conclude that Florida law made the trust company an indispensable party, it was under no obligation to give the Florida judgment any faith and credit—even against parties over whom Florida's jurisdiction was unquestioned.

It is suggested that this disposition is improper—that the Delaware case should be held while the Florida cause is remanded to give that court an opportunity to determine whether the trustee is an indispensable party in the circumstances of this case....

---

27. This conclusion makes unnecessary any consideration of appellants' contention that the contacts the trust agreement had with Florida were so slight that it was a denial of due process of law to determine its validity by Florida law. See Home Insurance Co. v. Dick, 281 U.S. 397. [Footnote by the Court.]

The rule of primacy to the first final judgment is a necessary incident to the requirement of full faith and credit. Our only function is to determine whether judgments are consistent with the Federal Constitution. In determining the correctness of Delaware's judgment we look to what Delaware was entitled to conclude from the Florida authorities at the time the Delaware court's judgment was entered. To withhold affirmance of a correct Delaware judgment until Florida has had time to rule on another question would be participating in the litigation instead of adjudicating its outcome.

The judgment of the Delaware Supreme Court is affirmed and the judgment of the Florida Supreme Court is reversed and the cause is remanded for proceedings not inconsistent with this opinion.

■ JUSTICE BLACK, whom JUSTICE BURTON and JUSTICE BRENNAN join, dissenting.

I believe the courts of Florida had power to adjudicate the effectiveness of the appointment made in Florida by Mrs. Donner with respect to all those who were notified of the proceedings and given an opportunity to be heard without violating the Due Process Clause of the Fourteenth Amendment. If this is correct, it follows that the Delaware courts erred in refusing to give the prior Florida judgment full faith and credit....

True the question whether the law of a State can be applied to a transaction is different from the question whether the courts of that State have jurisdiction to enter a judgment, but the two are often closely related and to a substantial degree depend upon similar considerations. It seems to me that where a transaction has as much relationship to a State as Mrs. Donner's appointment had to Florida its courts ought to have power to adjudicate controversies arising out of that transaction, unless litigation there would impose such a heavy and disproportionate burden on a nonresident defendant that it would offend what this Court has referred to as "traditional notions of fair play and substantial justice." ... So far as the nonresident defendants here are concerned I can see nothing which approaches that degree of unfairness....

■ JUSTICE DOUGLAS, dissenting.

... Distribution of the assets of the estate could not be made without determining the validity of the power of appointment. The power of appointment, being integrated with the will, was as much subject to construction and interpretation by the Florida court as the will itself. Of course one not a party or privy to the Florida proceedings is not bound by it and can separately litigate the right to assets in other States.... But we have no such situation here. The trustee of the trust was in privity with the deceased. She was the settlor; and under the trust, the trustee was to do her bidding.... So far as the present controversy is concerned the trustee was purely and simply a stakeholder or an agent holding assets of the settlor to dispose of as she designated. It had a community of interest with the deceased. I see no reason therefore why Florida could not say that the deceased and her executrix may stand in judgment for the trustee so far as the disposition of the property under the power of appointment and the will is concerned. The question in cases of this kind is whether the procedure is fair and just, considering the interests of the parties.... We must remember this is not a suit to impose liability on the Delaware trustee or on any other absent person. It is merely a suit to determine interests in those intangibles. Cf. Mullane v. Central Hanover Trust Co., supra, 339 U.S. at page 313. Under closely analogous facts the California Supreme Court held in Atkinson v. Superior Court, 49 Cal.2d 338, 316 P.2d 960, that California had jurisdiction over an absent trustee. I would hold the same here.

NOTES

1. In Kulko v. Superior Court of California, 436 U.S. 84 (1978), a child custody and support action, the Supreme Court reversed a state's assertion of judicial jurisdiction over the nonresident father on the ground that he had not purposefully availed himself of the benefits and protections of the forum state's law. In *Kulko*, the former spouses had resided in New York with their minor children. Upon their separation, the mother moved to California. A subsequent Haitian divorce obtained by her incorporated the New York separation agreement. It provided that the children were to live with the father during the school year and with the mother during vacations. The father made support payments while the children were in the mother's care. When the daughter requested permission to live with the mother, the father acquiesced and bought her a one-way ticket to California. She was subsequently joined by her younger brother. The mother then started an action in California against the father, seeking full custody, increased support payments and other relief. The California courts upheld personal jurisdiction. Held: reversed. "A father who agrees, in the interests of family harmony and his children's preferences, to allow them to spend more time in California than was required under a separation agreement can hardly be said to have 'purposefully availed himself' of the 'benefits and protections of California' laws...." The fact that the father now had fewer expenses than before, the Court noted, was the result of the absence of the children from New York and not of their presence in California.

See also Anderson v. Sonat Exploration Co., 523 So.2d 1024 (Miss.1988), noted 58 Miss.L.J. 177 (1988): by having an instrument notarized in Mississippi, the Louisiana defendant had purposefully availed herself of the benefits and protection of Mississippi law. The Mississippi court had personal jurisdiction in an action by the Mississippi plaintiff to have the instrument set aside or, in the alternative, to have it reformed.

2. Modern jurisdictional theory has moved beyond the "purposeful availment" and "benefits" test of Hanson v. Denckla. Instead, the modern focus is on the circumstances that affiliate the defendant with the forum state, together with the foreseeability of litigation there. Stewart, A New Litany of Personal Jurisdiction, 60 U.Colo.L.Rev. 5 (1989); Weber, Purposeful Availment, 39 S.C.L.Rev. 815 (1988); Symposium, Fifty Years of *International Shoe:* The Past and Future of Personal Jurisdiction, 28 U.C.Davis L.Rev. 513 (1995); Conference on Jurisdiction, Justice, and Choice of Law for the Twenty–First Century: Case Three—Personal Jurisdiction, 29 New England L.Rev. 627 (1995). For a more far-reaching proposal, premised on the proposition that the issue is really one of interstate venue and advocating "fairness without contacts" as the focus for the jurisdictional inquiry,

see Weintraub, A Map out of the Personal Jurisdiction Labyrinth, 28 U.C.Davis L.Rev. 531 (1995). This theme is also considered following the *Asahi* decision, infra p. 78.

Consider in this connection, and as an initial question, whether it would have been unfair to subject the father in *Kulko,* supra Note (1), to jurisdiction in California for the claim for support modification. In the European Union, there is judicial jurisdiction in the courts of the place where the person entitled to support is domiciled or habitually resident. Brussels Convention, supra p. 37, Art. 5 No. 2. Note that whether someone is entitled to support is in itself a conflicts question (i.e., a choice-of-law determination answers the jurisdictional question) and that "support" is not limited to child support. Jurisdiction at the residence of the claimant also is the rule in England, Sweden, Switzerland, and under the proposed Inter–American Convention on Support Obligations. See Martiny, Maintenance Obligations in the Conflict of Laws, Hague Academy, 247 Collected Courses 131, 251–54 (1994–III). In the United States, the new Uniform Interstate Family Support Act, infra at p. 913, provides for the *continuing* jurisdiction of the original court under certain circumstances, and federal law, supra p. 913, provides for interstate recognition of child support orders. *Kulko,* however, still determines when a court other than the original court has jurisdiction over an absent defendant to establish or to modify a support obligation.

3. In Hanson v. Denckla, Chief Justice Warren observed that, although the facts may have warranted Florida's applying its law to the transaction, the nonresident trustee's contact was too insubstantial to warrant exercising personal jurisdiction over it. Order 11, rule 1(1)(d)(iii) of the Rules of the Supreme Court of Judicature of England, as amended, provides for the jurisdiction over a nonresident for breach of a contract which is to be "governed by English law." Dicey & Morris, Conflict of Laws 331 (12th ed. by Collins 1993). The Brussels Convention on Jurisdiction and the Recognition of Judgments, in force in the European Communities, as well as the new Lugano Convention, provide for general jurisdiction at the defendant's domicile or, if an enterprise, at its principal place of business, and for specific jurisdiction in a number of enumerated cases as well as on the basis of a written stipulation by the parties (forum selection clause). They do not confer jurisdiction by inference from the applicability of the forum's substantive law. With respect to its European partner states, this is now also the law in England. Dicey & Morris, supra, 43. In the United States, the applicability of a particular state's law, even if as a result of a choice-of-law clause, does not ordinarily, without more, confer jurisdiction. Scoles and Hay, Conflict of Laws § 18.1 n. 6 (2d ed. 1992). However, a choice-of-law clause in a contract may be a *"contact"* and may also represent a party expectation which, together with other contacts, may serve to satisfy the *International Shoe* test: Burger King Corp. v. Rudzewicz, 471 U.S. 462 (1985), pp. 100–101, infra. Should a choice-of-law clause be deemed an *ipso facto* basis of jurisdiction? Conversely, should a forum-selection clause imply that the chosen forum's substantive law is to apply?

NOTE ON STATUTORY DEVELOPMENTS

The International Shoe decision made it clear that state court jurisdiction was considerably greater than hitherto supposed. It remained for each state to determine the extent to which it would authorize its courts to "reach out", consistent with due process. Illinois showed the way in 1955, and its type of "long-arm statute" was soon widely followed by other states, of course with individual differences. This type of statute provided detailed and specific guidance as to the defendant's activities or contacts that would permit the exercise of jurisdiction. Examples were: the "transaction of any business within this State; ... the commission of a tortious act ...;" contracts of insurance on local risks. Sec. 2–209 Illinois Code of Civil Procedure.

Detailed long-arm statutes can give rise to questions of interpretation. (1) May the nonresident defendant defeat jurisdiction by denying the commission of the alleged act? Early Illinois decisions answered this question in the negative. Nelson v. Miller, 11 Ill.2d 378, 143 N.E.2d 673 (1957); Gray v. American Radiator & Standard Sanitary Corp., 22 Ill.2d 432, 176 N.E.2d 761 (1961). (2) The same two decisions had to define what constitutes the commission of a tort, in particular whether action by the defendant outside Illinois (e.g., the manufacture of a defective product) that results in injury in Illinois permits the exercise of long-arm jurisdiction. The answer was in the affirmative, as it was elsewhere as well. A similar problem arose in the European Union where Art. 5 No. 3 of the Brussels Convention provides for specific jurisdiction at the place where the "damaging event occurred." Stretching the treaty language, the European Court held, consistent with the practice of prior national law, that jurisdiction exists at the place of acting and at the place of injury, at plaintiff's option. Case 21/76, Bier B.V. v. Mines de Potasse d'Alsace, [1976] ECR 1735. In the case of the publication of a libellous newspaper, it held that there was jurisdiction in the state of the publisher's principal place of business and in every other state in which the publication was distributed and there injured the plaintiff's reputation, as alleged by her. Case C–68/93, Shevill v. Presse Alliance SA, [1995] 2 W.L.R. 499, [1995] EWS 165, [1995] ECR ___.

New York's long-arm statute has given rise to interpretative difficulties with respect to what constitutes "transacting any business" in the state and whether committing a tortious act "causing injury" includes non-physical injuries. N.Y.Civil Practice Law and Rules § 302(a)(1) and (3), respectively. "Transacting business" has been extended to non-commercial transactions, (e.g., Elman v. Belson, 32 A.D.2d 422, 302 N.Y.S.2d 961 (2d Dep't 1969)) (retainer of N.Y. attorney) and § 302(a)(1) was amended in 1979 to remove mere shipment of goods from outside New York on the basis of an out-of-state contract from its purview.

Differences in coverage or interpretation of the various state long-arm statutes have become progressively less important. A number of states adopted omnibus long-arm statutes from the beginning, asserting jurisdiction "to the limits of due process." See, e.g., Cal.Civ.Proc.Code § 410.10 (West 1973). In other states, a detailed statute was subsequently replaced by such a general one. This was the case in Illinois. Ill.Ann.Stat. ch. 735 Art. 5 § 2–209 (Smith–Hurd Supp.1989). In still a third group, the detailed statute has been judicially interpreted to provide for the exercise of judicial jurisdiction to the limit of due process. See, e.g., Guardian Royal Exchange Assoc. Ltd. v. English China Clays, 815 S.W.2d 223 (Tex.1991); Northern Aircraft, Inc. v. Reed, 154 Vt. 36, 572 A.2d 1382 (1990). As a result, there are now relatively few states, probably fewer than ten, in which the long-arm statute, as interpreted and applied, will permit less jurisdiction to be asserted than due process would permit. See, e.g., Abbott v. Owens–Corning Fiberglass, 191 W.Va. 198, 444 S.E.2d 285 (1994). Moreover, in a number of these there is no recent case law addressing the issue. See e.g., Banco Ambrosiano, S.p.A. v. Artoc Bank & Trust Limited, 62 N.Y.2d 65, 476 N.Y.S.2d 64, 464 N.E.2d 432 (1984) (New York long-arm provision does not go to due process limits).

Both approaches have advantages and drawbacks. The detailed statute provides some specificity and foreseeability, subject to judicial construction, that general invocation of uncertain and changing standards of due process might not. The detailed statute keeps the issue one of (state) statutory construction; the general statute converts it even initially into one of constitutional law. At the same time, the detailed statute is more limiting and may lose sight of the principle underlying issue of fairness (see above p. 65). The European Union has chosen the style of a detailed statute and, may for that reason, draw jurisdictional competence too narrowly. See Lowenfeld, International Litigation and Reasonableness, Hague Academy of International Law, 245 Collected Courses 9, 121–22 (1994–I). American law may strike Europeans as too expansive and may make work on a common convention difficult. See Juenger, supra p. 631. See also Weintraub, Commentary on the Conflict of Laws 165–69 (3d ed. 1986); Scoles & Hay, Conflict of Laws § 8.33 (2d ed. 1992).

It will be observed that long-arm statutes do not in terms distinguish between natural persons and corporations in delineating the bases of personal jurisdiction. The courts adopt a similar approach. All bases for exercise of judicial jurisdiction over an individual, with the exception of presence, domicile and nationality or citizenship, will give a state judicial jurisdiction over a foreign corporation. Restatement, Second, Conflict of Laws §§ 42–52. In a diversity action, a federal court has been held bound, within constitutional limits, to follow state standards, in determining the amenability of a defendant to in personam jurisdiction. Arrowsmith v. United Press International, 320 F.2d 219 (2d Cir.1963), which overruled Jaftex Corporation v. Randolph Mills, Inc., 282 F.2d 508 (2d Cir.1960), noted, 77 Harv.L.Rev. 559 (1964). For claims arising under federal law, the 1993 amendment to the Federal Rules now gives federal courts nationwide jurisdiction within the limits of the Due Process Clause of the Fifth Amendment when the defendant is not subject to the jurisdiction of the courts of general jurisdiction of any state. FRCivProc. 4(k)(2).

See also Hazard, A General Theory of State–Court Jurisdiction, 1965 Supreme Court Review 241 (Kurland ed.); von Mehren and Trautman, Jurisdiction to Adjudicate: A Suggested Analysis, 79 Harv.L.Rev. 1121 (1966).

World–Wide Volkswagen Corp. v. Woodson, District Judge of Creek County, Oklahoma

Supreme Court of the United States, 1980.
444 U.S. 286, 100 S.Ct. 559, 62 L.Ed.2d 490.

■ JUSTICE WHITE delivered the opinion of the Court.

The issue before us is whether, consistently with the Due Process Clause of the Fourteenth Amendment, an Oklahoma court may exercise *in personam* jurisdiction over a nonresident automobile retailer and its wholesale distributor in a products liability action, when the defendants' only connection with Oklahoma is the fact that an automobile sold in New York to New York residents became involved in an accident in Oklahoma.

I

Respondents Harry and Kay Robinson purchased a new Audi automobile from petitioner Seaway Volkswagen, Inc. (Seaway) in Massena, N.Y., in 1976. The following year the Robinson family, who resided in New York, left that State for a new home in Arizona. As they passed through the State of Oklahoma, another car struck their Audi in the rear, causing a fire which severely burned Kay Robinson and her two children.[1]

The Robinsons subsequently brought a products liability action in the District Court for Creek County, Okla., claiming that their injuries resulted from defective design and placement of the Audi's gas tank and fuel system. They joined as defendants the automobile's manufacturer, Audi NSU Auto Union Aktiengesellschaft (Audi); its importer, Volkswagen of America, Inc. (Volkswagen); its regional distributor, petitioner World–Wide Volkswagen Corporation (World–Wide); and its retail dealer, petitioner Seaway. Seaway and World–Wide entered special appearances,[3] claiming that Oklahoma's exercise of jurisdiction over them would offend the limitations on the State's jurisdiction imposed by the Due Process Clause of the Fourteenth Amendment.

The facts presented to the District Court showed that World–Wide is incorporated and has its business office in New York. It distributes vehicles, parts and accessories, under contract with Volkswagen, to retail dealers in New York, New Jersey, and Connecticut. Seaway, one of these retail dealers, is incorporated and has its place of business in New York. Insofar as the record reveals, Seaway and World–Wide are fully independent corporations whose relations with each other and with Volkswagen and Audi are contractual only. Respondents adduced no evidence that either World–Wide or Seaway does any business in Oklahoma, ships or sells any products to or in that State, has an agent to receive process there, or purchases advertisements in any media calculated to reach Oklahoma. In fact, as respondents' counsel conceded at oral argument, ... there was no showing that any automobile sold by World–Wide or Seaway has ever entered Oklahoma with the single exception of the vehicle involved in the present case.

Despite the apparent paucity of contacts between petitioners and Oklahoma, the District Court rejected their constitutional claim and reaf-

---

1. The driver of the other automobile does not figure in the present litigation.

3. Volkswagen also entered a special appearance in the District Court, but unlike World–Wide and Seaway did not seek review in the Supreme Court of Oklahoma and is not a petitioner here. Both Volkswagen and Audi remain as defendants in the litigation pending before the District Court in Oklahoma.

firmed that ruling in denying petitioners' motion for reconsideration. Petitioners then sought a writ of prohibition in the Supreme Court of Oklahoma to restrain the District Judge, respondent Charles S. Woodson, from exercising *in personam* jurisdiction over them. They renewed their contention that because they had no "minimal contacts" ... with the State of Oklahoma, the actions of the District Judge were in violation of their rights under the Due Process Clause.

The Supreme Court of Oklahoma denied the writ, 585 P.2d 351 (1978), holding that personal jurisdiction over petitioners was authorized by Oklahoma's "Long–Arm" Statute, Okla.Stat., Tit. 12, § 1701.3(a)(4) (1961).[7] Although the Court noted that the proper approach was to test jurisdiction against both statutory and constitutional standards, its analysis did not distinguish these questions, probably because § 1701.03(a)(4) has been interpreted as conferring jurisdiction to the limits permitted by the United States Constitution. The Court's rationale was contained in the following paragraph, 585 P.2d, at 354:

> "In the case before us, the product being sold and distributed by the petitioners is by its very design and purpose so mobile that petitioners can foresee its possible use in Oklahoma. This is especially true of the distributor, who has the exclusive right to distribute such automobile [*sic*] in New York, New Jersey and Connecticut. The evidence presented below demonstrated that goods sold and distributed by the petitioners were used in the State of Oklahoma, and under the facts we believe it reasonable to infer, given the retail value of the automobile, that the petitioners derive substantial income from automobiles which, from time to time are used in the State of Oklahoma. This being the case, we hold that under the facts presented, the trial court was justified in concluding that the petitioners derive substantial revenue from goods used or consumed in this State."

. . .

II

. . .

As has long been settled, and as we reaffirm today, a state court may exercise personal jurisdiction over a nonresident defendant only so long as there exist "minimum contacts" between the defendant and the forum State. International Shoe Co. v. Washington [p. 47, supra]. The concept of minimum contacts, in turn, can be seen to perform two related, but distinguishable, functions. It protects the defendant against the burdens

---

7. This subsection provides: "A court may exercise personal jurisdiction over a person, who acts directly or by an agent, as to a cause of action or claim for relief arising from the person's ... causing tortious injury in this state by an act or omission outside this state if he regularly does or solicits business or engages in any other persistent course of conduct, or derived substantial revenue from goods used or consumed or services rendered, in this state...." The State Supreme Court rejected jurisdiction based on § 1701.03(a)(3), which authorizes jurisdiction over any person "causing tortious injury in this state by an act or omission in this state." Something in addition to the infliction of tortious injury was required.

of litigating in a distant or inconvenient forum. And it acts to ensure that the States, through their courts, do not reach out beyond the limits imposed on them by their status as coequal sovereigns in a federal system.

The protection against inconvenient litigation is typically described in terms of "reasonableness" or "fairness." ... Implicit in this emphasis on reasonableness is the understanding that the burden on the defendant, while always a primary concern, will in an appropriate case be considered in light of other relevant factors, including the forum State's interest in adjudicating the dispute, see McGee v. International Life Ins. Co. [p. 53, supra]; the plaintiff's interest in obtaining convenient and effective relief, see Kulko v. Superior Court [p. 63, supra] at least when that interest is not adequately protected by the plaintiff's power to choose the forum, cf. Shaffer v. Heitner [p. 136, infra]; the interstate judicial system's interest in obtaining the most efficient resolution of controversies; and the shared interest of the several States in furthering fundamental substantive social policies, see Kulko v. Superior Court, supra....

The limits imposed on state jurisdiction by the Due Process Clause, in its role as a guarantor against inconvenient litigation, have been substantially relaxed over the years....

Nevertheless, we have never accepted the proposition that state lines are irrelevant for jurisdictional purposes, nor could we and remain faithful to the principles of interstate federalism embodied in the Constitution. The economic interdependence of the States was foreseen and desired by the Framers. In the Commerce Clause, they provided that the Nation was to be a common market, a "free trade unit" in which the States are debarred from acting as separable economic entities. H.P. Hood & Sons, Inc. v. Du Mond, 336 U.S. 525, 538 (1949). But the Framers also intended that the States retain many essential attributes of sovereignty, including, in particular, the sovereign power to try causes in their courts. The sovereignty of each State, in turn, implied a limitation on the sovereignty of all of its sister States—a limitation express or implicit in both the original scheme of the Constitution and the Fourteenth Amendment.

Hence, even while abandoning the shibboleth that "[t]he authority of every tribunal is necessarily restricted by the territorial limits of the State in which it is established," Pennoyer v. Neff [p. 45, supra], we emphasized that the reasonableness of asserting jurisdiction over the defendant must be assessed "in the context of our federal system of government," International Shoe Co. v. Washington, supra, and stressed that the Due Process Clause ensures, not only fairness, but also the "orderly administration of the laws,"....

Even if the defendant would suffer minimal or no inconvenience from being forced to litigate before the tribunals of another State; even if the forum State has a strong interest in applying its law to the controversy; even if the forum State is the most convenient location for litigation, the Due Process Clause, acting as an instrument of interstate federalism, may sometimes act to divest the State of its power to render a valid judgment. Hanson v. Denckla [p. 56, supra].

III

Applying these principles to the case at hand, we find in the record before us a total absence of those affiliating circumstances that are a necessary predicate to any exercise of state-court jurisdiction. Petitioners carry on no activity whatsoever in Oklahoma. They close no sales and perform no services there. They avail themselves of none of the privileges and benefits of Oklahoma law. They solicit no business there either through salespersons or through advertising reasonably calculated to reach the State. Nor does the record show that they regularly sell cars at wholesale or retail to Oklahoma customers or residents or that they indirectly, through others, serve or seek to serve the Oklahoma market. In short, respondents seek to base jurisdiction on one, isolated occurrence and whatever inferences can be drawn therefrom: the fortuitous circumstances that a single Audi automobile, sold in New York to New York residents, happened to suffer an accident while passing through Oklahoma.

It is argued, however, that because an automobile is mobile by its very design and purpose it was "foreseeable" that the Robinsons' Audi would cause injury in Oklahoma. Yet "foreseeability" alone has never been a sufficient benchmark for personal jurisdiction under the Due Process Clause. In Hanson v. Denckla, supra, it was no doubt foreseeable that the settlor of a Delaware trust would subsequently move to Florida and seek to exercise a power of appointment there; yet we held that Florida courts could not constitutionally exercise jurisdiction over a Delaware trustee that had no other contacts with the forum State. In Kulko v. Superior Court, supra, it was surely "foreseeable" that a divorced wife would move to California from New York, the domicile of the marriage, and that a minor daughter would live with the mother. Yet we held that California could not exercise jurisdiction in a child-support action over the former husband who had remained in New York.

If foreseeability were the criterion, a local California tire retailer could be forced to defend in Pennsylvania when a blowout occurs there, see Erlanger Mills, Inc. v. Cohoes Fibre Mills, Inc., 239 F.2d 502, 507 (C.A.4 1956); a Wisconsin seller of a defective automobile jack could be haled before a distant court for damage caused in New Jersey, Reilly v. Phil Tolkan Pontiac, Inc., 372 F.Supp. 1205 (N.J.1974); or a Florida soft drink concessionaire could be summoned to Alaska to account for injuries happening there, see Upgren v. Executive Aviation Services, Inc., 304 F.Supp. 165, 170–171 (Minn.1969). Every seller of chattels would in effect appoint the chattel his agent for services of process. His amenability to suit would travel with the chattel. We recently abandoned the outworn rule of Harris v. Balk [p. 131, infra], that the interest of a creditor in a debt could be extinguished or otherwise affected by any State having transitory jurisdiction over the debtor. Shaffer v. Heitner [p. 136, infra]. Having interred the mechanical rule that a creditor's amenability to a *quasi in rem* action travels with his debtor, we are unwilling to endorse an analogous principle in the present case.[11]

This is not to say, of course, that foreseeability is wholly irrelevant. But the foreseeability that is critical to due process analysis is not the mere likelihood that a product will find its way into the forum State. Rather, it is that the defendant's conduct and connection with the forum State are such that he should reasonably anticipate being haled into court there. . . . The Due Process Clause, by ensuring the "orderly administration of the laws," International Shoe Co. v. Washington, supra, gives a degree of predictability to the legal system that allows potential defendants to structure their primary conduct with some minimum assurance as to where that conduct will and will not render them liable to suit.

When a corporation "purposefully avails itself of the privilege of conducting activities within the forum State," Hanson v. Denckla, supra, it has clear notice that it is subject to suit there, and can act to alleviate the risk of burdensome litigation by procuring insurance, passing the expected costs on to customers, or, if the risks are too great, severing its connection with the State. Hence if the sale of a product of a manufacturer or distributor such as Audi or Volkswagen is not simply an isolated occurrence, but arises from the efforts of the manufacturer or distributor to serve, directly or indirectly, the market for its product in other States, it is not unreasonable to subject it to suit in one of those States if its allegedly defective merchandise has there been the source of injury to its owner or to others. The forum State does not exceed its powers under the Due Process Clause if it asserts personal jurisdiction over a corporation that delivers its products into the stream of commerce with the expectation that they will be purchased by consumers in the forum State. Compare Gray v. American Radiator & Standard Sanitary Corp. [p. 65, supra].

But there is no such or similar basis for Oklahoma jurisdiction over World–Wide or Seaway in this case. Seaway's sales are made in Massena, N.Y. World–Wide's market, although substantially larger, is limited to dealers in New York, New Jersey, and Connecticut. There is no evidence of record that any automobiles distributed by World–Wide are sold to retail customers outside this tri-State area. It is foreseeable that the purchasers of automobiles sold by World–Wide and Seaway may take them to Oklahoma. But the mere "unilateral activity of those who claim some relation-

---

11. Respondents' counsel, at oral argument, see Tr. of Oral Arg. 19–22, 29, sought to limit the reach of the foreseeability standard by suggesting that there is something unique about automobiles. It is true that automobiles are uniquely mobile, see Tyson v. Whitaker & Son, Inc., 407 A.2d 1, 6, and n. 11 (Me.1979) (McKusick, C.J.), that they did play a crucial role in the expansion of personal jurisdiction through the fiction of implied consent, e.g., Hess v. Pawloski, 274 U.S. 352 (1927), and that some of the cases have treated the automobile as a "dangerous instrumentality." But today, under the regime of *International Shoe,* we see no difference for jurisdictional purposes between an automobile and any other chattel. The "dangerous instrumentality" concept apparently was never used to support personal jurisdiction; and to the extent it has relevance today it bears not on jurisdiction but on the possible desirability of imposing substantive principles of tort law such as strict liability.

ship with a nonresident defendant cannot satisfy the requirement of contact with the forum State." Hanson v. Denckla, supra.

In a variant on the previous argument, it is contended that jurisdiction can be supported by the fact that petitioners earn substantial revenue from goods used in Oklahoma. The Oklahoma Supreme Court so found, 585 P.2d, at 354–355, drawing the inference that because one automobile sold by petitioners had been used in Oklahoma, others might have been used there also. While this inference seems less than compelling on the facts of the instant case, we need not question the Court's factual findings in order to reject its reasoning.

This argument seems to make the point that the purchase of automobiles in New York, from which the petitioners earn substantial revenue, would not occur *but for* the fact that the automobiles are capable of use in distant States like Oklahoma. Respondents observe that the very purpose of an automobile is to travel, and that travel of automobiles sold by petitioners is facilitated by an extensive chain of Volkswagen service centers throughout the Country, including some in Oklahoma.[12] However, financial benefits accruing to the defendant from a collateral relation to the forum State will not support jurisdiction if they do not stem from a constitutionally cognizable contact with that State.... In our view, whatever marginal revenues petitioners may receive by virtue of the fact that their products are capable of use in Oklahoma is far too attenuated a contact to justify that State's exercise of *in personam* jurisdiction over them.

. . .

Reversed.

■ JUSTICE BRENNAN, dissenting.*

. . .

[T]he interest of [Oklahoma] and its connection to the litigation is strong. The automobile accident underlying the litigation occurred in Oklahoma. The plaintiffs were hospitalized in Oklahoma when they brought suit. Essential witnesses and evidence were in Oklahoma.... The State has a legitimate interest in enforcing its laws designed to keep its highway system safe, and the trial can proceed at least as efficiently in Oklahoma as anywhere else.

The petitioners are not unconnected with the forum. Although both sell automobiles within limited sales territories, each sold the automobile which in fact was driven to Oklahoma where it was involved in an

---

12. As we have noted, petitioners earn no direct revenues from these service centers....

* Justice Brennan combined his dissents in World–Wide Volkswagen and Rush v. Savchuk (p. 153, infra) into a single opinion. That part of his dissent dealing with the

accident.[8] It may be true, as the Court suggests, that each sincerely intended to limit its commercial impact to the limited territory, and that each intended to accept the benefits and protection of the laws only of those States within the territory. But obviously these were unrealistic hopes that cannot be treated as an automatic constitutional shield.[9]

An automobile simply is not a stationary item or one designed to be used in one place. An automobile is *intended* to be moved around. Someone in the business of selling large numbers of automobiles can hardly plead ignorance of their mobility or pretend that the automobiles stay put after they are sold. It is not merely that a dealer in automobiles foresees that they will move.... The dealer actually intends that the purchasers will use the automobiles to travel to distant States where the dealer does not directly "do business." The sale of an automobile does *purposefully* inject the vehicle into the stream of interstate commerce so that it can travel to distant States....

The Court accepts that a State may exercise jurisdiction over a distributor which "serves" that State "indirectly" by "deliver[ing] its products into the stream of commerce with the expectation that they will [be] purchased by consumers in other States." ... It is difficult to see why the Constitution should distinguish between a case involving goods which reach a distant State through a chain of distribution and a case involving goods which reach the same State because a consumer, using them as the dealer knew the customer would, took them there. In each case the seller purposefully injects the goods into the stream of commerce and those goods predictably are used in the forum State.

Furthermore, an automobile seller derives substantial benefits from States other than its own. A large part of the value of automobiles is the extensive, nationwide network of highways. Significant portions of that network have been constructed by and are maintained by the individual States, including Oklahoma. The States, through their highway programs, contribute in a very direct and important way to the value of petitioners' businesses. Additionally, a network of other related dealerships with their service departments operate throughout the country under the protection of the laws of the various States, including Oklahoma, and enhance the value of petitioners' businesses by facilitating their customers' traveling....

former case is set forth here. [Footnote by the Editors.]

8. On the basis of this fact the state court inferred that the petitioners derived substantial revenue from goods used in Oklahoma. The inference is not without support. Certainly, were use of goods accepted as a relevant contact, a plaintiff would not need to have an exact count of the number of petitioners' cars that are used in Oklahoma.

9. Moreover, imposing liability in this case would not so undermine certainty as to destroy an automobile dealer's ability to do business. According jurisdiction does not expand liability except in the marginal case where a plaintiff cannot afford to bring an action except in the plaintiff's own State. In addition, these petitioners are represented by insurance companies. They not only could, but did, purchase insurance to protect them should they stand trial and lose the case. The costs of the insurance no doubt are passed onto customers.

It may be that affirmance of the judgments in these cases would approach the outer limits of *International Shoe*'s jurisdictional principle. But that principle, with its almost exclusive focus on the rights of defendants, may be outdated....

In answering the question whether or not it is fair and reasonable to allow a particular forum to hold a trial binding on a particular defendant, the interests of the forum State and other parties loom large in today's world and surely are entitled to as much weight as are the interests of the defendant.... Certainly, I cannot see how a defendant's right to due process is violated if the defendant suffers no inconvenience.

... Assuming that a State gives a nonresident defendant adequate notice and opportunity to defend, I do not think the Due Process Clause is offended merely because the defendant has to board a plane to get to the site of the trial....

■ JUSTICE MARSHALL, with whom JUSTICE BLACKMUN joins, dissenting....

. . .

The majority apparently acknowledges that if a product is purchased in the forum State by a consumer, that State may assert jurisdiction over everyone in the chain of distribution.... With this I agree. But I cannot agree that jurisdiction is necessarily lacking if the product enters the State not through the channels of distribution but in the course of its intended use by the consumer. We have recognized the role played by the automobile in the expansion of our notions of personal jurisdiction.... Unlike most other chattels, which may find their way into States far from where they were purchased because their owner takes them there, the intended use of the automobile is precisely as a means of traveling from one place to another. In such a case, it is highly artificial to restrict the concept of the "stream of commerce" to the chain of distribution from the manufacturer to the ultimate consumer....

[T]he "quality and nature" of commercial activity is different, for purposes of the *International Shoe* test, from actions from which a defendant obtains no economic advantage. Commercial activity is more likely to cause effects in a larger sphere, and the actor derives an economic benefit from the activity that makes it fair to require him to answer for his conduct where its effects are felt....

■ JUSTICE BLACKMUN, dissenting.

I confess that I am somewhat puzzled why the plaintiffs ... are so insistent that the regional distributor and the retail dealer ... be named defendants. It would appear that the manufacturer, whose subjectability to Oklahoma's jurisdiction is not challenged ... ought not to be judgment-proof.*

* "The answer to Justice Blackmun's question is a simple tactical move familiar to any litigator. 'Creek County, Oklahoma ... is one of the best jurisdictions in the United States in which to try a plaintiff's lawsuit. It ranks on a par with Dade County, Florida,

[He emphasized that here the instrumentality of injury was an automobile, an intentionally far-ranging product. He saw nothing unfair to hold the dealer and distributors subject to Oklahoma's jurisdiction. He saw no material distinction between foreseeable use of a product in another state and foreseeable sale of it there].

. . .

World–Wide Volkswagen was followed in short order by three other decisions involving the question whether the defendant's forum contacts were sufficient in kind and quality to permit the exercise of personal jurisdiction. In Keeton v. Hustler Magazine, Inc., 465 U.S. 770 (1984), the issue of the magazine containing the allegedly libelous material had been distributed nationwide, including in the New Hampshire forum, the only state in which the statute of limitations had not yet run. In sustaining New Hampshire's jurisdiction, the Court acknowledged that "it is undoubtedly true that the bulk of the harm done to petitioner occurred outside New Hampshire. But that will be true in almost every libel action brought somewhere other than the plaintiff's domicile. There is no justification for restricting libel actions to the plaintiff's home forum. The victim of a libel, like the victim of any other tort, may choose to bring suit in any forum with which the defendant has 'certain minimum contacts. . . .' International Shoe. . . . Where, as in this case, respondent Hustler Magazine, Inc., has continuously and deliberately exploited the New Hampshire market, it must reasonably anticipate being haled into court there in a libel action based on the contents of its magazine." In addition to the fact that publication of the libel in New Hampshire resulted in the commission of a tort in New Hampshire (as well as elsewhere) and thus supported jurisdiction over the defendant, the majority also noted that New Hampshire had "a significant interest in redressing injuries that . . . occur within the State." Whether New Hampshire could apply its six-year statute of limitations and whether the plaintiff was allowed to recover damages for injury to her reputation throughout the country are questions that depend on material examined in chapters 7, 8 and 9, infra. Recall that the European Court also concluded that jurisdiction could be asserted in a number of different fora. Shevill v. Presse Alliance S.A., supra p. 65. However, it distinguished among these possible fora with respect to the scope of their jurisdiction: states in which jurisdiction was asserted because of injury to plaintiff's reputation may only entertain a claim for compensa-

and Cook County, Illinois . . .' Counsel for the Robinsons did not want the defendants to be able to remove the case from this plaintiffs' paradise to the Federal District Court in Tulsa. . . . [A]t the time suit was brought, the Robinsons were still domiciled in New York, because they had not yet arrived in Arizona. . . . By joining the dealer and regional distributor, both New York corporations, [counsel] could prevent complete diversity of citizenship . . . necessary for removal." Weintraub, Commentary on the Conflict of Laws 125 (3d ed. 1986), quoting letter to him from Jefferson G. Greer, Esq., counsel for plaintiffs. [Footnote by Eds.]

tion for the local harm. In contrast, the courts at the defendant's principal place of business may entertain a claim for the redress of all harm caused.

In Calder v. Jones, 465 U.S. 783 (1984), decided with *Keeton,* the Supreme Court held that nonresident employees acting on behalf of their employer-defendant in distributing allegedly defamatory material are not insulated from personal jurisdiction.

In Burger King Corp. v. Rudzewicz, 471 U.S. 462 (1985), the Supreme Court upheld the assertion of jurisdiction by Florida over a Michigan franchisee even though the latter had dealt mainly with the franchisor's Michigan district office. Florida-related contacts were: negotiation of some contract terms with the franchisor's Florida headquarters, the contractual obligation to make payments in Florida, the purchase of equipment for the franchise from Florida, the contractual obligation to accept supervision and direction from the franchisor's Florida headquarters, and the stipulation of Florida law (choice-of-law clause). The single contract was a sufficient contact for jurisdiction for claims arising from it, although the Court noted that the contract was to extend over twenty years, i.e. that the parties had contemplated a long term relationship. Relying on Hanson v. Denckla, supra, the Court of Appeals ruled that the choice-of-law provision in the contract was irrelevant to the question of whether Florida had personal jurisdiction. The Supreme Court disagreed: "Nothing in our cases, however, suggests that a choice-of-law *provision* should be ignored in considering whether a defendant has 'purposefully invoked the benefits and protections of a State's laws' for jurisdictional purposes. Although such a provision standing alone would be insufficient to confer jurisdiction, we believe that, when combined with the 20-year interdependent relationship Rudzewicz established with Burger King's Miami headquarters, it reinforced his deliberate affiliation with the forum State and the reasonable foreseeability of possible litigation there...." (original emphasis.)

In the European Union, there is specific jurisdiction at the place where the contractual obligation was or is to be performed. Brussels Convention Art. 5 No. 1. Quite clearly, a single contract will support jurisdiction. Moreover, the European Court has held that it is the contractual obligation *in issue* in the litigation that is relevant for the jurisdictional determination. Thus, depending on who sues whom on what aspect of a contract, different courts may have specific jurisdiction (in addition to the court with general jurisdiction at the defendant's domicile). The matter is made more difficult still because the legal systems of the member states may differ as to where a particular contract obligation is to be performed (and it is the place of performance that has jurisdiction). Thus, the questions a court must ask are: what is the obligation in issue; where—as determined by my (the forum's) conflicts law—is the place of performance of such an obligation; if that should turn out to be another state, would it determine the "place-of-performance" issue the same way or, under its law, have looked to yet another state or referred back to me (for "renvoi", see infra p. 500? Only after all these questions have been answered, will the court know whether it or another court has specific jurisdiction to proceed to the merits. Is this system a useful way to give jurisdiction to the state with the closest connection to the issue or is it too complicated to make sense? For comment and further references, see Hill, Jurisdiction in Matters Relating to a Contract under the Brussels Convention, 44 Int'l & Comp. L.Q. 591 (1995).

NOTE: DUE PROCESS AND FEDERALISM CONCERNS

Recall Justice Field's discussion of the sovereignty of the several states in Pennoyer v. Neff, supra p. 45. In Hanson v. Denckla, supra p. 56, Chief Justice Warren said that the restrictions on a state's asserting personal jurisdiction "are more than a guarantee of immunity from inconvenient or distant litigation." ... They are a consequence of territorial limitations on the power of the respective states. In World–Wide Volkswagen, supra p. 66, Justice White emphasized the "limits imposed on [the states] by their status as coequal sovereigns in the federal system." Thereafter, the Court's pronouncements are less clear.

INSURANCE CORP. v. COMPAGNIE DES BAUXITES DE GUINEE, 456 U.S. 694 (1982). In a diversity action against a group of foreign insurance companies for indemnity to cover losses resulting from interruptions of plaintiff's business, defendants raised various defenses including lack of personal jurisdiction. Plaintiff initiated discovery to establish minimum contacts. Defendants failed to comply with a series of court orders for production of requested information. After due warning, the district court invoked Rule 37(b)(2) as a basis for deeming the jurisdictional facts established by reason of petitioners' failure to make the required disclosures.

The Supreme Court upheld the district court's sanction—namely, presuming that a jurisdictional basis was present on account of defendant's failure to comply with the discovery orders. Justice White for the Court reasoned that since personal jurisdiction is a waivable defense, it can be established by regarding the defendants' failure to obey procedural requirements as tantamount to waiver. However, he was troubled by the fact that the waiver theory suggests that a defendant may confer personal jurisdiction on the court in circumstances where the absence of contacts would raise a territorial-sovereignty limitation on the reach of the court's jurisdiction (456 U.S. at p. 702, n. 10):

> "It is true that we have stated that the requirement of personal jurisdiction, as applied to state courts, reflects an element of federalism and the character of state sovereignty vis-a-vis other States....
>
> "The restriction on state sovereign power described in *World–Wide Volkswagen Corp.,* however, must be seen as ultimately a function of the individual liberty interest preserved by the Due Process Clause. That Clause is the only source of the personal jurisdiction requirement and the Clause itself makes no mention of federalism concerns. Furthermore, if the federalism concept operated as an independent restriction on the sovereign power of the court, it would not be possible to waive the personal jurisdiction requirement: Individual actions cannot change the powers of

sovereignty, although the individual can subject himself to powers from which he may otherwise be protected."

Justice Powell saw the Court's footnote as effecting "a potentially substantial change of law. For the first time it defines personal jurisdiction solely by reference to abstract notions of fair play" (456 U.S. at p. 714). The change, according to Justice Powell, was that: "Before today ... our cases had linked minimum contacts and fair play as *jointly* defining the 'sovereign' limits on state assertions of personal jurisdiction over unconsenting defendants. See World–Wide Volkswagen Corp. v. Woodson, supra, at 66; see Hanson v. Denckla, supra, at 56. The Court appears to abandon the rationale of these cases in a footnote."

In Keeton v. Hustler Magazine, Inc., 465 U.S. 770 (1984), Justice Rehnquist wondered whether a state's "'interest' in adjudicating the dispute is part of the Fourteenth Amendment due process equation." If so, he concluded that there was sufficient basis for New Hampshire to exercise jurisdiction. In his concurrence, Justice Brennan cited footnote 10 of *Insurance Corp. of Ireland* and concluded that the "interests of the state should be relevant only to the extent that they bear upon the liberty interests of the respondent that are protected by the Fourteenth Amendment." 465 U.S. at 782. In Asahi Metal Indus. Co. v. Superior Court, 480 U.S. 102 (1987), the Court states that "the interests of the 'several States'" as well as of foreign countries "are affected by the assertion of jurisdiction by a state court."

To what extent are concerns of federalism relevant to the determination of whether a state has judicial jurisdiction under due process? For an argument that they play no role see Redish, Due Process, Federalism, and Personal Jurisdiction: A Theoretical Evaluation, 75 Nw.U.L.Rev. 1112 (1981). See also the debate concerning the original (and continuing) authority of Pennoyer v. Neff with respect to this question. Supra p. 45. Should federalism concerns have relevance in the interstate conflict of laws only in choice of law, only in jurisdiction, or in both areas? Cf. Hay, Full Faith and Credit in Choice of Law, 34 Mercer L.Rev. 709 (1983).

Asahi Metal Industry Co., Ltd. v. Superior Court of California, Solano County

Supreme Court of the United States, 1987.
480 U.S. 102, 107 S.Ct. 1026, 94 L.Ed.2d 92.

■ JUSTICE O'CONNOR announced the judgment of the Court and delivered the unanimous opinion of the Court with respect to Part I, the opinion of the Court with respect to Part II–B, in which The Chief Justice, Justice Brennan, Justice White, Justice Marshall, Justice Blackmun, Justice Powell, and Justice Stevens join, and an opinion with respect to Parts II–A and III, in which The Chief Justice, Justice Powell, and Justice Scalia join.

This case presents the question whether the mere awareness on the part of a foreign defendant that the components it manufactured, sold, and delivered outside the United States would reach the forum state in the stream of commerce constitutes "minimum contacts" between the defendant and the forum state such that the exercise of jurisdiction "does not offend 'traditional notions of fair play and substantial justice.'" International Shoe Co. v. Washington, 326 U.S. 310, 316 (1945)....

I

On September 23, 1978, on Interstate Highway 80 in Solano County, California, Gary Zurcher lost control of his Honda motorcycle and collided with a tractor. Zurcher was severely injured, and his passenger and wife, Ruth Ann Moreno, was killed. In September 1979, Zurcher filed a product liability action in the Superior Court of the State of California in and for the County of Solano. Zurcher alleged that the 1978 accident was caused by a sudden loss of air and an explosion in the rear tire of the motorcycle, and alleged that the motorcycle tire, tube, and sealant were defective. Zurcher's complaint named, *inter alia,* Cheng Shin Rubber Industrial Co., Ltd. (Cheng Shin), the Taiwanese manufacturer of the tube. Cheng Shin in turn filed a cross-complaint seeking indemnification from its codefendants and from petitioner, Asahi Metal Industry Co., Ltd. (Asahi), the manufacturer of the tube's valve assembly. Zurcher's claims against Cheng Shin and the other defendants were eventually settled and dismissed, leaving only Cheng Shin's indemnity action against Asahi.

California's long-arm statute authorizes the exercise of jurisdiction "on any basis not inconsistent with the Constitution of this state or of the United States." Cal.Code Civ.Proc.Ann. § 410.10 (West 1973). Asahi moved to quash Cheng Shin's service of summons arguing the State could not exert jurisdiction over it consistent with the Due Process Clause of the Fourteenth Amendment.

In relation to the motion, the following information was submitted by Asahi and Cheng Shin. Asahi is a Japanese corporation. It manufactures tire valve assemblies in Japan and sells the assemblies to Cheng Shin, and to several other tire manufacturers, for use as components in finished tire tubes. Asahi's sales to Cheng Shin took place in Taiwan. The shipments from Asahi to Cheng Shin were sent from Japan to Taiwan. Cheng Shin bought and incorporated into its tire tubes 150,000 Asahi valve assemblies in 1978; 500,000 in 1979; 500,000 in 1980; 100,000 in 1981; and 100,000 in 1982. Sales to Cheng Shin accounted for 1.24 percent of Asahi's income in 1981 and 0.44 percent in 1982. Cheng Shin alleged that approximately 20 percent of its sales in the United States are in California. Cheng Shin purchases valve assemblies from other suppliers as well, and sells finished tubes throughout the world.

In 1983 an attorney for Cheng Shin conducted an informal examination of the valve stems of the tire tubes sold in one cyclery in Solano County. The attorney declared that of the approximately 115 tire tubes in the store, 97 were purportedly manufactured in Japan or Tawain, and of those 97, 21 valve stems were marked with the circled letter "A", apparently Asahi's trademark. Of the 21 Asahi valve stems, 12 were incorporated into Cheng Shin tire tubes. The store contained 41 other Cheng Shin tubes that incorporated the valve assemblies of other manufacturers....

Primarily on the basis of the above information, the Superior Court denied the motion to quash summons, stating that "Asahi obviously does business on an international scale. It is not unreasonable that they defend claims of defect in their product on an international scale."

. . .

The Court of Appeal of the State of California issued a peremptory writ of mandate commanding the Superior Court to quash service of summons. The court concluded that "it would be unreasonable to require Asahi to respond in California solely on the basis of ultimately realized foreseeability that the product into which its component was embodied would be sold all over the world including California." ...

The Supreme Court of the State of California reversed and discharged the writ issued by the Court of Appeal.... The court observed that "Asahi has no offices, property or agents in California. It solicits no business in California and has made no direct sales [in California]." ... Moreover, "Asahi did not design or control the system of distribution that carried its valve assemblies into California." ... Nevertheless, the court found the exercise of jurisdiction over Asahi to be consistent with the Due Process Clause.... The court considered Asahi's intentional act of placing its components into the stream of commerce—that is, by delivering the components to Cheng Shin in Taiwan—coupled with Asahi's awareness that some of the components would eventually find their way into California, sufficient to form the basis for state court jurisdiction under the Due Process Clause.

. . .

II
A

The Due Process Clause of the Fourteenth Amendment limits the power of a state court to exert personal jurisdiction over a nonresident defendant.... Most recently we have reaffirmed the oft-quoted reasoning of Hanson v. Denckla, 357 U.S. 235, 253 (1958), that minimum contacts must have a basis in "some act by which the defendant purposefully avails itself of the privilege of conducting activities within the forum State, thus invoking the benefits and protections of its laws." ...

Applying the principle that minimum contacts must be based on an act of the defendant, the Court in World–Wide Volkswagen Corp. v. Woodson, 444 U.S. 286 (1980), rejected the assertion that a *consumer's* unilateral act of bringing the defendant's product into the forum State was a sufficient constitutional basis for personal jurisdiction over the defendant. It had been argued in *World–Wide Volkswagen* that because an automobile retailer and its wholesale distributor sold a product mobile by design and purpose, they could foresee being haled into court in the distant States into which their customers might drive. The Court rejected this concept of foreseeability as an insufficient basis for jurisdiction under the Due Process Clause.... The Court disclaimed, however, the idea that "foreseeability is wholly irrelevant" to personal jurisdiction, concluding that "[t]he forum State does not exceed its powers under the Due Process Clause if it asserts personal jurisdiction over a corporation that delivers its products into the stream of commerce with the expectation that they will be purchased by consumers in the forum State." ...

In *World–Wide Volkswagen* itself, the state court sought to base jurisdiction not on any act of the defendant, but on the foreseeable unilateral actions of the consumer. Since *World–Wide Volkswagen,* lower courts have been confronted with cases in which the defendant acted by placing a product in the stream of commerce, and the stream eventually swept defendant's product into the forum State, but the defendant did nothing else to purposefully avail itself of the market in the forum state. Some courts have understood the Due Process Clause, as interpreted in *World–Wide Volkswagen,* to allow an exercise of personal jurisdiction to be based on no more than the defendant's act of placing the product in the stream of commerce. Other courts have understood the Due Process Clause and the above-quoted language in *World–Wide Volkswagen* to require the action of the defendant to be more purposefully directed at the forum State than the mere act of placing a product in the stream of commerce.

. . .

We now find this latter position to be consonant with the requirements of due process. The "substantial connection," ... between the defendant and the forum State necessary for a finding of minimum contacts must come about by *an action of the defendant purposefully directed toward the forum State*.... The placement of a product into the stream of commerce, without more, is not an act of the defendant purposefully directed toward the forum State. Additional conduct of the defendant may indicate an intent or purpose to serve the market in the forum State, for example, designing the product for the market in the forum State, advertising in the forum State, establishing channels for providing regular advice to customers in the forum State, or marketing the product through a distributor who has agreed to serve as the sales agent in the forum State. But a defendant's awareness that the stream of commerce may or will sweep the product into the forum State does not convert the mere act of placing the product into the stream into an act purposefully directed toward the forum State.

Assuming, *arguendo,* that respondents have established Asahi's awareness that some of the valves sold to Cheng Shin would be incorporated into tire tubes sold in California, respondents have not demonstrated any action by Asahi to purposefully avail itself of the California market. Asahi does not do business in California. It has no office, agents, employees, or property in California. It does not advertise or otherwise solicit business in

California. It did not create, control, or employ the distribution system that brought its valves to California. ... On the basis of these facts, the exertion of personal jurisdiction over Asahi by the Superior Court of California * exceeds the limits of Due Process.

B

The strictures of the Due Process Clause forbid a state court from exercising personal jurisdiction over Asahi under circumstances that would offend "traditional notions of fair play and substantial justice." International Shoe Co. v. Washington, 326 U.S., at 316, quoting Milliken v. Meyer, 311 U.S. at 463.

We have previously explained that the determination of the reasonableness of the exercise of jurisdiction in each case will depend on an evaluation of several factors. A court must consider the burden on the defendant, the interests of the forum state, and the plaintiff's interest in obtaining relief. It must also weigh in its determination "the interstate judicial system's interest in obtaining the most efficient resolution of controversies; and the shared interest of the several States in furthering fundamental substantive social policies." World–Wide Volkswagen, 444 U.S., at 292 (citations omitted).

A consideration of these factors in the present case clearly reveals the unreasonableness of the assertion of jurisdiction over Asahi, even apart from the question of the placement of goods in the stream of commerce.

Certainly the burden on the defendant in this case is severe. Asahi has been commanded by the Supreme Court of California not only to traverse the distance between Asahi's headquarters in Japan and the Superior Court of California in and for the County of Solano, but also to submit its dispute with Cheng Shin to a foreign nation's judicial system. The unique burdens placed upon one who must defend oneself in a foreign legal system should have significant weight in assessing the reasonableness of stretching the long arm of personal jurisdiction over national borders.

When minimum contacts have been established, often the interests of the plaintiff and the forum in the exercise of jurisdiction will justify even the serious burdens placed on the alien defendant. In the present case, however, the interests of the plaintiff and the forum in California's assertion of jurisdiction over Asahi are slight. All that remains is a claim for indemnification asserted by Cheng Shin, a Taiwanese corporation, against Asahi. The transaction on which the indemnification claim is based took

---

* We have no occasion here to determine whether Congress could, consistent with the Due Process Clause of the Fifth Amendment, authorize federal court personal jurisdiction over alien defendants based on the aggregate of *national* contacts, rather than on the contacts between the defendant and the State in which the federal court sits. See Max Daetwyler Corp. v. R. Meyer, 762 F.2d 290, 293–295 (CA3 1985); DeJames v. Magnificence Carriers, Inc., 654 F.2d 280, 283 (CA3 1981); see also Born, Reflections on Judicial Jurisdiction in International Cases, to be published in 17 Ga.J. Int'l & Comp.L. 1 (1987); Lilly, Jurisdiction Over Domestic and Alien Defendants, 69 Va.L.Rev. 85, 127–145 (1983). [Footnote by the Court. Eds.]

place in Taiwan; Asahi's components were shipped from Japan to Taiwan. Cheng Shin has not demonstrated that it is more convenient for it to litigate its indemnification claim against Asahi in California rather than in Taiwan or Japan.

Because the plaintiff is not a California resident, California's legitimate interests in the dispute have considerably diminished. The Supreme Court of California argued that the State had an interest in "protecting its consumers by ensuring that foreign manufacturers comply with the state's safety standards." ... The State Supreme Court's definition of California's interest, however, was overly broad. The dispute between Cheng Shin and Asahi is primarily about indemnification rather than safety standards. Moreover, it is not at all clear at this point that California law should govern the question whether a Japanese corporation should indemnify a Taiwanese corporation on the basis of a sale made in Taiwan and a shipment of goods from Japan to Taiwan.... The possibility of being haled into a California court as a result of an accident involving Asahi's components undoubtedly creates an additional deterrent to the manufacture of unsafe components; however, similar pressures will be placed on Asahi by the purchasers of its components as long as those who use Asahi components in their final products, and sell those products in California, are subject to the application of California tort law.

World–Wide Volkswagen also admonished courts to take into consideration the interests of the "several States," in addition to the forum state, in the efficient judicial resolution of the dispute and the advancement of substantive policies. In the present case, this advice calls for a court to consider the procedural and substantive policies of other *nations* whose interests are affected by the assertion of jurisdiction by the California court. The procedural and substantive interests of other nations in a state court's assertion of jurisdiction over an alien defendant will differ from case to case. In every case, however, those interests, as well as the Federal interest in its foreign relations policies, will be best served by a careful inquiry into the reasonableness of the assertion of jurisdiction in the particular case, and an unwillingness to find the serious burdens on an alien defendant outweighed by minimal interests on the part of the plaintiff or the forum State....

Considering the international context, the heavy burden on the alien defendant, and the slight interests of the plaintiff and the forum State, the exercise of personal jurisdiction by a California court over Asahi in this instance would be unreasonable and unfair.

III

Because the facts of this case do not establish minimum contacts such that the exercise of personal jurisdiction is consistent with fair play and substantial justice, the judgment of the Supreme Court of California is reversed, and the case is remanded for further proceedings not inconsistent with this opinion.

It is so ordered.

■ JUSTICE BRENNAN, with whom JUSTICE WHITE, JUSTICE MARSHALL, and JUSTICE BLACKMUN join, concurring in part and in the judgment.

I do not agree with the plurality's interpretation of the stream-of-commerce theory, nor with its conclusion that Asahi did not "purposely avail itself of the California market." ... I do agree, however, with the Court's conclusion in Part II–B that the exercise of personal jurisdiction over Asahi in this case would not comport with "fair play and substantial justice," International Shoe Co. v. Washington, 326 U.S. 310, 320 (1945). This is one of those rare cases in which "minimum requirements inherent in the concept of 'fair play and substantial justice' ... defeat the reasonableness of jurisdiction even [though] the defendant has purposefully engaged in forum activities." Burger King Corp. v. Rudzewicz, 471 U.S. 462, 477–478 (1985). I therefore join Parts I and II–B of the Court's opinion, and write separately to explain my disagreement with Part II–A.

The plurality states that "a defendant's awareness that the stream of commerce may or will sweep the product into the forum State does not convert the mere act of placing the product into the stream into an act purposefully directed toward the forum State." ... The plurality would therefore require a plaintiff to show "[a]dditional conduct" directed toward the forum before finding the exercise of jurisdiction over the defendant to be consistent with the Due Process Clause.... I see no need for such a showing, however. The stream of commerce refers not to unpredictable currents or eddies, but to the regular and anticipated flow of products from manufacture to distribution to retail sale. As long as a participant in this process is aware that the final product is being marketed in the forum State, the possibility of a lawsuit there cannot come as a surprise. Nor will the litigation present a burden for which there is no corresponding benefit. A defendant who has placed goods in the stream of commerce benefits economically from the retail sale of the final product in the forum State, and indirectly benefits from the State's laws that regulate and facilitate commercial activity.... Accordingly, most courts and commentators have found that jurisdiction premised on the placement of a product into the stream of commerce is consistent with the Due Process Clause, and have not required a showing of additional conduct.

The plurality's endorsement of what appears to be the minority view among Federal Courts of Appeals represents a marked retreat from its analysis in World–Wide Volkswagen v. Woodson, 444 U.S. 286 (1980)....

The Court in *World–Wide Volkswagen* ... took great care to distinguish "between a case involving goods which reach a distant State through a chain of distribution and a case involving goods which reach the same State because a consumer ... took them there." 444 U.S., at 306–307 (BRENNAN, J., dissenting). The California Supreme Court took note of this distinction, and correctly concluded that our holding in *World–Wide Volkswagen* preserved the stream-of-commerce theory....

In this case, the facts found by the California Supreme Court support its finding of minimum contacts. The Court found that "[a]lthough Asahi did not design or control the system of distribution that carried its valve assemblies into California Asahi was aware of the distribution system's operation, and it knew that it would benefit economically from the sale in California of products incorporating its components." ... Accordingly, I cannot join the plurality's determination that Asahi's regular and extensive sales of component parts to a manufacturer it knew was making regular sales of the final product in California is insufficient to establish minimum contacts with California.

■ JUSTICE STEVENS, with whom JUSTICE WHITE and JUSTICE BLACKMUN join, concurring in part and concurring in the judgment.

The judgment of the Supreme Court of California should be reversed for the reasons stated in Part II–B of the Court's opinion. While I join Parts I and II–B, I do not join Part II–A for two reasons. First, it is not necessary to the Court's decision. An examination of minimum contacts is not always necessary to determine whether a state court's assertion of personal jurisdiction is constitutional.... Part II–B establishes, after considering the factors set forth in World–Wide Volkswagen Corp. v. Woodson, 444 U.S. 286, 292 (1980), that California's exercise of jurisdiction over Asahi in this case would be "unreasonable and unfair." ... This finding alone requires reversal; this case fits within the rule that "minimum requirements inherent in the concept of 'fair play and substantial justice' may defeat the reasonableness of jurisdiction even if the defendant has purposefully engaged in forum activities." Burger King, 471 U.S., at 477–478.... Accordingly, I see no reason in this case for the Court to articulate "purposeful direction" or any other test as the nexus between an act of a defendant and the forum State that is necessary to establish minimum contacts.

Second, even assuming that the test ought to be formulated here, Part II–A misapplies it to the facts of this case. The Court seems to assume that an unwavering line can be drawn between "mere awareness" that a component will find its way into the forum State and "purposeful availment" of the forum's market.... Over the course of its dealings with Cheng Shin, Asahi has arguably engaged in a higher quantum of conduct than "[t]he placement of a product into the stream of commerce, without more...." ... Whether or not this conduct rises to the level of purposeful availment requires a constitutional determination that is affected by the volume, the value, and the hazardous character of the components. In most circumstances I would be inclined to conclude that a regular course of dealing that results in deliveries of over 100,000 units annually over a period of several years would constitute "purposeful availment" even though the item delivered to the forum State was a standard product marketed throughout the world.

"STREAM OF COMMERCE"

(1) With the Justices divided 4–4 on the question, the Asahi case left unclear whether merely placing an article in the stream of commerce makes a defendant amenable to jurisdiction of the state where the article

ultimately causes legal injury. Justice O'Connor thought that putting a product in the stream is not enough "without more," but did not say how much more is needed. Is Justice Stevens justified in rejecting the distinction between "mere awareness" that an article will get to the forum state and "purposeful availment" of the forum's market? See Hall v. Zambelli, 669 F.Supp. 753, 756 (S.D.W.Va.1987): "... the Supreme Court's endorsement of the [stream-of-commerce] theory in *World–Wide Volkswagen* taken together with the lack of consensus in *Asahi* convinces this Court that the theory continues to have precedential value." Accord: Dehmlow v. Austin Fireworks, 963 F.2d 941 (7th Cir.1992) (Illinois jurisdiction upheld over Kansas manufacturer of fireworks sold to Wisconsin company employing Illinois plaintiff for fireworks displays in Illinois; defendant had direct Illinois business contacts, unlike the defendant in *Asahi*.) But see: Gould v. P.T. Krakatau Steel, 957 F.2d 573 (8th Cir.1992), cert. denied 113 S.Ct. 304 (1992); Arguello v. Industrial Woodworking Machine Co., 838 P.2d 1120 (Utah 1992).

The federal courts of appeal that have considered it have split over the issue of whether "stream-of-commerce" jurisdiction continues. See, e.g., Irving v. Owens–Corning Fiberglass Corp., 864 F.2d 383 (5th Cir.), cert. denied, 493 U.S. 823 (1989); Boit v. Gar–Tec Prods., Inc., 967 F.2d 671, 683 (1st Cir.1992). For extensive discussion, see Weintraub, Commentary on the Conflict of Laws, 1991 Supp. to 3d ed. (1986), 22–36; Scoles & Hay, Conflict of Laws § 9.9–1 (2d ed. 1992 & 1995 Supp. with Borchers); Weintraub, Case Three: Personal Jurisdiction, 29 New England L.Rev. 664, 666 (1995).

(2) Realistically, can a defendant who has foreseen the likelihood of causing injury in the forum state be found not to have anticipated the likelihood of being haled into the forum state's courts? Would it be a "reasonable expectation" on the defendant's part to anticipate not being sued in the state where the product caused injury? Do we answer that question by inquiring whether the defendant's actual expectation was reasonable or by deciding what expectation the defendant would have been reasonable to entertain? If the former, should evidence be taken regarding what the defendant in fact expected?

(3) Should it make any difference in product liability cases of the Gray v. American Standard Radiator type (p. 65, supra), or World–Wide Volkswagen type that the nonresident defendant put the goods into interstate circulation through the consumer rather than through a distributor? In World–Wide Volkswagen Justice Brennan opined that the possible movement of an unsafe automobile to the forum was foreseeable in either case. Should it make a difference that in the distributor case it is definitely the defendant's desire and to its advantage that the goods reach the forum and be sold there; but that no similar direct advantage accrues to the defendant when a consumer takes the product to F?

(4) A New Jersey resident sued the American distributor of a German-made printing press for work injuries he sustained as a result of alleged defects in design and manufacture. The distributor invoked long-arm

jurisdiction in a third-party action against Heidelberger, the manufacturer. Heidelberger carried on no activities in the United States. It sold the printing press in Germany to the distributor, parting with title there and expecting the press would be resold in the United States but not knowing where. The New Jersey court upheld jurisdiction: "If [Heidelberger] wishes to benefit from American markets ... it is not unreasonable or fundamentally unfair for them to be required to submit to the jurisdiction of the state whose resident has allegedly been injured by its product." Certisimo v. Heidelberg Co., 122 N.J.Super. 1, 298 A.2d 298, 305 (1972).

(5) In Nelson v. Park Industries, Inc., 717 F.2d 1120 (7th Cir.1983), cert. denied 465 U.S. 1024 (1984), a manufacturer in Hong Kong produced all the flannel shirts Woolworth purchased for resale in the United States between 1973 and 1977. However, Woolworth had no direct commercial contact with the manufacturer. It bought the shirts from a third party, another Hong Kong corporation, which acted as purchasing agent and exporter from Hong Kong for several foreign buyers. The agent had bought the shirts "f.o.b. Hong Kong." A shipper, selected by Woolworth, arranged for the transportation of the shirts to several United States destinations. A shirt purchased in Wisconsin for the minor plaintiff caught fire and caused the injuries for which she brought a damage action against the manufacturer and the export agent. The Seventh Circuit reversed the trial court's order dismissing the action for lack of personal jurisdiction: "... [The defendants'] function in the distribution of flannel shirts place them at the start of the system. This case, thus, is distinguishable from the facts underlying ... *World–Wide Volkswagen* because [the defendants] are early actors in a distribution system which places and moves the product in the stream of commerce. *World–Wide Volkswagen* is also different because the ... product not only caused injury in the forum, but it was also purchased there.... [The defendants] maintain that the ... shirt ... was sold in Wisconsin only because of Woolworth's actions rather than theirs.... Further, [the manufacturer] submits that it had no control over the ... shirts once they were sold to [the exporter] and that it made no efforts to distribute the shirts anywhere. However, even though [the defendants] did not originate the distribution system and do not control it, they did place the ... shirts in and move them along the stream of commerce destined for retail sale throughout the United States in Woolworth's retail stores.... [A] critical factor is whether [the] defendants were aware of that distribution system. If they were aware, they were indirectly serving and deriving economic benefits from the national retail market established by Woolworth, and they should reasonably anticipate being subject to suit in any forum within that market where their product caused injury."

Is the defendant manufacturer in the same position as the manufacturer of the Audi in *World–Wide Volkswagen* (assuming that Audi, unlike the retailer, was subject to jurisdiction in Oklahoma)? See Castree v. E.R. Squibb & Sons Ltd., [1980] 1 W.L.R. 1248 (C.A.): "The substantial wrongdoing ... is putting *on the English market* a defective machine with no warning as to its defects" (emphasis added). In DeJames v. Magnificence

Carriers, Inc., 654 F.2d 280 (3d Cir.1981), the plaintiff longshoreman was injured while working on a vessel when it was moored in New Jersey. He sought damages, inter alia, from Hitachi, the Japanese company which had converted the vessel from a bulk carrier to an automobile carrier. In affirming the district court's dismissal, the court said: "... Were we to accept [the plaintiff's] foreseeability argument in this case, Hitachi would be amenable to suit in every forum where a ship on which it had done conversion work, and over which it exercised no control, could be found." The court also rejected the plaintiff's argument that Hitachi's contacts with the United States as a whole should be aggregated to support jurisdiction over Hitachi. With respect to national contacts and nationwide service see Omni Capital International v. Rudolf Wolff & Co., 484 U.S. 97 (1987), p. 89, infra.

(6) Compare Keeton v. Hustler Magazine, Inc., p. 78, supra, and Nelson v. Park Industries, Inc., p. 87, supra, with a 1977 decision of the German Supreme Court. The defendants were the publisher and editor of a magazine published in Vienna, Austria. The German plaintiff, resident in Berlin, learned that a particular issue carried allegedly libelous material. He obtained a copy through a friend and subsequently placed an order for an additional copy with a dealer. The Court held that the tort of libel is committed, and jurisdiction exists to entertain claims arising from it, where the magazine is published and where it is distributed. "It does not suffice that an occasional issue, through third parties, reaches an area not usually served by the publisher's distribution system.... It also does not amount to 'distribution' when someone places a special order for a copy of an issue in order to establish his domicile as the place of the commission of the tort for jurisdictional purposes.... It is thus decisive for the jurisdictional determination ... whether the magazine containing the article was distributed in Berlin.... If, upon remand, the [trial] court should find that copies of the particular issue ... were sold commercially in Berlin or sent there to subscribers, it need not require that a particularly substantial number of copies was involved in order to find the 'distribution' requirement satisfied." Decision of May 3, 1977, [1977] Neue Juristische Wochenschrift 1590, eds.' transl.

(7) In the European Union, Art. 5 No. 3 of the Brussels Convention, as interpreted by the European Court, provides for tort jurisdiction at the place of acting or of injury. See supra p. 535. There is no requirement of foreseeability or purposeful availment. Jurisdiction in tort is thus potentially more extensive than the formulation of German national tort jurisdiction by the German Supreme Court for non-Convention state cases. See also Professor Weintraub's suggestion, which parallels the German formulation, that "a defendant that releases a product for sale is subject to jurisdiction in any state where the product causes harm if the product comes there either in the normal course of commercial distribution or is brought into that state by someone using that product as it is intended to be used." Weintraub, supra Note (1), 29 New England L.Rev. at 666. Under the Brussels Convention, moreover, the state with jurisdiction over the principal defendant also has jurisdiction over a third-party defendant

for purposes of claims for contribution or liability over. No affiliation of the third-party defendant need be shown. Art. 6 No. 2. This provision is consistent with the wide reach of the principal tort provision of Art. 5. Some countries will not go this far. Thus, Germany, for instance, will not exercise jurisdiction on the basis of Art. 6 No. 2; however, it will recognize judgments of other Convention states based on that provision. Art. V, Protocol of Sept. 27, 1968, Official Journal EC 1989, No. L. 285, 1.

(8) For a stimulating debate on Professor Brilmayer's thesis that the basic question in specific jurisdiction situations is whether the contacts are substantively relevant to the plaintiff's claim, see Brilmayer, How Contacts Count: Due Process Limitations on State Court Jurisdiction, 1980 Sup.Ct. Rev. 77; Twitchell, The Myth of General Jurisdiction, 101 Harv.L.Rev. 610 (1988); Brilmayer, Related Contacts and Personal Jurisdiction, 101 Harv. L.Rev. 1444 (1988); Twitchell, A Rejoinder to Professor Brilmayer, 101 Harv.L.Rev. 1465 (1988).

"NATIONAL CONTACTS"

If it could be shown that valve stems manufactured by Asahi were also incorporated in tire tubes marketed in states other than California, could Asahi's "national contacts" be aggregated for the purpose of permitting the exercise of jurisdiction? See footnote * in the plurality opinion in *Asahi*. In Omni Capital International v. Rudolf Wolff & Co., 484 U.S. 97 (1987), suit was brought on a claim under the federal Commodity Exchange Act. The English defendants sought dismissal because service on them was not authorized by the law of the Louisiana forum nor by federal law. The lower courts had dismissed the action but the dissenters in the Court of Appeals had argued that, even if not provided for by Federal Rule, the federal courts could authorize service outside the state. The Supreme Court declined to adopt that suggestion. Justice Blackmun wrote that "statutes and rules have always provided the measures for service, courts are inappropriate forums for deciding whether to extend them.... We are not blind to the consequences of the inability to serve process on ... the English defendants. A narrowly tailored service of process provision, authorizing service on an alien in a federal-question case when the alien is not amenable to service under the applicable state long-arm statute, might well serve the ends of of the Commodity Exchange Act and other federal statutes."

In December 1993, Federal Rule of Civil Procedure 4(k)(2) was added:

> If the exercise of jurisdiction is consistent with the Constitution and laws of the United States, serving a summons or filing a waiver of service is also effective, with respect to claims arising under federal law, to establish personal jurisdiction over the person of any defendant who is not subject to the jurisdiction of the courts of general jurisdiction of any state.

Will the requirement that the defendant "is not subject to the jurisdiction of the courts of general jurisdiction of any state" cause plaintiff and defendant to reverse their usual contentions concerning jurisdiction over the defendant in state court? Is the Due Process standard of the Fifth Amendment, which applies to federal courts, the same as that of the Fourteenth, which applies to state courts?

In a case brought under the Federal Jones Act or in admiralty, must a state court apply the federal forum non conveniens doctrine or a local state statute describing the forum non conveniens doctrine to be unavailable in Jones Act and maritime case laws brought in the state courts? In American Dredging Company v. Miller, —— U.S. ——, 114 S.Ct. 981, 127 L.Ed.2d 285 (1994), the Supreme Court upheld application of the state statute. Does that decision seem sound?

NOTES

The 1993 amendment to the Federal Rules of course does not answer the question raised at the beginning of the textual Note above: what about "national contacts" as a basis for jurisdiction in a case based on diversity of citizenship and arising under state law? Consider that question further in the light of the following illustrative cases:

1. Erlanger Mills v. Cohoes Fibre Mills, 239 F.2d 502 (4th Cir.1956) involved a North Carolina statute (N.C.Gen.Stat. § 55–145) which makes a foreign corporation subject to personal jurisdiction on claims arising out of the "production, manufacture, or distribution of goods by such corporation with the reasonable expectation that those goods are to be used or consumed in this State and are so used or consumed...." In New York, plaintiff's agent contracted to purchase yarn from defendant, f.o.b. New York, and the goods were shipped to North Carolina. Plaintiff sued for damages, claiming the yarn was defective, but the action was dismissed on the ground that the statute could not constitutionally be applied to defendant. "To illustrate the logical and not too improbable extension of the problem, let us consider the hesitancy a California dealer might feel if asked to sell a set of tires to a tourist with Pennsylvania license plates, knowing that he might be required to defend in the courts of Pennsylvania a suit for refund of the purchase price or for heavy damages in case of accident attributed to a defect in the tires."

Should the California dealer not be subject to Pennsylvania jurisdiction in the hypothetical case posed in the Erlanger opinion? Suppose on similar facts that the Pennsylvania motorist had in California given a promissory note to the dealer in payment of the tires. Would the motorist be subject to California jurisdiction in an action on the note? Should there be a wider scope of jurisdiction over a defendant with respect to conduct that is multistate in character than with respect to conduct that is essentially local? Would it be correct to say in general that the more a defendant's activities are multistate in character the wider the scope of jurisdiction that can be exercised over him, and the less a plaintiff engages in multistate activity the narrower the scope of jurisdiction that should be exercised over the defendant in plaintiff's favor? See von Mehren and Trautman, Jurisdiction to Adjudicate: A Suggested Analysis, 79 Harv.L.Rev. 1121, 1167–1168 (1966).

2. Wright v. Yackley, 459 F.2d 287 (9th Cir.1972). While a resident of South Dakota, the plaintiff had been treated by the defendant, a South Dakota doctor, and at his direction had taken certain drugs. Plaintiff then moved to Idaho and wrote the defendant in South Dakota requesting that he confirm the prescription so that she could purchase an additional supply of the drugs. Defendant did so and plaintiff thereafter was allegedly injured by use of the drugs. She brought suit for malpractice against the defendant in the federal district court in Idaho.

Held: Idaho lacks judicial jurisdiction over the defendant.

"... [T]he idea that tortious rendition of [personal] services is a portable tort which can be deemed to have been committed wherever the consequences foreseeably were felt is wholly inconsistent with having services of this sort generally available. Medical services, in particular, should not be proscribed by the doctor's concerns as to where the patient may carry the consequences of his treatment and in what distant lands he may be called upon to defend it. The traveling public would be ill served were the treatment of local doctors confined to so much aspirin as would get the patient into the next state. The scope of medical treatment should be defined by the patient's needs, as diagnosed by the doctor, rather than by geography.... [T]he forum state's [Idaho's] natural interest in the protection of its citizens is here countered by an interest in their access to medical services whenever needed."

3. McGee v. Riekhof, 442 F.Supp. 1276 (D.Mont.1978). Having been operated on by the defendant doctor in Utah, plaintiff returned to his home in Montana. Sometime later the defendant told plaintiff's wife over the telephone that he could return to work in Montana. Allegedly as a result, the plaintiff suffered further injury. Held that the defendant was subject to the jurisdiction of the federal district court in Montana. "... [T]he defendant doctor did precisely what wasn't done in *Wright,* he provided a new diagnosis via telephone. This court recognizes the need to keep open the flow of medical and other personal services across state boundaries.... [Under the circumstances], it would be fundamentally unfair to patients to permit doctors to telephonically render services and treatment in Montana, yet shield them from suit in Montana."

4. Compare Tarango v. Pastrana, 94 N.M. 727, 616 P.2d 440 (App.1980), with the decisions summarized in Notes 2 and 3 above. A New Mexico patient sued Texas physicians and a Texas hospital alleging that the negligent performance of a tubal litigation in Texas subsequently resulted in the birth of a child in New Mexico. The defendants' only connection with New Mexico was the mailing there of statements for payment. Held: the New Mexico court lacked personal jurisdiction. "Unlike a case involving voluntary interstate or international economic activity ... which is directed at the forum state's markets, the residence of a recipient of personal services rendered elsewhere is irrelevant ... [W]hen ... a patient travels to receive professional services without having been solicited (which is prohibited by most professional codes of ethics), then the client, who originally traveled to seek services apparently not available at home, ought to expect that he will have to travel again if he thereafter complains that the services ... were rendered improperly....", quoting from Gelineau v. New York University Hospital, 375 F.Supp. 661 (D.N.J.1974).

Contracts that involve activities in different states during their negotiation, execution or performance are fertile sources of jurisdictional issues. How much contact and what kind must a nonresident have with the forum to be amenable to suit there? Are nonresident sellers more susceptible to long-arm jurisdiction than nonresident buyers? Does the relative size or financial strength of the parties play a significant role? What importance is attached to the nonresident's dealings in the forum that are unrelated to the contract sued upon? The Supreme Court has not addressed these questions in definitive terms since the International Shoe decision, although it has had opportunities to do so. In Lakeside Bridge & Steel Co. v. Mountain State Construction Co., Inc., 445 U.S. 907 (1980), the plaintiff, a Wisconsin seller, contracted to supply structural assemblies for a dam and reservoir in Virginia. The defendant was a West Virginia corporation whose dealings with the plaintiff were conducted by mail and telephone between West Virginia and Wisconsin. The Court of Appeals for the Seventh Circuit found the defendant's contacts with Wisconsin insufficient to support jurisdiction over it in the plaintiff's suit for part of the purchase price. Justice White, joined by Justice Powell, dissented from the Supreme Court's denial of certiorari, arguing that "the issue is one of considerable importance" and that the "disarray" among the federal and state courts might be having a disruptive effect on commercial relations that place a premium on certainty.

Buyers are often treated more gently than sellers in jurisdictional cases on the theory that the buyer is more likely to be weaker financially than the seller, especially when consumer goods are involved. Thus, "with few exceptions, in those cases where jurisdiction is extended over a nonresident defendant purchaser, that purchaser has either initiated the relationship or actively participated in negotiations and plans for production (*e.g.*, design specifications)." Vacu–Maid, Inc. v. Covington, 530 P.2d 137, 141, 143 (Okla.App.1975). See also Tube Turns Div. of Chemetron v. Patterson Co., 562 S.W.2d 99 (Ky.App.1978). When the buyer is not an individual but a large and sophisticated business, jurisdiction is more likely to be sustained. Nordberg Div. of Rex Chainbelt Inc. v. Hudson Eng. Corp., 361 F.Supp. 903 (E.D.Wis.1973). The big fish-little fish approach to jurisdiction drew criticism in Vencedor Mfg. Co. Inc. v. Gougler Industries, Inc., 557 F.2d 886, 894 (1st Cir.1977). The court said:

> ... To vary the minimum contacts needed for jurisdiction according to the character of the suit would lead plaintiffs into disingenuous manipulation of their pleadings, and it would plunge the courts into ever more difficult refinements of the categories. They would need to decide whether a contract action involving individuals should be treated like one between corporations; whether consumers' orders from mail order catalogues should be treated like commercial contracts; whether the tort of defamation or of interference with contract is to be treated like the negligent operation of an automobile.

Some courts have made the issue of jurisdiction turn on which party took the initiative in the transaction. See also Burger King Corp. v. Rudzewicz, 471 U.S. 462 (1985), p. 76, supra.

The Brussels Convention contains special jurisdictional provisions for consumer transactions. The consumer may be sued only in the state of his or her residence, while "the other party" may also be sued there as well as at its own domicile or business seat. Art. 14. Forum selection clauses that provide for jurisdiction elsewhere are permissible only in limited and specifically described circumstances, e.g., when the clause gives the consumer additional courts in which to sue the other party. Art. 15 No. 2.

Art. 13 defines "consumer transactions" for purposes of these provisions (e.g., installment sales, loans and credit transactions, sales of personal property and the rendition of services when the contract was preceded by advertising or the making of an offer in the state of the consumer's residence).

"GENERAL JURISDICTION"

NOTE

The closer a defendant's contacts with a state, the more likely it is that the state has judicial jurisdiction and the wider the scope of jurisdiction the state may exercise. So a state may entertain in its courts suit on any and all civil claims against a defendant who is domiciled in the state and, subject to considerations of reasonableness, may do the same against a defendant who is a resident or a national of the state. For historical reasons, the same is true of a defendant who is served with process while physically present in the state.

There is some uncertainty as to the circumstances in which a state may exercise jurisdiction over a nonresident which engages in commercial activity within its territory with respect to claims that do not arise from this business. Consider in this regard the statements on this subject by Chief Justice Stone in the International Shoe case (p. 47, supra). Consider also the following cases.

PERKINS V. BENGUET CONSOLIDATED MINING CO., 342 U.S. 437 (1952): The president of defendant, a Philippine corporation, was served with a summons in action in personam against the corporation filed in an Ohio state court by a non-resident of Ohio. The cause of action did not arise in Ohio and did not relate to the corporation's activities there. On motion, the service was quashed by the Ohio courts. The defendant owned mining properties in the Philippine Islands, but all its operations there halted during the Japanese occupation. The main activities in Ohio were carried on by the president, who was also general manager and principal stockholder of the company, and included: maintaining the files, corresponding, paying salaries of employees out of the company's local bank accounts, holding directors' meetings, and supervising rehabilitation of the corporation after the occupation. The Supreme Court of the United States held that the due process clause of the Fourteenth Amendment did not compel Ohio to open its courts to such a case. On the other hand, it held that the activities in Ohio were sufficiently "continuous and systematic" so that Ohio could, consistently with due process, (1) entertain the cause of action if it wished to do so, even though it was unrelated to the Ohio activities, or (2) refuse to hear the case, if that was its own local rule or policy. On remand, the Supreme Court of Ohio held that its courts should exercise jurisdiction. 158 Ohio St. 145, 107 N.E.2d 203 (1952).

FISHER GOVERNOR CO. V. SUPERIOR COURT, 53 Cal.2d 222, 1 Cal.Rptr. 1, 347 P.2d 1 (1959): An action was brought in California against the Fisher Company, a corporation of Iowa with its principal office and plants there, for wrongful death and personal injuries occurring in Idaho from alleged defective equipment manufactured by Fisher. Fisher's products were sold in California through manufacturers' agents who sold also similar products of other manufacturers, but the California agents had no connection with the sale of the Idaho machinery. Held, the action will not lie.

■ TRAYNOR, J. ... Although a foreign corporation may have sufficient contacts with a state to justify an assumption of jurisdiction over it to enforce causes of action having no relation to its activities in that state, ... more contacts are required for the assumption of such extensive jurisdiction than sales and sales promotion within the state by independent nonexclusive sales representatives.... Accordingly we must look beyond defendant's sales activities in this state to determine whether jurisdiction may constitutionally be assumed. The interests of the state in providing a forum for its residents, ... or in regulating the business involved; the relative availability of evidence and the burden of defense and prosecution in one place rather than another; ... the ease of access to an alternative forum; the avoidance of multiplicity of suits and conflicting adjudications; and the extent to which the cause of action arose out of defendant's local activities are all relevant to this inquiry....

Helicopteros Nacionales de Colombia, S.A. v. Hall

Supreme Court of the United States, 1984.
466 U.S. 408, 104 S.Ct. 1868, 80 L.Ed.2d 404.

■ JUSTICE BLACKMUN delivered the opinion of the Court.

I

Petitioner Helicopteros Nacionales de Colombia, S.A., (Helicol) is a Colombian corporation with its principal place of business in the city of Bogota in that country. It is engaged in the business of providing helicopter transportation for oil and construction companies in South America. On January 26, 1976, a helicopter owned by Helicol crashed in Peru. Four United States citizens were among those who lost their lives in the accident. Respondents are the survivors and representatives of the four decedents.

At the time of the crash, respondents' decedents were employed by Consorcio, a Peruvian consortium, and were working on a pipeline in Peru. Consorcio is the alter ego of a joint venture named Williams–Sedco–Horn (WSH). The venture had its headquarters in Houston, Tex. Consorcio had been formed to enable the venturers to enter into a contract with Petro Peru, the Peruvian state-owned oil company. Consorcio was to construct a pipeline for Petro Peru running from the interior of Peru westward to the Pacific Ocean. Peruvian law forbade construction of the pipeline by any non-Peruvian entity.

Consorcio/WSH needed helicopters to move personnel, materials, and equipment into and out of the construction area. In 1974, upon request of Consorcio/WSH, the chief executive officer of Helicol, Francisco Restrepo, flew to the United States and conferred in Houston with representatives of the three joint venturers. At that meeting, there was a discussion of prices, availability, working conditions, fuel, supplies, and housing. Restrepo represented that Helicol could have the first helicopter on the job in 15 days. The Consorcio/WSH representatives decided to accept the contract proposed by Restrepo. Helicol began performing before the agreement was formally signed in Peru on November 11, 1974. The contract was written in Spanish on official government stationery and provided that the residence of all the parties would be Lima, Peru. It further stated that controversies arising out of the contract would be submitted to the jurisdiction of Peruvian courts. In addition, it provided that Consorcio/WSH would make payments to Helicol's account with the Bank of America in New York City....

Aside from the negotiation session in Houston between Restrepo and the representatives of Consorcio/WSH, Helicol had other contacts with Texas. During the years 1970–1977, it purchased helicopters (approximately 80% of its fleet), spare parts, and accessories for more than $4,000,000 from Bell Helicopter Company in Fort Worth. In that period, Helicol sent prospective pilots to Fort Worth for training and to ferry the aircraft to South America. It also sent management and maintenance personnel to visit Bell Helicopter in Fort Worth during the same period in order to receive "plant familiarization" and for technical consultation. Helicol received into its New York City and Panama City, Fla., bank accounts over $5,000,000 in payments from Consorcio/WSH drawn upon First City National Bank of Houston.

Beyond the foregoing, there have been no other business contacts between Helicol and the State of Texas. Helicol never has been authorized to do business in Texas and never has had an agent for the service of process within the State. It never has performed helicopter operations in Texas or sold any product that reached Texas, never solicited business in Texas, never signed any contract in Texas, never had any employee based there, and never recruited an employee in Texas. In addition, Helicol never has owned real or personal property in Texas and never has maintained an office or establishment there. Helicol has maintained no records in Texas and has no shareholders in that State. None of the respondents or their decedents were domiciled in Texas ... but all of the decedents were hired in Houston by Consorcio/WSH to work on the Petro Peru pipeline project.

Respondents instituted wrongful death actions in the District Court of Harris County, Tex., against Consorcio/WSH, Bell Helicopter Company, and Helicol. Helicol filed special appearances and moved to dismiss the actions for lack of *in personam* jurisdiction over it. The motion was denied. After a consolidated jury trial, judgment was entered against Helicol on a jury verdict of $1,141,200 in favor of respondents.... [The

Texas Supreme Court upheld the trial court.] In ruling that the Texas courts had *in personam* jurisdiction, the Texas Supreme Court first held that the State's long-arm statute reaches as far as the Due Process Clause of the Fourteenth Amendment permits.... Thus, the only question remaining for the court to decide was whether it was consistent with the Due Process Clause for Texas courts to assert *in personam* jurisdiction over Helicol. Ibid.

II

... Due process requirements are satisfied when *in personam* jurisdiction is asserted over a nonresident corporate defendant that has "certain minimum contacts with [the forum] such that the maintenance of the suit does not offend 'traditional notions of fair play and substantial justice.'" International Shoe Co. v. Washington, 326 U.S. 310, 316 ... (1945), ... When a controversy is related to or "arises out of" a defendant's contacts with the forum, the Court has said that a "relationship among the defendant, the forum, and the litigation" is the essential foundation of *in personam* jurisdiction. Shaffer v. Heitner, 433 U.S. 186, 204 ... (1977).

Even when the cause of action does not arise out of or relate to the foreign corporation's activities in the forum State, due process is not offended by a State's subjecting the corporation to its *in personam* jurisdiction when there are sufficient contacts between the State and the foreign corporation. Perkins v. Benguet Consolidated Mining Co., 342 U.S. 437 ... (1952).

All parties to the present case concede that respondents' claims against Helicol did not "arise out of," and are not related to, Helicol's activities within Texas.[10] We thus must explore the nature of Helicol's contacts with the State of Texas to determine whether they constitute the kind of

---

10. See Brief for Respondents 14; Tr. of Oral Arg. 26–27, 30–31. Because the parties have not argued any relationship between the cause of action and Helicol's contacts with the State of Texas, we, contrary to the dissent's implication, assert no "view" with respect to that issue.

The dissent suggests that we have erred in drawing no distinction between controversies that "relate to" a defendant's contacts with a forum and those that "arise out of" such contacts.... This criticism is somewhat puzzling, for the dissent goes on to urge that, for purposes of determining the constitutional validity of an assertion of specific jurisdiction, there really should be no distinction between the two....

We do not address the validity or consequences of such a distinction because the issue has not been presented in this case. Respondents have made no argument that their cause of action either arose out of or is related to Helicol's contacts with the State of Texas. Absent any briefing on the issue, we decline to reach the questions (1) whether the terms "arising out of" and "related to" describe different connections between a cause of action and a defendant's contacts with a forum, and (2) what sort of tie between a cause of action and a defendant's contacts with a forum is necessary to a determination that either connection exists. Nor do we reach the question whether, if the two types of relationship differ, a forum's exercise of personal jurisdiction in a situation where the cause of action "relates to," but does not "arise out of," the defendant's contacts with the forum should be analyzed as an assertion of specific jurisdiction. [Some footnotes omitted. Eds.].

continuous and systematic general business contacts the Court found to exist in *Perkins*. We hold that they do not.

It is undisputed that Helicol does not have a place of business in Texas and never has been licensed to do business in the State. Basically, Helicol's contacts with Texas consisted of sending its chief executive officer to Houston for a contract-negotiation session; accepting into its New York bank account checks drawn on a Houston bank; purchasing helicopters, equipment, and training services from Bell Helicopter for substantial sums; and sending personnel to Bell's facilities in Fort Worth for training.

The one trip to Houston by Helicol's chief executive officer for the purpose of negotiating the transportation-services contract with Consorcio/WSH cannot be described or regarded as a contact of a "continuous and systematic" nature, as *Perkins* described it, see also International Shoe Co. v. Washington, 326 U.S., at 320 . . . and thus cannot support an assertion of *in personam* jurisdiction over Helicol by a Texas court. Similarly, Helicol's acceptance from Consorcio/WSH of checks drawn on a Texas bank is of negligible significance for purposes of determining whether Helicol had sufficient contacts in Texas. There is no indication that Helicol ever requested that the checks be drawn on a Texas bank or that there was any negotiation between Helicol and Consorcio/WSH with respect to the location or identity of the bank on which checks would be drawn. Common sense and everyday experience suggest that, absent unusual circumstances, the bank on which a check is drawn is generally of little consequence to the payee and is a matter left to the discretion of the drawer. Such unilateral activity of another party or a third person is not an appropriate consideration when determining whether a defendant has sufficient contacts with a forum State to justify an assertion of jurisdiction.

The Texas Supreme Court focused on the purchases and the related training trips in finding contacts sufficient to support an assertion of jurisdiction. We do not agree with that assessment, for the Court's opinion in Rosenberg Bros. & Co. v. Curtis Brown Co., 260 U.S. 516 . . . (1923) (Brandeis, J., for a unanimous tribunal), makes clear that purchases and related trips, standing alone, are not a sufficient basis for a State's assertion of jurisdiction.

. . . In accordance with *Rosenberg,* we hold that mere purchases, even if occurring at regular intervals, are not enough to warrant a State's assertion of *in personam* jurisdiction over a nonresident corporation in a cause of action not related to those purchase transactions. Nor can we conclude that the fact that Helicol sent personnel into Texas for training in connection with the purchase of helicopters and equipment in that State in any way enhanced the nature of Helicol's contacts with Texas. The training was a part of the package of goods and services purchased by Helicol from Bell Helicopter. The brief presence of Helicol employees in Texas for the purpose of attending the training sessions is no more a significant contact than were the trips to New York made by the buyer for the retail store in *Rosenberg*. . . .

III

We hold that Helicol's contacts with the State of Texas were insufficient to satisfy the requirements of the Due Process Clause of the Fourteenth Amendment.[13] Accordingly, we reverse the judgment of the Supreme Court of Texas.

It is so ordered.

■ JUSTICE BRENNAN, dissenting....

... I believe that the undisputed contacts in this case between petitioner Helicol and the State of Texas are sufficiently important, and sufficiently related to the underlying cause of action, to make it fair and reasonable for the State to assert personal jurisdiction over Helicol for the wrongful death actions filed by the respondents....

I

The Court expressly limits its decision in this case to "an assertion of general jurisdiction over a foreign defendant." ... Having framed the question in this way, the Court is obliged to address our prior holdings in Perkins v. Benguet Consolidated Mining Co., 342 U.S. 437 ... (1952), and Rosenberg Bros. & Co. v. Curtis Brown Co., 260 U.S. 516 ... (1923). In *Perkins,* the Court considered a State's assertion of general jurisdiction over a foreign corporation that "ha[d] been carrying on ... a continuous and systematic, but limited, part of its general business" in the forum. 342 U.S., at 438.... Under the circumstances of that case, we held that such contacts were constitutionally sufficient "to make it reasonable and just to subject the corporation to the jurisdiction" of that State. Id., at 445 ... (citing *International Shoe,* supra, 326 U.S., at 317–320 ...). Nothing in *Perkins* suggests, however, that such "continuous and systematic" contacts are a necessary minimum before a State may constitutionally assert general jurisdiction over a foreign corporation....

The vast expansion of our national economy during the past several decades has provided the primary rationale for expanding the permissible reach of a State's jurisdiction under the Due Process Clause. By broadening the type and amount of business opportunities available to participants in interstate and foreign commerce, our economy has increased the frequency with which foreign corporations actively pursue commercial transactions throughout the various States. In turn, it has become both necessary and, in my view, desirable to allow the States more leeway in

---

13. As an alternative to traditional minimum-contacts analysis, respondents suggest that the Court hold that the State of Texas had personal jurisdiction over Helicol under a doctrine of "jurisdiction by necessity." See Shaffer v. Heitner, 433 U.S. 186, 211, n. 37 (1977). We conclude, however, that respondents failed to carry their burden of showing that all three defendants could not be sued together in a single forum. It is not clear from the record, for example, whether suit could have been brought against all three defendants in either Colombia or Peru. We decline to consider adoption of a doctrine of jurisdiction by necessity—a potentially far-reaching modification of existing law—in the absence of a more complete record.

bringing the activities of these nonresident corporations within the scope of their respective jurisdictions....

Moreover, this "trend ... toward expanding the permissible scope of state jurisdiction over foreign corporations and other nonresidents," *McGee,* supra, 355 U.S., at 222, ... is entirely consistent with the "traditional notions of fair play and substantial justice," *International Shoe,* supra, 326 U.S., at 316 ... that control our inquiry under the Due Process Clause. As active participants in interstate and foreign commerce take advantage of the economic benefits and opportunities offered by the various States, it is only fair and reasonable to subject them to the obligations that may be imposed by those jurisdictions. And chief among the obligations that a nonresident corporation should expect to fulfill is amenability to suit in any forum that is significantly affected by the corporation's commercial activities.

As a foreign corporation that has actively and purposefully engaged in numerous and frequent commercial transactions in the State of Texas, Helicol clearly falls within the category of nonresident defendants that may be subject to that forum's general jurisdiction.... Taken together, [the defendant's many] contacts demonstrate that Helicol obtained numerous benefits from its transaction of business in Texas. In turn, it is eminently fair and reasonable to expect Helicol to face the obligations that attach to its participation in such commercial transactions. Accordingly, on the basis of continuous commercial contacts with the forum, I would conclude that the Due Process Clause allows the State of Texas to assert general jurisdiction over petitioner Helicol.

II

The Court also fails to distinguish the legal principles that controlled our prior decisions in *Perkins* and *Rosenberg.* In particular, the contacts between petitioner Helicol and the State of Texas, unlike the contacts between the defendant and the forum in each of those cases, are significantly related to the cause of action alleged in the original suit filed by the respondents. Accordingly, in my view, it is both fair and reasonable for the Texas courts to assert specific jurisdiction over Helicol in this case.

By asserting that the present case does not implicate the specific jurisdiction of the Texas courts, ... the Court necessarily removes its decision from the reality of the actual facts presented for our consideration. Moreover, the Court refuses to consider any distinction between contacts that are "related to" the underlying cause of action and contacts that "give rise" to the underlying cause of action. In my view, however, there is a substantial difference between these two standards for asserting specific jurisdiction. Thus, although I agree that the respondents' cause of action did not formally "arise out of" specific activities initiated by Helicol in the State of Texas, I believe that the wrongful death claim filed by the respondents is significantly related to the undisputed contacts between Helicol and the forum. On that basis, I would conclude that the Due

Process Clause allows the Texas courts to assert specific jurisdiction over this particular action.

The wrongful death action filed by the respondents was premised on a fatal helicopter crash that occurred in Peru. Helicol was joined as a defendant in the lawsuit because it provided transportation services, including the particular helicopter and pilot involved in the crash, to the joint venture that employed the decedents. Specifically, the respondents claimed in their original complaint that "Helicol is ... legally responsible for its own negligence through its pilot employee." ... Viewed in light of these allegations, the contacts between Helicol and the State of Texas are directly and significantly related to the underlying claim filed by the respondents. The negotiations that took place in Texas led to the contract in which Helicol agreed to provide the precise transportation services that were being used at the time of the crash. Moreover, the helicopter involved in the crash was purchased by Helicol in Texas, and the pilot whose negligence was alleged to have caused the crash was actually trained in Texas.... This is simply not a case, therefore, in which a state court has asserted jurisdiction over a nonresident defendant on the basis of wholly unrelated contacts with the forum. Rather, the contacts between Helicol and the forum are directly related to the negligence that was alleged in the respondents' original complaint. Because Helicol should have expected to be amenable to suit in the Texas courts for claims directly related to these contacts, it is fair and reasonable to allow the assertion of jurisdiction in this case....

Limiting the specific jurisdiction of a forum to cases in which the cause of action formally arose out of the defendant's contacts with the State would subject constitutional standards under the Due Process Clause to the vagaries of the substantive law or pleading requirements of each State. For example, the complaint filed against Helicol in this case alleged negligence based on pilot error. Even though the pilot was trained in Texas, the Court assumes that the Texas courts may not assert jurisdiction over the suit because the cause of action "did not 'arise out of,' and [is] not related to," that training.... If, however, the applicable substantive law required that negligent training of the pilot was a necessary element of a cause of action for pilot error, or if the respondents had simply added an allegation of negligence in the training provided for the Helicol pilot, then presumably the Court would concede that the specific jurisdiction of the Texas courts was applicable.

Our interpretation of the Due Process Clause has never been so dependent upon the applicable substantive law or the State's formal pleading requirements. At least since *International Shoe,* supra, the principal focus when determining whether a forum may constitutionally assert jurisdiction over a nonresident defendant has been on fairness and reasonableness to the defendant. To this extent, a court's specific jurisdiction should be applicable whenever the cause of action arises out of *or* relates to the contacts between the defendant and the forum. . . . I would affirm the judgment of the Supreme Court of Texas.

BRYANT V. FINNISH NAT. AIRLINE, 15 N.Y.2d 426, 260 N.Y.S.2d 625, 208 N.E.2d 439 (1965): A Finnish airline was held subject to jurisdiction in a New York action by a New York resident who was injured in Paris by the alleged negligence of the airline, on the ground that it was "doing business" in New York. Defendant had not qualified in New York; had no American stockholders, directors or officers; operated no aircraft in the United States and sold no tickets in New York. Its activities in New York were unrelated to the plaintiff's cause of action, consisting of receiving reservations for travel in Europe, transmitting information and publicizing and advertising defendant's European services.

NOTES

1. In *Helicopteros*, the Supreme Court adopts the distinction between "general" and "specific" jurisdiction which was implicit in such earlier decisions as *World–Wide Volkswagen, Kulko* (p. 63, supra), *Keeton* (p. 78, supra), and *Burger King* (p. 76, supra). The distinction is particularly sharp if "specific" jurisdiction requires that the claim "arise out of" the forum contact. The distinction is more fluid if, as Justice Brennan writes, a state may assert jurisdiction if the claim "relates" to the defendant's forum activities.

A sharp distinction between general and specific jurisdiction also may not take sufficient account of the way business is done. Suppose that a foreign car manufacturer has its principal U.S. establishment in California. It has divided the United States into regions. Each regional establishment supervises and directs retail outlets in a number of states. New Jersey parties, while vacationing in Florida, purchase a car from a local retailer. Because of a defect in the automobile, the purchasers are injured in an accident in North Carolina on their trip home. General jurisdiction presumably exists at the manufacturer's California U.S. headquarters. Specific jurisdiction over the same defendant will exist where the accident occurred, just as in *World–Wide Volkswagen* jurisdiction existed in Oklahoma over the manufacturer and the principal importer. Assuming, however, that the accident occurred neither in New Jersey nor in New York and that suit at the place of the accident or in California would be inconvenient, would there be jurisdiction over the manufacturer in the New York regional center? Arguably, New York is another "principal place of business," in that the defendant carries on "continuous and systematic" business there. Perkins v. Benquet Consolidated Mining Co., p. 93, supra. Would the defendant also be subject to jurisdiction in New Jersey on the theory that, having structured its business activity in the United States in a regional manner, the foreign enterprise should be subject to general jurisdiction not only at its headquarters and at the place where an office doing "continuous and systematic" business is physically located but also in any state of the *region* which it serves? For previous references to a "national contacts"-approach to jurisdiction, see supra p. 89.

2. In *Helicopteros*, Justice Blackmun relied on the U.S. Supreme Court's decision in *Rosenberg* (260 U.S. 516 (1923), supra p. 97). That decision had been urged upon the Court by the United States in its brief as amicus curiae. In *Rosenberg*,

the Court had held that the forum had no jurisdiction over a defendant, in default for the purchase price of goods ordered in person from the seller in the forum state, because the defendant corporation was not "present" in the forum at the time of suit. *Rosenberg* was decided twenty-two years before *International Shoe,* that decision refers to it (326 U.S. 310, 319) (1945), but also had not yet—see supra p. 53, Note 2—recognized and accepted the general/specific-jurisdiction dichotomy. In view of the latter, is *Rosenberg* authority for anything, under modern law, for fact situations such as in *Helicopteros?* See Weintraub, A Map Out of the Personal Jurisdiction Labyrinth, 28 U.C.Davis L.Rev. 531, 537–38 (1995).

3. The Bryant case goes far, perhaps too far, in allowing personal jurisdiction over a foreign corporation based on unrelated activities in the forum. Will jurisdiction be upheld on lesser contacts when an American plaintiff sues and the alternative forum is a foreign country? See Footnote 13 in the Supreme Court's decision in *Helicopteros,* p. 94, supra.

4. In Lee v. Walworth Valve Company, 482 F.2d 297 (4th Cir.1973), the court held that the federal district court of South Carolina had jurisdiction over an out-of-state manufacturer in a suit to recover for a wrongful death on the high seas which resulted from the rupture of a steam valve on a U.S. naval vessel. The defendant manufacturer maintained no place of business in South Carolina but solicited a considerable number of orders there through traveling salesmen. The decedent and his wife were both domiciled in the state. The court said: "The difficulty . . . arises out of the fact that the cause of action did not arise out of any of [the defendant's] activity in South Carolina. The cause of action did not even arise in that State, for the injury occurred on the high seas . . . . [T]here probably are only two states in the United States with any interest in the controversy, the state of [the defendant's incorporation] and South Carolina. . . . The interest of South Carolina is substantial, however, for it has a paternal interest in the recovery by one of its citizens of appropriate compensation . . . . Our holding in *Ratliff* [444 F.2d 745 (4th Cir.1971), cert. denied 404 U.S. 948 (1971)] was dictated by the fact that South Carolina had no interest or connection with the controversy . . . and, hence, there were no countervailing considerations of fairness to be placed in the scales when weighing the substantiality of the defendant's contacts." Is this decision valid after *World–Wide Volkswagen* and *Helicopteros?* See also de Reyes v. Marine Management and Consulting, Ltd., 586 So.2d 103 (La.1991) (Hong Kong company had continuous and systematic contacts with Louisiana through its New Orleans office, sufficient to support general jurisdiction) and United Rope Distributors, Inc. v. Kimberly Line, 785 F.Supp. 446 (S.D.N.Y.1992) (large New York bank account, though related to the claim and therefore perhaps sufficient for specific jurisdiction, held to satisfy New York's "doing business" statute for purposes of general jurisdiction).

In Carnival Cruise Lines, Inc. v. Shute, 499 U.S. 585 (1991), considered infra at p. 172, the Ninth Circuit held that "a tort can arise from prior business solicitation in the forum state." 897 F.2d 377, 384 (9th Cir.1990). It rejected the "stringent standard of causation" (*id.,* at 383) found in opinions of the First, Second, and Eighth Circuits and instead cited with approval decisions that "apply a 'but for' test of causality" (*id.*). State court decisions are similarly split. See Weintraub, A Map out of the Personal Jurisdiction Labyrinth, 28 U.C.Davis L.Rev. 531, 543 (1995). If limited (i.e., not "systematic and continuous") business solicitation furnishes the basis for jurisdiction in tort for injuries suffered elsewhere, does the distinction between specific and general jurisdiction become blurred? Should there be any such distinction or is it really only basic fairness that due process commands? See further infra at p. 119. See also infra chapter 4, at p. 174.

5. When we considered specific jurisdiction, especially in tort, the assertion of jurisdiction by states of the European Union seemed more extensive because not limited by notions of "availment" or "foreseeability". Supra p. 532. At the same time, European law has nothing comparable to our *general* jurisdiction on the basis of "doing business", no matter how "systematic and continuous" (in the sense of *Perkins,* supra p. 93) such business activity was. Under Art. 2 of the Brussels Convention, general jurisdiction exists *only* at the domicile of a person. For a legal person, i.e. a corporation (Art. 52), "domicile" is what national law determines it to be. In most countries, it is the place of the corporate headquarters. In some countries (those of the common law countries and in The Netherlands) it is the state of incorporation. In all other cases, the plaintiff must make out a case of specific jurisdiction, i.e. forum-relatedness (commission of a tort [Art. 5 No. 3, supra p. 88], performance of a contractual obligation [Art. 1 No. 1, supra p. 544], and others). The specific-jurisdiction emphasis of the Convention is heightened by the provision that a branch is subject only for claims arising from *its* activities (see Art. 5, No. 5 Brussels Convention). Separateness between parent and subsidiary under corporate law thus is also observed in the law of jurisdiction. The wider reach of American law on the basis of doing business is a source of conflict between the United States and Europe: see infra p. 66. The narrower European approach makes an exception from the principle of separateness of the main company and its branches in favor of consumers: if the consumer's "contracting party" has no seat (principal place of business) in the European Union (i.e., is a non-Member State company), but maintains an agency or other representation within the EU, it will be deemed to be "domiciled" there for purposes of jurisdiction. Brussels Convention, Art. 13(2). This is clearly a case of "piercing of the corporate veil" (see infra p. 105) in limited, specified circumstances. But these are narrower than a theory of general jurisdiction based on "systematic and continuous" (but not claim-related) business. For a European study, see H. Müller, Die Gerichtspflichtigkeit wegen "doing business" (1992). See further infra p. 110.

6. See also the exchange of views between Professors Brilmayer and Twitchell in 1980 Sup.Ct.Rev. 77, 101 Harv.L.Rev. 610, 1444, 1465 (1988).

In re DES Cases, 789 F.Supp. 552 (E.D.N.Y.1992), presents a far reaching and novel approach to judicial jurisdiction. New York bases the substantive liability in products liability on the defendant's national market share. In *DES Cases,* an action against manufacturers of the drug DES, it was accepted that the products of one of the defendants had never reached New York and could not have injured the New York plaintiffs. The court upheld its jurisdiction by resorting to the market share approach of substantive law: "Defendants' engagement in the national DES industry alerted them to the fact that their conduct in marketing generic DES in one part of the country would have economic and trade flow consequences in every other part, including New York." 789 F.Supp. at 572. Due process is satisfied in mass tort cases, in these circumstances, "if the forum state has an appreciable interest in the litigation." Id. at 587. How does this case differ from *Nelson* page 87, supra? From the hypothetical in Note (1), second paragraph, on page 101? Note that the national market share of the one defendant mentioned above amounted to 0.05%. Is this fact relevant? The court also noted that, if plaintiffs were forced to sue in another forum, the alternative court might not apply New York's market-share rule of substantive liability to injuries suffered in a state in which the defendant had not actually marketed its product: plaintiffs therefore might not have a remedy against that particular defendant. Should that make a difference? Consider the U.S. Supreme Court's statement in footnote 13 in *Helicopteros* (at page 98 supra) and its statement about possible differences in the law that another forum might apply, uttered in the context of forum non conveniens dismissals (*Piper,* page 184 infra).

It is often a question of some importance whether one member of a corporate family can be reached through another. In the typical case, the goal will be to reach an out-of-state parent corporation of an in-state subsidiary. If the claim relates to the subsidiary's activities, the case is one of *vicarious liability,* and the question becomes what standards should be applied to hold the parent liable, for instance, for the tortious conduct of the subsidiary. An example is the Bhopal disaster case, infra at p. 185. The Indian Union Carbide subsidiary, where the disaster had occurred, was capital-poor. Suit against Union Carbide Corporation, the parent, provided the solvent parent. See Note, Developments in the Law—International Environmental Law, 104 Harv.L.Rev. 1484, 1620 (1991); Lowenfeld, International Litigation and Arbitration 276 (1993). American-owned *maquiladoras,* shell corporations in Mexico for the local assembly of goods from American-supplied components, is another example. See Vaznaugh, Extraterritorial Jurisdiction—Environmental Muscle for the North American Trade Agreement, 17 Hastings Int'l & Comp.L.Rev. 207 (1993). "Enterprise theory" has long suggested that traditional principles of corporate separateness should yield to the needs of compensation when substantive liability is at stake. See Blumberg, The Corporate Personality in American Law, 38 Am.J.Comp.L. 49, 63–69 (Supplement 1990). The amount of control exercised by the parent over the subsidiary might be an appropriate standard for determining vicarious liability. See My Bread Baking Co. v. Cumberland Farms, Inc., 233 N.E.2d 748, 752 (Mass.1968). In the case of the tanker *M/V Amoco Cadiz,* whose breakup caused a vast oil spill off the coast of France, the court wrote: "As an integrated multinational corporation . . . , Standard is responsible for the tortious acts of its wholly owned subsidiaries and instrumentalities. . . ." In re Oil Spill by the Amoco Cadiz off the Coast of France on March 16, 1978, 1984 AMC 2123, 2194 (N.D.Ill.1984). For further discussion and illustrations, see Lowenfeld, International Litigation and the Quest for Reasonableness—General Course on Private International Law, Hague Academy, 245 Collected Courses 9, 129–152 (1994–I).

To reach the out-of-state parent, whether on claims relating to the subsidiary (vicarious liability) or for claims against itself, there must be *jurisdiction* over it. Assume that the case involves a claim against an out-of-state manufacturer of a product which it distributes through separately incorporated, but often wholly-owned subsidiaries. When the product causes injury in the forum state, is the manufacturer subject to jurisdiction there? The discussion concerning "stream-of-commerce" based jurisdiction suggests that there is jurisdiction over the manufacturer, and that the presence of the subsidiary is not a necessary prerequisite for this conclusion. But what if the stream-of-commerce theory is not followed? Or what about general jurisdiction? In these circumstances, the question becomes important whether the activities of the local subsidiary can be attributed to the parent and the latter be subjected to jurisdiction on the basis of those contacts. The United States Supreme Court wrote in the *Schlunk* case, infra at p. 105: "In the only cases in which it has considered the question, this Court held that the activities of a subsidiary are not necessarily enough to render a parent subject to a court's jurisdiction, for service of process or otherwise. Cannon Mfg. Co. v. Cudahy Packing Co., 267 U.S. 333, 336–337 (1925)," *Schlunk,* 486 U.S. 694, 705 n. 1 (1988). *Cannon* and many other cases addressed the question whether mere stock ownership, even 100%, by the parent of the subsidiary subjected the former to jurisdiction. See also Restatement Second, Conflict of Laws § 52, comment *b.* But what about the activities of the subsidiary that it undertakes for and on behalf of the parent, perhaps even at its direction? What does "not necessarily" in *Cannon* mean? The court in Gallagher v. Mazda Motor of America, 781 F.Supp. 1079 (E.D.Pa.1992), reviewed the case law and adopted a broadly phrased test: "jurisdictional contacts of [a] subsidiary ... should be imputed to ... [the] parent, for purposes of service of process when [the] subsidiary is engaged in functions that, but for the existence of [the] subsidiary, [the] parent would have to undertake."

The foregoing comments do not differentiate, and neither does the U.S. Supreme Court in its n. 1 in the *Schlunk* decision, infra at p. 105, between the standard appropriate for holding the parent liable for the subsidiary's actions and for attributing the subsidiary's forum standards to the parent for purposes of suing the parent for its wrongs. Is the standard necessarily the same? Does it depend on whether the issue is specific or general jurisdiction?

When courts subject the out-of-state parent to jurisdiction in the state in which the subsidiary acts or has acted, they may do so on agency principles or by disregarding the corporate separateness ("piercing the corporate veil"). If, as a result, of "piercing", the two are the same, service on the subsidiary is service on "the" company.

The Hague Convention on the Service Abroad of Judicial and Extrajudicial Documents in Civil and Commercial Matters, to which the United States is a party (20 U.S.T. 361, 28 U.S.C.A. Rule 4, provides specific and exclusive procedures for the transmission of documents to parties in foreign states. Does the Convention affect the problems discussed above?

Volkswagenwerk Aktiengesellschaft v. Schlunk

Supreme Court of the United States, 1988.
486 U.S. 694, 108 S.Ct. 2104, 100 L.Ed.2d 722.

■ JUSTICE O'CONNOR delivered the opinion of the Court....

I

The parents of respondent Herwig Schlunk were killed in an automobile accident in 1983. Schlunk filed a wrongful death action on their behalf in the Circuit Court of Cook County, Illinois. Schlunk alleged that Volkswagen of America, Inc. (VWoA) had designed and sold the automobile that his parents were driving, and that defects in the automobile caused or contributed to their deaths.... Schlunk successfully served his complaint on VWoA, and VWoA filed an answer denying that it had designed or assembled the automobile in question. Schlunk then amended the complaint to add as a defendant Volkswagen Aktiengesellschaft (VWAG), which is the petitioner here. VWAG, a corporation established under the laws of the Federal Republic of Germany, has its place of business in that country. VWoA is a wholly-owned subsidiary of VWAG. Schlunk attempted to serve his amended complaint on VWAG by serving VWoA as VWAG's agent.

VWAG filed a special and limited appearance for the purpose of quashing service. VWAG asserted that it could be served only in accordance with the Hague Service Convention, and that Schlunk had not complied with the Convention's requirements. The Circuit Court denied VWAG's motion. It first observed that VWoA is registered to do business in Illinois and has a registered agent for receipt of process in Illinois. The Court then reasoned that VWoA and VWAG are so closely related that VWoA is VWAG's agent for service of process as a matter of law, notwithstanding VWAG's failure or refusal to appoint VWoA formally as an agent. The court relied on the facts that VWoA is a wholly-owned subsidiary of VWAG, that a majority of the members of the board of directors of VWoA are members of the board of directors of VWAG, and that VWoA is by contract the exclusive importer and distributor of VWAG products sold in the United States. The court concluded that, because service was accomplished within the United States, the Hague Service Convention did not apply.... [The Illinois Appellate Court affirmed, and the Illinois Supreme Court denied leave to appeal.]

We granted certiorari to address this issue ... which has given rise to disagreement among the lower courts....

II

The Hague Service Convention is a multilateral treaty ... Thirty-two countries, including the United States and the Federal Republic of Germany, have ratified or acceded to the Convention....

The primary innovation of the Convention is that it requires each state to establish a central authority to receive requests for service of documents from other countries. Once a central authority receives a request in the proper form, it must serve the documents by a method prescribed by the internal law of the receiving state or by a method designated by the requester and compatible with that law....

Article 1 defines the scope of the Convention, which is the subject of controversy in this case. It says: "The present Convention shall apply in all cases, in civil or commercial matters, where there is occasion to transmit a judicial or extrajudicial document for service abroad." ... By virtue of the Supremacy Clause, U.S. Const., Art. VI, the Convention preempts inconsistent methods of service prescribed by state law in all cases to which it applies. Schlunk does not purport to have served his complaint on VWAG in accordance with the Convention. Therefore, if service of process in this case falls within Article 1 of the Convention, the trial court should have granted VWAG's motion to quash....

The Convention does not specify the circumstances in which there is "occasion to transmit" a complaint "for service abroad." But at least the term "service of process" has a well-established technical meaning. Service of process refers to a formal delivery of documents that is legally sufficient to charge the defendant with notice of a pending action.... The legal sufficiency of a formal delivery of documents must be measured against some standard. The Convention does not prescribe a standard, so we almost necessarily must refer to the internal law of the forum state. If the internal law of the forum state defines the applicable method of serving process as requiring the transmittal of documents abroad, then the Hague Service Convention applies....

VWAG correctly maintains that the Convention also aims to ensure that there will be adequate notice in cases in which there is occasion to serve process abroad. Thus compliance with the Convention is mandatory in all cases to which it applies.... Our interpretation of the Convention does not necessarily advance this particular objective, inasmuch as it makes recourse to the Convention's means of service dependent on the forum's internal law. But we do not think that this country, or any other country, will draft its internal laws deliberately so as to circumvent the Convention in cases in which it would be appropriate to transmit judicial documents for service abroad. For example, there has been no question in this country of excepting foreign nationals from the protection of our Due Process Clause. Under that Clause, foreign nationals are assured of either personal service, which typically will require service abroad and trigger the Convention, or substituted service that provides "notice reasonably calculated, under all the circumstances, to apprise interested parties of the pendency of the action and afford them an opportunity to present their objections." Mullane v. Central Hanover Bank & Trust Co., 339 U.S. 306 (1950).[1]

Furthermore, nothing that we say today prevents compliance with the Convention even when the internal law of the forum does not so require. The Convention provides simple and certain means by which to serve process on a foreign national. Those who eschew its procedures risk discovering that the forum's internal law required transmittal of documents for service abroad, and that the Convention therefore provided the exclusive means of valid service. In addition, parties that comply with the Convention ultimately may find it easier to enforce their judgments abroad.... For these reasons, we anticipate that parties may resort to the Convention voluntarily, even in cases that fall outside the scope of its mandatory application.

III

In this case, the Illinois long-arm statute authorized Schlunk to serve VWAG by substituted service on VWoA, without sending documents to Germany.... VWAG has not petitioned for review of the Illinois Appellate Court's holding that service was proper as a matter of Illinois law. VWAG contends, however, that service on VWAG was not complete until VWoA

---

1. The concurrence believes that our interpretation does not adequately guarantee timely notice, which it denominates the "primary" purpose of the Convention, albeit without authority. The concurrence instead proposes to impute a substantive standard to the words, "service abroad." Evidently, a method of service would be deemed to be "service abroad" within the meaning of Article 1 if it does not provide notice to the recipient "in due time." This due process notion cannot be squared with the plain meaning of the words, "service abroad." The contours of the concurrence's substantive standard are not defined and we note that it would create some uncertainty even on the facts of this case. If the substantive standard tracks the Due Process Clause of the Fourteenth Amendment, it is not self-evident that substituted service on a subsidiary is sufficient with respect to the parent. In the only cases in which it has considered the question, this Court held that the activities of a subsidiary are not necessarily enough to render a parent subject to a court's jurisdiction, for service of process or otherwise. Cannon Mfg. Co. v. Cudahy Packing Co., 267 U.S. 333, 336–337 (1925)....

transmitted the complaint to VWAG in Germany. According to VWAG, this transmission constituted service abroad under the Hague Service Convention. . . .

We reject this argument. Where service on a domestic agent is valid and complete under both state law and the Due Process Clause, our inquiry ends and the Convention has no further implications. . . .

Affirmed.

[Justice Brennan concurred in the judgment in an opinion joined by Justices Marshall and Blackmun.] Until the Convention was implemented, the contracting nations followed widely divergent practices for serving judicial documents across international borders, some of which did not ensure any notice, much less timely notice, and therefore often produced unfair default judgments. See generally International Co–Operation in Litigation: Europe (H. Smit ed. 1965); 3 1965 Conférence de la Haye de Droit International Privé, Actes et Documents de la Dixième Session (Notification) 11–12 (1965) (hereinafter 3 Actes et Documents). Particularly controversial was a procedure, common among civil-law countries, called *"notification au parquet,"* which permitted delivery of process to a local official who was then ordinarily supposed to transmit the document abroad through diplomatic or other channels. See S.Exec.Rep. No. 6, 90th Cong., 1st Sess., 11–12, 14–16 (1967) (S.Exec.Rep. No. 6); S.Doc. C, 90th Cong., 1st Sess., 5–6, 21 (1967) (S.Exec.Doc. C). Typically, service was deemed complete upon delivery of the document to the official whether or not the official succeeded in transmitting it to the defendant and whether or not the defendant otherwise received notice of the pending lawsuit.[1]

The United States delegation to the Convention objected to *notification au parquet* as inconsistent with "the requirements of 'due process of law' under the Federal Constitution." 3 Actes et Documents 128 (citations omitted). . . .

In response to this and other concerns, the Convention prescribes the exclusive means for service of process emanating from one contracting nation and culminating in another. As the Court observes, the Convention applies only when the document is to be "transmit[ted] . . . for service

---

1. The head of the United States delegation to the Convention described *notification au parquet* as follows:

> "This is a system which permits the entry of judgments in personam by default against a nonresident defendant without requiring adequate notice. There is also no real right to move to open the default judgment or to appeal, because the time to move to open judgment or to appeal will generally have expired before the defendant finds out about the judgment.
>
> "Under this system of service, the process-server simply delivers a copy of the writ to a public official's office. The time for answer begins to run immediately. Some effort is supposed to be made through the Foreign Office and through diplomatic channels to give the defendant notice, but failure to do this has no effect on the validity of the service. . . .
>
> "There are no . . . limitations and protections [comparable to due process or personal jurisdiction] under the *notification au parquet* system. Here jurisdiction lies merely if the plaintiff is a local national; nothing more is needed." S.Exec.Rep. No. 6, at 11–12 (statement by Philip W. Amram).

abroad"; it covers not every transmission of judicial documents abroad, but only those transmissions abroad that constitute formal "service." See *ante,* at 700. It is common ground that the Convention governs when the procedure prescribed by the internal law of the forum nation or state provides that service is not complete until the document is transmitted abroad. That is not to say, however, as does the Court, that the forum nation may designate any type of service "domestic" and thereby avoid application of the Convention.

Admittedly, as the Court points out, *ibid.,* the Convention's language does not prescribe a precise standard to distinguish between "domestic" service and "service abroad." But the Court's solution leaves contracting nations free to ignore its terms entirely, converting its command into exhortation. Under the Court's analysis, for example, a forum nation could prescribe direct mail service to any foreigner and deem service effective upon deposit in the mailbox, or could arbitrarily designate a domestic agent for any foreign defendant and deem service complete upon receipt domestically by the agent even though there is little likelihood that service would ever reach the defendant. In fact, so far as I can tell, the Court's interpretation permits any contracting nation to revive *notification au parquet* so long as the nation's internal law deems service complete domestically, but cf. *ante,* at 704, even though, as the Court concedes, "such methods of service are the least likely to provide a defendant with actual notice," and even though "[t]here is no question but that the Conference wanted to eliminate *notification au parquet,*" *ante,* at 703 (citation omitted)....

The negotiating history and the uniform interpretation announced by our own negotiators confirm that the Convention limits a forum's ability to deem service "domestic," thereby avoiding the Convention's terms. Admittedly, the Convention does not precisely define the contours. But that imprecision does not absolve us of our responsibility to apply the Convention mandatorily, any more than imprecision permits us to discard the words "due process of law," U.S. Const., Amdt. 14, § 1. And however difficult it might be in some circumstances to discern the Convention's precise limits, it is remarkably easy to conclude that the Convention does not prohibit the type of service at issue here. Service on a wholly owned, closely controlled subsidiary is reasonably calculated to reach the parent "in due time" as the Convention requires.... That is, in fact, what our own Due Process Clause requires, see Mullane v. Central Hanover Bank & Trust Co., 339 U.S. 306, 314–315 (1950), and since long before the Convention's implementation our law has permitted such service, see, e.g., Perkins v. Benguet Consolidated Mining Co., 342 U.S. 437, 444–445 (1952); ... This is significant because our own negotiators made clear to the Senate their understanding that the Convention would require no major changes in federal or state service-of-process rules. Thus, it is unsurprising that nothing in the negotiating history suggests that the contracting nations were dissatisfied with the practice at issue here, of which they were surely aware, much less that they intended to abolish it like they intended to abolish *notification au parquet.* And since notice served on a wholly owned domestic subsidiary is infinitely more likely to reach the foreign parent's attention than was notice served *au parquet* (or by any other procedure that the negotiators singled out for criticism) there is no reason to interpret the Convention to bar it....

NOTES

1. In United Electrical, Radio & Machine Workers v. 163 Pleasant Street Corp., 960 F.2d 1080 (1st Cir.1992), the court declined to pierce the corporate veil between the Scottish parent and its Massachusetts subsidiary for jurisdictional purposes when plaintiffs had not offered any proof that the separate corporations had been established for an improper purpose or that they had failed to maintain their separate corporate identities. In Vermeulen v. Renault, U.S.A., Inc., 965 F.2d 1014 (11th Cir.1992), the court employed an agency theory to uphold Georgia's assertion of jurisdiction over the French defendant car manufacturer on the basis of the activities of its wholly-owned distributor. The court held that the defendant purposefully availed itself of the American market by specifically designing cars for it, advertising in it, and setting the distribution system. However, after further appeals, the court concluded that jurisdiction—both subject matter and personal—were governed by a federal statute, the Foreign Sovereign Immunities Act, and that both kinds of jurisdiction existed. See Vermeulen v. Renault, U.S.A., Inc., 975 F.2d 746 (11th Cir.1992) and Vermeulen v. Renault, U.S.A., Inc., 985 F.2d 1534 (11th Cir.1993).

2. The *Schlunk* decision is equally relevant for an American defendant served by a foreign plaintiff. See Ackermann v. Levine, 788 F.2d 830 (2d Cir.1986) (enforcing a German default judgment against a U.S. defendant over the latter's objection to service of process).

3. See also Voxman, Jurisdiction over a Parent Corporation in Its Subsidiary's State of Incorporation, 141 U.Pa.L.Rev. 327 (1992).

4. The Brussels Convention of the European Union addresses only one aspect of the problems considered here: If litigation relates to the activities of a branch, agency or other establishment, (special) jurisdiction exists in the courts of the place where such a branch is located. Art. 5 No. 5. Recall that there is no general jurisdiction under European law for "systematic and continuous" doing of business. Supra p. 103. Except for stream-of-commerce cases, in which the parent can be reached by means of the tort provisions, jurisdiction over the out-of-state parent in the state of the subsidiary in other cases would therefore require analytically that the two be regarded as one (piercing of the corporate veil) and that the parent/subsidiary then be subjected to specific jurisdiction for its/their activity. Disregard of the separate personality of parent and subsidiary for *jurisdictional* purposes is generally not part of European law. See also Hofstetter, Parent Responsibility for Subsidiary Corporations: Evaluating European Trends, 39 Int'l & Comp.L.Q. 576 (1990).

5. The 1993 amendments to the Federal Rules of Civil Procedure made some changes with respect to the manner of "service upon an individual ... in a place not within any judicial district of the United States." Rule 4(f) now provides in part that such service may be effected:

> (1) by any internationally agreed means reasonably calculated to give notice, such as those authorized by the Hague Convention ...; or

(2) [in the manner prescribed by foreign law or by foreign authorities or, unless prohibited by foreign law, by personal delivery or by mail]; or

(3) by other means not prohibited by international agreement as may be directed by the court.

Does the new version of the Rule have any effect on the problems raised in *Schlunk*?

NOTE ON PARTNERSHIPS AND ASSOCIATIONS

Extraterritorial enforcement of in personam judgments against partnerships and other unincorporated associations raises a few special points stemming from historical oddities in local law treatment of those entities. One question, for example, is whether personal service upon a partner gives jurisdiction to bind partnership property outside the state. If the firm were owned by an individual, his presence in the state would be a sufficient basis for a valid personal judgment that could be enforced against his firm's property elsewhere. On the other hand, if the nonresident firm were incorporated, mere presence on personal business of a shareholder, officer, or director would not furnish a basis for an in personam judgment against the corporation. See Riverside & Dan River Cotton Mills v. Menefee, 237 U.S. 189 (1915); Goldey v. Morning News of New Haven, 156 U.S. 518 (1895). Shall a partnership be treated as amenable in the manner of an individual, or not amenable by analogy to a corporation? Further, under what circumstances may the members of a partnership be bound as to their personal property by a judgment against the firm?

RESTATEMENT, SECOND, CONFLICT OF LAWS: *

§ 40. Partnerships or Other Unincorporated Associations

(1) A state in which a partnership or other unincorporated association is subject to suit in the firm or common name has power to exercise judicial jurisdiction over the partnership or association if under the circumstances it could exercise judicial jurisdiction over an individual ....

(2) A valid judgment rendered against a partnership or association is a binding adjudication as to the liability of the partnership or association with respect to its assets in every state.

Comment: ...

d. Effect of judgment. A valid judgment rendered against a partnership or other unincorporated association under the circumstances stated in Subsection (1) will be recognized and enforced in other states, and, as between States of the United States, this result is required by full faith and credit. An action to enforce the judgment may be maintained against the partnership or association in another state, provided that it is subject to the

---

* Quoted with the permission of the copyright owner, The American Law Institute.

judicial jurisdiction of that state and by the local law of that state may be sued in its firm or common name. If by the local law of the second state the partnership or association is not subject to suit in its firm or common name, the action to enforce the judgment may be maintained against the members individually, but recovery will be permitted to be had only out of firm, as opposed to individual, property.

NOTES

1. In Sugg v. Thornton, 132 U.S. 524 (1889), personal service was had upon one member of a partnership and notice as provided by the state statute was sent to the other partner outside the state. The judgment rendered, purporting to be a personal judgment only against the partner personally served and a judgment against "the partnership as a distinct legal entity", was upheld against a due process attack. So far as the non-appearing partner who received only statutory service was concerned, the judgment "bound the firm assets only, and could not be proceeded on by execution against his individual property."

2. See Scoles and Hay, Conflict of Laws § 9.1 (2d ed. 1992). In England, service on one partner in England or abroad under Order 11, rule 1(1) of the Supreme Court, as amended, is good service on absent partners. North and Fawcett, Cheshire & North's Private International Law 187–88 (12th ed. 1992).

CONTACTS AND FAIRNESS REVISITED: THE CASE OF "TRANSIENT JURISDICTION"

Burnham v. Superior Court of California

Supreme Court of the United States, 1990.
495 U.S. 604, 110 S.Ct. 2105, 109 L.Ed.2d 631.

■ JUSTICE SCALIA announced the judgment of the Court.*

The question presented is whether the Due Process Clause of the Fourteenth Amendment denies California courts jurisdiction over a nonresident, who was personally served with process while temporarily in that State, in a suit unrelated to his activities in the State.

I

Petitioner Dennis Burnham married Francie Burnham in 1976, in West Virginia. In 1977 the couple moved to New Jersey, where their two children were born. In July 1987 the Burnhams decided to separate. They agreed that Mrs. Burnham, who intended to move to California, would take custody of the children. Shortly before Mrs. Burnham departed for California that same month, she and petitioner agreed that she would file for divorce on grounds of "irreconcilable differences."

In October 1987, petitioner filed for divorce in New Jersey state court on grounds of "desertion." Petitioner did not, however, obtain an issuance of summons against his wife, and did not attempt to serve her with process.

* Footnotes omitted.

Mrs. Burnham, after unsuccessfully demanding that petitioner adhere to their prior agreement to submit to an "irreconcilable differences" divorce, brought suit for divorce in California state court in early January 1988.

In late January, petitioner visited southern California on business, after which he went north to visit his children in the San Francisco Bay area, where his wife resided. He took the older child to San Francisco for the weekend. Upon returning the child to Mrs. Burnham's home on January 24, 1988, petitioner was served with a California court summons and a copy of Mrs. Burnham's divorce petition. He then returned to New Jersey.

Later that year, petitioner made a special appearance in the California Superior Court, moving to quash the service of process on the ground that the court lacked personal jurisdiction over him because his only contacts with California were a few short visits to the State for the purpose of conducting business and visiting his children. The Superior Court denied the motion, and the California Court of Appeal denied mandamus relief, rejecting petitioner's contention that the Due Process Clause prohibited California courts from asserting jurisdiction over him because he lacked "minimum contacts" with the State. The court held it to be "a valid jurisdictional predicate for in personam jurisdiction" that the "defendant [was] present in the forum state and personally served with process." . . . We granted certiorari. 493 U.S. 807 (1989).

II

A

The proposition that the judgment of a court lacking jurisdiction is void traces back to the English Year Books, see Bowser v. Collins, Y.B.Mich. 22 Edw. IV, f. 30, pl. 11, 145 Eng.Rep. 97 (1482), and was made settled law by Lord Coke in Case of the Marshalsea, 10 Co.Rep. 68b, 77 Eng.Rep. 1027, 1041 (K.B.1612). Traditionally that proposition was embodied in the phrase coram non judice, "before a person not a judge"— meaning, in effect, that the proceeding in question was not a judicial proceeding because lawful judicial authority was not present, and could therefore not yield a judgment. American courts invalidated, or denied recognition to, judgments that violated this common-law principle long before the Fourteenth Amendment was adopted. See, e.g., Grumon v. Raymond, 1 Conn. 40 (1814); Picquet v. Swan, 19 F.Cas. 609 (No. 11,134) (CC Mass.1828); Dunn v. Dunn, 4 Paige 425 (N.Y.Ch.1834); Evans v. Instine, 7 Ohio 273 (1835); Steel v. Smith, 7 Watts & Serg. 447 (Pa.1844); Boswell's Lessee v. Otis, 50 U.S. 336, 350 (1850). In Pennoyer v. Neff, 95 U.S. 714, 732 (1878), we announced that the judgment of a court lacking personal jurisdiction violated the Due Process Clause of the Fourteenth Amendment as well.

To determine whether the assertion of personal jurisdiction is consistent with due process, we have long relied on the principles traditionally followed by American courts in marking out the territorial limits of each State's authority. . . . In what has become the classic expression of the criterion, we said in International Shoe Co. v. Washington, 326 U.S. 310 (1945), that a State court's assertion of personal jurisdiction satisfies the Due Process Clause if it does not violate " 'traditional notions of fair play and substantial justice.' " Id., at 36, quoting Milliken v. Meyer, 311 U.S. 457, 463 (1940).... Since International Shoe, we have only been called upon to decide whether these "traditional notions" permit States to exercise jurisdiction over absent defendants.... The question we must decide today is whether due process requires a similar connection between the litigation and the defendant's contacts with the State in cases where the defendant is physically present in the State at the time process is served upon him.

B

Among the most firmly established principles of personal jurisdiction in American tradition is that the courts of a State have jurisdiction over nonresidents who are physically present in the State. The view developed early that each State had the power to hale before its courts any individual who could be found within its borders, and that once having acquired jurisdiction over such a person by properly serving him with process, the State could retain jurisdiction to enter judgment against him, no matter how fleeting his visit. See, e.g., Potter v. Allin, 2 Root 63, 67 (Conn.1793); Barrell v. Benjamin, 15 Mass. 354 (1819). That view had antecedents in English common-law practice, which sometimes allowed "transitory" actions, arising out of events outside the country, to be maintained against seemingly nonresident defendants who were present in England. See, e.g., Mostyn v. Fabrigas, 98 Eng.Rep. 1021 (K.B.1774)....

This American jurisdictional practice is, moreover, not merely old; it is continuing. ... We do not know of a single State or federal statute, or a single judicial decision resting upon State law, that has abandoned in-State service as a basis of jurisdiction. Many recent cases reaffirm it. See Hutto v. Plagens, 254 Ga. 512, 513, 330 S.E.2d 341, 342 (1985). ...

C

Despite this formidable body of precedent, petitioner contends, in reliance on our decisions applying the International Shoe standard, that in the absence of "continuous and systematic" contacts with the forum, ... a nonresident defendant can be subjected to judgment only as to matters that arise out of or relate to his contacts with the forum. This argument rests on a thorough misunderstanding of our cases.

. . .

Nothing in International Shoe or the cases that have followed it ... offers support for the very different proposition petitioner seeks to establish today: that a defendant's presence in the forum is not only unnecessary to validate novel, nontraditional assertions of jurisdiction, but is itself no longer sufficient to establish jurisdiction. That proposition is unfaithful to both elementary logic and the foundations of our due process jurisprudence. The distinction between what is needed to support novel procedures and what is needed to sustain traditional ones is fundamental. ...

The short of the matter is that jurisdiction based on physical presence alone constitutes due process because it is one of the continuing traditions of our legal system that define the due process standard of "traditional notions of fair play and substantial justice." That standard was developed by analogy to "physical presence," and it would be perverse to say it could now be turned against that touchstone of jurisdiction.

D

. . .

It goes too far to say, as petitioner contends, that Shaffer [v. Heitner, 433 U.S. 186 (1977)] compels the conclusion that a State lacks jurisdiction over an individual unless the litigation arises out of his activities in the State. Shaffer, like International Shoe, involved jurisdiction over an absent defendant, and it stands for nothing more than the proposition that when the "minimum contact" that is a substitute for physical presence consists of property ownership it must, like other minimum contacts, be related to the litigation. Petitioner wrenches out of its context our statement in Shaffer that "all assertions of state-court jurisdiction must be evaluated according to the standards set forth in International Shoe and its progeny." 433 U.S., at 212. When read together with the two sentences that preceded it, the meaning of this statement becomes clear:

> "The fiction that an assertion of jurisdiction over property is anything but an assertion of jurisdiction over the owner of the property supports an ancient form without substantial modern justification. Its continued acceptance would serve only to allow state-court jurisdiction that is fundamentally unfair to the defendant.
>
> "We *therefore conclude* that all assertions of state-court jurisdiction must be evaluated according to the standards set forth in International Shoe and its progeny." Ibid. (emphasis added).

Shaffer was saying, in other words, not that all bases for the assertion of in personam jurisdiction (including, presumably, in-state service) must be treated alike and subjected to the "minimum contacts" analysis of International Shoe; but rather that quasi in rem jurisdiction, that fictional "ancient form," and in personam jurisdiction, are really one and the same and must be treated alike—leading to the conclusion that quasi in rem jurisdiction, i.e., that form of in personam jurisdiction based upon a "property ownership" contact and by definition unaccompanied by personal, in-state service, must satisfy the litigation-relatedness requirement of International Shoe. ...

It is fair to say, however, that while our holding today does not contradict Shaffer, our basic approach to the due process question is different. We have conducted no independent inquiry into the desirability or fairness of the prevailing in-state service rule, leaving that judgment to the legislatures that are free to amend it; for our purposes, its validation is its pedigree. ... Shaffer did conduct such an independent inquiry, asserting that " 'traditional notions of fair play and substantial justice' can be as readily offended by the perpetuation of ancient forms that are no longer justified as by the adoption of new procedures that are inconsistent with the basic values of our constitutional heritage." 433 U.S., at 212. Perhaps that assertion can be sustained when the "perpetuation of ancient forms" is engaged in by only a very small minority of the States. Where, however, as in the present case, a jurisdictional principle is both firmly approved by tradition and still favored, it is impossible to imagine what standard we could appeal to for the judgment that it is "no longer justified." While in no way receding from or casting doubt upon the holding of Shaffer or any other case, we reaffirm today our time-honored approach. ... For new procedures, hitherto unknown, the Due Process Clause requires analysis to determine whether "traditional notions of fair play and substantial justice" have been offended. International Shoe, 326 U.S., at 316. But a doctrine of personal jurisdiction that dates back to the adoption of the Fourteenth Amendment and is still generally observed unquestionably meets that standard.

III

A few words in response to Justice Brennan's concurrence:

. . .

The subjectivity, and hence inadequacy, of this approach [which uses "contemporary notions of due process"] becomes apparent when the concurrence tries to explain why the assertion of jurisdiction in the present case meets its standard of continuing-American-tradition-plus-innate-fairness. Justice Brennan lists the "benefits" Mr. Burnham derived from the State of California—the fact that, during the few days he was there, "his health and safety [were] guaranteed by the State's police, fire, and emergency medical services; he [was] free to travel on the State's roads and waterways; he likely enjoy[ed] the fruits of the State's economy." ... Three days' worth of these benefits strike us as powerfully inadequate to establish, as an abstract matter, that it is "fair" for California to decree the ownership of all Mr. Burnham's worldly goods acquired during the ten years of his marriage, and the custody over his children. We dare say a contractual exchange swapping those benefits for that power would not survive the "unconscionability" provision of the Uniform Commercial Code. ...

. . .

The difference between us and Justice Brennan has nothing to do with whether "further progress [is] to be made" in the "evolution of our legal system." ... It has to do with whether changes are to be adopted as progressive by the American people or decreed as progressive by the Justices of this Court. Nothing we say today prevents individual States from limiting or entirely abandoning the in-state service basis of jurisdiction.

. . .

Because the Due Process Clause does not prohibit the California courts from exercising jurisdiction over petitioner based on the fact of in-state service of process, the judgment is Affirmed.

■ JUSTICE WHITE, concurring in part and concurring in the judgment.

I join Part I and Parts II–A, II–B, and II–C of Justice Scalia's opinion and concur in the judgment of affirmance. The rule allowing jurisdiction to be obtained over a non-resident by personal service in the forum state, without more, has been and is so widely accepted throughout this country that I could not possibly strike it down, either on its face or as applied in this case, on the ground that it denies due process of law guaranteed by the Fourteenth Amendment. Although the Court has the authority under the Amendment to examine even traditionally accepted procedures and declare them invalid, e.g., Shaffer v. Heitner, 433 U.S. 186 (1977), there has been no showing here or elsewhere that as a general proposition the rule is so arbitrary and lacking in common sense in so many instances that it should be held violative of Due Process in every case. Furthermore, until such a showing is made, which would be difficult indeed, claims in individual cases that the rule would operate unfairly as applied to the particular non-resident involved need not be entertained. At least this would be the case where presence in the forum state is intentional, which would almost always be the fact. Otherwise, there would be endless, fact-specific litigation in the trial and appellate courts, including this one. ...

■ JUSTICE BRENNAN with whom JUSTICE MARSHALL, JUSTICE BLACKMUN, and JUSTICE O'CONNOR join, concurring in the judgment.

I agree with Justice Scalia that the Due Process Clause of the Fourteenth Amendment generally permits a state court to exercise jurisdiction over a defendant if he is served with process while voluntarily present in the forum State. ... I do not perceive the need, however, to decide that a jurisdictional rule that " 'has been immemorially the actual law of the land,' " ... automatically comports with due process simply by virtue of its "pedigree." ... Unlike Justice Scalia, I would undertake an "independent inquiry into the ... fairness of the prevailing in-state service rule." ...

I

I believe that the approach adopted by Justice Scalia's opinion today—reliance solely on historical pedigree—is foreclosed by our decisions in International Shoe Co. v. Washington, 326 U.S. 310 (1945), and Shaffer v. Heitner, 433 U.S. 186 (1977). In International Shoe, we held that a state court's assertion of personal jurisdiction does not violate the Due Process Clause if it is consistent with " 'traditional notions of fair play and substantial justice.' " 326 U.S., at 316, quoting Milliken v. Meyer, 311 U.S. 457, 463 (1940). In Shaffer, we stated that "all assertions of state-court jurisdiction must be evaluated according to the standards set forth in

International Shoe and its progeny." 433 U.S., at 212 (emphasis added). The critical insight of Shaffer is that all rules of jurisdiction, even ancient ones, must satisfy contemporary notions of due process. No longer were we content to limit our jurisdictional analysis to pronouncements that "[t]he foundation of jurisdiction is physical power," McDonald v. Mabee, 243 U.S. 90, 91 (1917), and that "every State possesses exclusive jurisdiction and sovereignty over persons and property within its territory." Pennoyer v. Neff, 95 U.S. 714, 722 (1878). While acknowledging that "history must be considered as supporting the proposition that jurisdiction based solely on the presence of property satisfie[d] the demands of due process," we found that this factor could not be "decisive." 433 U.S., at 211–212. We recognized that " '[t]raditional notions of fair play and substantial justice' can be as readily offended by the perpetuation of ancient forms that are no longer justified as by the adoption of new procedures that are inconsistent with the basic values of our constitutional heritage." Id., at 212 (citations omitted). . . .

II

Tradition, though alone not dispositive, is of course relevant to the question whether the rule of transient jurisdiction is consistent with due process.

. . .

[H]owever murky the jurisprudential origins of transient jurisdiction, the fact that American courts have announced the rule for perhaps a century (first in dicta, more recently in holdings) provides a defendant voluntarily present in a particular State today "clear notice that [he] is subject to suit" in the forum. World–Wide Volkswagen Corp. v. Woodson, 444 U.S. 286, 297 (1980). . . .

By visiting the forum State, a transient defendant actually "avail[s]" himself, Burger King, [Corp. v. Rudzewicz, 471 U.S. 462, 476 (1985)] of significant benefits provided by the State. His health and safety are guaranteed by the State's police, fire, and emergency medical services; he is free to travel on the State's roads and waterways; he likely enjoys the fruits of the State's economy as well. Moreover, the Privileges and Immunities Clause of Article IV prevents a state government from discriminating against a transient defendant by denying him the protections of its law or the right of access to its courts. See Supreme Court of New Hampshire v. Piper, 470 U.S. 274, 281, n. 10 (1985); Baldwin v. Montana Fish and Game Comm'n of Montana, 436 U.S. 371, 387 (1978); see also Supreme Court of Virginia v. Friedman, 487 U.S. 59, 64–65 (1988). Subject only to the doctrine of forum non conveniens, an out-of-state plaintiff may use state courts in all circumstances in which those courts would be available to state citizens. Without transient jurisdiction, an asymmetry would arise; a transient would have the full benefit of the power of the forum State's courts as a plaintiff while retaining immunity from their authority as a defendant. . . .

The potential burdens on a transient defendant are slight. " '[M]odern transportation and communications have made it much less burdensome for a party sued to defend himself' " in a State outside his place of residence. Burger King, 471 U.S., at 474, quoting McGee v. International Life Insurance Co., 355 U.S. 220, 223 (1957). That the defendant has already journeyed at least once before to the forum—as evidenced by the fact that he was served with process there—is an indication that suit in the forum likely would not be prohibitively inconvenient. Finally, any burdens that do arise can be ameliorated by a variety of procedural devices. For these reasons, as a rule the exercise of personal jurisdiction over a defendant based on his voluntary presence in the forum will satisfy the requirements of due process.

In this case, it is undisputed that petitioner was served with process while voluntarily and knowingly in the State of California. I therefore concur in the judgment.

■ JUSTICE STEVENS, concurring in the judgment.

As I explained in my separate writing, I did not join the Court's opinion in Shaffer v. Heitner, 433 U.S. 186 (1977), because I was concerned by its unnecessarily broad reach. Id., at 217–219 (opinion concurring in judgment). The same concern prevents me from joining either Justice Scalia's or Justice Brennan's opinion in this case. For me, it is sufficient to note that the historical evidence and consensus identified by Justice Scalia, the considerations of fairness identified by Justice Brennan, and the common sense displayed by Justice White, all combine to demonstrate that this is, indeed, a very easy case.** Accordingly, I agree that the judgment should be affirmed.

NOTES

1. Does the *International Shoe* reference, supra at p. 47, to "minimum contacts ... [so that] 'traditional notions of fair play and substantial justice' " not be offended state a single test (i.e., minimum contacts assure fairness) or two? See *Asahi,* supra p. 78. What was lacking in *Helicopteros,* supra p. 94? What about *Bryant,* supra p. 101? Does not the hypothetical in Note (1) on p. 101 raise the same issues?

2. Should "fairness" also matter when the issue concerns *general* jurisdiction? See *Insurance Corp.* and its footnote 10, supra p. 77. Is the exercise of jurisdiction at the domicile always "fair"? Would the exercise of jurisdiction on the basis of personal presence be fair if service occurred in an airplane (*Grace,* supra p. 43 or was made on a foreign-country defendant attending an American trade show in a cause of action involving a foreign plaintiff and foreign facts (compare *Asahi,* supra p. 78? Was the exercise of jurisdiction over Mr. Burnham fair on the facts of the particular case, i.e. were there other "affiliating circumstances" (*World–Wide Volkswagen,* supra at p. 66? Why did not the Court inquire whether there were any? Does *Burnham* rest on *power* or history or both? Did not Delaware, in

---

** Perhaps the adage about hard cases making bad law should be revised to cover easy cases.

Shaffer v. Heitner, infra p. 136, have power over the defendant's property? If, in the same case, the decision only meant to remove, as Justice Scalia writes in *Burnham,* the artificial distinction between in rem and in personam bases of jurisdiction and subject both to scrutiny, why did not the fact that jurisdiction by attachment is also time-honored permit Delaware to exercise jurisdiction, the same as California could in *Burnham*? Is it relevant that Delaware exercised attachment jurisdiction over an intangible to which it itself had assigned a Delaware situs?

3. Should jurisdiction on the basis of personal presence be available notwithstanding inconvenience to the defendant because of the possibility of dismissal in favor of or transfer to a more convenient alternative forum?

4. Should state courts have nationwide jurisdiction: "while the defendant's contacts with the forum are not irrelevant, ... they are of central importance only after the defendant has shown that litigation in the forum raises a serious likelihood of unfairness to him"? Weintraub, Due Process Limitations on the Personal Jurisdiction of State Courts: Time for Change, 63 Or.L.Rev. 485, 523 (1984) and, with detailed suggestions, Weintraub, An Objective Basis for Rejecting Transient Jurisdiction, 22 Rutgers L.J. 611 (1991). Professor Weintraub opposes the result in *Burnham* because of the anomaly that a state can draw in some but not all defendants for unrelated causes of action. See also Weintraub, A Map out of the Personal Jurisdiction Labyrinth, 28 U.C.Davis L.Rev. 531, 558 (1995). Similarly Lowenfeld: "I believe that a consensus is emerging about the relevant criteria .... I believe the cause of action matters, the alternate fora matter, the reasonable expectations of the parties matter, the layers in a product liability suit between the defendant and the end-product matter." Lowenfeld, International Litigation and the Quest for Reasonableness—General Course on Private International Law, Hague Academy, 245 Collected Courses 9, 120–121 (1994–I). Does jurisdiction reduce to fairness in the individual case or should there be a number of predetermined objective standards, as in the Brussels Convention? See Hay, Flexibility versus Predictability and Uniformity in Choice of Law, Hague Academy, 226 Collected Courses 281, 327 (1991–I). "I realize that in supporting discretion and reasonableness, I seem to be inviting litigation about litigation. So far as I can see, however, litigation about judicial jurisdiction has been a favourite indoor sport in all States." Lowenfeld, supra, at 120.

Compare Cox, Case Three: Personal Jurisdiction, 29 New England L.Rev. 627, 648 (1995): "The replacement of territoriality by a more limited version of state sovereignty means that forums exercise limited, rather than plenary, jurisdiction over parties. ... A person should not be counted present before a court in abstract or in plenary fashion, but only as the particular suit gives the forum state legitimacy to intrude on that person's life. The mistake in allowing jurisdiction based on presence, convenience, or any basis other than litigation related contacts is that a court is given authority to decide something about a party without regard to why the party is before the court."

5. If the fact that the United States is one country should lend some support to the outcome in *Burnham,* should "transient jurisdiction" be also available as against foreign-country defendants casually present here on a fortnight's holiday at the time of service? See Restatement (Third), Foreign Relations Law of the United States § 421(2)(a) (1987): a state (country) has jurisdiction to adjudicate if a "person or thing is present in the ... state, other than transitorily." Comment *e* to § 421 states that the exercise of jurisdiction based on transient presence "is not generally acceptable under international "law." It is not in the European Union, supra p. 42 and infra Note (7). For the position that *Burnham* should be restricted to interstate defendants, see Hay, Transient Jurisdiction, Especially Over International Defendants: Critical Comments on *Burnham v. Superior Court,* 1990 U.Ill. L.Rev. 593. Accord: Lowenfeld, supra Note (4), at 120 n. 273; Weintraub, supra Note (4) ("A Map . . ."), at 559.

Suppose a state interprets its own constitution as prohibiting use of "transient" presence as a basis for personal jurisdiction. How long a stay in the state by a non-resident converts presence there into something more than transient presence for jurisdictional purposes? If the sojourn is unrelated to the claim sued upon, does it make any difference whether it is for pleasure rather than business?

6. Does *Burnham* apply to corporate defendants—for instance, if a corporate officer is casually present in the forum state at the time of service? Does it matter whether the officer was in the forum on business or on vacation? In Wenche Siemer v. Learjet Acquisition Corp., 966 F.2d 179 (5th Cir.1992), the court held that there was not general jurisdiction in Texas over a Delaware corporation with a principal place of business in Kansas just because the defendant had designated an agent in Texas for receipt of process. The defendant was licensed to do business in Texas, but maintained no offices or facilities there, and its Texas sales were about 1% of total sales. *Burnham,* the court reasoned, was based on a court's traditional power over the defendant's person. Corporations, in contrast, subject themselves to jurisdiction through their activities. The present defendant's activities did not satisfy the test for general jurisdiction over a corporation (*Perkins,* supra p. 93). There also was no specific jurisdiction (supra p. 119, Note (1)) because the claim arose from an airplane disaster in Egypt. Does the decision answer, or foreshadow an answer to, the question asked in the first two sentences? Note also that the decision is careful to avoid confusing the notice function of service and the basis for acquiring judicial jurisdiction (see pp. 160–167).

7. In England, the Civil Jurisdiction and Judgments Act of 1982 redefined "domicile" for jurisdictional purposes in connection with England's accession to the European Union's (Brussels) Convention: "[A]n individual is domiciled in the United Kingdom . . . if he is resident in, and the nature and circumstances of his residence indicate that he has a substantial connection with, the United Kingdom. . . ." Dicey & Morris, Conflict of Laws 290 (12th ed. by Collins 1993), citing to § 41(2), (3) of the Act. Would such a description of the required quality of a person's presence in the forum be helpful to answer the questions raised in the preceding Note?

As you recall the various bases of jurisdiction in the Brussels Convention (general jurisdiction at a person's domicile or the seat of a corporation, consent, specific jurisdiction in contract, tort, and for some other matters), consider the following statement: "I think the Brussels Convention, while correct in the catalogue of jurisdictional bases it condemns in Article 3 [e.g., "tag" jurisdiction, supra, and personal jurisdiction based on the presence of property unrelated to the claim], is a bit too limited in the bases of jurisdiction that it expressly permits. I think there is often justification for general jurisdiction, and also for some other bases . . ., such as jurisdiction on the basis of the place of making of a contract." Lowenfeld, supra Note (4), at 120. Do you agree? Reconsider the problems raised in Note (4).

8. For extensive discussion of Burnham, see Symposium: The Future of Personal Jurisdiction, 22 Rutgers L.J. 559 (1991), with contributions by Brilmayer, Silberman, Stein, Weintraub, Kogan, Twitchell, Redish, and Maltz.

C. Continuance of Jurisdiction

RESTATEMENT, SECOND, CONFLICT OF LAWS: *

§ 26. Continuance of Jurisdiction

If a state obtains judicial jurisdiction over a party to an action, the jurisdiction continues throughout all subsequent proceedings which arise out of the original cause of action. Reasonable notice and reasonable opportunity to be heard must be given the party at each new step in the proceeding.

Michigan Trust Co. v. Ferry
Supreme Court of the United States, 1913.
228 U.S. 346, 33 S.Ct. 550, 57 L.Ed. 867.

■ JUSTICE HOLMES delivered the opinion of the court:

These are suits brought in the Circuit Court for the District of Utah upon decrees of the Probate Court of Ottawa, Michigan. The defendant demurred to the complaints, the Circuit Court sustained the demurrers and gave judgments for the defendant, and these judgments were affirmed by the Circuit Court of Appeals. . . .

William M. Ferry died in 1867 domiciled in Ottawa County, Michigan. His will was proved, and the defendant, Edward P. Ferry, was appointed executor by the Ottawa Probate Court, qualified and entered upon his duties. In 1878 he removed to Utah and becoming incompetent was put under the guardianship of two sons, W. Mont Ferry and Edward S. Ferry, in 1892. In 1903 residuary legatees and devisees petitioned the Michigan Probate Court that the defendant be removed from his office of executor, that he be ordered to account for the unadministered residue of the estate and that the Michigan Trust Company be appointed administrator de bonis non with the will annexed. Notice of the petition and time and place of the hearing was given by publication and also was given to the defendant and his guardians personally in Utah. The guardians by order of the Utah court appeared and asked for the appointment of a guardian ad litem, which was made . . . There were various proceedings the end of which was that the plaintiff was appointed administrator de bonis non . . . and it was decreed that the defendant was indebted to the estate for $1,220,473.41. The defendant being entitled to one-fourth of the above sum as residuary legatee, he was declared liable for $915,355.08 and ordered to pay it over within sixty days to the Michigan Trust Company. . . .

Ordinarily jurisdiction over a person is based on the power of the sovereign asserting it to seize that person and imprison him to await the sovereign's pleasure. But when that power exists and is asserted by service at the beginning of a cause, or if the party submits to the

---

* Quoted with the permission of the copyright owner, The American Law Institute.

jurisdiction in whatever form may be required, we dispense with the necessity of maintaining the physical power and attribute the same force to the judgment or decree whether the party remain within the jurisdiction or not. This is one of the decencies of civilization that no one would dispute.... This is true not only of ordinary actions but of proceedings like the present. It is within the power of a State to make the whole administration of the estate a single proceeding, to provide that one who has undertaken it within the jurisdiction shall be subject to the order of the court in the matter until the administration is closed by distribution, and, on the same principle, that he shall be required to account for and distribute all that he receives, by the order of the Probate Court....

It follows from what we have said that a petition to the Probate Court that the defendant be ordered to account covered all his receipts as executor and that notice of the petition was notice that the accounting would have that scope. The decree upon the account was made with full jurisdiction and ... could be sued upon ... and was entitled to full faith and credit elsewhere....

Judgment reversed.

NOTES

1. In Fitzsimmons v. Johnson, 90 Tenn. 416, 17 S.W. 100 (1891), a decree of an Ohio court against the defendant, as executor qualified in Ohio, was enforced in Tennessee, even though the proceedings to reverse the initial judgment of the Ohio court, approving the defendant's account and discharging him, were instituted more than twenty years after the entry of that judgment, and the only service of process on the defendant, a nonresident of Ohio, was by publication. See also Blumle v. Kramer, 14 Okl. 366, 79 P. 215 (1904), involving jurisdiction to enter a judgment for a deficiency following a mortgage foreclosure, and after the defendant had moved away from the state.

2. In Ohlquist v. Nordstrom, 143 Misc. 502, 257 N.Y.S. 711 (1932), affirmed 238 App. Div. 766, 261 N.Y.S. 1039 (1933), affirmed 262 N.Y. 696, 188 N.E. 125 (1933), A recovered a judgment in New York against B and C as joint tortfeasors, whereupon C removed his residence to Pennsylvania. B paid the entire judgment and began the present suit for contribution, serving C's attorneys in New York and C personally outside the state. The service was held effective. Cf. New York Life Insurance Co. v. Dunlevy, p. 133, infra.

SECTION 3. JURISDICTION OVER "THINGS"

RESTATEMENT, SECOND, CONFLICT OF LAWS: *

    Chapter 3, Introductory Note to Topic 2:

---

* Quoted with the permission of the copyright owner, The American Law Institute.

CHAPTER 3   Jurisdiction of Courts

INTRODUCTORY NOTE

... [E]very valid exercise of judicial jurisdiction affects the interests of persons. It is possible, however, to affect the interests of persons in different ways, and it is convenient to divide the subject of judicial jurisdiction into three main categories: jurisdiction over persons, jurisdiction over things and jurisdiction over status.... When one or more of ... [the various bases for the exercise of judicial jurisdiction over persons] exists, a personal judgment may be rendered against the defendant. The effect of such a judgment, if it is one for money, is to make the defendant a judgment debtor of the plaintiff. This debt may be enforced against any property in the state subject to execution which the defendant then owns or subsequently acquires. An action to recover this debt may likewise be maintained against the defendant either in the same state or elsewhere. A personal judgment may also take the form of an equitable decree ordering the defendant either to do something or to refrain from action. In such a case, the defendant may be punished for contempt if he fails to obey the court's order.

Even though personal jurisdiction over the defendant is lacking, the state may affect any interests he may have in things subject to its jurisdiction. A judgment rendered in such a proceeding binds only the defendant's interests in the specific thing at which it is directed and thus has a more limited effect than a judgment rendered against the defendant personally. All that a defendant risks in a proceeding directed against a particular thing, if he is at no time personally subject to the judicial jurisdiction of the state, is the loss of his interests therein. An in personam judgment, on the other hand, may be enforced against any and all of his property which is not exempt from execution.

Where a thing is subject to the judicial jurisdiction of a state, an action may be brought to affect the interests in the thing of all persons in the world. Such an action is commonly referred to as a proceeding in rem. Or, as is usually the case, the action may be brought to affect the interests in the thing of particular persons only, in which case it is commonly referred to as a proceeding quasi in rem....

Proceedings quasi in rem are of two types. In the first type the plaintiff asserts an interest in a thing, and seeks to have his interest established against the claim of a designated person or persons. Of this type are actions to recover possession of land or to establish title to land, such as an action of ejectment, or one to quiet title or to remove a cloud on title, where the court has jurisdiction to give the relief asked because of its power over the land even though it has no power over the adverse claimant. Of this type also is an action to foreclose a mortgage.

In the second type of proceeding quasi in rem, the plaintiff does not assert that he has an interest in the thing, but asserts a claim against the defendant personally and seeks, by attachment or garnishment, to apply the thing to the satisfaction of his claim against the defendant.

Recent decisions by the Supreme Court of the United States have significantly affected the traditional distinctions between jurisdiction over persons and jurisdiction over things. A total merger of the concepts would be unfortunate, since the effect of a judgment still depends in important respects on whether it rests on jurisdiction over the defendant's person.

A. LAND

A classic statement of the nature of a proceeding *in rem* was provided by Justice Holmes in Tyler v. Judges of the Court of Registration, 175 Mass. 71, 76, 55 N.E. 812, 814 (1900):

"If ... [the object of the suit] is to bar indifferently all who might be minded to make an objection of any sort against the right sought to be established, and if any one in the world has a right to be heard on the strength of alleging facts which, if true, show an inconsistent interest, the proceeding is in rem.... All proceedings, like all rights, are really against persons. Whether they are proceedings or rights in rem depends on the number of persons affected."

The traditional concept of jurisdiction over land was based on the theory that only the state where the land was located had power to deal with it effectively; hence, only the situs state was thought to have jurisdiction to issue decrees "directly" affecting title to land. However, some courts permitted themselves to issue decrees ordering the defendant to pay damages with regard to foreign real estate, or even to convey interests in land outside the state. Penn v. Lord Baltimore, 1 Ves.Sr. 444, 27 Eng.Rep. 1132 (Ch. 1750) is perhaps the most famous example of the latter remedy. The principle was approved in Massie v. Watts, 10 U.S. (6 Cranch) 148 (1810), Chief Justice Marshall declaring that where the defendant "is liable to the plaintiff, either in consequence of contract, or as trustee, or as the holder of a legal title acquired by any species of mala fides practiced on the plaintiff, the principles of equity give a court jurisdiction wherever the person may be found, and the circumstance, that a question of title may be involved in the inquiry, and may even constitute the essential point on which the case depends, does not seem sufficient to arrest that jurisdiction."

NOTES

1. Should the fact that a great many people or "all the world" will be bound by the judgment, make it possible to utilize a more wholesale type of notification of the suit than if only one person is defendant? For the type of notice to adverse claimants, known and unknown, required by registration statutes, see McKinney's N.Y. Real Property Law § 385. Generally, as to notice, see Mullane v. Central Hanover Bank & Trust Co., 339 U.S. 306, 70 S.Ct. 652 (1950), p. 160, infra. The Supreme Court has upheld state statutes providing that title to real property within the state may be determined in a suit in which a non-resident defendant is served only by publication. See Arndt v. Griggs, 134 U.S. 316 (1890). But such decisions seem questionable in the light of more recent cases. See p. 166, note (1), infra.

2. A buyer of land is entitled to a decree for the conveyance of land in the state of the situs if the court has been made competent to grant such relief, even though the vendor is served outside the state. Garfein v. McInnis, 248 N.Y. 261, 162 N.E. 73 (1928).

3. Even though a court cannot directly affect interests in foreign land, it may exercise its personal jurisdiction over the parties before it to order appropriate relief. Incident to a divorce proceeding, for instance, a court may award real property in another state and, in the exercise of its equitable powers, compel one party to convey to the other. See Dority v. Dority, 645 P.2d 56, 58 (Utah 1982); Miller v. Miller, 109 Misc.2d 982, 441 N.Y.S.2d 339 (1981); Anno., Power of Divorce Court to Deal with Real Property Located in Another State, 34 A.L.R.3d 962 (1970). See also Hay, The Situs Rule in European and American Conflicts Law—Comparative Notes, in: Hay and Hoeflich (eds.), Property Law and Legal Education—Essays in Honor of John E. Cribbet 109 (1988). See Chapter 5, Sec. 3 for discussion of whether equitable decrees affecting foreign land are entitled to recognition at the situs under Full Faith and Credit principles.

4. A deed to land, executed by the owner in accordance with a decree of a foreign court, will be given effect as a valid conveyance in the state where the land lies. Deschenes v. Tallman, 248 N.Y. 33, 161 N.E. 321 (1928). Where a court, having jurisdiction over the defendant, orders a conveyance of foreign land, what effect will be given to the decree in the state where the land is located, if no conveyance is actually made? See Fall v. Eastin, set out at p. 254, infra.

Combs v. Combs
Supreme Court of Kentucky, 1933.
249 Ky. 155, 60 S.W.2d 368, 89 A.L.R. 1095.

■ THOMAS, J. The appellant, A.T. Combs, who was one of the defendants below, became indebted to the appellees and plaintiffs below, in a considerable sum. A lien to secure it was created on a tract of land in Washington county, Ark. Plaintiffs were and are residents of Kentucky and of other states, and all of them were and are nonresidents of the state of Arkansas. Appellant's brother, who was a joint defendant with him, is a resident of this commonwealth, and this action was filed by plaintiffs in the Breathitt circuit court against appellant and his brother to obtain a personal judgment against them for the amount of the debt. Personal process could not [be] and was not served on appellant for a considerable time after he was proceeded against and made a defendant in the action. During that time he filed an equity action in the chancery court of Washington county, Ark., in which the land in lien was situated, against the plaintiffs in this action, and proceeded against them exclusively by constructive process in accordance with the prescribed practice of the Arkansas forum. In his petition in that court he set forth the facts creating the indebtedness, as well as the lien on his land to secure it, and stated that he had paid part of the debt, leaving a named sum as the balance due, and that the lien to secure it was a cloud on the title to his land which he desired released, and he asked that court to enter judgment fixing the amount of the balance due by him to plaintiffs in this action (but defendants in that one) and to permit him to pay that amount into that court to be followed by a decree canceling the lien on his land. The Arkansas practice for that kind of procedure was followed, and upon submission, without any of the defendants therein entering their appearance in any manner, that court adjudged that plaintiff therein, appellant herein, was indebted to the defendants in that action (plaintiffs herein) in the sum admitted in his petition, and ordered him to pay it to the master commissioner of that court which he did, and when done, that the lien on his land should be released. Appellant then procured a copy of that proceeding and filed his answer in this action relying upon the Arkansas judgment in bar of a recovery herein. The court disallowed that defense and rendered judgment against appellant for the amount it found to be due plaintiffs, and to reverse it defendant prosecutes this appeal.

The only argument made, and the only possible one that could be made, against the propriety of the judgment appealed from is that the Arkansas judgment, under the provisions of section 1 of article 4 of the Federal Constitution, is entitled to full faith and credit in this state the same as if it had been rendered by a court of competent jurisdiction in this state, and that, since it is argued that the Arkansas court had jurisdiction to render the judgment relied on as a defense herein, it is binding on plaintiffs, and that they may not impeach it in this collateral attack. In making that argument, counsel assumes the correctness of the crucial point in this case, and we think erroneously so. It is, that the Arkansas court had jurisdiction, upon constructive process alone, to finally and conclusively adjudge the amount of plaintiff's debt owed to them by defendant, and then to assume to collect it through its master commissioner, or, more appropriately, to direct plaintiff in the Arkansas judgment to discharge it by paying the amount found to be due to the court's master commissioner, and to thereby completely discharge defendant from all further liability to plaintiffs. The error in the assumption of counsel for defendant lies in their failure to appraise and comprehend the nature of the relief granted by the Arkansas judgment and relied on as a defense in this case; confusing it with the power and jurisdiction of that court to deal with and adjudicate concerning the res within its jurisdiction, which in this case was the land in lien for plaintiff's debt.

[The court first questioned, without deciding, whether, under the doctrines of equity, an appropriate case for a bill to remove a cloud on title was made out in the Arkansas proceeding, since the alleged cloud was created by the debtor himself.]

... [I]n this case, conceding that there was no doubt of the proper cloud upon defendant's title to his Arkansas land so as to authorize the action in that state to remove it, the judgment rendered by the Arkansas court would be obligatory on plaintiffs herein in so far as it released their lien upon the land in that state. But, when the court undertook to grant additional relief strictly in personam, it transgressed its jurisdiction so as to render such unauthorized additional relief of no force and effect whatever. That relief in this case was the adjudication that defendant herein had paid to plaintiffs herein any part of his debt and thereby discharged a part of his obligation to them, and that the court could and did fix the amount due from him to plaintiffs herein and directed its payment to the commissioner of that court. The rights so attempted to be adjudicated were and are strictly personal. It may be that the Arkansas court was vested with authority to lift the lien from the land involved, and for that purpose to incidentally determine the amount of the lien, and whether or not it had been paid, but the only binding effect of such adjudications would be that of releasing the lien as an incumbrance upon the title to the res. Such adjudications in so far as they affected the personal obligations and rights of the parties were and are not binding upon plaintiffs herein, nor do they operate as a res adjudicata estoppel in any future action....

Wherefore the judgment is affirmed.

NOTES

1. If the creditors, after the entry of the Arkansas judgment, sued the debtor in Arkansas for the balance alleged to be due, and the Arkansas court held the prior judgment to be res judicata of the plaintiff's rights, would this constitute a denial of due process? On the conclusiveness of a judgment quasi in rem, see Restatement, Second, Judgments §§ 30, 32 (1982).

2. Freeman v. Alderson, 119 U.S. 185 (1886) determined that, in an action to try title to real estate and obtain a partition thereof against a non-resident defendant served only by publication, a personal judgment for costs could not be entered. Similarly, in State ex rel. Truitt v. District Court, 44 N.M. 16, 96 P.2d 710 (1939), a non-resident lessee of New Mexico land, sued by his sublessee for reformation of the lease, was held not subject to suit in New Mexico when notified by mail outside the state. Would there not have been jurisdiction over the non-resident in these cases under a modern statute taking advantage of all constitutionally permissible bases of personal jurisdiction, including "ownership, possession or use of real estate situated within the state?"

B. CHATTELS

RESTATEMENT, SECOND, CONFLICT OF LAWS: *

§ 60. Judicial Jurisdiction over Chattel

A state has power to exercise judicial jurisdiction to affect interests in a chattel in the state, which is not in the course of transit in interstate or foreign commerce, although a person owning or claiming an interest in the chattel is not personally subject to the judicial jurisdiction of the state.

Martin v. Better Taste Popcorn Co.

United States District Court, S.D.Iowa, 1950.
89 F.Supp. 754.

■ SWITZER, DISTRICT JUDGE. The petition [in the Iowa state court alleged that in Fremont County, Iowa] there is situated 4¼ million pounds of stored

---

* Quoted with the permission of the copyright owner, The American Law Institute.

popcorn, a part of which is the property of the plaintiffs, having been commingled with the remainder and unidentifiable therefrom.

Plaintiffs seek a decree determining the respective interests of each of the owners of said stored popcorn, claiming said popcorn cannot be divided or partitioned in kind; for a referee to take possession thereof, and preserve the same under order of this court, and further, that the court order an appearance and hearing and prescribe the method of notice on the defendant; for a judgment against the defendant and the popcorn, for the costs of the action and such further relief as the court may find proper. In short, this is an action to partition personal property, located in Fremont County, Iowa, in the custody of the defendant, a non-resident corporate defendant.

[After personal service pursuant to the state court's order, which allowed defendant five days to appear, defendant removed the action to the Federal court and attacked jurisdiction for "insufficiency of process and service" under state law and also for lack of "jurisdiction of the subject matter" because there were owners of interests in the popcorn who had not been joined as parties, also in violation of the requirements of state law.]

Did the five-days' notice prescribed by the State court to the defendant in this case in which to make an appearance and defend, allow a sufficient time in view of the residence of the defendant in the State of Indiana to satisfy the due process clause of the Constitution of the United States, Amend. 14 . . . ?

The real test of the sufficiency of the notice in the instant case is whether or not the defendant was informed of the claim and the nature thereof and the time and place of appearance to defend within a sufficient time to afford it an opportunity to make such defense. I believe the notice and service thereof under these tests are sufficient.

Defendant contends that the requirements of Section 616.4, Code of Iowa, 1946, I.C.A. . . . precludes the possibility of the State court obtaining jurisdiction of a nonresident defendant owning property in this State unless aided by attachment. I do not believe this reasoning to be sound. The District Court in the State of Iowa is a court of general jurisdiction. . . . Every state has uncontrolled jurisdiction over all property, real or personal, within its borders, and, as stated in Vol. 14 American Jurisprudence, Par. 189, p. 383: "Therefore, although a nonresident does not come within the territorial limits of a state, if he owns property therein the courts may acquire jurisdiction thereof which may be exercised on such property. Where property of a nonresident is thus brought within the jurisdiction of the court, notice of the proceedings may be given by publication, since the theory of the law is that the owner is always in possession of his property and that its seizure will warn him to look after his interests. . . ." See Perry v. Young, 133 Tenn. 522, 182 S.W. 577, L.R.A.1917B, 385.

Of course, no personal judgment can be rendered against such defendant and the court has jurisdiction only to the extent of adjudicating the interest in the thing itself, that is, the res or the property located within the State of Iowa. This, being an action to partition personal property in Fremont County, Iowa, is in the nature of a rem action, or, perhaps more correctly put, a "quasi-in-rem" proceeding, and the Iowa Supreme Court has ... held valid a decree on partition predicated only upon notice by publication to non-residents and without attachment of the property itself to aid such published notice....

And it is likewise true, as disclosed by the petition here itself, that all of the indispensable parties necessary to a final determination of this cause are not presently joined in this action. As such, it would not be possible or proper for this court, having assumed jurisdiction, to proceed to a final determination without first requiring that all indispensable parties be joined herein....

I must therefore conclude that this court has jurisdiction of the parties hereto and of the subject matter hereof and that the Special Appearance of the defendant should be overruled in all respects; that this is an action to partition personal property located in Fremont County, Iowa, and that all persons having an interest therein or lien thereon are necessary and indispensable parties to this suit and that they should be joined as parties, plaintiffs or defendants herein.

NOTES

1. Various parties involved in making and distributing a motion picture called "Race Track" asserted conflicting interests in the movie's negative and sound track, which had been placed in a studio in New Jersey for reproduction work. Not all the interested parties were before the court. It was held: "Where the Court of Chancery has jurisdiction, and there are conflicting equitable liens upon a chattel, and the chattel is in an incomplete and unmarketable condition, the court may, upon proper terms, permit it to be completed and sold, and the proceeds to be held in its place pending a final hearing, in order to avoid the risk of a poorer market then." Educational Studios v. Consolidated Film Industries, 112 N.J.Eq. 352, 164 A. 24 (1933). See also Cammell v. Sewell, p. 683, infra; Green v. Van Buskirk, p. 786, infra; 1 Beale, Conflict of Laws, sec. 102.1 (1935).

2. State courts have been allowed to exercise jurisdiction over a chattel habitually situated in the forum even though the chattel was temporarily beyond the territorial limits of the state when the proceedings were instituted. North Carolina Land & Lumber Co. v. Boyer, 191 Fed. 552 (6th Cir.1911); 1 Beale, Conflict of Laws, sec. 99.1 (1935). Has a court jurisdiction to attach or garnish chattels which the defendant, not subject to the jurisdiction of the forum, was induced by the fraudulent acts of the plaintiff to send into the forum so that they could be subjected to the jurisdiction of the forum? Even if it has jurisdiction, the court will refuse to exercise it. See Sea–Gate Tire & Rubber Co. v. Moseley, 161 Okl. 256, 18 P.2d 276 (1933).

3. In Connecticut and Digiovanni v. Doehr, 501 U.S. 1 (1991) a statute that permitted prejudgment attachment of real estate without providing for notice and a hearing was held to violate due process.

C. Intangibles

"The situs of intangibles is in truth a legal fiction, but there are times when justice or convenience requires that a legal situs be ascribed to them.

The locality selected is for some purposes, the domicile of the creditor; for others, the domicile or place of business of the debtor, the place, that is to say, where the obligation was created or was meant to be discharged; for others, any place where the debtor can be found. At the root of the selection is generally a common sense appraisal of the requirements of justice and convenience in particular conditions." Cardozo, J., in Severnoe Securities Corporation v. London & Lancashire Ins. Co., Ltd., 255 N.Y. 120, 123–124, 174 N.E. 299, 300 (1931).

Harris v. Balk

Supreme Court of the United States, 1905.
198 U.S. 215, 25 S.Ct. 625, 49 L.Ed. 1023.

[Harris, a North Carolina domiciliary, was indebted to Balk, another North Carolina domiciliary, in the amount of $180. Balk in turn owed more than $300 to Epstein, who lived in Baltimore, Maryland. One day Harris came to Baltimore for a short visit and while there was served in hand by Epstein with a writ attaching the debt which Harris owed Balk. In addition, in accordance with the Maryland practice, process against Balk was delivered to a Baltimore sheriff and then placed at the court house door. Harris did not contest the garnishment action and consented to the entry against him of a payment for $180 which he paid. Thereafter in North Carolina, Balk sued Harris on his debt. A judgment in Balk's favor was affirmed by the North Carolina Supreme Court on the ground that Maryland had no jurisdiction to garnish the debt Harris owed Balk "because Harris was but temporarily in the state, and the situs of the debt was in North Carolina."]

■ JUSTICE PECKHAM . . . delivered the opinion of the court.

. . . Attachment is the creature of the local law . . . If there be a law of the State providing for the attachment of the debt, then if the garnishee be found in that State, and process be personally served upon him therein, we think the court thereby acquires jurisdiction over him, and can garnish the debt due from him to the debtor of the plaintiff and condemn it, provided the garnishee could himself be sued by his creditor in that State. We do not see how the question of jurisdiction vel non can properly be made to depend upon the so-called original situs of the debt, or upon the character of the stay of the garnishee, whether temporary or permanent, in the State where the attachment is issued. Power over the person of the garnishee confers jurisdiction on the courts of the State where the writ issues. Blackstone v. Miller, 188 U.S. 189, 206. If, while temporarily there, his creditor might sue him there and recover the debt, then he is liable to process of garnishment, no matter where the situs of the debt was originally. . . . The obligation of the debtor to pay his debt clings to and accompanies him wherever he goes. He is as much bound to pay his debt in a foreign state when therein sued upon his obligation by his creditor, as he was in the state where the debt was contracted. We speak of ordinary debts, such as the one in this case. . . . [P]ossession cannot be taken of a debt or of the obligation to pay it, as tangible property might be taken possession of. Notice to the debtor (garnishee) of the commencement of the suit, and notice not to pay his creditor, is all that can be given, whether the garnishee be a mere casual and temporary comer, or a resident of the State where the attachment is laid. His obligation to pay to his creditor is thereby arrested and a lien created upon the debt itself. Cahoon v. Morgan, 38 Vermont 236; National Fire Ins. Co. v. Chambers, 53 N.J.Eq. 468, 483. We can see no reason why the attachment could not be thus laid, provided the creditor of the garnishee could himself sue in that State and its laws permitted the attachment....

It ... appears that Balk could have sued Harris in Maryland to recover his debt, notwithstanding the temporary character of Harris' stay there; it also appears that the municipal law of Maryland permits the debtor of the principal debtor to be garnished ...

It seems to us, therefore, that the judgment against Harris in Maryland, condemning the $180 which he owed to Balk, was a valid judgment, because the court had jurisdiction over the garnishee by personal service of process within the State of Maryland.

It ought to be and it is the object of courts to prevent the payment of any debt twice over. Thus, ... Harris ... should have the right to plead his payment under the Maryland judgment. It is objected, however, that the payment by Harris to Epstein was not under legal compulsion. Harris in truth owed the debt to Balk, which was attached by Epstein. He had, therefore, as we have seen, no defense to set up against the attachment of the debt. Jurisdiction over him personally had been obtained by the Maryland court. As he was absolutely without defense, there was no reason why he should not consent to a judgment impounding the debt ... There was no merely voluntary payment within the meaning of that phrase as applicable here.

[Justice Peckham went on to state that it is the garnishee's duty to take reasonable steps to notify his creditor of the pendency of the garnishment proceedings "so that the creditor may have the opportunity to defend himself against the claim of the person suing out the attachment." It did not appear that Harris had given Balk such notice and therefore his payment of the garnishment judgment would not under ordinary circumstances have constituted a defense to Balk's action against him. This was not true, however, in this particular case, because Balk did receive notice of the garnishment judgment shortly after its entry and under the peculiar Maryland practice had a year's time following such entry to establish that he was not indebted to Epstein in the amount claimed.]

The judgment of the Supreme Court of North Carolina must be reversed and the cause remanded for further proceedings not inconsistent with the opinion of this court.

Reversed.

■ JUSTICE HARLAN and JUSTICE DAY dissenting.

NOTES

1. Harris v. Balk's reasoning and result were severely questioned and perhaps overruled by the United States Supreme Court in Shaffer v. Heitner, p. 136, infra, but its influence, if not its authority, endures. It gave constitutional approval to garnishment proceedings.

2. Garnishment proceedings have been meeting with procedural as well as jurisdictional challenges. In Sniadach v. Family Finance Corp. of Bay View, 395 U.S. 337 (1969), the Supreme Court struck down as violative of due process provisions of the Wisconsin garnishment procedure under which wages are frozen when process in a garnishment action is served upon the employer of the alleged debtor and the latter "without any opportunity to be heard and to tender any defense he may have, whether it be fraud or otherwise" is thereby deprived of his earned wages until after the termination of the creditor's action against him. For essentially similar reasons the Georgia garnishment provisions were declared unconstitutional in North Georgia Finishing, Inc. v. DiChem, Inc., 419 U.S. 601 (1975). Analogous Supreme Court decisions are Fuentes v. Shevin, 407 U.S. 67 (1972) and Mitchell v. W.T. Grant Co., 416 U.S. 600 (1974). See generally Note, Foreign Attachment after *Sniadach* and *Fuentes,* 73 Colum.L.Rev. 342 (1973); Note, Quasi in Rem Jurisdiction and Due Process Requirements, 82 Yale L.J. 1023 (1973).

New York Life Insurance Co. v. Dunlevy

Supreme Court of the United States, 1916.
241 U.S. 518, 36 S.Ct. 613, 60 L.Ed. 1140.

■ JUSTICE MCREYNOLDS delivered the opinion of the court:

Respondent, Effie J. Gould Dunlevy, instituted this suit in the superior court, Marin county, California, January 14, 1910, against petitioner and Joseph W. Gould, her father, to recover $2,479.70, the surrender value of a policy on his life which she claimed had been assigned to her in 1893, and both were duly served with process while in that state. It was removed to the United States district court, February 16, 1910, and there tried by the judge in May, 1912, a jury having been expressly waived. Judgment for amount claimed was affirmed by the circuit court of appeals. 204 F. 670, 130 C.C.A. 473, 214 F. 1.

The insurance company by an amended answer filed December 7, 1911, set up in defense (1) that no valid assignment had been made, and (2) that Mrs. Dunlevy was concluded by certain judicial proceedings in Pennsylvania wherein it had been garnished and the policy had been adjudged to be the property of Gould. Invalidity of the assignment is not now urged; but it is earnestly insisted that the Pennsylvania proceedings constituted a bar.

In 1907 Boggs & Buhl recovered a valid personal judgment by default, after domiciliary service, against Mrs. Dunlevy, in the common pleas court at Pittsburgh, where she then resided. During 1909, "the tontine dividend period" of the life policy having expired, the insurance company became liable for $2,479.70, and this sum was claimed both by Gould, a citizen of Pennsylvania, and his daughter, who had removed to California. In November, 1909, Boggs & Buhl caused issue of an execution attachment on their judgment, and both the insurance company and Gould were summoned as garnishees. He appeared, denied assignment of the policy, and claimed the full amount due thereon. On February 5, 1910,—after this suit was begun in California,—the company answered, admitted its indebtedness, set up the conflicting claims to the fund, and prayed to be advised as to its rights. At the same time it filed a petition asking for a rule upon the claimants to show cause why they should not interplead and thereby ascertain who was lawfully entitled to the proceeds, and, further, that it might be allowed to pay amount due into court for benefit of proper party. An order granted the requested rule, and directed that notice be given to Mrs. Dunlevy in California. This was done, but she made no answer and did not appear. Later the insurance company filed a second petition, and, upon leave obtained thereunder, paid $2,479.70 into court, March 21, 1910. All parties except Mrs. Dunlevy having appeared, a feigned issue was framed and tried to determine validity of alleged transfer of the policy. The jury found, October 1, 1910, there was no valid assignment, and thereupon, under an order of court, the fund was paid over to Gould.

Beyond doubt, without the necessity of further personal service of process upon Mrs. Dunlevy, the court of common pleas of Pittsburgh had ample power through garnishment proceedings to inquire whether she held a valid claim against the insurance company, and, if found to exist, then to condemn and appropriate it so far as necessary to discharge the original judgment. Although herself outside the limits of the state, such disposition of the property would have been binding on her.... But the interpleader initiated by the company was an altogether different matter. This was an attempt to bring about a final and conclusive adjudication of her personal rights, not merely to discover property and apply it to debts. And unless in contemplation of law she was before the court, and required to respond to that issue, its orders and judgments in respect thereto were not binding on her....

Counsel maintain that having been duly summoned in the original suit instituted by Boggs & Buhl in 1907, and notwithstanding entry of final judgment therein, "Mrs. Dunlevy was in the Pennsylvania court and was bound by every order that court made, whether she remained within the jurisdiction of that court after it got jurisdiction over her person or not;" and hence, the argument is, "When the company paid the money into court where she was, it was just the same in legal effect as if it had paid it to her." This position is supposed to be supported by our opinion in Michigan Trust Co. v. Ferry, 228 U.S. 346 ... The judgment under consideration was fairly within the reasonable anticipation of the executor when he submitted himself to the probate court. But a wholly different and intolerable condition would result from acceptance of the theory that, after final judgment, a defendant remains in court and subject to whatsoever orders may be entered under title of the cause.... The interpleader proceedings were not essential concomitants of the original action by Boggs & Buhl against Dunlevy, but plainly collateral; and, when summoned to respond in that action, she was not required to anticipate them....

It has been affirmatively held in Pennsylvania that a judgment debtor is not a party to a garnishment proceeding to condemn a claim due him from a third person, and is not bound by a judgment discharging the garnishee (Ruff v. Ruff, 85 Pa. 333); and this is the generally accepted doctrine....

We are of opinion that the proceedings in the Pennsylvania court constituted no bar to the action in California, and the judgment below is accordingly affirmed.

NOTES

1. Are the Harris and Dunlevy cases distinguishable on a reasoned analysis—for example, by considering what values are furthered and what injuries are avoided by allowing the forum to affect the nonresident's interests?

2. Sanders v. Armour Fertilizer Works, 292 U.S. 190 (1934). Sanders, who was domiciled in Texas, was insured by two insurance companies against loss by fire of certain Texas property. The property was destroyed by fire and the insurance companies each admitted indebtedness to Sanders in stipulated amounts. Thereafter, garnishment proceedings seeking to attach the debts owed Sanders by the insurance companies were brought in Illinois by the Armour Fertilizer Works, a creditor of Sanders. While these proceedings were pending, the insurance companies brought an action in Texas under the Federal Interpleader Act against Sanders and Armour Fertilizer Works and paid into court the amounts owed by them under the policies. The court enjoined the Armour Fertilizer Company from proceeding further with the Illinois garnishment proceeding and, after a hearing, determined that Sanders was entitled to the sums due under the policies because these sums under Texas law were exempt from the claims of his creditors. *Held,* reversed on the ground that full faith and credit had been denied the Illinois garnishment proceedings. Under Illinois law, the commencement of a garnishment action imposes an "inchoate lien" upon the debt subject to defeat by certain subsequent events, none of which had transpired. Likewise, the Illinois courts would have rejected Sanders' claim of exemption under Texas law. "To hold that the District Court in Texas could enjoin the Fertilizer Works from proceeding further and then declare that because the last step had not been taken, Sanders, in some way, became entitled to priority, plainly would be inequitable. Moreover, it would deny to the garnishment proceedings the credit and effect accorded them in the State where taken." Four Justices dissented on the ground that under Illinois law garnishment does not create a lien upon the debt.

3. The difficulty encountered in obtaining jurisdiction over all claimants in state proceedings led to the adoption and gradual extension of federal interpleader proceedings. The classic treatment of the development and shortcomings of interpleader proceedings in the federal courts, as well as of state interpleader proceedings, is given by Professor Zechariah Chafee in the following articles: Modernizing Interpleader, 30 Yale L.J. 814 (1921); Interstate Interpleader, 33 Yale L.J. 685 (1924); Interpleader in the United States Courts, 41 Yale L.J. 1134 (1932); The Federal Interpleader Act of 1936, 45 Yale L.J. 963 (1936); Federal Interpleader Since the Act of 1936, 49 Yale L.J. 377 (1940); Broadening the Second Stage of Interpleader, 56 Harv.L.Rev. 541, 929 (1943). It will be observed that the advantage of federal interpleader over state interpleader inheres in the fact that while the jurisdiction of a state court over persons may be limited by the boundaries of the

state, the jurisdiction of the federal courts over persons may be extended throughout the whole of the United States, even in diversity cases in which the subject matter of the controversy is beyond the legislative jurisdiction of the federal government. Why should it be regarded as unfair imposition upon a non-resident defendant to be called to defend in a distant state court action, as in the Dunlevy case, supra, but entirely consistent with due process to impose the same burden upon the defendant by federal interpleader? Cf. Chapter 6, infra.

The statutory sources for federal interpleader are 28 U.S.C.A. §§ 1335, 1397, and 2361; Federal Rule of Civil Procedure 22.

Shaffer v. Heitner
Supreme Court of the United States, 1977.
433 U.S. 186, 97 S.Ct. 2569, 53 L.Ed.2d 683.

■ JUSTICE MARSHALL delivered the opinion of the Court.

The controversy in this case concerns the constitutionality of a Delaware statute that allows a court of that State to take jurisdiction of a lawsuit by sequestering any property of the defendant that happens to be located in Delaware. . . .

I

Appellee Heitner, a nonresident of Delaware, is the owner of one share of stock in the Greyhound Corporation, a business incorporated under the laws of Delaware with its principal place of business in Phoenix, Ariz. On May 22, 1974, he filed a shareholder's derivative suit in the Court of Chancery for New Castle County, Del., in which he named as defendants Greyhound, its wholly owned subsidiary Greyhound Lines, Inc., and 28 present or former officers or directors of one or both of the corporations. In essence, Heitner alleged that the individual defendants had violated their duties to Greyhound by causing it and its subsidiary to engage in actions that resulted in the corporations being held liable for substantial damages in a private antitrust suit and a large fine in a criminal contempt action. The activities which led to these penalties took place in Oregon.

Simultaneously with his complaint, Heitner filed a motion for an order of sequestration of the Delaware property of the individual defendants pursuant to 10 Del.C. § 366. . . . The requested sequestration order was signed the day the motion was filed. Pursuant to that order, the sequestrator "seized" approximately 82,000 shares of Greyhound common stock belonging to 19 of the defendants, and options belonging to another two defendants. . . . So far as the record shows, none of the certificates representing the seized property was physically present in Delaware. The stock was considered to be in Delaware, and so subject to seizure, by virtue of 8 Del.C. § 169, which makes Delaware the situs of ownership of all stock in Delaware corporations.

All 28 defendants were notified of the initiation of the suit by certified mail directed to their last known addresses and by publication in a New Castle County newspaper. The 21 defendants whose property was seized (hereafter referred to as appellants) responded by entering a special appearance [asserting] that under the rule of International Shoe Co. v. Washington, 326 U.S. 310 (1945), they did not have sufficient contacts with Delaware to sustain the jurisdiction of that State's courts....

II

The Delaware courts rejected appellants' jurisdictional challenge by noting that this suit was brought as a *quasi in rem* proceeding. Since *quasi in rem* jurisdiction is traditionally based on attachment or seizure of property present in the jurisdiction, not on contacts between the defendant and the State, the courts considered appellants' claimed lack of contacts with Delaware to be unimportant. This categorical analysis assumes the continued soundness of the conceptual structure founded on the century-old case of Pennoyer v. Neff, 95 U.S. 714 (1877).

[Justice Marshall here discussed the *Pennoyer* case and noted that it based 'authority to adjudicate ... on the jurisdiction's power over either persons or property.' He stated that with respect to judicial jurisdiction over persons the *Pennoyer* rule has been supplanted by the rule of *International Shoe*. He continued:]

No equally dramatic change has occurred in the law governing jurisdiction *in rem*. There have, however, been intimations that the collapse of the *in personam* wing of *Pennoyer* has not left that decision unweakened as a foundation for *in rem* jurisdiction. Well-reasoned lower court opinions have questioned the proposition that the presence of property in a State gives that State jurisdiction to adjudicate rights to the property regardless of the relationship of the underlying dispute and the property owner to the forum. [Citations omitted.]. The overwhelming majority of commentators have also rejected *Pennoyer's* premise that a proceeding "against" property is not a proceeding against the owners of that property. Accordingly, they urge that the "traditional notions of fair play and substantial justice" that govern a State's power to adjudicate *in personam* should also govern its power to adjudicate personal rights to property located in the State. [Citations omitted.] ...

Although this Court has not addressed this argument directly, we have held that property cannot be subjected to a court's judgment unless reasonable and appropriate efforts have been made to give the property owners actual notice of the action. Schroeder v. City of New York, 371 U.S. 208 (1962); Walker v. City of Hutchinson, 352 U.S. 112 (1956); Mullane v. Central Hanover Bank & Trust Co., 339 U.S. 306 (1950). This conclusion recognizes, contrary to *Pennoyer,* that an adverse judgment *in rem* directly affects the property owner by divesting him of his rights in the property before the court....

III

The case for applying to jurisdiction *in rem* the same test of "fair play and substantial justice" as governs assertions of jurisdiction *in personam* is simple and straightforward. It is premised on recognition that "[t]he phrase, 'judicial jurisdiction over a thing,' is a customary elliptical way of referring to jurisdiction over the interests of persons in a thing." Restatement (Second) of Conflict of Laws § 56, introductory note. This recognition leads to the conclusion that in order to justify an exercise of jurisdiction *in rem,* the basis for jurisdiction must be sufficient to justify exercising "jurisdiction over the interests of persons in a thing." The standard for determining whether an exercise of jurisdiction over the interests of persons is consistent with the Due Process Clause is the minimum contacts standard elucidated in *International Shoe.*

This argument, of course, does not ignore the fact that the presence of property in a State may bear on the existence of jurisdiction by providing contacts among the forum State, the defendant, and the litigation. For example, when claims to the property itself are the source of the underlying controversy between the plaintiff and the defendant, it would be unusual for the State where the property is located not to have jurisdiction. In such cases, the defendant's claim to property located in the State would normally indicate that he expected to benefit from the State's protection of his interest. The State's strong interests in assuring the marketability of property within its borders and in providing a procedure for peaceful resolution of disputes about the possession of that property would also support jurisdiction, as would the likelihood that important records and witnesses will be found in the State.[28] The presence of property may also favor jurisdiction in cases, such as suits for injury suffered on the land of an absentee owner, where the defendant's ownership of the property is conceded but the cause of action is otherwise related to rights and duties growing out of that ownership.[29]

It appears, therefore, that jurisdiction over many types of actions which now are or might be brought *in rem* would not be affected by a holding that any assertion of state court jurisdiction must satisfy the *International Shoe* standard.[30] For the type of *quasi in rem* action typified by Harris v. Balk [p. 146, supra] and the present case, however, accepting the proposed analysis would result in significant change. These are cases where the property which now serves as the basis for state court jurisdiction is completely unrelated to the plaintiff's cause of action. Thus, although the presence of the defendant's property in a State might suggest the existence of other ties among the defendant, the State, and the litigation, the presence of the property alone would not support the State's jurisdiction. If those other ties did not exist, cases over which the State is now thought to have jurisdiction could not be brought in that forum.

---

28. We do not suggest that these illustrations include all the factors that may affect the decision, nor that the factors we have mentioned are necessarily decisive.

29. Cf. Dubin v. City of Philadelphia, 34 Pa.D. & C. 61 (1938)....

30. Smit, The Enduring Utility of In Rem Rules: A Lasting Legacy of Pennoyer v. Neff, 48 Brooklyn L.Rev. 600 (1977). We do not suggest that jurisdictional doctrines other than those discussed in text, such as the particularized rules governing adjudications of status, are inconsistent with the standard of fairness....

Since acceptance of the *International Shoe* test would most affect this class of cases, we examine the arguments against adopting that standard as they relate to this category of litigation.[31] Before doing so, however, we note that this type of case also presents the clearest illustration of the argument in favor of assessing assertions of jurisdiction by a single standard. For in cases such as *Harris* and this one, the only role played by the property is to provide the basis for bringing the defendant into court.[32] Indeed, the express purpose of the Delaware sequestration procedure is to compel the defendant to enter a personal appearance. In such cases, if a direct assertion of personal jurisdiction over the defendant would violate the Constitution, it would seem that an indirect assertion of that jurisdiction should be equally impermissible.

The primary rationale for treating the presence of property as a sufficient basis for jurisdiction to adjudicate claims over which the State would not have jurisdiction if *International Shoe* applied is that a wrongdoer "should not be able to avoid payment of his obligations by the expedient of removing his assets to a place where he is not subject to an in personam suit." Restatement (Second) of Conflicts § 66, comment a.... This justification, however, does not explain why jurisdiction should be recognized without regard to whether the property is present in the State because of an effort to avoid the owner's obligations. Nor does it support jurisdiction to adjudicate the underlying claim. At most, it suggests that a State in which property is located should have jurisdiction to attach that property, by use of proper procedures, as security for a judgment being sought in a forum where the litigation can be maintained consistently with *International Shoe*.... Moreover, we know of nothing to justify the assumption that a debtor can avoid paying his obligations by removing his property to a State in which his creditor cannot obtain personal jurisdiction over him. The Full Faith and Credit Clause, after all, makes the valid *in personam* judgment of one State enforceable in all other States.[36]

It might also be suggested that allowing *in rem* jurisdiction avoids the uncertainty inherent in the *International Shoe* standard and assures a plaintiff of a forum.[37] ... We believe, however, that the fairness standard

---

31. Concentrating on this category of cases is also appropriate because in the other categories, to the extent that presence of property in the State indicates the existence of sufficient contacts under *International Shoe,* there is no need to rely on the property as justifying jurisdiction regardless of the existence of those contacts.

32. The value of the property seized does serve to limit the extent of possible liability, but that limitation does not provide support for the assertion of jurisdiction. ... In this cases, appellants' potential liability under the *in rem* jurisdiction exceeds one million dollars....

36. Once it has been determined by a court of competent jurisdiction that the defendant is a debtor of the plaintiff, there would seem to be no unfairness in allowing an action to realize on that debt in a State where the defendant has property, whether or not that State would have jurisdiction to determine the existence of the debt as an original matter....

37. This case does not raise, and we therefore do not consider, the question whether the presence of a defendant's property in a State is a sufficient basis for jurisdiction when no other forum is available to the plaintiff.

of *International Shoe* can be easily applied in the vast majority of cases. Moreover, when the existence of jurisdiction in a particular forum under *International Shoe* is unclear, the cost of simplifying the litigation by avoiding the jurisdictional question may be the sacrifice of "fair play and substantial justice." That cost is too high....

We are left, then, to consider the significance of the long history of jurisdiction based solely on the presence of property in a State. Although the theory that territorial power is both essential to and sufficient for jurisdiction has been undermined, we have never held that the presence of property in a State does not automatically confer jurisdiction over the owner's interest in that property. This history must be considered as supporting the proposition that jurisdiction based solely on the presence of property satisfies the demands of due process, ... but it is not decisive.... The fiction that an assertion of jurisdiction over property is anything but an assertion of jurisdiction over the owner of the property supports an ancient form without substantial modern justification. Its continued acceptance would serve only to allow state court jurisdiction that is fundamentally unfair to the defendant.

We therefore conclude that all assertions of state court jurisdiction must be evaluated according to the standards set forth in *International Shoe* and its progeny.[39]

IV

The Delaware courts based their assertion of jurisdiction in this case solely on the statutory presence of appellants' property in Delaware. Yet that property is not the subject matter of this litigation, nor is the underlying cause of action related to the property. Appellants' holdings in Greyhound do not, therefore, provide contacts with Delaware sufficient to support the jurisdiction of that State's courts over appellants. If it exists, that jurisdiction must have some other foundation.

Appellee Heitner did not allege and does not now claim that appellants have ever set foot in Delaware. Nor does he identify any act related to his cause of action as having taken place in Delaware. Nevertheless, he contends that appellants' positions as directors and officers of a corporation chartered in Delaware provide sufficient "contacts, ties, or relations," International Shoe Co. v. Washington, supra, at 319, with that State to give its courts jurisdiction over appellants in this stockholder's derivative action. This argument is based primarily on what Heitner asserts to be the strong interest of Delaware in supervising the management of a Delaware corporation. That interest is said to derive from the role of Delaware law in establishing the corporation and defining the obligations owed to it by its officers and directors. In order to protect this interest, appellee concludes,

---

39. It would not be fruitful for us to reexamine the facts of cases decided on the rationales of *Pennoyer* and *Harris* to determine whether jurisdiction might have been sustained under the standard we adopt today. To the extent that prior decisions are inconsistent with this standard, they are overruled.

Delaware's courts must have jurisdiction over corporate fiduciaries such as appellants.

This argument is undercut by the failure of the Delaware Legislature to assert the state interest appellee finds so compelling. Delaware law bases jurisdiction not on appellants' status as corporate fiduciaries, but rather on the presence of their property in the State. Although the sequestration procedure used here may be most frequently used in derivative suits against officers and directors, ... the authorizing statute evinces no specific concern with such actions. Sequestration can be used in any suit against a nonresident, ..., and reaches corporate fiduciaries only if they happen to own interests in a Delaware corporation, or other property in the State. But as Heitner's failure to secure jurisdiction over seven of the defendants named in his complaint demonstrates, there is no necessary relationship between holding a position as a corporate fiduciary and owning stock or other interests in the corporation. If Delaware perceived its interest in securing jurisdiction over corporate fiduciaries to be as great as Heitner suggests, we would expect it to have enacted a statute more clearly designed to protect that interest.

Moreover, even if Heitner's assessment of the importance of Delaware's interest is accepted, his argument fails to demonstrate that Delaware is a fair forum for this litigation. The interest appellee has identified may support the application of Delaware law to resolve any controversy over appellants' actions in their capacities as officers and directors. But [in Hanson v. Denckla, p. 56, supra] we ... rejected the argument that if a State's law can properly be applied to a dispute, its courts necessarily have jurisdiction over the parties to that dispute....

Appellee suggests that by accepting positions as officers or directors of a Delaware corporation, appellants performed the acts required by Hanson v. Denckla. He notes that Delaware law provides substantial benefits to corporate officers and directors, and that these benefits were at least in part the incentive for appellants to assume their positions. It is, he says, "only fair and just" to require appellants, in return for these benefits, to respond in the State of Delaware when they are accused of misusing their powers....

But like Heitner's first argument, this line of reasoning establishes only that it is appropriate for Delaware law to govern the obligations of appellants to Greyhound and its stockholders. It does not demonstrate that appellants have "purposefully avail[ed themselves] of the privilege of conducting activities within the forum State," Hanson v. Denckla, supra, at 253, in a way that would justify bringing them before a Delaware tribunal. Appellants have simply had nothing to do with the State of Delaware. Moreover, appellants had no reason to expect to be haled before a Delaware court. Delaware, unlike some States, has not enacted a statute that treats acceptance of a directorship as consent to jurisdiction in the State.... Appellants, who were not required to acquire interests in Greyhound in order to hold their positions, did not by acquiring those interests surrender their right to be brought to judgment only in States with which they had had "minimum contacts." . . .

. . . The judgment of the Delaware Supreme Court must, therefore, be reversed.

■ JUSTICE REHNQUIST took no part in the consideration or decision of this case.

■ JUSTICE POWELL, concurring.

I agree that the principles of International Shoe Co. v. Washington, 326 U.S. 310 (1945), should be extended to govern assertions of *in rem* as well as *in personam* jurisdiction in state court. I also agree that neither the statutory presence of appellants' stock in Delaware nor their positions as directors and officers of a Delaware corporation can provide sufficient contacts to support the Delaware courts' assertion of jurisdiction in this case.

I would explicitly reserve judgment, however, on whether the ownership of some forms of property whose situs is indisputably and permanently located within a State may, without more, provide the contacts necessary to subject a defendant to jurisdiction within the State to the extent of the value of the property. In the case of real property, in particular, preservation of the common law concept of *quasi in rem* jurisdiction arguably would avoid the uncertainty of the general *International Shoe* standard without significant cost to " 'traditional notions of fair play and substantial justice.' " . . .

Subject to that reservation, I join the opinion of the Court.

■ JUSTICE STEVENS, concurring in the judgment.

The Due Process Clause affords protection against "judgments without notice." . . . Throughout our history the acceptable exercise of in rem and quasi in rem jurisdiction has included a procedure giving reasonable assurance that actual notice of the particular claim will be conveyed to the defendant. Thus, publication, notice by registered mail, or extraterritorial personal service has been as essential ingredient of any procedure that serves as a substitute for personal service within the jurisdiction.

The requirement of fair notice also, I believe, includes fair warning that a particular activity may subject a person to the jurisdiction of a foreign sovereign. If I visit another State, or acquire real estate or open a bank account in it, I knowingly assume some risk that the State will exercise its power over my property or my person while there. My contact with the State, though minimal, gives rise to predictable risks.

Perhaps the same consequences should flow from the purchase of stock of a corporation organized under the laws of a foreign nation, because to some limited extent one's property and affairs then become subject to the laws of the nation of domicile of the corporation. As a matter of international law, that suggestion might be acceptable because a foreign investment is sufficiently unusual to make it appropriate to require the investor to study the ramifications of his decision. But a purchase of securities in the domestic market is an entirely different matter.

One who purchases shares of stock on the open market can hardly be expected to know that he has thereby become subject to suit in a forum remote from his residence and unrelated to the transaction. As a practical matter, the Delaware sequestration statute creates an unacceptable risk of judgment without notice. Unlike the 49 other States, Delaware treats the place of incorporation as the situs of the stock, even though both the owner and the custodian of the shares are elsewhere. Moreover, Delaware denies the defendant the opportunity to defend the merits of the suit unless he subjects himself to the unlimited jurisdiction of the court. Thus, it coerces a defendant either to submit to personal jurisdiction in a forum which could not otherwise obtain such jurisdiction or to lose the securities which have been attached. If its procedure were upheld, Delaware would, in effect, impose a duty of inquiry on every purchaser of securities in the national market. For unless the purchaser ascertains both the State of incorporation of the company whose shares he is buying, and also the idiosyncrasies of its law, he may be assuming an unknown risk of litigation. I therefore agree with the Court that on the record before us no adequate basis for jurisdiction exists and that the Delaware statute is unconstitutional on its face.

How the Court's opinion may be applied in other contexts is not entirely clear to me.... My uncertainty as to the reach of the opinion, and my fear that it purports to decide a great deal more than is necessary to dispose of this case, persuade me merely to concur in the judgment.

■ JUSTICE BRENNAN, concurring and dissenting.

I join Parts I–III of the Court's opinion. I fully agree that the minimum-contacts analysis developed in International Shoe Co. v. Washington, 326 U.S. 310 (1945), represents a far more sensible construct for the exercise of state court jurisdiction than the patchwork of legal and factual fictions that has been generated from the decision in Pennoyer v. Neff, 95 U.S. 714 (1877). It is precisely because the inquiry into minimum contacts is now of such overriding importance, however, that I must respectfully dissent from Part IV of the Court's opinion....

... I am convinced that as a general rule a state forum has jurisdiction to adjudicate a shareholder derivative action centering on the conduct and policies of the directors and officers of a corporation chartered by that State. Unlike the Court, I therefore would not foreclose Delaware from asserting jurisdiction over appellants were it persuaded to do so on the basis of minimum contacts.

It is well settled that a derivative lawsuit as presented here does not inure primarily to the benefit of the named plaintiff. Rather, the primary beneficiaries are the corporation and its owners, the shareholders....

Viewed in this light, the chartering State has an unusually powerful interest in insuring the availability of a convenient forum for litigating claims involving a possible multiplicity of defendant fiduciaries and for vindicating the State's substantive policies regarding the management of its domestic corporations. I believe that our cases fairly establish that the State's valid substantive interests are important considerations in assessing whether it constitutionally may claim jurisdiction over a given cause of action....

To be sure, the Court is not blind to these considerations. It notes that the State's interests "may support the application of Delaware law to resolve any controversy over appellants' actions in their capacities as officers and directors." ... But this, the Court argues, pertains to choice of law, not jurisdiction. I recognize that the jurisdictional and choice-of-law inquiries are not identical. Hanson v. Denckla, 357 U.S. 235, 254 (1958). But I would not compartmentalize thinking in this area quite so rigidly as it seems to me the Court does today, for both inquiries "are often closely related and to a substantial degree depend upon similar considerations." Id., at 258, 78 S.Ct., at 1242 (Black, J., dissenting). In either case an important linchpin is the extent of contacts between the controversy, the parties, and the forum state. While constitutional limitations on the choice of law are by no means settled, see, e.g., Home Ins. Co. v. Dick, 281 U.S. 397 (1930), important considerations certainly include the expectancies of the parties and the fairness of governing the defendants' acts and behavior by rules of conduct created by a given jurisdiction. See, e.g., Restatement (Second) Choice of Law § 6. These same factors bear upon the propriety of a State's exercising jurisdiction over a legal dispute. At the minimum, the decision that it is fair to bind a defendant by a State's laws and rules should prove to be highly relevant to the fairness of permitting that same State to accept jurisdiction for adjudicating the controversy.

Furthermore, I believe that practical considerations argue in favor of seeking to bridge the distance between the choice-of-law and jurisdictional inquiries.... a court will feel less knowledgeable and comfortable in interpretation, and less interested in fostering the policies of [a] foreign jurisdiction, than would the courts established by the State that provides the applicable law.... Obviously, ... choice-of-law problems cannot entirely be avoided in a diverse legal system such as our own. Nonetheless, when a suitor seeks to lodge a suit in a State with a substantial interest in seeing its own law applied to the transaction in question, we could wisely act to minimize conflicts, confusion, and uncertainty by adopting a liberal view of jurisdiction, unless considerations of fairness or efficiency strongly point in the opposite direction.

This case is not one where, in my judgment, this preference for jurisdiction is adequately answered. Certainly nothing said by the Court persuades me that it would be unfair to subject appellants to suit in Delaware. The fact that the record does not reveal whether they "set foot" or committed "acts related to [the] cause of action" in Delaware ... is not decisive, for jurisdiction can be based strictly on out-of-state acts having foreseeable effects in the forum state. E.g., McGee v. International Life

Ins. Co., supra; Gray v. American Radiator & Standard Sanitary Corp., supra; Restatement (Second) Conflicts of Law § 37. . . .

[I] . . . would approach the minimum contacts analysis differently than does the Court. Crucial to me is the fact that appellants voluntarily associated themselves with the State of Delaware, "invoking the benefits and protections of its laws," Hanson v. Denckla, supra, at 56; International Shoe Co. v. Washington, supra, at 47, by entering into a long term and fragile relationship with one of its domestic corporations. They thereby elected to assume powers and to undertake responsibilities wholly derived from that State's rules and regulations, and to become eligible for those benefits that Delaware law makes available to its corporations' officials. . . .

Despite its rejection of the theoretical underpinning of Harris v. Balk, the majority in Shaffer stopped short of explicitly overruling the decision. (See footnote 39.) Perhaps the Court was aware, as Professor Andreas F. Lowenfeld has observed, that the record in the Harris case shows that both Harris and Balk were customers of Epstein and that on the facts Balk probably would be subject to jurisdiction in Maryland by today's standards. See Lowenfeld, In Search of the Intangible: A Comment on Shaffer v. Heitner, 53 N.Y.U.L.Rev. 102, 103–107 (1978).

Does the Shaffer decision spell the end of *quasi in rem* attachments for jurisdictional purposes? Since the plaintiff's judgment in an attachment-for-jurisdiction case will be limited to the value of the attached property and since the required contacts are likely to be no more exacting, the plaintiff would usually do better to use the defendant's contacts with the forum to assert *in personam* jurisdiction. (See Silberman, Shaffer v. Heitner: The End of an Era, 53 N.Y.U.L.Rev. 33, 67–68 (1978).)

In Intermeat, Inc. v. American Poultry, Inc., 575 F.2d 1017 (2d Cir.1978), in applying the *Shaffer* principle to uphold jurisdiction to attach debts owing to defendant from a third party, the court relied on the nonresident buyer's contacts with the forum. The buyer had entered into at least five prior contracts for the purchase of imported meats from the New York plaintiff-importer. The contracts called for delivery to ports outside New York. On two occasions defendant-buyer signed and returned to plaintiff in New York contracts that committed it to arbitration in that state. On other occasions the defendant retained the seller's form contracts without signing them. The court said it was unnecessary to decide whether defendant was "doing business" (for general jurisdiction purposes), but only whether there were minimum contacts satisfying the International Shoe requirements. Is that correct?

A persistent question is whether a bank account maintained by a nonresident in the forum is subject to attachment. In Pennington v. Fourth National Bank, 243 U.S. 269 (1917), a nonresident husband's instate bank account was attached by the wife in a suit for alimony. The court upheld the attachment. Does the validity of an attachment of property unrelated to the cause of action survive the *Shaffer* decision? An affirmative answer was given in Feder v. Turkish Airlines, 441 F.Supp. 1273 (S.D.N.Y.1977). The presence of the Turkish corporation's bank account in New York was held sufficient to supply the required jurisdictional contact. *Shaffer* was distinguished on the basis that the defendants there had not voluntarily associated themselves with the forum state. But the fact that a nonresident Spanish corporation sent an aircraft engine to Arizona for repair, even though there may have been some relationship between the subject matter of the contract sued upon and the engine, did not suffice to warrant quasi-in-rem-style attachment. Omni Aircraft Sales, Inc. v. Actividades Aereas Aragonesas (D.Ariz.1977) (not reported).

In an earlier case, the United States government sued in a federal court in New York to recover income taxes allegedly owed by a Uruguayan corporation. To prevent the corporation (which had not been served with process) from withdrawing any assets that might be available to satisfy a tax liability, the government obtained a temporary injunction against the First National City Bank, restraining it from disbursing the Uruguayan's account at the Bank's branch in Montevideo. The Supreme Court sustained the injunction, holding that the Bank's obligation to the Uruguayan corporation could be reached in New York and rejecting the argument that the debt was not a property interest in the United States. "If it were clear that the debtor [the Uruguayan] were beyond reach of the District Court as far as personal service is concerned, we would have quite a different case—one on which we intimate no opinion." United States v. First National City Bank, 379 U.S. 378, 381 (1965).

NOTES

1. In Carolina Power & Light Co. v. Uranex, 451 F.Supp. 1044 (N.D.Cal.1977), the North Carolina plaintiff sought to attach a debt owed a French defendant by a California company. The debt was the defendant's only asset in the United States, and the attachment was sought to secure any award the plaintiff might receive in New York where its dispute with the French defendant was being arbitrated. There was no personal jurisdiction over the French company in California. The court sustained the attachment:

"This court has concluded that in circumstances such as these a fair reading of the Supreme Court's opinion in Shaffer v. Heitner requires that the application of notions of 'fair play and substantial justice' include consideration of both the jeopardy to plaintiff's ultimate recovery and the limited nature of the jurisdiction sought, that is, jurisdiction merely to order the attachment and not to adjudicate the underlying merits of the controversies. In some circumstances even limited jurisdiction to attach property would nonetheless violate standards of 'fair play and substantial justice,' for example, where the attached property was merely moving through the state in transit to another country. But where the facts show that the presence of defendant's property within the state is not merely fortuitous, and that the attaching jurisdiction is not an inconvenient arena for defendant to litigate the limited issues arising from the attachment, assumption of limited jurisdiction to issue the attachment pending litigation in another forum would be constitutionally permissible." Is this a correct reading of *Shaffer*? (See the majority opinion at

[136]). In the specific context of international commercial arbitration, the majority view is that the U.N. Arbitration Convention does not permit a court to exercise jurisdiction except to order arbitration or to review the validity of the arbitration agreement itself. See Drexel Burnham Lambert, Inc. v. Ruebsamen, 139 A.D.2d 323, 531 N.Y.S.2d 547 (1 Dep't 1988).

2. A "Mareva" injunction, in English practice, enjoins a defendant from removing assets from the jurisdiction while an action is pending against it. Mareva Cia Naviera SA v. International Bulk Carriers SA, [1980] 1 All E.R. 213 (C.A.). As a result of English accession to the Brussels Convention on Jurisdiction and the Recognition of Judgments, Mareva injunctions are now also granted in support of proceedings commenced in other EC countries. Republic of Haiti v. Duvalier, [1989] 1 All E.R. 456 (C.A.). Mareva injunctions may also issue to restrain a defendant over whom the court has personal jurisdiction from dealing with its assets worldwide. Republic of Haiti, supra; Derby & Co. Ltd. v. Weldon, [1989] 469 (C.A.). See Collins, The Territorial Reach of Mareva Injunctions, 105 L.Q.Rev. 262 (1989); Dicey & Morris, Conflict of Laws 189 (12th ed. by Collins, 1993). Would U.S. courts enforce a Mareva injunction against a defendant seeking to dispose of assets located in the United States? The "Babanaft proviso" in Mareva injunctions makes clear that "no person other than the defendants themselves shall ... be affected" and that there is no intent to attempt to affect the foreign property directly. Babanaft International Co. SA v. Bassatne, [1989] 1 All E.R. 433 (C.A.).

Note that Mareva injunctions may issue on the basis of information about the defendant's assets obtained by means of an "Anton Piller Order." The order takes its name from Anton Piller KG v. Manufacturing Process Ltd., [1976] Ch. 55, [1976] 1 All E.R. 779 (C.A.), and is now also part of discovery procedures in Australia and Canada. The order issues ex parte and permits the successful movant to search the opponent's premises to secure and safeguard evidence in danger of destruction or loss. During the search, however, the holder of the order may also discover bank account information and learn of the location of assets and then seek to freeze these by means of a Mareva injunction. See House of Spring Gardens Ltd. v. Waite, [1985] F.S.R. 173 (C.A.). See Dockray & Laddie, Piller Problems, 106 L.Q.Rev. 601 (1990); Collins, Anton Piller Orders and Fundamental Rights, *id.* at 173. Should recognition of a Mareva injunction (see preceding paragraph) depend on how the underlying information was obtained? Note that the European Court of Human Rights has held that the ex parte nature and lack of a public hearing in Anton Piller Order cases does not violate the European Convention on Human Rights, of which the United Kingdom is a contracting state. Chappell v. United Kingdom, 1989 Eur. Court of Human Rights, Series A, No. 152–A.

3. Compare footnote 37 in the Shaffer decision with footnote 13 in Helicopteros, p. 98, supra. Is it likely today that the Supreme Court would uphold jurisdiction based on the presence of property in the forum upon a showing that the defendant is not subject to personal jurisdiction anywhere else in the United States?

In *Burnham,* supra p. 113, Justice Scalia concluded that *Shaffer* did not require a reexamination of transient jurisdiction in the light of *International Shoe* -principles. Justice Brennan in contrast thought that all assertions of state court jurisdiction is subject to due process scrutiny but concluded, on the grounds of availment and lack of unfairness, that the exercise of jurisdiction over Mr. Burnham passed the constitutional test. Is *Shaffer* as limited as Justice Scalia writes? Recall the search for appropriate standards for the assertion of personal jurisdiction, supra p. 120, Note 4. If fairness and convenience were the principal or only focal points, should a case like *Shaffer* be decided differently today? What about *Rush,* the next principal case (infra p. 148)?

4. After the Supreme Court's decision in *Shaffer,* the Delaware Code was amended (Del.Code Title 10, § 3114) to provide that "every nonresident of [Delaware] who after September 1, 1977, accepts election or appointment as a director, trustee or member of the governing body of a [Delaware] corporation, ... or who after June 30, 1978 serves in such capacity ... shall, by such acceptance or by such service, be deemed thereby to have consented to the appointment of the registered agent of such corporation (or, if there is none, the Secretary of State) as his agent upon whom service of process may be made in all civil actions or proceedings brought in this state, by or on behalf of, or against such corporation, in which such director, trustee or member is a necessary or proper party, or in any action or proceeding against such director, trustee or member for violation of his duty in such capacity...."

Being appointed a director of a Delaware corporation is by itself a constitutionally sufficient basis for the application of this statute to a non-resident defendant. Armstrong v. Pomerance, 423 A.2d 174 (Del.1980).

5. Among the many articles written about Shaffer v. Heitner are: Lowenfeld, In Search of the Intangible: A Comment on Shaffer v. Heitner, 53 N.Y.U.L.Rev. 102 (1978); Riesenfeld, Shaffer v. Heitner: Holding, Implications, Forebodings, 30 Hast.L.J. 1183 (1979); Silberman, Shaffer v. Heitner, The End of an Era, 53 N.Y.U.L.Rev. 33 (1978); Slomanson, Real Property Unrelated to Claim: Due Process for Quasi in Rem Jurisdiction?, 83 Dickinson L.Rev. 51 (1978); Symposium, 1978 Wash.U.L.Q. 273; Symposium, 63 Iowa L.Rev. 991. For analysis of the effect of Shaffer v. Heitner on the interplay of principles of judicial jurisdiction and choice of law, see Hay, The Interrelations of Jurisdiction and Choice-of-Law in U.S. Conflicts Law, 28 Int'l and Comp.L.Q. 161 (1979).

6. Judge John Gibbons had gone a considerable distance in anticipating the Shaffer decision in a concurring opinion in Jonnet v. Dollar Savings Bank of The City of New York, 530 F.2d 1123 (3d Cir.1976), referred to by Justice Marshall in *Shaffer.*

Rush v. Savchuk

Supreme Court of the United States, 1980.
444 U.S. 320, 100 S.Ct. 571, 62 L.Ed.2d 516.

■ JUSTICE MARSHALL delivered the opinion of the Court.

This appeal presents the question whether a State may constitutionally exercise *quasi in rem* jurisdiction over a defendant who has no forum contacts by attaching the contractual obligation of an insurer licensed to do business in the State to defend and indemnify him in connection with the suit.

I

On January 13, 1972, two Indiana residents were involved in a single-car accident in Elkhart, Ind. Appellee Savchuk, who was a passenger in the car driven by appellant Rush, was injured. The car, owned by Rush's father, was insured by appellant State Farm Mutual Automobile Insurance Co. (State Farm) under a liability insurance policy issued in Indiana.

Indiana's guest statute would have barred a claim by Savchuk. Ind.Stat. § 9–3–3–1.

Savchuk moved with his parents to Minnesota in June 1973.[1] On May 28, 1974, he commenced an action against Rush in the Minnesota state courts.[2] As Rush had no contacts with Minnesota that would support *in personam* jurisdiction, Savchuk attempted to obtain *quasi in rem* jurisdiction by garnishing State Farm's obligation under the insurance policy to defend and indemnify Rush in connection with such a suit. State Farm does business in Minnesota. Rush was personally served in Indiana. The complaint alleged negligence and sought $125,000 in damages.

As provided by the state garnishment statute, Savchuk moved the trial court for permission to file a supplemental complaint-making the garnishee, State Farm, a party to the action after State Farm's response to the garnishment summons asserted that it owed the defendant nothing. Rush and State Farm moved to dismiss the complaint for lack of jurisdiction over the defendant. The trial court denied the motion to dismiss and granted the motion for leave to file the supplemental complaint.

On appeal, the Minnesota Supreme Court affirmed the trial court's decision. 311 Minn. 480, 245 N.W.2d 624 (1976) (*Savchuk I*). It held, first, that the obligation of an insurance company to defend and indemnify a nonresident insured under an automobile liability insurance policy is a garnishable res in Minnesota for the purpose of obtaining *quasi in rem* jurisdiction when the incident giving rise to the action occurs outside Minnesota but the plaintiff is a Minnesota resident when the suit is filed. Second, the court held that the assertion of jurisdiction over Rush was constitutional because he had notice of the suit and an opportunity to defend, his liability was limited to the amount of the policy, and the garnishment procedure may be used only by Minnesota residents. The court expressly recognized that Rush had engaged in no voluntary activity that would justify the exercise of *in personam* jurisdiction. The court found, however, that considerations of fairness supported the exercise of *quasi in rem* jurisdiction because in accident litigation the insurer controls the defense of the case, State Farm does business in and is regulated by the State, and the State has an interest in protecting its residents and providing them with a forum in which to litigate their claims.

Rush appealed to this Court. We vacated the judgment and remanded the cause for further consideration in light of Shaffer v. Heitner [136, supra].

On remand, the Minnesota Supreme Court held that the assertion of *quasi in rem* jurisdiction through garnishment of an insurer's obligation to

---

1. Savchuk moved to Pennsylvania after this appeal was filed.

2. The suit was filed after the two-year Indiana statute of limitations had run. 272 N.W.2d 888, 891, n. 5 (1978). [The Court here misconstrues n. 5 in the Minnesota court's opinion. Whether the Indiana statute had run before suit was filed (rather than, as the Minnesota opinion says, when the trial court ruled to make State Farm a party) is uncertain.—Eds.].

an insured complied with the due process standards enunciated in *Shaffer*. 272 N.W.2d 888 (Minn.1978) (*Savchuk II*). The court found that the garnishment statute differed from the Delaware stock sequestration procedure held unconstitutional in *Shaffer* because the garnished property was intimately related to the litigation and the garnishment procedure paralleled the asserted state interest in "facilitating recoveries for resident plaintiffs." Id., at 891.[8] This appeal followed.

II

The Minnesota Supreme Court held that the Minnesota garnishment statute embodies the rule stated in Seider v. Roth [17 N.Y.2d 111, 269 N.Y.S.2d 99, 216 N.E.2d 312 (1966)] that the contractual obligation of an insurance company to its insured under a liability insurance policy is a debt subject to attachment under state law if the insurer does business in the State. *Seider* jurisdiction was upheld against a due process challenge in Simpson v. Loehmann, 21 N.Y.2d 305, 234 N.E.2d 669 (1967), reargument denied 21 N.Y.2d 990, 238 N.E.2d 319 (1968). The New York court relied on Harris v. Balk, 198 U.S. 215 (1905), in holding that the presence of the debt in the State was sufficient to permit *quasi in rem* jurisdiction over the absent defendant. The court also concluded that the exercise of jurisdiction was permissible under the Due Process Clause because, "[v]iewed realistically, the insurer in a case such as the present is in full control of the litigation" and "where the plaintiff is a resident of the forum state and the insurer is present in and regulated by it, the State has a substantial and continuing relation with the controversy." Simpson v. Loehmann, supra, at 311, 234 N.E.2d, at 672.

The United States Court of Appeals for the Second Circuit gave its approval to *Seider* in Minichiello v. Rosenberg, 410 F.2d 106, adhered to en banc, 410 F.2d 117 (1968), cert. denied, 396 U.S. 844 (1969), although on a slightly different rationale. Judge Friendly construed *Seider* as "in effect a judicially created direct action statute. The insurer doing business in New York is considered the real party in interest and the nonresident insured is viewed simply as a conduit, who has to be named as a defendant in order to provide a conceptual basis for getting at the insurer." 410 F.2d at 109; see Donawitz v. Danek, 42 N.Y.2d 138, 142, 366 N.E.2d 253, 255 (1977). The court held that New York could constitutionally enact a direct action statute, and that the restriction of liability to the amount of the policy coverage made the policyholder's personal stake in the litigation so slight that the exercise of jurisdiction did not offend due process.

---

8. Minnesota would apply its own comparative negligence law, rather than Indiana's contributory negligence rule. See Schwartz v. Consolidated Freightways Corp., 300 Minn. 487, 221 N.W.2d 665 (1974). Appellants assert that Minnesota would also decline to apply the Indiana guest statute if this case were tried in Minnesota. Juris Statement 10, n 2; cf. Savchuk II, supra, at 891–892. The constitutionality of a choice-of-law rule that would apply forum law in these circumstances is not before us. Cf. Home Ins. Co. v. Dick, 281 U.S. 397, 74 L.Ed. 926, 50 S.Ct. 338, 74 A.L.R. 701 (1930).

New York has continued to adhere to *Seider*.[10] New Hampshire follows *Seider* if the defendant resides in a *Seider* jurisdiction,[11] but not in other cases.[12] Minnesota is the only other State that has adopted *Seider*-type jurisdiction. The Second Circuit recently reaffirmed its conclusion that *Seider* does not violate due process after reconsidering the doctrine in light of Shaffer v. Heitner. O'Connor v. Lee–Hy Paving Corp., 579 F.2d 194 (CA2), cert. denied, 439 U.S. 1034 (1978).

III

In Shaffer v. Heitner [p. 136, supra] we held that "all assertions of state-court jurisdiction must be evaluated according to the standards set forth in *International Shoe* and its progeny." . . .

It is conceded that Rush has never had any contacts with Minnesota, and that the auto accident that is the subject of this action occurred in Indiana and also had no connection to Minnesota. The only affiliating circumstance offered to show a relationship among Rush, Minnesota, and this lawsuit is that Rush's insurance company does business in the State. *Seider* constructed an ingenious jurisdictional theory to permit a State to command a defendant to appear in its courts on the basis of this factor alone. State Farm's contractual obligation to defend and indemnify Rush in connection with liability claims is treated as a debt owed by State Farm to Rush. The legal fiction that assigns a situs to a debt, for garnishment purposes, wherever the debtor is found is combined with the legal fiction that a corporation is "present," for jurisdictional purposes, wherever it does business to yield the conclusion that the obligation to defend and indemnify is located in the forum for purposes of the garnishment statute. The fictional presence of the policy obligation is deemed to give the State the power to determine the policyholder's liability for the out of state accident.

We held in *Shaffer* that the mere presence of property in a State does not establish a sufficient relationship between the owner of the property and the State to support the exercise of jurisdiction over an unrelated cause of action. The ownership of property in the State is *a* contact between the defendant and the forum, and it may suggest the presence of other ties. 433 U.S., at 209. Jurisdiction is lacking, however, unless there are sufficient contacts to satisfy the fairness standard of *International Shoe*.

Here, the fact that the defendant's insurer does business in the forum State suggests no further contacts between the defendant and the forum, and the record supplies no evidence of any. State Farm's decision to do business in Minnesota was completely adventitious as far as Rush was concerned. He had no control over that decision, and it is unlikely that he

---

10. Baden v. Staples, 45 N.Y.2d 889, 383 N.E.2d 110 (1978). The State has declined, however, to make the attachment procedure available to nonresident plaintiffs. Donawitz v. Danek, 42 N.Y.2d 138, 366 N.E.2d 253 (1977).

11. Forbes v. Boynton, 113 N.H. 617, 313 A.2d 129 (1973).

12. Camire v. Scieszka, 116 N.H. 281, 358 A.2d 397 (1976).

would have expected that by buying insurance in Indiana he had subjected himself to suit in any State to which a potential future plaintiff might decide to move. In short, it cannot be said that the *defendant* engaged in any purposeful activity related to the forum that would make the exercise of jurisdiction fair, just, or reasonable ... merely because his insurer does business there.

Nor are there significant contacts between the litigation and the forum. The Minnesota Supreme Court was of the view that the insurance policy was so important to the litigation that it provided contacts sufficient to satisfy due process. The insurance policy is not the subject matter of the case, however, nor is it related to the operative facts of the negligence action. The contractual arrangements between the defendant and the insurer pertain only to the conduct, not the substance, of the litigation, and accordingly do not affect the court's jurisdiction unless they demonstrate ties between the defendant and the forum.

In fact, the fictitious presence of the insurer's obligation in Minnesota does not, without more, provide a basis for concluding that there is *any* contact in the *International Shoe* sense between Minnesota and the insured. To say that "a debt follows the debtor" is simply to say that intangible property has no actual situs, and a debt may be sued on wherever there is jurisdiction over the debtor. State Farm is "found," in the sense of doing business, in all 50 States and the District of Columbia. Under appellee's theory, the "debt" owed to Rush would be "present" in each of those jurisdictions simultaneously. It is apparent that such a "contact" can have no jurisdictional significance.

An alternative approach for finding minimum contacts in *Seider*-type cases, referred to with approval by the Minnesota Supreme Court, is to attribute the insurer's forum contacts to the defendant by treating the attachment procedure as the functional equivalent of a direct action against the insurer. This approach views *Seider* jurisdiction as fair both to the insurer, whose forum contacts would support *in personam* jurisdiction even for an unrelated cause of action, and to the "nominal defendant." Because liability is limited to the policy amount, the defendant incurs no personal liability, and the judgment is satisfied from the policy proceeds which are not available to the insured for any purpose other than paying accident claims, the insured is said to have such a slight stake in the litigation as a practical matter that it is not unfair to make him a "nominal defendant" in order to obtain jurisdiction over the insurance company.

Seider actions are not equivalent to direct actions, however. The State's ability to exert its power over the "nominal defendant" is analytically prerequisite to the insurer's entry into the case as a garnishee. If the Constitution forbids the assertion of jurisdiction over the insured based on the policy, then there is no conceptual basis for bringing the "garnishee" into the action. Because the party with forum contacts can only be reached through the out of state party, the question of jurisdiction over the nonresident cannot be ignored. Moreover, the assumption that the defendant has no real stake in the litigation is far from self-evident.[20]

The Minnesota court also attempted to attribute State Farm's contacts to Rush by considering the "defending parties" together and aggregating their forum contacts in determining whether it had jurisdiction. The result was the assertion of jurisdiction over Rush based solely on the activities of State Farm. Such a result is plainly unconstitutional. Naturally, the parties' relationships with each other may be significant in evaluating their ties to the forum. The requirements of *International Shoe*, however, must be met as to each defendant over whom a state court exercises jurisdiction.

The justifications offered in support of *Seider* jurisdiction share a common characteristic: they shift the focus of the inquiry from the relationship among the defendant, the forum, and the litigation to that among the plaintiff, the forum, the insurer, and the litigation. The insurer's contacts with the forum are attributed to the defendant because the policy was taken out in anticipation of such litigation. The State's interests in providing a forum for its residents and in regulating the activities of insurance companies are substituted for its contacts with the defendant and the cause of action. This subtle shift in focus from the defendant to the plaintiff is most evident in the decisions limiting *Seider* jurisdiction to actions by forum residents on the ground that permitting nonresidents to avail themselves of the procedure would be unconstitutional.[22] In other words, the plaintiff's contacts with the forum are decisive in determining whether the defendant's due process rights are violated.

Such an approach is forbidden by *International Shoe* and its progeny.... The judgment of the Minnesota Supreme Court is, therefore,

Reversed.

■ JUSTICE STEVENS, dissenting.

... In this kind of case, the Minnesota statute authorizing jurisdiction is correctly characterized as the "functional equivalent" of a so-called direct action statute. The impact of the judgment is against the insurer. I

---

20. A party does not extinguish his legal interest in a dispute by insuring himself against having to pay an eventual judgment out of his own pocket. Moreover, the purpose of insurance is simply to make the defendant whole for the economic costs of the lawsuit; but noneconomic factors may also be important to the defendant. Professional malpractice actions, for example, question the defendant's integrity and competence and may affect his professional standing. Cf. Donawitz v. Danek, 42 N.Y.2d 138, 366 N.E.2d 253 (1977) (medical malpractice action premised on *Seider* jurisdiction dismissed because plaintiff was a nonresident). Further, one can easily conceive of cases in which the defendant might have a substantial economic stake in *Seider* litigation—if, for example, multiple plaintiffs sued in different States for an aggregate amount in excess of the policy limits, or if a successful claim would affect the policyholder's insurability. For these reasons, the defendant's interest in the adjudication of his liability cannot reasonably be characterized as *de minimis*.

22. See, e.g., Farrell v. Piedmont Aviation, Inc., 411 F.2d 812 (C.A.2 1969); Rintala v. Shoemaker, 362 F.Supp. 1044 (Minn.1973); Donawitz v. Danek, 42 N.Y.2d 138, 366 N.E.2d 253 (1977); *Savchuk I*.

believe such a direct action statute is valid as applied to a suit brought by a forum resident, ... even if the accident giving rise to the action did not occur in the forum State, ... so long as it is understood that the forum may exercise no power whatsoever over the individual defendant. As so understood it makes no difference whether the insurance company is sued in its own name or, as Minnesota law provides, in the guise of a suit against the individual defendant.

In this case, although appellant may have a contractual obligation to his insurer to appear in court to testify and generally to cooperate in the defense of the lawsuit, it is my understanding that Minnesota law does not compel him to do so through the contempt power or otherwise. Moreover, any judgment formally entered against the individual defendant may only be executed against the proceeds of his insurance policy. In my opinion, it would violate the Due Process Clause to make any use of such a judgment against the individual—for example, by giving the judgment collateral estoppel effect in a later action against him arising from the same accident.... But we are not now faced with any problem concerning use of a *quasi-in-rem* judgment against an individual defendant personally. I am therefore led to the conclusion that the Federal Constitution does not require the Minnesota courts to dismiss this action.

■ JUSTICE BRENNAN, dissenting.*

... [A] number of considerations suggest that Minnesota is an interested and convenient forum. The action was filed by a bona fide resident of the forum. Consequently, Minnesota's interests are similar to, even if lesser than, the interests of California in *McGee,* "in providing a forum for its residents and in regulating the activities of insurance companies" doing business in the State.... Moreover, Minnesota has "attempted to assert [its] particularized interest in trying such cases in its courts by ... enacting a special jurisdictional statute." *Kulko,* [p. 63, supra]; *McGee,* [p. 53, supra]. As in *McGee,* a resident forced to travel to a distant State to prosecute an action against someone who has injured him could, for lack of funds, be entirely unable to bring the cause of action. The plaintiff's residence in the State makes the State one of a very few convenient fora for a personal injury case (the others usually being the defendant's home State and the State where the accident occurred).[5]

In addition, the burden on the defendant is slight.... Here the real impact is on the defendant's insurer, which is concededly amenable to suit in the forum State. The defendant is carefully protected from financial liability because the action limits the prayer for damages to the insurance

---

* Justice Brennan combined in a single opinion his dissents in Rush v. Savchuk and in World–Wide Volkswagen Corporation v. Woodson (page 66, supra). That part of his opinion dealing with Rush v. Savchuk is set forth here. [Footnote by the Editors].

5. In every *International Shoe* inquiry, the defendant, necessarily, is outside the forum State. Thus it is inevitable that either the defendant or the plaintiff will be inconvenienced. The problem existing at the time of Pennoyer v. Neff, that a resident plaintiff could obtain a binding judgment against an unsuspecting, distant defendant, has virtually disappeared in this age of instant communication and virtually instant travel.

policy's liability limit. The insurer will handle the case for the defendant. The defendant is only a nominal party who need be no more active in the case than the cooperation clause of his policy requires. Because of the ease of airline transportation, he need not lose significantly more time than if the case were at home. Consequently, if the suit went forward in Minnesota, the defendant would bear almost no burden or expense beyond what he would face if the suit were in his home State. The real impact on the named defendant is the same as it is in a direct action against the insurer, which would be constitutionally permissible.... The only distinction is the formal, "analytical prerequisite," ..., of making the insured a named party. Surely the mere addition of appellant's name to the complaint does not suffice to create a due process violation.

Finally, even were the relevant inquiry whether there are sufficient contacts between the forum and the named defendant, I would find that such contacts exist. The insurer's presence in Minnesota is an advantage to the defendant that may well have been a consideration in his selecting the policy he did. An insurer with offices in many States makes it easier for the insured to make claims or conduct other business that may become necessary while traveling. It is simply not true that "State Farm's decision to do business in Minnesota was completely adventitious as far as Rush was concerned." ... By buying a State Farm policy, the defendant availed himself of the benefits he might derive from having an insurance agent in Minnesota who could, among other things, facilitate a suit for appellant against a Minnesota resident. It seems unreasonable to read the Constitution as permitting one to take advantage of his nationwide insurance network but not to be burdened by it.

In sum, I would hold that appellant is not deprived of due process by being required to submit to trial in Minnesota, first because Minnesota has a sufficient interest in and connection to this litigation and to the real and nominal defendants, and second because the burden on the nominal defendant is sufficiently slight.

NOTES

1. Justice Marshall argued that Rush should not be bound by State Farm's decision to do business in Minnesota or Savchuk's action in moving there since he had no control over those decisions. Is there an analogy between that argument and Justice White's insistence in World–Wide Volkswagen (p. 66, supra) that the nonresident defendants were not made amenable to personal jurisdiction by reason of the presence of the Audi automobile in Oklahoma, since they had not placed it in a stream of commerce that ran to Oklahoma?

2. The Court might have taken note of a point made in Brilmayer, How Contacts Count: Due Process Limitations on State Court Jurisdiction, 1980 Supreme Court Review 77, 103 (1980), namely, that neither Minnesota nor New York allows a direct action in a non-conflicts case. Both states require that an unsatisfied judgment against the insured exist before the insurer is suable in a domestic case. Is there any good reason for the courts to dispense with the requirement in a multistate case?

3. What is the impact of Rush v. Savchuk on statutory direct actions against insurers when the insured is not subject to personal jurisdiction in the forum? The major permutations include: (a) the state where the injury occurred provides for a direct action but the forum does not; (b) the converse; (c) the plaintiff is a forum resident; (d) the plaintiff is a nonresident. These questions are considered in Ch. 7, at p. 375, infra.

4. In Minichiello v. Rosenberg, 410 F.2d 106 (2d Cir.1968), adhered to en banc, 410 F.2d 117 (1968), discussed in the Rush case, Judge Friendly in his opinion for the panel rested his argument for the constitutionality of Seider's "judicially created direct action" procedure on Watson v. Employers Liability Corp., [p. 343, infra], which the dissenters in Rush also relied upon. However, in his majority opinion for the Second Circuit en banc in Minichiello Judge Friendly shifted to reliance on Harris v. Balk, arguing that as long as it stood, the nonresident defendant's claim of unfair burden in having to defend in the forum was unpersuasive. Was reliance on Watson justified? Notice that Judge Friendly's court did not think either Watson or Minichiello would support a Seider-type proceeding brought by a nonresident plaintiff. Farrell v. Piedmont Aviation, Inc., 411 F.2d 812 (1969) cert. denied 396 U.S. 840 (1969).

5. The demise of Seider attachments dissolved a knotty issue that had troubled the court in Minichiello: if the Seider-type action determined after trial that the nonresident defendant was at fault, would that finding bind the defendant as res judicata (collateral estoppel) in a later in personam suit in another state? That question will be considered in connection with Harnischfeger Sales Corp. v. Sternberg Dredging Co., p. 235, infra.

SECTION 4. COMPETENCE OF COURT AND NOTICE

RESTATEMENT, SECOND, CONFLICT OF LAWS: *

§ 105. Judgment Rendered By Court Lacking Competence

A judgment rendered by a court lacking competence to render it and subject to collateral attack for that reason in the state of rendition will not be recognized or enforced in other states.

Thompson v. Whitman

Supreme Court of the United States, 1874.
85 U.S. (18 Wall.) 457, 21 L.Ed. 897.

■ JUSTICE BRADLEY delivered the opinion of the court:

This is an action of trespass for taking and carrying away goods, originally brought in the superior court of New York City, and removed by the defendant, now plaintiff in error, into the circuit court of the United States. The declaration charges that, on the 26th of September, 1862, the defendant, with force and arms on the high seas, in the outward vicinity of

---

* Quoted with the permission of the copyright owner, The American Law Institute.

the Narrows of the Port of New York, and within the southern district of New York, seized and took the sloop Ann L. Whitman, with her tackle, furniture, etc., the property of the plaintiff, and carried away and converted the same. The defendant pleaded "Not guilty" and a special plea in bar. The latter plea justified the trespass by setting up that the plaintiff, a resident of New York, on the day of seizure was raking and gathering clams with said sloop in the waters of New Jersey, to wit: within the limits of the county of Monmouth, contrary to the law of that state; and that, by virtue of said law, the defendant, who was sheriff of said county, seized the sloop within the limits thereof, and informed against her before two justices of the peace of said county, by whom she was condemned and ordered to be sold. In answer to this plea the plaintiff took issue as to the place of seizure, denying that it was within the state of New Jersey or the county of Monmouth, thus challenging the jurisdiction of the justices, as well as the right of the defendant to make the seizure. On the trial conflicting testimony was given upon this point, but the defendant produced a record of the proceedings before the justices which stated the offense as having been committed and seizure as made within the county of Monmouth, with a history of the proceedings to the condemnation and order of sale. The defendant claimed that this record was conclusive, both as to the jurisdiction of the court and the merits of the case, and that it was a bar to the action, and requested the court so to charge the jury. But this was refused, and the court charged that the said record was only prima facie evidence of the facts therein stated, and threw upon the plaintiff the burden of proving the contrary. The defendant excepted, and the jury, under the direction of the court, found for the plaintiff generally, and in answer to certain questions framed by the court found specially: first, that the seizure was made within the state of New Jersey; second, that it was not made in the county of Monmouth; third, that the plaintiff was not engaged on the day of the seizure in taking claims within the limits of the county of Monmouth. Judgment being rendered for the plaintiff, the case is brought here for review.

The main question in the cause is, whether the record produced by the defendant was conclusive of the jurisdictional facts therein contained. It stated, with due particularity, sufficient facts to give the justices jurisdiction under the law of New Jersey. Could that statement be questioned collaterally in another action brought in another State? If it could be, the ruling of the court was substantially correct. If not, there was error....

Without that provision of the Constitution of the United States which declares that "full faith and credit shall be given in each State to the public acts, records, and judicial proceedings of every other State," and the act of Congress passed to carry it into effect, it is clear that the record in question would not be conclusive as to the facts necessary to give the justices of Monmouth County jurisdiction, whatever might be its effect in New Jersey. In any other State it would be regarded like any foreign judgment; and as to a foreign judgment it is perfectly well settled that the inquiry is always open, whether the court by which it was rendered had jurisdiction of the person or the thing....

Justice Story, who pronounced the judgment in Mills v. Duryee [7 Cranch 484], in his Commentary on the Constitution (Sec. 1313), after stating the general doctrine established by that case with regard to the conclusive effect of judgments of one State in every other State, adds: "But this does not prevent an inquiry into the jurisdiction of the court in which the original judgment was given, to pronounce it; or the right of the State itself to exercise authority over the person or the subject-matter. The Constitution did not mean to confer [upon the States] a new power or jurisdiction, but simply to regulate the effect of the acknowledged jurisdiction over persons and things within their territory."...

But if it is once conceded that the validity of a judgment may be attacked collaterally by evidence showing that the court had no jurisdiction, it is not perceived how any allegation contained in the record itself, however strongly made, can affect the right so to question it. The very object of the evidence is to invalidate the paper as a record. If that can be successfully done no statements contained therein have any force. If any such statements could be used to prevent inquiry, a slight form of words might always be adopted so as effectually to nullify the right of such inquiry. Recitals of this kind must be regarded like asseverations of good faith in a deed, which avail nothing if the instrument is shown to be fraudulent. The records of the domestic tribunals of England and some of the States, it is true, are held to import absolute verity as well in relation to jurisdictional as to other facts, in all collateral proceedings. Public policy and the dignity of the courts are supposed to require that no averment shall be admitted to contradict the record. But, as we have seen, that rule has no extra-territorial force....

On the whole, we think it clear that the jurisdiction of the court by which a judgment is rendered in any State may be questioned in a collateral proceeding in another State, notwithstanding the provision of the fourth article of the Constitution and the law of 1790, and notwithstanding the averments contained in the record of the judgment itself.

This is decisive of the case; for, according to the findings of the jury, the justices of Monmouth County could not have had any jurisdiction to condemn the sloop in question. It is true she was seized in the waters of New Jersey; but the express finding is, that the seizure was not made within the limits of the county of Monmouth, and that no clams were raked within the county on that day. The authority to make the seizure and to entertain cognizance thereof is given by the ninth section of the act, as follows:

> "It shall be the duty of all sheriffs and constables, and may be lawful for any other person or persons, to seize and secure any such canoe, flat, scow, boat, or other vessel as aforesaid, and immediately thereupon give information thereof to *two justices of the peace of the county where such seizure shall have been made,* who are hereby empowered and required to meet at such time and place as they shall appoint for the trial thereof, and hear and determine the same; and in case the same shall be condemned, it shall be sold by the order of and under the direction of the said justices, who, after deducting all legal costs and charges, shall pay one-half of the

proceeds of said sale to the collector of the county in which such offense shall have been committed, and the other half to the person who shall have seized and prosecuted the same."

From this it appears that the seizure must be made in a county, and that the case can only be heard by justices of the county where it is made— "two justices of the peace of the county where such seizure shall have been made." The seizure in this case as specially found by the jury was not made in Monmouth County; but the justices who tried the case were justices of that county. Consequently the justices had no jurisdiction, and the record had no validity.

It is argued that the seizure was continuous in its character, and became a seizure in Monmouth County when the sloop was carried into that county. This position is untenable. Suppose the seizure had been made in Cumberland County, in Delaware Bay, could the sloop have been carried around to Monmouth County and there condemned, on the ground that the seizure was continuous, and became finally a seizure in Monmouth County? This would hardly be contended. But it is said that the seizure was made within the State, off the county of Monmouth, and not within the limits of any county; and, hence, that Monmouth County was the first county in which the seizure took place. If this had been true (as it undoubtedly was), and the jury had so found, still it would not have helped the case. The major proposition is not correct. A seizure is a single act, and not a continuous fact. Possession, which follows seizure, is continuous. It is the seizure which must be made within the county where the vessel is to be proceeded against and condemned. The case may have been a casus omissus in the law; it is certainly not included in it.

As this disposes of all the errors which have been assigned, the judgment must be

Affirmed.

NOTES

1. In his assertion, "the justices [of Monmouth County] had no jurisdiction," what meaning did Justice Bradley intend to convey by the word "jurisdiction"? Would "competence" have been an accurate word? Or should he have said the "venue" was incorrect? If the latter, should the New Jersey judgment have been vulnerable to collateral attack?

2. In Pemberton v. Hughes, [1889] 1 Ch. 781, the validity of a Florida divorce decree was in question in an English court. The defendant asserted the decree was void because the return day of appearance in court was only nine days after the service of process, while under the rules of the Florida court the period should have been ten days. The court held that the divorce was valid, since the tests of "international jurisdiction" were met. What is the dividing line between a defect that can be corrected only by appeal and a defect that impairs jurisdiction?

3. In Aldrich v. Aldrich, 378 U.S. 540 (1964), a Florida alimony decree that purported to bind the estate of the obligor was entitled to recognition in West Virginia when the Florida Supreme Court, upon certification by the U.S. Supreme Court, responded that the decree, though entered without subject matter jurisdiction, "passed into verity, became final" for lack of appeal, and was no longer subject to collateral attack.

Mullane v. Central Hanover Bank & Trust Co.
Supreme Court of the United States, 1950.
339 U.S. 306, 70 S.Ct. 652, 94 L.Ed. 865.

■ JUSTICE JACKSON delivered the opinion of the Court.

This controversy questions the constitutional sufficiency of notice to beneficiaries on judicial settlement of accounts by the trustee of a common trust fund established under the New York Banking Law. The New York Court of Appeals considered and overruled objections that the statutory notice contravenes requirements of the Fourteenth Amendment and that by allowance of the account beneficiaries were deprived of property without due process of law. . . .

Common trust fund legislation is addressed to a problem appropriate for state action. Mounting overheads have made administration of small trusts undesirable to corporate trustees. In order that donors and testators of moderately sized trusts may not be denied the service of corporate fiduciaries, the District of Columbia and some thirty states other than New York have permitted pooling small trust estates into one fund for investment administration. The income, capital gains, losses and expenses of the collective trust are shared by the constituent trusts in proportion to their contribution. By this plan, diversification of risk and economy of management can be extended to those whose capital standing alone would not obtain such advantage.

Statutory authorization for the establishment of such common trust funds is provided in the New York Banking Law, § 100–c (c. 687, L.1937, as amended by c. 602, L.1943 and c. 158, L.1944). Under this Act a trust company may, with approval of the State Banking Board, establish a common fund and, within prescribed limits, invest therein the assets of an unlimited number of estates, trusts or other funds of which it is trustee. Each participating trust shares ratably in the common fund, but exclusive management and control is in the trust company as trustee, and neither a fiduciary nor any beneficiary of a participating trust is deemed to have ownership in any particular asset or investment of this common fund. The trust company must keep fund assets separate from its own, and in its fiduciary capacity may not deal with itself or any affiliate. Provisions are made for accountings twelve to fifteen months after the establishment of a fund and triennially thereafter. The decree in each such judicial settlement of accounts is made binding and conclusive as to any matter set forth in the account upon everyone having any interest in the common fund or in any participating estate, trust or fund.

In January, 1946, Central Hanover Bank and Trust Company established a common trust fund in accordance with these provisions, and in March, 1947, it petitioned the Surrogate's Court for settlement of its first account as common trustee. During the accounting period a total of 113 trusts, approximately half *inter vivos* and half testamentary, participated in the common trust fund, the gross capital of which was nearly three million dollars. The record does not show the number or residence of the beneficiaries, but they were many and it is clear that some of them were not residents of the State of New York.

The only notice given beneficiaries of this specific application was by publication in a local newspaper in strict compliance with the minimum requirements of N.Y.Banking Law § 100–c(12): "After filing such petition (for judicial settlement of its account) the petitioner shall cause to be issued by the court in which the petition is filed and shall publish not less than once in each week for four successive weeks in a newspaper to be designated by the court a notice or citation addressed generally without naming them to all parties interested in such common trust fund and in such estates, trusts or funds mentioned in the petition, all of which may be described in the notice or citation only in the manner set forth in said petition and without setting forth the residence of any such decedent or donor of any such estate, trust or fund." Thus the only notice required, and the only one given, was by newspaper publication setting forth merely the name and address of the trust company, the name and the date of establishment of the common trust fund, and a list of all participating estates, trusts or funds.

At the time the first investment in the common fund was made on behalf of each participating estate, however, the trust company, pursuant to the requirements of § 100–c(9), had notified by mail each person of full age and sound mind whose name and address were then known to it and who was "entitled to share in the income therefrom . . . (or) . . . who would be entitled to share in the principal if the event upon which such estate, trust or fund will become distributable should have occurred at the time of sending such notice." Included in the notice was a copy of those provisions of the Act relating to the sending of the notice itself and to the judicial settlement of common trust fund accounts.

Upon the filing of the petition for the settlement of accounts, appellant was, by order of the court pursuant to § 100–c(12), appointed special guardian and attorney for all persons known or unknown not otherwise appearing who had or might thereafter have any interest in the income of the common trust fund; and appellee Vaughan was appointed to represent those similarly interested in the principal. There were no other appearances on behalf of any one interested in either interest or principal.

Appellant appeared specially, objecting that notice and the statutory provisions for notice to beneficiaries were inadequate to afford due process under the Fourteenth Amendment, and therefore that the court was without jurisdiction to render a final and binding decree. Appellant's objections were entertained and overruled, the Surrogate holding that the notice required and given was sufficient. 75 N.Y.S.2d 397. A final decree accepting the accounts has been entered, affirmed by the Appellate Division of the Supreme Court, 275 App.Div. 769, 88 N.Y.S.2d 907, and by the Court of Appeals of the State of New York, 299 N.Y. 697, 87 N.E.2d 73.

The effect of this decree, as held below, is to settle "all questions respecting the management of the common fund." We understand that every right which beneficiaries would otherwise have against the trust company, either as trustee of the common fund or as trustee of any individual trust, for improper management of the common trust fund during the period covered by the accounting is sealed and wholly terminated by the decree. . . .

We are met at the outset with a challenge to the power of the State—the right of its courts to adjudicate at all as against those beneficiaries who reside without the State of New York. It is contended that the proceeding is one *in personam* in that the decree affects neither title to nor possession of any *res,* but adjudges only personal rights of the beneficiaries to surcharge their trustee for negligence or breach of trust. Accordingly, it is said, under the strict doctrine of Pennoyer v. Neff, 95 U.S. 714, the Surrogate is without jurisdiction as to nonresidents upon whom personal service of process was not made. . . .

Judicial proceedings to settle fiduciary accounts have been sometimes termed *in rem,* or more indefinitely *quasi in rem,* or more vaguely still, "in the nature of a proceeding *in rem.*" It is not readily apparent how the courts of New York did or would classify the present proceeding, which has some characteristics and is wanting in some features of proceedings both *in rem* and *in personam.* But in any event we think that the requirements of the Fourteenth Amendment to the Federal Constitution do not depend upon a classification for which the standards are so elusive and confused generally and which, being primarily for state courts to define, may and do vary from state to state. Without disparaging the usefulness of distinctions between actions *in rem* and those *in personam* in many branches of law, or on other issues, or the reasoning which underlies them, we do not rest the power of the State to resort to constructive service in this proceeding upon how its courts or this Court may regard this historic antithesis. It is sufficient to observe that, whatever the technical definition of its chosen procedure, the interest of each state in providing means to close trusts that exist by the grace of its laws and are administered under the supervision of its courts is so insistent and rooted in custom as to establish beyond doubt the right of its courts to determine the interests of all claimants, resident or nonresident, provided its procedure accords full opportunity to appear and be heard.

Quite different from the question of a state's power to discharge trustees is that of the opportunity it must give beneficiaries to contest. Many controversies have raged about the cryptic and abstract words of the Due Process Clause but there can be no doubt that at a minimum they require that deprivation of life, liberty or property by adjudication be preceded by notice and opportunity for hearing appropriate to the nature of the case.

In two ways this proceeding does or may deprive beneficiaries of property. It may cut off their rights to have the trustee answer for negligent or illegal impairments of their interests. Also, their interests are presumably subject to diminution in the proceeding by allowance of fees and expenses to one who, in their names but without their knowledge, may conduct a fruitless or uncompensatory contest. Certainly the proceeding is one in which they may be deprived of property rights and hence notice and hearing must measure up to the standards of due process.

Personal service of written notice within the jurisdiction is the classic form of notice always adequate in any type of proceeding. But the vital interest of the State in bringing any issues as to its fiduciaries to a final settlement can be served only if interests or claims of individuals who are outside of the State can somehow be determined. A construction of the Due Process Clause which would place impossible or impractical obstacles in the way could not be justified.

Against this interest of the State we must balance the individual interest sought to be protected by the Fourteenth Amendment. This is defined by our holding that "The fundamental requisite of due process of law is the opportunity to be heard." Grannis v. Ordean, 234 U.S. 385, 394. This right to be heard has little reality or worth unless one is informed that the matter is pending and can choose for himself whether to appear or default, acquiesce or contest.

The Court has not committed itself to any formula achieving a balance between these interests in a particular proceeding or determining when constructive notice may be utilized or what test it must meet. Personal service has not in all circumstances been regarded as indispensable to the process due to residents, and it has more often been held unnecessary as to nonresidents. We disturb none of the established rules on these subjects. No decision constitutes a controlling or even a very illuminating precedent for the case before us. But a few general principles stand out in the books.

An elementary and fundamental requirement of due process in any proceeding which is to be accorded finality is notice reasonably calculated, under all the circumstances, to apprise interested parties of the pendency of the action and afford them an opportunity to present their objections.... The notice must be of such nature as reasonably to convey the required information ... and it must afford a reasonable time for those interested to make their appearance.... But if with due regard for the practicalities and peculiarities of the case these conditions are reasonably met, the constitutional requirements are satisfied. "The criterion is not the possibility of conceivable injury but the just and reasonable character of the requirements, having reference to the subject with which the statute deals." American Land Co. v. Zeiss, 219 U.S. 47, 67; and see Blinn v. Nelson, 222 U.S. 1, 7.

But when notice is a person's due, process which is a mere gesture is not due process. The means employed must be such as one desirous of actually informing the absentee might reasonably adopt to accomplish it. The reasonableness and hence the constitutional validity of any chosen method may be defended on the ground that it is in itself reasonably certain to inform those affected, compare Hess v. Pawloski, 274 U.S. 352, with Wuchter v. Pizzutti, 276 U.S. 13,* or, where conditions do not reasonably permit such notice, that the form chosen is not substantially less likely to bring home notice than other of the feasible and customary substitutes.

It would be idle to pretend that publication alone, as prescribed here, is a reliable means of acquainting interested parties of the fact that their rights are before the courts. It is not an accident that the greater number of cases reaching this Court on the question of adequacy of notice have been concerned with actions founded on process constructively served through local newspapers. Chance alone brings to the attention of even a local resident an advertisement in small type inserted in the back pages of a newspaper, and if he makes his home outside the area of the newspaper's normal circulation the odds that the information will never reach him are large indeed. The chance of actual notice is further reduced when, as here, the notice required does not even name those whose attention it is supposed to attract, and does not inform acquaintances who might call it to attention. In weighing its sufficiency on the basis of equivalence with actual notice, we are unable to regard this as more than a feint.

Nor is publication here reinforced by steps likely to attract the parties' attention to the proceeding. It is true that publication traditionally has been acceptable as notification supplemental to other action which in itself may reasonably be expected to convey a warning. The ways of an owner with tangible property are such that he usually arranges means to learn of any direct attack upon his possessory or proprietary rights. Hence, libel of a ship, attachment of a chattel or entry upon real estate in the name of law may reasonably be expected to come promptly to the owner's attention. When the state within which the owner has located such property seizes it for some reason, publication or posting affords an additional measure of notification....

This Court has not hesitated to approve of resort to publication as a customary substitute in another class of cases where it is not reasonably possible or practicable to give more adequate warning. Thus it has been recognized that, in the case of persons missing or unknown, employment of an indirect and even a probably futile means of notification is all that the situation permits and creates no constitutional bar to a final decree foreclosing their rights....

Those beneficiaries represented by appellant whose interests or whereabouts could not with due diligence be ascertained come clearly within this category. As to them the statutory notice is sufficient. However great the odds that publication will never reach the eyes of such unknown parties, it is not in the typical case much more likely to fail than any of the choices open to legislators endeavoring to prescribe the best notice practicable.

---

* In Wuchter v. Pizzutti, the defendant had received notice by personal service outside the state but was nevertheless allowed to attack successfully the New Jersey nonresident motorist statute on the ground that it did not require that anyone inform defendant of the commencement of suit in a way making it "reasonably probable" that he would receive actual notice. [Footnote by the Editors.]

Nor do we consider it unreasonable for the State to dispense with more certain notice to those beneficiaries whose interests are either conjectural or future or, although they could be discovered upon investigation, do not in due course of business come to knowledge of the common trustee. Whatever searches might be required in another situation under ordinary standards of diligence, in view of the character of the proceedings and the nature of the interests here involved we think them unnecessary. We recognize the practical difficulties and costs that would be attendant on frequent investigations into the status of great numbers of beneficiaries, many of whose interests in the common fund are so remote as to be ephemeral; and we have no doubt that such impracticable and extended searches are not required in the name of due process. The expense of keeping informed from day to day of substitutions among even current income beneficiaries and presumptive remaindermen, to say nothing of the far greater number of contingent beneficiaries, would impose a severe burden on the plan, and would likely dissipate its advantages. These are practical matters in which we should be reluctant to disturb the judgment of the state authorities.

Accordingly, we overrule appellant's constitutional objections to published notice insofar as they are urged on behalf of any beneficiaries whose interests or addresses are unknown to the trustee.

As to known present beneficiaries of known place of residence, however, notice by publication stands on a different footing. Exceptions in the name of necessity do not sweep away the rule that within the limits of practicability notice must be such as is reasonably calculated to reach interested parties. Where the names and postoffice addresses of those affected by a proceeding are at hand, the reasons disappear for resort to means less likely than the mails to apprise them of its pendency.

The trustee has on its books the names and addresses of the income beneficiaries represented by appellant, and we find no tenable ground for dispensing with a serious effort to inform them personally of the accounting, at least by ordinary mail to the record addresses. Cf. Wuchter v. Pizzutti, supra. Certainly sending them a copy of the statute months and perhaps years in advance does not answer this purpose. The trustee periodically remits their income to them, and we think that they might reasonably expect that with or apart from their remittances word might come to them personally that steps were being taken affecting their interests.

We need not weigh contentions that a requirement of personal service of citation on even the large number of known resident or nonresident beneficiaries would, by reasons of delay if not of expense, seriously interfere with the proper administration of the fund. Of course personal service even without the jurisdiction of the issuing authority serves the end of actual and personal notice, whatever power of compulsion it might lack. However, no such service is required under the circumstances. This type of trust presupposes a large number of small interests. The individual interest does not stand alone but is identical with that of a class. The rights of each in the integrity of the fund and the fidelity of the trustee are shared by many other beneficiaries. Therefore notice reasonably certain to reach most of those interested in objecting is likely to safeguard the interests of all, since any objection sustained would inure to the benefit of all. We think that under such circumstances reasonable risks that notice might not actually reach every beneficiary are justifiable....

The statutory notice to known beneficiaries is inadequate, not because in fact it fails to reach everyone, but because under the circumstances it is not reasonably calculated to reach those who could easily be informed by other means at hand. However it may have been in former times, the mails today are recognized as an efficient and inexpensive means of communication. Moreover, the fact that the trust company has been able to give mailed notice to known beneficiaries at the time the common trust fund was established is persuasive that postal notification at the time of accounting would not seriously burden the plan.

In some situations the law requires greater precautions in its proceedings than the business world accepts for its own purposes. In few, if any, will it be satisfied with less. Certainly it is instructive, in determining the reasonableness of the impersonal broadcast notification here used, to ask whether it would satisfy a prudent man of business, counting his pennies but finding it in his interest to convey information to many persons whose names and addresses are in his files. We are not satisfied that it would. Publication may theoretically be available for all the world to see, but it is too much in our day to suppose that each or any individual beneficiary does or could examine all that is published to see if something may be tucked away in it that affects his property interests. We have before indicated in reference to notice by publication that, "Great caution should be used not to let fiction deny the fair play that can be secured only by a pretty close adhesion to fact." McDonald v. Mabee, 243 U.S. 90, 91.

We hold that the notice of judicial settlement of accounts required by the New York Banking Law § 100–c(12) is incompatible with the requirements of the Fourteenth Amendment as a basis for adjudication depriving known persons whose whereabouts are also known of substantial property rights. Accordingly the judgment is reversed and the cause remanded for further proceedings not inconsistent with this opinion.

Reversed.

■ [A dissenting memorandum by JUSTICE BURTON is omitted.]

NOTES

1. Does *Mullane* require any particular form of notice? See Federal Rule of Civil Procedure 4(e): service is to be effected either in accordance with the law of the state in which the federal district court sits or by delivery of the complaint to the individual personally or by leaving copies at his place of residence or with a "person of suitable age and discretion" there. See also Hanna v. Plumer, 380 U.S. 460 (1965), considered infra at p. 678.

In a series of cases the Supreme Court has held that publication in a newspaper, with or without posted notice, is insufficient to comply with the Mullane standards of due process. In Mennonite Board of Missions v. Adams, 462 U.S. 791 (1983), a notice of tax sale was posted in the county courthouse and published once a week for three weeks. This was held inadequate notice to a mortgagee of the property despite the dissenters' argument that the notification satisfied Mullane's "balancing" test. Similarly, in Tulsa Professional Collection Services, Inc. v. Pope, 485 U.S. 478 (1988), the Court required notice by a better method than publication to bar the creditor of a decedent's estate by a two month non-claim period. Cf. Schroeder v. City of New York, 371 U.S. 208 (1962) and Walker v. City of Hutchinson, 352 U.S. 112 (1956), invalidating newspaper and posted notices in condemnation cases where the owner's address was known to the city. In Greene v. Lindsey, 456 U.S. 444 (1982), the court held that posting a summons on the tenant's apartment door was inadequate notice for a forcible entry and detainer.

2. The common forms of notice in an action in personam are: handing the process to the person to be served; leaving it at his place of residence (with a person of a described class or affixed to the door, etc.); sending it by registered mail after service on a designated statutory agent, such as a registrar. Should registered mail alone always be sufficient?

3. Dobkin v. Chapman, 21 N.Y.2d 490, 289 N.Y.S.2d 161, 236 N.E.2d 451 (1968). Involved were three cases arising from automobile accidents in New York. In two of the cases, defendants were domiciled in New York while in the third they were domiciled in another state. In each case, the defendants' whereabouts were unknown and it was therefore impossible to give them actual notice. Nevertheless in each case the plaintiff was permitted to proceed after having given notice in a form prescribed by the court, in one case by publishing the summons and order in a local newspaper and in another by mailing the process and order to defendants' last known address from which they were known to have moved. Held affirmed. The plaintiffs should not be deprived of their rights after having done all that they reasonably could to inform the defendants. These are "situations in which insistence on actual notice, or even on the high probability of actual notice, would be both unfair to plaintiffs and harmful to the public interest."

CHAPTER 4

LIMITATIONS ON THE EXERCISE OF JURISDICTION

INTRODUCTORY NOTE

This chapter examines situations where states choose not to exercise judicial jurisdiction they undoubtedly have. This may result because of an agreement between the parties purporting to give exclusive jurisdiction to the courts of another state or because the court deems itself to be an inconvenient forum for the trial of the action or to be incapable of granting appropriate relief. Another question treated in this chapter is whether, when a state seeks by statute to restrict to its own courts jurisdiction to entertain particular actions, the courts of other states will give effect to the former state's desires. On some occasions, a state which has judicial jurisdiction in the due process sense may be required by other provisions of the United States Constitution either to hear or to refrain from hearing a case.

SECTION 1. LIMITATIONS IMPOSED BY CONTRACT

A state has judicial jurisdiction over a defendant who appears or has consented in advance to the court's jurisdiction. Section 2 of the Model Choice of Forum Act, reprinted at p. 43, supra, states the conditions upon which courts will usually exercise jurisdiction when the parties have made a contractual choice of the local forum. The *conferral* of jurisdiction by means of a contractual choice-of-court clause is also known as *"prorogation."* Suppose, however, that the plaintiff brings an action in a court other than the chosen forum and that it is now the defendant who seeks to enforce the exclusive choice-of-court stipulation: will a court refrain from exercising jurisdiction it possesses? Such a jurisdiction-*limiting* effect of a choice-of-court clause is known as *"derogation."* The Brussels Convention (Art. 17), infra p. 178, Note 9, does not distinguish between the prorogation and derogation effects of these clauses, except by generally proscribing their use in certain transactions. In contrast, American courts have drawn a distinction and, in the past, have often disregarded the parties' choice of another forum on the ground that parties cannot by private argument "oust" a court of jurisdiction given it by law. Of late, effect has usually been given to these agreements except when it would be "unfair or unreasonable" to do so. Restatement, Second, Conflict of Laws § 80.

Section 3 of the Model Choice of Forum Act [†] states more precisely the circumstances making it "unfair or unreasonable" to give effect to the parties' agreement.

Section 3. [*Action in Another Place by Agreement.*] If the parties have agreed in writing that an action shall on a controversy be brought only in another state and it is brought in a court of this state, the court will dismiss or stay the action, as appropriate, unless

(1) the court is required by statute to entertain the action;
(2) the plaintiff cannot secure effective relief in the other state, for reasons other than delay in bringing the action;
(3) the other state would be a substantially less convenient place for the trial of the action than this state;
(4) the agreement as to the place of the action was obtained by misrepresentation, duress, the abuse of economic power, or other unconscionable means; or
(5) it would for some other reason be unfair or unreasonable to enforce the agreement.

Comment

. . .

Clause (4): A significant factor to be considered in determining whether there was an "abuse of economic power or other unconscionable means" is whether the choice of forum agreement was contained in an adhesion, or "take-it-or-leave-it," contract.

M/S Bremen v. Zapata Off-Shore Co.

Supreme Court of the United States, 1972.
407 U.S. 1, 92 S.Ct. 1907, 32 L.Ed. 513.

The defendant, a German corporation, agreed to tow a drilling rig of Zapata, an American corporation, from Louisiana to a point off Ravenna, Italy. The contract provided that "any dispute arising must be treated before the London Court of Justice" and also contained two clauses purporting to exculpate the defendant from liability for damages to the rig. These latter provisions were valid under English law, and, according to the uncontradicted testimony of a British legal expert, would have been applied to exonerate the defendant if suit had been brought in England. On the other hand, these latter provisions were invalid under the law of the United States. The rig was damaged while being towed in the Gulf of Mexico. Suit to recover for this damage was brought in a federal district court in Florida. The lower courts refused to dismiss the action despite the fact that it had been brought in violation of the choice-of-forum clause. The Supreme Court reversed.

[†] After having been adopted in four states, this model act was withdrawn in 1975. (Handbook of the Conference of Commissioners on Uniform State Laws 351 (1976)).

■ CHIEF JUSTICE BURGER delivered the opinion of the Court.

... The expansion of American business and industry will hardly be encouraged if, notwithstanding solemn contracts, we insist on a parochial concept that all disputes must be resolved under our laws and in our courts....

Forum-selection clauses have historically not been favored by American courts. Many courts, federal and state, have declined to enforce such clauses on the ground that they were "contrary to public policy," or that their effect was to "oust the jurisdiction" of the court. Although this view apparently still has considerable acceptance, other courts are tending to adopt a more hospitable attitude toward forum-selection clauses. This view ... is that such clauses are prima facie valid and should be enforced unless enforcement is shown by the resisting party to be 'unreasonable' under the circumstances. We believe this is the correct doctrine to be followed by federal district courts sitting in admiralty. ... This approach is substantially that followed in other common-law countries including England. ... It accords with ancient concepts of freedom of contract and reflects an appreciation of the expanding horizons of American contractors who seek business in all parts of the world. Not surprisingly, foreign businessmen prefer, as do we, to have disputes resolved in their own courts, but if that choice is not available, then in a neutral forum with expertise in the subject matter. Plainly, the courts of England meet the standards of neutrality and long experience in admiralty litigation. The choice of that forum was made in an arm's-length negotiation by experienced and sophisticated businessmen, and absent some compelling and countervailing reason it should be honored by the parties and enforced by the courts.

The argument that such clauses are improper because they tend to "oust" a court of jurisdiction is hardly more than a vestigial legal fiction. It appears to rest at core on historical judicial resistance to any attempt to reduce the power and business of a particular court and has little place in an era when all courts are overloaded and when businesses once essentially local now operate in world markets. It reflects something of a provincial attitude regarding the fairness of other tribunals. No one seriously contends in this case that the forum-selection clause "ousted" the District Court of jurisdiction over Zapata's action. The threshold question is whether that court should have exercised its jurisdiction to do more than give effect to the legitimate expectations of the parties, manifested in their freely negotiated agreement, by specifically enforcing the forum clause.

There are compelling reasons why a freely negotiated private international agreement, unaffected by fraud, undue influence, or overweening bargaining power, such as that involved here, should be given full effect. ... Manifestly much uncertainty and possibly great inconvenience to both parties could arise if a suit could be maintained in any jurisdiction in which an accident might occur or if jurisdiction were left to any place where the *Bremen* or *Unterweser* might happen to be found. The elimination of all such uncertainties by agreeing in advance on a forum acceptable to both parties is an indispensable element in international trade, commerce, and contracting.

[I]t seems reasonably clear that the District Court and the Court of Appeals placed the burden on Unterweser to show that London would be a more convenient forum than Tampa, although the contract expressly resolved that issue. The correct approach would have been to enforce the forum clause specifically unless Zapata could clearly show that enforcement would be unreasonable and unjust, or that the clause was invalid for such reasons as fraud or overreaching. Accordingly, the case must be remanded for reconsideration.

We note, however, that there is nothing in the record presently before us that would support a refusal to enforce the forum clause. The Court of Appeals suggested that enforcement would be contrary to the public policy of the forum under Bisso v. Inland Waterways Corp., 349 U.S. 85 (1955), because of the prospect that the English courts would enforce the clauses of the towage contract purporting to exculpate Unterweser from liability for damages to the [rig]. A contractual choice-of-forum clause should be held unenforceable if enforcement would contravene a strong public policy of the forum in which suit is brought, whether declared by statute or by judicial decision. It is clear, however, that whatever the proper scope of the policy expressed in *Bisso,* it does not reach this case. *Bisso* rested on considerations with respect to the towage business strictly in American waters, and those considerations are not controlling in an international commercial agreement.

Courts have also suggested that a forum clause, even though it is freely bargained for and contravenes no important public policy of the forum, may nevertheless be "unreasonable" and unenforceable if the chosen forum is *seriously* inconvenient for the trial of the action. Of course, where it can be said with reasonable assurance that at the time they entered the contract, the parties to a freely negotiated private international commercial agreement contemplated the claimed inconvenience, it is difficult to see why any such claim of inconvenience should be heard to render the forum clause unenforceable.... [S]election of a remote forum to apply differing foreign law to an essentially American controversy might contravene an important public policy of the forum. For example, so long as *Bisso* governs American courts with respect to the towage business in American waters, it would quite arguably be improper to permit an American tower to avoid that policy by providing a foreign forum for resolution of his disputes with an American towee.

This case, however, involves a freely negotiated international commercial transaction between a German and an American corporation for towage of a vessel from the Gulf of Mexico to the Adriatic Sea.

[T]o allow Zapata opportunity to carry its heavy burden of showing not only that the balance of convenience is strongly in favor of trial in Tampa (that is, that it will be far more inconvenient for Zapata to litigate in London than it will be for Unterweser to litigate in Tampa), but also that a London trial will be so manifestly and gravely inconvenient to Zapata that it will be effectively deprived of a meaningful day in court, we remand for further proceedings.

■ JUSTICE DOUGLAS dissented primarily on the ground that the parties should not be permitted to escape the strong policy expressed in the *Bisso* case by means of a choice-of-forum clause.]

NOTES

1. So far as appears, England had no contact in the Zapata case with the parties or the transaction. Under these circumstances, would a choice-of-law clause calling for application of English law have been given effect? See cases at pp. 325–367 infra. Can the parties by means of a choice-of-forum clause obtain application of a law which could not have been made applicable by a choice-of-law clause?

2. The needs of international trade were also emphasized in Scherk v. Alberto–Culver Co., 417 U.S. 506 (1974), p. 646 infra, where the Supreme Court enforced an arbitration clause in a contract calling for the purchase by an American manufacturer of foreign enterprises owned by a German citizen. This was done despite the fact that the Court had previously held that an arbitration clause in an analogous agreement with only United States contacts was unenforceable by reason of the Securities and Exchange Act. Zapata was cited as an important precedent in the Alberto–Culver opinion. Similarly, the Supreme Court held in Mitsubishi Motors Corp. v. Soler Chrysler–Plymouth, Inc., 473 U.S. 614, 629 (1985), that an antitrust claim was covered by the parties' agreement to arbitrate, even though such an agreement would not be enforceable in the interstate context: "[C]oncerns of international comity, respect for the capacities of foreign and international tribunals, and sensitivity to the need of the international commercial system for predictability in the resolution of disputes require that we enforce the parties' agreement, even assuming that a contrary result would be forthcoming in a domestic context."

3. In Rodriguez de Quijas v. Shearson/American Express, Inc., 490 U.S. 477 (1989), the Court found that a predispute agreement to arbitrate claims under the Securities Act of 1933 was enforceable. Resolution of such claims only in a judicial forum is not required.

Carnival Cruise Lines, Inc. v. Shute

Supreme Court of the United States, 1991.
499 U.S. 585, 111 S.Ct. 1522, 113 L.Ed.2d 622.

[The Shutes, a Washington State couple, bought tickets for a cruise through a local travel agent from Carnival Cruise Lines, a Panamanian corporation with its principal place of business in Miami, Florida. Payment was forwarded to Miami, the tickets were issued there. They also constituted the Contract of Passage which contained a forum-selection clause in favor of Florida. The cruise departed from Los Angeles. Mrs. Shute was injured as a result of a fall when the ship was in international waters. The Shutes sued in Washington. The Court of Appeals held that the forum-selection clause was unenforceable because it was not freely bargained for and because enforcement of the clause would deprive the Shutes of their day in court inasmuch as they were physically and financially unable to pursue litigation in Florida. The Court of Appeals also held that Carnival Lines' Washington contacts were sufficient for the exercise of specific jurisdiction.]

■ BLACKMUN, J., delivered the opinion of the Court, in which REHNQUIST, C.J., and WHITE, O'CONNOR, SCALIA, KENNEDY, and SOUTER, JJ., joined. STEVENS, J., filed a dissenting opinion, in which MARSHALL, J., joined.

[T]he Court of Appeals acknowledged that a court concerned with the enforceability of such a clause must begin its analysis with The Bremen v. Zapata Off-Shore Co., 407 U.S. 1 (1972), where this Court held that forum-selection clauses, although not "historically . . . favored," are "prima facie valid." The appellate court concluded that the forum clause should not be enforced because it "was not freely bargained for." As an "independent justification" for refusing to enforce the clause, the Court of Appeals noted that there was evidence in the record to indicate that "the Shutes are physically and financially incapable of pursuing this litigation in Florida" and that the enforcement of the clause would operate to deprive them of their day in court and thereby contravene this Court's holding in *The Bremen.*

We begin by noting the boundaries of our inquiry. First, this is a case in admiralty, and federal law governs the enforceability of the forum-selection clause we scrutinize. Second, we do not address the question whether respondents had sufficient notice of the forum clause before entering the contract for passage. Respondents essentially have conceded that they had notice of the forum-selection provision. Brief for Respondent 26 ("The respondents do not contest the incorporation of the provisions nor [sic] that the forum selection clause was reasonably communicated to the respondents, as much as three pages of fine print can be communicated."). Additionally, the Court of Appeals evaluated the enforceability of the forum clause under the assumption, although "doubtful," that respondents could be deemed to have had knowledge of the clause.

In evaluating the reasonableness of the forum clause at issue in this case, we must refine the analysis of *The Bremen* to account for the realities of form passage contracts. As an initial matter, we do not adopt the Court of Appeals' determination that a non-negotiated forum-selection clause in a form ticket contract is never enforceable simply because it is not the subject of bargaining. Including a reasonable forum clause in a form contract of this kind well may be permissible for several reasons: First, a cruise line has a special interest in limiting the fora in which it potentially could be subject to suit. Because a cruise ship typically carries passengers from many locales, it is not unlikely that a mishap on a cruise could subject the cruise line to litigation in several different fora. Additionally, a clause establishing *ex ante* the forum for dispute resolution has the salutary effect of dispelling any confusion about where suits arising from the contract must be brought and defended, sparing litigants the time and expense of pretrial motions to determine the correct forum, and conserving judicial resources that otherwise would be devoted to deciding those motions. Finally, it stands to reason that passengers who purchase tickets containing a forum clause like that at issue in this case benefit in the form of reduced fares reflecting the savings that the cruise line enjoys by limiting the fora in which it may be sued.

We also do not accept the Court of Appeals' "independent justification" for its conclusion that *The Bremen* dictates that the clause should not be enforced because "there is evidence in the record to indicate that the Shutes are physically and financially incapable of pursuing this litigation in Florida." We do not defer to the Court of Appeals' findings of fact.... The Court of Appeals' conclusory reference to the record provides no basis for this Court to validate the finding of inconvenience. Furthermore, the Court of Appeals did not place in proper context this Court's statement in *The Bremen* that "the serious inconvenience of the contractual forum to one or both of the parties might carry greater weight in determining the reasonableness of the forum clause." 407 U.S., at 17. The Court made this statement in evaluating a hypothetical "agreement between two Americans to resolve their essentially local disputes in a remote alien forum." Ibid. In the present case, Florida is not a "remote alien forum," nor—given the fact that Mrs. Shute's accident occurred off the coast of Mexico—is this dispute an essentially local one inherently more suited to resolution in the State of Washington than in Florida. In light of these distinctions, and because respondents do not claim lack of notice of the forum clause, we conclude that they have not satisfied the "heavy burden of proof" required to set aside the clause on grounds of inconvenience.

It bears emphasis that forum-selection clauses contained in form passage contracts are subject to judicial scrutiny for fundamental fairness. In this case, there is no indication that petitioner set Florida as the forum in which disputes were to be resolved as a means of discouraging cruise passengers from pursuing legitimate claims. Any suggestion of such a bad-faith motive is belied by two facts: petitioner has its principal place of business in Florida, and many of its cruises depart from and return to Florida ports. Similarly, there is no evidence that petitioner obtained respondents' accession to the forum clause by fraud or overreaching. Finally, respondents have conceded that they were given notice of the forum provision and, therefore, presumably retained the option of rejecting the contract with impunity. In the case before us, therefore, we conclude that the Court of Appeals erred in refusing to enforce the forum-selection clause.

[Reversed.]

■ JUSTICE STEVENS, joined by JUSTICE MARSHALL, dissented on the grounds inter alia that the Shutes did not have notice of the clause and that it was not freely bargained for.

CARNIVAL CRUISE LINES, INC. v. SUPERIOR COURT, 234 Cal.App.3d 1019, 286 Cal.Rptr. 323 (2d Dist.1991). Two hundred thirty-eight cruise passengers sought damages for injuries sustained during a storm. The trial court refused to honor a forum-selection clause in favor of Florida, identical to the clause involved in the *Shute* case, and Carnival Cruise Lines petitioned for a writ of mandamus. The appellate court denied the writ on the basis of the considerations advanced by the Court of Appeals in *Shute*. The United States Supreme Court ultimately reversed and remanded for reconsideration in the light of its decision in *Shute*. On remand, held: "[T]he forum-selection clause is unenforceable as to any particular plaintiff if the [trial] court determines that such plaintiff did not have sufficient notice of the forum-selection clause prior to entering into the contract for passage. Absent such notice, the requisite mutual consent to that contractual term is lacking and no valid contract with respect to such clause thus exists. [Remanded to the trial court for a determination of this issue.]"

NOTES

1. Two-thirds of the plaintiffs in the California Carnival Cruise case were California residents, close to one half of the remaining plaintiffs were residents of Western states. Not a single plaintiff was from Florida, Carnival Cruise Lines' place of business. The court had originally stressed this fact to emphasize the "unreasonableness" of the forum-selection clause. Obviously wishing to provide the plaintiffs with a local forum, the court seized on the notice issue that the United States Supreme Court had expressly left open. Is it not likely that the notice issue will swallow up the *Shute* decision's endorsement of forum-selection clauses in standard form contracts?

2. If the forum-selection clause is unenforceable in the California case, the California court obviously has jurisdiction: the cruise in question departed from and was to end in Los Angeles. If the forum-selection clause had been unenforceable in *Shute*, would the Washington court have had jurisdiction? Carnival Cruise Lines had no offices and no exclusive agents in Washington, is not registered to do business there, and does not pay taxes there. It did advertise in local media, conducted promotional seminars, and paid commissions to local travel agents. It issued cruise tickets in Florida. The Court of Appeals held that these facts permitted the exercise of specific jurisdiction: "... Carnival's solicitation of business in Washington attracted the Shutes (through their travel agent) to the Carnival cruise. In the absence of Carnival's activity, the Shutes would not have taken the cruise, and Mrs. Shute's injury would not have occurred. It was Carnival's forum-related activities that put the parties within 'tortious striking distance' of one another." Shute v. Carnival Cruise Lines, 897 F.2d 377, 386 (9th Cir.1990). Is the court's "but for" test consistent with the United States Supreme Court's approach in *Helicopteros,* supra p. 94, particularly at p. 96, n. 10? In *Shute,* the Ninth Circuit Court of Appeals rejected opinions from the First, Second, and Eighth Circuits that had held that negligent injuries elsewhere did not "arise out of" solicitation of forum vacationers. Decisions in state courts have reflected this split in the federal circuits concerning the "but for, arising out of" argument. See Tatro v. Manor Care, Inc., 416 Mass. 763, 625 N.E.2d 549, 554 (1994) (accepting the "but for" test in a suit against a hotel); Munley v. Second Judicial Dist. Court, 104 Nev. 492, 761 P.2d 414, 415 (1988) (holding no jurisdiction over ski resort because the injury there did not "arise out of" forum solicitations). For an argument that a "but for" test would have provided specific jurisdiction in *Helicopteros,* see Seidelson, Recasting *World–Wide Volkswagen* as a Source of Longer Jurisdictional Reach, 19 Tulsa L.J. 1; 27 n. 105 (1983). Wilson v. Humphreys (Cayman) Ltd., 916 F.2d 1239 (7th Cir.1990), cert. denied, 499 U.S. 947 (1991), upheld jurisdiction over a

Cayman Island hotel without reaching the "arising out of" issue, perhaps assisted by the fact that the complaint pleaded not only negligence, but also breach of express and implied warranties, and breach of contract.

3. Forum-selection clauses have won widespread approval. From among the extensive contributions to the literature, see Mullenix, Another Choice of Forum, Another Choice of Law: Consensual Adjudicatory Procedure in Federal Court, 57 Fordham L.Rev. 291 (1988); Note, Forum Selection Clauses in Light of the Erie Doctrine and Federal Common Law: Stewart Organization v. Ricoh Corporation, 72 Minn.L.Rev. 1090 (1988); Juenger, American Jurisdiction: A Story of Comparative Neglect, 65 Colo.L.Rev. 1 (1993); Heiser, Forum Selection Clauses in State Courts: Limitations on Enforcement after Stewart and Carnival Cruise, 45 Fla.L.Rev. 361 (1993), and: Forum Selection Clauses in Federal Courts: Limitations on Enforcement after *Stewart* and Carnival Cruise, 45 Fla.L.Rev. 553 (1993); Note, Viva Zapata!: Toward a Rational System of Forum–Selection Clause Enforcement in Diversity Cases, 66 N.Y.U.L.Rev. 422 (1991); Note, Forum Selection Clauses: Substantive or Procedural for Erie Purposes, 89 Colum.L.Rev. 1068 (1989). For case law, see: Dougherty, Validity of Contractual Provision Limiting Place or Court in Which Action May be Brought, 31 A.L.R.4th 404 (1984); Fusco, Effect, on Application of 28 U.S.C.S. § 1404(a) or Forum Non Conveniens in Diversity Case, of Contractual Provision Fixing Forum for Enforcement or Laws Governing Interpretation—Post–Bremen Cases, 123 A.L.R.Fed. 323 (1995).

4. Choice-of-forum agreements have sometimes been denied effect. For instance, because it was "clearly and palpably unreasonable," the court in Calzavara v. Biehl & Co., 181 So.2d 809 (La.App.1966) ignored a provision purporting to give an Italian court exclusive jurisdiction over any action on a ticket for transportation from New Orleans to Italy. Plaintiff was a Louisiana resident and the defendant a Louisiana corporation. See also Kolendo v. Jerell, Inc., 489 F.Supp. 983 (S.D.W.Va. 1980); Lulling v. Barnaby's Family Inns, Inc., 482 F.Supp. 318 (E.D.Wis.1980); Carefree Vacations, Inc. v. Brunner, 615 F.Supp. 211 (W.D.Tenn.1985) (choice of Texas forum in contract executed in Illinois and Tennessee held to be unreasonable).

Some states adhere to the older view that forum-selection clauses represent an attempt to oust a court of jurisdiction given it by law, therefore violate public policy and are unenforceable. See, e.g., Redwing Carriers, Inc. v. Foster, 382 So.2d 554, 556 (Ala.1980); Stewart Organization, Inc. v. Ricoh Corporation, 487 U.S. 22 (1987).

Several lower federal courts had looked to the Zapata decision as providing a federal common law standard for the enforceability of forum selection clauses in diversity cases, regardless of whether the law of the forum state favored or was hostile to such clauses. In Stewart Organization, Inc. v. Ricoh Corp., 487 U.S. 22 (1988), the Supreme Court agreed that "federal law ... governs the District Court's decision whether to give effect to the parties' forum-selection clause and transfer this case to a court in Manhattan." The issue arose on a motion to transfer, and the Court viewed the case as one of "statutory construction"—turning on whether the parties' own stipulation should be given weight and, if so, how much, in the application of the federal transfer statute. The Court noted that, by providing rules of venue for diversity actions, Congress showed it wanted federal standards to apply, obviating the need to evaluate the issue in light of the "twin aims" that animate the *Erie* doctrine. 487 U.S. at 32 n. 11. In holding that transfer to the selected forum was proper, Justice Marshall said (487 U.S., at 29–31):

> "Section 1404(a) is intended to place discretion in the District Court to adjudicate motions for transfer [on a consideration of fairness and convenience.] ... Congress has directed that multiple considerations govern transfer within the federal court system and a state statute focusing on a single concern or a subset of the factors identified in § 1404(a) would defeat that command. Its application would impoverish the flexible and multifaceted analysis that Congress intended to govern motions to transfer within the federal systems. The forum-selection clause, which represents the parties' agreement as to the most proper forum, should receive neither dispositive consideration (as respondent might have it) nor no consideration (as Alabama law might have it), but rather the consideration for which Congress provided in § 1404(a)...."

As to what law governs the enforceability of forum-selection clauses when the federal transfer statute does not apply (to wit, in international cases) several decisions have adopted the view expressed by Justice Kennedy in his concurrence in *Stewart* that the clause should be given controlling effect in all but the most exceptional cases. See *e.g.*, Manetti–Farrow, Inc. v. Gucci America, Inc., 858 F.2d 509, 513 (9th Cir.1988); Scoles and Hay, Conflict of Laws 364–366 (2d ed. 1992). See also: Rindal v. Seckler Co., 786 F.Supp. 890 (D.Mont.1992) (Montana law applied under which forum selection clauses are presumptively unenforceable because contrary result would lead to forum shopping).

For critical discussion of the *Stewart* and *Carnival Cruise* decisions, see Borchers, Forum Selection Agreements in the Federal Courts After *Carnival Cruise*: A Proposal for Congressional Reform, 67 Wash.L.Rev. 55 (1992): by statute, forum selection clauses would be enforceable in all cases except employment contracts, individual insurance contracts, consumer contracts, and agreements involving less than $50,000. For consumer protection with respect to cognovit notes, see supra p. 178. For protection of the weaker party in the context of contractual choice of law, see infra p. 178. See also Goldman, My Way and the Highway: The Law and Economics of Choice of Forum Clauses in Consumer Form Contracts, 86 Nw.L.Rev. 700 (1992).

5. Choice-of-forum clauses frequently appear in maritime and other transportation contracts. Indussa Corp. v. S.S. Ranborg, 377 F.2d 200 (2d Cir.1967), held that Section 3(8) of the Carriage of Goods by Sea Act (46 U.S.C.A. § 1303(8)) invalidated such clauses in bills of lading involving commerce with the United States. Continuing its *Zapata* approach, the U.S. Supreme Court disapproved of *Indussa* in Vimar Seguros Y Reaseguros v. M/V Sky Reefer, 115 S.Ct. 2322 (1995).

6. A choice-of-forum clause providing for suit in the courts of a certain state has been held to bar a diversity action in a federal court sitting in the same jurisdiction. Spatz v. Nascone, 364 F.Supp. 967 (W.D.Pa.1973).

7. For general discussion of the effect given choice-of-forum clauses in the United States and in other countries, see Gruson, Forum–Selection Clauses in International and Interstate Commercial Agreements, 1982 U.Ill.L.Rev. 133; Gilbert, Choice of Forum Clauses in International and Interstate Contracts, 65 Ky.L.J. 1 (1977); The Validity of Forum Selecting Clauses, 13 Am.J.Comp.L. 157–192 (1964). For English practice see North and Fawcett, Cheshire and North's Private International Law 234–239 (12th ed. 1992).

8. In D.H. Overmyer Co. v. Frick Co., 405 U.S. 174 (1972), which involved a corporate debtor, the U.S. Supreme Court held that cognovit notes, supra p. 44, do not *per se* violate due process. The decision in Swarb v. Lennox, 405 U.S. 191 (1972), rendered on the same day, clarified that the rule extends to individual debtors as well. The Court emphasized that *Overmyer* had only decided that "under appropriate circumstances, a cognovit debtor may be held effectively and legally to have waived those rights he would possess if the document he signed had contained no cognovit provision." The Court had no occasion to speak to those circumstances that might make it "inappropriate" to assume or to give effect to a waiver of rights. In particular, it did not have occasion to review that part of the decision of the district court that considered the Pennsylvania practice to be unconstitutional with regards to debtors with annual incomes of less than $10,000.

9. In the European Union, Art. 17 of the Brussels Convention allows parties (one of whom must be habitually resident in a member state) to select, by agreement, a member state court for the resolution of a present or future dispute. The court so selected then has jurisdiction, even if it otherwise would not have. (Art. 17(1)). Its jurisdiction is exclusive and other courts must honor the stipulation and decline to entertain an action sought to be brought in violation of it. Exceptions apply when the stipulation contravenes special provisions protective of consumers and insureds (supra p. 37 or an exclusive jurisdiction established by the Convention (Art. 16). For discussion of the European rule, see Dicey & Morris, Conflict of Laws 419 et seq. (12th ed. by Collins, 1993); B. Ancel, La clause attributive de juridiction selon l'article 17 de la convention de Bruxelles, Riv. dir. int. priv. proc. 1991, 263; Kropholler, Internationales Privatrecht 510 et seq. (2d ed. 1994).

How would the *Carnival Cruise* cases come out under the Brussels Convention? Specifically: would the consumer-protection provision (Art. 13) have limited the parties' freedom to stipulate the forum to the courts at the passengers' domicile(s) (Art. 14(2)) or to courts more convenient *to them* (see Art. 15, No. 2)? First, Art. 13 does not apply to transportation contracts (Art. 13(3)) and therefore would not be a limitation on the parties' freedom of choice under Art. 17. Did the parties contract for transportation or for entertainment (services)? Assuming that the contract concerned mainly services, did it meet the requirements for the applicability of Art. 13 to contracts for "services" (Art. 13(1), No. 3)? These are that the making of the contract was preceded by an offer or by advertising in the state of the consumer's domicile and that the consumer undertook the necessary legal steps for the formation of the contract in that state.

The distinction between contracts for transportation and for services is difficult. The Rome Convention on the Law Applicable to Contractual Obligations, infra p. 547, addresses it this way: contracts for transportation are excluded from the provision specifying the law applicable to consumer contracts, but not (i.e., they are *included*) if the contract is one for "travel" and offers, for one overall price, both transportation and lodging and related services (Rome Convention, Art. 5(5)). The Brussels Convention lacks this further clarification. However, there is support for a uniform construction of parallel provisions of the two conventions. See Tizzano in [1990] Official Journal E.C. No. C 219/1. If Art. 13(3) of the Brussels Convention thus would not exclude travel contracts, Arts. 14 and 15 would limit the parties' freedom to stipulate the forum if the prerequisites of Art. 13(1), summarized in the preceding paragraph, were met. Were they in one or both of the two *Carnival Cruise* cases?

SECTION 2. FRAUD, FORCE AND PRIVILEGE *

Terlizzi v. Brodie
Supreme Court, Appellate Division, Second Department, 1972.
38 A.D.2d 762, 329 N.Y.S.2d 589.

■ MEMORANDUM BY THE COURT. ...

. . .

In May or June, 1968 defendants, New Jersey residents, were in an automobile collision in New Jersey which caused plaintiffs, New York residents, to sustain injuries. In February, 1971 defendants were called at home and told that they had been chosen to receive two tickets to a Broadway show as a promotional venture to get their opinion on a questionnaire of the new 7:30 P.M. curtain time. After the performance and while still in the theatre, defendants were served with a summons in this action by a man who had been sitting behind them. No questionnaire had been given them. Plaintiffs have presented no facts concerning the service to refute defendants' claim and have not submitted an affidavit of the investigator retained to effect service.

It has long been held that where a defendant has been lured into this jurisdiction by fraud or deceit in order that he may be served, the service so effected is invalid . . .

In our opinion, the service was invalid and the [defendants'] motion [to vacate service of process] should have been granted.

NOTES

1. Where the defendant's presence in the state was obtained by fraudulent use of extradition procedure, it has been held that service on him is not effective to support a civil judgment against him. Klaiber v. Frank, 9 N.J. 1, 86 A.2d 679 (1952). However, the mere fact that the defendant is a non-resident and is under arrest for a criminal charge does not make him immune from the valid service of civil process. State ex rel. Sivnksty v. Duffield, 137 W.Va. 112, 71 S.E.2d 113 (1952).

2. Suppose the defendant is kidnapped and brought into the state by force. If he is then served with civil process, does the state get jurisdiction over him? See Restatement, Second, Conflict of Laws, § 82, Comments *e-f.*

3. The Uniform Criminal Extradition Act, now enacted in 47 states, Puerto Rico and the U.S. Virgin Islands, (see 11 Uniform Laws Ann. 51) provides (in § 25) that where a person is brought into a state on extradition, or after waiver of extradition he shall not be subject to service of process "in civil actions arising out of the same facts as the criminal proceedings . . . until he has been convicted in the criminal

---

* See Restatement, Second, Conflict of Laws §§ 82–83.

proceeding, or if acquitted, until he has had reasonable opportunity to return to the state from which he was extradited." In Bubar v. Dizdar, 240 Minn. 26, 60 N.W.2d 77 (1953), the defendant waived extradition, came into the state, and pleaded guilty. Later the same day, but before sentence was imposed, he was served with process. It was held that this was after conviction, and valid.

4. In criminal cases, the jurisdiction of the court over the defendant is usually held not to be impaired by the fact that he was unlawfully extradited, or brought in by force. State v. Waitus, 226 S.C. 44, 83 S.E.2d 629 (1954), overruled on other grounds 406 S.E.2d 315 (1991). The Supreme Court has held that a state may prosecute a person brought into the state by force even though this was a violation of the Federal Kidnapping Act. Frisbie v. Collins, 342 U.S. 519 (1952). See Scott, Criminal Jurisdiction of a State over a Defendant Based upon Presence Secured by Force or Fraud, 37 Minn.L.Rev. 91 (1953).

The question of criminal jurisdiction based on removing a person by force arose in dramatic form when the Nazi war criminal Adolf Eichmann was abducted from Argentina by Israeli agents, taken to Israel, there tried for war crimes and executed. Israel asserted that genocide and war crimes are subject to universal jurisdiction, and Argentina acquiesced. Attorney General v. Eichmann, 36 Int'l L.Rep. 18 (Dist.Ct.Israel 1961), affirmed 36 Int'l L.Rep. 277 (Sup.Ct.Israel 1962). Section 404 of the Restatement, Third, Foreign Relations Law of the United States (1987) now also adopts this view. See also in Matter of Demjanjuk, 603 F.Supp. 1468 (N.D.Ohio 1985), affirmed 776 F.2d 571 (6th Cir.1985), cert. denied 457 U.S. 1016 (1986) (approving Israeli request for extradition of person charged with murder alleged to have been committed in Nazi camps in Eastern Europe). After Demjanjuk's acquittal of charges in Israel, the Sixth Circuit Court of Appeals reopened the case and found prosecutorial misconduct in failing to disclose exculpatory information. Demjanjuk v. Petrovsky, 10 F.3d 338 (6th Cir.1993).

A number of recent cases have involved persons who were brought by force from foreign countries to the United States to stand trial on criminal charges. In these cases, jurisdiction to try the defendant was ultimately upheld even though it was alleged that the defendant had been forcefully abducted at the instigation of agents of the United States. United States v. Lira, 515 F.2d 68 (2d Cir.1975); United States v. Gengler, 510 F.2d 62 (2d Cir.1975); United States v. Cotten, 471 F.2d 744 (9th Cir.1973); United States v. Marzano, 388 F.Supp. 906 (N.D.Ill.1975); see Annotation, 28 A.L.R.Fed. 685 (1976). In United States v. Toscanino, 500 F.2d 267 (2d Cir.1974), the court held that jurisdiction would be lacking and the defendant's conviction void if he could establish that he had not only been kidnapped but also tortured and interrogated abroad by U.S. agents and that the United States attorney was at all times aware of these activities. The court said that Frisbie v. Collins must be read in the light of such supervening Supreme Court decisions as Mapp, Miranda, etc. which hold that "due process not only requires a fair trial but also protects the accused against pretrial illegality by denying to the government the fruits of its exploitation of any deliberate and unnecessary lawlessness on its part." After remand to the District Court, however, Toscanino failed to establish that United States officials had participated in his abduction or torture. Accordingly, his motion to vacate his judgment of conviction was denied. United States v. Toscanino, 398 F.Supp. 916 (E.D.N.Y.1975). See LaFave, Search and Seizure § 1.9(a) (2d ed. 1987); see also, Epstein, 33 A.L.R. Fed. 344 (1977) for the applicability of the 4th Amendment exclusionary rule to evidence obtained from searches conducted abroad by officials of foreign governments.

5. Privilege and Immunity. A foreign sovereign is generally immune from suit. Foreign Sovereign Immunities Act, 28 U.S.C.A. § 1605. There are exceptions, for instance when the foreign sovereign engages in commercial (non-governmental) activity. Foreign diplomats enjoy absolute immunity from criminal as well as civil and administrative jurisdiction. However, the sending state can waive the immunity of its envoys. Arts. 31, 32, para. 4, Vienna Convention on Diplomatic Relations, 23 U.S.T. 3227, T.I.A.S. No. 7502, 500 U.N.T.S. 95. See Fernandez v. Fernandez, 208 Conn. 329, 545 A.2d 1036 (1988), noted 102 Harv.L.Rev. 1403 (1989), interpreting partial waiver of immunity allowing the exercise of divorce jurisdiction to confer authority to entertain petitioner's claim for the marital residence.

6. "It is customary for a state to grant immunity from service of process to nonresidents whose presence it deems necessary for the proper conduct of a judicial proceeding. Such immunity is usually granted to witnesses and to lawyers and in some states to parties as well. The immunity ceases when the need for protection ends. It is lost, for example, when the person fails to leave the state within a reasonable time after his presence there has ceased to be necessary." Restatement, Second, Conflict of Laws § 83, Comment *b*.

7. Immunity from service of process in a civil action is usually granted to persons who enter the state, either voluntarily or under subpoena, for the purpose of appearing as a witness in a state or federal proceeding. See, e.g., Shapiro & Son Curtain Corp. v. Glass, 348 F.2d 460 (2d Cir.1965), cert. denied 382 U.S. 942 (1965); Celanese Corporation v. Duplan Corporation, 502 F.2d 188 (4th Cir.1974), cert. den. 420 U.S. 929 (1974). NASL Marketing, Inc. v. de Vries, 94 F.R.D. 309 (S.D.N.Y. 1982); Viking Penguin, Inc. v. Janklow, 98 F.R.D. 763 (S.D.N.Y.1983).

In Youpe v. Strasser, 113 F.Supp. 289 (D.D.C.1953), it was held that a witness subpoenaed to appear before a Congressional investigating committee was immune from service in a civil suit.

Section 3. Forum Non Conveniens

American jurisdictional law provides plaintiffs with a wide choice of fora in which to sue. Individuals are subject to jurisdiction at their domicile and in any state where personal service can be effected. For a discussion of "transient" service, see p. 41, supra.

In addition, a state has jurisdiction when the nonresident defendant's contact with that state gave rise to the plaintiff's cause of action. For discussion of "specific" jurisdiction, see pp. 47–92, supra. Similarly, a corporation is subject to "general" jurisdiction where it does "continuous and systematic business" and to "specific" jurisdiction where its acts or contacts give rise to the cause of action, supra at p. 101. Although rare, there may be circumstances where an individual might be subject to general jurisdiction on the basis of "continuous and systematic" activities as well. See, e.g., Schlobohn v. Shapiro, 784 S.W.2d 355 (Tex.1990).

A plaintiff thus has considerable opportunity to "shop around" for a forum. Reasons may include geographic convenience, but also advantages of procedural law (e.g. a longer statute of limitations) or of the substantive law that the chosen court could be expected to apply. See Allstate, infra, p.

349. As to the jurisdiction side, the doctrine of *forum non conveniens* affords an avenue for relief in jurisdictionally hard cases.

The doctrine of *forum non conveniens* has by now been widely accepted throughout the common law world, from the doctrine's first recognition in Scotland in 1866. The United States Supreme Court accepted the use of forum non conveniens in 1947, in the lead case below.

More recently, however, the Supreme Court has limited the applicability of the doctrine, on the federal level, to situations where the alternative forum is not in the United States. Where the parties' choices of fora are both in the United States on the other hand, the federal transfer statute (28 U.S.C.A. § 1404(a)) provides the proper remedy. Some decisions, however, still confuse the two. For clarification of the difference, see Jhong, Application of Common-law Doctrine of Forum Non Conveniens in Federal Courts after Enactment of 28 U.S.C.A. § 1404(a) Authorizing Transfer to Another District, 10 A.L.R.Fed. 352 (1972).

Gulf Oil Corp. v. Gilbert

Supreme Court of the United States, 1947.
330 U.S. 501, 67 S.Ct. 839, 91 L.Ed. 1055.

[A resident of Virginia brought an action in a federal district court in New York against a Pennsylvania corporation. The cause of action was based on a fire in Virginia alleged to have resulted from the defendant's negligence. The defendant was qualified to do business in Virginia, and could have been sued there. The defendant moved to dismiss on grounds of forum non conveniens.

The opinion of the Court, by Justice Jackson, contains the following passages:]

I

It is conceded that the venue statutes of the United States permitted the plaintiff to commence his action in the Southern District of New York and empower that court to entertain it. But that does not settle the question whether it must do so. Indeed the doctrine of *forum non conveniens* can never apply if there is absence of jurisdiction or mistake of venue.... In all cases in which the doctrine of *forum non conveniens* comes into play, it presupposes at least two forums in which the defendant is amenable to process; the doctrine furnishes criteria for choice between them.

II

The principle of *forum non conveniens* is simply that a court may resist imposition upon its jurisdiction even when jurisdiction is authorized by the letter of a general venue statute. These statutes are drawn with a necessary generality and usually give a plaintiff a choice of courts, so that he may be quite sure of some place in which to pursue his remedy. But the open door may admit those who seek not simply justice but perhaps justice blended with some harassment. A plaintiff sometimes is under temptation to resort to a strategy of forcing the trial at a most inconvenient place for an adversary, even at some inconvenience to himself.

Many of the states have met misuse of venue by investing courts with a discretion to change the place of trial on various grounds, such as the convenience of witnesses and the ends of justice. The federal law contains no such express criteria to guide the district court in exercising its power. But the problem is a very old one affecting the administration of the courts as well as the rights of litigants, and both in England and in this country the common law worked out techniques and criteria for dealing with it.

Wisely, it has not been attempted to catalogue the circumstances which will justify or require either grant or denial of remedy. The doctrine leaves much to the discretion of the court to which plaintiff resorts, and experience has not shown a judicial tendency to renounce one's own jurisdiction so strong as to result in many abuses.

If the combination and weight of factors requisite to given results are difficult to forecast or state, those to be considered are not difficult to name. An interest to be considered, and the one likely to be most pressed, is the private interest of the litigant. Important considerations are the relative ease of access to sources of proof; availability of compulsory process for attendance of unwilling, and the cost of obtaining attendance of willing, witnesses; possibility of view of premises, if view would be appropriate to the action; and all other practical problems that make trial of a case easy, expeditious and inexpensive. There may also be questions as to the enforceability of a judgment if one is obtained. The court will weigh relative advantages and obstacles to fair trial. It is often said that the plaintiff may not, by choice of an inconvenient forum, "vex," "harass," or "oppress" the defendant by inflicting upon him expense or trouble not necessary to his own right to pursue his remedy. But unless the balance is strongly in favor of the defendant, the plaintiff's choice of forum should rarely be disturbed.

Factors of public interest also have place in applying the doctrine. Administrative difficulties follow for courts when litigation is piled up in congested centers instead of being handled at its origin. Jury duty is a burden that ought not to be imposed upon the people of a community which has no relation to the litigation. In cases which touch the affairs of many persons, there is reason for holding the trial in their view and reach rather than in remote parts of the country where they can learn of it by report only. There is a local interest in having localized controversies decided at home. There is an appropriateness, too, in having the trial of a diversity case in a forum that is at home with the state law that must govern the case, rather than having a court in some other forum untangle problems in conflict of laws, and in law foreign to itself.

The law of New York as to the discretion of a court to apply the doctrine of *forum non conveniens,* and as to the standards that guide discretion is, so far as here involved, the same as the federal rule....

[The Court held that the district court had acted properly in dismissing the suit.]

PIPER AIRCRAFT CO. v. REYNO, 454 U.S. 235 (1981). Action in a Pennsylvania federal district court against the manufacturers of an aircraft and its propellers to recover for the wrongful death of persons killed in an airplane crash in Scotland. At the time, the plane was registered in Great Britain and was being operated by a Scottish air taxi service. All of the decedents were Scottish subjects and residents. As plaintiff, the appointed administratrix of the decedents' estates was frank to admit, the suit had been brought in the United States because its laws regarding liability, capacity to sue and damages were more favorable to her cause than those of Scotland. Held: The action should be dismissed on *forum non conveniens* grounds. "The possibility of a change in substantive law should ordinarily not be given conclusive or even substantial weight in the *forum non conveniens* inquiry ... [Otherwise] American courts, which are already extremely attractive to foreign plaintiffs, would become even more attractive. The flow of litigation into the United States would increase and further congest already crowded courts. ... The Court of Appeals' approach is not only inconsistent with the purpose of the *forum non conveniens* doctrine, but also poses substantial practical problems. If the possibility of a change in law were given substantial weight, deciding motions to dismiss would become quite difficult. Choice-of-law analysis would become extremely important, and the courts would frequently be required to interpret the law of foreign jurisdictions. First, the trial court would have to determine what law would apply if the case were tried in the chosen forum, and what law would apply if the case were tried in the alternative forum. It would then have to compare the rights, remedies, and procedures available under the law that would be applied in each forum. Dismissal would be appropriate only if the court concluded that the law applied by the alternative forum is as favorable to the plaintiff as that of the chosen forum. The doctrine of *forum non conveniens,* however, is designed in part to help courts avoid conducting complex exercises in comparative law.... The Court of Appeals based its decision, at least in part, on an analogy between dismissals on grounds of *forum non conveniens* and transfers between federal courts pursuant to § 1404(a).... Congress enacted § 1404(a) to permit change of venue between federal courts. Although the statute was drafted in accordance with the doctrine of *forum non conveniens,* it was intended to be a revision rather than a codification of the common law.... District courts were given more discretion to transfer under § 1404(a) than they had to dismiss on grounds of *forum non conveniens*.... Of course, if the remedy provided by the alternative forum is so clearly inadequate or unsatisfactory that it is no remedy at all, the unfavorable change in law may be given substantial weight."

NOTE

In American Dredging Co. v. Miller, 114 S.Ct. 981 (1994) the Supreme Court succinctly recognized, at note 2, what was already implicitly understood: "the federal doctrine of forum non conveniens has continuing application only in cases where the alternative forum is abroad"; otherwise, the proper route is 28 U.S.C. § 1404(a).

The development of forum non conveniens through the Court's decision in *Piper* has been criticized as allowing a simple reasonableness test, committed to the sound discretion of the trial court, considering many factors, including, most noticeably, docket congestion. Consider pundits' detractions with respect to the following decision, controversial in many respects.

In re Union Carbide Corporation Gas Plant Disaster at Bhopal, India in December, 1984

United States District Court, S.D. New York.
634 F.Supp. 842 (1986).

[In the aftermath of the most devastating industrial catastrophe in history, some 145 actions by victims were started in federal courts in the United States against Union Carbide Corporation, a Connecticut corporation. The disaster occurred when a lethal gas known as methyl isocyanate escaped from a chemical plant operated by Union Carbide India Limited (UCIL) in Bhopal, India. More than 2,000 people were killed and hundreds of thousands injured. A few months later the Union of India (UOI) enacted the Bhopal Gas Leak Disaster (Processing of Claims) Act, granting the Indian government the exclusive right to represent the victims.

The Indian government, acting as *parens patriae,* filed a complaint in the federal court for the Southern District of New York on behalf of all victims of the Bhopal disaster, similar to the class action complaints filed by individuals in the United States. Under multi-district procedures, the Southern District of New York was designated the court for resolution of all the federal actions. UOI asserted it had to sue in the United States because the Indian courts did not have jurisdiction over UCC, which is the American parent of UCIL by virtue of ownership or control of 50.9% of its stock. Of the balance of UCIL's stock, 22% is in the hands of the government of India and the rest is owned by 23,500 members of the Indian public].

"This Court is firmly convinced that the Indian legal system is in a far better position than the American courts to determine the cause of the tragic event and thereby fix liability. Further, the Indian courts have greater access to all the information needed to arrive at the amount of the compensation to be awarded the victims.

The presence in India of the overwhelming majority of the witnesses and evidence, both documentary and real, would by itself suggest that India is the most convenient forum for this consolidated case. The additional presence in India of all but the less than a handful of claimants underscores the convenience of holding trial in India. All of the private interest factors described in *Piper* and *Gilbert* weigh heavily toward dismissal of this case on the grounds of *forum non conveniens.*

The public interest factors set forth in *Piper* and *Gilbert* also favor dismissal. The administrative burden of this immense litigation would unfairly tax this or any American tribunal. The cost to American taxpayers of supporting the litigation in the United States would be excessive. When another, adequate and more convenient forum so clearly exists, there is no reason to press the United States judiciary to the limits of its capacity. No American interest in the outcome of this litigation outweighs the interest of India in applying Indian law and Indian values to the task of resolving this case.

The Bhopal plant was regulated by Indian agencies. The Union of India has a very strong interest in the aftermath of the accident which affected its citizens on its own soil. Perhaps Indian regulations were ignored or contravened. India may wish to determine whether the regulations imposed on the chemical industry within its boundaries were sufficiently stringent. The Indian interests far outweigh the interests of citizens of the United States in the litigation."

In Re Union Carbide Corporation Gas Plant Disaster at Bhopal, India in December, 1984

United States Court of Appeals, Second Circuit, 1987.
809 F.2d 195, cert. denied 484 U.S. 871, 108 S.Ct. 199, 98 L.Ed.2d 150 (1987).

[UCC moved to dismiss the complaints of the Indian plaintiffs and UOI on *forum non conveniens* and other grounds. The district judge granted the motion on condition that UCC:

(1) consent to the jurisdiction of the courts of India and continue to waive defenses based on the statute of limitations,

(2) agree to satisfy any judgment rendered by an Indian court against it and upheld on appeal, provided the judgment and affirmance "comport with minimal requirements of due process," and

(3) be subject to discovery under the Federal Rules of Civil Procedure of the United States.

Relying on the standards laid down in Piper Aircraft Co. v. Reyno, 454 U.S. 235 (1981), the Court of Appeals affirmed the dismissal, but modified two of the conditions.]

■ MANSFIELD, CIRCUIT JUDGE. The first condition, that UCC consent to the Indian court's personal jurisdiction over it and waive the statute of limitations as a defense, are not unusual and have been imposed in numerous cases where the foreign court would not provide an adequate alternative in the absence of such a condition. The remaining two conditions, however, pose problems.

In requiring that UCC consent to enforceability of an Indian judgment against it, the district court proceeded at least in part on the erroneous assumption that, absent such a requirement, the plaintiffs, if they should succeed in obtaining an Indian judgment against UCC, might not be able to enforce it against UCC in the United States. The law, however, is to the contrary. Under New York law, which governs actions brought in New York to enforce foreign judgments, see Island Territory of Curacao v. Solitron Devices, Inc., 489 F.2d 1313, 1318 (2d Cir.1973), cert. denied, 416 U.S. 986 (1974), a foreign-country judgment that is final, conclusive and enforceable where rendered must be recognized and will be enforced as "conclusive between the parties to the extent that it grants or denies recovery of a sum of money" except that it is not deemed to be conclusive if:

> "1. the judgment was rendered under a system which does not provide impartial tribunals or procedures compatible with the requirements of due process of law;
>
> "2. the foreign court did not have personal jurisdiction over the defendant."

Art. 53, Recognition of Foreign Country Money Judgments, 7B N.Y.Civ.Prac.L. & R. § 5301–09 (McKinney 1978). Although § 5304 further provides that under certain specified conditions a foreign country judgment need not be recognized, none of these conditions would apply to the present cases except for the possibility of failure to provide UCC with sufficient notice of proceedings or the existence of fraud in obtaining the judgment, which do not presently exist but conceivably could occur in the future.

UCC contends that Indian courts, while providing an adequate alternative forum, do not observe due process standards that would be required as a matter of course in this country. As evidence of this apprehension it points to the haste with which the Indian court in Bhopal issued a temporary order freezing its assets throughout the world and the possibility of serious prejudice to it if the UOI is permitted to have the double and conflicting status of both plaintiff and co-defendant in the Indian court proceedings. It argues that we should protect it against such denial of due process by authorizing Judge Keenan to retain the authority, after *forum non conveniens* dismissal of the cases here, to monitor the Indian court proceedings and be available on call to rectify in some undefined way any abuses of UCC's right to due process as they might occur in India.

UCC's proposed remedy is not only impractical but evidences an abysmal ignorance of basic jurisdiction principles, so much that it borders on the frivolous. The district court's jurisdiction is limited to proceedings before it in this country. Once it dismisses those proceedings on grounds of *forum non conveniens* it ceases to have any further jurisdiction over the matter unless and until a proceeding may some day be brought to enforce here a final and conclusive Indian money judgment. Nor could we, even if we attempted to retain some sort of supervisory jurisdiction, impose our due process requirements upon Indian courts, which are governed by their laws, not ours. The concept of shared jurisdictions is both illusory and unrealistic. The parties cannot simultaneously submit to both jurisdictions the resolution of the pre-trial and trial issues when there is only one consolidated case pending in one court. Any denial by the Indian courts of due process can be raised by UCC as a defense to the plaintiffs' later attempt to enforce a resulting judgment against UCC in this country.

We are concerned, however, that as it is written the district court's requirement that UCC consent to the enforcement of a final Indian judgment, which was imposed on the erroneous assumption that such a judgment might not otherwise be enforceable in the United States, may create misunderstandings and problems of construction. Although the order's provision that the judgment "comport with *minimal* requirements of due process" (emphasis supplied) probably is intended to refer to "due process" as used in the New York Foreign Country Money Judgments Law and others like it, there is the risk that it may also be interpreted as providing for a lesser standard than we would otherwise require. Since the court's condition with respect to enforceability of any final Indian judgment is predicated on an erroneous legal assumption and its "due process" language is ambiguous, and since the district court's purpose is fully served by New York's statute providing for recognition of foreign-country money judgments, it was error to impose this condition upon the parties.

We also believe that the district court erred in requiring UCC to consent (which UCC did under protest and subject to its right of appeal) to broad discovery of it by the plaintiffs under the Federal Rules of Civil Procedure when UCC is confined to the more limited discovery authorized under Indian law. We recognize that under some circumstances, such as when a moving defendant unconditionally consents thereto or no undiscovered evidence of consequence is believed to be under the control of a plaintiff or co-defendant, it may be appropriate to condition a *forum non conveniens* dismissal on the moving defendant's submission to discovery under the Federal Rules without requiring reciprocal discovery by it of the plaintiff. See, e.g., Piper Aircraft v. Reyno, supra, 454 U.S. at 257 n. 25 (suggesting that district courts can condition dismissal upon a defendant's agreeing to provide all relevant records); Ali v. Offshore Co., 753 F.2d 1327, 1334, n. 16 (5th Cir.1985) (same); Boskoff v. Transportes Aereos Portugueses, 17 Av.Cas. (CCH) 18,613, at 18,616 (N.D.Ill.1983) (accepting defendant's voluntary commitment to provide discovery in foreign forum according to Federal Rules). Basic justice dictates that both sides be treated equally, with each having equal access to the evidence in the possession or under the control of the other. Application of this fundamental principle in the present case is especially appropriate since the UOI, as the sovereign government of India, is expected to be a party to the Indian litigation, possibly on both sides.

For these reasons we direct that the condition with respect to the discovery of UCC under the Federal Rules of Civil Procedure be deleted without prejudice to the right of the parties to have reciprocal discovery of each other on equal terms under the Federal Rules, subject to such approval as may be required of the Indian court in which the cases will be pending. If, for instance, Indian authorities will permit mutual discovery pursuant to the Federal Rules, the district court's order, as modified in accordance with this opinion, should not be construed to bar such procedure. In the absence of such a court-sanctioned agreement, however, the parties will be limited by the applicable discovery rules of the Indian court in which the claims will be pending.

NOTES

1. Under the Indian Bhopal Gas Leak Disaster Act, enacted in 1985, the Government of India had the exclusive right to represent victims of the Bhopal disaster. The Government pursued claims in the courts of India until the Supreme Court of India approved a settlement in February of 1989. Under the terms of the settlement, Union Carbide India Limited and its parent corporation agreed to pay $470 million to the Indian Government for the benefit of the victims of the disaster. The Supreme Court of India found the settlement just and reasonable, see Union Carbide Corp. v. Union of India, 1989 [Supp.] S.C.A.L.E. 89.

2. In support of the contention that a successful forum non conveniens motion may be the ultimate defense tactic, see Robertson, Forum Non Conveniens in America and England: "A Rather Fantastic Fiction," 103 L.Q.R. 398 (1987), and Robertson, The Federal Doctrine of Forum Non Conveniens, 29 Tex.Int'l L.J. 353 (1994). See also, "Carbide got off easy in Bhopal Disaster," New York Times, December 18, 1994, p. 14, sec. 4, col. 4. But see p. 190 Note 6 for the suggestion that the forum-non-conveniens dismissal perhaps averted an improper "piercing the corporate veil," i.e., placing liability for the subsidiary's actions at the feet of the parent. Query further whether the dismissal had the aforementioned effect: note that the settlement was ten times the value of the subsidiary and twenty times Union Carbide's share of the equity in the subsidiary.

3. In recent years, suits have often been dismissed on forum non conveniens grounds in situations where the more convenient forum was a foreign country. See, e.g., Gonzalez v. Naviera Neptuno A.A., 832 F.2d 876 (5th Cir.1987); Vaz Borralho v. Keydril Co., 696 F.2d 379 (5th Cir.1983); Panama Processes, S.A. v. Cities Service Co., 650 F.2d 408 (2d Cir.1981); Dahl v. United Technologies Corp., 632 F.2d 1027 (3d Cir.1980); Vargas v. M/V Mini Lama, 709 F.Supp. 117 (E.D.La. 1989). For an erudite and entertaining opinion see Syndicate 420 at Lloyd's London v. Early Am. Ins., 796 F.2d 821 (5th Cir.1986) (drawing on Greek drama and mythology). For validity and propriety of conditions imposed on a foreign court, see Thomas, 89 A.L.R.Fed. 238 (1988).

Dismissals have been ordered even when the plaintiff was a United States citizen. See, e.g., Pain v. United Technologies Corp., 637 F.2d 775 (D.C.Cir.1980) cert. den. 454 U.S. 1128 (1981); Alcoa Steamship Co. v. M/V Nordic Regent, 453 F.Supp. 10 (S.D.N.Y.1978), judgment affirmed 654 F.2d 165 (2d Cir.1979) cert. den. 449 U.S. 890 (1980). It has been said, however, that the presumption in favor of the plaintiff's chosen forum is "even stronger" when the plaintiff is an American citizen and the alternative forum is a foreign country. Olympic Corp. v. Societe Generale, 462 F.2d 376, 378 (2d Cir.1972).

When litigation is already pending in a foreign forum, an American court may abstain from exercising jurisdiction and dismiss in favor of the foreign forum. See Rolls Royce (Canada), Ltd. v. Cayman Airways, Ltd., 617 F.Supp. 17 (S.D.Fla.1985). But see American Home Assur. Co. v. Insurance Corp. of Ireland, 603 F.Supp. 636 (S.D.N.Y.1984) (when the plaintiffs are U.S. citizens or residents and trial in the United States is merely inconvenient but not oppressive for the foreign defendant, the court may decline to dismiss but instead enjoin the simultaneous prosecution of the foreign litigation). In English practice, multiplicity of proceedings which may result from the pendency of litigation elsewhere ("lis alibi pendens") now is also an important element to be taken into account in ruling on forum non conveniens motions. See The Abidin Daver, [1984] AC 398, [1984] 1 All E.R. 470 (H.L.). In Canada, see Amchem Products Inc. v. Worker's Comp Bd., 102 D.L.R. (4th) 96 (1993). On "lis pendens", see textual Note infra.

4. Dismissals on forum non conveniens grounds have been denied in a variety of circumstances. Lake v. Richardson–Merrell, Inc., 538 F.Supp. 262 (N.D.Ohio 1982) (court believed that action would be dismissed in Quebec on the ground of prescription, a defense that, under Quebec law, could not be waived by the defendant); In re Air Crash Disaster Near Bombay, etc., 531 F.Supp. 1175 (W.D.Wash.1982) (statute of limitations had run in India and there was a substantial possibility that the Bombay court would not accept defendant's waiver of the statute); Canadian Overseas Ores, Limited v. Compania, etc., 528 F.Supp. 1337 (S.D.N.Y.1982) (court feared that fair trial could not be had in Chile).

5. A factor that militates against dismissal of a case on forum non conveniens grounds is that the forum may be the only state where jurisdiction can be obtained over all defendants. See Watson v. Merrell Dow Pharmaceuticals, Inc., 769 F.2d 354, 356 (6th Cir.1985); Varkonyi v. S.A. Empresa De Viacao A.R.G., 22 N.Y.2d 333, 292 N.Y.S.2d 670, 239 N.E.2d 542 (1968). Cf. Islamic Republic of Iran v. Pahlavi, 62 N.Y.2d 474, 478 N.Y.S.2d 597, 467 N.E.2d 245 (1984) cert. den. 469 U.S. 1108 (1984). See also Pacific Employers Ins. Co. v. M/V Capt. W.D. Cargill, 751 F.2d 801 (5th Cir.1985).

The availability of an alternate forum is "the essential predicate for dismissal": Liaw Su Teng v. Skaarup Shipping Corp., 743 F.2d 1140, 1147 (5th Cir.1984). The fact that the other forum would apply a different substantive law or that procedural advantages which the plaintiff would enjoy in the local forum are not available in the foreign court, or that the foreign legal system does not provide punitive damages should not defeat a dismissal for forum non conveniens that is otherwise indicated. See, e.g., Piper Aircraft Co. v. Reyno, 454 U.S. 235 (1981), p. 184, supra (no strict liability under Scottish law); Coakes v. Arabian American Oil Co., 831 F.2d 572 (5th Cir.1987) (no contingent-fee system in England); de Melo v. Lederle Laboratories, 801 F.2d 1058 (8th Cir.1986) (no punitive damages in Brazil). See Sibaja v. Dow Chemical Co., 757 F.2d 1215, 1219 (11th Cir.1985), rehearing denied 765 F.2d 154 (11th Cir.1985): "The *forum non conveniens* doctrine is a rule of venue, not a rule of decision." The trial court therefore did not transgress the limitations imposed by *Erie* when it applied the federal and not the Florida standard. See also Scoles and Hay, Conflict of Laws § 11.10 (2d ed. 1992). Cf. Stewart Organization, Inc. v. Ricoh Corp., 487 U.S. 22 (1988), p. 176 supra.

6. A number of long-arm statutes expressly authorize the court to dismiss the case on forum non conveniens grounds. See, e.g., Wis.Stat.Ann. § 801.63(1). It makes "substantial justice" the standard for the exercise of the court's discretion in the area. It expressly provides that forum non conveniens may be invoked even where the defendant would not have been subject to jurisdiction in the more convenient forum, provided that the moving party (1) stipulates consent to jurisdiction in the new forum, and (2) waives any statute of limitations that may have run therein. Section 801.63(3) lists four criteria to be followed by the court: (a) amenability of the parties to personal jurisdiction in this and the other forum; (b) convenience of witnesses; (c) differences in conflict of laws rules; and (d) "any other factors having substantial bearing upon the selection of a convenient, reasonable, and fair place of trial."

Should the court entertain a motion to dismiss on forum non conveniens grounds when the parties had executed a forum selection clause in favor of the local forum? In England, the forum selection clause is prima facie evidence that England is the convenient forum. See North and Fawcett, Cheshire and North's Private International Law 234–239 (12th ed. 1992). New York law goes further: a New York court may not dismiss for forum non conveniens in the face of a forum selection clause in favor of New York when the case involves obligations of $1 million in the aggregate and when New York law has been chosen as the applicable law. N.Y.McKinney's Gen.Oblig.Law § 5–1402. In New York, the legislative policy gives the parties the opportunity to select a sophisticated body of commercial law and a judicial system with substantial experience in administering it and thereby enhances the importance of New York as an international commercial center. 1984 McKinney's Sess. Law News A–689–A–690. Absent legislative directive, in what circumstances should a court disregard the forum selection clause and dismiss or stay for reasons of forum non conveniens?

7. *Forum non conveniens in other common law jurisdictions.* The doctrine of forum non conveniens is widely recognized throughout the common law world. Of all countries, *Australia* likely recognizes the purest approach to forum non conveniens determinations, see Voth v. Milandra Flour Mills, [1990] 171 C.L.R. 538. For *England,* see Spiliada Maritime Corp. v. Cansulex Ltd. (The Spiliada), [1986] 3 All ER (HL) 843; for *Canada,* see Amchem Products Inc. v. Worker's Comp. Bd., 102 D.L.R. (4th) 96 (1993); for *New Zealand,* see VanDyck v. VanDyck, [1990] 3 NZLR 624 (High Ct. Whangarei); for *South Africa,* see Great River Shipping Inc. v. Sunnyface Marine Ltd., 1992 (4) SA 291; for *Scotland,* see the original use of forum non conveniens in Clements v. Macauley, 4 Mac Pherson (Sess. Cas. 3rd Serv.) 583 (1866), and more recently, Shell UK v. Andrew Innes, 1994 Outer House Cases; for *Ireland,* see Doe and Dowling v. Armour Pharmaceutical Co., [1994] 1 ILRM 416; for *Northern Ireland,* see Macrete v. Guardian Royal Exchange Plc., [1988] NI 332; and for the *Philippines,* see Hong Kong & Shanghai Banking Corp. v. Sherman, 176 Sup.Ct.Rep.Ann. 331 (1989). For comparative treatment, see also Reus, Die "forum non conveniens-doctrine" in Großbritannien und den USA in Zukunft auch in Deutschland?, [1991] Recht der Internationalen Wirtschaft 542.

8. The Brussels Convention of the European Community contains detailed jurisdictional rules, as we have seen, and also deals with the problem of potential multiplicity of litigation. It does not provide for judicial discretion to decline to exercise jurisdiction. Forum non conveniens is generally unknown to civil-law systems and, it is widely thought, is not part of the law established by the Convention. Cheshire & North, Private International Law, p. 331 (12th ed. 1992); Kropholler, Europäisches Zivilprozessrecht anno. 19 preceding Art. 2 (3d ed. 1991).

But what about England where the doctrine has a long tradition (supra, note 7)? In re Harrods (Buenos Aires) Ltd., [1992] Ch. 72 (C.A.), the Court of Appeal decided that section 49 of the 1982 Civil Jurisdiction and Judgments Act was not inconsistent with the Brussels Convention and that an English court could therefore dismiss, in favor of Argentina, an action against a defendant domiciled in England on forum non conveniens grounds. The House of Lords referred the question to the European Court of Justice which has jurisdiction to render binding decisions of interpretation of the Brussels Convention. When the case was settled, the matter was removed from the Court's docket and no decision issued on the question submitted. Another decision, not reviewed on appeal and not submitted to the European court followed *In Re Harrods* and dismissed in favor of Brazil. The Po, [1991] 2 Lloyd's Rep. 206, critically noted by North, IPRax 1992, 183. For comprehensive discussion, see Huber, Die englische forum-non-conveniens Doktrin und ihre Anwendung im Rahmen des EuGVÜ (1994).

THE RACE TO A JUDGMENT

The Full Faith and Credit Clause of the federal Constitution requires the interstate recognition of judgments rendered by courts of competent jurisdiction. Parallel litigation in a second forum may therefore be a means to obtain a quick determination of an issue in order to preclude further consideration of it in the first court or in other fora. It may be used by the plaintiff or, as a preemptive strike, by the defendant, in both cases often for perceived procedural or choice-of-law advantages. For obvious reasons, such tactics are often referred to as a "race to judgment," or "race to the courthouse."

In *federal* practice and when the claim arises under federal law, most federal circuits follow a "first filed" rule: "[a]ll the issues are, or can be ... joined [in the first forum] and the balance of convenience appears to be in favor of that action. Moreover, it was the first suit brought, and absent the showing of balance of convenience in favor of the second action, it should have priority," Remington Products Corp. v. American Aerovap, 192 F.2d 872 (2d Cir.1951). "In deciding between competing jurisdictions, it has often been stated that the balancing of convenience should be left to the sound discretion of the trial courts.... [An] example [of when departure from the 'first filed rule' is justified] is where forum shopping alone motivated the choice of the situs for the first suit," Gluckin & Co. v. Int'l Playtex Corp., 407 F.2d 177 (2d Cir.1969). Thus, the second-filed action may be entertained when the first-filed action was brought in anticipation of the second: non-application of the "first filed rule" in these circumstances protects the "real plaintiff," as it were, in his traditional right to choose a forum. Conversely, the first forum may seek to protect its jurisdiction by enjoining litigation elsewhere. See New York v. Exxon Corp., 932 F.2d 1020 (2d Cir.1991).

When the pendency of a state-law action in another forum is invoked in *state* court or in a federal court exercising *diversity jurisdiction,* state law will determine whether the second action should be dismissed or stayed. In interstate cases, the common law "plea in abatement" has been broadened in some states to allow dismissal of an action when the cause is pending in the same or in another state. The effect is that of a "first-filed" rule. However, abatement remains discretionary. See A.E. Staley Mfg. Co. v. Swift & Co., 84 Ill.2d 245, 50 Ill.Dec. 156, 419 N.E.2d 23 (1980).

When state courts enjoin parallel litigation in state or federal courts of other states, violation of the injunction may result in the imposition of penalties in the first state; however, recognition and enforcement by the second state does not seem to be required. James v. Grand Trunk Western Railroad Co., 14 Ill.2d 356, 152 N.E.2d 858 (1958). The Supreme Court has not had occasion to determine whether an injunction against suit in another state is entitled to full faith and credit. Usually courts have disregarded the sister state injunction and have permitted the action to proceed. The Illinois Supreme Court recently revisited the issue and found that an injunction against suit in another state rested on the court's equitable power to "restrain a person over whom it has jurisdiction from instituting a suit or proceeding with a suit in a foreign state.... [However,] Courts do not, in such cases, pretend to direct or control the foreign court, but the decree acts solely on the party," Pfaff v. Chrysler Corp., 155 Ill.2d 35, 182 Ill.Dec. 627, 610 N.E.2d 51 (1992).

In *international* litigation, the balancing of litigants' and public interests is particularly difficult. In Laker Airways v. Sabena, Belgian World Airlines, 731 F.2d 909 (D.C.Cir.1984), the court upheld an injunction in favor of an English plaintiff, restraining defendants from participating in an English action in turn designed to enjoin the plaintiff from pursuing the U.S. action. As part and parcel of the complexity of transnational litigation, the Laker court noted that "mere filing of a suit in one forum does not cut off the preexisting right of an independent forum to regulate matters subject to its prescriptive jurisdiction," so "injunctions are most often necessary to protect the jurisdiction of the enjoining court, or to prevent the litigant's evasion of the important public policies of the forum," at 927. In Turner Entertainment Co. v. Degeto Film GmBH, 25 F.3d 1512 (11th Cir.1994), the Eleventh Circuit held that international comity *requires* a stay of the proceedings when a foreign action is pending, while the United States District Court for the Southern District of New York has held that international comity *allows* dismissal of an action. 1994 US Dist. Lexis 12535.

The American forum may also use the forum-non-conveniens doctrine and dismiss the local action in favor of an action pending abroad. Some decisions, however, give little or no insight to the fact that a foreign action is pending as they weigh and balance interest. American Cyanamid Co. v. Picaso–Anstalt, 741 F.Supp. 1150 (D.N.J.1990) (French defendants, prior action pending in Paris); American Home Assurance Co. v. Ins. Corp. of Ireland, 603 F.Supp. 636 (S.D.N.Y.1984) (motion to dismiss or stay pending outcome of litigation in the United Kingdom denied, parties enjoined from pursuing simultaneous litigation abroad).

In the Brussels Convention of the European Union, as in civil law systems generally, specific provisions deal with the problem of "lis alibi pendens," literally, "the suit is pending elsewhere."

> **Article 21:** Where proceedings involving the same cause of action and between the same parties are brought in the courts of different Contracting States, any court other than the court first seized shall of its own motion stay its proceedings until such time as the jurisdiction of the court first seized is established. Where the jurisdiction of the court first seized is established, any court other than the court first seized shall decline jurisdiction in favor of that court.
>
> **Article 22:** Where related actions are brought in the courts of different Contracting States, any court other than the court first seized may, while the actions are pending at first instance, stay its proceedings.

A court other than the court first seized may also, on the application of one of the parties, decline jurisdiction if the law of that court permits the consolidation of related actions and the court first seized has jurisdiction over both actions. For the purposes of this Article, actions are deemed to be related where they are so closely connected that it is expedient to hear and determine them together to avoid the risk of irreconcilable judgments resulting from separate proceedings.

The European Court held Arts. 21 and 22 inapplicable in a case in which parallel proceedings in Italy and England concerned the recognition of a judgment from a non-member state. The policy against parallel or duplicative litigation represented by Arts. 21 and 22 is not involved in such a case: since the Convention does not mandate the recognition of non-member state judgments but leaves recognition to the national law of each member state, the Italian and English proceedings test the compatibility of the non-member state judgment (and whether it is entitled to recognition) under the respective national law. With different national laws and policies involved, the proceedings are therefore not "parallel." Case C–129/92, [1994] 1 All E.R. 336, [1994] 2 W.L.R. 759 (Court of Justice, on referral from the House of Lords). What happens once one of the proceedings concludes and grants recognition to the non-member state's judgment: is the recognition by a member state a "judgment" within the meaning of the Brussels Convention and now entitled to recognition in all other member states (thus also effectively cutting off the recognition proceeding(s) still pending in such member states)? The traditional European answer is "no". For further discussion, see infra at p. 228.

See also, Reynolds, The Iron Law of Full Faith and Credit, 53 Maryland L.Rev. 412 (1994), and Reynolds, The Proper Forum for a Suit: Transnational Forum Non Conveniens and Counter–Suit Injunctions in the Federal Courts, 70 Tex.L.Rev. 1663 (1992); Note, Anti-suit and Anti–Anti–suit Injunctions: a Proposed Texas Approach, 45 Baylor L.Rev. 499 (1993). See also, Reichert, Problems with Parallel and Duplicate Proceedings: the Litispendence Principle and International Arbitration, 8 Arbitration International 237 (1992); Juenger, What's Wrong with Forum Shopping?, 18 Sydney L.Rev. 5 (1994); Opeskin, The Price of Forum Shopping—A Reply to Professor Juenger, 18 Sydney L.Rev. 14 (1994), with a Rejoinder by Juenger, at 28; Herzog, Brussels and Lugano, Should You Race to the Courthouse or Race for a Judgment, 43 Am.J.Comp.L. 379 (1995).

FEDERAL TRANSFER

In 1948, Congress adopted a revision of the Judicial Code, known as Title 28, United States Code. Section 1404(a) of this Act provides, with respect to the Federal district courts:

"For the convenience of parties and witnesses, in the interest of justice, a district court may transfer any civil action to any other district or division where it might have been brought."

This provision has been before the Supreme Court in a number of cases. In Norwood v. Kirkpatrick, 349 U.S. 29 (1955), the Court observed that under section 1404(a) the district court has "broader discretion in the application of the statute than under the doctrine of *forum non conveniens*." It pointed out that a transfer under section 1404(a) does not involve a dismissal of the proceeding, and it held that Congress, by enacting the transfer statute, "intended to permit courts to grant transfers on a lesser showing of inconvenience." For a recent application see Harris Trust & Sav. Bank v. SLT Warehouse, 605 F.Supp. 225, 227 (N.D.Ill.1985).

In Ex parte Collett, 337 U.S. 55 (1949), the Court held that a case brought under the Federal Employers' Liability Act could be transferred under § 1404(a) even though the original forum was appropriate under the special venue provision of the Act and dismissal would not be appropriate under the local state rule of forum non conveniens.

In Hoffman v. Blaski, 363 U.S. 335 (1960), the Court held that a civil action may be transferred only to a district where the plaintiff could have brought it without the consent of the defendant, that is, ordinarily, in a district where the defendant could have been served, and where venue lies.

See also Stewart Organization Inc. v. Ricoh Corp., supra p. 176, and Ferens v. John Deere Co., infra p. 693.

NOTES

1. A federal court may not dismiss under forum non conveniens if there is a convenient district to which the case may be transferred under § 1404(a). Headrick v. Atchison, Topeka & Santa Fe Railroad Co., 182 F.2d 305 (10th Cir.1950); Nieves v. American Airlines, 700 F.Supp. 769 (S.D.N.Y.1988). As clarified recently by the Supreme Court, dismissals on forum non conveniens grounds are impermissible unless the only convenient forum is in a foreign country or is a state court. American Dredging Co. v. Miller, 114 S.Ct. 981 (1994).

In Gross v. Owen, 221 F.2d 94 (C.A.D.C.1955) dismissal under forum non conveniens was held justified because a federal court sitting in the convenient state would not have had jurisdiction to hear the case by reason of lack of diversity.

For a more complete understanding of 28 U.S.C.A. § 1404(a), see Anno., Questions as to Convenience and Justice of Transfer under Forum Non Conveniens Provision of 28 U.S.C.A. § 1404(a), 1 A.L.R. Fed. 15 (1969); Jhong, Construction and Application of Change of Venue or Transfer Provision of 28 U.S.C.A. § 1404(a), Apart from Questions of Convenience and Justice of Transfer, 7 A.L.R. Fed. 9 (1971); Kelner, "Adrift on an Uncharted Sea": A Survey of Section 1404(a) Transfer in the Federal System, 67 N.Y.U.L.Rev. 612 (1992).

2. Some decisions state that a plaintiff may obtain a transfer under § 1404(a) only if, after bringing the action, he discovers good reason for the transfer. EMI Film Distributors, Limited v. L.D.S. Film Co., 404 F.Supp. 204 (S.D.N.Y.1975); Philip Carey Manufacturing Co. v. Taylor, 286 F.2d 782 (6th Cir.1961), cert. denied 366 U.S. 948 (1961). Contra: Cordis Corp. v. Siemens–Pacesetter, Inc., 682 F.Supp. 1200 (S.D.Fla.1987) (reviewing case law and concluding that there is no additional requirement of changed circumstances when the plaintiff is the moving party).

Many of the problems arising out of federal transfer under sec. 1404(a) were resolved by the Supreme Court in Van Dusen v. Barrack, 376 U.S. 612 (1964). That case arose out of an airplane accident which occurred in Boston, Massachusetts. The plane was scheduled to fly from Boston to Philadelphia. As a result more than 100 actions were brought against various defendants in the United States District Court for the District of Massachusetts, and more than 45 actions were brought in the United States District Court for the Eastern District of Pennsylvania. Most of the latter actions were brought by executors and administrators appointed in Pennsylvania, who were not qualified to act in Massachusetts.

The defendants moved in the Pennsylvania court that most of the actions be transferred to Massachusetts under sec. 1404(a). The Court of Appeals for the Third Circuit held that the proceedings could not be transferred. It relied on the fact that since the plaintiffs in Pennsylvania were not qualified to act in Massachusetts, the actions were not ones which "might have been brought" in Massachusetts. Barrack v. Van Dusen, 309 F.2d 953 (3d Cir.1962), noted in 76 Harv.L.Rev. 1679 (1963).

The Supreme Court reversed this decision, and remanded the case to the District Court in Pennsylvania for further consideration. It held that the phrase "might have been brought" related to the suability of the defendant, and not to the capacity of the plaintiff. It also held, that, "where the defendants seek transfer, the transferee district court must be obligated to apply the state law that would have been applied if there had been no change of venue. A change of venue under § 1404(a) generally should be, with respect to state law, but a change of courtrooms." The Court added:

> ... we do not and need not consider whether in all cases § 1404(a) would require the application of the law of the transferor, as opposed to the transferee, State. We do not attempt to determine whether, for example, the same considerations would govern if a plaintiff sought transfer under § 1404(a) or if it was contended that the transferor State would simply have dismissed the action on the ground of *forum non conveniens*....

The case was remanded to the District Court to determine whether on the actual facts a transfer to Massachusetts could be justified on the grounds of "convenience and fairness." On this point, the Supreme Court noted:

> ... it has long been recognized that: "There is an appropriateness ... in having the trial of a diversity case in a forum that is at home with the state law that must govern the case, rather than having a court in some other forum untangle problems in conflict of laws, and in law foreign to itself." Gulf Oil Corp. v. Gilbert, 330 U.S. 501, 509. Thus, to the extent that Pennsylvania laws are difficult or unclear and might not defer to Massachusetts laws, it may be advantageous to retain the actions in Pennsylvania where the judges possess a more ready familiarity with the local laws....
> We do not suggest that elements of uncertainty in transferor state law would alone justify a denial of transfer; but we do think that the uncertainty is one factor, among others, to be considered in assessing the desirability of transfer....

Thus if a case were transferred from Pennsylvania to Massachusetts, the Massachusetts District Court, subject perhaps to a few rare exceptions, would sit as if it were a federal court in Pennsylvania. Under Erie Railroad v. Tompkins, 304 U.S. 64 (1938), it would be required to apply the law of Pennsylvania, including the conflict of laws of Pennsylvania. Klaxon Co. v. Stentor Electric Manufacturing Co., Inc., 313 U.S. 487 (1941). This would mean that it would apply the Pennsylvania law to determine the qualification of the plaintiff, and thus the Pennsylvania executors and administrators would be competent to sue in the case transferred to Massachusetts. Whether the conflict of laws of Pennsylvania would refer to the law of Massachusetts for the substantive rules applicable to the accident would have to be determined by the Massachusetts District Court sitting as if it were a District Court in Pennsylvania, and applying Pennsylvania law.

NOTES

1. Prominent among the articles discussing § 1404(a) and written prior to Van Dusen are Currie, Change of Venue and the Conflict of Laws, 22 U.Chi.L.Rev. 405 (1955), and Currie, Change of Venue and the Conflict of Laws: A Retraction, 27 U.Chi.L.Rev. 341 (1960). The latter article is reprinted in Currie, Selected Essays on the Conflict of Laws (1963), Chapter 9, p. 431.

2. The rule of *Van Dusen*—that the law of the transferor forum should be applied—is a complicating factor in situations where a number of cases originally brought in various Federal districts in several states are consolidated for trial in a single district court under § 1407. See, e.g., In re Paris Air Crash of March 3, 1974, 399 F.Supp. 732 (C.D.Cal.1975); In re Air Crash Disaster at Boston, Mass., July 31, 1973, 399 F.Supp. 1106 (D.Mass.1975); Symposium: Conflict of Laws and Complex Litigation Issues in Mass Tort Litigation, Introduction, 1989 U. of Ill. L.Rev. 35. The American Law Institute's Complex Litigation Project gave extensive consideration to the problem. Under the ALI's proposed rules, the transferee court will select the applicable law. The proposals are considered infra at p. 624.

3. Courts and commentators were long divided over what law should be applied after the plaintiff has obtained a transfer under § 1404(a). In Ferens v. John Deere Co., 494 U.S. 516 (1990), the Supreme Court held that the rule of *Van Dusen* also applies in this situation. The decision is considered at p. 693 below.

4. When the case raises issues of *federal* law, the transferee court follows its own circuit's interpretation of the federal law and not that of the transferor's circuit. In re Korean Airlines Disaster of Sept. 1, 1983, 829 F.2d 1171 (D.C.Cir.1987), affirmed 490 U.S. 122, 109 S.Ct. 1676 (1989). See Marcus, Conflicts Among Circuits and Transfers Within the Federal Judicial System, 93 Yale L.J. 677, 686, 702, 721 (1984).

5. Where the case is initially brought in a court lacking proper venue, the case is governed by 28 U.S.C.A. § 1406(a), which provides that the district court "shall dismiss, or if it be in the interest of justice, transfer such case to any district in which it could have been brought." The courts are agreed that where the transferor forum lacks either jurisdiction or proper venue, the law of the transferee forum will be applied regardless of whether the plaintiff or the defendant sought the transfer. LaVay Corp. v. Dominion Federal Sav. & Loan Ass'n, 830 F.2d 522 (4th Cir.1987) cert. den. 484 U.S. 1065 (1987); Manley v. Engram, 755 F.2d 1463 (11th

Cir.1985). 28 U.S.C.A. § 1631, as interpreted, clarified that not only must the transferee court apply its own law, but that it must accept the date on which the action was removed as the filing date. Ross v. Colorado Outward Bound School, Inc., 822 F.2d 1524 (10th Cir.1987).

SECTION 4. OTHER LIMITATIONS IMPOSED BY THE FORUM

RESTATEMENT, SECOND, CONFLICT OF LAWS: *

§ 53. Decree to Be Carried Out in Another State

b. *When jurisdiction exercised.* A person will be ordered to do an act in another state when this relief is required by the demands of justice and convenience. The reluctance of the courts to issue such orders stems primarily from (1) the fear of interfering unduly with the affairs of the other state and (2) the possible difficulty of enforcing obedience to an order that the defendant do an act in a place beyond the effective control of the court. Because of the first factor, the defendant will not, except on extremely rare occasions, be ordered to do an act which violates the law of the other state ... there is greater likelihood of the defendant's being ordered to do an act in another state if the court has some means at its disposal of insuring compliance with the decree, such as by requiring the defendant to post a bond or to act in the other state through the medium of an agent....

United States v. First National City Bank

United States Court of Appeals, Second Circuit, 1968.
396 F.2d 897.

[In aid of a grand jury investigation of suspected antitrust violations, a subpoena was served upon the First National City Bank requiring it to produce all documents in its office in Frankfurt, Germany, which involved certain of its customers. The Bank refused to comply on the ground that production of these documents would subject it to civil liability to these customers under German law. The District Court held the Bank liable for contempt, and it appealed.]

■ KAUFMAN, CIRCUIT JUDGE ... It is no longer open to doubt that a federal court has the power to require the production of documents located in foreign countries if the court has *in personam* jurisdiction of the person in possession or control of the material.... Thus, the task before us, as Citibank concedes, is not one of defining power but of developing rules governing the proper exercise of power.... This problem is particularly acute where the documents are sought by an arm of a foreign government. The complexities of the world being what they are, it is not surprising to

---

* Quoted with the permission of the copyright owner, The American Law Institute.

discover nations having diametrically opposed positions with respect to the disclosure of a wide range of information. It is not too difficult, therefore, to empathize with the party or witness subject to the jurisdiction of two sovereigns and confronted with conflicting commands....

... Where, as here, the burden of resolution ultimately falls upon the federal courts, the difficulties are manifold because the courts must take care not to impinge upon the prerogatives and responsibilities of the political branches of the government in the extremely sensitive and delicate area of foreign affairs.... Mechanical or overbroad rules of thumb are of little value; what is required is a careful balancing of the interests involved and a precise understanding of the facts and circumstances of the particular case.

With these principles in mind, we turn to the specific issues presented by this appeal. Citibank concedes, as it must, that compliance with the subpoena does not require the violation of the criminal law of a foreign power ... or risk the imposition of sanctions that are the substantial equivalent of criminal penalties ... or even conflict with the public policy of a foreign state as expressed in legislation .... Instead, all that remains, as we see it, is a possible prospective civil liability flowing from an implied contractual obligation between Citibank and its customers that, we are informed, is considered implicit in the bank's license to do business in Germany.

... In the instant use, the obvious, albeit troublesome, requirement for us is to balance the national interests of the United States and Germany and to give appropriate weight to the hardship, if any, Citibank will suffer.

The important interest of the United States in the enforcement of the subpoena warrants little discussion.... [T]he antitrust laws ... have long been considered cornerstones of this nation's economic policies, have been vigorously enforced and the subject of frequent interpretation by our Supreme Court. We would have great reluctance, therefore, to countenance any device that would place relevant information beyond the reach of this duly impaneled Grand Jury or impede or delay its proceedings....

We examine the importance of bank secrecy within the framework of German public policy with full recognition that it is often a subtle and difficult undertaking to determine the nature and scope of the law of a foreign jurisdiction. There is little merit, however, in Citibank's suggestion that the mere existence of a bank secrecy doctrine requires us to accept on its face the bank's assertion that compliance with the subpoena would violate an important public policy of Germany.... While we certainly do not intend to deprecate the importance of bank secrecy in the German scheme of things, neither can we blind ourselves to the doctrine's severe limitations as disclosed by the expert testimony. We have already made the assumption that the absence of criminal sanctions is not the whole answer to or finally determinative of the problem. But, it is surely of considerable significance that Germany considers bank secrecy simply a privilege that can be waived by the customer and is content to leave the matter of enforcement to the vagaries of private litigation. Indeed, bank secrecy is not even required by statute.... [Likewise, the Bank could not assert bank secrecy in a criminal investigation in Germany.]

In addition, it is noteworthy that neither the Department of State nor the German Government has expressed any view on this case or indicated that, under the circumstances present here, enforcement of the subpoena would violate German public policy or embarrass German–American relations....

[Finally, the court turned to the hardship, if any, which the Bank would suffer if it complied with the subpoena. The Court found little merit in the contention that compliance by the Bank would result in the loss of foreign business or in economic reprisals by its customers. The Court further found that the chance of the Bank being held liable for civil damages under German law was "slight and speculative."]

Affirmed.

NOTE

On occasion, courts in this country have ordered a person to testify or to bring documents from a foreign country even though compliance with the order would violate the law of that country. In re Grand Jury Proceedings, 694 F.2d 1256 (11th Cir.1982) (attorney-client privilege); In re Grand Jury Proceedings, 691 F.2d 1384 (11th Cir.1982) cert. den. 462 U.S. 1119 (1982) (bank secrecy law); In re Grand Jury Proceedings, 532 F.2d 404 (5th Cir.1976) (bank secrecy law); cf. Civil Aeronautics Board v. Deutsche Lufthansa Aktiengesellschaft, 591 F.2d 951 (D.C.Cir. 1979) (defendant ordered to use all good faith efforts to obtain government permission for release of documents).

On other occasions, the courts have refused to issue an order that would require violation of the law of a foreign country. In re Westinghouse Electric Corp. Uranium, etc., 563 F.2d 992 (10th Cir.1977) (interests of the foreign country held to be more seriously involved than those of the United States); Application of Chase Manhattan Bank, 297 F.2d 611 (2d Cir.1962).

For a general discussion of the problem, see Note, Extraterritorial Discovery: An Analysis Based on Good Faith, 83 Colum.L.Rev. 1320 (1983).

The problem addressed by Section 53 of the Restatement, Second, and in *First National City Bank* today arises most frequently in the context of pretrial discovery in international cases. Foreign legal systems do not provide for extensive pretrial discovery, and foreign countries have therefore become increasingly sensitive about what they regard as intrusive and overreaching American discovery orders. In recent years, a number of foreign countries have adopted "blocking statutes" forbidding the production of documents located in their territories in response to foreign orders or requests. Examples include the English Protection of Trading Interests Act of 1980, the Canadian Foreign Extraterritorial Measures Act of 1985, and the Australian Foreign Proceedings (Excess of Jurisdiction) Act of 1984. In Société Nationale Industrielle Aerospatiale v. United States District Court for the Southern District of Iowa, 482 U.S. 522 (1987), the defendant resisted a pretrial discovery order for the production of documents located in France on the ground that the Hague Convention on the Taking of Evidence Abroad provided the exclusive, or at least the primary means for obtaining such documents. In support of its argument, the defendant also pointed to the existence of a French blocking statute. The Supreme Court rejected the argument: "It is well-settled that such statutes do not deprive an American court of the power to order a party subject to its jurisdiction to produce evidence even though the act of production may violate that statute.... Extraterritorial assertions of jurisdiction are not one-sided. While the District Court's discovery orders arguably have some impact in France, the French blocking statute asserts similar authority over acts to take place in this country.... The blocking statute ... is relevant to the court's particularized comity analysis only to the extent that its terms and its enforcement identify the nature of the sovereign interests in nondisclosure.... 482 U.S. at 544 n. 29.

NOTES

1. The subject is discussed further at pp. 744–746 infra.

2. See Note, A Comparative Study of U.S. and British Approaches to Discovery Conflicts: Achieving a Uniform System of Extraterritorial Discovery, 18 Fordham Int'l L.J. 1340 (1995). For extensive and comparative discussion of discovery of documents and inspection of objects in civil litigation, see Hay, Informationsbeschaffung über schriftliche Unterlagen und Augenscheinsobjekte in Zivilprozess, ___ Veröffentlichungen der Wissenschaftlichen Vereinigung für Prozessrecht ___ (1996).

3. For a discussion of the factors that should be considered by a court in a situation where two or more states have power to require a person to engage in inconsistent courses of conduct, see Restatement, Third, Foreign Relations Law of the United States § 403 and Reporters' Notes Nos. 6–7 (1987).

4. A court of equity will be less reluctant to issue a decree affecting interests in property outside the state when the act ordered may be performed without the party leaving the state. See authorities set forth on p. 257, Note (2), infra, and Weesner v. Weesner, p. 258, Note (5), infra.

Slater v. Mexican National R. Co.
Supreme Court of the United States, 1904.
194 U.S. 120, 24 S.Ct. 581, 48 L.Ed. 900.

■ MR. JUSTICE HOLMES delivered the opinion of the court.

This is an action brought in the United States Circuit Court for the Northern District of Texas by citizens and residents of Texas against a Colorado corporation operating a railroad from Texas to the City of Mexico. The plaintiffs are the widow and children of William H. Slater, who was employed by the defendant as a switchman on its road and was killed through the defendant's negligence while coupling two freight cars at Nuevo Laredo, in Mexico. This action is to recover damages for the death. The laws of Mexico were set forth in the plaintiffs' petition, and the defendant demurred on the ground that the cause of action given by the

Mexican laws was not transitory, for reasons sufficiently stated. The demurrer was overruled, and the defendant excepted. A similar objection was taken also by plea setting forth additional sections of the Mexican statutes. A demurrer to this plea was sustained, subject to exception. The same point was raised again at the trial by a request to direct a verdict for the defendant. The judge who tried the case instructed the jury that the damages to be recovered, if any, were to be measured by the money value of the life of the deceased to the widow and children, and the jury returned a verdict for a lump sum, apportioned to the several plaintiffs. The judge and jury in this regard acted as prescribed by the Texas Rev.Stat. Art. 3027. The case then was taken to the Circuit Court of Appeals, where the judgment was reversed and the action ordered to be dismissed. 115 F. 593, 53 C.C.A. 239.

There is no need to encumber the reports with all the statutes in the record.... We assume for the moment that it was sufficiently alleged and proved that the killing of Slater was a negligent crime within the definition of Article 11 of the Penal Code, and, therefore, if the above sections were the only law bearing on the matter, that they created a civil liability to make reparation to any one whose rights were infringed.

As Texas has statutes which give an action for wrongfully causing death, of course there is no general objection of policy to enforcing such a liability there, although it arose in another jurisdiction. Stewart v. Baltimore & Ohio R.R., 168 U.S. 445. But when such a liability is enforced in a jurisdiction foreign to the place of the wrongful act, obviously that does not mean that the act in any degree is subject to the lex fori, with regard to either its quality or its consequences. On the other hand, it equally little means that the law of the place of the act is operative outside its own territory. The theory of the foreign suit is that although the act complained of was subject to no law having force in the forum, it gave rise to an obligation, an *obligatio,* which, like other obligations, follows the person, and may be enforced wherever the person may be found. Stout v. Wood, 1 Blackf. (Ind.) 71; Dennick v. Railroad Co., 103 U.S. 11, 18. But as the only source of this obligation is the law of the place of the act, it follows that the law determines not merely the existence of the obligation, Smith v. Condry, 1 How. 28, but equally determines its extent. It seems to us unjust to allow a plaintiff to come here absolutely depending on the foreign law for the foundation of his case, and yet to deny the defendant the benefit of whatever limitations on his liability that law would impose. In Northern Pacific R.R. v. Babcock, 154 U.S. 190, 199, an action was brought in the District of Minnesota for a death caused in Montana, and it was held that the damages were to be assessed in accordance with the Montana statute. Therefore we may lay on one side as quite inadmissible the notion that the law of the place of the act may be resorted to so far as to show that the act was a tort, and then may be abandoned, leaving the consequences to be determined according to the accident of the place where the defendant may happen to be caught.... We are aware that expressions of a different tendency may be found in some English cases. But they do not cover the question before this court, and our opinion is based ... as it seems to us upon the only theory by which actions fairly can be allowed to be maintained for foreign torts. As the cause of action relied upon is one which is supposed to have arisen in Mexico under Mexican laws, the place of the death and the domicile of the parties have no bearing upon the case.

The application of these considerations now is to be shown.... By Article 318 [of the Penal Code of Mexico] civil responsibility for a wrongful homicide includes, besides the expenses of medical attendance and burial and damages to the property of the deceased, the expenses "of the support not only of the widow, descendants and ascendants of the deceased, who were being supported by him, he being under legal obligations to do so, but also to the posthumous descendants that he may leave." Then, by Art. 319, the obligation to support shall last during the time that the deceased might have lived, calculated by a given life table, but taking the state of his health before the homicide into consideration, but "the obligation shall cease: 1. At whatever time it shall not be absolutely necessary for the subsistence of those entitled to receive it. 2. When those beneficiaries get married. 3. When the minor children become of age. 4. In any other case in which, according to law, the deceased, if alive; would not be required to continue the support." It is unnecessary to set forth the detailed provisions as to support in other parts of the statutes. It is sufficiently obvious from what has been quoted that the decree contemplated by the Mexican law is a decree analogous to a decree for alimony in divorce proceedings—a decree which contemplates periodical payments and which is subject to modification from time to time as the circumstances change. See, also, Arts. 1376, 1377, of the Code of Procedure, and Penal Code, Bk. 2, Art. 363.

The present action is a suit at common law and the court has no power to make a decree of this kind contemplated by the Mexican statutes. What the Circuit Court did was to disregard the principles of the Mexican statute altogether and to follow the Texas statute. This clearly was wrong and was excepted to specifically. But we are of opinion further that justice to the defendant would not permit the substitution of a lump sum, however estimated, for the periodical payments which the Mexican statute required. The marriage of beneficiaries, the cessation of the absolute necessity for the payments, the arising of other circumstances in which, according to law, the deceased would not have been required to continue the support, all are contingencies the chance of which cannot be estimated by any table of probabilities. It would be going far to give a lump sum in place of an annuity for life, the probable value of which could be fixed by averages based on statistics. But to reduce a liability conditioned as this was to a lump sum would be to leave the whole matter to a mere guess. We may add that by Art. 225, concerning alimony, the right cannot be renounced, nor can it be subject to compromise between the parties. There seems to be no possibility in Mexico of capitalizing the liability. Evidently the Texas courts would deem the dissimilarities between the local law and that of Mexico too great to permit an action in the Texas state courts. Mexican National Ry. v. Jackson, 89 Tex. 107; St. Louis, Iron Mountain & Southern

Ry. v. McCormick, 73 Tex. 660. The case is not one demanding extreme measures like those where a tort is committed in an uncivilized country. The defendant always can be found in Mexico, on the other side of the river, and it is to be presumed that the courts there are open to the plaintiffs, if the statute conferred a right upon them notwithstanding their absence from the jurisdiction, as we assume that it did, for the purposes of this part of the case. See Mulhall v. Fallon, 176 Mass. 266. . . .

Judgment affirmed.

■ CHIEF JUSTICE FULLER dissented in an opinion, in which JUSTICE HARLAN and JUSTICE PECKHAM concurred.

NOTES

1. The Supreme Court of Texas finally abolished "dissimilarity" as a basis for refusing to entertain cases applying Mexican personal injury law, Gutierrez v. Collins, 583 S.W.2d 312 (Tex.1979).

2. Phrantzes v. Argenti, [1960] 2 Q.B. 19, [1960] 1 All Eng.L.R. 778, was a suit brought by a daughter, under Greek law, claiming a dowry from her father. The court refused to entertain the suit, saying that the Greek "machinery by way of remedies" was entirely different from the English machinery.

CONSTITUTIONAL LIMITATIONS ON POWER OF STATE TO REFUSE TO ENTERTAIN CASE

Query, are there any circumstances in which a state may refrain from enforcing a Federal cause of action? Suppose, for example, it enforces no wrongful death actions, either arising in its own state or in other states. Could it refuse to entertain an action for death brought under the Federal Employers' Liability Act?

MONDOU V. NEW YORK, NEW HAVEN & HARTFORD RAILROAD CO., 223 U.S. 1 (1912): An action was brought in a Connecticut state court by the personal representative of an employee who was killed in Connecticut in the course of his employment in interstate commerce. The action was brought under the Federal Employers' Liability Act which increased the liabilities of employers by abolishing certain common law defenses. It also provided that the jurisdiction of the courts of the United States and of the states should be concurrent under the Act. The defendant demurred to the complaint, and this was sustained by the Connecticut state court on the ground, among others, that the Act, in so extending liability, was contrary to the public policy of Connecticut.

The Supreme Court of the United States reversed. After holding the Act constitutional, the Court stated that federal action within its sphere is paramount to and supersedes state law. Consequently, the Act established a policy binding on all states, and if the court in which the action is brought is otherwise competent, it is under a duty to exercise its jurisdiction.

McKnett v. St. Louis & San Francisco Railroad Co., 292 U.S. 230 (1934): Held that Alabama could not refuse to enforce Federal Employers' Liability Act claims when it would entertain suits based on wrongful death statutes of other states under similar circumstances.

Missouri ex rel. Southern Railway Co. v. Mayfield, 340 U.S. 1 (1950): A Missouri state court was held free to apply the forum non conveniens doctrine to a Federal Employers' Liability Act case brought before it where the plaintiff and defendant were nonresidents, and the accident had occurred in another state.[1] In American Dredging Co. v. Miller, 114 S.Ct. 981 (1994), the Supreme Court held that Louisiana was free to apply state law motions of forum non conveniens in an action arising under the federal Jones Act.

Testa v. Katt, 330 U.S. 386 (1947): A suit was brought in a state court in Rhode Island to recover triple damages for an overcharge on the sale of goods, contrary to the Emergency Price Control Act. Sec. 205(e) of that Act authorized a suit "in any court of competent jurisdiction," and sec. 205(c) provided that federal district courts should have jurisdiction of such suits "concurrently with State and Territorial courts."

The Supreme Court of Rhode Island held that the statute allowing recovery of treble damages was a penal statute, and could not be enforced in the Rhode Island courts. This was reversed by the Supreme Court of the United States, which said that "the State courts are not free to refuse enforcement of petitioners' claim."

NOTE

See Brilmayer and Underhill, Congressional Obligation to Provide a Forum for Constitutional Claims: Discriminatory Jurisdictional Rules and the Conflict of Laws, 39 Va.L.Rev. 819 (1983); See Note, State Remedies for Federally-Created Rights, 47 Minn.L.Rev. 815 (1963). See Hughes v. Fetter, 326, infra.

1. But, on remand, the Missouri state court held that the forum non conveniens rule did not apply and, hence refused to dismiss the case. State ex rel. Southern Railway Co. v. Mayfield, 362 Mo. 101, 240 S.W.2d 106 (1951). *Mayfield* was subsequently overruled: State v. Riederer, 454 S.W.2d 36 (1970).

Section 5. Limitations Imposed by the State of the Transaction *

Buttron v. El Paso Northeastern Ry. Co.
Court of Civil Appeals of Texas, 1906.
93 S.W. 676.

Action by Louis Buttron against the El Paso Northeastern Railway Co. and others. From a judgment for defendants, plaintiff appeals.

■ JAMES, C.J. This action was brought by Buttron in the district court of El Paso county, Tex., against the above-named appellee and two other railway companies, to recover damages for injury alleged to have been caused him by their negligence. The court directed the jury to find for defendants, stating as its reason for so doing that defendants had introduced in evidence a valid and subsisting judgment of the Sixth judicial district court of the territory of New Mexico, adjudicating the issues involved. The said territorial judgment was rendered in a proceeding begun and prosecuted by the defendants herein against Buttron, under the provisions of the second and fourth sections of the following act of the Legislature Assembly of the said territory (Laws 1903, p. 51, c. 33). . . .

There are peculiar and radical features in this law, which appellant says affect its validity.[1] These are stated by appellant to be: (1) It provides that no suit for personal injuries incurred within the territory shall be brought in another jurisdiction, provided the defendant can be served within the territory. (2) The right of action is taken away from the claimant, unless within ninety days after the injury, and thirty days before commencing his action he shall serve upon his adversary a sworn statement giving the details of his case and the names and addresses of his witnesses. (3) The suit must be brought in one year after the injury. (4) The party who has inflicted the injury can compel the one he has injured to come into the court for the district in which the wrongdoer lives and set up his claim there, and, in case he does not do it, then the court will try the case on the statement of the wrongdoer, and upon that statement of the claim render judgment, which shall be final. (5) On its appearing to the court that any such suit has been begun in a court outside the territory, the court in the territory where an action is pending, under the act, may try the latter case upon such short notice as the court may direct, and compel the parties to plead on such short day as the court may fix, and the institution of such suit outside the territory shall be construed by the court as a waiver of a jury in the case pending in the territorial court. (6) On showing made that

---

* See Restatement, Second, Conflict of Laws § 91.

1. The text of the carefully drawn Act, which was included in full in the opinion, is omitted. It was "disapproved and declared null and of no effect" by an Act of Congress. Act of May 13, 1908, 35 Stat. 573, 575.

a party injured contemplates bringing suit outside the territory, or has already instituted such a suit, the court may perpetually enjoin the claimant from prosecuting or maintaining his suit outside the territory....

The Court gave effect to a judgment of the territorial court rendered under the provisions of section 2 of the act.... Section 2 allows the person or corporation inflicting the injury, or causing the death, to commence a proceeding against the injured party, in the district court for the county in the territory where it has its principal office, if a corporation, and requires the injured party to appear and litigate his claim. The defendants in the case resorted to such a proceeding, and plaintiff, a resident of the territory, was personally served with the prescribed summons. He failed to appear, and, the court proceeding in the prescribed manner, judgment was rendered against him in favor of these defendants on his cause of action, upon the hearing required by the act. The only point of objection which we perceive possible in reference to section 2 is that it gives to one who is accustomed to figure as a defendant, and who has heretofore invariably occupied that attitude in the courts, the right to anticipate the ordinary action, and to himself begin a proceeding requiring the injured party to appear and submit his cause of action to adjudication. Why is this not due exercise of power vested in a legislative body? It consisted in giving the person or corporation charged with committing a wrong remedy which it otherwise would not have had. Ordinarily such party would have had to await the bringing of the action by the claimant at his convenience, within the period of limitations. Such delay, it can readily be conceived, might often work a hardship on the former, by the loss of testimony. It is true there generally are statutes enabling a party to perpetuate testimony, but it is well known that written testimony is not always as effective as oral, which might not be obtainable in the course of time. Viewing the matter abstractly, what justice is there, after all, in forcing a party interested in the settlement of a controversy to await the pleasure of his adversary as to the time of its adjudication? Why should they not have equal right and opportunity to bring the matter to issue in the courts? There may be reasons of a substantial nature for such legislation. If they were sufficient in the minds of the legislators to dictate the wisdom of policy of a statute conferring on a prospective defendant such a remedy, it is for the courts to give effect to the will of the people thus expressed, though the wisdom and policy may be doubted by some. There is no obstacle of a constitutional nature, to the adoption of such a rule. It concerns merely procedure which is a proper subject of legislative action. Our courts are required to give full faith and credit to the judgment of the territorial court. Therefore we think the judgment appealed from should be affirmed.

Affirmed.

NOTES

1. Compare Atchison, Topeka & Santa Fe Railway Co. v. Sowers, 213 U.S. 55 (1909), which involved Sec. 1 of the same New Mexico statute and is outlined in the opinion of the court in Tennessee Coal, Iron & Railroad Co. v. George, infra.

2. A considerable number of states have adopted declaratory judgment acts. See 12 Uniform Laws Annotated 109 (1975). See also 28 U.S.C.A. § 2201. May the declaratory judgments acts be utilized by the alleged obligor to have a controversy tried (a) in the normal forum, or (b) in any forum selected by him that has jurisdiction over the alleged obligee? Will the courts exercise the same type of discretion in taking jurisdiction to render a declaratory judgment as they have done in other cases?

Tennessee Coal, Iron & Railroad Co. v. George

Supreme Court of the United States, 1914.
233 U.S. 354, 34 S.Ct. 587, 58 L.Ed. 997.

■JUSTICE LAMAR delivered the opinion of the court.

Wiley George, the defendant in error, was an engineer employed by the Tennessee Coal, Iron and Railroad Company at its steel plant in Jefferson County, Alabama. While he was under a locomotive repairing the brakes, a defective throttle allowed steam to leak into the cylinder causing the engine to move forward automatically in consequence of which he was seriously injured. He brought suit by attachment, in the City Court of Atlanta, Georgia, founding his action on sec. 3910 of the Alabama Code of 1907, which makes the master liable to the employe when the injury is "caused by reason of any defect in the condition of the ways, works, machinery or plant connected with or used in the business of the master or employer."

The defendant filed a plea in abatement in which it was set out that sec. 6115 of that Code also provided that "all actions under said section 3910 must be brought in a court of competent jurisdiction within the State of Alabama and not elsewhere." The defendant thereupon prayed that the action be abated because "to continue said case on said statutory cause of action given by the statutes of Alabama and restricted by said statutes to the courts of Alabama, ... would be a denial so far as the rights of this defendant are concerned, of full faith and credit to said public acts of the State of Alabama in the State of Georgia, contrary to the provisions of Art. 4, sec. 1 of the Constitution of the United States." A demurrer to the plea in abatement was sustained and the judgment for the plaintiff thereafter entered was affirmed by the Court of Appeals. The case was then brought to this court.

The record raises the single question as to whether the full faith and credit clause of the Constitution prohibited the courts of Georgia from enforcing a cause of action given by the Alabama Code, to the servant against the master, for injuries occasioned by defective machinery, when another section of the same Code provided that suits to enforce such liability "must be brought in a court of competent jurisdiction within the State of Alabama *and not elsewhere.*"

There are many cases where right and remedy are so united that the right cannot be enforced except in the manner and before the tribunal designated by the act. For the rule is well settled that "where the provision for the liability is coupled with a provision for a special remedy, that remedy, and that alone, must be employed." Pollard v. Bailey, 20 Wall. 520, 527....

But that rule has no application to a case arising under the Alabama Code relating to suits for injuries caused by defective machinery. For, whether the statute be treated as prohibiting certain defenses, as removing common law restrictions or as imposing upon the master a new and larger liability, it is in either event evident that the place of bringing the suit is not part of the cause of action,—the right and the remedy are not so inseparably united as to make the right dependent upon its being enforced in a particular tribunal. The cause of action is transitory and like any other transitory action can be enforced "in any court of competent jurisdiction within the State of Alabama." But the owner of the defective machinery causing the injury may have removed from the State and it would be a deprivation of a fixed right if the plaintiff could not sue the defendant in Alabama because he had left the State nor sue him where the defendant or his property could be found because the statute did not permit a suit elsewhere than in Alabama. The injured plaintiff may likewise have moved from Alabama and for that, or other, reason may have found it to his interest to bring suit by attachment or in personam in a State other than where the injury was inflicted.

The courts of the sister State trying the case would be bound to give such faith and credit to all those substantial provisions of the statute which inhered in the cause of action or which name conditions on which the right to sue depend. But venue is no part of the right; and a State cannot create a transitory cause of action and at the same time destroy the right to sue on that transitory cause of action in any court having jurisdiction. That jurisdiction is to be determined by the law of the court's creation and cannot be defeated by the extraterritorial operation of a statute of another State, even though it created the right of action.

The case here is controlled by the decision of this court in Atchison & C. Ry. v. Sowers, 213 U.S. 55, 59, 70, where the New Mexico statute, giving a right of action for personal injuries and providing that suits should be brought after certain form of notice in a particular district, was preceded by the recital that "it has become customary for persons claiming damages for personal injuries received in this Territory to institute and maintain suits for the recovery thereof in other States and Territories to the increased cost and annoyance and manifest injury and oppression of the business interests of this Territory and in derogation of the dignity of the courts thereof." Despite this statement of the public policy of the Territory, the judgment obtained by the plaintiff in Texas was affirmed by this court in an opinion wherein it was said that where an action is brought in "another jurisdiction based upon common law principles, although having certain statutory restrictions, such as are found in this [territorial] act as to the making of an affidavit and limiting the time of prosecuting the suit, full faith and credit is given to the law, when the recovery is permitted, subject to the restrictions upon the right of action imposed in the Territory enacting the statute. When it is shown that the court in the other jurisdiction observed such conditions, and that a recovery was permitted after such conditions had been complied with, the jurisdiction thus invoked is not defeated because of the provision of the statute" requiring the suit to be brought in the district where the plaintiff resides or where the defendant, if a corporation, has its principal place of business.

It is claimed, however, that the decision in the Sowers Case is not in point because the plaintiff was there seeking to enforce a common law liability, while here he is asserting a new and statutory cause of action. But that distinction marks no difference between the two cases because in New Mexico, common law liability is statutory liability—the adopting statute (Complied Laws sec. 1823) providing that "the common law as recognized in the United States of America shall be the rule of practice and decision."

The decision in the Sowers Case, however, was not put upon the fact that the suit was based on a common law liability. The court there announced the general rule that a transitory cause of action can be maintained in another State even though the statute creating the cause of action provides that the action must be brought in local domestic courts.

In the present case the Georgia court gave full faith and credit to the Alabama act and its judgment is

Affirmed.

■ JUSTICE HOLMES dissents.

NOTES

1. If in the principal case the Georgia court had refused to entertain the plaintiff's action, would its refusal have been in violation of any provision of the Constitution? Would the Constitution require that the plaintiff's action be entertained in Georgia despite the wishes of both Alabama and Georgia, the only two states of interest? Compare Hughes v. Fetter, 318 infra.

2. Note Justice Lamar's statement in the *George* case that "[t]he courts of the sister state trying the case would be bound to give such faith and credit to all those substantial provisions of the statute which inhered in the cause of action or which name conditions on which the right to sue depend." In connection with this statement, consider the following:

In Pearson v. Northeast Airlines, Inc., 309 F.2d 553 (2d Cir.1962), a majority of the court, sitting en banc, held it constitutional for a state to apply the wrongful death statute of a sister state to determine whether the defendant was liable for the death and at the same time refuse to apply the limitation contained in that statute as to the amount of recovery. Speaking for a minority of three, Judge Friendly wrote a dissent in which he said:

"An important reason why a forum state may not do this is that it thereby interferes with the proper freedom of action of the legislature of the sister state. The terms and conditions of a claim created by statute inevitably reflect the legislature's balancing of those considerations that favor and of those that oppose the imposition of liability. The legislature may be quite unwilling to create the claim on terms allowing it to be enforced without limit of amount as most common law rights can be, or for a period bounded only by statutes of limitations ordinarily applicable. The Full Faith and Credit Clause insures that, in making its choice, the legislature creating the claim need not have to weigh the risk that the courts of sister states looking to its 'public acts' as a source of rights will disregard substantial conditions which it has imposed.... This consideration is inapplicable to instances where the forum, looking solely to its own substantive law, wholly disregards that of the sister state.... True, conduct in the enacting state has been given consequences different from what the legislators of that state desired; but that is the inevitable result of the duplicate law-making jurisdiction that can never be wholly avoided even in our federal system...."

In Nevada v. Hall, 440 U.S. 410 (1979), reh. den. 441 U.S. 917 (1978), p. 348, infra, the Court rejected Nevada's argument that the Full Faith and Credit Clause required California to respect Nevada's limitation on its waiver of immunity from suit and the Nevada $25,000 cap on the amount of damages recoverable against the state.

3. Crider v. Zurich Insurance Co., 380 U.S. 39 (1965), involved an action brought in an Alabama court by a resident of that state to recover under the Georgia Workmen's Compensation Act for injuries suffered in Alabama. Georgia decisions had previously held that the remedy provided by the Georgia act is "an exclusive one which can be afforded only" by the Georgia Compensation Board. Nevertheless, the Supreme Court held that Alabama was not prohibited from entertaining the action. In the course of his majority opinion, Justice Douglas stated that the rule of the Georgia case "has been eroded" to the extent that it would limit the courts of a second state to the award of a "special remedy" that is "coupled" with the provision for liability on which the action is based.

4. Judge Friendly's dissent in *Pearson,* supra, expressed the concern that the majority was giving less than *full* faith and credit to the law of a sister state. Would he have had the same concern about *Hall?* Does *Crider* raise a different issue?

The Crider case is discussed in Greenspan, Crider v. Zurich Insurance Co.: Decline of Conceptualism in Conflict of Laws, 27 U.Pitt.L.Rev. 49 (1965). The question of whether it is a denial of full faith and credit to rely on a sister-state law as the basis for enforcing a claim while at the same time rejecting a limitation provided in that law is considered in Chapter 6, infra.

James v. Grand Trunk Western Railroad Co.

Supreme Court of Illinois, 1958.
14 Ill.2d 356, 152 N.E.2d 858, Cert. den. 358 U.S. 915 (1958).

[The case involved a Michigan injunction and an Illinois counterinjunction. A resident of Michigan was killed in that state by the defendant railroad company. His widow, appointed administratrix in Michigan, brought an action in Illinois under the Michigan wrongful death statute, alleging the death was caused by the negligence of the railroad.

In Michigan, where the administratrix resided, the defendant obtained a temporary injunction restraining her from proceeding with the action in Illinois.

The administratrix then filed a supplemental complaint in the Illinois court, which alleged she believed she could not obtain a fair trial in the county in Michigan where she resided, and the railroad's injunction suit in Michigan was for the purpose of preventing her from obtaining a fair trial in Illinois and of forcing her into an unjust settlement to her irreparable injury. She moved for an injunction restraining the enforcement of the Michigan injunction. The motion was denied by the Illinois trial court and the Appellate Court, and their action is the subject of the present appeal to the Supreme Court of Illinois.]

■ BRISTOW, JUSTICE.... The issues are essentially whether the Illinois court, having prior jurisdiction of a wrongful death action instituted by a nonresident plaintiff, must recognize an out-of-State injunction restraining the plaintiff from proceeding with that action; and whether the Illinois court, to protect its jurisdiction of the wrongful death action, may issue a counterinjunction restraining defendant from enforcing its injunction against plaintiff in the State of her residence....

In the instant case it is uncontroverted that the Illinois trial court had proper jurisdiction of the parties.... Moreover, it is the undisputed policy of this State to keep its courts open to residents and nonresidents alike.

[W]hile we quite agree with defendant's repeated assertion that a court of equity has power to restrain persons within its jurisdiction from instituting or proceeding with foreign actions (Cole v. Cunningham, 133 U.S. 107, 6 A.L.R.2d 896), we note that the exercise of such power by equity courts has been deemed a matter of great delicacy, invoked with great restraint to avoid distressing conflicts and reciprocal interference with jurisdiction....

Conversely, where other States have enjoined litigants from proceeding with a previously instituted Illinois action, this jurisdiction has followed the overwhelming judicial opinion that neither the full-faith-and-credit clause nor rules of comity require compulsory recognition of such injunctions so as to abate or preclude the disposition of the pending case....

Therefore, [we are not required] to recognize the Michigan injunction, and we may retain jurisdiction and proceed with plaintiff's wrongful death action. Such a course, however, is not practicable in the instant case, unless plaintiff, who is subject to imprisonment and other coercive tactics if she fails to dismiss her Illinois action, is protected by enjoining defendant from enforcing the Michigan injunction by contempt proceedings. A plaintiff cannot be expected or required to risk imprisonment so that the court may retain jurisdiction of a cause.

This brings us to the ultimate issue in this case: whether the court which first acquires jurisdiction of the parties and of the merits of the cause can issue a counterinjunction restraining a party before it from enforcing an out-of-State injunction which requires the dismissal of the local cause and ousts the forum of jurisdiction....

... [W]e cannot close our eyes to the fact that the intended effect of the Michigan injunction, though directed at the parties and not at this court, is to prevent the Illinois court from adjudicating a cause of action of which it had proper jurisdiction. For it is patent that if the litigants are coerced to dismiss the Illinois action, it is our rightfully acquired jurisdiction that is thereby destroyed. Therefore, the Michigan injunction was in everything but form an order restraining the Illinois court and determining the cases, it may properly try.

... [T]his court need not, and will not, countenance having its right to try cases, of which it has proper jurisdiction, determined by the courts of other States, through their injunctive process. We are not only free to disregard such out-of-State injunctions, and to adjudicate the merits of the pending action, but we can protect our jurisdiction from such usurpation by the issuance of a counterinjunction restraining the enforcement of the out-of-State injunction....

Reversed and remanded, with directions.

■ SCHAEFER, JUSTICE (dissenting)....

So far as I have been able to ascertain, no court has as yet held that such an injunction is entitled to full faith and credit in the sense that the action toward which the injunction is directed must be abated. When such injunctions have been recognized, it has been because the State in which the action is pending has chosen to do so as a matter of comity, and not because it was required to do so by constitutional command....

In part this view appears to rest upon the ground that to recognize the injunction is to recognize the claim of the enjoining State to exclusive cognizance of a transitory cause of action, which might abridge constitutional privileges.... In part it appears to rest upon the ground that to recognize the injunction would "mean in effect that the courts of one State can control what goes on in another." ... For these reasons I agree with the majority that the Michigan injunction is not entitled to full faith and credit.

But the question in this case goes a step beyond the issue as to full faith and credit. What is here sought is a counter-injunction to restrain the railroad from enforcing the injunction entered by the Michigan court.... Just as the first injunction sired the second, so the second might sire a third. The ultimate end is not foreseeable.

The place to stop this unseemly kind of judicial disorder is where it begins. The peculiar preference of one State for a particular venue in a single class of cases does not, it seems to me, afford a basis for indirect interference with litigation pending in another jurisdiction. The salutary power of a court of equity to restrain the prosecution of inequitable actions in a foreign court originated and developed upon more substantial considerations. But we are not called upon to review the propriety of the Michigan injunction. Plaintiff did not seek to review it in the Michigan courts.... Illinois has no connection whatever with the occurrences out of which the administrator's claim arose. The policy of Illinois with respect to the maintenance of foreign wrongful death actions was expressed in section 2 of the Injuries Act (Ill.Rev.Stat.1955, chap. 70, par. 2) which prohibited them. While it is true that this prohibition is no longer effective, the policy that it expressed is also of significance in determining whether or not a counter-injunction should have been issued.

I think that the trial court and the Appellate Court were right, and so I would affirm.

NOTES

1. Pound, The Progress of the Law—Equity, 33 Harv.L.Rev. 420, 426–427 (1920): "Three types of cases may be distinguished in which courts have enjoined litigation in foreign jurisdictions. In one the foreign court had no jurisdiction, but the threatened foreign judgment would embarrass plaintiff in the assertion of his rights, the legal remedy of collateral attack on the judgment when set up against plaintiff involved danger of impairment of the evidence by which its invalidity could be made to appear, and to compel plaintiff to go to the foreign state to defend or attack the threatened judgment directly involved compelling him to litigate abroad with a wrongdoer whom he could reach at home. In a second type concurrent litigation between the same parties over the same subject matter was in progress or was threatened. In some of the cases of this type there was simply a vexatious multiplicity of actions. Here courts were cautious about interposing. In others, one court was not in as good a position to do complete justice as another. In still others, the defendant was seeking to obtain an inequitable advantage over other creditors by means of concurrent litigation abroad. In a third type there was an attempt of domestic creditors to reach exempt property of a domestic debtor by means of an action outside of the state. To these some courts are adding a fourth: Cases where the foreign court has jurisdiction, in which there is no concurrent litigation or vexatious multiplicity of actions, and in which there is no attempt to reach anything which the policy of the local legislation seeks to secure to the plaintiff, but in which a domestic creditor seeks to sue a domestic debtor, as he has full legal power to do, in another state, where the latter has property, because of more favorable procedure or more favorable views as to what is a defense in the latter jurisdiction. In these cases it cannot be said that plaintiff (in equity) has a legal right only to be sued at home, nor may he claim a legal interest in the procedure or substantive law of his domicile. Doctrines of Conflict of Laws may sometimes require the court in the other state to judge the cause by the laws of the jurisdiction where the parties are domiciled. But that is a matter for that court to consider and does not give to the latter jurisdiction any claim to exclusive cognizance of the cause nor to its citizens any legal claim to make their defense solely at their domicile. As between a plaintiff and a defendant, each seeking the tribunal more favorable to him, why should not equity leave the matter to the law? ..."

2. The unwillingness manifested by a court having jurisdiction of the parties to an action to give effect to a foreign decree enjoining the institution or maintenance of that action has its counterpart in the reluctance to treat the pendency of a foreign action on the same cause of action as a defense. A plea in abatement based on the pendency of a prior personal action in another state has often been held to be ineffective. Fitch v. Whaples, 220 A.2d 170 (Me.1966). However, since the granting of a stay does not have the effect of sustaining a plea in abatement in terminating the action, a stay may be allowed when a plea in abatement would be unavailable. See Mahaffey v. Bechtel Associates Professional Corp., 699 F.2d 545 (D.C.Cir.1983); Evans Transp. Co. v. Scullin Steel Co., 693 F.2d 715 (7th Cir.1982); A.E. Staley Mfg. Co. v. Swift & Co., 84 Ill.2d 245, 50 Ill.Dec. 156, 419 N.E.2d 23 (1980). See also Restatement, Second, Conflict of Laws § 86. For further discussion of *lis pendens* in the context of forum non conveniens, see p. 189, Note (3), supra.

SECTION 6. EFFECT OF INTERSTATE COMMERCE

For many years, in a variety of circumstances, the Supreme Court has held that the States cannot unreasonably "burden" interstate commerce. Many of these decisions are in the general field of constitutional law, and they are not dealt with here. In some cases, however, the question arises with respect to the jurisdiction of the state courts. See Restatement, Second, Conflict of Laws § 84, Comment *i* (1971).

An example may be found in Sioux Remedy Co. v. Cope, 235 U.S. 197 (1914). This was an action by an Iowa corporation brought in a South Dakota court. It arose out of a contract made in South Dakota for goods to be shipped by the plaintiff from Iowa to South Dakota. The plaintiff had not "qualified" to do business in South Dakota, and a statute of the latter state provided that if a foreign corporation did business in the state without qualifying (which included the appointment of an agent for the service of process on any and all claims), the foreign corporation could not maintain any action in the South Dakota courts.

The Supreme Court held that this statute, requiring a general consent to the jurisdiction of the South Dakota courts, was unreasonable and an undue burden on interstate commerce. It held that the South Dakota courts must entertain the action.

Suppose the South Dakota statute had required the filing of a consent limited to suits arising out of the business done in South Dakota? Would that have been valid? Would a requirement of filing a consent in such a case be necessary? Would the decision in the Sioux Remedy Co. case have been different if the plaintiff had been transacting all or a substantial part of its business in South Dakota? Compare Union Brokerage Co. v. Jensen, which is set forth at p. 993, infra.

Another problem was presented in Davis v. Farmers' Co-op. Equity Co., 262 U.S. 312 (1923). The Atchison, Topeka and Santa Fe Railroad is a Kansas corporation. It does not operate any railroad in Minnesota, but does maintain there an agent for the solicitation of traffic. A Minnesota statute provided that when a railroad maintained such an agent it could be served by delivering a summons to the agent. Acting under this statute, the plaintiff, a Kansas corporation, brought suit against the railroad in Minnesota. The cause of action arose over a bill of lading for the shipment of grain from one point in Kansas to another point in the same state. After extensive consideration, the Court held that the Minnesota statute, as applied to these facts, violated the commerce clause of the Constitution. The Court said "It may be that a statute like that here assailed would be valid, although applied to suits in which the cause of action arose elsewhere, if the transaction out of which it arose had been entered upon within the State, or if the plaintiff was, when it arose, a resident of the State.... But orderly effective administration of justice clearly does not require that a foreign carrier shall submit to a suit in a State in which the cause of action did not arise, in which the transaction giving rise to it was not entered upon, in which the carrier neither owns nor operates a railroad, and in which the plaintiff does not reside."

This was soon followed by Atchison, Topeka & Santa Fe Railway Co. v. Wells, 265 U.S. 101 (1924), which was a suit in a federal court in Texas to enjoin the enforcement of a judgment obtained in a Texas state court. The plaintiff in the original action, a resident of Colorado, had been injured in New Mexico while in the employ of the defendant, a Kansas corporation which neither did business nor had an agent in Texas. Unable to secure personal service on the defendant in Texas the plaintiff garnisheed traffic balances due the defendant and attached rolling stock in the possession of a Texas railroad. Judgment for the plaintiff was rendered by default, the defendant not having entered an appearance. On certiorari from a decree dismissing the bill for an injunction, held, reversed. "The writ of garnishment is void because of the purpose for which it was invoked. . . . Seizure of the rolling stock and credits for the purpose of compelling the Santa Fe to submit to the jurisdiction of the court in the Wells (original) suit interfered unreasonably with interstate commerce." Today, the assertion of jurisdiction on this basis would also be considered as violative of the defendant's due process rights. See Shaffer v. Heitner, supra p. 136.

INTERNATIONAL MILLING CO. v. COLUMBIA TRANSPORTATION CO., 292 U.S. 511 (1934): The plaintiff and the defendant were both Delaware corporations. The plaintiff's principal place of business was in Minnesota, the defendant's in Ohio. The defendant was an interstate and foreign carrier by water. When one of its ships was unloading in Minnesota, it was attached by the plaintiff, on account of damage which had been sustained to a shipment previously made by the plaintiff. This damage had occurred somewhere between Chicago and Buffalo.

The defendant moved to vacate the attachment on the ground that prosecution of the action in Minnesota "would impose a serious burden upon interstate commerce, in contravention of Article I, Section 8, of the Constitution of the United States." This was granted by the state courts.

On appeal, the Supreme Court reversed this judgment. The court held that the defendant was regularly engaged in business in Minnesota. Its ships were often there. The court said: "Viewing all of these circumstances together, we find ourselves unable to conclude that by the prosecution of this suit there has been laid upon the carrier a burden so heavy and so unnecessary as to be oppressive and unreasonable. . . . Such a suit may be a burden, but oppressive and unreasonable it is not."

NOTES

1. Does the commerce clause objection go to the judicial jurisdiction of the state? If so, will the objection be deemed to have been waived, if not seasonably made? Cf.

Atchison, Topeka & Santa Fe Railway Co. v. Wells, p. 216, supra, and Baldwin v. Iowa State Traveling Men's Association, p. 284, infra.

2. Later cases have given little effect to any commerce clause limitation on the exercise of jurisdiction. In Baltimore & Ohio Railroad Co. v. Kepner, 314 U.S. 44 (1941), the following statement appears: "Davis v. Farmers Cooperative Co., 262 U.S. 312, is limited to its particular facts, 292 U.S. 511 at 517; ..." The citation is to the International Milling case, where it is stated that the Davis "decision was confined narrowly within the bounds of its own facts." For a more recent case taking a similar view, see Scanapico v. Richmond, Fredericksburg & Potomac Railroad Co., 439 F.2d 17 (2d Cir.1970).

CHAPTER 5

FOREIGN JUDGMENTS

SECTION 1. POLICIES UNDERLYING THE RECOGNITION AND ENFORCEMENT OF FOREIGN JUDGMENTS

"Public policy dictates that there be an end of litigation; that those who have contested an issue shall be bound by the result of the contest, and that matters once tried shall be considered forever settled as between the parties."[1] This policy, embodied in the doctrine of res judicata, prevents the parties from relitigating issues that have been determined between them by a valid local judgment. It also forms the basis for the firmly established principle of Anglo–American law that foreign judgments, subject to only a few exceptions, are not open to reexamination on the merits when placed in issue before a local court. This latter principle, however, is frequently explained by the courts in terms other than that of res judicata. Thus, in cases which do not fall within the constitutional mandate of full faith and credit, the American courts have often talked in terms of "comity,"[2] while those of England usually phrase their opinions in terms of the "legal obligation of foreign judgments."[3] These modes of expression merely state but do not explain the result; they should not be permitted to obscure the underlying policy involved.

In this country, an express constitutional mandate calls for the extraterritorial recognition and enforcement of sister state and federal judgments. This mandate is embodied in the full faith and credit clause and its implementing statute, which, in the words of Chief Justice Stone, were designed to

". . . establish throughout the federal system the salutary principle of the common law that a litigation once pursued to judgment shall be as conclusive of the rights of the parties in every other court as in that where the judgment was rendered.... The full faith and credit clause like the commerce clause thus became a nationally unifying force. It altered the status of the several states as independent foreign sovereignties, each free to ignore rights and obligations created under the laws or established by the judicial proceedings of the others, by making each an integral part of a single nation, in which rights judicially established in any part are given nation-wide application. Because there is a full faith and credit clause a defendant may not a second time challenge the validity of plaintiff's right

---

1. Roberts, J., in Baldwin v. Iowa State Travelling Men's Association, 283 U.S. 522, 525 (1931).

2. See, e.g., Hilton v. Guyot, infra.

3. See, e.g., Godard v. Gray, L.R. 6 Q.B. 139 (1870).

which has ripened into a judgment and a plaintiff may not for his single cause of action secure a second or a greater recovery...."[4]

NOTES

1. The full faith and credit clause and its implementing statute are quoted at pp. 39–40, supra.

For general consideration of the problems of this Chapter, see Scoles and Hay, Conflict of Laws 950–1024 (2nd ed. 1992); Leflar, McDougal and Felix, American Conflicts Law 215–253 (4th ed. 1986).

2. Are all questions relating to the extraterritorial respect owed to federal and state judgments governed by the full faith and credit clause and its implementing statute? Or is there still room in this field for the occasional application by the states of their individual conflict of laws rules? See, for example, pp. 293–295, infra.

3. Is the implementing statute constitutional? Note that whereas the full faith and credit clause only requires extraterritorial respect for the acts, records and judicial proceedings of the several states, the statute also includes within its scope those of every "Territory, or Possession of the United States." From what source, if any, did Congress derive power so to enact? See Embry v. Palmer, 107 U.S. 3 (1883).

It is well established that federal court judgments are entitled to the same full faith and credit as those of the state courts. Stoll v. Gottlieb, 305 U.S. 165 (1938); Hancock National Bank v. Farnum, 176 U.S. 640 (1900); Metcalf v. City of Watertown, 153 U.S. 671 (1894). Can such a requirement be spelled out of the language of the implementing statute?

4. Federal courts are required by the implementing statute to give full faith and credit to the judgments of state and territorial courts. Kremer v. Chemical Construction Corp., infra p. 246; Huron Holding Corp. v. Lincoln Mine Operating Co., 312 U.S. 183 (1941); Davis v. Davis, 305 U.S. 32 (1938). A Puerto Rican judgment is covered by the implementing statute. Americana of Puerto Rico, Inc. v. Kaplus, 368 F.2d 431 (3d Cir.1966).

Hilton v. Guyot
Supreme Court of the United States, 1895.
159 U.S. 113, 16 S.Ct. 139, 40 L.Ed. 95.

[Action in a circuit court of the United States upon a judgment of a French court against citizens of the United States, and in favor of a French firm, the plaintiffs in the French proceeding. The answer, setting forth the original dealings between the parties, alleged that the defendants were not indebted to the plaintiffs. The defendants also contended that the French judgment should not be enforced without an examination of the merits of the case, since the courts of France would examine anew the merits of a controversy if an American judgment against a French national were sued on in France. Other objections of the defendants are specified in the

---

4. Magnolia Petroleum Co. v. Hunt, 320 U.S. 430, 439–40 (1943).

court's opinion. The circuit court entered a judgment and a decree for the French firm without examining the merits.]

■ JUSTICE GRAY, after stating the case, delivered the opinion of the court....

No law has any effect, of its own force, beyond the limits of the sovereignty from which its authority is derived. The extent to which the law of one nation, as put in force within its territory, whether by executive order, by legislative act, or by judicial decree, shall be allowed to operate within the dominion of another nation, depends upon what our greatest jurists have been content to call "the comity of nations." Although the phrase has been often criticized, no satisfactory substitute has been suggested.

"Comity," in the legal sense, is neither a matter of absolute obligation, on the one hand, nor of mere courtesy and good will, upon the other. But it is the recognition which one nation allows within its territory to the legislative, executive or judicial acts of another nation, having due regard both to international duty and convenience, and to the rights of its own citizens or of other persons who are under the protection of its laws....

In order to appreciate the weight of the various authorities cited at the bar, it is important to distinguish different kinds of judgments. Every foreign judgment, of whatever nature, in order to be entitled to any effect, must have been rendered by a court having jurisdiction of the cause, and upon regular proceedings and due notice. In alluding to different kinds of judgments, therefore, such jurisdiction, proceedings and notice will be assumed. It will also be assumed that they are untainted by fraud, the effect of which will be considered later.

A judgment in rem, adjudicating the title to a ship or other movable property within the custody of the court, is treated as valid everywhere.... The most common illustrations of this are decrees of courts of admiralty and prize, which proceed upon principles of international law.... But the same rule applies to judgments in rem under municipal law.

A judgment affecting the status of persons, such as a decree confirming or dissolving a marriage, is recognized as valid in every country, unless contrary to the policy of its own law....

Other judgments, not strictly in rem, under which a person has been compelled to pay money, are so far conclusive that the justice of the payment cannot be impeached in another country, so as to compel him to pay it again. For instance a judgment in foreign attachment is conclusive, as between the parties, of the right to the property or money attached. Story on Conflict of Laws (2d ed.), sec. 592a....

The extraterritorial effect of judgments in personam, at law or in equity, may differ, according to the parties to the cause. A judgment of that kind between two citizens or residents of the country, and thereby subject to the jurisdiction, in which it is rendered, may be held conclusive as between them everywhere. So, if a foreigner invokes the jurisdiction by bringing an action against a citizen, both may be held bound by a judgment in favor of either. And if a citizen sues a foreigner, and judgment is rendered in favor of the latter, both may be held equally bound....

The effect to which a judgment purely executory, rendered in favor of a citizen or resident of the country, in a suit there brought by him against a foreigner, may be entitled in an action thereon against the latter in his own country—as is the case now before us—presents a more difficult question, upon which there has been some diversity of opinion.... [The court reviewed the common-law cases.]

In view of all the authorities upon the subject, and of the trend of judicial opinion in this country and in England, following the lead of Kent and Story, we are satisfied that, where there has been opportunity for a full and fair trial abroad before a court of competent jurisdiction, conducting the trial upon regular proceedings, after due citation or voluntary appearance of the defendant, and under a system of jurisprudence likely to secure an impartial administration of justice between the citizens of its own country and those of other countries, and there is nothing to show either prejudice in the court or in the system of laws under which it was sitting, or fraud in procuring the judgment, or any other special reason why the comity of this nation should not allow it full effect, the merits of the case should not, in an action brought in this country upon the judgment, be tried afresh, as on a new trial or an appeal, upon the mere assertion of the party that the judgment was erroneous in law or in fact. The defendants, therefore, cannot be permitted, upon that general ground, to contest the validity or the effect of the judgment sued on.

But they have sought to impeach that judgment upon several other grounds, which require separate consideration.

It is objected that the appearance and litigation of the defendants in the French tribunals were not voluntary, but by legal compulsion, and therefore that the French courts never acquired such jurisdiction over the defendants, that they should be held bound by the judgment.... [The court found that the French court had acquired jurisdiction of the person of the defendants.]

It is next objected that in those courts one of the plaintiffs was permitted to testify not under oath, and was not subjected to cross-examination by the opposite party, and that the defendants were, therefore, deprived of safeguards which are by our law considered essential to secure honesty and to detect fraud in a witness; and also that documents and papers were admitted in evidence, with which the defendants had no connection, and which would not be admissible under our own system of jurisprudence. But it having been shown by the plaintiffs, and hardly denied by the defendants, that the practice followed and the method of examining witnesses were according to the laws of France, we are not prepared to hold that the fact that the procedure in these respects differed from that of our own courts is, of itself, a sufficient ground for impeaching the foreign judgment....

When an action is brought in a court of this country, by a citizen of a foreign country against one of our own citizens, to recover a sum of money adjudged by a court of that country to be due from the defendant to the plaintiff, and the foreign judgment appears to have been rendered by a competent court, having jurisdiction of the cause and of the parties, and upon due allegations and proofs, and opportunity to defend against them, and its proceedings are according to the course of a civilized jurisprudence, and are stated in a clear and formal record, the judgment is prima facie evidence, at least, of the truth of the matter adjudged; and it should be held conclusive upon the merits tried in the foreign court, unless some special ground is shown for impeaching the judgment, as by showing that it was affected by fraud or prejudice, or that, by the principles of international law, and by the comity of our own country, it should not be given full credit and effect.

There is no doubt that both in this country, as appears by the authorities already cited, and in England, a foreign judgment may be impeached for fraud....

But whether those decisions can be followed in regard to foreign judgments, consistently with our own decisions as to impeaching domestic judgments for fraud, it is unnecessary in this case to determine, because there is a distinct and independent ground upon which we are satisfied that the comity of our nation does not require us to give conclusive effect to the judgments of the courts of France; and that ground is, the want of reciprocity, on the part of France, as to the effect to be given to the judgments of this and other foreign countries.... [The court quoted the French statutes as to the effect of foreign judgments.]

The defendants, in their answer, cited the above provisions of the statutes of France, and alleged, and at the trial offered to prove, that, by the construction given to these statutes by the judicial tribunals of France, when the judgments of tribunals of foreign countries against the citizens of France are sued upon in the courts of France, the merits of the controversies upon which those judgments are based are examined anew, unless a treaty to the contrary effect exists between the Republic of France and the country in which such judgment is obtained, (which is not the case between the Republic of France and the United States,) and that the tribunals of the Republic of France give no force and effect, within the jurisdiction of that country, to the judgments duly rendered by courts of competent jurisdiction of the United States against citizens of France after proper personal service of the process of those courts has been made thereon in this country. We are of the opinion that this evidence should have been admitted.... [The court's lengthy review of the laws of many countries as to the enforcement of foreign judgments is omitted.]

It appears, therefore, that there is hardly a civilized nation on either continent, which, by its general law, allows conclusive effect to an executory foreign judgment for the recovery of money. In France, and in a few smaller States—Norway, Portugal, Greece, Monaco, and Haiti—the merits of the controversy are reviewed, as of course, allowing to the foreign judgment, at the most, no more effect than of being prima facie evidence of the justice of the claim. In the great majority of the countries on the continent of Europe—in Belgium, Holland, Denmark, Sweden, Germany, in many cantons of Switzerland, in Russia and Poland, in Roumania, in Austria and Hungary, (perhaps in Italy,) and in Spain—as well as in Egypt, in Mexico, and in a great part of South America, the judgment rendered in a foreign country is allowed the same effect only as the courts of that country allow to the judgments of the country in which the judgment in question is sought to be executed.

... [T]he rule of reciprocity has worked itself firmly into the structure of international jurisprudence.

The reasonable, if not the necessary, conclusion appears to us to be that judgments rendered in France, or in any other foreign country, by the laws of which our own judgments are reviewable upon the merits, are not entitled to full credit and conclusive effect when sued upon in this country, but are prima facie evidence only of the justice of the plaintiff's claim.

In holding such a judgment, for want of reciprocity, not to be conclusive evidence of the merits of the claim, we do not proceed upon any theory of retaliation upon one person by reason of injustice done to another; but upon the broad ground that international law is founded upon mutuality and reciprocity, and that by the principles of international law recognized in most civilized nations, and by the comity of our own country, which it is our judicial duty to know and to declare, the judgment is not entitled to be considered conclusive....

[The judgment and the decree were reversed.]

■ CHIEF JUSTICE FULLER, with whom concurred JUSTICE HARLAN, JUSTICE BREWER, and JUSTICE JACKSON, dissenting.

I cannot yield my assent to the proposition that because by legislation and judicial decision in France that effect is not there given to judgments recovered in this country which, according to our jurisprudence, we think should be given to judgments wherever recovered, (subject, of course, to the recognized exceptions,) therefore we should pursue the same line of conduct as respects the judgments of French tribunals. The application of the doctrine of res judicata does not rest in discretion; and it is for the government, and not for its courts, to adopt the principle of retorsion, if deemed under any circumstances desirable or necessary.

As the court expressly abstains from deciding whether the judgment is impeachable on the ground of fraud, I refrain from any observations on that branch of the case.

NOTES

1. Apart from the question of reciprocity, what defenses, according to the principal case, can be raised in this country to a suit seeking the enforcement of a foreign country judgment?

2. In Ritchie v. McMullen, 159 U.S. 235 (1895), decided the same day as Hilton v. Guyot, the Supreme Court held that an Ontario judgment should be enforced without an examination of its merits, as Canada would give conclusive effect to a judgment rendered by a court in the United States.

3. The doctrine of *révision au fond* has been abandoned in France in matters relating to status. In Munzer v. Dame Munzer–Jacoby, decided by the Cour de Cassation on January 7, 1964, it was held that no such doctrine exists. See Nadelmann, French Courts Recognize Foreign Money–Judgments: One Down and More to Go, 13 Am.J.Comp.L. 1 (1964); Batiffol & Lagarde, Traité de droit international privé, vol. 2, 593–95 (7th ed. 1983).

4. In 1992, the German Supreme Court adopted a liberal view with respect to the recognition and enforcement of American money judgments in Germany. Judgment of June 4, 1992, [1992] Wertpapiermitteilungen 1451. It had previously been uncertain whether Germany would recognize awards for expenses not yet incurred (e.g., future medical expenses), awards for pain and suffering far in excess of what a German court would have awarded, and for punitive damages. In its decision, the Court accepted the first of these in recognition of the American rule that a plaintiff cannot split his cause of action. It also accepted the award of pain and suffering in an amount 11 times greater than a comparable domestic award, [and] declaring that German public policy is not offended by the application of California law and practice to a case that arose there, between parties domiciled there at the time; an interposition of German public policy concerns presupposes German "contacts" and they were lacking. However, the Court declined, in keeping with general Continental practice, to recognize the award of punitive damages. Punishment is within the province of the criminal justice system which also affords defendants different rights and protections than obtain in civil litigation. The Court left open whether punitive damages would be recognized to the extent that they contain identifiable compensatory aspects, e.g., the plaintiff's attorney's contingent fee. For discussion see Hay, The Recognition and Enforcement of American Money–Judgments in Germany, 40 Am.J.Comp.L. 1001 (1992).

In a defamation action brought by Princess Caroline of Monaco against a German tabloid, the German Supreme Court held that she was entitled to have the defendant print a retraction, but that the extent and print size of such a retraction had to be determined by balancing her interests against the defendant's freedom-of-press rights to publish additional material on the front page. Because such a balancing might not adequately redress the plaintiff's injury, the award of damages should take into account what it would take to give her satisfaction for her injury, focus on the egregious nature of defendant's conduct of "marketing" the plaintiff's private life, and the need to deter such conduct by others in the future. The remedy, the court said, was not based on or an enlargement of § 847 of the Civil Code (damages for pain and suffering) but is (judicially) derived from the constitutional guarantee of the right of personality (the right of privacy). Arts. 1, 21, German Constitution. German Federal Supreme Court (BGH). Judgment of Nov. 11, 1994, [1995] Neue Juristische Wochenschrift 861. Despite the court's narrow focus on the constitutional right of privacy and the express disclaimer of the applicability of its ruling in the general context of damages for pain and suffering, is this decision not an example of an award of punitive damages? If such an award becomes possible, albeit in limited and specified circumstances, can this type of relief, when awarded by an American court, still violate German public policy as a matter of principle?

In the European Union, the Brussels Convention, supra p. 37, governs the recognition and enforcement of judgments in civil and commercial matters rendered by courts of member states. The Lugano Convention, supra p. 37, extends this system to Iceland, Norway, and Switzerland. From among the extensive contributions to the literature see Hartley, Civil Jurisdiction and Judgments (1984); Dicey & Morris, Conflict of Laws 298 (12th ed. 1993 by Collins). A comprehensive bibliography (all languages) can be found in Kegel, Internationales Privatrecht 822–28 (7th ed. 1995). National law with respect to jurisdiction and the recognition and enforcement of judgments remains in force with respect to non-member states of the European Union. The Conventions expressly prohibit *révision au fond*. Art. 29. The only exception (which defers to national law) is Art. 27, No. 4: if a decision depended on a preliminary decision regarding personal status, matrimonial property, or succession, the F–2 court may review the F–1 court's determination of the law applicable to the preliminary matter on the basis of the forum's (F–2's) conflicts law. The reason? The subjects listed are beyond the scope of the Conventions and their jurisdictional prescriptions (Art. 1(2)) and therefore not subject to a recognition requirement.

5. Also in 1992, the United States proposed that the Hague Conference on Private International Law resume work toward the drafting of a recognition and enforcement of judgments convention that would be open for potentially worldwide acceptance. A Working Group of the Hague Conference has endorsed the suggestion and the proposal for such a project will now be submitted to the Conference for its approval. For an evaluation, see Schack, Perspektiven eines weltweiten Anerkennungs–Und Vollstreckungsabkommen, 1 Zeitschrift für Europäisches Privatrecht 306 (1993).

6. A proposed U.K.–U.S. convention on the reciprocal recognition and enforcement of their judgments was prepared during the 1970's but never went into effect. See Hay and Walker, The Proposed Recognition-of-Judgments Convention between the United States and the United Kingdom, 11 Texas Int.L.J. 421 (1976); North, Draft U.K./U.S. Judgments Convention: A British Viewpoint, 1 N.W.J.Int.L. & Bus. 219 (1979).

7. Application of the law of a foreign state is rarely if ever limited by any requirement of reciprocity. What is the justification for a stricter attitude toward the enforcement of foreign judgments than toward the application of foreign law?

8. The defense of lack of reciprocity has today been widely discarded. See, e.g., Somportex Limited v. Philadelphia Chewing Gum Corp., 453 F.2d 435 (3d Cir.1971); Royal Bank of Canada v. Trentham Corp., 491 F.Supp. 404 (S.D.Tex.1980); Nicol v. Tanner, 310 Minn. 68, 256 N.W.2d 796 (1976). Some states require reciprocity by statute. This is the case in the Massachusetts and Texas versions of the Uniform Foreign Money–Judgments Recognition Act: Mass.Gen.Laws Ann. ch. 235, § 23A; Tex.Civ.Prac. & Rem.Code Ann. ch. 36. The Colorado provision (Col.Rev.Stat.Ann. § 13–62–102(1)) in effect nullifies the Act. It defines "foreign state" in § 1(1) as a "governmental unit [that] has entered into a reciprocal agreement with the United States recognizing any judgment of a court of record of the United States...." There is no such foreign state. Other statutes requiring reciprocity are: O.C.Ga. Ann. § 9–12–114(10); Idaho Code § 10–1404(2)(g); N.H.Rev.Stat.Ann. § 524.11 (with respect to Canadian judgments); Ohio Rev.Code Ann. § 2329.92(B). In Texas, the defense of lack of reciprocity failed in the context of Canadian and English judgments. See Norkan Lodge Co. Ltd. v. Gillum, 587 F.Supp. 1457

(N.D.Tex.1984) (Canada); Hunt v. BP Exploration Co. (Libya) Ltd., 580 F.Supp. 304 (N.D.Tex.1984).

COWANS V. TICONDEROGA PULP & PAPER CO., 219 App.Div. 120, 219 N.Y.S. 284 (1927), affirmed on opinion below 246 N.Y. 603, 159 N.E. 669 (1927): Action brought in a New York court to enforce a money judgment recovered in the Province of Quebec, Canada. Plaintiffs appealed from an order of the trial court denying their motion for judgment on the pleadings. Held, reversed. Van Kirk, J. . . . "The question presented here is whether this Quebec judgment is in our court merely prima facie proof of liability, against which any defense which could have been used at the trial in the Quebec court is available to defeat recovery here, or is it conclusive, subject only to the recognized exceptions. The respondent's proposition is that the judgment is only prima facie evidence, because, under the Quebec law (Code Civ.Proc. of Quebec § 210): 'Any defense which was or might have been set up to the original action may be pleaded to an action brought upon a judgment rendered out of Canada' . . ."

"The force and effect which is to be given to a foreign judgment is for each sovereign power to determine for itself. . . . The general rule in this State is settled as follows: A judgment recovered in a foreign country, when sued upon in the courts of this State, is conclusive so far as to preclude a retrial of the merits of the case, subject, however, to certain well-recognized exceptions, namely, where the judgment is tainted with fraud, or with an offense against the public policy of the State, or the foreign court had no jurisdiction.

". . . The respondent does not question the general rule as above stated, but urges that the denial of reciprocity in the Province of Quebec furnishes a further exception to the general rule. It rests its contention confidently on the decision in Hilton v. Guyot. . . ."

". . . Our Court of Appeals [in Johnston v. Compagnie Generale Transatlantique, 242 N.Y. 381, 152 N.E. 121 (1926)] has we think definitely refused to accept that holding as the policy of this State; and, without reciprocity, would give to the foreign judgment the full effect to which its persuasiveness entitles it. The decision in the Hilton case would deprive a party of the private rights he has acquired by reason of a foreign judgment because the country in whose courts that judgment was rendered has a rule of evidence different from that which we have and does not give the same effect as this State gives to a foreign judgment.

"We think the general rule as above stated must be applied to this case, and that the proposition which the respondent would maintain is in conflict with the policy and law of this State. . . ."

NOTES

1. What law determines the effect to be given the judgments of foreign countries by American courts? Is this a question of national law or one to be decided by the

conflict of laws rules of the individual states? The consensus today is that state law controls. Somportex Limited v. Philadelphia Chewing Gum Corp., 453 F.2d 435 (3d Cir.1971), cert. denied 405 U.S. 1017 (1972); Toronto–Dominion Bank v. Hall, 367 F.Supp. 1009 (E.D.Ark.1973). See also, McCord v. Jet Spray Int'l Corp., 874 F.Supp. 436 (D.Mass.1994); Banque Libanaise Pour Le Commerce v. Khreich, 915 F.2d 1000 (5th Cir.1990). Accordingly, if the question presented in the Hilton case were to arise today in a federal court sitting in New York, the court would presumably follow Cowans v. Ticonderoga Pulp and Paper Co. rather than Hilton. Consider, however, Banco Nacional de Cuba v. Sabbatino, 376 U.S. 398 (1964) (p. 740, infra); see generally Kulzer, Recognition of Foreign Country Judgments in New York: The Uniform Foreign Money–Judgments Recognition Act, 18 Buff. L.Rev. 1 (1969); Brand, Enforcement of Judgments in the United States and Europe, 13 Journal of Law and Commerce 193 (1994); Brand, Enforcement of Foreign Money–Judgments in the United States: In Search of Uniformity and International Acceptance, 67 Notre Dame L.Rev. 253 (1991); Annotation, 100 A.L.R.3d 792. For an extensive bibliography, see Ebke & Parker, Foreign Country Money–Judgments and Arbitral Awards and the Restatement (Third) of the Foreign Relations Law of the United States: A Conventional Approach, 24 International Lawyer 21 (1990).

2. Foreign-country causes of action and foreign-country claims may present currency problems. The traditional rule in this country was that an American court could express a judgment only in dollars. The Uniform Foreign–Money Claims Act (1989 Act) now provides in its § 10 that "if an action is brought to enforce a judgment of another jurisdiction expressed in a foreign money and the judgment is recognized in this State as enforceable, the enforcing judgment must be entered as provided in Section 7 ..." The latter provides that "a judgment or award on a foreign-money claim must be stated in an amount of the money of the claim." The debtor then has the option to pay in the foreign money or in U.S. dollars on the rate in effect on the "conversion date," defined by § 1(3) as "the banking day next preceding" the payment date. As of January 1995, the Act was in force in thirteen states and in the Virgin Islands. For discussion from a European perspective, see Hay, Fremdwährungsansprüche and -urteile nach dem US-amerikanischen Uniform Act, 41 Recht der Internationalen Wirtschaft 113 (1995).

3. For a comparison of the effects accorded in this country to sister state and foreign country judgments, see pp. 311–314, infra. See Wurfel, Recognition of Foreign Judgments, 50 N.Car.L.Rev. 21 (1971).

4. For a general discussion of the recognition and enforcement of foreign country judgments, see Scoles and Hay, Conflict of Laws 996–1017 (2nd ed. 1992).

SECTION 2. RECOGNITION AND ENFORCEMENT IN GENERAL

In this section and the one immediately succeeding, we examine the effects which a state or federal judgment carries in the state of rendition and those which under full faith and credit must be accorded it in other states. Here, consideration is given to a judgment's basic effects as res judicata and to methods of enforcing a foreign judgment. In Section 3 attention is directed to other questions relating to the parties and issues concluded by a judgment and to various special matters.

A. IN PERSONAM JUDGMENTS

In the state of rendition, an in personam judgment for a sum certain can normally be enforced by a levy of execution against any local property of the defendant. All in personam judgments also have one or more of the following effects: (1) *Merger,* by which the plaintiff's original claim (cause of action) is merged in a judgment for a sum certain, so that the original claim is extinguished and a claim on the judgment takes its place.[1] (2) *Bar,* by which a judgment for the defendant extinguishes the original claim. (3) *Issue preclusion,*[2] by which issues of fact and perhaps of law actually litigated in the action are conclusively determined in subsequent proceedings in which the same issues arise, even though the claim may be different. If the subsequent proceedings are on the same claim, this is sometimes known as direct estoppel. If the question arises in connection with another claim, this has commonly been called collateral estoppel. Further reference to the problem of issue preclusion is made in Section 3B, infra.

The rule was concisely put in Mendez v. Bowie, 118 F.2d 435 (1st Cir.1941), at p. 440, as follows:

"The effect of a judgment or decree as res judicata depends upon whether the second action or suit is upon the same or a different cause of action. If upon the same cause of action, the judgment or decree upon the merits in the first case is an absolute bar to the subsequent action or suit between the same parties or those in privity with them, not only in respect of every matter which was actually offered and received to sustain the demand or to make out a defense, but also as to every ground of recovery or defense which might have been presented.... But if the second case be upon a different cause of action, the prior judgment or decree operates as an estoppel only as to matters actually in issue or points controverted, upon the determination of which the judgment or decree was rendered, and not as to matters or points which might have been litigated and determined."

Obviously, much depends on whether the term "claim" (cause of action) is given a broad or a narrow definition. See Restatement, Second, Judgments §§ 24–26 (1982); James, Hazard and Leubsdorf, Civil Proce-

---

1. It has been held, however, that the rule of merger does not apply to a judgment of a foreign country. Eastern Townships Bank v. H.S. Beebe & Co., 53 Vt. 177 (1880). The Restatement, Second, Conflict of Laws § 95, Comment (c)(1) retains this view. The rule has been changed in England: unless the foreign judgment is not entitled to recognition in England, a plaintiff who obtained a valid judgment in his favor abroad may not bring another action on the same claim in England. Civil Jurisdiction and Judgments Act (1982) § 34. See Dicey & Morris, 1 Conflict of Laws 499 et seq. (12th ed. 1993 by Collins). For criticism of the American non-merger rule, see Scoles, Interstate and International Distinctions in Conflict of Laws in the United States, 54 Calif.L.Rev. 1599, 1607 (1966); Scoles & Hay, Conflict of Laws 957 (2nd ed. 1992). The English rule is also to the effect that the underlying cause of action is not merged in the judgment of a foreign country. Borm–Reid, Recognition and Enforcement of Foreign Judgments, 3 Int. & Comp.L.Q. 49, 50 (1954).

2. This is the terminology adopted by the Restatement, Second, Judgments § 17, now widely accepted in American law.

dure 578–641 (4th ed. 1992); Rosenberg, Collateral Estoppel in New York, 44 St. John's L.Rev. 165 (1969). The broader the definition, the more will a plaintiff be required to seek relief in a single action for his various complaints against the defendant. The present trend, according to Section 24, comment *a.*, of the Restatement of Judgments, Second, is to define "claim" to embrace all the remedial rights of the plaintiff against the defendant growing out of the relevant transaction or series of connected transactions.

An important problem is whether the definition of claim is to be sought in the law of F–1 or of F–2. Should a distinction be made in this connection between a judgment rendered in a state of the United States and one rendered in a foreign country?

Lynde v. Lynde

Supreme Court of the United States, 1901.
181 U.S. 183, 21 S.Ct. 555, 45 L.Ed. 810.

[In 1892 Mrs. Lynde filed a bill in New Jersey asking for a divorce on the ground of desertion and for reasonable alimony. Service was had by publication. The decree of divorce was granted but no provision for alimony was made. In 1896 Mrs. Lynde asked that the decree be amended to provide for alimony, alleging an oversight on the part of her attorney in failing to include such a provision in the original decree. In the interim her divorced husband had married again in New York but he now appeared generally in the proceeding and contested the alimony request. The court, however, awarded the wife $7,840 back alimony and further alimony at the rate of $80 a week. A receiver of the husband's New Jersey property was appointed but was able to find no property in New Jersey. The second New Jersey decree also provided for security, which the husband failed to give, and for an injunction against disposal of property to evade the decree. (Lynde v. Lynde, 54 N.J.Eq. 473.)

The wife then brought suit in New York asking for past due alimony, counsel fees, and $80 weekly as allowed her by the New Jersey court. She also asked that her ex-husband be directed to give security, and that the order provide for sequestration, receivership, and an injunction. The New York court (Lynde v. Lynde, 162 N.Y. 405) conceded the New Jersey court's jurisdiction to grant an in personam decree against the husband for alimony because of his general appearance in the later New Jersey proceedings. The judgment was enforced only as to counsel fees and past due alimony; since future alimony remained subject to modification in the discretion of the New Jersey chancellor, the judgment on that point was not final and could not be enforced in New York. The collateral means of enforcement provided in the New Jersey decree and asked for by the plaintiff were also denied since the Constitution does not require such action to be taken, being a mode of effectuating the decree and not part of the decree itself.

Each party to the New York proceeding then sued out a writ of error from the Supreme Court of the United States, which rendered the following opinion.]

■ GRAY, J. The husband, as the record shows, having appeared generally in answer to the petition for alimony in the Court of Chancery in New Jersey, the decree of that court for alimony was binding upon him.... The court of New York having so ruled, thereby deciding in favor of the full faith and credit claimed for that decree under the Constitution and laws of the United States, its judgment on that question cannot be reviewed by this court on writ of error.... The husband having appeared and been heard in the proceeding for alimony, there is no color for his present contention that he was deprived of his property without due process of law.... His writ of error, therefore, must be dismissed.

By the Constitution and the act of Congress, requiring the faith and credit to be given to a judgment of the court of another State that it has in the State where it was rendered, it was long ago declared by this court: "The judgment is made a debt of record, not examinable upon its merits; but it does not carry with it, into another State, the efficacy of a judgment upon property or persons, to be enforced by execution. To give it the force of a judgment in another State, it must be made a judgment there; and can only be executed in the latter as its laws may permit." McElmoyle v. Cohen, 13 Pet. 312, 325; Thompson v. Whitman, 18 Wall. 457, 463....

The decree of the Court of Chancery of New Jersey, on which this suit is brought, provides, first, for the payment of $7840 for alimony already due, and $1000 counsel fee; second, for the payment of alimony since the date of the decree at the rate of $80 per week; and third, for the giving of a bond to secure the payment of these sums, and, on default of payment or of giving bond, for leave to apply for a writ of sequestration, or a receiver and injunction.

The decree for the payment of $8840 was for a fixed sum already due, and the judgment of the court below was properly restricted to that. The provision of the payment for alimony in the future was subject to the discretion of the Court of Chancery of New Jersey, which might at any time alter it, and was not a final judgment for a fixed sum. The provisions for bond, sequestration, receiver and injunction, being in the nature of execution, and not of judgment, could have no extraterritorial operation; but the action of the courts of New York in these respects depended on the local statutes and practice of the State, and involved no Federal question.

On the writ of error of the wife, therefore, the judgment is affirmed.

Emery v. Hovey

Supreme Court of New Hampshire, 1931.
84 N.H. 499, 153 A. 322.

Assumpsit, for attorney's fees and disbursements. The defendant pleaded a former adjudication in the supreme judicial court for the state of Maine.

At a trial before Young, J., the plaintiff put in evidence a Maine statute to the effect that one not admitted to practice there cannot recover "any remuneration for his professional services rendered in this state," and that at the trial of his cause in Maine the defendant's motion for a directed verdict, based upon the statute, was granted. The services in question were rendered partly in Maine and partly in this state.

In the present suit, the court ordered judgment for the defendant on her plea, and allowed the plaintiff's bill of exceptions.

■ PEASLEE, C.J. The record shows that the plaintiff had previously sued the same cause of action in the supreme judicial court of the state of Maine, that a trial by jury was had, that upon direction of the presiding justice the jury returned a verdict for the defendant and that judgment was entered upon the verdict. This judgment was pleaded in bar of the present action. The ruling that the plea stated a good defense was correct. Const. of U.S., Art. IV, sec. 1.

Whatever error there may have been in the ruling of the justice presiding at the trial in the Maine suit was correctible only in the Maine courts. The ruling having been submitted to and a final judgment having been entered in accordance therewith, the whole subject is foreclosed in the courts of any other state. The historic case, Kittredge v. Emerson, 15 N.H. 227, established in this jurisdiction the doctrine that the judgment of a court of record, having jurisdiction of the parties and the cause, is conclusive in the courts of every other state and of the United States, no matter how erroneous in law or in fact that judgment may be....

There is no suggestion that the Maine judgment is not a complete bar to any further action in that state. It is equally effective here. "Thus and thus only can the full faith and credit prescribed by the Constitution of the United States and the act of Congress be secured." Hancock National Bank v. Farnum, 176 U.S. 640....

Exception overruled.

NOTE ON METHODS OF ENFORCEMENT

In this country, the original method of enforcing an F–1 judgment was to bring an action in the nature of debt upon the judgment in F–2. That method has persisted. Only after a new judgment has been obtained in F–2 can execution there be had against the property of the defendant. This requirement is time-consuming; it also results in the efficacy of a judgment being greatly decreased when enforcement is sought in other states. For example, although a foreign judgment, since it establishes the existence of a debt, may be filed as a claim against an insolvent estate, it does not have the priority over simple contract debts in the distribution of assets which it had in F–1 or which F–2 gives to domestic judgments. Trionics Research Sales Corp. v. Nautec Corp., 21 N.Y.2d 574, 289 N.Y.S.2d 745, 237 N.E.2d 68 (1968). To acquire such a priority, the judgment creditor must obtain a new judgment in F–2 in the manner set forth above.

The problems and burdens presented by this method of enforcement are mitigated by the availability in the great majority of states of summary judgment procedures for the enforcement of foreign judgments. Leflar, The New Uniform Foreign Judgments Act, 24 N.Y.U.L.Q. 336 (1949).

In 1948, Congress made provision for the registration in any federal district court of a judgment rendered in any other district. This statute (28 U.S.C.A. § 1963, as amended) reads as follows:

"A judgment in an action for the recovery of money or property entered in any district court or in the Court of International Trade may be registered by filing a certified copy of such judgment in any other district or, with respect to the Court of International Trade, in any judicial district, when the judgment has become final by appeal or expiration of the time for appeal or when ordered by the court that entered the judgment for good cause shown. Such a judgment entered in favor of the United States may be so registered any time after judgment is entered. A judgment so registered shall have the same effect as a judgment of the district court of the district where registered and may be enforced in like manner.

"A certified copy of the satisfaction of any judgment in whole or in part may be registered in like manner in any district in which the judgment is a lien."

Congress has likewise provided that a judgment entered in the United States Claims Court in favor of the United States may be registered and enforced in any district court. 28 U.S.C.A. § 2508.

NOTES

1. Section 1963 applies only to judgments in "an action for the recovery of money or property." In Stiller v. Hardman, 324 F.2d 626 (2d Cir.1963), the court held that a judgment for money could be registered, even though it was rendered on a counterclaim in a suit originally brought for a declaratory judgment. The court also held that the judgment could not be registered insofar as it involved an injunction. It pointed out that "The mandate of an injunction issued by a Federal district court runs throughout the United States. Leman v. Krenlier–Arnold Hinge Last Co., 284 U.S. 448 (1932)." Thus there is no need to register judgments of district courts in so far as they involve injunctions.

2. Originally, § 1963 only applied to judgments that had become final by appeal or expiration of the time for appeal. A 1988 revision added an exception for non-final judgments with "good cause shown". On what constitutes "good cause" see Schreiber v. Kellogg, 839 F.Supp. 1157 (E.D.Pa.1993); Associated Business Telephone Systems Corp. v. Greater Capital Corp., 128 F.R.D. 63 (D.N.J.1989).

3. A judgment registered in a second federal district under § 1963 becomes in effect a new F–2 judgment subject to the rules of F–2. So the judgment will be subject to the F–2 statute of limitations rather than to that of F–1. Matanuska Valley Lines, Inc. v. Molitor, 365 F.2d 358 (9th Cir.1966); Stanford v. Utley, 341 F.2d 265 (8th Cir.1965). Similarly, the law of F–2 will be applied to determine the circumstances under which the judgment may be stayed. United States, etc. v. Home Indemnity Co., 549 F.2d 10 (7th Cir.1977).

Uniform Enforcement of Foreign Judgments Act (Revised 1964 Act)

13 Uniform Laws Ann. 149 (1986)

§ 1. Definition. In this Act "foreign judgment" means any judgment, decree, or order of a court of the United States or of any other court which is entitled to full faith and credit in this state.

§ 2. Filing and Status of Foreign Judgments. A copy of any foreign judgment authenticated in accordance with the act of Congress or the statutes of this state may be filed in the office of the Clerk of any [District Court of any city or county] of this state. The Clerk shall treat the foreign judgment in the same manner as a judgment of the [District Court of any city or county] of this state. A judgment so filed has the same effect and is subject to the same procedures, defenses and proceedings for reopening, vacating, or staying as a judgment of a [District Court of any city or county] of this state and may be enforced or satisfied in like manner.

§ 3. Notice of Filing. (a) At the time of the filing of the foreign judgment, the judgment creditor or his lawyer shall make and file with the Clerk of Court an affidavit setting forth the name and last known post office address of the judgment debtor, and the judgment creditor.

(b) Promptly upon the filing of the foreign judgment and the affidavit, the Clerk shall mail notice of the filing of the foreign judgment to the judgment debtor at the address given and shall make a note of the mailing in the docket. The notice shall include the name and post office address of the judgment creditor and the judgment creditor's lawyer, if any, in this state. In addition, the judgment creditor may mail a notice of the filing of the judgment to the judgment debtor and may file proof of mailing with the Clerk. Lack of mailing notice of filing by the Clerk shall not affect the enforcement proceedings if proof of mailing by the judgment creditor has been filed.

[(c) No execution or other process for enforcement of a foreign judgment filed hereunder shall issue until [ ] days after the date the judgment is filed.]

§ 4. Stay. (a) If the judgment debtor shows the [District Court of any city or county] that an appeal from the foreign judgment is pending or will be taken, or that a stay of execution has been granted, the court shall stay enforcement of the foreign judgment until the appeal is concluded, the time for appeal expires, or the stay of execution expires or is vacated, upon proof that the judgment debtor has furnished the security for the satisfaction of the judgment required by the state in which it was rendered.

(b) If the judgment debtor shows the [District Court of any city or county] any ground upon which enforcement of a judgment of any [District Court of any city or county] of this state would be stayed, the court shall stay enforcement of the foreign judgment for an appropriate period, upon requiring the same security for satisfaction of the judgment which is required in this state.

. . .

§ 6. Optional Procedure. The right of a judgment creditor to bring an action to enforce his judgment instead of proceeding under this Act remains unimpaired.

. . .

NOTES

1. The 1964 Revision of the Uniform Act has been adopted in 45 states. It is discussed in Homburger, Recognition and Enforcement of Foreign Judgments, 18 Am.J.Comp.L. 367 (1970). See also, Brand, Enforcement of Judgments in the United States and Europe, 13 Journal of Law and Commerce 193 (1994); Brand, Enforcement of Foreign Money–Judgments in the United States: In Search of Uniformity and International Acceptance, 67 Notre Dame L.Rev. 253 (1991); Annotation, 100 A.L.R.3d 792.

2. Undoubtedly, Congress has power to provide in the case of sister state judgments for a system of registration under which a duly registered judgment could be enforced just like a domestic judgment. See Note, Constitutionality of a Uniform Reciprocal Registration of Judgments Statute, 36 N.Y.U.L.Rev. 488 (1961); Cook, The Powers of Congress under the Full Faith and Credit Clause, 28 Yale L.J. 421 (1919).

3. Australia, which has a federal system much like our own, has provided by an act of its Parliament for the registration throughout the Commonwealth of local state judgments. This act applies not only to judgments for money but also to those which order or forbid the doing of acts. Service and Execution of Process Act, 1901–1963 (11 Commonwealth Acts 359 (1901–1963)). In the United Kingdom, statutes provide for a similar system of registration in the case of judgments rendered in any division of the United Kingdom and also, where the court thinks it "just and convenient," in the case of those rendered in Commonwealth countries. Administration of Justice Act, 1920, 10 & 11 Geo. 5, c. 81. Moreover, the Foreign Judgments (Reciprocal Enforcement) Act, 1933, 23 Geo. 5, c. 13, authorizes the extension by Order in Council of the registration system to money judgments rendered in foreign countries which are prepared to give substantial reciprocity of treatment to judgments originally handed down in the United Kingdom.[1] Thus, the enforcement of intra-Commonwealth and, in some cases, of international judgments in the United Kingdom is easier than the method that generally prevails in this country for the enforcement of sister state judgments. See also, Private International Law (Miscellaneous Provisions) Act 1995 (c. 42).

For a discussion of the British statutory system of registration, see Cheshire and North, Private International Law 392–410 (12th ed. 1992) by North and Fawcett); Graveson, Conflict of Laws 235–245 (7th ed. 1974); 1 Dicey and Morris, Conflict of Laws 453 et seq. (12th ed. 1993 by Collins).

1. A number of countries have been so specified: Australian capital territory, Austria, France, West Germany, Guernsey, India, Isle of Man, Israel, Jersey, The Netherlands and Norway and Pakistan. The provisions of the Foreign Judgments Act, 1933, have been extended to apply to judgments of the supreme courts of these countries.

B. JUDGMENTS BASED ON JURISDICTION OVER THINGS OR OVER STATUS

Judgments of this sort do not impose a personal obligation upon the defendant and hence, unlike in personam judgments, cannot be enforced by action in other states. Their basic effects in the state of rendition are set forth in the Restatement, Second, Judgments:

§ 30. Judgments Based on Jurisdiction to Determine Interests in Things *

A valid and final judgment in an action based only on jurisdiction to determine interests in a thing:

(1) Is conclusive as to those interests with regard to all persons, if the judgment purports to have that effect (traditionally described as "in rem"), or with regard to the named parties, if the judgment purports to have that effect (traditionally described as "quasi in rem"); and

(2) Does not bind anyone with respect to a personal liability; and

(3) Is conclusive between parties, in accordance with the rules of issue preclusion, as to any issues actually litigated by them and determined in the action.

Sec. 31 states an analogous rule with respect to judgments determining status.

These being the basic effects of such judgments in F–1, to what extent, if at all, do they differ when the judgment is placed in issue in F–2?

Combs v. Combs

Supreme Court of Kentucky, 1933.
249 Ky. 155, 60 S.W.2d 368.

[The case appears p. 126, supra.]

Harnischfeger Sales Corp. v. Sternberg Dredging Co.

Supreme Court of Mississippi, 1939.
189 Miss. 73, 191 So. 94.

[Harnischfeger Sales Corporation sold a dredge to Sternberg Dredging Company, taking notes secured by a chattel mortgage for a part of the purchase price. Thereafter, Harnischfeger started a suit in Louisiana to enforce the chattel mortgage, and prayed a personal judgment for $16,000

---

* Quoted with the permission of the copyright owner, The American Law Institute.

on the notes. Sternberg appeared and moved to dismiss for want of jurisdiction. This plea was overruled. Sternberg then pleaded that the dredge was defective and did not meet warranties which were given at the time of sale. The trial court in Louisiana, after a full trial on the merits of this question, entered a decree that the machine be sold and also rendered a personal judgment against Sternberg for the amount due on the notes. The Supreme Court of Louisiana affirmed the judgment enforcing the lien of the chattel mortgage, but held that the trial court did not have jurisdiction to enter a personal judgment and reversed that part of its judgment. See Harnischfeger Sales Corp. v. Sternberg Dredging Co., 179 La. 317, 154 So. 10 (1934).

Harnischfeger then started the present suit in Mississippi, where it obtained personal jurisdiction over Sternberg. The suit in Mississippi was to recover the balance due on the notes after making allowance for the amount obtained through the sale of the dredge in the Louisiana proceedings. Sternberg defended on the ground of breach of warranty and fraud, and Harnischfeger replied that that issue was res judicata as a result of the Louisiana judgment. The trial court struck out the plea of res judicata, and on the merits held in favor of Sternberg on the defense of breach of warranty. Harnischfeger then appealed.]

■ McGOWAN, JUSTICE. ... At the outset we will state that the effect of the estoppel by the final decree of the Supreme Court of Louisiana is to be determined by the laws of that state where the decree was rendered, and this seems to be an accepted and universal rule....

... The ultimate facts as to whether or not a debt existed that would authorize the enforcement of a lien are the same in both the Louisiana and the Mississippi courts. The litigation was between the same parties, the same subject, the only difference in the pleas and proof in the two courts being a change in the name of the pleading. The same cause of action was alleged in the Louisiana Court as was interposed and allowed by the lower court in this state, and that cause of action was, when the case is stripped to the bone, that the machine delivered would not and did not carry a two-yard bucket, and by this we understand it to mean that the machine was not capacitated to be filled with two yards of earth and successfully dumped therefrom....

It is said that the Louisiana decree cannot operate as res adjudicata or estoppel because the Supreme Court held that the proceeding was in rem. 179 La. 317, 154 So. 10. The appellant, Harnischfeger Sales Corporation, is not seeking here to bring a suit on the contention that the Louisiana judgment and action of that court, on the defense thereto, operated as a judgment which concluded the parties as to the amount of the judgment. The contention of the appellant is, as we understand it, that the Sternberg Dredging Company interposed the same defense in the Louisiana court as it interposed in the case at bar, and as to that defense the doctrine of res adjudicata is interposed and effective to conclude it, even though the proceedings in Louisiana to enforce a chattel mortgage on the thing mortgaged in that state were in rem. The appellee had its option to stand on the want of jurisdiction of the Court, but it did not do so. It appeared there. Sternberg, the main witness in both trials, testified to the same salient facts as to this defense in the Louisiana Court as was testified by him in the Mississippi Court in the case at bar. We are of the opinion that the defense was adjudged and concluded as to that defense and that every court everywhere would be bound to so hold....

When the Sternberg Dredging Company decided and elected to resist the entry of any decree in rem against the machine and to interpose the breach-of-warranty defense, it thereby concluded itself irrevocably. Suppose the Louisiana Court had taken the opposite view and had determined in the court of last resort that the defense was valid in that it extinguished the debt? By that decree it would have retained the machine free from the lien; and, certainly where both parties appeared and contested the issue, debt or no debt, because of a breach of warranty, that decree would be final and conclusive on that issue actually litigated, and we think under the statute controlling in Louisiana would be res adjudicata. Such statute is as follows: "The authority of the thing adjudged takes place only with respect to what was the object of the judgment. The thing demanded must be the same; the demand must be founded on the same cause of action; the demand must be between the same parties, and formed by them against each other in the same quality." Art. 2286, Louisiana Civil Code....

We are, therefore, of the opinion that the court below erred in striking the plea of res adjudicata and declining to allow it as an estoppel to the defense here involved....

Reversed, and judgment for appellant.

NOTES

1. In a further opinion in 189 Miss. 73, 195 So. 322 (1940), the court refused to modify this opinion against the contention that the issue raised in the Louisiana proceeding was breach of warranty, while in the Mississippi suit the defendant relied on fraud. The court held that the same evidence bore on the questions of fraud and breach of warranty, and that the two defenses were really the same though "here the name given the counterclaim is different from that given it in the Louisiana court."

2. What accounts for the different effect given the judgment of F–1 (Arkansas) in the Combs case, p. 126, supra, and the judgment of F–1 (Louisiana) in the Harnischfeger case?

3. The defendant is faced with a dilemma when suit is brought in a state whose sole basis of jurisdiction is the presence there of the defendant's property. If the defendant does not appear and defend on the merits, he stands a strong risk of losing the property. He will not be bound, however, under principles of res judicata by any finding of fact that the court may have made. On the other hand, if he enters a defense on the merits, he runs the risk that the findings made by the court will be binding upon him everywhere. It has been argued that to place the defendant in such a position is so unfair as to violate due process. Taintor, Foreign Judgments in Rem: Full Faith and Credit v. Res Judicata *in Personam,* 8 U.Pitt. L.Rev. 223, 226 (1942).

In order to mitigate this problem, a fair number of courts permit the defendant to make a so-called limited appearance. By means of this device, the defendant can appear and resist on the merits and yet be protected from the entry of a personal judgment against him. In some states, he may further be protected from being collaterally bound as to issues actually litigated. It seems probable that the practical significance of a limited appearance has been diminished substantially by the ruling of the Supreme Court in Shaffer v. Heitner, 433 U.S. 186 (1977), p. 136, supra. This is because the property owner may now invoke the principles of International Shoe (p. 47, supra) in an attempt to have the action wholly terminated. Restatement, Second, Judgments § 8, Comment g.

Section 3. Particular Effects

A. Persons Affected *

Sovereign Camp v. Bolin
Supreme Court of the United States, 1938.
305 U.S. 66, 59 S.Ct. 35, 83 L.Ed. 45, 119 A.L.R. 478.

■ Justice Roberts delivered the opinion of the Court.

We granted certiorari because of the claim that the judgment of the court below failed to accord full faith and credit to the public acts, records, and judicial proceedings of the State of Nebraska as required by Article IV, Section 1 of the Constitution.

The petitioner is a fraternal beneficiary association organized under the laws of Nebraska, having a lodge system, a ritualistic form of work, and a representative form of government. It has no capital stock, and transacts its affairs without profit and solely for the mutual benefit of its members and their beneficiaries. It makes provision for the payment of death benefits by assessments upon its members and issues to members certificates assuring payment of such benefits.

In 1895 the petitioner adopted a by-law authorizing the issue of life membership certificates. Under this by-law a member entering the order at an age greater than 43 years was entitled to life membership without the payment of further dues and assessments when the certificate had been outstanding 20 years. In June 1896, while the by-law remained unrepealed, Pleasant Bolin, who was over 43 years of age, joined a Missouri lodge of the petitioner and received a certificate of membership which recited that while in good standing he would be entitled to participate in the beneficial fund to the amount of $1,000 payable to his beneficiaries and to the sum of $100 for placing a monument at his grave. The certificate recited that it was issued subject to all the conditions named in the constitution and laws of the fraternity and was endorsed with the words "Payments to cease after 20 years."

---

* See generally Restatement, Judgments, Second §§ 34–63.

After Bolin's death, the respondents, as beneficiaries, brought action to recover upon the certificate. The petitioner's answer set up that Bolin had ceased to pay the required dues and assessments in July 1916, and his certificate had therefore become void; that the by-law making the certificate fully paid after twenty years was *ultra vires* the association and had been so declared by the Supreme Court of Nebraska in a class suit brought by one Trapp, the holder of a certificate similar to that of Bolin [Trapp v. Sovereign Camp of the Woodmen of the World, 102 Neb. 562, 168 N.W. 191]; that, under Article IV, Section 1, of the Constitution, full faith and credit must be given by the courts of Missouri to this decision of the Supreme Court of Nebraska. The respondents replied that the contract was made and delivered in Missouri and was to be construed and enforced according to Missouri law; that, at the date of its consummation, the petitioner had no license or authority to transact business in Missouri as a corporation or otherwise, and the certificate was therefore to be considered as issued pursuant to, and governed by, the general insurance laws of Missouri; that Bolin having fully performed in accordance with the terms of the certificate, the petitioner was estopped to plead *ultra vires;* and that in truth the contract was not *ultra vires* the petitioner....

[The Missouri courts found for the respondents. They] refused to give force or effect to the decision of the Supreme Court of Nebraska in Trapp v. Woodmen, supra, saying that ... the contract being a Missouri contract its *ultra vires* character must be adjudged by the local law irrespective of what the courts of the domicile had held; that the respondents in the present case relied on an estoppel of the petitioner to plead *ultra vires,* whereas no such issue was presented or decided in the Trapp case.

We hold that the judgment denied full faith and credit to the public acts, records, and judicial proceedings of the State of Nebraska.

First. The beneficiary certificate was not a mere contract to be construed and enforced according to the laws of the state where it was delivered. Entry into membership of an incorporated beneficiary society is more than a contract; it is entering into a complex and abiding relation and the rights of membership are governed by the law of the state of incorporation. Another state, wherein the certificate of membership was issued, cannot attach to membership rights against the society which are refused by the law of the domicile.[1]

Second. ...

The court below was not at liberty to disregard the fundamental law of the petitioner and turn a membership beneficiary certificate into an old line policy to be construed and enforced according to the law of the forum. The decision that the principle of *ultra vires* contracts was to be applied as if the petitioner were a Missouri old line life insurance company was erroneous in the light of the decisions of this court which have uniformly held

---

1. Modern Woodmen v. Mixer, 267 U.S. 531, 542. 544, 551; Royal Arcanum v. Green, 237 U.S.

that the rights of members of such associations are governed by the definition of the society's powers by the courts of its domicile.[2]

Third. The doctrine of estoppel was erroneously invoked to avoid the force and effect of the Nebraska judgment. The court below was of the opinion that, as the petitioner had issued a "payments to cease after 20 years" certificate, and as Bolin had fully performed on his part by paying all dues and assessments over the named period, the petitioner was estopped to plead its lack of power to issue such a certificate. This again was on the theory that whatever might be the nature of the petitioner's organization in Nebraska, for the purposes of this action it must be treated as an old line insurance company in Missouri. It was further held that no question of estoppel was decided in the Trapp case.

As to the first of these positions, it need only be said that the Trapp case was a class suit in which it was determined that the petitioner lacked power, under the law of Nebraska, to issue such certificates. In such a suit the association represents all its members and stands in judgment for them, and even though the suit had a different object than the instant one it is conclusive upon all the members of the association with respect to all rights, questions, or facts therein determined.[3]

With respect to the second position, it appears from the record that Trapp, in the suit in Nebraska, pleaded that the association was estopped to deny its power to issue the form of certificate in question and the opinion of the Nebraska court, by reference to a case decided on the same day, clearly indicates that the issue of estoppel was considered and determined adversely to the plaintiff.

Fourth. Under our uniform holdings the court below failed to give full faith and credit to the petitioner's charter embodied in the statutes of Nebraska as interpreted by its highest court.[4]

The judgment is reversed and the cause is remanded for further proceedings not inconsistent with this opinion.

NOTES

1. Was the doctrine of class suits properly invoked in the principal case? The Trapp case cited in the opinion was an ordinary action brought by a single claimant under another certificate.

2. How does the court get jurisdiction to affect the rights of non-residents in so-called class or representative suits? Cf. Hansberry v. Lee, 311 U.S. 32 (1940), involving a suit brought to enjoin the breach of a restrictive covenant against selling

---

2. Hartford Life Insurance Company v. Ibs, 237 U.S. 662; Hartford Life Insurance Co. v. Barber, 245 U.S. 146; Royal Arcanum v. Green, 237 U.S. 531; Modern Woodmen v. Mixer, 267 U.S. 544.

3. Hartford Life Insurance Company v. Ibs, supra, [footnote 2 at] p. 673.

4. Royal Arcanum v. Green, supra, pp. 540, 543, 546; Hartford Life Ins. Co. v. Ibs, supra, [footnote 2 at] p. 669; Hartford Life Insurance Co. v. Barber, supra, [footnote 2 at] p. 151; Modern Woodmen v. Mixer, supra, [footnote 2 at] p. 551. [The footnotes to the case are from the Court's opinion.]

land to black persons. The covenant by its terms was not effective unless it had been signed by the owners of 95 per cent of the frontage within the area. The defense was that the required 95 per cent had not signed. This was answered with a plea of res judicata based on an earlier suit. The defendants were not parties in this suit, but the Supreme Court of Illinois held that the earlier suit was a "class" or "representative" suit, and that all members of the class were bound by the decree. The Supreme Court of the United States reversed, holding that under the facts of the case there was not a "class" since all persons concerned did not have the same interest. It recognized, however, the possibility of binding absent parties in a class suit. It said (pp. 40–42):

"It is a principle of general application in Anglo–American jurisprudence that one is not bound by a judgment *in personam* in a litigation in which he is not designated as a party or to which he has not been made a party by service of process...

"To these general rules there is a recognized exception that, to an extent not precisely defined by judicial opinion, the judgment in a 'class' or 'representative' suit, to which some members of the class are parties, may bind members of the class or those represented who were not made parties to it.

"... there is scope within the framework of the Constitution for holding in appropriate cases that a judgment rendered in a class suit is *res judicata* as to members of the class who are not formal parties to the suit.... With a proper regard for divergent local institutions and interests, ..., the Court is justified in saying that there has been a failure of due process only in those cases where it cannot be said that the procedure adopted, fairly insures the protection of the interests of absent parties who are to be bound by it ..."

Phillips Petroleum Co. v. Shutts, 472 U.S. 797 (1985), involved the question of the jurisdiction of a Kansas court to entertain a class action when the great majority of the plaintiff class were nonresidents of the state. The suit was to recover interest on delayed royalty payments for natural gas extracted from land located in 11 states. The class consisted of some 28,000 members who resided in all 50 states, in the District of Columbia and in several foreign countries. Fewer than 1,000 members of the class were residents of Kansas. Each member had been notified by mail of the pendency of the action and invited to attend in person or by counsel. Otherwise, the absent members would be represented by the class members who initiated the action and would be bound by the judgment unless they "opted out" of the action by returning a "request for exclusion." Held that the Kansas court had jurisdiction over those members of the class who had not "opted out." The Court declared that the defendant was in error in arguing that Kansas could not exert jurisdiction over absentees' claims unless the absentees have sufficient minimum contacts with Kansas. The Court said that fewer burdens and fewer risks are placed upon class plaintiffs than upon defendants. Due process requires only that class plaintiffs be given notice of the action, an opportunity to appear in person or by counsel, adequate representation and an opportunity to "opt out." They need not be required affirmatively to "opt into" the class. "The interests of the absent plaintiffs are sufficiently protected by the forum State when those plaintiffs are provided with a request for exclusion that can be returned within a reasonable time to the court." (472 U.S. at p. 812.)

For an extensive discussion of Phillips Petroleum see Miller and Crump, Jurisdiction and Choice of Law in Multistate Actions After Phillips Petroleum Co. v. Shutts, 96 Yale L.J. 1 (1986).

Riley v. New York Trust Co.
Supreme Court of the United States, 1942.
315 U.S. 343, 62 S.Ct. 608, 86 L.Ed. 885.

Certiorari to the Supreme Court of Delaware.

■ JUSTICE REED delivered the opinion of the Court.

Coca–Cola International Corporation, incorporated in Delaware, filed a bill of interpleader in a Delaware Court of Chancery against Julian Riley and Hughes Spalding, petitioners here, the Executors of Mrs. Julia M. Hungerford, with letters testamentary issued by the Court of Ordinary of Fulton County, Georgia, and against the New York Trust Company, the respondent, a New York corporation, as temporary administrator (afterward administrator c.t.a.) of the same decedent, appointed by the Surrogate's Court for New York County, New York.

The Georgia executors and the New York administrator each claim the right to have transferred to them, in their representative capacity, stock in the Coca–Cola Corporation now on its books in the name of the decedent. The outstanding certificates are in Georgia, in the hands of the Georgia executors. The parties are agreed, and it is therefore assumed, that Delaware is the situs of the stock. In accordance with the prayer of the bill, the Delaware court directed the adversary claimants to interplead between themselves as to their respective claims.

The Georgia executors assert that original domiciliary probate of Mrs. Hungerford's will in solemn form was obtained by them in Georgia, with all beneficiaries and heirs at law of testatrix, including her husband, Robert Hungerford, actual parties by personal service. These, it is conceded, were all the parties under the law of Georgia entitled to be heard on the probate of the will. The respondent administrator c.t.a. was not a party. The record of probate includes a determination by special finding, over the objection of the caveator, the husband, that the testatrix was domiciled in Georgia. The special finding was specifically approved as an essential fact to determine the jurisdiction of the Court of Ordinary by the highest court of Georgia in its affirmance of the probate. Hungerford v. Spalding, 183 Ga. 547, 189 S.E. 2. ...

From the facts alleged, petitioners inferred the conclusive establishment of the place for domiciliary distribution against "all persons," and prayed the issue to them of new certificates. An offer was made to pay all Delaware taxes or charges on the stock.

Respondent admitted that all parties entitled under the law of Georgia to be heard in opposition to probate were actually before the Georgia courts. It denied that Mrs. Hungerford was domiciled in Georgia or that the Georgia judgment of domicile and probate was binding on it, and averred testatrix's domicile at death was New York. It further averred that there were New York creditors of the estate interested in the proper and lawful administration of the estate, and that New York had certain claims for inheritance and estate taxes. Its own subsequent appointment by the Surrogate's Court of New York County, New York, on the suggestion of testatrix's husband and the State Tax Commission, was pleaded with applicable provisions of New York probate and estate tax law. By stipulation it was established that petitioners and the heirs and beneficiaries of testatrix, except her husband, who was an actual party, were notified of the New York proceedings for probate only by publication or substituted service of the citation in Georgia, and did not appear. As a domiciliary administrator c.t.a., the respondent prayed the issue to it of new certificates for the stock in controversy.

The trial court concluded from the evidence adduced at the hearings that the testatrix was domiciled in Georgia. It was therefore, as the court stated, unnecessary for it to consider the binding effect of the Georgia judgment. The Supreme Court of Delaware reversed this finding of fact, determined that New York was testatrix's domicile and denied petitioners' contention that Article IV, § 1, of the Constitution required the award of the certificates of stock to the Georgia executors. The Coca–Cola Corporation was directed to issue its stock certificate to the respondent, the New York administrator c.t.a. New York Trust Co. v. Riley, 16 A.2d 772....

The constitutional effect of the Georgia decree on a claim in his own name in another state by a party to the Georgia proceedings is not here involved. The question we are to decide is whether this Georgia judgment on domicile conclusively establishes the right of the Georgia executors to demand delivery to them of personal assets of their testatrix which another state is willing to surrender to the domiciliary personal representative, when another representative, appointed by a third state, asserts a similar domiciliary right. For the purpose of this review, the conclusion of Delaware that the testatrix was in fact domiciled in New York is accepted. The answer to the question lies in the extent to which Article IV, § 1, of the Constitution, as made applicable by R.S. § 905, nevertheless controls Delaware's action.

This clause of the Constitution brings to our Union a useful means for ending litigation. Matters once decided between adverse parties in any state or territory are at rest. Were it not for this full faith and credit provision, so far as the Constitution controls the matter, adversaries could wage again their legal battles whenever they met in other jurisdictions. Each state could control its own courts but itself could not project the effect of its decisions beyond its own boundaries. Cf. Pennoyer v. Neff, 95 U.S. 714, 722. That clause compels that controversies be stilled, so that, where a state court has jurisdiction of the parties and subject matter, its judgment controls in other states to the same extent as it does in the state where rendered. Roche v. McDonald, 275 U.S. 449, 451.... By the Constitutional provision for full faith and credit, the local doctrines of *res judicata*, speaking generally, become a part of national jurisprudence, and therefore federal questions cognizable here.

... The full faith and credit clause allows Delaware, in disposing of local assets, to determine the question of domicile anew for any interested party who is not bound by participation in the Georgia proceeding [Citing cases.] It must be admitted that this re-examination may result in conflicting decisions upon domicile, but that is an inevitable consequence of the existing federal system, which endows its citizens with the freedom to choose the state or states within which they desire to carry on business, enjoy their leisure or establish their residences. Worcester County Co. v. Riley, 302 U.S. 292, 299. But, while allowing Delaware to determine domicile for itself, where any interested party is not bound by the Georgia proceedings, the full faith and credit clause and R.S. § 905, do require that Delaware shall give Georgia judgments such faith and credit "as they have by law or usage" in Georgia. . . .

We find nothing in [Tant v. Wigfall, 65 Ga. 412 (1880), and Wash v. Dickson, 147 Ga. 540, 94 S.E. 1009 (1918)] which would lead to the conclusion that, in Georgia, the New York administrator c.t.a. was in privity, so far as the sequestration of assets for the payment of death taxes or indebtedness of decedent or her estate is concerned, with any parties before the Georgia court, or that the New York representative could not take steps in Georgia courts which might result in its getting possession of any assets which under the Georgia law of administration would be properly deliverable to a foreign domiciliary administrator. . . . Hence, if the Georgia judgment is to bind the New York administrator, it can be considered to do so only *in rem*.

. . . It may be assumed that the judgment of probate and domicile is a judgment *in rem* . . . But this does not bar litigation anew by a stranger, of facts upon which the decree *in rem* is based. . . . While the Georgia judgment is to have the same faith and credit in Delaware as it does in Georgia, that requirement does not give the Georgia judgment extraterritorial effect upon assets in other states. So far as the assets in Georgia are concerned, the Georgia judgment of probate is *in rem;* so far as it affects personalty beyond the state, it is *in personam* and can bind only parties thereto or their privies. This is the result of the ruling in Baker v. Baker, Eccles & Co., 242 U.S. 394, 400.[1] Phrased somewhat differently, if the effect of a probate decree in Georgia *in personam* was to bar a stranger

---

1. Illustrative state cases.

A will is admitted to original domiciliary probate in state A. Thereafter an ancillary proceeding is commenced in state B based upon the domiciliary determination of A. At that point a beneficiary, a stranger to the proceeding in A, appears and asserts that the decedent was domiciled in B. The determination of domicile by state A will not be recognized by state B, but state B will take evidence and redetermine the issue of domicile. Estate of Clark, 148 Cal. 108, 82 P. 760. . . .

If the objector was privy to the proceeding in state A, state B will not redetermine the issue of domicile. Willetts' Appeal, 50 Conn. 330. . . .

Where the proceeding in state B is by a stranger to the proceedings for original domiciliary probate in state A upon the theory that the domicile is actually B, state B will determine domicile for itself. Scripps v. Wayne Probate Judge, 131 Mich. 265, 90 N.W. 1061. . . .

Where the person seeking to establish domicile in state B, and to have original domiciliary probate there, was a party to the proceeding in state A, state B will not redetermine domicile. Hopper v. Nicholas, 106 Ohio 292, 140 N.E. 186. . . . [Footnote by the Court. Other footnotes omitted.]

to the decree from later asserting his rights, such a holding would deny procedural due process.

It seems quite obvious that the administrator c.t.a., appears in Delaware as an agency of the State of New York, and not as the *alter ego* of the beneficiaries of the Hungerford estate. In its answer to the petitioners' statement of claim, it established its status by alleging that not merely the beneficiaries but creditors residing in New York and the State of New York were interested in the estate, that its appointment as temporary administrator had been sought by the New York Tax Commissioner "to protect the claim of the State of New York to inheritance and succession taxes," that the State of New York was asserting such claims in substantial amount on the theory that the domicile was New York....

Georgia and New York might each assert its right to administer the estates of its domiciliaries to protect its sovereign interests, and Delaware was free to decide for itself which claimant is entitled to receive the portion of Mrs. Hungerford's personalty within Delaware's borders.

Affirmed.

■ CHIEF JUSTICE STONE: I concur upon the single ground that the New York administrator was not bound by the Georgia judgment. He was not a party to the Georgia proceedings, nor was he represented by any of those who were parties. As administrator appointed under the New York statutes, he was charged with the duty of administering the estate of the decedent and paying inheritance taxes upon it. His interest so far as he owes duties to the state is therefore adverse to that of the husband and the next of kin, who alone were parties to the Georgia proceeding. To have bound him by representation of those so adverse in interest would have been a denial of due process. Hansberry v. Lee, 311 U.S. 32. A judgment so obtained is not entitled to full faith and credit with respect to those not parties.... Any other conclusion would foreclose New York from litigating its right to collect taxes lawfully due, by the simple expedient of a probate by the next of kin of the will of the decedent as the domiciled resident of another state, without notice to any representative of New York or opportunity to be heard.

It is unnecessary to consider the other questions discussed by the opinion.

■ JUSTICE FRANKFURTER and JUSTICE JACKSON concur in this opinion.

NOTES

1. RESTATEMENT, SECOND, CONFLICT OF LAWS: *

§ 94. Persons Affected

What persons are bound by a valid judgment is determined, subject to constitutional limitations, by the local law of the State where the judgment was rendered.

---

* Quoted with the permission of the copyright owner, The American Law Institute.

Comment:

. . .

d. Privies. Subject to constitutional limitations (see Comment b), the local law of the State where the judgment was rendered determines which persons are in privity with the parties to the action and hence are bound by and entitled to the benefits of the rules of res judicata. This law determines whether the judgment was rendered in a class action and, if so, which persons are members of the class and the extent to which the interests of these persons are affected by the judgment. This law likewise determines, for example, whether the term "privies" includes those who control an action although not parties to it, those whose interests are represented by a party to the action and those who are successors in interest to a party to the action. . . .

2. The various situations where privity is commonly found to exist in local law are set forth in Restatement, Second, Judgments c. 4.

Kremer v. Chemical Construction Corp.

Supreme Court of the United States, 1982.
456 U.S. 461, 102 S.Ct. 1883, 72 L.Ed.2d 262.

[The plaintiff filed a complaint with the Equal Employment Opportunity Commission (EEOC) under Title VII of the Civil Rights Act of 1964, complaining that his discharge from employment had been caused by illegal discrimination. As required by the Civil Rights Act, the Commission referred the charge to the New York State Division of Human Rights (NYHRD), the agency charged with enforcing the New York law against discrimination. The NYHRD rejected the claim as meritless and, on appeal to the New York Appellate Division, this decision was unanimously affirmed. The plaintiff then brought a Title VII action in a federal district court which dismissed the complaint on res judicata grounds and the Court of Appeals affirmed. This decision was in turn affirmed by the Supreme Court with four Justices dissenting.]

■ JUSTICE WHITE delivered the opinion of the Court.

. . . Section 1738 [quoted on p. 39, supra] requires federal courts to give the same preclusive effect to state court judgments that those judgments would be given in the courts of the state from which the judgments emerged. Here the Appellate Division of the New York Supreme Court has issued a judgment affirming the decision of the NYHRD Appeals Board that the discharge and failure to rehire Kremer were not the product of the discrimination that he had alleged. There is no question that this judicial determination precludes Kremer from bringing "any other action, civil or criminal, based upon the same grievance" in the New York courts. N.Y.Exec.Law § 300 (McKinney 1972). By its terms, therefore, § 1738 would appear to preclude Kremer from relitigating the same question in federal court.

Kremer . . . suggests that in Title VII cases Congress intended that federal courts be relieved of their usual obligation to grant finality to state court decisions. . . .

... The petitioner ... contends that the judgment should not bar his Title VII action because the New York courts did not resolve the issue that the District Court must hear under Title VII—whether Kremer had suffered discriminatory treatment—and because the procedures provided were inadequate. Neither contention is persuasive. Although the claims presented to the NYHRD and subsequently reviewed by the Appellate Division were necessarily based on New York law, the alleged discriminatory acts are prohibited by both federal and state laws. The elements of a successful employment discrimination claim are virtually identical; petitioner could not succeed on a Title VII claim consistently with the judgment of the NYHRD that there is no reason to believe he was terminated or not rehired because of national origin or religion. The Appellate Division's affirmance of the NYHRD's dismissal necessarily decided that petitioner's claim under New York law was meritless, and thus it also decided that a Title VII claim arising from the same events would be equally meritless. . . .

Our previous decisions have not specified the source or defined the content of the requirement that the first adjudication offer a full and fair opportunity to litigate. But for present purposes, where we are bound by the statutory directive of § 1738, state proceedings need do no more than satisfy the minimum procedural requirements of the Fourteenth Amendment's Due Process Clause in order to qualify for the full-faith-and-credit guaranteed by federal law. It has long been established that § 1738 does not allow federal courts to employ their own rules of res judicata in determining the effect of state judgments. Rather, it ... commands a federal court to accept the rules chosen by the state from which the judgment is taken. . . .

The State must, however, satisfy the applicable requirements of the Due Process Clause. A state may not grant preclusive effect in its own courts to a constitutionally infirm judgment and other state and federal courts are not required to accord full-faith-and-credit to such a judgment. Section 1738 does not suggest otherwise; other state and federal courts would still be providing a state court judgment with the "same" preclusive effect as the courts of the state from which the judgment emerged. In such a case, there could be no constitutionally recognizable preclusion at all.

We have little doubt that Kremer received all the process that was constitutionally required in rejecting his claim that he had been discriminatorily discharged contrary to the statute. . . .

In our system of jurisprudence the usual rule is that merits of a legal claim once decided in a court of competent jurisdiction are not subject to redetermination in another forum. Such a fundamental departure from traditional rules of preclusion, enacted into federal law, can be justified only if plainly stated by Congress. Because there is no "affirmative showing" of a "clear and manifest" legislative purpose in Title VII to deny res judicata or collateral estoppel effect to a state court judgment affirming that a claim of employment discrimination is unproven, and because the procedures provided in New York for the determination of such claims offer a full and fair opportunity to litigate the merits, the judgment of the Court of Appeals is

Affirmed.

[The dissenters' position was that the New York courts had decided only that the NYHRC's finding of no discrimination was a rational conclusion, not that it was correct in fact. Hence, they said, there was no judicial determination of the issue in the instant proceeding, and Section 1738 did not bar a federal district court from adjudicating the issue.]

NOTES

1. All of the Justices, including the dissenters, were apparently agreed that the obligation of the federal courts to respect state court decisions is based on Section 1738. Does this mean that they thought that the federal courts are not bound by the full faith and credit clause itself (Article IV, Section 1) and that Congress would be free to limit the conclusive effect of state court judgments in such cases?

2. In the eyes of the dissenting Justices, would a judicial affirmance of an administrative decision ever be entitled to full faith and credit?

3. In Davis v. United States Steel Supply, Etc., 688 F.2d 166 (3d Cir.1982) (en banc), the facts were much the same as in the Kremer case, except that it was the defendant rather than the plaintiff who appealed from the administrative decision to a state court. It was held that once the state court had decided the appeal, the plaintiff was barred from seeking relief in a federal court. There were dissents.

4. Allen v. McCurry, 449 U.S. 90 (1980) (en banc). At his trial in a state court for possession of heroin and assault with intent to kill, McCurry sought to suppress evidence that he claimed had been obtained by an illegal search and seizure. This motion was denied, and McCurry was convicted. He later brought a damage suit in a federal court against the officers who had entered his home and seized the evidence. The federal court granted summary judgment against McCurry on the ground that collateral estoppel prevented him from relitigating the search and seizure question that had been decided against him in the criminal trial. On writ of certiorari, this decision was affirmed by the Supreme Court since McCurry had received a "full and fair hearing" on the issue of illegal search and seizure in the state court. The dissent, written by Justice Blackmun and joined by Justices Brennan and Marshall, concluded that "The criminal defendant is an involuntary litigant in the state trial.... To force him to a choice between forgoing either a potential defense or a federal forum for hearing his constitutional civil claim is fundamentally unfair."

Marrese v. American Academy of Ortho. Surgeons

Supreme Court of the United States, 1985.
470 U.S. 373, 105 S.Ct. 1327, 84 L.Ed.2d 274.

[Plaintiffs, orthopedic surgeons, applied for membership in the American Academy of Orthopedic Surgeons. Their application was denied, and they then filed suit in the Illinois courts claiming that the Academy had violated their associational rights protected by Illinois law. Upon being denied relief in the state courts, plaintiffs filed a federal antitrust suit in the Illinois federal courts. Here again they were denied relief on the ground that under federal law their claims were precluded by the earlier Illinois judgment. The Supreme Court reversed.]

■ JUSTICE O'CONNOR delivered the opinion of the Court....

The issue presented by this case is whether a state court judgment may have preclusive effect on a federal antitrust claim that could not have been raised in the state proceeding. Although federal antitrust claims are within the exclusive jurisdiction of the federal courts, ... the Court of Appeals ruled that the dismissal of petitioners' complaints in state court barred them from bringing a claim based on the same facts under the Sherman Act. The Court of Appeals erred by suggesting that in these circumstances a federal court should determine the preclusive effect of a state court judgment without regard to the law of the State in which judgment was rendered.

The preclusive effect of a state court judgment in a subsequent federal lawsuit generally is determined by the full faith and credit statute....

The fact that petitioners' antitrust claim is within the exclusive jurisdiction of the federal courts does not necessarily make § 1738 inapplicable to this case. Our decisions indicate that a state court judgment may in some circumstances have preclusive effect in a subsequent action within the exclusive jurisdiction of the federal courts. ...

To be sure, a state court will not have occasion to address the specific question whether a state judgment has issue or claim preclusive effect in a later action that can be brought only in federal court. Nevertheless, a federal court may rely in the first instance on state preclusion principles to determine the extent to which an earlier state judgment bars subsequent litigation....

With respect to matters that were not decided in the state proceedings, we note that claim preclusion generally does not apply where "[t]he plaintiff was unable to rely on a certain theory of the case or to seek a certain remedy because of the limitations on the subject matter jurisdiction of the courts...." Restatement (Second) of Judgments § 26(1)(c) (1982). If state preclusion law includes this requirement of prior jurisdictional competency, which is generally true, a state judgment will not have claim preclusive effect on a cause of action within the exclusive jurisdiction of the federal courts....

Reference to state preclusion law may make it unnecessary to determine if the federal court, as an exception to § 1738, should refuse to give preclusive effect to a state court judgment. The issue whether there is an exception to § 1738 arises only if state law indicates that litigation of a particular claim or issue should be barred in the subsequent federal proceeding.... Unless application of Illinois preclusion law suggests, contrary to the usual view, that petitioners' federal antitrust claim is somehow barred, there will be no need to decide in this case if there is an exception to § 1738.

The Court of Appeals did not apply the approach to § 1738 that we have outlined. It expressed the view that § 1738 allows a federal court to give a state court judgment greater preclusive effect than the state courts themselves would give to it....

We are unwilling to create a special exception to § 1738 for federal antitrust claims that would give state court judgments greater preclusive effect than would the courts of the State rendering the judgment....

... [W]e have parallel systems of state and federal courts, and the concerns of comity reflected in § 1738 generally allow States to determine the preclusive scope of their own courts' judgments.... These concerns certainly are not made less compelling because state courts lack jurisdiction over federal antitrust claims....

In this case the Court of Appeals should have first referred to Illinois law to determine the preclusive effect of the state judgment. Only if state law indicates that a particular claim or issue would be barred, is it necessary to determine if an exception to § 1738 should apply. Although for purposes of this case, we need not decide if such an exception exists for federal antitrust claims, we observe that the more general question is whether the concerns underlying a particular grant of exclusive jurisdiction justify a finding of an implied partial repeal of § 1738. Resolution of this question will depend on the particular federal statute as well as the nature of the claim or issue involved in the subsequent federal action. Our previous decisions indicate that the primary consideration must be the intent of Congress....

The judgment of the Court of Appeals is reversed, and the case is remanded for further proceedings consistent with this opinion.

NOTES

1. For extensive comment see 71 Iowa L.Rev. 609 (1986). See, also, Migra v. Warren City School District Board of Educ., 465 U.S. 75 (1984); Parsons Steel, Inc. v. First Alabama Bank, 474 U.S. 518 (1986), on remand 785 F.2d 929 (11th Cir.1986), affirmed 825 F.2d 1475 (11th Cir.1987), cert. denied 484 U.S. 1060 (1988).

2. The difficulties inherent in the application of the Marrese holding are illustrated by the comment of the district court judge upon remand of the case. In his view, he was required to decide "a nearly metaphysical question." Marrese v. American Academy of Ortho. Surgeons, 628 F.Supp. 918, 919 (N.D.Ill.1986). The Second Circuit encountered similar problems in Gargiul v. Tompkins, 790 F.2d 265 (2d Cir.1986).

3. Marrese is discussed in Burbank, Interjurisdictional Preclusion, Full Faith and Credit and Federal Common Law: A General Approach, 71 Cornell L.Rev. 733 (1986); Shreve, Preclusion and Federal Choice of Law, 64 Tex.L.Rev. 1209 (1986). See also, Weinberg, The Federal–State Conflict of Laws: "Actual" Conflicts, 70 Tex.L.Rev. 1743 (1992).

B. Issues Affected

Restatement, Second, Conflict of Laws: *

§ 95. Issues Affected

What issues are determined by a valid judgment is determined, subject to constitutional limitations, by the local law of the State where the judgment was rendered.

NOTES

1. Section 95 is in line with opinions of the Supreme Court. See, e.g., Magnolia Petroleum Co. v. Hunt, p. 266, infra; Riley v. New York Trust Co., p. 242, supra. See also, as to splitting a cause of action, Cheatham, Res Judicata and the Full Faith and Credit Clause: Magnolia Petroleum Co. v. Hunt, 44 Colum.L.Rev. 330, 346–348 (1944). And as to collateral estoppel, United States v. Silliman, 167 F.2d 607 (3d Cir.1948), cert. denied 335 U.S. 825 (1948).

2. When F–1 is a foreign country, what will be the res judicata or collateral estoppel effect in this country of the F–1's determination? See p. 233, supra.

3. Compulsory counterclaims. DeGroot, Kalliel, Traint & Conklin v. Camarota, 169 N.J.Super. 338, 404 A.2d 1211 (1979). Suit by Michigan attorneys to enforce a default judgment obtained in Michigan for professional services rendered. Defendant counterclaimed for legal malpractice in connection with these services. Held that the counterclaim was properly dismissed. Under the Michigan compulsory joinder rule, the claim for malpractice should have been asserted by way of defense or counterclaim. Since the malpractice claim could no longer be asserted in Michigan, it could not, under full faith and credit, be asserted in New Jersey.

Compare Chapman v. Aetna Finance Co., 615 F.2d 361 (5th Cir.1980), where the question was whether plaintiffs' claims under the federal Truth-in-Lending law should be dismissed because of failure to assert them as compulsory counterclaims in prior Georgia state court foreclosure proceedings. Under Georgia law the unasserted claims would have been barred, but the court held that they were not precluded from relitigation by the full faith and credit clause. After noting that the purpose of the Georgia rule was to promote judicial economy and thus was "local in scope," the court said: "We think that Georgia's compulsory counterclaim, for full faith and credit purposes, is more properly analyzed as a legislative act than as an element of that state's judicial proceedings." Is that a justifiable distinction?

Mutuality of Estoppel

A question of increasing importance is the impact of full faith and credit in situations where F–1 and F–2 have different rules with respect to the collateral estoppel effect of a judgment in a later action between a party to the judgment and a stranger seeking to rely on it (*offensive collateral estoppel*). A case in point is Hart v. American Airlines, Inc., 61 Misc.2d 41, 304 N.Y.S.2d 810 (1969). That case arose out of a crash in Kentucky of an

---

* Quoted with the permission of the copyright owner, The American Law Institute.

American Airlines plane in which most of the passengers were killed. Of the various actions involving the crash, the first to go to judgment was an action brought in Texas. The crash was found to have been caused by the negligence of American Airlines and accordingly a judgment was rendered for the plaintiff. Thereafter, in a New York action involving different passengers, the plaintiffs contended that under principles of collateral estoppel American Airlines was precluded by the Texas judgment from denying that its negligence had caused the accident. This was the New York rule of collateral estoppel but not the Texas rule which imposed the requirement of mutuality, namely that one party is not collaterally estopped by a former adjudication if the other party would not have been estopped by a contrary outcome in the earlier suit. The court upheld the plaintiffs' contention, stating that New York's "superior interest in the issue of collateral estoppel" was established by the fact that the plaintiffs and their decedents were New York domiciliaries. The court continued that the defendant's reliance on full faith and credit was "misplaced", since this was not an action to enforce the Texas judgment and that what was here involved was New York's policy determination that "one who has had his day in court should not be permitted to relitigate the question anew." Is this case consistent with Marrese, p. 248 supra?

Suppose that the New York judgment had been the first to be handed down. Some cases suggest that in this situation Texas would have been required to apply the New York rule of collateral estoppel and hold American Airlines barred from relitigating the question of its negligence although the Airline would have been free to do so under the Texas rule of mutuality. United States v. United Air Lines, Inc., 216 F.Supp. 709 (E.D.Wash., D.Nev.1962), affirmed as to issue of mutuality of collateral estoppel sub nom. United Air Lines, Inc. v. Wiener, 335 F.2d 379 (9th Cir.1964); Cummings v. Dresher, 18 N.Y.2d 105, 271 N.Y.S.2d 976, 218 N.E.2d 688 (1966). Non-mutual offensive use of collateral estoppel was approved in Parklane Hosiery Co. v. Shore, 439 U.S. 322 (1979). For an exception, where the federal government was the party against which the estoppel was sought to be raised, see United States v. Mendoza, 464 U.S. 154 (1984).

Can the Hart decision be sustained on the reasoning that the New York court gave the Texas judgment greater, rather than less, effect than it would have in Texas and thereby accorded it more full faith and credit, not less? Similar questions can be raised as to the preclusive effect of an F–1 judgment with respect to splitting a cause of action.

Besides the question of just what full faith requires of F–2 when its rules of res judicata (and collateral estoppel) differ from those of F–1, there are the following issues: (1) If F–1 is a federal diversity court, is the res judicata effect of its judgment determined pursuant to federal law or pursuant to the rules of the state that created the underlying claim? (2) If F–2 is a federal diversity court, is it obliged to give the same effect to the F–1 judgment that would be given in the state in which it sits? In Degnan, Federalized Res Judicata, 85 Yale L.J. 741, 773 (1976), the author asserts that the emerging principle of the res judicata scope of full faith and credit is that

> "A valid judgment rendered in any judicial system within the United States must be recognized by all other judicial systems within the United States.... [T]he claims and issues precluded by that judgment, and the parties bound thereby, are determined by the law of the system which rendered the judgment."

In accord, see Stovall v. Price Waterhouse Co., 652 F.2d 537 (5th Cir.1981) holding that federal law should be applied to determine the res judicata effect of a judgment rendered by a federal court. Restatement, Second, Judgments § 87 is also in accord.

On the full-faith, Erie and choice-of-law aspects of the problem when different doctrines of mutuality of collateral estoppel prevail in the concerned jurisdictions, see Note, Collateral Estoppel: The Changing Role of the Mutuality Rule, 41 Mo.L.Rev. 521, 538–42 (1976).

NOTE

See generally Carrington, Collateral Estoppel and Foreign Judgments, 24 Ohio St.L.J. 381 (1963); Lewis, Mutuality in Conflict—Flexibility and Full Faith and Credit, 23 Drake L.Rev. 364 (1974); Overton, The Restatement of Judgments, Collateral Estoppel and the Conflict of Laws, 44 Tenn.L.Rev. 927 (1977); Rosenberg, Collateral Estoppel in New York, 44 St. John's L.Rev. 165 (1969); Note, Collateral Estoppel in Multistate Litigation, 68 Colum.L.Rev. 1590 (1968); Note, Collateral Estoppel Effects of Administrative Agency Determinations: Where Should Federal Courts Draw the Line?, 73 Cornell L.Rev. 817 (1988).

WARNER v. BUFFALO DRYDOCK CO., 67 F.2d 540 (2d Cir.1933), cert. denied 291 U.S. 678 (1934): Action in a federal court in New York to recover for damages to plaintiffs' steamer caused by defendant's servants. One of the defendant's pleas in bar was that prior to the commencement of this action plaintiffs had filed a libel action in a federal court in Ohio based upon the same cause of action, and that the libel action had been dismissed "because of laches on the part of libellants in pursuing the alleged claim." Augustus N. Hand, J. "The decisions of the Supreme Court and the English cases all indicate that the judgment of the court of a foreign state which dismisses a cause of action because of the statute of limitations of the forum is not a decision upon the merits and is not a bar to a new action upon the identical claim in the courts of another state.... All the court in Ohio decided was that the remedy was barred there because of laches.... The Ohio decree does not fail to bar the remedy in the present action because it is not res judicata as to everything which it decided, but because it did not decide that the plaintiffs' claim was extinguished, but only that they could not sue in Ohio on account of the local statute of limitations.... In our opinion, the dismissal of the libel by the Ohio court was not a bar to the present action."

NOTES

1. The *Warner* rule has the support of Restatement of Conflicts, Second, § 110, Comment *b*. But compare Shoup v. Bell & Howell Co., 872 F.2d 1178 (4th Cir.1989), where a federal court's summary judgment dismissing an action on statute of limitations grounds was held to preclude suit on the same claim in a second federal court. The decision was based entirely on the court's interpretation of the Federal Rules of Civil Procedure.

2. Would not the Ohio decree in *Warner* have effectively barred the plaintiffs from again suing the defendant in that state on the same cause of action? How then can the result reached in the principal case be reconciled with the statutory command that F–2 must accord F–1 judicial proceedings "such faith and credit ... as they have by law or usage in the courts" of F–1?

3. Would an F–1 judgment dismissing plaintiff's suit on the ground of public policy be binding in F–2 whose public policy was different? If not, why should not F–2 also be permitted to apply its own rule as to collateral estoppel and the splitting of a cause of action? Compare Mertz v. Mertz, p. 379, infra.

4. Does a judgment dismissing plaintiff's suit on the ground that it is barred by the forum's statute of limitations occupy, of necessity, the same status as one basing the dismissal upon the forum's public policy? Is a judgment of the latter type more likely to go to the merits of the cause of action? See Paulsen and Sovern, "Public Policy" in the Conflict of Laws, 56 Colum.L.Rev. 969, 1010–1012 (1956); Restatement, Second, Judgments §§ 19–20.

C. Limitations on Full Faith and Credit

Fall v. Eastin

Supreme Court of the United States, 1909.
215 U.S. 1, 30 S.Ct. 3, 54 L.Ed. 65, 23 L.R.A.,N.S., 924, 17 Ann.Cas. 853.

■ Justice McKenna delivered the opinion of the Court:

The question in this case is whether a deed to land situate in Nebraska, made by a commissioner under the decree of a court of the state of Washington in an action for divorce, must be recognized in Nebraska under the due faith and credit clause of the Constitution of the United States.

[The plaintiff and E.W. Fall were married in Indiana in 1876 and subsequently moved to Nebraska, where E.W. Fall acquired title to the land in controversy. In 1889 they moved to Washington, where in 1895 the plaintiff obtained a divorce on a cross-petition filed by her. The divorce decree, in accordance with a Washington statute concerning the property of divorced parties, was accompanied by a decree awarding plaintiff the Nebraska land and ordering her husband to convey that portion to her. E.W. Fall did not comply with the decree, but a commissioner appointed by the Washington court executed to her a deed to the land. Thereafter, E.W. Fall executed to third parties, W.H. Fall and Elizabeth Eastin, a mortgage on the land and a deed to the land. Plaintiff then brought the present suit in the state court of Nebraska to quiet her title to the land and to cancel the mortgage and the deed executed by E.W. Fall. She set up the

Washington decree and the commissioner's deed, and contended that Fall's conveyances were ineffective to impair the rights she claimed under that decree and the deed. E.W. Fall was never served personally in the Nebraska proceedings and did not appear, though his conveyees were duly served. The trial court gave a decree in favor of the plaintiff. The Supreme Court of Nebraska first affirmed (75 Neb. 104, 106 N.W. 412), but on rehearing, it reversed the decree of the trial court (75 Neb. 120, 113 N.W. 175).]

... Plaintiff urges the equities which arose between her and her husband, on account of their relation as husband and wife, in the state of Washington, and under the laws of that state. The defendant urges the policy of the state of Nebraska, and the inability of the court of Washington, by its decree alone or the deed executed through the commissioner, to convey the land situate in Nebraska....

... The supreme court of the state concedes, as we understand its opinion, the jurisdiction in the Washington court to render the decree. The court said:

"We think there can be no doubt, where a court of chancery has, by its decree, ordered and directed persons properly within its jurisdiction to do or refrain from doing a certain act, it may compel obedience to this decree by appropriate proceedings, and that any action taken by reason of such compulsion is valid and effectual wherever it may be assailed. In the instant case, if Fall had obeyed the order of the Washington court, and made a deed of conveyance to his wife of the Nebraska land, even under the threat of contempt proceedings, or after duress by imprisonment, the title thereby conveyed to Mrs. Fall would have been of equal weight and dignity with that which he himself possessed at the time of the execution of the deed."

But Fall, not having executed a deed, the court's conclusion was, to quote its language, that "neither the decree nor the commissioner's deed conferred any right or title upon her.... The decree is inoperative to affect the title to the Nebraska land ... it remained in E.W. Fall until divested by operation of law or by his voluntary act. He has parted with it to Elizabeth Eastin; and whether any consideration was ever paid for it or not is immaterial so far as the plaintiff is concerned, for she is in no position to question the transaction, whatever a creditor of Fall might be able to do." ...

The territorial limitation of the jurisdiction of courts of a state over property in another state has a limited exception in the jurisdiction of a court of equity, but it is an exception well defined. A court of equity, having authority to act upon the person, may indirectly act upon real estate in another state, through the instrumentality of this authority over the person....

Whether the doctrine that a decree of a court rendered in consummation of equities, or the deed of a master under it, will not convey title, and that the deed of a party coerced by the decree will have such effect, is illogical or inconsequent, we need not inquire, nor consider whether the other view would not more completely fulfil the Constitution of the United States....

But, however plausibly the contrary view may be sustained, we think that the doctrine that the court, not having jurisdiction of the res, cannot affect it by its decree, nor by a deed made by a master in accordance with the decree, is firmly established....

This doctrine is entirely consistent with the provision of the Constitution of the United States, which requires a judgment in any state to be given full faith and credit in the courts of every other state. This provision does not extend the jurisdiction of the courts of one state to property situated in another, but only makes the judgment rendered conclusive on the merits of the claim or subject-matter of the suit....

Plaintiff seems to contend for a greater efficacy for a decree in equity affecting real property than is given to a judgment at law for the recovery of money simply. The case of Burnley v. Stevenson, 24 Ohio St. 474, in a sense sustains her.... [In that case, action was brought in an Ohio court to recover possession of local realty. By way of defense, the defendant relied upon a deed executed by a master commissioner in Kentucky in pursuance of a decree for specific performance rendered by a court of the latter state. The court found for the defendant, holding that, although the commissioner's deed must "be regarded as a nullity," it would recognize the validity of the actual decree "in so far as it determined the equitable rights of the parties in the land in controversy. In our judgment, the parties, and those holding under them with notice are still bound thereby."]

... There is ... much temptation in the facts of this case to follow the ruling of the supreme court of Ohio ... but, as the ruling of the [Nebraska] court, that the decree in Washington gave no such equities as could be recognized in Nebraska as justifying an action to quiet title, does not offend the Constitution of the United States, we are constrained to affirm its judgment.

So ordered.

■ JUSTICE HARLAN and JUSTICE BREWER dissent.

■ JUSTICE HOLMES, concurring specially:

I am not prepared to dissent from the judgment of the court, but my reasons are different from those that have been stated.

The real question concerns the effect of the Washington decree. As between the parties to it, that decree established in Washington a personal obligation of the husband to convey to his former wife. A personal obligation goes with the person. If the husband had made a contract, valid by the law of Washington, to do the same thing, I think there is no doubt that the contract would have been binding in Nebraska. Ex parte Pollard, 4 Deacon, Bankr. 27, 40; Polson v. Stewart, 167 Mass. 211. So I conceive that a Washington decree for the specific performance of such a contract would be entitled to full faith and credit as between the parties in Nebraska. But it does not matter to its constitutional effect what the ground of the decree may be, whether a contract or something else. Fauntleroy v. Lum, 210 U.S. 230. (In this case it may have been that the wife contributed equally to the accumulation of the property, and so had an equitable claim.) A personal decree is equally within the jurisdiction of a court having the person within its power, whatever its ground and whatever it orders the defendant to do. Therefore I think that this decree was entitled to full faith and credit in Nebraska.

But the Nebraska court carefully avoids saying that the decree would not be binding between the original parties, had the husband been before the court. The ground on which it goes is that to allow the judgment to affect the conscience of purchasers would be giving it an effect in rem. It treats the case as standing on the same footing as that of an innocent purchaser. Now, if the court saw fit to deny the effect of a judgment upon privies in title, or if it considered the defendant an innocent purchaser, I do not see what we have to do with its decision, however wrong. I do not see why it is not within the power of the state to do away with equity or with the equitable doctrine as to purchasers with notice if it sees fit. Still less do I see how a mistake as to notice could give us jurisdiction. If the judgment binds the defendant, it is not by its own operation, even with the Constitution behind it, but by the obligation imposed by equity upon a purchaser with notice. The ground of decision below was that there was no such obligation. The decision, even if wrong, did not deny to the Washington decree its full effect. Bagley v. General Fire Extinguisher Co., 212 U.S. 477, 480.

NOTES

1. Does the majority opinion hold that that part of the Washington decree which ordered Fall to convey the Nebraska land to the plaintiff was entirely without extraterritorial effect? Or can the decision be explained on the ground that the plaintiff had misconceived her remedy? For extensive discussion of the powers of the non-situs court and of the decision in Fall v. Eastin, see Eckard v. Eckard, 333 Md. 531, 636 A.2d 455 (1994). Rejecting the argument that the non-situs court lacked subject matter jurisdiction to compel acts with respect to out-of-state land, the court held that an equity court may "by virtue of its power over a person properly before it ... compel him to act in relation to property not within the jurisdiction." 636 A.2d at 462.

2. Suppose that the defendant Fall had executed a conveyance to the Nebraska land in order to avoid punishment for contempt at the hands of the Washington court. Such deeds have generally been held effective in passing title to the land. Phillips v. Phillips, 224 Ark. 225, 272 S.W.2d 433 (1954) (defendant signed deed in order to be released from jail); Deschenes v. Tallman, 248 N.Y. 33, 161 N.E. 321 (1928); Scoles & Hay, Conflict of Laws 352 (2nd ed. 1992). Why should a title deed rendered under duress be valid if the court that exercised the duress could not itself have transferred title?

3. Restatement, Second, Conflict of Laws § 102, Comment b * reads:

b. *Recognition.* A valid foreign judgment that orders the doing of an act other than the payment of money or that enjoins the doing of an act will be given the same degree of recognition as any other judgment (see §§ 93–97). This means that such a judgment will be given the same res judicata effect with respect to the persons, the subject matter of the action and the issues involved that it has in the state of rendition.... So, if a court of State X finds that the defendant has broken his contract to convey land in State Y and orders the defendant to make the conveyance, a court of State Y, where the enforcement of the X judgment is sought, must give conclusive effect to the finding of the X court that the defendant has been guilty of breach of contract. Similarly if a court of State X finds that the defendant has procured a judgment in State Y by fraud and enjoins its enforcement, a court of State Y must give conclusive effect to the finding of the X court that the judgment was procured by fraud.

4. *Enforcement.* The great majority of cases dealing with the enforcement of equity decrees that order the doing of an act other than the payment of money have involved an order to convey land in F–2. At one time it was generally believed that such decrees would not be enforced extraterritorially. This conclusion was based on the ground either that (a) since equity decrees are discretionary in nature, F–2 could not be required to accept the relief that F–1 had found appropriate and (b) in any event no action was available for the enforcement of a foreign judgment other than one in the nature of debt. These notions were found baseless in Currie, Full Faith and Credit to Foreign Land Decrees, 21 U.Chi.L.Rev. 620 (1964). He concluded that an action could be brought in F–2 to establish the F–1 decree as one of F–2 or for a judgment declaring the interests of the parties in the F–2 land in light of the F–1 decree or, if neither of these alternatives was available, an action on the original claim with the F–2 court being required to give res judicata effect to the findings made in F–1. See also Scoles and Hay, Conflict of Laws 964–968 (2nd ed. 1992); Hay, The Situs Rule in European and American Conflicts Law, in Hay & Hoeflich, eds., Property Law and Legal Education, Essays in Honor of John E. Cribbet 109 (1988).

5. Most of the recent cases have enforced foreign equity decrees ordering the conveyance of local land. See Andre v. Morrow, 106 Idaho 455, 680 P.2d 1355 (1984). Varone v. Varone, 359 F.2d 769 (7th Cir.1966); Cuevas v. Cuevas, 191 So.2d 843 (Miss.1966); Higginbotham v. Higginbotham, 92 N.J.Super. 18, 222 A.2d 120 (1966). In Weesner v. Weesner, 168 Neb. 346, 95 N.W.2d 682 (1959), the Nebraska court did what it had refused to do in Fall v. Eastin, namely, entertained a cross-petition to quiet title to Nebraska land on the basis of an F–1 decree that ordered conveyance of this land. The F–1 defendant was subjected to the personal jurisdiction of the court in F–2. See also Day v. Wiswall, 11 Ariz.App. 306, 464 P.2d 626 (1970).

6. As to the recognition of decisions with respect to *interests* in land, see Hay, supra note 4; Note, Modernizing the Situs Rule for Real Property Conflicts, 65 Tex.L.Rev. 585 (1987); Weintraub, Commentary on the Conflict of Laws 428 (3d ed. 1986). In Matter of Estate of Mack, 373 N.W.2d 97 (Iowa 1985), the court recognized a Missouri divorce court's decree setting off, to the former wife, a farm in the Iowa forum. Even though the former husband had not been ordered to

* Quoted with the permission of the copyright owner, The American Law Institute.

convey and the former wife had taken no steps to have the Iowa land put in her name, the court adopted the "preferable" view of Section 43 of the Restatement, Second, Conflict of Laws, that a "judgment in an action determining interests in real or personal property conclusively determines the claims of the parties ..."

Yarborough v. Yarborough
Supreme Court of the United States, 1933.
290 U.S. 202, 54 S.Ct. 181, 78 L.Ed. 269, 90 A.L.R. 924.

■ JUSTICE BRANDEIS delivered the opinion of the Court.

On August 10, 1930, Sadie Yarborough, then 16 years of age, was living with her maternal grandfather, R.D. Blowers, at Spartanburg, South Carolina. Suing by him as guardian ad litem, she brought this action in a court of that State to require her father, W.A. Yarborough, a resident of Atlanta, Georgia, to make provision for her education and maintenance. She alleged "that she is now ready for college and is without funds and, unless the defendant makes provision for her, will be denied the necessities of life and an education, and will be dependent upon the charity of others." Jurisdiction was obtained by attachment of defendant's property. Later he was served personally within South Carolina.

In bar of the action, W.A. Yarborough set up, among other defences, a judgment entered in 1929 by the Superior Court of Fulton County, Georgia, in a suit for divorce brought by him against Sadie's mother. He alleged that by the judgment the amount thereafter to be paid by him for Sadie's education and maintenance had been determined; that the sum so fixed had been paid; and that the judgment had been fully satisfied by him. He claimed that in Georgia the judgment was conclusive of the matter here in controversy; that having been satisfied, it relieved him, under the Georgia law, of all obligation to provide for the education and maintenance of their minor child; and that the full faith and credit clause of the Federal Constitution (Art. 4, sec. 1) required the South Carolina court to give to that judgment the same effect in this proceeding which it has, and would have in Georgia. The trial court denied the claim; ordered W.A. Yarborough to pay to the grandfather, as trustee, fifty dollars monthly for Sadie's education and support; and to pay $300 as fees of her counsel. It directed that the property held under the attachment be transferred to R.D. Blowers, trustee, as security for the performance of the order. The judgment was affirmed by the Supreme Court of South Carolina. A petition for rehearing was denied, with opinion. 168 S.C. 46, 166 S.E. 877. This Court granted certiorari. 289 U.S. 718.

For sometime prior to June, 1927, W.A. Yarborough, his wife and their daughter Sadie had lived together at Atlanta, Georgia, where he then was, and ever since has been, domiciled. In that month, Sadie's mother left Atlanta for Hendersonville, N.C., where she remained during the summer. Sadie joined her there, after a short stay at a camp. In September, 1927, while they were at Hendersonville, W.A. Yarborough brought in the Superior Court for Fulton County, at Atlanta, suit against his wife for a total divorce on the ground of mental and physical cruelty.... An order, several times modified, awarded to the wife the custody of Sadie and as temporary alimony, sums "for the support and maintenance of herself and her minor daughter Sadie." Hearings were held from time to time at Atlanta. At some of these, Sadie (and also her grandfather) was personally present. But she was not formally made a party to the litigation; she was not served with process; and no guardian ad litem was appointed for her therein.

"Two concurring verdicts favoring a total divorce to plaintiff having been rendered," a decree of total divorce, with the right in each to remarry, was entered on June 7, 1929; the wife was ordered to pay the costs; and jurisdiction of the case "was retained for the purpose of further enforcement of the orders of the court theretofore passed." Among such orders, was the provision for the maintenance and education of Sadie here relied upon as res judicata....

W.A. Yarborough complied fully with this order.

By the law of Georgia, it is the duty of the father to provide for the maintenance and education of his child until maturity.... In case of total divorce, the court is authorized to make, by its decree, final or permanent provision for the maintenance and education of children during minority, and thus fix the extent of the father's obligation. But even if the decree for total divorce fails to include a provision for the support of minor children, they cannot maintain in their own names, or by guardian ad litem, or by next friend, an independent suit for an allowance for education and maintenance....

[The court found, first, that the Georgia decree was "intended to relieve the father from all further liability to support Sadie"; second, that the decree conformed to Georgia law; and, third that the failure to make the child a formal party to the divorce suit did not destroy the effectiveness of the decree as to her.]

Fourth. It is contended that the order for permanent alimony is not binding upon Sadie because she was not a resident of Georgia at the time it was entered. Being a minor, Sadie's domicile was Georgia, that of her father; and her domicile continued to be in Georgia until entry of the judgment in question. She was not capable by her own act of changing her domicile. Neither the temporary residence in North Carolina at the time the divorce suit was begun, nor her removal with her mother to South Carolina before entry of the judgment, effected a change of Sadie's domicile....

Fifth. The fact that Sadie has become a resident of South Carolina does not impair the finality of the judgment. South Carolina thereby acquired the jurisdiction to determine her status and the incidents of that status. Upon residents of that State it could impose duties for her benefit. Doubtless, it might have imposed upon her grandfather who was resident there a duty to support Sadie. But the mere fact of Sadie's residence in South Carolina does not give that State the power to impose such a duty upon the father who is not a resident and who long has been domiciled in Georgia. He has fulfilled the duty which he owes her by the law of his domicile and the judgment of its court. Upon that judgment he is entitled to rely. It was settled by Sistare v. Sistare, 218 U.S. 1, that the full faith and credit clause applies to an unalterable decree of alimony for a divorced wife. The clause applies, likewise, to an unalterable decree of alimony for a minor child. We need not consider whether South Carolina would have power to require the father, if he were domiciled there, to make further provision for the support, maintenance, or education of his daughter.

Reversed.

■ JUSTICE STONE, dissenting.

I think the judgment should be affirmed.

The divorce decree of the Georgia court purported to adjudicate finally, both for the present and for the future, the right of a minor child of the marriage to support and maintenance, by directing her father to make a lump sum payment for that purpose. More than two years later, after the minor had become a domiciled resident of South Carolina, and after the sum paid had been exhausted, a court of that State, on the basis of her need as then shown, has rendered a judgment directing further payments for her support out of property of the father in South Carolina, in addition to that already commanded by the Georgia judgment.

For the present purposes we may take it that the Georgia decree, as the statutes and decisions of the State declare, is unalterable and, as pronounced, is effective to govern the rights of the parties in Georgia. But there is nothing in the decree itself, or in the history of the proceedings which led to it to suggest that it was rendered with any purpose or intent to regulate or control the relationship of parent and child, or the duties which flow from it, in places outside the State of Georgia where they might later come to reside.... But if we are to read the decree as though it contained a clause, in terms, restricting the power of any other state, in which the minor might come to reside, to make provision for her support, then, in the absence of some law of Congress requiring it, I am not persuaded that the full faith and credit clause gives sanction to such control by one state of the internal affairs of another.[1] ...

Between the prohibition of the due process clause, acting upon the courts of the state from which such proceedings may be taken, and the mandate of the full faith and credit clause, acting upon the state to which they may be taken, there is an area which federal authority has not occupied. As this Court has often recognized, there are many judgments which need not be given the same force and effect abroad which they have at home, and there are some, though valid in the state where rendered, to which the full faith and credit clause gives no force elsewhere. In the assertion of rights, defined by a judgment of one state, within the territory of another there is often an inescapable conflict of interest of the two

---

1. It may be assumed for present purposes that the child was sufficiently represented in the Georgia proceedings. But the point is doubtful....

states, and there comes a point beyond which the imposition of the will of one state beyond its own borders involves a forbidden infringement of some legitimate domestic interest of the other. That point may vary with the circumstances of the case, and in the absence of provisions more specific than the general terms of the congressional enactment [2] this Court must determine for itself the extent to which one state may qualify or deny rights claimed under proceedings or records of other states....

■ [JUSTICE STONE enumerated the situations in which the Supreme Court had held that the full faith and credit clause does not compel recognition by one state of the public acts, records, and judicial proceedings of a sister state.]

Just as due process of law will not permit a state by its judgment to inflict parties "with a perpetual contractual paralysis" which will prevent them from altering outside the state their contracts or ordinary business relations entered into within it, New York L. Ins. Co. v. Head, supra (234 U.S. 161), so full faith and credit does not command that the obligations attached to a status, because once appropriately imposed by one state, shall be forever placed beyond the control of every other state, without regard to the interest in it and the power of control which the other may later acquire. See Bradford Electric Light Co. v. Clapper, 286 U.S. 145, 157, note 7. Whatever difference there may be between holding that a judgment is invalid under the Fourteenth Amendment because it is "extraterritorial," and in holding that it is not entitled to full faith and credit although it does not infringe the Fourteenth Amendment, is one of degree, or of a difference in circumstances which may prevent the operation of the latter provision of the Constitution. The Georgia judgment with which we are now concerned does not infringe the Fourteenth Amendment, for Georgia had "jurisdiction" of the parties and subject matter at the time its judgment was rendered. The possibility of conflict of the Georgia judgment with the interest of South Carolina first arose when the minor transferred her domicile to South Carolina, long after the Georgia judgment was given.

---

2. The mandatory force of the full faith and credit clause as defined by this Court may be, in some degree not yet fully defined, expanded or contracted by Congress. Much of the confusion and procedural deficiencies which the constitutional provision alone has not avoided may be remedied by legislation. Cook, "Powers of Congress under the Full Faith and Credit Clause," 28 Yale L.J. 421; Corwin, "The Full Faith and Credit Clause," 81 University of Pa.L.Rev. 371; cf. 33 Columbia L.Rev. 854, 866. The constitutional provision giving Congress power to prescribe the effect to be given to acts, records and proceedings would have been quite unnecessary had it not been intended that Congress should have a latitude broader than that given the courts by the full faith and credit clause alone. It was remarked on the floor of the Constitutional Convention that without the extension of power in the legislature, the provision "would amount to nothing more than what now takes place among all Independent Nations." Hunt and Scott, Madison's Reports of the Debates in the Federal Convention of 1787, p. 503. The play which has been afforded for the recognition of local public policy in cases where there is called in question only a statute of another state, as to the effect of which Congress has not legislated, compared with the more restricted scope for local policy where there is a judicial proceeding, as to which Congress has legislated, suggests the Congressional power.

The question presented here is whether the support and maintenance of a minor child, domiciled in South Carolina, is so peculiarly a subject of domestic concern that Georgia law can not impair South Carolina's authority.... The maintenance and support of children domiciled within a state, like their education and custody, is a subject in which government itself is deemed to have a peculiar interest and concern.... The states very generally make some provision from their own resources for the maintenance and support of orphans or destitute children, but in order that children may not become public charges the duty of maintenance is one imposed primarily upon the parents, according to the needs of the child and their ability to meet those needs.... Hence, it is no answer in such a suit that at some earlier time provision was made for the child, which is no longer available or suitable because of his greater needs, or because of the increased financial ability of the parent to provide for them, or that the child may be maintained from other sources....

Even though the Constitution does not deny to Georgia the power to indulge in such a policy for itself, it by no means follows that it gives to Georgia the privilege of prescribing that policy for other states in which the child comes to live.[19] South Carolina has adopted a different policy. It imposes on the father or his property located within the state the duty to support his minor child domiciled there. It enforces the duty by criminal prosecution and also permits suit by the minor child maintained by guardian ad litem. The measure of the duty is the present need of the child and the ability of the parent to provide for it....

The opinion of this Court leaves it uncertain whether it is thought that the Constitution commands that the duty of support prescribed by Georgia, the domicile of the father, shall be dominant over that enjoined by South Carolina, the domicile of the child, in any event, or only after the duty has been defined by a judgment of Georgia.[21] It is attested by eminent authority that the Fourteenth Amendment, at least, does not prevent the state of the child's domicile from imposing the duty ... a view confirmed by the uniform rulings that the father is liable to the criminal process of the state of the child's residence, though before, and at all times during his failure to conform to the duty demanded by that state, he has been domiciled elsewhere. [Citing cases.] The Fourteenth Amendment does not enable a father by the expedient of choosing a domicile other than the state where the child is rightfully domiciled, to avoid the duty which that state may impose for support of his child. The reason seems plain. The locality of the child's residence must see to his welfare.... The conclusion must be the same when the issue is that of the credit to be given the prior Georgia judgment....

---

19. In the custody cases a very similar situation is presented. As conventionally stated the rule has been that the most the full faith and credit clause can require is that the prior ruling shall be deemed conclusive in the absence of an asserted change in circumstances....

21. Cf. Home Ins. Co. v. Dick, 281 U.S. 397, with Kryger v. Wilson, 242 U.S. 171.

... Here the Georgia decree did not end the relationship of parent and child, as a decree of divorce may end the marriage relationship. Had the infant continued to reside in Georgia, and had she sought in the courts of South Carolina to compel the application of property of her father, found there, to her further maintenance and support, full faith and credit to the Georgia decree applied to its own domiciled resident might have required the denial of any relief. [Citing cases.] But when she became a domiciled resident of South Carolina a new interest came into being, the interest of the State of South Carolina as a measure of self preservation to secure the adequate protection and maintenance of helpless members of its own community and its prospective citizens. That interest was distinct from any which Georgia could conclusively regulate or control by its judgment even though rendered while the child was domiciled in Georgia. The present decision extends the operation of the full faith and credit clause beyond its proper function of affording protection to the domestic interests of Georgia and makes it an instrument for encroachment by Georgia upon the domestic concerns of South Carolina.

■ JUSTICE CARDOZO concurs in this opinion.

NOTES

1. Elkind v. Byck, 68 Cal.2d 453, 67 Cal.Rptr. 404, 439 P.2d 316 (1968). In that case, the parties had been divorced in Georgia pursuant to a decree under which the husband paid a lump sum for the maintenance and support of his wife and child. Under the Georgia law, his payment was in full satisfaction of the husband's obligation and no further liability could be imposed upon him. Following the divorce, the wife made her home in New York and the husband moved to California. Thereafter, the wife sought additional support from the husband, and it was held that the California court had power to grant her request. Yarborough was said not to stand in the way "[s]ince that decision was based upon the father's continued domicile and residence in Georgia." In this case, the husband's "substantial relationship" with California "justifies the application of its law of support." The court concluded that the facts of the case served to demonstrate "why the divorce state should not be permitted to determine the welfare of the child for all time and in all states. More than ten years following the divorce, none of the parties appears to have any connection at all with Georgia: the mother and child reside in New York and the father resides in California."

2. RESTATEMENT, SECOND, CONFLICT OF LAWS.*

§ 103. Limitations on Full Faith and Credit

A judgment rendered in one State of the United States need not be recognized or enforced in a sister State if such recognition or enforcement is not required by the national policy of full faith and credit because it would involve an improper interference with important interests of the sister State.

* Quoted with the permission of the copyright owner, The American Law Institute.

3. Section 103 was approved in Thompson v. Thompson, 645 S.W.2d 79 (Mo.App. 1982). In that case, a divorce decree rendered by a Kansas court had ordered the husband to provide child support. By Kansas statute, a parent's obligation to support a child ceases when the child attains eighteen years. Thereafter, all parties moved to Missouri and there the wife sought to compel the husband to support a son who was then over eighteen years old. The Missouri court found for the wife, holding that an exception should be made to the normal command of full faith and credit in order to protect Missouri's "overriding domestic interests." It relied upon Justice Stone's dissent in Yarborough, upon Elkind v. Byck, and upon § 103. Was it necessary for the court to rely upon an exception to full faith and credit to reach the desired result?

4. See generally Reese and Johnson, The Scope of Full Faith and Credit to Judgments, 49 Colum.L.Rev. 153 (1949).

KUBON v. KUBON, 51 Cal.2d 229, 331 P.2d 636 (1958): A controversy between parents over children began in a Nevada proceeding in which the court, with jurisdiction over both parents, gave custody of the two children to the mother, ordered the father to pay $100 a month for child support, and reserved jurisdiction to make further orders as to custody and support. The Nevada court modified its order so as to allow the husband physical custody during the summer vacation. During the vacation while the children were with the father in California, he filed a petition in California seeking appointment of himself as guardian, and the California court issued a temporary restraining order restraining the mother from taking the children from the father's home or custody pending the hearing of the guardianship petition. Nevertheless, the mother took the children from the father's home and carried them back to Nevada with her. The Nevada court then modified its order again, taking away from the father the right to the summer custody of the children but giving him the right of reasonable visitation in Nevada. The father ceased his payments for support when he secured the California restraining order. Ten months later the mother sought a judgment in Nevada for the accrued installments for support, and the Nevada court after notice by mail to the father in California entered a judgment for the accrued installments of $1,000 and attorney's fees. The mother sued on the Nevada judgment in California. She was met by the defense that in taking the children from California she had violated the California restraining order and so was in contempt of the court from which she sought relief. The majority of the Supreme Court of California upheld the defense. A minority were of the opinion the defense was bad.

■ TRAYNOR, J. (dissenting). "It is my opinion that recognition of such defense violates the full faith and credit clause ... The United States Supreme Court has repeatedly held that a state may not vindicate its own policy by refusing enforcement of a sister state judgment for the payment of money on the ground that its recognition would violate the policy of the state where enforcement is sought ... Accordingly, ... we cannot invoke that policy as a rule of procedure to sustain a plea in abatement to a suit on that judgment.... even had the California order such dignity as to compel its recognition in Nevada under the full faith and credit clause, a final judgment entered in disregard of it could not now be denied enforcement here.... Even if we were not constitutionally compelled to reject defendant's plea in abatement based on plaintiff's contempt of the temporary restraining order, we should reject it on its own merits.... The Nevada court did not err in placing the welfare of the children above the desirability of compelling plaintiff to respect the order of the California court."

NOTE

As to the status of custody decrees under full faith and credit, see pp. 887–901, infra.

Magnolia Petroleum Co. v. Hunt
Supreme Court of the United States, 1943.
320 U.S. 430, 64 S.Ct. 208, 88 L.Ed. 149, 150 A.L.R. 413.

Certiorari to the Court of Appeal, First Circuit, of Louisiana.

■ CHIEF JUSTICE STONE delivered the opinion of the Court.

The question for decision is whether, under the full faith and credit clause, Art. IV, § 1 of the Constitution of the United States, an award of compensation for personal injury under the Texas Workmen's Compensation Law, Title 130 of the Revised Civil Statutes of Texas, bars a further recovery of compensation for the same injury under the Louisiana Workmen's Compensation Law, Title 34, Chapter 15 of the Louisiana General Statutes.

Magnolia Petroleum Company, petitioner here, employed respondent in Louisiana as a laborer in connection with the drilling of oil wells. In the course of his employment respondent, a Louisiana resident, went from Louisiana to Texas, and while working there for petitioner on an oil well, he was injured by a falling drill stem. He sought and procured in Texas an award of compensation for his injury under its Workmen's Compensation Law, and petitioner's insurer made payments of compensation as required by the statute and the award. The award became final in accordance with the terms of the Texas statute.

Respondent then brought the present proceeding in the Louisiana District Court to recover compensation for his injury under the Louisiana Workmen's Compensation Law. Petitioner filed exceptions to respondent's petition on the ground that the recovery sought was barred as res judicata by the Texas award which, by virtue of the constitutional command, was entitled in the Louisiana courts to full faith and credit. The District Court overruled the exceptions and gave judgment for the amount of the compensation fixed by the Louisiana statute, after deducting the amount of the Texas payments. The Louisiana Court of Appeal affirmed 10 So.2d 109, and the Supreme Court of Louisiana refused writs of certiorari and review for the reason that it found "no error of law in the judgment complained of." ...

In Texas a compensation award against the employer's insurer ... is explicitly made by statute in lieu of any other recovery for injury to the employee, since Art. 8306, § 3 provides that employees subject to the Act "shall have no right of action against their employer or against any agent, servant or employé of said employer for damages for personal injuries ... but such employés ... shall look for compensation solely to the association [the insurer]." A compensation award which has become final "is entitled to the same faith and credit as a judgment of a court." ...

It does not appear, nor is it contended, that Louisiana more than Texas allows in its own courts a second recovery of compensation for a single injury. The contention is that since Louisiana is better satisfied with the measure of recovery allowed by its own laws, it may deny full faith and credit to the Texas award, which respondent has procured by his election to pursue his remedy in that state. In thus refusing, on the basis of state law and policy, to give effect to the Texas award as a final adjudication of respondent's claim for compensation for his injury suffered in Texas, the Louisiana court ignored the distinction, long recognized and applied by this Court ... between the faith and credit required to be given to judgments and that to which local common and statutory law is entitled under the Constitution and laws of the United States.

In the case of local law, since each of the states of the Union has constitutional authority to make its own law with respect to persons and events within its borders the full faith and credit clause does not ordinarily require it to substitute for its own law the conflicting law of another state, even though that law is of controlling force in the courts of that state with respect to the same persons and events.... It was for this reason that we held that the state of the employer and employee is free to apply its own compensation law to the injury of the employee rather than the law of another state where the injury occurred. Alaska Packers Assn. v. Industrial Accident Comm'n, [294 U.S. 532 at] 544–550. And for like reasons we held also that the state of the place of injury is free to apply its own law to the exclusion of the law of the state of the employer and employee. Pacific Employers Ins. Co. v. Industrial Accident Comm'n, [306 U.S. 493 at] 502–505.

But it does not follow that the employee who has sought and recovered an award of compensation in either state may then have recourse to the laws and courts of the other to recover a second or additional award for the same injury. Where a court must make choice of one of two conflicting statutes of different states and apply it to a cause of action which has not been previously litigated, there can be no plea of res judicata. But when the employee who has recovered compensation for his injury in one state seeks a second recovery in another he may be met by the plea that full faith and credit requires that his demand, which has become res judicata in one state, must be recognized as such in every other.

The full faith and credit clause and the Act of Congress implementing it have, for most purposes, placed a judgment on a different footing from a statute of one state, judicial recognition of which is sought in another....

These consequences flow from the clear purpose of the full faith and credit clause to establish throughout the federal system the salutary principle of the common law that a litigation once pursued to judgment shall be as conclusive of the rights of the parties in every other court as in that where the judgment was rendered, so that a cause of action merged in a judgment in one state is likewise merged in every other. The full faith and credit clause like the commerce clause thus became a nationally unifying force. It altered the status of the several states as independent foreign sovereignties, each free to ignore rights and obligations created under the laws or established by the judicial proceedings of the others, by making each an integral part of a single nation, in which rights judicially established in any part are given nation-wide application.... Because there is a full faith and credit clause a defendant may not a second time challenge the validity of the plaintiff's right which has ripened into a judgment and a plaintiff may not for his single cause of action secure a second or a greater recovery....

We have no occasion to consider what effect would be required to be given to the Texas award if the Texas courts held that an award of compensation in another state would not bar an award in Texas, for ... Texas does not allow such a second recovery. And if the award of compensation in Texas were not res judicata there, full faith and credit would, of course, be no bar to the recovery of an award in another state. Chicago, R.I. & P.R. Co. v. Elder, 270 U.S. 611, 622–623.

Whether the proceeding before the State Industrial Accident Board in Texas be regarded as a "judicial proceeding," or its award as a "record" within the meaning of the full faith and credit clause and the Act of Congress, the result is the same. For judicial proceedings and records of the state are both required to have "such faith and credit given to them in every court within the United States as they have by law or usage in the courts of the State from which they are taken."

The decision of the state court is not supported by the suggestion that the Texas award is not res judicata in Louisiana because respondent's suit there was on a different cause of action. When a state court refuses credit to the judgment of a sister state because of its opinion of the nature of the cause of action or the judgment in which it is merged, an asserted federal right is denied and the sufficiency of the grounds of denial are for this Court to decide.... Respondent's injury in Texas did not give rise to two causes of action merely because recovery in each state is under a different statute, or because each affords a different measure of recovery.... The grounds of recovery are the same in one state as in the other—the injury to the employee in the course of his employment.... Respondent was free to pursue his remedy in either state but, having chosen to seek it in Texas, where the award was res judicata, the full faith and credit clause precludes him from again seeking a remedy in Louisiana upon the same grounds....*

■ JUSTICE DOUGLAS, dissenting.

---

* A concurring opinion by Justice Jackson is omitted.

... We are dealing here with ... a clash between the policies of two sovereign States. The question is not which policy we prefer; it is whether the two conflicting policies can somehow be accommodated. The command of the full faith and credit clause frequently makes a reconciliation of the two interests impossible. One must give way in the larger interest of the federal union. The question in each case is whether as a practical matter there is room for adjustment, consistent with the requirements of full faith and credit....

... If the Texas award had undertaken to adjudicate the rights and duties of the parties under the Louisiana contract of employment, which we are told carries the right to compensation under the Louisiana Act (10 So.2d 109, 112), the result would be quite different. Then the judgment, ... would undertake to regulate the relationship of the parties, or their rights and duties which flow from it, as respects their undertakings in another State.... But there is nothing in the Texas proceeding or in the Texas award to indicate that that was either intended or done. The most charitable construction is that Texas undertook to adjust the rights and duties of the parties and to regulate their relationship only so long as they remained subject to the jurisdiction of Texas.

... But even if the Texas award were less clear than I think it is, I would resolve all doubts against an inference that rights under the Louisiana contract were adjudicated in Texas. Such a course seems to me essential so that the greatest possible accommodations of the interests of the two States, consistent with the requirements of full faith and credit, may be had whether the matter be divorce, workmen's compensation or any other subject on which state policies differ....

■ JUSTICE MURPHY joins in this dissent.

■ JUSTICE BLACK, dissenting:

The respondent Hunt is a resident of Louisiana, employed in that state by the petitioner and sent by the petitioner to do work in Texas. While in Texas he was seriously injured in the course of his employment. Confined to a hospital he was told that he could not recover compensation unless he signed two forms presented to him. As found by the Louisiana trial judge there was printed on each of the forms "in small type" the designation "Industrial Accident Board, Austin, Texas." To get his compensation Hunt signed the forms and the Texas insurer began to pay. Returning to his home in Louisiana Hunt apparently discovered that his interest would be more fully protected under Louisiana law and notified the insurer of an intention to claim under the statute of that state. The insurer immediately stopped payment to him and notified the Texas Board to that effect. Four days later, without any request from Hunt, the Board notified him at his Louisiana home that a hearing would be held in Texas within two and a half weeks "to determine the liability of the insurance company" under Texas law. Hunt did not participate in that proceeding. The Texas Board thereafter made an award to him which, under the law of Texas, was equivalent to a judgment against the insurer. Before the Texas award became final, Hunt, who had declined to accept any money under it, filed suit against his employer in the courts of Louisiana under the Workmen's Compensation Law of Louisiana. He recovered a judgment for a substantially larger sum than had been allowed him under the Texas award, from which the Louisiana court deducted the sum he had already received from the Texas insurer....

As I see it, this case properly involves two separate legal questions: (1) Did Texas intend the award of its Industrial Accident Board against the insurer to bar the right granted the employee by the Louisiana Workmen's Compensation Law to collect from his employer for the same injury the difference between the compensation allowed by Texas and the more generous compensation allowed by Louisiana? (2) Assuming the Texas award was intended to constitute such a bar, does the interest of Louisiana in regulating the employment contracts of its residents nevertheless permit it to grant that larger measure of compensation which as a matter of local policy it believes necessary? The decision of the Court on both of these issues appears to me to be wrong.

Where a state court refuses to recognize the judgment of a sister state as a bar to an asserted cause of action, the full faith and credit clause cannot raise a federal question unless the judgment would have been a bar to a similar suit in that sister state.... Whether Texas intended that its award should bar the employee here from recovering compensation under the Louisiana law is an issue upon which Texas courts have not spoken. In fact, they absolutely refuse to entertain any suits at all based on the Louisiana Workmen's Compensation Law....

In the absence of compelling language this Court should not construe the statutes of Texas in such a manner that grave questions of their constitutionality are raised. Cf. Yarborough v. Yarborough, [290 U.S. at] 213, 214. It is extremely doubtful whether Texas has the power, by any legal device, to preclude a sister state from granting to its own residents employed within its own borders that measure of compensation for occupational injuries which it deems advisable.... I "am not persuaded that the full faith and credit clause gives sanction to such control by one state of the internal affairs of another." Yarborough v. Yarborough, supra, 214.

It is apparently conceded that Louisiana would not have been required to apply the Texas statute had there not been a judgment in the particular case by the Texas tribunal. This freedom of the state to apply its own policy in workmen's compensation cases despite a conflicting statute in the state in which the accident occurs rests on the theory that the state where the workman is hired or is domiciled has a genuine and special interest in the outcome of the litigation.... The argument of state interest is hardly less compelling when Louisiana chooses to reject as decisive of the issues of the case a foreign judgment than when it rejects a foreign statute.

The interest of Texas in providing compensation for an injured employee who like respondent was only temporarily employed in the state is not the same as that of Louisiana where the respondent was domiciled and where the contract of employment was made. Someone has to take care of an individual who has received, as has respondent, an injury which permanently disables him from performance of his work.... If it chooses to be more generous to injured workmen than Texas, no Constitutional issue is presented....

Today's decision is flatly in conflict with accepted law and practice. The Restatement of Conflict of Laws, sec. 403 states categorically that an "award already had under the Workmen's Compensation Act of another state will not bar a proceeding under an Applicable Act, but the amount paid on a prior award in another state will be credited on the second award," and one of the foremost studies of workmen's compensation states the same rule.

... There should be no Constitutional barrier preventing a state in effect from increasing the workmen's compensation award of another state in a case in which it has jurisdiction over the participants and the social responsibility for the results. Where two states both have a legitimate interest in the outcome of workmen's compensation litigation, the question of whether the second state which considers the case should abide by the decision of the first is a question of policy which should be decided by the state legislatures and courts.... State laws vary, and uniformity is not the highest value in the law of workmen's compensation....

■ JUSTICE DOUGLAS, JUSTICE MURPHY, and JUSTICE RUTLEDGE concur in this opinion.

Industrial Commission of Wisconsin v. McCartin

Supreme Court of the United States, 1947.
330 U.S. 622, 67 S.Ct. 886, 91 L.Ed. 1140, 169 A.L.R. 1179.

[Kopp and McCartin were both Illinois residents. Pursuant to a contract made in Illinois, Kopp worked for McCartin on a building job in Wisconsin and there suffered an eye injury in the course of his employment. Kopp sought workmen's compensation in both Illinois and Wisconsin. The Illinois award, which was the first to be handed down, provided that it "does not affect any rights" which Kopp might have under the Workmen's Compensation Statute of Wisconsin. Thereafter, the Wisconsin Commission gave Kopp an additional award but on appeal the Wisconsin courts set aside the award on the authority of the Magnolia decision. The Supreme Court granted certiorari.]

■ JUSTICE MURPHY delivered the opinion of the Court....

If it were apparent that the Illinois award was intended to be final and conclusive of all the employee's rights against the employer and the insurer growing out of the injury, the decision in the Magnolia Petroleum Co. case would be controlling here....

But there is nothing in the [Illinois award or in the underlying] statute or in the decisions thereunder to indicate that it was designed to preclude any recovery by proceedings brought in another state for injuries received there in the course of an Illinois employment.... And in light of the rule that workmen's compensation laws are to be liberally construed in furtherance of the purpose for which they were enacted ... we should not readily interpret such a statute so as to cut off an employee's right to sue under other legislation passed for his benefit. Only some unmistakable language by a state legislature or judiciary would warrant our accepting such a construction....

We need not rest our decision, however, solely upon the absence of any provision or construction of the Illinois Workmen's Compensation Act forbidding an employee from seeking alternative or additional relief under the laws of another state. There is even stronger evidence that the employee is free to ask for additional compensation in Wisconsin....

Here the employer and the employee entered into a settlement contract fixing the amount of compensation to which the employee was entitled under the Illinois statute....

One of the provisions in the settlement contract which became the award was the statement that "This settlement does not affect any rights that applicant may have under the Workmen's Compensation Act of the State of Wisconsin." That statement was made a part of the contract at the request of the employee, who had been informed by the Wisconsin Commission that he was entitled to claim an additional amount of compensation in Wisconsin after recovering in Illinois....

This contract provision saving the rights of the employee in Wisconsin thus became part of the Illinois award.... [And] when the reservation in this award is read against the background of the Illinois Workmen's Compensation Act, it becomes clear that the reservation spells out what we believe to be implicit in that Act—namely, that an Illinois workmen's compensation award of the type here involved does not foreclose an additional award under the laws of another state....

Since this Illinois award is final and conclusive only as to rights arising in Illinois, Wisconsin is free under the full faith and credit clause to grant an award of compensation in accord with its own laws. Magnolia Petroleum Co. v. Hunt, supra, thus does not control this case.

Reversed.

■ JUSTICE RUTLEDGE concurs in the result.

NOTES

1. Suppose that a contract made in State X is by its terms to be performed in State Y. Under their respective conflict of laws rules, the courts of State X look to the law of the place of making to determine the validity of a contract, those of State Y to that of the place of performance; the particular contract in question would be invalid under the local law of State X but valid under that of State Y. Suppose further that the plaintiff, domiciled in State Y, brings suit for breach of the contract in State X and loses. Does the existence of this judgment preclude him from thereafter pressing his claim in State Y even though he would almost certainly have won if he had originally brought suit in that state? If the answer to this question is in the affirmative, does it also follow that the result reached by the majority in the Magnolia case was correct?

2. Semler v. Psychiatric Institute of Washington, D.C., 575 F.2d 922 (D.C.Cir. 1978). The plaintiff's decedent had been murdered in Virginia by a person who had been placed by the defendant Psychiatric Institute in a generally unsupervised outpatient program. The plaintiff initially brought suit in Virginia and recovered $25,000 under that state's wrongful death act. She then sought recovery in the District of Columbia under the District's survival act. Held that full faith and credit required that the second suit be barred by the Virginia judgment. "Under District of Columbia law, negligent conduct resulting in death gives rise to two independent rights of action, one under the Wrongful Death Act and the other under the Survival Act." On the other hand, the Virginia Wrongful Death Act provides the "exclusive right of action in wrongful death cases" and "exists in lieu of an action based on the survival of the deceased's original claim." The court concluded that initially the plaintiff could have brought her action in either Virginia or the District of Columbia and that presumably a greater recovery for the death could have been obtained under District of Columbia law than under that of Virginia. "Either state could have properly applied its law in the first instance. But having elected to seek her remedy in Virginia, where the [effect of the judgment was to bar any further recovery for the wrongful death], the full faith and credit clause precludes her from again seeking a remedy in the District of Columbia upon the same grounds."

3. Compare Ellis v. Garwood, 168 Ohio St. 241, 152 N.E.2d 100 (1958), where the decedent employee resided and was employed in New York. While driving in Ohio on business, with the defendant, another employee, the decedent was killed. The plaintiff, his wife, received workmen's compensation benefits under the New York statute, which, under New York law, precludes any recovery against a fellow employee. The Ohio court held that the action in Ohio could be maintained. The court relied heavily on the fact that the injury occurred in Ohio, and was thus subject to Ohio law.

Thomas v. Washington Gas Light Co.

Supreme Court of the United States, 1980.
448 U.S. 261, 100 S.Ct. 2647, 65 L.Ed.2d 757.

■ JUSTICE STEVENS announced the judgment of the Court and delivered an opinion in which JUSTICE BRENNAN, JUSTICE STEWART, and JUSTICE BLACKMUN join....

Petitioner is a resident of the District of Columbia and was hired by respondent in the District of Columbia. During the year that he was employed by respondent, he worked primarily in the District but also worked in Virginia and Maryland. He sustained a back injury while at work in Arlington, Va., on January 22, 1971. Two weeks later he entered into an "Industrial Commission of Virginia Memorandum of Agreement as to Payment of Compensation" providing for benefits of $62 per week....

In 1974, petitioner notified the Department of Labor of his intention to seek compensation under the District of Columbia Act. Respondent opposed the claim primarily on the ground that since, as a matter of Virginia law, the Virginia award excluded any other recovery "at common law or otherwise" on account of the injury in Virginia, the District of Columbia's obligation to give that award full faith and credit precluded a second, supplemental award in the District.

[A second award granted the petitioner in administrative proceedings in the District of Columbia was reversed by the United States Court of Appeals. This judgment, however, was reversed by the Supreme Court.]

I

Respondent contends that the District of Columbia was without power to award petitioner additional compensation because of the Full Faith and Credit Clause of the Constitution or, more precisely, because of the federal statute implementing that Clause. An analysis of this contention must begin with two decisions from the 1940's that are almost directly on point: Magnolia Petroleum Co. v. Hunt and Industrial Commission of Wisconsin v. McCartin.

[Justice Stevens here reviewed the Magnolia and McCartin decisions]

[In its *McCartin*] opinion, the Court ... stated that "[o]nly some unmistakable language by a state legislature or judiciary would warrant our accepting ... a construction" that a workmen's compensation statute "is designed to preclude any recovery by proceedings brought in another state." Id., at 627–628....

The Virginia Workmen's Compensation Act ... contains no "unmistakable language" directed at precluding a supplemental compensation award in another State.... Consequently, *McCartin* by its terms, rather than the earlier *Magnolia* decision, is controlling as between the two precedents....

II

We cannot fail to observe that, in the Court's haste to retreat from *Magnolia*, it fashioned a rule that clashes with normally accepted full faith and credit principles. It has long been the law that "the judgment of a state court should have the same credit, validity, and effect, in every other court in the United States, which it had in the state where it was pronounced." Hampton v. McConnel, 3 Wheat. 234, 235 (Marshall, C.J.)....

The *McCartin* rule, however, focusing as it does on the extraterritorial intent of the rendering State, is fundamentally different. It authorizes a State, by drafting or construing its legislation in "unmistakable language," directly to determine the extraterritorial effect of its workmen's compensation awards....

[This] rule represents an unwarranted delegation to the States of this Court's responsibility for the final arbitration of full faith and credit questions.[15] ... To vest the power of determining the extraterritorial

---

15. See ... Reese and Johnson. The Scope of Full Faith and Credit to Judgment, 49 Colum.L.Rev. 153, 161–162 (1949) (hereinafter Reese and Johnson):

effect of a State's own laws and judgments in the State itself risks the very kind of parochial entrenchment on the interests of other States that it was the purpose of the Full Faith and Credit Clause and other provisions of Art. IV of the Constitution to prevent....

Thus, a re-examination of *McCartin's* unmistakable language test reinforces our tentative conclusion that it does not provide an acceptable basis on which to distinguish *Magnolia*. But if we reject that test, we must decide whether to overrule either *Magnolia* or *McCartin*....

III

... It is ... appropriate to begin the inquiry by considering whether a rule that permits, or a rule that forecloses, successive workmen's compensation awards is more consistent with settled practice. The answer to this question is pellucidly clear.

It should first be noted that *Magnolia,* by only the slimmest majority, ... effected a dramatic change in the law that had previously prevailed throughout the United States.... Of greater importance is the fact that as a practical matter the "unmistakable language" rule of construction announced in *McCartin* left only the narrowest area in which *Magnolia* could have any further precedential value. For the exclusivity language in the Illinois Act construed in *McCartin* was typical of most state workmen's compensation laws. Consequently, it was immediately recognized that *Magnolia* no longer had any significant practical impact. Moreover, since a state legislature seldom focuses on the extraterritorial effect of its enactments,[21] and since a state court has even less occasion to consider whether an award under its State's law is intended to preclude a supplemental award under another State's workmen's compensation act, the probability that any State would thereafter announce a new rule against supplemental awards in other States was extremely remote. As a matter of fact,

"Full faith and credit is a national policy, not a state policy. Its purpose is not merely to demand respect from one state for another, but rather to give us the benefits of a unified nation by altering the status of otherwise 'independent, sovereign states.' Hence it is for federal law, not state law, to prescribe the measure of credit which one state shall give to another's judgment. In this regard, it is interesting to note that in dealing with full faith and credit to statutes the Supreme Court in recent years has accorded no weight to language which purported to give a particular statute extraterritorial effect. There is every reason why a similar attitude should be taken with respect to judgments."

. . .

21. Apparently only Nevada's workmen's compensation act contains the unmistakable language required under the *McCartin* rule. Nev.Rev.Stat. § 616.525 (1979) provides in part:

"... [I]f an employee who has been hired or is regularly employed in this state receives personal injury by accident arising out of and in the course of such employment outside this state, and he ... accepts any compensation or benefits under the provisions of this chapter, the acceptance of such compensation shall constitute a waiver by such employee ... of all rights and remedies against the employer at common law *or given under the laws of any other state,* and shall further constitute a full and complete release of such employer from any and all liability arising from such injury...." (Emphasis added.) ...

subsequent cases in the state courts have overwhelmingly followed *McCartin* and permitted successive state workmen's compensation awards....

IV

Three different state interests are affected by the potential conflict between Virginia and the District of Columbia. Virginia has a valid interest in placing a limit on the potential liability of companies that transact business within its borders. Both jurisdictions have a valid interest in the welfare of the injured employee—Virginia because the injury occurred within that State, and the District because the injured party was employed and resided there. And finally, Virginia has an interest in having the integrity of its formal determinations of contested issues respected by other sovereigns.

. . .

It is ... perfectly clear that petitioner could have sought a compensation award in the first instance either in Virginia, the State in which the injury occurred ... or in the District of Columbia, where petitioner resided, his employer was principally located and the employment relation was formed ... Thus ... respondent and its insurer would have had to measure their potential liability exposure by the more generous of the two workmen's compensation schemes in any event. It follows that a State's interest in limiting the potential liability of businesses within the State is not of controlling importance.

It is also manifest that the interest in providing adequate compensation to the injured worker would be fully served by the allowance of successive awards. In this respect the two jurisdictions share a common interest and there is no danger of significant conflict.

The ultimate issue, therefore, is whether Virginia's interest in the integrity of its tribunal's determinations forecloses a second proceeding to obtain a supplemental award in the District of Columbia....

We are ... persuaded that ... the proposition [set forth in *Magnolia*] that workmen's compensation awards stand on the same footing as court judgments was unwarranted. To be sure ... the factfindings of state administrative tribunals are entitled to the same res judicata effect in the second State as findings by a court. But the critical differences between a court of general jurisdiction and an administrative agency with limited statutory authority forecloses the conclusion that constitutional rules applicable to court judgments are necessarily applicable to workmen's compensation awards.

A final judgment entered by a court of general jurisdiction normally establishes not only the measure of the plaintiff's rights but also the limits of the defendant's liability. A traditional application of res judicata principles enables either party to claim the benefit of the judgment insofar as it resolved issues the court had jurisdiction to decide. Although a Virginia court is free to recognize the perhaps paramount interests of another State by choosing to apply that State's law in a particular case, the Industrial

Commission of Virginia does not have that power. Its jurisdiction is limited to questions arising under the Virginia Workmen's Compensation Act.... Typically, a workmen's compensation tribunal may only apply its own State's law.... The Virginia Commission could and did establish the full measure of petitioner's rights under Virginia law, but it neither could nor purported to determine his rights under the law of the District of Columbia. Full faith and credit must be given to the determination that the Virginia Commission had the authority to make; but by a parity of reasoning, full faith and credit need not be given to determinations that it had no power to make. Since it was not requested, and had no authority, to pass on petitioner's rights under District of Columbia law, there can be no constitutional objection to a fresh adjudication of those rights....

... whether or not the worker has sought an award from the less generous jurisdiction in the first instance, the vindication of that State's interest in placing a ceiling on employers' liability would inevitably impinge upon the substantial interests of the second jurisdiction in the welfare and subsistence of disabled workers—interests that a court of general jurisdiction might consider, but which must be ignored by the Virginia Industrial Commission....

We simply conclude that the substantial interests of the second State in these circumstances should not be overridden by another State through an unnecessarily aggressive application of the Full Faith and Credit Clause, as was implicitly recognized at the time of *McCartin*.

... The Full Faith and Credit Clause should not be construed to preclude successive workmen's compensation awards. Accordingly, Magnolia Petroleum Co. v. Hunt should be overruled.

The judgment of the Court of Appeals is reversed.

■ JUSTICE WHITE, with whom THE CHIEF JUSTICE and JUSTICE POWELL join, concurring in the judgment.

... Although the plurality argues strenuously that the rule of today's decision is limited to awards by state workmen's compensation boards, it seems to me that the underlying rationale goes much further....

The plurality contends that unlike courts of general jurisdiction, workmen's compensation tribunals generally have no power to apply the law of another State and thus cannot determine the rights of the parties thereunder.... Yet I see no reason why a judgment should not be entitled to full res judicata effect under the Full Faith and Credit Clause merely because the rendering tribunal was obligated to apply the law of the forum—provided, of course, as was certainly the case here, that the forum could constitutionally apply its law. The plurality's analysis seems to grant state legislatures the power to delimit the scope of a cause of action for federal full faith and credit purposes merely by enacting choice of law rules binding on the State's workmen's compensation tribunals....

As a matter of logic, the plurality's analysis would seemingly apply to many everyday tort actions. I see no difference for full faith and credit purposes between a statute which lays down a forum-favoring choice of law rule and a common-law doctrine stating the same principle. Hence when a court, having power in the abstract to apply the law of another State, determines by application of the forum's choice of law rules to apply the substantive law of the forum, I would think that under the plurality's analysis the judgment would not determine rights arising under the law of some other State. Suppose, for example, that in a wrongful death action the court enters judgment on liability against the defendant, and determines to apply the law of the forum which sets a limit on the recovery allowed. The plurality's analysis would seem to permit the plaintiff to obtain a subsequent judgment in a second forum for damages exceeding the first forum's liability limit....

Perhaps the major purpose of the Full Faith and Credit Clause is to act as a nationally unifying force.... The plurality's rationale would substantially undercut that function. When a former judgment is set up as a defense under the Full Faith and Credit Clause, the court would be obliged to balance the various state interests involved. But the State of the second forum is not a neutral party to this balance. There seems to be a substantial danger—not presented by the firmer rule of res judicata—that the court in evaluating a full faith and credit defense would give controlling weight to its own parochial interests in concluding that the judgment of the first forum is not res judicata in the subsequent suit....

[Justice White concluded that he would not overrule either *Magnolia* or *McCartin,* although, in his opinion, "*Magnolia* states the sounder doctrine" and *McCartin* rests "on questionable foundations." *McCartin,* however, had been on the books for over thirty years and had been widely interpreted as substantially limiting *Magnolia. McCartin* would clearly permit a second award in the instant case, because the Virginia Workmen's Compensation Act lacked the "unmistakable language" which *McCartin* requires if a workers' compensation award is to preclude a further award in a second state.]

■ JUSTICE REHNQUIST, with whom JUSTICE MARSHALL joins, dissenting....

. . .

One might suppose that, having destroyed McCartin's ratio decidendi, the plurality would return to the eminently defensible position adopted in Magnolia. But such is not the case....

[Justice Rehnquist concluded that a balancing of state interests as done by Justice Stevens in his plurality opinion could not properly be used in determining the respect owed under full faith and credit to sister-state judgments. Such a balancing would, however, be appropriate in determining questions of constitutional control of choice of law.]

NOTES

1. Pettus v. American Airlines, Inc., 587 F.2d 627 (4th Cir.1978). Pettus, an employee of American Airlines, sustained injury in Virginia while acting in the scope of his employment. He was awarded benefits under the Virginia Workmen's

Compensation Act, but these benefits were terminated following a finding that he had unjustifiably refused to undergo surgery in order to correct his ailment. Pettus then sought and was awarded compensation for the same injury under the District of Columbia Workmen's Compensation Act. On appeal, this latter award was reversed on grounds of full faith and credit and res judicata. The District of Columbia also provides for the termination of benefits if the employee unreasonably refuses to undergo surgery. Should the outcome have been different if the District of Columbia Act had not contained that provision? Would a different result be reached today in the light of the Thomas case?

2. *Pettus* was strongly questioned in Director, Office of Wkrs' Comp., Etc. v. National Van Lines, Inc., 613 F.2d 972 (D.C.Cir.1979).

3. For a discussion of whether a balancing of state interests is appropriate in the case of full faith and credit to judgments, see Sterk, Full Faith and Credit, More or Less, to Judgments: Doubts About Washington Gas Light Co. v. Thomas, 69 Geo.L.J. 1329 (1981).

SECTION 4. DEFENSES

A. NATURE OF THE ORIGINAL PROCEEDINGS

A prerequisite to recognition of a judgment both at common law and under the full faith and credit clause is that it be rendered in the course of proper judicial proceedings. Such proceedings may be said to comprehend all action taken in the name of a state by a duly authorized representative or representatives in the settlement of an individual controversy. However, it has been held that a judgment obtained by confession under a warrant of attorney is not a "judicial proceeding" within the meaning of full faith and credit. Atlas Credit Corporation v. Ezrine, 25 N.Y.2d 219, 303 N.Y.S.2d 382, 250 N.E.2d 474 (1969). Although a state ordinarily exercises judicial jurisdiction through its courts, it may also do so, if it sees fit, through its legislature and its executive and administrative bodies as well. A decision rendered by an administrative tribunal in the course of its judicial functions is entitled to full faith and credit (Magnolia Petroleum Co. v. Hunt, p. 266, supra; City of New York v. Shapiro, p. 309, note (1), infra, and so too is an arbitration award which is dignified in the state of rendition with the status of a judgment. Wernwag v. Pawling, 5 G. & J. 500 (Md.1833)). A divorce granted by the Danish king personally to two of his subjects has also been recognized as a judgment in this country. Sorenson v. Sorenson, 122 Misc. 196, 202 N.Y.S. 620 (1924), affirmed 219 App.Div. 344, 220 N.Y.S. 242 (1927). See Note, 53 Minn.L.Rev. 612 (1969). See also A.I. Credit Corp. v. Liebman, 791 F.Supp. 427 (S.D.N.Y.1992) questioning the continued validity of *Atlas Credit.*

On the other hand, the mere fact that something is termed a "judgment" by the state of rendition does not entitle it to full faith and credit as such. Thus, for example, the constitutional protection was denied to a commissioner's report appraising the value of property for probate purposes even though the state in which the report was filed denominated it as a judgment and treated it as binding unless appealed from (Taylor v.

Barron, 30 N.H. 78 (1855)) and to a bond given in stay of execution which under the law of F–1 had the effect of a judgment confessed if forfeited. Foote v. Newell, 29 Mo. 400 (1860).

NOTES

1. In the European Union, the drafters of the Brussels Convention, supra p. 225, faced the problem of defining "judgment" broadly enough to ensure wide recognition of judicial or equivalent acts of courts of member states. Art. 25 accordingly now provides that "judgment" includes *any* judicial determination, however labelled. The provision lists a number of examples, including orders of execution and decisions as to court costs. Art. V(a) of the 1968 Protocol ([1989] Official Journal EC No. L285, 1) specifically clarifies that, for purposes of support decrees, the term "courts" also encompasses Danish administrative agencies. Art. 24 provides that interlocutory measures of relief of national law shall be available to all litigants of EU states. A result of these provisions is, for instance, that Germany is obligated to recognize non-final decrees of other EU states when its national law (see §§ 722, 723, 328 Code of Civil Procedure)—still in effect with respect to nonmember states—presupposes that the foreign judgment sought to be recognized and enforced is final. Case law of the European Court has restricted "judgments" entitled to recognition and enforcement under Art. 25 to those that issued in an adversary proceeding. Case 125/79, Denilauler v. SNC Couchet Freres, [1980] ECR 1553, [1981] CMLR 62. An English decision goes further: interlocutory decisions obtained ex parte are not entitled to recognition even if the party affected had an opportunity to seek its stay or reversal but failed to avail itself of this opportunity. EMI Records, Ltd. v. Modern Music GmbH, [1992] 1 All E.R. 616 (Q.B.). This means that an English "Anton Piller Order," supra p. ___, may be sought and obtained ex parte in England by another EU litigant but that the Order is not necessarily entitled to recognition and enforcement in other EU states.

2. The fact that the rendering court committed error, either of fact or of law, is not an adequate reason for a failure to recognize the judgment either under full faith and credit or at common law. See in this regard Milliken v. Meyer, 311 U.S. 457 (1940) (p. 42, supra) where a Colorado judgment was reversed for failure to give full faith and credit to a Wyoming decree despite the unrebutted contention that there was "an irreconcilable contradiction between the findings [of the Wyoming court] and the decree." Likewise an English court has enforced a French judgment even though the latter was based upon a misinterpretation of English law. Godard v. Gray, L.R., 6 Q.B. 139 (1870). In effect, these rulings reject, as do legal systems generally today, the notion of *"révision au fond"*, supra p. 225, Note 4 whereby the second court would judge the correctness of the first court's determinations of law.

3. A judgment, of course, is not entitled to recognition or enforcement either at common law or under full faith and credit if the rendering court lacked jurisdiction or if the defendant was not given reasonable notice and a reasonable opportunity to be heard. Schibsby v. Westenholz, L.R. 6 Q.B. 155 (1870) (p. 35, supra); Pennoyer v. Neff, 95 U.S. 714 (1878) (p. 45, supra); cf. Mullane v. Central Hanover Bank & Trust Co., 339 U.S. 306 (1950) (p. 160, supra). Where is the line between prohibited review of another court's findings of law and fact (*"révision au fond"*) and a finding that the first court lacked jurisdiction so that its determination is not entitled to recognition for that reason? Under the Brussels Convention, even review of the first court's jurisdiction is generally not allowed. Exceptions are judgments in consumer and insurance transactions or when the Convention provides for the exclusive jurisdiction of a specified court. In these cases, the second court may review the first court's jurisdiction but is bound by that court's determinations of the underlying facts. Art. 28(2). However, a judgment is not entitled to recognition at all when the defendant, who did not submit the rendering court's jurisdiction, did not receive the documents commencing suit or did not receive them in sufficient time to prepare a defense. Art. 27, No. 2. Does American law reach a similar result? See Adam v. Saenger, immediately following, *Baldwin,* infra p. 284, and *Treinies,* infra p. 286.

Adam v. Saenger

Supreme Court of the United States, 1938.
303 U.S. 59, 58 S.Ct. 454, 82 L.Ed. 649.

■ JUSTICE STONE delivered the opinion of the Court.

The question for decision is whether the action, in this case, of the Texas state courts, in dismissing a suit founded upon a judgment of the Supreme Court of California, denied to the judgment the faith and credit which the Constitution, article 4, § 1, commands.

Petitioner, as assignee of a California judgment against the Beaumont Export & Import Company, a Texas corporation, brought the present suit in the Texas state district court against respondents, directors of the corporation acting as its trustees in dissolution, and against its stockholders as transferees of corporate assets, to collect the judgment....

It appears that the corporation brought suit in the superior court of California, a court of general jurisdiction, against Montes, petitioner's predecessor in interest, to recover a money judgment for goods sold and delivered. Thereupon Montes, following what is alleged to be the California practice, with leave of the court brought a cross-action against the corporation, by service of a cross-complaint upon the corporation's attorney of record in the pending suit, to recover for the conversion of chattels. Judgment in the cross-action, taken by default, was followed by dismissal of the corporation's suit and is the judgment which is the subject of the present suit....

The trial court sustained a general demurrer to the complaint and gave judgment dismissing the cause, which the Texas Court of Civil Appeals affirmed, 101 S.W.2d 1046. Petition to the Texas Supreme Court for a writ of error was denied for want of jurisdiction....

The Texas Court of Civil Appeals rested its decision on a single ground, want of jurisdiction of the California court over the corporation in the cross-action in which the judgment was rendered. Construing the California statutes and decisions which the complaint set out, it concluded that they did not authorize service of the complaint in the cross-action upon the plaintiff's attorney of record. It held further that in any case as the corporation was not present within the state no jurisdiction could be acquired over it by the substituted service, and the California judgment was consequently without due process and a nullity beyond the protection of the full faith and credit clause. To review these rulings we brought the case here....

Congress has not prescribed the manner in which the legal effect of the judgment and the proceedings on which it is founded in the state where rendered are to be ascertained by the courts of another state. It has left that to the applicable procedure of the courts in which they are drawn in question. Where they are in issue this Court, in the exercise of its appellate jurisdiction to review cases coming to it from state courts, takes judicial notice of the law of the several states to the same extent that such notice is taken by the court from which the appeal is taken....

In the present suit petitioner, in conformity to the state procedure, has set out in his complaint the California statutes and the citations of the decisions of California courts which he contends establish the law of that state that a cross-action in a pending suit may be begun by service of a cross-complaint upon the plaintiff's attorney. The question thus raised upon demurrer for decision by the court is the legal effect in California of the service, and hence of the judgment founded upon it.

Whether the question be regarded as one of fact or more precisely and accurately as a question of law to be determined as are other questions of law ... it is one arising under the Constitution and a statute of the United States which commands that such faith and credit shall be given by every court to the California proceedings "as they have by law or usage" of that state. And since the existence of the federal right turns on the meaning and effect of the California statute, the decision of the Texas court on that point, whether of law or of fact, is reviewable here....

While this Court re-examines such an issue with deference after its determination by a state court, it cannot, if the laws and Constitution of the United States are to be observed, accept as final the decision of the state tribunal as to matters alleged to give rise to the asserted federal right. This is especially the case where the decision is rested, not on local law or matters of fact of the usual type, which are peculiarly within the cognizance of the local courts, but upon the law of another state, as readily determined here as in a state court....

In ruling that the service in the California suit was unauthorized, the Texas Court of Civil Appeals said: "The cross-action was not an ancillary proceeding, but an independent suit in which a final judgment could be rendered without awaiting a decision in the original suit. Farrar v. Steenbergh, 173 Cal. 94, 159 P. 707. It is well settled in this state that a cross-action occupies the attitude of an independent suit and requires service of the cross-action upon the cross-defendant. Harris v. Schlinke, 95 Tex. 88, 65 S.W. 172. This being so, in the absence of a waiver of service, or an appearance by the cross-defendant, personal service on the cross-defendant must be had to confer jurisdiction upon the court to determine the matter and render judgment in the case."

But the question presented by the pleadings is the status of a cross-action under the California statutes, not under those of Texas. We think its status is adequately disclosed by the California statutes and decisions pleaded by petitioner, and is that for which he contends.

[The Court then reviewed the pertinent California statutes.]

There is nothing in the Fourteenth Amendment to prevent a state from adopting a procedure by which a judgment in personam may be rendered in a cross-action against a plaintiff in its courts, upon service of process or of appropriate pleading upon his attorney of record. The plaintiff having, by his voluntary act in demanding justice from the defendant, submitted himself to the jurisdiction of the court, there is nothing arbitrary or unreasonable in treating him as being there for all purposes for which justice to the defendant requires his presence. It is the price which the state may exact as the condition of opening its courts to the plaintiff. . . .

[Reversed.]

NOTE

The full faith and credit clause does not compel F–2 to take judicial notice of F–1 law in determining the effect of a judgment. Treinies v. Sunshine Mining Co., p. 286, infra.

Thompson v. Whitman

Supreme Court of the United States, 1874.
85 U.S. (18 Wall.) 457, 21 L.Ed. 897.

[The case appears supra, p. 156.]

NOTES

1. Does the opinion in Thompson v. Whitman proceed on the basis that, since the New Jersey court exceeded the power accorded it by local law, the judgment condemning the sloop was legally ineffective? If so, did the Supreme Court ascertain that the judgment did in fact have no binding effect under New Jersey law? Or is there some other explanation for the result reached? See Restatement, Second, Judgments § 30, quoted p. 235, supra.

2. Consider the following elements of the F–1 proceedings or judgment to determine whether any of them will preclude F–2 from examining into the jurisdiction of the F–1 court:

(a) Recital of jurisdiction.

(b) Recital of the jurisdictional facts on which the jurisdiction was based.

(c) Recital of a hearing on the jurisdictional facts.

(d) Opportunity to litigate the jurisdictional facts in F–1.

(e) Actual contest and litigation of the jurisdictional facts.

BALDWIN v. IOWA STATE TRAVELING MEN'S ASSOCIATION, 283 U.S. 522 (1931): Suit in the federal District Court for Southern Iowa to enforce a judgment rendered in the federal District Court for Western Missouri. The defendant had made a special appearance in the Missouri proceedings to claim that the court lacked in personam jurisdiction. This claim was rejected and judgment on the merits rendered in the plaintiff's favor. In defense of the enforcement proceeding in Iowa, the defendant contended that the Missouri judgment had been rendered without jurisdiction. The lower federal courts found for the defendant on this issue, but, on certiorari, the Supreme Court reversed. In the course of his opinion, Justice Roberts said:

The [plaintiff] suggests that Article IV, Section 1 of the Constitution forbade the retrial of the question determined on respondent's motion in the Missouri District Court; but the full faith and credit required by that clause is not involved since neither of the courts concerned was a state court....

The substantial matter for determination is whether the judgment amounts to res judicata on the question of the jurisdiction of the court which rendered it over the person of the respondent. It is of no moment that the appearance was a special one expressly saving any submission to such jurisdiction. The fact would be important upon appeal from a judgment, and would save the question of the propriety of the court's decision on the matter even though after the motion had been overruled the respondent had proceeded, subject to a reserved objection and exception, to a trial on the merits.... The special appearance gives point to the fact that the respondent entered the Missouri court for the very purpose of litigating the question of jurisdiction over its person. It had the election not to appear at all. If, in the absence of appearance, the court had proceeded to judgment and the present suit had been brought thereon, respondent could have raised and tried out the issue in the present action, because it would never have had its day in court with respect to jurisdiction.... It had also the right to appeal from the decision of the Missouri District Court.... It elected to follow neither of those courses, but, after having been defeated upon full hearing in its contention as to jurisdiction, it took no further steps, and the judgment in question resulted.

Public policy dictates that there be an end of litigation; that those who have contested an issue shall be bound by the result of the contest, and that matters once tried shall be considered forever settled as between the parties. We see no reason why this doctrine should not apply in every case where one voluntarily appears, presents his case and is fully heard, and why he should not, in the absence of fraud, be thereafter concluded by the judgment of the tribunal to which he has submitted his cause....

NOTE

A decision of a state court in a proceeding begun by a motion to set aside a judgment for lack of jurisdiction over the parties is res judicata and is entitled to full faith and credit in a federal court where the defeated movant sought an injunction against enforcement of the judgment of the state court. American Surety Co. v. Baldwin, 287 U.S. 156 (1932).

In DURFEE V. DUKE, 375 U.S. 106 (1963), there was first a suit to quiet title in Nebraska with both parties before the court. The land involved lay in the Missouri River, and the question of title turned on the question whether the land was in Nebraska or in Missouri. This depended on whether a shift in the river's course was a result of avulsion or accretion. The Nebraska court decided that the land was in Nebraska, and quieted title in the Nebraska claimant. This was affirmed on appeal by the Nebraska Supreme Court.

Then the Missouri claimant started a suit in Missouri, which was removed to the federal court. The United States Court of Appeals for the Eighth Circuit held that the land was in Missouri, and that the Nebraska decree need not be given full faith and credit, since the Nebraska court did not have jurisdiction over the subject matter.

On certiorari to the Supreme Court, this decision was reversed. The Supreme Court held that the issue had been litigated by the parties in Nebraska, both of whom were before the Nebraska court, and that the Nebraska decision was res judicata between them. Speaking through Mr. Justice Stewart, the Court said:

> Full faith and credit thus generally requires every State to give to a judgment at least the *res judicata* effect which the judgment would be accorded in the State which rendered it....
>
> It is argued that an exception to this rule of jurisdictional finality should be made with respect to cases involving real property because of this Court's emphatic expressions of the doctrine that courts of one State are completely without jurisdiction directly to affect title to land in other States. This argument is wide of the mark. Courts of one State are equally without jurisdiction to dissolve the marriages of those domiciled in other States. But the location of land, like the domicile of a party to a divorce action, is a matter "to be resolved by judicial determination." Sherrer v. Sherrer, 334 U.S., at 349. The question remains whether, once the matter has been fully litigated and judicially determined, it can be retried in another State in litigation between the same parties. Upon the reason and authority of the cases we have discussed, it is clear that the answer must be in the negative.
>
> It is to be emphasized that all that was ultimately determined in the Nebraska litigation was title to the land in question as between the parties to the litigation there. Nothing there decided, and nothing that could be decided in litigation between the same parties or their privies in Missouri, could bind either Missouri or Nebraska with respect to any controversy they might have, now or in the future, as to the location of the boundary between them, or as to their respective sovereignty over the land in question.... Either State may at any time protect its interest by initiating independent judicial proceedings here. Cf. Missouri v. Nebraska, 196 U.S. 23.

NOTES

1. For a discussion of Durfee v. Duke, see B. Currie, Full Faith and Credit, Chiefly to Judgments: A Role for Congress, 1964 Sup.Ct.Rev. 89, 105. Suppose that a court, having jurisdiction over the parties, goes ahead and decides the case. Does this constitute an adjudication that the court had jurisdiction of the subject matter so that the question cannot be reopened in a later case? It was so held in Chicot County Drainage District v. Baxter State Bank, 308 U.S. 371 (1940), but not in Kalb v. Feuerstein, 308 U.S. 433 (1940). For cases raising the question in a conflict of laws setting, see Sherrer v. Sherrer, p. 836, infra; Coe v. Coe, p. 859 infra; cf. Davis v. Davis, p. 856, infra. With respect to foreign in personam decrees affecting forum land, see supra p. 258, Notes 4–6.

2. In Hodge v. Hodge, 621 F.2d 590 (3d Cir.1980), the Court said in the course of its opinion:

"Reflecting the heightened concern for finality of judgments in post-*Chicot* developments in the law, the Second Restatement of Judgments replaced the First Restatement's simple listing of factors to be considered in weighing finality against validity with a presumption of finality followed by limited, enumerated exceptions. A party is foreclosed from litigating subject matter jurisdiction in a subsequent lawsuit except if the lack of jurisdiction was so clear that its assumption 'was a manifest abuse of authority,' the challenged judgment 'would substantially infringe the authority of another tribunal or [governmental] agency,' or the rendering court was incapable of making an adequately informed assessment of its own jurisdiction."

3. See Dobbs, The Validity of Void Judgments: The Bootstrap Principle, 53 Va.L.Rev. 1003, 1241 (1967); Reynolds, The Iron Law of Full Faith and Credit, 53 Md.L.Rev. 412 (1994).

Treinies v. Sunshine Mining Co.

Supreme Court of the United States, 1939.
308 U.S. 66, 60 S.Ct. 44, 84 L.Ed. 85.

[This case involved a dispute between Mrs. Mason and Evelyn Treinies, and her assignor John Pelkes, with respect to the ownership of a block of Sunshine Mining Company stock which had originally formed part of the estate of Pelkes' wife. The first step in the complicated proceedings was an action brought by Mrs. Mason against Pelkes and Treinies in an Idaho state court in which she sought to have the stock awarded to her. Before the Idaho court had rendered judgment, Mrs. Mason filed a petition in the probate proceedings in Washington seeking to have Pelkes removed as executor of his wife's estate. Pelkes by cross-petition claimed the stock and despite the protests of Mrs. Mason that it lacked jurisdiction, the Washington court held that Pelkes was the owner. In the meantime, the Idaho litigation continued and, after an appeal to the Supreme Court of Idaho, a final judgment in Mrs. Mason's favor was handed down more than a year after the contrary decision of the Washington court. Pelkes and Treinies thereupon filed suit against Mrs. Mason in the Washington court claiming that the Idaho judgment was void for lack of jurisdiction. At this point, the Sunshine Mining Company took the initiative and brought an interpleader proceeding under the Federal Interpleader Act against all of the contestants in a federal court in Idaho. This court found in favor of Mrs. Mason and its judgment was affirmed by the federal Court of Appeals and by the Supreme Court.]

■ JUSTICE REED delivered the opinion of the Court....

On the merits petitioner's [Treinies'] objection to the decree below is that it fails to consider and give effect to the Washington judgment ... awarding the property in question to Pelkes, petitioner's assignor. It is petitioner's claim that the Washington judgment must be considered as effective in this litigation because the question of the jurisdiction of the Washington court was actually litigated before the Supreme Court of Washington and determined favorably to petitioner by the refusal to grant a writ of prohibition against the exercise of jurisdiction by the Washington Superior Court in probate. This failure to give effect to the judgment is said to infringe the full faith and credit clause of the Constitution. The decree of the Court of Appeals is based upon the doctrine of *res judicata*. The applicability of that doctrine arises from a determination of pertinent matters by the Supreme Court of Idaho....

The [federal] Court of Appeals held that the Idaho suit settled that the stock was distributed in 1923 and that therefore the Idaho court had jurisdiction to determine rights under the alleged oral trust. It was further of the view that the Idaho court's invalidation of the Washington judgment and its decree upholding Mrs. Mason's claim to the disputed property were *res judicata* in this action. Petitioner's only ground for objection to the conclusion that the Idaho decree is *res judicata* rests on the argument that by such ruling below the "judgment of the courts of the State of Washington affecting the same subject matter and parties" is ignored.

In the Idaho proceeding the Washington judgment awarding the stock and dividends to Pelkes was pleaded in bar to Mrs. Mason's suit to recover the stock. The effectiveness of the Washington judgment as a bar depended upon whether the court which rendered it had jurisdiction, after an order of distribution, to deal with settlements of distributees with respect to the assets of an estate. On consideration it was determined in the Idaho proceeding that the Washington court did not have this jurisdiction and that the stock of the Mining Company became the property of Mrs. Mason. In declining to give effect to the Washington decree for lack of jurisdiction over the subject matter, the Idaho court determined also the basic question raised by petitioner in the interpleader action. The contention of petitioner in the interpleader proceedings that the Idaho court did not have jurisdiction of the stock controversy because that controversy was in the exclusive jurisdiction of the Washington probate court must fall, because of the Idaho decision that the Washington probate court did not have exclusive jurisdiction. This is true even though the question of the Washington jurisdiction had been actually litigated and decided in favor of Pelkes in the

Washington proceedings. If decided erroneously in the Idaho proceedings, the right to review that error was in those (the Idaho) proceedings. While petitioner sought review from the decree of the Supreme Court of Idaho by petition for certiorari to this Court, which was denied, no review was sought from the final decree of the Idaho District Court of August 18, 1936, on new findings of fact and conclusions of law on remittitur from the Supreme Court of Idaho.[1]

The [federal] Court of Appeals correctly determined that the issue of jurisdiction *vel non* of the Washington court could not be relitigated in this interpleader. As the Idaho District Court was a court of general jurisdiction, its conclusions are unassailable collaterally except for fraud or lack of jurisdiction. The holding by the Idaho court of no jurisdiction in Washington necessarily determined the question raised here as to the Idaho jurisdiction against Miss Treinies' contention. She is bound by that judgment.

The power of the Idaho court to examine into the jurisdiction of the Washington court is beyond question.[2] Even where the decision against the validity of the original judgment is erroneous, it is a valid exercise of judicial power by the second court.[3]

One trial of an issue is enough.[4] "The principles of *res judicata* apply to questions of jurisdiction as well as to other issues,"[5] as well to jurisdiction of the subject matter as of the parties.[6]

Decree affirmed.

1. It is unnecessary to consider whether the Idaho determination as to the jurisdiction of the Washington court was properly made. As the procedure by which a state court examines into the question of the jurisdiction of the court of a sister state is a matter within the control of the respective states (Adam v. Saenger, 303 U.S. 59, 63), it need only be added that such procedure is subject to question only on direct appeal.

It was stipulated by all parties to the Idaho cause that the Idaho courts might take judicial notice of the statutes and decisions of Washington. Some constitutional and statutory provisions relating to the jurisdiction of the Superior Court were pleaded and admitted. It has long been the rule in Idaho that its courts do not take judicial notice of the laws of another state and that without allegation and evidence it will be assumed the laws are the same as those of Idaho. [Citing cases.] While none of these cases involved a stipulation, the decision of the Supreme Court of Idaho (57 Idaho 10) declares the law of that jurisdiction. It follows from the Idaho court's refusal to look into the statutes of Washington that the jurisdiction of the Washington court was presumed to be governed by Idaho law. Under proper proof, the Idaho court would have been compelled to examine the jurisdiction of the Washington court under Washington law.

2. Old Wayne Life Ass'n v. McDonough, 204 U.S. 8, 15; Thompson v. Whitman, 18 Wall. 457, 468; Adam v. Saenger, 303 U.S. 59, 62.

3. Chicago Life Ins. Co. v. Cherry, 244 U.S. 25, 30; Stoll v. Gottlieb, 305 U.S. 165, 172; Roche v. McDonald, 275 U.S. 449, 454.

4. Baldwin v. Traveling Men's Ass'n, 283 U.S. 522, 525.

5. American Surety Co. v. Baldwin, 287 U.S. 156, 166.

6. Stoll v. Gottlieb, supra, Note 3, 172.

No decision or statute relative to the reexamination of the decree or judgment of an Idaho court on a contested issue of jurisdiction has been found or called to our attention. It is concluded that the rule here expressed states too the law of Idaho.

NOTES

1. RESTATEMENT, SECOND, CONFLICT OF LAWS: *

    § 114. Inconsistent Judgments

    A judgment rendered in a State of the United States will not be recognized or enforced in sister States if an inconsistent, but valid, judgment is subsequently rendered in another action between the parties and if the earlier judgment is superseded by the later judgment under the local law of the State where the later judgment was rendered.

2. It has been suggested that the *Treinies* rule with respect to inconsistent judgments should not be applied in situations where it is not possible to obtain review by the Supreme Court of the second inconsistent judgment. Ginsburg, Judgments in Search of Full Faith and Credit: The Last-in-Time Rule for Conflicting Judgments, 82 Harv.L.Rev. 798 (1969). This would be true where the second judgment is that of a foreign country or where the Supreme Court denies certiorari.

3. For a case applying the *Treinies* rule to inconsistent judgments of foreign countries, see Ambatielos v. Foundation Co., 203 Misc. 470, 116 N.Y.S.2d 641 (1952).

4. Colby v. Colby, 78 Nev. 150, 369 P.2d 1019 (1962), cert. denied 371 U.S. 888 (1962). We obtained an ex parte divorce in Nevada after H had been served with process in Washington, D.C. but did not appear. Thereafter, H was awarded a separation in Maryland. W appeared in this action and contended that the relief sought could not be granted because of the Nevada divorce. The Maryland court found, however, that W had not been domiciled in Nevada and that therefore the Nevada divorce was not entitled to full faith and credit. H then brought an action in Nevada to have the divorce set aside. Held for W. The divorce decree is still valid in Nevada. A divorce that is not entitled to full faith and credit may nevertheless have satisfied due process requirements and be valid in the state of rendition. Can this result be reconciled with Treinies v. Sunshine Mining Co., p. 286, supra and Sutton v. Leib, p. 881, infra? See Rodgers and Rodgers, The Disparity between Due Process and Full Faith and Credit: The Problem of the Somewhere Wife, 67 Colum.L.Rev. 1363 (1967), Note, 55 Tex.L.Rev. 127 (1976). For an interesting attempt to apply *Colby* outside the area of divorce, see Campion v. State, Department of Community and Regional Affairs, 876 P.2d 1096 (Alaska 1994).

5. The Brussels Convention of the European Union, supra p. 37, and the national laws of Continental countries do not follow a last-in-time rule; instead, they give priority to the judgment that was first in time (cf. Brussels Convention Art. 27 No. 5), modified by an exception in favor of inconsistent forum-state judgments (Id., Art 27, No. 3). Europeans criticize the last-in-time rule on the ground that it legitimizes a judgment that itself failed to give respect to the first court's decision. See Schack, Internationales Zivilverfahrensrecht anno. 856, P. 312 (1991). Is this criticism justified? Does *Treinies* suggest an answer? American law contains no rule providing for a general forum-judgment advantage (whether prior or subsequent in time): why not? Is such a rule any more consistent or acceptable in a

---

* Quoted with the permission of the copyright owner, The American Law Institute.

system such as that provided by the Brussels Convention? See Art. 25, supra p. 280.

RESTATEMENT, SECOND, CONFLICT OF LAWS: *

§ 112. Vacated Judgment

. . .

b. Proceedings on appeal. Whether proceedings on appeal or error vacate a judgment is determined by the local law of the state of rendition. At common law, a pending writ of error does not vacate a judgment, while an appeal in equity vacates a decree. In the United States, the rule has frequently been changed by statute. If appellate proceedings do not, by the local law of the state of rendition, vacate the judgment, suit to enforce the judgment may be brought in another state. Usually, however, the courts of the state in which enforcement of the judgment is sought will either stay their judgment, or stay execution thereof, pending the determination of the appeal (see § 107, Comment *e*). As between States of the United States, full faith and credit does not prevent in such circumstances either stay of the judgment, or stay of execution, pending determination of the appeal.

NOTES

1. For cases applying this rule, see Maner v. Maner, 412 F.2d 449 (5th Cir.1969); Nowell v. Nowell, 157 Conn. 470, 254 A.2d 889 (1969); Fehr v. McHugh, 413 A.2d 1285 (D.C.App.1980).

2. See generally on the question of the finality of judgments, Restatement, Second, Conflict of Laws § 107.

Lynde v. Lynde

Supreme Court of the United States, 1901.
181 U.S. 183, 21 S.Ct. 555, 45 L.Ed. 810.

[The case appears supra, p. 229.]

Barber v. Barber

Supreme Court of the United States, 1944.
323 U.S. 77, 65 S.Ct. 137, 89 L.Ed. 82.

■ CHIEF JUSTICE STONE delivered the opinion of the Court.

The question for decision is whether the Supreme Court of Tennessee, in a suit brought upon a North Carolina judgment for arrears of alimony, rightly denied full faith and credit to the judgment, on the ground that it

---

* Quoted with the permission of the copyright owner, The American Law Institute.

lacks finality because, by the law of North Carolina, it is subject to modification or recall by the court which entered it.

In 1920 petitioner secured in the Superior Court of North Carolina for Buncombe County, a court of general jurisdiction, a judgment of separation from respondent, her husband. The judgment directed payment to petitioner of $200 per month alimony, later reduced to $160 per month. In 1932 respondent stopped paying the prescribed alimony. In 1940, on petitioner's motion in the separation suit for a judgment for the amount of the alimony accrued and unpaid under the earlier order, the Superior Court of North Carolina gave judgment in her favor. It adjudged that respondent was indebted to petitioner in the sum of $19,707.20, under its former order, that petitioner have and recover of respondent that amount, and "that execution issue therefor".

Petitioner then brought the present suit in the Tennessee Chancery Court to recover on the judgment thus obtained. Respondent, by his answer, put in issue the finality, under North Carolina law, of the judgment sued upon....

The Tennessee Chancery Court held the judgment sued upon to be entitled to full faith and credit, and gave judgment for petitioner accordingly. The Supreme Court of Tennessee reversed on the ground that the judgment was without the finality entitling it to credit under the full faith and credit clause of the Constitution, Art. IV, § 1. 180 Tenn. 353, 175 S.W.2d 324. We granted certiorari because of an asserted conflict with Sistare v. Sistare, 218 U.S. 1, ...

In Sistare v. Sistare, supra, this Court considered whether a decree for future alimony, brought to a sister state, was entitled to full faith and credit as to installments which had accrued, but which had not been reduced to a further judgment. The Court held that a decree for future alimony is, under the Constitution and the statute, entitled to credit as to past due installments, if the right to them is "absolute and vested," even though the decree might be modified prospectively by future orders of the court. See also Barber v. Barber, 21 How. 582. The Sistare case also decided that such a decree was not final, and therefore not entitled to credit, if the past due installments were subject retroactively to modification or recall by the court after their accrual....

The Sistare case considered the applicability of the full faith and credit clause, only as to decrees for future alimony some of the installments of which had accrued. The present suit was not brought upon a decree of that nature, but upon a money judgment for alimony already due and owing to the petitioner, as to which execution was ordered to issue. The Supreme Court of Tennessee applied to this money judgment the distinction taken in the Sistare case as to decrees for future alimony. It concluded that by the law of North Carolina the judgment for the specific amount of alimony already accrued, was subject to modification by the court which awarded it, that it was not a final judgment under the rule of the Sistare case, and therefore was not entitled to full faith and credit.

As we are of opinion that the Tennessee Supreme Court erroneously construed the law of North Carolina as to the finality of the judgment sued upon here, it is unnecessary to consider whether the rule of the Sistare case as to decrees for future alimony is also applicable to judgments subsequently entered for arrears of alimony.... For the same reason, it is unnecessary to consider whether a decree or judgment for alimony already accrued, which is subject to modification or recall in the forum which granted it, but is not yet so modified, is entitled to full faith and credit until such time as it is modified....

We assume for present purposes that petitioner's judgment for accrued alimony is not entitled to full faith and credit, if by the law of North Carolina it is subject to modification....

... Our examination of the North Carolina law on this subject must be in the light of the admonition of Sistare v. Sistare, supra, 218 U.S. 22, that "every reasonable implication must be resorted to against the existence of" a power to modify or revoke installments of alimony already accrued "in the absence of clear language manifesting an intention to confer it." The admonition is none the less to be heeded when the debt has been reduced to a judgment upon which execution has been directed to issue.

[The Court then considered the relevant North Carolina statutes and decisions.]

Upon full consideration of the law of North Carolina we conclude that respondent has not overcome the prima facie validity and finality of the judgment sued upon. We cannot say that the statutory authority to modify or recall an order providing for future allowances of installments of alimony extends to a judgment for overdue installments or that such a judgment is not entitled to full faith and credit.

Reversed.

■ JUSTICE JACKSON, concurring.

I concur in the result, but I think that the judgment of the North Carolina court was entitled to faith and credit in Tennessee even if it was not a final one. On this assumption I do not find it necessary or relevant to examine North Carolina law as to whether its judgment might under some hypothetical circumstances be modified.

Neither the full faith and credit clause of the Constitution nor the Act of Congress implementing it says anything about final judgments or, for that matter, about any judgments. Both require that full faith and credit be given to "judicial proceedings" without limitation as to finality. Upon recognition of the broad meaning of that term much may some day depend.

Whatever else this North Carolina document might be, no one denies that it is a step in a judicial proceeding, instituted validly under the strictest standards of due process. On its face it is final and by its terms it awards a money judgment in a liquidated amount, presently collectible, and provides "that execution issue therefor." Tennessee should have rendered substantially the same judgment that it received from the courts of North

Carolina. If later a decree is made in North Carolina which modifies or amends its judgment, that modification or amendment will also be entitled to faith and credit in Tennessee.

Of course a judgment is entitled to faith and credit for just what it is, and no more. But its own terms constitute a determination by the rendering court as to what it is, and an enforcing court may not search the laws of the state to see whether the judgment terms are erroneous. Of course, if a judgment by its terms reserves power to modify or states conditions, a judgment entered upon it could appropriately make like reservations or conditions. No such appear in this judgment unless they are to be annexed to it by a study of the law of North Carolina. Any application for such relief should be addressed to the North Carolina court and not to the Tennessee court nor to this one. The purpose of the full faith and credit clause is to lengthen the arm of the state court and to eliminate state lines as a shelter from judicial proceedings. . . .

NOTE

Is not Justice Jackson correct? How can it be consistent with the mandate of full faith and credit for F–2 to refuse to enforce an F–1 decree merely because it remains subject to modification at the hands of the F–1 court? Such action certainly does not accord the judgment the same effect that it enjoys by "law or usage" in F–1. But, on the other hand, if the F–2 court were to enforce the F–1 decree without question, might it not thereby accord the judgment creditor a greater recovery than he would have obtained in F–1? Would such a result be thought inconsistent with full faith and credit? See also Keeton v. Hustler Magazine, Inc., 815 F.2d 857 (2d Cir.1987) (registration of New Hampshire judgment in New York permitted under New York law despite pendency of an appeal in New Hampshire); Irving L. Young Foundation, Inc. v. Damrell, 607 F.Supp. 705 (D.Me.1985) (pendency of a motion for relief from a default judgment in the state of rendition does not deprive the judgment of its finality and therefore does not preclude its enforcement in F–2). Note also that European recognition law—including under the Lugano Convention—no longer requires finality of the F–1 judgment. Supra p. 289, Note 5.

What recourse does the original judgment debtor have if, after recognition and enforcement of the F–1 judgment against him in F–2, the appeal (or the motion to set aside) is successful in F–1?

Worthley v. Worthley

Supreme Court of California, 1955.
44 Cal.2d 465, 283 P.2d 19.

[Suit by a wife against her husband to recover accrued arrearages under a New Jersey decree for separate maintenance and to have the New Jersey decree "established as a California decree" and the husband ordered to pay her $9 a week (the amount specified in the New Jersey decree) until further order of the court. The trial court entered judgment for the husband and the wife appealed to the Supreme Court of California.]

■ TRAYNOR, JUSTICE. ... Since the New Jersey decree is both prospectively and retroactively modifiable, N.J.S.A. § 2A:34–23, we are not constitutionally bound to enforce defendant's obligations under it. Sistare v. Sistare, 218 U.S. 1 ... Nor are we bound *not* to enforce them. People of State of New York ex rel. Halvey v. Halvey, 330 U.S. 610, 615.... The United States Supreme Court has held, however, that if such obligations are enforced in this state, at least as to accrued arrearages, due process requires that the defendant be afforded an opportunity to litigate the question of modification. Griffin v. Griffin, 327 U.S. 220, 233–234.... It has also clearly indicated that as to either prospective or retroactive enforcement of such obligations, this state "has at least as much leeway to disregard the judgment, to qualify it, or to depart from it as does the State where it was rendered." People of State of New York ex rel. Halvey v. Halvey, supra....

In Biewend v. Biewend, 17 Cal.2d 108, 113–114, 109 P.2d 701, 704 ... it was held that the California courts will recognize and give prospective enforcement to a foreign alimony decree, even though it is subject to modification under the law of the state where it was originally rendered, by establishing it "as the decree of the California court with the same force and effect as if it had been entered in this state, including punishment for contempt if the defendant fails to comply...." Similar holdings in reference to both alimony and support decrees have repeatedly been made by the District Courts of Appeal ... and by the courts of other states....

Although the question of retroactive modification has been seldom litigated.... there is no valid reason, in a case in which both parties are before the court, why the California courts should refuse to hear a plaintiff's prayer for enforcement of a modifiable sister-state decree and the defendant's plea for modification of his obligations thereunder. If the accrued installments are modified retroactively, the judgment for a liquidated sum entered after such modification will be final and thus will be entitled to full faith and credit in all other states.... If the installments are modified prospectively, the issues thus determined will be res judicata so long as the circumstances of the parties remain unchanged.... Moreover, the interests of neither party would be served by requiring the plaintiff to return to the state of rendition and reduce her claim for accrued installments to a money judgment.... Repeated suits for arrearages would have to be brought in New Jersey as installments accrued, to be followed by repeated actions in California to enforce the New Jersey judgments for accrued installments, with the net result that the costs of litigation and the dilatoriness of the recovery would substantially reduce the value of the support to which plaintiff is entitled.

Furthermore, there is no merit to the contention that as a matter of practical convenience the issue of modification should be tried in the courts of the state where the support decree was originally rendered. [Proof of changed circumstances can be presented to the California court]. Moreover, in most states the problem of modification is dealt with according to general equitable principles, and the law of the state in which the support obligation originated can be judicially noticed, Code Civ.Proc. § 1875, and applied by the California courts.

Accordingly, we hold that foreign-created alimony and support obligations are enforceable in this state. In an action to enforce a modifiable support obligation, either party may tender and litigate any plea for modification that could be presented to the courts of the state where the alimony or support decree was originally rendered.

The judgment is reversed.

. . .

■ SPENCE, JUSTICE, I dissent. ... the New Jersey judgment which plaintiff seeks to enforce in California is modifiable retroactively, as well as prospectively, under the law of New Jersey; but the majority opinion nevertheless requires its enforcement and modification by the courts of this state. This will result in confusion worse confounded, as the courts of each of several states, including New Jersey, might be called upon to modify the same decree, both retroactively as well as prospectively. In my opinion, the New Jersey decree, until made final by the courts of that state, is based upon shifting sands, which furnish no firm foundation upon which to predicate a judgment in any other jurisdiction....

LIGHT V. LIGHT, 12 Ill.2d 502, 147 N.E.2d 34 (1957): Proceeding in Illinois to register, under the Uniform Enforcement of Foreign Judgments Act, a divorce decree of Missouri, which ordered the defendant husband to pay alimony in gross and thereafter to pay $100 and $50 a month for alimony and for support of the child. The trial court gave a decree for past due installments only, and "the plaintiff contends [on appeal] ... that the decree is entitled to full faith and credit as to future installments." Held, the decree is entitled to the protection the plaintiff seeks.

■ SCHAEFER, J. ... Policy considerations argue strongly that such decrees are entitled to full faith and credit. Unless they receive interstate recognition, the insulated judicial systems of the several States may become sanctuaries within which obligations that have been fully and fairly adjudicated in another jurisdiction may be escaped. These policy considerations have found expression in the decisions of many State courts which, on the grounds of comity, have given full effect, ... Strong as are the considerations of policy, the argument that derives from the language of the constitution itself is at least as strong.... We hold, therefore, that the decree is entitled to full faith and credit as to future payments....

NOTES

1. The majority of the recent cases follow the approach taken in Worthley v. Worthley with respect to foreign alimony decrees that are subject to modification in the state of rendition. See chapter 11, at 907, infra.

2. The Supreme Court of the United States has not yet passed upon the relationship of the full faith and credit clause to installments of alimony that have not yet accrued in the extremely rare situation where these installments are not subject to modification in the state of rendition.

3. The special problems of recognition and enforcement raised by sister-state custody decrees are considered at pp. 887–901, infra.

Levin v. Gladstein
Supreme Court of North Carolina, 1906.
142 N.C. 482, 55 S.E. 371, 32 L.R.A., N.S., 905, 115 Am.St.Rep. 747.

This was a suit upon a judgment obtained in the Superior Court of Baltimore City, Maryland.... At the beginning of the trial ... counsel for defendant stated he admitted the regularity of the judgment sued upon and withdrew all pleas and defenses to said action, save ... that the judgment ... was procured by a fraud practiced by plaintiffs upon the defendant.... [Defendant] testified ... that he knew Philip Levin and Simon Levin, and had bought goods of them. That some time prior to his going to Baltimore he bought a bill of goods of plaintiffs, but had shipped some of them back to Baltimore because they were not up to sample. That plaintiffs had refused to take the goods out of the depot in Baltimore. That upon his visit to Baltimore summons was served upon him in the action brought there by the plaintiffs; but after said summons was served upon him, and before the return day, he saw one of the plaintiffs [who] agreed ... to withdraw said suit and return the goods to him at Durham, provided he would, upon their receipt pay the plaintiffs a sum of money which they agreed upon, to-wit, $133, and freight and storage not to exceed $3. That relying upon his agreement he returned to Durham and made no defense to the action. Plaintiffs never returned the goods to him at Durham. That the first time he knew of the judgment was when called upon by attorneys for plaintiffs to pay said judgment.

There was testimony contradicting defendant. After hearing testimony from both parties, the Court submitted the following issue to the jury: "Was the alleged judgment ... obtained by the fraud of plaintiffs?" To which the jury responded "Yes." Judgment was thereupon rendered that the plaintiffs take nothing by their action, and that the defendant go without day, etc. Plaintiffs excepted and appealed.

■ CONNOR, J., after stating the case: ... The plaintiffs, relying upon the provision of the Constitution of the United States, Article IV, section 1, that "Full faith and credit shall be given in each State to the public acts, records and judicial proceedings of every other State," earnestly contend that the defense is not open to the courts of this State. That the remedy for the fraud in procuring the judgment, if any, must be sought in the courts of Maryland....

In Allison v. Chapman, 19 Fed.Rep. 488, Nixon, J. says: "... the allegation, *in a plea,* that a judgment was procured through fraud, is not a good common law defense to a suit brought upon it in the same or a sister State." This conclusion is fully supported by all of the authorities....

Notwithstanding the well-settled rule that the judgment when sued upon in another State cannot be impeached or attacked for fraud by any plea known to the common law system of pleading, it is equally clear that upon sufficient allegation and proof defendant is entitled, in a court of equity, to enjoin the plaintiff from suing upon or enforcing his judgment....

The underlying principle is that the judgment of a sister State will be given the *same faith* and credit which is given domestic judgments. It is contended, however, and with force, that the "faith and credit" to be given such judgment is measured by the law of the State in which it is rendered. We find upon examining the decisions made by the Maryland Court that in that State a court of equity will enjoin the enforcement of a judgment obtained by fraud.... It is thus apparent that the judgment obtained by the fraud of plaintiffs ... would be open to attack in the courts of Maryland ... and in giving the defendant relief we are giving the judgment the same "faith and credit" which it has in that State....

The plaintiff says, however this may be, the defendant can have this relief only in Maryland; that he must go into that State and attack the judgment or enjoin the plaintiff. Mr. Freeman says: "If the judgment was procured under circumstances requiring its enforcement to be enjoined in equity, the question will arise whether these circumstances may be interposed as a defense to an action on the judgment in another State. Notwithstanding expressions to the contrary, we apprehend that in bringing an action in another State, the judgment creditor must submit to the law of the forum, and must meet the charge of fraud in its procurement, when presented in any form in which fraud might be urged in an action on a domestic judgment. If, in the State in which the action is pending, fraud can be pleaded to an action on a domestic judgment, it is equally available and equally efficient in actions on judgments of other States...."

[Affirmed.]

NOTES

1. Accord: Leflar, McDougal & Felix, American Conflicts Law 240–41 (4th ed. 1986); Scoles and Hay, Conflict of Laws 977–978 (2nd ed. 1992); Pryles, The Impeachment of Sister State Judgments for Fraud, 25 Sw.L.J. 697 (1971).

2. See Pryles, Impeachment of Sister State Judgment for Fraud, 25 Sw.L.J. 697 (1971).

3. The various situations wherein local law affords equitable relief against enforcement of a judgment on the ground of fraud in its procurement are discussed in Restatement, Second, Judgments § 70.

B. NATURE OF ORIGINAL CAUSE OF ACTION

Huntington v. Attrill

Supreme Court of the United States, 1892.
146 U.S. 657, 13 S.Ct. 224, 36 L.Ed. 1123.

■ JUSTICE GRAY delivered the opinion of the court.

This was a bill in equity, filed March 21, 1888, in the Circuit Court of Baltimore City, by Collis P. Huntington, a resident of New York, against the Equitable Gas Light Company of Baltimore, a corporation of Maryland, and against Henry Y. Attrill, his wife and three daughters, all residents of Canada, to set aside a transfer of stock in that company, made by him for their benefit and in fraud of his creditors, and to charge that stock with the payment of a judgment recovered by the plaintiff against him in the State of New York, upon his liability as a director in a New York corporation, under the statute of New York of 1875, c. 611, . . .

The bill alleged that on June 15, 1886, the plaintiff recovered, in the Supreme Court of the State of New York, in an action brought by him against Attrill on March 21, 1883, a judgment for the sum of $100,240, which had not been paid, secured or satisfied; and that the cause of action on which that judgment was recovered was as follows: On February 29, 1880, the Rockaway Beach Improvement Company, Limited, of which Attrill was an incorporator and a director, became a corporation under the law of New York, with a capital stock of $700,000. On June 15, 1880, the plaintiff lent that company the sum of $100,000 to be repaid on demand. On February 26, 1880, Attrill was elected one of the directors of the Company, and accepted the office, and continued to act as a director until after January 29, 1881. On June 30, 1880, Attrill, as a director of the company, signed and made oath to, and caused to be recorded, as required by the law of New York, a certificate, which he knew to be false, stating that the whole of the capital stock of the corporation had been paid in, whereas in truth no part had been paid in; and by making such false certificate became liable, by the law of New York, for all the debts of the company contracted before January 29, 1881, including its debt to the plaintiff. On March 8, 1882, by proceedings in a court of New York, the corporation was declared to be insolvent and to have been so since July, 1880, and was dissolved. A duly exemplified copy of the record of that judgment was annexed to and made part of the bill. . . .

[The bill further alleged that Attrill was insolvent, and that he had transferred the shares of stock to himself as trustee for his wife and daughters in order to hinder, delay, and defraud the plaintiff and other creditors.]

One of the daughters demurred to the bill, because it showed that the plaintiff's claim was for the recovery of a penalty against Attrill arising under a statute of the State of New York. . . .

The Circuit Court of Baltimore City overruled the demurrer. On appeal to the Court of Appeals of the State of Maryland, the order was reversed, and the bill dismissed. 70 Maryland 191. . . .

The question whether due faith and credit were thereby denied to the judgment rendered in another State is a Federal question, of which this court has jurisdiction on this writ of error. . . .

In order to determine this question, it will be necessary, in the first place, to consider the true scope and meaning of the fundamental maxim of international law, stated by Chief Justice Marshall in the fewest possible words: "The courts of no country execute the penal laws of another." The Antelope, 10 Wheat. 66, 123. In interpreting this maxim, there is danger of being misled by the different shades of meaning allowed to the word "penal" in our language.

In the municipal law of England and America, the words "penal" and "penalty" have been used in various senses. Strictly and primarily, they denote punishment, whether corporal or pecuniary, imposed and enforced by the State, for a crime or offence against its laws.... But they are also commonly used as including any extraordinary liability to which the law subjects a wrongdoer in favor of the person wronged, not limited to the damages suffered. They are so elastic in meaning as even to be familiarly applied to cases of private contracts, wholly independent of statutes, as when we speak of the "penal sum" or "penalty" of a bond....

The test whether a law is penal, in the strict and primary sense, is whether the wrong sought to be redressed is a wrong to the public, or a wrong to the individual....

The question whether a statute of one State, which in some aspects may be called penal, is a penal law in the international sense, so that it cannot be enforced in the courts of another State, depends upon the question whether its purpose is to punish an offense against the public justice of the State, or to afford a private remedy to a person injured by the wrongful act....

The provision of the statute of New York, now in question, making the officers of a corporation, who sign and record a false certificate of the amount of its capital stock, liable for all its debts, is in no sense a criminal or quasi criminal law. The statute, while it enables persons complying with its provisions to do business as a corporation, without being subject to the liability of general partners, takes pains to secure and maintain a proper corporate fund for the payment of the corporate debts. With this aim, it makes the stockholders individually liable for the debts of the corporation until the capital stock is paid in and a certificate of the payment made by the officers; and makes the officers liable for any false and material representation in that certificate. The individual liability of the stockholders takes the place of a corporate fund, until that fund has been duly created; and the individual liability of the officers takes the place of the fund, in case their statement that it has been duly created is false. If the officers do not truly state and record the facts which exempt them from liability, they are made liable directly to every creditor of the company, who by reason of their wrongful acts has not the security, for the payment of his debt out of the corporate property, on which he had a right to rely. As the statute imposes a burdensome liability on the officers for their wrongful act, it may well be considered penal, in the sense that it should be strictly construed. But as it gives a civil remedy, at the private suit of the creditor only, and measured by the amount of his debt, it is as to him clearly remedial. To maintain such a suit is not to administer a punishment imposed upon an offender against the State, but simply to enforce a private right secured under its laws to an individual. We can see no just ground, on principle, for holding such a statute to be a penal law, in the sense that it cannot be enforced in a foreign state or country.

The decisions of the Court of Appeals of New York, so far as they have been brought to our notice, fall short of holding that the liability imposed upon the officers of the corporation by such statutes is a punishment or penalty which cannot be enforced in another State.

In Garrison v. Howe, [17 N.Y. 458] the court held that the statute was so far penal that it must be construed strictly, and therefore the officers could not be charged with a debt of the corporation, which was neither contracted nor existing during a default in making the report required by the statute; . . .

The other cases in that court, cited in the opinion of the Court of Appeals of Maryland in the present case, adjudged only the following points: Within the meaning of a statute of limitations applicable to private actions only, the action against an officer is not "upon a liability created by statute, other than a penalty or forfeiture," which would be barred in six years, but is barred in three years as "an action upon a statute for a penalty or forfeiture where action is given to the party aggrieved," because the provisions in question, said the court, "impose a penalty, or a liability in that nature." Merchants' Bank v. Bliss, 35 N.Y. 412, 417. A count against a person as an officer for not filing a report cannot be joined with one against him as a stockholder for debts contracted before a report is filed, that being "an action on contract." Wiles v. Suydam, 64 N.Y. 173, 176. The action against an officer is an action ex delicto, and therefore does not survive against his personal representatives. Stokes v. Stickney, 96 N.Y. 323.

In a later case than any of these, the court, in affirming the very judgment now sued on, and adjudging the statute of 1875 to be constitutional and valid, said that "while liability within the provision in question is in some sense penal in its character, it may have been intended for the protection of creditors of corporations created pursuant to that statute." Huntington v. Attrill, 118 N.Y. 365, 378. . . .

We do not refer to these decisions as evidence in this case of the law of New York, because in the courts of Maryland that law could only be proved as a fact, and was hardly open to proof on the demurrer, and, if not proved in those courts, could not be taken judicial notice of by this court on this writ of error. . . . Nor, for reasons to be stated presently, could those decisions, in any view, be regarded as concluding the courts of Maryland, or this court, upon the question whether this statute is a penal law in the international sense. But they are entitled to great consideration, because made by a court of high authority, construing the terms of a statute with which it was peculiarly familiar; and it is satisfactory to find no adjudication of that court inconsistent with the view which we take of the liability in question. . . .

The true limits of the international rule are well stated in the decision of the Judicial Committee of the Privy Council of England, upon an appeal from Canada, in an action brought by the present plaintiff against Attrill in the Province of Ontario upon the judgment to enforce which the present suit was brought....[1]

In the Privy Council, Lord Watson, speaking for Lord Chancellor Halsbury and other judges, as well as for himself, delivered an opinion in favor of reversing the judgment below, and entering a decree for the appellant, upon the ground that the action "was not, in the sense of international law, penal, or, in other words, an action on behalf of the government or community of the State of New York for punishment of an offence against their municipal law." ...

He had already, in an earlier part of the opinion, observed: "Their lordships could not assent to the proposition that, in considering whether the present action was penal in such sense as to oust their jurisdiction, the courts of Ontario were bound to pay absolute deference to any interpretation which might have been put upon the statute of 1875 in the State of New York. They had to construe and apply an international rule.... The court appealed to must determine for itself, in the first place, the substance of the right sought to be enforced, and, in the second place, whether its enforcement would, either directly or indirectly, involve the execution of the penal law of another State. Were any other principle to guide its decision, a court might find itself in the position of giving effect in one case, and denying effect in another, to suits of the same character, in consequence of the causes of action having arisen in different countries; or in the predicament of being constrained to give effect to laws which were, in its own judgment, strictly penal."

In this view that the question is not one of local, but of international, law, we fully concur. The test is not by what name the statute is called by the legislature or the courts of the State in which it was passed, but whether it appears to the tribunal which is called upon to enforce it to be, in its essential character and effect, a punishment of an offence against the public, or a grant of a civil right to a private person.

... [I]f the original liability has passed into judgment in one State, the courts of another State, when asked to enforce it, are bound by the Constitution and laws of the United States to give full faith and credit to that judgment, and if they do not, their decision, as said at the outset of this opinion, may be reviewed and reversed by this court on writ of error....

If a suit to enforce a judgment rendered in one State ... is brought in the courts of another State, this court, in order to determine, on writ of error, whether the highest court of the latter State has given full faith and credit to the judgment, must determine for itself whether the original cause of action is penal in the international sense....

---

1. [Huntington v. Attrill, [1893] A.C. 150.]

The Court of Appeals of Maryland, therefore, in deciding this case against the plaintiff, upon the ground that the judgment was not one which it was bound in any manner to enforce, denied to the judgment the full faith, credit and effect to which it was entitled under the Constitution and laws of the United States.

[Judgment reversed.]

NOTES

1. In City of Philadelphia v. Austin, 86 N.J. 55, 429 A.2d 568 (1981), the New Jersey Supreme Court held that full faith and credit required enforcement of a Pennsylvania judgment for a fine for failure to file tax returns required by the Philadelphia Wage Tax Ordinance. The Court noted that the United States Supreme Court has never decided whether sister state money judgments on penal claims were entitled to full faith and credit. It reserved the question whether full faith and credit was owed to all sister state money judgments for violations other than tax laws.

2. The fact that the plaintiff is a sovereign state does not of itself make the action one for a penalty. The action is not penal where it is brought by the state to vindicate its proprietary interests, and a judgment rendered in such an action is entitled to full faith and credit. Connolly v. Bell, 286 App.Div. 220, 141 N.Y.S.2d 753 (1st Dep't 1955), affirmed 309 N.Y. 581, 132 N.E.2d 852 (1956).

3. For a discussion of the problems involved when the suit is on the original liability created by a foreign statute alleged to be penal, see pp. 375–379 infra.

Fauntleroy v. Lum
Supreme Court of the United States, 1908.
210 U.S. 230, 28 S.Ct. 641, 52 L.Ed. 1039.

By law the State of Mississippi prohibited certain forms of gambling in futures, and inhibited its courts from giving effect to any contract or dealing made in violation of the prohibitive statute. In addition, it was made criminal to do any of the forbidden acts. With the statutes in force two citizens and residents of Mississippi made contracts in that State which were performed therein, and which were in violation of both the civil and criminal statutes referred to. One of the parties asserting that the other was indebted to him because of the contracts, both parties, in the State of Mississippi, submitted their differences to arbitration, and on an award being made in that State the one in whose favor it was made sued in a state court in Mississippi to recover thereon. In that suit, on the attention of the court being called to the prohibited and criminal nature of the transactions, the plaintiff dismissed the case. Subsequently, in a court of the State of Missouri the citizen of Mississippi, in whose favor the award had been made, brought an action on the award, and succeeded in getting personal service upon the other citizen of Mississippi, the latter being temporarily in the State of Missouri. The action was put at issue. Rejecting evidence offered by the defendant to show the nature of the transactions, and that under the laws of Mississippi the same were illegal and criminal, the Missouri court submitted the cause to a jury, with an instruction to find for the plaintiff if they believed that the award had been made as alleged. A verdict and judgment went in favor of the plaintiff. Thereupon the judgment so obtained was assigned by the plaintiff to his attorney, who sued upon the same in a court of Mississippi, where the facts upon which the transaction depended were set up and the prohibitory statutes of the State were pleaded as a defense. Ultimately the case went to the Supreme Court of the State of Mississippi, where it was decided that the Missouri judgment was not required, under the due faith and credit clause, to be enforced in Mississippi, as it concerned transactions which had taken place exclusively in Mississippi, between residents of that State, which were in violation of laws embodying the public policy of that State, and to give effect to which would be enforcing transactions which the courts of Mississippi had no authority to enforce.*

■ JUSTICE HOLMES delivered the opinion of the court....

The main argument urged by the defendant to sustain the judgment below is addressed to the jurisdiction of the Mississippi courts.

The laws of Mississippi make dealing in futures a misdemeanor, and provide that contracts of that sort, made without intent to deliver the commodity or to pay the price, "shall not be enforced by any court." Annotated Code of 1892, secs. 1120, 1121, 2117. The defendant contends that this language deprives the Mississippi courts of jurisdiction, and that the case is like Anglo–American Provision Co. v. Davis Provision Co. No. 1, 191 U.S. 373. There the New York statutes refused to provide a court into which a foreign corporation could come, except upon causes of action arising within the State, etc., and it was held that the State of New York was under no constitutional obligation to give jurisdiction to its Supreme Court against its will. One question is whether that decision is in point.

No doubt it sometimes may be difficult to decide whether certain words in a statute are directed to jurisdiction or to merits, but the distinction between the two is plain. One goes to the power, the other only to the duty of the court. Under the common law it is the duty of a court of general jurisdiction not to enter a judgment upon a parol promise made without consideration; but it has power to do it, and, if it does, the judgment is unimpeachable, unless reversed. Yet a statute could be framed that would make the power, that is, the jurisdiction of the court dependent upon whether there was a consideration or not. Whether a given statute is intended simply to establish a rule of substantive law, and thus to define the duty of the court, or is meant to limit its power, is a question of construction and common sense. When it affects a court of general jurisdiction and deals with a matter upon which that court must pass, we naturally are slow to read ambiguous words, as meaning to leave the judgment open to dispute, or as intended to do more than to fix the rule by which the court should decide.

---

* The statement of the facts is taken from the dissenting opinion.

The case quoted concerned a statute plainly dealing with the authority and jurisdiction of the New York court. The statute now before us seems to us only to lay down a rule of decision. The Mississippi court in which this action was brought is a court of general jurisdiction and would have to decide upon the validity of the bar if the suit upon the award or upon the original cause of action had been brought there. The words "shall not be enforced by any court" are simply another, possibly less emphatic, way of saying that an action shall not be brought to enforce such contracts.... We regard this question as open under the decisions below, and we have expressed our opinion upon it independent of the effect of the judgment, although it might be that, even if jurisdiction of the original cause of action was withdrawn, it remained with regard to a suit upon a judgment based upon an award, whether the judgment or award was conclusive or not. But it might be held that the law as to jurisdiction in one case followed the law in the other, and therefore we proceed at once to the further question, whether the illegality of the original cause of action in Mississippi can be relied upon there as a ground for denying a recovery upon a judgment of another State.

The doctrine laid down by Chief Justice Marshall was "that the judgment of a state court should have the same credit, validity, and effect in every other court in the United States, which it had in the State where it was pronounced, and that whatever pleas would be good to a suit thereon in such State, and none others, could be pleaded in any other court of the United States." Hampton v. McConnel, 3 Wheat. 234....

Whether the award would or would not have been conclusive, and whether the ruling of the Missouri court upon that matter was right or wrong, there can be no question that the judgment was conclusive in Missouri on the validity of the cause of action.... A judgment is conclusive as to all the media concludendi, United States v. California & Oregon Land Co., 192 U.S. 355; and it needs no authority to show that it cannot be impeached either in or out of the State by showing that it was based upon a mistake of law. Of course a want of jurisdiction over either the person or the subject-matter might be shown.... But as the jurisdiction of the Missouri court is not open to dispute the judgment cannot be impeached in Mississippi even if it went upon a misapprehension of the Mississippi law....

We feel no apprehensions that painful or humiliating consequences will follow upon our decision. No court would give judgment for a plaintiff unless it believed that the facts were a cause of action by the law determining their effect. Mistakes will be rare. In this case the Missouri court no doubt supposed that the award was binding by the law of Mississippi. If it was mistaken it made a natural mistake. The validity of its judgment, even in Mississippi, is, as we believe, the result of the Constitution as it always has been understood, and is not a matter to arouse the susceptibilities of the States, all of which are equally concerned in the question and equally on both sides.

Judgment reversed.

■ JUSTICE WHITE, with whom concurred JUSTICE HARLAN, JUSTICE MCKENNA, and JUSTICE DAY, dissenting.

... Although not wishing in the slightest degree to weaken the operation of the due faith and credit clause as interpreted and applied from the beginning, it to me seems that this ruling so enlarges that clause as to cause it to obliterate all state lines, since the effect will be to endow each State with authority to overthrow the public policy and criminal statutes of the others, thereby depriving all of their lawful authority.... The whole theory upon which the Constitution was framed, and by which alone, it seems to me, it can continue, is the recognition of the fact that different conditions may exist in the different States, rendering necessary the enactment of regulations of a particular subject in one State when such subject may not in another be deemed to require regulation; in other words, that in Massachusetts, owing to conditions which may there prevail, the legislature may deem it necessary to make police regulations on a particular subject, although like regulations may not obtain in other States....

... Now it cannot be denied that under the rules of comity recognized at the time of the adoption of the Constitution, and which at this time universally prevail, no sovereignty was or is under the slightest moral obligation to give effect to a judgment of a court of another sovereignty, when to do so would compel the State in which the judgment was sought to be executed to enforce an illegal and prohibited contract, when both the contract and all the acts done in connection with its performance had taken place in the latter State. This seems to me conclusive of this case, since both in treatises of authoritative writers (Story, Conflict of Law, sec. 609), and by repeated adjudications of this court it has been settled that the purpose of the due faith and credit clause was not to confer any new power, but simply to make obligatory that duty which, when the Constitution was adopted rested, as has been said, in comity alone....

NOTES

1. If an appeal to the Supreme Court of the United States had been taken from the decision of the Missouri court (assuming the decision of the Missouri trial court had been affirmed by the Supreme Court of Missouri), would the decision of that court have been reversed on constitutional grounds? See p. 325 et seq., infra.

2. For a discussion of the doctrine that a court will refuse to assume jurisdiction of a suit on an original cause of action because the action is opposed to the public policy of the forum, see pp. 375–392 infra.

ROCHE V. MCDONALD, 275 U.S. 449 (1928): Action in Washington to enforce an Oregon judgment. The Oregon judgment was based on a prior Washington judgment and was rendered after the expiration of the Washington period of limitation. The Washington court, relying on the Washington statute which provided that "No suit, action, or other proceeding shall ever be had on any judgment rendered in this state by which ... the duration of such judgment ... shall be extended or continued in force for any greater or longer period than six years from the date of the entry of the original judgment," refused to enforce the Oregon judgment. On appeal, held, reversed. "The Oregon judgment, being valid and conclusive between the parties in that state, was equally conclusive in the courts of Washington, and under the full faith and credit clause should have been enforced by them."

NOTES

1. Union National Bank of Wichita, Kansas v. Lamb, 337 U.S. 38 (1949). Suit in Missouri to enforce a Colorado judgment obtained in 1927 and revived in 1945, in accordance with the Colorado practice, on personal service upon the defendant in Missouri. Enforcement was refused by the Missouri courts because of their local statute of limitations which (a) limited the effective life of a judgment to ten years and (b) provided that no judgment could be revived after ten years from its rendition. Held, reversed. "Roche v. McDonald is dispositive of the merits.... In this case it is the 1945 Colorado judgment that claims full faith and credit in Missouri. No Missouri statute of limitations is tendered to cut off a cause of action based on judgments of that vintage." The dissenting opinion contended that the judgment should be vacated and the cause remanded to the Missouri court for an initial determination whether the revival proceedings had "created a new Colorado judgment, or whether they merely had the effect of extending the Colorado statute of limitations on the old judgment. Only in the former case would Roche v. McDonald be 'dispositive of the merits'; in the latter case it is equally clear that McElmoyle for Use of Bailey v. Cohen, supra, 13 Pet. 312 ... would be controlling." See Note, Revival Judgments under the Full Faith and Credit Clause, 17 U.Chi. L.Rev. 520 (1950). A modern application of the point is Johnson Brothers Wholesale Liquor v. Clemmons, 233 Kan. 405, 661 P.2d 1242 (1983).

2. In the European Union, the Brussels Convention mandates the recognition of member state judgments, as noted earlier. Does this requirement apply to judgments recognizing a prior judgment of another member state or, for that matter, of a non-member state? What if, in the case of the American judgment sought to be enforced in Germany (and discussed supra at p. 280, Note (1)), the plaintiff had first sought and obtained its recognition in England, including of its punitive damage part: would Germany have had to recognize the English recognition judgment? In traditional European conflicts law, recognition and enforcement of a judgment (the grant of "exequatur") has only territorial effect, and another state will not adopt that effect as its own. If it were otherwise, the argument goes, State A (England, in the example) could undermine the public policy of State B (Germany) by making effective in State B—through the recognition of a State C judgment (the American judgment in our case)—something which State B abhors (punitive damages): "One trusts one's friends [England], but not the friends [U.S.] of one's friends." Kegel, Exequatur sur exequatur ne vaut, Festschrift für Müller–Freienfels 377, 392 (1986). Was Mississippi's policy undermined in Fauntleroy, supra p. 302, or Washington's in Roche? Is there or should there be a difference in the answer one gives to the basic question ("is prior recognition in turn entitled to recognition?"), depending on whether States A and B are wholly independent and unrelated jurisdictions or are bound together through a constitutional or treaty-based full-faith-and-credit mandate?

3. McElmoyle, for Use of Bailey v. Cohen, 38 U.S. (13 Pet.) 312 (1839) held it consistent with full faith and credit for F–2 to refuse to enforce an F–1 judgment on the ground that suit was barred under the F–2 statute of limitations applicable to judgments even though the judgment would still have been enforceable in F–1.

Watkins v. Conway
Supreme Court of the United States, 1966.
385 U.S. 188, 87 S.Ct. 357, 17 L.Ed.2d 286.

■ PER CURIAM. This litigation began when appellant Watkins brought a tort action against Conway in a circuit court of Florida. On October 5, 1955, that court rendered a $25,000 judgment for appellant. Five years and one day later, appellant sued upon this judgment in a superior court of Georgia. Appellee raised § 3–701 of the Georgia Code as a bar to the proceeding:

> "Suits upon foreign judgments.—All suits upon judgments obtained out of this State shall be brought within five years after such judgments shall have been obtained."

The Georgia trial court gave summary judgment for appellee. In so doing, it rejected appellant's contention that § 3–701, when read against the longer limitation period on domestic judgments set forth in Ga.Code §§ 110–1001, 1002 (1933), was inconsistent with the Full Faith and Credit and Equal Protection Clauses of the Federal Constitution. The Georgia Supreme Court affirmed, also rejecting appellant's constitutional challenge to § 3–701. 221 Ga. 374, 144 S.E.2d 721 (1965).

Although appellant lays his claim under two constitutional provisions, in reality his complaint is simply that Georgia has drawn an impermissible distinction between foreign and domestic judgments. He argues that the statute is understandable solely as a reflection of Georgia's desire to handicap out-of-state judgment creditors. If appellant's analysis of the purpose and effect of the statute were correct, we might well agree that it violates the Federal Constitution. For the decisions of this Court which appellee relies upon do not justify the discriminatory application of a statute of limitations to foreign actions.[1]

But the interpretation which the Georgia courts have given § 3–701 convinces us that appellant has misconstrued it. The statute bars suits on foreign judgments only if the plaintiff cannot revive his judgment in the State where it was originally obtained. For the relevant date in applying § 3–701 is not the date of the original judgment, but rather it is the date of the latest revival of the judgment. Fagan v. Bently, 32 Ga. 534 (1861); Baty v. Holston, 108 Ga.App. 359, 133 S.E.2d 107 (1963). In the case at

---

1. The case most directly on point, McElmoyle for Use of Bailey v. Cohen, 13 Pet. 312, upheld the Georgia statute with which we deal today. But the parties in that case did not argue the statute's shorter limitation for foreign judgments as the ground of its invalidity. Instead, the issue presented to this Court concerned the power of the States to impose any statute of limitations upon foreign judgments. See argument for plaintiff, 13 Pet., at 313–320.

bar, for example, all appellant need do is return to Florida and revive his judgment.[2] He can then come back to Georgia within five years and file suit free of the limitations of § 3–701.

It can be seen, therefore, that the Georgia statute has not discriminated against the judgment from Florida. Instead, it has focused on the law of that State. If Florida had a statute of limitations of five years or less on its own judgments, the appellant would not be able to recover here. But this disability would flow from the conclusion of the Florida Legislature that suits on Florida judgments should be barred after that period. Georgia's construction of § 3–701 would merely honor and give effect to that conclusion. Thus, full faith and credit is insured, rather than denied, the law of the judgment State. Similarly, there is no denial of equal protection in a scheme that relies upon the judgment State's view of the validity of its own judgments. Such a scheme hardly reflects invidious discrimination.

Affirmed.

In MILWAUKEE COUNTY V. M.E. WHITE CO., 296 U.S. 268 (1935), the Supreme Court held that a sister state judgment for taxes must be enforced under full faith and credit. In the course of his opinion, Justice Stone said:

... Such exception as there may be to [the] all-inclusive command [of full faith and credit] is one which is implied from the nature of our dual system of government, and recognizes that consistently with the full-faith and credit clause there may be limits to the extent to which the policy of one state, in many respects sovereign, may be subordinated to the policy of another. That there are exceptions has often been pointed out ... and in some instances decided. See Haddock v. Haddock, 201 U.S. 562; Maynard v. Hill, 125 U.S. 190; Hood v. McGehee, 237 U.S. 611; Olmsted v. Olmsted, 216 U.S. 386; Fall v. Eastin, 215 U.S. 1. Without attempting to say what their limits may be, we assume for present purposes that the command of the Constitution and of the statute is not all-embracing, and direct our inquiry to the question whether a state to which a judgment for taxes is taken may have a policy against its enforcement meriting recognition as a permissible limitation upon the full-faith and credit clause. Of that question this court is the final arbiter....

Whether one state must enforce the revenue laws of another remains an open question in this court. See Moore v. Mitchell, 281 U.S. 18....

A cause of action on a judgment is different from that upon which the judgment was entered. In a suit upon a money judgment for a civil cause of action, the validity of the claim upon which it was founded is not open to inquiry, whatever its genesis....

---

2. The Florida statute of limitations on domestic judgments is 20 years. Fla.Stat. Ann. § 95.11(1) (1960). Thus, it appears that appellant still has ample time to revive his judgment and bring it back to Georgia....

We can perceive no greater possibility of embarrassment in litigating the validity of a judgment for taxes and enforcing it than any other for the payment of money. The very purpose of the full-faith and credit clause was to alter the status of the several states as independent foreign sovereignties, each free to ignore obligations created under the laws or by the judicial proceedings of the others, and to make them integral parts of a single nation throughout which a remedy upon a just obligation might be demanded as of right, irrespective of the state of its origin. That purpose ought not lightly to be set aside out of deference to a local policy which, if it exists, would seem to be too trivial to merit serious consideration when weighed against the policy of the constitutional provision and the interest of the state whose judgment is challenged. In the circumstances here disclosed, no state can be said to have a legitimate policy against payment of its neighbor's taxes, the obligation of which has been judicially established by courts to whose judgments in practically every other instance it must give full faith and credit....

We conclude that a judgment is not to be denied full faith and credit in state and federal courts merely because it is for taxes.

We intimate no opinion whether a suit upon a judgment for an obligation created by a penal law, in the international sense, see Huntington v. Attrill, supra, 146 U.S. 657, 677, is within the jurisdiction of the federal District Courts, or whether full faith and credit must be given to such a judgment even though a suit for the penalty before reduced to judgment could not be maintained outside of the state where imposed. See Wisconsin v. Pelican Insurance Co., 127 U.S. 265 (1888).

NOTES

1. City of New York v. Shapiro, 129 F.Supp. 149 (D.Mass.1954). Action by the City of New York to recover a sum assessed by the City Comptroller against the defendants for unpaid use and business taxes, penalties and interest. Held: this administrative determination is entitled to full faith and credit. There is no "reason of policy for distinguishing between a State's duty to give effect to a sister State's binding administrative determination of taxes." To similar effect, see State of Ohio v. Kleitch Brothers, Inc., 357 Mich. 504, 98 N.W.2d 636 (1959).

2. On the question of the enforcement of foreign tax claims, not reduced to judgment, see p. 389, infra.

3. In United States v. Harden, [1963] S.C.R. 366, 41 D.L.R.2d 721 (1963), the Supreme Court of Canada refused to enforce a United States judgment for taxes, relying primarily on British authority holding that, "[i]t is perfectly elementary that a foreign government cannot come here" to enforce its tax claims even when reduced to judgment.

Her Majesty the Queen in Right of the Province of British Columbia v. Gilbertson, 433 F.Supp. 410 (D.Or.1977), affirmed 597 F.2d 1161 (9th Cir.1979). Suit by the Province of British Columbia to enforce a judgment for taxes obtained in its courts against certain citizens of Oregon. Enforcement of the judgment was refused. The court said "Apparently this is the first time in American legal history that a foreign government has sought enforcement of a tax judgment in a court of the United States. The best explanation for this seems to be that the 'well established rule' that it cannot be done has deterred all attempts."

For a thorough discussion of the enforcement of foreign country tax judgments, see Note, The Nonrecognition of Foreign Tax Judgments, International Tax Evasion, (1981) U. of Ill.L.Rev. 241. For public policy concerns in international recognition practice see Carter, Rejection of Foreign Law: Some Private International Law Inhibitions, 55 Brit.Ybk. Int'l L. 1984, p. 111 (1985).

4. In Titus v. Wallick, 306 U.S. 282 (1939), suit was brought in Ohio on a judgment obtained in New York by an assignee of a cause of action. The Ohio suit was defended on the ground that the judgment creditor was not the real party in interest, and that in procuring the judgment, he had suppressed and withheld that fact from the defendant and the New York courts. The Ohio court sustained this defense on the ground that the New York judgment was impeachable there for fraud and was to the same extent impeachable in Ohio. The Supreme Court of the United States reversed, holding that the judgment creditor was entitled to maintain the suit under the law of New York. It also held that the Ohio court must recognize the judgment creditor as the real party in interest, since he held the judgment, even though he might not have been the real party in interest if he had sued in Ohio on the original cause of action.

C. Lack of a Competent Court

Kenney v. Supreme Lodge of the World, Loyal Order of Moose

Supreme Court of the United States, 1920.
252 U.S. 411, 40 S.Ct. 371, 64 L.Ed. 638, 10 A.L.R. 716.

■ Justice Holmes delivered the opinion of the court.

This is an action of debt brought in Illinois upon a judgment recovered in Alabama. The defendant pleaded to the jurisdiction that the judgment was for negligently causing the death of the plaintiff's intestate in Alabama. The plaintiff demurred to the plea, setting up Article IV, secs. 1 and 2 of the Constitution of the United States. A statute of Illinois provided that no action should be brought or prosecuted in that State for damages occasioned by death occurring in another State in consequence of wrongful conduct. The Supreme Court of Illinois held that as by the terms of the statute the original action could not have been brought there, the Illinois Courts had no jurisdiction of a suit upon the judgment. The Circuit Court of Kane County having ordered that the demurrer be quashed its judgment was affirmed. 285 Ill. 188.

In the court below and in the argument before us reliance was placed upon Anglo-American Provision Co. v. Davis Provision Co., No. 1, 191 U.S. 373, and language in Wisconsin v. Pelican Insurance Co., 127 U.S. 265, the former as showing that the clause requiring full faith and credit to be given to judgments of other States does not require a State to furnish a court, and the latter as sanctioning an inquiry into the nature of the original cause of action in order to determine the jurisdiction of a court to enforce a foreign judgment founded upon it. But we are of opinion that the conclusion sought to be built upon these premises in the present case cannot be sustained.

Anglo–American Provision Co. v. Davis Provision Co. was a suit by a foreign corporation on a foreign judgment against a foreign corporation. The decision is sufficiently explained without more by the views about foreign corporations that had prevailed unquestioned since Bank of Augusta v. Earle, 13 Pet. 519, 589–591, cited 191 U.S. 375. Moreover, no doubt there is truth in the proposition that the Constitution does not require the State to furnish a court. But it also is true that there are limits to the power of exclusion and to the power to consider the nature of the cause of action before the foreign judgment based upon it is given effect.

In Fauntleroy v. Lum, 210 U.S. 230, it was held that the courts of Mississippi were bound to enforce a judgment rendered in Missouri upon a cause of action arising in Mississippi and illegal and void there. The policy of Mississippi was more actively contravened in that case than the policy of Illinois is in this. Therefore the fact that here the original cause of action could not have been maintained in Illinois is not an answer to a suit upon the judgment. See Christmas v. Russell, 5 Wall. 290; Converse v. Hamilton, 224 U.S. 243. But this being true, it is plain that a State cannot escape its constitutional obligations by the simple device of denying jurisdiction in such cases to courts otherwise competent.... [T]he Illinois statute ... read as [the Illinois courts] read it ... attempted to achieve a result that the Constitution of the United States forbade....

Judgment reversed.*

NOTE

Does the principal case in effect overrule Anglo–American Provision Co. v. Davis Provision Co., 191 U.S. 373 (1903)? Cf. Weidman v. Weidman, 274 Mass. 118, 174 N.E. 206 (1931). In that case a wife got a judgment against her husband in New York for alimony in an unsuccessful annulment suit. She then sued the husband on the judgment in Massachusetts where she was denied recovery. The court stated that it had no jurisdiction to entertain the case since Massachusetts law did not allow suit between spouses.

D. FOREIGN COUNTRY JUDGMENTS

We have now considered the various defenses that can be raised under full faith and credit to the recognition and enforcement of a sister state judgment. How do these defenses differ from those that are available when the judgment of a foreign country is involved? Consider in this connection the discussion of defenses to the enforcement of foreign country

---

* "I also had a case in which Illinois tried to dodge the Constitutional requirement of due faith and aids to judgments in other states by denying jurisdiction to Courts otherwise competent. They laid hold of a statement of mine in an earlier case that the Constitution did not oblige States to furnish a Court, but we said the dodge wouldn't do." Letter from O.W. Holmes to Sir Frederick Pollock, April 25, 1920, in 2 Holmes–Pollock Letters (1941) 41.

judgments in Schibsby v. Westenholz (p. 35, supra); Hilton v. Guyot (p. 219, supra) and Cowans v. Ticonderoga Pulp & Paper Co. (p. 226, supra). See also Restatement, Second, Conflict of Laws § 98.

Consider also § 4 of the Uniform Foreign Money–Judgments Recognition Act.

Section 4. [*Grounds for Non–Recognition.*]

(a) A foreign judgment is not conclusive if

(1) the judgment was rendered under a system which does not provide impartial tribunals or procedures compatible with the requirements of due process of law;

(2) the foreign court did not have personal jurisdiction over the defendant; or

(3) the foreign court did not have jurisdiction over the subject matter.

(b) A foreign judgment need not be recognized if

(1) the defendant in the proceedings in the foreign court did not receive notice of the proceedings in sufficient time to enable him to defend;

(2) the judgment was obtained by fraud;

(3) the [cause of action] [claim for relief] on which the judgment is based is repugnant to the public policy of this state;

(4) the judgment conflicts with another final and conclusive judgment;

(5) the proceeding in the foreign court was contrary to an agreement between the parties under which the dispute in question was to be settled otherwise than by proceedings in that court; or

(6) in the case of jurisdiction based only on personal service, the foreign court was a seriously inconvenient forum for the trial of the action.

Which of the defenses listed in Section 4(a), above, would be effective against a sister state judgment?

NOTES

1. As of 1995 the Uniform Foreign Money–Judgments Recognition Act had been adopted in 26 states. The Act is discussed in Homburger, Recognition and Enforcement of Foreign Judgments, 18 Am.J.Comp.L. 367 (1970); Kulzer, Recognition of Foreign Country Judgments in New York: The Uniform Foreign Money–Judgments Recognition Act, 18 Buff.L.Rev. 1 (1969). Brand, Enforcement of Judgments in the United States and Europe, 13 Journal of Law and Commerce 193 (1994); Brand, Enforcement of Foreign Money–Judgments in the United States: In Search of Uniformity and International Acceptance, 67 Notre Dame L.Rev. 253 (1991); Westerheim, The Uniform Foreign–Money Claims Act: No Solution to an Old Problem, 69 Texas L.Rev. (1991); 100 A.L.R.3d 792.

For a comprehensive discussion of the recognition and enforcement of foreign country judgments, see Restatement, Third, Foreign Relations Law of the United States §§ 481–486. For the current proposal that the Hague Conference begin work on a worldwide recognition-of-judgments convention, see supra p. 225, Note 5. Such a convention would assure the reciprocity still required by a few states (for a list, see supra p. 225, Note (8)).

The problem addressed by *Fauntleroy,* supra p. 302, and by *Kenney,* supra p. 310, of course arises also in the international context. With the Full Faith and Credit requirement not applicable, what should be the role and effect of the foreign country judgment? For the German answer in the reverse setting, focusing on the quantity and quality of forum contacts, see supra p. 222, Note 4. See also infra p. 313, Note (1).

In three states, Massachusetts, Texas, and New Hampshire (the latter, solely as to Canadian judgments), recognition of the foreign judgment is conditional on reciprocity. The defense or lack of reciprocity failed in Norkan Lodge Co. Ltd. v. Gillum, 587 F.Supp. 1457 (N.D.Tex.1984) (Canada) and in Hunt v. BP Exploration Co. (Libya) Ltd., 580 F.Supp. 304 (N.D.Tex.1984) (England).

2. Expanding notions of jurisdiction in this country have led American courts to take a more tolerant view of assertions of jurisdiction by foreign-country courts. Compare in this regard Ross v. Ostrander, 192 Misc. 140, 79 N.Y.S.2d 706 (1948) with Porisini v. Petricca, 90 A.D.2d 949, 456 N.Y.S.2d 888 (1982). Both cases involved attempts to enforce in New York English judgments obtained by default against defendants who had engaged in transactions in England. Enforcement was refused in Ross because the "requirement of jurisdiction according to the laws of this forum" had not been met. On the other hand, enforcement was granted in Porisini. By that time New York law had been amended (CPLR § 302) to permit New York courts to entertain an action in similar circumstances. Is it correct to make decision as to the jurisdiction of a foreign court depend upon local rules of competence?

3. For currency problems associated with foreign-country claims and judgments, see the Uniform Foreign–Money Claims Act (1989 Act), see supra p. 746.

4. A foreign country judgment in an action for alienation of affections and criminal conversation has been enforced by a state which gives no right of action for such matters under its local law. Neporany v. Kir, 5 A.D.2d 438, 173 N.Y.S.2d 146 (1st Dep't 1958) (Canadian judgment).

5. See generally Scoles and Aarnas, The Recognition and Enforcement of Foreign Nations' Judgments: California, Oregon and Washington, 57 Ore.L.Rev. 377 (1978).

A question that remains relatively unexplored by the courts is the extent to which a foreign-country judgment will be given a lesser res judicata or collateral estoppel effect in this country than that to which a sister state judgment would be entitled under full faith and credit. The question has been much discussed in the law reviews. Some writers believe that the difference in treatment should be quite marked. See Smit, International Res Judicata and Collateral Estoppel in the United States, 9 U.C.L.A.Rev. 44 (1962); von Mehren and Trautman, Recognition of Foreign Adjudications: A Survey and Suggested Approach, 81 Harv.L.Rev. 1601 (1968). See also Kulzer, Some Aspects of Enforceability of Foreign Judgments, 16 Buff.L.Rev. 84 (1966); Reese, The Status in this Country of Judgments Rendered Abroad, 50 Colum.L.Rev. 783 (1950); Nadelmann, Enforcement of Foreign Judgments in Canada, 38 Can.Bar Rev. 68 (1960).

NOTES

1. In Ackerman v. Levine, 788 F.2d 830 (2d Cir.1986), a West German judgment for attorneys' fees was recognized and partially enforced despite the fact that it violated New York's public policy because the German attorneys had failed adequately to assure that the defendant understood the fee arrangement. In Matusevitch v. Telnikoff, 877 F.Supp. 1 (D.D.C.1995), the court held an English judgment in a libel action not to be entitled to recognition and enforcement on constitutional and on public policy grounds. Citing to the public-policy exception in Maryland's version of the Uniform Foreign–Money Judgments Recognition Act (Md.Code Ann., Cts. & Jud.Proc. § 10–704(b)(2), the court considered the English standards for libel underlying the judgment to violate Maryland public policy and to deprive the judgment debtor of his First and Fourth Amendment rights. See similarly, Bachchan v. India Abroad Publications Inc., 154 Misc.2d 228, 585 N.Y.S.2d 661 (1992).

In interstate practice, the claim merges in the judgment. See Scoles & Hay, Conflict of Laws §§ 24.1, 24.3 (2d ed. 1992). The merger idea also helps to explain the result in *Fauntleroy,* supra p. 302. A foreign country judgment traditionally does not merge the underlying claim. This explains why the claim and its legal basis remain reviewable in the second court. Does this make sense? See Scoles & Hay, supra, § 24.3.

2. Recent cases in which an American court has given collateral estoppel effect to the judgment of a foreign country include Clarkson Co., Limited v. Shaheen, 544 F.2d 624 (2d Cir.1976); Fairchild, Arabatzis & Smith, Inc. v. Prometco (Produce & Metals) Co., Limited, 470 F.Supp. 610 (S.D.N.Y.1979); Leo Feist, Inc. v. Debmar Publishing Co., 232 F.Supp. 623 (E.D.Pa.1964). Seetransport Wiking Trader Schiffartgesellschaft, MBH and Co. v. Navimpex Centrala Navala, 837 F.Supp. 79 (S.D.N.Y.1993); Scheiner v. Wallace, 832 F.Supp. 687 (S.D.N.Y.1993); Ma v. Continental Bank N.A., 905 F.2d 1073 (7th Cir.1990); In–Tech Marketing, Inc. v. Hasbro, Inc., 719 F.Supp. 312 (D.N.J.1989). The opinions normally are silent on whether they are applying American rules of collateral estoppel or those of the state of rendition. See Peterson, Foreign Country Judgments and the Second Restatement of Conflict of Laws, 72 Colum.L.Rev. 220, 259–64 (1972).

What reasons can be advanced that would justify an American court in giving a foreign country judgment either greater or less collateral estoppel effect than it would have in the state of rendition?

E. Matters Subsequent to F–1 Judgment

A judgment's effectiveness as an enforceable obligation can be affected or destroyed by events which take place thereafter. One obvious example is the running of the forum's statutory period of limitations. McElmoyle for Use of Bailey v. Cohen, p. 307, Note (3), supra. Here we consider the consequences of other supervening occurrences; namely (1) payment or other discharge, (2) the rendition of a second judgment which may either be consistent or inconsistent with the first and (3) the effect on a judgment of the reversal of an earlier one upon which it was based.

(a) Payment or Other Discharge

Payment, release and accord and satisfaction are, of course, valid defenses to the enforcement of a judgment. And where a second judgment has been rendered upon the first, discharge of the obligation created by either of these judgments in one of the foregoing ways, will also operate to extinguish that created by the other. Restatement, Second, Conflict of Laws § 116. This latter principle has been applied to a situation where payment of the second judgment was made in depreciated currency. Matter of James' Will, 248 N.Y. 1, 161 N.E. 201 (1928). In that case, suit to enforce a New York judgment in the amount of $65,000 was brought in France, and, according to the French procedure, an exequatur was issued which directed the payment of some 2,300,000 francs, the equivalent of the dollar judgment at the date the French proceeding was begun in 1922. This sum of francs was paid in 1925, and the judgment debtor then moved to have the New York judgment discharged as paid. This was opposed on the ground that, since the value of the franc vis-a-vis the dollar had declined in the intervening years, the francs received in 1925 were not worth $65,000. It was therefore argued that the francs should be valued as of the date of payment and treated only as a payment on account. The court held (4 to 3, with Chief Judge Cardozo dissenting) that the New York judgment was discharged. Is such a result either necessary or desirable? For a discussion of the problem, see Reese, The Status in this Country of Judgments Rendered Abroad, 50 Colum.L.Rev. 783, 798–99 (1950).

(b) Successive Judgments

A second judgment, in the sense here used, can be handed down in any one of four situations: (1) in a suit brought to enforce the first judgment, or (2) but less frequently, in one based upon the underlying cause of action,* or (3) where the first judgment was for the defendant and constituted a bar to the prosecution of the second action, or (4) where under the principles of collateral estoppel the first judgment has already determined one or more of the relevant issues involved. Such a judgment may either be consistent or inconsistent with the first. It is consistent so long as it accords the first judgment the same res judicata effect (either by way of merger, bar or collateral estoppel) that the latter would enjoy at home, or, even if it fails to do this, where it reaches the same result with respect to the particular issue involved. It is inconsistent with the first judgment in all other situations. Common examples of the latter sort are where the second court refuses to enforce the first judgment on the ground that it was rendered without jurisdiction or where it permits the issues to be relitigated afresh and then determines them differently.

Where the second judgment is consistent with the first, the legal effectiveness of the latter remains unaffected. The doctrine of merger is inapplicable to judgments, so that the first judgment, even after it has been reduced to a second judgment in another state, continues in full force and effect and can be used, if the judgment creditor so elects, as the basis for a suit in a third state. The first judgment also retains all of its original effect as res judicata. Restatement, Second, Judgments § 18, comment *j*.

The converse is true, however, in situations where the second court hands down an inconsistent judgment. Here the second judgment—assum-

---

* Such an eventuality might occur in a case where the first judgment was rendered in a foreign country (Eastern Townships Bank v. H.S. Beebe & Co., 53 Vt. 177 (1880)), or where the first judgment was not drawn to the attention of the court in the second action.

ing always that the court had jurisdiction and that review by the Supreme Court was available—is controlling and destroys the legal effectiveness of the first judgment, so long as it remains unreversed and to the extent that it is inconsistent with the latter. Thus, the plaintiff can no longer maintain an action, or otherwise rely, upon a judgment rendered in his favor once it has been denied enforcement in a second state because of lack of jurisdiction on the part of the original court. And this is true even though the second court violated the mandate of full faith and credit; its finding of no jurisdiction is nevertheless res judicata and binding upon the parties. Plaintiff's remedy in such a case is by way of appeal from the second judgment. Treinies v. Sunshine Mining Co., p. 286, supra; Restatement, Second, Conflict of Laws § 114.

(c) Reversal of Earlier Judgment

What is the effect on the second judgment of a subsequent reversal of the earlier one upon which it was based? Assuming that the second court had jurisdiction its judgment was a valid exercise of judicial power and remains res judicata of the issues involved despite the reversal of the other. Reed v. Allen, 286 U.S. 191 (1932). The judgment debtor, however, is not remediless. Dependent upon the particular law of the second state, he can in that state either have the second judgment vacated or reversed on appeal or else have its enforcement enjoined by means of an independent action in equity. Restatement, Second, Judgments § 16. As to the debtor's right to restitution on account of any benefits conferred in compliance with a judgment that has subsequently been reversed, see Restatement, Restitution § 74 (1937).

Suppose now that the second judgment is sought to be enforced, or is otherwise placed in issue, in the courts of a third state and that, while these proceedings are pending, the first judgment is reversed. What is the status of the second judgment in F–3 upon the happening of this event? Presumably, it cannot under full faith and credit be treated as a nullity so long as it remains valid and effective in F–2. But so long as it is subject to impeachment in F–2 on account of the F–1 reversal, it should likewise be subject to attack on this ground in F–3. And by analogy to the rule prevailing in the case of judgments procured by fraud (Levin v. Gladstein, p. 296, supra), F–3 law would presumably govern the particular method of attack—i.e., whether the issue could be raised by way of defense to the plaintiff's action or only in an independent proceeding in equity for an injunction against the enforcement of the F–2 judgment. Cf. Ellis v. McGovern, 153 App.Div. 26, 137 N.Y.S. 1029 (1st Dep't 1912).

CHAPTER 6

The Impact of the Constitution

INTRODUCTORY NOTE

The bulk of this course, and particularly the material that follows, is devoted to problems in choice of law. However, before plunging into that subject, we pause to examine overriding limitations and obligations that may deprive state courts of options they would otherwise enjoy in ruling on conflicts issues.

The constraints and compulsions that may literally override state court conflicts policies flow from the United States Constitution, directly or indirectly. The most important Constitutional provisions in this regard appear at page 39, supra. First comes the Supremacy Clause (Art. VI), compelling state law to give way to the United States Constitution and valid national statutes, treaties, etc. In addition, controls are exerted by the Full Faith and Credit Clause (Article IV, § 1), the Privileges and Immunities Clause (Article IV, § 2), the Due Process Clauses of the Fifth and Fourteenth Amendments and the Equal Protection Clause of the Fourteenth Amendment. The Interstate Commerce Clause (Article I, § 8), also warrants mention even though it rarely influences decision in conflicts cases.

Sometimes the Constitution compels a state to provide a forum for suit on the claim arising in a sister state. On occasion it prohibits a state from applying its own rule of decision to resolve an issue in a multistate case, for the reason that the state does not have adequate ties, relations, concerns, or interests in the issue and its resolution to warrant applying its own rule of decision. The same prohibition may prevent application of the rule of decision of some other state, equally unconcerned or removed from legitimate interest in the outcome of the disputed issue. On rare occasions the Constitution may affirmatively mandate that the law of a particular state be applied to decide the issue presented. Less rarely, a state will be constitutionally prohibited from discriminating unreasonably against citizens of sister states or from dealing unequally with persons in its jurisdiction who are similarly situated.

Section 1. The Obligation to Provide or to Refuse a Forum

Hughes v. Fetter
Supreme Court of the United States, 1951.
341 U.S. 609, 71 S.Ct. 980, 95 L.Ed. 1212.

■ Justice Black delivered the opinion of the Court.

Basing his complaint on the Illinois wrongful death statute, appellant administrator brought this action in the Wisconsin state court to recover damages for the death of Harold Hughes, who was fatally injured in an automobile accident in Illinois. The allegedly negligent driver and an insurance company were named as defendants. On their motion the trial court entered summary judgment "dismissing the complaint on the merits." It held that a Wisconsin statute, which creates a right of action only for deaths caused in that state, establishes a local public policy against Wisconsin's entertaining suits brought under the wrongful death acts of other states.[2] The Wisconsin Supreme Court affirmed,[*] notwithstanding the contention that the local statute so construed violated the Full Faith and Credit Clause of Art. IV, § 1 of the Constitution. The case is properly here on appeal under 28 U.S.C. § 1257.

We are called upon to decide the narrow question whether Wisconsin, over the objection raised, can close the doors of its courts to the cause of action created by the Illinois wrongful death act. Prior decisions have established that the Illinois statute is a "public act" within the provision of Art. IV, § 1 that "Full Faith and Credit shall be given in each State to the public Acts ... of every other State." It is also settled that Wisconsin cannot escape this constitutional obligation to enforce the rights and duties validly created under the laws of other states by the simple device of removing jurisdiction from courts otherwise competent. We have recognized, however, that full faith and credit does not automatically compel a forum state to subordinate its own statutory policy to a conflicting public act of another state; rather, it is for this Court to choose in each case between the competing public policies involved. The clash of interests in cases of this type has usually been described as a conflict between the

---

2. Wis.Stat., 1949, § 331.03. This section contains language typically found in wrongful death acts but concludes as follows: "provided, that such action shall be brought for a death caused in this state."

* The Wisconsin court stated in Hughes v. Fetter, 257 Wis. 35, 42 N.W.2d 452 (1950): "It has been repeatedly declared to be the law that it was not intended by the provisions of the Federal Constitution referred to [the full faith and credit clause and the privileges and immunities clause] to give to the laws of one state any operation in other states except by permission, express or implied, by those states.... The statute in another state cannot be made the basis of furnishing a remedy for action in Wisconsin whose maintenance would be wholly inconsistent with the public policy of our state as declared by the legislature." [Eds.]

public policies of two or more states. The more basic conflict involved in the present appeal, however, is as follows: On the one hand is the strong unifying principle embodied in the Full Faith and Credit Clause looking toward maximum enforcement in each state of the obligations or rights created or recognized by the statutes of sister states;[9] on the other hand is the policy of Wisconsin, as interpreted by its highest court, against permitting Wisconsin courts to entertain this wrongful death action.[10]

We hold that Wisconsin's policy must give way. That state has no real feeling of antagonism against wrongful death suits in general. To the contrary, a forum is regularly provided for cases of this nature, the exclusionary rule extending only so far as to bar actions for death not caused locally. The Wisconsin policy, moreover, cannot be considered as an application of the *forum non conveniens* doctrine, whatever effect that doctrine might be given if its use resulted in denying enforcement to public acts of other states. Even if we assume that Wisconsin could refuse, by reason of particular circumstances, to hear foreign controversies to which nonresidents were parties, the present case is not one lacking a close relationship with the state. For not only were appellant, the decedent and the individual defendant all residents of Wisconsin, but also appellant was appointed administrator and the corporate defendant was created under Wisconsin laws. We also think it relevant, although not crucial here, that Wisconsin may well be the only jurisdiction in which service could be had as an original matter on the insurance company defendant. And while in the present case jurisdiction over the individual defendant apparently could be had in Illinois by substituted service, in other cases Wisconsin's exclusionary statute might amount to a deprivation of all opportunity to enforce valid death claims created by another state.

Under these circumstances, we conclude that Wisconsin's statutory policy which excludes this Illinois cause of action is forbidden by the national policy of the Full Faith and Credit Clause.[16] The judgment is

---

9. This clause "altered the status of the several states as independent foreign sovereignties, each free to ignore rights and obligations created under the laws or established by the judicial proceedings of the others, by making each an integral part of a single nation...." Magnolia Petroleum Co. v. Hunt, 320 U.S. 430, 439. See also Milwaukee County v. White, 296 U.S. 268, 276–277; Order of Travelers v. Wolfe, 331 U.S. 586.

10. The present case is not one where Wisconsin, having entertained appellant's lawsuit, chose to apply its own instead of Illinois' statute to measure the substantive rights involved. This distinguishes the present case from those where we have said that "*Prima facie* every state is entitled to enforce in its own courts its own statutes, lawfully enacted." Alaska Packers Ass'n v. Industrial Acc. Commission, 294 U.S. 532; see, also, Williams v. State of North Carolina, 317 U.S. 287, 295–296.

16. In certain previous cases, e.g., Pacific Employers Ins. Co. v. Industrial Accident Commission, 306 U.S. 493, 502; Alaska Packers Ass'n v. Industrial Accident Commission, 294 U.S. 532, 547, this Court suggested that under the Full Faith and Credit Clause a forum state might make a distinction between statutes and judgments of sister states because of Congress' failure to prescribe the extra-state effect to be accorded public acts. Subsequent to these decisions the Judicial Code was revised so as to provide: "Such Acts [of the legislature of any state] ... and judicial proceedings ... shall have the same full faith and credit in every court within the United States ... as they have ... in the courts of such State ... from which they are

reversed and the cause is remanded to the Supreme Court of Wisconsin for proceedings not inconsistent with this opinion.

Reversed and remanded.

■ JUSTICE FRANKFURTER, with whom JUSTICE REED, JUSTICE JACKSON, and JUSTICE MINTON join, dissenting.

. . . In the present case, the decedent, the plaintiff, and the individual defendant were residents of Wisconsin. The corporate defendant was created under Wisconsin law. The suit was brought in Wisconsin. No reason is apparent—and none is vouchsafed in the opinion of the Court— why the interest of Illinois is so great that it can force the courts of Wisconsin to grant relief in defiance of their own law.

Finally, it may be noted that there is no conflict here in the policies underlying the statute of Wisconsin and that of Illinois. The Illinois wrongful death statute has a proviso that "no action shall be brought or prosecuted in this State to recover damages for a death occurring outside of this State where a right of action for such death exists under the laws of the place where such death occurred and service of process in such suit may be had upon the defendant in such place." . . . Thus, in the converse of the case at bar—if Hughes had been killed in Wisconsin and suit had been brought in Illinois—the Illinois courts would apparently have dismissed the suit. There is no need to be "more Roman than the Romans."

NOTES

1. For a full discussion of the principal case, see Reese, Full Faith and Credit to Statutes: The Defense of Public Policy, 19 U.Chi.L.Rev. 339 (1952). To what did the Wisconsin court fail to give full faith and credit? Note in this connection Justice Black's intimation in the third footnote—that the Wisconsin court would not have violated full faith and credit if it had decided the "substantive rights" of the parties by application of the Wisconsin wrongful death statute. Professor Brainerd Currie suggested that the proper basis for the decision was the equal protection clause of the Fourteenth Amendment in that the Wisconsin statute discriminated unreasonably between Wisconsin citizens killed in Wisconsin and those killed in other states. In his view, Wisconsin could not constitutionally have denied plaintiff a forum if, the facts otherwise being the same, the Wisconsin decedent had met his death in a foreign country rather than in a sister state. Currie, The Constitution and the "Transitory" Cause of Action, 73 Harv.L.Rev. 36, 268 (1959), reprinted in Currie, Selected Essays on the Conflict of Laws, Chap. 6 (1963). See also Weinberg, Against Comity, 80 Georgetown L.J. 53 (1991); Weintraub, Who's Afraid of Constitutional Limitations on Choice of Law?, 10 Hofstra L.Rev. 17 (1981); and Chief Justice Vinson's explanation of the Hughes decision in Wells v. Simonds Abrasive Co., below. In support of the court's rationale, is the argument sound that the full faith and credit clause, as a basic instrument of federalism, may be given a non-literal meaning to require that a state under certain

taken." 28 U.S.C. (1946 ed., Supp. III), § 1738. In deciding the present appeal, however, we have found it unnecessary to rely on any changes accomplished by the Judicial Code revision.

circumstances must make its courts available for the enforcement of claims arising in sister states?

2. First National Bank of Chicago v. United Air Lines, 342 U.S. 396 (1952) was an action in the Federal court in Illinois for wrongful death in an airplane crash in Utah. An Illinois statute (quoted in Justice Frankfurter's dissent in Hughes v. Fetter, supra) was similar to the Wisconsin statute but applied only when the defendant was subject to suit in the place where the death occurred. The majority of the court held the Illinois statute could not bar the action. Black, J.: "Nor is it crucial here that Illinois only excludes cases that can be tried in other states. We hold again that the Full Faith and Credit Clause forbids such exclusion."

3. Assuming Hughes v. Fetter was properly based on full faith and credit, may it lead to decisions by the Supreme Court that there are constitutional limitations upon the power of a state to refuse to entertain suit on a claim arising in a sister state on the ground of forum non conveniens; or because the state considers the claim to be penal or contrary to its public policy? Does the Constitution limit the power of a state to refuse to entertain suit on a claim that arose in a sister state by reason of congestion in the local courts?

4. As to the power of a state to refuse to entertain a suit on forum non conveniens grounds, see Missouri ex rel. Southern Railway Co. v. Mayfield, 340 U.S. 1 (1950), p. 205 supra, and Douglas v. New York, New Haven & Hartford Railroad Co., 279 U.S. 377 (1929).

5. In Broderick v. Rosner, 294 U.S. 629 (1935), p. 967, infra, New Jersey was held to have violated full faith and credit by imposing unreasonable procedural restrictions upon the ability of the New York Superintendent of Banks to recover assessments against New Jersey shareholders of an insolvent New York bank.

6. By reason of the Supremacy Clause (Article VI), a state cannot discriminate against claims arising under federal law. McKnett v. St. Louis & San Francisco Railway Co., 292 U.S. 230 (1934), p. 205, supra. Likewise, a state cannot refuse to entertain suit on a federal claim on the ground that it is penal (Testa v. Katt, 330 U.S. 386 (1947), p. 205, supra), or is contrary to the state's public policy, Mondou v. New York, New Haven & Hartford Railroad Co., 223 U.S. 1 (1912), p. 204, supra.

WELLS v. SIMONDS ABRASIVE CO.
Supreme Court of the United States, 1953.
345 U.S. 514, 73 S.Ct. 856, 97 L.Ed. 1211.

[A resident of Alabama, while at work with a grinding wheel in the state, was killed by the bursting of the wheel. The wheel was manufactured by respondent, a Pennsylvania corporation, with its principal place of business in Pennsylvania. The administratrix of the decedent, finding it impossible to serve process on the respondent in Alabama, brought an action for the death under the wrongful death statute of Alabama in the federal court in Pennsylvania. The action was brought more than one year, but less than two years, after the death. The Alabama wrongful death statute permitted the action to be brought within two years from the death, but the Pennsylvania death statute required the action be brought within one year. The Pennsylvania conflict of laws rule called for the application of its own period of limitation. The district judge, deeming himself bound by the Pennsylvania conflicts rule, gave summary judgment for the defendant, and the Court of Appeals affirmed.]

■ CHIEF JUSTICE VINSON delivered the opinion of the Court.

We granted certiorari limited to the question whether this Pennsylvania conflicts rule violates the Full Faith and Credit Clause of the Federal Constitution.

... The Full Faith and Credit Clause does not compel a state to adopt any particular set of rules of conflict of laws; it merely sets certain minimum requirements which each state must observe when asked to apply the law of a sister state.

Long ago, we held that applying the statute of limitations of the forum to a foreign substantive right did not deny full faith and credit, ... Recently we referred to "... the well established principle of conflict of laws that 'If action is barred by the statute of limitations of the forum, no action can be maintained though action is not barred in the state where the cause of action arose.' Restatement, Conflict of Laws, § 603 (1934)." ...

The rule that the limitations of the forum apply (which this Court has said meets the requirements of full faith and credit) is the usual conflicts rule of the states. However, there have been divergent views when a foreign statutory right unknown to the common law has a period of limitation included in the section creating the right. The Alabama statute here involved creates such a right and contains a built-in limitation. The view is held in some jurisdictions that such a limitation is so intimately connected with the right that it must be enforced in the forum state along with the substantive right.

... Our prevailing rule is that the Full Faith and Credit Clause does not compel the forum state to use the period of limitation of a foreign state. We see no reason in the present situation to graft an exception onto it. Differences based upon whether the foreign right was known to the common law or upon the arrangement of the code of the foreign state are too unsubstantial to form the basis for constitutional distinctions under the Full Faith and Credit Clause.

. . .

Our decisions in Hughes v. Fetter, 1951, 341 U.S. 609, and First National Bank v. United Air Lines, 1952, 342 U.S. 396, do not call for a change in the well-established rule that the forum state is permitted to apply its own period of limitation. The crucial factor in those two cases was that the forum laid an uneven hand on causes of action arising within and without the forum state. Causes of action arising in sister states were discriminated against. Here Pennsylvania applies her one-year limitation to all wrongful death actions wherever they may arise. The judgment is affirmed.

Affirmed.

. . .

■ JUSTICE JACKSON, with whom JUSTICE BLACK and JUSTICE MINTON join, dissenting.

... I believe the United States District Court, though sitting in Pennsylvania should apply the law of Alabama, both as to liability and as to limitation.

The respondent relies upon the line of cases that began with Erie R. Co. v. Tompkins, 304 U.S. 64. A careful reading of the Erie decision will show that, so far as it applies at all, it is authority for the plaintiff's and not the defendant's position. The Erie injury occurred in Pennsylvania, but the action was brought in a United States District Court in New York. Although the trial court sat in New York, this Court held that it must decide liability by Pennsylvania law, that is, by the law of the state of injury, not that of the forum state, which holding, if applied here, would require that this case be adjudged by the law of Alabama even though it is brought in a federal court sitting in another state. That opinion, by Mr. Justice Brandeis, will be searched in vain for any hint that this result depended on the New York law of conflicts, which is not even paid the respect of mention. Erie R. Co. v. Tompkins held that there is no federal common law of torts and that federal courts must not improvise one of their own but must follow that state's law *which is applicable to the case.*

That the applicable state law was that of Pennsylvania, instead of that of the forum, was assumed without discussion of the reason because it was pursuant to what is probably the best-settled rule of conflicts in tort cases....

[The opinion reviews cases in which the law of the place of the tort was used and in which the federal court followed the conflict of laws rule of the forum state.]

Most of these decisions are actuated by a laudable but undiscriminating yen for uniformity within the forum state. Thus, "Otherwise the accident of diversity of citizenship would constantly disturb equal administration of justice in coordinate state and federal courts sitting side by side." Klaxon Co. v. Stentor Electric Mfg. Co., supra, 313 U.S. [487] at page 688, citing the Erie case; and the Court's opinion here refers to it as a "crucial factor" that "the forum laid an uneven hand on causes of action arising within and without the forum state."

But the essence of the Full Faith and Credit Clause of the Constitution is that uniformities other than just those within the state are to be observed in a federal system. The whole purpose and the only need for requiring full faith and credit to foreign law is that it does differ from that of the forum. But that disparity does not cause the type of evil aimed at in Erie R. Co. v. Tompkins, supra, namely, that the same event may be judged by two different laws, depending upon whether a state court or a federal forum within that state is available. Application of the Full Faith and Credit Clause prevents this disparity by requiring that the law where the cause of action arose will follow the cause of action in whatever forum it is pursued.

. . .

This case is in United States Court, not by grace of Pennsylvania, but by authority of Congress, and what I said in 342 U.S. 396, 398, seems to me applicable here. I had supposed, before Hughes v. Fetter, 341 U.S. 609, that the Commonwealth of Pennsylvania could close its courts to trial of this case. But no one would have questioned, I should think, that if the cause were entertained it must be tried in accordance with the law of the place of the wrong. . . .

Whether the principle of full faith and credit and of the law of conflicts will carry a general statute of limitations into the state of the forum along with the right is a more difficult question in the light of our precedents. McElmoyle v. Cohen, 13 Pet. 312.

. . .

But whatever may be the argument concerning general statutes of limitations as applied to common-law causes, this Court long ago recognized a distinction as to limitations on the action created by statutes in the pattern of the Lord Campbell Act. This Court early held such an action in federal court to be barred by the limitation contained in the applicable state statute. The reasoning of Mr. Chief Justice Waite is just as valid when it leads to a contrary result. . . .

. . .

The Supreme Court of Alabama has held the same doctrine applicable to the very statute in question, saying, "This is not a statute of limitations, but of the essence of the cause of action, to be disclosed by averment and proof." Parker v. Fies & Sons, 243 Ala. 348, 350, 10 So.2d 13, 15. The doctrine is well recognized in the literature of the law of conflicts.

. . .

We think that the better view of the case before us would be that it is Alabama law which giveth and only Alabama law that taketh away.

NOTES

1. Would Pennsylvania have been equally free to apply its statute of limitations if it had provided for a longer period than the Alabama statute? What policy or purpose of Pennsylvania would be served by application of its statute of limitations in such a case? The policies and purposes of statutes of limitations are treated in Chapter 7, Section 3.

2. See generally Currie, The Constitution and the "Transitory" Cause of Action, 73 Harv.L.Rev. 36, 268 (1959), reprinted in Currie, Selected Essays on the Conflict of Laws, Chap. 6 (1963).

3. On the history of the full faith and credit clause, especially as it is directed to public acts, see Nadelmann, Full Faith and Credit to Judgments and Public Acts, 56

Mich.L.Rev. 33 (1957). See also Hay, Full Faith and Credit and Federalism in Choice of Law, 34 Mercer L.Rev. 709 (1983).

Section 2. Choice of Law

Home Insurance Co. v. Dick
Supreme Court of the United States, 1930.
281 U.S. 397, 50 S.Ct. 338, 74 L.Ed. 926, 74 A.L.R. 701.

Appeal from the Supreme Court of Texas.

■ Justice Brandeis delivered the opinion of the Court.

Dick, a citizen of Texas, brought this action in a court of that State against Compania General Anglo–Mexicana de Seguros S.A., a Mexican corporation, to recover on a policy of fire insurance for the total loss of a tug. Jurisdiction was asserted in rem through garnishment, by ancillary writs issued against the Home Insurance Company and Franklin Fire Insurance Company, which reinsured, by contracts with the Mexican corporation, parts of the risk which it had assumed. The garnishees are New York corporations. Upon them, service was effected by serving their local agents in Texas.

. . .

Their defense rests upon the following facts: This suit was not commenced till more than one year after the date of the loss. The policy provided: "It is understood and agreed that no judicial suit or demand shall be entered before any tribunal for the collection of any claim under this policy, unless such suits or demands are filed within one year counted as from the date on which such damage occurs." This provision was in accord with the Mexican law to which the policy was expressly made subject. It was issued by the Mexican company in Mexico to one Bonner, of Tampico, Mexico, and was there duly assigned to Dick prior to the loss. It covered the vessel only in certain Mexican waters. The premium was paid in Mexico; and the loss was "payable in the City of Mexico in current funds of the United States of Mexico, or their equivalent elsewhere." At the time the policy was issued, when it was assigned to him, and until after the loss, Dick actually resided in Mexico, although his permanent residence was in Texas. The contracts of reinsurance were effected by correspondence between the Mexican company in Mexico and the New York companies in New York. Nothing thereunder was to be done, or was in fact done, in Texas.

. . . To this defense Dick demurred, on the ground that article 5545 of the Texas Revised Civil Statutes (1925) provides: "No person, firm, corporation, association or combination of whatsoever kind shall enter into any stipulation, contract, or agreement, by reason whereof the time in which to sue thereon is limited to a shorter period than two years. And no stipulation, contract, or agreement for any such shorter limitation in which to sue shall ever be valid in this State."

The trial court sustained Dick's contention and entered judgment against the garnishees. On appeal, both in the Court of Civil Appeals (8 S.W.2d 354) and in the Supreme Court of the state (15 S.W.2d 1028), the garnishees asserted that, as construed and applied, the Texas statute violated the due process clause of the Fourteenth Amendment and the contract clause. Both courts treated the policy provision as equivalent to a foreign statute of limitation; held that article 5545 related to the remedy available in Texas courts; concluded that it was validly applicable to the case at bar; and affirmed the judgment of the trial court. The garnishees appealed to this Court on the ground that the statute, as construed and applied, violated their rights under the Federal Constitution. Dick moved to dismiss the appeal for want of jurisdiction. Then the garnishees filed, also, a petition for a writ of certiorari. Consideration of the jurisdiction of this Court on the appeal, and of the petition for certiorari, was postponed to the hearing of the case on the merits.

First. Dick contends that this Court lacks jurisdiction of the action, because the errors assigned involve only questions of local law and of conflict of laws. The argument is that, while a provision requiring notice of loss within a fixed period is substantive because it is a condition precedent to the existence of the cause of action, the provision for liability only in case suit is brought within the year is not substantive because it relates only to the remedy after accrual of the cause of action; that, while the validity, interpretation, and performance of the substantive provisions of a contract are determined by the law of the place where it is made and is to be performed, matters which relate only to the remedy are unquestionably governed by the lex fori; and that, even if the Texas court erred in holding the statute applicable to this contract, the error is one of state law or of the interpretation of the contract, and is not reviewable here.

The contention is unsound. There is no dispute as to the meaning of the provision in the policy. It is that the insurer shall not be liable unless suit is brought within one year of the loss.... Nor are we concerned with the question whether the provision is properly described as relating to remedy or to substance. However characterized, it is an express term in the contract of the parties by which the right of the insured and the correlative obligation of the insurer are defined. If effect is given to the clause, Dick cannot recover from the Mexican corporation, and the garnishees cannot be compelled to pay. If, on the other hand, the statute is applied to the contract, it admittedly abrogates a contractual right and imposes liability, although the parties have agreed that there should be none.

The statute is not simply one of limitation. It does not merely fix the time in which the aid of the Texas courts may be invoked. Nor does it govern only the remedies available in the Texas courts. It deals with the powers and capacities of persons and corporations. It expressly prohibits the making of certain contracts. As construed, it also directs the disregard in Texas of contractual rights and obligations wherever created and assumed; and it commands the enforcement of obligations in excess of those contracted for. Therefore, the objection that, as applied to contracts made and to be performed outside of Texas, the statute violates the Federal Constitution, raises federal questions of substance; and the existence of the federal claim is not disproved by saying that the statute, or the one-year provision in the policy, relates to the remedy and not to the substance.

... The case is properly here on appeal. The motion to dismiss the appeal is overruled; and the petition for certiorari is therefore denied.

Second. The Texas statute as here construed and applied deprives the garnishees of property without due process of law. A state may, of course, prohibit and declare invalid the making of certain contracts within its borders. Ordinarily, it may prohibit performance within its borders, even of contracts validly made elsewhere, if they are required to be performed within the state and their performance would violate its laws. But, in the case at bar, nothing in any way relating to the policy sued on, or to the contracts of reinsurance, was ever done or required to be done in Texas. All acts relating to the making of the policy were done in Mexico. All in relation to the making of the contracts of reinsurance were done there or in New York. And, likewise, all things in regard to performance were to be done outside of Texas. Neither the Texas laws nor the Texas courts were invoked for any purpose, except by Dick in the bringing of this suit. The fact that Dick's permanent residence was in Texas is without significance. At all times here material he was physically present and acting in Mexico. Texas was therefore without power to affect the terms of contracts so made. Its attempt to impose a greater obligation than that agreed upon and to seize property in payment of the imposed obligation violates the guaranty against deprivation of property without due process of law. Compania General De Tabacos v. Collector of Internal Revenue, 275 U.S. 87; Aetna Life Ins. Co. v. Dunken, 266 U.S. 389; New York Life Ins. Co. v. Dodge, 246 U.S. 357. Compare Modern Woodmen of America v. Mixer, 267 U.S. 544, 551.[1]

The cases relied upon, in which it was held that a state may lengthen its statute of limitations, are not in point. See Atchafalaya Land Co. v. Williams Cypress Co., 258 U.S. 190; National Surety Co. v. Architectural Decorating Co., 226 U.S. 276; Vance v. Vance, 108 U.S. 514. In those cases, the parties had not stipulated a time limit for the enforcement of their obligations. It is true that a state may extend the time within which

---

1. The division of this court in the Tabacos and Dodge Cases was not on the principle here stated, but on the question of fact whether there were in those cases things done within the state of which the state could properly lay hold as the basis of the regulations there imposed. Compare Bothwell v. Buckbee, Mears Co., 275 U.S. 274; Palmetto Fire Ins. Co. v. Conn, 272 U.S. 295. In the absence of any such things, as in this case, the Court was agreed that a state is without power to impose either public or private obligations on contracts made outside of the state and not to be performed there. Compare Mutual Life Insurance Co. of New York v. Liebing, 259 U.S. 209; E. Merrick Dodd, Jr., "The Power of the Supreme Court to Review State Decisions in the Field of Conflict of Laws," 39 Harv.L.Rev. (1926) 533, 548. [Footnote by the Court.]

suit may be brought in its own courts, if, in doing so, it violates no agreement of the parties. And, in the absence of a contractual provision, the local statute of limitation may be applied to a right created in another jurisdiction even where the remedy in the latter is barred.[2] In such cases, the rights and obligations of the parties are not varied. When, however, the parties have expressly agreed upon a time limit on their obligation, a statute which invalidates the agreement and directs enforcement of the contract after the time has expired increases their obligation and imposes a burden not contracted for.

. . .

Third. Dick urges that article 5545 of the Texas law is a declaration of its public policy; and that a state may properly refuse to recognize foreign rights which violate its declared policy. Doubtless, a state may prohibit the enjoyment by persons within its borders of rights acquired elsewhere which violate its laws or public policy; and under some circumstances, it may refuse to aid in the enforcement of such rights. Bothwell v. Buckbee, Mears Co., 275 U.S. 274, 277, 279; Union Trust Co. v. Grosman, 245 U.S. 412; compare Fauntleroy v. Lum, 210 U.S. 230. But the Mexican corporation never was in Texas; and neither it nor the garnishees invoked the aid of the Texas courts or the Texas laws. The Mexican corporation was not before the court. The garnishees were brought in by compulsory process. Neither has asked favors. They ask only to be let alone. We need not consider how far the state may go in imposing restrictions on the conduct of its own residents, and of foreign corporations which have received permission to do business within its borders; or how far it may go in refusing to lend the aid of its courts to the enforcement of rights acquired outside its borders. It may not abrogate the rights of parties beyond its borders having no relation to anything done or to be done within them.

Fourth. Finally, it is urged that the Federal Constitution does not require the states to recognize and protect rights derived from the laws of foreign countries—that as to them the full faith and credit clause has no application. See Aetna Life Ins. Co. v. Tremblay, 223 U.S. 185. The claims here asserted are not based upon the full faith and credit clause. Compare Royal Arcanum v. Green, 237 U.S. 531; Modern Woodmen of America v. Mixer, 267 U.S. 544. They rest upon the Fourteenth Amendment. Its protection extends to aliens. Moreover, the parties in interest here are American companies. The defense asserted is based on the provision of the policy and on their contracts of reinsurance. The courts of the state confused this defense with that based on the Mexican Code. They held that, even if the effect of the foreign statute was to extinguish the right, Dick's removal to Texas prior to the bar of the foreign statute removed the cause of action from Mexico, and subjected it to the Texas statute of

---

2. Whether a distinction is to be drawn between statutes of limitation which extinguish or limit the right and those which merely bar the remedy, we need not now determine. Compare Davis v. Mills, 194 U.S. 451, and Texas Portland Cement Co. v. McCord, 233 U.S. 157, with Canadian Pac. Ry. Co. v. Johnston, 61 F. 738. [Footnote by the Court.]

limitation. And they applied the same rule to the provision in the policy. Whether or not that is a sufficient answer to the defense based on the foreign law we may not consider; for no issue under the full faith and credit clause was raised. But in Texas, as elsewhere, the contract was subject to its own limitations.

Fifth.... Since we hold that the Texas statute, as construed and applied, violates the due process clause, we have no occasion to consider [the contract clause] contention....

Reversed.

NOTE ON HOME INSURANCE CO. v. DICK

Home Insurance Co. v. Dick is a landmark. It stands as a warning that at some point the due process clause prevents a state deciding a multistate case from making whatever choice of law it is minded to. When is that point reached? That question requires identifying the critical factors in the Dick case. Which factor or combination of factors was critical?

- The nearly total absence of connections to Texas?
- The stipulation in the parties' contract limiting the time within which suit had to be brought?
- The fact that the Texas statute purported to prohibit the parties from making agreements shortening the time-to-sue period to less than two years?

The Dick case is sometimes said to stand for the proposition that a naked forum may not apply its own rules of decision to a multistate case. However, Professor Russell J. Weintraub has pointed out that although the policy was issued to Bonner of Tampico, Mexico, the loss was payable to a firm in Texas and Dick, as their interests might appear; and many years before the boat burned the policy was assigned to Dick with defendant's written consent. See R. Weintraub, Commentary on the Conflict of Laws (3d ed. 1986), p. 401, n. 28. By today's standards, do those facts sufficiently clothe Texas with connections to the case to give it constitutional basis for applying the statute in question?

Consider Justice Brandeis's statement that in the absence of a contrary agreement by the parties, a state may extend the time within which suit may be brought in its own courts even when the right is created in another jurisdiction. Are the implications that (a) a state may never extend the time when the parties have made an agreement for a shorter time? (b) a state may virtually always extend the time to sue in tort cases, where there are seldom agreements as to time-to-sue limits? (c) a state may always extend the time to sue in contract cases if the only time limits applicable are those supplied by the law of another state rather than the agreement of the parties? Cf. Clay v. Sun Insurance Office, Limited, 377 U.S. 179 (1964), p. 346, infra.

Under Shaffer v. Heitner, p. 136, supra, and Rush v. Savchuk, p. 148, supra, would there be judicial jurisdiction today on the facts of the Dick case?

NOTES

1. Justice Brandeis' strongly expressed reliance on a due-process limitation in the Dick case repudiated the Court's earlier position—also articulated by Justice Brandeis—that choice of law was not a matter with which the Court was concerned. See Kryger v. Wilson, 242 U.S. 171, 176 (1916).

2. For an excellent discussion of the problem, see Currie, The Constitution and Choice of Law, 26 U.Chi.L.Rev. 9 (1958), reprinted in Currie, Selected Essays on the Conflict of Laws, Chap. 5 (1963). See also Restatement, Second, Conflict of Laws § 9; Reese, Legislative Jurisdiction, 78 Colum.L.Rev. 1587 (1978). Laycock, Equal Citizens of Equal and Territorial States: The Constitutional Foundations of Choice of Law, 92 Columbia L.Rev. 249 (1992).

JOHN HANCOCK MUTUAL LIFE INSURANCE CO. v. YATES, 299 U.S. 178 (1936): Suit upon a life insurance policy which had been applied for and issued in New York. The insured was a New York domiciliary who was being treated for cancer at the time. In his insurance application, the insured stated that he had not recently been under medical care. Under the law of New York this false statement constituted a material misrepresentation that voided the policy. Following the insured's death, his widow moved to Georgia and there brought suit on the policy. She recovered judgment by application of the Georgia rule that a false statement in an insurance policy is not material if the agent who solicited the policy was aware of the facts. Application of the Georgia rule was justified by the Georgia courts on the ground that the jury had found that the insurance agent knew that the insured was suffering from cancer and that it is for forum law to determine as a question of procedure whether the materiality of a misrepresentation is a question of fact to be decided by the jury. The Supreme Court reversed, holding that the Georgia courts had denied full faith and credit to the laws of New York and that "there was no occurrence, nothing done, to which the law of Georgia could apply." The Court also said (299 U.S., at 183):

> "... Because the statute is a 'public act,' faith and credit must be given to its provisions as fully as if the materiality of this specific misrepresentation in the application, and the consequent non-existence of liability, had been declared by a judgment of a New York court...."

NEW YORK LIFE INSURANCE CO. v. DODGE, 246 U.S. 357 (1918): The Court held (5–4) that it was an unconstitutional impairment of contract for the Missouri courts to apply a local statute that kept life insurance in force after non-payment of premiums. Even though the insured had taken out the policy in Missouri, the court ruled that the fact that his application for a loan on the policy had been sent to New York and acted on there by the company made it a New York contract. Under the New York law the policy lapsed for non-payment of premiums and was not saved from forfeiture, as was true in Missouri. In declaring the New York rule applicable the Court said that to "hold otherwise would permit destruction of the right ... freely to borrow money upon policy ... and ... sanction the impairment of that liberty of contract guaranteed to all by the Fourteenth Amendment."

In dissent, Justice Brandeis argued that the loan agreement was a "Missouri contract" because every act done by the insured was done in Missouri. However, he insisted, even if the loan agreement was made in New York, Missouri was not powerless to affect it (246 U.S. at pp. 382–83):

> "The test of constitutionality to be applied here is that commonly applied when the validity of a statute limiting the right of contract is questioned, namely: Is the subject-matter within the reasonable scope of regulation? Is the end legitimate? Are the means appropriate to the end sought to be obtained? If so, the act must be sustained, unless the court is satisfied that it is clearly an arbitrary and unnecessary interference with the right of the individual to his personal liberty. Here the subject is insurance; a subject long recognized as being within the sphere of regulation of contracts. The specific end to be attained was the protection of the net value of insurance policies by prohibiting provisions for forfeiture; an incident of the insurance contract long recognized as requiring regulation. The means adopted was to prescribe the limits within which the parties might agree to dispose of the net value of the policy otherwise than by commutation into extended insurance; a means commonly adopted in nonforfeiture laws, only the specific limitation in question being unusual. The insurance policy sought to be protected was a contract made within the state, between a citizen of the state and a foreign corporation also resident or present there. The protection was to be afforded while the parties so remained subject to the jurisdiction of the State. The protection was accomplished by refusing to permit the courts of the State to give to acts done within it by such residents (Dodge did no act elsewhere), the effect of nullifying in part that nonforfeiture provision, which the legislature deemed necessary for the welfare of the citizens of the State and for their protection against acts of insuring corporations. The statute does not invalidate any part of the loan; it leaves intact the ordinary remedies for collecting debts. The statute merely prohibits satisfying a part of the debt out of the reserve in a manner deemed by the legislature destructive of the protection devised against forfeiture. The provision may be likened to homestead and exemption laws by which creditors are limited in respect to the property out of which their claims may be enforced. When the New York Life Insurance Company sought and obtained permission to do business within the State, and when the policy in question and the loan agreement were entered into, this statute was in existence and was of course known to the company. It has no legal ground of complaint, when the Missouri courts refuse to give to the loan agreement effect in a manner

and to an extent inconsistent with the express prohibition of the statute...."

MUTUAL LIFE INSURANCE CO. v. LIEBING, 259 U.S. 209 (1922): [The issues and the facts in this case were almost precisely parallel to those in the Dodge case next above, except for a difference in the wording of the loan provision in the insurance policy. The Supreme Court of the United States unanimously affirmed a judgment of the Missouri court in favor of the beneficiary against the insurance company.]

■ HOLMES, J. ... In New York L. Ins. Co. v. Dodge, supra, it was held that when the later transaction was consummated in New York, Missouri could not prohibit a citizen within her borders from executing it. But if the later contract was made in Missouri, then by the present and earlier decisions, notwithstanding any contrary agreement, the statute does govern the case. See 246 U.S. 366.

The policy now sued upon contained a positive promise to make the loan if asked, whereas, in the one last mentioned, it might be held that some discretion was reserved to the company. For here the language is, "the company will ... loan amounts within the limits of the cash surrender value," etc., where as there it was, "cash loans can be obtained." On this distinction the Missouri court seems to have held that, as soon as the application was delivered to a representative of the company in Missouri, the offer in the policy was accepted and the new contract complete, and therefore subject to Missouri law. If, however, the application should be regarded as only an offer, the effective acceptance of it did not take place until the check was delivered to Blees, which again was in Missouri, where he lived. In whichever way regarded, the facts lead to the same conclusion; and although the circumstances may present some temptation to seek a different one by ingenuity, the Constitution and the first principles of legal thinking allow the law of the place where a contract is made to determine the validity and the consequences of the act.

HARTFORD ACCIDENT & INDEMNITY CO. v. DELTA & PINE LAND CO., 292 U.S. 143 (1934): An action was brought in a Mississippi court on a fidelity bond covering the insured's employees in any position and anywhere they worked, of course including Mississippi. The bond was issued in Tennessee. The defalcation which was the subject of the action occurred in Mississippi. The bond had a provision that claim under it must be made within fifteen months from the termination of the suretyship on the defaulting employee, and the claim sued on was not made within that period. The provision was valid under the law of Tennessee. A Mississippi statute provided "All contracts of insurance on property, lives or interests in this state shall be deemed to be made therein". Another statute struck down the kind of limitation contained in the bond. The courts of Mississippi applied the Mississippi statutes and gave judgment for the plaintiff. The Supreme Court of the United States reversed the judgment, saying "A state may limit or prohibit the making of certain contracts within its own territory ... but it cannot extend the effect of its laws beyond its borders so as to destroy or impair the rights of citizens of other states to make a contract not operative within its jurisdiction and lawful where made.... it may not, on grounds of policy, ignore a right which has lawfully vested elsewhere, if, as here, the interest of the forum has but slight connection with the substance of the contract obligations. A legislative policy which attempts to draw to the state of the forum control over the obligations of contracts elsewhere validly consummated and to convert them for all purposes into contracts of the forum, regardless of the relative importance of the interests of the forum as contrasted with those created at the place of the contract, conflicts with the guaranties of the Fourteenth Amendment." The Court said it was unnecessary to reach the defendant's arguments based on the full faith and credit and contract clauses.

NOTES

1. The Delta & Pine case has had a checkered career in the Supreme Court. Its current status must be diagnosed on the basis of close reading of the Justices' opinions in Clay v. Sun Insurance Office, Limited, p. 346, infra and Allstate Insurance Co. v. Hague, p. 349, infra.

2. What factors might argue for a different standard in determining the constitutionality of assertions of legislative power in the international context compared with the interstate? See Jones, An Interest Analysis Approach to Extraterritorial Application of Rule 10b–5, 52 Tex.L.Rev. 983 (1974); Comment, 12 Houston L.Rev. 924 (1975).

Order of United Commercial Travelers v. Wolfe

Supreme Court of the United States, 1947.
331 U.S. 586, 67 S.Ct. 1355, 91 L.Ed. 1687, 173 A.L.R. 1107.

■ JUSTICE BURTON delivered the opinion of the Court.

This is an action in a circuit court of the State of South Dakota, brought by an Ohio citizen against a fraternal benefit society incorporated in Ohio, to recover benefits claimed to have arisen under the constitution of that society as a result of the death of an insured member who had been a citizen of South Dakota throughout his membership. The case presents the question whether the full faith and credit clause of the Constitution of the United States required the court of the forum, South Dakota, to give effect to a provision of the constitution of the society prohibiting the bringing of an action on such a claim more than six months after the disallowance of the claim by the Supreme Executive Committee of the society, when that provision was valid under the law of the state of the society's incorporation, Ohio, but when the time prescribed generally by

South Dakota for commencing actions on contracts was six years and when another statute of South Dakota declared that—

"Every stipulation or condition in a contract, by which any party thereto is restricted from enforcing his rights under the contract by the usual legal proceedings in the ordinary tribunals, or which limits the time within which he may thus enforce his rights, is void."

We hold that, under such circumstances, South Dakota, as the state of the forum, was required, by the Constitution of the United States, to give full faith and credit to the public acts of Ohio under which the fraternal benefit society was incorporated, and that the claimant was bound by the six-month limitation upon bringing suit to recover death benefits based upon membership rights of a decedent under the constitution of the society. This has been the consistent view of this Court. [Citing in a footnote Royal Arcanum v. Green, 237 U.S. 531; Modern Woodmen v. Mixer, 267 U.S. 544; Broderick v. Rosner, 294 U.S. 629; Sovereign Camp v. Bolin, 305 U.S. 66; Pink v. A.A.A. Highway Express, 314 U.S. 201.]

. . .

... These public acts have created and regulated the society and the rights and obligations of its members. They are reflected in its articles of incorporation, constitution and by-laws. They make possible uniformity of rights and obligations among all members throughout the country, provided full faith and credit are given also to the constitution and by-laws of the society insofar as they are valid under the law of the state of incorporation. If full faith and credit are not given to these provisions, the mutual rights and obligations of the members of such societies are left subject to the control of each state. They become unpredictable and almost inevitably unequal.

. . .

The relationship thus established between a member and his fraternal benefit society differs from the ordinary contractual relationship between a policyholder and a separately owned corporate or "stock" insurance company. It differs also from that between an insured member of the usual business form of a mutual insurance company and that company. The fact of membership in the Ohio fraternal benefit society is the controlling and central feature of the relationship.... The foundation of the society is the law of Ohio. It provides the unifying control over the rights and obligations of its members....

The decisions passing upon this comparatively narrow issue are to be distinguished from those which deal only with the well established principle of conflict of laws that "If action is barred by the statute of limitations of the forum, no action can be maintained though action is not barred in the state where the cause of action arose." Restatement, Conflict of Laws § 603 (1934)....

. . .

Accepting the view ..., that this Court should not give what Mr. Justice Stone called a mere "automatic effect to the full faith and credit clause," [Alaska Packers Assn. v. Industrial Acc. Comm'n, 294 U.S. 532, at page 547], this Court consistently has upheld, on the basis of evaluated public policy, the law of the state of incorporation of a fraternal benefit society as the law that should control the validity of the terms of membership in that corporation. The weight of public policy behind the general statute of South Dakota, which seeks to avoid certain provisions in ordinary contracts, does not equal that which makes necessary the recognition of the same terms of membership for members of fraternal benefit societies wherever their beneficiaries may be.

. . .

Reversed.

■ JUSTICE BLACK, with whom JUSTICE DOUGLAS, JUSTICE MURPHY, and JUSTICE RUTLEDGE join, dissenting.

. . .

Until today I had never conceived of the Federal Constitution as requiring the forty-eight states to give full faith and credit to the laws of private corporations on the theory that a policyholder-member's ability to protect himself through intra-corporate politics makes state protection of him unnecessary and unconstitutional. . . .

. . .

... Hereafter, if today's doctrine should be carried to its logical end, the state in which the most powerful corporations are concentrated, or those corporations themselves, might well be able to pass laws which would govern contracts made by the people in all of the other states.

NOTE

1. The Wolfe case has remained a rare instance of the use of the full faith and credit clause to strike down a choice of the forum's rule in preference to a sister state's. Compare Clay v. Sun Ins. Office, Ltd., p. 346, infra; Wells v. Simonds Abrasive Co., p. 321, supra.

2. See Hay, Full Faith and Credit and Federalism in Choice of Law, 34 Mercer L.Rev. 709 (1983) (arguing that the Due Process clause should be construed to impose limits on judicial jurisdiction only—see *Insurance Co.*, supra p. 77—while interstate (federalism) concerns should be addressed through resort to the Full Faith and Credit Clause). Professor James A. Martin argued that the policies of the Full Faith and Credit Clause should be the sole measures of the constitutional limits on choice of law. See Martin, Constitutional Limitations on Choice of Law, 61 Corn.L.Rev. 185 (1976). Compare Kirgis, The Rules of Due Process and Full Faith and Credit in Choice of Law, 62 Corn.L.Rev. 94 (1976). If the forum does not violate due process in applying its decisional norm to a multistate case is the full-faith-and-credit requirement automatically satisfied?

ALASKA PACKERS ASSOCIATION v. INDUSTRIAL ACCIDENT COMMISSION OF CALIFORNIA, 294 U.S. 532 (1935): A non-resident alien executed in California a written contract of employment under which he agreed to work for his employer in Alaska during the salmon canning season. The employer agreed to transport him to and from Alaska and to pay him his stipulated wages in California on his return. The contract recited that the employee had elected to be bound by the Alaska Workmen's Compensation Law. The employee was injured in Alaska and on his return to California he sought an award under that state's compensation act and was granted it. The employer attacked the award as made in violation of the due process and full faith and credit clauses. The Supreme Court of the United States upheld the award.

Justice Stone: "The probability is slight that injured workmen, once returned to California, would be able to retrace their steps to Alaska, and there successfully prosecute their claims for compensation. Without a remedy in California, they would be remediless, and there was the danger that they might become public charges, both matters of grave public concern to the state.

"California, therefore, had a legitimate public interest in controlling and regulating this employer-employee relationship....

"... [T]he conflict is to be resolved, not by giving automatic effect to the full faith and credit clause, compelling the courts of each state to subordinate its own statutes to those of the other, but by appraising the governmental interests of each jurisdiction, and turning the scale of decision according to their weight.

"... [O]nly if it appears that, in the conflict of interests which have found expression in the conflicting statutes, the interest of Alaska is superior to that of California, is there rational basis for denying to the courts of California the right to apply the laws of their own state."

Pacific Employers Insurance Co. v. Industrial Accident Commission

Supreme Court of the United States, 1939.
306 U.S. 493, 59 S.Ct. 629, 83 L.Ed. 940.

■ JUSTICE STONE delivered the opinion of the Court.

The question is whether the full faith and credit which the Constitution requires to be given to a Massachusetts workmen's compensation statute precludes California from applying its own workmen's compensation act in the case of an injury suffered by a Massachusetts employee of a Massachusetts employer while in California in the course of his employment.

. . .

The injured employee, a resident of Massachusetts, ... instituted the present proceeding before the California Commission for the award of compensation under the California Act ..., naming petitioner as insurance carrier under that Act.... The California Commission directed petitioner to pay the compensation prescribed by the California Act, including the amounts of lien claims filed in the proceeding for medical, hospital and nursing services and certain further amounts necessary for such services in the future.

By the applicable Massachusetts statute, sections 24, 26, c. 152, Mass. Gen.Laws (Ter.Ed.1932), an employee of a person insured under the Act, as was the employer in this case, is deemed to waive his "right of action at common law or under the law of any other jurisdiction" to recover for personal injuries unless he shall have given appropriate notice to the employer in writing that he elects to retain such rights. Section 26 directs that without the notice his right to recover be restricted to the compensation provided by the Act for injuries received in the course of his employment, "whether within or without the commonwealth." ...

... Section 27(a) [of California's Workmen's Compensation Act] provides that "No contract, rule, or regulation shall exempt the employer from liability for the compensation fixed by this act." And section 58 provides that the commission shall have jurisdiction over claims for compensation for injuries suffered outside the state when the employee's contract of hire was entered into within the state.... The California Act is compulsory. Section 6(a). The Massachusetts Act is similarly effective unless the employee gives notice not to be bound by it, which in this case he did not do. Section 24.

Petitioner, which as insurance carrier has assumed the liability of the employer under the California Act, relies on the provisions of the Massachusetts Act that the compensation shall be that prescribed for injuries suffered in the course of the employment, whether within or without the state. It insists that since the contract of employment was entered into in Massachusetts and the employee consented to be bound by the Massachusetts Act, that, and not the California statute, fixes the employee's right to compensation whether the injuries were received within or without the state, and that the Massachusetts statute is constitutionally entitled to full faith and credit in the courts of California.

We may assume that these provisions are controlling upon the parties in Massachusetts, and that since they are applicable to a Massachusetts contract of employment between a Massachusetts employer and employee, they do not infringe due process.... Similarly the constitutionality of the provisions of the California statute awarding compensation for injuries to an employee occurring within its borders, ... is not open to question....

While in the circumstances now presented, either state, if its system for administering workmen's compensation permitted, would be free to adopt and enforce the remedy provided by the statute of the other, here each has provided for itself an exclusive remedy for a liability which it was constitutionally authorized to impose. But neither is bound, apart from the compulsion of the full faith and credit clause, to enforce the laws of the other....

To the extent that California is required to give full faith and credit to the conflicting Massachusetts statute it must be denied the right to apply in its own courts its own statute, constitutionally enacted in pursuance of its policy to provide compensation for employees injured in their employment within the state.... We cannot say that the full faith and credit clause goes so far.

While the purpose of that provision was to preserve rights acquired or confirmed under the public acts and judicial proceedings of one state by requiring recognition of their validity in other states, the very nature of the federal union of states, to which are reserved some of the attributes of sovereignty, precludes resort to the full faith and credit clause as the means for compelling a state to substitute the statutes of other states for its own statutes dealing with a subject matter concerning which it is competent to legislate. As was pointed out in Alaska Packers Assn. v. Industrial Accident Comm'n, [294 U.S. 532, 547]: "A rigid and literal enforcement of the full faith and credit clause, without regard to the statute of the forum, would lead to the absurd result that, wherever the conflict arises, the statute of each state must be enforced in the courts of the other, but cannot be in its own." And in cases like the present it would create an impasse which would often leave the employee remediless. Full faith and credit would deny to California the right to apply its own remedy, and its administrative machinery may well not be adapted to giving the remedy afforded by Massachusetts....

. . .

This Court must determine for itself how far the full faith and credit clause compels the qualification or denial of rights asserted under the laws of one state, that of the forum, by the statute of another state.... But there would seem to be little room for the exercise of that function when the statute of the forum is the expression of domestic policy, in terms declared to be exclusive in its application to persons and events within the state. Although Massachusetts has an interest in safeguarding the compensation of Massachusetts employees while temporarily abroad in the course of their employment, and may adopt that policy for itself, that could hardly be thought to support an application of the full faith and credit clause which would override the constitutional authority of another state to legislate for the bodily safety and economic protection of employees injured within it. Few matters could be deemed more appropriately the concern of the state in which the injury occurs or more completely within its power....

Bradford Electric Light Co. v. Clapper [286 U.S. 145 (1932)], on which petitioner relies, fully recognized this limitation on the full faith and credit clause. It was there held that a federal court in New Hampshire, in a suit brought against a Vermont employer by his Vermont employee to recover for an injury suffered in the course of his employment while temporarily in New Hampshire, was bound to apply the Vermont Compensation Act rather than the provision of the New Hampshire Compensation Act which permitted the employee, at his election, to enforce his common law remedy.

But the Court was careful to point out that there was nothing in the New Hampshire statute, the decisions of its courts, or in the circumstances of the case, to suggest that reliance on the provisions of the Vermont statute, as a defense to the New Hampshire suit, was obnoxious to the policy of New Hampshire. The Clapper case cannot be said to have decided more than that a state statute applicable to employer and employee within the state, which by its terms provides compensation for the employee if he is injured in the course of his employment while temporarily in another state, will be given full faith and credit in the latter when not obnoxious to its policy....

Here, California legislation ... expressly provides, ... that "No contract, rule or regulation shall exempt the employer from liability for the compensation fixed by this Act." The Supreme Court of California has declared in its opinion in this case that ... "It would be obnoxious to [the policy of the California Act] to deny persons who have been injured in this state the right to apply for compensation when to do so might require physicians and hospitals to go to another state to collect charges for medical care and treatment given to such persons."

Full faith and credit does not here enable one state to legislate for the other or to project its laws across state lines so as to preclude the other from prescribing for itself the legal consequences of acts within it.

Affirmed.

NOTE

In the Pacific Employers case Justice Stone seemingly shifted away from the interest-appraising and weighing approach to full faith and credit that he asserted so forcefully in Alaska Packers. Instead, he advanced a view based on reading Bradford Electric v. Clapper to mean that the full faith and credit clause does not require the forum state to apply another state's laws if it finds them "obnoxious" to the forum law's policy. Since the forum court presumably will not often balk at applying sister-state law that is congenial to its own, does this approach in effect read full faith and credit out of the picture? Notice what happens to the interest-weighing and "obnoxious" tests in later Supreme Court decisions, such as Carroll v. Lanza and Watson.

Carroll v. Lanza

Supreme Court of the United States, 1955.
349 U.S. 408, 75 S.Ct. 804, 99 L.Ed. 1183.

■ JUSTICE DOUGLAS delivered the opinion of the Court.

Carroll, the petitioner, was an employee of Hogan, an intervenor, who in turn was a subcontractor doing work for the respondent Lanza, the general contractor. Carroll and Hogan were residents of Missouri; and Carroll's employment contract with Hogan was made in Missouri. The work, however, was done in Arkansas; and it was there that the injury occurred.

Carroll, not aware that he had remedies under the Arkansas law, received 34 weekly payments for the injury under the Missouri Compensation Act.

[The Missouri workmen's compensation act, so the Court found, was applicable to injuries received outside the state if the employment contract was made in the state, as here, and the act in terms excluded "all other rights and remedies ... at common law or otherwise" on account of an injury or death. The Arkansas workmen's compensation act also purported to provide the exclusive remedy of the employee against the employer but not against a third party as the general contractor, Lanza.

While receiving weekly payments under the Missouri act Carroll sued Lanza for common law damages in an Arkansas state court, and on removal to the federal court recovered a judgment. The Court of Appeals, while agreeing with the District Court that the judgment was sustainable as a matter of Arkansas law, reversed on the ground the Full Faith and Credit Clause of the Constitution barred recovery. The Supreme Court of the United States granted certiorari because of doubts raised by the Pacific Employers Insurance Co. case, p. 336 supra.]

The Pacific Employers Insurance Co. case allowed the Compensation Act of the place of the injury to override the Compensation Act of the home State. Here it is a common-law action that is asserted against the exclusiveness of the remedy of the home State; and that is seized on as marking a difference. That is not in our judgment a material difference. Whatever deprives the remedy of the home State of its exclusive character qualifies or contravenes the policy of that State and denies it full faith and credit, if full faith and credit is due. But the Pacific Employers Insurance Co. case teaches that in these personal injury cases the State where the injury occurs need not be a vassal to the home State and allow only that remedy which the home State has marked as the exclusive one.... Her interests are large and considerable and are to be weighed not only in the light of the facts of this case but by the kind of situation presented. For we write not only for this case and this day alone, but for this type of case. The State where the tort occurs certainly has a concern in the problems following in the wake of the injury. The problems of medical care and of possible dependents are among these ... Arkansas therefore has a legitimate interest in opening her courts to suits of this nature, even though in this case Carroll's injury may have cast no burden on her or on her institutions.

... Arkansas, the State of the forum, is not adopting any policy of hostility to the public Acts of Missouri. It is choosing to apply its own rule of law to give affirmative relief for an action arising within its borders.

... Were it otherwise, the State where the injury occurred would be powerless to provide any remedies or safeguards to nonresident employees working within its borders. We do not think the Full Faith and Credit Clause demands that subserviency from the State of the injury.

Reversed.

■ JUSTICE FRANKFURTER, whom JUSTICE BURTON and JUSTICE HARLAN join, dissenting.

In order to place the problems presented by this case in the proper context for adjudication, it has seemed to me desirable to examine the course of the Court's decisions touching the constitutional requirement for giving full faith and credit to statutes of a sister State.

The cases fall into three main groups:

(1) Those in which the forum was called upon to give effect to a sister-state statute and declined to do so.

... From these cases it appears that, the forum cannot, by statute or otherwise, refuse to enforce a sister-state statute giving a transitory cause of action, whether in contract or tort. E.g., Broderick v. Rosner, [294 U.S. 629 (1935)]; Hughes v. Fetter, [341 U.S. 609 (1951)]. Indeed, the forum may permissibly go a step in the other direction and disregard the venue provisions of an out-of-state statute which would have prevented the forum from enforcing the right. Tennessee Coal, Iron & R. Co. v. George, [233 U.S. 354 (1914)]. The forum may, however, apply its own more restrictive statute of limitations to an outside wrongful death action, Wells v. Simonds Abrasive Co., [345 U.S. 514 (1953)] and dicta indicate that it may refuse to enforce a penal law, a law found antagonistic to the forum's public policy, or a law which requires specialized proceedings or remedies not available in the forum, ...

(2) Those in which the forum applied its own statute rather than that of a sister State because the latter was not of limiting exclusiveness, or in which the forum applied the sister-state statute because the forum's was not exclusive....

These cases prove that where the statute of either the forum or the outside State is not found to be exclusive regarding remedies or rights elsewhere, the statute need not be accorded exclusive effect....

(3) Those in which the forum applied its own substantive law, statutory or judicial, when clearly in conflict with the out-of-state statute. [The opinion here cites twenty-one cases.]

These cases have arisen in three principal fields: (a) commercial law; (b) insurance; and (c) workmen's compensation. As a statistical matter, in 21 cases of direct conflict the Court held for the forum 10 times and for the sister State 11 times.

(a) In commercial law a number of cases have involved statutory assessment against out-of-state shareholders under the laws of the State of incorporation of an insolvent corporation. The Court's consistent position has been that the law of the incorporating State must be given effect by the forum....

(b) The insurance cases reflect considerations similar to those in the commercial cases. The Court has found in fraternal benefit societies an "indivisible unity" among the members and a resultant need for uniform construction of rights and duties in the common fund....

As to ordinary insurance contracts, the forum has had a much wider scope. The Court has balanced the interests of the competing jurisdictions, including factors such as the residence of the insured, where premiums were paid or payable, where the policy was applied for and delivered, where the insured died, what law the policy itself provided should govern, and whether loan agreements and new policies were ancillary to the initial policy. The forum has been permitted to protect its residents against insurance companies, but the Court has required the forum to have more than a casual interest....

(c) In workmen's compensation cases the Court has likewise adopted an interests-weighing approach....

In applying to the immediate situation the fair guidance offered by the past decisions of the Court regarding full faith and credit, a number of considerations become apparent: (1) Unlike the other workmen's compensation cases—or, for that matter, any of the cases in which the forum has prevailed in a conflict between the forum and the outside law—the interest of the forum here is solely dependent on the occurrence of the injury within its borders. No rights of Arkansas residents are involved, since none of the parties is an Arkansan; the workman was removed immediately to a Missouri hospital and has, so far as appears, remained in Missouri. What might be regarded as the societal interest of Arkansas in the protection of the bodily safety of workers within its borders is an interest equally true of any jurisdiction where a workman is injured and exactly the sort of interest which New Hampshire had in Clapper. [Bradford Electric Light Co. v. Clapper, 286 U.S. 145 (1932).] (2) Thus, the Court is squarely faced with the Clapper problem. To make the interest of Arkansas prevail over the interest of Missouri on the basis of the Full Faith and Credit Clause would require that Clapper be explicitly overruled and that, in the area of workmen's compensation law, the place of injury be decisive. And if Clapper is to be overruled, on which I and those who join me express no opinion, it should be done with reasons making manifest why Justice Brandeis' long-matured, weighty opinion in that case was ill-founded. It should not be cast aside on the presupposition that full faith and credit need not be given to a sister-state workmen's compensation statute if the law of the forum happens to be more favorable to the claimant. (3) Furthermore, the new provision of 28 U.S.C. § 1738, cannot be disregarded. In 1948 Congress for the first time dealt with the full faith and credit effect to be given statutes. The absence of such a provision was used by Justice Stone to buttress the Court's opinions both in Alaska Packers, 294 U.S. at page 547, and Pacific Employers, 306 U.S. at page 502. Hence, if § 1738 has any effect, it would seem to tend toward respecting Missouri's legislation. See Reese, Full Faith and Credit to Statutes: The Defense of Public Policy, 19 U. of Chi.L.Rev. 339, 343 et seq.

There is, however, a readily available alternative short of overruling Clapper, which dispenses with the difficulties inherent in applying the Full Faith and Credit Clause.

[The alternative preferred in the dissent was that the Missouri law itself might not bar a right of action against the general contractor, and the case should be remanded to the Court of Appeals for a determination of the Missouri law on this matter.]

NOTES

1. How should former law professor Frankfurter's opinion be graded as an exposition of the command of full faith and credit to sister-state law as of 1955?

2. Bradford Electric v. Clapper seemed to have identified the place where the employment was entered into and centered as *the* critical factor selected by full faith and credit in implementing workmen's compensation laws. Is there anything left of that implication—or of the holding in Clapper—after Carroll v. Lanza?

3. In Posnak, Choice of Law: A Very Well–Curried Leflar Approach, 34 Mercer L.Rev. 731 (1983), the author argues that the Carroll case may go over the edge constitutionally because it seems to allow a state with no actual interest in the aftermath of an injury (or any other element of the transaction) to apply its own rule in derogation of the contrary law of a state with strong interests in the case. See also Kramer, Rethinking Choice of Law, 90 Columbia L.Rev. 277 (1990).

Watson v. Employers Liability Assurance Corp., Limited

Supreme Court of the United States, 1954.
348 U.S. 66, 75 S.Ct. 166, 99 L.Ed. 74.

■ JUSTICE BLACK delivered the opinion of the Court.

Louisiana has an insurance code which comprehensively regulates the business of insurance in all its phases. This case brings to us challenges to the constitutionality of certain provisions of that code allowing injured persons to bring direct actions against liability insurance companies that have issued policies contracting to pay liabilities imposed on persons who inflict injury. Cf. Lumbermen's Mutual Casualty Co. v. Elbert, 348 U.S. 48. This is such a direct action brought by the appellants, Mr. and Mrs. Watson, in a Louisiana state court claiming damages against the appellee, Employers Liability Assurance Corporation, Ltd., on account of alleged personal injuries suffered by Mrs. Watson. The complaint charged that the injuries occurred in Louisiana when Mrs. Watson bought and used in that State "Toni Home Permanent," a hair-waving product alleged to have contained a highly dangerous latent ingredient put there by its manufacturer. The manufacturer is the Toni Company of Illinois, a subsidiary of the Gillette Safety Razor Company which has its headquarters in Massachusetts.

The particular problem presented with reference to enforcing the Louisiana statute in this case arises because the insurance policy sued on was negotiated and issued in Massachusetts and delivered in Massachusetts and Illinois. This Massachusetts-negotiated contract contains a clause, recognized as binding and enforceable under Massachusetts and Illinois law, which prohibits direct actions against the insurance company until *after* final determination of the Toni Company's obligation to pay personal injury damages either by judgment or agreement. Contrary to this contractual "no action" clause, the challenged statutory provisions permit injured persons to sue an insurance company *before* such final determination. As to injuries occurring in Louisiana, one provision of the State's direct action statute makes it applicable, even though, as here, an insurance contract is made in another state and contains a clause forbidding such direct actions. Another Louisiana statutory provision, with which Employers long ago complied, compels foreign insurance companies to consent to such direct suits in order to get a certificate to do business in the State. The basic issue raised by the attack on both these provisions is whether the Federal Constitution forbids Louisiana to apply its own law and compels it to apply the law of Massachusetts or Illinois.

. . .

[The defendant contended the two Louisiana provisions contravened the Equal Protection, Contract, Due Process, and Full Faith and Credit clauses of the Constitution. The United States District Court, to which the case had been removed, dismissed the case, holding the statutory provisions unconstitutional under the Due Process Clause as to policies written and delivered outside Louisiana. The Court of Appeals affirmed the dismissal and the plaintiff appealed.]

Some contracts made locally, affecting nothing but local affairs, may well justify a denial to other states of power to alter those contracts. But, as this case illustrates, a vast part of the business affairs of this Nation does not present such simple local situations. Although this insurance contract was issued in Massachusetts, it was to protect Gillette and its Illinois subsidiary against damages on account of personal injuries that might be suffered by users of Toni Home Permanents anywhere in the United States, its territories, or in Canada. As a consequence of the modern practice of conducting widespread business activities throughout the entire United States, this Court has in a series of cases held that more states than one may seize hold of local activities which are part of multistate transactions and may regulate to protect interests of its own people, even though other phases of the same transactions might justify regulatory legislation in other states....

Louisiana's direct action statute is not a mere intermeddling in affairs beyond her boundaries which are no concern of hers. Persons injured or killed in Louisiana are most likely to be Louisiana residents, and even if not, Louisiana may have to care for them. Serious injuries may require treatment in Louisiana homes or hospitals by Louisiana doctors. The injured may be destitute. They may be compelled to call upon friends, relatives, or the public for help. Louisiana has manifested its natural interest in the injured by providing remedies for recovery of damages. It has a similar interest in policies of insurance which are designed to assure ultimate payment of such damages. Moreover, Louisiana courts in most instances provide the most convenient forum for trial of these cases. But modern transportation and business methods have made it more difficult to serve process on wrongdoers who live or do business in other states. In this case efforts to serve the Gillette Company were answered by a motion to dismiss on the ground that Gillette had no Louisiana agent on whom process could be served. If this motion is granted, Mrs. Watson, but for the direct action law, could not get her case tried without going to Massachusetts or Illinois although she lives in Louisiana and her claim is for injuries from a product bought and used there. What has been said is enough to show Louisiana's legitimate interest in safeguarding the rights of persons injured there. In view of that interest, the direct action provisions here challenged do not violate due process.

What we have said above goes far toward answering the Full Faith and Credit Clause contention. That clause does not automatically compel a state to subordinate its own contract laws to the laws of another state in which a contract happens to have been formally executed. Where, as here, a contract affects the people of several states, each may have interests that leave it free to enforce its own contract policies.... We have already pointed to the vital interests of Louisiana in liability insurance that covers injuries to people in that State. Of course Massachusetts also has some interest in the policy sued on in this case. The insurance contract was formally executed in that State and Gillette has an office there. But plainly these interests cannot outweigh the interest of Louisiana in taking care of those injured in Louisiana. Since this is true, the Full Faith and Credit Clause does not compel Louisiana to subordinate its direct action provisions to Massachusetts contract rules....

Reversed.

■ [JUSTICE FRANKFURTER concurred in a separate opinion in which he relied on "the practically arbitrary power of a State in dealing with the desire of a foreign corporation not privileged to do so by federal authority to do business within its bounds."]

NOTES

1. "Since," the Court said, Massachusetts' interests "cannot outweigh the interests of Louisiana in taking care of those injured in Louisiana," full faith does not compel Louisiana to enforce the no action clause of the "Massachusetts contract." The clear implication is that the full faith and credit clause would come into play if the forum state's interests were outweighed by the other state's interests. On the other hand, the position taken in the Pacific Employers case before Watson and the Carroll case after Watson was that there is no need for interest weighing; a state is privileged to apply its own law under full faith and credit provided only it has power to do so under due process.

2. In the years since the Watson case was decided, long-arm jurisdiction has expanded so greatly it is no longer necessary to use the direct action statute as a jurisdictional device, except in circumstances dealt with by the Seider procedure. With the invalidation of that procedure by Rush v. Savchuk, p. 146, supra, the question is what contacts the forum state must have in order to permit a direct action against an insurer when the insurance contract contains a no action clause that is valid in the state where the contract was made.

3. In Hoopeston Canning Co. v. Cullen, 318 U.S. 313 (1943), the Court held that Illinois reciprocal insurance associations could be made subject to the laws of New York as a condition of insuring property in that state against fire and related risks. The insurance contracts were completed in Illinois, and the associations contended that under the due process clause New York could not make them subject to the laws of New York. Justice Black responded that a state other than the state where the contract was made could have a substantial interest, "measured by highly realistic considerations such as the protection of the citizen insured or the protection of the state from the incidents of loss." *Hoopeston Canning* was questioned in Silver v. Garcia, 592 F.Supp. 495 (D.Puerto Rico 1984).

4. The usual rule is that the forum will apply its own law in determining whether or not to grant a divorce. Can this rule constitutionally be applied in a situation where neither spouse has a close relationship to the forum state? This question is discussed by Judge Hastie in his dissenting opinion in Alton v. Alton, 207 F.2d 667 (3d Cir.1953), p. 839, infra.

Are the tests of judicial jurisdiction and of legislative jurisdiction the same or different? See, in this connection, the following statement in Leflar, McDougal & Felix, American Conflicts Law 164 (4th ed. 1986):

> ... Contacts sufficient to satisfy "fair play and substantial justice" for judicial jurisdiction under the due process clause will often satisfy whatever test (perhaps the same test) the same clause prescribes for legislative jurisdiction. It cannot be concluded, however, that identical *facts* automatically mark the outer limits of "fair play and substantial justice" for *both* constitutional purposes. The "fairness" and "justice" which the due process clause requires depend upon the purposes and functions of the law's operation in each specific separated context. Fairness and justice are relative things, not absolutes. The questions of what law may govern and what court may act are similar though not the same. The lines that delineate the answers to the questions seem to be converging but they have not merged. (Italics as in original text.) *

See, also, the Symposium, 59 Col.L.Rev. 1–104 (1988), comparing the constitutional limits on the exercise of long-arm jurisdiction with those limiting a court in its choice of law. The Symposium articles consisted of: Hay, Judicial Jurisdiction and Choice of Law: Constitutional Limitations, 9–36; Peterson, Jurisdiction and Choice of Law Revisited, 37–66; Weinberg, The Place of Trial and the Law Applied: Overhauling Constitutional Theory, 67–104.

Clay v. Sun Insurance Office, Limited
Supreme Court of the United States, 1964.
377 U.S. 179, 84 S.Ct. 1197, 12 L.Ed.2d 229.

■ JUSTICE DOUGLAS delivered the opinion of the Court.

This case, which invoked the diversity jurisdiction of the Federal District Court in a suit to recover damages under an insurance policy, was

---

* Quoted with the permission of the copyright owner, The Michie Company.

here before. 363 U.S. 207. The initial question then as now is whether the 12-month-suit clause in the policy governs, in which event the claim is barred, or whether Florida's statutes nullifying such clauses if they require suit to be filed in less than five years are applicable and valid, in which event the suit is timely. The policy was purchased by petitioner in Illinois while he was a citizen and resident of that State. Respondent, a British company, is licensed to do business in Illinois, Florida, and several other States.

A few months after purchasing the policy, petitioner moved to Florida and became a citizen and resident of that State; and it was in Florida that the loss occurred two years later. When the case reached here, the majority view was that the underlying constitutional question—whether consistently with due process, Florida could apply its five-year statute to this Illinois contract—should not be reached until the Florida Supreme Court, through its certificate procedure, had construed that statute and resolved another local law question. On remand the Court of Appeals certified the two questions to the Florida Supreme Court, which answered both questions in petitioner's favor. 133 So.2d 735. Thereafter the Court of Appeals held that it was not compatible with due process for Florida to apply its five-year statute to this contract and that judgment should be entered for respondent. 319 F.2d 505. We again granted certiorari....

While there are Illinois cases indicating that parties may contract—as here—for a shorter period of limitations than is provided by the Illinois statute, we are referred to no Illinois decision extending that rule into other States whenever claims on Illinois contracts are sought to be enforced there. We see no difficulty whatever under either the Full Faith and Credit Clause or the Due Process Clause. We deal with an ambulatory contract on which suit might be brought in any one of several States. Normally, as the Court held in Pacific Employers Ins. Co. v. Industrial Accident Comm'n, 306 U.S. 493, 502, a State having jurisdiction over a claim deriving from an out-of-state employment contract need not substitute the conflicting statute of the other State (workmen's compensation) for its own statute (workmen's compensation)—where the employee was injured in the course of his employment while temporarily in the latter State....

The Court of Appeals relied in the main on Hartford Accident & Indemnity Co. v. Delta & Pine Land Co., 292 U.S. 143, and Home Ins. Co. v. Dick, 281 U.S. 397. Those were cases where the activities in the State of the forum were thought to be too slight and too casual, as in the Delta & Pine Land Co. case ... to make the application of local law consistent with due process, or wholly lacking, as in the Dick case. No deficiency of that order is present here. As Justice Black, dissenting, said when this case was here before:

"Insurance companies, like other contractors, do not confine their contractual activities and obligations within state boundaries. They sell to customers who are promised protection in States far away from the place where the contract is made. In this very case the policy was sold to Clay with knowledge that he could take his property anywhere in the world he saw fit without losing the protection of his insurance. In fact, his contract was described on its face as a 'Personal Property Floater Policy (World Wide)'. The contract did not even attempt to provide that the law of Illinois would govern when suits were filed anywhere else in the country. Shortly after the contract was made, Clay moved to Florida and there he lived for several years. His insured property was there all that time. The company knew this fact. Particularly since the company was licensed to do business in Florida, it must have known it might be sued there...." 363 U.S. at 221.

. . .

Reversed.

NOTES

1. Were all of the Florida contacts mentioned by Justice Douglas necessary to give Florida legislative jurisdiction? Note in this connection that the policy had been issued at a time when neither the insured nor his property had any contact with Florida.

2. Can the Clay decision be satisfactorily distinguished from John Hancock Mutual Life Insurance Co. v. Yates, p. 330, supra? Would the decision have been different in Yates if, following the issuance of the policy, the insured had moved to Georgia and had died while domiciled there?

3. What if the insured risk is immovable? In Burger King Corp. v. Continental Insurance Co., 359 F.Supp. 184 (W.D.Pa.1973), suit was brought in Florida on a casualty policy for property loss and loss of income as a result of damage to a fast-food restaurant because of earth movement. The insured was a Florida corporation, while the defendant was a New York corporation which wrote the insurance policy in New York on property owned by plaintiff in Pennsylvania. The policy provided that no action could be brought on it more than 12 months after the loss. This suit was commenced in Florida approximately 18 months after the loss and transferred to the Pennsylvania federal court. In denying defendant's motion for summary judgment the court applied the Florida statute that declared contractual provisions "illegal and void" as contrary to Florida's public policy if they fixed the period for suit at less than the state's five-year statute of limitations.

The court noted that the constitutionality of the Florida rule had been upheld by the Supreme Court in the Clay case. It stressed that in contrast to Quarty v. Insurance Company of North America, 244 So.2d 181 (Fla.App.1971), denying applicability of the Florida rule to a suit for loss by burglary in New York on a policy issued in New York by a New York insurer to a New York resident who became a Florida resident within the 12–month policy claim period but did not sue until later, Burger King was a Florida corporation, with its principal place of business in Florida and at the time of the transaction defendant had a licensed agent in Florida. If the instant decision had been reviewed on appeal, should it have been reversed?

NEVADA V. HALL, 440 U.S. 410 (1979): Suit brought by California residents in the courts of that state to recover for injuries sustained in

California in a collision with an automobile owned by the state of Nevada and being driven on state business. Nevada interposed two defenses: sovereign immunity and that full faith and credit was owed to a Nevada statute limiting recovery against the state to $25,000. The California courts rejected both defenses and plaintiffs were awarded judgment of $1,150,000. The Supreme Court granted certiorari and, in an opinion by Justice Stevens, affirmed. On the subject of full faith and credit, Justice Stevens said:

"[T]his Court's decision in Pacific Insurance Company v. Industrial Accident Commission [supra p. 336] clearly establishes that the Full Faith and Credit Clause does not require a State to apply another State's law in violation of its own legitimate public policy.

"... In this case, California's interest is the closely related and ... substantial one of providing 'full protection to those who are injured on its highways through the negligence of both residents and nonresidents.' Hall v. University of Nevada (appendix to petition at 7). To effectuate this interest, California has provided by statute for jurisdiction in its courts over residents and nonresidents alike to allow those injured on its highways through the negligence of others to secure full compensation for their injuries in the California courts.

"In further implementation of that policy, California has unequivocally waived its own immunity from liability for the torts committed by its own agents and authorized full recovery even against the sovereign. As the California courts have found, to require California either to surrender jurisdiction or to limit respondents' recovery to the $25,000 maximum of the Nevada statute would be obnoxious to its statutorily based policies of jurisdiction over nonresident motorists and full recovery. The Full Faith and Credit Clause does not require this result.[1]"

[Three Justices dissented with respect to the denial of Nevada's claim to sovereign immunity.]

Allstate Insurance Co. v. Hague
Supreme Court of the United States, 1981.
449 U.S. 302, 101 S.Ct. 633, 66 L.Ed.2d 521.

■ JUSTICE BRENNAN announced the judgment of the Court and an opinion in which JUSTICE WHITE, JUSTICE MARSHALL, and JUSTICE BLACKMUN join.

This Court granted certiorari to determine whether the Due Process Clause of the Fourteenth Amendment or the Full Faith and Credit Clause of Art. 4, § 1, of the United States Constitution bars the Minnesota

---

1. California's exercise of jurisdiction in this case poses no substantial threat to our constitutional system of cooperative federalism. Suits involving traffic accidents occurring outside of Nevada could hardly interfere with Nevada's capacity to fulfill its own sovereign responsibilities. We have no occasion, in this case, to consider whether different state policies, either of California or of Nevada, might require a different analysis or a different result. [Footnote renumbered; other footnotes omitted.]

Supreme Court's choice of substantive Minnesota law to govern the effect of a provision in an insurance policy issued to respondent's decedent....

I

Respondent's late husband, Ralph Hague, died of injuries suffered when a motorcycle on which he was a passenger was struck from behind by an automobile. The accident occurred in Pierce County, Wis., which is immediately across the Minnesota border from Red Wing, Minn. The operators of both vehicles were Wisconsin residents, as was the decedent who, at the time of the accident, resided with respondent in Hager City, Wis., which is one and one-half miles from Red Wing. Mr. Hague had been employed in Red Wing for the 15 years immediately preceding his death and had commuted daily from Wisconsin to his place of employment.

Neither the operator of the motorcycle nor the operator of the automobile carried valid insurance. However, the decedent held a policy issued by petitioner Allstate Insurance Company covering three automobiles owned by him and containing an uninsured motorist clause insuring him against loss incurred from accidents with uninsured motorists. The uninsured motorist coverage was limited to $15,000 for each automobile.[3]

After the accident, but prior to the initiation of this lawsuit, respondent moved to Red Wing. Subsequently, she married a Minnesota resident and established residence with her new husband in Savage, Minn. At approximately the same time, a Minnesota Registrar of Probate appointed respondent personal representative of her deceased husband's estate. Following her appointment, she brought this action in Minnesota District Court seeking a declaration under Minnesota law that the $15,000 uninsured motorist coverage on each of her late husband's three automobiles could be "stacked" to provide total coverage of $45,000. Petitioner defended on the ground that whether the three uninsured motorist coverages could be stacked should be determined by Wisconsin law, since the insurance policy was delivered in Wisconsin, the accident occurred in Wisconsin, and all persons involved were Wisconsin residents at the time of the accident.

The Minnesota Supreme Court, sitting en banc, affirmed the District Court [and], ... interpreting Wisconsin law to prohibit stacking, applied Minnesota law after analyzing the relevant Minnesota contacts and interests within the analytical framework developed by Professor Leflar. See Leflar, Choice–Influencing Considerations in Conflicts Law, 41 N.Y.U.L.Rev. 267 (1966). [Professor Leflar's analytical approach, discussed at p. 515, infra, focuses on five considerations as the key factors in choice of law. The Minnesota Supreme Court determined that the fifth consideration—"applying the better rule of law"—called for use of Minnesota's stacking law. The court stressed that most states allow stacking, recent court decisions favor it, and the practice works well by spreading accident

---

3. Ralph Hague paid a separate premium for each automobile including an additional separate premium for each uninsured motorist coverage.

costs more broadly. Since insurance companies know that automobiles move freely across state lines, applying the Minnesota rule would not offend due process as too arbitrary or unreasonable.]

II

It is not for this Court to say whether the choice-of-law analysis suggested by Professor Leflar is to be preferred or whether we would make the same choice-of-law decision if sitting as the Minnesota Supreme Court. Our sole function is to determine whether the Minnesota Supreme Court's choice of its own substantive law in this case exceeded federal constitutional limitations. Implicit in this inquiry is the recognition, long accepted by this Court, that a set of facts giving rise to a lawsuit, or a particular issue within a lawsuit, may justify, in constitutional terms, application of the law of more than one jurisdiction.... As a result, the forum State may have to select one law from among the laws of several jurisdictions having some contact with the controversy.

In deciding constitutional choice-of-law questions, whether under the Due Process Clause or the Full Faith and Credit Clause,[10] this Court has traditionally examined the contacts of the State, whose law was applied, with the parties and with the occurrence or transaction giving rise to the litigation.... In order to ensure that the choice of law is neither arbitrary nor fundamentally unfair, ... the Court has invalidated the choice of law of a State which has had no significant contact or significant aggregation of contacts, creating state interests, with the parties and the occurrence or transaction.[11]

---

10. This Court has taken a similar approach in deciding choice-of-law cases under both the Due Process Clause and the Full Faith and Credit Clause. In each instance, the Court has examined the relevant contacts and resulting interests of the State whose law was applied. See, e.g., Nevada v. Hall, 440 U.S. 410, 424 (1979). Although at one time the Court required a more exacting standard under the Full Faith and Credit Clause than under the Due Process Clause for evaluating the constitutionality of choice-of-law decisions, see Alaska Packers Assn. v. Industrial Accident Comm'n, 294 U.S. 532, 549–550 (1935) (interest of State whose law was applied was no less than interest of State whose law was rejected), the Court has since abandoned the weighing of interests requirement. Carroll v. Lanza, 349 U.S. 408 (1955); see Nevada v. Hall, supra; Weintraub, Due Process and Full Faith and Credit Limitations on a State's Choice of Law, 44 Iowa L.Rev. 449 (1959). Different considerations are of course at issue when full faith and credit is to be accorded to acts, records and proceedings outside the choice-of-law area, such as in the case of sister state court judgments.

11. Prior to the advent of interest analysis in the state courts as the "dominant mode of analysis in modern choice of law theory," Silberman, Shaffer v. Heitner: The End of an Era, 53 N.Y.U.L.Rev. 33, 80, n. 259 (1978)..., the prevailing choice of law methodology focused on the jurisdiction where a particular event occurred. See, e.g., Restatement of the Law, Conflict of Laws (1934) (hereinafter cited as "Restatement First")....

Hartford Accident and Indemnity Co. v. Delta & Pine Land Co., 292 U.S. 143 (1934), ... has scant relevance for today. It implied a choice-of-law analysis which, for all intents and purposes, gave an isolated event—the writing of the bond in Tennessee—controlling constitutional significance, even though there might have been contacts with another State (there Mississippi) which would make application of its law neither unfair nor unexpected. See Martin, Personal Jurisdiction and Choice of Law, 78 Mich.L.Rev. 872, 874, and n. 11 (1980).

Two instructive examples of such invalidation are Home Insurance Company v. Dick [p. 325, supra] and John Hancock Mutual Life Insurance Co. v. Yates [p. 330, supra]. In both cases, the selection of forum law rested exclusively on the presence of one nonsignificant forum contact.

... [Justice Brennan here reviewed the Dick and Yates decisions.]

Dick and *Yates* stand for the proposition that if a State has only an insignificant contact with the parties and the occurrence or transaction, application of its law is unconstitutional. *Dick* concluded that nominal residence—standing alone—was inadequate; *Yates* held that a post-occurrence change of residence to the forum State—standing alone—was insufficient to justify application of forum law. Although instructive as extreme examples of selection of forum law, neither *Dick* nor *Yates* governs this case. For in contrast to those decisions, here the Minnesota contacts with the parties and the occurrence are obviously significant. Thus, this case is like *Alaska Packers,* [p. 339, supra] Cardillo v. Liberty Mutual Insurance Co., 330 U.S. 469 (1947), and *Clay II* [p. 346, supra]—cases where this Court sustained choice-of-law decisions based on the contacts of the State, whose law was applied, with the parties and occurrence.

In *Alaska Packers,* the Court ... held that the choice of California law was not "so arbitrary or unreasonable as to amount to a denial of due process," 294 U.S., at 542, because "without a remedy in California, [he] would be remediless," ibid., and because of California's interest that the worker not become a public charge, ibid.[15] ...

The lesson from *Dick* and *Yates,* which found insufficient forum contacts to apply forum law, and from *Alaska Packers, Cardillo,* and *Clay II,* which found adequate contacts to sustain the choice of forum law, is that for a State's substantive law to be selected in a constitutionally permissible manner, that State must have a significant contact or significant aggregation of contacts, creating state interests, such that choice of its law is neither arbitrary nor fundamentally unfair. Application of this principle to the facts of this case persuades us that the Minnesota Supreme Court's choice of its own law did not offend the Federal Constitution.

III

Minnesota has three contacts with the parties and the occurrence giving rise to the litigation. In the aggregate, these contacts permit selection by the Minnesota Supreme Court of Minnesota law allowing the stacking of Mr. Hague's uninsured motorist coverages.

First, and for our purposes a very important contact, Mr. Hague was a member of Minnesota's workforce, having been employed by a Red Wing,

---

15. The Court found no violation of the Full Faith and Credit Clause, since California's interest was considered to be no less than Alaska's, Alaska Packers Assn. v. Industrial Accident Comm'n, supra, 294 U.S. at 547–548, 549–550, even though the injury occurred in Alaska while the employee was performing his contract obligations there. While *Alaska Packers* balanced the interests of California and Alaska to determine the full faith and credit issue, such balancing is no longer required. See Nevada v. Hall, supra, 440 U.S. at 424; n. 10, supra.

Minn., enterprise for the 15 years preceding his death. While employment status may implicate a state interest less substantial than does resident status, that interest is nevertheless important. The State of employment has police power responsibilities towards the nonresident employee that are analogous, if somewhat less profound, than towards residents. Thus, such employees use state services and amenities and may call upon state facilities in appropriate circumstances.

In addition, Mr. Hague commuted to work in Minnesota, a contact which was important in Cardillo v. Liberty Mutual Co., supra, ... (daily commute between residence in District of Columbia and workplace in Virginia), and was presumably covered by his uninsured motorist coverage during the commute. The State's interest in its commuting nonresident employees reflects a state concern for the safety and well-being of its workforce and the concomitant effect on Minnesota employers.

That Mr. Hague was not killed while commuting to work or while in Minnesota does not dictate a different result. To hold that the Minnesota Supreme Court's choice of Minnesota law violated the Constitution for that reason would require too narrow a view of Minnesota's relationship with the parties and the occurrence giving rise to the litigation. An automobile accident need not occur within a particular jurisdiction for that jurisdiction to be connected to the occurrence. Similarly, the occurrence of a crash fatal to a Minnesota employee in another State is a Minnesota contact. If Mr. Hague had only been injured and missed work for a few weeks the effect on the Minnesota employer would have been palpable and Minnesota's interest in having its employee made whole would be evident. Mr. Hague's death affects Minnesota's interest still more acutely, even though Mr. Hague will not return to the Minnesota workforce. Minnesota's workforce is surely affected by the level of protection the State extends to it, either directly or indirectly. Vindication of the rights of the estate of a Minnesota employee, therefore, is an important state concern.

Mr. Hague's residence in Wisconsin does not—as Allstate seems to argue—constitutionally mandate application of Wisconsin law to the exclusion of forum law. If, in the instant case, the accident had occurred in Minnesota between Mr. Hague and an uninsured Minnesota motorist, if the insurance contract had been executed in Minnesota covering a Minnesota registered company automobile which Mr. Hague was permitted to drive, and if a Wisconsin court sought to apply Wisconsin law, certainly Mr. Hague's residence in Wisconsin, his commute between Wisconsin and Minnesota, and the insurer's presence in Wisconsin should be adequate to apply Wisconsin's law.[22] ... Employment status is not a sufficiently less

---

22. Of course, Allstate could not be certain that Wisconsin law would necessarily govern any accident which occurred in Wisconsin, whether brought in the Wisconsin courts or elsewhere. Such an expectation would give controlling significance to the wooden *lex loci delicti* doctrine. While the place of the accident is a factor to be considered in choice-of-law analysis, to apply blindly the traditional, but now largely abandoned, doctrine, Silberman, supra, 53 N.Y.U.L.Rev., at 80, n. 259; see n. 11, supra, would fail to distinguish between the relative importance of various legal issues involved in a lawsuit as

important status than residence . . . when combined with Mr. Hague's daily commute across state lines and the other Minnesota contacts present, to prohibit the choice-of-law result in this case on constitutional grounds.

Second, Allstate was at all times present and doing business in Minnesota.[23] By virtue of its presence, Allstate can hardly claim unfamiliarity with the laws of the host jurisdiction and surprise that the state courts might apply forum law to litigation in which the company is involved. "Particularly since the company was licensed to do business in [the forum], it must have known it might be sued there, and that [the forum], courts would feel bound by [forum] law."[24] Clay v. Sun Insurance Office Limited, 363 U.S. 207, 221 (1960) (Black, J., dissenting). Moreover, Allstate's presence in Minnesota gave Minnesota an interest in regulating the company's insurance obligations insofar as they affected both a Minnesota resident and court appointed representative—respondent—and a longstanding member of Minnesota's workforce—Mr. Hague. . . .

Third, respondent became a Minnesota resident prior to institution of this litigation. The stipulated facts reveal that she first settled in Red Wing, Minn., the town in which her late husband had worked. She subsequently moved to Savage, Minn., after marrying a Minnesota resident who operated an automobile service station in Bloomington, Minn. Her move to Savage occurred "almost concurrently," 289 N.W.2d, at 45, with the initiation of the instant case. There is no suggestion that Mrs. Hague moved to Minnesota in anticipation of this litigation or for the purpose of finding a legal climate especially hospitable to her claim. The stipulated facts, sparse as they are, negate any such inference.

While John Hancock Mutual Life Insurance Company v. Yates, supra, held that a postoccurrence change of residence to the forum State was insufficient in and of itself to confer power on the forum State to choose its law, that case did not hold that such a change of residence was irrelevant. Here, of course, respondent's bona fide residence in Minnesota was not the sole contact Minnesota had with this litigation. And in connection with

---

well as the relationship of other jurisdictions to the parties and the occurrence or transaction. . . .

23. The Court has recognized that examination of a State's contacts may result in divergent conclusions for jurisdiction and choice-of-law purposes. See Kulko v. Superior Court, 436 U.S. 84, 98 (1978); Shaffer v. Heitner, supra, 433 U.S., at 215; cf. Hanson v. Denckla, 357 U.S. 235, 254, and n. 27 (no jurisdiction in Florida; the "issue is personal jurisdiction, not choice of law," an issue which the Court found no need to decide). Nevertheless, "both inquiries 'are often closely related and to a substantial degree depend upon similar considerations.'" 433 U.S., at 224–225 (Brennan, J., concurring in part and dissenting in part). . . .

24. There is no element of unfair surprise or frustration of legitimate expectations as a result of Minnesota's choice of its law. Because Allstate was doing business in Minnesota and was undoubtedly aware that Mr. Hague was a Minnesota employee, it had to have anticipated that Minnesota law might apply to an accident in which Mr. Hague was involved. . . . Indeed, Allstate specifically anticipated that Mr. Hague might suffer an accident either in Minnesota or elsewhere in the United States, outside of Wisconsin, since the policy it issued offered continental coverage. . . . At the same time, Allstate did not seek to control construction of the contract since the policy contained no choice-of-law clause dictating application of Wisconsin law. . . .

her residence in Minnesota, respondent was appointed personal representative of Mr. Hague's estate by the Registrar of Probate for the County of Goodhue, Minn. Respondent's residence and subsequent appointment in Minnesota as personal representative of her late husband's estate constitute a Minnesota contact which gives Minnesota an interest in respondent's recovery, an interest which the court below identified as full compensation for "resident accident victims" to keep them "off welfare rolls" and able "to meet financial obligations." 289 N.W.2d, at 49.

In sum, Minnesota had a significant aggregation [29] of contacts with the parties and the occurrence, creating state interests, such that application of its law was neither arbitrary nor fundamentally unfair. Accordingly, the choice of Minnesota law by the Minnesota Supreme Court did not violate the Due Process Clause or the Full Faith and Credit Clause.

Affirmed.

■ JUSTICE STEWART took no part in the consideration or decision of this case.

■ JUSTICE STEVENS, concurring in the judgment.

As I view this unusual case—in which neither precedent nor constitutional language provides sure guidance—two separate questions must be answered. First, does the Full Faith and Credit Clause *require* Minnesota, the forum State, to apply Wisconsin law? Second, does the Due Process Clause of the Fourteenth Amendment *prevent* Minnesota from applying its own law? The first inquiry implicates the federal interest in ensuring that Minnesota respect the sovereignty of the State of Wisconsin; the second implicates the litigants' interests in a fair adjudication of their rights.

I realize that both this Court's analysis of choice-of-law questions [4] and scholarly criticism of those decisions have treated these two inquiries as though they were indistinguishable. Nevertheless, I am persuaded that the two constitutional provisions protect different interests and that proper analysis requires separate consideration of each.

I

The Full Faith and Credit Clause is one of several provisions in the Federal Constitution designed to transform the several States from independent sovereignties into a single, unified Nation.... The Full Faith and Credit Clause implements this design by directing that a State, when acting as the forum for litigation having multistate aspects or implications, respect the legitimate interests of other States and avoid infringement upon their sovereignty. The Clause does not, however, rigidly require the forum State to apply foreign law whenever another State has a valid

---

29. We express no view whether the first two contacts, either together or separately, would have sufficed to sustain the choice of Minnesota law made by the Minnesota Supreme Court.

4. Although the Court has struck down a state court's choice of forum law on both due process, see e.g., Home Insurance Co. v. Dick, 281 U.S. 397 (1930), and full faith and credit grounds, see e.g., John Hancock Insurance Co. v. Yates, 299 U.S. 178 (1936), no clear analytical distinction between the two constitutional provisions has emerged....

interest in the litigation.... On the contrary, in view of the fact that the forum State is also a sovereign in its own right, in appropriate cases it may attach paramount importance to its own legitimate interests. Accordingly, the fact that a choice-of-law decision may be unsound as a matter of conflicts law does not necessarily implicate the federal concerns embodied in the Full Faith and Credit Clause. Rather in my opinion, the Clause should not invalidate a state court's choice of forum law unless that choice threatens the federal interest in national unity by unjustifiably infringing upon the legitimate interests of another State.

In this case, I think the Minnesota courts' decision to apply Minnesota law was plainly unsound as a matter of normal conflicts law. Both the execution of the insurance contract and the accident giving rise to the litigation took place in Wisconsin. Moreover, when both of those events occurred the plaintiff, the decedent, and the operators of both vehicles were all residents of Wisconsin. Nevertheless, I do not believe that any threat to national unity or Wisconsin's sovereignty ensues from allowing the substantive question presented by this case to be determined by the law of another State.

... Since the policy provided coverage for accidents that might occur in other States, it was obvious to the parties at the time of contracting that it might give rise to the application of the law of States other than Wisconsin. Therefore, while Wisconsin may have an interest in ensuring that contracts formed in Wisconsin in reliance upon Wisconsin law are interpreted in accordance with that law, that interest is not implicated in this case.

Petitioner has failed to establish that Minnesota's refusal to apply Wisconsin law poses any direct or indirect threat to Wisconsin's sovereignty. In the absence of any such threat, I find it unnecessary to evaluate the forum State's interest in the litigation in order to reach the conclusion that the Full Faith and Credit Clause does not require the Minnesota courts to apply Wisconsin law to the question of contract interpretation presented in this case.

II

It may be assumed that a choice-of-law decision would violate the Due Process Clause if it were totally arbitrary or if it were fundamentally unfair to either litigant. I question whether a judge's decision to apply the law of his own State could ever be described as wholly irrational. For judges are presumably familiar with their own state law and may find it difficult and time consuming to discover and apply correctly the law of another State. The forum State's interest in the fair and efficient administration of justice is therefore sufficient, in my judgment, to attach a presumption of validity to a forum State's decision to apply its own law to a dispute over which it has jurisdiction.

The forum State's interest in the efficient operation of its judicial system is clearly not sufficient, however, to justify the application of a rule of law that is fundamentally unfair to one of the litigants. Arguably, a litigant could demonstrate such unfairness in a variety of ways. Concern about the fairness of the forum's choice of its own rule might arise if that rule favored residents over nonresidents, if it represented a dramatic departure from the rule that obtains in most American jurisdictions, or if the rule itself was unfair on its face or as applied.

The application of an otherwise acceptable rule of law may result in unfairness to the litigants if, in engaging in the activity which is the subject of the litigation, they could not reasonably have anticipated that their actions would later be judged by this rule of law. A choice-of-law decision that frustrates the justifiable expectations of the parties can be fundamentally unfair. This desire to prevent unfair surprise to a litigant has been the central concern in this Court's review of choice-of-law decisions under the Due Process Clause.

Neither the "stacking" rule itself, nor Minnesota's application of that rule to these litigants, raises any serious question of fairness. As the plurality observes, "[s]tacking was the rule in most States at the time the policy was issued." ... Moreover, the rule is consistent with the economics of a contractual relationship in which the policyholder paid three separate premiums for insurance coverage for three automobiles, including a separate premium for each uninsured motorist coverage.... Nor am I persuaded that the decision of the Minnesota courts to apply the "stacking" rule in this case can be said to violate due process because that decision frustrates the reasonable expectations of the contracting parties....

... [T]he decision of the Minnesota courts to apply the law of the forum in this case does not frustrate the reasonable expectations of the contracting parties, and I can find no fundamental unfairness in that decision requiring the attention of this Court.

In terms of fundamental fairness, it seems to me that two factors relied upon by the plurality—the plaintiff's post-accident move to Minnesota and the decedent's Minnesota employment—are either irrelevant to or possibly even tend to undermine the plurality's conclusion. When the expectations of the parties at the time of contracting are the central due process concern, as they are in this case, an unanticipated post-accident occurrence is clearly irrelevant for due process purposes....

III

Although I regard the Minnesota courts' decision to apply forum law as unsound as a matter of conflicts law, and there is little in this record other than the presumption in favor of the forum's own law to support that decision, I concur in the plurality's judgment. It is not this Court's function to establish and impose upon state courts a federal choice-of-law rule, nor is it our function to ensure that state courts correctly apply whatever choice-of-law rules they have themselves adopted. Our authority may be exercised in the choice-of-law area only to prevent a violation of the Full Faith and Credit or the Due Process Clause. For the reasons stated above, I find no such violation in this case.

■ JUSTICE POWELL, with whom THE CHIEF JUSTICE and JUSTICE REHNQUIST join, dissenting.

My disagreement with the majority is narrow. I accept with few reservations Part II of the majority opinion, which sets forth the basic principles that guide us in reviewing state choice-of-law decisions under the Constitution. The Court should invalidate a forum State's decision to apply its own law only when there are no significant contacts between the State and the litigation. This modest check on state power is mandated by the Due Process Clause of the Fourteenth Amendment and the Full Faith and Credit Clause of Art. 4, § 1. I do not believe, however, that the Court adequately analyzes the policies such review must serve. In consequence, it has found significant what appear to me to be trivial contacts between the forum State and the litigation.

I

... The significance of asserted contacts must be evaluated in light of the constitutional policies that oversight by this Court should serve. Two enduring policies emerge from our cases.

First, the contacts between the forum State and the litigation should not be so "slight and casual" that it would be fundamentally unfair to a litigant for the forum to apply its own State's law. Clay v. Sun Ins. Office, Ltd. [p. 346, supra]. The touchstone here is the reasonable expectation of the parties. See Weintraub, Due Process and Full Faith and Credit Limitations on a State's Choice of Law, 44 Iowa L.Rev. 449, 445–457 (1959).

Second, the forum State must have a legitimate interest in the outcome of the litigation before it. Pacific Ins. Co. v. Industrial Accident Comm'n [p. 336, supra]. The Full Faith and Credit Clause addresses the accommodation of sovereign power among the various States. Under limited circumstances, it requires one State to give effect to the statutory law of another State. Nevada v. Hall, 440 U.S. 410, 423 (1979). To be sure, a forum State need not give effect to another State's law if that law is in "violation of its own legitimate public policy." Id., at 624. Nonetheless, for a forum State to further its legitimate public policy by applying its own law to a controversy, there must be some connection between the facts giving rise to the litigation and the scope of the State's lawmaking jurisdiction.

Both the Due Process and Full Faith and Credit Clauses ensure that the States do not "reach out beyond the limits imposed on them by their status as coequal sovereigns in a federal system." World–Wide Volkswagen Corp. v. Woodson, 444 U.S. 286, 292 (1980) (addressing Fourteenth Amendment limitations on state court jurisdiction)....

In summary, the significance of the contacts between a forum State and the litigation must be assessed in light of these two important constitutional policies. A contact, or a pattern of contacts, satisfies the Constitution when it protects the litigants from being unfairly surprised if the forum State applies its own law, and when the application of the forum's law reasonably can be understood to further a legitimate public policy of the forum State.

II

Recognition of the complexity of the constitutional inquiry requires that this Court apply these principles with restraint. Applying these principles to the facts of this case, I do not believe, however, that Minnesota had sufficient contacts with the "persons and events" in this litigation to apply its rule permitting stacking. I would agree that no reasonable expectations of the parties were frustrated. The risk insured by petitioner was not geographically limited....

The more doubtful question in this case is whether application of Minnesota's substantive law reasonably furthers a legitimate state interest. The Court attempts to give substance to the tenuous contacts between Minnesota and this litigation. Upon examination, however, these contacts are either trivial or irrelevant to the furthering of any public policy in Minnesota.

First, the post-accident residence of the plaintiff-beneficiary is constitutionally irrelevant to the choice-of-law question. John Hancock Mut. Life Ins. Co. v. Yates, supra.... Any possible ambiguity in the Court's view of the significance of a post-occurrence change of residence is dispelled by Home Ins. Co. v. Dick, supra, cited by the *Yates* Court, where it was held squarely that Dick's post-accident move to the forum State was "without significance." ...

This rule is sound. If a plaintiff could choose the substantive rules to be applied to an action by moving to a hospitable forum, the invitation to forum shopping would be irresistible. Moreover, it would permit the defendant's reasonable expectations at the time the cause of action accrues to be frustrated, because it would permit the choice-of-law question to turn on a post-accrual circumstance. Finally, post-accrual residence has nothing to do with facts to which the forum State proposes to apply its rule; it is unrelated to the substantive legal issues presented by the litigation.

Second, the Court finds it significant that the insurer does business in the forum State.... The State does have a legitimate interest in regulating the practices of such an insurer. But this argument proves too much. The insurer here does business in all 50 States. The forum State has no interest in regulating that conduct of the insurer unrelated to property, persons or contracts executed within the forum State.... The Court recognizes this flaw and attempts to bolster the significance of the local presence of the insurer by combining it with the other factors deemed significant: the presence of the plaintiff and the fact that the deceased worked in the forum State. This merely restates the basic question in the case.

Third, the Court emphasizes particularly that the insured worked in the forum State.... The insured's place of employment is not, however, significant in this case. Neither the nature of the insurance policy, the events related to the accident, nor the immediate question of stacking coverage are in any way affected or implicated by the insured's employment status. The Court's opinion is understandably vague in explaining how trebling the benefits to be paid to the estate of a nonresident employee furthers any substantial state interest relating to employment. Minnesota does not wish its workers to die in automobile accidents, but permitting stacking will not further this interest. The substantive issue here is solely one of compensation, and whether the compensation provided by this policy is increased or not will have no relation to the State's employment policies or police power. . . .

Neither taken separately nor in the aggregate do the contacts asserted by the Court today indicate that Minnesota's application of its substantive rule in this case will further any legitimate state interest.[6] The Court focuses only on physical contacts *vel non,* and in doing so pays scant attention to the more fundamental reasons why our precedents require reasonable policy-related contacts in choice-of-law cases. Therefore, I dissent.

After Allstate v. Hague, what is the impact of due process and full faith and credit on choice of law? Perhaps it is not realistic to view full faith as retaining any significant function in this context considering that the Supreme Court, despite frequent reference to the full faith command has not since 1947 struck down a choice of law for violating that command. This suggests that the only serious test is due process. Once due process is satisfied the full-faith requirement fades away. But there is a possibility, is there not, that the forum's choice might be the equivalent of a "forbidden infringement" on a sister state's interests of the kind that Justice Stone referred to in the judgments area. If so, what are the indicia of such an infringement? Is using part of a sister state statute while rejecting an unmistakably interrelated part an example of a forbidden infringement?

The law reviews have published floods of commentary on Allstate v. Hague. A major collection is Symposium: Choice of Law Theory After Allstate Insurance Co. v. Hague, 10 Hofstra L.Rev. 1 (1981), containing comments by Professors Cavers, Davies, Leflar, Martin, Reese, Sedler, Silberman, Trautman, Twerski, von Mehren, and Weintraub.

6. The concurring opinion of Justice Stevens supports my view that the forum State's application of its own law to this case cannot be justified by the existence of relevant minimum contacts. As Justice Stevens observes, the principal factors relied on by the Court are "either irrelevant or possibly even tend to undermine the [Court's] conclusion." . . . The interesting analysis he proposes to uphold the State's judgment is, however, difficult to reconcile with our prior decisions and may create more problems than it solves. For example, it seems questionable to measure the interest of a State in a controversy by the degree of conscious reliance on that State's law by private parties to a contract. . . . Moreover, scrutinizing the strength of the interests of a nonforum State may draw this Court back into the discredited practice of weighing the relative interests of various States in a particular controversy. . . .

Among other useful commentaries are Hay, Full Faith and Credit and Federalism in Choice of Law, 34 Mercer L.Rev. 709 (1983); Hill, Choice of Law and Jurisdiction in the Supreme Court, 81 Colum.L.Rev. 960 (1981); Kozyris, Reflections on Allstate—The Lessening of Due Process in Choice of Law, 14 U.C.D.L.Rev. 889 (1981); Weinberg, Choice of Law and Minimal Scrutiny, 49 U.Chi.L.Rev. 440 (1982); Note, Legislative Jurisdiction, State Policies and Post–Occurrence Contacts in Allstate Insurance Co. v. Hague, 81 Colum.L.Rev. 1134 (1981).

Jepson v. General Cas. Co. of Wisconsin, 513 N.W.2d 467 (Minn.1994). Jepson, a Minnesota resident, purchased a policy through a Minnesota insurance agency covering seven motor vehicles. The named insureds were Jepson, his wife, and a corporation. The address of the named insureds was listed as the North Dakota address of the corporation and the premium was calculated at North Dakota rates, which were lower than Minnesota rates. Six vehicles were registered and garaged in North Dakota and one in Indiana. Two years after the decision in *Allstate,* Jepson was injured in a collision in Arizona while a passenger in a real estate agent's automobile. Jepson settled his claim against the driver of the other automobile for that driver's policy limits and also received compensation from the insurer covering the real estate agent's car. Jepson then sued his insurer seeking underinsured motorist benefits under his policy, contending that the benefits should be stacked. Jepson's policy provided for $100,000 per person underinsured motorist coverage, but it also contained a provision prohibiting stacking of the underinsured benefits. At the time of the accident, as in *Allstate,* the anti-stacking provision was invalid under Minnesota law. The provision was, however, valid under the law of North Dakota. Held that North Dakota law applied. Considerations of "predictability and maintenance of the interstate order" pointed to application of North Dakota law and these considerations were more compelling than "our governmental interest in compensating a tort victim." The court noted that after the accident, a Minnesota statute took effect that prohibited stacking. The statute applied only to policies issued after the statute's effective date. The opinion commented on the "better law" basis for choice of law, which the court had used in *Allstate* to choose Minnesota law: "From our present day vantage point, neither the law Minnesota had then, nor the law we have now, is clearly better. Sometimes different laws are neither better nor worse in an objective way, just different."

THE RESTATEMENT, SECOND, CONFLICT OF LAWS, SECTION 9, READS:

§ 9. Limitations on Choice of Law

A court may not apply the local law of its own state to determine a particular issue unless such application of this law would be reasonable in light of the relationship of the state and of other states to the person, thing or occurrence involved.

Is that as accurate and precise a statement of the law as we can make after Allstate v. Hague?

NOTES

1. McCluney v. Joseph Schlitz Brewing Co., 649 F.2d 578 (8th Cir.1981), affirmed 454 U.S. 1071. The plaintiff was originally employed by the defendant to work in Missouri. Thereafter, he was transferred to a number of states and finally five years later, while working in Wisconsin, he was discharged. He requested a "service letter" in the form provided for in a Missouri statute, but the defendant refused to supply one. Plaintiff then moved to Missouri and there brought suit against the defendant under Missouri law. Held on appeal that the Missouri statute could not be applied under due process for lack of any significant contact with the parties and the contract of employment. The "significant contacts" analysis of the Supreme Court in the Hague case "addresses the traditional concerns of due process: preventing unfairness to the parties and promoting interstate relations." The defendant performs no manufacturing or processing operations in Missouri although some of its distributors are located there. Missouri's "one relevant contact" is that the plaintiff moved there after his discharge. This contact is not of itself sufficient to permit application of Missouri law. The dissenting judge emphasized that defendant was doing business in Missouri through its distributors and there was nothing to indicate that plaintiff had moved to Missouri in order to obtain application of Missouri law. He also pointed to the fact that plaintiff's original contract of employment had called for application of Missouri law and "no later agreement expressly modified that arrangement." The dissenting judge concluded that he knew of no Supreme Court case "more recent than 1936 striking down a state's choice of law under the federal Constitution." What about Commercial Travelers v. Wolfe in 1947, p. 333, supra?

2. See Reese, Legislative Jurisdiction, 78 Colum.L.Rev. 1587 (1978); Müller–Freienfels, Conflicts of Law and Constitutional Law, 45 U.Chi.L.Rev. 598 (1978). As to federal control of choice of law, Justice Jackson, in The Supreme Court in the American System of Government 41–44 (1955), said: "It seems to me that disagreement as to which of conflicting or competing state laws applies raises a federal question under the Full Faith and Credit Clause and that our hope for a better general legal system would be well served by wider application of that clause." Is that the best path in light of Allstate v. Hague? See Scoles & Hay, Conflict of Laws § 3.23 (2d ed. 1992).

Phillips Petroleum Co. v. Shutts
Supreme Court of the United States, 1985.
472 U.S. 797, 105 S.Ct. 2965, 86 L.Ed.2d 628.

■ JUSTICE REHNQUIST delivered the opinion of the Court.

Petitioner is a Delaware corporation which has its principal place of business in Oklahoma. During the 1970's it produced or purchased natural gas from leased land located in 11 different States, and sold most of the gas in interstate commerce. Respondents are some 28,000 of the royalty owners possessing rights to the leases from which petitioner produced the gas; they reside in all 50 States, the District of Columbia, and several foreign countries. Respondents brought a class action against petitioner in the Kansas state court, seeking to recover interest on royalty payments which had been delayed by petitioner. They recovered judgment in the trial court, and the Supreme Court of Kansas affirmed the judgment over petitioner's contentions that the Due Process Clause of the Fourteenth Amendment prevented Kansas from adjudicating the claims of all the respondents, and that the Due Process Clause and the Full Faith and Credit Clause of Article IV of the Constitution prohibited the application of Kansas law to all of the transactions between petitioner and respondents. 235 Kan. 195, 679 P.2d 1159 (1984). We granted certiorari to consider these claims. 469 U.S. 879 (1984). We reject petitioner's jurisdictional claim, but sustain its claim regarding the choice of law.

[The part of the Court's decision holding that the Kansas court had jurisdiction to entertain the class action is summarized at page 241, supra.]

III

The Kansas courts applied Kansas contract and Kansas equity law to every claim in this case, notwithstanding that over 99% of the gas leases and some 97% of the plaintiffs in the case had no apparent connection to the State of Kansas except for this lawsuit. Petitioner protested that the Kansas courts should apply the laws of the States where the leases were located, or at least apply Texas and Oklahoma law because so many of the leases came from those States. The Kansas courts disregarded this contention and found petitioner liable for interest on the suspended royalties as a matter of Kansas law, and set the interest rates under Kansas equity principles.

... We must first determine whether Kansas law conflicts in any material way with any other law which could apply. There can be no injury in applying Kansas law if it is not in conflict with that of any other jurisdiction connected to this suit.

[At this point, the court determined that Kansas law might differ in material aspects from the law of the other states.]

Four Terms ago we addressed a similar situation in Allstate Ins. Co. v. Hague, 449 U.S. 302 (1981)....

The plurality in *Allstate* noted that a particular set of facts giving rise to litigation could justify, constitutionally, the application of more than one jurisdiction's laws. The plurality recognized, however, that the Due Process Clause and the Full Faith and Credit Clause provided modest restrictions on the application of forum law. These restrictions required "that for a State's substantive law to be selected in a constitutionally permissible manner, that State must have a significant contact or significant aggregation of contacts, creating state interests, such that choice of its law is neither arbitrary nor fundamentally unfair." Id., at 312–313, 101 S.Ct., at 639–640. The dissenting Justices were in substantial agreement with this principle. Id., at 332, 101 S.Ct., at 650 (opinion of Powell, J.).... Kansas' contacts to this litigation, as explained by the Kansas Supreme Court, can be gleaned from the opinion below.

Petitioner owns property and conducts substantial business in the State, so Kansas certainly has an interest in regulating petitioner's conduct in Kansas. 235 Kan., at 210, 679 P.2d, at 1174. Moreover, oil and gas extraction is an important business to Kansas, and although only a few leases in issue are located in Kansas, hundreds of Kansas plaintiffs were affected by petitioner's suspension of royalties; thus the court held that the State has a real interest in protecting "the rights of these royalty owners both as individual residents of [Kansas] and as members of this particular class of plaintiffs." Id., at 211–212, 679 P.2d, at 1174. The Kansas Supreme Court pointed out that Kansas courts are quite familiar with this type of lawsuit, and "[t]he plaintiff class members have indicated their desire to have this action determined under the laws of Kansas." Id., at 211, 222, 679 P.2d, at 1174, 1181. Finally, the Kansas court buttressed its use of Kansas law by stating that this lawsuit was analogous to a suit against a "common fund" located in Kansas. Id., at 201, 211–212, 679 P.2d, at 1168, 1174.

We do not lightly discount this description of Kansas' contacts with this litigation and its interest in applying its law. There is, however, no "common fund" located in Kansas that would require or support the application of only Kansas law to all these claims. See, e.g., Hartford Life Ins. Co. v. Ibs, 237 U.S. 662 (1915). As the Kansas court noted, petitioner commingled the suspended royalties with its general corporate accounts. 235 Kan. 201, 679 P.2d, at 1168. There is no specific identifiable res in Kansas, nor is there any limited amount which may be depleted before every plaintiff is compensated. Only by somehow aggregating all the separate claims in this case could a "common fund" in any sense be created, and the term becomes all but meaningless when used in such an expansive sense.

We also give little credence to the idea that Kansas law should apply to all claims because the plaintiffs, by failing to opt out, evinced their desire to be bound by Kansas law. Even if one could say that the plaintiffs "consented" to the application of Kansas law by not opting out, plaintiff's desire for forum law is rarely, if ever controlling. In most cases the plaintiff shows his obvious wish for forum law by filing there.... Even if a plaintiff evidences his desire for forum law by moving to the forum, we have generally accorded such a move little or no significance. John Hancock Mut. Life Ins. Co. v. Yates, 299 U.S. 178, 182 (1936); Home Ins. Co. v. Dick, 281 U.S. 397, 408 (1930). In *Allstate* the plaintiff's move to the forum was only relevant because it was unrelated and prior to the litigation. 449 U.S., at 318–319, 101 S.Ct., at 643. Thus the plaintiffs' desire for Kansas law, manifested by their participation in this Kansas lawsuit, bears little relevance.

The Supreme Court of Kansas in its opinion in this case expressed the view that by reason of the fact that it was adjudicating a nationwide class action, it had much greater latitude in applying its own law to the transactions in question than might otherwise be the case:

"The general rule is that the law of the forum applies unless it is expressly shown that a different law governs, and in case of doubt, the law of the forum is preferred.... Where a state court determines it has jurisdiction over a nationwide class action and procedural due process guarantees of notice and adequate representation are present, we believe the law of the forum should be applied unless compelling reasons exist for applying a different law.... 235 Kan., at 221–222, 679 P.2d, at 1181.

We think that this is something of a "bootstrap" argument.... While a state may, for the reasons we have previously stated, assume jurisdiction over the claims of plaintiffs whose principal contacts are with other States, it may not use this assumption of jurisdiction as an added weight in the scale when considering the permissible constitutional limits on choice of substantive law....

The issue of personal jurisdiction over plaintiffs in a class action is entirely distinct from the question of the constitutional limitations on choice of law; the latter calculus is not altered by the fact that it may be more difficult or more burdensome to comply with the constitutional limitations because of the large number of transactions which the State proposes to adjudicate and which have little connection with the forum.

Kansas must have a "significant contact or aggregation of contacts" to the claims asserted by each member of the plaintiff class, contacts "creating state interests" in order to ensure that the choice of Kansas law is not arbitrary or unfair. *Allstate,* supra, 449 U.S., at 312–313, 101 S.Ct., at 639–640. Given Kansas' lack of "interest" in claims unrelated to that State, and the substantive conflict with jurisdictions such as Texas, we conclude that application of Kansas law to every claim in this case is sufficiently arbitrary and unfair as to exceed constitutional limits.

When considering fairness in this context, an important element is the expectation of the parties. See *Allstate,* supra, 449 U.S., at 333, 101 S.Ct., at 650 (opinion of POWELL, J.). There is no indication that when the leases involving land and royalty owners outside of Kansas were executed, the parties had any idea that Kansas law would control. Neither the Due Process Clause nor the Full Faith and Credit Clause requires Kansas "to substitute for its own [laws], applicable to persons and events within it, the conflicting statute of another state," Pacific Employers Insurance Co. v. Industrial Accident Comm'n, 306 U.S. 493, 502, 59 S.Ct. 629, 633, 83 L.Ed. 940 (1939), but Kansas "may not abrogate the rights of parties beyond its borders having no relation to anything done or to be done within them." Home Insurance Co. v. Dick, supra, 281 U.S., at 410, 50 S.Ct., at 342.

... We make no effort to determine for ourselves which law must apply to the various transactions involved in this lawsuit, and we reaffirm our observation in *Allstate* that in many situations a state court may be free to apply one of several choices of law. But the constitutional limitations laid down in cases such as *Allstate* and Home Insurance Co. v. Dick, supra, must be respected even in a nationwide class action....

■ JUSTICE STEVENS, concurring in part and dissenting in part.

... I agree that the Kansas courts properly exercised jurisdiction over this class action....

... [I]t has long been settled that "a mere misconstruction by the forum of the laws of a sister State is not a violation of the Full Faith and Credit Clause." Carroll v. Lanza, 349 U.S. 408, 414, n. 1, 75 S.Ct. 804, 807, n. 1, 99 L.Ed. 1183 (1955) (Frankfurter, J., dissenting). That clause requires only that States accord "full faith and credit" to other States' laws—that is, acknowledge the validity and finality of such laws and attempt in good faith to apply them when necessary as they would be applied by home state courts....

... [T]he Kansas court made a careful survey of the relevant laws of Oklahoma and Texas, the only other states whose law is proffered as relevant to this litigation. But, as the Court acknowledges, ... no other State's laws or judicial decisions were precisely on point, and, in the Kansas court's judgment, roughly analogous Texas and Oklahoma cases supported the results the Kansas court reached. The Kansas court expressly declared that, in a multistate action, a "court should also give careful consideration, as we have attempted to do, to any possible conflict of law problems".... While a common law judge might disagree with the substantive legal determinations made by the Kansas court (although nothing in its opinion seems erroneous to me), that court's approach to the possible choices of law evinces precisely the "full faith and credit" that the Constitution requires.

It is imaginable that even a good faith review of another State's law might still "unjustifiably infring[e] upon the legitimate interests of another State" so as to violate the Full Faith and Credit Clause.... If, for example, a Texas oil company or a Texas royalty owner with an interest in a Texas lease were treated directly contrary to a stated policy of the State of Texas by a Kansas court through some honest blunder, the Constitution might bar such "parochial entrenchment" on Texas' interests.... But this case is so distant from such a situation that I need not pursue this theoretical possibility. Even Phillips does not contend that any stated policies of other States have been plainly contravened, and the Court's discussion is founded merely on an *absence* of reported decisions and the Court's speculation of what Oklahoma or Texas courts might "most likely" do in a case like this.... There is simply no demonstration here that the Kansas Supreme Court's decision has impaired the legitimate interests of any other States or infringed on their sovereignty in the slightest.

III

It is nevertheless possible for a State's choice of law to violate the Constitution because it is so "totally arbitrary or ... fundamentally unfair" to a litigant that it violates the Due Process Clause. *Allstate,* 449 U.S., at 326 (Stevens, J., concurring in judgment). If the forum court has no connection to the lawsuit other than its jurisdiction over the parties, a decision to apply the forum State's law might so "frustrat[e] the justifiable expectations of the parties" as to be unconstitutional. Id., at 327.

Again, however, a constitutional claim of "unfair surprise" cannot be based merely upon an unexpected choice of a particular State's law—it must rest on a persuasive showing of an unexpected *result* arrived at by application of that law. Thus, absent any *conflict* of laws, in terms of the results they produce, the Due Process Clause simply has not been violated. This is because the underlying theory of a choice-of-law due process claim must be that parties plan their conduct and contractual relations based upon their legitimate expectations concerning the subsequent legal consequences of their actions....

The crux of my disagreement with the Court is over the standard applied to evaluate the sufficiency of allegations of choice-of-law conflicts necessary to support a constitutional claim. Rather than potential, "putative," or even "likely" conflicts, I would require demonstration of an *unambiguous* conflict with the *established* law of another State as an essential element of a constitutional choice-of-law claim. Arguments that a State court has merely applied general common law principles in a novel manner, or reconciled arguably conflicting laws erroneously in the face of unprecedented factual circumstances should not suffice to make out a constitutional issue....

NOTES

1. For a discussion of the case and its effect on choice of law, see Miller and Crump, Jurisdiction and Choice of Law in Multistate Class Actions After Phillips Petroleum Co. v. Shutts, 96 Yale L.J. 1 (1986).

2. In Quill Corp. v. North Dakota, 504 U.S. 298 (1992), the constitutional due process requisites for personal jurisdiction and jurisdiction to tax were equated, but the commerce clause was held to require more than "minimum contacts." The result was to invalidate the state use tax on sales of goods by a non-resident business that had no sales force in the state and little tangible property.

The Control of Choice of Law by Federal Statutes

The Constitution of the United States gives to the Congress wide powers over conflict of laws. This is done in the clearest form by the words of the full faith and credit clause: "And the Congress may by General Laws prescribe the Manner in which such Acts, Records and Proceedings shall be proved, and the Effect thereof." Perhaps, similar power is also conferred by other parts of the Constitution, as, the interstate and foreign commerce clause and the due process clauses.

This power has been sweepingly exercised by the Congress in the field of state judgments, as shown in Chapter 5, supra.

Until 1948 there seems to have been no similar federal statute on choice of law. The statute enacted in 1790 under the full faith and credit clause had dealt with the protection of "records" and "judicial proceedings", but not with "acts". In 1948 the provision was amended, as shown on p. 39, supra, to include "acts" within the scope of its protection.

The Supreme Court has not yet determined the effect, if any, of the amendment. Note, in this connection, that the Court adverted to the question, but did not decide it, in Hughes v. Fetter, p. 318, supra. Note also Justice Frankfurter's statement in his dissent in Carroll v. Lanza, p. 339, supra, that the amendment "cannot be disregarded."

Section 3. Unreasonable Discrimination

By reason of the privileges and immunities clause (Art. IV, § 2) and the equal protection clause of the Fourteenth Amendment, a state cannot discriminate unreasonably against citizens of sister states or against persons within its jurisdiction. Up to this point we have seen the problem raised in Douglas v. New York, New Haven & Hartford Railroad Co., 279 U.S. 377 (1929), p. 321, supra, where it was held that a state does not violate the privileges and immunities clause by dismissing on a forum non conveniens grounds a suit between residents of sister states that is based on a foreign occurrence. Other cases in the book that raise problems of privileges and immunities or of equal protection are Canadian Northern Railway Co. v. Eggen, 252 U.S. 553 (1920); Blake v. McClung, 172 U.S. 239 (1898), p. 955, infra, and Kentucky Finance Corp. v. Paramount Auto Exchange, 262 U.S. 544 (1923), p. 995, infra.

It has also come to be recognized that some of the more recent approaches to choice of law reveal a tendency to extend the protection of forum law to forum residents and not to do so for nonresidents, thereby giving rise to privileges and immunities and equal protection problems. For example, suppose that the owner and driver of an automobile, who is domiciled in state X, is involved in an accident in state Y and thereafter is sued in X by two injured guest passengers, one of whom is domiciled in X and the other in Y. Would it be appropriate in these circumstances for the X court to apply X law to determine the rights of the X passenger in a favorable way, but refuse to apply X law to determine the Y passenger's rights on the ground that a state has no interest in favorable treatment of a nonresident but, on the ground that it has no interest in him, to apply Y law to determine the rights of the Y passenger? Problems of this kind are considered (particularly at pp. 504–511) in the chapters which follow. The field is intensively discussed in two articles by Professors Currie and Schreter, Unconstitutional Discrimination in the Conflict of Laws: Privileges and Immunities, 69 Yale L.J. 1323 (1960), and Unconstitutional Discrimination in The Conflict of Laws: Equal Protection, 28 U.Chi.L.Rev. 1 (1960). These articles are reprinted in Currie, Selected Essays on the Conflict of Laws, Chs. 11, 12 (1963). See also Note, Unconstitutional Discrimination in Choice of Law, 77 Colum.L.Rev. 272 (1977).

Section 4. Privileges and Immunities

Supreme Court of New Hampshire v. Piper
Supreme Court of the United States, 1985.
470 U.S. 274, 105 S.Ct. 1272, 84 L.Ed.2d 205.

■ Justice Powell delivered the opinion of the Court.

The Rules of the Supreme Court of New Hampshire limit bar admission to state residents. We here consider whether this restriction violates the Privileges and Immunities Clause of the United States Constitution, Art. IV, § 2.

I

A

Kathryn Piper lives in Lower Waterford, Vermont, about 400 yards from the New Hampshire border. In 1979, she applied to take the February 1980 New Hampshire bar examination. Piper submitted with her application a statement of intent to become a New Hampshire resident. Following an investigation, the Board of Bar Examiners found that Piper was of good moral character and met the other requirements for admission. She was allowed to take, and passed, the examination. Piper was informed by the Board that she would have to establish a home address in New Hampshire prior to being sworn in.

On May 7, 1980, Piper requested from the Clerk of the New Hampshire Supreme Court a dispensation from the residency requirement. Although she had a "possible job" with a lawyer in Littleton, New Hampshire, Piper stated that becoming a resident of New Hampshire would be inconvenient. Her house in Vermont was secured by a mortgage with a favorable interest rate, and she and her husband recently had become parents. According to Piper, these "problems peculiar to [her] situation ... warrant[ed] that an exception be made." ...

On May 13, 1980, the Clerk informed Piper that her request had been denied. She then formally petitioned the New Hampshire Supreme Court for permission to become a member of the bar.... The Supreme Court denied Piper's formal request on December 31, 1980.

. . .

... [Piper] alleged that Rule 42 of the New Hampshire Supreme Court, that excludes nonresidents from the bar,[1] violates the Privileges and Immunities Clause of Art. IV, § 2, of the United States Constitution.

II

A

Article IV, § 2, of the Constitution provides that the "Citizens of each State shall be entitled to all Privileges and Immunities of Citizens in the several States."[2] This Clause was intended to "fuse into one Nation a collection of independent, sovereign States." Toomer v. Witsell, 334 U.S. 385, 395 (1948). Recognizing this purpose, we have held that it is "[o]nly

---

1. Rule 42 does not provide explicitly that only New Hampshire residents may be admitted to the bar. It does require, however, that an applicant either be a resident of New Hampshire or file a statement of intent to reside there.... [Some footnotes omitted or renumbered, Eds.]

2. Under this Clause, the terms "citizen" and "resident" are used interchangeably....

with respect to those 'privileges' and 'immunities' bearing on the vitality of the Nation as a single entity" that a State must accord residents and nonresidents equal treatment. Baldwin v. Montana Fish & Game Comm'n, supra, [436 U.S. 371 (1978)] at 383. In *Baldwin,* for example, we concluded that a State may charge a nonresident more than it charges a resident for the same elk-hunting license. Because elk hunting is "recreation" rather than a "means of a livelihood," we found that the right to a hunting license was not "fundamental" to the promotion of interstate harmony. 436 U.S., at 388.

Derived, like the Commerce Clause, from the fourth of the Articles of Confederation, the Privileges and Immunities Clause was intended to create a national economic union. It is therefore not surprising that this Court repeatedly has found that "one of the privileges which the Clause guarantees to citizens of State A is that of doing business in State B on terms of substantial equality with the citizens of that State." Toomer v. Witsell, supra, at 396. In Ward v. Maryland, 12 Wall. 418 (1871), the Court invalidated a statute under which nonresidents were required to pay $300 per year for a license to trade in goods not manufactured in Maryland, while resident traders paid a fee varying from $12 to $150. Similarly, in *Toomer,* supra, the Court held that nonresident fishermen could not be required to pay a license fee of $2,500 for each shrimp boat owned when residents were charged only $25 per boat. Finally, in Hicklin v. Orbeck, 437 U.S. 518 (1978), we found violative of the Privileges and Immunities Clause a statute containing a resident hiring preference for all employment related to the development of the State's oil and gas resources.

There is nothing in *Ward, Toomer,* or *Hicklin* suggesting that the practice of law should not be viewed as a "privilege" under Art. IV, § 2. Like the occupations considered in our earlier cases, the practice of law is important to the national economy. As the Court noted in Goldfarb v. Virginia State Bar, 421 U.S. 773, 788 (1975), the "activities of lawyers play an important part in commercial intercourse."

The lawyer's role in the national economy is not the only reason that the opportunity to practice law should be considered a "fundamental right." We believe that the legal profession has a noncommercial role and duty that reinforce the view that the practice of law falls within the ambit of the Privileges and Immunities Clause. Out-of-state lawyers may—and often do—represent persons who raise unpopular federal claims. In some cases, representation by nonresident counsel may be the only means available for the vindication of federal rights.... The lawyer who champions unpopular causes surely is as important to the "maintenance or well-being of the Union," *Baldwin,* 436 U.S., at 388, as was the shrimp fisherman in *Toomer* or the pipeline worker in *Hicklin.*

. . .

III

The conclusion that Rule 42 deprives nonresidents of a protected privilege does not end our inquiry. The Court has stated that "[l]ike many other constitutional provisions, the privileges and immunities clause is not an absolute." Toomer v. Witsell, 334 U.S., at 396; see United Building & Construction Trades Council v. Mayor & Council of Camden, 465 U.S. 208, 222 (1984). The Clause does not preclude discrimination against nonresidents where (i) there is a substantial reason for the difference in treatment; and (ii) the discrimination practiced against nonresidents bears a substantial relationship to the State's objective. Ibid. In deciding whether the discrimination bears a close or substantial relationship to the State's objective, the Court has considered the availability of less restrictive means.

The Supreme Court of New Hampshire offers several justifications for its refusal to admit nonresidents to the bar. It asserts that nonresident members would be less likely (i) to become, and remain, familiar with local rules and procedures; (ii) to behave ethically; (iii) to be available for court proceedings; and (iv) to do *pro bono* and other volunteer work in the State. We find that none of these reasons meets the test of "substantiality," and that the means chosen do not bear the necessary relationship to the State's objectives.

IV

We conclude that New Hampshire's bar residency requirement violates the Privileges and Immunities Clause of Art. IV, § 2, of the United States Constitution. The nonresident's interest in practicing law is a "privilege" protected by the Clause. Although the lawyer is "an officer of the court," he does not hold a position that can be entrusted only to a "full-fledged member of the political community." A State may discriminate against nonresidents only where its reasons are "substantial," and the difference in treatment bears a close or substantial relation to those reasons. No such showing has been made in this case. Accordingly, we affirm the judgment of the Court of Appeals.

■ [JUSTICE WHITE concurred in the result. JUSTICE REHNQUIST dissented.]

SECTION 5. GOVERNMENT SEIZURE; INTERSTATE COMMERCE

Under the abandoned property laws enacted in many states, after a stated time elapses, unclaimed intangible property such as bank deposits, stock dividends, insurance benefits, telephone equipment deposits, etc., become property of the state by escheat. Questions arose when states having different connections to the debtor escheated the same property. In Western Union Telegraph Co. v. Pennsylvania, 368 U.S. 71 (1961), the Court confirmed that it had the power, and the state courts did not have jurisdiction, to decide which of the competing escheat claims of various states should prevail. The Court declared that this was necessary in order to protect the debtor from having to pay twice on a single obligation. Its decision did not resolve the issue of which state was entitled to escheat the property.

A few years later the question was answered in Texas v. New Jersey, 379 U.S. 674 (1965). In that case, Texas, invoking the Supreme Court's original jurisdiction, brought an action against several sister states and the Sun Oil Company to determine which state could escheat small debts totaling about $26,500 which the Sun Oil Company owed to approximately 1,730 creditors. Texas contended that the state with the "most significant contacts" with the debt should be allowed to escheat it. This contention was rejected by the Court on the ground that:

> ... the rule ... would serve only to leave in permanent turmoil a question which should be settled once and for all by a clear rule which will govern all types of intangible obligations like these and to which all States may refer with confidence. The issue before us is not whether a defendant has had sufficient contact with a State to make him or his property rights subject to the jurisdiction of its courts, a jurisdiction which need not be exclusive.... Since this Court has held in Western Union Tel. Co. v. Com. of Pennsylvania, ... that the same property cannot constitutionally be escheated by more than one State, we are faced here with the very different problem of deciding which State's claim to escheat is superior to all others. The "contacts" test as applied in this field is not really any workable test at all—it is simply a phrase suggesting that this Court should examine the circumstances surrounding each particular item of escheatable property on its own peculiar facts and then try to make a difficult, often quite subjective, decision as to which State's claim to those pennies or dollars seems stronger than another's.... The uncertainty of any test which would require us in effect either to decide each escheat case on the basis of its particular facts or to devise new rules of law to apply to ever-developing new categories of facts, might in the end create so much uncertainty and threaten so much expensive litigation that the States might find that they would lose more in litigation expenses than they might gain in escheats....

The Court likewise rejected arguments favoring the state of the debtor's incorporation or that where its principal offices were located and concluded:

> ... since a debt is property of the creditor, not of the debtor, fairness among the States requires that the right and power to escheat the debt should be accorded to the State of the creditor's last known address as shown by the debtor's books and records. Such a solution would be in line with one group of cases dealing with intangible property for other purposes in other areas of the law. Adoption of such a rule involves a factual issue simple and easy to resolve, and leaves no legal issue to be decided. It takes account of the fact that if the creditor instead of perhaps leaving behind an uncashed check had negotiated the check and left behind the cash, this State would have been the sole possible escheat claimant; in other words, the rule recognizes that the debt was an asset of the creditor. The rule ... will tend to distribute escheats among the States in the proportion of the commercial activities of their residents. And by using a standard of last known address, rather than technical legal concepts of residence and domicile, administration and application of escheat laws should be simplified. It may well be that some addresses left by vanished creditors will be in States other than those in which they lived at the time the obligation arose or at the time of the escheat. But such situations probably will be

the exception, and any errors thus created, if indeed they could be called errors, probably will tend to a large extent to cancel each other out....

The Court finally held that debts owed persons whose address is unknown to the debtor or is in a state which does not provide for escheat should be subject to escheat by the state of the debtor's incorporation "provided that another State could later escheat upon proof that the last known address of the creditor was within its borders."

■ JUSTICE STEWART dissented. In his view, only the state of the debtor's incorporation should have power to escheat.

NOTES

1. In New Jersey v. Amsted Industries, 48 N.J. 544, 226 A.2d 715 (1967), New Jersey claimed that as the state of incorporation it should be permitted to escheat amounts owed creditors residing in states where jurisdiction could not be obtained over the corporate debtor. This argument was rejected on the ground that escheat claims are not penal and hence the New Jersey courts would be open to a suit by the claimant states against the corporate debtor.

2. A United States statute, which provides that a veteran's personal property shall vest in the United States when he dies without a will or legal heirs in a veterans' hospital, overrides a state statute of escheat. United States, Trustee v. Oregon, 366 U.S. 643 (1961). Accord as to federal war pension funds, In re Hammond's Estate, 3 N.Y.2d 567, 170 N.Y.S.2d 505, 147 N.E.2d 777 (1958).

3. See generally Lake, Escheat, Federalism and State Boundaries, 24 Ohio St.L.J. 322 (1963); Santell, Escheat, Unclaimed Property and the Supreme Court, 17 West.Res.L.Rev. 50 (1965); Note, 16 Sw.L.J. 660 (1962).

UNITED STATES BREWERS ASSOCIATION, INC. v. HEALY, 692 F.2d 275 (2d Cir.1982): In 1981 Connecticut amended its comprehensive statute regulating the sale and distribution of liquors in an effort to lower the retail price of beer. The historically higher beer prices in Connecticut had led its residents to buy their beer in contiguous states, costing Connecticut tax revenues. Under the amended statute manufacturers and importers of beer were required to file a sworn affirmation that prices charged Connecticut wholesalers were no higher than prices for comparable units of beer in any bordering state. The Court upheld the brewers' attack on the beer price affirmation provisions for violating the Commerce Clause of the United States Constitution (p. 281):

> Notwithstanding the greater scope permitted to the states for regulation of traffic in intoxicating beverages, nothing in the Twenty-first Amendment suggests that a state may regulate the sale of liquor outside of its own territory. The Amendment itself speaks only of the "transportation or importation *into* any State ... for delivery or use *therein*." (Emphasis added.) ... We are aware of no authority to the effect that the Twenty-first Amendment modifies the traditional Commerce Clause principles that bar a state from regulating the transport, sale, or use of products outside of its own territory.

In Bendix Autolite Corp. v. *Midwesco* Enterprises, Inc., 486 U.S. 888 (1988), the Supreme Court held an Ohio tolling statute unconstitutional for unduly burdening interstate commerce. The diversity action, commenced more than four years after the alleged breach of contract, was against a non-resident corporation. Under the Ohio statute the limitations period did not run while the defendant was out of the state; further, the defendant had not designated an agent. The Court noted the impossible situation defendant would be in if such an interpretation prevailed. The Court held in a later decision that *Midwesco* must be applied retroactively to claims accruing prior to that decision. Reynoldsville Casket Co. v. Hyde, 115 S.Ct. 1745 (1995). Compare the decisions of the Supreme Court in Skiriotes v. Florida, 313 U.S. 69 (1941), affirming a decision by the Florida Supreme Court, 144 Fla. 220, 197 So. 736 (1940), and Steele v. Bulova Watch Co., 344 U.S. 280 (1952). Is their distinguishing feature the fact that the "extraterritorial" application of the forum's law in those cases did not collide with the law of any other state?

CHAPTER 7

THRESHOLD PROBLEMS OF THE FORUM IN CHOICE OF LAW

INTRODUCTORY NOTE

This chapter focuses on four problems that any system for choosing law must resolve. (1) When choice-of-law analysis selects foreign law, under what circumstances should the court or other adjudicating agency (the "forum") reject that law? If the forum rejects the otherwise applicable law, should it dismiss the case without deciding the merits? (2) When and how should the forum take notice of foreign law? (3) When is choice-of-law analysis unnecessary because the issue is "procedural" and therefore properly decided under forum rules without regard to foreign contacts or policies? (4) When should the forum refer to the choice-of-law rules of another jurisdiction?

The materials raise two questions. How does a territorial choice-of-law system, which chooses law based on the location of some event in a transaction, deal with these problems? Second, should the treatment of these issues change if the forum abandons a territorial system for one that takes account of the content and purposes of conflicting laws?

SECTION 1. ADMITTING OR REJECTING THE ACTION OR DEFENSE

Loucks v. Standard Oil Co. of New York
Court of Appeals of New York, 1918.
224 N.Y. 99, 120 N.E. 198.

■ CARDOZO, J. The action is brought to recover damages for injuries resulting in death. The plaintiffs are the administrators of the estate of Everett A. Loucks. Their intestate, while traveling on a highway in the state of Massachusetts, was run down and killed through the negligence of the defendant's servants then engaged in its business. He left a wife and two children, residents of New York. A statute of Massachusetts (R.L. ch. 171, sec. 2, as amended by L.1907, ch. 375) provides that "if a person or corporation by his or its negligence, or by the negligence of his or its agents and servants while engaged in his or its business, causes the death of a person who is in the exercise of due care, and not in his or its employment or service, he or it shall be liable in damages in the sum of not less than $500, nor more than $10,000, to be assessed with reference to the degree of his or its culpability, or that of his or its servants, to be recovered in an action of tort commenced within two years after the injury which caused the death by the executor or administrator of the deceased; one-half thereof to the use of the widow and one-half to the use of the children of the deceased, or if there are no children, the whole to the use of the widow, or if there is no widow, the whole to the use of the next of kin." The question is whether a right of action under that statute may be enforced in our courts.

"The courts of no country execute the penal laws of another" (The Antelope, 10 Wheat. 66, 123, 6 L.Ed. 268). The defendant invokes that principle as applicable here. Penal in one sense, the statute indisputably is. The damages are not limited to compensation; they are proportioned to the offender's guilt. A minimum recovery of $500 is allowed in every case. But the question is not whether the statute is penal in some sense. The question is whether it is penal within the rules of private international law. A statute penal in that sense is one that awards a penalty to the state, or to a public officer in its behalf, or to a member of the public, suing in the interest of the whole community to redress a public wrong.... The purpose must be, not reparation to one aggrieved, but vindication of the public justice (Huntington v. Attrill [p. 297, supra]; Brady v. Daly, [175 U.S. 148, 20 S.Ct. 62, 44 L.Ed. 109]). The Massachusetts statute has been classified in some jurisdictions as penal, and in others as remedial.... The courts of Massachusetts have said that the question is still an open one (Boott Mills v. B. & M. R. R., 218 Mass. 582, 592, 106 N.E. 680). No matter how they may have characterized the act as penal, they have not meant to hold that it is penal for every purpose (218 Mass. 592, 106 N.E. 680)....

We think the better reason is with those cases which hold that the statute is not penal in the international sense. On that branch of the controversy, indeed, there is no division of opinion among us. It is true that the offender is punished, but the purpose of the punishment is reparation to those aggrieved by his offense (Comm. v. B. & A. R. R. Co., 121 Mass. 36, 37; Comm. v. Eastern R. R. Co., 5 Gray, 473, 474). The common law did not give a cause of action to surviving relatives.... In the light of modern legislation, its rule is an anachronism. Nearly everywhere, the principle is now embodied in statute that the next of kin are wronged by the killing of their kinsman.... They sue to redress an outrage peculiar to themselves.

We cannot fail to see in the history of the Massachusetts statutes a developing expression of this policy and purpose. The statutes have their distant beginnings in the criminal law. To some extent the vestiges of criminal forms survive. But the old forms have been filled with a new content. The purpose which informs and vitalizes them is the protection of the survivors....

Through all this legislation there runs a common purpose (Boott Mills v. B. & M. R. R. Co., supra, 586; Brown v. Thayer, 212 Mass. 392, 99 N.E. 237). It is penal in one element and one only: the damages are punitive.... But the punishment of the wrongdoer is not designed as atonement for a crime; it is solace to the individual who has suffered a private wrong. This is seen in many tokens. The employer may be innocent himself.... The executor or administrator who sues under this statute is not the champion of the peace and order and public justice of the commonwealth of Massachusetts. He is the representative of the outraged family. He vindicates a private right.

Another question remains. Even though the statute is not penal, it differs from our own. We must determine whether the difference is a sufficient reason for declining jurisdiction.

A tort committed in one state creates a right of action that may be sued upon in another unless public policy forbids. That is the generally accepted rule in the United States.... The question is whether the enforcement of a right of action for tort under the statutes of another state is to be conditioned upon the existence of a kindred statute here....

A foreign statute is not law in this state, but it gives rise to an obligation, which, if transitory, "follows the person and may be enforced wherever the person may be found".... "No law can exist as such except the law of the land; but ... it is a principle of every civilized law that vested rights shall be protected" (Beale, Conflict of Laws, sec. 51). The plaintiff owns something, and we help him to get it.... We do this unless some sound reason of public policy makes it unwise for us to lend our aid. "The law of the forum is material only as setting a limit of policy beyond which such obligations will not be enforced there" (Cuba R. R. Co. v. Crosby, [222 U.S. 473–478]).... If aid is to be withheld here, it must be because the cause of action in its nature offends our sense of justice or menaces the public welfare.... Our own scheme of legislation may be different. We may even have no legislation on the subject. That is not enough to show that public policy forbids us to enforce the foreign right. A right of action is property. If a foreign statute gives the right, the mere fact that we do not give a like right is no reason for refusing to help the plaintiff in getting what belongs to him. We are not so provincial as to say that every solution of a problem is wrong because we deal with it otherwise at home. Similarity of legislation has indeed this importance: its presence shows beyond question that the foreign statute does not offend the local policy. But its absence does not prove the contrary. It is not to be exalted into an indispensable condition. The misleading word "comity" has been responsible for much of the trouble. It has been fertile in suggesting a discretion unregulated by general principles (Beale, Conflict of Laws, sec. 71).... The courts are not free to refuse to enforce a foreign right at the pleasure of the judges, to suit the individual notion of expediency or fairness. They do not close their doors unless help would violate some fundamental principle of justice, some prevalent conception of good morals, some deep-rooted tradition of the common weal.

This test applied, there is nothing in the Massachusetts statute that outrages the public policy of New York. We have a statute which gives a civil remedy where death is caused in our own state. We have thought it so important that we have now embedded it in the Constitution (Const. art. 1, sec. 18). The fundamental policy is that there shall be some atonement for the wrong. Through the defendant's negligence, a resident of New York has been killed in Massachusetts. He has left a widow and children who are also residents. The law of Massachusetts gives them a recompense for his death. It cannot be that public policy forbids our courts to help in collecting what belongs to them. We cannot give them the same judgment that our law would give if the wrong had been done here. Very likely we cannot give them as much. But that is no reason for refusing to give them what we can. We shall not make things better by sending them to another state, where the defendant may not be found, and where suit may be impossible. Nor is there anything to shock our sense of justice in the possibility of a punitive recovery. The penalty is not extravagant.... We shall not feel the pricks of conscience if the offender pays the survivors in proportion to the measure of his offense. We have no public policy that prohibits exemplary damages or civil penalties. We give them for many wrongs. To exclude all penal actions would be to wipe out the distinction between the penalties of public justice and the remedies of private law....

We hold, then, that public policy does not prohibit the assumption of jurisdiction by our courts, and that this being so, mere differences of remedy do not count.... We must apply the same rules that are applicable to other torts; and the tendency of those rules today is toward a larger comity, if we must cling to the traditional term (Walsh v. B. & M. R. R., 201 Mass. 527, 533, 88 N.E. 12). The fundamental public policy is perceived to be that rights lawfully vested shall be everywhere maintained. At least, that is so among the states of the Union (Walsh v. N. Y. & N. E. R. R. Co., 160 Mass. 571, 573, 36 N.E. 584, 39 Am.St.Rep. 514; Walsh v. B. & M. R. R., supra; Beach, Uniform Interstate Enforcement of Vested Rights, 27 Yale Law Journal, 656). There is a growing conviction that only exceptional circumstances should lead one of the states to refuse to enforce a right acquired in another.... The test of similarity has been abandoned there. If it has ever been accepted here, we think it should be abandoned now.

The judgment of the Appellate Division should be reversed, and the order of the Special Term affirmed, with costs in the Appellate Division and in this court.

NOTES

1. In the course of deciding whether the Massachusetts statute was "penal" in the international sense, Judge Cardozo made only passing reference to Huntington v. Attrill, p. 297, supra, clearly not treating it as binding or dispositive in the Loucks case. Why not? After all, the Supreme Court in the Huntington case addressed precisely the question "whether a statute of one State, which in some aspects may be called penal, is a penal law in the international sense." For a thorough discussion of the concept of penality in a conflict-of-laws sense, see Kutner, Judicial Identification of "Penal Laws" in the Conflict of Laws, 31 Okla.L.Rev. 590 (1978).

2. In Doggrell v. Southern Box Co., 208 F.2d 310 (6th Cir. 1953), the court affirmed a judgment of the federal district court in Tennessee imposing on a

stockholder of an Arkansas corporation liability for the price of goods sold to the corporation. The ground was failure of the defendant and others to comply with the corporate organization laws of Arkansas. Soon after, the Supreme Court of Tennessee held in another case that the Arkansas statute should not be applied in a Tennessee action because it was a "penal" statute. Thereupon the federal court of appeals withdrew its ruling and reversed the district court, in part because it believed the doctrine of Erie R. Co. v. Tompkins, p. 665, infra, compelled a Federal court in Tennessee wielding diversity jurisdiction to apply the ruling of the state's Supreme Court. The Doggrell case is set out, p. 702, infra.

3. When, if ever, does a court's refusal to enforce a claim resting on sister-state law on grounds of "penality" or for contravening the forum's public policy violate the United States Constitution? Does Hughes v. Fetter, p. 318, supra, shed any light on that question?

4. Is there any inconsistency between the position that the dissimilarity of the law of a sister state is not a ground for refusing to entertain a claim based on that law and the position that the dissimilar rule should not be applied to decide the case?

5. Judge Cardozo's opinion is a classic statement of the "vested rights" theory of choice of law. Under this theory, did the court even consider the possibility that it could apply New York law? After Babcock v. Jackson, 12 N.Y.2d 473, 240 N.Y.S.2d 743, 191 N.E.2d 279 (1963), p. 520, infra, would a New York court consider that possibility?

Mertz v. Mertz

Court of Appeals of New York, 1936.
271 N.Y. 466, 3 N.E.2d 597, 108 A.L.R. 1120.

■ LEHMAN, JUDGE. The plaintiff has brought an action in this state against her husband to recover damages for personal injuries which, she alleges, she sustained in the state of Connecticut through her husband's negligent operation of an automobile, owned and controlled by him. Under the law of New York the rule is well established that a husband is not liable to his wife for personal injuries caused by his negligence.... The complaint alleges that under the law of the state of Connecticut a husband is liable for such injuries. The parties are residents of the state of New York. The problem presented upon this appeal is whether a wife residing here may resort to the courts of this state to enforce liability for a wrong committed outside of the state, though under the laws of this state a husband is immune from such liability....

The Legislature of Connecticut has chosen to remove the common-law disability. There a wife may maintain an action against her husband for damages caused by his wrong, and no exception has been engrafted there upon the general rule that "illegality established, liability ensues." ... A cause of action for personal injuries is transitory. Liability follows the person and may be enforced wherever the person may be found. Nonetheless, a cause of action arising in one state may be enforced in another state only by the use of remedies afforded by the law of the forum where enforcement is sought. The courts of the state of New York are not concerned with the wisdom of the law of Connecticut or of the internal policy back of that law. They must enforce a transitory cause of action arising elsewhere, unless enforcement is contrary to the law of this state....

"The term 'public policy' is frequently used in a very vague, loose or inaccurate sense. The courts have often found it necessary to define its juridical meaning, and have held that a state can have no public policy except what is to be found in its Constitution and laws.... Therefore, when we speak of the public policy of the state, we mean the law of the state whether found in the Constitution, the statutes or judicial records." (People v. Hawkins, 157 N.Y. 1, 12, 51 N.E. 257.) * ... There is nothing in the opinion in Loucks v. Standard Oil Co. of New York supra, which could indicate that in the field of conflict of laws the "juridical meaning" of the vague concept of public policy is different.

In that case the administrator of a resident of this state who was killed in Massachusetts sued here to recover the damages caused by his death.... This court then held only that in such case the courts may not read into the law a limitation created by a supposed public policy, founded on its own notion of expediency and justice. It did not hold that the courts might disregard a limitation, contained in the law of the state, established by authority and tradition, because the court could not discern a sound public policy back of the law.

The law of the forum determines the jurisdiction of the courts, the capacity of parties to sue or to be sued, the remedies which are available to suitors and the procedure of the courts. Where a party seeks in this state enforcement of a cause of action created by foreign law, he can avail himself only of the remedies provided by our law, and is subject to the general limitations which are part of our law.... The law of this state attaches to the marriage status a reciprocal disability which precludes a suit by one spouse against the other for personal injuries. It recognizes the wrong, but denies remedy for such wrong by attaching to the person of the spouse a disability to sue. No other state can, outside of its own territorial limits, remove that disability or provide by its law a remedy available in our courts which our law denies to other suitors. So we said in Herzog v. Stern, 264 N.Y. 379, 191 N.E. 23. A disability to sue which arises solely from the marital status and which has no relation to a definition of wrong or the quality of an act from which liability would otherwise spring may perhaps be an anachronistic survival of a common-law rule. Even then the courts should not transform an anachrony into an anomaly, and a disability to sue attached by our law to the person of a wife becomes an anomaly if another state can confer upon a wife, even though residing here, capacity to sue in our courts upon a cause of action arising there.

---

* In People v. Hawkins there was an indictment for offering for sale a scrub brush which was convict-made but not so labeled, in violation of a state statute which required the label. The brush had been made in an Ohio prison and shipped to New York. The Court of Appeals struck down the statute as in violation of the interstate commerce clause of the United States Constitution. Does the quotation on "public policy" given in this context, guide or control its meaning for conflict of laws purposes?—Eds.

The judgment should be affirmed with costs.

■ CROUCH, JUDGE (dissenting).... The Appellate Division affirmed a judgment dismissing the complaint for insufficiency and lack of jurisdiction. It was held that "the cause of action asserted offends our public policy to so great an extent that the court is without jurisdiction to entertain it." 247 App.Div. 713, 285 N.Y.S. 590.

Without pausing to inquire whether the word "jurisdiction" was accurately used, we accept it as a convenient symbol applying to a refusal to enforce a claim created by a foreign law. In approaching the question whether the refusal was justified, certain general principles may be dogmatically stated. The cause of action rests primarily upon the law of Connecticut. If we entertain it, whether we say we are enforcing the original foreign law or a copy of it incorporated in our own rule of conflicts, is immaterial as a practical matter. It is not penal; it is transitory; and our courts will enforce it according to the substantive law of Connecticut unless it "is contrary to the strong public policy" of our own state. Restatement of Law of Conflict of Laws, section 612. We are left, then, to determine whether the law of Connecticut, which permits a wife to sue a husband for personal injuries, is contrary to some strong public policy of New York.

The public policy concept is a vague and variable phenomenon. When we find it necessary, in a general way, to embody it in words, we are apt to ... say ... "we mean the law of the state, whether found in the Constitution, the statutes or judicial records." We go further, sometimes, and in explanation say that the law so found evidences "the will of the Legislature," Straus & Co. v. Canadian Pacific Ry. Co., 254 N.Y. 407, 413, 173 N.E. 564, 566, and so, perhaps, represents an inarticulate public opinion on the specific matter involved. In that broad sense it may be true to say that back of every law there is something which is conventionally referred to as public policy. Obviously, however, the bulk of public policy, so defined, relates to "minor morals of expediency and debatable questions of internal policy." Hence the difference between our own public policy and that of our sister states is for the most part disregarded by our own law of conflict of laws....

It may be freely conceded that back of the New York rule which withholds from the wife the right to sue the husband for personal injuries is a public policy of the kind which is back of every other rule of law. But neither in the history of the rule nor in its operation is there anything to indicate that that policy is founded upon a definite view—or even upon some vague feeling—that justice or the public welfare would be affected by a contrary rule.... It is enough to say that the rule exists merely as a product of judicial interpretation, is vestigial in character, and embodies no tenable policy of morals or of social welfare. To urge that it survives because it is an aid to conjugal peace disregards reality. Conjugal peace would be as seriously jarred by an action for breach of contract, or on a promissory note, or for an injury to property, real or personal, all of which the law permits, as by one for personal injury. In short, even though we assume that there is some shadowy element of policy back of the rule, it should give way to "the controlling public policy . . . that the courts of each State shall give effect to all valid causes of action created by the laws of another State except possibly in extreme cases." Hubbs, J., in Herzog v. Stern, 264 N.Y. 379, 387, 191 N.E. 23, 26. . . .

■ CRANE, C.J., and O'BRIEN, HUBBS, and LOUGHRAN, JJ. concur with LEHMAN, J.

■ CROUCH, J., dissents in opinion, in which FINCH, J., concurs.

Judgment affirmed.

NOTES

1. Does Judge Lehman's definition of public policy and its sources contradict Judge Cardozo's assertion in the Loucks case that "similarity" is not a valid test of the enforceability in New York of claims based on the law of other states? Consider the following quotation:

"The defendant's position is that the policy of the state—the forum of the action—is to be found in its laws; and when a law of the locus of the action differs from and therefore (she says) contravenes a corresponding law of the forum, the law of the former state will not be enforced. . . . If this were strictly true there would be no question on the subject, for then the courts of one state would, aside from considerations of comity, never enforce different laws of another state, when as a matter of fact, the books are full of cases where state courts have, without regard to their own laws, enforced contracts and permitted recovery for torts according to the laws of the state where the contracts were made and the torts committed." Curtis v. Campbell, 76 F.2d 84, 85 (3d Cir. 1935).

2. D held a contract franchise from P in the business of providing temporary help. In the contract the parties stipulated that Wisconsin law was to govern. D covenanted not to compete with P in the business for two years after termination of the franchise. P sued in a federal court in Florida to enforce the covenant. Rejecting the defense that enforcement of the restriction would violate Florida's statute banning "[e]very contract" in restraint of trade, the court said that failure of the Florida statute to expressly except from the ban a covenant like the one in suit did not mean it therefore contravened Florida's public policy. Wilkinson v. Manpower, Inc., 531 F.2d 712 (5th Cir. 1976).

3. In the *Mertz* case the dissenting opinion states that the trial court dismissed the complaint "for [1] insufficiency and [2] lack of jurisdiction". What difference would it make for res judicata purposes in a later action in the same or a different state that the decision went on one or the other of the two grounds? When it is unclear whether a dismissal of an action was "on the merits" for res judicata purposes, what factors and circumstances are persuasive one way or the other? Compare Davis v. Furlong, 328 N.W.2d 150 (Minn.1983), p. 407 infra; Angel v. Bullington, p. 705, infra, and Warner v. Buffalo Drydock Co., p. 253, supra.

Intercontinental Hotels Corp. (Puerto Rico) v. Golden
Court of Appeals of New York, 1964.
15 N.Y.2d 9, 254 N.Y.S.2d 527, 203 N.E.2d 210.

■ BURKE, JUDGE. On this appeal by the plaintiff from a judgment dismissing the complaint, the only issue is whether the courts of this State must deny access to a party seeking to enforce obligations validly entered into in the Commonwealth of Puerto Rico and enforceable under Puerto Rican law.

Plaintiff, the owner and operator of a government-licensed gambling casino in Puerto Rico, seeks to recover the sum of $12,000 evidenced by defendant's check and I.O.U.'s given in payment of gambling debts incurred in Puerto Rico.

Once again we are faced with the question of when our courts may refuse to enforce a foreign right, though valid where acquired, on the ground that its "enforcement is contrary to [the public] policy of the forum" (Straus & Co. v. Canadian Pacific Ry. Co., 254 N.Y. 407, 414, 173 N.E. 564, 567). . . .

Substantially all of the commentators agree that foreign-based rights should be enforced unless the judicial enforcement of such a contract would be the approval of a transaction which is inherently vicious, wicked or immoral, and shocking to the prevailing moral sense. (Beach, Uniform Interstate Enforcement of Vested Rights, 27 Yale L.J. 656, 662; Goodrich, Conflict of Laws [3d ed., 1949], 305; 2 Rabel, Conflict of Laws: A Comparative Study [1947], 555–575; Paulsen and Sovern, "Public Policy" in the Conflict of Laws, 56 Col.L.Rev. 969; 3 Beale, Conflict of Laws [1935], 1649.)

Applying this test we find decisions in this State involving gambling transactions which put this reasoning into practice. Over 100 years ago this court held in Thatcher v. Morris, 11 N.Y. 437 [1854] that a contract involving lottery tickets if legal and valid without the State would be upheld though illegal in New York. In Harris v. White, 81 N.Y. 532 [1880] suit was permitted for wages earned in out-of-State horse races at a time when horse racing was illegal in the State of New York. In Ormes v. Dauchy, 82 N.Y. 443 [1880] suit was upheld for commissions earned by placing extrastate lottery advertisements in out-of-State newspapers. Thus, aware of the common-law rule which barred the enforcement of gambling contracts and conscious that they were illegal and void in almost all the States of this country, the courts of this State took the position, even in Victorian times, that there was no strong public policy to prevent the enforcement of such contracts according to the law of the place of performance. There is nothing suggested by the respondent which should persuade us that Judge CARDOZO was wrong when he said in Loucks v. Standard Oil Co. [p. 375, supra]: "The courts are not free to refuse to enforce a foreign right at the pleasure of the judges, to suit the individual notion of expediency or fairness. They do not close their doors, unless help would violate some . . . prevalent conception of good morals".

It has, however, been urged that suits on gambling debts contracted validly elsewhere are contrary to two public policies of this State, i.e., in this jurisdiction gamblers are outlaws, and all gambling contracts made with them are void. Worthy though such considerations be, they apply only to transactions governed by our domestic law. . . .

Public policy is not determinable by mere reference to the laws of the forum alone. Strong public policy is found in prevailing social and moral attitudes of the community. In this sophisticated season the enforcement of the rights of the plaintiff in view of the weight of authority would not be considered repugnant to the "public policy of this State". It seems to us that, if we are to apply the strong public policy test to the enforcement of the plaintiff's rights under the gambling laws of the Commonwealth of Puerto Rico, we should measure them by the prevailing social and moral attitudes of the community which is reflected not only in the decisions of our courts in the Victorian era, but sharply illustrated in the changing attitudes of the People of the State of New York. The legalization of pari-mutuel betting and the operation of bingo games, as well as a strong movement for legalized off-track betting, indicate that the New York public does not consider authorized gambling a violation of "some prevalent conception of good morals [or] some deep-rooted tradition of the common weal." (Loucks v. Standard Oil Co. [p. 375, supra]).

The trend in New York State demonstrates an acceptance of *licensed* gambling transactions as a morally acceptable activity, not objectionable under the prevailing standards of lawful and approved social conduct in a community. Our newspapers quote the odds on horse races, football games, basketball games and print the names of the winners of the Irish Sweepstakes and the New Hampshire lottery. Informed public sentiment in New York is only against unlicensed gambling, which is unsupervised, unregulated by law and which affords no protection to customers and no assurance of fairness or honesty in the operation of the gambling devices.

In the present case there is no indication that the evils of gambling, which New York prohibits and Puerto Rico has licensed, will spill over into our community if these debts are enforced in New York courts. The New York constitutional provisions were adopted with a view toward protecting the family man of meager resources from his own imprudence at the gaming tables. (See Carter and Stone, Proceedings and Debates of the Convention, 567 [Hosford, 1821].)

Puerto Rico has made provision for this kind of imprudence by allowing the court to reduce gambling obligations or even decline to enforce them altogether, if the court in its discretion finds that the losses are "[in an] amount [which] may exceed the customs of a good father of a family." (Laws of Puerto Rico Ann., tit. 31, § 4774.) This regulation is consistent with New York policy and would be properly considered in any case before a New York court which may be asked to enforce a Puerto Rican gambling debt.

There is nothing immoral per se in the contract before us, but injustice would result if citizens of this State were allowed to retain the benefits of the winnings in a State where such gambling is legal, but to renege if they were losers.

The cases relied on by the respondent miss the mark.

In the case of Mertz v. Mertz [p. 379, supra], Judge LEHMAN, writing for the court, said that "a disability to sue attached by our law to the person of a wife becomes an anomaly if another state can confer upon a wife, *even though residing here,* capacity to sue in our courts upon a cause of action arising there".... As distinguished from the present case, in Mertz the court was faced with this State's interest in the marital status situated here. As a practical matter, all the significant contacts of the case were with New York and the language of the opinion indicates that the court was in reality there making a *choice of law* decision of the kind that this court today follows under the nominal heading of the "contacts" doctrine....

We think, therefore, that this case falls within the consistent practice of enforcing rights validly created by the laws of a sister State which do not tend to disturb our local laws or corrupt the public.

Accordingly, the judgment of the Appellate Division should be reversed ...

■ DESMOND, CHIEF JUDGE (dissenting).

. . .

Plaintiff, a Delaware corporation and operator of a Commonwealth-licensed gambling room or casino in its hotel in Puerto Rico, sued defendant, a New York resident, on a $3,000 check and 13 "I. O. U.'s" totaling $9,000. The $12,000 total covered defendant's gambling losses at plaintiff's casino where defendant had been allowed to gamble on credit....

The issue: are our courts open to suits by gambling house proprietors who let their customers run up debts; or do such transactions so offend our concept of good morals that our settled public policy prompts us to reject the suit? Closing our doors to such a lawsuit is in principle and under our decisions and statues the only possible course. It is not a matter of choice of law as between the Puerto Rican and domestic brands. We refuse the suit not because Puerto Rico's law differs from ours but because we cannot in good conscience use our judicial processes to recognize the gamester's claim by giving him a judgment. (Mertz v. Mertz, 271 N.Y. 466, 3 N.E.2d 597, 108 A.L.R. 1120)....

We are here asked to enforce a gambling contract, unenforceable at common law (Ruckman v. Pitcher, 1 N.Y. 392; Meech v. Stoner, 19 N.Y. 26; Irwin v. Williar, 110 U.S. 499) and made void and illegal in our State (and almost every other State, see Irwin v. Williar, supra) under specific statutes (Penal Law, Consol.Laws, c. 40, §§ 991–996). In truth, not one but two public policies of ours are offended when we give judgment for plaintiff. First, operating a gambling business (as distinguished from casual betting between individuals) was an indictable public nuisance at common law, has always been held criminal conduct in New York State, and professional gamblers are "outlaws" in New York.... Second, from earliest times in this State all gambling contracts and loans for gambling have been void and denied enforcement by the professional gambler even to the extent that the bettor-customer may sue for the amount he lost (Penal Law, § 994....)

The conclusion that settled New York policy bars suit on a claim like this one is not disproved by pointing to our legalization of bingo games and pari-mutuel betting on horse races (N.Y.Const. art. I, § 9). The people of the State in amending their Constitution and the legislators in adopting and revising the statutes have found and acted on important differences between those two forms of gambling and the operation of gambling houses. That these differences are widely recognized elsewhere is evident from the fact that while pari-mutual betting is lawful in 24 States and bingo is legalized in 11 States (lottery in one) nevertheless only one State (Nevada) licenses gambling rooms and even in Nevada gambling-house debts are not suable in court (Nevada Tax Comm. v. Hicks, 73 Nev. 115, 310 P.2d 852)....

NOTES

1. The court decided the preceding case a year and a half after it decided Babcock v. Jackson, 12 N.Y.2d 473, 240 N.Y.S.2d 743, 191 N.E.2d 279 (1963), p. 520, infra. In Babcock, the court referred to the content and purposes of the conflicting laws and decided to apply New York law even though the defendant injured the plaintiff in Ontario. Is the choice-of-law analysis in Intercontinental Hotels consistent with Babcock? How would the Babcock approach require both the majority and the dissent to rewrite their opinions? For an example of such mock opinions, see Weintraub, Choosing Law with an Eye on the Prize, 15 Mich.J. Int'l L. 705, 716–17 (1994). In Zurich Ins. Co. v. Shearson Lehman Hutton, 84 N.Y.2d 309, 618 N.Y.S.2d 609, 642 N.E.2d 1065 (1994), the court used New York "public policy" to choose New York law and preclude insurance indemnity for punitive damages awarded in a Texas judgment. When should a court use public policy to refuse to apply law selected by a process that has already taken account of the content of that law?

2. Professor Lorenzen said: "The doctrine of public policy in the Conflict of Laws ought to have been a warning that there was something the matter with the reasoning upon which the rules to which it is the exception were supposed to be based." Lorenzen, Territoriality, Public Policy and the Conflict of Laws, 33 Yale L.J. 736, 747 (1924). For of the argument that a court should use the "public policy" underlying legal rules to choose law rather than to reject law chosen without knowledge of its contents, see Katzenbach, Conflicts on an Unruly Horse: Reciprocal Claims and Tolerances in Interstate and International Law, 65 Yale L.J. 1087 (1956). The reference, in the title, to an "unruly horse," is taken from Judge Burrough's opinion in Richardson v. Mellish, 2 Bing. 229, 252, 130 Eng.Rep. 294, 303 (C.P.1824), in which he rejected the argument that a contract was unenforceable because against public policy and said: "I for one, protest ... against arguing too strongly upon public policy;—it is a very unruly horse, and when once you get astride of it, you never know where it will carry you."

3. The statement at the end of the case, that no state permits suit on gambling debts, is no longer true. Both Nevada and New Jersey license gambling casinos and allow such actions. Moreover, both states have long-arm statutes creating jurisdiction over tourist gamblers who have left the state. Judgments against gamblers are entitled to full faith and credit. See, e.g., Marina Associates v. Barton, 206

Ill.App.3d 122, 151 Ill.Dec. 4, 563 N.E.2d 1110 (1990) (New Jersey judgment for gambling debt); MGM Desert Inn, Inc. v. Holz, 104 N.C.App. 717, 411 S.E.2d 399 (1991), rev. denied, 313 N.C. 384, 417 S.E.2d 790 (1992) (Nevada judgment). International Recovery Systems Inc. v. Gabler, 208 Mich.App. 49, 527 N.W.2d 20 (1994) refused to enforce a Nevada gambling judgment, erroneously invoking the "public policy" exception of the Uniform Foreign Money–Judgments Act, which applies to foreign countries, not sister states. On rehearing, the court reversed itself. 210 Mich.App. 422 (1995). That Puerto Rico, even after it became a commonwealth in 1952, remained a "territory" within the meaning of 28 U.S.C.A. § 1738 and its judgments are entitled to full faith and credit, see Americana of Puerto Rico, Inc. v. Kaplus, 368 F.2d 431 (3d Cir.1966), cert. denied, 386 U.S. 943 (1967).

The Tokyo District Court has ordered Japan to reimburse a Nevada gambling casino for money collected in Japan from Japanese who had incurred debts at the casino. The casino's Japanese agents collected the money and were arrested on charges of issuing threats and violating exchange controls. The casino's agents waived any claim to the money, which was deposited in the state treasury. The court stated, "we hold that there is no ground [on the basis of public policy] to exclude the application of the law of Nevada to the contract between the plaintiff and the Japanese tourists." The holding was limited to the facts of the case—recovery on the basis of unjust enrichment from money having reverted to the state treasury. Desert Palace Inc. v. State of Japan, [1993] H.J. (1444) 41, [1993] H.T. (818) 56; summarized 37 Japanese Annual of Int'l L. 163 (1994).

Wong v. Tenneco

Supreme Court of California, 1985.
39 Cal.3d 126, 216 Cal.Rptr. 412, 702 P.2d 570.

[Wong, a United States citizen residing in California and best known for his green onions, conducted farming operations in Mexico through a local front-man in order to get around Mexican law. When the farming venture failed, Wong sued Tenneco's subsidiary, a California produce broker, and others, for misrepresentation, breach of contract and additional causes of action. The Tenneco group cross-complained for money owed by Wong. After trial and verdict awarding various forms of damages to plaintiff on his complaint and also awarding damages on the defendants' cross-complaint, the trial court set the verdicts aside and dismissed all claims. Holding the underlying transaction illegal under Mexican law, the trial court declined to afford relief to either party. Finding the Mexican law barring foreign ownership of land in Mexico to be contrary to California public policy, and applying the California law allowing ownership of property without regard to citizenship, the District Court of Appeal reversed and ordered judgment on the verdicts. Invoking comity, however, the Supreme Court of California threw out both verdicts on the ground that the whole venture was illegal. The Supreme Court did permit Tenneco to keep $108,816 from the sale of Wong's property in California, on which Tenneco held a mortgage. Tenneco had spent that sum to prevent foreclosure by others, and pay for taxes, insurance, and repairs.

The court said that Tenneco was entitled to this money to "prevent unjust enrichment."]

■ REYNOSO, JUSTICE. Comity teaches that "a contract ... made with a view of violating the laws of another country, though not otherwise obnoxious to the law ... of the forum ... will not be enforced." (15 Williston on Contracts (3d ed. 1972) § 1748, p. 121.) ...

The "public policy" exception to the comity doctrine is inapplicable in the present case. That exception precludes application of a foreign state's law where to do so would violate California's public policy. [Citations omitted.]

The standard, however, is not simply that the law is contrary to our public policy, but that it is so offensive to our public policy as to be "prejudicial to recognized standards of morality and to the general interests of the citizens...." (Knodel v. Knodel (1975) 14 Cal.3d 752, 765, fn. 15, 122 Cal.Rptr. 521, 537 P.2d 353, quoting Biewend v. Biewend (1941) 17 Cal.2d 108, 113, 109 P.2d 701.)....

California public policy is not offended by the application of Mexican law in the present case. California constitutional and statutory law expressly provide that noncitizens may own land within the state. However, the land with which we deal is situated in Mexico and it is a fundamental principle of the law of conflicts that questions relating to control of real property are to be determined by the law of the jurisdiction in which the property is located. (See Barber v. Barber (1958) 51 Cal.2d 244, 247, 331 P.2d 628; Estate of Patmore (1956) 141 Cal.App.2d 416, 424, 296 P.2d 863; Cummings v. Bullock (9th Cir., 1966) 367 F.2d 182, 183.) Mexico's history, we have noted, has led to a different approach. That California public policy regarding land ownership differs from the equivalent Mexican policy does not suggest that long-established conflicts principles should be abandoned.

Moreover, we cannot say that the Mexican law is so antagonistic to California public policy interests as to preclude the extension of comity in the present case. The protectionist sentiment that the law reflects has no prejudicial impact upon "recognized standard of morality" in this state. Nor does it adversely affect the "general interests of Californians." Law abiding Californians wishing to invest in Mexico or California will be unimpeded by application of Mexican law in this instance.

. . .

NOTES

1. Taken together, what do the Loucks, Mertz and Golden cases teach with regard to (a) the definition and (b) the source of "public policy" as a factor in denying enforcement of rights claimed to rest upon rules of law drawn from other states?

2. Is Judge Burke correct in his conclusion that in Mertz v. Mertz the court made a "choice of law" decision—that is, rejected Connecticut's permissive rule and applied New York's rule that one spouse was without capacity to sue the other—

rather than that it refused access to the New York courts for Mrs. Mertz' Connecticut-based cause of action? A refusal to entertain an action may leave the plaintiff with the possibility of suit in a different forum, thus serving as a dismissal without prejudice. On the other hand, a choice-of-law decision may preclude further action anywhere.

3. When public policy (*ordre public*) is used to deny a defense rather than to refuse to entertain a cause of action, there is no ambiguity regarding the res judicata consequences. Why? Does it follow that a disallowed defense is more likely to raise constitutional questions than a dismissed claim? See Chapter 6, especially Home Insurance Co. v. Dick, p. 325, supra.

4. In a much-cited article, Paulsen and Sovern, "Public Policy" in the Conflict of Laws, 56 Colum.L.Rev. 969 (1956), the authors warned that the use of the concept is especially insidious and dangerous if it is invoked by a forum court that has only slight contacts with the occurrence or the parties. Often, its use in those circumstances has been for parochial reasons—to give protection to interests of residents. They cautioned that the "principal vice of the public policy concepts is that they provide a substitute for analysis."

5. Wong raises several questions. What is the California policy toward enforcement of contracts that are illegal under California law? Does this same policy apply to contracts that are legal under California law but illegal under Mexican law? What is the Mexican policy toward enforcement of contracts illegal under Mexican law? How many of these questions did the court answer? Whether acts in Mexico violated Mexican law, is a matter of determining internal Mexican law. In Wong, majority and dissent disagreed on this last issue.

6. Public policy is a widely recognized basis for refusing to apply the law selected after choice-of-law analysis. See Convention on the Law Applicable to Contractual Obligations (80/934/EEC), in force among members of the European Union, Art. 16: "The application of a rule of the law of any country specified by this Convention may be refused only if such application is manifestly incompatible with the public policy ('ordre public') of the forum."

TAX CLAIMS

Until relatively recently suits by one state to collect its taxes in another state's courts were dismissed by analogy to the ban on enforcing another state's penal laws. For nearly a century and a half the question of the enforcement by the courts of one country (or state) of the tax claims of another country (or state) was dominated by the influence of Lord Mansfield's statement in Holman v. Johnson, 1 Cowp. 341, 343 (K.B.1775), where he said: "No country ever takes notice of the revenue laws of another." In 1935, Milwaukee County v. M. E. White Co., p. 308, supra, holding full faith and credit due a sister state judgment for taxes, said it was an "open question" whether an unadjudicated tax claim was subject to similar constitutional compulsion. After a period of chipping away at the old doctrine, state courts have tended to enforce sister states' revenue claims. See, e.g., City of Detroit v. Gould, 12 Ill.2d 297, 146 N.E.2d 61 (1957) (personal property tax); State ex rel. Oklahoma Tax Commission v. Rodgers, 238 Mo.App. 1115, 193 S.W.2d 919 (1946) (income tax). See, also, Scoles, Interstate and International Distinctions in Conflict of Laws in the United States, 54 Calif.L.Rev. 1599, 1607–1608 (1966).

By 1977 some 44 states had enacted reciprocal statutes for enforcement of tax claims. See Greenberg, Extrastate Enforcement of Tax Claims and Administrative Tax Determinations Under the Full Faith and Credit Clause, 43 Bklyn.L.Rev. 630, 642 (1977). Judicial decisions in Nevada and Wyoming have enforced extrastate tax claims without statutory authority while several other states with reciprocal statutes have gone beyond their provisions in enforcing claims. Id. at 643. Is there any likelihood that the doctrine of Hughes v. Fetter, p. 318, supra, compels enforcement of sister-state tax claims in a non-discriminatory way when the forum state itself levies identical taxes?

The United States has ratified the Council of Europe–Organization for Economic Co–Operation and Development Convention on mutual administrative assistance in tax matters, with a reservation that rejects enforcement of another signatory's tax claims. See Andersen, OECD Mutual Assistance Convention to Amplify Members' Tax Treaties, 1 J. Int'l Tax'n 252 (1990).

Holzer v. Deutsche Reichsbahn–Gesellschaft

Court of Appeals of New York, 1938.
277 N.Y. 474, 14 N.E.2d 798.

■ PER CURIAM. The complaint alleges two causes of action arising out of a contract between plaintiff, a German national, and Schenker & Co. G.m.b.H., a German corporation, for services to be performed by plaintiff for three years from January 1, 1932, in Germany and in other locations outside this state. Defendants, German corporations, controlled either through stock ownership or otherwise, the transportation system known as Schenker & Co.

Both causes of action allege that the contract provides that "in the event the plaintiff should die or become unable, without fault on his part, to serve during the period of the contract the defendants would pay to him or his heirs the sum of 120,000 marks, in discharge of their obligations under the hiring aforesaid."

The first cause of action alleges that on June 21, 1933, defendants discharged plaintiff as of October 31, 1933, upon the sole ground that he is a Jew and that as the result of such discharge he was damaged in a sum upwards of $50,000.

The second cause of action alleges that in April, 1933, the German government incarcerated plaintiff in prison and in a concentration camp for about six months, that his imprisonment was not brought about by any act or fault of plaintiff but solely by reason of the policy of the government which required the elimination of all persons of Jewish blood from leading commercial, industrial and transportation enterprises, that as a result *"plaintiff became unable, without any fault on his part, to continue his services from the month of April 1933,"* and has been damaged in the sum of $50,000.

The second separate defense of defendant Deutsche Reichsbahn-Gesellschaft alleges that the contract of hiring was made and was to be performed in Germany, was terminated in Germany and is governed by the laws of Germany, that subsequent to April 7, 1933, the government of Germany adopted and promulgated certain laws, decrees, and orders which required persons of non-Aryan descent, of whom plaintiff is one, to be retired.

The Special Term granted plaintiff's motion to strike out this defense, the Appellate Division affirmed and certified these questions: "(1) Is the second separate defense contained in the answer of the defendant, Deutsche Reichsbahn-Gesellschaft, sufficient in law upon the face thereof? (2) Does the complaint herein state facts sufficient to constitute a cause of action?"

The courts of this state are empowered to entertain jurisdiction of actions between citizens of foreign countries or other states of this Union based upon contracts between nonresidents to be performed outside this state.... Under the decisions of this court and of the Supreme Court of the United States, the law of the country or state where the contract was made and was to be performed by citizens of that country or state governs. Salimoff & Co. v. Standard Oil Co. of New York, 262 N.Y. 220, 186 N.E. 679, 89 A.L.R. 345. Within its own territory every government is supreme (United States v. Belmont, 301 U.S. 324) and our courts are not competent to review its actions. Wulfsohn v. Russian Socialist Federated Soviet Republic, 234 N.Y. 372, 138 N.E. 24. We have so held, "however objectionable" we may consider the conduct of a foreign government. Dougherty v. Equitable Life Assur. Soc. of United States, 266 N.Y. 71, 83, 193 N.E. 897. "Every sovereign State is bound to respect the independence of every other sovereign State, and the courts of one country will not sit in judgment on the acts of the government of another done within its own territory." Oetjen v. Central Leather Co., 246 U.S. 297, 303. In the Dougherty Case, supra, 266 N.Y. 71, at page 90, 193 N.E. 897, 903, we have held: "It cannot be against the public policy of this State to hold nationals to the contracts which they have made in their own country to be performed there according to the laws of that country."

Therefore, in respect to the first cause of action, we are bound to decide, as a matter of pleading, that the complaint does not state facts sufficient to constitute a cause of action and that the second separate defense of the answer is sufficient in law upon its face. Defendants did not breach their contract with plaintiff. They were forced by operation of law to discharge him.

In respect to the second cause of action, the result is necessarily different. We are dealing merely with pleadings. Assuming, as alleged, that plaintiff became unable without any fault on his part to continue his services subsequent to April, 1933, that part of the agreement which is alleged to provide "that in the event the plaintiff should die *or become unable, without fault on his part,* to serve during the period of the contract the defendants would pay to him or his heirs the sum of 120,000 marks, in discharge of their obligations, under the hiring aforesaid," must be interpreted according to German law and the meaning of German words. What that law is depends upon the solution of questions of fact which must be determined on the trial. If the English words "become unable" are a correct translation of the German words employed in the contract, then they would not appear to be limited to inability caused by physical illness but might be intended to apply to any factor which might prevent his service.

The order should be modified by reversing so much thereof as grants plaintiff's motion to strike out the second separate defense in the answer as applied to the first cause of action. It should be affirmed as to the second cause of action and the certified questions answered as follows: (1) As to the first cause of action, "Yes." As to the second cause of action, "No." (2) As to the first cause of action, "No." As to the second cause of action, "Yes."

NOTES

1. If Holzer had won on the basis that New York's public policy would not countenance the defense relying upon the Nazi regime's Aryan laws, would the defendant have been entitled to a reversal in the Supreme Court of the United States on the ground that its property had been taken without due process of law? Cf. Home Insurance Co. v. Dick, p. 325, supra.

In Bradford Elec. Light Co. v. Clapper, 286 U.S. 145, 160 (1932), the Court said:

> ... A State may, on occasion, decline to enforce a foreign cause of action. In so doing, it merely denies a remedy, leaving unimpaired the plaintiff's substantive right, so that he is free to enforce it elsewhere. But to refuse to give effect to a substantive defense under the applicable law of another State, as under the circumstances here presented, subjects the defendant to irremediable liability. This may not be done....

2. What is the relationship between the problem of the principal case and the "act of state" doctrine discussed in Banco Nacional de Cuba v. Sabbatino, 376 U.S. 398, 84 S.Ct. 923 (1964), p. 740, infra?

Section 2. Notice and Proof of Foreign Law

Notice and proof of foreign law raises two issues. (1) Must one of the parties inform the court that another jurisdiction has law different from that of the forum and persuade the court that forum law should be displaced with that foreign law? (2) Whether the burden is on a party, or whether the court will, on its own motion, notice and apply foreign law, does the forum have an efficient procedure for determining the content of foreign law?

The answer to the first question may depend on the forum's tradition concerning the role of a judge. The common law view, that it is the parties' responsibility to raise and brief issues, contrasts with the civil law maxim "jura novit curia"—"the court knows the law." Nevertheless, as indicated by James v. Powell, 19 N.Y.2d 249, 279 N.Y.S.2d 10, 225 N.E.2d 741 (1967), p. 399, infra, sometimes a common law court takes an active role in compelling application of foreign law.

The answer to the second question, as indicated by note 3, page 402, is "yes" in most states. A desirable procedure for determining foreign law has two elements. First and most important, the determination of foreign law should be a task for the judge, not jury, and should be reviewable de novo as a question of law. Second, the method for determining foreign law should minimize expenditures of time and money. Article IV of the Uniform Interstate and International Procedure Act, page 401, meets these requirements. Unlike many state rules, the Uniform Act avoids use of the term "judicial notice" when referring to foreign law. The court does not take "judicial notice" of foreign law in the same sense that it takes notice of generally known facts, such as that New York City is in the United States.

Walton v. Arabian American Oil Co.
United States Court of Appeals, Second Circuit, 1956.
233 F.2d 541.*

■ FRANK, CIRCUIT JUDGE. Plaintiff is a citizen and resident of Arkansas, who, while temporarily in Saudi Arabia, was seriously injured when an automobile he was driving collided with a truck owned by defendant, driven by one of defendant's employees. Defendant is a corporation incorporated in Delaware, licensed to do business in New York, and engaged in extensive business activities in Saudi Arabia. Plaintiff's complaint did not allege pertinent Saudi Arabian "law," nor at the trial did he prove or offer to prove it. Defendant did not, in its answer, allege such "law," and defendant did not prove or offer to prove it. There was evidence from which it might have been inferred, reasonably, that, under well-established New York decisions, defendant was negligent and therefore liable to plaintiff. The trial judge, saying he would not take judicial notice of Saudi-Arabian "law," directed a verdict in favor of the defendant and gave judgment against the plaintiff.

1. As jurisdiction here rests on diversity of citizenship, we must apply the New York rules of conflict of laws. It is well settled by the New York decisions that the "substantive law" applicable to an alleged tort is the "law" of the place where the alleged tort occurred....

It has been suggested that, where suit is brought in an American court by an American plaintiff against an American defendant, complaining of alleged tortious conduct by the defendant in a foreign country, and that conduct is tortious according to the rules of the forum, the court, in some circumstances, should apply the forum's tort rules. See Morris, The Proper Law of a Tort, 64 Harv.L.Rev. (1951) 881, criticizing, inter alia, Slater v. Mexican National Railroad, 194 U.S. 120. There, and in 12

---

* Cert. denied, 352 U.S. 872 (1956).

Modern L.Rev. (1949) 248, Morris decries, as "mechanical jurisprudence," the invariable reference to the "law" of the place where the alleged tort happened. There may be much to Morris' suggestion; and a court—particularly with reference to torts where conduct in reliance on precedents is ordinarily absent—should not perpetuate a doctrine which, upon re-examination, shows up as unwise and unjust.... But we see no signs that the New York decisions pertinent here are obsolescent.[5]

2. The general federal rule is that the "law" of a foreign country is a fact which must be proved. However, under Fed.Rules Civ.Proc. rule 43(a), 28 U.S.C.A., a federal court must receive evidence if it is admissible according to the rules of evidence of the state in which the court sits. At first glance, then, it may seem that the judge erred in refusing to take judicial notice of Saudi Arabian "law" in the light of New York Civil Practice Act, § 344–a.[7] In Siegelman v. Cunard White Star, 2 Cir., 221 F.2d 189, 196–197, applying that statute, we took judicial notice of English "law" which had been neither pleaded nor proved. Our decision, in that respect, has been criticized; but it may be justified on the ground that an American court can easily comprehend, and therefore, under the statute, take judicial notice of, English decisions, like those of any state in the United States.[9] However, where, as here, comprehension of foreign "law" is, to say the least, not easy, then, according to the somewhat narrow interpretation of the New York statute by the New York courts, a court "abuses" its discretion under that statute perhaps if it takes judicial notice of foreign "law" when it is not pleaded, and surely does so unless the party, who would otherwise have had the burden of proving that "law," has in some way adequately assisted the court in judicially learning it.

3. Plaintiff, however, argues thus: The instant case involves such rudimentary tort principles, that the judge, absent a contrary showing, should have presumed that those principles are recognized in Saudi Arabia; therefore the burden of showing the contrary was on the defendant, which did not discharge that burden.[12] But we do not agree that the applicable tort principles, necessary to establish plaintiff's claim, are "rudimentary": In countries where the common law does not prevail, our doctrines relative to negligence, and to a master's liability for his servant's acts, may well not

5. Were this not a diversity case, it might perhaps be appropriate to suggest that the Supreme Court should reconsider the accepted doctrine (as to the complete dominance of the "law" of the place where the alleged tort occurred) which seems to have been unduly influenced by notions of sovereignty a la Hobbes....

7. It reads, in part:

"A. Except as otherwise expressly required by law, any trial or appellate court, in its discretion, may take judicial notice of the following matters of law:

"1. A law, statute, proclamation, edict, decree, ordinance, or the unwritten or common law of a sister state, a territory or other jurisdiction of the United States, or of a foreign country or political subdivision thereof...."

9. An American court may go astray even in taking judicial notice of English "law." The similarity in language may be deceptive by concealing significant differences....

12. Cuba R. Co. v. Crosby, 222 U.S. 473, 478....

exist or be vastly different. Consequently, here plaintiff had the burden of showing, to the trial court's satisfaction, Saudi Arabian "law."

This conclusion seems unjust for this reason: Both the parties are Americans. The plaintiff was but a transient in Saudi Arabia when the accident occurred and has not been there since that time. The defendant company engages in extensive business operations there, and is therefore in a far better position to obtain information concerning the "law" of that country. But, under the New York decisions which we must follow, plaintiff had the burden. As he did not discharge it, a majority of the court holds that the judge correctly gave judgment for the defendant.

4. In argument, plaintiff's counsel asserted that Saudi Arabia has "no law or legal system," and no courts open to plaintiff, but only a dictatorial monarch who decides according to his whim whether a claim like plaintiff's shall be redressed, i.e., that Saudi Arabia is, in effect, "uncivilized." According to Holmes, J.—in Slater v. Mexican National R. Co., 194 U.S. 120, 129, in American Banana Co. v. United Fruit Co., 213 U.S. 347, 355–356, and in Cuba R. Co. v. Crosby, 222 U.S. 473, 478—the *lex loci* does not apply "where a tort is committed in an uncivilized country" or in one "having no law that civilized countries would recognize as adequate." If such were the case here, we think the New York courts would apply (and therefore we should) the substantive "law" of the country which is most closely connected with the parties and their conduct—in this case, American "law." But plaintiff has offered no data showing that Saudi Arabia is thus "uncivilized." We are loath to and will not believe it, absent such a showing....

Since the plaintiff deliberately refrained from establishing an essential element of his case, the complaint was properly dismissed. The majority of the court thinks that, for the following reasons, it is inappropriate to remand the case so that the plaintiff may have another chance: He had abundant opportunity to supply the missing element and chose not to avail himself of it.... The judgment of dismissal must therefore be affirmed.

The writer of the opinion thinks we should remand for this reason: Apparently neither the trial judge nor the parties were aware of New York Civil Practice Act, § 344–a; consequently, in the interests of justice, we should remand with directions to permit the parties, if they so desire, to present material which may assist the trial judge to ascertain the applicable "law" of Saudi Arabia.

Affirmed.

NOTES

1. See Schlesinger, A Recurrent Problem in Transnational Litigation: The Effect of a Failure to Invoke or Prove the Applicable Foreign Law, 59 Corn.L.Rev. 1 (1973). Requiring English law to be proved as fact, see Byrne v. Cooper, 11 Wn.App. 549, 523 P.2d 1216 (1974); but cf. Frummer v. Hilton Hotels International, Inc., p. 411, infra (English law judicially noticed). See Currie, On the Displacement of the Law of the Forum, 58 Colum.L.Rev. 964 (1958), reprinted in B. Currie,

Selected Essays on the Conflict of Laws, Chap. 1 (1963), which considers closely the Walton case and its problems.

2. Helpful treatments of this subject are: Pollack, Proof of Foreign Law, 26 Am.J.Comp.L. 470 (1978); Alexander, The Application and Avoidance of Foreign Law in the Law of Conflicts, 70 Nw.L.Rev. 602 (1975); Miller, Federal Rule 44.1 and the "Fact" Approach to Determining Foreign Law, 65 Mich.L.Rev. 613 (1967).

3. In Walton, Judge Frank indicates that if he were free to fashion a choice-of-law rule, he might apply the "American" rule of respondeat superior as the "proper law" of the tort. Instead he decides that under Klaxon Co. v. Stentor Electric Manufacturing Co., 313 U.S. 487 (1941), p. 688, infra, he must apply New York conflicts rules and he sees "no signs that the New York decisions [applying the law of the place of injury] are obsolescent." This is only five years before Kilberg v. Northeast Airlines, Inc., 9 N.Y.2d 34, 211 N.Y.S.2d 133, 172 N.E.2d 526 (1961), p. 503, infra, avoided the place-of-injury rule and seven years before Babcock v. Jackson, 12 N.Y.2d 473, 240 N.Y.S.2d 743, 191 N.E.2d 279 (1963), p. 520, infra, supplied a rationale for displacing that rule.

If you were an attorney arguing a case in a state that, like New York at the time of Walton, still adhered to a territorial choice-of-law rule, but you wished to argue that the rule should be abandoned, where would you prefer to make that argument—in a state court or in a federal court sitting in the state? If you would prefer to be in state court, how would you prevent removal to federal court? In Griffith v. United Air Lines, Inc., 203 A.2d 796 (Pa.1964), which abrogated lex loci delicti, Lee Kreindler, plaintiff's attorney, joined the airline's mechanics who had serviced the plane, guessing correctly that at least one of them would prove to be a citizen of Pennsylvania preventing removal to federal court by United Air Lines, which was a Delaware corporation with its principal place of business in Illinois. Kreindler, Luncheon Address, American Association of Law Schools Workshop on Conflict of Laws, Program 8032R Tape 10, July 9, 1988.

Many states have statutes or rules of court permitting a federal court to certify to a state supreme court questions of state law on which there are no controlling precedents. Is this certification procedure useful for assisting a federal court in determining whether state precedent is ripe for overruling?

4. Under a choice-of-law system in which law is chosen by taking account of its contents and purposes, will the problem of noticing foreign law change? If there are contacts with the forum that are relevant to a policy underlying forum law, should the court apply forum law unless a party who wishes to displace that law establishes that a foreign jurisdiction has different law and that forum law should be displaced by the foreign law? If there are no contacts with the forum that are relevant to any policy underlying forum law, does the answer to the preceding question change? For a discussion approving of the result in Walton and disagreeing with the argument that forum law should be applied in default of proof of foreign law, see Kramer, Interest Analysis and the Presumption of Forum Law, 56 U.Chi.L.Rev. 1301 (1989).

Leary v. Gledhill
Supreme Court of New Jersey, 1951.
8 N.J. 260, 84 A.2d 725.

[This is an action between two Americans based on an alleged loan of money which was made in France and which, so it was assumed, was governed by the law of France. At the trial the defendant moved that the action be dismissed because the law of France was neither pleaded nor proved. The action of the trial court in denying the motion was affirmed on appeal.]

■ VANDERBILT, C. J. ... Under the common law of England as adopted in this country, ... the law of other countries, including sister states, would not be ... noticed and applied by a court, but it was deemed an issue of fact to be pleaded and proved as other material facts had to be ...

The courts, however, were reluctant to dismiss an action for a failure to plead and prove the applicable foreign law as they would have dismissed it for a failure to prove other material facts necessary to establish a cause of action or a defense. Accordingly the courts frequently indulged in one or another of several presumptions: that the common law prevails in the foreign jurisdiction; that the law of the foreign jurisdiction is the same as the law of the forum, be it common law or statute; or that certain fundamental principles of the law exist in all civilized countries. As a fourth alternative, instead of indulging in any presumption as to the law of the foreign jurisdiction, the courts would merely apply the law of the forum as the only law before the court on the assumption that by failing to prove the foreign law the parties acquiesce in having their controversy determined by reference to the law of the forum, be it statutory or common law. By the application of these various presumptions the courts have in effect treated the common law rule that foreign law could not be noticed but must be pleaded and proved as if it were a matter of fact merely as a permissive rule whereby either party could, if it were to his advantage, plead and prove the foreign law. Thus the failure to plead and prove the foreign law has not generally been considered as fatal....

In the instant case the transaction occurred in France. Our courts may properly take judicial knowledge that France is not a common law, but rather a civil jurisdiction. It would, therefore, be inappropriate and indeed contrary to elementary knowledge to presume that the principles of the common law prevail there. This does not mean, however, that the plaintiff must fail in his cause of action because of the absence of any proof at the trial as to the applicable law of France. In these circumstances any one of the other three presumptions may be indulged in, i.e., that the law of France is the same as the law of the forum; that the law of France, like all civilized countries, recognizes certain fundamental principles, as, e.g., that the taking of a loan creates an obligation upon the borrower to make repayment; that the parties by failing to prove the law of France have acquiesced in having their dispute determined by the law of the forum.

The court below based its decision upon the presumption that the law of France in common with that of other civilized countries recognizes a liability to make repayment under the facts here present, and its decision is not without substantial merit in reason and support in the authorities ... The utilization of this presumption has decided limitations, however, for in many cases it would be difficult to determine whether or not the question presented was of such a fundamental nature as reasonably to warrant the assumption that it would be similarly treated by the laws of all civilized countries. The presumption that in the absence of proof the parties acquiesce in the application of the law of the forum, be it statutory law or common law, does not present any such difficulties for it may be universally applied regardless of the nature of the controversy.... We are of the opinion, therefore, that in the instant case the rights of the parties are to be determined by the law of New Jersey which unquestionably permits recovery on the facts proven.

NOTES

1. Would any legal obstacle have stood in the way of the Walton court's adopting an approach and reaching a conclusion like that in Leary v. Gledhill? In Cavic v. Grand Bahama Development Co., Limited, 701 F.2d 879 (11th Cir. 1983), plaintiffs claimed they had been defrauded in a land sale deal in the Bahamas. Although the land was situated there and the misrepresentations were made there, Bahamian law was not relied on by any of the parties, each of whom "seems to have assumed that Florida [forum] law governs." The court ruled that the law of Florida would be applied.

See, also, Belanger v. Keydril Co., 596 F.Supp. 823 (E.D.La.1984), affirmed 772 F.2d 902 (5th Cir.1985) (age discrimination claim arising from alleged wrongful discharge in Zaire was governed by Louisiana law in the absence of a showing that Zaire law differed).

2. In an action arising out of an intersection collision in Nuremberg, Germany, both sides agreed that New York law would be applied. The plaintiff asked the district court to charge the jury that the New York Vehicle and Traffic Law required the defendant to slow down when approaching an intersection. The court refused and the court of appeals affirmed, stating: "It is unlikely ... in a case arising out of an accident in Germany, that the courts would add the statutory refinements to the standard of care to include the apparent slight extra duty of care in approaching intersections. Although New York law may be applicable in the absence of proof of German law, strict statutory refinements in New York should not be held binding as the standard of care for operation of a vehicle in Germany." Loebig v. Larucci, 572 F.2d 81 (2d Cir. 1978).

3. In a contest in the New York courts over succession to funds in a New York joint bank account opened by a husband and wife domiciled in France, the issue turned on the res judicata effects of a prior French judgment involving the same underlying controversy. Neither side pleaded or offered to rely on the French rules of res judicata, either assuming or agreeing that the preclusive effect of the judgment in France would be the same as a similar New York judgment would enjoy at home. In ascribing "New York" effect to the judgment, the court explained its acceptance of the litigants' submission on the basis that "under modern principles a failure to raise or prove foreign law, without objection, should not automatically, in the absence of a manifest injustice, prevent the application of forum law on the theory that the parties have consented that the forum law be applied to the controversy." Watts v. Swiss Bank Corp., 27 N.Y.2d 270, 265 N.E.2d 739 (1970). Can a court know whether "manifest injustice" results from acquiescence in applying forum law without determining on a prima facie basis what the foreign law provides?

James v. Powell

New York Court of Appeals, 1967.
19 N.Y.2d 249, 279 N.Y.S.2d 10, 225 N.E.2d 741.

■ FULD, CH.J.—The parties in this litigation are not strangers to our court. In July, 1964, we affirmed a libel judgment for $46,500 that had been granted to the plaintiff against the defendant, Congressman Adam Clayton Powell (14 N.Y.2d 881; see also 18 N.Y.2d 931). And now we are called upon to review an award of damages to the plaintiff against the defendant and his wife, Yvette Powell, based upon the charge that they had transferred real property owned by them in order to frustrate collection of the original libel judgment.

That judgment was entered in the office of the Clerk of the County of New York on April 5, 1963, and execution was duly issued on the same day, to be returned wholly unsatisfied two months later. On April 17, 1963, defendant Yvette Powell, "acting in her own capacity and as the holder of power of attorney from her ... husband," transferred certain real estate which they owned in Puerto Rico to her uncle and aunt, Gonzalo and Carmen Diago. The plaintiff never docketed the libel judgment in Puerto Rico nor, since she could find no property listed in Powell's name in Puerto Rico, did she institute any proceedings for the purpose of levying execution there.

Instead, she sued the defendants ... in New York alleging as a cause of action ... that the conveyance of the Puerto Rican property was made without consideration and with intent to defraud the plaintiff by preventing the collection of her judgment....

A Supreme Court Justice, sitting without a jury, awarded the plaintiff compensatory damages against both defendants in the sum of $75,000, inclusive of the costs of the litigation and attorney's fees, plus punitive damages in the amount of $500,000 against the defendant Powell and in the sum of $25,000 against Mrs. Powell. The Appellate Division, on appeal, ... modified the final judgment by reducing the award of compensatory damages against both defendants to slightly less than $56,000 and the award of punitive damages against Powell to $100,000 and by entirely eliminating the punitive damages assessed against his wife.

The parties have assumed that the substantive law of New York is completely dispositive of the appeal, and the courts below have in fact decided the case under such law. In so doing, they have overlooked the applicable choice of law principle which establishes that the issue of whether the plaintiff was defrauded must be determined under the law of Puerto Rico. The rule is that the validity of a conveyance of a property interest is governed by the law of the place where the property is located....

Whatever right the plaintiff had to levy execution on the land in question necessarily arose solely under the law of Puerto Rico, the jurisdiction empowered to deal with the res. Puerto Rico might have regarded the property, when it was owned by the defendants, as not being subject to attachment . . . and, if that were the case, manifestly the plaintiff could not be heard to complain about the conveyance no matter what the defendants' motives. The same would be true if the land were subject to attachment prior to its transfer and if under the law of Puerto Rico the plaintiff's right to proceed against the property were unaffected by the conveyance to the Diagos. On the other hand, it is clear that, if the plaintiff did have a right initially to proceed against the land and that right was frustrated, impaired or made more costly to enforce, her remedy, if any, must itself arise under the law of Puerto Rico. . . .

One point remains—whether there is legitimate basis for an award of punitive damages against Mr. Powell. Although it is clear that the measure of compensatory damages is determined by the same law under which the cause of action arises . . . this is not necessarily true with regard to exemplary damages. An award of compensatory damages depends upon the *existence* of wrongdoing—in this case an issue for resolution under the lex situs of the property alleged to have been fraudulently conveyed. An award of punitive damages, on the other hand, depends upon the *object or purpose* of the wrongdoing, and on this issue we should look to the "law of the jurisdiction with the strongest interest in the resolution of the particular issue presented" (Babcock v. Jackson, 12 N.Y.2d 473, 484 . . .). If the conveyance were invalid, the particular wrong which would serve as a predicate for punitive damages is the attempt to frustrate satisfaction of a New York judgment. It cannot be disputed that New York has the "strongest interest" in the protection of its judgment creditors and, accordingly, New York law should govern as to whether the judgment debtor's conduct in the case before us—if it should prove wrongful under Puerto Rican law—warranted an award of punitive damages.

We do not believe that [under the law of New York] this case involves the type of behavior for which punitive damages may be justified. . . .

To recapitulate—the Appellate Division erred in awarding compensatory damages under the law of New York, since the applicable law on that issue is the law of Puerto Rico. In view of the fact that the parties have not previously litigated the law of Puerto Rico they should be given an opportunity to do so. Under the law of New York, which is controlling on the question of punitive damages, such an award would not, in any event, be justified here. . . .

NOTE

In James v. Powell, the court refuses to allow the parties to acquiesce in the application of New York law and remands the case for determination and application of the law of Puerto Rico, even though the court does not know the content of that law. The court says that the law of Puerto Rico must decide three issues. (1) Before defendants conveyed the land, did the plaintiff have the right to levy execution on it? (2) If the plaintiff had such a right, did the conveyance impair it? (3) If the answers to the first two questions are "yes," what remedy, if any, does plaintiff have for the harm caused by the conveyance? Do you agree that the law of Puerto Rico should apply to all three issues?

On the issue of whether the realty is exempt from execution, should Puerto Rico apply New York law? See Uniform Exemptions Act, 13 ULA § 3(a): "Residents of this State are entitled to the exemptions provided by this Act. Nonresidents are entitled to the exemptions provided by the law of the jurisdiction of their residence." Cf. Restatement (Second) Conflict of Laws § 132 (forum law determines exemptions unless another state, such as the common domicile of creditor and debtor, "has the dominant interest in the question of exemption.")

RESTATEMENT, SECOND, CONFLICT OF LAWS:*

§ 136. Notice and Proof of Foreign Law

(1) The local law of the forum determines the need to give notice of reliance on foreign law, the form of notice and the effect of a failure to give such notice.

(2) The local law of the forum determines how the content of foreign law is to be shown and the effect of a failure to show such content.

UNIFORM INTERSTATE AND INTERNATIONAL PROCEDURE ACT.

ARTICLE IV, DETERMINATION OF FOREIGN LAW.**

Section 4.01 [Notice.] A party who intends to raise an issue concerning the law of any jurisdiction or governmental unit thereof outside this state shall give notice in his pleadings or other reasonable written notice.

Section 4.02 [Materials to be Considered.] In determining the law of any jurisdiction or governmental unit thereof outside this state, the court may consider any relevant material or source, including testimony, whether or not submitted by a party or admissible under the rules of evidence.

Section 4.03 [Court Decision and Review.] The court, not jury, shall determine the law of any governmental unit outside this state and its determination shall be subject to review on appeal as a ruling on a question of law.

Section 4.04 [Other Provisions of Law Unaffected.] This Article does not repeal or modify any other law of this state permitting another procedure for the determination of foreign law.

NOTES

1. Article IV is an improved version of the Uniform Judicial Notice of Foreign Law Act, which has been enacted in more than half the states. See Smit, The Uniform Interstate and International Procedure Act Approved by the National Conference of Commissioners on Uniform State Laws: A New Era Commences, 11 Am.Comp.L. 415, 416 (1962). Are Section 136 of the Restatement and Article IV on sound ground in failing to refer explicitly to judicial notice? Is there any utility in

---

* Quoted with the permission of the copyright owner, The American Law Institute.

** The Act, with the Commissioners' Prefatory Note and Comments, section by section, are published in 13 U.L.A. 279 (1975) and 11 Amer.J.Comp.L. 415 (1962).

encouraging courts to do their own research in order to learn the contents of foreign-country or sister-state law?

2. Rule 44.1, Fed.Rules Civ.Proc., effective in 1966 is an even shorter rendering of the basic provisions of a useful rule on this subject. See Miller, Federal Rule 44.1 and the "Fact" Approach to Determining Foreign Law: Death Knell for a Die-Hard Doctrine, 65 Mich.L.Rev. 613 (1967). For a criticism of the prolix and lengthy provisions of New York CPLR Rules 3016 and 4511, see Smit, Report of the Adm. Board of the N.Y.Jud.Conf. 170–181 (1967).

3. Regarding the overall situation, the following is a useful summary:

> "Almost three-quarters of the states, including all but one of those in which transnational litigation occurs with some frequency, have enacted statutes or Rules [sic] either providing for 'judicial notice' of foreign-country law or in other ways authorizing the court, in determining foreign law, to consider any relevant material or source, regardless of admissibility under technical rules of evidence, and regardless also of whether or not such material was submitted by a party. These judicial notice statutes are, however, superimposed on common-law doctrines, which may retain some vitality in situations in which the statutory provisions do not lead to actual notice being taken of the foreign law....
>
> ... [S]ituations arise in which the court either lacks the power to take judicial notice, or as a matter of discretion will refuse to do so. In every case of this sort, the judicial notice statute in effect becomes inoperative; and just as in the old common-law days, the court is then faced with the question of how it should react to the parties' failure to invoke or prove the foreign law. Most of the statutes are silent on this point. To find an answer, the court must turn to decisional rules—the same rules which would govern in the absence of a judicial notice statute."

Schlesinger, Baade, Damaska & Herzog, Comparative Law 108–109 (5th ed. 1988).

SECTION 3. USE OF THE FORUM'S "PROCEDURAL" RULES

A. INTRODUCTION

When a court labels a rule "procedural" for choice-of-law purposes, the court applies local law without further analysis and without reference to the content or purposes of the rule of another jurisdiction on the same issue. What justifies such insistence on local law? Two variables affect the answer—the difficulty of finding and applying the foreign rule and the likelihood that the foreign rule will change the outcome. The more inconvenient it would be to find and apply a foreign rule and the less likely it is that the rule will affect the result, the greater the justification for a "procedural" label. Examples of procedural rules under this analysis, are the proper methods of pleading the action and of preserving objections during trial. Of course even these rules may "affect the result" if a party does not obey them. Neither party, however, is likely to obtain any tactical advantage by application of forum rather than foreign rules on these issues, and local judges and lawyers will avoid the effort of learning and applying the foreign law. On the other hand, the easier it is to find and apply the foreign rule and the greater the likelihood that the rule will affect the result, the greater the justification for a complete choice-of-law analysis before deciding whether to apply that rule.

As the materials in this section indicate, under traditional conflict-of-laws analysis, many rules that were easy to find and apply, and that had high potential for affecting the result, were nevertheless labeled as "procedural." The increased emphasis on the content and purposes of local and foreign rules, which has changed many traditional choice-of-law rules, is also affecting what rules courts regard as "procedural."

Noe v. United States Fidelity & Guaranty Co.*
Supreme Court of Missouri, Division No. 2, 1966.
406 S.W.2d 666.

■ STOCKARD, COMMISSIONER. The issue here presented is whether an action may be maintained in the courts of this State under a Louisiana statute which gives a right of direct action by an injured person against a liability insurer for the damages he has sustained, irrespective of whether or not a judgment has been first obtained against the insured.

The Louisiana statute (La.Rev.Stat. 22:655), in its parts here material, provides that an "injured person . . . shall have a right of direct action against the insurer within the terms and limits of the policy; and such action may be brought against the insurer alone, or against both the insured and insurer jointly and in solido, in the parish in which the accident or injury occurred or in the parish in which an action could be brought against either the insured or the insurer under the general rules of venue prescribed by Art. 42, Code of Civil Procedure. This right of direct action shall exist whether the policy of insurance sued upon was written or delivered in the State of Louisiana or not and whether or not such policy contains a provision forbidding such direct action, provided the accident or injury occurred within the State of Louisiana."

Plaintiffs' petition is in two counts. The first is on behalf of Jerry L. Noe who alleged that he was injured in the State of Louisiana as the result of the negligence of Dr. Hugh Lamensdorf who was insured by a policy of liability insurance issued by defendant. The second count is on behalf of Shirley Ann Noe, wife of Jerry, for loss of consortium. Defendant contends that no action by a wife for loss of consortium exists under the Law of Louisiana, but we need not rule that question. . . .

There is no statute in Missouri comparable to the direct action statute of Louisiana, and there is no contention that plaintiffs are entitled to maintain this suit in this State except on the basis of the Louisiana statute. Plaintiffs contend that the statute is substantive, and that pursuant to the full faith and credit provision of the federal Constitution they are entitled to maintain in this State this direct action against the alleged tort-feasor's

---

* Footnotes omitted. Eds.

liability insurer. Defendant, on the other hand, contends that the statute is procedural only and has no extra-territorial effect.

It is the general rule that the court at the forum determines, according to its own rules as to conflict of laws, whether a given foreign law is substantive or procedural, but in making this determination it will give consideration to the interpretation of the foreign law by the courts of that state. Hopkins v. Kurn, 351 Mo. 41, 171 S.W.2d 625, 149 A.L.R. 762; Restatement, Conflict of Laws, § 584. In our examination of the Louisiana direct action statute, we are immediately impressed with the fact that it does not in express terms impose liability on or create a new cause of action against the insurer. Instead, it purports to create a method or procedure for enforcing in the courts of that State the cause of action which came into being by the tortious act of the insured. Following the provisions of the statute quoted above, it is further provided that it is the "intent" of the statute that "all liability policies within their terms and limits are executed for the benefit of all injured persons, his or her survivors or heirs, to whom the insured is liable". Thus it recognizes that the cause of action is based on the liability of the insured, and that the statute is designed to afford a procedural remedy to enforce that liability. In addition, the language of the statute creating the right of action directly against the insurer to enforce the liability of the insured to the injured person expressly provides where the remedy there authorized may be exercised, and it limits that right to the courts of Louisiana in certain designated parishes. Although the direct action statute, by amendment, now provides that the action may be brought in additional parishes in Louisiana than previously authorized, the effect of such a limitation contained in the statute creating the right of action was expressly recognized in Morton v. Maryland Casualty Company, 1 A.D.2d 116, 148 N.Y.S.2d 524, affirmed 4 N.Y.2d 488, 176 N.Y.S.2d 329, 151 N.E.2d 881; Pearson v. Globe Indemnity Company, 5 Cir., 311 F.2d 517; and Oltarsh v. Aetna Insurance Company, 15 N.Y.2d 111, 256 N.Y.S.2d 577, 204 N.E.2d 622. In the Morton case it was held that "the right and the remedy are so united that the right cannot be enforced except in the manner and before the tribunal designated by the act."

We shall consider now what the courts of Louisiana have had to say concerning the rights created by this direct action statute. In Finn v. Employers' Liability Assurance Corporation, La.App., 141 So.2d 852, the court said this: "Nor do we find any merit in the contention that the direct-action statute created separate and distinct causes of action, one against the insurer alone and another against the insurer and the insured. The statute is remedial in character, rather than substantive, and does not create causes of action." [Citations omitted.] We have found no court of appeal decision to the contrary. In Burke v. Massachusetts Bonding & Insurance Co., 209 La. 495, 24 So.2d 875, the Supreme Court of Louisiana had the issue squarely before it. There the plaintiff was injured in Mississippi as the result of the negligence of her husband, and under the law of Mississippi one spouse had no cause of action against the other for tort, and Mississippi had no direct action statute. The Louisiana Supreme Court said this: "It is conceded that Act 55 of 1930 [the direct action statute] is procedural and not substantive, and it is only by virtue of the statute that plaintiff brought her suit in Louisiana. Plaintiff insists that since the statute creates no substantive right, the case must be governed by the law of the place where the remedy is sought. But the statute merely gives a claimant a direct right of action against the liability insurer when he has a cause of action against the insured, or where the insured would be liable but for immunity personal to him. The statute does not give plaintiff any more rights than she has under the law of Mississippi. It only furnishes her with a method to enforce in Louisiana whatever rights she has in Mississippi. Since she has no cause of action under the law of Mississippi, necessarily Act 55 of 1930 confers upon her no cause of action in Louisiana. The mere fact that under the statute plaintiff was able to obtain jurisdiction against her husband's liability insurer in a direct action in this State does not create, as against her husband, or as against his insurer, a substantive cause of action that does not exist under the law of the State where the wrongful act occurred." ...

Courts of other jurisdictions have held the Louisiana direct action statute to be procedural. See ... Goodin v. Gulf Coast Oil Company, 241 Miss. 862, 133 So.2d 623; Penny v. Powell, 162 Tex. 497, 347 S.W.2d 601; and Pearson v. Globe Indemnity Company, 5 Cir., 311 F.2d 517.

The only basis for any different view concerning the Louisiana statute is West v. Monroe Bakery, 217 La. 189, 46 So.2d 122. In that case the insurer was sued in Louisiana for an injury occurring in Louisiana, and the insurer claimed it was released from its liability under the terms of its policy of insurance because the insured had failed to comply with the cooperation clause. The court said this: "An analysis of our jurisprudence considered by the Appellate Court [which had sustained the contention of the insurer] in reaching its conclusion discloses that with two exceptions Act 55 of 1930 has been treated consistently as conferring *substantive rights* on third parties to contracts of public liability insurance, which become vested at the moment of the accident in which they are injured," subject only to such defenses as the tort-feasor himself may legally interpose. The two cases referred to, Howard v. Rowan, La.App., 154 So. 382, and State Farm Mut. Automobile Ins. Co. v. Grimmer, D.C., 47 F.Supp. 458, held that under the facts of each case the failure of the insured to notify the insurer of the accident, as was required by the terms of the policy, relieved the insurer from liability on its contract. When we read the West case, we conclude that it dealt only with the question of whether the failure of the insured to give reasonable notice to his insurer resulted in the injured person being denied the right granted by the direct action statute to enforce directly his cause of action for his injuries against the insurer. The court held in the West case that it would be contrary to the public policy of that State as set forth in the direct action statute for the existence of that right to depend upon the actions of another. While the opinion referred to "substantive rights," we agree with the statement in Penny v. Powell, supra, that the "case did not involve a conflict of laws" issue, and we also agree with the conclusion in Morton v. Maryland Casualty Company, 1 A.D.2d 116, 148 N.Y.S.2d 524, that the vesting of the right to bring the action at the moment of the accident, as held in the West case, "was the vesting of a right to bring the action in the parishes named." Whether the creating of an additional remedy to enforce an otherwise existing cause of action creates a right that has "vested," or creates something which may in one sense be classified as "substantive" is a matter of the use of words. In any event, the fact remains that neither in the West case nor in any other Louisiana case have the Louisiana courts ruled that the direct action statute creates a separate cause of action against the insurer, as distinguished from a right to invoke the authorized procedure in Louisiana to enforce the cause of action which arose by reason of the tortious act of the insured. We note in the West case the court did not overrule the numerous previous cases which had expressly held that the direct action statute did not affect substantive rights but provided only a procedure to enforce an existing cause of action.... [S]ubsequent to the West case in Home Insurance Co. v. Highway Insurance Underwriters [222 La. 540, 62 So.2d 828], the Louisiana Supreme Court, without overruling, criticising or distinguishing the West case, expressly held that the direct action statute "is purely remedial." ...

Plaintiffs cite numerous cases, but rely principally, according to the statement in their brief, on two: Collins v. American Automobile Insurance Company of St. Louis, 2 Cir., 230 F.2d 416, and Oltarsh v. Aetna Insurance Company, 15 N.Y.2d 111, 256 N.Y.S.2d 577, 204 N.E.2d 622. [T]he Collins case refused to follow the applicable New York law ... and relied on a statement in Lumbermen's Mutual Casualty Co. v. Elbert, 348 U.S. 48, that "The Louisiana courts have characterized the statute as creating a separate and distinct cause of action against the insurer which an injured party may elect *in lieu* of his action against the tort feasor." ...

We do not consider the Collins case to be persuasive authority that the Louisiana direct action statute is entitled to enforcement by the courts of Missouri.

The Oltarsh case construed the direct action statute of Puerto Rico and held it to be substantive and entitled to enforcement in New York. However, in doing so it distinguished the Puerto Rican statute from the Louisiana statute this way: "Unlike the Louisiana statute ... the statute before us contains no built-in venue provision, no clause even remotely resembling the 'localizing' provision in the Louisiana statute, or any other language which could possibly be read as a limitation restricting to the courts of Puerto Rico the direct action it authorizes." In this manner the Oltarsh case re-affirms the result of the Morton case, and in fact supports the conclusion we have reached.

We do not rule [on] defendant's contention that to enforce the Louisiana statute would be contrary to the public policy of this State, but by not doing so we do not discredit it. The position we have taken makes such ruling unnecessary.

We conclude that the direct action statute of Louisiana does not create a separate and distinct cause of action against the liability insurer which may be enforced in the courts of this State, but in accord with what we consider to constitute a proper construction of the language of the statute and the numerous pronouncements of the Louisiana courts, it provides a separate remedy available in that State alone to enforce the cause of action against the insurer which arose by reason of tortious conduct of the insured. For that reason the statute is what is termed procedural, as distinguished from substantive, and is not enforceable in the courts of this State.

The judgment is affirmed.

NOTES

1. In Romero v. State Farm Mutual Automobile Insurance Co., 277 So.2d 649 (La.1973), the Louisiana direct action statute was held to be available in Louisiana to a plaintiff injured in an automobile accident in Texas. That case relied on a similar result in Webb v. Zurich Insurance Co., 251 La. 558, 205 So.2d 398 (1967), a wrongful death action in Louisiana based upon the fatal crash of an airplane in Michigan, to which the plane had flown from Baton Rouge, La. The insurance contracts were made in Louisiana.

2. Would a suit in Louisiana be barred by res judicata if the plaintiff previously had sued the insurance company in the state of the accident and suffered a dismissal? No, according to McNeal v. State Farm Mutual Automobile Insurance Co., 278 So.2d 108 (La.1973), in which the dismissal in the first suit had also been put on the ground that the family immunity doctrine of the lex loci prevented the mother and child from suing for the husband-father's tort. Cf. Mertz v. Mertz, p. 379, supra.

3. In Oltarsh v. Aetna Insurance Co., 15 N.Y.2d 111, 256 N.Y.S.2d 577, 204 N.E.2d 622 (1965), the Puerto Rican direct action statute (Laws of Puerto Rico, tit. 26, §§ 2001, 2003) was held a sufficient basis for a New York resident's direct suit against the liability insurer of Puerto Rican premises in which Mrs. Oltarsh was injured in a fall. The court said the direct action statute "went beyond merely providing a procedural shortcut" by allowing immediate suit against the insurer, and created a "separate and distinct right of action against the insurer where no such right had previously existed." Compare Davis v. Furlong, 328 N.W.2d 150 (Minn.1983), involving a similar fact pattern: automobile accident in Wisconsin, which permits direct actions; suit in Minnesota by Minnesota resident. The court held, 5-4, that forum law should be applied since the issue of whether a direct action lay was procedural. The dissenters favored applying the same methodology as Minnesota employs in resolving substantive choice-of-law issues. This would in their view have permitted the direct action to be maintained. By contrast the Illinois Supreme Court characterized the Wisconsin direct action statute as substantive, but refused to enforce it as contrary to the forum's public policy. Marchlik v. Coronet Insurance Co., 40 Ill.2d 327, 239 N.E.2d 799 (1968).

4. Does the principal case convincingly distinguish Oltarsh as a decision that dealt with a statute containing (at that time) no venue-limiting provisions? Are venue-restricting provisions in direct action statutes valid under Tennessee Coal, Iron & Railroad Co. v. George, 233 U.S. 354, p. 208, supra?

5. In permitting a victim of allegedly negligent operation of a motor vehicle to sue the car owner's liability insurer as a third party beneficiary of the insurance contract, a court creates a judicially sanctioned direct action. See, e.g., Shingleton v. Bussey, 223 So.2d 713 (Fla.1969). Is there any doubt that the remedy is

"exportable" in the sense of permitting direct suits in other jurisdictions based upon Florida highway accidents? What is the significance of the point noted in Davidson v. Garden Properties, Inc., 386 F.Supp. 900 (N.D.Fla.1975) that "Florida decisions ... hold that the [Shingleton decision] effected no change in the substantive law of Florida," but merely brought about a procedural change. What of direct actions for injuries resulting from alleged negligence on public premises? See Barrios v. Dade County, 310 F.Supp. 744 (S.D.N.Y.1970). After two unsuccessful tries the Florida legislature overruled the Shingleton decision by statute. VanBibber v. Hartford Acc. & Indem. Insurance Corp., 439 So.2d 880 (Fla.1983) upheld the validity of the law.

B. Presumptions and Burden of Proof

Levy v. Steiger

Supreme Judicial Court of Massachusetts, 1919.
233 Mass. 600, 124 N.E. 477.

■ De Courcy, J. The plaintiffs were injured in a collision between an automobile, in which they were riding as guests, and a car driven by the defendant. Although the parties are residents of this Commonwealth, the accident occurred in the town of East Providence in the State of Rhode Island. The judge of the Superior Court ruled that the Massachusetts St.1914, c. 553, was applicable to the cases on trial; and accordingly instructed the jury that the defendant had the burden of showing contributory negligence on the part of the plaintiffs. The defendant's exception to this ruling and instruction raises the single question before us.

It is elementary that the law of the place where the injury was received determines whether a right of action exists; and that the law of the place where the action is brought regulates the remedy and its incidents, such as pleading, evidence and practice. Davis v. New York & New England Railroad, 143 Mass. 301. Hoadley v. Northern Transportation Co., 115 Mass. 304. While there may be cases where it is difficult to decide whether a particular enactment relates to procedure or to substantive rights, it was settled in Duggan v. Bay State Street Railway, 230 Mass. 370, where its construction and constitutionality were in question, that this "due care" statute, so called, is one of procedure. As the court expressly said, in construing the statute, with a view to determining its constitutionality (page 377): "These two parts of the statute do not undertake to change the substantive law of negligence in any respect. The tribunal hearing the case must still be satisfied on all the evidence that the plaintiff was in the exercise of due care and did not by his own acts of omission or commission help to produce his injury, and that the defendant was negligent." And again (page 380): "The present statute simply affects procedure and the burden of proof. It does not work any modification of fundamental rights."
... In Lemieux v. Boston & Maine Railroad, 219 Mass. 399, 106 N.E. 992, relied on by the defendant, it was expressly stated: "By the common law of Vermont, as proved at the trial, an employee assumes not only the risks ordinarily incident to his employment but such unusual and extraordinary

risks as he knows and comprehends. And the burden is on him to prove as part of his case that he did not know and comprehend the danger. [Citing cases.] This affects the right of action, and does not relate merely to the matter of evidence or procedure...."

Exceptions overruled.

NOTES

1. Duggan v. Bay State Street Railway Co., relied on in the principal case, was a nonconflicts case in which the court upheld the constitutionality of a statute that shifted to the defendant the burden of proving contributory negligence. The opinion concluded that "it hardly can be said that the inference of due care on the part of the person injured ... is purely arbitrary or irrational." The court also said: "The present statute simply affects procedure and the burden of proof." Should the characterization of burden of proof in Duggan control the characterization in the principal case?

2. Under the standards proposed in the Note introducing this section, is burden of proof "procedural"? If the court applied choice-of-law analysis to the issue, would it apply Massachusetts law, not because the rule is procedural, but because Massachusetts has "the most significant relationship" to the issue?

3. The substance-procedure dichotomy arises in federal-state as well as state-state contexts. See Chapter 9, infra. Is there any relationship between the standards applicable in the two types of problems? Cf. Sedler, The Erie Outcome Test as a Guide to Substance and Procedure in the Conflict of Laws, 37 N.Y.U.L.Rev. 813 (1962).

NOTE ON BURDEN OF PROOF

The term "burden of proof" sometimes refers to the burden of coming forward with, or producing, sufficient evidence to avoid a directed verdict. More commonly in the conflicts context it refers to the burden of persuasion. This is the burden cast on one side to persuade the jury to the required level of conviction on one or more issues. That level is frequently cast in terms like the following (N.Y. Pattern Jury Instructions 1:23):

PJI 1:23. Burden of Proof.

The burden of proof rests on the plaintiff. That means that it must be established by a fair preponderance of the credible evidence that the claim plaintiff makes is true. The credible evidence means the testimony or exhibits that you find to be worthy to be believed. A preponderance means the greater part of such evidence. That does not mean the greater number of witnesses or the greater length of time taken by either side. The phrase refers to the quality of the evidence, that is, its convincing quality, the weight and the effect that it has on your minds. The law requires that, in order for the plaintiff to prevail, the evidence that supports his claim must appeal to you as more nearly representing what took place than that opposed to his claim. If it does not, or if it weighs so evenly that you are unable to say that there is a preponderance on either side, then you must resolve the question in favor of the defendant. It is only if the evidence favoring the plaintiff's claim outweighs the evidence opposed to it that you can find in favor of plaintiff.

FITZPATRICK v. INTERNATIONAL RAILWAY CO., 252 N.Y. 127, 169 N.E. 112 (1929): Plaintiff was hurt in Ontario while working for the Niagara Gorge Railway Company, a New York corporation. He relied on the Ontario comparative fault statute that reduced plaintiff's recovery for defendant's negligence by the degree his own fault contributed to his injuries. The jury found the plaintiff 10 per cent negligent. Defendant claimed error in the trial judge's instruction that it had the burden of proving contributory negligence, relying on the New York rule that in personal injury actions plaintiffs have the burden of proving freedom from contributory negligence. Defendant argued that the burden of proof rule was procedural, but the Court of Appeals disagreed, saying:

The Contributory Negligence Act of Ontario does more than touch or affect a matter of procedure; it goes beyond directing who shall first proceed to prove that the act of the defendant was *solely* responsible for the act or the damage. The act gives a right to recover not recognized by the common law. It provides that even if the plaintiff be guilty of contributory negligence he may yet recover, if the defendant were more negligent, the recovery, however, being limited to the surplus degree of negligence, as figured out by a jury. The law of the State of New York has no application under such circumstances; it is impossible of application. If the Ontario act had merely dealt with this order of proof or burden of proof, and provided that the defendant, in common-law actions for negligence, had the burden of proving the plaintiff's contributory negligence, we would have another question. There would then be the same substantial right as at common law, the change merely being in the procedure at the trial or in the burden of proof. Under such circumstances our courts might feel called upon to apply our own rule.

The appellant suggests that as this act does not refer to the burden of proof, the plaintiff, under our form of procedure, should have the burden of proving either freedom from contributing negligence or else the degree to which his own negligence contributed. We have no such law in this State. To follow the appellant's suggestion would still require our courts to adopt a portion of the Ontario statute. If we are to adopt a part we must apply it as a whole, because it affects the substantial rights of the parties. Under our rule, it would be impossible for the plaintiff to prove his own contributing neglect, without proving himself out of court, as we have no comparative negligence rule for actions at common law. As has been stated more than once, this action is under the Ontario statute.

NOTES

1. By what instruction could the court have explained to the jurors how they were to apply the New York burden of proof rule in determining the degree of plaintiff's

contributory fault? Does the New York instruction on burden of proof do anything more than tell the jurors that the party with the burden is to lose if the jury cannot decide which side's evidence is more convincing? If the instruction meant that defendant had to prove the degree of plaintiff's fault by a preponderance of the evidence or the jury would be obliged to find a lesser degree of fault on plaintiff's part, in what sense was that a "substantive" matter?

2. Reaching a similar result without getting involved in burdens of proof or resorting to the substance-procedure characterization is Frummer v. Hilton Hotels International, Inc., 60 Misc.2d 840, 304 N.Y.S.2d 335, 344 (Sup.Ct.1969). Plaintiff slipped and fell in defendant's London hotel while taking a shower. At the time New York still had the contributory negligence rule but England had comparative negligence. The court said: "England's interest is ... greater than New York's, which certainly has no interest in applying its own law and probably has an interest in seeing England's rule used as the rule of decision."

C. Rules of Evidence: Privilege

Rules on the admissibility of evidence are among the most arcane and diverse of any of the rules that differentiate the way litigation is conducted from forum to forum. The variations from one country to another in the rules for gathering and presenting proof are understandably great. But even among States of the Union the variations are immense and thus far the differences have not been effectively harmonized by wide adoption of a uniform system, such as has occurred in other areas of litigation management by adoption in most states of large portions of the Federal Rules of Civil Procedure.

In the interests of efficiency and convenience, the local law of the forum is usually applied to determine admissibility of evidence. Familiarity of lawyers and judges with their local rules permits them to deal with evidentiary issues with some measure of assurance, a necessary capability, if trials are to proceed swiftly and smoothly. These considerations undoubtedly apply to issues of hearsay, "best evidence," establishing authenticity of documents; and to limitations on leading or cross-examining a witness on the stand, among other matters. Those issues may influence the outcome of a trial in some cases, but they are not as deeply affected by values of the substantive law as issues of relevance and materiality. Certainly, they do not raise policy considerations as deep as those involved in creating areas of privileged communication and preventing disclosure under compulsion of matter learned in confidence.

RULES OF EVIDENCE FOR UNITED STATES COURTS AND MAGISTRATES [*]

ARTICLE V. PRIVILEGES

Rule 501

. . .

---

[*] Effective July 1, 1975.

General Rule

Except as otherwise required by the Constitution of the United States or provided by the Act of Congress or in rules prescribed by the Supreme Court pursuant to statutory authority, the privilege of a witness, person, government, State, or political subdivision thereof shall be governed by the principles of the common law as they may be interpreted by the courts of the United States in the light of reason and experience. However, in civil actions and proceedings, with respect to an element of a claim or defense as to which State law supplies the rule of decision, the privilege of a witness, person, government, State, or political subdivision thereof shall be determined in accordance with State law.

Samuelson v. Susen

United States Court of Appeals, Third Circuit, 1978.
576 F.2d 546.

■ SEITZ, CHIEF JUDGE.

. . .

Plaintiff, Dr. Gene H. Samuelson, a resident of Steubenville, Ohio, and a neurosurgeon, asserted a claim based upon defamation and tortious interference with business and professional relationships. He alleged that defendants, Drs. Anthony F. Susen and Peter J. Jannetta, published defamatory statements, either by mail, orally or both, to certain physicians at Ohio Valley Hospital, and other persons, including physicians at St. John Medical Center and Harrison Community Hospital (all in the Steubenville area) and at Weirton General Hospital, Weirton, West Virginia. He seeks damages based on his claim that defendants' conduct has resulted in his being refused privileges at two Ohio hospitals and his staff privileges severely limited at the remaining hospitals.

During the course of discovery, plaintiff sought to depose six physicians and administrators of two Steubenville, Ohio hospitals. All of the proposed deponents (appellees) filed motions for protective orders, which were granted by the district court in Pennsylvania on the basis of Ohio Revised Code § 2305.251, which provides:

> Proceedings and records of all review committees described in section 2305.25 of the Revised Code [1] shall be held in confidence and shall not be subject to discovery or introduction in evidence in any civil action against a health care professional or institution arising out of matters which are the subject of evaluation and review by such committee. No person within

---

1. Section 2305.25 provides in pertinent part:

No member or employee of a utilization review committee ... shall be deemed liable in damages to any person for any action taken or recommendation made within the scope of the functions of such committee....

This section shall also apply to any member or employee of a ... hospital board or committee reviewing professional qualifications or activities of its medical staff or applicants for admission thereto.

attendance at a meeting of such committee shall be permitted or required to testify in any civil action as to any evidence or other matters produced or presented during the proceedings of such committee or as to any finding, recommendation, evaluation, opinion or other action of such committee or member thereof. Information, documents, or records otherwise available from original sources are not to be construed as being unavailable for discovery or for use in any civil action merely because they were presented during proceedings of such committee nor should any person testifying before such committee or who is any member of such committee be prevented from testifying as to matters within his knowledge, but the witness cannot be asked about his testimony before such committee or opinion formed by him as a result of such committee hearing.

[The district court entered an order designating four questions as controlling questions of law pursuant to 28 U.S.C. § 1292(b), the first of which is relevant]:

(1) Do conflicts of law principles require the application of Ohio law to the instant matter? . . .

I

. . .

Rule 501 provides that with respect to state issues in "civil actions and proceedings" any privilege "shall be determined in accordance with State law." However, that Rule provides no explicit guidance as to which state's law regarding privilege is to be applied in a diversity case.

Plaintiff argues that under Rule 501 a federal court must apply the privilege law of the forum, whether or not state courts of the forum would apply their own privilege law. We cannot agree. We believe Rule 501 requires a district court exercising diversity jurisdiction to apply the law of privilege which would be applied by the courts of the state in which it sits.

[The court's reasoning in deciding to apply the privilege rule that would be applied by a Pennsylvania state court in this case appears in Chapter 9.]

We thus look to Pennsylvania's conflict-of-laws rules to determine whether Ohio's or Pennsylvania's privilege law applies. We do so even though, it might be argued that the law, of the two jurisdictions, controlling the resolution of the privilege question is essentially the same.

There are no precise Pennsylvania precedents to guide us as to how Pennsylvania courts would rule with respect to the questions before us: consequently, we must predict how Pennsylvania courts would rule. We do know that Pennsylvania has, generally speaking, adopted the "interest analysis" approach to conflict-of-law questions. Griffith v. United Air Lines, 416 Pa. 1, 203 A.2d 796 (1964); Cipolla v. Shaposka, 439 Pa. 563, 267 A.2d 854 (1970). Under that approach "we should apply the law of the predominantly concerned jurisdiction, measuring the depth and breadth of that concern by the relevant contacts each affected jurisdiction had with . . . 'the policies and interests underlying the particular issue before the court.'" Suchomajcz v. Hummel Chemical Company, 524 F.2d 19, 23 (3d Cir. 1975).

Here the review committee proceedings were held in Ohio. The participants were Ohio residents. The proceedings were those of an Ohio body seeking to effectuate policies respecting an Ohio physician's use of Ohio medical facilities. Presumably, the proceedings were for the protection of Ohio residents. Under all these circumstances, it seems clear that the district court was justified in concluding that Ohio had the more "significant relationship" to the dispute. It was therefore warranted in prophesying that the Pennsylvania courts would apply Ohio law to the resolution of the conflicts question, particularly since both states have adopted a non-disclosure policy with respect to medical review committee proceedings.[4]

The approach of applying the law of the jurisdiction with the more significant relationship to the dispute is also consistent with that of the Restatement 2d, Conflict of Laws § 139(2).

II

The district court, concluding that Ohio law should apply, granted deponents' motions for protective orders under O.R.C. § 2305.251. Plaintiff contends that it was erroneous to apply O.R.C. § 2305.251 in this litigation because it did not take effect until July 28, 1975, subsequent to plaintiff's February 21, 1975 filing of his complaint in this action.

Article II, Section 28 of the Ohio Constitution denies to the General Assembly the power to enact retroactive legislation. Ohio courts, however, have held that this inhibition applies only to statutes affecting substantive rights, and has no reference to laws of a remedial or procedural nature....

In the context of these proceedings, § 2305.251 works to keep possibly relevant and otherwise admissible evidence from the trier of facts, and is thus clearly procedural. It does not impair the substantive law of defamation, or the substantive right of the plaintiff to bring a cause of action thereon. Therefore, it may be invoked by these deponents even though this action was commenced prior to the effective date of the statute.

[The court considered and rejected plaintiff's contentions that the statute was intended to apply only in malpractice actions and that its application here would abridge federal due process.]

The protective order of the district court dated November 3, 1976, interpreted in its memorandum order denying a motion for reconsideration will be affirmed.

---

4. Compare O.R.C. § 2305.251 with Pennsylvania Peer Review Protection Act, 63 P.S. & 425.1 *et seq.*

ARMOUR INTERNATIONAL CO. v. WORLDWIDE COSMETICS, INC., 689 F.2d 134 (7th Cir. 1982): In a diversity action in a federal court in Illinois to enforce a contract obligating defendant to purchase the shares of a corporation in Japan, the defense was misrepresentation of the financial condition of the Japanese business. Defendant obtained a subpoena duces tecum requiring Touche Ross & Co., the accounting firm that audited the Japanese corporation, to produce relevant papers. Touche Ross resisted compliance on the basis of the accountants' privilege created by the Illinois Public Accountants Act, 1943 Ill.Laws 999, § 27, providing for examinations, registration and rules of conduct. The privilege provision declares: "A public accountant shall not be required by any court to divulge information or evidence which has been obtained by him in his confidential capacity as a public accountant." Japanese law did not recognize an accountant's privilege. The court denied the claim of privilege, describing the Illinois statute as one that "protects citizens and business from unqualified accountants and questionable accounting practices" and along with those protections,

> ... Illinois grants confidential information given to accountants an immunity from the inquiries of the judicial process. But accountants not subject to and in compliance with Illinois protective regulation can be considered not similarly deserving of that special privileged status. The same assumptions about the qualifications and methods of those accountants cannot be made and, consequently, the conclusion that those accountants have the same need for privileged information is unfounded. The balance between the search for truth and the attempt to improve the audit accuracy of Illinois accountants swings to the former and, therefore, to the side of full disclosure. The Illinois courts need not be impeded in their attempts to gather information useful—in this case possibly essential—to the fair resolution of the pending dispute. In sum, the context of the privilege indicates that the privilege is intended to apply to accountants registered to practice under and subject to the other provisions of the Illinois Act....

NOTES

1. See Application of Cepeda, 233 F.Supp. 465 (S.D.N.Y.1964) for an analysis of the journalists' privilege in a conflicts setting in a federal diversity suit before the adoption in 1975 of the Federal Rules of Evidence, including Rule 501.

2. For extensive discussion of the marital privilege, see United States v. Byrd, 750 F.2d 585 (7th Cir.1984).

RESTATEMENT, SECOND, CONFLICT OF LAWS: *

§ 139. Privileged Communications

(1) Evidence that is not privileged under the local law of the state which has the most significant relationship with the communication will be admitted, even though it would be privileged under the local law of the

---

* Quoted with the permission of the copyright owner, The American Law Institute.

forum, unless the admission of such evidence would be contrary to the strong public policy of the forum.

(2) Evidence that is privileged under the local law of the state which has the most significant relationship with the communication but which is not privileged under the local law of the forum will be admitted unless there is some special reason why the forum policy favoring admission should not be given effect.

NOTES

1. If evidence is not admitted under Restatement (Second) § 139(1), should the case be dismissed without reaching the merits? Does § 139(2) adequately take account of the policy underlying the foreign privilege?

Ford Motor Co. v. Leggat, 904 S.W.2d 643 (Tex.1995), applied the Michigan attorney-client privilege to bar admission of a report made in Michigan by Ford's general counsel to Ford's Policy and Strategy Committee. Commenting on § 139(2), the court said: "The Restatement ... goes on to explain that 'the forum will be more inclined to give effect to a foreign privilege that is well established and recognized in many states,' and if the privilege 'was probably relied upon by the parties.' [Section 139 cmt. d.] The purpose of the attorney-client privilege and the reliance placed by the client on the confidential nature of the communications create special reasons why Texas should defer to the broader attorney-client privilege of Michigan in this case.... Although we may reach a different result when confronted with other privileges, in view of the nature and purpose of the attorney-client privilege, we hold that it will be governed by the law of the state with the most significant relationship to the communication."

See generally Reese and Leiwant, Testimonial Privileges and Conflict of Laws, 41 Law & Contemp.Prob. 85 (1977); Sterk, Testimonial Privileges: An Analysis of Horizontal Choice of Law Problems, 61 Minn.L.Rev. 461 (1977).

2. In state X, suit is brought for benefits under a life insurance policy issued in X where the insured resided. The insurance company contests on the ground of alleged material misrepresentation in the application for the insurance policy. Under the Restatement rule, may a doctor in Y testify in a deposition in Y regarding emergency cardiac treatment he gave to the insured prior to the application, there being a statutory physician-patient privilege in X but not in Y? Cf. Levy v. Mutual Life Insurance Co., 56 N.Y.S.2d 32 (Sup.Ct., N.Y.Co.1945), in which the doctor was allowed to testify under analogous circumstances.

3. In another suit for proceeds of a life insurance policy, issued to a resident of Y in favor of a beneficiary residing in Y, suit is brought in Y, which does not have the physician-patient privilege. A doctor in state X, who treated the insured in state X, could supply material evidence if permitted to depose in X, which has a physician-patient privilege. Under the reasoning of the Samuelson decision or under Restatement, Second, Conflict of Laws § 139 should the doctor be permitted to testify? If the doctor is called as a witness at the trial in Y, will he be permitted to testify to patient's communications that would have been privileged in X? Will it be decisive that the only sources of material evidence are privileged under the law of X? That the privilege is widely recognized, rather than confined to a few states?

4. If the principal rights and duties under a contract between the litigants are to be determined by the law of state X rather than Y, will it improperly modify the

rights and duties thus prescribed if Y's rule of admission or exclusion of a crucial communication is applied? See generally Weinstein, Recognition in the United States of the Privileges of Another Jurisdiction, 56 Colum.L.Rev. 535 (1956); Sedler, The Erie Outcome Test as a Guide to Substance and Procedure in the Conflict of Laws, 37 N.Y.U.L.Rev. 813, 870 (1962).

BURGE v. STATE, 443 S.W.2d 720 (Tex.Cr.App.1969): Prosecution in Texas for burglary of a home with intent to rape. The victim testified to a struggle with the defendant, during which she managed to "bite him and spit out a piece of the sweater he was wearing." The piece of material was recovered at the scene. Defendant's wife agreed to allow police officers to search their Oklahoma residence without a search warrant. The search uncovered a sweater belonging to Burge, from which a piece of material was missing. It matched the scrap found in the victim's home and was admitted at the Texas trial, which resulted in conviction.

Burge complained that the Oklahoma rule giving each spouse a separate and independent right to insist that a warrant be obtained before search of the home should have been applied to bar the incriminating evidence. The Texas court overruled the objection, holding the issue "procedural," hence governed by the forum's rule even though the search occurred in Oklahoma.

NOTES

1. Under the rules and criteria earlier discussed, is Texas the state of "most significant relationship" to the question of privilege asserted by Burge? See Leflar, Choice of Law in Criminal Cases, 25 Case Wes.L.Rev. 44 (1974).

2. In People v. Saiken, 49 Ill.2d 504, 275 N.E.2d 381 (1971), the police in Indiana learned that a body was buried on defendant's farm, obtained a search warrant from an Indiana judge, searched the farm and found the body. The warrant was based on hearsay information and conclusions that were insufficient under Indiana law although adequate in Illinois, the forum state. The Illinois Supreme Court upheld the defendant's conviction for conspiracy to obstruct justice by concealing the body. Burge was cited by the court en route to holding that Illinois had the significant relationship for choice-of-law purposes.

3. Defendant was accused of murder in New York. He fled, leaving items of evidence in New Jersey and Florida. In an interesting opinion the court ruled that New York state had the greatest interest in the case, "including the New Jersey searches, the Florida arrest, searches and confessions or admissions." The interests of the other two states were said to pale before the "overwhelming New York interests in prosecution of such heinous crimes as here committed against its own residents on its own soil." People v. Graham, 90 Misc.2d 1019, 396 N.Y.S.2d 966, 974 (Co.Ct.Sullivan Co.1977).

D. TIME LIMITATION

Common law conflicts analysis characterized statutes of limitations as procedural. This opened the way for plaintiffs to hunt for a forum in which they could obtain jurisdiction over the defendant and which had an unexpired limitations period. An example is Ferens v. John Deere Co., 494 U.S. 516 (1990), page 693, infra. There were two exceptions to this procedural treatment of limitations, one statutory, the so-called "borrowing statute," and one judge-made. These exceptions existed in most, but not all states. Many courts that have adopted modern choice-of-law techniques in other areas have applied these techniques to statutes of limitations. Ironically, the borrowing statute, intended to avoid undesirable consequences of the procedural classification of limitations, may prevent modern conflicts analysis of the issue.

THORNTON V. CESSNA AIRCRAFT CO., 886 F.2d 85 (4th Cir.1989). The South Carolina deceased died when his 1972 Cessna airplane crashed in Tennessee. His widow, as executrix, brought a wrongful death action in South Carolina, alleging negligence, breach of implied warranty, and strict liability. The trial court, following South Carolina's *lex loci* rule, dismissed the negligence and strict liability counts as barred under Tennessee's statute of repose which provided that "any action against a manufacturer ... must be brought ... within ten (10) years" from the time the product was first purchased. It applied South Carolina's statute of limitations to the warranty claim. On appeal, held: Affirmed. "As this court has previously recognized, statutes of limitation are critically different from statutes of repose. Goad v. Celotex Corp., 831 F.2d 508, 510–11 (4th Cir.1987).... In Goad, the court stated that: 'Statutes of limitation ... are primarily instruments of public policy and of court management, and do not confer upon defendants any right to be free from liability, although this may be their effect. In contrast ..., statutes of repose serve primarily to relieve potential defendants from anxiety over liability for acts committed long ago. Statutes of repose make the filing of suit within a specified time a substantive part of plaintiff's cause of action.' Thus, statutes of limitation are procedural in that they 'serve interests peculiar to the forum, and are considered as going to the remedy and not the fundamental right itself.' However, statutes of repose are substantive since 'the time for filing suit is engrafted onto a substantive right created by law.'"

The warranty claim, in contrast, was held to arise under the Uniform Commercial Code. The court interpreted § 1–105(1) (infra, page 543) to call for the application of the law of the state of the most significant relationship to the parties and the issues and found that state to be South Carolina.

NOTE

Do you agree that statutes of limitations, unlike statutes of repose, do not have, as one of their purposes, ending the threat of litigation? Though most courts, like *Thornton*, distinguish between repose and limitations for conflicts purposes, some have classified statutes of repose as procedural. See, e.g., Baxter v. Sturm, Ruger & Co., 230 Conn. 335, 644 A.2d 1297 (1994); Etheredge v. Genie Industries, Inc., 632 So.2d 1324 (Ala.1994).

Bournias v. Atlantic Maritime Co., Limited

United States Court of Appeals, Second Circuit, 1955.
220 F.2d 152.

■ HARLAN, CIRCUIT JUDGE. Libelant, a seaman, was employed on respondents' vessel at the time she was changed from Panamanian to Honduran registry. As originally filed the libel contained two causes of action. The first was based on several Articles of the Panama Labor Code, under which the libelant claimed an extra three-months' wages payable to seaman upon change of registry, and other amounts for vacation, overtime and holiday pay. The second was for penalties under 46 U.S.C.A. § 596 for failure to pay these amounts promptly. [The district court ruled that the one-year Panama statute of limitations barred all the claims under the Labor Code.]

Article 623 of the Labor Code of Panama, applicable to Articles 127, 154, 166 and 170 of the Code, upon which the libelant based his first cause of action, reads:

> "Actions and rights arising from labor contracts not enumerated in Article 621 shall prescribe [i.e., shall be barred by the Statute of Limitations] in a year from the happening of the events from which arise or are derived the said actions and rights."

The libelant's employment terminated on December 27, 1950, and since his libel was not filed until December 29, 1952, his first cause of action would be barred by Article 623 if it is controlling in this action.

In actions where the rights of the parties are grounded upon the law of jurisdictions other than the forum, it is a well-settled conflict-of-laws rule that the forum will apply the foreign substantive law, but will follow its own rules of procedure.... While it might be desirable, in order to eliminate "forum-shopping," for the forum to apply the entire foreign law, substantive and procedural—or at least, as much of the procedural law as might significantly affect the choice of forum, it has been recognized that to do so involves an unreasonable burden on the judicial machinery of the forum ... and perhaps more significantly, on the local lawyers involved....

The general rule appears established that for the purpose of deciding whether to apply local law or foreign law, statutes of limitations are classified as "procedural." ... Hence the law of the forum controls.... This rule has been criticized as inconsistent with the rationale expressed above, since the foreign statute, unlike evidentiary and procedural details, is generally readily discovered and applied, and a difference in periods of limitation would often be expected to influence the choice of forum....

But as might be expected, some legislatures and courts, perhaps recognizing that in light of the rationale of the underlying conflict-of-laws doctrine it is anomalous to classify across-the-board statutes of limitation as "procedural," have created exceptions to the rule so categorizing such statutes. A legislative example are the so-called "borrowing statutes" which require the courts of the forum to apply the statute of limitations of another jurisdiction, often that where the cause of action arose, when the forum's statute has been tolled.... A court-made exception, and the one with which we are concerned here, is that where the foreign statute of limitations is regarded as barring the foreign right sued upon, and not merely the remedy, it will be treated as conditioning that right and will be enforced by our courts as part of the foreign "substantive" law....

It is not always easy to determine whether a foreign statute of limitations should be regarded as "substantive" or "procedural," for the tests applied by the courts are far from precise. In The Harrisburg, 1886, 119 U.S. 199, the Supreme Court held "substantive" a limitation period contained in a wrongful death statute, emphasizing that "the liability and the remedy are created by the same statutes, and the limitations of the remedy are therefore to be treated as limitations of the right." 119 U.S. at page 214.... The rule was also carried a step further in Davis v. Mills, 1904, 194 U.S. 451. Suggesting that in the instances where courts have found some statutes of limitation to be "substantive" they were seeking a "reasonable distinction" for escaping from the anomaly of the rule that limitations are generally to be regarded as "procedural," Mr. Justice Holmes continued, "The common case [where limitations are treated as 'substantive'] is where a statute creates a new liability, and in the same section or in the same act limits the time within which it can be enforced, whether using words of condition or not. The Harrisburg, 119 U.S. 199. But the fact that the limitation is contained in the same section or the same statute is material only as bearing on construction. It is merely a ground for saying that the limitation goes to the right created, and accompanies the obligation everywhere. The same conclusion would be reached if the limitation was in a different statute, provided it was directed to the newly created liability so specifically as to warrant saying that it qualified the right." ...

Two other approaches to the problem were suggested in our opinion in Wood & Selick, Inc., v. Compagnie Generale Transatlantique, 2 Cir., 1930, 43 F.2d 941. First, that the foreign law might be examined to see if the defense possessed the attributes which the forum would classify as "procedural" or "substantive"; that is, for example, whether the defense need be pleaded, as a "substantive" period of limitations need not be in this country. Second, the foreign law might be examined to see if the operation of limitation completely extinguished the right, in which case limitation would be regarded as "substantive." Still other tests are suggested by Goodwin v. Townsend, 3 Cir., 1952, 197 F.2d 970—namely, whether the foreign limitation is regarded as "procedural" or "substantive" by the courts of the foreign state concerned, and possibly whether the limitation is cast in language commonly regarded as "procedural."

Which, then, of these various tests should be applied here? It appears to us that it should be the one which Davis v. Mills, 1904, 194 U.S. 451, suggests for use where the right and its limitation period are contained in separate statutes, viz.: Was the limitation "directed to the newly created liability so *specifically* as to warrant saying that it qualified the right"? 194 U.S., at page 454, 24 S.Ct. at page 694, italics supplied. ...

Even though the limitation period here is contained in the same statute as enacts the right sought to be enforced, The Harrisburg, supra, still, as noted later, because of the breadth of the Panama Labor Code, as contrasted with the limited scope of the statute involved in The Harrisburg, the limitation period should not automatically be regarded as "substantive." Nor would it be appropriate to make this case turn on the fact that the right sued upon was unknown at common law ... when we are dealing with the statutes of a country where the common law does not exist. And we do not think that it should matter whether the foreign court has interpreted its statute as being "procedural" or "substantive" for some other purpose, which may have happened in Goodwin, supra, or whether the foreign practice requires that limitation be pleaded, Wood & Selick, supra. "The tendency to assume that a word which appears in two or more legal rules, and so in connection with more than one purpose, has and should have precisely the same scope in all of them, runs all through legal discussions. It has all the tenacity of original sin and must constantly be guarded against." Cook, Substance and Procedure in the Conflict of Laws, 42 Yale L.J. 333, 337 (1933). No more should it matter whether the foreign right is extinguished altogether by the mere passage of time, or is instead only repressed into a dormant state, subject to "revival" if the defense of limitation is waived or renounced, Wood & Selick, supra. Such a distinction would generally be difficult to apply, and might also lead to results out of the pattern of the precedents; that is, if the defense could be waived under foreign law, a limitation period might be considered "procedural" even though it was contained in a specific statute giving a remedy for wrongful death. ... And whether the wording of the limitation period seems more like "procedural" or "substantive" language, Goodwin, supra, does not appear to have been generally considered important.

It is true that the test we prefer leaves much to be desired. It permits the existence of a substantial gray area between the black and the white. But it at least furnishes a practical means of mitigating what is at best an artificial rule in the conflict of laws, without exposing us to the pitfalls inherent in prolonged excursions into foreign law; and it permits us to avoid the short-comings discussed above. We conclude, therefore, that the "specificity" test is the proper one to be applied in a case of this type, without deciding, of course, whether the same test would also be controlling in cases involving domestic or other kinds of foreign statutes of limitations.

Applying that test here it appears to us that the libelant is entitled to succeed, for the respondents have failed to satisfy us that the Panamanian period of limitation in question was specifically aimed against the particular rights which the libelant seeks to enforce. The Panama Labor Code is a statute having broad objectives, viz.: "The present Code regulates the relations between capital and labor, placing them on a basis of social justice, so that, without injuring any of the parties, there may be guaranteed for labor the necessary conditions for a normal life and to capital an equitable return for its investment." In pursuance of these objectives the Code gives laborers various rights against their employers. Article 623 establishes the period of limitation for *all* such rights, except certain ones which are enumerated in Article 621. And there is nothing in the record to indicate that the Panamanian legislature gave special consideration to the impact of Article 623 upon the particular rights sought to be enforced here, as distinguished from the other rights to which that Article is also applicable. Were we confronted with the question of whether the limitation period of Article 621 (which carves out particular rights to be governed by a shorter limitation period) is to be regarded as "substantive" or "procedural" under the rule of "specificity" we might have a different case; but here on the surface of things we appear to be dealing with a "broad," and not a "specific," statute of limitations....

We therefore conclude that under the proper test the respondents have not made out their defense. In so holding we reach the same result as we did in the similar situation involved in Wood & Selick, 1930, 43 F.2d 941....

Reversed.

NOTE

The distinction between procedural and substantive statutes of limitations, adopted by Judge Harlan in Bournias, sometimes produced interesting results. In Nelson v. Eckert, 231 Ark. 348, 329 S.W.2d 426 (1959), Arkansas residents were in an automobile returning to Arkansas from Texas. The car crashed in Texas, killing driver and passengers. The administrator of the deceased passengers brought a wrongful death action in Arkansas against the administrator of the deceased driver. This suit was commenced more than two years but less than three years after the fatal crash. Both Texas and Arkansas had two-year statutes of limitations for wrongful death. Nevertheless, the action was held to be timely. The Arkansas two-year statute did not apply because it was part of the Arkansas wrongful death act and therefore substantive, applying only to wrongful death occurring in Arkansas. The Texas limitation was not part of the Texas death act. Therefore it was procedural and inapplicable outside of a Texas forum. This left the general Arkansas five-year statute of limitations for personal injury, which the court held to be procedural and applicable.

At the time of the accident, under Arkansas law, the cause of action for wrongful death did not survive the death of the defendant, but the action did survive under Texas law. The court characterized survival as "substantive" and permitted suit.

Heavner v. Uniroyal, Inc.

Supreme Court of New Jersey, 1973.
63 N.J. 130, 305 A.2d 412.

■ HALL, J.

This product liability case presents two important questions concerning the statute of limitations. The first, a choice-of-law question, is whether New Jersey, as the forum state, should apply its limitations statute or that of North Carolina—the state where all the parties are and where the cause of action arose and all preceding incidents occurred. The second question is whether, in any product liability case in this state in which our limitations law is applicable, the appropriate period is governed by our general statutes of limitations or is four years after the tender of delivery of the defective product as provided in the sales chapter of the Uniform Commercial Code, [§ 2-725].

In the complaint plaintiff Roy Heavner, the purchaser of a truck tire from defendant Pullman which had been manufactured by defendant Uniroyal, sought recovery from both for personal injuries to himself and contemporaneous damage to his vehicle. His wife, plaintiff Rebecca Heavner, sought a per quod recovery for loss of consortium. All three claims were alleged to have resulted from a defect in the tire, which blew out while Heavner was driving the rig, causing it to crash into an abutment. Each was stated, in separate counts, on the theories of negligence, breach of express and implied warranty, strict liability in tort and strict liability for misrepresentation as to quality by advertising and otherwise.

Defendants moved in the Law Division before answer filed to dismiss the personal injury and per quod counts on the ground that our two-year personal injury statute of limitations applied rather than the Uniform Commercial Code four-year provision and that, on the face of the complaint, action thereon was consequently barred. The motion was granted and the Appellate Division affirmed on the same basis. We granted certification on plaintiffs' petition....

Plaintiffs were at the time of the accident, and have been since, residents of North Carolina. Defendant Uniroyal is a New Jersey corporation engaged in the manufacture, sale and distribution of truck tires throughout the United States. Defendant Pullman, a Delaware corporation, is a retailer of trailers equipped with Uniroyal truck tires, likewise doing business throughout the nation.

On October 21, 1966, plaintiff Roy Heavner purchased a truck trailer, having the Uniroyal tire in question mounted on one of its wheels, from Pullman in Charlotte, North Carolina. Presumably the vehicle was registered there. The accident occurred on April 17, 1967 in that state. No suit has ever been instituted in North Carolina. There is agreement that jurisdiction could have been obtained over both defendants in that state and no explanation has been offered why a timely action was not begun there. The present suit was started here on September 25, 1970—more than three years after the accident, but less than four years from the delivery of the tire by Pullman to Heavner.

We take it to be conceded that, at the time of commencement of this suit, the applicable North Carolina statute of limitations had expired and any action was barred in that state. The limitations period there for actions for tortious injuries to the person or chattels and upon contract at the times here involved was three years from the accrual of the cause of action, the latest possible date for which would be the date of the accident. The Uniform Commercial Code did not become effective in that state until July 1, 1967. (The four-year limitation section specifically provides, 2–

725(4), that it shall not apply to causes of action which have accrued before the act becomes effective.)

I

Choice of Law as to the Statute of Limitations

Sound sense and practical reasons dictate that a suit on a foreign cause of action should be processed and tried according to the procedural rules of the forum state. It would be an impossible task for the court of such a state to conform to procedural methods and diversities of the state whose substantive law is to be applied. The determination of that law is a difficult enough burden to impose upon a foreign tribunal.

A statute of limitations is, however, not subject to the same problems as strictly procedural matters. The limitation period of the foreign state can generally be ascertained even more easily and certainly than foreign substantive law. It came to be included in the category of procedure on the theory that the passage of the period destroys only the remedy and not the right and remedy is considered procedural and governed by the law of the forum. Historically, the thesis developed in England more than two centuries ago when English common law judges restricted as much as possible all reference to or reliance upon the law of foreign countries. In any event, the rule fitted very neatly into basic principles of early conflicts law which rather arbitrarily compartmentalized the incidents found in a foreign cause of action into fixed characteristics and mechanical rules in the supposed interests of uniformity and certainty, almost regardless of the justice or good sense of the particular situation—an approach recently abandoned in this and many other states, at least with respect to the substantive law to be applied.

This law-of-the-forum rule as to the applicable period of limitations has been almost universally criticized by legal commentators, especially in recent times when the whole field of conflicts law has been undergoing so much reevaluation by both scholars and American courts....

Courts have been indeed slow to follow the scholarly lead and candidly change the rule....

General dissatisfaction with the rule has however, found concrete expression in ways other than by outright judicial change. The first of these is the judge-made principle which has developed that the foreign limitations period will be applicable where a statute creating the cause of action bars the right and not merely the remedy. Wrongful death statutes are a common example....

The other method which has been utilized to counteract the law-of-the-forum rule is the enactment, by about three-quarters of the states, of so-called "borrowing statutes." Generally these statutes either bar the action if it is barred by the state where the defendant, or both of the parties, resided or [by] the place where the cause of action arose. In modern days, they serve a purpose of preventing forum shopping. Although undoubtedly intended to be mechanical and certain in operation, these statutes are exceedingly diverse and complex and may well be said to have created more problems than they have solved. New Jersey has never had such a statute....

We are convinced the time has come, for the reasons previously outlined, to discard the mechanical rule that the limitations law of this state must be employed in every suit on a foreign cause of action. We need go no further now than to say that when the cause of action arises in another state, the parties are all present in and amenable to the jurisdiction of that state, New Jersey has no substantial interest in the matter, the substantive law of the foreign state is to be applied, and its limitation period has expired at the time suit is commenced here, New Jersey will hold the suit barred. In essence, we will "borrow" the limitations law of the foreign state. We presently restrict our conclusion to the factual pattern identical with or akin to that in the case before us, for there may well be situations involving significant interest of this state where it would be inequitable or unjust to apply the concept we here espouse.

[In an alternative holding, the court ruled that the four-year period of UCC § 2–725 did not apply to the action for personal injury. Therefore, that action would be barred under New Jersey's two-year period for personal injury suits, even if New Jersey law applied.]

■ The judgment of the Appellate Division is affirmed.

For affirmance: CHIEF JUSTICE WEINTRAUB, JUSTICES JACOBS, PROCTOR, HALL and MOUNTAIN, and JUDGE CONFORD–6.

For reversal: None.

PINE V. ELI LILLY & CO., 201 N.J.Super. 186, 492 A.2d 1079 (1985). Mr. Pine's mother had ingested the drug Diethylstilbestrol (DES) while pregnant with Mr. Pine. He was born in New York and lived there except for the time he attended law school in Massachusetts. He underwent surgery for testicular cancer. His doctor advised him that his condition was related to the in utero exposure to DES. Mr. Pine then moved to New Jersey, where he sued eight pharmaceutical companies that had marketed DES when his mother ingested it. His action would be barred under New York, but not under New Jersey, limitations. New Jersey, unlike New York, started the limitations period when Mr. Pine reasonably discovered the basis for his action. The court held that if Mr. Pine in fact had become domiciled in New Jersey, New Jersey limitations applied and the action could proceed. The court distinguished Heavner v. Uniroyal, stating: "New Jersey's interest in compensating its domiciliary is paramount [and] outweighs our policy of discouraging forum shopping."

NOTES

1. Other courts have abandoned the "procedural" characterization of statutes of limitations and have applied modern conflicts analysis to the issue. See, e.g., Industrial Indemnity Co. v. Chapman & Cutler, 22 F.3d 1346 (5th Cir.1994) (applying the conflicts law of California, from which the case had been transferred); Tomlin v. Boeing Co., 650 F.2d 1065 (9th Cir.1981) (Washington conflicts law); Gianni v. Fort Wayne Air Serv., Inc., 342 F.2d 621 (7th Cir.1965) (Indiana conflicts law); Johnson v. Pischke, 108 Idaho 397, 700 P.2d 19 (1985); Cameron v. Hardisty, 407 N.W.2d 595 (Iowa 1987); Air Prod. & Chem., Inc. v. Fairbanks Morse, Inc., 58 Wis.2d 193, 206 N.W.2d 414 (1973).

2. Responding to the cases in Note (1), the American Law Institute revised the Restatement (Second) of Conflict of Laws:

RESTATEMENT, SECOND, CONFLICT OF LAWS *

1988 REVISIONS

§ 142. Statute of Limitations

Whether a claim will be maintained against the defense of the statute of limitations is determined under the principles stated in § 6. In general, unless the exceptional circumstances of the case make such a result unreasonable:

(1) The forum will apply its own statute of limitations barring the claim.

(2) The forum will apply its own statute of limitations permitting the claim unless:

(a) maintenance of the claim would serve no substantial interest of the forum; and

(b) the claim would be barred under the statute of limitations of a state having a more significant relationship to the parties and the occurrence.

Does the revision adequately provide for a most-significant-relationship analysis of the limitations issue? Should § 142(1) distinguish between a forum that applies its own shorter statute of limitations to close its courts, but not prevent suit elsewhere, and a forum that dismisses the action on the merits to protect a forum defendant? Does § 142(2) permit a local plaintiff to sue a foreign defendant under forum limitations, when the defendant's contacts with the forum are sufficient for personal jurisdiction but are unrelated to the cause of action?

Cropp v. Interstate Distributor Co.

Court of Appeals of Oregon, 1994.
129 Or.App. 510, 880 P.2d 464, review denied, 887 P.2d 791 (Or.1994).

■ Before ROSSMAN, P.J., and De MUNIZ and LEESON, JJ.

■ De MUNIZ, JUDGE.

Plaintiffs brought this action against defendants seeking money damages for personal injuries and property damage that they sustained when a truck, owned by defendant Interstate Distributor Company (Interstate) and operated by defendant Rust, collided with their parked truck in California. Plaintiffs appeal from a summary judgment that their action was barred by California's one-year statute of limitations. We affirm....

* Quoted with the permission of the copyright owner, The American Law Institute.

Plaintiffs are self-employed truck drivers. They live in Gervais, Oregon, which is also their principal place of business. In 1990, they worked in Oregon, Washington, California, Nevada and Arizona. Rust is a resident of Nevada and an employee of Interstate. He works mainly in California, but also works in Colorado, Wyoming, Montana, Washington and Oregon. He works in Oregon about twice a month and uses Interstate's maintenance and fueling facility in Wilsonville, Oregon. Occasionally, he uses another company's facility in White City, Oregon. Interstate is a Washington corporation with its principal office in Tacoma. It transacts most of its business in California.

On December 18, 1990, plaintiffs were returning to Oregon with a load of lime from Napa Valley, California. Near Doyle, California, they pulled to the side of Highway 395 to change drivers. Rust was also traveling on Highway 395, transporting merchandise north in an Interstate truck. His truck struck plaintiffs' parked truck.

Plaintiffs retained counsel within one month of the accident. They began, but did not complete, the process of filing a lawsuit in Washington. Instead, in April, 1992, they filed this action, and the trial court granted summary judgment for defendants.

In their two assignments of error, which challenge the granting of defendants' motion for summary judgment and the denial of their motion for partial summary judgment, plaintiffs assert that the trial court erred in concluding that, because the "greater contacts are outside of Oregon," California's one-year statute of limitations, applied and barred plaintiffs' claims. Plaintiffs assert that Oregon's two-year statute of limitations, ORS 12.110(1), applies to their personal injury claims, because only Oregon has a substantial interest in having its law applied, and, thus, there is no conflict of laws issue. Alternatively, they assert that ORS 12.110(1) applies according to Oregon tort conflict of laws rules.

We begin with the requirements of ORS 12.430 in the Uniform Conflict of Laws–Limitations Act: "(1) Except as provided by ORS 12.450, if a claim is substantively based: (a) Upon the law of one other state, the limitation period of that state applies; or (b) Upon the law of more than one state, the limitation period of one of those states, chosen by the law of conflict of laws of this state, applies. (2) The limitation period of this state applies to all other claims." ... In short, the statute requires us to apply the statute of limitations that corresponds to the substantive law forming the basis of plaintiffs' claims.... Plaintiffs allege that Rust was negligent in failing to keep a proper lookout, failing to keep his vehicle under control, driving his truck at a speed that was greater than reasonable and prudent under the circumstances and operating his truck "in violation of PUC regulations." Those allegations concern the parties' rights and responsibilities in operating motor vehicles on highways in California. California law, including its Vehicle Code, defines and regulates those rights. Oregon motor vehicle laws do not define or regulate the operation of motor vehicles in California and thus have no bearing on plaintiffs' claims. Therefore, we conclude that those claims are substantively based on California law only. Accordingly, California's one-year statute of limitations applies and bars plaintiffs' claims....

Affirmed.

■ ROSSMAN, PRESIDING JUDGE, dissenting....

I agree with the majority that the answer to this case depends on which state's substantive law governs the claims. Determining, in turn, whether the claims are based on the substantive law of Oregon or California requires a choice of laws analysis, which the majority does not make. I disagree with the majority's view that the claims here are based on the substantive law of the State of California because the accident took place there. Under a choice of law analysis, I would conclude that plaintiff's tort claims are substantively based only on the law of Oregon. Accordingly, I would conclude that, pursuant to ORS 12.430(2), Oregon's statute of limitations applies....

For there to be a choice of law issue, there must be a choice to make. Oregon law and another state's law must be different on the disputed issue. Here, there are two different laws on the disputed issue of whether plaintiffs' personal injury claims were timely filed. In Oregon, plaintiffs had to file their action within two years of December 18, 1990. ORS 12.110(1). In California, plaintiffs had to file their action within one year. Thus, the answer to ... whether there is an actual conflict between Oregon and California law, is yes.

Even if there is a difference between Oregon law and the law of the other state on the disputed issue, there is no choice of law issue unless both states have a substantial interest in having their law apply. Whether a state has a substantial interest in having its law applied to a disputed issue involves identifying that state's interests in the case, and an examination of the policy behind the state's law on the disputed issue and how that policy would be affected by application or non-application of its law in the case.

Perhaps one of the strongest interests that a state can have in a case arises when the parties to the dispute are residents of the state or are to be regarded as such. Here, plaintiffs are Oregonians. Additionally, defendants are considered to be Oregon domiciliaries. According to the Restatement (Second) Conflicts of Law § 145, comment i (1971), when certain contacts involving a tort are located in two or more states with identical local law rules on the issue in question, then the case will be treated, for choice-of-law purposes, as if those contacts were grouped in a single state. Nevada, where Rust lived, and Washington, where Interstate was incorporated and had its principal place of business, each have personal injury statutes of limitations equal to or longer than ORS 12.110(1). Accordingly, for purposes of resolving the conflict, defendants are considered to be Oregon domiciliaries. Additionally, part of the conduct related to the accident—the freight contracts and dispatch instructions—occurred in Oregon, Nevada and Washington, each of which have statutes of limitations similar to ORS 12.110(1). Therefore, at least in part, the conduct causing plaintiffs' personal injuries is considered to have occurred in Oregon. The economic consequences of plaintiff's recovery or lack of recovery would be felt in Oregon, not California. Finally, defendants do business in Oregon. All of those factors require the conclusion that Oregon has a substantial interest in the outcome of the disputed issue.

In contrast, the relevant factors show that any interest that California has in the outcome of the dispute is, at best, minor. Neither plaintiffs nor defendants are, or are considered to be, California domiciliaries for the purpose of resolving the conflict. The majority's holding seems to be based primarily on its view that, because the allegations of the complaint concern the parties' rights and responsibilities in operating motor vehicles on the highways, only California substantive law is implicated. Although California has an interest in maintaining traffic safety in its state, that interest is met by enforcement of its traffic laws. As between California and Oregon, the only relationship that California has to this action is the entirely fortuitous event that it happened to be the site of the crash. That in itself is not a substantial interest. Additionally, the economic impact of denying plaintiffs the right to recover on their personal injury claims would not be felt in California. Finally, the purpose underlying California's one-year statute of limitations, to make sure that tort claims are brought before they become stale, would not be frustrated by application of Oregon's two-year limitation period. California simply has no substantial interest that would be offended by applying Oregon's statute of limitations to a California automobile accident that does not involve California residents.

In short, the important contacts—where the parties live or are deemed to live and the economic impact of the litigation—are Oregon contacts. The less consequential contact—where the accident occurred—is a California contact. I would conclude that that contact does not create a substantial interest in California. Accordingly, I would conclude that ... Oregon substantive law therefore applies....

NOTES

1. The principal case reveals the problems encountered when the limitations issue is linked to other issues and not given an independent conflict-of-laws analysis. ORS § 12.450, the exception referred to in the opinion, is § 4 of the Uniform Act. It provides for application of Oregon law if "the limitation period of another state [otherwise applicable under the Act] is substantially different from the limitation of this State and has not afforded a fair opportunity to sue upon, or imposes an unfair burden in defending against, the claim." As of January 1, 1994, the Uniform Act had been adopted in six states.

2. On January 1, 1992, a new comprehensive conflict-of-laws code took effect in Louisiana. La.C.C. arts. 3515–3549. Article 3549 provides for application of Louisiana time limitations unless (1) the action would be barred under Louisiana law but not "in the state whose law would be applicable to the merits and maintenance of the action in this state is warranted by compelling considerations of remedial justice"; or (2) the action "would be barred in the state whose law is applicable to the merits and maintenance of the action in this state is not warranted by the policies of this state and its relationship to the parties or the dispute nor by any compelling considerations of remedial justice."

In Smith v. ODECO (UK), Inc., 615 So.2d 407 (La.App.1993), writ denied 618 So.2d 412 (La.1993), the court found that "compelling considerations of remedial justice" permitted a resident and domiciliary of the United Kingdom to sue in Louisiana when the Louisiana period of limitations had expired but the United Kingdom period had not. Louisiana was the only forum in which jurisdiction could be obtained over all defendants. For a discussion of Art. 3549 of the Louisiana conflicts code and of cases applying it, see Symeonides, Louisiana Conflicts Law: Two "Surprises," 54 La.L.Rev. 497, 530–548 (1994).

3. The Foreign Limitation Periods Act 1984, applicable to England and Wales, provides that if the law of a foreign country applies, then the time limitations of that country for bringing of proceedings shall also apply. Civil law countries characterize limitations as substantive for choice-of-law purposes. See Rabel, 3 The Conflict of Laws: A Comparative Study 511–512 (2d ed. 1964 by Bernstein). See also Convention on the Law Applicable to Contractual Obligations (80/934/EEC), in force between members of the European Union, Art. 10: "1. The law applicable to a contract by virtue of Articles 3 to 6 and 12 of this Convention shall govern in particular: . . . (d) the various ways of extinguishing obligations, and prescription and limitation of actions."

Trzecki v. Gruenewald

Supreme Court of Missouri, En Banc., 1976.
532 S.W.2d 209.

■ HOLMAN, JUDGE.

In this suit for damages for personal injuries the trial court sustained the separate motions of defendants to dismiss plaintiff's action. Plaintiff appealed to the St. Louis District of the Court of Appeals. That court adopted an opinion which held that plaintiff's claim was not barred by the statute of limitations and reversed the judgment of dismissal. Upon application of respondents we ordered the case transferred to this court. . . . We affirm [the trial court and reverse the Court of Appeals].

This suit was filed on November 20, 1972. The petition alleged that all of the parties were residents of Missouri and that plaintiff was injured near Springfield, Illinois; that he and defendant David Gruenewald were on a trip which was intended to begin and end in Missouri; that on June 23, 1970, in Illinois, their automobile became inoperative and that David telephoned a request that Steven come to the place of their difficulty and tow the car and transport them back to St. Louis County. Shortly after the tow-trip began Steven's car was overturned and plaintiff was injured. Both of the automobiles involved were licensed and garaged in Missouri. Under the Illinois guest statute a cause of action against an automobile driver accrues to a guest occupant only if his injuries are caused by the willful and wanton misconduct of the driver. No such misconduct was alleged.

Section 15, Chap. 83, Ill.Rev.Stat. provides that, "Actions for damages for an injury to the person . . . shall be commenced within two years next after the cause of action accrued." And the Missouri "borrowing statute," Section 516.190 provides that, "Whenever a cause of action has been fully barred by the laws of the state, territory or country in which it originated, said bar shall be a complete defense to any action thereon, brought in any of the courts of this state."

In their motions to dismiss, defendants pleaded the foregoing statutes of limitation and alleged that since the action was not commenced within two years it was barred. The trial court agreed.

It is plaintiff's contention that the Missouri five year statute of limitation is applicable to this action and hence the trial court erred in dismissing the suit. His rather ingenious theory is that since he did not charge defendants with willful and wanton misconduct no cause of action accrued to him under Illinois law and his claim for relief is therefore based on the common law of Missouri. This, he says, is in accord with the "dominant interest or principal contacts" doctrine adopted in Kennedy v. Dixon, 439 S.W.2d 173 (Mo.1969).

Defendants, on the contrary, say that the Missouri "borrowing statute" made the two year Illinois statute of limitation, in effect, a Missouri statute for purposes of this case and thus bars the action....

At this point it should be mentioned that in *Kennedy,* supra, we abandoned the inflexible lex loci delicti rule in favor of the rule stated in Section 145 of Restatement 2d on Conflict of Laws. That rule permits a choice of law based upon the most significant relationships and contacts. We chose not to apply the Indiana guest law in that case. However, we do not think Kennedy has any application in the instant case because we are not concerned with a conflict of laws question....

Since *Kennedy* adopted the Restatement rule we think it particularly significant that the Restatement is in accord with the conclusion we have heretofore stated. 1 Restatement of Conflict of Laws 2d, p. 10, Section 6(1) states that, "A court, subject to constitutional restrictions, will follow a statutory directive of its own state on choice of law," and Section 142(1) reads, "An action will not be maintained if it is barred by the statute of limitations of the forum, including a provision borrowing the statute of limitations of another state." ...

In his reply brief plaintiff contends that our borrowing statute should be construed as applying only in cases involving nonresident parties. The reasoning seems to be that otherwise there is a conflict between our borrowing statute and our tolling statute, Sec. 516.200, [which suspends the running of Missouri limitations in an action against a Missouri resident, while the resident is out of the state] in that an action could be barred under the borrowing statute even though the facts would cause it to be tolled under Sec. 516.200. The idea for his contention no doubt came from the case of Coan v. Cessna Aircraft, 53 Ill.2d 526, 293 N.E.2d 588 (1973) wherein the Illinois court reached that result under statutory provisions somewhat different from ours. We see no reasonable basis for holding that Missouri's borrowing and tolling statutes are in conflict. This contention is accordingly disallowed.

As indicated, we think the foregoing authorities are applicable to and decisive of the question presented in this case and hence that the trial court ruled correctly in dismissing the action.

Judgment affirmed.

All concur.

NOTES

1. Restatement (Second) Conflicts of Laws § 142, quoted by the court in the principal case, was revised in 1988 as indicated in Note (2), p. 426. Comment b to the revised § 142 states: "In the light of the recommendation of this Section to give statutes of limitations the same analysis as other substantive choice-of-law issues, borrowing statutes should probably either be repealed or amended to conform to the policies of this Section."

2. In Coan v. Cessna Aircraft, 53 Ill.2d 526, 293 N.E.2d 588 (1973), referred to in the principal case, the Illinois statute suspending the running of limitations while the defendant is out of the state, provided that it did not apply if neither plaintiff nor defendant were Illinois residents at the time the action accrued. The Illinois Supreme Court held that the tolling statute exception for Illinois residents required reading a similar exception into the Illinois borrowing statute. Otherwise, the two statutes might conflict if an Illinois defendant who committed a wrong in another state, was absent from Illinois during the limitations period. Haughton v. Haughton, 76 Ill.2d 439, 31 Ill.Dec. 183, 394 N.E.2d 385 (1979), cert. denied 444 U.S. 1102 (1980), held the exception for nonresidents in the Illinois tolling statute violated the equal protection clauses of both the United States and Illinois constitutions. Canadian Northern Ry. v. Eggen, 252 U.S. 553 (1920), held that a borrowing statute exception for forum residents did not violate the Privileges and Immunities clause of Art. IV § 2 of the United States Constitution. Canadian Northern Ry. was not cited in Haughton.

Bendix Autolite Corp. v. Midwesco Enterprises, 486 U.S. 888 (1988), invalidated, as an unreasonable burden on interstate commerce, the Ohio rule that suspended the running of the statute of limitations against a foreign corporation. The suspension operated even when the corporation was subject to long-arm jurisdiction. To avoid tolling of limitations, the foreign corporation would have to obtain a license to do business in Ohio and appoint a resident agent for service of process. Reynoldsville Casket Co. v. Hyde, 115 S.Ct. 1745 (1995) holds that Bendix applies retroactively to actions accruing before Bendix was decided.

Statutes are common that suspend limitations while an action is pending, if suit is terminated without deciding the merits. There is a split of authority whether such statutes apply to actions brought in another state. See Muzingo v. Vaught, 887 S.W.2d 693 (Mo.App.1994), collecting authority and holding that the Missouri statute applies only if the dismissed action was brought in Missouri.

3. In the principal case, how could the cause of action have "originated" in Illinois, within the meaning of the Missouri borrowing statute, if the Illinois guest statute would have deprived the plaintiff of any cause of action? Bates v. Cook, Inc., 509 So.2d 1112 (Fla.1987), held that where a cause of action "arose," under the Florida borrowing statute, was determined by the same "significant relationships test" used to choose law in tort actions.

4. Malone v. Jackson, 652 S.W.2d 170 (Mo.App.1993), held that the Missouri borrowing statute does not apply to the special statute of limitations contained in the Missouri wrongful death act and, under a most significant relationship test, the forum's wrongful death act applied. The holding was based on a provision in the chapter of the Missouri code that contained the borrowing statute, that the chapter does not apply "to any action which is or shall be otherwise limited by statute." Even without this provision, should the borrowing statute, which was enacted to prevent the undesirable consequences of characterizing limitations as "procedural," apply if the Missouri statute of limitations is "substantive." Most states agree with Bournias v. Atlantic Maritime Co., Ltd., 220 F.2d 152 (2d Cir.1955), p. 419, supra, that limitations are substantive if part of the same statute creating the cause of action.

5. Do the words "laws of the state" in the Missouri borrowing statute refer to the conflict-of-laws rules of that state? Suppose a court of that state would not apply its own shorter statute of limitations to an action between Missouri residents? Ledesma v. Jack Stewart Produce, Inc., 816 F.2d 482 (9th Cir.1987), permitted a California resident to sue Arizona and Oklahoma residents who injured the plaintiff in Arizona. The California one-year limitation had expired, but not the Arizona or Oklahoma two-year limitations. For disagreement with Ledesma, see Weinberg, Choosing Law: The Limitations Debates, 1991 U.Ill.L.Rev. 683, 720–721.

Drudge v. Overland Plazas Co., 670 F.2d 92 (8th Cir.1982) held that the Iowa borrowing statute language, "laws ... where the defendant has previously resided," referred to the whole law of that place, including its borrowing statute, which borrowed the law of the state in which the action "originated." Hobbs v. Firestone Tire & Rubber Co., 195 F.Supp. 56 (N.D.Ind.1961), however, rejected a reference to the borrowing statute of the state referred to by the forum's borrowing statute. Rescildo by Rescildo v. R.H. Macy's, 187 A.D.2d 112, 594 N.Y.S.2d 139 (1st Dept.1993) rejected plaintiff's argument that the reference in New York's borrowing statute to the "laws" of Connecticut included Connecticut's characterization of statutes of limitations as procedural. This holding is distinguishable from the argument above that reference should be made to another state's substantive preference for the longer limitations of the forum.

The Foreign Limitation Periods Act 1984, supra page 430, Note 3, § 1(5): "In this section 'law', in relation to any country, shall not include rules of private international law applicable by the courts of that country...."

Uniform Conflict of Laws–Limitations Act, supra p. 427, Note 1: "If the statute of limitations of another state applies to the assertion of a claim in this State, the other state's relevant statutes and other rules of law governing tolling and accrual apply in computing the limitation period, but its statutes and other rules of law governing conflict of laws do not apply."

6. Some borrowing statutes that refer to the law of the state where the action "arose" or "originated," state that they do not apply if the plaintiff has been a resident of the forum and has held the cause of action since its inception. Some statutes do not apply if either the plaintiff or defendant is a resident. Are these exceptions for forum residents sufficient to prevent the application of the law of a state that does not have the most significant relationship to the issue? Assume that Plaintiff and Defendant reside in X. X has a borrowing statute that refers to the law of the state where the action "arose," but does not apply if either party was an X resident at that time. Defendant injures Plaintiff while driving in Y with Plaintiff as passenger. Defendant then moves to F, which has the same borrowing statute as X. F and X have two-year limitations, but Y has a one-year period.

Plaintiff sues Defendant in F more than one year but less than two years after the accident. What result?

Sun Oil Company v. Wortman

Supreme Court of the United States, 1988.
486 U.S. 717, 108 S.Ct. 2117, 100 L.Ed.2d 743

[Action in the Kansas courts to recover interest on royalties whose payment had been deferred. The royalties were from properties located in Texas, Oklahoma and Louisiana and the action was barred by the statutes of limitation of each of those states. Nevertheless, the Kansas courts entertained the action by application of the longer Kansas statute of limitations. The Kansas courts also found that the defendant should pay interest at the rate it had implicitly agreed to pay although this rate was higher than the maximum rate specified by statutes in Texas, Oklahoma and Louisiana. The Supreme Court affirmed.]

■ JUSTICE SCALIA delivered the opinion of the court:

. . .

This Court has long and repeatedly held that the Constitution does not bar application of the forum State's statute of limitations to claims that in their substance are and must be governed by the law of a different State.... We granted certiorari to reexamine this issue. We conclude that our prior holdings are sound.

. . .

Petitioner initially argues that M'Elmoyle v. Cohen, [p. 307, supra] was wrongly decided when handed down. The holding of *M'Elmoyle,* that a statute of limitations may be treated as procedural and thus may be governed by forum law even when the substance of the claim must be governed by another State's law, rested on two premises, one express and one implicit. The express premise was that this reflected the rule in international law at the time the Constitution was adopted.... The implicit premise, which petitioner does challenge, was that this rule from international law could properly have been applied in the interstate context consistently with the Full Faith and Credit Clause.

. . .

The reported state cases in the decades immediately following ratification of the Constitution show that courts looked without hesitation to international law for guidance in resolving the issue underlying this case: which State's law governs the statute of limitations. The state of international law on that subject being as we have described, these early decisions uniformly concluded that the forum's statute of limitations governed even when it was longer than the limitations period of the State whose substantive law governed the merits of the claim....

Moreover, this view of statutes of limitation as procedural for purposes of choice of law followed quite logically from the manner in which they were treated for domestic-law purposes. At the time the Constitution was adopted the rule was already well established that suit would lie upon a promise to repay a debt barred by the statute of limitations—on the theory, as expressed by many courts, that the debt constitutes consideration for the promise, since the bar of the statute does not extinguish the underlying right but merely causes the remedy to be withheld.... This is the same theory, of course, underlying the conflicts rule: the right subsists, and the forum may choose to allow its courts to provide a remedy, even though the jurisdiction where the right arose would not....

Unable to sustain the contention that under the original understanding of the Full Faith and Credit Clause statutes of limitations would have been considered substantive, petitioner argues that we should apply the modern understanding that they are so. It is now agreed, petitioner argues, that the primary function of a statute of limitations is to balance the competing substantive values of repose and vindication of the underlying right; and we should apply that understanding here, as we have applied it in the area of choice of law for purposes of federal diversity jurisdiction, where we have held that statutes of limitation are substantive, see Guaranty Trust Co. v. York, 326 U.S. 99 (1945).

To address the last point first: Guaranty Trust itself rejects the notion that there is an equivalence between what is substantive under the Erie doctrine and what is substantive for purposes of conflict of laws.... In the context of our Erie jurisprudence, see Erie R. Co. v. Tompkins, 304 U.S. 64 (1938), that purpose is to establish (within the limits of applicable federal law, including the prescribed Rules of Federal Procedure) substantial uniformity of predictable outcome between cases tried in a federal court and cases tried in the courts of the State in which the federal court sits.... The purpose of the substance-procedure dichotomy in the context of the Full Faith and Credit Clause, by contrast, is not to establish uniformity but to delimit spheres of state legislative competence....

But to address petitioner's broader point of which the Erie argument is only a part—that we should update our notion of what is sufficiently "substantive" to require full faith and credit: We cannot imagine what would be the basis for such an updating. As we have just observed, the words "substantive" and "procedural" themselves (besides not appearing in the Full Faith and Credit Clause) do not have a precise content, even (indeed especially) as their usage has evolved. And if one consults the purpose of their usage in the full-faith-and-credit context, that purpose is quite simply to give both the forum State and other interested States the legislative jurisdiction to which they are entitled. If we abandon the currently applied, traditional notions of such entitlement we would embark upon the enterprise of constitutionalizing choice-of-law rules, with no compass to guide us beyond our own perceptions of what seems desirable. There is no more reason to consider recharacterizing statutes of limitation as substantive under the Full Faith and Credit Clause than there is to consider recharacterizing a host of other matters generally treated as procedural under conflicts law, and hence generally regarded as within the forum State's legislative jurisdiction. See, e.g., Restatement (Second) of Conflict of Laws § 131 (remedies available), § 133 (placement of burden of proof), § 134 (burden of production), § 135 (sufficiency of the evidence), § 139 (privileges) (1971).

In sum, long established and still subsisting choice-of-law practices that come to be thought, by modern scholars, unwise, do not thereby become unconstitutional. If current conditions render it desirable that forum States no longer treat a particular issue as procedural for conflict of laws purposes, those States can themselves adopt a rule to that effect, ... or it can be proposed that Congress legislate to that effect under the second sentence of the Full Faith and Credit Clause. It is not the function of this Court, however, to make departures from established choice-of-law precedent and practice constitutionally mandatory. We hold, therefore, that Kansas did not violate the Full Faith and Credit Clause when it applied its own statute of limitations.

. . .

Petitioner also makes a due process attack upon the Kansas court's application of its own statute of limitations. Here again neither the tradition in place when the constitutional provision was adopted nor subsequent practice supports the contention. At the time the Fourteenth Amendment was adopted, this Court had not only explicitly approved (under the Full Faith and Credit Clause) forum-state application of its own statute of limitations, but the practice had gone essentially unchallenged. And it has gone essentially unchallenged since. "If a thing has been practiced for two hundred years by common consent, it will need a strong case for the Fourteenth Amendment to affect it." Jackman v. Rosenbaum Co., 260 U.S. 22, 31 (1922).

A State's interest in regulating the work load of its courts and determining when a claim is too stale to be adjudicated certainly suffices to give it legislative jurisdiction to control the remedies available in its courts by imposing statutes of limitations. Moreover, petitioner could in no way have been unfairly surprised by the application to it of a rule that is as old as the Republic. . . .

III

In *Shutts III,* [p. 362, supra] we held that Kansas could not apply its own law to claims for interest by nonresidents concerning royalties from property located in other States. The Kansas Supreme Court has complied with that ruling, but petitioner claims that it has unconstitutionally distorted Texas, Oklahoma, and Louisiana law ...

To constitute a violation of the Full Faith and Credit Clause or the Due Process Clause, it is not enough that a state court misconstrue the law of another State. Rather, our cases make plain that the misconstruction must contradict law of the other State that is clearly established and that has been brought to the court's attention....

[Justice Scalia then held that the Kansas court had acted constitutionally when it "anticipated" that the courts of Oklahoma, Texas and Louisiana would have enforced the rate of interest that the parties had implicitly agreed upon although statutes in these three states did provide for the payment of a lower rate of interest.]

. . .

■ JUSTICE BRENNAN, with whom JUSTICE MARSHALL and JUSTICE BLACKMUN join, concurring in part and concurring in the judgment.

I ... agree with the result the Court reaches in Part II [although with respect to the statute of limitations] I reach that result through a somewhat different path of analysis.

For 150 years, this Court has consistently held that a forum State may apply its own statute of limitations period to out-of-state claims even though it is longer or shorter than the limitations period that would be applied by the State out of which the claim arose....

... The constitutional issue in this case is somewhat more complicated than usual because the question is not the typical one of whether a State can constitutionally apply its substantive law where both it and another State have certain contacts with the litigants and the facts underlying the dispute. Rather the question here is whether a forum State can constitutionally apply its limitations period, which has mixed substantive and procedural aspects, where its contacts with the dispute stem only from its status as the forum.

... Statutes of limitations ... defy characterization as either purely procedural or purely substantive. The statute of limitations a State enacts represents a balance between, on the one hand, its substantive interest in vindicating substantive claims and, on the other hand, a combination of its procedural interest in freeing its courts from adjudicating stale claims and its substantive interest in giving individuals repose from ancient breaches of law. A State that has enacted a particular limitations period has simply determined that after that period the interest in vindicating claims becomes outweighed by the combination of the interests in repose and avoiding stale claims. One cannot neatly categorize this complicated temporal balance as either procedural or substantive.

Given the complex of interests underlying statutes of limitations, I conclude that the contact a State has with a claim simply by virtue of being the forum creates a sufficient procedural interest to make the application of its limitations period to wholly out-of-state claims consistent with the Full Faith and Credit Clause. This is clearest when the forum State's limitations period is shorter than that of the claim State. A forum State's procedural interest in avoiding the adjudication of stale claims is equally applicable to in-state and out-of-state claims....

The constitutional question is somewhat less clear where, as here, the forum State's limitations period is longer than that of the claim State. In this situation, the claim State's statute of limitations reflects its policy judgment that at the time the suit was filed the combination of the claim State's procedural interest in avoiding stale claims and its substantive interest in repose outweighs its substantive interest in vindicating the plaintiff's substantive rights. Assuming, for the moment, that each State has an equal substantive interest in the repose of defendants, then a forum State that has concluded that its procedural interest is less weighty than that of the claim State does not act unfairly or arbitrarily in applying its longer limitations period. The claim State does not, after all, have any substantive interest in not vindicating rights it has created. Nor will it do to argue that the forum State has no interest in vindicating the substantive rights of nonresidents: the forum State cannot discriminate against nonresidents, and if it has concluded that the substantive rights of its citizens outweigh its procedural interests at that period then it cannot be faulted for applying that determination evenhandedly.

If the different limitations periods also reflect differing assessments of the substantive interests in the repose of defendants, however, the issue is more complicated. It is, to begin with, not entirely clear whether the interest in the repose of defendants is an interest the State has as a forum or wholly as the creator of the claim at issue. Even if one assumes the latter, determining whether application of the forum State's longer limitations period would thwart the claim State's substantive interest in repose requires a complex assessment of the relative weights of both States' procedural and substantive interests. For example, a claim State may have a substantive interest in vindicating claims that, at a particular period, outweighs its substantive interest in repose standing alone but not the combination of its interests in repose and avoiding the adjudication of stale claims. Such a State would not have its substantive interest in repose thwarted by the claim's adjudication in a State that professed no procedural interest in avoiding stale claims, even if the forum State had less substantive interest in repose than the claim State, because the forum State would be according the claim State's substantive interests all the weight the claim state gives them. Such efforts to break down and weigh the procedural and substantive components and interests served by the various States' limitations periods would, however, involve a difficult, unwieldy and somewhat artificial inquiry that itself implicates the strong procedural interest any forum State has in having administrable choice-of-law rules.

In light of the forum State's procedural interests and the inherent ambiguity of any more refined inquiry in this context, there is some force to the conclusion that the forum State's contacts give it sufficient procedural interests ... to have a per se rule of applying its own limitations period to out-of-state claims—particularly where, as here, the states out of which the claims arise view their statutes of limitations as procedural.... The issue, after all, is not whether the decision to apply forum limitations law is wise as a matter of choice-of-law doctrine but whether the decision is within the range of constitutionally permissible choices, . . . any merely arguable inconsistency with our current full faith and credit jurisprudence surely does not merit deviating from 150 years of precedent holding that choosing the forum State's limitations period over that of the claim State is constitutionally permissible.

The Court's technique of avoiding close examination of the relevant interests by wrapping itself in the mantle of tradition is as troublesome as it is conclusory. It leads the Court to assert broadly (albeit in dicta) that States do not violate the Full Faith and Credit Clause by adjudicating out-of-state claims under the forum's own law on, inter alia, remedies, burdens of proof, and burdens of production.... The constitutionality of refusing to apply the law of the claim State on such issues was not briefed or argued before this Court, and whether, as the Court asserts without support, there are insufficient reasons for "recharacterizing" these issues (at least in part) as substantive is a question that itself presents multiple issues of enormous difficulty and importance which deserve more than the offhand treatment the Court gives them.

. . .

In short, I fear the Court's rationale will cause considerable mischief with no corresponding benefit. This mischief is all the more unfortunate because it appears to stem from the misperception that this case cannot be resolved without conclusively labeling statutes of limitations as either "procedural" or "substantive." Having asked the wrong question (and an unanswerable one), it is no wonder the Court resorts to tradition rather than analysis to answer it. . . .

■ JUSTICE O'CONNOR, with whom THE CHIEF JUSTICE joins, concurring in part and dissenting in part.

The Court properly concludes that Kansas did not violate the Full Faith and Credit Clause or the Due Process Clause when it chose to apply its own statute of limitations in this case. Different issues might have arisen if Texas, Oklahoma, or Louisiana regarded its own shorter statute of limitations as substantive. Such issues, however, are not presented in this case, and they are appropriately left unresolved. . . .

In my view, however, the Supreme Court of Kansas violated the Full Faith and Credit Clause when it concluded that the three States in question would apply the interest rates set forth in the regulations of the Federal Power Commission (FPC). The Court correctly states that misconstruing those States' laws would not by itself have violated the Constitution, for the Full Faith and Credit Clause only required the Kansas court to adhere to law that was clearly established in those States and that had been brought to the Kansas court's attention. . . . Under the standard the Court articulates, however, the Clause was violated. Each of the three States has a statute setting an interest rate that is different from the FPC rate, and the Supreme Court of Kansas offered no valid reason whatsoever for ignoring those statutory rates. Neither has this Court suggested a colorable argument that could support the Kansas court's decision, and its affirmance of that decision effectively converts an important constitutional guarantee into a precatory admonition.

. . .

At bottom, the Kansas court's insistence on its equitable theory seems based on nothing more than its conviction that it *would* have been "fair" for the parties to agree that the oil and gas company should pay the same interest rates for suspended royalty payments arising from approved price increases that the company would have had to pay its customers for refunds arising from disapproved price increases. That is a wholly inadequate basis for concluding that three other States would conclude that the parties *did* make such an agreement.... Even assuming that the result imposed on the parties by the Kansas court was "fair," which is not at all obvious, neither that court nor this Court has given any reason for concluding that the parties to the case before us agreed either to adopt the FPC interest rates or to be bound by the Kansas judiciary's notions of equity.

The majority does not discuss the Kansas court's analysis of its sister States' statutes, which clearly indicate that rates of 6% or 7% were applicable. Indeed, the Court appears to think that no analysis was necessary because the Kansas court was not bound by the language of the statutes with which it was confronted.... This suggestion is inconsistent with the language of the Full Faith and Credit Clause and is not dictated by the holding in any of our previous cases. Nor is the Court on firmer ground when it imagines that the Kansas court merely read "standard contract law" into the statutes of its sister States.... The "industry practice" of complying with FPC regulations where they are applicable hardly implies an "industry usage" or "common understanding" under which the terms of those regulations are to be applied in other situations where they are *not* applicable. Neither the Kansas court nor this Court has pointed to a single instance—let alone an "industry practice"—in which an oil company and its lessor agreed that the FPC interest rates would apply in circumstances like those presented here. Unless "industry usage" means "practices that the Supreme Court of Kansas thinks are fair," neither standard contract law nor standard logic will support the majority's attempted defense of the Kansas court's result.

Today's decision discards important parts of our decision in *Shutts III*.... Faced with the constitutional obligation to apply the substantive law of another State, a court that does not like that law apparently need take only two steps in order to avoid applying it. First, invent a legal theory so novel or strange that the other State has never had an opportunity to reject it; then, on the basis of nothing but unsupported speculation, "predict" that the other State would adopt that theory if it had the chance. To call this giving full faith and credit to the law of another State ignores the language of the Constitution and leaves it without the capacity to fulfill its purpose....

KEETON V. HUSTLER MAGAZINE, INC., 549 A.2d 1187 (N.H.1988). Following reversal by the Supreme Court and remand to the lower federal courts (Keeton v. Hustler Magazine, Inc., 465 U.S. 770 (1984)), the United States Court of Appeals certified two questions to the New Hampshire Supreme Court, namely (1) would the New Hampshire courts apply the interstate single publication rule in the case at hand and (2) would the New Hampshire courts apply their longer (6 year) statute of limitations. The Supreme Court of New Hampshire answered both questions in the affirmative.

The Supreme Court of New Hampshire justified its application of the New Hampshire statute of limitations on a number of points. It found particularly that application of the statute would be constitutional under the Supreme Court decision in Sun Oil Co. v. Wortman, 486 U.S. 717 (1988), (2) would further New Hampshire's interest since a substantial number of the defendant's magazines had been sold there and (3) would be in line with precedent and hence would simplify the judicial task.

There were two dissents.

NOTE

The interstate single publication rule, referred to in Keeton v. Hustler Magazine, would permit the plaintiff to recover for harm suffered from publication of the libel in all jurisdictions. Shevill v. Presse Alliance S.A., [1995] 2 W.L.R. 499, (Court of Justice of the European Communities, Case C–68/93) interpreted art. 5(3) of the European Union Convention on Jurisdiction and Enforcement of Judgments, in the context of multistate libel. Article 5(3) permits suit "in matters relating to tort, delict or quasi-delict, in the courts of the place where the harmful event occurred." The Court stated that "the victim of a libel by a newspaper article distributed in several contracting states may bring an action for damages against the publisher either before the courts ... of the place where the publisher ... is established, which have jurisdiction to award damages for all the harm caused by the defamation, or before the courts of each contracting state in which the publication was distributed and where the victim claims to have suffered injury to his reputation, which have jurisdiction to rule solely in respect of the harm caused in the state of the court seised." Id. at 542.

SECTION 4. REFERENCE TO THE CHOICE-OF-LAW RULES OF ANOTHER JURISDICTION

In Re Annesley

Chancery Division, 1926. [1926] Ch. 692.

[Summons to determine distribution of personal property in England. This turned on the validity of a will, which depended upon whether the decedent was domiciled in England or France.

The decedent was a widow over 80 years old at her death in 1924. She was married in England in 1860 to an Army officer, with whom she lived in England until 1866, and then in France until his death in 1884. She then purchased a chateau in Orthez, France, and resided there until her death, making only a few short visits back to England. After 1866 she had no place of residence in England. Two daughters survived her, but she left a will giving most of her estate to others. Under the French law she could dispose by will of only one third of her personal property. Under the English law she could dispose of all of it.]

RUSSELL, J. stated the facts and continued: The first question to be decided is whether the domicil of the testatrix was English or French. But for the fact that Mrs. Annesley took no steps to obtain a formal French domicil according to French law, and both in her will and in a codicil to it declared that it was not her intention to abandon her domicil of origin— namely, England, there could not, I conceive, be any room for doubt as to the position according to English law. She died having acquired a French domicil of choice. To use the language of Lord Westbury in Udny v. Udny, L.R. 1 H.L.Sc. 441, 458, Mrs. Annesley fixed voluntarily her sole residence in France, with an intention of continuing to reside there for an unlimited time. The domicil flows from the combination of fact and intention, the fact of residence and the intention of remaining for an unlimited time. The intention required is not an intention specifically directed to a change of domicil, but an intention of residing in a country for an unlimited time. The above recited facts in my opinion clearly establish both the necessary fact and the necessary intention.

Those who seek to establish an English domicil naturally place much reliance on the declarations in her will and codicil. They contend that we have here two statements made at different times by the lady herself, that she had never intended and did not intend to abandon her English domicil, and that in the face of these statements it is impossible for the Court to hold that a French domicil of choice had in fact or in law arisen. The contention is a tempting one to accede to in view of the fact that the finding of an English domicil would solve sundry other knotty points of difficulty which lurk in the background. But I feel unable to accede to it.

It must I think be conceded that domicil cannot depend upon mere declaration, though the fact of the declaration having been made must be one of the elements to be weighed in arriving at a conclusion on the question of domicil. But if a particular domicil clearly emerges from a consideration of the other relevant facts, a declaration of intention to retain some other domicil will not suffice to destroy the result of those facts. If (as I think she had) Mrs. Annesley had by the factum of long residence and by her animus manendi acquired before the date of her codicil a French domicil of choice, her statement that she never intended to abandon her English domicil will not prevent the acquisition of a French domicil of choice, unless weighing the statement with the other relevant facts the Court comes to the conclusion that the animus manendi had not been established....

It was however contended that assuming that all the relevant facts do establish a French domicil, yet in the particular case it was according to English law impossible for Mrs. Annesley to have acquired a French domicil—because not having taken the steps prescribed by art. 13 of the Civil Code she was not and could not be a domiciled Frenchwoman in the eyes of the law of France. In other words the proposition is that no one can, according to English law, acquire a domicil of choice in a foreign country unless that person has also acquired a domicil there according to the law of the foreign country. The contention is founded upon one branch of the judgment of Farwell J. in the well known case In re Johnson, [1903] 1 Ch. 821.

Such a contention appears to me inconsistent with many decisions in the Courts of this country. In In re Martin, [1900] P. 211, 227, Lindley M. R. clearly lays it down that domicil is to be determined by English law. His judgment is no doubt a dissenting judgment, but the effect of his views upon this particular point is not weakened or affected by that fact. "The domicil ... must be determined by the English Court ... according to those legal principles applicable to domicil which are recognized in this country and are part of its law." If it were otherwise the question whether an individual were domiciled in France (or in any other country which requires the fulfilment of certain legal requirements before a person can be considered by the Court of that country as domiciled in that country) would be solved quite easily in every case by ascertaining whether those legal requirements had or had not been fulfilled. Yet there have been numerous cases (some of which appear in the books) in which the question has always been considered and answered by an elaborate consideration of the various facts and circumstances in each case....

... [I]f I am free—and I think I am—to follow my own view, I would prefer to follow what I have always considered the true view—namely, that the question whether a person is or is not domiciled in a foreign country is to be determined in accordance with the requirements of English law as to domicil, irrespective of the question whether the person in question has or has not acquired a domicil in the foreign country in the eyes of the law of that country....

I accordingly decide that the domicil of the testatrix at the time of her death was French. French law accordingly applies, but the question remains: what French law? According to French municipal law, the law applicable in the case of a foreigner not legally domiciled in France is the law of that person's nationality, in this case British. But the law of that nationality refers the question back to French law, the law of the domicil; and the question arises, will the French law accept this reference back, or *renvoi*, and apply French municipal law?

Upon this question arises acute conflict of expert opinion. Two experts took the view that the *renvoi* would not be accepted, but that a French Court would distribute the movables of the testatrix in accordance with English municipal law. One expert equally strongly took the view that a French Court would accept the *renvoi* and distribute in accordance with French municipal law. I must come to a conclusion as best I can upon this question of fact upon the evidence after considering and weighing the reasons given by each side in support of their respective views. It is a case rather of views expressed by the experts as to what the French law ought to be, than what it is. Although there is in France no system of case law such as we understand it here—the decisions of higher Courts not being binding upon inferior tribunals—yet I think I must pay some attention to the fact that this question of *renvoi* has at different times come for consideration before the Cour de Cassation, the highest Court in France, and each time with the same result—namely, the acceptance of the *renvoi* and the application of the French municipal law. It is true that the Cour de Cassation is quite free to take the opposite view on a future occasion, but it has never done so. I refer to the cases which were discussed and expounded before me—namely, the Forgo case [Clunet (1883), 64] in 1882, and the Soulié case [Clunet (1910), 888] in 1910. In the former case a decision of the Cour de Cassation, the *renvoi* was accepted, and French municipal law was applied to the disposition of the estate of a Bavarian national domiciled de facto in France (but not domiciled there according to French law), because according to Bavarian law the law of the domicil or usual residence was applicable. The Forgo case gave rise to grave differences of opinion among French jurists and was followed by many conflicting decisions in lower Courts, some favouring the "Théorie du Renvoi," others against it. The matter again came under the consideration of the branch of the Cour de Cassation entitled Chambre de Requêtes, one of whose functions is to decide whether or not an appeal to the Cour de Cassation should be allowed to proceed. That was the Soulié case, in which the Court below had held that French municipal law governed the succession to the movable property of an American subject who had died in France with a de facto domicil in that country. The Chamber declined to allow an appeal to the Cour de Cassation to proceed. This decision, coming as it did after the grave differences of opinion which resulted from the Forgo case, strikes me as of great importance. As is pointed out in a note to the report in Clunet [Clunet (1910), 888, 892] it shows that the Supreme Court persists with energy in its former view, notwithstanding the views of text writers to the contrary.

In these circumstances, and after careful consideration of the evidence of the experts called before me, I have come to the conclusion that I ought to accept the view that according to French law the French Court, in administering the movable property of a deceased foreigner who, according to the law of his country, is domiciled in France, and whose property must, according to that law, be applied in accordance with the law of the country in which he was domiciled, will apply French municipal law, and that even though the deceased had not complied with art. 13 of the Code.

The result is that as regards her English personal estate and her French movable property the testatrix in this case had power only to dispose of one-third thereof by her will.

Speaking for myself, I should like to reach the same conclusion by a much more direct route along which no question of *renvoi* need be encountered at all. When the law of England requires that the personal estate of a British subject who dies domiciled, according to the requirements of English law, in a foreign country shall be administered in accordance with the law of that country, why should this not mean in accordance with the law which that country would apply, not to the propositus, but to its own nationals legally domiciled there? In other words, when we say that French law applies to the administration of the personal estate of an Englishman who dies domiciled in France, we mean that French municipal law which France applies in the case of Frenchmen. This appears to me a simple and rational solution which avoids altogether that endless oscillation which otherwise would result from the law of the country of nationality invoking the law of the country of domicil, while the law of the country in turn invokes the law of the country of nationality, and I am glad to find that this simple solution has in fact been adopted by the Surrogates' Court of New York.[1] ...

NOTES

1. Matter of Tallmadge, 109 Misc. 696, 181 N.Y.S. 336 (1919), cited at the end of the principal case, is the opinion of a referee in a surrogate's court. It involved the will of a United States citizen, formerly of New York, who died domiciled in France. His will, written in English in New York, left ten dollars to his brother who was his only heir. It left all of the residue of his estate to an aunt and to a cousin, share and share alike. It appeared that the cousin predeceased the testator, and the question was whether the brother took the cousin's share as intestate property according to New York law, or whether the aunt took the whole of the residue under sec. 1044 of the French Civil Code. It was held that the French internal law should be applied.

2. In re Annesley raises the question of why, when the conflicts law of the forum points to another jurisdiction, a forum court should refer to the choice-of-law rules of that jurisdiction. This problem is called "renvoi," which means "sending back" or "sending away," and occurs when the other state's conflicts rule points back to the forum or to a third state. The first Restatement of Conflict of Laws (1934), which contained territorial rules that selected law according to the location of one element in a transaction, rejected reference to another jurisdiction's conflicts rules, except on questions of title to land and validity of a divorce. Id. §§ 7, 8.

The Restatement (Second) of Conflict of Laws, which chooses law by taking account, among other things, of the policies underlying the laws of "interested states" (Id. § 6(2)(b), (c)), suggests three reasons for the forum to refer to the conflicts rules of other jurisdictions.

(i) The forum wishes to reach the same result as the other jurisdiction. Id. § 8(2). An example of this would be a court adjudicating interests in realty in another country. Suppose that the courts in the other country would insist on determining those rights under the law of the situs and would not recognize a

---

1. Re Tallmadge, New York Law Journal, Oct. 17, 1919, ...: see 36 Law Quarterly Review 91.

different determination by a non-situs court. There is no point in the non-situs court attempting to reach a different result, unless there are other assets in the forum that can be distributed to take account of the disposition in the foreign situs. In re Schneider's Estate, 198 Misc. 1017, 96 N.Y.S.2d 652 (Sur.Ct.1950), referred to the Swiss choice-of-law rule to validate the testamentary disposition of realty in Switzerland. The testator was an American citizen who died domiciled in New York. Under Swiss internal law, the testator's heirs were entitled to portions of the estate beyond the portion devised to them. The Swiss conflicts rule, however, applied the law of the domicile at death of a foreign national. A similar result was reached in Matter of Estate of Wright, 637 A.2d 106 (Me.1994). The testator was an American who died domiciled in Switzerland. A Swiss statute permitted a foreigner domiciled in Switzerland to elect the law of his nationality to determine the validity of his will. The testator's will chose Maine law to govern the administration of his estate. The court held that the decedent's children were not entitled to take a forced share of the estate—a power they had under internal Swiss law.

(ii) "[T]he state of the forum has no substantial relationship to the particular issue or the parties and the courts of all interested states would concur in selecting the local law rule applicable to this issue...." Restatement (Second) Conflict of Laws § 8(3). Matter of Zietz' Estate, 198 Misc. 77, 96 N.Y.S.2d 442 (Sur.Ct.1950), is an illustration. A national of Liechtenstein died in Austria. If he was domiciled in Austria, New York conflicts law would refer to that law to determine which foreign administrator should control ancillary administration in New York, but under a treaty between Austria and Liechtenstein, the law of the nationality controlled. The court stated that under these circumstances it would "accept that reference to the law of the nationality."

(iii) The forum wishes to determine whether the other jurisdiction asserts an "interest" in the application of the other jurisdiction's law. Restatement (Second) Conflict of Laws § 8, comment k. In Annesley, can the French rule referring to the law of the nationality, be interpreted as an indication that France disclaims any interest in applying its forced-share rule to a domiciliary who was a national of another country? If so, did it make any sense to insist on applying the French forced-share rule because English conflicts rules pointed to France? Does the extent to which another jurisdiction's choice-of-law rule indicates that state's "interest" in the application of law depend upon whether that rule itself takes account of policies underlying the law chosen? In Pfau v. Trent Aluminum Co., 55 N.J. 511, 263 A.2d 129 (1970), a New Jersey driver, with a Connecticut passenger, crashed in Iowa. The passenger sued the driver. Although the laws of both states have since changed, Iowa had a guest statute, which prevented the passenger from recovering for the driver's ordinary negligence, and Connecticut's choice-of-law rule applied the law of the place of injury. The Supreme Court of New Jersey held that the Iowa guest statute did not apply: "[W]e see no reason for applying Connecticut's choice-of-law rule.... Connecticut's choice-of-law rule does not identify that state's interest in the matter. *Lex loci delicti* was born in an effort to achieve simplicity and uniformity, and does not relate to a state's interest in having its law applied to given issues in a tort case."

For a discussion of reference to foreign choice-of-law rules as an aid in determining the purposes underlying foreign internal law, see Kramer, Return of the Renvoi, 66 N.Y.U.L.Rev. 979 (1991).

3. Another reason to refer to the choice-of-law rule of another jurisdiction is to avoid a statutory choice-of-law rule of the forum. See supra p. 433, Note 5, suggesting use of this technique in construing borrowing statutes. Richards v.

United States, 369 U.S. 1 (1962), construed the Federal Tort Claims Act's reference to "law of the place where the act or omission occurred," to mean the whole law of that place, including its choice-of-law rules. The Court stated: "[T]his interpretation of the Act provides a degree of flexibility to the law to be applied in federal courts.... Recently there has been a tendency on the part of some States to depart from the general conflict rule [which, chose the law of the place of injury] in order to take into account the interests of the State having significant contact with the parties to the litigation. We can see no compelling reason to saddle the Act with an interpretation that would prevent the federal courts from implementing this policy in choice-of-law rules where the State in which the negligence occurred has adopted it."

4. The classic European position is to consider the foreign conflicts rule and to follow its reference forward to the law of a third state, or back to the law of the forum. The principal exception, for signatories of the European Union's Convention on the Law Applicable to Contractual Obligations, is Article 15 of that Convention: "Exclusion of renvoi. The application of the law of any country specified by this Convention means the application of the rule of law in force in that country other than its rules of private international law."

Below are provisions concerning renvoi from various European codes. In practice, the difference between the Swiss approach and that of a country such as Germany may not be as great as appears on the surface. Switzerland starts with a presumption against renvoi subject to numerous exceptions. Germany starts out with reference to the choice-of-law rules of other states, subject to numerous exceptions including the vague exception in the basic renvoi provision itself (Intro. Law to Civil Code, Article 4, below). Which system results in more frequent references to the conflicts rules of other states, depends on a detailed examination of these rules in action.

Switzerland, Statute on Private International Law, entered into force January 1, 1989. Article 14. "1. If the law applicable refers back to Swiss Law or to foreign law, the referral in question is only taken into account if the present Law has such a provision. 2. As to family status, the reference back to Swiss law shall be respected." Following are examples of provisions of the Swiss statute in which foreign choice-of-law rules are "taken into account." Article 91(1): "The inheritance of a person who had his or her last domicile abroad, is governed by the law designated by the provisions of international private law of the State in which the deceased was domiciled." Article 119(3): "[T]he form of [a contract relating to immovables] is governed by the law of the State in which the immovable asset is located, unless this law allows the application of some other law."

Austria, Federal Statute of 15 June 1978 on Private International Law. Section 5: "(1) Reference to a foreign legal order includes also its conflicts rules. (2) If the foreign legal order refers back, Austrian internal rules (rules excepting conflicts rules) shall be applied; if reference is made to a third jurisdiction, further reference shall be considered, but the internal rules of the legal order which itself does not refer to any other law or to which another law refers back for the first time shall be determinative."

Germany, Intro. Law to the Civil Code [EGBGB] (as revised 1986), Federal Gazette Part III, 400–1. Article 4: "(1) If reference is made to the law of another state, its private international law shall also be applied so far as it does not contradict the meaning of the renvoi. If the law of the other state refers back to German law, German substantive provisions shall apply."

CHAPTER 8

THE PROBLEM OF CHOOSING THE RULE OF DECISION

SECTION 1. THE RECEIVED SYSTEM AND TRADITION

A. TERRITORIALITY AND THE JURISDICTION-SELECTING PROCESS

RESTATEMENT, SECOND, CONFLICT OF LAWS: *

1. *The Position Taken by the Original Restatement*

The original Restatement stated that, with minor exceptions, all substantive questions relating to the existence of a tort claim are governed by the local law of the "place of wrong." This was described (in Section 377) as "the state where the last event necessary to make an actor liable for an alleged tort takes place." Since a tort is the product of wrongful conduct and of resulting injury and since the injury follows the conduct, the state of the "last event" is the state where the injury occurred. This rule of the original Restatement was derived from the vested rights doctrine which called for the enforcement everywhere of rights that had been lawfully created under the local law of a state. In effect, the doctrine provided for the application of the local law of the state in which had occurred the last act necessary to bring a legal obligation into existence. In the case of torts, the state of the last act, for reasons stated above, was the state where the injury had occurred. In the case of contracts, it was the state where the contract was made....

"The theory ... is that, although the act complained of was subject to no law having force in the forum, it gave rise to an obligation, an *obligatio*, which, like other obligations, follows the person, and may be enforced wherever the person may be found.... But as the only source of this obligation is the law of the place of the act, it follows that that law determines not merely the existence of the obligation, ... but equally

---

* Quoted with the permission of the copyright owner, The American Law Institute.

determines its extent." Justice Holmes in Slater v. Mexican National Railroad Co., 194 U.S. 120, 126 (1904), which is set forth at p. 201 supra.

"It would be as unjust to apply a different law as it would be to determine the rights of the parties by a different transaction." Story, Conflict of Laws 38 (8th ed. 1883).

■ CAVERS, THE CHOICE-OF-LAW PROCESS (1965), pp. 5–9: *

In Anglo-American jurisdictions, the development of choice-of-law doctrine has been greatly influenced by the works of the English scholar and jurist, A.V. Dicey, and the American law professor, Joseph H. Beale. Dicey adopted the theory that the task of the court in a choice-of-law case was the enforcement of vested rights. Professor Beale coupled this with the territorial concepts that Story had drawn from Huber and thereby organized a system of choice-of-law rules, simple in structure, which could be applied without regard to the content of the particular laws between which choice had to be made. This theory dominated the American Law Institute's *Restatement of Conflict of Laws* for which Professor Beale served as Reporter.

Professor Beale confronted the welter of conflicting conflicts decisions with bland determination. "Most of the statements in this work will be dogmatic," he wrote at the start of his treatise and then asked—rhetorically: "Does not the Bar desire dogmatic statements?" I need quote only two propositions from the treatise to convey the character of his doctrine and his thought. Thus, at the outset of his discussion of the choice of law as to contracts, he declared: "The question whether a contract is valid ... can on general principles be determined by no other law than that which applies to the acts [of the parties], that is, by the law of the place of contracting.... If ... the law of the place where the agreement is made annexes no legal obligation to it, *there is no other law which has power to do so.*"

And in expounding choice of law as to torts, Professor Beale explained, "It is impossible for a plaintiff to recover in tort unless he has been given by some law a cause of action in tort; and *this cause of action can be given only by the law of the place where the tort was committed.* That is the place where the injurious event occurs, and its law is the law *therefore* which applies to it."

While the *Conflicts Restatement* was still in gestation, Beale's basic conceptions came under attack by what he termed "an ephemeral school"

---

* Quoted with the permission of the copyright owner, The University of Michigan Press.

of "self-styled realists." Among these Professor Ernest Lorenzen and Professor Walter Wheeler Cook were the foremost. Professor Charles Wesley Hohfeld, famed for his analysis of jural relations, had also been a dissenter from conflicts orthodoxy of his day, and Professor Lorenzen has credited him with the origin of the "local law" theory that, particularly as championed by Professor Cook, became the principal rival of Professor Beale's "vested rights" theory. These critics challenged the logic of the vested rights theory which they found question-begging, but they also challenged its practicality. They complained of its failure to reflect social and economic needs and policies, though they were seldom specific in identifying these....

... Though I joined them in asking, in Professor Lorenzen's words: "What are the demands of justice in the particular situation; what is the controlling policy?" I insisted, nevertheless, that these questions could not be answered as long as the questioners continued to seek what I termed "a jurisdiction-selecting" rule,[24] that is, a rule indicating the source of the law to be applied without regard to the law's content. Without taking the content of the conflicting laws into account, how could one know what would satisfy the demands of justice or the requirements of policy?

---

3 BEALE, A TREATISE ON THE CONFLICT OF LAWS 1929 (1935):

[E]very law has both a territorial and a personal application; and where a conflict arises, it is because one sovereign wishes to apply his own law to a juridical relation arising on his territory, while another wishes to throw around his own subject, who is one of the parties to the relation, the protection of his personal law. Which of the two independent sovereigns should yield is a question not susceptible of a solution upon which all parties would agree.

NOTE

This excerpt from Professor Beale's treatise, published the year after the first Restatement of Conflict of Laws, may be taken as a response to the critics referred to by Professor Cavers. In order to rebut Professor Beale, it is necessary to establish two propositions. First, there are occasions on which a sovereign should not seek "to apply his own law to a juridical relation arising on his territory." Second, when two or more sovereigns do wish their own laws applied, there is a method of resolving this conflict that is more satisfactory than selecting some one event in a multi-state transaction and applying the law of the geographical location of that event. The first proposition may be easier to establish than the second.

24. Cavers, [A Critique of the Choice-of-Law Problem, 47 Harv.L.Rev. 173,] 194 (1933): This concept, launched in the article cited, is gradually becoming current. The jurisdiction-selecting rule makes a *state* the object of choice; in theory it is only after the rule has selected the governing state by reference to the "contact" prescribed in the rule that the court ascertains the content of the state's law....

As the materials in this chapter indicate, Professor Beale's territorial conflicts system has been largely superseded by methods that take into account the content and purposes of domestic rules before choosing between them. What cases created the greatest dissatisfaction with the territorial rules? If Professor Beale's rule for unintentional torts had been, "if both parties have the same domicile, apply that law, otherwise apply the law of the place of injury," would there have been a "conflicts revolution?"

B. EXAMPLES OF THE SYSTEM IN OPERATION

1. THE FORUM APPLIES ITS OWN RULE OF DECISION

Divorce is an area in which ordinary choice-of-law concepts do not apply. A migratory divorce can be granted in any forum in which one spouse establishes domicil, a feat readily accomplished by residing for a specified number of weeks or months in the forum state. In Torlonia v. Torlonia, 108 Conn. 292, 142 A. 843 (1928), p. 33, supra, the court enunciated the accepted doctrine:

"... [T]he rule is well established that the courts of the State of the domicil may grant a divorce for any cause allowed by its laws, without regard to the place of the commission of the offense for which it is granted or to whether such offense constitutes a ground for divorce in the state in which it was committed...."

Under other legal systems, the forum does not invariably apply its own divorce law. See Federal Republic of Germany Act on the Revision of Private International Law, art. 17(1) (1986), 27 I.L.M. 1 (1988):

> (1) Divorce is governed by the law which, at the time that the pendancy of the petition for divorce begins, controls the general legal effects of the marriage. [Under art. 14, the legal effects of the marriage are governed by the law of the state of which both spouses were last nationals, if one of them is still a national of that state, otherwise by the law of the state which was the last habitual residence of both spouses, or the law of that state with which the spouses are mutually most closely connected.] If the marriage cannot be dissolved under that law, the divorce is subject to German law if the spouse seeking divorce is a German national at that time or was a German national at the time of marriage.

WORKERS' COMPENSATION

RESTATEMENT, SECOND, CONFLICT OF LAWS *

CHAPTER 7—TOPIC 3

INTRODUCTORY NOTE

A workmen's compensation statute, as the term is used in this Topic, is a statute which makes an employer, and sometimes other persons as well,

---

* Quoted with the permission of the copyright owner, The American Law Institute.

liable without regard to any question of fault for injuries suffered by an employee in the course of his employment....

A peculiarity of this area is that usually relief under a particular statute may be obtained only in the state of its enactment. This is because the statutes normally provide for their enforcement by special administrative tribunals and such tribunals do not consider themselves competent to give relief under any statute but their own. Hence the principal problem in this area is not one of choice of law but rather what range of application to persons and things without the state will be given by a state to its own workmen's compensation statute....

Problems posed by workers' compensation laws are considered at greater length at pp. 644–648, infra.

People v. Olah
Court of Appeals of New York, 1949.
300 N.Y. 96, 89 N.E.2d 329.

■ FULD, JUDGE. ... Section 1941 of the Penal Law, Consol. Laws, c. 40, provides that a defendant, convicted of a felony in New York, is to be punished as a second felony offender if he was "previously" *convicted* ... under the laws of any other state ... *of a crime* which, if committed within this state, would be a felony. (Emphasis supplied.) ...

In the present case, Olah was convicted in New Jersey following his plea of guilty to an indictment accusing him of having stolen a watch and a wallet containing $200, "all of the value of over Twenty Dollars." He was given a suspended sentence and placed on probation.

... To ascertain [the] "crime" [of which he was convicted], we must of necessity consider the statute which created and defined it and upon which the indictment was based.

The indictment was founded upon a New Jersey statute which, creating the "crime" of larceny as "a high misdemeanor", defined it as the theft of "Money, or personal goods" having a "value ... of or above twenty dollars" (N.J.Stat.Ann. 2:145–2). Since section 1941 of the Penal Law renders vital the "crime" of which a defendant was convicted and since the "crime" in New Jersey was that of stealing $20 of more, it follows that such a crime would not have been a felony in this State—for it is the theft of more than $100 that is here denominated a felony. Penal Law, §§ 1296, 1299....

. . .

... [S]ection 1941 of the Penal Law does not provide that a defendant should be treated as a second felony offender if he did something in another State which might furnish the basis for a felony prosecution in New York or—relating the problem to larceny cases—if he stole an amount which might justify a prosecution for grand larceny in this State....

The orders should be reversed and the matter remitted to the Court of General Sessions, with directions to vacate and set aside the judgment of conviction and to take such further proceedings as may be necessary, not inconsistent with this opinion.

NOTES

1. Is People v. Olah a choice-of-law case? Was the question whether the law of New York or of New Jersey should be applied to determine the nature of Olah's crime? Or was it clear that only the law of New York was applicable and that the law of New Jersey was considered solely for the purpose of determining whether Olah had committed a felony within the meaning of New York law? Under this latter view, New Jersey's penal law was referred to as a "datum" to give meaning to the New York statute. Cf. B. Currie, p. 513, infra.

2. A potential choice-of-law problem evaporates if there is no essential difference in the relevant rules of decision of the interested states. Pahmer v. The Hertz Corp., 32 N.Y.2d 119, 343 N.Y.S.2d 341, 296 N.E.2d 243 (1973), was a suit for injuries sustained in a California accident while the plaintiff was a passenger in a car rented by her fellow employee, Cullen. Among the defenses was the California guest statute. After the appeal to the New York Court of Appeals on that issue had been "extensively briefed and argued ... on choice of law principles," the Supreme Court of California declared the guest statute unconstitutional as a denial of the equal protection clauses of the California and United States constitutions. Brown v. Merlo, 8 Cal.3d 855, 106 Cal.Rptr. 388, 506 P.2d 212 (1973). This effectively disposed of the choice-of-law issue.

Sometimes courts have created conflicts where none existed. See Nelson v. Eckert, 231 Ark. 348, 329 S.W.2d 426 (1959), discussed p. 422, supra, in which the court held that although both Arkansas and Texas had two-year statutes of limitations for wrongful death, neither applied, and that the Arkansas five-year limit for personal injury made the action timely.

2. TRADITIONAL RULES

(a) Tort

Alabama Great Southern Railroad Co. v. Carroll

Supreme Court of Alabama, 1892.
97 Ala. 126, 11 So. 803, 18 L.R.A. 433, 38 Am.St.Rep. 163.

[Plaintiff was a brakeman on defendant's railroad. Both parties were residents of Alabama and plaintiff was hired there. Plaintiff was injured in Mississippi due to a break in a defective car link. The evidence showed negligence on the part of railroad employees who had a duty to inspect the links at various places in Alabama.]

■ McCLELLAN, J. ... This was the negligence not of the master, the defendant, but of fellow-servants of the plaintiff, for which at common-law the defendant is not liable.... We feel entirely safe in declaring that plaintiff has shown no cause of action under the common-law as it is understood and applied both here and in Mississippi.

It is, however, further contended that the plaintiff ... has made out a case for the recovery sought under the Employer's Liability Act of Alabama, it being clearly shown that there is no such ... law ... in the State of Mississippi. Considering this position in the abstract, that is dissociated from the facts of this particular case which are supposed to exert an important influence upon it, there cannot be two opinions as to its being unsound and untenable. So looked at, we do not understand appellee's counsel even to deny either the proposition or its application to this case, that there can be no recovery in one State for injuries to the person sustained in another unless the infliction of the injuries is actionable under the law of the State in which they were received. Certainly this is the well established rule of law subject in some jurisdictions to the qualification that the infliction of the injuries would also support an action in the State where the suit is brought, had they been received within that State....

But it is claimed that the facts of this case take it out of the general rule ... and authorize the courts of Alabama to subject the defendant to the payment of damages under section 2590 of the Code, although the injuries counted on were sustained in Mississippi under circumstances which involved no liability on the defendant by the laws of that State.

This insistence is in the first instance based on that aspect of the evidence which goes to show that the negligence which produced the casualty transpired in Alabama, and the theory that wherever the consequence of that negligence manifested itself, a recovery can be had in Alabama. We are referred to no authority in support of this proposition, and exhaustive investigation on our part has failed to disclose any....

It is admitted, or at least cannot be denied, that negligence of duty unproductive of damnifying results will not authorize or support a recovery. Up to the time this train passed out of Alabama no injury had resulted. For all that occurred in Alabama, therefore, no cause of action whatever arose. The fact which created the right to sue, the injury without which confessedly no action would lie anywhere, transpired in the State of Mississippi. It was in that State, therefore, necessarily that the cause of action, if any, arose; and whether a cause of action arose and existed at all or not must in all reason be determined by the law which obtained at the time and place when and where the fact which is relied on to justify a recovery transpired. Section 2590 of the Code of Alabama had no efficiency beyond the lines of Alabama.... Section 2590 of the Code, in other words, is to be interpreted in the light of universally recognized principles of private international or interstate law, as if its operation had been expressly limited to this State and as if its first line read as follows: "When a personal injury is *received in Alabama* by a servant or employee," &c., &c.... We have not been inattentive to the suggestions of counsel in this connection, which are based upon that rule of the statutory and common criminal law under which a murderer is punishable where the fatal blow is delivered, regardless of the place where death ensues.—Green

v. State, 66 Ala. 40. This principle is patently without application here. There would be some analogy if the plaintiff had been stricken in Alabama and suffered in Mississippi, which is not the fact. There is, however, an analogy which is afforded by the criminal law, but which points away from the conclusion appellee's counsel desire us to reach. This is found in that well established doctrine of criminal law, that where the unlawful act is committed in one jurisdiction or State and takes effect—produces the result which it is the purpose of the law to prevent, or, it having ensued, punish for—in another jurisdiction or State, the crime is deemed to have been committed and is punished in that jurisdiction or State in which the result is manifested, and not where the act was committed. . . .

[Plaintiff argued that since the contract of employment was entered into in Alabama between Alabama citizens the Alabama Employer's Liability Act became a part of the contract and the defendant was under a contractual duty to the plaintiff. On this point the court said, inter alia, . . . "that the duties and liabilities incident to the relation between the plaintiff and the defendant which are involved in this case, are not imposed by and do not rest in or spring from the contract between the parties. The only office of the contract, under section 2590 of the Code, is the establishment of a relation between them, that of master and servant; and it is upon that relation, that incident or consequence of the contract, and not upon the rights of the parties under the contract, that our statute operates. The law is not concerned with the contractual stipulations, except in so far as to determine from them that the relation upon which it is to operate exists. Finding this relation the statute imposes certain duties and liabilities on the parties to it wholly regardless of the stipulations of the contract as to the rights of the parties under it, and, it may be, in the teeth of such stipulations."]

For the error in refusing to instruct the jury to find for the defendant if they believed the evidence, the judgment is reversed and the cause will be remanded.

NOTES

1. What if the train in Carroll's case had been negligently coupled in Mississippi and his injury had occurred in Alabama? Presumably, on these facts, the Alabama court would have applied the law of Alabama. But should a simple shift in the location of conduct and injury lead to such a total reversal of result? Yet, what would be the alternative if simple, uniform, forum-proof, even-handed answers are to be reached in multistate cases? Is there a better choice-of-law rule than "place of the wrong"?

2. The words "in Alabama" did not appear in § 2590 of the Alabama Code. The Alabama Employers' Liability Act was subsequently amended to cover out-of-state injury if the contract of employment was made in Alabama. Ala.Code Ann. § 7540 (1928).

3. The "doctrine of criminal law" that the court refers to is no longer "well established." See Model Penal Code § 1.03(1), 10 U.L.A. 433, 452–53: "[A] person may be convicted under the law of this State of an offense . . . if: (a) either the conduct which is an element of the offense or the result which is such an element occurs within this State...."

4. D's dog strayed from Massachusetts to New Hampshire and there bit P. By New Hampshire law, D was liable only upon proof that he knew his dog was accustomed to bite (there was no such proof). By statute in Massachusetts, D was absolutely liable. P was denied recovery. LeForest v. Tolman, 117 Mass. 109 (1875). Assume identical canine behavior, but switch the rules in the two states. Cf. Fischl v. Chubb, 30 Pa.D. & C. 40 (1937), where the turnabout case arose and P was allowed to recover.

In Siegmann v. Meyer, 100 F.2d 367 (2d Cir. 1938), plaintiff was assaulted by defendant's wife in Florida, where she had gone without the defendant. He, indeed, had never been in Florida, which, unlike defendant's New York domicile, held a husband liable for his wife's torts. Defendant was held not liable. Is the case different in principle from the dog-bite case?

5. In Dallas v. Whitney, 118 W.Va. 106, 188 S.E. 766 (1936), plate glass stored by P in Ohio was shattered by the force of an explosion caused by D's blasting in West Virginia. The West Virginia court determined D's liability by reference to Ohio law, which imposed liability without fault. If under West Virginia law D would be liable only if negligent, was it fair to apply Ohio's strict rule?

In Hunter v. Derby Foods, 110 F.2d 970 (2d Cir. 1940), an action for wrongful death was brought in the federal district court in New York. The deceased died in Ohio as a result of eating unwholesome canned meat which he had purchased and eaten in Ohio. The defendant, a New York distributor, has secured the meat from a concern which had processed and canned it in South America. The defendant sold it to a wholesaler in Ohio who in turn sold it to the grocer from whom the deceased purchased it. An Ohio statute made it negligence per se to sell unwholesome food without disclosure of that fact to the buyer. Held: P may recover on a showing of a violation of the statute and need not prove lack of due care. Is that a fair result?

Victor v. Sperry

District Court of Appeal, Fourth District, California, 1958.
163 Cal.App.2d 518, 329 P.2d 728.

■ MUSSELL, JUSTICE. This is an action for personal injuries sustained by plaintiff in an automobile accident which occurred on the San Quintin highway, approximately 44 kilometers south of Tiajuana, Baja California, Republic of Mexico.

At the time of the collision on July 3, 1955, defendant John C. Sperry, with the permission and consent of defendant John M. Sperry, was driving a Mercury automobile northerly on said highway when the Mercury collided with a Chevrolet automobile being driven in a southerly direction on said highway by defendant Edward Thornton. Plaintiff Rudolph Victor was an occupant of the Thornton vehicle and was severely injured in the collision. Plaintiff and the drivers of both cars were and now are residents and citizens of the State of California. The accident was the result of the negligence (and of the equivalent of negligence under Mexican law) of the drivers of both cars involved in the accident.

Article 1910 of the Civil Code of 1928 for the Federal District and Territories of Mexico, as amended, which had been adopted by the State of Baja California del Norte and which was in effect at the time of the accident, provided as follows: "A person who, acting illicitly or contrary to good customs, causes damages to another, is obligated to repair it, unless it is shown that the damage was produced as a consequence of the guilt or inexcusable negligence of the victim." Neither said code nor the general law of said state or of said Republic distinguished between guests and passengers in motor vehicles nor did they impose any restrictions upon the right of a guest to recover damages from the negligent operator of a motor vehicle in which he was riding.

Prior to the accident plaintiff had been employed as a house mover and his weekly wage was $99. He had not returned to work at the time of the trial and will not be able to engage in the same occupation or any occupation requiring a substantial amount of physical activity.

The trial court found (and it is not disputed) that as a result of the accident plaintiff's spinal cord was damaged. He suffered a paralysis of the left upper and lower extremities and the disability in his left upper extremity is permanent and total. The disability in his lower extremity is permanent and partial. He is and will continue to be unable to walk without a limp or for protracted periods. The court further found that plaintiff suffered the following actual damages as a result of the accident:

Medical and hospital expenses	$ 2,962.05
Loss of earnings	7,500.00
Impairment of earning capacity	15,000.00
Pain, suffering and mental anguish	15,000.00
	$40,462.05

At the time of the accident the Mexican law in effect imposed restrictions on the recovery of damages for personal injuries regardless of their nature or extent. Under the Mexican law in effect at the time a victim of the negligent conduct of another could recover his medical and hospital expenses. For a temporary total disability he could recover only 75 per cent of his lost wages for a period not to exceed one year. Wages in excess of 25 pesos, or $2 per day, could not be taken into account in computing the amount allowed. If he suffered a permanent and total disability, he could recover lost earnings for only 818 days and, even though he earned more than 25 pesos per day, only that amount could be taken into account in computing the amount of the recovery. Where the disability was permanent but not total, the recovery was scaled down. For a permanent disability of an upper extremity the victim could recover only from 50 to 70 per cent of $2 per day for 918 days, the exact percentage depending upon age, the importance of the disability, and the extent to which the disability prevented the victim from engaging in his occupation. If the injured extremity was the "least useful", the indemnity was reduced by 15 per cent. In addition, "moral damages" up to a maximum of one-third of the other recoverable damages might, in the discretion of the court, be awarded. "Moral damages" are defined as "damages suffered by a person in his honor, reputation, personal tranquility or spiritual integrity of his life, and as damages which are not of a physical nature and not capable of exact monetary evaluation." The trial court concluded that enforcement of these restrictions on the recovery of damages is not contrary to the public policy of this State or to abstract justice or injurious to the welfare of the people of this State and that plaintiff was not entitled to recover his actual damages in the amount of $40,462.05. Judgment was thereupon rendered against defendants John C. Sperry and Edward Thornton in the amount of $6,135.96. The recovery was computed as follows:

Medical and hospital expenses	$2,962.05
Temporary total disability (75% of $2.00 for 365 days)	547.50
Permanent partial disability (70% of $2.00 for 918 days less 15%)	1,092.42
Sub–Total	4,601.97
Moral damages	1,533.99
Total	$6,135.96

Under Article 1913 of the Civil Code of 1928 for the Mexican Federal District and Territories, if a person has the use of mechanisms or instruments which are dangerous per se, by the speed they develop, or otherwise, he is obligated to answer for the damages he causes, even though he does not act illicitly, unless the damage is caused by the guilt or inexcusable negligence of the victim. The Mexican courts hold that an automobile is a dangerous mechanism or instrument within the meaning of this section and that a person injured by a motor vehicle is entitled to recover damages without regard to fault or negligence from both the owner and driver of the automobile. However, if liability exists only under Article 1913 "moral damages" are not recoverable. Since liability under Article 1910 was found to exist on the part of the drivers of both automobiles, it became immaterial whether liability under Article 1913 was found to exist as to them. Plaintiff, however, sought a judgment against John M. Sperry, owner of the Chevrolet automobile, for $4,601.97, under Article 1913. The trial court concluded that this article is contrary to the public policy of this State, is in substantial conflict with the law of this State, and should not be enforced. Judgment was entered in favor of defendant John M. Sperry.

Rudolph Victor appeals from the judgment (a) Insofar as it fails to award damages in excess of $6,135.96 as against defendants John C. Sperry and Edward Thornton; and (b) Insofar as it fails to award any damages against defendant John M. Sperry....

In the instant case, since the accident occurred in Mexico, plaintiff's cause of action arose there and the character and measure of his damages are governed by the laws of Mexico. The measure of damages is inseparably connected to the cause of action and cannot be severed therefrom. The limitation upon the amount of damages imposed by the laws of Mexico is not contrary to the public policy of the State of California or injurious to the welfare of the people thereof.

The trial court herein held that the application of Article 1913 of the Civil Code of 1928 for the Federal District and Territories of Mexico, which provides for liability without fault, was in opposition to the public policy of the State of California and refused to enforce that article against John M. Sperry, owner of one of the automobiles involved in the collision. We find no reversible error in this refusal. . . .

Since no right of action exists in California for damages for liability without fault under the circumstances set forth herein and in Article 1913 of the Civil Code of 1928 for the Mexican Federal District and Territories, the trial court herein properly concluded that this article should not be enforced as against John M. Sperry as owner of one of the automobiles involved.

Judgment affirmed.

■ GRIFFIN, P.J., and COUGHLIN, J. pro tem., concur.

■ Hearing denied; CARTER, J., dissenting.

NOTES

1. At the end of its opinion, the court states that "no right of action exists in California for damages for liability without fault under the circumstances set forth herein." Under California Code of 1935, § 402(a), in force at the time of the accident, the owner of a motor vehicle was liable for death or injury resulting from the negligence of "any person using or operating the same with the permission express or implied, of the owner." The court found that "[t]he accident was the result of the negligence ... of the drivers of both cars." If the owner of the automobile in which the plaintiff was a passenger would have been liable under the law of either California or Mexico, is there a rational basis on which a different result could be reached in the principal case?

2. If the plaintiff becomes a public charge as the result of his injuries, on which society will the burden fall, Mexico or California?

Without special arrangements with his insurer, the owner's California liability insurance did not cover him "44 kilometers south of Tiajuana," which was more than 25 miles from the United States border. If the court had indicated that it was considering applying the California measure of damages in order to enforce California's "interests," did the owner have a cogent argument that he was unfairly surprised? Would this argument be cogent after the California Supreme Court had adopted interest analysis in Reich v. Purcell, 67 Cal.2d 551, 63 Cal.Rptr. 31, 432 P.2d 727 (1967), page 606, infra?

3. The court did not mention the California "guest statute" in force at the time of the accident. This statute, since repealed, required a showing of "intoxication or willful misconduct" of the driver in order for a guest passenger to recover against the driver or "any person legally liable for the conduct of the driver." California Code of 1935, § 403. Should this statute have been applied?

4. Other classic applications of the place-of-wrong rule occurred in marital immunity and guest statute cases. If spouses or host and guest are domiciled in a state that permits them to sue one another for negligence, does it make sense to apply the immunity rule of the place of injury to bar suit in their home state? This was the result reached in many of the cases decided before wide-spread abandonment of the place-of-wrong rule. For marital immunity cases, see, e.g., Dawson v. Dawson, 224 Ala. 13, 138 So. 414 (1931); Landers v. Landers, 153 Conn. 303, 216 A.2d 183 (1966), abrogated by statute, Conn.Gen.Stat.Ann. § 52–527d; Gray v. Gray, 87 N.H. 82, 174 A. 508 (1934), overruled, Thompson v. Thompson, 105 N.H. 86, 193 A.2d 439 (1963) (abandoning place-of-wrong rule). For guest statute cases see, e.g., Sharp v. Johnson, 248 Minn. 518, 80 N.W.2d 650 (1957), overruled, Kopp v. Rechtzigel, 273 Minn. 441, 141 N.W.2d 526 (1966) (abandoning place-of-wrong rule); Naphtali v. Lafazan, 8 A.D.2d 22, 186 N.Y.S.2d 1010 (1959); overruled, Babcock v. Jackson, 12 N.Y.2d 473, 240 N.Y.S.2d 743, 191 N.E.2d 279 (1963) (abandoning place-of-wrong rule).

Gordon v. Parker

United States District Court D. Massachusetts, 1949.
83 F.Supp. 40, aff'd, 178 F.2d 888 (1st Cir.1949).

■ WYZANSKI, DISTRICT JUDGE. Plaintiff and his wife Naomi are citizens of and domiciled in Pennsylvania. During his service as Lt. Colonel in India, she came to Massachusetts and met defendant who is a citizen and domiciliary of Massachusetts. Plaintiff's complaint alleges that defendant, intending "to deprive him of comfort, society, aid and assistance of Naomi," enticed her to continue absent from his home.... The parties have stipulated "that the alleged acts upon which the plaintiff is bringing this action are alleged to have been committed in * * * Massachusetts".

Defendant moves for summary judgment on the basis of Pa. Act of June 22, 1935, Pamphlet Law 450, ... as amended by Pa. Act of June 25, 1937, Pamphlet Law 2317, ... which, so far as material, provides:

§ 170—" * * * all civil causes of action for alienation of affections of husband or wife * * * are hereby abolished * * *."

§ 172—"No act hereafter done within this Commonwealth shall operate to give rise, either within or without this Commonwealth, to any of the causes of action abolished by this act. * * * It is the intention of this section to fix the effect, status, and character of such acts * * * and to render them ineffective to support or give rise to any such causes of action within or without this Commonwealth."

Since this is an action brought in this Court solely by virtue of the diversity jurisdiction statute, 28 U.S.C.A. § 1332(a)(1), this Court must apply the law of Massachusetts, including its rule of conflict of laws. Klaxon Co. v. Stentor Electric Mfg. Co., 313 U.S. 487–497, 61 S.Ct. 1020, 85 L.Ed. 1477....

With respect to an action for alienation of affections there is a difference between the two Commonwealths. Massachusetts has retained in modified form the husband's common law right to hold liable a defendant who has induced his wife to deprive him of her consortium. But Pennsylvania has enacted that in that state all actions for alienation of affections are abolished and that no act within Pennsylvania shall give rise to an action for alienation of affections. The question is whether Massachusetts would extend the asserted underlying policy of the Pennsylvania statute to bar a suit brought in the courts of Massachusetts by a Pennsylvania husband against a Massachusetts paramour on account of conduct within Massachusetts.

In the literal sense of the phrase this is not a question of "conflict of laws." For though Pennsylvania has a law governing suits in her courts and conduct within her borders, she has no law purporting to regulate her domiciliaries' right to bring actions in other states based on conduct outside Pennsylvania. Yet, because of the somewhat divergent policies of the different states whose interests are involved, the problem is one which would properly be called one of private international law.

Like most other American states, Massachusetts generally applies the law of the state where an alleged wrong has occurred in deciding whether a person has sustained a legal injury. However, these and other Massachusetts cases have dealt with the type of injuries to body and mind caused by the negligent or wilful misconduct of persons such as employers, fellow servants and automobile drivers. There appears to be no conflict of laws case dealing with injury to consortium, or to any other marital relationship, or even to a contractual relationship or other advantageous business relationship.

Defendant's argument is that where the asserted damage has been inflicted on a marital relationship Massachusetts would recognize that the existence of liability should be determined by the policy not of the forum, or of the place of wrong, but of the state of marital domicil. It is there, so the contention runs, that the alienator's act has its chief and indeed its final legal consequences. That is the state that has the most sustained and profound interest in the marriage. If it does not give the husband a legal interest in protecting his wife's affections and consortium from strangers, no other state should. To do so amounts to conferring upon a husband a property right in his wife's affections to which he would not be entitled at the seat of the marriage. And it is virtually to impose a restriction upon the freedom which the wife enjoys at home.

There are, it seems to me, sufficient reasons for believing that Massachusetts would reject these arguments as applied to this case.

This is not a situation in which the interests of Pennsylvania plainly outweigh those of Massachusetts. The social order of each is implicated. As the place of matrimonial domicil, Pennsylvania has an interest in whether conduct in any part of the world is held to affect adversely the marriage relationship between its domiciliaries. But, as the place where the alleged misconduct occurred and as the place where the alleged wrongdoer lives, Massachusetts also has an interest. She is concerned with conduct within her borders which in her view lowers the standards of the community where they occur. She also is concerned when her citizens intermeddle with other people's marriages. But admittedly she has little interest in the degree of affection one Pennsylvania spouse has for another. It so happens that this distinction in interest finds a parallel in the substantive law of Massachusetts. For under her rules a defendant is liable for alienation of affections only if his conduct produces physical results—either adultery or separation. Massachusetts does not hold a defendant liable when all that is involved are emotional upsets in a domestic or foreign marriage and the decreased loyalty of domestic or foreign spouses.

If the choice between Pennsylvania's interests and Massachusetts' interests presented in the case at bar were laid before a Massachusetts court, it seems to me probably that it would strike a balance in favor of its own Commonwealth. It could point out that the interests of Massachusetts were perhaps the most fundamental ones in the development certainly of tort law and perhaps of all private law. Tort law, like its younger brother criminal law, was sired by a policy of regulating the social order and substituting legal process for self-help. To be sure, tort law also always has a compensatory element. But that is of secondary consequence where, as in the tort of alienation of affections, the principal reason why the state stamps conduct as wrongful is that so many people regard it as sinful, so many regard it as offensive to public morals, and so many are likely to take matters into their own hands if public tribunals are not available.

Moreover, departures from the territorial view of torts ought not to be lightly undertaken. There was a time in Anglo–American history when persons from abroad did not have the full benefit or burden of local private law. Thus, foreign merchants in England in the Fifteenth Century were "not bound to sue according to the law of the land * * * but * * * the matter shall be determined by the law of nature." Y.B. 13 Edw. III f. 9, Pasch. pl. 5, quoted in 2 Pollock & Maitland, History of English Law, 1st Ed., 449. 9 Holdsworth, History of English Law, 95, n. 4. However, it was regarded as an advance when "by the end of the Sixteenth Century, the alien could bring personal actions * * * just as a subject." 9 Holdsworth, supra, p. 97. It is, therefore, not necessarily a forward step for courts now to adopt a doctrine that in all matrimonial tort cases the right to maintain a suit against a local defendant on account of local conduct turns on the matrimonial domicil of the plaintiff. To be sure, technically this will not reintroduce a doctrine of personal disability. For the doctrine will make the applicable rule depend not on the person of the plaintiff or his lack of local citizenship, but on a relationship involving him, his foreign spouse and his foreign state. Yet the lay plaintiff will regard the distinction as involving a personal discrimination against him rather than as a step toward comity between states. This would be particularly true if the rule should be applied to a plaintiff who was formally domiciled in one state but who spent most of his time with his wife in the state where the misconduct occurred.

Furthermore, up to now I have assumed what is by no means clear, that the present case involves some implied Pennsylvania policy. So far as appears, Pennsylvania has no general policy that injured spouses should bear their suffering in silence and rely exclusively upon the forces of social ostracism and religious discipline. Pennsylvania was concerned with not having Pennsylvania courts hear this sordid type of controversy and not having Pennsylvania citizens and visitors called upon to defend actions which have so often been motivated by spiteful or ulterior purposes. That is, Pennsylvania has spoken qua possible forum and qua possible state of defendant's domicil, but not qua state of matrimonial domicil. In any event, its policy is not connected with the purification of Massachusetts courts or the immunization of Massachusetts defendants who have been acting illicitly in Massachusetts. . . .

Motion for summary judgment denied. . . .

NOTES

1. According to Judge Wyzanski, when does the place where the defendant acts advance its policies by conferring liability? Does it have a similar "interest" in denying liability? Does the answer in both circumstances turn on the nature of the tort?

2. Judge Wyzanski suggests that a spouse might regard application of the law of the marital domicile to defeat a cause of action under the law of the place of injury, "as involving a personal discrimination against him rather than as a step toward comity between states." Might a defendant similarly deprived of a defense have a similar reaction? Are these attitudes justified?

(b) Contract

Unlike the monolithic place-of-wrong rule for torts, the traditional choice-of-law rules applicable to contracts were more diverse and some were not territorial. Moreover, judges applying the contract rules were more likely than in tort cases to address practical reasons for choosing law.

Contract choice-of-law issues arise in two contexts—validity and construction. If the issue is one of validity, then no matter how clearly the parties have expressed their intention, one state whose law might be applicable would refuse to give effect to that intention. If the issue is solely one of construction, then any state that has a contact with the parties or the transaction would give effect to the parties' intention if clearly expressed. The problem is that the parties have left a hole in their agreement and the laws of the contact states fill in that hole in different ways. An example of a construction problem is excuse for impossibility or frustration of purpose. Suppose Seller from X promises to manufacture goods and sell them to Buyer in Y. Seller's factory burns down and Buyer obtains the goods from another source but at a higher price. If the contract had specifically addressed this circumstance and stated which party would bear the risk, the courts of X and Y would have enforced the agreement. The contract is silent on the issue, however, and X law excuses Seller, but Y law does not.

Should it make a difference for choice-of-law purposes whether the issue is one of validity or construction? Restatement (Second) Conflict of Laws § 187, page 541, infra, allows the parties to choose any law to govern construction, but limits their freedom to choose law for validity.

Milliken v. Pratt

Supreme Judicial Court of Massachusetts, 1878.
125 Mass. 374, 28 Am.Rep. 241.

Contract to recover $500 and interest from January 6, 1872. Writ dated June 30, 1875. The case was submitted to the Superior Court on agreed facts, in substance as follows:

The plaintiffs are partners doing business in Portland, Maine, under the firm name of Deering, Milliken & Co. The defendant is and has been since 1850, the wife of Daniel Pratt, and both have always resided in Massachusetts. In 1870, Daniel, who was then doing business in Massachusetts, applied to the plaintiffs at Portland for credit, and they required of him, as a condition of granting the same a guaranty from the defendant to the amount of five hundred dollars, and accordingly he procured from his wife the following instrument:

"Portland, January 29, 1870. In consideration of one dollar paid by Deering, Milliken & Co., receipt of which is hereby acknowledged, I guarantee the payment to them by Daniel Pratt of the sum of five hundred dollars, from time to time as he may want—this to be a continuing guaranty. Sarah A. Pratt."

This instrument was executed by the defendant two or three days after its date, at her home in Massachusetts, and there delivered by her to her husband, who sent it by mail from Massachusetts to the plaintiffs in Portland; and the plaintiffs received it from the post-office in Portland early in February, 1870.

The plaintiffs subsequently sold and delivered goods to Daniel from time to time until October 7, 1871, and charged the same to him, and, if competent, it may be taken to be true, that in so doing they relied upon the guaranty.... This action is brought for goods sold from September 1, 1871, to October 7, 1871, inclusive, amounting to $860.12, upon which he paid $300, leaving a balance due of $560.12. The one dollar mentioned in the guaranty was not paid, and the only consideration moving to the defendant therefor was the giving of credit by the plaintiffs to her husband. Some of the goods were selected personally by Daniel at the plaintiffs' store in Portland, others were ordered by letters mailed by Daniel from Massachusetts to the plaintiffs at Portland, and all were sent by the plaintiffs by express from Portland to Daniel in Massachusetts, who paid all express charges....

Payment was duly demanded of the defendant before the date of the writ, and was refused by her.

The Superior Court ordered judgment for the defendant; and the plaintiffs appealed to this court.

■ GRAY, C.J. The general rule is that the validity of a contract is to be determined by the law of the state in which it is made; if it is valid there, it is deemed valid everywhere, and will sustain an action in the courts of a state whose laws do not permit such a contract. Scudder v. Union National

Bank, 91 U.S. 406. Even a contract expressly prohibited by the statutes of the state in which the suit is brought, if not in itself immoral, is not necessarily nor usually deemed so invalid that the comity of the state, as administered by its courts, will refuse to entertain an action on such a contract made by one of its own citizens abroad in a state the laws of which permit it. Greenwood v. Curtis, 6 Mass. 358. M'Intyre v. Parks, 3 Metc. 207.

If the contract is completed in another state, it makes no difference in principle whether the citizen of this state goes in person, or sends an agent, or writes a letter across the boundary line between the two states.... So if a person residing in this state signs and transmits, either by a messenger or through the post-office, to a person in another state, a written contract, which requires no special forms or solemnities in its execution, and no signature of the person to whom it is addressed, and is assented to and acted on by him there, the contract is made there, just as if the writer personally took the executed contract into the other state, or wrote and signed it there....

... The sales of the goods ordered by him from the plaintiffs at Portland, and there delivered by them to him in person or to a carrier for him, were made in the State of Maine.... The contract between the defendant and the plaintiffs was complete when the guaranty had been received and acted on by them at Portland, and not before. Jordan v. Dobbins, 122 Mass. 168. It must therefore be treated as made and to be performed in the State of Maine.

The law of Maine authorized a married woman to bind herself by any contract as if she were unmarried. St. of Maine of 1866, c. 52. Mayo v. Hutchinson, 57 Maine 546. The law of Massachusetts, as then existing, did not allow her to enter into a contract as surety or for the accommodation of her husband or of any third person. Gen.Sts. c. 108, sec. 3. Nourse v. Henshaw, 123 Mass. 96....

The question therefore is, whether a contract made in another state by a married woman domiciled here, which a married woman was not at the time capable of making under the law of this Commonwealth, but was then allowed by the law of that state to make, and which she could now lawfully make in this Commonwealth, will sustain an action against her in our courts.

It has been often stated by commentators that the law of the domicil, regulating the capacity of a person, accompanies and governs the person everywhere. But this statement, in modern times at least, is subject to many qualifications; and the opinions of foreign jurists upon the subject ... are too varying and contradictory to control the general current of the English and American authorities in favor of holding that a contract, which by the law of the place is recognized as lawfully made by a capable person, is valid everywhere, although the person would not, under the law of his domicil, be deemed capable of making it....

In Pearl v. Hansborough, 9 Humph. 426, the rule was carried so far as to hold that where a married woman domiciled with her husband in the State of Mississippi, by the law of which a purchase by a married woman was valid and the property purchased went to her separate use, bought personal property in Tennessee, by the law of which married women were incapable of contracting, the contract of purchase was void and could not be enforced in Tennessee. Some authorities, on the other hand, would uphold a contract made by a party capable by the law of his domicil, though incapable by the law of the place of the contract. In re Hellmann's Will [L.R. 2 Eq. 363], and Saul v. His Creditors [17 Martin (La.) 569], above cited. But that alternative is not here presented.

The principal reasons on which continental jurists have maintained that personal laws of the domicil, affecting the status and capacity of all inhabitants of a particular class, bind them wherever they may go, appear to have been that each state has the rightful power of regulating the status and condition of its subjects ... that laws limiting the capacity of infants or of married women are intended for their protection, and cannot therefore be dispensed with by their agreement; that all civilized states recognize the incapacity of infants and married women; and that a person, dealing with either, ordinarily has notice, by the apparent age or sex, that the person is likely to be of a class whom the laws protect, and is thus put upon inquiry how far, by the law of the domicil of the person, the protection extends.

. . .

In the great majority of cases, especially in this country, where it is so common to travel, or to transact business through agents, or to correspond by letter, from one state to another, it is more just, as well as more convenient, to have regard to the law of the place of the contract, as a uniform rule operating on all contracts of the same kind, and which the contracting parties may be presumed to have in contemplation when making their contracts, than to require them at their peril to know the domicil of those with whom they deal, and to ascertain the law of that domicil, however remote, which in many cases could not be done without such delay as would greatly cripple the power of contracting abroad at all. . . .

It is possible also that in a state where the common law prevailed in full force, by which a married woman was deemed incapable of binding herself by any contract whatever, it might be inferred that such an utter incapacity, lasting throughout the joint lives of husband and wife, must be considered as so fixed by the settled policy of the state, for the protection of its own citizens, that it could not be held by the courts of that state to yield to the law of another state in which she might undertake to contract.

But it is not true at the present day that all civilized states recognize the absolute incapacity of married women to make contracts. The tendency of modern legislation is to enlarge their capacity in this respect, and in many states they have nearly or quite the same powers as if unmarried. In Massachusetts, even at the time of the making of the contract in question, a married woman was vested by statute with a very extensive power to carry on business by herself, and to bind herself by contracts with regard to her own property, business and earnings; and, before the bringing of the present action, the power had been extended so as to include the making of all kinds of contracts, with any person but her husband, as if she were unmarried. There is therefore no reason of public policy which should prevent the maintenance of this action.

Judgment for the plaintiffs.

NOTES

1. Under the reasoning of the court in the principal case, would the decision have been different if the seller had delivered the goods by the seller's own wagon or truck to the buyer in Massachusetts? Did the change in Massachusetts law affect the outcome? Should it?

2. Should the rules of contract law with respect to the time *when* a binding contract is made be deemed determinative of the question *where* the contract was made for choice-of-law purposes? What are the policies that underlie the rule prescribing the point in time when an agreement becomes binding?

3. Union National Bank v. Chapman, 169 N.Y. 538, 62 N.E. 672 (1902). Defendant wife, a resident of Alabama, signed in that state a note as surety for the firm of which her husband was a member. The note was subsequently discounted by the plaintiff bank in Illinois. It was found at the trial that "while it was the intention of the firm that the note should be negotiated and discounted in the state of Illinois she [the defendant] did not know of such intention...." Under the law of Alabama, the defendant had no capacity to make the contract in question, but the law of Illinois was otherwise, and the plaintiff contended that this latter law should be applied since the note had "no legal inception" until it was discounted in Illinois. Held for the defendant. "... it seems clear that the capacity of Mrs. Chapman to contract must be determined by the law of the state where the contract was executed unless it can fairly be said that she ... clearly understood and intended that it should be governed by the laws of another state."

In Chemical National Bank v. Kellogg, 183 N.Y. 92, 75 N.E. 1103 (1905), the defendant wife was held liable on facts analogous to those in the Chapman case on the ground that "since the defendant's endorsement gave no notice which would put a purchaser on guard, she is estopped from claiming that her endorsement was a New Jersey contract and therefore void." If domicile and "place of contract" are both unsatisfactory connecting factors, what choice-of-law rule would be fair and acceptable in this type of case?

4. In New York P telephoned D in Pennsylvania accepting an offer to enter into a reinsurance contract for which the New York Statute of Frauds required a writing because it was not to be performed in a year. Under the law of Pennsylvania the oral agreement was enforceable. The court acknowledged that the sounder view in contract law theory was Williston's position that "the place of contracting is where the acceptance is heard," but ruled that it would promote "uniformity" and discourage "forum-shopping" to "hold that acceptance by telephone of an offer takes place where the words are spoken." Linn v. Employer Reinsurance Corp., 392 Pa. 58, 139 A.2d 638 (1958).

Louis–Dreyfus v. Paterson Steamships, Limited

United States Circuit Court of Appeals, Second Circuit, 1930.
43 F.2d 824.

Appeal from the District Court of the United States for the Western District of New York.

Libel by Louis–Dreyfus and another doing business under the firm name and style of Louis–Dreyfus & Company, against Paterson Steamships, Limited. The libel was dismissed (35 F.2d 353), and libellants appeal.

■ L. HAND, CIRCUIT JUDGE. The libellants at Duluth shipped a parcel of wheat upon two ships of the respondent and received in exchange bills of lading, Duluth to Montreal, "with transshipment at Port Colbourne, Ontario." These contained an exception for "dangers of navigation, fire and collision," but nothing further which is here relevant. The respondent exercised its right of reshipment, unladed the wheat at Port Colbourne, stored it in an elevator, and reladed thirty-five thousand bushels in another ship, the Advance, belonging to one Webb, chartered by the respondent's agent, the Hall Shipping Company, for that purpose. This ship safely carried her cargo until she reached the entrance to the Cornwall Canal in the St. Lawrence River, where she took the ground, stove in her bottom and sank. The suit is for the resulting damage to the wheat.

The respondent ... relied upon the Harter Act (46 U.S.C.A. secs. 190–195) and the Canadian Water–Carriage of Goods Act (9–10 Edward VII, Chap. 81), which covers among other ships those "carrying goods from any port in Canada to any other port in Canada" (section 3)....

We shall assume arguendo that section three of the Harter Act (46 U.S.C.A. sec. 192) did not cover the case; verbally it only includes "vessels transporting merchandise or property to or from any port in the United States." [Under this section, the owner of a vessel is relieved of liability "for damage or loss resulting from faults or error in navigation" if the owner exercises due diligence to make the vessel seaworthy.] ...

The important question is whether we should look to Canadian law at all. Here is a contract of carriage, made in Minnesota without any relevant exceptions, to be performed partly in the United States and partly in Canada; the carrier fails in performing that part of it which is to take place in Canada; he does not safely transport the grain from the entrance of the canal to Montreal. The law of the place of that performance excuses him for those faults in navigation which have caused the loss. Does that law control? Liverpool & G.W.S. Co. v. Phenix Ins. Co., 129 U.S. 397, decided that the validity of a provision in a contract of carriage, limiting the carrier's common-law duty, was to be determined by the law of the place where the contract was made, and this is well-settled law.... It is of course only an instance of the usual rule that the law of the place where promises are made determines whether they create a contract ...; that law alone attaches any legal consequences to acts within its territory.

On the other hand, it is always said that as to matters of performance the law of the place of performance controls. Andrews v. Pond, 13 Pet. 65, 78; Scudder v. Union National Bank, 91 U.S. 408; Pritchard v. Norton, 106 U.S. 124; Hall v. Cordell, 142 U.S. 116, though in application the boundaries of this doctrine are not easy to find, as the last two cases cited illustrate very well. An exchange of mutual promises, or whatever other acts may create a contract for future performance, do not put the obligor under any immediate constraint, except so far as the doctrine of anticipatory breach demands. A present obligation arises only in the sense that it is then determined that when the time for performance arrives, his conduct shall not be open to his choice. For the present nothing is required of him; he can commit no fault and incur no liability. When the time comes for him to perform, if he fails, the law requires him to give the equivalent of the neglected performance; that compulsion is the sanction imposed by the state and the measure of the obligation. The default must indeed be at the place of performance, but the promisor need not himself be there, nor may he there have any property to respond. In such cases it is impossible to say that any liability arises under the law of that place; yet it would be exceedingly inconvenient to hold that it depended upon the law of the place where the promisor chanced to be at the time of performance, especially if such a doctrine were extended to all places where he has any property. In the interest of certainty and uniformity there must be some definite place fixed whose law shall control, wherever the suit arises. Whether the place of performance is chosen because of the likelihood that the obligor will be there present at the time of performance, or—what is nearly the same thing—because the agreement presupposes that he shall be, is not important. All we need say here is that the same law which determines what liabilities shall arise upon nonperformance, must determine any excuses for nonperformance, which are no more than exceptions to those liabilities.

The authorities in general support this view; as, for example, in the case of a moratorium (Rouquette v. Overmann, L.R. 10 Q.B. 525); of payment upon a forged indorsement (Kessler v. Armstrong Cork Co., 158 F. 744 (C.C.A.2); Belestin v. First National Bank, 177 Mo.App. 300, 164 N.Y.S. 160); of the delivery of a note as payment (Tarbox v. Childs, 165 Mass. 408, 43 N.E. 124) . . . In the case at bar, the Canadian law says that performance of the contract of carriage, as respects navigation, shall be excused if the owner uses due care to examine his ship and make her fit for her voyage, to man and victual her and the like. The conduct so specified is thus made an excuse for his failure to carry the goods safely to their destination as he has promised to do. That is exactly like any other excuse for such failure; delay is as much a breach as default; payment not specified is no payment; delivery to another, no delivery. . . .

We conclude that if the Advance was in fact seaworthy, the respondent was excused by virtue of the Canadian statute, and in that event we need not consider the issue of due diligence. . . .

[The court found there was an issue of fact as to defect in construction, which called for new proof.]

Decree reversed; cause remanded to be reheard upon the issue above mentioned.

NOTES

1. Would Judge Hand have held that American law governed in the Louis–Dreyfus case if the ship had sunk in American waters? Did it make any difference whether United States or Canadian law applied?

2. It is generally recognized that the law of the place of performance regulates matters involving the mode of performance, as, for example, the proper medium of payment and in the case of negotiable instruments the time and form of presentment, protest and notice. For other examples, see Restatement, Second, Conflict of Laws § 206 (1971).

Pritchard v. Norton

Supreme Court of the United States, 1882.
106 U.S. 124, 1 S.Ct. 102, 27 L.Ed. 104.

[Pritchard had become surety on an appeal bond in Louisiana on behalf of a defendant railroad company against which a judgment had been rendered in Louisiana. McComb and Norton executed and delivered to Pritchard in New York an indemnity bond in which they promised to indemnify him against all losses arising from his liability on the appeal bond. McComb and Norton had not requested Pritchard to become a surety. The judgment against the railroad company was affirmed and Pritchard was compelled to satisfy the bond. Pritchard's executrix sued McComb and Norton in Louisiana on the indemnity bond. Under Louisiana law the preexisting liability of Pritchard as surety was sufficient consideration to support the promise of indemnity, although Pritchard's obligation was not incurred at the defendant's request. The law of New York was otherwise. The lower court, the Circuit Court of the United States for the District of Louisiana, accepted the defendants' contention that the law of New York governed. The plaintiff appealed.]

■ Mr. Justice Matthews delivered the opinion of the court....

The argument in support of the judgment is simple, and may be briefly stated. It is, that New York is the place of the contract, both because it was executed and delivered there, and because no other place of performance being either designated or necessarily implied, it was to be performed there....

The phrase lex loci contractus is used, in a double sense, to mean, sometimes, the law of the place where a contract is entered into; sometimes, that of the place of its performance. And when it is employed to describe the law of the seat of the obligation, it is, on that account, confusing. The law we are in search of, which is to decide upon the nature, interpretation, and validity of the engagement in question, is that which the parties have, either expressly or presumptively, incorporated into their contract as constituting its obligation. It has never been better described than it was incidentally by Mr. Chief Justice Marshall in Wayman v. Southard, 10 Wheat. 1, 48, where he defined it as a principle of universal law,—"The principle that in every forum a contract is governed by the law with a view to which it was made." ...

So, Phillimore says: ...

"As all the foregoing rules rest upon the presumption that the obligor has voluntarily submitted himself to a particular local law, that presumption may be rebutted, either by an express declaration to the contrary, or by the fact that the obligation is illegal by that particular law, though legal by another. The parties cannot be presumed to have contemplated a law which would defeat their engagements." 4 Int.Law, sect. DCLIV, pp. 470, 471.

This rule, if universally applicable, which perhaps it is not, ... would be decisive of the present controversy, as conclusive of the question of the application of the law of Louisiana, by which alone the undertaking of the obligor can be upheld.

At all events, it is a circumstance, highly persuasive in its character, of the presumed intention of the parties, and entitled to prevail, unless controlled by more express and positive proofs of a contrary intent....

If now we examine the terms of the bond of indemnity, and the situation and relation of the parties, we shall find conclusive corroboration of the presumption, that the obligation was entered into in view of the laws of Louisiana.

The antecedent liability of Pritchard, as surety for the railroad company on the appeal bond, was confessedly contracted in that State, according to its laws, and it was there alone that it could be performed and discharged. Its undertaking was, that Pritchard should, in certain contingencies, satisfy a judgment of its courts. That could be done only within its territory and according to its laws. The condition of the obligation, which is the basis of this action, is, that McComb and Norton, the obligors, shall hold harmless and fully indemnify Pritchard against all loss or damage arising from his liability as surety on the appeal bond. A judgment was, in fact, rendered against him on it in Louisiana. There was but one way in which the obligors in the indemnity bond could perfectly satisfy its warranty. That was, the moment the judgment was rendered against Pritchard on the appeal bond, to come forward in his stead, and, by payment, to extinguish it. He was entitled to demand this before any payment by himself, and to require that the fund should be forthcoming at the place where otherwise he could be required to pay it. Even if it should be thought that Pritchard was bound to pay the judgment recovered against himself, before his right of recourse accrued upon the bond of indemnity, nevertheless he was entitled to be reimbursed the amount of his advance at the same place where he had been required to make it. So that it is clear, beyond any doubt, that the obligation of the indemnity was to be fulfilled in Louisiana, and, consequently, is subject, in all matters affecting its construction and validity, to the law of that locality....

We do not hesitate, therefore, to decide that the bond of indemnity sued on was entered into with a view to the law of Louisiana as the place for the fulfillment of its obligation; and that the question of its validity, as depending on the character and sufficiency of the consideration, should be determined by the law of Louisiana, and not that of New York. For error in its rulings on this point, consequently, the judgment of the Circuit Court is reversed, with directions to grant a new trial.

NOTES

1. Is the search for "presumed intention" of the parties any more than an effort by the court to pick the rule it thinks should apply, regardless of whether the parties intended anything in that respect, or what they intended? Consider this quotation:

"... the question of intent can hardly be said to involve the actual mental operations of the parties. For, as a matter of fact, they probably did not stop to consider what was the legal effect of their agreement, or whether there was any diversity in the law of the two States; and, therefore, when we speak of the 'question of intent' we are making use of what may perhaps be termed a 'legal fiction'; but, nevertheless, the law does look at the acts of the parties and the circumstances surrounding them which may possibly have exerted some influence upon their actions, and then assumes that their intention is in harmony with such acts and circumstances." Grand v. Livingston, 4 App.Div. 589, 595, 38 N.Y.S. 490, 494 (4th Dep't 1896).

2. Is there a "Basic Rule of Validation" of such compelling force that the courts must nearly always choose the law which upholds and enforces the parties' "engagements"? See Ehrenzweig, Contracts and the Conflict of Laws, 59 Colum.L.Rev. 973, 1171 (1959). Or is that suggestion an example of a penchant for "transmuting a tendency into a doctrine"? See Cavers, Re–Restating the Conflict of Laws: The Chapter on Contracts, XXth Century Comparative and Conflict Laws 349, 358 (1961).

Seeman v. Philadelphia Warehouse Co.

Supreme Court of the United States, 1927.
274 U.S. 403, 47 S.Ct. 626, 71 L.Ed. 1123.

■ Mr. Justice Stone delivered the opinion of the court.

Respondent brought suit in the district court for Southern New York to recover for the conversion of a quantity of canned salmon pledged to it as security for a loan. The pledgor, who had fraudulently regained possession, sold the salmon to petitioners. The defense set up was that the transaction between respondent and the pledgor was usurious and therefore void under the law of New York, where the pledgor conducted its business and where petitioners contend the pledge agreement was made.

The trial court charged the jury that the New York law was applicable. The jury returned a verdict for petitioners. The judgment on the verdict was reversed by the court of appeals for the second circuit. 7 F.2d 999. This Court granted certiorari. 269 U.S. 543.

Respondent is a Pennsylvania corporation having its only office or place of business in Philadelphia. It has an established credit and for many years has engaged in a business which is carried on according to the routine followed in the present case which respondent contends, results in loans of credit and not of money. To applicants in need of funds it delivers its promissory note, payable to its own order and then endorsed. The applicant in exchange gives the required security—here warehouse receipts for the salmon—and a pledge agreement by which he undertakes to pay the amount of the note at maturity to respondent at its office in Philadelphia, and agrees that the collateral pledged shall be security for all obligations present and prospective. At the same time the applicant pays to respondent a "commission" for its "services" and for the "advance of its credit" computed at the rate of 3 per cent. per annum on the face of the note. He is then free to discount the note, and to use the proceeds. In practice, as in the present case, respondent usually, with the consent of the borrower, delivers the note to its own note broker in Philadelphia, receives from him the proceeds of the note less discount and brokerage, and pays or forwards the amount so received to the borrower. At maturity he must pay the face value of the note to respondent, or, as was the case here, renew the note by paying a new commission and the amount of the discount on the matured note. On each transaction the applicant thus pays, in addition to the amount of the proceeds of the note, the commission and the discount. Respondent, after taking up its note, retains the commission alone as the net compensation for its part in the transaction. In addition, the applicant may, as was the case here, pay the fees of the note broker and the fee or compensation of a loan broker, acting as intermediary in securing the accommodation by respondent, a total amount far exceeding 6 per cent., the legal rate of interest in New York. The commission and discount paid here varied from 8½ to 10½ per cent. per annum of the face amount of the notes, taking no account of fees paid to brokers.

In Pennsylvania, the exaction of interest on loans of money in excess of 6 per cent., the lawful rate, does not invalidate the entire transaction, but excess interest may be recovered by the borrower.... The business carried on by respondent as described, was considered and upheld by the Supreme Court of Pennsylvania as not usurious in Righter, Cowgill & Co. v. Philadelphia Warehouse Co., 99 Pa.St. 289.

To avoid the application of the Pennsylvania law ... petitioners at the trial relied on evidence that preliminary negotiations were had in New York City between the pledgor and the agent of respondent from which it might be inferred that the agreement was in fact made there, although the formal documents were dated at Philadelphia and respondent actually executed its note and delivered it to the note broker there. Petitioners also relied on the special circumstances of the case, particularly the fact that respondent itself procured the proceeds of the note in Philadelphia and forwarded them to the borrower in New York, as ground for the inference by the jury that the real transaction was a loan of money thinly disguised as a loan or a sale of credit....

... in the view we take, we think it immaterial whether the contract was entered into in New York or Pennsylvania, and it may be assumed for the purposes of our decision that the jury might have found that in fact the parties stipulated for a loan of money rather than of credit.... as we said in Andrews v. Pond, 13 Pet. 65, 77–78, "The general principle in relation to contracts made in one place, to be executed in another, is well settled. They are to be governed by the law of the place of performance, and if the interest allowed by the laws of the place of performance, is higher than that permitted at the place of contract, the parties may stipulate for the higher interest, without incurring the penalties of usury." ...

In support of a policy of upholding contractual obligations assumed in good faith, this Court has adopted the converse of the rule quoted from Andrews v. Pond, supra. "If the rate of interest be higher at the place of contract than at the place of performance, the parties may lawfully contract in that case also for the higher rate." [Citing cases.]

A qualification of these rules, as sometimes stated, is that the parties must act in good faith, and that the form of the transaction must not "disguise its real character." ... As thus stated, the qualification, if taken too literally, would destroy the rules themselves for they obviously are to be invoked only to save the contract from the operation of the usury laws of the one jurisdiction or the other. The effect of the qualification is merely to prevent the evasion or avoidance at will of the usury law otherwise applicable, by the parties' entering into the contract or stipulating for its performance at a place which has no normal relation to the transaction and to whose law they would not otherwise be subject. Wharton, in his Conflict of Laws, Section 510o, in discussing this qualification says: "Assuming that their real, bona fide intention was to fix the situs of the contract at a certain place which has a natural and vital connection with the transaction, the fact that they were actuated in so doing by an intention to obtain a higher rate of interest than is allowable by the situs of some of the other elements of the transaction does not prevent the application of the law allowing the higher rate." ...

Here respondent, organized and conducting its business in Pennsylvania, was subject to laws of that state and had a legitimate interest in seeking their benefit. The loan contract which stipulated for repayment there and which thus chose that law as governing its validity cannot be condemned as an evasion of the law of New York which might otherwise be deemed applicable....

Judgment affirmed.

RESTATEMENT, SECOND, CONFLICT OF LAWS: *

§ 203. Usury

The validity of a contract will be sustained against the charge of usury if it provides for a rate of interest that is permissible in a state to which the contract has a substantial relationship and is not greatly in excess of the rate permitted by the general usury law of the state of the otherwise applicable law under the rule of § 188.

Kinney Loan & Finance Co. v. Sumner

Supreme Court of Nebraska, 1954.
159 Neb. 57, 65 N.W.2d 240.

[Action by a Colorado corporation against a resident of Nebraska to replevy a trailer coach. The trial court sustained a general demurrer to plaintiff's petition and entered judgment for the defendant. The plaintiff appealed.

The petition alleged that plaintiff was authorized to do business by the State of Colorado under its small loan laws which, as the petition stated, were similar in principle to the regulatory small loan laws of Nebraska. The defendant, being indebted to the plaintiff, executed and delivered in Colorado his installment promissory note for $2,712 with interest at 2% per month on unpaid balances in conformity with the laws of Colorado. On the same day the defendant executed and delivered to the plaintiff in Colorado a chattel mortgage on the trailer coach then in Nebraska, as security for payment of the note. The chattel mortgage was filed with the appropriate recording official in Nebraska and the chattel mortgage lien was entered on the certificate of title to the trailer. The defendant paid nothing on the note. So the plaintiff, as provided in the note, and mortgage, declared the whole amount due, and brought this action for the trailer.]

■ CHAPPELL, JUSTICE. ... Assuming as we must upon demurrer, that such note and mortgage were not usurious under the laws of Colorado where they were made and to be performed, and that they were valid under the laws of that state, the sole question presented here for determination is whether or not they are enforceable in this state simply because they both reserved a rate of interest higher than that permitted by law in this state. The trial court concluded that they were not, but we conclude otherwise.

. . .

... Provisions relating to "installment loans" now appear as sections 45–114 to 45–158, R.R.S.1943. Such 1943 act included section 9, page 375, now section 45–158, R.R.S.1943, which provides: "No loan, made outside this state, in the amount or of the value of one thousand dollars or less, for which a greater rate of interest, consideration or charges than is permitted

---

* Quoted with the permission of the copyright owner, The American Law Institute.

by section 45–138 has been charged, contracted for or received, shall be enforced in this state and every person, in anywise participating therein in this state, shall be subject to the provisions of this act; Provided, that the foregoing shall not apply to loans legally made in any state under and in accordance with a regulatory small loan law similar in principle to this act."

. . .

[The court reviewed the Nebraska and Colorado statutes applicable to small loans. The applicable Nebraska statute fixes the maximum interest rate at 9% per annum on loans exceeding $1,000.]

To meticulously compare each section of such Colorado statutes under which the loan here involved was made with our own relating to installment loans would serve no useful purpose and unduly prolong this opinion. It is sufficient for us to say that they are not identical, but they are "similar in principle" with our own act within the meaning of section 45–158, R.R.S.1943.

. . .

... By use of the phrase "a regulatory small loan law similar in principle to this act" in section 45–158, R.R.S.1943, our Legislature clearly did not mean "identical" or "precisely like," or the statute would be of little use. It meant a regulatory small loan law resembling our own installment loan act in origin, purpose, and result, which licenses, controls, and regulates those engaged in lending money at conventional higher rates of interest in order to combat the reservation of extortionate and oppressive rates.

. . .

In the light of the foregoing rules and circumstances presented in this case, we conclude that the loan here involved came within the purview of the proviso and that, unless there are other defenses thereto, which are not an issue here, the public policy of this state permits its enforcement in this state. . . .

Reversed and remanded.

NOTE

In London Finance Co. v. Shattuck, 221 N.Y. 702, 117 N.E. 1075 (1917), the defendant, a resident of New York, executed at the office of the Star Finance Company in New York an application for a loan of twenty-five dollars addressed to the plaintiff in Massachusetts, a promissory note bearing interest at the rate of three per cent per month, and a confession of judgment. Shortly thereafter, the defendant received a check from the plaintiff, mailed in Massachusetts. On nonpayment judgment by confession was entered in New York for $43.70. The Special Term vacated the judgment because "it was apparent the contract was made in the state of New York and that the claim that it had been made in the state of

Massachusetts was a mere subterfuge for the purpose of evading the usury laws of the state of New York." On appeal, held, affirmed.

REVIEW BY RHEINSTEIN OF FALCONBRIDGE, ESSAYS ON THE CONFLICT OF LAWS (1947), in 15 U.Chi.L.Rev. 478, 485–487 (1948).

... [T]here cannot be found any reason why a state, through its legislature or its courts, should not lay down the following rule: Whenever parties to a situation which is alleged by one to have given rise to a legally enforceable contract, have in some ascertainable way expressed the opinion that disputes which may later arise out of that relation shall be decided under the legal system of some particular state or country, such law shall be resorted to whenever such a dispute actually arises.... If a state adopts that rule, then the law thus determined by the parties is the proper law of the contract and it is inconsistent to say that, by their understanding, they cannot exempt their contract from the prohibitive or restrictive provisions of the proper law. The law to whose prohibitive, restrictive, and other provisions the alleged contract is subject is the law referred to by the parties, just because it is the proper law and it is the proper law simply because the choice of law rule of the forum declares it to be such.

... If we agree that it is one of the very basic policies of the conflict of laws to prevent the application of a legal system of which the parties could not have thought, or, to express the same idea in a positive way, if we regard it as one of the principal purposes of the conflict of laws to protect the justified expectations of the parties, then the intention of the parties rule is the one which fulfills that purpose better than any rival rule....

... [O]pposition to the intention of the parties rule has been motivated by the fear that the rule might too easily lend itself to evasion of the law. But which law is it that the opponents fear might be evaded? All the prohibitive and restrictive provisions of the law chosen by the parties apply.... There are also applicable all those prohibitive and restrictive rules of ... the forum ... which are regarded ... as sufficiently important to merit classification as rules of public policy. If a state thinks that a contract should not be enforced because it was made in contravention of an important prohibition of the place where the agreement was made ... it can perfectly well do so by an appropriate exception to the general intention of the parties rule.... Whether we should ... [limit] the parties' choice to those laws with which their transaction has some factual connection is not a question of logic but of legal policy.... The choice of some unknown law may have been imposed upon one party to the transaction by the other, especially where the latter is occupying an economically or otherwise dominant position. That danger may be guarded against however, by the application of rules against duress, undue influence, or similar abuses.... There also remains the practical difficulty with which the court may be faced when it is asked to ascertain and interpret some foreign, conceivably exotic, law. This effort should not be asked of the court unless there are some good, objective reasons. It ought to be considered, however, that ... [if] parties to a transaction stipulate some law other than that of their respective places of business or domicile, they will hardly do so without cause.

NOTES

1. For a discussion of contractual autonomy, see Gruson, Governing Law Clauses in Commercial Agreements—New York's Approach, 18 Colum.J.Transnat'l L. 323 (1980); Prebble, Choice of Law to Determine the Validity and Effect of Contracts: A Comparison of English and American Approaches to the Conflict of Laws, 58 Cornell L.Rev. 433, 491–536 (1973); Johnston, Party Autonomy in Contracts Specifying Foreign Law, 7 Wm. & Mary L.Rev. 37 (1966).

2. Trautman, Some Notes on the Theory of Choice of Law Clauses, 35 Mercer L.Rev. 535 (1984).

Siegelman v. Cunard White Star, Limited

United States Court of Appeals, Second Circuit, 1955.
221 F.2d 189.

[This is an action by the husband of a dead woman, brought in his own right and as administrator of her estate, against a British steamship company to recover for injuries suffered by her during a trip on one of the defendant's vessels.

On September 9, 1949, an agent of the defendant company sold to the husband and wife in New York a "Contract Ticket" for a voyage from New York to Cherbourg. The printed ticket was a document about a foot long and almost as wide and on its back it contained extensive notices to passengers. On the front there was conspicuously printed a notice directing attention to the ticket's "terms and conditions". Three of its provisions were:

"10. ... No suit, action, or proceeding against the Company or the ship, or the Agents of either, shall be maintainable for loss of life of or bodily injury to any passenger unless ... (b) ... the suit, action or proceeding is commenced within one year from the day when the death or injury occurred.

"11. The price of passage hereunder has been fixed partly with reference to the liability assumed by the Company as defined by this contract, and no agreement, alteration or amendment creating any other or different liability shall be valid unless made in writing and signed for the Company by its Chief Agent at the port of embarkation.

"20. All questions arising on this contract ticket shall be decided according to English Law with reference to which this contract is made."

The injuries in question were suffered on the vessel on the high seas, September 24, 1949. On August 31, 1950, the defendant made an offer of $800 in settlement. Her lawyer, noticing the requirement of suit within a year, asked Swaine, a claim agent of the defendant, whether it would be necessary to begin suit to protect his client's rights. Swaine replied, so it is testified, that suit was not necessary and there was no point in commencing it, as it appeared the chance of settlement was excellent.

Later the injured woman died. On January 4, 1951, the defendant withdrew its offer, stating it could be tendered only to the injured party. On June 7, 1951, the plaintiff was appointed administrator of his wife's estate. On December 14, 1951, the present action was begun in a New York state court. It was removed on diversity grounds to the federal district court.

As one defense, the defendant relied on the failure of the plaintiff to bring the action within a year of the date of the injury. The district court sustained the defense and dismissed the complaint, and the plaintiff appeals.]

■ Before CLARK, CHIEF JUDGE, and FRANK and HARLAN, CIRCUIT JUDGES.

■ HARLAN, CIRCUIT JUDGE. ... Before reaching the merits of the plaintiff's claim, we must deal with a number of preliminary questions: (1) Are federal or state choice-of-laws rules to be applied here? (2) What is the applicable choice-of-law rule of the proper authority? (3) If the applicable choice-of-law rule points to the use of English law, what difference is made by the facts that English law was not pleaded or proved below, and that the plaintiff made no attempt to supply affidavits of experts on English law, after the trial Judge had offered him an opportunity to do so?

I

This case involves a claim based on a tort, committed on the high seas, and a defense based on a contract made in New York, to be performed there, on the high seas, and abroad. Our first question, though, is not what law governs the issues involved, but rather what law, federal or New York, controls the choice of the governing law. This is not a question of choice of laws, properly speaking, but rather a question of the division of competence between federal and state authority.

[The court held that since the federal judicial power extends under the Constitution "to all Cases of admiralty and maritime Jurisdiction", and Federal statutes have implemented this power, the doctrine of Erie R.R. Co. v. Tompkins, p. 665, infra, and Klaxon v. Stentor, p. 688, infra, did not apply and the federal court sitting in New York would not have to use New York conflict of laws rules.]

... Instead, ... the federal choice-of-law rule might well be binding on the state courts, if either rule is to be binding in both sets of courts....

II

Our next question is: under the federal choice-of-law rule, what law governs the issues here? We are not concerned with the law applicable to the accident. Instead we must decide what law applies to the validity and interpretation of certain provisions of the "Contract Ticket," and to the effect of Swaine's conduct upon Cunard's right to resort to the one-year limitation period in the contract.

The ticket stipulated that "All questions arising on this contract ticket shall be decided according to English Law with reference to which this contract is made." Considering, as we do, the ticket to be a contract—see Foster v. Cunard White Star, 2 Cir. 1941, 121 F.2d 12—the provision that English law should govern must be taken to represent the intention of both parties. Therefore, this provision, if effective under the federal choice-of-law rule, renders English law applicable here, even though, absent the provision, some other law would govern under the applicable federal conflicts rule....

... [S]ince we cannot assume that the parties' choice of law will always foreclose the court from applying another law, our question is whether the contract provision here should have the effect, under federal conflicts rules, of making the English law applicable to the particular questions posed by this case. While this question may appear on the surface to be purely one of conflict of laws, we think it also involves interpretation of the contract. For it is not altogether free from doubt what is meant by the stipulation that "All questions arising on this contract ticket shall be decided according to English Law...." See 40 Col.L.Rev. 518, 522–23 (1940), criticizing one interpretation of a similar provision.

Our issue, then, involves two lines of inquiry: (1) What questions did the parties intend to be controlled by English law? and (2) Will the federal conflicts rule give effect to their intention? In pursuing the first inquiry, we must examine more closely the provision of the ticket quoted above.

Three questions as to the scope of this provision arise under its language. *First,* are questions to be decided by the "whole" English law, including its conflicts rules, or just by the substantive English law? That is, are questions to be decided according to the law of England, or instead, as an English court might decide them, applying where appropriate the law of some other country? We think the provision must be read as referring to the substantive law alone, for surely the major purpose of including the provision in the ticket was to assure Cunard of a uniform result in any litigation no matter where the ticket was issued or where the litigation arose, and this result might not obtain if the "whole" law of England were referred to. *Second,* does the provision intend that questions of validity of the contract and its provisions, as well as questions of interpretation, are to be governed by English law? The language of the clause, covering "all questions," indicates that validity as well as interpretation is embraced. *Third,* is the recital meant to require the application of English law to the question of what conduct may amount to a waiver of its provisions? Although the wording of the clause—relating to questions arising "on" the contract—may indicate that such a question was not meant to be covered, it appears unnatural to hold that all questions of validity and interpretation were intended to be governed by English law but that this question was not. We therefore consider that the question of what conduct was sufficient to operate as a waiver of the ticket's provisions was also meant to be determined by English law.

We now come to the inquiry as to the extent to which this provision, so construed, is to be given effect in deciding the particular issues before us. Those issues are: (1) Is the one-year limitation period provided in the contract for the bringing of suits valid? (2) Does Swaine's conduct prevent Cunard from using the period as a defense? and (3) How is this matter affected by the clause requiring alterations of the contract to be in writing? It appears not to be contested that the ticket should be treated as a contract and that failure to bring the action within the contract limitation period would be a defense under English law—see Jones v. Oceanic Steam Navigation Co., [1924] 2 K.B. 730, but since the same result would follow under American law—see 46 U.S.C.A. § 183(b); Scheibel v. Agwilines, Inc., 2 Cir. 1946, 156 F.2d 636—we need not decide whether English law is applicable to the first of these issues. As to the second and third issues—where English and American law may differ—in the view which we take of the case, we need really only deal with applicability of English law to the second issue—viz., whether Swaine's conduct prevents Cunard from using the one-year limitations provision as a defense—although in light of what we say below we think that English law would clearly control the third issue—viz., the effect of the "alterations" clause.

As we have said, we construe the contract as establishing the intention of the parties that English law should govern both the interpretation and validity of its terms. And we think it clear that the federal conflicts rule will give effect to the parties' intention that English law is to be applied to the *interpretation* of the contract. Stipulating the governing law for this purpose is much like stipulating that words of the contract have the meanings given in a particular dictionary. See Cheatham, Goodrich, Griswold & Reese, Cases on Conflict of Laws 461 (1951). On the other hand, there is much doubt that parties can stipulate the law by which the *validity* of their contract is to be judged. Beale, Conflict of Laws, § 332.2 (1935). To permit parties to stipulate the law which should govern the validity of their agreement would afford them an artificial device for avoiding the policies of the state which would otherwise regulate the permissibility of their agreement. It may also be said that to give effect to the parties' stipulation would permit them to do a legislative act, for they rather than the governing law would be making their agreement into an enforceable obligation. And it may be further argued that since courts have not always been ready to give effect to the parties' stipulation, no real uniformity is achieved by following their wishes. See Beale, op. cit. supra, at page 1085.

Here, of course, the question is neither one of interpretation nor one of validity, but instead involves the circumstances under which parties may be said to have partially rescinded their agreements or to be barred from enforcing them. The question is, however, more closely akin to a question of validity.... Instead of viewing the parties as usurping the legislative function, it seems more realistic to regard them as relieving the courts of the problem of resolving a question of conflict of laws. Their course might be expected to reduce litigation, and is to be commended as much as good draftsmanship which relieves courts of problems of resolving ambiguities. To say that there may be no reduction in litigation because courts may not honor the provision is to reason backwards. A tendency toward certainty in commercial transactions should be encouraged by the courts. Furthermore, in England, where much if the litigation on these contracts might be expected to arise, the parties' stipulation would probably be respected. Vita Food Products, Inc. v. Unus Shipping Co., Ltd., [1939] A.C. 277 (P.C.) (similar provision in bill of lading given effect; construed, however, as referring to England's whole law, including its conflicts rules).

Where the law of the parties' intention has been permitted to govern the validity of contracts, it has often been said (1) that the choice of law must be *bona fide,* and (2) that the law chosen must be that of a jurisdiction having some relation to the agreement, generally either the place of making or the place of performance. The second of these conditions is obviously satisfied here. The fact that a conflicts question is presented in the absence of a stipulation is some indication that the first condition is also satisfied. Furthermore, there does not appear to be an attempt here to evade American policy....

This is not to suggest that English and American policies on this subject are identical. Any difference in law reflects some difference in policy. Consequently, to the extent English and American policies may differ on this question, we would consider that the parties may choose to have the English policies apply. But we express no opinion on what result would follow if we had stronger policies at stake, or if the parties had attempted a feigned rather than a genuine solution of the conflicts problem.

III

We must next decide whether it is within our competence to apply English law, which was neither pleaded nor proved below.

Pleading the foreign law was clearly unnecessary. The Federal Rules of Civil Procedure, 28 U.S.C.A., apply here....

Rule 43(a) of the Federal Rules of Civil Procedure permits the presentation of evidence according to the most convenient method prescribed in (1) the statutes of the United States, (2) the rules of evidence formerly applied in suits in equity by federal courts, or (3) the rules of evidence applied in the courts of general jurisdiction of the state in which the federal court is held....

The District Judge in this case appears to have exercised both his options under the New York law. He took notice of the English law and stated what he believed it to be. He also offered the parties an opportunity to submit affidavits of experts on English law, if it was thought that his understanding was incorrect. So far as appears, no affidavits were submitted....

Finally we come to the substantive question whether Swaine's conduct prevents Cunard from successfully invoking the contractual limitation period as a defense.

[The court found Cunard could invoke the contractual time limitation.]

Affirmed.

■ FRANK, CIRCUIT JUDGE (dissenting)....

Disregarding for the moment clause 20 of the ticket (referring to "English law"), I think it clear that, under federal and New York decisions, the defendant waived (or is estopped to assert) the one-year provision (clause 10) and thereby completely abandoned it.

... My colleagues, in holding that there was no waiver or estoppel, rely principally ... on clause 20 which reads: "All questions arising on this contract ticket shall be decided according to English Law with reference to which this contract is made."

I think this clause does not import "English law" concerning a waiver after the injury occurred. For, at best, as my colleagues apparently concede, the words "*on* this contract" are ambiguous, i.e., do not (to say the least) unambiguously cover the post-injury conduct, in New York, of defendant's claim agent.

Because the contract was made in New York, for a journey beginning in New York, the usual rule is that its provisions must be interpreted according to New York "law," or by the "maritime law" which, as previously noted, must (absent decisions on the subject) be learned from federal "law" as to internal transactions. What, then, of a provision, clause 20, which ambiguously refers to "English law"? Surely, in interpreting that ambiguous provision, we should not look to English decisions. Thus to consult "English law," in interpreting an American contract ambiguously referring to "English law," would indeed be a pulling-yourself-up-by-your-own-bootstraps device. Especially is this true here, since the interpretation of a clause in a contract like this involves an important internal public policy. For, since the document was a fixed printed form prepared by defendant and tendered to the passenger, clause 20, under New York and federal decisions, must be construed most strongly against defendant....

... Although I think the foregoing sufficient to render "English law" inapplicable to the issue before us, the following factors are also pertinent:

... Consider a suit brought in this country on a contract made in England to be performed in England, and where a breach of the contract happened in England. Under the usual "conflict" rule, English "law" would be ordinarily decisive as to the interpretation of the contract. That "law" would not govern, I think, with reference to acts, in New York, asserted to be a discharge—by way of release, rescission, accord and satisfaction, or an account stated; see Restatement of Conflict of Laws, Section 373, Comments a and b. Accordingly, I think "American law" governs the legal effect, as a waiver, of the New York conduct of defendant after the injury occurred.

[Judge Frank indicated his belief that clause 20 referred "to 'English law' as a 'whole' " and not to English local law.]

... I call attention to another factor which, while unnecessary to my conclusion, I think supports it: The ticket is what has been called a "contract of adhesion" or a "take-it-or-leave-it" contract. In such a standardized or mass-production agreement, with one-sided control of its terms, when the one party has no real bargaining power, the usual contract rules, based on the idea of "freedom of contract," cannot be applied rationally.... The commentators on "adhesion" contracts do not at all suggest that all standardized contracts be stricken down, for they recognize that such contracts often serve a highly useful purpose where the parties are not markedly unequal in bargaining power (as in many "commercial" contracts).

An ordinary contract has been called a sort of private statute, mutually made by the parties and governing their relations. But in a take-it-or-leave-it contract, absent actual freedom to contract, the parties do not "legislate" by mutual agreement; the dominant party "legislates" for both....

All this has special pertinence here: A party, like the passenger here, having no real choice about the matter, cannot in fairness be said to have joined in a "choice of law" merely because the carrier has inserted a provision that some particular foreign "law" shall govern; therefore it would seem that that party should not be bound by such a provision. I shall not elaborate this point, since it is amply discussed in a recent excellent article, Ehrenzweig, "Adhesion Contracts in The Conflict of Laws," 53 Col.L.Rev. (1953) 1072, where most of the authorities are cited and considered.

... I grant that, in this context, I am stressing the need to do justice in particular instances. I do so unashamedly. For it is generally agreed that the decisions of conflict-of-laws cases by mechanized rules, without regard to particularized justice, cannot be defended on the ground that they have promoted certainty and uniformity, since such results have not been thus achieved. Several wise commentators have urged that the element of justice should have a dominating influence.

NOTES

1. Does Judge Frank have the better of the argument? What about his point that New York law should determine the effect of the alleged discharge, agreed to in New York, of the one-year limitation? Cf. Restatement, Second, Conflict of Laws § 212.

2. The English view is that a contractual provision calling for arbitration in England provides a strong, but not conclusive, indication that the parties intended to have English law govern their contract. This is so even though neither the parties nor the transaction had any other contact with England. Compagnie Tunisienne de Navigation S.A. v. Compagnie d'Armement Maritime S.A., [1971]

A.C. 572; 1 Dicey and Morris, The Conflict of Laws 577–578 (12th ed. by Collins, 1993).

3. A steamship ticket in the English language was issued in Germany to the German plaintiff and called for application of "United States" law. The court, ruling on the defense that the claim was time barred under United States law, declared that "unilaterally imposed provisions of this nature should not be enforced unless the party urging enforcement provided the other, illiterate in the language of the contract, with knowledge of what was intended." Fricke v. Isbrandtsen Co., 151 F.Supp. 465, 468 (S.D.N.Y.1957).

4. A provision that the contract in question was made "under the law of Indiana", was held not to carry the meaning that the validity and interpretation of the contract should be governed by Indiana law. McCabe v. Great Pacific Century, 222 N.J.Super. 397, 537 A.2d 303 (A.D.1988).

(c) Real Property

For issues involving interests in real property, once again a monolithic choice-of-law rule emerges—apply the law of the situs. In his typically colorful fashion, Judge Henry Lamm expressed the almost mystical acceptance of this rule: "It follows that the right to redemption as of course under a foreclosure sale is a rule of property in the State of Iowa. It has no extra-territorial force, but dies at the State boundary, as the trees about Troy, under the mandate of the gods, grew no higher than the walls." Hughes v. Winkleman, 243 Mo. 81, 147 S.W. 994, 996 (1912). Moreover, the situs rule for real estate is the territorial rule that has proven most resistant to change.

Sinclair v. Sinclair
Supreme Court of New Hampshire, 1954.
99 N.H. 316, 109 A.2d 851.

Probate Appeal in the estate of Epps E. Sinclair brought by the appellant, brother of the decedent against the appellee, widow of the decedent. The following reserved case was transferred by Griffith, J.:

"The appeal is from a decree of the Judge of Probate for the County of Merrimack dated January 7, 1954, setting off and assigning to the widow $10,000 in value of the real estate of the deceased located in Concord, New Hampshire and one-half in value of the remainder thereof and appointing a committee of three persons pursuant to Chapter 361, Revised Laws, to make a division thereof.

"Epps E. Sinclair died domiciled in Rutland, Vermont on September 6, 1951, leaving no surviving issue. He was survived by his widow, the appellee and by his brother the appellant, who are the sole persons who appear to be interested in his estate. His widow, Edith M. Sinclair, was duly appointed administratrix of his estate by decree of the Probate Court for the District of Rutland, Vermont, dated September 17, 1951. His brother, Quincy V. Sinclair was duly appointed Administrator of his estate in New Hampshire by decree of the Probate Court for Merrimack County, dated October 19, 1951.

"At the time of his death, the deceased owned certain real estate in Concord, New Hampshire, consisting of two tenement properties in Concord proper and an undivided one-half interest in a summer cottage on the Contoocook River.

"The appellee, Edith M. Sinclair, duly filed in the Registry of Probate for Merrimack County, her waiver of dower and homestead and claim of her distributive share in the decedent's real estate in the value of $10,000 outright and one half in value in excess of said sum, remaining after the payment of debts and expenses of administration. This waiver was filed and recorded seasonably within one year after the decease of the decedent.

"By his probate appeal, the appellant has placed in issue the question whether the amount of real estate to be awarded to the appellee as widow is governed by the law of the State of Vermont or the law of the State of New Hampshire.

"It appearing that justice requires the determination of a certain question of law in advance of further proceedings, the following question of law is reserved and transferred without ruling:

"Should the law of New Hampshire or the law of Vermont be applied in determining what share of the real estate of the decedent situated in Concord, New Hampshire is to be awarded to the widow, Edith M. Sinclair?"

■ KENISON, CHIEF JUSTICE. It is a rule of general application that the descent of real property is governed by the law of the state where the property is located. Since the law of the situs controls, the domicile of the intestate is unimportant. This rule finds specific application in determining the rights of a widow in the real estate of her intestate husband. "The existence and extent of a common law or statutory interest of a surviving spouse in the land of a deceased spouse are determined by the law of the state where the land is." Restatement, Conflict of Laws, § 248(1). While it has been said that there are logical reasons and policy arguments for a different rule, the great weight of authority supports the views of the Restatement.

The widow by proceeding to assert her rights in the ancillary administration in New Hampshire, obtains a larger share of the value of the real estate than she would in the domiciliary administration in Vermont. This fact is immaterial in deciding whether the governing law is in New Hampshire or Vermont. The law of the situs of the real estate has been applied in determining the procedure and time limitations that a widow must conform with in order to claim dower or its statutory equivalent in the real estate of her deceased husband. Although there is limited authority on the point, the cases generally hold that in computing the value or interest due the surviving spouse the value of the real property of the decedent in other states is not to be taken into consideration. This is based on the proposition that only the state where the land is determines the method, extent and amount of succession thereto.

While an estate is a single thing for practical purposes and its unitary character should be emphasized for the convenient administration of estates at the domicile, there are persuasive reasons why the law of the domicile has not been applied to determine rights in real estate. "Any supposed desirability or convenience in the administration of estates arising from this would certainly be counterbalanced by the inconvenience of searching title and the impossibility of determining the validity of title if such foreign judgments are considered as directly affecting the title to land * * *. The domicil theory would make difficult, even impossible, the tracing of title to land." Stimson, Conflict of Laws and the Administration of Decedents' Real Estate, 6 Vanderbilt L.Rev. 545, 548 (1953).

Accordingly we conclude that the appellee's share in the real estate of the decedent is determined by the law of New Hampshire.

Remanded. All concurred.

NOTES

1. What are the "logical reasons and policy arguments for a different rule," referred to by the court? For testate and intestate succession of both personalty and realty, The Convention on the Law Applicable to Succession to the Estates of Deceased Persons, promulgated under the auspices of the Hague Conference on Private International Law on October 20, 1988, refers to the country in which the decedent was "habitually resident" at death, with alternative references under some circumstances to the law of the decedent's nationality. A survey of countries that are members of the Conference revealed that most civil law jurisdictions applied the same law to both personal and real property (unity principle) for testate and intestate succession. Most applied the law of the decedent's nationality, but some applied the law of the decedent's domicile at death. Droz, Commentary on the Questionnaire on Succession in Private International Law, and Van Loon, Update of the Commentary, in Proceedings of the Sixteenth Session of the Hague Conference on Private International Law.

2. Is it true, as stated in the quotation at the end of the opinion, that applying the law of the decedent's domicile to determine intestate succession to land in another state "would make difficult, even impossible, the tracing of title to land"? What if innocent third parties would be unfairly surprised if this were done in the principal case? If there are none and the law of Vermont is applied to determine interests in the New Hampshire land, can this be recorded in the New Hampshire land records?

Toledo Society for Crippled Children v. Hickok

Supreme Court of Texas, 1953.
152 Tex. 578, 261 S.W.2d 692.

[Mr. Hickok died domiciled in Ohio survived by a wife and two children, also Ohio domiciliaries. In a will that he executed within one year of his death, he established a trust, the income to be paid to his widow and two adult children for twenty years and then the corpus to be divided among twenty charities. The charities asserted their rights under the will to certain land and mineral interests in Texas. Some of the land and mineral interests were owned by Mr. Hickok individually at his death, but the most valuable interest were owned by a partnership of which he was a member. Before his death, Mr. Hickok had contracted with his partner to form a corporation and to convey the partnership assets to the corporation in exchange for stock. His will incorporated this contract by reference and directed compliance with it. By the time of trial in the Texas probate proceedings, his executors had carried out Mr. Hickok's instructions and all of this interest in the partnership had been conveyed to the corporation in exchange for stock. As to the land and mineral interest that Mr. Hickok owned individually at his death, the trustees of the testamentary trust were given the power, but not directed, to sell any assets and reinvest the proceeds.]

■ GARWOOD, JUSTICE. Our petitioners—sundry charitable, religious and similar enterprises, including the Toledo Society for Crippled Children—seek in this suit against the respondents, who are the two children, widow, executors and trustees of the late Arthur S. Hickok, an Ohio resident, to establish their rights specified in Mr. Hickok's will, but only to the extent of certain lands, and mineral estates in land, located in Texas. All of the parties to the suit appear to reside in Ohio or have their corporate offices there. The facts are without substantial dispute. The sole obstacle to the enjoyment by the petitioners of the benefits conferred by the will is that the latter was executed less than a year before the testator died leaving issue surviving. Under such circumstances, an Ohio statute (which has no counterpart in our law) declares testamentary gifts to enterprises such as the petitioners to be invalid. In previous litigation between the same parties, the Ohio courts have in general terms adjudged the statute to be applicable. In the instant suit, the District Court of Eastland County, on motion for summary judgment, held the gifts valid in respect of part of the Texas property in question and invalid as to the rest. The Eastland Court of Civil Appeals reformed that judgment so as to deny the petitioners any relief whatever—stating that their interest was contingent rather than vested. We granted writ of error upon rehearing of the petition therefor. . . .

It is perhaps appropriate to observe at this point that, minerals in land or "in place" being, by our local law, land, we are admittedly well within our rights in characterizing the mineral estates here in question as Texas land for purposes of the Conflict of Laws as well as for purely domestic purposes. . . .

Assuming, for purposes of discussion, that we are dealing with the simple case of an Ohioan, who dies seized of Texas lands free of any obligation to sell, and whose will makes an ordinary devise of a remainder in such lands to beneficiaries such as the Toledo Society for Crippled Children, it is not disputed or disputable that under proper principles of the Conflict of Laws the validity of the devise is to be determined by reference to Texas law (which permits it) and not by the domiciliary statute (which forbids it). Nor would the above conclusion be varied by the bare fact that the devise runs to a trustee rather than to the beneficiary direct....

In the [Ohio] probate court, the executors and trustees did apparently make the point that there was an equitable conversion—and no doubt with the object of securing a declaration that the Ohio statute governed even as to foreign lands of the testator, but the judge, while apparently of the opinion that we would or should hold that the Ohio statute governs as the result of an equitable conversion, rather clearly indicated that the final answer lay with the Texas law and Texas courts....

The ... thesis of the respondents is that these circumstances, by the law of Texas as well as that of Ohio, present a case of equitable conversion of all the testator's estate into personalty, with the result that we must regard the will as involving only personalty. Similarly, they appear to say that the will left the petitioners no interest in the Texas property (or other specific property of any kind). Either approach, they argue, forecloses application of any law except that of the testator's domicile to the matter of validity of the trust remainder.

We will consider first the partnership property. The fact since the testator's death, it has been put into the form of corporate stock does not of itself affect the problem, because we are dealing with the validity of what the testator himself did, as judged by the applicable law which depends on what kind of property he had at his death, rather than what kind exists at the time of litigation. As to what happened before his death, it may doubtless be conceded that the will alone, without aid of the subsequent conduct of the testator himself in the organization of the corporation, shows a clear intent that his interest in the partnership should be put into the form of corporate stock at the earliest practical date after his death. The situation is thus comparable to one wherein the testator instructs his executor to trade his land for corporate stock and give the stock to the beneficiary. Or, looking at the contract between the testator and his partner, it is not unnaturally argued that this alone, and aside from the will, was enough to change into a movable or personalty that which had previously been an interest in immovables or land, as would obviously have been the case had the testator sold his interest and received, before his death, stock, cash or an unsecured promissory note in return. That, but for the contract, the testator had, through his partnership interest, an interest in land, does not seem to be contested.

Assuming the theory of equitable conversion to be relevant to the process of determining the applicable law, then, looking at the case from the standpoint of either the will itself or the contract or both, there are presented situations of the type in which our courts, for at least certain domestic law purposes, declare a conversion to have been effected. In Hardcastle v. Sibley, Tex.Civ.App., 107 S.W.2d 432 (writ of error refused) a direction in the will of Mrs. Crosby to sell land and distribute the proceeds to the beneficiary (Mrs. Wood) was held to convert the land in question into personalty so as thereafter to pass as such by the will of the beneficiary herself. (The fact that Mrs. Crosby's executors had actually sold the land after her death was said to be immaterial). The case is also authority for the point that where the testator's contract of sale of his land is virtually carried out during his lifetime, the land is treated as personalty for the purposes of the will....

There appear to be no Texas decisions on the point of whether rules of equitable conversion are to be used in determining whether the nature of the property in question is such as to invoke the law of the situs or that of the domicile. And those very few cases from other jurisdictions, which seem to consider such rules as relevant, apparently follow the same principles exemplified in our Texas decisions in deciding whether a given set of facts is one of conversion or otherwise. The Wisconsin and Michigan decisions in connection with the same will, Ford v. Ford, 70 Wis. 19, 33 N.W. 188; Id., 80 Mich. 42, 44 N.W. 1057, held that the direction to the executors to sell land situated in those states and invest the proceeds in Missouri land to be held in trust, effected a double conversion from land to money to Missouri land, with the result that the Wisconsin and Michigan rules against perpetuities, which would otherwise have invalidated the trusts as to the Wisconsin and Michigan lands of the testator, had no application. But, as to the property which the will gave no positive direction to sell, it was held that no conversion occurred. Penfield v. Tower, 1 N.D. 216, 46 N.W. 413 actually held that no conversion was effected by the terms of a testamentary trust of North Dakota land and personalty for several beneficiaries, not greatly different from that of the Hickok will, and accordingly applied the North Dakota rule against perpetuities, as against that of Pennsylvania, the testator's domicile, thus defeating the trust to the extent of the North Dakota land. But the implication is rather clear that, had the will necessarily disclosed an 'intent' for the land to be sold, the court would have applied the domiciliary law, on the conversion theory....

Contrary to the decisions, or implications thereof, last mentioned are the English and Canadian cases of Re Berchtold (1923), 1 Ch. 192, and Re Burke (1928), 1 D.L.R. 318, each of which, both in result and words, and with considerable citation of English authority, clearly refuses to base the choice between conflicting laws of the situs and domicile upon the principle of equitable conversion. In the first, English land was devised by a Hungarian in trust for the very purpose of being converted to money and thus distributed to two Hungarian beneficiaries, both of whom died intestate before the sale was made. It was held that: (a) the nature of the interests of these beneficiaries as movables or immovables should be determined by English law; (b) by that law the interests were immovables; (c) their distribution was accordingly to be made without regard to the law of the domicile of the two deceased owners and according to English law; (d) the latter requiring that such interests be distributed as personalty (although immovables) they should go to the persons who by English law would take the personalty of a deceased English intestate. Thus, although by English law, the interests in question were personalty for distribution purposes, they were yet immovables for purposes of determining whether the laws of England or those of Hungary applied. In discussing the latter question, the court said that the point of whether the interests were regarded as realty or personalty under principles of conversion or otherwise had nothing to do with the choice of which of the conflicting laws of England and Hungary should govern....

Re Burke, supra, held that where an American contracted to sell his Canadian land and then died intestate, the distribution of his estate was governed by the law of Canada, rather than the domiciliary law, to the extent of this land or its proceeds, including the money which had been actually paid after his death for one particular tract. The court not only declared the fiction of equitable conversion to be irrelevant to the choice between conflicting laws, but also rejected the suggestion that, as a result of actual conversion, the intestate died possessed of merely a chose in action for money, while the purchaser was the owner of the land, thus holding the interest of the intestate at death to be an interest in land, subject to the contract....

We are disposed to agree with the majority of the text writers, whose view appears to be also the view of the Restatement, that the fiction of equitable conversion from realty to personalty or vice versa, 'can have no place in the Conflict of Laws'. The generally stated reason seems a sound one, to wit, that this body of law is really private international law and not merely a system for operation between the common or English law states of the United States or between these and common or English law nations. Thus to use as a basis for selection of a particular law between conflicting laws a doctrine which may not even exist in some jurisdictions is obviously less desirable than a more realistic basis such as the movable or immovable character of the object in question. As argued by the petitioners, it would in some cases result in state or nation A deferring to the law of state or nation B, when the latter in a converse situation would not reciprocate. It would thus also be more likely to produce unnecessary confusion in particular instances.... If the instant case were varied so that Mr. Hickok had no land, but directed by his will that all his stocks and bonds should be forthwith converted into Texas land and the land conveyed to the petitioners, one is inclined to doubt if the Ohio courts would uphold the gift on the theory that an equitable conversion made the Texas law applicable. Or were our case one of a Texas testator, who by will directed conversion of his Texas cattle into Ohio land for the use of these Ohio petitioners, we are disposed to question that the Ohio courts would consider the gift invalid on the theory that equitable conversion made the Ohio statute applicable....

We need not, therefore, decide whether in a proper case for the domestic application of equitable conversion, the partnership mineral interests here in question would be regarded as personal property for the purposes of the will. It is enough to say that at Mr. Hickok's death he was the owner of a half interest in these minerals, subject to a contract that they should be converted into corporate stock.... And the circumstances that the will, in effect, directs the contract to be carried out, does not change the fact that, on Mr. Hickok's death, what passed for the benefit of the petitioners and others was his interest in the minerals ... If this view should impress some as legalistic in the sense of excluding the intent of the testator that his mineral interest should become corporate stock, it is hardly more of a "technical" approach than that of regarding "as done" that which was not done, in order to deprive the petitioners of the last remnant of benefits the testator obviously intended them to have, and, in effect, to enforce here a legislative policy of Ohio, which is contrary to the policy of our own Legislature....

A fortiori we conclude also that our law governs the validity of the trust remainder with respect to the Texas interests owned by Mr. Hickok individually at his death. Indeed, as to these interests, there is insufficient ground on which to claim equitable conversion....

The effect of the foregoing being to hold that as to all the above mentioned lands, and mineral interests in lands, situated in this state, the will of Arthur S. Hickok is valid and passed to the petitioners the interests in trust which it purports to pass, it follows that the judgment of the Court of Civil Appeals should be reversed and the judgment of the trial court modified so as to conform to our holding.

It is so ordered.

■ GRIFFIN, J., dissenting.

NOTES

1. The court states that applying the Ohio statute to invalidate the bequest to charities would be "contrary to the policy of our own Legislature." Would it? In the Ohio proceedings, the Supreme Court of Ohio stated that the purpose of the Ohio statute is "to prevent undue influence enhanced by the apprehension of approaching death." Kirkbride v. Hickok, 155 Ohio St. 293, 98 N.E.2d 815, 820 (1951). Was this policy applicable to the bequest of the Texas realty?

2. In Lowe v. Plainfield Trust Co., 216 A.D. 72, 215 N.Y.S. 50 (1st Dep't 1926), the law of the situs was applied to invalidate half of a bequest to charity that would have been valid under the law of the testator's domicile at death. The situs statute prohibited any person having a spouse or child from devising more than one-half of their estate to a charity.

3. If the doctrine of "equitable conversion," discussed in the principal case, were applied in the conflicts context, would the results give greater effect to the policy of the state that had to live with the long-range consequences of validating or invalidating a will? If so, should the principal case have accepted the doctrine? Hancock, Conceptual Devices for Avoiding the Land Taboo in Conflict of Laws: The Disadvantages of Disingenuousness, 20 Stan.L.Rev. 1 (1967) opposes application of the law of the situs in cases like the principal case, but states that use of the equitable conversion fiction may obscure the "real ground" for decision and mislead judges in subsequent cases. What should be the "real ground" for decision?

4. If only courts at the situs of real estate had the power to adjudicate interests in the realty, the traditional choice-of-law rule could be defended as efficient. The only possible forum would apply its own law. Can courts in other states adjudicate the interests that parties before them have in other states and are these judgments entitled to full faith and credit at the situs? See Fall v. Eastin, 215 U.S. 1 (1909), page 254, supra, and the Notes following that case.

Section 2. Escape Devices

A. Characterization

1. SUBSTANCE VS. PROCEDURE

Grant v. McAuliffe

Supreme Court of California, 1953.
41 Cal.2d 859, 264 P.2d 944, 42 A.L.R.2d 1162.

[Pullen died shortly after and as a result of the collision of two automobiles in Arizona. After his death, plaintiffs sued the California administrator of Pullen's estate for injuries sustained as a result of Pullen's alleged negligence which caused the accident. All parties were residents of California.

Under Arizona law tort actions do not survive the tortfeasor's death; under California law they do. The court below granted a motion to abate the suits on the ground that Arizona law applied and the causes of action did not survive.]

■ TRAYNOR, JUSTICE. ... the answer to the question whether the causes of action against Pullen survived and are maintainable against his estate depends on whether Arizona or California law applies. In actions on torts occurring abroad, the courts of this state determine the substantive matters inherent in the cause of action by adopting as their own the law of the place where the tortious acts occurred, unless it is contrary to the public policy of this state.... "[N]o court can enforce any law but that of its own sovereign, and, when a suitor comes to a jurisdiction foreign to the place of the tort, he can only invoke an obligation recognized by that sovereign. A foreign sovereign under civilized law imposes an obligation of its own as nearly homologous as possible to that arising in the place where the tort occurs." Learned Hand, J., in Guinness v. Miller, D.C., 291 F. 769, 770. But the forum does not adopt as its own the procedural law of the place where the tortious acts occur. It must, therefore, be determined whether survival of causes of action is procedural or substantive for conflict of laws purposes.

This question is one of first impression in this state. The precedents in other jurisdictions are conflicting.... Before his death, the injured person himself has a separate and distinct cause of action and, if it survives, the same cause of action can be enforced by the personal representative of the deceased against the tortfeasor. The survival statutes do not create a new cause of action, as do the wrongful death statutes.... They merely prevent the abatement of the cause of action of the injured person, and provide for its enforcement by or against the personal representative of the deceased. They are analogous to statutes of limitation, which are procedural for conflict of laws purposes and are governed by the domestic law of the forum....

Defendant contends, however, that the characterization of survival of causes of action as substantive or procedural is foreclosed by Cort v. Steen, 36 Cal.2d 437, 442, 224 P.2d 723, where it was held that the California survival statutes were substantive and therefore did not apply retroactively. The problem in the present proceeding, however, is not whether the survival statutes apply retroactively, but whether they are substantive or procedural for purposes of conflict of laws. " 'Substance' and 'procedure,' ... are not legal concepts of invariant content." ... and a statute or other rule of law will be characterized as substantive or procedural according to the nature of the problem for which a characterization must be made....

Defendant also contends that a distinction must be drawn between survival of causes of action and revival of actions, and that the former are substantive but the latter procedural.... The distinction urged by defendant is not a valid one.... in most "revival" statutes, substitution of a personal representative in place of a deceased party is expressly conditioned on the survival of the cause of action itself....

Since we find no compelling weight of authority for either alternative, we are free to make a choice on the merits. We have concluded that survival of causes of action should be governed by the law of the forum. Survival is not an essential part of the cause of action itself but relates to the procedures available for the enforcement of the legal claim for damages. Basically the question is one of the administration of decedents' estate, which is a purely local proceeding. The problem here is whether the causes of action that these plaintiffs had against Pullen before his death survive as liabilities of his estate.... Decedent's estate is located in this state, and letters of administration were issued to defendant by the courts of this state. The responsibilities of defendant, as administrator of Pullen's estate, for injuries inflicted by Pullen before his death are governed by the laws of this state.... Today, tort liabilities of the sort involved in these actions are regarded as compensatory. When, as in the present case, all of the parties were residents of this state, and the estate of the deceased tortfeasor is being administered in this state, plaintiffs' right to prosecute their causes of action is governed by the laws of this state relating to administration of estates....

■ SCHAUER, JUSTICE. I dissent.... [E]ven more regrettable than the failure to either follow or unequivocally overrule the cited cases ... is the character of the "rule" which is now promulgated: the majority assert that henceforth "a statute or other rule of law will be characterized as substantive or procedural according to the nature of the problem for which a characterization must be made," thus suggesting that the court will no longer be bound to consistent enforcement or uniform application of "a statute or other rule of law" but will instead apply one "rule" or another as the untrammeled whimsy of the majority may from time to time dictate, "according to the nature of the problem" as they view it in a given case.

This concept of the majority strikes deeply at what has been our proud boast that ours was a government of laws rather than of men.

Although any administration of an estate in the courts of this State is local in a procedural sense, the rights and claims both in favor of and against such an estate are substantive in nature, and vest irrevocably at the date of death....

NOTES

1. Justice Traynor said the dispositive question in the case was "whether survival of causes of action is procedural or substantive for conflict of laws purposes." Did his opinion answer the question? If so, in what words? On the basis of the materials in Chapter 7, what are the best arguments pro and con?

2. If Pullen had been a resident of Arizona instead of California and all else had been the same (with ancillary administration of the Pullen estate permitted in California), should the result have been different? What if suit had been brought in Arizona? If the plaintiffs, but not Pullen, had been Arizona residents, what result in each state? The rule as to survival of the place of injury has generally been applied in the cases, despite the steady waning of the non-survival rule. See Nelson v. Eckert, 231 Ark. 348, 329 S.W.2d 426 (1959); Allen v. Nessler, 247 Minn. 230, 76 N.W.2d 793 (1956); Tice v. E. I. DuPont de Nemours & Co., 144 W.Va. 24, 106 S.E.2d 107 (1958).

3. "It may not be amiss to add a postscript that although the opinion [Grant v. McAuliffe] is my own, I do not regard it as ideally articulated, developed as it had to be against the brooding background of a petrified forest. Yet I would make no more apology for it than that in reaching a rational result it was less deft than it might have been to quit itself of the familiar speech of choice of law." Traynor, Is This Conflict Really Necessary?, 37 Texas L.Rev. 657, 670 (1959). How could the opinion have been made more "deft"? Consider the opinion by the same judge in Bernkrant v. Fowler, p. 568, infra.

2. NATURE OF THE ACTION

Haumschild v. Continental Casualty Co.

Supreme Court of Wisconsin, 1959.
7 Wis.2d 130, 95 N.W.2d 814.

[A woman brought this action against her husband for personal injuries sustained through his negligence in a California motor accident. The couple were domiciled in Wisconsin. The trial court dismissed the action because under the local law of California the plaintiff could not recover. The plaintiff appealed.]

■ CURRIE, JUSTICE. This appeal presents a conflict of laws problem with respect to interspousal liability for tort growing out of an automobile accident. Which law controls, that of the state of the forum, the state of the place of wrong, or the state of domicile? Wisconsin is both the state of the forum and of the domicile while California is the state where the alleged wrong was committed. Under Wisconsin law a wife may sue her husband in tort. Under California law she cannot....

This court was first faced with this question in Buckeye v. Buckeye, 1931, 203 Wis. 248, 234 N.W. 342....

The principle enunciated in the Buckeye case and followed in subsequent Wisconsin cases, that the law of the place of wrong controls as to whether one spouse is immune from suit in tort by the other, is the prevailing view in the majority of jurisdictions in this country....

[The court referred to the writings of Messrs. Cook, Rheinstein, Rabel and Ford, and outlined and quoted from Emery v. Emery, 45 Cal.2d 421, 289 P.2d 218 [1955], "the first case to break the ice", and Koplik v. C.P. Trucking Corp., 27 N.J. 1, 141 A.2d 34.]

... [I]t is our considered judgment that this court should adopt the rule that, whenever the courts of this state are confronted with a conflict of laws problem as to which law governs the capacity of one spouse to sue the other in tort, the law to be applied is that of the state of domicile. We, therefore, expressly overrule ... Buckeye v. Buckeye, supra; ... the instant decision should not be interpreted as a rejection by this court of the general rule that ordinarily the substantive rights of parties to an action in tort are to be determined in the light of the law of the place of wrong. This decision merely holds that incapacity to sue because of marital status presents a question of family law rather than tort law....

... While the appellant's counsel did not request that we overrule Buckeye v. Buckeye, supra, and the subsequent Wisconsin cases dealing with this particular conflict of laws problem, he did specifically seek to have this court apply California's conflict of laws principle, that the law of the domicile is determinative of interspousal capacity to sue, to this particular case....

Wisconsin certainly should not adopt the much criticized renvoi principle in order not to overrule the Buckeye v. Buckeye line of cases, and still permit the plaintiff to recover. Such a result we believe would contribute far more to produce chaos in the field of conflict of laws than to overrule the Buckeye v. Buckeye line of cases and adopt a principle the soundness of which has been commended by so many reputable authorities.

Judgment reversed and cause remanded for further proceedings not inconsistent with this opinion.

■ FAIRCHILD, JUSTICE (concurring). I concur in the reversal of the judgment, but do not find it necessary to re-examine settled Wisconsin law in order to do so....

1. *Solution of this case without overruling previous decisions....* It has been the rule in Wisconsin that the existence or nonexistence of immunity because of family relationship is substantive and not merely procedural, and is to be determined by the law of the locus state. The law of California is that the existence or nonexistence of immunity is a substantive matter, but that it is an element of the law of status, not of

tort.... Thus it makes no difference under the facts of this case whether we look directly to the law of Wisconsin to determine that immunity is not available as a defense or look to the law of Wisconsin only because California, having no general tort principle as to immunity, classifies immunity as a matter of status....

I would dispose of the present case upon the theory that California law governs the existence of the alleged cause of action and that in California the immunity question can not be decided by resort to the law of torts but rather the law of status. I would leave to a later case the consideration of whether the Wisconsin rule of choice of law as to the defense of family immunity should remain as heretofore or, if it is to be changed, which rule will be best.

NOTES

1. It will be noted that the Haumschild case would invariably call for application of the law of the state of the couple's domicile to determine issues of interspousal immunity. Is that rule overly broad? Should a distinction be drawn between a situation where, as in the Haumschild case, there is no immunity under the law of the state of domicile but immunity under the law of the state of injury and the converse situation? What would be the rationale of such a distinction? Most of the later cases have applied the domicile's rule even in a case where there was immunity under the law of the domicile. See, e. g., Zurzola v. General Motors Corp., 503 F.2d 403 (3d Cir. 1974); Wartell v. Formusa, 34 Ill.2d 57, 213 N.E.2d 544 (1966); Balts v. Balts, 273 Minn. 419, 142 N.W.2d 66 (1966); Gordon v. Gordon, 118 N.H. 356, 387 A.2d 339 (1978); McSwain v. McSwain, 420 Pa. 86, 215 A.2d 677 (1966); but cf. Purcell v. Kapelski, 444 F.2d 380 (3d Cir. 1971).

2. In Haynie v. Hanson, 16 Wis.2d 299, 114 N.W.2d 443 (1962), the wife was injured in Wisconsin as a result of a collision between automobiles driven by her husband and by one Hanson. The wife brought suit against Hanson and he sought contribution from the husband's liability insurer. Hanson's cross-complaint was dismissed on the ground that under the law of Illinois, where the spouses were domiciled, one spouse has no capacity to sue the other spouse in tort. Haynie was in effect overruled *sub silentio* in Zelinger v. State Sand and Gravel Co., 38 Wis.2d 98, 156 N.W.2d 466 (1968), where the court applied an interests analysis.

Garza v. Greyhound Lines, Inc.

Court of Civil Appeals of Texas, San Antonio, 1967.
418 S.W.2d 595, no writ.

■ CADENA, JUSTICE. This suit was filed by plaintiff, Efrain C. Garza, a resident citizen of Texas, in a district court of Bexar County against defendant, Greyhound Lines, Inc., a Texas corporation having its home office in Houston, to recover for personal injuries sustained by him in the Republic of Mexico while he was a passenger on a bus. Plaintiff appeals from an order of the trial court sustaining defendant's plea to the "jurisdiction" and dismissing plaintiff's suit on the ground that the applicable substantive law of the place of injury is so dissimilar to the Texas law that our courts will not undertake to adjudicate the rights of the parties.

Plaintiff's petition alleged the following: In May, 1965, a contract was entered into in this State between defendant, a common carrier, and the Good Neighbor Bowling League of San Antonio, calling for transportation by defendant of members of the bowling league, including plaintiff, from San Antonio, Texas, to the City of Monterrey, Mexico, and back to San Antonio. The entire trip, including arrangements for an unnamed connecting carrier to carry plaintiff and the other bowlers from the City of Laredo, Texas, to Monterrey and back to Laredo, Texas, was planned by defendant. On June 20, 1965, plaintiff, while a passenger on a bus marked "Transportes del Norte," was injured as the result of the negligence of the driver of the bus. The place of injury and of the driver's negligence was in the Republic of Mexico, between the cities of Nuevo Laredo and Monterrey.

In the alternative, plaintiff alleged that he was a third party beneficiary of the contract between the bowling league and defendant, and that defendant breached its implied contractual obligation to carry plaintiff safely....

We ... decline plaintiff's invitation to re-examine the rule, well established in Texas as of this date, that in a tort action the law of the place of the tort, or the lex loci delicti, must be looked to in determining the substantive rights of the parties. Our reluctance is not based on a head-in-the-sand assumption that defendant, in subsequent proceedings, will abandon its insistence that our courts close their doors to plaintiff. We find nothing in the Texas decisions which may be characterized as a trend away from the lex loci rule in tort actions, or which has the effect of lessening, in any way, the precedential weight of the Texas decisions applying that rule....

Plaintiff further assigns as error the dismissal of his alternative cause of action, based on defendant's breach of its implied contractual duty to carry plaintiff safely, pointing out that, under applicable choice-of-law rules, this portion of his suit is governed by the laws of the State of Texas, the place where the contract was made. Under the holding in Hudson v. Continental Bus System, Inc., 317 S.W.2d 584 (Tex.Civ.App., 1958, writ ref'd n.r.e.), which involved facts strikingly similar to those before us, this alternative ground of recovery is governed by the law of this State, and the trial court erred in refusing to take jurisdiction thereof.

The judgment of the trial court is reversed and the cause is remanded with instructions that the case be reinstated upon the docket for further proceedings not inconsistent with this opinion.

NOTE

For a Holmes opinion dismissing an action in Texas under the "dissimilarity" doctrine discussed in the principal case, see Slater v. Mexican National R. Co., 194 U.S. 120 (1904), p. 201, supra.

LEVY v. DANIELS' U–DRIVE AUTO RENTING CO., 108 Conn. 333, 143 A. 163, 61 A.L.R. 846 (1928): Defendant, a Connecticut automobile rental agency, rented a car in that state. The Connecticut lessee's negligent driving in Massachusetts caused injury to plaintiff, his guest, who was also a Connecticut resident. Plaintiff sued under a Connecticut statute which made the lessor of a motor vehicle "liable for any damage to any person or property caused by the operation of such motor vehicle while so rented or leased." Judgment for the plaintiff was affirmed.

■ WHEELER, C.J. ... It is the defendant's contention ... that the action set forth in the complaint is one of tort and since Massachusetts has no statute like, or substantially like, the Connecticut Act it must be determined by the common law of that State, under which the plaintiff must prove, to prevail, the negligence of the defendant in renting a defective motor vehicle and in failing to disclose the defect. If this were the true theory of the complaint, the conclusion thus reached must have followed.... The plaintiff concedes the correctness of this. His counsel, however, construe the complaint as one in its nature contractual....

... The statute gives, in terms, the injured person a right of action against the defendant which rented the automobile to Sack, though the injury occurred in Massachusetts. It was a right which the statute gave directly, not derivatively, to the injured person as a consequence of the contract of hiring. The purpose of the statute was not primarily to give the injured person a right of recovery against the tortious operator of the car, but to protect the safety of traffic upon highways by providing an incentive to him who rented motor vehicles to rent them to competent and careful operators by making him liable for damage resulting from the tortious operation of the rented vehicles.... The rental of motor vehicles to any but competent and careful operators, or to persons of unknown responsibility, would be liable to result in injury to the public upon or near highways, and this imminent danger justified, as a reasonable exercise of the police power, this statute, which requires all who engage in this business to become responsible for any injury inflicted upon the public by the tortious operation of the rented motor vehicle.... The statute made the liability of the person renting motor vehicles a part of every contract of hiring of a motor vehicle in Connecticut....

If the liability of this defendant under this statute is contractual, no question can arise as to the plaintiff's right to enforce this contract, provided the obligation imposed upon this defendant was for the "direct, sole and exclusive benefit" of the plaintiff. The contract was made in Connecticut; at the instant of its making the statute made a part of the contract of hiring the liability of the defendant which the plaintiff seeks to enforce. The law inserted in the contract this provision. The statute did not create the liability; it imposed it in case the defendant voluntarily rented the automobile.... The right of the plaintiff as a beneficiary of this contract to maintain this action is no longer an open question in this State.... The contract was made for him and every other member of the public.

NOTES

1. Suppose Connecticut law had allowed the rental agency to sue the driver-lessee for indemnity and he had pleaded as a defense that under Massachusetts law he would not have been liable to his guest passenger because of a defense given by the Massachusetts guest statute. Would the defense be allowable in the Connecticut third-party action? Cf. Haynie v. Hanson, 16 Wis.2d 299, 114 N.W.2d 443 (1962), p. 497, note 2, supra.

2. As the court analyzed the problem in Levy, would it have made any difference if the plaintiff had been a Massachusetts resident? Should it make a difference?

3. For a modern echo of Levy v. Daniels' U–Drive, see Cortes v. Ryder Truck Rental, Inc., 220 Ill.App.3d 632, 163 Ill.Dec. 50, 581 N.E.2d 1 (1991), appeal dism'd, 143 Ill.2d 637, 167 Ill.Dec. 398, 587 N.E.2d 1013 (1992). The court applied the lessor liability statute of Wisconsin, where the rental agreement was executed, to hold the rental company liable for injures suffered in Indiana: "Although choice-of-law principles might indicate that ... Indiana law applied to the tort of negligence ..., Ryder's liability was not based on negligence, directly or vicariously. Ryder's liability ... arose ... through its contractual relationship as lessor." The court identified the policy underlying the statute as assuring compensation to a person injured by the rented vehicle.

B. RENVOI

American Motorists Insurance Co. v. ARTRA Group, Inc.

Court of Appeals of Maryland, 1995.
338 Md. 560, 659 A.2d 1295.

[ARTRA sold a paint manufacturing factory in Maryland to Sherwin–Williams. The Maryland Department of the Environment ordered Sherwin–Williams to investigate and remedy hazardous waste contamination at the site. Sherwin–Williams sued ARTRA to recover the costs of investigation and remediation. ARTRA was insured by American Motorists under a general liability policy. The policy excluded coverage for pollution unless the release of the pollutants "is sudden and accidental". ARTRA requested that American Motorists defend and indemnify ARTRA in the Sherwin–Williams suit. American Motorists refused and sued in the Circuit Court for Baltimore City for a determination that the policy did not cover ARTRA's liability to Sherwin–Williams. ARTRA and American Motorists were both headquartered in Illinois and the policy was countersigned on behalf of American Motorists in Illinois.

Under Maryland law, the pollution exclusion was not ambiguous and did not cover ARTRA's liability to Sherwin–Williams. Under Illinois law, the exclusion was ambiguous and the ambiguity would be construed in favor of ARTRA.

The Circuit Court applied Maryland law and granted American Motorists' motion for summary judgment. The Court of Special Appeals reversed on the grounds that under Maryland choice-of-law rules, the law of Illinois as the *lex loci contractus* governed and that it was irrelevant, as the trial court had found, that an Illinois court would apply Maryland law. The trial court's finding that an Illinois court would apply Maryland law was based on the adoption in Illinois of the "most significant relationship" approach of the Restatement (Second) of Conflict of Laws and on § 193 of the Restatement, under which the rights created by a liability insurance policy are determined by "the local law of the state which the parties understood was to be the principal location of the insured risk during the term of the policy, unless with respect to the particular issue, some other state has a more significant relationship ... to the transaction and the parties...." The Maryland Court of Appeals reversed, holding that Maryland law applied and that the trial court had properly granted summary judgment for American Motorists.]

■ CHASNOW, J. ... [F]or the purpose of this opinion we must assume that Illinois choice-of-law rules would dictate the application of Maryland law to the substantive issues in the present case [because the trial judge had so found and ARTRA did not contest this finding].

American Motorists's first suggestion is that we recognize that the rule of *lex loci contractus* is antiquated and should be abandoned in favor of some form of the more modern approaches to choice of law such as the one advocated by Restatement (Second) Conflict of Laws.... Based on our holding on the *renvoi* issue, we need not give any consideration to the intriguing question of whether Maryland's traditional *lex loci contractus* test should be abandoned in favor of one of the "modern" most significant relationship tests. American Motorists's second suggestion is that we engraft the doctrine of *renvoi* to our body of conflict of law rules. We need not determine today how far we should go in incorporating the doctrine of *renvoi,* but we do adopt a limited form of *renvoi* which will direct the application of Maryland law to resolve the substantive issues in the instant case....

It has been suggested that the doctrine of *renvoi* was formulated to avoid the harshness of the traditional common law choice-of-law principles. Rhoda S. Barish, Comment, Renvoi and the Modern Approaches to Choice-of-Law, 30 Am.U.L.Rev. 1049, 1061–62 (1981)....

A persuasive case for adopting *renvoi* is made by two law school professors in their text on conflict of laws.... "[A] mechanical use of renvoi by all concerned jurisdictions could theoretically produce the problem of circularity. In this case, however, it is suggested that the forum accept the reference to its own law, refer no further, and apply its own law. This is the practice of most jurisdictions that do employ renvoi. This is good policy: the foreign conflict rule itself discloses a disinterest to have its own substantive law applied, indeed it recognizes the significance of the forum's law for the particular case; the case therefore probably presents a 'false conflict.' Furthermore, since uniformity in result would not otherwise be achieved in these circumstances, ease in the administration of justice is furthered by the application of forum law rather than by the use of foreign law." Scoles & Hay, Conflict of Laws § 3.13, at 67–70 (2d ed. 1992)....

In the absence of some reason to apply foreign law, Maryland courts would ordinarily apply Maryland substantive law, and there is no reason to apply the substantive law of a foreign state if that foreign state recognizes that Maryland has the most significant interest in the issues and that Maryland substantive law ought to be applied to the contract issues....

The limited *renvoi* exception which we adopt today will allow Maryland courts to avoid the irony of applying the law of a foreign jurisdiction when that jurisdiction's conflict of law rules would apply Maryland law. Under this exception, Maryland courts should apply Maryland substantive law to contracts entered into in foreign states' jurisdictions in spite of the doctrine of *lex loci contractus* when:

1) Maryland has the most significant relationship, or, at least, a substantial relationship with respect to the contract issue presented; and

2) The state where the contract was entered into would not apply its own substantive law, but instead would apply Maryland substantive law to the issue before the court.

Our holding ... is not a total jettisoning of *lex loci contractus*.... *Lex loci contractus* is still the law in the majority of jurisdictions, although there is a significant modern erosion of the rule. If that erosion continues, however, this Court may, in the proper case, have to reevaluate what the best choice-of-law rules ought to be to achieve simplicity, predictability, and uniformity....

NOTES

1. Note 2(iii), p. 446, supra, states that a forum court should refer to the choice-of-law rules of another jurisdiction when "[t]he forum wishes to determine whether the other jurisdiction asserts an 'interest' in the application of the other jurisdiction's law." Is the principal case an example of this use of renvoi? Why is a forum concerned with another state's assertion of an interest if the forum has not adopted a choice-of-law approach that takes account of such interests? If a court does refer to another state's choice-of-law rule to determine that state's interest, should it do so, as in the principal case, based on an agreement by the parties as to the content of the foreign rule, or should the court make an independent determination of what law the foreign court would apply and of the reasons for that application?

2. University of Chicago v. Dater, 277 Mich. 658, 270 N.W. 175 (1936) applied Michigan law to hold that a Michigan wife lacked capacity to guarantee her husband's debt to an Illinois bank. Under Illinois law, the guarantee was valid and the Michigan choice-of-law rule pointed to Illinois as the place of making of the contract. An Illinois court, however, would apply Michigan law because on the facts of the case, an Illinois court would consider the contract "made" in Michigan. But see House v. Lefebvre, 303 Mich. 207, 6 N.W.2d 487 (1942), which determined the capacity of a wife solely with reference to the internal law of Ohio where a promissory note was delivered to the creditor.

3. For discussion of renvoi as a device for escaping from a statutory choice-of-law rule, see Note (3), p. 446, supra.

C. Public Policy

Kilberg v. Northeast Airlines, Inc.
Court of Appeals of New York, 1961.
9 N.Y.2d 34, 172 N.E.2d 526.

[Kilberg, a New York domiciliary, purchased in New York a ticket from the defendant airline, which was incorporated in Massachusetts, for transportation from New York to Nantucket, Massachusetts. The airplane crashed in Nantucket and Kilberg was killed. Both Massachusetts and New York have wrongful death statutes. The Massachusetts statute limited recovery against a common carrier to not less than $2,000 or more than $15,000 assessed with reference to the defendant's culpability. By way of contrast, the New York Constitution forbade any limitation on the amount of recovery. Kilberg's administrator brought suit in New York for the death. Two of the three causes of action pleaded in the complaint were considered on appeal. The first was a cause of action under the Massachusetts wrongful death statute; the second was a cause of action for breach of an alleged contract of safe carriage asking for $150,000 in damages. The trial court denied a motion to dismiss the second cause of action on the ground that, as it was in contract, the law of New York, the place of contracting, governed. The Appellate Division reversed and dismissed the second cause of action because, however labeled, it was in tort for negligently causing death and was subject to the Massachusetts limitation. The Court of Appeals unanimously affirmed the dismissal of the second cause of action, but a majority of the court stated that the first cause of action for wrongful death was not subject to the Massachusetts limitation of damages.]

■ DESMOND, C.J. . . . If the alleged contract breach had caused injuries not resulting in death, a New York-governed contract suit would, we will assume, be available. . . . But it is law long settled that wrongful death actions, being unknown to the common law, derive from statutes only and that the statute which governs such an action is that of the place of wrong. . . .

This does not mean, however, that for the alleged wrong plaintiff cannot possibly recover more than the $15,000 maximum specified in the Massachusetts act. Modern conditions make it unjust and anomalous to subject the traveling citizen of this State to the varying laws of other States through and over which they move. The number of States limiting death case damages has become smaller over the years but there are still 14 of them. . . . An air traveler from New York may in a flight of a few hours' duration pass through several of those commonwealths. His plane may meet with disaster in a State he never intended to cross but into which the plane has flown because of bad weather or other unexpected developments, or an airplane's catastrophic descent may begin in one State and end in another. The place of injury becomes entirely fortuitous. Our courts should if possible provide protection for our own State's people against unfair and anachronistic treatment of the lawsuits which result from these disasters....

Since both Massachusetts ... and New York ... authorize wrongful death suits against common carriers, the only controversy is as to amount of damages recoverable. New York's public policy prohibiting the imposition of limits on such damages is strong, clear and old. Since the Constitution of 1894, our basic law has been (N.Y.Const., art. I, § 16; N.Y.Const. [1894], art. I, § 18) that "The right of action now existing to recover damages for injuries resulting in death, shall never be abrogated; and the amount recoverable shall not be subject to any statutory limitation." Each later revision of the State Constitution has included this same prohibition against limitations of death action damages.... We will still require plaintiff to sue on the Massachusetts statute but we refuse on public policy grounds to enforce one of its provisions as to damages....

As to conflict of law rules it is of course settled that the law of the forum is usually in control as to procedures including remedies ... As to whether the measure of damages should be treated as a procedural or a substantive matter in wrongful death cases, there is ... no controlling New York decision.... It is open to us, therefore, particularly in view of our own strong public policy as to death action damages, to treat the measure of damages in this case as being a procedural or remedial question controlled by our own State policies....

From all of this it follows that while plaintiff's second or contract cause of action is demurrable, his first count declaring under the Massachusetts wrongful death action is not only sustainable but can be enforced, if the proof so justifies, without regard to the $15,000 limit. Plaintiff, therefore, may apply if he be so advised for leave to amend his first cause of action accordingly.... *

■ FULD, J., concurred in the decision on the second count. He felt foreclosed by earlier decisions, though if the matter were of first impression New York might be deemed the jurisdiction having "the most significant contact or contacts".

■ FROESSEL, JUDGE (concurring). We concur for affirmance of the judgment appealed from, dismissing plaintiff's second cause of action. We should reach no other question....

Plaintiff's right to maintain this action must ... stem from the provisions of the Massachusetts statute (Mass.Gen.Stat., ch. 229, § 2). That statute, however, expressly limits the extent of the right given, and declares that the damages assessed thereunder shall not be more than $15,000.... The majority, by giving extraterritorial effect to our prohibition against the limitation of recovery in such actions, would permit plaintiff to recover on the basis of the foreign law, and yet not be bound by its express limitation....

---

* Kilberg's administrator ultimately settled for less than $15,000 and did not seek leave to amend his first cause of action. Presumably, this was because he did not believe he could prove greater damages. [Footnote by the editors.]

No sound reason appears why our courts, in enforcing such a right at all, should not enforce it in its entirety....

The position adopted by the majority may result in the situation where, in a single airplane crash in which numerous passengers from various States are killed, a different law will be applied in each action resulting therefrom....

NOTES

1. In Davenport v. Webb, 11 N.Y.2d 392, 230 N.Y.S.2d 17, 183 N.E.2d 902 (1962), the court retracted the "procedural" basis of the Kilberg decision. That case involved an action for the wrongful death of persons domiciled in New York in an automobile collision in Maryland. A New York statute provided that a judgment for the plaintiff in a wrongful death action should include interest from the date of death. Maryland law did not authorize prejudgment interest. The Court of Appeals held that the New York statute could not properly be applied to provide for the inclusion of interest in the judgment, and that the Kilberg decision "must be held merely to express this State's strong public policy with respect to limitations in wrongful death actions."

2. Kilberg was followed in Pearson v. Northeast Airlines, Inc., 309 F.2d 553 (2d Cir. 1962; en banc opinion), overturning the decision of the panel, 307 F.2d 131 (1962). Erie Railroad Co. v. Tompkins, p. 665, infra, and its conflicts progeny were thought to compel the Federal court to echo the New York court's view of the wrongful death damage ceiling question, but no enthusiasm was registered for Chief Judge Desmond's sledgehammer use of the "public policy" argument. Judge Friendly's dissent from the en banc opinion is excerpted at p. 210, note 2, supra.

D. PROPERTY: EQUITABLE CONVERSION AND THE CONTRACT-CONVEYANCE DISTINCTION

The materials in section 1(B)(2)(c), supra this chapter, indicate that the traditional rule for issues affecting real property is to apply the law of the situs. Toledo Society for Crippled Children v. Hickok, 152 Tex. 578, 261 S.W.2d 692 (1953), page 487, supra, discusses and rejects one possible device for escaping from this rule—equitable conversion. This doctrine, which is rooted in the notion that the law will regard as done what ought to have been done, may be applicable if an inter vivos or testamentary document directs the sale of realty and its conversion into personalty. If the realty is regarded as "equitably converted" into personalty, then the relevant choice-of-law rule for personalty would apply. For many issues concerning decedents' estates, the reference would then be to the domicile at death, rather than the situs.

Another device for avoiding the law of the situs is the contract-realty distinction. Courts have distinguished between the contract to convey and the conveyance itself (Polson v. Stewart, 167 Mass. 211, 45 N.E. 737 (1897, Holmes, J.)), between a promissory note and the mortgage securing the note (Thompson v. Kyle, 39 Fla. 582, 23 So. 12 (1897)), and between covenants personal to the parties and those running with the land (Beauchamp v. Bertig, 90 Ark. 351, 119 S.W. 75 (1909)). The effect of these distinctions has often been to treat the second item in each set as a "land" problem to which the law of the situs applies, and the first item as a "contract" problem to be resolved by the contract choice-of-law rule—typically the law of the place of making of the contract.

SECTION 3. TRANSITION: THE SEARCH FOR NEW APPROACHES

A. EARLY GROPINGS

Schmidt v. Driscoll Hotel, Inc.

Minnesota Supreme Court, 1957.
249 Minn. 376, 82 N.W.2d 365.

■ GALLAGHER, JUSTICE. Plaintiff, Herbert G. Schmidt . . . instituted this action against the Driscoll Hotel, Inc., doing business as The Hook-Em-Cow Bar and Cafe in South St. Paul . . .

The complaint alleged that defendant illegally sold intoxicating liquors to Sorrenson to the extent of causing him to become intoxicated in defendant's establishment in South St. Paul so that shortly thereafter, as a proximate result thereof, plaintiff sustained injuries when an automobile driven by Sorrenson, in which plaintiff was a passenger, was caused to turn over near Prescott, Wisconsin.

Defendant . . . moved to dismiss the action on the ground that the pleadings failed to state a claim against the defendant . . .

On April 28, 1956, the trial court made its order granting defendant's motion . . . [on the ground] that "No penalty by way of collecting damages arose under M.S.A 340.95 [Civil Damage Act] . . . unless the illegal sale in the state was followed by an injury in the state. . . ."

This is an appeal from the judgment entered pursuant to the foregoing order.

1. . . . M.S.A. 340.95, commonly known as the Civil Damage Act, provides that: "Every *** person who is injured in person or property, *** by any intoxicated person, or by the intoxication of any person, has a right of action, in his own name, against any person who, by illegally selling, bartering or giving intoxicating liquors, caused the intoxication of such person, for all damages, sustained; ***." . . .

2. It is defendant's position that the action is governed by the law of torts and that, since the last act in the series of events for which plaintiff instituted his action occurred in Wisconsin, which has no Civil Damage Act similar to § 340.95, the latter can have no application in determining plaintiff's rights or defendant's liability. In support thereof defendant cites Restatement, Conflict of Laws, § 377, which states:

"The place of wrong is in the state where the last event necessary to make an actor liable for an alleged tort takes place."

And § 378, which states:

"The law of the place of wrong determines whether a person has sustained a legal injury."

3. ... plaintiff's damages are the result of two distinct wrongs—one committed by defendant in Minnesota when it sold Sorrenson intoxicating liquors in violation of M.S.A. 340.14, subd. 1; and one committed by Sorrenson in Wisconsin when his negligence caused the car in which plaintiff was riding to turn over. It cannot be disputed that, had plaintiff's action been against Sorrenson for his negligence, his rights would be governed by the law of Wisconsin applicable in tort actions of this kind.... But, even if at the time of the accident there had been in effect in Wisconsin a statute similar to § 340.95, it is doubtful if it could be applied to ascertain plaintiff's rights against defendant since there is nothing here to support a claim that defendant ever consented to be bound by Wisconsin law....

4. ...

5. We feel that the principles in Restatement, Conflict of Laws, §§ 377 and 378, should not be held applicable to fact situations such as the present to bring about the result described and that a determination to the opposite effect would be more in conformity with principles of equity and justice. Here all parties involved were residents of Minnesota. Defendant was licensed under its laws and required to operate its establishment in compliance therewith. Its violation of the Minnesota statutes occurred here, and its wrongful conduct was complete within Minnesota when, as a result thereof, Sorrenson became intoxicated before leaving its establishment. The consequential harm to plaintiff, a Minnesota citizen, accordingly should be compensated for under M.S.A. 340.95 which furnishes him a remedy against defendant for its wrongful acts. By this construction, no greater burden is placed upon defendant than was intended by § 340.95.

6. In arriving at this conclusion, we have in mind decisions of a number of jurisdictions which have reached similar results in situations, which, though not involving civil damage acts, presented factual circumstances comparable to those here. Gordon v. Parker, D.C.D.Mass., 83 F.Supp. 40.... [page 460, supra].

Reversed.

NOTE

Two constitutional issues arise when a retail liquor seller is located just across the boundary of a state in which an automobile driven by a customer of the seller crashes. If suit is brought against the seller where the crash occurred, can the court obtain in personam jurisdiction over the seller and can the court apply the law of the state in which it sits to impose civil liability on the seller? West American Ins. Co. v. Westin, Inc., 337 N.W.2d 676 (Minn.1983), held that under World–Wide Volkswagen Corp. v. Woodson, 444 U.S. 286 (1980), page 66, supra, jurisdiction could not be obtained over a bar across the state line. Do you agree? BLC Insurance Co. v. Westin, Inc., 359 N.W.2d 752 (Minn.App.1985), cert. denied, 474

U.S. 844 (1985), another suit against the same bar, reached a different result in the light of advertising in the forum since the prior decision.

Applying the materials in Chapter 6, supra, can the state where the drunken driver causes harm apply its law to the liquor seller to create civil liability, if the seller would not be liable under the law of the state where the liquor was sold?

Auten v. Auten

Court of Appeals of New York, 1954.
308 N.Y. 155, 124 N.E.2d 99.

[This is an action by Mrs. Auten against Mr. Auten to recover installments owing under a separation agreement executed in New York in 1933.

The parties, married in England in 1917, continued to live there with their two children until 1931, when he deserted her and came to the United States. He obtained a Mexican divorce and married another woman. In 1933 Mrs. Auten came to New York to make some arrangement with the defendant, and there they executed a separation agreement under which he promised to pay 50 pounds a month for the support of herself and the children. In addition the agreement provided that the parties would continue to live apart, that neither should sue "in any action relating to their separation" and that the wife should not "cause any complaint to be lodged against . . . [the husband], in any jurisdiction by reason of the said alleged divorce or remarriage". The plaintiff immediately returned to England where she has continued to live with her children.

The defendant failed to live up to the agreement, making only a few payments. In 1934 the plaintiff filed a petition for separation in an English court, charging the defendant with adultery, and in 1938 an order was entered against him to pay alimony. The English action was instituted upon the advice of English counsel that it was the plaintiff's only means of obtaining support.

Having realized nothing through the English action, the plaintiff in 1947 instituted the present suit to recover the amounts alleged to be due under the 1933 separation agreement. The defendant claimed that the institution of the English suit was a repudiation of the agreement and ended plaintiff's right to payments under it. The trial court, agreeing with the defense, dismissed the complaint, and the Appellate Division affirmed the dismissal.]

■ FULD, J. . . . Both of the courts below, concluding that New York law was to be applied, held that under such law plaintiff's commencement of the English action and the award of temporary alimony constituted a rescission and repudiation of the separation agreement, requiring dismissal of the complaint. Whether that is the law of this state, or whether something more must be shown to effect a repudiation of the agreement . . . need not detain us, since in our view it is the law of England, not that of New York which is here controlling.

Choosing the law to be applied to a contractual transaction with elements in different jurisdictions is a matter not free from difficulty. The New York decisions evidence a number of different approaches to the question. See, e.g., Jones v. Metropolitan Life Ins. Co., 158 Misc. 466, 286 N.Y.S. 4.*

Most of the cases rely upon the generally accepted rules that "All matters bearing upon the execution, the interpretation and the validity of contracts ... are determined by the law of the place where the contract is made", while "all matters connected with its performance ... are regulated by the law of the place where the contract, by its terms, is to be performed." ... What constitutes a breach of the contract and what circumstances excuse a breach are considered matters of performance, governable, within this rule, by the law of the place of performance....

Many cases appear to treat these rules as conclusive. Others consider controlling the intention of the parties and treat the general rules merely as presumptions or guideposts, to be considered along with all the other circumstances.... And still other decisions, including the most recent one in this court, have resorted to a method—first employed to rationalize the results achieved by the courts in decided cases, see Barber Co. v. Hughes, 223 Ind. 570, 586, 63 N.E.2d 417,—which has come to be called the "center of gravity" or the "grouping of contacts" theory of the conflict of laws. Under this theory, the courts, instead of regarding as conclusive the parties' intention or the place of making or performance, lay emphasis rather upon the law of the place "which has the most significant contacts with the matter in dispute". Rubin v. Irving Trust Co., 305 N.Y. 288, 305, 113 N.E.2d 424, 431 ...

Although this "grouping of contacts" theory may, perhaps, afford less certainty and predictability than the rigid general rules ..., the merit of its approach is that it gives to the place "having the most interest in the problem" paramount control over the legal issues arising out of a particular factual context, thus allowing the forum to apply the policy of the jurisdiction "most intimately concerned with the outcome of [the] particular litigation". 3 Utah L.Rev., pp. 498–499. Moreover, by stressing the significant contacts, it enables the court, not only to reflect the relative interests of the several jurisdictions involved ..., but also to give effect to the probable intention of the parties and consideration to "whether one rule or the other produces the best practical result". Swift & Co. v. Bankers Trust Co., supra, 280 N.Y. 135, 141, 19 N.E.2d 992, 995; ...

---

* The opinion in the Jones case stated: "The cases in New York take various positions on the question of which law governs the validity of a contract. In some, the place where the contract was made is said to be determinative....

"Other cases maintain that the contract is governed by the law of the place of performance.... Still other cases rely on the intention of the parties to determine which law governs the contract.... The last position that the cases take is the one which assumes that it is the grouping of the various elements which have gone to make up the contract that determines which law governs."— Eds.

Turning to the case before us, examination of the respective contacts with New York and England compels the conclusion that it is English law which must be applied to determine the impact and effect to be given the wife's institution of the separation suit. It hardly needs stating that it is England which has all the truly significant contacts, while this state's sole nexus with the matter in dispute—entirely fortuitous, at that—is that it is the place where the agreement was made and where the trustee, to whom the moneys were in the first instance to be paid, had his office. The agreement effected a separation between British subjects, who had been married in England, had children there and lived there as a family for fourteen years....

In short, then, the agreement determined and fixed the marital responsibilities of an English husband and father and provided for the support and maintenance of the allegedly abandoned wife and children who were to remain in England. It merely substituted the arrangements arrived at by voluntary agreement of the parties for the duties and responsibilities of support that would otherwise attach by English law. There is no question that England has the greatest concern in prescribing and governing those obligations, and in securing to the wife and children essential support and maintenance....

It is, perhaps, not inappropriate to note that, even if we were not to place our emphasis on the law of the place with the most significant contacts, but were instead simply to apply the rule that matters of performance and breach are governed by the law of the place of performance, the same result would follow. Whether or not there was a repudiation, essentially a form of breach ..., is also to be determined by the law of the place of performance, cf. Wester v. Casein Co. of America, 206 N.Y. 506, 100 N.E. 488; Restatement, Conflict of Laws, § 370, Caveat, and that place, so far as the wife's performance is concerned, is England. Whatever she had to do under the agreement—"live separate and apart from" her husband, "maintain, educate and support" the children and refrain from bringing "any action relating to [the] separation"—was to be done in England. True, the husband's payments were to be made to a New York trustee for forwarding to plaintiff in England, but that is of no consequence in this case. It might be if the question before us involved the manner or effect of payment to the trustee, but that is not the problem; we are here concerned only with the effect of the wife's performance....

Since, then, the law of England must be applied, and since, at the very least, an issue exists as to whether the courts of that country treat the commencement of a separation action as a repudiation of an earlier-made separation agreement, summary judgment should not have been granted....

Judgments reversed, etc.*

---

* The principal case is discussed in M. Traynor, Conflict of Laws: Professor Currie's Restrained and Enlightened Forum, 49 Calif.L.Rev. 845 (1961); Reese, Chief Judge Fuld and Choice of Law, 71 Colum.L.Rev. 548 (1971).—Eds.

NOTES

1. It will be noted that Judge Fuld detoured the issue of whether a correct construction of New York's contract law rules would have produced the same result as applying the English rule. Does by-passing that issue put the cart before the horse by treating as a choice-of-law problem an issue to which the supposedly "conflicting" rules may in fact give a single answer?

2. If the "center of gravity" or "grouping of contacts" called for application of English law and if that law would hold the wife had effectively repudiated the agreement, she would have lost. Would that have been a just result?

3. By what tests did the court determine which contacts were "significant" or which state had the greatest "interest" or the most "intimate concern" in Auten v. Auten?

4. In Haag v. Barnes, 9 N.Y.2d 554, 216 N.Y.S.2d 65, 175 N.E.2d 441 (1961), an unwed mother sued to establish paternity and support for her child. The putative father set up an Illinois agreement which provided support and which was valid under Illinois law, where it was executed, defendant resided, the child was born and payments were made. The agreement provided that it was to be governed by Illinois law. Purporting to follow Auten, the court, per Fuld, J., upheld the agreement under Illinois law even though under New York local law it would have been ineffective because it had not been approved by a court. For critical comment on the decision, see Ehrenzweig, The "Bastard" in the Conflict of Laws—A National Disgrace, 29 U.Chi.L.Rev. 498 (1962); Currie, Conflict, Crisis and Confusion in New York, 1963 Duke L.J. 1, reprinted in B. Currie, Selected Essays on the Conflict of Laws, Ch. 14, at pp. 727–739 (1963).

B. Scholarly Camps

One of the most thorough changes in the judge-made rules applied in any area has occurred in the past three decades in choice-of-law rules. The writings of conflicts scholars heavily influenced this change. The first tentative draft of the Second Restatement of Conflict of Laws was distributed in 1953, when there was little indication from the courts of the dramatic changes that were to come. The Reporter was Willis Reese, one of the scholars whose work is represented below. Under his guidance, the Restatement responded to the early indications of a shift from territorial rules and the drafts of the Restatement, in turn, influenced the courts. In many respects the Restatement became a Pre–Statement. Although, as in any field, more persons are doing useful work than can be represented in any short selection, this section presents the theories of some conflicts scholars who had a major role in influencing the conflicts revolution.

Elliott E. Cheatham and Willis L.M. Reese, "Choice of the Applicable Law," 52 Colum.L.Rev. 959 (1952).

When an occurrence has substantial elements in two or more states having different local laws, it is necessary to determine which of these laws shall govern the rights of the parties. The problem of choice thus presented is the most difficult one in conflict of laws. This difficulty is primarily a consequence of the youth and fluidity of the subject. Not only is precedent relatively sparse in this area; that which exists is frequently misleading. Guidance therefore cannot be sought, as in many other branches of the law, from an accepted body of settled rules. Rather the judge frequently finds himself forced to pursue the inquiry into basic questions of policy and value....

The ... policies, [that are] of significance in the great majority of cases where there is no express legislative direction on the subject of choice of law are discussed in what is conceived to be the order of their relative importance—subject to the constant warning that in large part this latter question depends on the facts of the particular case.

I. THE NEEDS OF THE INTERSTATE AND INTERNATIONAL SYSTEMS

Except in the comparatively rare situation where a court must follow the explicit directions of its legislature, the smooth functioning of the interstate and international systems in private law matters should be the basic consideration in the decision of every choice of law case. In no country are the needs of the interstate system more important than in the United States where business and social activities almost ignore state lines....

Of necessity, this overriding policy is so vaguely worded as to be difficult of application. Frequently, it is well-nigh impossible to determine whether the needs of the interstate or international system would best be served by the resolution of a given dispute one way or the other....

[In the rest of their article the authors listed in order of importance the policies they thought salient. A court should: apply its own local law, with which it is more familiar and adept, unless impelled by good reason not to; try to advance its local law purposes in deciding the choice-of-law question; try to advance certainty, predictability and uniformity of result; try to protect justified expectations; try to advance the policies of the state of dominant interest in the case; try to formulate rules of choice of law that will be easy for the court to apply; try to implement the broader local law substantive values involved; and try to achieve justice in the individual case.]

Currie: *The Governmental Interest Methodology*

One of the most influential conflicts scholars of the mid-20th century was the late Professor Brainerd Currie. He developed the governmental interests analysis, postulating that a choice-of-law case confronts a court with the problem of analyzing the policies that are in competition in the local law rules vying for application. His work fired the imagination and interest of many of the oncoming generation of conflicts scholars and attracted the support of a number of courts. For the 1964 edition of this book,* he prepared a succinct statement of his theory, the substance of which follows:

Currie begins by observing that a court may refer to foreign law for quite different purposes. One purpose is to find the "rule of decision"—the answer to such questions as: Is this a valid contract? Does this injury constitute an actionable wrong? On what principle is the estate of this decedent to be distributed? Another purpose is to find some "datum" made relevant by a known rule of decision [see, e.g., People v. Olah, p. 452, supra]. Thus a case otherwise wholly domestic may involve mistake of foreign law. The rule of decision is unquestionably supplied by the law of the forum, but it is necessary to refer to foreign law to establish the fact of mistake. Putting aside for further study all such references to foreign law for other purposes, Currie concentrates on the problem of reference to the foreign law as the source of the rule of decision. In this context he finds choice-of-law rules of the traditional type unacceptable, and suggests as a substitute for all such rules the following guides:

1. When a court is asked to apply the law of a foreign state different from the law of the forum, it should inquire into the policies expressed in the respective laws, and into the circumstances in which it is reasonable for the respective states to assert an interest in the application of those policies. In making these determinations the court should employ the ordinary processes of construction and interpretation.

2. If the court finds that one state has an interest in the application of its policy in the circumstances of the case and the other has none, it should apply the law of the only interested state.

3. If the court finds an apparent conflict between the interests of the two states it should reconsider. A more moderate and restrained interpretation of the policy or interest of one state or the other may avoid conflict.

4. If, upon reconsideration, the court finds that a conflict between the legitimate interests of the two states is unavoidable, it should apply the law of the forum.

5. If the forum is disinterested, but an unavoidable conflict exists between the interests of two other states, and the court cannot with justice decline to adjudicate the case, it should apply the law of the forum, at least if that law corresponds with the law of one of the other states. Alternatively, the court might decide the case by a candid exercise of legislative discretion, resolving the conflict as it believes it would be resolved by a supreme legislative body having power to determine which interest should be required to yield.

6. The conflict of interest between states will result in different dispositions of the same problem, depending on where the action is brought. If with respect to a particular problem this appears seriously to

---

* Currie originally set out his theories in an article, Currie, Notes on Methods and Objectives in the Conflict of Laws, 1959 Duke L.J. 171, 178. These he modified quite quickly in a series of articles and statements, culminating in the present statement. See also B. Currie, Selected Essays on the Conflict of Laws (1963).

infringe a strong national interest in uniformity of decision, the court should not attempt to improvise a solution sacrificing the legitimate interest of its own state, but should leave to Congress, exercising its powers under the full faith and credit clause, the determination of which interest shall be required to yield.

Step 2, above, in Professor Currie's methodology has become known as the technique of identifying "false conflicts" and eliminating the spurious issues they involve. This proved to be one of the most attractive features of Currie's methodology. However, analysis of the "false conflict" concept has persuaded some writers that it is a misbegotten idea. Professor Leflar has said that it confuses cases of no conflict with cases in which opposed rules of internal law appear to by vying for application, but where the claim of one of the rules to being invoked is so slender that the conflict is easily resolved in favor of the other rule. A more trenchant attack has been mounted by a student writer, who pointed out that the term has at least a half-dozen meanings which shift from case to case and from user to user. See Comment, False Conflicts, 55 Calif.L.Rev. 74 (1967). Perhaps the principal notion of "false conflicts" can be put in one sentence. When rules of two or more states are phrased in terms that literally construed would lead to opposed results, they pose a gratuitous conflict if, on according them their intended scope, the rules would produce the same decision on the issue presented.

Professor Currie's work triggered many responses and criticisms. Three criticisms are (1) the method slights transjurisdictional policies, such as facilitating and encouraging interstate and international transactions; (2) preferring forum law when there is a clash of state policies will be another incentive for forum shopping and reflects interstate chauvenism rather than cooperation; (3) the work represents an approach to resolving choice-of-law problems, but does not provide substitute rules. Professor Currie wrote that "[w]e would be better off without choice-of-law rules." B. Currie, Notes on Methods and Objectives in the Conflict of Laws, 1959 Duke L.J. 171, 177. If a court uses Professor Currie's method to decide a series of cases in the same substantive area, will the court or conflicts scholars inevitably attempt to summarize the results of those cases? Will this summary be a choice-of-law rule?

NOTES

1. For an interesting article which espouses the Currie approach, subject to rather substantial limitations, see Traynor, War and Peace in the Conflict of Laws, 25 Int. and Comp.L.Q. 121 (1976).

2. Among commentaries discussing Professor Currie's approach are Brilmayer, Interest Analysis and the Myth of Legislative Intent, 78 Mich.L.Rev. 392 (1980); Hill, Governmental Interest and the Conflict of Laws—a Reply to Professor Currie, 27 U.Chi.L.Rev. 463 (1960); Juenger, Conflict of Law: A Critique of Interest Analysis, 32 Am.J.Comp.L. 1 (1984); Rosenberg, The Comeback of Choice-of-Law

Rules, 81 Colum.L.Rev. 946 (1981); M. Traynor, Professor Currie's Restrained and Enlightened Forum, 49 Calif.L.Rev. 845 (1961).

Leflar: *Choice-Influencing Considerations*

Professor Robert A. Leflar's American Conflicts Law (4th ed. 1986, with L. McDougal & R. Felix) provides a summary and refinement of the work that he produced in the conflicts field for many years. He reviews the work of other conflicts scholars "to systematize and correlate the choice-influencing considerations" that are useful in resolving choice-of-law problems. Id. § 95. Professor Leflar finds that this produces "a list of five, which seem to incorporate all that are in the longer lists: (A) Predictability of results; (B) Maintenance of interstate and international order; (C) Simplification of the judicial task; (D) Advancement of the forum's governmental interests; (E) Application of the better rule of law." A major ingredient of this last "better rule" is whether one of the competing domestic rules, when compared with the other, "is anachronistic, behind the times." Id. § 107.

Several courts have been attracted to the Leflar formula, with the opinion in Clark v. Clark, 107 N.H. 351, 222 A.2d 205 (1966), showing the way. See, e.g., Satchwill v. Vollrath Co., 293 F.Supp. 533 (E.D.Wis.1968); Schneider v. Nichols, 280 Minn. 139, 158 N.W.2d 254 (1968); Mitchell v. Craft, 211 So.2d 509 (Miss.1968); Tiernan v. Westext Transport, Inc., 295 F.Supp. 1256 (D.R.I.1969); Conklin v. Horner, 38 Wis.2d 468, 157 N.W.2d 579 (1968). See also Allstate Ins. Co. v. Hague, p. 349, supra.

NOTES

1. Courts that engage in a search for the "better rule of law" usually end by applying their own local rule in the decision of the case. An exception is Frummer v. Hilton Hotels International Inc., 60 Misc.2d 840, 304 N.Y.S.2d 335 (Sup.Ct., Kings Co. 1969), which involved an action brought by a New York resident to recover for personal injuries suffered when he slipped and fell while showering in a London hotel. Using an interest analysis approach, the court rejected the forum's contributory negligence rule in favor of the lex loci's comparative negligence rule.

2. Suppose a court determines that the forum's rule is not the "better rule." If forum law is judge-made and can be changed by judicial decision, is the forum's highest court likely to eliminate the conflicts problems by changing forum law to accord with the rule of the other state? If forum law is statutory, ought a court have more latitude to reject the rule in a multistate case than in a local case? If forum law is found in judicial precedents, ought a trial or intermediate appellate court have more latitude to reject the rule in a multistate case than in a local case?

von Mehren & Trautman: *The Functional Analysis*

Professors Arthur von Mehren and Donald Trautman, in The Law of Multistate Problems (1965), set forth "a functional approach or analysis, one that aims at solutions that are the rational elaboration and application of the policies and purposes underlying specific legal rules and the legal system as a whole." Id. at 76. They first locate each concerned jurisdiction, which is one that "in view either of its thinking about the particular substantive issue raised or of its more general legal policies, such as concern for members of the community, can be taken to have expressed some interest in regulating an aspect of the multistate transaction in question." Id. Then Professors von Mehren and Trautman construct for each concerned jurisdiction a "regulating rule" that takes "account both of relevant policies expressed through the jurisdiction's domestic rules and policies peculiar to (or of special importance in) multistate transactions...." Id. at 77. Many of the conflicts that remain after these steps, the authors believe can "be resolved by applying the rule of the jurisdiction predominantly concerned." Resolution is available on this basis when "one jurisdiction has ultimate, effective control ... and in cases in which all concerned jurisdictions agree that one has predominant concern." Id. If this is not so, it may be that "the claims of one jurisdiction are so clearly superior that its rule should be recognized." Id. For conflicts that persist, resolution may be possible by applying "the more salutary rule from the standpoint of facilitating multistate activity." Id. at 407. In contrast to Professor Currie, Professors von Mehren and Trautman thus recognize and give effect to multistate policies, as distinguished from the policies underlying the laws of each concerned jurisdiction. See also Singer, Real Conflicts, 69 B.U.L.Rev. 1, 91 (1989): "False conflict analysis rests, to a large extent, on an impoverished conception of state interests."

Cavers: *Principles of Preference*

On the eve of publication of the first Restatement of Conflict of Laws, Professor David F. Cavers wrote a penetrating critique of the whole conceptual apparatus of the choice-of-law system the American Law Institute was to embrace. See Cavers, A Critique of the Choice-of-Law Problem, 47 Harv.L.Rev. 173 (1933). His message was that the traditional rules were bent on "jurisdiction-selecting"—choosing a body of governing law or a legal system—instead of on choosing the decisional norm whereby to resolve the issue presented.

He argued that choice-of-law rules should not be oblivious to the contents of the rules of decision whose application they dictated and urged a revised body of choice-of-law rules. In 1965, he presented a limited set of "principles of preference" that he had carefully worked out on the basis of diverse fact-law multistate combinations and that he proposed as guidelines for courts concerned with reaching principled decisions that were neither completely result-selectively ad hoc nor yet blind to consequences.

One example will suffice to illustrate his view of the problem and the path to solution. In his words, the "problem we face today is not how to exorcise choice-of-law rules and principles but how to develop them." D. Cavers, The Choice-of-Law Process 113 (1965). Using tort cases as his chief subjects, he offered the following as an example of principles of preference (p. 138):

"1. Where the liability laws of the state of injury set a *higher* standard of conduct or of financial protection against injury than do the laws of the state where the person causing the injury has acted or had his home, the laws of the state of injury should determine the standard and the protection applicable to the case, at least where the person injured was not so related to the person causing the injury that the question should be relegated to the law governing their relationship."

Professor Cavers admitted to greater confidence in the idea that principles of preference are necessary than in the particular formulations he has advanced. He was satisfied that as courts consciously strive for principled decisions and as precedents accumulate, better principles and a more just choice-of-law process will evolve.

Weintraub: *A Pragmatic Approach*

Another respected writer in the field is Professor Russell Weintraub of the University of Texas School of Law. In his Commentary on the Conflict of Laws (3d ed. 1986), he proposes the following as an approach to choice of law in torts (p. 360):

> 1. "False conflict" cases: If, in the light of its contacts with the parties or the transaction, only one state will have the policies underlying its tort rule advanced, apply the law of that state.
>
> 2. "True conflict" cases: If two or more states having contacts with the parties or the transaction will have the policies underlying their different tort rules advanced, apply the law that will favor the plaintiff unless one or both of the following factors is present:
>
>   a. That law is anachronistic or aberrational.
>
>   b. The state with that law does not have sufficient contact with the defendant or the defendant's actual or intended course of conduct to make application of its law reasonable.
>
> 3. "No interest" cases: If none of the states having contacts with the parties or the transaction will have the policies underlying its tort rule advanced, apply the law that will favor the plaintiff unless one or both of the following factors is present:
>
>   a. That law is anachronistic or aberrational.
>
>   b. The state with that law does not have sufficient contact with the defendant or the defendant's actual or intended course of conduct to make application of its law reasonable.

These rules are sympathetically, but critically, discussed in Seidelson, Interest Analysis: The Quest for Perfection and the Frailties of Man, 19 Duq.L.Rev. 207 (1981).

Professor Weintraub first proposed this rule in 1977, and justified the preference for the rule favoring the plaintiff on an "objective better law" basis. The Future of Choice of Law for Torts: What Principles Should be Preferred? 41 L. & Contemp.Prob. 146 (1977). He argued that the rule preventing or limiting recovery was likely to be anachronistic and waning in acceptance, such as a guest statute, marital immunity, or limits on wrongful death recovery. When, in the face of the tort reform movement, this was no longer so, he stated that the plaintiff-preference rules should not be applied to cases of products liability or generally to enterprise liability. For these cases he suggested applying the law of the plaintiff's habitual residence. If this law favored the plaintiff, its application would have to be justified by some reasonable and foreseeable contact with the defendant or the defendant's course of conduct. Commentary on the Conflict of Laws. 1991 Supp. 74–75. If the defendant's conduct was sufficiently outrageous that policies of deterrence and punishment were relevant, the law of any state in which that conduct occurred could be selected for punitive or compensatory damages.

Juenger: *Multistate Justice*

In Choice of Law and Multistate Justice (1993), Professor Friedrich K. Juenger summarizes his work of many years. He suggests that law be chosen from the best the world has to offer and that the choice not be limited to states that have contacts with the parties and the transaction. Id. 192–94. As a fall-back approach, he suggests the use of alternative references to select, from among states connected to the parties and the transaction, the law that best reflects modern trends and doctrine. Id. 195. He provides an example of such an alternative reference rule for conflicts cases involving products liability:

> In selecting the rules of decision applicable to any issue a multistate liability case presents the court will take into account the laws of the following jurisdictions:
>
>> (a) the place where the injury occurred,
>>
>> (b) the place where the conduct causing the injury occurred, and
>>
>> (c) the home state (habitual residence, place of incorporation or principal place of business) of the parties.
>
> As to each issue, the court shall select from the laws of these jurisdictions the rule of decision that most closely accords with modern products liability standards.

Professor Juenger's book is reviewed in Weintraub, Choosing Law with an Eye on the Prize, 15 Mich.J.Int'l L. 705 (1994).

NOTE

A survey of various scholarly perspectives on interest analysis appears in a symposium in 46 Ohio State L.J. 457–568 (1985).

Restatement, Second, Conflict of Laws

The basic section on choice of law principles in general (§ 6) and the introductory section on torts (§ 145) of the Restatement Second are set forth below:

§ 6. Choice-of-Law Principles*

(1) A court, subject to constitutional restrictions, will follow a statutory directive of its own state on choice of law.

(2) When there is no such directive, the factors relevant to the choice of the applicable rule of law include

(a) the needs of the interstate and international systems,

(b) the relevant policies of the forum,

(c) the relevant policies of other interested states and the relative interests of those states in the determination of the particular issue,

(d) the protection of justified expectations,

(e) the basic policies underlying the particular field of law,

(f) certainty, predictability and uniformity of result, and

(g) ease in the determination and application of the law to be applied.

---

§ 145. The General Principle

(1) The rights and liabilities of the parties with respect to an issue in tort are determined by the local law of the state which, with respect to that issue, has the most significant relationship to the occurrence and the parties under the principles stated in § 6.

(2) Contacts to be taken into account in applying the principles of § 6 to determine the law applicable to an issue include:

(a) the place where the injury occurred,

(b) the place where the conduct causing the injury occurred,

(c) the domicil, residence, nationality, place of incorporation and place of business of the parties, and

(d) the place where the relationship, if any, between the parties is centered.

These contacts are to be evaluated according to their relative importance with respect to the particular issue.

"... Although it is printed in black letters, section 145 is not much of a rule since it fails to offer a definition of the central word 'significant.' ** Thus, the Restatement provisions on tort choice of law appear to be programmatic rather than normative...." Juenger, Choice of Law in Interstate Torts, 118 U.Pa.L.Rev. 202, 212 (1969). With regard to the

---

* Quoted with the permission of the copyright owner, The American Law Institute.

** Do the references in the Restatement's black-letter rules to the choice-of-law factors listed in section 6 provide definitional guidance? [Eds.]

latter sentence, Professor Juenger quotes from the Reporter for the Second Restatement this observation: "This rule of most significant relationship, at the very least, will not stand in the way of progress." Reese, Conflict of Laws and the Restatement Second, 28 Law & Contemp.Prob. 679, 697 (1963).

If we grant that the "most significant relationship" doctrine is not part of the problem, does that mean it is part of the solution? An affirmative answer is suggested on the ground that the Restatement's provisions direct attention to the right questions. Although they do not for the most part supply firm answers to these questions, they may set the stage for decisions that in time can be synthesized into workable rules that take account of the significant underlying considerations.

Section 4. The New Era

A. Adopting New Choice-of-Law Rules

Babcock v. Jackson

Court of Appeals of New York, 1963.
12 N.Y.2d 473, 240 N.Y.S.2d 743, 191 N.E.2d 279.

FULD, JUDGE. On Friday, September 16, 1960, Miss Georgia Babcock and her friends, Mr. and Mrs. William Jackson, all residents of Rochester, left that city in Mr. Jackson's automobile, Miss Babcock as guest, for a weekend trip to Canada. Some hours later, as Mr. Jackson was driving in the Province of Ontario, he apparently lost control of the car; it went off the highway into an adjacent stone wall, and Miss Babcock was seriously injured. Upon her return to this State, she brought the present action against William Jackson, alleging negligence on his part in operating his automobile.

At the time of the accident, there was in force in Ontario a statute providing that "the owner or driver of a motor vehicle, other than a vehicle operated in the business of carrying passengers for compensation, is not liable for any loss or damage resulting from bodily injury to, or the death of any person being carried in ... the motor vehicle" (Highway Traffic Act of Province of Ontario [Ontario Rev.Stat. (1960), ch. 172], § 105, subd. [2]). Even though no such bar is recognized under this State's substantive law of torts ... the defendant moved to dismiss the complaint on the ground that the law of the place where the accident occurred governs and that Ontario's guest statute bars recovery. The court at Special Term, agreeing with the defendant, granted the motion and the Appellate Division ... affirmed the judgment of dismissal without opinion.

The question presented is simply drawn. Shall the law of the place of the tort [2] *invariably* govern the availability of relief for the tort or shall the applicable choice of law rule also reflect a consideration of other factors which are relevant to the purposes served by the enforcement or denial of the remedy?

The traditional choice of law rule, embodied in the original Restatement of Conflict of Laws (§ 384), and until recently unquestioningly followed in this court ... has been that the substantive rights and liabilities arising out of a tortious occurrence are determinable by the law of the place of the tort.... It had its conceptual foundation in the vested rights doctrine, namely, that a right to recover for a foreign tort owes its creation to the law of the jurisdiction where the injury occurred and depends for its existence and extent solely on such law.... [T]he vested rights doctrine has long since been discredited.... More particularly, as applied to torts, the theory ignores the interest which jurisdictions other than that where the tort occurred may have in the resolution of particular issues. It is for this very reason that, despite the advantages of certainty, ease of application and predictability which it affords ... there has in recent years been increasing criticism of the traditional rule by commentators and a judicial trend towards its abandonment or modification.

. . .

In Auten v. Auten, 308 N.Y. 155, 124 N.E.2d 99, ... this court ... applied what has been termed the "center of gravity" or "grouping of contacts" theory of the conflict of laws. "Under this theory," we declared in the Auten case, "the courts, instead of regarding as conclusive the parties' intention or the place of making or performance, lay emphasis rather upon the law of the place 'which has the most significant contacts with the matter in dispute'" (308 N.Y., at p. 160, 124 N.E.2d, at pp. 101–102)....

The "center of gravity" or "grouping of contacts" doctrine adopted by this court in conflicts cases involving contracts impresses us as likewise affording the appropriate approach for accommodating the competing interests in tort cases with multi-State contacts. Justice, fairness and "the best practical result" (Swift & Co. v. Bankers Trust Co., 280 N.Y. 135, 141, 19 N.E.2d 992, 995 ...) may best be achieved by giving controlling effect to the law of the jurisdiction which, because of its relationship or contact with the occurrence or the parties, has the greatest concern with the specific issue raised in the litigation....

Comparison of the relative "contacts" and "interests" of New York and Ontario in this litigation, vis-a-vis the issue here presented, makes it clear that the concern of New York is unquestionably the greater and more direct and that the interest of Ontario is at best minimal. The present

---

2. In this case, as in nearly all such cases, the conduct causing injury and the injury itself occurred in the same jurisdiction. The phrase "place of the tort," as distinguished from "place of wrong" and "place of injury," is used herein to designate the place where both the wrong and the injury took place.

action involves injuries sustained by a New York guest as the result of the negligence of a New York host in the operation of an automobile, garaged, licensed and undoubtedly insured in New York, in the course of a week-end journey which began and was to end there. In sharp contrast, Ontario's sole relationship with the occurrence is the purely adventitious circumstance that the accident occurred there.

New York's policy of requiring a tort-feasor to compensate his guest for injuries caused by his negligence cannot be doubted—as attested by the fact that the Legislature of this State has repeatedly refused to enact a statute denying or limiting recovery in such cases (see, e.g., 1930 Sen.Int.No. 339, Pr.No. 349; 1935 Sen.Int.No. 168, Pr.No. 170; 1960 Sen.Int.No. 3662, Pr.No. 3967)—and our courts have neither reason nor warrant for departing from that policy simply because the accident, solely affecting New York residents and arising out of the operation of a New York based automobile, happened beyond its borders. Per contra, Ontario has no conceivable interest in denying a remedy to a New York guest against his New York host for injuries suffered in Ontario by reason of conduct which was tortious under Ontario law. The object of Ontario's guest statute, it has been said, is "to prevent the fraudulent assertion of claims by passengers, in collusion with the drivers, against insurance companies" (Survey of Canadian Legislation, 1 U.Toronto L.J. 358, 366) and, quite obviously, the fraudulent claims intended to be prevented by the statute are those asserted against Ontario defendants and their insurance carriers, not New York defendants and their insurance carriers. Whether New York defendants are imposed upon or their insurers defrauded by a New York plaintiff is scarcely a valid legislative concern of Ontario simply because the accident occurred there, any more so than if the accident had happened in some other jurisdiction.

It is hardly necessary to say that Ontario's interest is quite different from what it would have been had the issue related to the manner in which the defendant had been driving his car at the time of the accident. Where the defendant's exercise of due care in the operation of his automobile is in issue, the jurisdiction in which the allegedly wrongful conduct occurred will usually have a predominant, if not exclusive, concern. In such a case, it is appropriate to look to the law of the place of the tort so as to give effect to that jurisdiction's interest in regulating conduct within its borders, and it would be almost unthinkable to seek the applicable rule in the law of some other place.

The issue here, however, is not whether the defendant offended against a rule of the road prescribed by Ontario for motorists generally or whether he violated some standard of conduct imposed by that jurisdiction, but rather whether the plaintiff, because she was a guest in the defendant's automobile, is barred from recovering damages for a wrong concededly committed. As to that issue, it is New York, the place where the parties resided, where their guest-host relationship arose and where the trip began and was to end, rather than Ontario, the place of the fortuitous occurrence of the accident, which has the dominant contacts and the superior claim for application of its law. Although the rightness or wrongness of defendant's conduct may depend upon the law of the particular jurisdiction through which the automobile passes, the rights and liabilities of the parties which stem from their guest-host relationship should remain constant and not vary and shift as the automobile proceeds from place to place. Indeed, such a result, we note, accords with "the interests of the host in procuring liability insurance adequate under the applicable law, and the interests of his insurer in reasonable calculability of the premium." (Ehrenzweig, Guest Statutes in the Conflict of Laws, 69 Yale L.J. 595, 603.)

Although the traditional rule has in the past been applied by this court in giving controlling effect to the guest statute of the foreign jurisdiction in which the accident occurred ... it is not amiss to point out that the question here posed was neither raised nor considered in those cases and that the question has never been presented in so stark a manner as in the case before us with a statute so unique as Ontario's. Be that as it may, however, reconsideration of the inflexible traditional rule persuades us, as already indicated, that, in failing to take into account essential policy considerations and objectives, its application may lead to unjust and anomalous results. This being so, the rule, formulated as it was by the courts, should be discarded....

In conclusion, then, there is no reason why all issues arising out of a tort claim must be resolved by reference to the law of the same jurisdiction. Where the issue involves standards of conduct, it is more than likely that it is the law of the place of the tort which will be controlling but the disposition of other issues must turn, as does the issue of the standard of conduct itself, on the law of the jurisdiction which has the strongest interest in the resolution of the particular issue presented.

The judgment appealed from should be reversed, with costs, and the motion to dismiss the complaint denied.

■ VAN VOORHIS, JUDGE (dissenting). The decision about to be made of this appeal changes the established law of this State.... The decision in Auten v. Auten rationalized and rendered more workable the existing law of contracts.... The difference between the present case and Auten v. Auten is that Auten did not materially change the law, but sought to formulate what had previously been decided. The present case makes substantial changes in the law of torts....

In my view there is no overriding consideration of public policy which justifies or directs this change in the established rule or renders necessary or advisable the confusion which such a change will introduce....

NOTES

1. Is Judge Fuld's opinion internally consistent? Can a court consistently call for application of the law of the state that has the greatest interest in the issue to be decided and also declare that "the rights and liabilities of the parties which stem from the guest-host relationship should ... not vary and shift as the automobile proceeds from place to place"?

2. The principal case produced a torrent of commentary, mostly approving, starting with a symposium, Comments on Babcock v. Jackson, 63 Colum.L.Rev. 1212 (1963). Professors Cavers, Cheatham, Currie, Leflar and Reese all found the result pleasing, but they gave different reasons for doing so. Each tended to find in the opinion support for his own theories.

3. The principal case compares rules regulating conduct with rules affecting compensation. In subsequent New York cases, this concept developed into a distinction between "conduct regulating" rules and "loss allocating" rules. If a rule was conduct regulating, the law of the place where the defendant acted was applicable. If a rule was loss allocating, choice of law followed that approach in the principal case. A case that epitomizes this distinction is Padula v. Lilarn Properties Corp., 84 N.Y.2d 519, 620 N.Y.S.2d 310, 644 N.E.2d 1001 (1994). A worker, domiciled in New York, was injured by a fall from a scaffold at a construction site in Massachusetts. The site was owned by a New York corporation. The scaffold did not conform with specifications promulgated under New York law for worker safety. The New York Labor Law provided "strict and vicarious liability of the owner of the property" if a worker was injured because of a non-conforming scaffold. The court affirmed a summary judgment for the property owner, holding that because the scaffold requirements were "conduct regulating" rather than "loss allocating," Massachusetts law applied. For comment on this case, see Borchers, The Return of Territorialism to New York's Conflict Law: Padula v. Lilarn Properties Corp., 58 Albany L.Rev. 775 (1995).

Is the distinction between "conduct regulating" and "loss allocating" rules sound? There are some rules so directly conduct regulating, such as speed limits and rules of the road, that the applicable rules must be those where the regulated conduct occurs. Brainerd Currie distinguished between "a rule of decision," which he would select by interest analysis, and a "rule of conduct," which provides the factual "datum" on which the rule of decision will operate. Currie, Selected Essays on the Conflict of Laws 69 (1963). The recent Louisiana conflicts code provides separately for "issues of conduct and safety" (La.Civ.C. art. 3543) and "issues of loss distribution and financial protection" (art. 3544). If conduct and injury occur in the same state, issues of conduct and safety are governed by the law of that state. Issues of loss distribution and financial protection are governed by the law of the domicile of the injured person and the person who caused the injury if both are domiciled in the same state or in different states that have "substantially identical" laws on the relevant issue. Whether violation of a rule of conduct constitutes negligence per se is treated as a rule of conduct. Art. 3543, Revision Comment (e). Should it be? For comments on these and other aspects of the Louisiana conflicts code, see Symeonides, Louisiana's New Law of Choice of Law for Tort Conflicts: An Exegesis, 66 Tul.L.Rev. 677 (1992); Weintraub, The Contributions of Symeonides and Kozyris in Making Choice of Law Predictable and Just: An Appreciation and Critique, 38 Am.J.Comp.L. 511 (1990).

4. The principal case is typical of the cases in other states that followed its lead to avoid a rule of the place of injury which excluded or limited liability and was perceived to be an anachronistic rule that most states had abandoned. Classic examples were provided by guest statutes, marital immunity rules, and wrongful death statutes that contained a low cap on damages. See, e.g., Griffith v. United Air Lines, Inc., 416 Pa. 1, 203 A.2d 796 (1964) (limit on wrongful death recovery); Mellk v. Sarahson, 49 N.J. 226, 229 A.2d 625 (1967) (guest statute); White v. White, 618 P.2d 921 (Okl.1980) (spousal immunity). Some of the opinions abandoning the place-of-wrong rule, however, do not fit this pattern.

Chambers v. Dakota Charter, Inc., 488 N.W.2d 63 (S.D.1992) applies the law of the forum, rather than the Missouri law to deprive a South Dakota resident of a cause of action against a South Dakota corporation. Under South Dakota law, recovery is barred "if the plaintiff's negligence is more than slight in comparison with the negligence of the defendant." (Id. 64). "Under Missouri law, if a plaintiff is determined to be contributorily negligent in any degree, the plaintiff may still recover, but the plaintiff's damages are reduced by the percentage of fault that is attributed to plaintiff's conduct." Id.

Hataway v. McKinley, 830 S.W.2d 53 (Tenn.1992). A Tennessee resident was killed during a scuba dive at a diving class taught in Arkansas by another Tennessee resident. Tennessee barred recovery if the decedent was contributorily negligent, but Arkansas had a doctrine of comparative fault. Held: Tennessee law applied because "Arkansas has no interest in applying its laws to this dispute between Tennessee residents." Id. at 60.

5. Following the decision in the principal case, New York's highest court did not live happily ever after with its new approach to choice of law for torts. In the next nine years, the court would decide four more cases in which the issue was whether a guest passenger could recover against a New York host driver under New York's ordinary negligence rule or was required to meet stricter liability standards under the law of the place of injury. Dym v. Gordon, 16 N.Y.2d 120, 262 N.Y.S.2d 463, 209 N.E.2d 792 (1965), page 583, infra, denied recovery to a New York guest suing a New York host for injuries resulting from a collision in Colorado. The court distinguished *Babcock* on the ground that this was a two-car accident and one purpose of the Colorado guest statute was to preserve the host's assets for the injured parties in the other car. Moreover, the relationship between host and guest was formed in Colorado, where they met at summer school. Macey v. Rozbicki, 18 N.Y.2d 289, 274 N.Y.S.2d 591, 221 N.E.2d 380 (1966), applied New York law to a suit between sisters who lived in Buffalo but were vacationing at the host's summer home in Ontario, where the collision occurred during a local trip. The court stated that the relationship between host and guest had been established in New York. Tooker v. Lopez, 24 N.Y.2d 569, 301 N.Y.S.2d 519, 249 N.E.2d 394 (1969), overruled Dym v. Gordon and applied New York law to a death caused in Michigan, where the New York host and passenger were students at Michigan State University. The court declined to rest its decision on the fact that, unlike Dym v. Gordon, the death was caused by the car overturning, not by a collision with another car.

At this point New York conflicts rules for tort appeared to be in chaos. Understandably, in the next principal case, the court sought to clarify matters.

Neumeier v. Kuehner

Court of Appeals of New York, 1972.
31 N.Y.2d 121, 335 N.Y.S.2d 64, 286 N.E.2d 454.

■ FULD, CHIEF JUDGE. A domiciliary of Ontario, Canada, was killed when the automobile in which he was riding, owned and driven by a New York resident, collided with a train in Ontario. That jurisdiction has a guest statute, and the primary question posed by this appeal is whether in this action brought by the Ontario passenger's estate, Ontario law should be applied and the New York defendant permitted to rely on its guest statute as a defense.

The facts are quickly told. On May 7, 1969, Arthur Kuehner, the defendant's intestate, a resident of Buffalo, drove his automobile from that city to Fort Erie in the Province of Ontario, Canada, where he picked up Amie Neumeier, who lived in that town with his wife and their children. Their trip was to take them to Long Beach, also in Ontario, and back again to Neumeier's home in Fort Erie. However, at a railroad crossing in the Town of Sherkston—on the way to Long Beach—the auto was struck by a train of the defendant Canadian National Railway Company. Both Kuehner and his guest-passenger were instantly killed.

Neumeier's wife and administratrix, a citizen of Canada and a domiciliary of Ontario, thereupon commenced this wrongful death action in New York against both Kuehner's estate and the Canadian National Railway Company. The defendant estate pleaded, as an affirmative defense, the Ontario guest statute and the defendant railway also interposed defenses in reliance upon it. In substance, the statute provides that the owner or driver of a motor vehicle is not liable for damages resulting from injury to, or the death of, a guest-passenger unless he was guilty of gross negligence (Highway Traffic Act of Province of Ontario [Ont.Rev.Stat. (1960), ch. 172], § 105, subd. [2], as amd. by Stat. of 1966, ch. 64, § 20, subd. [2]). It is worth noting, at this point, that, although our court originally considered that the sole purpose of the Ontario statute was to protect Ontario defendants and their insurers against collusive claims (see Babcock v. Jackson, 12 N.Y.2d 473, 482–483, 240 N.Y.S.2d 743, 749–750, 191 N.E.2d 279, 283–284[,]) "Further research ... has revealed the distinct possibility that one purpose, and perhaps the only purpose, of the statute was to protect owners and drivers against ungrateful guests." (Reese, Chief Judge Fuld and Choice of Law, 71 Col.L.Rev. 548, 558; see Trautman, Two Views on Kell v. Henderson: A Comment, 67 Col.L.Rev. 465, 469.)*

The plaintiff, asserting that the Ontario statute "is not available ... in the present action", moved, pursuant to CPLR 3211 (subd. [b]), to dismiss the affirmative defenses pleaded. The court at Special Term holding the guest statute applicable, denied the motions (63 Misc.2d 766, 313 N.Y.S.2d 468) but, on appeal, a closely divided Appellate Division reversed and directed dismissal of the defenses (37 A.D.2d 70, 322 N.Y.S.2d 867). It was the court's belief that such a result was dictated by Tooker v. Lopez, 24 N.Y.2d 569, 301 N.Y.S.2d 519, 249 N.E.2d 394.

In reaching that conclusion, the Appellate Division misread our decision in the *Tooker* case—a not unnatural result in light of the variant views expressed in the three separate opinions written on behalf of the majority. It is important to bear in mind that in *Tooker*, the guest-passenger and the host-driver were both domiciled in New York, and our decision—that New York law was controlling—was based upon, and limited to, that fact situation. Indeed [both] ... Judge Keating (24 N.Y.2d at p. 580, 301

---

* Another scholar's research into the legislative history of the Ontario statute has led him to the conclusion that the statute was only intended to protect insurance companies. Baade, The Case of The Disinterested Two States: Neumeier v. Kuehner, 1 Hofstra L.Rev. 150, 152–154 (1973). [Footnote by the Editors.]

N.Y.S.2d at p. 528, 249 N.E.2d at p. 400) and Judge Burke (at p. 591, 301 N.Y.S.2d at p. 537, 249 N.E.2d at p. 407) expressly noted that the determination then being made left open the question whether New York law would be applicable if the plaintiff passenger happened to be a domiciliary of the very jurisdiction which had a guest statute.[1] Thus, Tooker v. Lopez did no more than hold that, when the passenger and driver are residents of the same jurisdiction and the car is there registered and insured, its law, and not the law of the place of accident, controls and determines the standard of care which the host owes to his guest.

What significantly and effectively differentiates the present case is the fact that, although the host was a domiciliary of New York, the guest, for whose death recovery is sought, was domiciled in Ontario, the place of accident and the very jurisdiction which had enacted the statute designed to protect the host from liability for ordinary negligence. It is clear that although New York has a deep interest in protecting its own residents, injured in a foreign state, against unfair or anachronistic statutes of that state, it has no legitimate interest in ignoring the public policy of a foreign jurisdiction—such as Ontario—and in protecting the plaintiff guest domiciled and injured there from legislation obviously addressed, at the very least, to a resident riding in a vehicle traveling within its borders.

To distinguish *Tooker* on such a basis is not improperly discriminatory. It is quite true that, in applying the Ontario guest statute to the Ontario-domiciled passenger, we, in a sense, extend a right less generous than New York extends to a New York passenger in a New York vehicle with New York insurance. That, though, is not a consequence of invidious discrimination; it is, rather, the result of the existence of disparate rules of law in jurisdictions that have diverse and important connections with the litigants and the litigated issue.

The fact that insurance policies issued in this State on New York-based vehicles cover liability, regardless of the place of the accident (Vehicle and Traffic Law, Consol.Laws, c. 71 § 311, subd. 4), certainly does not call for the application of internal New York law in this case. The compulsory insurance requirement is designed to cover a car-owner's liability, not create it; in other words, the applicable statute was not intended to impose liability where none would otherwise exist. This being so, we may not properly look to the New York insurance requirement to dictate a choice-of-law rule which would invariably impose liability....

When, in Babcock v. Jackson (12 N.Y.2d 473, 240 N.Y.S.2d 743, 191 N.E.2d 279, supra), we rejected the inexorable choice-of-law rule in personal injury cases because it failed to take account of underlying policy considerations, we were willing to sacrifice the certainty provided by the old rule for the more just, fair and practical result that may best be achieved by giving controlling effect to the law of the jurisdiction which has

---

1. In the other concurring opinion (24 N.Y.2d at p. 585, 301 N.Y.S.2d at p. 533, 249 N.E.2d at p. 404), I wrote that in such a case—where the passenger is a resident of the state having a guest statute—"the applicable rule of decision will [normally] be that of the state where the accident occurred". [Footnote by the court.]

the greatest concern with, or interest in, the specific issue raised in the litigation.... In consequence of the change effected—and this was to be anticipated—our decisions in multi-state highway accident cases, particularly in those involving guest-host controversies, have, it must be acknowledged, lacked consistency. This stemmed, in part, from the circumstance that it is frequently difficult to discover the purposes or policies underlying the relevant local law rules of the respective jurisdictions involved. It is even more difficult, assuming that these purposes or policies are found to conflict, to determine on some principled basis which should be given effect at the expense of the others.

The single all-encompassing rule which called, invariably, for selection of the law of the place of injury was discarded, and wisely, because it was too broad to prove satisfactory in application. There, is, however, no reason why choice-of-law rules, more narrow than those previously devised, should not be successfully developed, in order to assure a greater degree of predictability and uniformity, on the basis of our present knowledge and experience.... "The time has come," I wrote in Tooker (24 N.Y.2d, at p. 584, 301 N.Y.S.2d, at p. 532, 249 N.E.2d, at p. 403), "to endeavor to minimize what some have characterized as an *ad hoc* case-by-case approach by laying down guidelines, as well as we can, for the solution of guest-host conflicts problems." *Babcock* and its progeny enable us to formulate a set of basic principles that may be profitably utilized, for they have helped us uncover the underlying values and policies which are operative in this area of the law.... "Now that these values and policies have been revealed, we may proceed to the next stage in the evolution of the law—the formulation of a few rules of general applicability, promising a fair level of predictability." Although it was recognized that no rule may be formulated to guarantee a satisfactory result in every case, the following principles were proposed as sound for situations involving guest statutes in conflicts settings (24 N.Y.2d, at p. 585, 301 N.Y.S.2d, at p. 532, 249 N.E.2d, at p. 404):

> "1. When the guest-passenger and the host-driver are domiciled in the same state, and the car is there registered, the law of that state should control and determine the standard of care which the host owes to his guest.
>
> "2. When the driver's conduct occurred in the state of his domicile and that state does not cast him in liability for that conduct, he should not be held liable by reason of the fact that liability would be imposed upon him under the tort law of the state of the victim's domicile. Conversely, when the guest was injured in the state of his own domicile and its law permits recovery, the driver who has come into that state should not—in the absence of special circumstances—be permitted to interpose the law of his state as a defense.
>
> "3. In other situations, when the passenger and the driver are domiciled in different states, the rule is necessarily less categorical. Normally, the applicable rule of decision will be that of the state where the accident occurred but not if it can be shown that displacing that normally applicable rule will advance the relevant substantive law purposes without

impairing the smooth working of the multi-state system or producing great uncertainty for litigants. (Cf. Restatement, 2d, Conflict of Laws, P.O.D., pt. II, §§ 146, 159 [later adopted and promulgated May 23, 1969].)"

The variant views expressed not only in *Tooker* but by Special Term and the divided Appellate Division in this litigation underscore and confirm the need for these rules. Since the passenger was domiciled in Ontario and the driver in New York, the present case is covered by the third stated principle. The law to be applied is that of the jurisdiction where the accident happened unless it appears that "displacing [that] normally applicable rule will advance the relevant substantive law purposes" of the jurisdictions involved. Certainly, ignoring Ontario's policy requiring proof of gross negligence in a case which involves an Ontario-domiciled guest at the expense of a New Yorker does not further the substantive law purposes of New York. In point of fact, application of New York law would result in the exposure of this State's domiciliaries to a greater liability than that imposed upon resident users of Ontario's highways. Conversely, the failure to apply Ontario's law would "impair"—to cull from the rule set out above—"the smooth working of the multi-state system [and] produce great uncertainty for litigants" by sanctioning forum shopping and thereby allowing a party to select a forum which could give him a larger recovery than the court of his own domicile. In short, the plaintiff has failed to show that this State's connection with the controversy was sufficient to justify displacing the rule of *lex loci delictus*....

In each action, the Appellate Division's order should be reversed, that of Special Term reinstated, without costs, and the questions certified answered in the negative.

BREITEL, JUDGE (concurring).

I agree that there should be a reversal, but would place the reversal on quite narrow grounds. It is undesirable to lay down prematurely major premises based on shifting ideologies in the choice of law. True, Chief Judge Fuld in his concurring opinion in the *Tooker* case ... took the view that there had already occurred sufficient experience to lay down some rules of law which would reduce the instability and uncertainty created by the recent departures from traditional *lex loci delictus*. This case, arising so soon after, shows that the permutations in accident cases, especially automobile accident cases, is disproof that the time has come.

Problems engendered by the new departures have not gone unnoticed and they are not confined to the courts of this State (Juenger, Choice of Law in Interstate Torts, 118 U.Pa.L.Rev. 202, 214–220). They arise not merely because any new departure of necessity creates problems, but much more because the departures have been accompanied by an unprecedented competition of ideologies, largely of academic origin, to explain and reconstruct a whole field of law, each purporting or aspiring to achieve a single universal principle.

Babcock v. Jackson, 12 N.Y.2d 473, 240 N.Y.S.2d 743, 191 N.E.2d 279, an eminently correctly and justly decided case, applied the then current new doctrine of grouping of contacts. Troubles arose only when the universality of a single doctrine was assumed.... By the time of Miller v. Miller, 22 N.Y.2d 12, 290 N.Y.S.2d 734, 237 N.E.2d 877 and the *Tooker* case, supra, the new doctrine had been displaced by a still newer one, that of governmental interests developed most extensively by the late Brainerd Currie, and the court was deeply engaged in probing the psychological motivation of legislatures of other States in enacting statutes restricting recoveries in tort cases. Now, evidently, it is suggested that this State and other States may have less parochial concerns in enacting legislation restricting tort recoveries than had been believed only a short time ago. The trouble this case has given the courts below and now this court stems, it is suggested, more from a concern in sorting out ideologies than in applying narrow rules of law in the traditional common-law process (Juenger, op. cit., supra, at p. 233).

What the *Babcock* case ... taught and what modern day commentators largely agree is that *lex loci delictus* is unsoundly applied if it is done indiscriminately and without exception. It is still true, however, that the *lex loci delictus* is the normal rule, as indeed Chief Judge Fuld noted in the *Tooker* case, ... to be rejected only when it is evident that the situs of the accident is the least of the several factors or influences to which the accident may be attributed.... Certain it is that States are not concerned only with their own citizens or residents. They are concerned with events that occur within their territory, and are also concerned with the "stranger within the gates" (Juenger, op. cit., supra, at pp. 209–210).

In this case, none would have ever assumed that New York law should be applied just because one of the two defendants was a New York resident and his automobile was New York insured, except for the overbroad statements of Currie doctrine in the *Tooker* case....

Consequently, I agree that there should be a reversal and the defenses allowed to stand. The conclusion, however, rests simply on the proposition that plaintiff has failed by her allegations to establish that the relationship to this State was sufficient to displace the normal rule that the *lex loci delictus* should be applied, the accident being associated with Ontario, from inception to tragic termination, except for adventitious facts and where the lawsuit was brought.

■ BERGAN, JUDGE (dissenting)....

There is a difference of fundamental character between justifying a departure from *lex loci delictus* because the court will not, as a matter of policy, permit a New York owner of a car licensed and insured in New York to escape a liability that would be imposed on him here; and a departure based on the fact a New York resident makes the claim for injury. The first ground of departure is justifiable as sound policy; the second is justifiable only if one is willing to treat the rights of a stranger permitted to sue in New York differently from the way a resident is treated. Neither because of "interest" nor "contact" nor any other defensible ground is it proper to say in a court of law that the rights of one man whose suit is accepted shall be adjudged differently on the merits on the basis of where he happens to live....

... What the court is deciding today is that although it will prevent a New York car owner from asserting the defense of a protective foreign statute when a New York resident in whose rights it has an "interest" sues; it has no such "interest" when it accepts the suit in New York of a nonresident. This is an inadmissible distinction.

NOTES

1. On occasion, Judge Fuld's principles may produce results that some may think unpalatable. See, e.g., Foster v. Leggett, 484 S.W.2d 827 (Ky.1972). The defendant driver was legally domiciled in Ohio, which has a guest statute, but he was employed in Kentucky and spent much of his time there. He and his guest set out from Kentucky for Columbus, Ohio, intending to "have dinner, go to a show or the races" and then return to Kentucky "the night of the same day." In Ohio the car was in an accident and the passenger was killed. The Kentucky court refused to apply the Ohio guest statute and found for the plaintiff by applying Kentucky's common law standard of negligence. Judge Fuld's second principle would apparently call for application of the law of Ohio. Foster v. Leggett is the subject of a symposium in 61 Ky.L.J. 368–428 (1973).

On the other hand, see Cipolla v. Shaposka, 439 Pa. 563, 267 A.2d 854 (1970). A Delaware host was driving his Pennsylvania guest back to Pennsylvania when the car crashed in Delaware. The court applied the Delaware guest statute declaring that "it seems only fair to permit a defendant to rely on his home state's law when he is acting within that state." Would there be anything unfair about applying the Pennsylvania rule of ordinary negligence when the trip was intended to reach there?

Should *Neumeier* Rule 2 have provided an exception for cases like *Foster* and *Cipolla*? If rules are desirable to provide reasonable predictability, are the *Neumeier* rules good rules for this purpose? Do they sufficiently provide for the most likely variations in host-guest cases? What purpose is served by including the state where the car is "registered" in Rule 1?

The *Neumeier* rules provide for possible exceptions in the second sentence of Rule 2 and in Rule 3. Are these exceptions carefully drafted? Why should there be an exception in the second sentence of Rule 2, but not in the first sentence? For a discussion of the art of drafting exceptions when codifying choice-of-law rules, see Symeonides, Exception Clauses in American Conflicts Law, 42 Am.J.Comp.L. 813 (1994).

2. Subsequent cases in the New York courts have apparently only been concerned with Chief Judge Fuld's third principle. Pursuant to this principle, the law of the place of injury was applied and judgment rendered in the defendant's favor in Croft v. National Car Rental, 56 N.Y.2d 989, 453 N.Y.S.2d 631, 439 N.E.2d 346 (1982) (vicarious liability of owner for negligence of driver); Towley v. King Arthur Rings, Inc., 40 N.Y.2d 129, 386 N.Y.S.2d 80, 351 N.E.2d 728 (1976) (guest-passenger statute); Blais v. Deyo, 92 A.D.2d 998, 461 N.Y.S.2d 471 (3rd Dept.1983) (limit on amount of recovery); Rogers v. U-Haul Co., 41 A.D.2d 834, 342 N.Y.S.2d 158 (1973) (vicarious liability of owner for negligence of driver).

3. The New York Court of Appeals cited Neumeier in an opinion in which it said by way of dictum that "*lex loci delicti* remains the general rule in tort cases to be displaced only in extraordinary circumstances." Cousins v. Instrument Flyers, Inc., 44 N.Y.2d 698, 699, 405 N.Y.S.2d 441, 376 N.E.2d 914, 915 (1978).

4. A "modern" dog-bite case (purporting to apply the third rule in *Neumeier*) is Bader v. Purdom, 841 F.2d 38 (2d Cir.1988). While New York plaintiffs were visiting Ontario defendants at their farm one of the New York children was bitten by defendants' dog. In the resulting diversity action in New York defendants impleaded the New York parents as liable over because of negligent supervision of their child. Ontario law was applied to permit the impleader claim, though under New York the parents would not have been liable.

5. Action by a guest-passenger to recover for injuries resulting from an automobile accident in Ohio. The plaintiff was domiciled in New Jersey and the defendant driver in New York. The automobile was registered, principally garaged and "presumably insured" in New York. *Held*: The Ohio guest-passenger statute was not available to the defendant as a defense. Chief Judge Fuld's third principle would not require application of Ohio law in this instance, since "none of the litigants reside in a state having a guest statute, nor presumably did the insurer calculate the defendants' insurance premiums with a guest statute in mind." Chila v. Owens, 348 F.Supp. 1207 (S.D.N.Y.1972).

See also Diehl v. Ogorewac, 836 F.Supp. 88 (E.D.N.Y.1993). A driver from New Jersey crashed in North Carolina killing one New York passenger and injuring another. Neither passenger was wearing a seat belt. Under North Carolina law, this fact was not admissible in evidence as proof of contributory negligence, but it was admissible under both New Jersey and New York law. The court held the evidence admissible as comporting "with the policies served by the first *Neumeier* rule" and, in any event, within the exception in Rule 3. Should Rule 1 have expressly included cases in which host and guest live in different states but there is no difference in the laws of the two states?

6. Other states have given Chief Judge Fuld's Neumeier principles a mixed reception. First National Bank in Fort Collins v. Rostek, 514 P.2d 314 (Colo.1973), adopted the first two principles; but in Labree v. Major, 111 R.I. 657, 306 A.2d 808 (1973), Note 2, page 623, infra, the court applied the Rhode Island ordinary negligence rule rather than the Massachusetts gross negligence standard, to permit recovery by a Massachusetts guest passenger, injured in Massachusetts by a Rhode Island host driver.

7. Neumeier v. Kuehner is the subject of a symposium, consisting of articles by Professors Twerski, Sedler, Baade, Shapira and King, in 1 Hofstra L.Rev. 104–182 (1973). All of the writers, with the exception of the last mentioned, criticize the decision on a variety of grounds. Compare the view of a Dutch conflicts scholar, who wrote with respect to *Neumeier*, "It is too facile to dismiss the labor of American courts and writers as a waste of effort which did not produce a workable ... method and ... rules right away." DeBoer, Beyond Lex Loci Delicti 196 (1987).

8. For a lengthy and scholarly critique of *Neumeier* see Korn, The Choice-of-Law Revolution: A Critique, 83 Colum.L.Rev. 772 (1983). See generally Reese, Chief Judge Fuld and Choice of Law, 71 Colum.L.Rev. 548 (1971); Reese, Choice of Law: Rules or Approach, 57 Corn.L.Q. 315 (1972); Powers, Formalism and Nonformalism in Choice of Law Methodology, 52 Wash.L.Rev. 27 (1976); Haworth, The Mirror Image Conflicts Case, 1974 Wash.U.L.Q. 1.

CHANGES IN THE CONFLICTS RULES OF OTHER COUNTRIES

As of January 1, 1995, thirty-seven states plus the District of Columbia and Puerto Rico have adopted a method of choosing law for torts that takes into account the content and purposes of the laws of the states that have contacts with the parties and the transaction. See p. 5, n. 8, supra. A similar change has occurred abroad.

United Kingdom Law

Red Sea Insurance Co. v. Bouygues SA, [1994] 3 W.L.R. 926, [1994] 3 All.E.R. 749 (P.C.1994) (appeal taken from Hong Kong). A number of companies were engaged in a joint venture to construct buildings in Saudi Arabia. The joint venturers discovered structural damage to the buildings and, when their insurers rejected a claim for compensation, the joint venturers sued the insurer at its place of incorporation, Hong Kong. The insurer counterclaimed against one member of the joint venture contending the member had supplied faulty materials that caused the damage. The counterclaim was based on the insurer's subrogation to the rights of the other insured members of the venture. Under the law of Saudi Arabia, the insurer could bring its subrogation action before paying the claim, but under Hong Kong law, the insurer first had to pay, which it had not done. The Hong Kong courts, at trial and on appeal, held that the insurer could not bring the subrogation claim in Hong Kong, because under the English rule, the wrong had to be actionable under both the lex loci delicti and the lex fori. The Privy Council reversed on the ground that on the issue of the right to subrogation, the most significant relationship with the occurrence and the parties was with Saudi Arabia and therefore Saudi law applied. Although double actionability remained the usual rule, in order to avoid injustice in particular cases, the law of the place of most significant relationship could be applied either to a single issue and to replace the lex loci delicti (as in Chaplin v. Boys, [1969] 3 W.L.R. 322, [1969] 2 All E.R. 1085), or to all issues and to replace the lex fori (as in this case).

In Chaplin v. Boys, a motor vehicle collision in Malta involved two English servicemen who were stationed there. Under Maltese law, the injured serviceman could not recover for his pain and suffering, but under English law he could. The five-member panel of the House of Lords decided unanimously that English law should apply. Two of the five law Lords based their analysis on the respective interests of Malta and England in the issue. Three of the panel characterized damages as "procedural," but two of the three indicated that this would not permit English damages law to apply if, unlike this case, the plaintiff was forum shopping. Could a judge determine whether a plaintiff was forum shopping without inquiring into whether the plaintiff's contacts with England gave England a reasonable interest in applying its law?

On November 8, 1995, Parliament passed The Private International Law (Miscellaneous Provisions) Act. Part III of the Act abolishes the double actionability rule for tort or delict (§ 10) and replaces it with a presumption that the applicable law is that of the place of injury (§ 11). This presumption is rebutted as to one or more issues arising in a case, if it is "substantially more appropriate" to apply the law of another country (§ 12). The Act applies to "acts or omissions giving rise to a claim which occur" after the Act takes effect (§ 14(1)). There is a "public policy" exception (§ 14(3)(a)(i)). The Act does not affect choice of law for defamation (§ 13).

German Law

The codification noted p. 448, supra, does not include torts. German decisions apply the law of the place where the tortfeasor acted. If, however, the injury occurs in another jurisdiction, the law of either the place of acting or of injury is applied, whichever is more favorable to the victim. A 1942 regulation provided that German law applies to tort claims arising abroad between German nationals. Judicial extension of this regulation provides for the application of the common home-State law to foreign nationals for torts committed in Germany. See Hay, Flexibility Versus Predictability and Uniformity in Choice of Law, 226 Academy of International Law Recueil des cours (Collection of Courses) 365–67 (1991–I).

Austria

Federal Statute of 15 June 1978 on Private International Law

§ 1(1). Factual situations with foreign contacts shall be judged, in regard to private law, according to the legal order to which the strongest connection exists.

§ 48(1). Noncontractual damage claims shall be judged according to the law of the state in which the damage-causing conduct occurred. However, if the persons involved have a stronger connection to the law of one and the same other state, that law shall be determinative.

Switzerland

Statute on Private International Law, Entered Into for January 1, 1989, 29 I.L.M. 1254, Article 133

1. When the tortfeasor and the injured party have their habitual residence in the same State, claims based on tort are governed by the law of that State.

2. When the tortfeasor and the injured party have no habitual residence in the same state, these claims are governed by the law of the State where the tort was committed. However, if the result occurred in another State, the law of this State shall be applied if the tortfeasor could have foreseen that the damage would be suffered in that State.

3. Notwithstanding the preceding paragraphs, if and when a tort violates a judicial relationship between the tortfeasor and the injured party, claims based on this act are governed by the law applying to this judicial relationship.

For product liability, article 135 allows the injured party to choose either the law of the tortfeasor's place of business or, if the product was sold there with the tortfeasor's permission, the law where the product was acquired. If foreign law applies, "no compensation can be awarded in Switzerland other than the compensation that would be granted for such damage pursuant to Swiss law."

Hungary

Decree 13 of the Presidential Council of the Hungarian People's Republic: The International Private Law, effective July 1, 1979

Section 32

(3) If the domicile of the tortfeasor and the injured party is in the same State, the law of that State shall be applied.

(4) If, according to the law governing the tortious act or omission, liability is conditioned on a finding of culpability, the existence of culpability can be determined by either the personal law of the tortfeasor or the law of the place of injury.

Hague Convention on the Law Applicable to Traffic Accidents, 4 May 1971 (As of August 1, 1994, in force in Austria, Belgium, Czech Republic, Fyrom, France, Luxembourg, Netherlands, Slovak Republic, Slovenia, Spain, Switzerland, Bosnia and Herzegovinia, and Croatia; signed but not ratified in Portugal.)

Article 4

Subject to Article 5 [liability for damage to goods] the following exceptions are made to the provisions of Article 3 [applying the "internal law of the State where the accident occurred."]

(a) where only one vehicle is involved ... and it is registered in a State other than that where the accident occurred, the internal law of the State of registration is applicable to determine liability—towards the driver, owner or any other person having control of or an interest in the vehicle irrespective of their habitual residence—towards a victim who is a passenger and whose habitual residence is in a State other than that where the accident occurred—towards a victim who is outside the vehicle at the place of the accident and whose habitual residence is in the State of registration....

(b) Where two or more vehicles are involved ... the provisions of (a) are applicable only if all the vehicles are registered in the same State....

Hague Convention on the Law Applicable to Products Liability, 2 October 1973 (As of August 1, 1994, in force in Finland, Fyrom, France, Luxembourg, Netherlands, Norway, Slovenia, Spain, and Croatia. Signed but not ratified in Belgium, Italy and Portugal.)

Article 4

The applicable law shall be the internal law of the State of the place of injury, if that state is also—(a) the place of the habitual residence of the person directly suffering damage, or (b) the principal place of business of the person claimed to be liable, or (c) the place where the product was acquired by the person directly suffering damage.

Article 5

Notwithstanding the provisions of Article 4, the applicable law shall be the internal law of the State of the habitual residence of the person directly suffering damage, if that State is also—(a) the principal place of business of the person claimed to be liable, or (b) the place where the product was acquired by the person directly suffering damage.

Article 6

Where neither of the laws designated in Articles 4 and 5 applies, the applicable law shall be the internal law of the State of the principal place of business of the person claimed to be liable, unless the claimant bases his claim upon the internal law of the State of the place of injury.

Article 7

Neither the law of the State of the place of injury nor the law of the State of the habitual residence of the person directly suffering damages shall be applicable by virtue of Articles 4, 5 and 6 if the person claimed to be liable establishes that he could not reasonably have foreseen that the product or his own product of the same type would be made available in that State through commercial channels.

NOTE

Do these codes and conventions compare favorably or unfavorably with the *Neumeier* rules? Under the Products Liability Convention, if the product is foreseeably sold through commercial channels at the victim's habitual residence, should it matter whether the victim acquired it there? Under the Traffic Accidents Convention, should it make a difference that a victim or another car is not from the same state as that where the other car is registered, if they are from a state that has the same law as the state of registration?

Duncan v. Cessna Aircraft Company

Supreme Court of Texas, 1984.
665 S.W.2d 414.

■ SPEARS, JUSTICE.... Carolyn Parker Duncan, individually and on behalf of her minor children, brought this wrongful death action against Cessna Aircraft Company ("Cessna") for damages suffered when an airplane crash killed her husband, James Parker. The jury returned a verdict of $1,000,-000 for Duncan, but the trial court rendered judgment non obstante veredicto for Cessna. The court of appeals reversed the trial court's judgment and remanded the cause for a partial new trial. 632 S.W.2d 375. We reverse the judgments of the court of appeals and the trial court and render judgment for Duncan on the jury verdict.

This case presents three questions. The first is whether Texas or New Mexico law controls the construction of a release executed by Duncan in favor of the owner of the airplane, Air Plains West, Inc. We hold that the release must be construed according to Texas law because Texas has the most significant relationship to this issue.

The second question is whether, under Texas law, the release discharged Cessna's liability to Duncan. We hold that Cessna was not discharged because it was not specifically identified in the release.

The final question before us is whether Cessna, a strictly liable manufacturer, is entitled to contribution from Smithson's estate based on proof that his pilot negligence caused the fatal crash. We hold that in products liability cases tried after July 13, 1983, the date of our former opinion, a defendant may obtain a jury allocation of the plaintiff's damages according to the plaintiff's, defendants', and third parties' respective percentages of causation of those damages. We also hold, however, that Cessna did not preserve its claim for contribution against Smithson's estate. [The portion of the opinion dealing with the "final question" is omitted.]

I. BACKGROUND

Benjamin Smithson and James Parker died in the crash of a Cessna 150 airplane in New Mexico in 1976. At the time of the crash, Smithson was employed as an instructor pilot for Air Plains West, Inc., which owned the airplane, and was giving Parker flying lessons.

Parker's widow, Carolyn Duncan, individually and on behalf of her minor children, filed a wrongful death action in Federal District Court for the Northern District of Texas against Air Plains West and Smithson's estate. She alleged that their negligence proximately caused the crash and her husband's death. The suit was terminated when Duncan settled with Air Plains West for $90,000 and executed a release ("Duncan release") that stated, in pertinent part, "we [Duncan and her minor children] ... do hereby release, discharge and forever quitclaim Air Plains West, Inc., its agents, servants and employees, and the Estate of Benjamin A. Smithson, Jr., deceased, *or any other corporations or persons whomsoever responsible therefor, whether named herein or not,* from any and all claims of every kind and character whatsoever ... on account of the fatal injuries sustained by the said James E. Parker, which resulted in his death, as the result of an airplane crash occurring on or about October 19, 1976...." (emphasis added).

Duncan and Mrs. Smithson subsequently instituted wrongful death actions against Cessna. They alleged that design and manufacturing defects in the legs of the cockpit seats caused the legs to break during the crash, causing the deaths of their husbands.

Cessna responded with a counterclaim against Smithson's estate....

In addition, in its first amended original answer to Duncan's petition, Cessna claimed that its liability to the Duncan family was discharged by the Duncan release of Air Plains West....

The trial court ... granted Cessna's motion for judgment non obstante veredicto on the ground that the release executed in favor of Air Plains West and Smithson's estate also discharged Cessna's liability.

II. THE CONFLICTS PROBLEM

Cessna argues that in determining the effect of the Duncan release on Cessna's liability, we should apply New Mexico law, not Texas law. Cessna further argues that the New Mexico courts would construe the Duncan release to bar Duncan's cause of action against Cessna for damages arising out of the plane crash.

Duncan, on the other hand, contends that this case presents no true conflicts problem. She argues that we do not need to decide which state's law applies because under either Texas or New Mexico law, the general language in her release did not discharge Cessna. In order to resolve the effect of the release, therefore, we must first determine whether there is a difference between the rules of Texas and New Mexico on this issue.

A. Effect of the Release Under Texas Law

... We hold that under Texas law, the mere naming of a general class of tortfeasors in a release does not discharge the liability of each member of that class. A tortfeasor can claim the protection of a release only if the release refers to him by name or with such descriptive particularity that his identity or his connection with the tortious event is not in doubt. In this case, the release does not name Cessna, nor does it provide some specific description of Cessna. Since the reference to "all corporations" does not supply the descriptive particularity necessary to specifically identify Cessna, the release does not bar Duncan's action if Texas law applies to its construction.

B. Effect of the Release Under New Mexico Law

Section 4 of New Mexico's version of the Uniform Contribution Among Tortfeasors Act provides, "A release by the injured party of one joint tortfeasor, whether before or after judgment, does not discharge the other tortfeasor *unless the release so provides.*" N.M.Stat.Ann. § 41–3–4 (emphasis added).

In Johnson v. City of Las Cruces, 86 N.M. 196, 521 P.2d 1037 (Ct.App.1974), a New Mexico Court of Appeals interpreted this statute and held that a release discharges any tortfeasor who is named or who comes within a named general class.... Because Johnson is contrary to [Texas decisions], we must decide whether Texas or New Mexico law applies in construing the release.

C. The Law Applicable to Construction of the Release

One week before trial, Cessna moved the court to take judicial notice of certain statutes and case law of New Mexico. The court granted Cessna's motion and ruled that New Mexico law, to the extent that it differed from Texas law, applied to all substantive issues in the case. The court of appeals, however, held that Texas law governed the construction of the release because the release was a contract executed in Texas and, in accordance with the rule of lex loci contractus, the law of the place of the making of the contract applied to its construction.

Cessna and Duncan both argue that the court of appeals erred in applying the rule of lex loci contractus. They contend that the correct approach is the most significant relationship methodology of the Restatement (Second) of Conflict of Laws, which we adopted in Gutierrez v. Collins, 583 S.W.2d 312 (Tex.1979), for tort choice of law issues.[4]

In Gutierrez, this court strongly criticized the traditional tort choice of law rule of lex loci delecti (i.e., apply the law of the place where the wrong occurred). We decided that the rule's ease of application and uniformity of result did not justify its arbitrary and often inequitable results. Additionally, we noted that the traditional rule did not meet the demands of our highly mobile modern society. Primarily for these reasons, we abandoned lex loci delecti and replaced it with the most significant relationship approach set forth in §§ 6 and 145 of the Restatement (Second) of Conflict of Laws. The significant relationship methodology was selected because it offers a "rational yet flexible approach to conflicts problems, ... represents a collection of the best thinking on this subject ... [and] include[s] 'most of the substance' of all the modern theories." Id. at 318.

Most of the numerous inadequacies inherent in lex loci delecti also exist in the other traditional lex loci rules, including lex loci contractus. Each of these traditional rules sacrifices just and reasoned results for the ease and predictability of mechanistic decision making. However, "[e]ase of administration alone is a wholly inadequate reason for retention of an unjust rule." Id. at 317. By contrast, use of the most significant relationship approach in accordance with the general principles stated in § 6 produces reasoned choice of law decisions grounded in those specific governmental policies relevant to the particular substantive issue. Consequently, the lex loci rules will no longer be used in this state to resolve conflicts problems. Instead, in all choice of law cases, except those contract cases in which the parties have agreed to a valid choice of law clause, the law of the state with the most significant relationship to the particular substantive issue will be applied to resolve that issue.

---

4. Cessna also argues that § 170(1) of the Second Restatement applies. Section 170(1) provides, "The law selected by application of the rule of § 145 [governing tort issues] determines the effect of a release ... given to one joint tortfeasor upon the liability of the other." Because Cessna was not a party to the Duncan release, however, its liability to Duncan implicates policies underlying both contract and tort law. See generally R. Leflar, American Conflicts Law § 134, at 273 (3d ed. 1977). We therefore decline to adopt § 170(1).

In applying § 6 to this case, we must first identify the state contacts that should be considered. Once these contacts are established, the question of which state's law will apply is one of law. Moreover, the number of contacts with a particular state is not determinative. Some contacts are more important than others because they implicate state policies underlying the particular substantive issue. Consequently, selection of the applicable law depends on the qualitative nature of the particular contacts.

The following undisputed state contacts are present in this case: Cessna is a Kansas corporation; the plane's defective seats were designed and manufactured in Kansas; the plane was put into the stream of commerce in Texas; decedent James Parker lived in Texas and worked in New Mexico; decedent Benjamin Smithson lived and worked in New Mexico; Air Plains West is a New Mexico corporation; and the release was executed in Texas as a settlement of a lawsuit filed in a federal district court in Texas. The beginning point for evaluating these contacts is the identification of the policies or "governmental interests," if any, of each state in the application of its rule.

Since under New Mexico law, the Duncan release would discharge Cessna, New Mexico has no governmental interest in the resolution of this issue. Its rule, set forth in Johnson, reflects policies of effectuating the intent of the parties to the release and of protecting New Mexico defendants. Here, however, no New Mexico defendant or injured party is involved. Cessna is a Kansas corporation seeking the benefit of a release executed in Texas by an injured Texas resident as part of a settlement of a suit filed in Texas. We can conceive of no legitimate reason why the New Mexico legislature should be concerned with the application of its statute to a Texas settlement to cut off a Texas resident's claim against a Kansas corporation.[6]

Texas, on the other hand, has direct and important interests in the effect given to the Duncan release. Our purposes in abolishing the "unity of release" rule and requiring specific identification of nonsettling tortfeasors were to encourage both partial and full settlements; to avoid unfairly depriving injured Texas residents of their full satisfactions; to avoid providing an incentive to tortfeasors to delay or to stay out of early settlement negotiations; and to ensure that Texas claimants do not inadvertently lose their valuable rights against unnamed and perhaps unknown tortfeasors by settling with only one of the wrongdoers. See Knutson v. Morton Foods, Inc., 603 S.W.2d 805, 807–08 (Tex.1980); McMillen v. Klingensmith, 467 S.W.2d at 195–96. To effectuate these policies, we must narrowly construe general, categorical release clauses. A nonsettling tortfeasor should not fortuitously escape compensating his Texas victim simply because of settlement arrangements that did not encompass him or his conduct and to which he contributed nothing. If Cessna obtains the

---

6. As for the application of Kansas law, since Cessna has not asserted any error in the trial court's application of New Mexico law, we need not decide whether the resolution of this issue will impair any policies expressed in Kansas law.

benefit of the Duncan release, then the policies underlying McMillen will obviously be frustrated.

Texas has an additional interest. Duncan could reasonably have expected that the laws of Texas would govern the effect on third parties of a settlement agreement negotiated and executed in Texas. She certainly had no reason to believe that New Mexico law would apply to cut off her cause of action against Cessna or some other unknown tortfeasor. Texas has an interest in protecting Duncan's reasonable contractual expectations.

An analysis of the relevant state contacts reveals that New Mexico has no underlying interest in the application of its law, while Texas has important interests in allowing Duncan's action against Cessna. In this situation, known as a "false conflict," it is an established tenet of modern conflicts law that the law of the interested state should apply. See, e.g., J. Martin, Perspectives on Conflict of Laws: Choice of Law 85 (1980); Scoles & Hay, Conflict of Laws § 2.6, at 15 (2d ed. 1992); R. Weintraub, Commentary on the Conflict of Laws § 3.1, at 48, § 6.2, at 267–68 (2d ed. 1980). Accordingly, we hold that Texas law applies to the determination of the effect of the Duncan release on Cessna. We further hold that Cessna's liability to Duncan is not discharged....

The judgments of the trial court and court of appeals [which had remanded for a new trial on the contribution issue] are reversed, and judgment is here rendered on the jury verdict for Duncan, subject to a credit for the $90,000 already received in settlement.

NOTE

Is the contract issue in the principal case one of construction or validity?

The court states that "no New Mexico defendant or injured party is involved." Is that so in the light of Cessna's counterclaim?

The court states that it need not decide whether Kansas law should be applied, because Cessna did not request it. Would it be reasonable to apply Kansas law?

RESTATEMENT, SECOND, CONFLICT OF LAWS (1971):*

§ 187. Law of the State Chosen by the Parties

(1) The law of the state chosen by the parties to govern their contractual rights and duties will be applied if the particular issue is one which the parties could have resolved by an explicit provision in their agreement directed to that issue.

(2) The law of the state chosen by the parties to govern their contractual rights and duties will be applied, even if the particular issue is one which the parties could not have resolved by an explicit provision in their agreement directed to that issue, unless either

---

* Quoted with the permission of the copyright owner, The American Law Institute.

(a) the chosen state has no substantial relationship to the parties or the transaction and there is no other reasonable basis for the parties' choice, or

(b) application of the law of the chosen state would be contrary to a fundamental policy of a state which has a materially greater interest than the chosen state in the determination of the particular issue and which, under the rule of § 188, would be the state of the applicable law in the absence of an effective choice of law by the parties.

(3) In the absence of a contrary indication of intention, the reference is to the local law of the state of the chosen law.

---

§ 188. Law Governing in Absence of Effective Choice by the Parties

(1) The rights and duties of the parties with respect to an issue in contract are determined by the local law of the state which, with respect to that issue, has the most significant relationship to the transaction and the parties under the principles stated in § 6.

(2) In the absence of an effective choice of law by the parties (see § 187), the contacts to be taken into account in applying the principles of § 6 to determine the law applicable to an issue include:

(a) the place of contracting,

(b) the place of negotiation of the contract,

(c) the place of performance,

(d) the location of the subject matter of the contract, and

(e) the domicil, residence, nationality, place of incorporation and place of business of the parties.

These contacts are to be evaluated according to their relative importance with respect to the particular issue.

(3) If the place of negotiating the contract and the place of performance are in the same state, the local law of this state will usually be applied, except as otherwise provided in §§ 189–199 and 203.

NOTES

1. Are the exceptions in § 187 necessary and workable? They are extensively considered in Reese, Power of Parties to Choose Law Governing Their Contract, 1960 Proc.Am.Soc.Int'l Law 49. See also Weinberger, Party Autonomy and Choice-of-Law: The Restatement (Second), Interest Analysis, and the Search for a Methodological Synthesis, 4 Hofstra L.Rev. 605 (1976); Note, Effectiveness of Choice-of-Law Clauses in Contract Conflicts of Law: Party Autonomy or Objective Determination?, 82 Colum.L.Rev. 1659 (1982).

2. Professor Weintraub believes that choice-of-law clauses should only control issues of construction and that, with respect to issues of validity, there should be a rebuttable presumption that the validating law will be applied unless certain factors, which he enumerates, point in a contrary direction. Among these factors are that the invalidating rule is protective of the party in the inferior bargaining position and that it differs in basic policy from the validating rule. Weintraub, Commentary on the Conflict of Laws 369–77, 409–11 (3d ed. 1986).

3. The American Law Institute reports "uncertainty" as to dépeçage—whether the parties should be permitted to select the local law of two or more states to govern different aspects of a contract. Restatement, Second, Conflict of Laws § 187, Comment *i*. What contentions might be made?

4. What should be the result when a choice-of-law clause calls for application of a law that would invalidate a contract? Section 187, Comment *e* of the Restatement, Second, states that in such circumstances the court should disregard the choice-of-law provision and, instead, apply the law of the state which would otherwise be applicable.

UNIFORM COMMERCIAL CODE § 1–105. TERRITORIAL APPLICATION OF THE ACT; PARTIES' POWER TO CHOOSE APPLICABLE LAW

(1) Except as provided hereafter in this section, when a transaction bears a reasonable relation to this state and also to another state or nation the parties may agree that the law either of this state or of such other state or nation shall govern their rights and duties. Failing such agreement this Act applies to transactions bearing an appropriate relation to this state.

(2) Where one of the following provisions of this Act specifies the applicable law, that provision governs and a contrary agreement is effective only to the extent permitted by the law (including the conflict of laws rules) so specified:

Rights of creditors against sold goods. Section 2–402.

Applicability of the Article on Leases. Sections 2A–105 and 2A–106.

Applicability of the Article on Bank Deposits and Collections. Section 4–102.

Governing law in the Article on Funds Transfers. Section 4A–507.

Bulk sales subject to the Article on Bulk Sales. Section 6–103.

Applicability of the Article on Investment Securities. Section 8–110.

Perfection provisions of the Article on Secured Transactions. Section 9–103.

NOTES

1. How should the second sentence of § 1–105(1) be construed. See Siegel, The U.C.C. and Choice of Law: Forum Choice or Forum Law, 21 Am.U.L.Rev. 494 (1972), taking the position that it should be construed to mean only that the forum should apply its usual choice-of-law rules; and that any other interpretation would lead to forum-shopping. In re Merritt Dredging Co., 839 F.2d 203 (4th Cir.1988), takes this position.

2. Section 1–105, along with the rest of Article 1, is in the process of being revised. Drafts indicate that the revised section will emphasize party autonomy and include a provision enforcing the parties' choice of forum.

Uniform Commercial Code, Article 4A, Funds Transfers § 4A–507(b): "If the parties ... have made an agreement selecting the law of a particular jurisdiction to govern rights and obligations between each other, the law of that jurisdiction governs those rights and obligations, whether or not the payment order or the funds transfer bears a reasonable relation to that jurisdiction."

Louisiana Civil Code

Art. 3537.   General Rule

Except as otherwise provided in this Title, an issue of conventional obligations is governed by the law of the state whose policies would be most seriously impaired if its law were not applied to that issue....

Art. 3540.   Party Autonomy

All other issues [other than form and capacity to contract] of conventional obligations are governed by the law expressly chosen or clearly relied upon by the parties, except to the extent that law contravenes the public policy of the state whose law would otherwise be applicable under Article 3537.

COMPARATIVE PERSPECTIVE: "CLOSEST CONNECTION" AND "CHARACTERISTIC PERFORMANCE"

The Restatement, Second, § 188 calls for the application of the law of the place of the "most significant relationship" and lists a number of contacts to be taken into account in making this determination. For some contracts, such as insurance, it provides rules, which may be displaced upon a showing that another law is more significantly related to the transaction and the parties. Modern European law, in analogy to § 188, calls for the application of the "most closely connected" law. Instead of "contacts," European law uses the concept of the "characteristic performance" for the determination of that law.

European Community Convention on the Law Applicable to Contractual Obligations

Article 4.   Applicable Law in the Absence of Choice

1. To the extent that the law applicable to the contract has not been chosen in accordance with Article 3, the contract shall be governed by the law of the country with which it is most closely connected. Nevertheless, a severable part of the contract which has a closer connection with another country may by way of exception be governed by the law of that other country.

2. Subject to the provisions of paragraph (5) of this Article, it shall be presumed that the contract is most closely connected with the country where the party who is to effect the performance which is characteristic of the contract has, at the time of conclusion of the contract, his habitual residence, or, in the case of a body corporate or unincorporated, its central administration. However, if the contract is entered into in the course of that party's trade or profession, that country shall be the country in which the principal place of business is situated or, where under the terms of the contract the performance is to be effected through a place of business other

than the principal place of business, the country in which that other place of business is situated.

3. Notwithstanding the provisions of paragraph (2) of this Article, to the extent that the subject matter of the contract is a right in immovable property or a right to use immovable property it shall be presumed that the contract is most closely connected with the country where the immovable property is situated.

4. A contract for the carriage of goods shall not be subject to the presumption in paragraph (2). In such a contract if the country in which, at the time the contract is concluded, the carrier has his principal place of business is also the country in which the place of loading or the place of discharge or the principal place of business of the consignor is situated it shall be presumed that the contract is most closely connected with that country. In applying this paragraph single voyage charter-parties and other contracts the main purpose of which is the carriage of goods shall be treated as contracts for the carriage of goods.

5. Paragraph (2) shall not apply if the characteristic performance cannot be determined, and the presumptions in paragraphs (2), (3) and (4) shall be disregarded if it appears from the circumstances as a whole that the contract is more closely connected with another country.

NOTES

1. The Convention's provisions are now in force. The "closest connection," as evidenced by the "characteristic performance," is a concept first developed by Swiss doctrine and case law. BGE 60, II, 294 (1934). Schnitzer, Handbuch des internationalen Privatrechts I, 52 and II, 639 (4th ed. 1957–58). It is now part of the Swiss Conflicts Statute of 1988 (Art. 117); see, also, Note (4), infra. The Austrian Conflicts Statute of 1978 adopts the "closest connection" as the basic principle for choice of law (§ 1) and provides specific contract choice-of-law rules in its §§ 36 et seq., which, in effect, derive from presumptions of what performance is "characteristic." Government bill Regierungsvorlage) 784–XIV. GP, anno. to § 36. For discussion of the Convention and comparison with the Restatement (Second), see Hay, Flexibility versus Uniformity and Predictability in Choice of Law, Hague Academy of International Law, 226 Collected Courses 281 (1991–I).

2. Art. 4(3) of the European Convention has its counterpart in Restatement, Second, §§ 189–190. For transportation contracts (Art. 4(4) of the Convention), the Restatement, Second, § 197 selects the law of the place of dispatch or departure or, in the case of round trips, of initial departure. The rule is intended to provide certainty and predictability as well as to comport with party expectations since "there can be no absolute certainty ... that the passenger or the goods will reach ..." the state of destination. Restatement, Second, § 197, comment (b). Does the Convention rule also achieve these goals?

3. The Convention severely limits the parties' freedom to choose the applicable law in consumer and employment contracts. Thus, a choice-of-law clause may not deprive a consumer of the mandatory rules of law of his habitual residence, and an employee may invoke the benefit of the mandatory rules of the law which would be applicable in the absence of the choice-of-law clause. When the parties have not made a choice, Art. 5(3) calls for the application of the law of the consumer's

habitual residence (assuming that the seller has one of the specified contacts with that country); in the main, the law of the place of the employee's habitual employment applies to the employment contract (Art. 6(2)). The Restatement, Second, § 196 provides for the law of the state "where the contract requires that the services ... be rendered." In a decision rendered before Dutch ratification of the Convention, the Netherlands Supreme Court took a narrow view of what constitutes a mandatory rule of Dutch law. A United States employer and a United States employee had concluded an employment contract in Texas and had stipulated the application of Texas law. The employee worked in the Netherlands for five years, when he was dismissed. Dutch law provides better protection against dismissal than does Texas law. Held: Texas law applies. Dutch public policy does not require displacement of the chosen law. Sorenson v. De vennootshap ... Aramco Overseas Co., [1987] NJ 2824. Would the Convention require a different result?

4. Except for the provisions of Arts. 4(3) and (4), 5(2), and 6(2), the Convention does not define "characteristic performance." What is the "characteristic performance" in a contract for the sale of goods (delivery of the goods or payment of the price) or in a loan (extension of the loan or repayment)?

The Austrian and Swiss Conflicts Statutes parallel the European Convention with respect to employment and consumer contracts and those regarding an interest in land. The Swiss statute (§ 117) provides an additional list of "characteristic" performances. In the sale of goods, the seller's performance is that which is "characteristic" for the contract; lease: the lessor's performance; rendition of services: performance of the services; bailment: bailee's performance; surety: surety's performance. These examples have in common that the payment of money is ordinarily not regarded as the characteristic performance. Rather, the focus is on the party obligated to do something: to sell the goods, perform the service, and so forth. Even when the transaction involves money on both sides, e.g., a loan, one performance may be said to be more characteristic than the other: the repayment with interest. However, many types of transactions are subject to regulation (e.g., insurance), so that the "characteristic performance" analysis will be affected by the existence of "mandatory" rules of law. See, e.g., Article 7 of the European Convention. Thus, even though the insured only pays money (the premium) while the insurance carrier provides the protection, it may well be that the law of the place of the insured's domicile will apply to life insurance contracts, while the location of the risk furnishes the applicable law in fire and casualty insurance. See Restatement, Second, §§ 192–193, respectively. Reciprocal performances which do not involve money are also hard to classify under the test. The focus on the "characteristic performance" has been criticized as tending to lead to the application of the law of the economically "stronger party: employers, banks, insurance companies, the closed professions." D'Oliveira, "Characteristic Obligation" in the Draft EEC Obligation Convention, 25 Am.J.Comp.L. 303, 327 (1977). Note, however, that the European Convention leaves "characteristic performance" largely undefined, that the Swiss statute only "presumes" the characteristic performance to be that of the party identified in its Art. 117, and that the basic principle of the "closest connection" in the European Convention and in the Austrian and Swiss statutes therefore still permits an evaluation of the individual circumstances of the parties' transaction.

5. Section 188 of the Restatement, Second, is an early proponent of a "closest connection" test ("place of the most significant relationship"). The Restatement's §§ 188(3), 189–199, and 203 suggest specific rules, in the manner of Arts. 4(3–4), 5(3), 6(2) of the European Convention, as supplemented by further definitions of

the "characteristic performance" in Art. 117 of the Swiss statute. Do the general provisions of § 188(1) and (2) provide enough guidance for other cases or would a central concept, such as that of the "characteristic performance," be helpful? In contrast, does the reference to the "characteristic performance" inject an unnecessary additional analytic step? Is there a danger of mechanical, i.e. inflexible choices? See also Article 4(5) of the Convention, supra and Hay, supra Note (1).

6. The 1986 Hague Convention on the Law Applicable to Contracts for the International Sale of Goods (not yet in force) calls for the application of the law of the seller's place of business. However, buyer's law is to be applied if the contract expressly calls for delivery at the buyer's place of business or if the buyer had opened the sale for bids and had controlled the terms of the transaction. If the transaction is, nonetheless, "more closely connected" with the law of another country, that law applies. This provision does not apply if the respective countries where the parties are located have declared that they do not accept this alternative reference or if these countries are members of the Vienna Convention (Note (7), infra) and the particular issue is covered by it. Mandatory provisions of forum law are not displaced by the Convention, and the forum will not apply foreign law which violates its public policy. For further detail see McLachlan, The New Hague Sales Convention and the Limits of the Choice of Law Process, 102 L.Q.Rev. 591 (1986).

7. One convention provides substantive rules of law. The United Nations Convention on Contracts for the International Sale of Goods (CISG), also known as the "Vienna Convention," entered into force for the United States on January 1, 1988. 53 Fed.Reg. 6262 (1987); 15 U.S.C.A.1988 Pocket Part. The Convention applies when the parties to the contract have their places of business in different Convention countries or if the forum's choice-of-law rules or the parties' own stipulation refer to a contracting state. The Convention provides rules of substantive law on formation of contracts (offer and acceptance) and the rights and obligations of sellers and buyers and, when it applies, therefore displaces the corresponding provisions of the UCC. See Bianca & Bonnell, eds., Commentary on the International Sales Law (1987).

CONTRACT AUTONOMY ABROAD

Foreign legal systems also permit the parties to stipulate the applicable law, with various limitations. The Austrian Conflicts Statute of 1978 does not require that the chosen law be related to the transaction but will not enforce a choice in consumer, employment, and lease contracts which would avoid mandatory provisions of law designed to protect consumers, employees, or lessees. The 1988 Swiss statute generally provides for party autonomy (Art. 116), but limits the parties' choices in employment contracts to the law of the employee's usual residence or to the employer's place of business or habitual or usual residence (Art. 121). The parties may not stipulate the applicable law in consumer contracts (Art. 120).

The European Union Convention on the Law Applicable to Contractual Obligations, Article 3, provides generally that the parties are free in their choice and refers to Articles 8, 9, and 11 for the determination of whether consent was validly given. These provisions, in turn, address the existence and validity of a contract in the first place (chosen law governs), compliance with formal requirements (place of execution if a single country, otherwise chosen law or of the law of a connected country), and capacity (place of execution). Other provisions of the Convention, however, limit Article 3. Thus, Article 5 imposes restrictions on choice-of-law clauses in consumer transactions, and Article 6 does the same with respect to employment contracts. Article 7 is unusual and potentially far-reaching: First, "when applying under this Convention the law of [another] country" (including one chosen by the parties), "effect may be given to the mandatory rules of the law of [a different] country with which the situation has a close connection." Second, "nothing in this Convention shall restrict the application of the rules of law of the forum in a situation where they are mandatory irrespective of the law otherwise applicable to the contract." In reverse, Article 16 provides that the forum may refuse to apply any rule of law "manifestly incompatible with [its] public policy."

Compare § 187 of the Restatement, Second, with the European statutory rules: is there a difference in the parties' freedom to stipulate the applicable law? For a representative decision in a mail order installment purchase case see Whitaker v. Spiegel, Inc., 95 Wn.2d 408, 623 P.2d 1147 (1981) (Washington usury law applied, despite choice-of-law clause stipulating Illinois law, on the basis of a Washington statute making Washington law applicable to all loans extended to Washington residents).

The 1986 Hague Convention on the Law Applicable to Contracts for the International Sale of Goods (not yet in force in any country) is intended to replace the 1955 Convention, which had been adopted by only nine countries. The new Convention also permits the parties to stipulate the applicable law. The validity of the stipulation is to be determined by reference to the chosen law. The parties may not exclude the mandatory rules of law of the forum, and the forum need not apply foreign law which is "manifestly" contrary to its public policy. It is unlikely that the countries of the European Community will adopt this convention in addition to their own (e.g., to apply to contracts involving non-Community countries).

The Inter–American Convention on the Law Applicable to International Contracts, opened for signature in 1994, 33 I.L.M. 732, except for "mandatory requirements" of forum law and "mandatory provisions of the law of another State with which the contract has close ties" (Art. 11), provides for complete party autonomy: "The contract shall be governed by the law chosen by the parties." Art. 7. "If the parties have not selected the applicable law, or if their selection proves ineffective, the contract shall be governed by the law of the State with which it has the closest ties." Art. 9. Article 10 reflects provisions often found in international commercial agreements: "In addition to the provisions in the foregoing articles, the guidelines, customs, and principles of international commercial law as well as commercial usage and practices generally accepted shall apply in order to discharge the requirements of justice and equity in the particular case." For discussion of the Convention, see Juenger, The Inter–American Convention on the Law Applicable to International Contracts: Some Highlights and Comparisons, 42 Am.J.Comp.L. 381 (1994).

NOTES

1. May the parties stipulate the law applicable to a *tort* claim? Such a stipulation will probably be effective for a claim that sounds in tort but arises out of the parties' contractual relationship and could have been brought as a contract claim. Hoes of America, Inc. v. Hoes, 493 F.Supp. 1205 (C.D.Ill.1979) (tortious interference with business claimed after termination of distributorship agreement). In general, however, this is still an open question in most jurisdictions. Compare Twohy v. First Nat. Bank of Chicago, 758 F.2d 1185 (7th Cir.1985) (stipulation upheld) with Ezell v. Hayes Oilfield Const. Co., Inc., 693 F.2d 489 (5th Cir.1982), certiorari denied 464 U.S. 818 (1983) (stipulation ineffective).

See also Nedlloyd Lines B.V. v. Superior Court, 3 Cal. 4th 459, 11 Cal.Rptr.2d 330, 834 P.2d 1148 (1992) construing a provision that the "agreement shall be governed by and construed in accordance with Hong Kong Law," as including a tort claim for breach of fiduciary duty, and enforcing it as so construed. Two dissenters found that the clause did not cover torts, but indicated that if it did, they would enforce it.

A choice-of-law clause will not cover statutes of limitations unless it expressly includes this issue. Financial Bancorp Inc. v. Pingree & Dahle, Inc., 880 P.2d 14 (Utah App.1994).

2. Under the Austrian statute (§ 35), the parties' freedom to stipulate the applicable law extends to tort claims. The government document supporting the bill cited as reasons that parties might wish to have a single law apply to all claims that might arise between them and that it might be desirable, in a given case, to stipulate for the application to the claim of the same law which would subsequently govern indemnification under insurance. German law permits the parties to select the applicable law for an existing tort claim. Kegel, Internationales Privatrecht 471 (6th ed. 1987).

3. Is it more likely or less likely that a choice-of-law clause relating to a tort claim will implicate the public policy of the forum than one relating to contract? See M/S Bremen v. Zapata Off–Shore Co., 407 U.S. 1 (1972), supra at 169 (choice-of-*court* clause in favor of English courts honored in a contract also containing exculpatory clauses valid under English law but not under American law).

4. "Floating" forum-selection or choice-of-law clauses or both give the plaintiff optional fora and, if choice of law is part of the stipulation, provide that the selected forum shall apply its own law. English law was long hostile to such "floating" clauses, principally on the ground that there had to be some law that applied to the question of validity of the contract (including its forum-selection clause) in the first place. For a review, see North, Reform, not Revolution, Hague Academy of International Law, 220 Collected Courses 9, 157–160 (1990–I). Art. 3(II)(1) of the Rome Convention permits the parties to make a subsequent choice of law; this includes changing an earlier choice. The English should now have less objection to an (initially) floating clause. Since the parties are permitted to make an alternative choice later on, there should be no objection to their providing for alternative choices *ab initio*. For an American decision enforcing floating jurisdictional and choice-of-law clauses in combination, see Musgrave v. HCA Mideast, Ltd., 856 F.2d 690 (4th Cir.1988).

Rudow v. Fogel

Appeals Court of Massachusetts, Essex, 1981.
12 Mass.App.Ct. 430, 426 N.E.2d 155.

■ Before ARMSTRONG, ROSE and DREBEN, JJ.

■ DREBEN, JUSTICE. This dispute ... involves a parcel of real estate located in Rockport, Massachusetts, which has been the subject of litigation since the death of the plaintiff's mother in 1963. The principal issue in this appeal is what law should Massachusetts apply in determining whether the defendant, the plaintiff's uncle, holds the property in constructive trust for the plaintiff. The trial judge found that the property was transferred to the defendant in New York on an oral trust at a time when the plaintiff, his mother, and the defendant were all domiciled in New York. We hold that, in the circumstances of this case, Massachusetts should look to New York law.

We state the relevant facts found by the trial judge. Marvin and Florence Rudow, the parents of the plaintiff William Rudow, purchased the Rockport property in 1958, taking title as tenants by the entirety. They operated a jewelry store in Rockport during the summer but lived in New York City during the rest of the year, where Florence taught school. In 1961, William's parents separated, Florence brought divorce proceedings in New York, and Marvin moved to Rockport. The plaintiff and Florence lived in New York with Florence's mother and with the defendant Albert Fogel, who was Florence's brother.

Great animosity developed between Marvin and Florence. Nevertheless, in 1962, while Florence was hospitalized for cancer, Marvin conveyed his interest in the Rockport property to Florence. The judge found this was done "out of a sense of remorse over the failure of the marriage and also because he felt sorry for his wife." The conveyance was a gift to Florence without any promise on her part of any kind.

In May, 1962, Florence made a will which, after several small gifts, left the residue of her property in trust for the plaintiff to be distributed to him at age twenty-five. Thereafter, on July 27, 1962, "anxious to keep the property away from her husband, then and in the future," Florence conveyed the Rockport property to the defendant in New York. The transfer was without consideration. The judge found, and his finding is not clearly erroneous, that at the time of transfer the defendant orally agreed that he would hold the property for the benefit of the plaintiff and "would turn it over to the plaintiff when (he) reached maturity." The judge also found that there was no fraud on the part of the defendant.

It appears that there is a difference between Massachusetts local law and New York law as to when a confidential (fiduciary) relationship may be found between close family members so as to impose a constructive trust. While recognizing that "respectable authority", including the State of New York, imposes a constructive trust on the principle "that a confidential relationship arises where the conveyance is made between members of a family," Ranicar v. Goodwin, 326 Mass. 710, 713, 96 N.E.2d 853 (1951), the Supreme Judicial Court has ruled, as a matter of Massachusetts local law, that "a confidential relationship does not arise merely because the conveyance was made between members of the family, even if the transferee promised to hold the land in trust." ...

The trial judge, applying Massachusetts local law, ruled that there was no constructive trust. Although he refused specific performance, he held that the plaintiff was not without remedy, and entered judgment for the plaintiff in the amount of the fair value of the property less expenses incurred by the defendant. The award to the plaintiff in the amount of the value of the property, less reasonable expenses, is in accord with Massachusetts law.

In determining that there was no constructive trust, the judge followed the traditional conflicts rule which looks to the law of the situs for determining all material questions involving legal or beneficial interests in land.

The Supreme Judicial Court has, however, in a series of cases, rejected the notion that a single test is appropriate for determining which law governs all questions relating to a transaction. The court can be said to have adopted a "more functional approach." See Choate, Hall & Stewart v. SCA Servs., Inc., 378 Mass. 535, 392 N.E.2d 1045 (1979). See also Restatement (Second) of Conflict of Laws § 6(2) (1971).

Thus, although the traditional torts conflicts rule provides for reference to the law of the place where the tort occurred, in Pevoski v. Pevoski, 371 Mass. 358, 360, 358 N.E.2d 416 (1976), the court recognized that "another jurisdiction may sometimes be more concerned and more involved with certain issues than the State in which the conduct occurred." In that case, which involved a three-car collision in New York State, the Pevoski automobile was registered in Massachusetts (as apparently were the other two) and all three vehicles were driven by Massachusetts residents. The plaintiff, a passenger in the car driven by her husband, brought an action against him for damages, and he defended on the ground of interspousal tort immunity. The court held that Massachusetts law governed that question. After pointing out that "the economic and social impact of this litigation will fall on Massachusetts domiciliaries and a Massachusetts insurer," the court concluded, "New York has an undoubted interest in enforcing its traffic laws and in making its highways safe for travel but it has no legitimate interest in regulating the interspousal relationships of Massachusetts domiciliaries who chance to be injured within its borders." Ibid....

While the court has not recently ruled on choice-of-law questions concerning trusts involving land, it has rejected the law of the situs as the only criterion for resolving all questions pertaining to an inter vivos trust. This is true even if the trust expressly directs that the trust shall be governed by and construed in accordance with internal Massachusetts law. In First Natl. Bank v. Shawmut Bank, 378 Mass. 137, 389 N.E.2d 1002 (1979), a Connecticut settlor created a revocable inter vivos trust in Massachusetts and directed her trustees to pay from the trust all estate and inheritance taxes imposed by reason of her death. Her will, executed while she was a resident of Connecticut but probated in Florida, her domicile at the time of her death, provided that such taxes were to be paid from the residue of her estate. In sending the matter back for more findings, the court found a significant choice of law question despite earlier Massachusetts cases which appeared to have rejected a reference to any law, other than Massachusetts local law, to determine tax apportionment questions for Massachusetts trusts....

We think these recent Massachusetts cases suggest that a trial court should examine the interests of both concerned jurisdictions, here Massachusetts and New York, and the interest of our interstate system before deciding what law is appropriate for Massachusetts to apply. See Restatement (Second) of Conflict of Laws § 6(2) (1971). See generally, A.T. Von Mehren & D.T. Trautman, The Law of Multistate Problems, 193–200, 59–65, 76–79 (1965); Hancock, Conceptual Devices for Avoiding the Land Taboo in Conflict of Laws: The Disadvantages of Disingenuousness, 20 Stan.L.Rev. 1, especially 39 (1967).

The most important interest of the situs in land transactions is the protection of bona fide purchasers or other persons who rely on the record title. Additionally, it is desirable for purposes of convenience that a purchaser and his title searchers need consult only the law of one jurisdiction. Here there are no such persons involved as these proceedings are solely between the defendant, the record holder of the real estate, and the plaintiff. Massachusetts also has an interest in upholding its Statute of Frauds; however, the policy underlying the Statute of Frauds is not here involved to any greater degree than in any other situation involving a constructive trust.

The concern at stake is not related to the situs of property but is analogous to the one recognized in Pevoski v. Pevoski, 371 Mass. at 360–361, 358 N.E.2d 416. Massachusetts is interested in establishing for its domiciliaries the obligations of family members to one another. New York has a similar interest for its domiciliaries. Here, New York "has the dominant contacts and the superior claim for application of its law." Id. at 360, 358 N.E.2d 416.

The defendant, his sister and the plaintiff were domiciled in New York at the time the property was transferred to the defendant in that State. It appears that Florence Rudow had an attorney for the transaction. She knew that she was not yet divorced. Both her will and the judge's findings indicate that a primary reason for the transfer was to prevent Marvin from having any interest in the form of marital rights or otherwise in the property. Florence's legitimate expectation, enforceable under New York local law, was that her brother would hold the property for her son.

In estate or commercial planning areas, the intentions of the settlor-testator or the contracting parties are significant both for local law and choice-of-law decisions....

Moreover, the interests of our interstate system as well as the interests of New York and Massachusetts are furthered by applying a single law in determining whether a given situation creates a fiduciary relationship. It is desirable that the same law apply to all property involved in the same transaction wherever situated....

There are no policy considerations against applying [New York] law here. Massachusetts is not opposed to constructive trusts. To the contrary, in Kelly v. Kelly, 358 Mass. at 156, 260 N.E.2d 659, which held Massachusetts does not find a fiduciary relationship merely because the parties are family members, the court recognized the need for imposing constructive trusts to avoid unjust enrichment where legal title is obtained "in violation of a fiduciary relation." Massachusetts would impose no legal impediment even if the defendant were a Massachusetts domiciliary, had he wished to honor his promise, Twomey v. Crowley, 137 Mass. 184, 185 (1884), and, indeed, as the court below correctly ruled, Massachusetts law does impose an obligation on the promisor to return the value of the property. Kemp v. Kemp, 248 Mass. at 357–358....

The matter is remanded to the Superior Court for further proceedings consistent with this opinion, including a determination whether there was, in fact, a confidential relationship between Florence Rudow and the defendant....

So ordered.

NOTES

1. Although the situs rule for determining interests in realty has proved to be the traditional rule most resistant to change, a few other courts have indicated that they will no longer apply it.

In re Estate of Janney, 498 Pa. 398, 446 A.2d 1265 (1982), applied Pennsylvania law to uphold the validity of a will of a Pennsylvania domiciliary as to the disposition of New Jersey land, although under New Jersey law the will would have been invalid because the main devisee was also an attesting witness.

Dority v. Dority, 645 P.2d 56 (Utah 1982), awarded a divorce to a husband who had moved to Utah from Pennsylvania, the marital domicile. Under Pennsylvania law, only one half of Pennsylvania realty, owned by the spouses as tenants by the entireties, could go to the wife. Under Utah law, the court could make such disposition of the property as was equitable. The court affirmed an award of all the Pennsylvania realty to the wife and rejected the husband's contention that the law of the situs must be applied.

Williams v. Williams, 390 A.2d 4 (D.C.App.1978), did apply the law of the situs to determine marital property rights on divorce, but the court made it clear that it was applying that law, not because it was that of the situs, but because that state had been the marital domicile, was still the domicile of the husband, and its "policy would be most advanced by having its law applied...." Id. at 6.

Wendelken v. Superior Court, 137 Ariz. 455, 671 P.2d 896 (1983), applied interest analysis to choose Arizona law, rather than Mexican law, to determine what compensation a person with a possessory interest in Mexican realty owed to a guest injured on the land. Both parties were domiciled in Arizona.

2. For attacks on the situs rule, see Hancock, In the Parish of St. Mary le Bow, in the Ward of Cheap, 16 Stan.L.Rev. 561 (1964); Weintraub, In Inquiry into the Utility of "Situs" As a Concept in Conflicts Analysis, 52 Cornell L.Q. 1 (1966). Professor Reese has also repudiated the situs rule. See Reese, Review of M. Hancock, Studies in Modern Choice of Law, 9 Dalhousie L.J. 181, 183–84 (1984) (stating that courts "have fared worse when they have disregarded [the purposes underlying conflicting laws] and unthinkingly applied some broad choice-of-law rule, such as one calling for application of the law of the situs"); Professor Leflar, also reviewing the same book, notes that the view that "rigid reliance on situs law ... is wrong" is "gradually achieving acceptance." Leflar, Review, 34 Am.J.Comp.L. 387 (1986).

B. The Courts at Work

Schultz v. Boy Scouts of America, Inc.
Court of Appeals of New York, 1985.
65 N.Y.2d 189, 491 N.Y.S.2d 90, 480 N.E.2d 679.

OPINION OF THE COURT

■· Simons, Judge....

I

In 1978 plaintiffs were residents of Emerson, New Jersey, where their two sons, Richard, age 13, and Christopher, age 11, attended Assumption School, an institution owned and operated by the Roman Catholic Archdiocese of Newark. By an agreement with the Archdiocese, defendant Brothers of the Poor of St. Francis, Inc., supplied teachers for the school. One of those assigned was Brother Edmund Coakeley, who also served as the scoutmaster of Boy Scout Troop 337, a locally chartered Boy Scout troop sponsored and approved by defendant Boy Scouts of America. Richard and Christopher attended Coakeley's class and were members of his scout troop.

In July 1978 Coakeley took Christopher Schultz to Pine Creek Reservation, a Boy Scout camp located in upstate New York near the Oneida County community of Foresport. The camp was located on land owned by Peter Grandy, who was also a resident of Emerson, New Jersey. The complaint alleges that while at the camp, Coakeley sexually abused Christopher [and Richard], that he continued to do so when the boys returned to Assumption School in New Jersey that fall and that he threatened the boys with harm if [they] revealed what had occurred.... Plaintiffs claim that as a result of Coakeley's acts both boys suffered severe psychological, emotional and mental pain and suffering and that as a result of the distress Coakeley's acts caused, Christopher Schultz committed suicide by ingesting drugs on May 29, 1979. They charge both defendants with negligence in assigning Coakeley to positions of trust where he could molest young boys and in failing to dismiss him despite actual or constructive notice that Coakeley had previously been dismissed from another Boy Scout camp for similar improper conduct....

After answering, defendants moved for summary judgment, urging that plaintiffs' claims were barred by New Jersey's charitable immunity statute (N.J.Stat.Ann. § 2A:53A–7).... Special Term granted defendants' motions.... A divided Appellate Division affirmed.

II

A

The choice-of-law question presented in the action against defendant Boy Scouts of America is whether New York should apply its law in an action involving codomiciliaries of New Jersey when tortious acts were committed in New York. This is the posture of the appeal although defendant is a Federally chartered corporation created exclusively for educational and charitable purposes pursuant to an act of Congress (see, 36 U.S.C. § 21) that originally maintained its national headquarters in New Brunswick, New Jersey, but moved to Dallas, Texas, in 1979. New Jersey is considered defendant's domicile because its national headquarters was in that State.... Its change of domicile after the commission of the wrongs from New Jersey to Texas, which no longer recognizes the doctrine of charitable immunity ... provides New York with no greater interest in this action than it would have without the change. Our decision recognizing a postaccident change in domicile in Miller v. Miller, 22 N.Y.2d 12, 290 N.Y.S.2d 734, 237 N.E.2d 877, is distinguishable because in that case the defendant's domicile was changed to New York, which was the forum and also the plaintiff's domicile.

The question presented in the action against defendant Franciscan Brothers is what law should apply when the parties' different domiciles have conflicting charitable immunity rules. The Franciscan order is incorporated in Ohio and it is a domiciliary of that State.... At the time these causes of action arose Ohio, like New Jersey, recognized charitable immunity.... The Ohio rule denied immunity in actions based on negligent hiring and supervision, however ... whereas New Jersey does not.... For this reason, no doubt, defendant Franciscan Brothers does not claim Ohio law governs and the choice is between the law of New York and the law of New Jersey.

As for the locus of the tort, both parties and the dissent implicitly assume it is New York because most of Coakeley's acts were committed here....

B

Historically, choice-of-law conflicts in tort actions have been resolved by applying the law of the place of the wrong. In Babcock v. Jackson, 12 N.Y.2d 473, 240 N.Y.S.2d 743, 191 N.E.2d 279, supra, we departed from traditional doctrine, however, and refused to invariably apply the rule of *lex loci delicti* to determine the availability of relief for commission of a tort....

The analysis was flexible and to the extent that it may have placed too much emphasis on contact-counting without specifying the relative significance of those contacts, the necessary refinements were added in later decisions of this court.... [In later cases] the court rejected the indiscriminate grouping of contacts, which in *Babcock* had been a consideration coequal to interest analysis, because it bore no reasonable relationship to the underlying policies of conflicting rules of recovery in tort actions.... Interest analysis became the relevant analytical approach to choice of law in tort actions in New York. "[T]he law of the jurisdiction having the greatest interest in the litigation will be applied and * * * the [only] facts or contacts which obtain significance in defining State interests are those which relate to the purpose of the particular law in conflict" (Miller v. Miller, supra, at pp. 15–16, 290 N.Y.S.2d 734, 237 N.E.2d 877 ...). Under this formulation, the significant contacts are, almost exclusively, the parties' domiciles and the locus of the tort....

Thus, under present rules, most of the nondomicile and nonlocus contacts relied on in Babcock v. Jackson (supra), such as where the guest-host relationship arose and where the journey was to begin and end, are no longer controlling in tort actions involving guest statutes....

[Our] decisions also establish that the relative interests of the domicile and locus jurisdictions in having their laws apply will depend on the particular tort issue in conflict in the case. Thus, when the conflicting rules involve the appropriate standards of conduct, rules of the road, for example, the law of the place of the tort "will usually have a predominant, if not exclusive, concern" ... because the locus jurisdiction's interests in protecting the reasonable expectations of the parties who relied on it to govern their primary conduct and in the admonitory effect that applying its law will have on similar conduct in the future assume critical importance and outweigh any interests of the common-domicile jurisdiction.... Conversely, when the jurisdictions' conflicting rules relate to allocating losses that result from admittedly tortious conduct, as they do here, rules such as those limiting damages in wrongful death actions, vicarious liability rules, or immunities from suit, considerations of the State's admonitory interest and party reliance are less important. Under those circumstances, the locus jurisdiction has at best a minimal interest in determining the right of recovery or the extent of the remedy in an action by a foreign domiciliary for injuries resulting from the conduct of a codomiciliary that was tortious under the laws of both jurisdictions.... Analysis then favors the jurisdiction of common domicile because of its interest in enforcing the decisions of both parties to accept both the benefits and the burdens of identifying with that jurisdiction and to submit themselves to its authority....

C

As to defendant Boy Scouts, this case is but a slight variation of our *Babcock* line of decisions and differs from them on only two grounds: (1) the issue involved is charitable immunity rather than a guest statute, and (2) it presents a fact pattern which one commentator has characterized as a "reverse" *Babcock* case because New York is the place of the tort rather than the jurisdiction of the parties' common domicile (see, Korn, The Choice-of-Law Revolution: A Critique, 83 Colum.L.Rev. 772, 789)....

... Both plaintiffs and defendant Boy Scouts in this case have chosen to identify themselves in the most concrete form possible, domicile, with a jurisdiction that has weighed the interests of charitable tort-feasors and their victims and decided to retain the defense of charitable immunity. Significantly, the New Jersey statute excepts from its protection actions by nonbeneficiaries of the charity who suffer injuries as a result of the negligence of its employees or agents (see, N.J.Stat.Ann. § 2A:53A–7). Plaintiffs and their sons, however, were beneficiaries of the Boy Scouts' charitable activities in New Jersey and should be bound by the benefits and burdens of that choice. Additionally, the State of New Jersey is intimately interested in seeing that the parties' associational interests are respected and its own loss-distributing rules are enforced so that the underlying policy, which is undoubtedly to encourage the growth of charitable work within its borders, is effectuated.

Thus, if this were a straight *Babcock* fact pattern, rather than the reverse, we would have no reason to depart from the first *Neumeier* rule and would apply the law of the parties' common domicile. Because this case presents the first case for our review in which New York is the forum-locus rather than the parties' common domicile, however, we consider the reasons most often advanced for applying the law of the forum-locus and those supporting application of the law of the common domicile.

The three reasons most often urged in support of applying the law of the forum-locus in cases such as this are: (1) to protect medical creditors who provided services to injured parties in the locus State, (2) to prevent injured tort victims from becoming public wards in the locus State and (3) the deterrent effect application of locus law has on future tort-feasors in the locus State.... The first two reasons share common weaknesses. First, in the abstract, neither reason necessarily requires application of the locus jurisdiction's law, but rather invariably mandates application of the law of the jurisdiction that would either allow recovery or allow the greater recovery.... They are subject to criticism, therefore, as being biased in favor of recovery. Second, on the facts of this case neither reason is relevant since the record contains no evidence that there are New York medical creditors or that plaintiffs are or will likely become wards of this State. Finally, although it is conceivable that application of New York's law in this case would have some deterrent effect on future tortious conduct in this State, New York's deterrent interest is considerably less because none of the parties is a resident and the rule in conflict is loss-allocating rather than conduct-regulating.

Conversely, there are persuasive reasons for consistently applying the law of the parties' common domicile. First, it significantly reduces forum-shopping opportunities, because the same law will be applied by the common-domicile and locus jurisdictions, the two most likely forums. Second, it rebuts charges that the forum-locus is biased in favor of its own laws and in favor of rules permitting recovery. Third, the concepts of mutuality and reciprocity support consistent application of the common-domicile law. In any given case, one person could be either plaintiff or defendant and one State could be either the parties' common domicile or the locus, and yet the applicable law would not change depending on their status. Finally, it produces a rule that is easy to apply and brings a modicum of predictability and certainty to an area of the law needing both.

As to defendant Franciscan Brothers, this action requires an application of the third of the rules set forth in *Neumeier* because the parties are domiciled in different jurisdictions with conflicting loss-distribution rules and the locus of the tort is New York, a separate jurisdiction. In that situation the law of the place of the tort will normally apply, unless displacing it " 'will advance the relevant substantive law purposes without impairing the smooth working of the multi-state system or producing great uncertainty for litigants.' " (Neumeier v. Kuehner, supra, 31 N.Y.2d at p. 128, 335 N.Y.S.2d 64, 286 N.E.2d 454). For the same reasons stated in our analysis of the action against defendant Boy Scouts, application of the law of New Jersey in plaintiffs' action against defendant Franciscan Brothers would further that State's interest in enforcing the decision of its domiciliaries to accept the burdens as well as the benefits of that State's loss-distribution tort rules and its interest in promoting the continuation and expansion of defendant's charitable activities in that State. Conversely, although application of New Jersey's law may not affirmatively advance the substantive law purposes of New York, it will not frustrate those interests because New York has no significant interest in applying its own law to this dispute. Finally, application of New Jersey law will enhance "the smooth working of the multistate system" by actually reducing the incentive for forum shopping and it will provide certainty for the litigants whose only reasonable expectation surely would have been that the law of the jurisdiction where plaintiffs are domiciled and defendant sends its teachers would apply, not the law of New York where the parties had only isolated and infrequent contacts as a result of Coakeley's position as Boy Scout leader. Thus, we conclude that defendant Franciscan Brothers has met its burden of demonstrating that the law of New Jersey, rather than the law of New York, should govern plaintiffs' action against it.

III

Plaintiffs contend that even if the New Jersey charitable immunity statute is applicable to this action, it should not be enforced because it is contrary to the public policy of New York....

The party seeking to invoke the doctrine ... must establish that there are enough important contacts between the parties, the occurrence and the New York forum to implicate our public policy and thus preclude enforcement of the foreign law....

... [A]lthough New York discarded the doctrine of charitable immunity long ago ... and enforcement of New Jersey's statute might well run counter to our fundamental public policy, we need not decide that issue because there are not sufficient contacts between New York, the parties and the transactions involved to implicate our public policy and call for its enforcement....

Accordingly, the order of the Appellate Division should be affirmed, with costs.

■ JASEN, JUDGE (dissenting)....

New Jersey's interests ... are hardly pressing under the circumstances. While it is true that laws providing for charitable immunity typically are intended to serve the purpose of protecting and promoting the charities incorporated within a state's jurisdiction, that function is virtually irrelevant in this case. Presently, neither corporate defendant is a resident of New Jersey. The Brothers of the Poor of St. Francis (the Franciscan Brothers) has at all relevant times been a resident of the State of Ohio, a jurisdiction which recognizes only a limited charitable immunity that does not extend to negligence in the selection and retention of personnel.... The Boy Scouts of America, although originally incorporated in New Jersey at the time of its alleged tortious conduct, has since relocated to Texas, a State which has wholly rejected charitable immunity.... While ordinarily a change in residence subsequent to the events upon which a lawsuit is predicated ought not to affect the rights and liabilities of the parties in order to avoid forum-shopping, there is no such reason to deny giving effect to the change in residence here. Rather, a defendant's post-tort change in residence—as opposed to that of a plaintiff—is often critical insofar as it affects state interest analysis....

. . .

It simply cannot be disputed that New Jersey presently has a much diminished interest, if any at all, in shielding the Boy Scouts of America from liability—let alone the Franciscan Brothers which has never been a New Jersey resident. The majority does not question that conclusion, but merely states that the change in residence does not enhance New York's interest....

Consequently, because the majority cannot in actuality rely upon New Jersey's interest in protecting resident charities—into which category neither corporate defendant now falls—the decision today is, in effect, predicated almost exclusively upon the plaintiffs' New Jersey domicile. What emerges from the majority's holding is an entirely untoward rule that nonresident plaintiffs are somehow less entitled to the protections of this State's law while they are within our borders. Besides smacking of arbitrary and injudicious discrimination against guests in this State and before our courts ... such a position, without more, has severely limited, if any, validity in resolving conflicts questions....

This is especially so where, as here, the defendants' contacts with the foreign State are insignificant for the purposes of interest analysis while, at the same time, the parties' contacts with New York are so clear and direct, and the resulting interests of this State so strong.

There can be no question that this State has a paramount interest in preventing and protecting against injurious misconduct within its borders. This interest is particularly vital and compelling where, as here, the tortious misconduct involves sexual abuse and exploitation of children, regardless of the residency of the victims and the tort-feasors....

As the majority stresses, a charitable immunity law such as New Jersey's typically serves a loss-distribution purpose reflecting a legislative paternalism toward resident charities. But that is obviously not true with regard to a rule, such as New York's, which denies charitable immunity. Consequently, it is mistaken to adjudge the propriety of applying the latter law by giving weight only to the interests served by the former.... A closer attention to the specific policy purposes of New York's charitable nonimmunity rule is essential to a more appropriate resolution of the conflict.

These purposes, to which the majority refuses to accord any significance ... are preventive, protective and compensatory....

... While the majority mentions New York's interest in deterrence, it dismisses that interest in short fashion by referring to the "rule in conflict" as being "loss-allocating rather than conduct-regulating." ... Of course, there is not one but two rules at issue, and the majority's characterization is accurate only with regard to New Jersey's law granting immunity, not with regard to New York's rule denying the same....

Moreover, New York's strong interest in deterring injurious misconduct, as well as in providing compensatory justice and protection to persons victimized by wrongdoing within this State, is reflected in the traditional principle of *lex loci* which, despite the majority's *sub silentio* disavowal, remains in this State "the general rule in tort cases to be displaced only in extraordinary circumstances". (Cousins v. Instrument Flyers, 44 N.Y.2d 698, 699, 405 N.Y.S.2d 441, 376 N.E.2d 914 ...). Indeed, despite the so-called "choice of law revolution" ... *lex loci* is still acknowledged almost universally as a central factor in determining the state, or states, in which the significant interests lie. (See, Restatement [Second] of Conflict of Laws § 145[2][a], [b]; § 146.) This rule ought not to be applied mechanically or rigidly to reach absurd results. But, neither ought it to be disregarded indiscriminately, without giving due consideration to the nature or extent of the relationship which accrues between the tort in question and a particular jurisdiction because that jurisdiction is the locus state....

This is clearly not a case in which the locus can be discounted as purely fortuitous or adventitious.... The infant plaintiffs and the defendants' tortfeasor were not merely *in transitu* in New York. Rather, they were here for a stay, albeit a short one, and as such they deliberately submitted themselves to the protections and responsibilities of this State's laws which should now govern the consequences of the tortious conduct committed while within New York's borders.

Contrary to what the majority states, it is hardly clear that the parties' only reasonable expectation was that New Jersey's law would apply despite the contacts with this State. Indeed, it would surely seem that the parties who came to New York, and those who sponsored their visit here, would have been quite surprised to learn that their conduct while in New York, or that which had a direct impact in New York, was not governed by the laws of this State. In any event, this court has unequivocally rejected the notion that the fictional expectation of the parties should determine the choice of law in tort cases.... Consequently, in my view, the majority does not adequately explain why the law of New York, the locus state, ought not to govern this case.

Additionally, apart from the foregoing, I believe that this court ought not to apply New Jersey's law of charitable immunity by reason of its incompatibility with this State's settled public policy. Almost 30 years ago, when this court abolished charitable immunity for this State, we explained that the rule was inherently incongruous, contrary to both good morals and sound law, out of tune with modern day needs, unfair and confused. (Bing v. Thunig, 2 N.Y.2d 656, at pp. 663, 666–667, 163 N.Y.S.2d 3, 143 N.E.2d 3,....) Surely, a rule deemed so archaic and anachronistic by this court ought not now to be given effect and, thereby, insulate defendants from whatever responsibility they should bear for the heinous acts of misconduct performed in this State....

Schultz clarifies that the *Neumeier* rules have general applicability and are not so restricted as the court in *Rosenthal,* infra page 613 at 615, had thought. In reviewing and confirming *Neumeier,* the *Schultz* Court focused on the additional criteria of conduct-regulating versus loss-allocating rules of law. Are these helpful additions? See Note 3, p. 524, supra.

Most states that have abandoned the rules of the First Restatement do not articulate *rules,* but follow one or the other of the *approaches* that have been discussed. The question arises whether, over time, the case law even in these states will begin to display definite patterns. If patterns can be identified, "approach" states will be very close to "rules" states, bearing in mind that even "rules" states today preserve a significant amount of flexibility in applying rules to a specific case, as illustrated by *Neumeier* rule 3. For a survey of the practice of a number of states against the background of the New York *Neumeier* Rules, see Hay and Ellis, Bridging the Gap Between Rules and Approaches in Tort Choice of Law in the United States: A Survey of Current Case Law, 27 International Lawyer 369 (1993).

Cooney v. Osgood Machinery, Inc.

Court of Appeals of New York, 1993.
81 N.Y.2d 66, 595 N.Y.S.2d 919, 612 N.E.2d 277.

■ KAYE, CHIEF JUDGE.

The issue on this appeal is whether a Missouri statute barring contribution claims against an employer—which conflicts with New York law permitting such claims—should be given effect in a third-party action pending here. Applying relevant choice of law principles, we conclude that the Missouri workers' compensation statute should be given effect, and therefore affirm the dismissal of the third-party complaint seeking contribution against a Missouri employer.

I

The facts relevant to this appeal are essentially undisputed. In 1957 or 1958, Kling Brothers, Inc. (succeeded in interest by third-party defendant Hill Acme Co.) manufactured a 16-foot wide "Pyramid Form Bending Roll," a machine to shape large pieces of metal. The device was sold in 1958 to a Buffalo company, American Standard Inc., through a New York sales agent, defendant Osgood Machinery, Inc., which assisted American in the setup and initial operation of the machine. American closed its Buffalo plant around 1961, and the history of the bending roll is obscured until 1969, when Crouse Company—which obtained the equipment in some unknown manner—sold the machine to Paul Mueller Co., a Missouri domiciliary.

Mueller installed the bending roll in its Springfield, Missouri, plant and subsequently modified it by adding a foot switch. In October 1978, plaintiff Dennis J. Cooney, a Missouri resident working at the Missouri plant, was injured while cleaning the machine. The machine was running at the time—a piece of wood having been wedged in the foot switch—and Cooney was unable to reach the switch to stop the machine and avoid injury.

In Missouri, Cooney filed for and received workers' compensation benefits. Because under Missouri law an employer providing such benefits "shall be released from all other liability whatsoever, whether to the employee or any other person" (Mo.Rev.Stat. § 287.120[1]), he could not additionally sue his employer, Mueller, in tort. Cooney did, however, bring a products liability action against Osgood—the machine's initial sales agent—in Supreme Court, Erie County. (Missouri apparently would not have had personal jurisdiction over Osgood.)

Seeking contribution from parties it deems more culpable in the event it is found liable to Cooney, Osgood brought a third-party action against Mueller, American Standard, and Hill Acme. Mueller invoked the Missouri statute shielding employers from both direct claims by employees and contribution claims by others, and moved for summary judgment dismissing Osgood's third-party complaint. In light of the conflict between the Missouri statute and New York law permitting contribution claims against employers, Supreme Court undertook a choice of law analysis and concluded that New York law should apply. The Appellate Division unanimously reversed and dismissed the third-party complaint as well as all cross claims against Mueller. 179 A.D.2d 240, 582 N.Y.S.2d 873. We now affirm.

II

... We conclude ... that this State has sufficient interest in the litigation so that if we chose to apply New York law on the contribution issue, that decision would not run afoul of the Federal Constitution. Accordingly, we turn to a choice of law analysis.

III

... In Neumeier v. Kuehner, 31 N.Y.2d 121, 335 N.Y.S.2d 64, 286 N.E.2d 454, ... the Court in seeking to return greater predictability and uniformity to the law, adopted a series of three rules that had been proposed by Chief Judge Fuld (see, Tooker v. Lopez, 24 N.Y.2d, at 585, 301 N.Y.S.2d 519, 249 N.E.2d 394 [Fuld, Ch. J., concurring]). Although drafted in terms of guest statutes—drivers and passengers—these rules could, in appropriate cases, apply as well to other loss allocation conflicts (see, Schultz, 65 N.Y.2d, at 200–201, 491 N.Y.S.2d 90, 480 N.E.2d 679 [applying first and third Neumeier rules to conflicting charitable immunity laws]).

The Neumeier Rules

[Chief Judge Kaye reviewed the "Neumeier Rules and concluded:]

Assuming that the interest of each State in enforcement of its law is roughly equal—a judgment that, insofar as guest statutes are concerned, is implicit in the second and third Neumeier rules—the situs of the tort is appropriate as a "tie breaker" because that is the only State with which both parties have purposefully associated themselves in a significant way....

... Contribution rules—as involved in the present case—are loss allocating, not conduct regulating. Had conduct regulating been at issue here, our analysis would be greatly simplified, for the traditional rule of lex loci delicti almost invariably obtains. Similarly, if the parties shared the same domicile, we would generally apply that jurisdiction's loss distribution law. Instead, our analysis is necessarily more complicated, calling upon us to evaluate the relative interests of jurisdictions with conflicting laws and, if neither can be accommodated without substantially impairing the other, finding some other sound basis for resolving the impasse.

Interest Analysis

The general scheme of workers' compensation acts is that an employer regardless of culpability is required to make specified payments to an injured employee and in exchange, the law immunizes the employer from further liability. Immunity "is part of the quid pro quo in which the sacrifices and gains of employees and employers are to some extent put in balance, for, while the employer assumes a new liability without fault, [it] is relieved of the prospect of large damage verdicts" (2A Larsen, Workmen's Compensation Law § 65.11 [1993]).

Some States immunize employers only from direct actions by injured workers; others extend protection from third-party contribution actions as well. The Missouri Supreme Court, in rejecting State and Federal constitutional challenges to the Missouri statute at issue here, noted that immunity " 'is the heart and soul of this legislation which has, over the years been of highly significant social and economic benefit to the working [person], the employer and the State.' " (State ex rel. Maryland Hgts. Concrete Contrs. v. Ferriss, 588 S.W.2d 489, 491 [Mo.], quoting Seaboard Coast Line R.R. Co. v. Smith, 359 So.2d 427, 429 [Fla.].) The court, quoting further from the Florida case, also observed that " ' "the right to contribution is not a vested right on which legislation may not impinge" ' " (588 S.W.2d, at 491).

Missouri's decision to shield employers from contribution claims is thus a policy choice implicating significant State interests: "to deny a person the immunity granted by a work[er]'s compensation statute of a given state would frustrate the efforts of that state to restrict the cost of industrial accidents and to afford a fair basis for predicting what these costs will be." (Restatement [Second] of Conflict of Laws § 184, comment b, at 547.) Indeed, as the Restatement concluded in a related context, for another State "to subject a person who has been held liable in work[er]'s compensation to further unlimited liability in tort or wrongful death would frustrate the work[er]'s compensation policy of the State in which the award was rendered." (Restatement [Second] of Conflict of Laws § 183, comment c, at 544.)

Arrayed against Missouri's interest in maintaining the integrity of its workers' compensation scheme is New York's interest in basic fairness to litigants. Under traditional joint and several liability rules, when more than one tortfeasor was responsible for plaintiff's injury, each was potentially liable for the entire judgment, irrespective of relative culpability. Indeed, plaintiff was not even required to sue all the wrongdoers, but could recover the entire judgment from the "deep pocket," who then had no recourse (Sommer v. Federal Signal Corp., 79 N.Y.2d 540, 556, 583 N.Y.S.2d 957, 593 N.E.2d 1365).

In Dole v. Dow Chem. Co., 30 N.Y.2d 143, 148–149, 331 N.Y.S.2d 382, 282 N.E.2d 288 [1972], this Court mitigated the inequity by allowing a defendant that pays more than its fair share of a judgment, as apportioned by the fact finder in terms of relative fault, to recover the difference from a codefendant. The Legislature, also recognizing the desirability of contribution, subsequently codified the Dole principles in CPLR article 14 (L.1974, ch. 742). Stated simply, the "goal of contribution, as announced in Dole and applied since, is fairness to tortfeasors who are jointly liable." (Sommer v. Federal Signal Corp., 79 N.Y.2d, at 556–557, 583 N.Y.S.2d 957, 593 N.E.2d 1365).

Manifestly, the interests of Missouri and New York are irreconcilable in this case. To the extent we allow contribution against Mueller, the policy underlying the Missouri workers' compensation scheme will be offended. Conversely, to the extent Osgood is required to pay more than its equitable share of a judgment, the policy underlying New York's contribution law is affronted. It is evident that one State's interest cannot be accommodated without sacrificing the other's, and thus an appropriate method for choosing between the two must be found.

This is a true conflict in the mold of Neumeier's second rule, where the local law of each litigant's domicile favors that party, and the action is pending in one of those jurisdictions. Under that rule, the place of injury governs, which in this case means that contribution is barred. This holding is consistent with the result reached historically, and reflects application of a neutral factor that favors neither the forum's law nor its domiciliaries. Moreover, forum shopping by defendants—who might attempt to invoke CPLR 1403 and bring a separate action for contribution in New York if sued elsewhere (compare, Grant Co. v. Uneeda Doll Co., 19 A.D.2d 361, 243 N.Y.S.2d 428, affd. 15 N.Y.2d 571, 254 N.Y.S.2d 834, 203 N.E.2d 299)—is eliminated.[2]

A primary reason that locus tips the balance, of course, is that ordinarily it is the place with which both parties have voluntarily associated themselves. In this case, there is some validity to Osgood's argument that it did nothing to affiliate itself with Missouri. Indeed, a decade after Osgood's last contact with the bending roll, the machine wound up in Missouri through no effort, or even knowledge, of Osgood. Moreover, the record establishes that Osgood was not in the business of distributing goods nationwide, but limited its activities to New York and parts of Pennsylvania, and thus Osgood may not have reasonably anticipated becoming embroiled in litigation with a Missouri employer.

For this reason, our decision to apply Missouri law rests as well on another factor that should, at times, play a role in choice of law: the protection of reasonable expectations (see, Restatement [Second] of Conflict of Laws § 6[2][d]; Allstate Ins. Co. v. Hague, 449 U.S. 302, 327 [Stevens, J., concurring]; Schultz, 65 N.Y.2d, at 198, 491 N.Y.S.2d 90, 480 N.E.2d 679 ["protecting the reasonable expectations of the parties" is one reason locus law is generally preferred when there are conflicting conduct-regulating rules]).[3] In view of the unambiguous statutory language barring third-party liability and the Missouri Supreme Court's holding in Ferriss, Mueller could hardly have expected to be haled before a New York court to respond in damages for an accident to a Missouri employee at the Missouri plant. By contrast, in ordering its business affairs Osgood could have had no reasonable expectation that contribution would be available in a products liability action arising out of the sale of industrial equipment. Indeed, Osgood's activity in connection with the bending roll occurred in 1958, some 14 years before Dole was decided and the principles of full contribution were introduced into our law. Moreover, even under present law, contribution is not foolproof. A defendant, for example, may be unable to obtain jurisdiction over a joint tortfeasor; the joint tortfeasor may be insolvent or defunct (like Kling Bros. here); or defendant's own assets may be insufficient to pay its share of the judgment (see, Klinger v. Dudley, 41 N.Y.2d 362, 369, 393 N.Y.S.2d 323, 361 N.E.2d 974).

2. New York law permitting contribution against an employer is clearly a minority view (see generally, Annotation, Modern Status of Effect of State Workmen's Compensation Act on Right of Third–Person Tortfeasor to Contribution or Indemnity From Employer of Injured or Killed Workman, 100 A.L.R.3d 350). A result that might impose New York law on the carefully structured workers' compensation schemes of other States—especially when the accident occurred there—is undesirable.

3. We have eschewed reliance on the fictional expectation of the parties based on mere contact with the locus of an accident (Miller v. Miller, 22 N.Y.2d, at 20, 290 N.Y.S.2d 734, 237 N.E.2d 877), but reasonable, justifiable expectations are another matter.

In sum, we conclude that Missouri law should apply because, although the interests of the respective jurisdictions are irreconcilable, the accident occurred in Missouri, and unavailability of contribution would more closely comport with the reasonable expectations of both parties in conducting their business affairs.

IV

[Chief Judge Kaye then considered and rejected the argument that New York's public policy should defeat application of the Missouri rule].

■ SIMONS, TITONE, HANCOCK, BELLACOSA and SMITH, JJ., concur.

Order affirmed, with costs.

NOTE

Cooney has stimulated much comment. There is a symposium on the case in 59 Brooklyn L.Rev. 1323 (1994), with articles by professors Sedler, Silberman, and Twerski. Another symposium, Conference on Jurisdiction, Justice, and Choice of Law for the Twenty-First Century, Case Four: Choice of Law Theory, 29 New England L.Rev. 669 (1995), presents a hypothetical variation of *Cooney* decided in mock judicial opinions by professors Borchers, Cox, Kramer, Maier, Silberman, Singer, and Weintraub.

Trailways, Inc. v. Clark

Court of Appeals of Texas, Corpus Christi, 1990.
794 S.W.2d 479, writ denied.

■ Before NYE, C.J., and KENNEDY and SEERDEN, JJ.

■ KENNEDY, JUSTICE.... The decedents, Eulalia Mayorga and Emma Trejo, while traveling on a bus in Mexico, were killed when the bus left the highway and overturned. Their survivors and the representatives of their estates brought the present suit to recover wrongful death and survival damages from Transportes Del Norte (TDN), the Mexican bus line on which the decedents were traveling, as well as from Trailways, Inc. (Trailways), a bus line operating out of Texas which plaintiffs also sought to hold responsible for the deaths. The jury found TDN negligent and assessed the amount of damages resulting to each plaintiff from the wrongful deaths. The trial court awarded judgment for plaintiffs against both TDN and Trailways, based on its own findings that Trailways was also liable for the damages resulting from TDN's negligence. [TDN and Trailways appeal. The judgment against TDN applying Texas law, is affirmed. The judgment against Trailways is reversed on the ground the plaintiffs sued the parent corporation instead of its Texas subsidiaries and the parent was not liable.]
. . .

By its second point of error, TDN complains that the trial court erred in applying Texas law, as opposed to Mexican law, to the issues of wrongful death damages....

In Gutierrez v. Collins, 583 S.W.2d 312 (Tex.1979), the Texas Supreme Court discarded the traditional lex loci delicti, or place of the wrong, approach to resolving conflicts of law in tort actions and adopted the "most significant relationship" test of sections 6 and 145 of the Restatement (Second) of Conflict of Laws (1971)....

In the simplest case, when the only identifiable competing state interests are that the plaintiffs are residents of one state and the defendants are residents of another, and no other factors would make the interests of one state any more significant than those of the other, wrongful death damages will generally be determined according to the law of the place of injury.

However, when additional considerations favor one state or the other, the place of injury is no longer the controlling factor. The next task is to determine the relative significance of the states' interests to the particular case and issues. Moreover, in Gutierrez, 583 S.W.2d at 319, the Court emphasized that the application of the "most significant relationship" analysis should not turn on the number of contacts any state has to the case but more importantly should turn on the qualitative nature of those contacts. There is no set formula for determining the significance of any particular contact, which must generally be weighed on a case-by-case basis and balanced against other such contacts. The trial judge, therefore, should have some latitude in balancing legitimate competing state interests. See Gutierrez, 583 S.W.2d at 319.

In the present case, the decedents and their survivors, plaintiffs in the present wrongful death suit, are Texas residents. The present controversy began when decedents bought round trip bus tickets to Mexico City from a subsidiary of Trailways in Corpus Christi, Texas. Trailways, which does not provide bus service in Mexico, had what is termed an "interlining" agreement with certain Mexican bus lines, including TDN, whereby Trailways would issue tickets to destinations in Mexico and TDN would honor the Trailways tickets from the border to the passenger's destination in Mexico and would then reclaim from Trailways the price of the ticket for the Mexican portion of the journey, less a 12% commission for Trailways. In turn, TDN had similar rights under the agreement to sell tickets to destinations in the United States which Trailways would honor.

The decedents boarded a Trailways bus in Corpus Christi and traveled to Brownsville, Texas, where they boarded a TDN bus and continued their journey across the border and chose to "interline" with TDN to Mexico City. The accident causing their deaths occurred in Mexico as an alleged result of TDN's negligent operation of the bus on which the decedents were traveling.

In wrongful death cases, Texas has an interest in protecting the rights of its citizens to recover adequate compensation for the wrongful death of their relatives in foreign lands. Mexico has a competing interest in protecting its residents from what it may consider to be excessive liability to foreigners for actions occurring on Mexican soil. Were these the only interests involved in the present case, we would be compelled to hold that neither Texas nor Mexico had a more significant interest and that the law of Mexico as the place of the injury applies.

However, the relationship between the decedents and TDN began in Corpus Christi, Texas, at the time they purchased bus tickets granting them the option of traveling on TDN from the Texas border to Mexico City. The initial negotiation and agreements leading to an entrustment by Texas residents of their safety to the foreign national occurred on Texas soil. This negotiation centered, or at least initiated, the relationship between decedents and TDN in Texas, which has at least as much significance to the overall duty to compensate the survivors as the actual place of the negligence or death. When a foreign corporation, by itself or through its agents, solicits business in Texas with Texas residents, as TDN did in effect through the interlining agreement, Texas has an interest in compelling the foreign corporation to pay adequate compensation for injuries to those residents, even if they occur in the foreign state or country....

[I]n the present case, we hold that there was no injustice in requiring TDN to be responsible according to Texas law for the death of passengers who bought round trip tickets to Mexico City in Corpus Christi and that the trial court did not err in weighing Texas' contacts as the most significant. TDN's second point of error is overruled....

NOTE

The principal case completes a cycle of suits in Texas courts for injury or death in Mexico. When Texas courts applied the place-of-wrong rule, the suits were dismissed on the ground that Mexican law was too "dissimilar" from Texas law to be applied in a Texas court. See Slater v. Mexican National R.R., 194 U.S. 120 (1904), page 201, supra, and the Texas cases discussed in that opinion. Next, plaintiffs avoided Mexican law by characterizing the claim as one based on contract, thereby triggering a different territorial choice-of-law rule pointing to Texas law. See Garza v. Greyhound Line, Inc., 418 S.W.2d 595 (Tex.Civ.App., San Antonio, 1967, no writ), p. 497, supra. Then Gutierrez v. Collins, 583 S.W.2d 312 (Tex. 1979), discussed in the principal case and in Duncan v. Cessna Aircraft Co., 665 S.W.2d 414 (Tex.1984), page 536, supra, abandoned the place-of-wrong rule and overruled the dissimilarity cases. Finally the principal case applies Texas law without the need to resort to re-characterization. Do you agree that it was fair to apply Texas law to TDN?

Bernkrant v. Fowler

Supreme Court of California, 1961.
55 Cal.2d 588, 12 Cal.Rptr. 266, 360 P.2d 906.

[A vendor named Granrud, whose installments of deferred purchase money were secured by a second deed of trust on the Nevada land purchased, asked the purchasers to refinance their obligations and to pay a substantial part of their indebtedness before the due date. He promised orally that if the purchasers would do this he would provide by will that any part of the purchase price remaining unpaid on his death would be cancelled. In compliance with the request the purchasers arranged a new loan and paid to the vendor a substantial sum in advance on their obligation. The vendor died with about $6,000 of the purchase money unpaid, but his will made no provision for cancellation of the debt. The purchasers brought an action in California against the vendor's executor to enforce the oral agreement. Under Nevada law, so the Supreme Court of California found, the oral agreement was valid. A California statute provided: "An agreement which by its terms is not to be performed during the lifetime of the promisor, or an agreement to devise or bequeath any property, or to make any provision by will" is "invalid unless the same, or some note or memorandum thereof, is in writing, and subscribed by the party to be charged or his agent." The trial court gave judgment for the defendant and the purchasers appealed.]

■ TRAYNOR, J. ... We are therefore confronted with a contract that is valid under the law of Nevada but invalid under the California statute of frauds if that statute is applicable. We have no doubt that California's interest in protecting estates being probated here from false claims based on alleged oral contracts to make wills is constitutionally sufficient to justify the Legislature's making our statute of frauds applicable to all such contracts sought to be enforced against such estates .... The Legislature, however, is ordinarily concerned with enacting laws to govern purely local transactions, and it has not spelled out the extent to which the statute of frauds is to apply to a contract having substantial contacts with another state. Accordingly, we must determine its scope in the light of applicable principles of the law of conflict of laws. See People v. One 1953 Ford Victoria, 48 Cal.2d 595, 598–599, 311 P.2d 480; 2 Corbin on Contracts, p. 67; Currie, Married Women's Contracts, 25 U.Chi.L.Rev. 227, 230–231; Cheatham and Reese, Choice of the Applicable Law, 52 Col.L.Rev. 959, 961.

In the present case plaintiffs were residents of Nevada, the contract was made in Nevada, and plaintiffs performed it there. If Granrud was a resident of Nevada at the time the contract was made, the California statute of frauds, in the absence of a plain legislative direction to the contrary, could not reasonably be interpreted as applying to the contract even though Granrud subsequently moved to California and died here.... The basic policy of upholding the expectations of the parties by enforcing contracts valid under the only law apparently applicable would preclude an interpretation of our statute of frauds that would make it apply to and thus invalidate the contract because Granrud moved to California and died here. Such a case would be analogous to People v. One 1953 Ford Victoria, 48 Cal.2d 595, 311 P.2d 480, where we held that a Texas mortgagee of an automobile mortgaged in Texas did not forfeit his interest when the automobile was subsequently used to transport narcotics in California although he had failed to make the character investigation of the mortgagor required by California law. A mortgagee entering into a purely local transaction in another state could not reasonably be expected to take cognizance of the law of all the other jurisdictions where the property might possibly be taken, and accordingly, the California statute requiring an investigation to protect his interest could not reasonably be interpreted to apply to such out of state mortgagees. Another analogy is found in the holding that the statute of frauds did not apply to contracts to make wills entered into before the statute was enacted (Rogers v. Schlotterback, 167 Cal. 35, 45, 138 P. 728). Just as parties to local transactions cannot be expected to take cognizance of the law of other jurisdictions, they cannot be expected to anticipate a change in the local statute of frauds. Protection of rights growing out of valid contracts precludes interpreting the general language of the statute of frauds to destroy such rights whether the possible applicability of the statute arises from the movement of one or more of the parties across state lines or subsequent enactment of the statute. See Currie and Schreter, Unconstitutional Discrimination in the Conflict of Laws: Privileges and Immunities, 69 Yale L.J. 1323, 1334.

In the present case, however, there is no finding as to where Granrud was domiciled at the time the contract was made. Since he had a bank account in California at that time and died a resident here less than two years later it may be that he was domiciled here when the contract was made. Even if he was, the result should be the same. The contract was made in Nevada and performed by plaintiffs there, and it involved the refinancing of obligations arising from the sale of Nevada land and secured by interests therein. Nevada has a substantial interest in the contract and in protecting the rights of its residents who are parties thereto, and its policy is that the contract is valid and enforcable. California's policy is also to enforce lawful contracts. That policy, however, must be subordinated in the case of any contract that does not meet the requirements of an applicable statute of frauds. In determining whether the contract herein is subject to the California statute of frauds we must consider both the policy to protect the reasonable expectations of the parties and the policy of the statute of frauds. See Cheatham and Reese, Choice of the Applicable Law, 52 Col.L.Rev. 959, 978–980. It is true that if Granrud was domiciled here at the time the contract was made, plaintiffs may have been alerted to the possibility that the California statute of frauds might apply. Since California, however, would have no interest in applying its own statute of frauds unless Granrud remained here until his death, plaintiffs were not bound to know that California's statute might ultimately be invoked against them. Unless they could rely on their own law, they would have to look to the laws of all of the jurisdictions to which Granrud might move regardless of where he was domiciled when the contract was made. We conclude, therefore, that the contract herein does not fall within our statute of frauds.... Since there is thus no conflict between the law of California and the law of Nevada, we can give effect to the common policy of both states to enforce lawful contracts and sustain Nevada's interest in protecting its residents and their reasonable expectations growing out of a transaction substantially related to that state without subordinating any legitimate interest of this state.

The judgment is reversed.

NOTES

1. In Rubin v. Irving Trust Co., 305 N.Y. 288, 113 N.E.2d 424 (1953), decedent was alleged to have made an oral contract in Florida to bequeath his shares of stock

to his brother. Both brothers were residents of New York. The promise was enforceable under Florida law, but not under New York law. Following Emery v. Burbank, supra, the court held that the contract was invalid, New York being the testator's domicile. Is the Bernkrant case distinguishable on the ground that it involved an arms-length business transaction rather than family-related finances? See Cavers, American Law Institute, Study of the Division of Jurisdiction Between State and Federal Courts (Tentative Draft No. 1, 1963), p. 169. If the Rubin brothers had orally agreed that Florida law should apply, would the outcome of the case have been different?

2. In the Bernkrant case, Justice Traynor said that, considering the California legislature's silence as to the reach of the statute of frauds in multistate cases, the court was obliged to "determine its scope in the light of applicable principles of the law of conflict of laws." What are those "applicable principles"?

3. Ehrenzweig, The Statute of Frauds in the Conflict of Laws, 59 Colum.L.Rev. 874, 876 (1959): "Contracts having foreign contacts quite generally have been upheld by American courts where such contracts have satisfied either the formality requirements of the forum, or those of another jurisdiction provided that the state of the validating law had sufficient contacts with the transaction to justify application of its law."

RESTATEMENT, SECOND, CONFLICT OF LAWS (1971) *

CHAPTER 8.   CONTRACTS

§ 199.   Requirements of a Writing—Formalities

(1) The formalities required to make a valid contract are determined by the law selected by application of the rules of §§ 187–188.

(2) Formalities which meet the requirements of the place where the parties execute the contract will usually be acceptable.

NOTES

1. If Bernkrant v. Fowler had been decided pursuant to Restatement, Second, Conflict of Laws § 199, what might the reasoning and the result have been?

2. See Intercontinental Planning, Limited v. Daystrom, Inc., 24 N.Y.2d 372, 300 N.Y.S.2d 817, 248 N.E.2d 576 (1969), which utilized an interest analysis to grant summary judgment under New York's statute of frauds against the plaintiff who claimed that by reason of an oral agreement he was entitled to a finder's fee. The oral agreement would have been enforceable in New Jersey where it was made and where numerous other contacts with the transaction were located.

3. Bushkin Associates, Inc. v. Raytheon Company, 393 Mass. 622, 473 N.E.2d 662 (1985). This case also involved a suit for a finder's fee. As in the *Daystrom* case, the alleged promise to pay the fee was oral, the plaintiff was from New York and the contract was made in another state, in this case, Massachusetts. The defendant moved for summary judgment relying on New York law. Its motion was denied on

---

* Quoted with the permission of the copy-right owner, The American Law Institute.

the ground that Massachusetts law governed. The court explicitly refused to base its decision on the fact that the contract was made in Massachusetts. Instead it concluded that when the "relevant contacts and considerations are balanced, or nearly so," the law to be applied is the one that would validate the transaction and thus protect the justified expectations of the parties.

4. Both the European Convention and the Swiss Conflicts Statute, above at pp. 544, 546, Note 4 contain alternative references, intended to validate the parties' contract. Under Art. 9(1) of the Convention, for instance, the contract is valid if it satisfies the law of the place of execution or of the law applicable under the Convention. If the parties acted in different countries, validity results from the satisfaction of either country's requirements (Art. 9(2)). "[T]he law which governs ... under this Convention ...," moreover, includes the law which *the parties may have chosen:* Art. 3, above at page 547. Exceptions apply to contracts regarding rights in immovable property and consumer contracts (Art. 9(5) and (6)). "Mandatory rules" of law, above at [p. 548], may exceptionally also apply. Swiss law is essentially the same.

SUBSTANCE–PROCEDURE AND THE STATUTE OF FRAUDS

Under the traditional choice-of-law regime, a court deciding a conflicts case involving a statute of frauds, confronted the issue of whether the statute was "substantive" or "procedural." The results in two classic cases seem to turn, not on that issue, but on the courts' perception of the need to validate in order to encourage interstate commercial transactions, or the need to protect forum interests in preventing fraud.

In Lams v. F.H. Smith Co., 36 Del. 477, 178 A. 651 (1935), a Delaware corporation sold securities to the plaintiffs. The contract of sale and sale were made in New York. An agent of the seller had written a letter giving the buyers a three-year resale option. The buyers sought to exercise their option and, when the Delaware corporation refused to buy, brought suit. The defendant pleaded the Delaware Statute of Frauds provision that "no action shall be brought" on any agreement not to be performed within one year from the making thereof unless the agreement is in writing signed by the party to be charged or by an agent "authorized in writing." New York had a similar statute of frauds, but did not require that the agent's authority be in writing. The agent's authority was not in writing. The court held that the Delaware statute did not apply, stating that despite the statute's apparently procedural wording, maximum protection of Delaware residents would result from construing the statute as substantive and therefore applicable to contracts made in Delaware. This contract, however, was made in New York.

In Emery v. Burbank, 163 Mass. 326, 39 N.E. 1026 (1895), a testatrix, domiciled in Massachusetts, was alleged to have orally agreed in Maine that if the plaintiff would care for her in Massachusetts, the testatrix would bequeath property to the plaintiff. The bequest was not made and plaintiff sued. Massachusetts, but not Maine, required a contract to make a will to be in writing. Judge Holmes applied Massachusetts law, stating that, despite the apparently "substantive" wording of the Massachusetts statute ("no agreement ... shall be binding, unless ... in writing"), in view of the strong interest of Massachusetts, as the domicile of the testatrix, in protecting her estate from fraud and mistake, the Massachusetts statute "implied a rule of procedure broad enough to cover this case." Id. at 1027.

Peugeot Motors of America, Inc. v. Eastern Auto Distributors, Inc.

United States Court of Appeals, Fourth Circuit, 1989.
892 F.2d 355, cert. denied, 497 U.S. 1005 (1990).

■ Before WIDENER, HALL, and WILKINS, CIRCUIT JUDGES.

■ WIDENER, CIRCUIT JUDGE. In 1971, Eastern Auto Distributors, Inc. (Eastern) entered into a Distributor Agreement with the corporate predecessor of Peugeot Motors of America, Inc. (Peugeot). On October 14, 1987, Peugeot sent a notice of non-renewal to Eastern. On November 9, 1987, Peugeot filed its complaint asking for a declaratory judgment that it properly exercised its rights under the contract not to renew. Eastern filed a ... counterclaim alleging [in addition to other claims] that Peugeot's action violated §§ 197 and 197–a of New York's General Business Law; and the New York Franchised Motor Vehicle Dealer Act (N.Y.Veh. & Traf.Law 460–471). The district court granted Eastern summary judgment on Peugeot's declaratory judgment claim. It also granted Peugeot's motion for summary judgment on ... all the remaining parts of Eastern's case....

Peugeot argues that the district court erred as it applied the New York regulatory law in this case, that New York common law permits the non-renewal, that the contract's specific non-renewal terms should be applied, and that even if the New York regulatory law applies, there was no violation under these facts.... Being of the opinion that the New York regulatory law was not properly applied in this case and that New York's common law permits the challenged non-renewal, we vacate the district court's summary judgment in favor of Eastern in Peugeot's declaratory judgment action....

Peugeot, a Delaware corporation with its principal place of business in New Jersey, imports Peugeot automobiles into the United States and distributes them through a network of enfranchised dealers in states where Eastern is not the distributor. For over twenty-five years, Eastern, a Virginia corporation, has distributed Peugeot products in West Virginia, Virginia, North Carolina, South Carolina, Maryland, Kentucky, Tennessee, Delaware, the District of Columbia, and the northern part of Georgia. Eastern has never sold or distributed vehicles in New York. Eastern has never registered under New York's regulatory laws to be a dealer in New York, nor has it qualified to do business as a foreign corporation in New York.

On January 1, 1971, Peugeot and Eastern entered into the Distributor Agreement which is the subject of the present dispute. There are two relevant contractual provisions. The first is the non-renewal provision, paragraph thirty-two of the contract, which states: "Unless terminated by any other provision, this agreement shall continue for a period of one year from the effective date set forth at the foot of the agreement [January 1, 1971] and shall be renewed automatically from year to year thereafter unless either party gives at least 60 days' written notice to the other that it shall not be so renewed." The second relevant provision is paragraph thirty-nine, the choice of law provision, and provides that "[i]t is the express intention of the parties hereto that this agreement shall be governed by the laws of the State of New York."

The relationship between Peugeot and Eastern became strained in the late 1970's.... The relationship continued to be strained. On October 14, 1987, as stated, Peugeot sent notice of non-renewal to Eastern stating that pursuant to the non-renewal clause of the Distributor Agreement the contract would not be renewed on its expiration on January 1, 1988. The current action followed.

We first decide which state law is applicable. A federal court sitting in diversity must apply the choice of law rules of the forum state. Klaxon Co. v. Stentor Elect. Mfg. Co., 313 U.S. 487, 496–97, 61 S.Ct. 1020, 1021–22, 85 L.Ed. 1477 (1941). Since the action was filed in the Eastern District of Virginia, Virginia's choice of law rules apply. Virginia gives effect to parties' choice of law in a contract unless circumstances show a fraudulent purpose. Tate v. Hain, 181 Va. 402, 25 S.E.2d 321, 324 (1943). There being no fraudulent purposes shown we give effect to the parties' choice to have New York law apply to the contract.

We next address the proper application of New York law. Absent some controlling statutory scheme, New York has traditionally enforced unrestricted termination clauses in contracts as written. A.S. Rampell Inc. v. Hyster Co., 3 N.Y.2d 369, 165 N.Y.S.2d 475, 144 N.E.2d 371, 379 (1957). Although the case at bar deals with a non-renewal clause as opposed to a termination clause, we believe New York would treat the two very similar situations the same. Eastern argues that §§ 197 and 197–a of New York's General Business Law as well as the New York Franchised Motor Vehicle Dealer Act apply and control over the contract's non-renewal clause. Given that N.Y.Business Law §§ 197, 197–a and the N.Y.Franchised Motor Vehicle Dealer Act are very similar, we will address their applicability to the dispute together. Both of these regulatory acts have explicit geographic limitations. Section 197–a prohibits a non-renewal of a motor vehicle franchise contract to a distributor except in good faith. Section 195 defines a distributor as one who "sells or distributes in this state." Likewise, § 463(2)(d)(1) prohibits non-renewal of a franchise of any "franchised motor vehicle dealer" except for due cause. Section 462(7) defines "franchised motor vehicle dealer" as "any person required to be registered pursuant to section four hundred fifteen of this chapter." Section 415(3) requires registration only if the dealer intends to engage in business "in this state." Eastern has never done business in New York. It has never registered pursuant to New York law as a motor vehicle dealer or distributor. The New York regulatory schemes with explicit geographical limitations do not apply to this contract between two parties outside the state of

New York. Given that the two New York regulatory schemes by their own terms do not apply to the dispute, New York common law controls, and there is nothing in New York law to indicate that Peugeot did not act properly under the contract regarding its notice of non-renewal.... [The court reversed the judgment under the New York statutes for Eastern, affirmed judgment for Peugeot on some of Eastern's claims, and remanded for further proceedings on others.]

■ K.K. HALL, CIRCUIT JUDGE, concurring in part and dissenting in part. I respectfully dissent from the majority opinion to the extent that it vacates the lower court's declaratory judgment because I believe that the parties' choice of New York law should be interpreted to include an agreement to be bound by New York's statutes governing the non-renewal of automobile dealerships. The majority's refusal to apply the New York non-renewal statutes, based on "explicit geographical limitations" in the definition section of that state's code, is the result of a strained statutory construction and of a failure to focus on the intent of the contracting parties.

The majority recognizes, and I agree, that the contractual choice of New York law should, under the forum state's (Virginia) choice of law rules, be given effect. I also agree with the majority's determination that, absent a controlling statute to the contrary, New York law would uphold the unrestricted termination clause in the Peugeot–Eastern dealership contract. My disagreement stems from the majority's constrictive reading of the New York statutes to limit the parties' contractual choice of law to only that state's common law and those statutes which can somehow be read to have been intended by New York to have no territorial limitation.

The majority declines to give effect to the parties' choice of New York law with regard to the non-renewal statutes because the definition section of the regulatory scheme defines "distributor" as one who "sells or distributes in this state" and "franchised motor vehicle dealer" as one who is "required to be registered in this state." ... Aside from the bare language of the definitional provisions of New York's statutes, however, no showing has been made that New York affirmatively intended to deprive outside parties from choosing New York law. If anything, New York has clearly evinced a desire to have its laws chosen as governing contracts.[2] Even if it

---

2. N.Y.Gen.Obligations Law § 5–1401 (1984) provides as follows: 1. The parties to any contract, agreement or undertaking, contingent or otherwise, in consideration of, or relating to any obligation arising out of a transaction covering in the aggregate not less than two hundred fifty thousand dollars, including a transaction otherwise covered by subsection one of section 1–105 of the uniform commercial code, may agree that the law of this state shall govern their rights and duties in whole or in part, whether or not such contract, agreement or undertaking bears a reasonable relation to this state. This section shall not apply to any contract, agreement or undertaking (a) for labor or personal services, (b) relating to any transaction for personal, family or household services, or (c) to the extent provided to the contrary in subsection two of section 1–105 of the uniform commercial code. 2. Nothing contained in this section shall be construed to limit or deny the enforcement of any provision respecting choice of law in any other contract, agreement, or undertaking.

is assumed that a state legislature may act to withhold its enactments from use by contracting parties, New York has not done so....

The choice of New York law essentially amounts to an agreement to incorporate that state's laws, both statutory and common, into the contract itself. Accordingly, I would affirm the declaratory judgment of the district court on the ground that the New York non-renewal statutes apply to Peugeot's attempted termination of its distributorship agreement with Eastern....

NOTES

1. In the principal case, the majority avoids applying the chosen law to invalidate the non-renewal provision in the contract. In other cases, however, the chosen law has been applied to invalidate a provision of the contract. See, e.g., Milanovich v. Costa Crociere S.p.A., 954 F.2d 763 (D.C.Cir.1992) (choice of Italian law invalidates a cruise ticket's stated time limit for suit); Moyer v. Citicorp Homeowners, Inc., 799 F.2d 1445 (11th Cir.1986) (under Georgia conflicts rules, apply chosen law to invalidate for usury); Boatland, Inc. v. Brunswick Corp., 558 F.2d 818 (6th Cir.1977) (under Tennessee conflicts law, apply chosen law to invalidate non-renewal term in dealership contract); Foreman v. George Foreman Associates, Ltd., 517 F.2d 354 (9th Cir.1975) (under California conflicts law, apply chosen law to invalidate boxing contract).

The Restatement counsels ignoring the choice-of-law clause under these circumstances as an obvious mistake. Restatement (Second) Conflict of Laws § 187 comment e. Professor Kramer contends that the assumption that the choice of an invalidating law was inadvertent is not always warranted. Kramer, Rethinking Choice of Law, 90 Colum.L.Rev. 277, 332 (1990) (stating that the invalidated portion may be unintended boilerplate or the dispute may concern the validity of an oral modification).

2. Choice-of-law clauses in arbitration agreements present problems when the chosen law limits the powers of arbitrators or otherwise affects enforcement. In Mastrobuono v. Shearson Lehman Hutton, Inc., 115 S.Ct. 1212 (1995), arbitrators awarded punitive damages, but the agreement chose New York law, which allows only courts, not arbitrators to award punitive damages. The Court held that the award should be enforced, stating that the choice-of-law clause "might include only New York's substantive rights and obligations, and not the State's allocation of power between alternative tribunals." Id. at 1217. In Volt Information Sciences, Inc. v. Board of Trustees of the Leland Stanford Junior University, 489 U.S. 468 (1989), a contract for construction on the Stanford campus chose "the law of the place where the Project is located" and also provided for the arbitration of all disputes arising out of the contract. When a dispute arose, Volt demanded arbitration. Stanford then filed an action against Volt in a California state court and also sought indemnity from two other parties involved in the construction project, with whom it did not have arbitration agreements. California law allows a stay of arbitration pending resolution of related litigation between a party to the arbitration agreement and third parties not bound by it. The Court affirmed a stay of arbitration stating that the California Court of Appeal's conclusion that the parties intended the choice-of-law clause to incorporate the California arbitration rules is a question of state law, which would not be set aside.

3. What is the purpose of N.Y.Gen.Obligations Law § 5–1401, quoted in footnote 2 of the dissent in the principal case? Is it sound policy?

Bledsoe v. Crowley
United States Court of Appeals, District of Columbia Circuit, 1988.
849 F.2d 639.

■ Harry T. Edwards, Circuit Judge:

This appeal concerns the question whether the trial court, in a diversity action brought in the District Court for the District of Columbia, correctly applied a Maryland statute requiring arbitration of medical malpractice claims. Appellant Theodore Bledsoe, a District of Columbia resident who sought treatment in Maryland, argues that the District Court erred in dismissing his suit for failure to comply with the Maryland statute....

Appellant Theodore Bledsoe, a medical doctor, brought suit in the District Court against Dr. Brian Crowley and Dr. Sylvia Friedman, alleging negligence in their failure to diagnose his brain tumor during the twelve years they treated him for psychiatric disorders. Bledsoe first consulted Dr. Crowley, a psychiatrist, in 1969, because of "occasional inability to control impulsive behavior." He underwent psychoanalysis with Crowley for the next eleven years. In 1979, Crowley referred Bledsoe to another psychiatrist, Dr. Friedman, with whom he engaged in group therapy for two and one-half years. In 1984, some time after Bledsoe had discontinued therapy with both doctors, he was admitted to St. Elizabeth's Hospital in Washington, D.C., where a CAT scan revealed a brain tumor. According to the complaint, the tumor had been present and growing for many years. While Bledsoe's condition improved following removal of the tumor, he allegedly suffered permanent brain damage and loss of vision, which prevented him from pursuing his practice of radiology.

Although Bledsoe resided in Maryland when he began seeing Dr. Crowley, he moved to the District of Columbia at some time thereafter and was a District resident at the time the suit was filed. His radiology practice was at all times in Maryland. Drs. Crowley and Friedman both resided in Maryland. Their practice was located in Maryland, although both were also licensed to practice in the District of Columbia. All of Bledsoe's therapy sessions with both doctors took place in Maryland.

The Maryland Health Care Malpractice Claims Statute, Md.Cts. & Jud.Proc.Code Ann. §§ 3–2A–01 to –09 (1984 & Supp.1987), provides that all medical malpractice claims alleging damages in excess of a certain jurisdictional amount must be submitted initially to an arbitration panel established pursuant to the statute's provisions. Either party is free to reject the arbitration award, but in such a case the award is admissible in a subsequent court action as the presumptively correct judgment. The party rejecting the award bears the burden of rebutting the presumption and must pay court costs if the verdict ultimately obtained is not more favorable than was the arbitration award. The statute provides, in section 3–

2A–02(a)(2), that "[a]n action or suit of [the type covered by the statute] may not be brought or pursued in any court of this State except in accordance with this subtitle." . . .

Appellant now advances three points in pursuit of this appeal: (1) District of Columbia law, not that of Maryland, should apply; (2) even assuming Maryland law controls, the arbitration provisions should not apply because they were intended to be applied only in Maryland courts, because they are "procedural," and because it would be unconstitutional to apply them here; and (3) the defendants waived application of the arbitration provisions by failing to raise this defense at an early stage of the proceedings.

A. *Choice of Law*

To determine the applicable law in a diversity case, a federal court must follow the choice of law rules of the forum state. Klaxon Co. v. Stentor Elec. Mfg. Co., 313 U.S. 487, 496 (1941). Therefore, in this case, . . . [a]dhering to the rules of the District of Columbia, we must apply a "governmental interest analysis," which requires a court "to evaluate the governmental policies underlying the applicable conflicting laws and to determine which jurisdiction's policy would be most advanced by having its law applied to the facts of the case under review." . . . [1]

The District Court resolved the conflict in favor of the application of Maryland law by determining that Maryland, through passage of the arbitration statute, had manifested a strong public policy concerning the manner in which malpractice claims should be resolved. It found that the District of Columbia, by contrast, had expressed no such interest, because it had adopted no legislation on the subject. The District Court thus decided that there was no true conflict, and that since no other factor outweighed Maryland's strong interest, Maryland law should be applied.

Appellant maintains that the District Court's analysis was defective because it failed to inquire into the law that a court in the *foreign* jurisdiction would apply; in other words, if a Maryland court, applying that state's choice of law principles, would apply District of Columbia law in this case, then Maryland's interest to be weighed against the District's would be much diminished. While we agree that such an inquiry has a place in the governmental interest analysis, see [Biscoe v. Arlington County, 738 F.2d 1352, 1360 (D.C.Cir.1984), cert. denied 469 U.S. 1159 (1985)]; Tramontana v. S.A. Empresa de Viacao Aerea Rio Grandense, 350 F.2d 468, 473–75 (D.C.Cir.1965), cert. denied, 383 U.S. 943 (1966), we reject appellant's contention that Maryland would apply the law of the District of Columbia in this case. Maryland—unlike the District of Columbia—adheres to the more traditional principle of *lex loci delicti,* which determines the applicable law in tort actions according to the place "where the wrong occurs." Hauch v. Connor, 295 Md. 120, 453 A.2d 1207, 1209 (1983). Appellant

---

1. If the interests of the two jurisdictions in the application of their law are equally weighty, the law of the forum will be applied. Kaiser–Georgetown Community Health Plan, Inc. v. Stutsman, 491 A.2d 502, 509 & n. 10 (D.C.1985).

argues that "[w]hile defendants' negligence here occurred primarily in Maryland, Dr. Bledsoe's injury occurred in the District of Columbia." ...

We disagree. Appellant's attempt to separate the place where the injury occurred from the place where the negligence took place makes no sense in the context of an alleged failure to diagnose a slowly growing brain tumor. Since it is impossible to make such a distinction, a Maryland court would, we believe, apply the general principle that the applicable law is that of the place where the "wrong" occurred. If Dr. Bledsoe was wronged anywhere, it was certainly in Maryland.

Appellant also argues that the District Court gave insufficient weight to the District of Columbia's interests in having its own law applied. He contends that the District government's silence on the question of malpractice reform does not necessarily, as the District Court thought, indicate a lack of interest in the question, for it could equally well support an inference that the District wished to assure its citizens the full remedies of traditional tort law. In the absence of further documentation of the District's putative interest, this argument remains speculative. Even were we to give it full credence, however, we would conclude that Maryland is "the jurisdiction with the stronger interest." *Biscoe,* 738 F.2d at 1360. Where the entire relationship between the parties was centered in Maryland and the allegedly tortious conduct occurred in that state, Maryland's interest in regulating the activity must be deemed the stronger one .... It is simply not possible to maintain in this case that "important interests of the forum would be sacrificed to advance *equal or lesser* interests of another jurisdiction...." Mazza v. Mazza, 475 F.2d 385, 391 (D.C.Cir. 1973) (emphasis added).[6] ...

Appellant also argues that the Maryland statute was not intended to have "extraterritorial" application because it "is procedural and is not part of the substantive law of Maryland for choice of law purposes." ... Appellant relies here on section 3–2A–09, which specifies that "[t]he provisions of this subtitle shall be deemed procedural in nature...." The context of this statement makes clear, however ... that it "was merely intended to indicate that the legislature was not attempting to create a new

---

6. Kaiser-Georgetown Community Health Plan, Inc. v. Stutsman, 491 A.2d 502 (D.C.1985), is not to the contrary. In that case the District of Columbia Court of Appeals determined that the District's interest in application of its law was stronger than Virginia's, despite the fact that the plaintiff was a resident of Virginia and the allegedly negligent medical treatment had taken place there. The court's decision was based largely on three factors: (1) the two defendants were District of Columbia corporations, and the District therefore had a significant interest in holding them fully liable for their negligence; (2) the plaintiff was employed in the District, the health plan under which she was treated was a benefit of that employment, and, therefore, the District's interest in the protection of its workforce was implicated; and (3) Virginia's interest in imposing a liability cap was primarily in protecting Virginia health care providers, and that interest was weaker where the defendants were foreign corporations with their principal places of business outside Virginia. Id. at 509–11. In the present case, none of these factors would point to a stronger interest for the District of Columbia.

cause of action in passing this statute." [Davison v. Sinai Hospital, 462 F.Supp. 778, 780 (D.Md.1978), aff'd 617 F.2d 361 (4th Cir.1980).] [8]

We have some difficulty comprehending the precise nature of appellant's argument. The only way in which the substantive/procedural distinction makes sense in the context in which appellant raises it is as an argument that the Maryland provision is a "procedural" one, which a federal court would not apply under the doctrine of Erie R.R. Co. v. Tompkins, 304 U.S. 64 (1938).[9] This argument was considered and properly rejected by *Davison*. That court found that the Maryland arbitration requirement should be treated as a "substantive" provision in order to comply with the policies underlying *Erie* that (1) the character or result of litigation not differ materially because the suit was brought in federal court, and (2) incentives to forum shopping be avoided....

As far as we can discern it, however, appellant's argument appears to be based solely on Maryland choice of law principles, according to which the law of the forum is applied to "procedural" matters. The legislature, it is argued, by defining the statute as procedural, intended to deny it "extraterritorial" application: while a federal court sitting in Maryland might apply the arbitration statute, a federal court sitting in another state could not do so. See Appellant's Brief at 16–19. This is a strange argument indeed. The only relevant difference between a federal court sitting in the District of Columbia and one sitting in Maryland is in the starting point of applying the choice of law principles of the forum state. Once it has been determined, through application of those principles, that Maryland law governs, a D.C. federal court would apply Maryland law no differently than would a Maryland federal court....

Finally, we reject appellant's contention that application of the Maryland statute in this context violates the privileges and immunities clause of the Fourteenth Amendment because it denies a citizen of the District of Columbia access to a District of Columbia court.... Appellant has not been barred from pursuing a remedy in the District of Columbia courts but rather is merely required first to submit to arbitration pursuant to the Maryland statute. Cf. Oxtoby v. McGowan, 294 Md. 83, 447 A.2d 860, 865 (1982) (analogizing the arbitration requirement to the doctrine of exhaustion of administrative remedies).

. . .

---

8. Section 3–2A–09 reads in full: "The provisions of this subtitle shall be deemed procedural in nature and shall not be construed to create, enlarge, or diminish any cause of action not heretofore existing, except the defense of failure to comply with the procedures required under this subtitle."

9. The adjectives "substantive" and "procedural" cannot be understood in the *Erie* context by reference to their common-sense meanings; rather, a federal court must look to the policies underlying *Erie* in order to determine whether to apply state or federal law. See Guaranty Trust Co. v. York, 326 U.S. 99, 109 (1945); Hanna v. Plumer, 380 U.S. 460, 465–68 (1965). Nonetheless, the terms "procedural" and "substantive" provide a convenient shorthand.

[Although it affirmed the district court's judgment on the merits, the court of appeals remanded the case for a stay pending the Maryland arbitration, rather than a dismissal.]

■ WILLIAMS, CIRCUIT JUDGE, concurring:

I concur wholeheartedly in Judge Edward's excellent opinion and write separately only to consider an additional element in the choice of laws problem.

The Restatement (Second) of Conflict of Laws (1971), to which District of Columbia courts often turn for guidance, lists as the first relevant "factor" in interest analysis "the needs of the interstate ... system." § 6(2)(a). This of course suggests—quite rightly—that states have shared, non-parochial interests. In the medical malpractice context, with which we deal here, there are systemic interests in (1) states' being able to develop coherent policies governing medical malpractice liability and (2) individuals' being able to take advantage of medical services outside their home jurisdictions.

For realization of the first interest, a state that seeks to reduce medical costs by reducing the burden of malpractice liability must be able to assure providers that the state's rules will actually apply to all (or virtually all) cases. For example, if Maryland places limits on malpractice recoveries but its medical providers are exposed to liability under the laws of states without such controls, the charges of persons providing medical services in Maryland will rise to carry the burden of expected liabilities to out-of-staters. This result thwarts not only the ability of each state to establish a policy and secure whatever benefits it may offer, but also the system's capacity to conduct and evaluate experiments in liability policy.

The above analysis assumes that the Maryland rule here at issue—requiring arbitration as a precondition to litigation and giving the arbitration result the weight of a presumption in any later suit—is directed at reducing at least the total costs of medical malpractice liability. That inference seems inescapable, and is independent of whether the rule is expected to affect net plaintiff recoveries.

Applying the rule of the patient's domicile might at first blush seem easily reconciled with the interest in state development of liability policy. If courts apply the law of the patient's domicile, medical associations can be expected to promptly inform Maryland providers, who in turn can reject would-be out-of-state patients. By contrast, potential out-of-state patients may not so readily learn that use of Maryland providers entails special malpractice rules.

On balance, though, the law of the jurisdiction where the services are provided seems to better accommodate the systemic values. For medical providers to screen out incoming patients altogether would completely destroy individuals' ability to seek out expert medical help throughout the United States. The Mayo Clinic in Minnesota is simply the most prominent of many providers whose reputation draws patients from the entire country. A system depriving the ill of these benefits would seem a tragic waste.

A more limited response to control by the law of the patient's domicile would be for providers to accept out-of-state patients, but insist on agreements binding them to local law. But such a practice might founder on rules refusing to enforce agreements waiving rights to recover in tort—including partial waivers such as would be entailed by application of the Maryland rule here. This difficulty might, of course, be salvaged by a halfway rule: that the law of the state where the services are provided would govern the validity of waivers. Such a halfway rule seems an irreducible minimum for achievement of basic systemic goals.

But the stronger rule—that substantive liability is defined by the law of the place services are rendered—seems preferable. While medical associations can readily communicate with members as to liability hazards, and alert them to possible responses, patients are inherently on notice that journeying to new jurisdictions may expose them to new rules. The maxim "When in Rome do as the Romans do" bespeaks the common sense view that it is the traveler who must adjust.

Here of course we act only as surrogates for the District of Columbia courts, and the District's only case on conflicts in medical malpractice law rejected the law of Virginia, where the services were provided. Kaiser-Georgetown Community Health Plan, Inc. v. Stutsman, 491 A.2d 502 (D.C.1985). Judge Edwards amply distinguishes the case.... For purposes of considering § 6(2)(a) of the Restatement, however, it appears that no one even brought the systemic values to the attention of the court. The opinion did note that Virginia's limitation on liability aimed in part at reducing the medical fees charged Virginia residents, 491 A.2d at 510, but assumed Virginia's primary interest lay in benefitting providers as opposed to consumers, id. Reasoning from that assumption, the court stated that Virginia's "interest in the application of its statute becomes attenuated when its intended beneficiaries are foreign corporations with principal places of business outside the State." Id. at 511. Such a characterization ignores the systemic interest in states' being able to adopt policies reducing health care costs for consumers. That interest is little affected by the domicile of the defendant provider. It is true that so long as purely domestic Virginia medical providers can count on the application of Virginia law in all cases arising out of provision of services there, their rates will reflect benefits due to Virginia restrictions; regardless of the conflicts rule, out-of-state firms, if they are to operate in Virginia, will have to match them. (A motel chain cannot charge New York City rates for rooms in Arkansas because it is incorporated or headquartered in New York.) But adoption of a conflicts rule that subjects out-of-state providers to more costly tort regimes effects a troubling discrimination, and if these firms are an important part of the potential supply of medical services in Virginia (i.e., if the purely domestic supply is inelastic), the presence of the burden will increase the market price of all those services.

Thus it seems unlikely that the location of the provider's incorporation or headquarters undermines the systemic analysis militating in favor of applying the law of the state where the services are provided. (This is a neutral principle and holds equally true if the state of provision has policies favoring high malpractice recoveries.) For our purposes it is enough to note that, given the D.C. courts' practice of looking to the Restatement for guidance on conflicts matters, there is no reason to suppose that they would not recognize the systemic concerns if properly brought to their attention.

NOTE

What argument could be based on the Maryland statute's designation of the relevant subtitle as "procedural," other than the *Erie* argument that Judge Edwards rejects?

C. PROBLEMS EMERGED AND EMERGING

Traditional territorial choice-of-law rules provided reasonable certainty, somewhat diminished by the escape devices examined on pages 493–506, supra. The problem with these rules is that sometimes they compelled application of the law of a state that would not have to bear the consequences of the decision and prevented application of the law of a state that would have to live with those consequences. The adoption of choice-of-law rules that take account of the content and purposes of domestic law, seeks to avoid this effect of the traditional rules, but in turn creates new problems. Six such problems are presented in this section. (1) Will the new method permit reasonable predictability and certainty? (2) If more than one state with conflicting laws will have to live with the consequences of decision, how can this "true" conflict be resolved? (3) After the event in litigation, how should a change in circumstances, such as a move by a party to another state, affect the analysis? (4) What factors other than state "interests" affect the cogency and fairness of the result? (5) If the law of plaintiff's state favors the defendant and the law of defendant's state favors the plaintiff, how should this "no interest" case be resolved? (6) Can the new methods be adapted to complex litigation involving many parties from different states with different laws?

1. PREDICTABILITY

Dym v. Gordon

Court of Appeals of New York, 1965.
16 N.Y.2d 120, 262 N.Y.S.2d 463, 209 N.E.2d 792.

[Plaintiff and defendant, New York residents, attended summer school at the University of Colorado in Boulder, Colorado. Defendant offered plaintiff a ride to a nearby town in Colorado and en route collided with another car, injuring plaintiff and, possibly, others. The Appellate Division ruled that ordinary negligence was not a sufficient basis for recovery, since the Colorado guest statute applied, requiring "willful and wanton disregard" of the passenger's safety.]

■ BURKE, J. ... Following our approach in Babcock, it is necessary first to isolate the issue, next to identify the policies embraced in the laws in conflict, and finally to examine the contacts of the respective jurisdictions to ascertain which has a superior connection with the occurrence and thus would have a superior interest in having its policy or law applied. The issue here is simply whether in an automobile host-guest relationship a negligent driver should be liable to his injured passenger. The New York law finds nothing in the host-guest relationship which warrants a digression from the usual negligence rule of ordinary care. In Colorado, however, this relationship is treated specially and, while ordinary negligence is usually enough for recovery in that state, injuries arising out of this relationship are compensable only if they result from "willful and wanton" conduct. Contrary to the narrow view advanced by plaintiff, the policy underlying Colorado's law is threefold: the protection of Colorado drivers and their insurance carriers against fraudulent claims, the prevention of suits by "ungrateful guests", and the priority of injured parties in other cars in the assets of the negligent defendant. Examining Colorado's interest in light of its public policy we find that over and above the usual interest which Colorado may bring to bear on all conduct occurring within its boundaries, Colorado has an interest in seeing that the negligent defendant's assets are not dissipated in order that the persons in the car of the blameless driver will not have their right to recovery diminished by the present suit.

Finally we come to the question of which state has the more significant contacts with the case such that its interest should be upheld. In this regard, the factual distinctions between this case and Babcock do have considerable influence. Babcock did not involve a collision between two cars; thus only New Yorkers were involved and it was unnecessary for us to consider the interest of Ontario in the rights of those in a car of a nonnegligent driver. In Babcock we pointed out that the host-guest relationship was seated in New York and that the place of the accident was "entirely fortuitous". In this case the parties were dwelling in Colorado when the relationship was formed and the accident arose out of Colorado based activity; therefore, the fact that the accident occurred in Colorado could in no sense be termed fortuitous. Thus it is that in this case where Colorado has such significant contacts with the *relationship itself* and the *basis of its formation* the application of its law and underlying policy are clearly warranted.

Of compelling importance in this case is the fact that here the parties had come to rest in the State of Colorado and had thus chosen to live their daily lives under the protective arm of Colorado law. Having accepted the benefits of that law for such a prolonged period, it is spurious to maintain that Colorado has no interest in a relationship which was formed there. In Babcock the New Yorkers at all times were *in transitu* and we were impressed with the fundamental unfairness of subjecting them to a law which they in no sense had adopted.

To say that this relationship was formed in Colorado implies that the parties had acquired so sufficient a nexus with that jurisdiction that relationships formed there were in the real sense Colorado relationships. In other words, it is neither the physical situs where the relationship was created nor the time of its creation which is controlling but rather these factors in conjunction with the general intent of the parties as inferred from their actions....

The alleged contacts referred to by plaintiff may be classified under the heading of domicile. Certainly it is merely a long-handed method of reciting that the parties were domiciled in New York to state that the car was registered here and that the insurance was written here. These and many other factors may usually be presumed from the fact of domicile; they have no independent significance as regards the host-guest relationship apart from their inclusion as natural incidents of domicile.

Judicial hostility to "guest" statutes and a preoccupation with New York social welfare problems and the relative liability of insurers should not be treated as "contacts" which are found then to outweigh the factual contacts....

Here, necessarily, the only valid competing consideration bearing on the host-guest relationship is that of domicile. However appealing it might seem to give effect to our own public policy on this issue, merely because the negligent driver of the car in the collision, and his guest, are domiciled here, to do so would be to totally neglect the interests of the jurisdiction where the accident occurred, where the relationship arose and where the parties were dwelling.... To give domicile or an alleged public policy such a preferred status is to substitute a conflicts rule every bit as inflexible and arbitrary as its *lex loci* predecessor. Such was not our intention in Babcock. It is suggested that New York has a dominant governmental interest in seeing that the plaintiff receives compensation because it is this State that she will look to for welfare payments should she become a public charge as a result of her injuries. Such an argument is hardly a legal one. Were we to give our attention to such considerations we might just as well speculate about the possibility that the New York defendant could become a public charge if the plaintiff were to be given recovery. There is no guarantee that the recovery will not far exceed the insurance coverage in this or in any other case. A reflection on the import of this argument gives one the feeling that a preference for whatever law will compensate the New York tort plaintiff lurks in the background. The suggestion that our courts should apply this State's policy of compensation for innocent tort victims to all cases of returning domiciliaries is tantamount to saying that different rules or interests of other jurisdictions should be denied application in a New York forum on the ground of their not suiting our public policy. The principles justifying our refusal to apply foreign law on the ground of public policy are well defined, and a mere difference between the foreign rule and our own will not warrant such refusal.

Public policy, per se, plays no part in a *choice* of law problem....

The present decision represents no departure from the rule announced in Babcock; merely an example of its application....

Accordingly, the order of the Appellate Division should be affirmed, without costs.

■ FULD, JUDGE (dissenting).

. . .

The [Babcock] rule is not, and does not profess to be, a talisman of legal certainty, nor does it of itself provide a formulary means for resolving conflicts problems. What it does provide is a method, a conceptual framework, for the disposition of tort cases having contacts with more than one jurisdiction. Although the majority in this case reaffirms Babcock's abandonment of the prior inflexible rule of *lex loci delicti*, its decision, nevertheless, in essence, reflects the adoption of an equally mechanical and arbitrary rule that, in litigation involving a special relationship, controlling effect must be given to the law of the jurisdiction in which the relationship originated, notwithstanding that that jurisdiction may not have the slightest concern with the specific issue raised or that some other state's relationship or contact with the occurrence or the parties may be such as to give it the predominant interest in the resolution of that issue.

There is, indeed, no material distinction between the factual situation here presented and that in the Babcock case....

... Under the circumstances of the present case, then, Colorado, to paraphrase what we wrote in Babcock, "has no conceivable interest in denying a remedy to a New York guest against his New York host for injuries suffered in [Colorado] by reason of conduct which was tortious under [Colorado] law" (12 N.Y.2d, at p. 482, 240 N.Y.S.2d, at p. 750, 191 N.E.2d, at p. 284).

Nor is the majority's position advanced by its further suggestion ... that the Colorado statute also reflects (1) an antipathy on the part of Colorado to suits by "ungrateful" guests (see Dobbs v. Sugioka, 117 Colo. 218, 220, 185 P.2d 784,) and (2) a policy to assure "the priority of injured parties in other cars in the assets of the negligent defendant." Indeed, as regards the latter asserted policy, there does not appear to be any Colorado pronouncement even to intimate that the Colorado Legislature was motivated by any such objective. In any event, though, Colorado would be legitimately concerned with the application of these alleged policies only in relation to matters within its legislative competence, such as the burdens of the Colorado courts, the regulation of the affairs and relationships of Colorado citizens or the protection of Colorado claimants or insurers....

■ CHIEF JUDGE DESMOND (dissenting).... What we did in the [Babcock, p. 520, supra and Kilberg, p. 503, supra] decisions was to announce for New York a modern public policy which abandoned the old sweeping rule that the law to be applied in every tort case was the law of the place of the wrong. Babcock and Kilberg (supra) together should be the law of this present case.

. . . .

No guides satisfactory to me are found in the concepts currently favored by teachers and writers on conflict of laws, such as "significant contacts", "center of gravity", and "interests of the respective states".... Counting up "contacts" or locating the "center of gravity" or weighing the respective "interests" of two states can never be a satisfactory way of deciding actual lawsuits....

NOTE

As described in Note 5, page 525, supra, the principal case marked the beginning of a chaotic period in New York choice-of-law decisions. Was this an inevitable consequence of the new approach adopted in Babcock v. Jackson, 12 N.Y.2d 473, 240 N.Y.S.2d 743, 191 N.E.2d 279 (1963), page 520, supra, or was it the result of misunderstanding and misapplying that approach? If it was misapplication, where did the principal case go wrong?

DeSantis v. Wackenhut Corporation

Supreme Court of Texas, 1990.
793 S.W.2d 670, cert. denied, 498 U.S. 1048 (1991).

■ HECHT, JUSTICE. ... This case involving a noncompetition agreement between an employer and employee presents three principal issues: first, whether the law of the state chosen by the parties to govern their agreement should be applied; second, whether the noncompetition agreement is enforceable; third, if the agreement is not enforceable, whether damages for its attempted enforcement are recoverable under the Texas Free Enterprise and Antitrust Act of 1983 or for wrongful injunction, fraud, or tortious interference with contract.

The trial court applied the law of the state of Florida, chosen by the parties to govern the noncompetition agreement, to hold the agreement valid but overly broad as to the geographical territory in which competition was restricted. Based upon a jury finding that the employee breached the agreement, the trial court enjoined any further violation of the agreement within a smaller territory, and denied the employee's claims for damages. The court of appeals affirmed. 732 S.W.2d 29. We hold that Texas law, not Florida law, applies in this case, and that under Texas law, the noncompetition agreement is unenforceable. We further hold that the employee is not entitled to recover damages for his employer's wrongfully obtaining an injunction against him, and that the employee has failed to show fraud, tortious interference, or a violation of the Texas Free Enterprise and Antitrust Act entitling him to damages. We accordingly reverse the judgment of the court of appeals and render judgment in accordance with this opinion.

I

A

Edward DeSantis has been providing international and corporate security services, both in the CIA and the private sector for his entire career. In June 1981, while employed by R.J. Reynolds Industries in North Carolina, DeSantis interviewed for a position with Wackenhut Corporation. At that time, Wackenhut, which was chartered and headquartered in Florida, was the third largest company in the nation specializing in furnishing security guards for businesses throughout the country. DeSantis met with Wackenhut's president, founder, and majority stockholder, George Wackenhut, at the company's offices in Florida, and the two agreed that DeSantis would immediately assume the position of Wackenhut's Houston area manager. According to DeSantis, George Wackenhut promised him that the area manager's position was only temporary, and that he would soon be moved into a top executive position. George Wackenhut denies that he made any such promises to DeSantis, admitting only that he mentioned advancement to an executive position as a possible opportunity.

At Wackenhut's request, DeSantis signed a noncompetition agreement at the inception of his employment. The agreement recites that it was "made and entered into" on August 13, 1981, in Florida, although DeSantis signed it in Texas. It also recites consideration "including but not limited to the Employee's employment by the Employer". In the agreement DeSantis covenanted that as long as he was employed by Wackenhut and for two years thereafter, he would not compete in any way with Wackenhut in a forty-county area in south Texas. DeSantis expressly acknowledged that Wackenhut's client list "is a valuable, special and unique asset of [Wackenhut's] business" and agreed never to disclose it to anyone. DeSantis also agreed never to divulge any confidential or proprietary information acquired through his employment with Wackenhut. Finally, DeSantis and Wackenhut agreed "that any questions concerning interpretation or enforcement of this contract shall be governed by Florida law."

DeSantis remained manager of Wackenhut's Houston office for nearly three years, until March 1984, when he resigned under threat of termination. DeSantis contends that he was forced to quit because of disagreements with Wackenhut's senior management over the profitability of the Houston office. Wackenhut contends that DeSantis was asked to resign because of his unethical solicitation of business.

Following his resignation, DeSantis invested in a company which marketed security electronics. He also formed a new company, Risk Deterrence, Inc. ("RDI"), to provide security consulting services and security guards to a limited clientele. The month following termination of his employment with Wackenhut, DeSantis sent out letters announcing his new ventures to twenty or thirty businesses, about half of which were Wackenhut clients. He added a postscript to letters to Wackenhut clients in which he disclaimed any intent to interfere with their existing contracts with Wackenhut. Within six months, however, one of Wackenhut's clients, Marathon Oil Company, had terminated its contract with Wackenhut and signed a five-year contract with RDI, and a second Wackenhut client, TRW–Mission Drilling Products, was considering doing the same. Wackenhut claims that DeSantis was acquiring its clients in violation of the noncompetition agreement. DeSantis claims that these clients began considering other security service providers only after the quality of Wackenhut's services declined, following DeSantis' departure.

B

Wackenhut sued DeSantis and RDI in October 1984 to enjoin them from violating the noncompetition agreement, and to recover damages for breach of the agreement and for tortious interference with business relations. Wackenhut alleged that DeSantis and RDI were soliciting its clients' business using confidential client and pricing information which DeSantis obtained through his employment with Wackenhut. The trial court issued an ex parte temporary restraining order against DeSantis and RDI, and fixed the amount of the requisite bond which Wackenhut filed at $5,000. Following a hearing, the trial court issued a temporary injunction upon a $75,000 bond, which Wackenhut also filed. DeSantis and RDI counterclaimed against Wackenhut, alleging that Wackenhut had fraudulently induced DeSantis to sign the noncompetition agreement, that the agreement violated state antitrust laws, and that enforcement of the agreement by temporary injunction was wrongful and tortiously interfered with DeSantis and RDI's contract and business relationships. RDI claimed damages for loss of the Marathon contract, which Marathon terminated after the injunction issued, for loss of the TRW business, and for injury to its reputation. DeSantis claimed damages for lost salary, impaired reputation, and mental anguish. DeSantis and RDI both sought statutory damages under the Texas Free Enterprise and Antitrust Act, Texas Business and Commerce Code Annotated sections 15.01–15.51 (Vernon 1987 and Supp. 1990), and exemplary damages.

The trial court granted Wackenhut's motion for summary judgment on DeSantis' and RDI's claim for tortious interference, and directed a verdict against them on their fraud claim. At trial, Wackenhut withdrew its tortious interference claim. A jury found that DeSantis breached the noncompetition agreement by competing with Wackenhut.... The jury also failed to find that Wackenhut had ever been unfair, unjust, misleading or deceptive to DeSantis so as to cause him any injury....

The trial court concluded that irreparable harm to Wackenhut was either presumed from DeSantis' breach of the agreement under Florida law, or established as a matter of law because of the absence of an adequate legal remedy for breach of the agreement under Texas law. Accordingly, the trial court permanently enjoined DeSantis from competing with Wackenhut, and RDI from employing DeSantis to compete with Wackenhut, for two years from the date DeSantis left Wackenhut in an area reduced by the trial court from the forty counties stated in the agreement to the thirteen counties found by the trial court to be reasonably necessary to protect Wackenhut's interest. The trial court also permanently enjoined DeSantis from divulging Wackenhut's client list or proprietary information, and RDI from using any proprietary information of Wackenhut's acquired through DeSantis. The trial court denied all relief requested by DeSantis and RDI, based upon the jury's finding that DeSantis had breached his agreement with Wackenhut. The trial court awarded Wackenhut attorney's fees and costs.

The court of appeals affirmed the judgment of the trial court in all respects.

II

We first consider what law is to be applied in determining whether the noncompetition agreement in this case is enforceable. Wackenhut contends that Florida law applies, as expressly agreed by the parties. DeSantis argues that Texas law applies, despite the parties' agreement.

A

... When parties to a contract reside or expect to perform their respective obligations in multiple jurisdictions, they may be uncertain as to what jurisdiction's law will govern construction and enforcement of the contract. To avoid this uncertainty, they may express in their agreement their own choice that the law of a specified jurisdiction apply to their agreement. Judicial respect for their choice advances the policy of protecting their expectations. This conflict of laws concept has come to be referred to as party autonomy. See R. Weintraub, Commentary on the Conflict of Laws 269–271 (1971) ["Weintraub"]. However, the parties' freedom to choose what jurisdiction's law will apply to their agreement cannot be unlimited. They cannot require that their contract be governed by the law of a jurisdiction which has no relation whatever to them or their agreement. And they cannot by agreement thwart or offend the public policy of the state the law of which ought otherwise to apply. So limited, party autonomy furthers the basic policy of contract law. With roots deep in two centuries of American jurisprudence, limited party autonomy has grown to be the modern rule in contracts conflict of laws. See Scoles & Hay, Conflict of Laws § 18.1, p. 657 et seq. (2d ed. 1992); Weintraub, supra at 269–275; Restatement (Second) of Conflict of Laws ["The Restatement"] § 187 (1971)....

B

[The court quotes Restatement § 187, page 541, supra, and concludes that this case falls under § 187(2) rather than under § 187(1).]

The parties in this case chose the law of Florida to govern their contract. Florida has a substantial relationship to the parties and the transaction because Wackenhut's corporate offices are there, and some of the negotiations between DeSantis and George Wackenhut occurred there. Thus, under section 187(2) Florida law should apply in this case unless it falls within the exception stated in section 187(2)(b). Whether that exception applies depends upon three determinations: first, whether there is a state the law of which would apply under section 188 of the Restatement absent an effective choice of law by the parties, or in other words, whether a state has a more significant relationship with the parties and their transaction than the state they chose; second, whether that state has a materially greater interest than the chosen state in deciding whether this noncompetition agreement should be enforced; and third, whether that state's fundamental policy would be contravened by the application of the law of the chosen state in this case. More particularly, we must determine: first, whether Texas has a more significant relationship to these parties and their transaction than Florida; second, whether Texas has a materially greater interest than Florida in deciding the enforceability of the noncompetition agreement in this case; and third, whether the application of Florida law in this case would be contrary to fundamental policy of Texas.

1

Section 188 of the Restatement [page 542, supra] provides that a contract is to be governed by the law of the state that "has the most significant relationship to the transaction and the parties", taking into account various contacts in light of the basic conflict of laws principles of section 6 of the Restatement. In this case, that state is Texas. Wackenhut hired DeSantis to manage its business in the Houston area. Although some of the negotiations between DeSantis and Wackenhut occurred in Florida, the noncompetition agreement was finally executed by DeSantis in Houston. The place of performance for both parties was Texas, where the subject matter of the contract was located. Wackenhut may also be considered to have performed its obligations in part in Florida, from where it supervised its various operations, including its Houston office. Still, the gist of the agreement in this case was the performance of personal services in Texas. As a rule, that factor alone is conclusive in determining what state's law is to apply. See Restatement § 196 (1971).[4] In this case, the relationship of the transaction and parties to Texas was clearly more significant than their relationship to Florida.

2

Texas has a materially greater interest than does Florida in determining whether the noncompetition agreement in this case is enforceable. At stake here is whether a Texas resident can leave one Texas job to start a competing Texas business. Thus, Texas is directly interested in DeSantis as an employee in this state, in Wackenhut as a national employer doing business in this state, in RDI as a new competitive business being formed in the state, and in consumers of the services furnished in Texas by

4. Section 196 states: "Contracts for the Rendition of Services. The validity of a contract for the rendition of services and the rights created thereby are determined, in the absence of an effective choice of law by the parties, by the local law of the state where the contract requires that the services, or a major portion of the services, be rendered, unless, with respect to the particular issue, some other state has a more significant relationship under the principles stated in § 6 to the transaction and the parties, in which event the local law of the other state will be applied."

Wackenhut and RDI and performed by DeSantis. Texas also shares with Florida a general interest in protecting the justifiable expectations of entities doing business in several states. Florida's direct interest in the enforcement of the noncompetition agreement in this case is limited to protecting a national business headquartered in that state. Although it is always problematic for one state to balance its own interests fairly against those of another state, the circumstances of this case leave little doubt, if any, that Texas has a materially greater interest than Florida in deciding whether the noncompetition agreement in this case should be enforced.

3

Having concluded that Texas law would control the issue of enforceability of the noncompetition agreement in this case but for the parties' choice of Florida law, and that Texas' interest in deciding this issue in this case is materially greater than Florida's, we must finally determine under section 187(2)(b) of the Restatement whether application of Florida law to decide this issue would be contrary to fundamental policy of Texas. The Restatement offers little guidance in making this determination. Comment g states only that a "fundamental" policy is a "substantial" one, and that "[t]he forum will apply its own legal principles in determining whether a given policy is a fundamental one within the meaning of the present rule...."

Comment g to section 187 does suggest that application of the law of another state is not contrary to the fundamental policy of the forum merely because it leads to a different result than would obtain under the forum's law. We agree that the result in one case cannot determine whether the issue is a matter of fundamental state policy for purposes of resolving a conflict of laws. Moreover, the fact that the law of another state is materially different from the law of this state does not itself establish that application of the other state's law would offend the fundamental policy of Texas. In analyzing whether fundamental policy is offended under section 187(2)(b), the focus is on whether the law in question is a part of state policy so fundamental that the courts of the state will refuse to enforce an agreement contrary to that law, despite the parties' original intentions, and even though the agreement would be enforceable in another state connected with the transaction.

Neither the Restatement nor the cases which have followed section 187 have undertaken a general definition of "fundamental policy", and we need not make the attempt in this case; for whatever its parameters, enforcement of noncompetition agreements falls well within them. This Court has held that "[a]n agreement not to compete is in restraint of trade and will not be enforced unless it is reasonable." Frankiewicz v. National Comp. Assoc., 633 S.W.2d 505, 507 (Tex.1982). Moreover, that policy is fundamental in that it ensures a uniform rule for enforcement of noncompetition agreements in this state. See Restatement § 187 comment g (1971) ("a fundamental policy may be embodied in a statute which makes one or more kinds of contracts illegal or which is designed to protect a person against the oppressive use of superior bargaining power"). Absent such a policy, agreements involving residents of other states would be controlled by the law and policy of those states. An employee of one out-of-state employer might take a competing job and escape enforcement of a covenant not to compete because of the law of another state, while a neighbor suffered enforcement of an identical covenant because of the law of a third state. The resulting disruption of orderly employer-employee relations, as well as competition in the marketplace, would be unacceptable. Employers would be encouraged to attempt to invoke the most favorable state law available to govern their relationship with their employees in Texas or other states.

These same considerations and others have led virtually every court that has addressed the question of whether enforcement of noncompetition agreements is a matter of fundamental or important state policy to answer affirmatively. Not many of these courts have considered the matter specifically in the context of section 187 of the Restatement, and yet, rather remarkably, many have nevertheless expressed similar conclusions.

We likewise conclude that the law governing enforcement of noncompetition agreements is fundamental policy in Texas, and that to apply the law of another state to determine the enforceability of such an agreement in the circumstances of a case like this would be contrary to that policy. We therefore hold that the enforceability of the agreement in this case must be judged by Texas law, not Florida law.

III

We now consider whether the noncompetition agreement between DeSantis and Wackenhut is enforceable under Texas law. [The court finds the agreement unenforceable because there is insufficient evidence that DeSantis was able to appropriate good will he had developed with customers while working for Wackenhut. Only one customer left Wackenhut for RDI and another was contemplating leaving. Moreover, there was evidence that these customers were dissatisfied with Wackenhut's services. Nor was there a showing that there is a need to protect confidential information relating to Wackenhut's business. DeSantis could have learned of Wackenhut's customers and their needs without working for Wackenhut and there is no showing that Wackenhut's pricing and bidding strategies are unique. DeSantis and RDI cannot recover on the injunction bond because the temporary restraining order and temporary injunction were never dissolved. There was no evidence to support the claim of malicious prosecution.]

NOTES

1. Would a Florida Court have agreed "that Texas has a materially greater interest than Florida in deciding whether the noncompetition agreement in this case should be enforced"? If not, what planning and litigation strategy does this suggest for an employer like Wackenhut?

2. Restatement (Second) Conflict of Laws § 187, comment g: "To be 'fundamental' within the meaning of the present rule, a policy need not be as strong as would be required to justify the forum in refusing to entertain suit upon a foreign cause of action under the rule of § 90 [Action Contrary to Public Policy]."

3. After the decision in the principal case, Texas law firms had difficulty writing "opinion letters" passing on the validity of interstate and international transactions involving Texas parties. An Ad Hoc Committee on Choice of Law of the Business Law Section of the State Bar of Texas drafted legislation, which provided that in a commercial transaction having "an aggregate value of at least $1,000,000 . . . if the parties . . . agree in writing that the law of a particular jurisdiction governs an issue relating to the transaction, including the validity or enforceability of an agreement relating to the transaction or a provision of the agreement, and the transaction bears a reasonable relation to that jurisdiction, the law, other than conflict of laws rules, of that jurisdiction governs the issue regardless of whether the application of that law is contrary to a fundamental or public policy of this state or of any other jurisdiction." The draft was enacted as Texas Business & Commerce Code § 35.51. If you were a member of the legislature, would you have voted for this bill?

2. RESOLVING POLICY CLASHES

Lilienthal v. Kaufman
Supreme Court of Oregon, 1964.
239 Or. 1, 395 P.2d 543.

■ DENECKE, JUSTICE. This is an action to collect two promissory notes. The defense is that the defendant maker has previously been declared a spendthrift by an Oregon court and placed under a guardianship and that the guardian has declared the obligations void. The plaintiff's counter is that the notes were executed and delivered in California, that the law of California does not recognize the disability of a spendthrift, and that the Oregon court is bound to apply the law of the place of the making of the contract. The trial court rejected plaintiff's argument and held for the defendant.

This same defendant spendthrift was the prevailing party in our recent decision in Olshen v. Kaufman, 235 Or. 423, 385 P.2d 161 (1963). In that case the spendthrift and the plaintiff, an Oregon resident, had gone into a joint venture to purchase binoculars for resale. For this purpose plaintiff had advanced moneys to the spendthrift. The spendthrift had repaid plaintiff by his personal check for the amount advanced and for plaintiff's share of the profits of such venture. The check had not been paid because the spendthrift had had insufficient funds in his account. The action was for the unpaid balance of the check.

The evidence in that case showed that the plaintiff had been unaware that Kaufman was under a spendthrift guardianship. The guardian testified that he knew Kaufman was engaging in some business and had bank accounts and that he had admonished him to cease these practices; but he could not control the spendthrift.

The statute applicable in that case and in this one is ORS 126.335:

"After the appointment of a guardian for the spendthrift, all contracts, except for necessaries, and all gifts, sales and transfers of real or personal estate made by such spendthrift thereafter and before the termination of the guardianship are voidable." (Repealed 1961, ch. 344, § 109, now ORS 126.280).

We held in that case that the voiding of the contract by the guardian precluded recovery by the plaintiff and that the spendthrift and the guardian were not estopped to deny the validity of plaintiff's claim. Plaintiff does not seek to overturn the principle of that decision but contends it has no application because the law of California governs, and under California law the plaintiff's claim is valid.

The facts here are identical to those in Olshen v. Kaufman, supra, except for the California locale for portions of the transaction. The notes were for the repayment of advances to finance another joint venture to sell binoculars. The plaintiff was unaware that defendant had been declared a spendthrift and placed under guardianship. The guardian, upon demand for payment by the plaintiff, declared the notes void. The issue is solely one involving the principles of conflict of laws.

. . .

Plaintiff contends that the substantive issue of whether or not an obligation is valid and binding is governed by the law of the place of making, California. This court has repeatedly stated that the law of the place of contract "must govern as to the validity, interpretation, and construction of the contract." . . .

This principle, that *lex loci contractus* must govern, however, has been under heavy attack for years. . . .

There is no need to decide that our previous statements that the law of the place of contract governs were in error. Our purpose is to state that this portion of our decision is not founded upon that principle because of our doubt that it is correct if the *only* connection of the state whose law would govern is that it was the place of making.

In this case California had more connection with the transaction than being merely the place where the contract was executed. The defendant went to San Francisco to ask the plaintiff, a California resident, for money for the defendant's venture. The money was loaned to defendant in San Francisco, and by the terms of the note, it was to be repaid to plaintiff in San Francisco.

On these facts, apart from *lex loci contractus,* other accepted principles of conflict of laws lead to the conclusion that the law of California should be applied. Sterrett v. Stoddard Lumber Co., 150 Or. 491, 504, 46 P.2d 1023 (1935), rests, at least in part, on the proposition that the validity of a note is determined by the law of the place of payment. . . .

There is another conflict principle calling for the application of California law. Stumberg terms it the application of the law which upholds the contract. Stumberg, supra, at 237. Ehrenzweig calls it the "Rule of Validation." Ehrenzweig, Conflict of Laws, 353 (1962)....

Thus far all signs have pointed to applying the law of California and holding the contract enforceable. There is, however, an obstacle to cross before this end can be logically reached. In Olshen v. Kaufman, supra, we decided that the law of Oregon, at least as applied to persons domiciled in Oregon contracting in Oregon for performance in Oregon, is that spendthrifts' contracts are voidable. Are the choice-of-law principles of conflict of laws so superior that they overcome this principle of Oregon law?

To answer this question we must determine, upon some basis, whether the interests of Oregon are so basic and important that we should not apply California law despite its several intimate connections with the transaction. The traditional method used by this court and most others is framed in the terminology of "public policy." The court decides whether or not the public policy of the forum is so strong that the law of the forum must prevail although another jurisdiction, with different laws, has more and closer contacts with the transaction. Included in "public policy" we must consider the economic and social interests of Oregon. When these factors are included in a consideration of whether the law of the forum should be applied this traditional approach is very similar to that advocated by many legal scholars. This latter theory is "that choice-of-law rules should rationally advance the policies or interests of the several states (or of the nations in the world community)." Hill, Governmental Interest and the Conflict of Laws—A Reply to Professor Currie, 27 Chi.L.Rev. 463, 474 (1960); Currie, Selected Essays on the Conflict of Laws, 64–72 (1963), reprint from 58 Col.L.Rev. 964 (1958)....

Some of the interests of Oregon in this litigation are set forth in Olshen v. Kaufman, supra. The spendthrift's family which is to be protected by the establishment of the guardianship is presumably an Oregon family. The public authority which may be charged with the expense of supporting the spendthrift or his family, if he is permitted to go unrestrained upon his wasteful way, will probably be an Oregon public authority. These, obviously, are interests of some substance.

Oregon has other interests and policies regarding this matter which were not necessary to discuss in Olshen. As previously stated, Oregon, as well as all other states, has a strong policy favoring the validity and enforceability of contracts. This policy applies whether the contract is made and to be performed in Oregon or elsewhere.

The defendant's conduct,—borrowing money with the belief that the repayment of such loan could be avoided—is a species of fraud. Oregon and all other states have a strong policy of protecting innocent persons from fraud....

It is in Oregon's commercial interest to encourage citizens of other states to conduct business with Oregonians. If Oregonians acquire a reputation for not honoring their agreements, commercial intercourse with Oregonians will be discouraged. If there are Oregon laws, somewhat unique to Oregon, which permit an Oregonian to escape his otherwise binding obligations, persons may well avoid commercial dealings with Oregonians.

The substance of these commercial considerations, however, is deflated by the recollection that the Oregon Legislature has determined, despite the weight of these considerations, that a spendthrift's contracts are voidable.

California's most direct interest in this transaction is having its citizen creditor paid.... California probably has another, although more intangible, interest involved. It is presumably to every state's benefit to have the reputation of being a jurisdiction in which contracts can be made and performance be promised with the certain knowledge that such contracts will be enforced. Both of these interests, particularly the former, are also of substance.

We have, then, two jurisdictions, each with several close connections with the transaction, and each with a substantial interest, which will be served or thwarted, depending upon which law is applied. The interests of neither jurisdiction are clearly more important than those of the other. We are of the opinion that in such a case the public policy of Oregon should prevail and the law of Oregon should be applied; we should apply that choice-of-law rule which will "advance the policies or interests of" Oregon. Hill, supra, 27 Chi.L.Rev. at 474.

Courts are instruments of state policy. The Oregon Legislature has adopted a policy to avoid possible hardship to an Oregon family of a spendthrift and to avoid possible expenditure of Oregon public funds which might occur if the spendthrift is required to pay his obligations. In litigation Oregon courts are the appropriate instrument to enforce this policy. The mechanical application of choice-of-law rules would be the only apparent reason for an Oregon court advancing the interests of California over the equally valid interests of Oregon. The present principles of conflict of laws are not favorable to such mechanical application.

We hold that the spendthrift law of Oregon is applicable and the plaintiff cannot recover.

Judgment affirmed.

■ O'CONNELL, JUSTICE (specially concurring)....

In the Olshen case we had to choose between two competing policies; on one hand the policy of protecting the interest of persons dealing with spendthrifts, which, broadly, may be described as the interest in the security of transactions, and on the other hand the policy of protecting the interests of the spendthrift, his family and the county. It was decided that the Oregon Legislature adopted the latter policy in preference to the former.

... To distinguish the Olshen case it would be necessary to assume that although the legislature intended to protect the interest of the spendthrift, his family and the county when local creditors were harmed, the same protection was not intended where the transaction adversely affected foreign creditors. I see no basis for making that assumption. There is no reason to believe that our legislature intended to protect California creditors to a greater extent than our own.

■ GOODWIN, JUSTICE (dissenting)....

In the case before us, I believe that the policy of both states, Oregon and California, in favor of enforcing contracts, has been lost sight of in favor of a questionable policy in Oregon which gives special privileges to the rare spendthrift for whom a guardian has been appointed.

The majority view in the case at bar strikes me as a step backward toward the balkanization of the law of contracts. Olshen v. Kaufman, 235 Or. 423, 385 P.2d 161 (1963), held that there was a policy in this state to help keep spendthrifts out of the almshouse. I can see nothing, however, in Oregon's policy toward spendthrifts that warrants its extension to permit the taking of captives from other states down the road to insolvency.

I would enforce the contract.

Casey v. Manson Construction And Engineering Co.
Supreme Court of Oregon, 1967.
247 Or. 274, 428 P.2d 898.

[Action by a wife to recover for the loss of consortium sustained as a result of an injury suffered by her husband in the State of Washington. The Caseys were domiciled in Oregon. Manson Construction was a Washington corporation which did business in Oregon. Plaintiff's husband, a business invitee, was injured by reason of a defective road while driving a tractor on Manson's property in Washington. Washington adhered to the common law rule which denied to a wife a right of action for the loss of her husband's consortium. Oregon conferred such a right by statute. The trial court found against the wife by application of Washington law.]

This court has heretofore been committed to the traditional choice-of-law rule that in tort cases the law of the place of wrong—*lex loci delicti*—governs: Nadeau v. Power Plant Engr. Co., 216 Or. 12, 20, 337 P.2d 313 (1959). In Lilienthal v. Kaufman, 239 Or. 1, 395 P.2d 543 (1964), however, we abandoned the mechanical application of the corresponding rule in contract cases—*lex loci contractus*....

Careful consideration of [the] decisions, as well as of the extensive writings on the subject, persuade us that we should adopt for tort actions the rule of "most significant relationship with the occurrence and with the parties" as set forth in the Tentative Draft of the Restatement.

... It cannot be said, ... that we are dealing here with an easy case. It differs in important particulars from any of those which we have examined in which the courts have refused to apply the law of the place of the wrong. There was nothing fortuitous here about the place of the accident; it could not have happened anywhere except on the negligently constructed and maintained road in the State of Washington.

As to the underlying policies involved and the interests of the respective states, it is to be presumed that the Oregon Legislature deemed it desirable that an anachronistic common law rule ... should be removed, and a wife accorded the same right as a husband to recover for a similar injury, though not to the same extent, because, with regard to the service element of consortium, in order to prevent a double recovery, the husband's recovery would be taken into account in measuring the wife's damages.... Since it must be presumed that if the wife is entitled to recover for loss of consortium the husband is also entitled to recover for his personal injury, this state's chief concern is that a wife's loss of her husband's society and affection should not go uncompensated.

Washington's policy is in one aspect rather negative than affirmative. Her highest court announced more than 13 years ago that no such action could be maintained unless the legislature provided for it and the legislature has not done so. Washington, of course, has no concern with whether an Oregon wife recovers for loss of consortium in an Oregon court, but Washington has a legitimate concern in whether she recovers against Washington residents when the wrong giving rise to the action occurs in Washington in circumstances such as those we deal with here. Washington has a legitimate concern with whether her residents engaged in a construction job there—in this case a job related to the public interest—should be disappointed in their reasonable expectation that the extent of their liability for negligent conduct in Washington be governed by the law of that state, regardless of the domicile of an injured plaintiff. It bears repetition that this case is to be distinguished from those in which the place of injury is a mere happenstance.

. . .

While consideration should be given, we assume, to the interest of Oregon arising from the fact that the effects of the injury are experienced by the plaintiff in this state, we, nevertheless, have a case in which both conduct and injury occurred in Washington when the plaintiff's husband was a business invitee of the defendants on land in their possession and control.

We conclude that Washington has the most significant relationship with the occurrence and with the parties and that Washington's law should govern the issue presented by the demurrer to the complaint....

The judgment is affirmed.

■ HOLMAN, JUSTICE (concurring).

After consideration of all the circumstances and the situation as a whole, it seems more logical to apply the law of the State of Washington. If it were otherwise, Washington citizens carrying on activities in Washington would have to lift their financial protection to an unaccustomed level and one which would be dependent upon the locality from which the injured party might come. Theoretically, citizens of Washington could be subjected to 49 different levels of responsibility for acts done within their state of residence, and this seems to me highly undesirable. It seems more reasonable that under the present circumstances "... By entering the state or nation, the visitor has exposed himself to the risks of the territory and should not expect to subject persons living there to a financial hazard that their law had not created."

At this time I am doubtful that I desire to be finally wedded to the methods of the second restatement as set forth in the majority opinion.

■ GOODWIN, J., concurs in this opinion.

NOTE

Are the Lilienthal and Casey decisions consistent? Is there more justice in subjecting the California lender in the former case to Oregon's unusual spendthrift trust law than in subjecting the Washington engineering firm to the increasingly common rule that negligent injury of a husband produces actionable injury to the wife deprived of his consortium? Was it a violation of due process for the court in Lilienthal to apply the Oregon spendthrift law?

BERNHARD V. HARRAH'S CLUB

Supreme Court of California, 1976.
16 Cal.3d 313, 128 Cal.Rptr. 215, 546 P.2d 719, cert. denied 429 U.S. 859, 97 S.Ct. 159, 50 L.Ed.2d 136.

[Action against defendant Harrah's Club, a Nevada corporation, to recover for personal injuries suffered in California. The plaintiff alleged that defendant owned and operated gambling and drinking establishments in Nevada and solicited business for such establishments in California "knowing and expecting that many California residents would use the public highways in going to and from defendant's ... establishments." In response to defendant's advertisements, two Californians patronized one of defendant's clubs in Nevada where they were served numerous alcoholic beverages "progressively reaching a point of obvious intoxication rendering them incapable of safely driving a car." After they had entered California on their way home, the car, while being driven by one of these Californians in an intoxicated state, collided head-on with a motorcycle operated by plaintiff Bernhard, also a California domiciliary, who suffered severe injuries. Defendant demurred to the complaint on the ground that Nevada law gave no right to recover against a tavern keeper for injuries caused by the selling of alcoholic beverages to an intoxicated person and that Nevada law governed since defendant's alleged tort had been committed in Nevada. The trial court sustained the demurrer and plaintiff appealed.]

■ SULLIVAN, JUSTICE:

We face a problem in the choice of law governing a tort action. As we have made clear on other occasions, we no longer adhere to the rule that the law of the place of the wrong is applicable in a California forum regardless of the issues before the court.... Rather we have adopted in its place a rule requiring an analysis of the respective interests of the states involved—the objective of which is "to determine the law that most appropriately applies to the issue involved." . . .

We observe at the start that the laws of the two states—California and Nevada—applicable to the issue involved are not identical. California imposes liability on tavern keepers in this state for conduct such as here alleged. In Vesely v. Sager, . . . 5 Cal.3d 153, 166, 95 Cal.Rptr. 623, 486 P.2d 151 (1971), this court [held that such liability should be imposed since not to do so would be] patently unsound and totally inconsistent with the principles of proximate cause established in other areas of negligence law. [Also] the Legislature has expressed its intention in this area with the adoption of Business and Professions Code § 25602 [making it a misdemeanor to sell to an obviously intoxicated person], a statute to which this presumption [of negligence, Evidence Code § 669] applies. . . . Nevada on the other hand refuses to impose such liability. In Hamm v. Carson City Nuggett, Inc., 85 Nev. 99, 450 P.2d 358, 359 (1969), the court held it would create neither common law liability nor liability based on the criminal statute banning sale of alcoholic beverages to a person who is drunk, because "if civil liability is to be imposed, it should be accomplished by legislative act after appropriate surveys, hearings, and investigations to ascertain the need for it and the expected consequences to follow. . . ."

Although California and Nevada, the two "involved states" . . . have different laws governing the issue presented in the case at bench, we encounter a problem in selecting the applicable rule of law only if *both* states have an interest in having their respective laws applied. . . .

Defendant contends that Nevada has a definite interest in having its rule of decision applied in this case in order to protect its resident tavern keepers like defendant from being subjected to a civil liability which Nevada has not imposed either by legislative enactment or decisional law. . . .

Plaintiff on the other hand points out that California also has an interest in applying its own rule of decision to the case at bench. California imposes on tavern keepers civil liability to third parties injured by persons to whom the tavern keeper has sold alcoholic beverages when they are obviously intoxicated "for the purpose of protecting members of the general public from injuries to person and damage to property resulting from the excessive use of intoxicating liquor." (Vesely v. Sager, supra, 5 Cal.3d 153, 165, 95 Cal.Rptr. 623, 486 P.2d 151 (1971).) California, it is urged, has a special interest in affording this protection to all California residents injured in California.

Thus, since the case at bench involves a California resident (plaintiff) injured in this state by intoxicated drivers and a Nevada resident tavern keeper (defendant) which served alcoholic beverages to them in Nevada, it is clear that each state has an interest in the application of its respective law of liability and nonliability. It goes without saying that these interests conflict. Therefore, unlike Reich v. Purcell, supra, 67 Cal.2d 551, 63 Cal.Rptr. 31, 432 P.2d 727 (1967), and Hurtado v. Superior Court, supra, 11 Cal.3d 574, 114 Cal.Rptr. 106, 522 P.2d 666 (1974), where we were faced with "false conflicts," in the instant case for the first time since applying a governmental interest analysis as a choice of law doctrine in *Reich*, we are confronted with a "true" conflicts case. We must therefore determine the appropriate rule of decision in a controversy where each of the states involved has a legitimate but conflicting interest in applying its own law in respect to the civil liability of tavern keepers.

The search for the proper resolution of a true conflicts case, while proceeding within orthodox parameters of governmental interest analysis, has generated much scholarly examination and discussion. The father of the governmental interest approach, Professor Brainerd Currie, originally took the position that in a true conflicts situation the law of the forum should always be applied. (Currie, Selected Essays on Conflicts of Laws p. 184 (1963).) However, upon further reflection, Currie suggested that when under the governmental interest approach a preliminary analysis reveals an apparent conflict of interest upon the forum's assertion of its own rule of decision, the forum should reexamine its policy to determine if a more restrained interpretation of it is more appropriate.... This process of reexamination ... can be approached under principles of "comparative impairment." (Baxter, Choice of Law and the Federal System, supra, 16 Stan.L.Rev. 1–22; Horowitz, The Law of Choice of Law in California—A Restatement, supra, 21 U.C.L.A. L.Rev. 719, 748–758.)

... [T]he "comparative impairment" approach to the resolution of such conflict seeks to determine which state's interest would be more impaired if its policy were subordinated to the policy of the other state. This analysis proceeds on the principle that true conflicts should be resolved by applying the law of the state whose interest would be the more impaired if its law were not applied. Exponents of this process of analysis emphasize that it is very different from a weighing process. The court does not "'weigh' the conflicting governmental interests in the sense of determining which conflicting law manifested the 'better' or the 'worthier' social policy on the specific issue...."

Mindful of the above principles governing our choice of law, we proceed to reexamine the California policy underlying the imposition of civil liability upon tavern keepers. At its broadest limits this policy would afford protection to all persons injured in California by intoxicated persons who have been sold or furnished alcoholic beverages while intoxicated regardless of where such beverages were sold or furnished. Such a broad policy would naturally embrace situations where the intoxicated actor had been provided with liquor by out-of-state tavern keepers. Although the State of Nevada does not impose such *civil* liability on its tavern keepers, nevertheless they are subject to *criminal* penalties under a statute making it unlawful to sell or give intoxicating liquor to any person who is drunk or known to be an habitual drunkard. (See Nev.Rev.Stats. 202.100; see Hamm v. Carson City Nuggett, Inc., supra, 85 Nev. 99, 450 P.2d 358 (1969).)

We need not, and accordingly do not here determine the outer limits to which California's policy should be extended, for it appears clear to us that it must encompass defendant, who as alleged in the complaint, "advertis[es] for and otherwise solicit[s] in California the business of California residents at defendant Harrah's Club Nevada drinking and gambling establishments, knowing and expecting said California residents, in response to said advertising and solicitation, to use the public highways of the State of California in going and coming from defendant Harrah's Club Nevada drinking and gambling establishments." Defendant by the course of its chosen commercial practice has put itself at the heart of California's regulatory interest, namely to prevent tavern keepers from selling alcoholic beverages to obviously intoxicated persons who are likely to act in California in the intoxicated state. It seems clear that California cannot reasonably effectuate its policy if it does not extend its regulation to include out-of-state tavern keepers such as defendant who regularly and purposely sell intoxicating beverages to California residents in places and under conditions in which it is reasonably certain these residents will return to California and act therein while still in an intoxicated state. California's interest would be very significantly impaired if its policy were not applied to defendant.

Since the act of selling alcoholic beverages to obviously intoxicated persons is already proscribed in Nevada, the application of California's rule of civil liability would not impose an entirely new duty requiring the ability to distinguish between California residents and other patrons. Rather the imposition of such liability involves an increased economic exposure, which, at least for businesses which actively solicit extensive California patronage, is a foreseeable and coverable business expense. Moreover, Nevada's interest in protecting its tavern keepers from civil liability of a boundless and unrestricted nature will not be significantly impaired when as in the instant case liability is imposed only on those tavern keepers who actively solicit California business.

... [W]e conclude that California has an important and abiding interest in applying its rule of decision to the case at bench, that the policy of this state would be more significantly impaired if such rule were not applied and that the trial court erred in not applying California law.

Defendant argues, however, that even if California law is applied, the demurrer was nonetheless properly sustained because the tavern keeper's duty stated in Vesely v. Sager, supra, 5 Cal.3d 153, 95 Cal.Rptr. 623, 486 P.2d 151 (1971), is based on Business and Professions Code section 25602, which is a criminal statute and thus without extraterritorial effect....

However, our decision in *Vesely* was much broader than defendant would have it.

... [O]ur opinion in *Vesely* struck down the old common law rule of nonliability constructed on the basis that the consumption, not the sale, of alcoholic beverages was the proximate cause of the injuries inflicted by the intoxicated person. Although we chose to impose liability on the *Vesely* defendant on the basis of his violating the applicable statute, the clear import of our decision was that there was no bar to civil liability under modern negligence law....

The judgment is reversed and the cause is remanded to the trial court with directions to overrule the demurrer and to allow defendant a reasonable time within which to answer.

NOTES

1. Was the court right to conclude that Nevada's policies were not impaired substantially by the imposition of civil liability on Harrah's Club? "If Nevada protects its taverns from liability to its own residents, it has an even greater interest in preventing their liability to out-of-state residents." Note, Conflict of Laws, 65 Calif.L.Rev. 290, 296 (1977). In a thoughtful article focusing on the principal case Professor Kanowitz criticized the comparative-impairment method for imprecision, manipulability and a tendency toward interest counting. Kanowitz, Comparative Impairment and Better Law: Grand Illusions in the Conflict of Laws, 30 Hastings L.J. 255, 293 (1979).

An Ontario husband and wife sued, respectively, for personal injury and consortium damages when he hurt his arm in a meat grinder while at work. Under the Ontario Workmen's Compensation Act the only benefits allowed were those provided in the Act; under the law of California, which was the forum and place of manufacture of the meat grinder, a common law recovery could be had. Held: Although California had some interest in deterring manufacture of defective machines, its interests would be less impaired than Ontario's if the plaintiffs failed to recover. Paulo v. Bepex Corp., 792 F.2d 894 (9th Cir.1986).

2. In 1978 the California legislature amended Cal.Bus.&Prof.Code § 25602 (West Cum.Supp.1979) to absolve bartenders and hosts at private parties from civil liability for acts of drunken patrons or guests. It remains a misdemeanor to serve a person who is obviously intoxicated. The statute overruled by name the *Vesely* and *Bernhard* decisions.

3. Cable v. Sahara Tahoe Corp., 93 Cal.App. 384, 155 Cal.Rptr. 770 (1979). The issue was the same as in the Bernhard case and so too were the facts, except that the plaintiff, who was assumed to be domiciled in California, had been employed by the defendant bar in Nevada and had been injured while driving from her place of employment to a destination in Nevada. Following the accident the plaintiff returned to California and, by reason of her injuries, has become and presumably will remain a public charge. Held for the defendant. Nevada's interests would be more impaired by application of California law than would California's interests be impaired by the application of the law of Nevada. "The state with the 'predominant' interest in controlling conduct normally is the state in which such conduct occurs and is most likely to cause injury." The policy that was given effect in the Bernhard case is applicable only to injuries that occur in California. Also, by statute enacted after the occurrence of the accident in question, California has repudiated the rule that a bartender is liable for injuries caused by intoxicated patrons. "Though an existing cause of action would not be nullified by the [statute], it is obvious that the impairment of such a repudiated policy [by application of Nevada law] has a minimal effect upon California's governmental interest."

4. For a decision using modern interest analysis on facts paralleling Schmidt v. Driscoll Hotel, Inc., p. 506, supra, see Rong Yao Zhou v. Jennifer Mall Rest., 534 A.2d 1268 (D.C.App.1987).

OFFSHORE RENTAL CO. v. CONTINENTAL OIL CO., 22 Cal.3d 157, 148 Cal.Rptr. 867, 583 P.2d 721 (1978). The case involved a suit by a California corporation to recover for the loss of services of a "key" employee who, it was alleged, had been negligently injured by the defendant in Louisiana. Recovery could be had under California law, but not under the law of Louisiana. Applying what it said to be its "comparative impairment" approach, the Supreme Court of California held that Louisiana law was applicable and affirmed a judgment for the defendant. The court said in part:

In sum, the comparative impairment approach to the resolution of true conflicts attempts to determine the relative commitment of the respective states to the laws involved. The approach incorporates several factors for consideration: the history and current status of the states' laws; the function and purpose of those laws.

Applying the comparative impairment analysis to the present case, we first probe the history and current status of the laws before us. The majority of common law states that have considered the matter do not sanction actions for harm to business employees, recognizing that even if injury to the master-servant relationship were at one time the basis for an action at common law, the radical change in the nature of that relationship since medieval times nullifies any right by a modern corporate employer to recover for negligent injury to his employees.... Louisiana law accords with the common law's consistent refusal generally to recognize a cause of action based on negligent, as opposed to intentional, conduct which interferes with the performance of a contract between third parties or renders its performance more expensive or burdensome....

... We therefore conclude that the trial judge in the present case correctly applied Louisiana, rather than California, law, since California's interest in the application of its unusual and outmoded statute is comparatively less strong than Louisiana's corollary interest ... in its "prevalent and progressive" law.

An examination of the function and purpose of the respective laws before us provides additional support for our limitation of the reach of California law in the present case. The accident in question occurred within Louisiana's borders; although the law of the place of the wrong is not necessarily the applicable law for all tort actions ... the situs of the injury remains a relevant consideration. At the heart of Louisiana's denial of liability lies the vital interest in promoting freedom of investment and enterprise *within Louisiana's borders*, among investors incorporated both in Louisiana and elsewhere. The imposition of liability on defendant, therefore, would strike at the essence of a compelling Louisiana law.

Furthermore, in connection with our search for the proper law to apply based on the "maximum attainment of underlying purpose by all governmental entities," we note the realistic fact that insurance is available to guard against the exigencies of the present case. As one commentator has remarked, "[T]he fact that the potential [tort] victim does not usually calculate his risk and plan his insurance program accordingly, hardly detracts from the consideration that he can fairly be made to bear the consequences of not doing so." (Ehrenzweig, A Treatise on the Conflict of Laws (1962) pp. 575–576.) The present plaintiff, a business corporation, is a potential "victim" peculiarly able to calculate such risks and to plan accordingly. Plaintiff could have obtained protection against the occurrence of injury to its corporate vice-president by purchasing key employee insurance, certainly a reasonable and foreseeable business expense. By entering Louisiana, plaintiff "exposed [it]self to the risks of the territory," and should not expect to subject defendant to a financial hazard that Louisiana law had not created. (Cavers, The Choice-of-Law Process (1965) p. 147.)

Although it is equally true that defendant is a business corporation able to calculate the risks of potential tort liability and to plan accordingly, because defendant's operations in Louisiana presumably involved dealing with key employees of companies incorporated in diverse states defendant would most reasonably have anticipated a need for the protection of premises' liability insurance based on Louisiana law. Accordingly, under these circumstances, we conclude that the burden of obtaining insurance for the loss at issue here is most properly borne by the plaintiff corporation....

The judgment is affirmed.

NOTE

The principal case is criticized for relying on a "better law" analysis despite the court's insistence that it was following the comparative-impairment approach in Kanowitz, Comparative Impairment and Better Law: Grand Illusions in the Conflict of Laws, 30 Hastings L.J. 255 (1979).

3. CHANGES IN CIRCUMSTANCES

Reich v. Purcell
Supreme Court of California, 1967.
67 Cal.2d 551, 63 Cal.Rptr. 31, 432 P.2d 727.*

■ TRAYNOR, CHIEF JUSTICE. This wrongful death action arose out of a head-on collision of two automobiles in Missouri. One of the automobiles was owned and operated by defendant Joseph Purcell, a resident and domiciliary of California who was on his way to a vacation in Illinois. The other automobile was owned and operated by Mrs. Reich, the wife of plaintiff Lee Reich. The Reichs then resided in Ohio and Mrs. Reich and the Reichs' two children, Jay and Jeffry, were on their way to California, where the Reichs were contemplating settling. Mrs. Reich and Jay were killed in the collision, and Jeffry was injured.

* A symposium devoted to this case appears in Comments on Reich v. Purcell, 15 U.C.L.A.L.Rev. 551 (1968).

Plaintiffs, Lee Reich and Jeffry Reich, are the heirs of Mrs. Reich and Lee Reich is the heir of Jay Reich. Plaintiffs moved to California and became permanent residents here after the accident. The estates of Mrs. Reich and Jay Reich are being administered in Ohio.

The parties stipulated that judgment be entered in specified amounts for the wrongful death of Jay, for the personal injuries suffered by Jeffry, and for the damages to Mrs. Reich's automobile. For the death of Mrs. Reich they stipulated that judgment be entered for $55,000 or $25,000 depending on the court's ruling on the applicability of the Missouri limitation of damages to a maximum of $25,000. (Vernon's Ann.Mo.Stats. § 537.090.) Neither Ohio nor California limit recovery in wrongful death actions. The trial court held that the Missouri limitation applied because the accident occurred there and entered judgment accordingly. Plaintiffs appeal.

For many years courts applied the law of the place of the wrong in tort actions regardless of the issues before the court, e.g., whether they involved conduct, survival of actions, applicability of a wrongful death statute, immunity from liability, or other rules determining whether a legal injury has been sustained.... It was assumed that the law of the place of the wrong created the cause of action and necessarily determined the extent of the liability. (Slater v. Mexican National R.R. Co., 194 U.S. 120, 126, 24 S.Ct. 581, 48 L.Ed. 900.) Aside from procedural difficulties (see Currie, Selected Essays on Conflict of Laws (1963) pp. 10–18), this theory worked well enough when all the relevant events took place in one jurisdiction, but the action was brought in another. In a complex situation involving multistate contacts, however, no single state alone can be deemed to create exclusively governing rights.... The forum must search to find the proper law to apply based upon the interests of the litigants and the involved states. Such complex cases elucidate what the simpler cases obscured, namely, that the forum can only apply its own law.... When it purports to do otherwise, it is not enforcing foreign rights but choosing a foreign rule of decision as the appropriate one to apply to the case before it. Moreover, it has now been demonstrated that a choice of law resulting from a hopeless search for a governing foreign law to create a foreign vested right may defeat the legitimate interests of the litigants and the states involved. (See generally, Cavers, The Choice of Law Process (1965); Currie, Selected Essays on Conflict of Laws, supra; Ehrenzweig, Conflict of Laws (1962).)

Accordingly, when application of the law of the place of the wrong would defeat the interests of the litigant and of the states concerned, we have not applied that law. (Grant v. McAuliffe [p. 493, supra] ...; Emery v. Emery, 45 Cal.2d 421, 428, 289 P.2d 218.) *Grant* was an action for personal injuries arising out of an automobile accident in Arizona between California residents. The driver whose negligence caused the accident died, and the court had to choose between the California rule that allowed an action against the personal representative and the Arizona rule that did not. We held that since "all of the parties were residents of this state, and the estate of the deceased tortfeasor is being administered in this state, plaintiffs' right to prosecute their causes of action is governed by the laws of this state relating to administration of estates." Under these circumstances application of the law of the place of the wrong would not only have defeated California's interest and that of its residents but would have advanced no interest of Arizona or its residents. (Grant v. McAuliffe, supra . . .). In *Emery* members of a California family were injured in Idaho when another member of the family who was driving lost control of the car and it went off the road. The question was whether Idaho or California law determined when one member of a family was immune from tort liability to another. We applied the law of the family domicile rather than the law of the place of the wrong. "That state has the primary responsibility for establishing and regulating the incidents of the family relationship and it is the only state in which the parties can, by participation in the legislative processes, effect a change in those incidents. Moreover, it is undesirable that the rights, duties, disabilities, and immunities conferred or imposed by the family relationship should constantly change as members of the family cross state boundaries during temporary absences from their home." (45 Cal.2d at p. 428, 289 P.2d at p. 223.)

Defendant contends, however, that there were compelling reasons in the *Grant* and *Emery* cases for departing from the law of the place of the wrong and that such reasons are not present in this case. He urges that application of that law promotes uniformity of decisions, prevents forum shopping, and avoids the uncertainties that may result from ad hoc searches for a more appropriate law in this and similar cases.

Ease of determining applicable law and uniformity of rules of decision, however, must be subordinated to the objective of proper choice of law in conflict cases, i.e., to determine the law that most appropriately applies to the issue involved (see Leflar, Choice-Influencing Considerations In Conflicts Law (1966) 41 N.Y.U.L.Rev. 267, 279–282). Moreover, as jurisdiction after jurisdiction has departed from the law of the place of the wrong as the controlling law in tort cases, regardless of the issue involved . . ., that law no longer affords even a semblance of the general application that was once thought to be its great virtue. We conclude that the law of the place of the wrong is not necessarily the applicable law for all tort actions brought in the courts of this state . . . [and] cases to the contrary are overruled.

As the forum we must consider all of the foreign and domestic elements and interests involved in this case to determine the rule applicable. Three states are involved. Ohio is where plaintiffs and their decedents resided before the accident and where the decedents' estates are being administered. Missouri is the place of the wrong. California is the place where defendant resides and is the forum. Although plaintiffs now reside in California, their residence and domicile at the time of the accident are the relevant residence and domicile. At the time of the accident the plans to change the family domicile were not definite and fixed, and if the choice of law were made to turn on events happening after the accident, forum shopping would be encouraged. (See Cavers, op. cit., supra, p. 151, fn. 16.) Accordingly, plaintiffs' present domicile in California does not give this state any interest in applying its law, and since California has no limitation of damages, it also has no interest in applying its law on behalf of defendant. As a forum that is therefore disinterested in the only issue in dispute, we must decide whether to adopt the Ohio or the Missouri rule as the rule of decision for this case.

Missouri is concerned with conduct within her borders and as to such conduct she has the predominant interest of the states involved. Limitations of damages for wrongful death, however, have little or nothing to do with conduct. They are concerned not with how people should behave but with how survivors should be compensated. The state of the place of the wrong has little or no interest in such compensation when none of the parties reside there. Wrongful death statutes create causes of action in specified beneficiaries and distribute the proceeds to those beneficiaries. The proceeds in the hands of the beneficiaries are not distributed through the decedent's estate and, therefore, are not subject to the claims of the decedent's creditors and consequently do not provide a fund for local creditors. Accordingly, the interest of a state in a wrongful death action insofar as plaintiffs are concerned is in determining the distribution of proceeds to the beneficiaries and that interest extends only to local decedents and beneficiaries. (Currie, op. cit., supra, pp. 690, 702). Missouri's limitation on damages expresses an additional concern for defendants, however, in that it operates to avoid the imposition of excessive financial burdens on them. That concern is also primarily local and we fail to perceive any substantial interest Missouri might have in extending the benefits of its limitation of damages to travelers from states having no similar limitation. Defendant's liability should not be limited when no party to the action is from a state limiting liability and when defendant, therefore, would have secured insurance, if any, without any such limit in mind. A defendant cannot reasonably complain when compensatory damages are assessed in accordance with the law of his domicile and plaintiffs receive no more than they would have had they been injured at home. (See Cavers, op. cit., supra, pp. 153–157.) Under these circumstances giving effect to Ohio's interests in affording full recovery to injured parties does not conflict with any substantial interest of Missouri. (Cf. Bernkrant v. Fowler, 55 Cal.2d 588, 595, 12 Cal.Rptr. 266, 360 P.2d 906.) Accordingly, the Missouri limitation does not apply....

The part of the judgment appealed from is reversed with directions to the trial court to enter judgment for the plaintiffs in the amount of $55,000 in accordance with the stipulations of the parties.

NOTE

Is the court correct in stating that "if the choice of law were made to turn on events happening after the accident, forum shopping would be encouraged"? Is this likely on the facts of the principal case? If California law permitted greater recovery than the laws of either Ohio or Missouri, could the court have decided that

California law applied without confronting the question of the effect of changed residence? See pp. 621–624, infra.

Miller v. Miller
Court of Appeals of New York, 1968.
22 N.Y.2d 12, 290 N.Y.S.2d 734, 237 N.E.2d 877.

[Action to recover for a wrongful death resulting from an automobile accident in Maine which occurred in the course of what was intended to be a short business trip from one point in Maine to another. The defendant driver and the decedent were brothers. At the time of the accident the defendant resided in Maine while the decedent was a resident of New York. Shortly after the accident, however, the defendant moved to New York. The question presented on appeal was the applicability of a Maine statute which imposed a $20,000 limitation on recovery for wrongful death. The statute was repealed subsequent to the accident but it was assumed that the Maine courts would have continued to apply it to pre-enactment deaths.]

■ KEATING, JUDGE.

... Prior to the adoption of the [New York] Constitution of 1894, recoveries for wrongful death were limited to the sum of $5,000 (Code of Civ.Pro. [1894], § 1904). The Record of Debates of the Constitutional Convention of 1894 (Vol. 2, pp. 581–595, 651, 652, 947–962) indicates that the framers of the constitutional provision regarded the arbitrary limitation of $5,000 as absurd and unjust....

Our inquiry as to the choice of an appropriate law cannot, however, stop merely in defining a New York interest—albeit a substantial one—in the application of the particular law which is the object of the conflict. We must recognize that, in addition to the interest in affording the plaintiff full recovery, there may be other more general considerations which should concern "a justice-dispensing court in a modern American state". (Leflar, Choice-Influencing Considerations in Conflicts Law, 41 N.Y.U.L.Rev. 267, 295). Among other considerations are the "fairness" of applying our law where a nonresident or even a resident has patterned his conduct upon the law of the jurisdiction in which he was acting (Babcock v. Jackson, 12 N.Y.2d 473, 483, ...) as well as the possible interest of a sister State in providing the remedy for injuries sustained as a result of conduct undertaken within its borders....

As we view the facts in this case, however, we perceive no substantial countervailing considerations of the kind described above which would warrant the rejection of our own law in favor of that of Maine. The Maine statute with which we are concerned here, dealing as it does with the nature of the remedy for concededly tortious conduct, is obviously not the kind of statute which regulates conduct and, therefore, is not the kind of statute upon which a person would rely in governing his conduct. The only justifiable reliance which could be present here would involve the purchase of liability insurance in light of the remedies available to an injured person.

No such reliance is claimed here and, as a more careful examination of the problem reveals, this is not without good reason.

Under Maine law as it existed at the time of the accident, the defendants would have been fully liable for compensatory damages, had the decedent not been killed but merely injured and this no matter how serious his injuries. We have been advised by the Insurance Department of the State of Maine that, despite the limitation on recovery in wrongful death actions, the standard automobile liability policies issued in Maine drew no distinction between liability coverage for wrongful death and personal injuries. It would, therefore, appear that no proper claim that the defendants relied upon the limitation in purchasing insurance can be made here and, as we have noted, no such claim is made....

With respect to the liability insurer—the real party in interest—a somewhat different situation obtains. The insurer may have expected that Maine's limitation on death recoveries would apply to accidents in Maine. But here in determining whether any unfairness will result by virtue of the application of New York law, we may also consider the fact that the policy in question was not and could not have been limited to affording protection only to accidents occurring in the State of Maine (Maine Rev.Stat.Ann., tit. 29, § 781 et seq.) and that, therefore, the possibility of liability in excess of $20,000 was certainly not unexpected and was insured against. Moreover, an analysis of the actuarial process as well as an inquiry to the Insurance Commission of the State of Maine reveals that the presence of the limitations had no substantial effect on insurance premiums, and a refusal to apply Maine law here will have an infinitesimal effect, if that, on insurance rates in Maine (see Morris, Enterprise Liability and the Actuarial Process—The Insignificance of Foresight, 70 Yale L.J. 554, 560–581).

... [W]e turn next to the question of whether the application of New York law here will unduly interfere with a legitimate interest of a sister State in regulating the rights of its citizens, at least with regard to conduct within its borders. Here again we perceive no reason to deny application of our own law. To the extent that the Maine limitation evinced a desire to protect its residents in wrongful death actions, that purpose cannot be defeated here since no judgment in this action will be entered against a Maine resident. Maine would have no concern with the nature of the recovery awarded against defendants who are no longer residents of that State and who are, therefore, no longer proper objects of its legislative concern. It is true that, at the time of the accident, the defendants were residents of Maine but they would have no vested right to the application of the law of their former residence unless it could be demonstrated that they had governed their conduct in reliance upon it ... a reliance which is neither present nor claimed in the case at bar. Any claim that Maine has a paternalistic interest in protecting its residents against liability for acts committed while they were in Maine, should they move to another jurisdiction, is highly speculative and ignores the fact that for the very same acts committed today Maine would now impose the same liability as New York.

There may be times where policy considerations such as a desire to prevent forum shopping would require us to ignore changes in domicile after the accident (Gore v. Northeast Airlines, [373 F.2d 717 (2d Cir. 1967)]; Reich v. Purcell [p. 606, supra]). In the instant case, however, the change in domicile has nothing whatever to do with a desire to achieve a more favorable legal climate, and we see no reason to ignore the facts as they are presented at the time of the litigation....

■ BREITEL, JUDGE (dissenting).

. . .

Infusing the old territorial rules as well as the newer theories of grouping of contacts or interest analysis is a desire to satisfy the reasonable expectations of persons participating in transactions. This is perhaps the dominant motif in the adjudication of multistate transactions, and therefore generally leads to the "justice" of the determination (see Rheinstein, Book Review, 32 U.Chi.L.Rev. 369).

Justice favors the fulfillment of expectations for two reasons. First, parties may have acted in reliance upon their assumption that courts would apply a certain rule of decision, and application of a different rule to their detriment would then be unjust. Of course, this pragmatic significance of expectations varies with the type of legal rule involved. It is undoubtedly strongest in contract cases (see, e.g., Auten v. Auten, 308 N.Y. 155; Ehrenzweig, Conflict of Laws, §§ 175–184). But it exists even in tort cases....

Justified expectations are also relevant in a second, more intangible, way: it is jurisprudentially significant that parties' rights be determined by the law or system of rules which they most probably believed would control their relationship. In this respect, the application of the proper law of the tort exercises an influence in "promoting an unconscious acceptance of legality and legal order" (Kegel, [The Crisis of Conflict of Laws, 112 Recueil des Cours], pp. 91, 184). Thus, in guest-statute cases, courts have applied a rule of guest-host liability which, in effect, reflects the parties' unexpressed but undoubted assumption that a single system of rules will control guest-host liability no matter where the accident happens to take place. For this reason there is much to be said for applying the rule of the seat of the relationship, or, alternatively, that of the common domicile of guest and host....

NOTES

1. Was the Court right to give weight to post-accident events in deciding a question of choice of law? A negative answer was given by Chief Justice Traynor in Reich v. Purcell, p. 606, supra. On the other hand, see Note, Post Transaction or Occurrence Events in Conflict of Laws, 69 Colum.L.Rev. 843, 865 (1969), which concludes:

> The logic of interest analysis requires that governmental interests be weighed as they exist at the time of trial rather than at the time of the

transaction or occurrence in issue. At the same time, ... [c]onsiderations of fairness, predictability, and the existence of forum shopping should all be considered. Consequently, it is as wrong categorically to give effect to post occurrence events as it is categorically to deny their relevance.

2. In Huddy v. Freuhauf Corp., 953 F.2d 955 (5th Cir.1992), cert. denied, 113 S.Ct. 89 (1992), a Texas resident, driving a truck from Texas to Georgia, was injured in an accident in Georgia. He sued the truck manufacturer in Texas. Four years later, the driver moved to New Jersey. The manufacturer had its principal place of business in Michigan. Texas, but not Michigan, recognized the doctrine of strict liability for defective products. The district court applied Michigan law to this issue, but the Fifth Circuit reversed. "The fact that [the question of whether the move affects choice of law] arises at all is testimony to the slow pace of justice in today's courts.... To hold that Texas loses its interest in this case because [the driver] chose to move to another state during the litigation process would chain litigants to the state of residence at the time of the accident lest they lose the protection of its laws." Id. at 957.

3. *Conflict of laws in time.* What is the crucial time for ascertaining the content of a state's law? The time of the occurrence? The time of the trial? Some other time? In Berghammer v. Smith, 185 N.W.2d 226 (Iowa 1971), suit was brought by Minnesota plaintiffs against an Illinois defendant to recover for damages arising out of an Iowa accident. One question was whether the wife of the injured plaintiff could recover for loss of consortium. The Iowa court determined that Minnesota law governed this issue since "only Minnesota is concerned with the marital status of plaintiff and the interspousal rights and duties arising therefrom." At the time of the accident, Minnesota did not recognize a wife's cause of action for loss of consortium. By the time of the trial, however, the Minnesota courts had changed the rule to permit such an action, but had stated that the new rule should be given only a prospective application. Nevertheless, the Iowa court applied the new Minnesota rule retroactively and permitted recovery by the wife. The court justified its decision by stating that the policy which had led the Minnesota courts to make the new rule solely prospective would not be furthered by applying this limitation in the present case. The court said: "The prospective application was apparently to permit those relying on the old rule to protect themselves against enlarged liability by securing additional insurance coverage.... But that element is not present here. Defendant, a resident of Illinois, cannot claim either surprise or injustice about the application of a rule which his own state recognized.... Certainly, Minnesota's purpose was not to protect non-resident motorists who had not relied upon the old rule at the expense of its own citizens." The dissenting judge thought it wrong to apply the new Minnesota rule without at the same time adhering to its provisions as to prospectivity and retroactivity.

4. FAIRNESS

Rosenthal v. Warren

United States Circuit Court of Appeals, Second Circuit, 1973.
475 F.2d 438, cert. denied, 414 U.S. 856 (1973).

■ OAKES, CIRCUIT JUDGE: This appeal in a diversity case raises the question whether New York would apply a Massachusetts damage limitation to the death of a New York domiciliary occurring in Massachusetts. The appeal, taken before final judgment pursuant to 28 U.S.C. § 1292(b), is from an order of the district court granting partial summary judgment in favor of the plaintiff in an action for wrongful death. The partial summary judgment struck the affirmative defense based upon the Massachusetts wrongful death statute limiting recoverable damages to "... not less than Five Thousand Dollars nor more than Fifty Thousand Dollars, to be assessed with reference to the degree of [the tortfeasor's] culpability...."[1] The district court held that New York law was applicable. That law places no fixed value on wrongful death or limitation upon the damages in a wrongful death action. N.Y. Estates, Powers & Trust Law, § 5–4.3; N.Y.Const. art. 1, sec. 16. We affirm.

The relevant facts are simple, the legal issue difficult. The decedent, Dr. Martin C. Rosenthal, was a citizen of New York. Decedent and his wife, who as executrix is plaintiff here, went to Boston where he was examined and diagnosed by Dr. Warren, whom the plaintiff describes as a world-renowned physician and surgeon treating patients from all over the world. On March 27, 1969, eight days after an operation performed by Dr. Warren at the New England Baptist Hospital, decedent died in the hospital while under the care of the defendant Warren.

Suit, alleging malpractice and asking for $1,250,000 in damages, was brought in New York state court. Jurisdiction of Dr. Warren to the extent of his insurance coverage was obtained by attachment levied on the St. Paul Fire & Marine Insurance Company, a Minnesota corporation doing business in New York, the malpractice insurer of a clinic where Dr. Warren is employed.[2] Jurisdiction of New England Baptist Hospital, of which Dr. Warren is surgeon in chief, a trustee, a member of the planning committee and an officer of the corporation, was obtained by service upon another officer of the hospital while soliciting funds in New York City. Defendants removed the suit to the federal district court on the basis of diversity of citizenship.

It is undisputed that although the hospital is a Massachusetts corporation, approximately one-third of its patients in 1969 came from outside Massachusetts and approximately 8 per cent of its patients in the same year were from New York. Indeed, the hospital claimed in its 1969 annual report that it was "not a local or community hospital in the usual sense because its patients come from literally everywhere." An affidavit of the head of the casualty underwriting department of the Boston office of St. Paul Fire & Marine, which issued the liability policy under which defendant Warren was covered, indicates that a general surgeon's liability policy in Massachusetts has a basic limit premium of $192, while a New York City surgeon pays a basic limit premium of $1,139, and that one factor contributing to the difference is the "dollar exposure" in New York, which has no wrongful death limitation. Dr. Warren's policy, however, makes no reference to coverage limitation in wrongful death cases.

1. M.G.L.A. c. 229 § 2 (1959).

2. Jurisdiction was obtained under Seider v. Roth, 17 N.Y.2d 111, 216 N.E.2d 312, 269 N.Y.S.2d 99 (1966). [p. 150, supra].

This being a diversity case, it is, of course, elemental that we must look to the choice of law rules of the forum state, that is, to New York law. [Judge Oakes here reviewed Kilberg v. Northeast Airlines, Inc. (p. 503, supra); Babcock v. Jackson (p. 520, supra); Miller v. Miller (p. 610, supra); Tooker v. Lopez (Note 5, p. 525, supra).]

The most recent conflict of laws tort case to reach the New York Court of Appeals, Neumeier v. Kuehner [p. 525, supra], did hold the Ontario guest law applicable in a suit by an *Ontario* decedent's executrix against a New York driver's estate arising from an accident in Ontario, the court saying that New York has "no legitimate interest in ignoring the public policy of [the] foreign jurisdiction . . . and in protecting the plaintiff guest domiciled and injured there from legislation obviously addressed, at the very least, to a resident riding in a vehicle traveling within its borders." 31 N.Y.2d at 125–26, 286 N.E.2d at 456, 335 N.Y.S.2d at 68. In no way, however, did the court retreat from the position it had staked out in *Kilberg* and *Miller*, refusing to apply other states' wrongful death limitations in the case of the death of a New York domiciliary. . . .

This review of the relevant case law leaves us with the overwhelming conclusion that . . . the strong New York public policy against damage limitations has triumphed over the contrary policies of sister states in every case where a New York domiciliary has brought suit. This conclusion is particularly striking in wrongful death actions where the New York policy, embedded in a state constitutional prohibition against damage limitations, has without exception been applied in suits brought for New York decedents since *Kilberg*. One might well inquire whether it would be anomalous to permit Dr. Rosenthal's heirs to recover without damage limitation if he died in a plane crash en route to Boston's Logan International Airport (*Kilberg*) or in a taxi cab from Logan to New England Baptist (*Miller*) but not once he stepped into the hospital itself. But to do so would substitute "a domiciliary conceptualism that rested on a vested right accruing from the fact of domicile," Miller v. Miller, supra, 22 N.Y.2d at 29, 237 N.E.2d at 887, 290 N.Y.S.2d at 748 (dissenting opinion), for New York's sophisticated "interest analysis" approach to choice of law problems. The New York precedents require more.

Appellants contend that Massachusetts is the situs of the events leading to this law suit and, in effect, that the intent, either actual or constructive, of the parties was for the Massachusetts limitation on damages to govern in the event of a malpractice claim. This argument fails for many reasons. Quite probably it never occurred to Dr. Rosenthal, Dr. Warren or to the New England Baptist Hospital that a choice of law problem would arise; at least one does not ordinarily think of wrongful death limitations even when undertaking surgery. This is not a case where the conduct of the Massachusetts doctor or hospital vis-a-vis the decedent was patterned upon the Massachusetts death limitation. It is therefore not unfair to apply New York's compensatory policy to them. Cf. Babcock v. Jackson, supra, 12 N.Y.2d at 483, 191 N.E.2d at 284, 240 N.Y.S.2d at 750–

51. Additionally, it cannot be said that the defendants purchased insurance with the expectation Massachusetts law would govern damage recovery in this case. As in Miller v. Miller, supra, the specific insurance policy here does not distinguish between liability coverage for wrongful death and personal injuries, nor does it distinguish between medical practice on Massachusetts and out of state citizens. Finally, neither the hospital nor the doctor named here as defendants operate provincially; the doctor has a world-wide following and the hospital actively solicits funds from outside the Commonwealth of Massachusetts (including New York) and treats patients from "literally everywhere." It is thus impossible to say with any certainty what the parties' actual "expectations" as to choice of law were.

Even if expectations, real or constructive, could be hypothesized, they would be legally irrelevant. Despite the argument that looking to the expectations of the parties to solve choice of law problems promotes " 'an unconscious acceptance of legality and the legal order,' " Miller v. Miller, supra, 22 N.Y.2d at 28, 237 N.E.2d at 886, 290 N.Y.S.2d at 747 (dissenting opinion), this contractual type of approach to multistate tort problems has been "summarily rejected" by the New York Court of Appeals. Tooker v. Lopez, supra, 24 N.Y.2d at 577, 249 N.E.2d at 399, 301 N.Y.S.2d at 526; Miller v. Miller, supra, 22 N.Y.2d at 20, 237 N.E.2d at 881, 290 N.Y.S.2d at 741....

Rather, as we view it, the New York courts would balance against the New York interest in protecting its domiciliaries against wrongful death limitations the interests of Massachusetts in limiting damages for wrongful deaths allegedly caused by Massachusetts citizens or occurring in Massachusetts. Consideration of Massachusetts' interests in this case should, however, be from the perspective that the damage limitation is not confined to wrongful deaths resulting from medical malpractice but applies to all wrongful deaths however caused. Thus, any interest Massachusetts has in keeping medical liability insurance premiums down so as to avoid passing the increased costs on to Massachusetts citizens in the form of higher medical fees is simply one facet of whatever larger interest it may have in limiting in death as distinguished from personal injury cases the size of damage recovery against its citizens generally.[8] ...

That interest we think the New York courts would say is one not based upon logic, reason or social policy, but is really the vestigial remains of the mistaken view that there was no common law action for wrongful death. We say "mistaken," for Massachusetts has only recently held precisely

---

8. If this case presented the converse fact situation where the decedent was a Massachusetts domiciliary and defendant doctor and hospital New York based, it is by no means clear a New York court would apply the Massachusetts wrongful death limitation. For, in addition to its interest in providing adequate compensation to those New York domiciliaries who suffer a wrongful demise, the unlimited nature of the possible recovery in New York can be said to deter resident doctors and medical facilities from acts of malpractice. Thus, New York would have an interest in regulating the conduct of the tortfeasors and "it would be almost unthinkable to seek the applicable rule in the law of some other place." Babcock v. Jackson, 12 N.Y.2d 473, 483, 191 N.E.2d 279, 284, 240 N.Y.S.2d 743, 751 (1962).

that, as of now, "the right to recovery for wrongful death is of common law origin ...," Gaudette v. Webb, 362 Mass. 60, 284 N.E.2d 222, 229 (1972) .... In any event, it is our considered view that the New York Court of Appeals would view the Massachusetts limitation ... as so "absurd and unjust" that the New York policy of fully compensating the harm from wrongful death would outweigh any interest Massachusetts has in keeping down in this limited type of situation the size of verdicts (and in some cases insurance premiums). If as *Kilberg* pointed out, "The absurdity and injustice [of wrongful death recovery limitations] have become increasingly apparent [since 1894] ...," ... since *Kilberg* they have become even more so. Since *Kilberg*, a number of states have repealed their wrongful death limitations or increased the amounts so that at the present time there are only seven which have an outright limit, although some jurisdictions place a limit on a component of the damages [10] and various states impose a limit in suits against certain governmental bodies.[11] Indeed, Massachusetts itself recently increased its limits.[12] Our examination indicates that Massachusetts is unique, moreover, in both imposing minimum and maximum damage limitations and assessing damages in proportion to the degree of the wrongdoer's culpability.[13] Thus, the "absurdity and injustice" of death recovery limitations in general is heightened insofar as Massachusetts is concerned, because it relates damages recoverable not to the damages sustained, but to the degree of culpability, however that can be measured, on the part of the defendant. A respected, famous surgeon like Dr. Warren might well be held liable, were the Massachusetts statute applicable, for only $5,000 in damages, regardless of the damages sustained by the decedent's survivors. Thus the anachronistic concept embodied in the Massachusetts act is hardly one that the New York courts can be expected to embrace in the case of the death of a New York domiciliary with whose wife and children New York is "vitally concerned ..." Miller v. Miller, supra, 22 N.Y.2d at 18, 237 N.E.2d at 880, 290 N.Y.S.2d at 739....

The constitutional argument, skillfully set forth in the dissent, was not raised by the parties below or on this appeal. We believe that in this case ... New York has a significant interest—its domiciliary is the one who died and his next of kin are New York's charges—and the "incident" in Massachusetts is not purely "a local one," ... since the decedent was from out of state, and the defendant hospital is a national one in terms of its patients, its staff, its reputation and its efforts to obtain out-of-state contributions. In these circumstances, the refusal by New York to apply the Massachusetts death act's qualitative and quantitative limitations, even

10. E.g., Michie's Md.Code, art. 93 § 4–401(n) (1971) ($2,000 limit on recovery for funeral expenses); Wis.Stat. § 895.04 (1971) ($5,000 limit on recovery for loss of consortium).

11. E.g., S.C.Code of Laws, tit. 33, § 926 (1962) ($5,000 limit for wrongful death action against a county based on defectively maintained roads).

12. 7A Mass.Anno.Laws ch. 229, § 2 (Supp.1971) ($5,000 to $100,000 limit depending on tortfeasor's degree of culpability).

13. Alabama assesses damages in proportion to the culpability of the tortfeasor but has no limit on maximum recovery. See S. Speiser, Recovery for Wrongful Death 71 (1966).

as it applies the remainder of the death act, is not so unreasonable as to violate the full faith and credit clause.... The fact that Massachusetts was the situs of the tort and the residence of the defendant would not be sufficient to require as a matter of full faith and credit that the limitations in the Massachusetts law control, in light of the very strong New York policy against wrongful death limitations in connection with its citizens and next of kin and in light of the interstate aspects of the transaction. *Pearson* established that the Massachusetts death statute could be constitutionally sued upon in New York absent its penal quality and its damage limitations. Given a legitimate forum state interest—as is here present— we see no *constitutional* difference between death on the *Pearson* airplane, death in a taxicab on the way from the airport and death on the operating table.

We agree with the court below and affirm the judgment.

■ LUMBARD, CIRCUIT JUDGE—(dissenting): ... I must dissent both because I do not agree that [the majority's] is a proper appraisal of applicable New York law and because I believe that the full faith and credit clause of the United States Constitution bars the New York courts, and federal district courts sitting in diversity, from refusing to apply the Massachusetts limitation on the facts of this case....

The majority purports to decide this case on interest-analysis grounds. However, the sole interest that it has found in New York emanates from the facts of plaintiff's and decedent's New York residence. Such an analysis simply proves too much; for it is tantamount to a per se rule that the courts will not apply such foreign damage limitations when the plaintiff is a resident of the forum state. Thus, I believe the majority's approach amounts to an insupportable abandonment of interest-analysis principles with regard to foreign damage limitations.

... New York's only connection with this occurrence was the patient's permanent residence in New York. I do not see that New York's interest in this occurrence is enhanced by the fact that this Massachusetts physician and Massachusetts institution have such an eminent reputation that a substantial number of their patients, many from New York, are not Massachusetts residents and choose to come into Massachusetts and undergo treatment there; for there is no evidence that either defendant solicited patients from outside Massachusetts—their popularity is due solely to their reputation and the choice of the individual patients.

In my opinion the Massachusetts interests and contacts with the occurrence underlying this litigation should predominate. In addition to its interest in protecting its citizens and institutions from excessive recoveries, an important consideration behind the Massachusetts limitation is its policy of keeping liability premiums as low as possible for its residents. The significant differential that the majority has noted between malpractice insurance premiums in New York and those in Massachusetts is some testimony to the success of this policy. This interest of Massachusetts is fortified by the fact that the insurance policy from which any recovery will be paid was issued in Massachusetts. The fact that the policy has no coverage limitation in wrongful death cases, as noted by the majority, is irrelevant; for the difference in premiums makes it clear that the Massachusetts damage limitation is considered by insurance companies in calculating premiums for liability insurance issued in Massachusetts. Therefore, if we are to take the New York courts at their word that they follow an interest-analysis approach to torts conflict of laws problems, I can see no escape from the conclusion that Massachusetts interests predominate here and that the New York Court would on these facts be impelled to apply the Massachusetts damage limitation....

In any event, even if the majority were correct that the New York courts would refuse to apply the Massachusetts damage limitation against a New York plaintiff, I would hold that such an approach, when applied to a case in which the contacts with Massachusetts are as great as they are here, violates the full faith and credit clause of the United States Constitution....

Accordingly, I would reverse the order of the district court.

NOTES

1. Is the decision in the principal case consistent with Neumeier v. Kuehner? Are *Kilberg* and *Miller* correctly invoked for support? Is *Babcock*?

2. Under interest analysis may a court properly refuse to apply another state's rule because it considers the rule "absurd and unjust?"

3. As noted in Judge Oakes' opinion, Dr. Rosenthal's executrix also brought suit for malpractice against the New England Baptist Hospital which raised the defense of the charitable immunity it enjoyed under Massachusetts law. The defense was stricken by the trial court on the plaintiff's motion. The court relied heavily on the Court of Appeals decision involving Dr. Warren and held that in view of New York's interest in the wellbeing of the surviving family of Dr. Rosenthal, who were New York domiciliaries, a New York court would refuse to give effect to the Massachusetts charitable immunity doctrine on the ground that "it is unfair, out of step with the times and abhorrent to [New York] public policy." The court also said that Massachusetts had no "current interest in perpetuating the charitable immunity doctrine," having abolished it by legislation after Dr. Rosenthal's death. Rosenthal v. Warren, 374 F.Supp. 522 (S.D.N.Y.1974).

4. If the malpractice insurance policy excluded coverage for claims of non-residents of Massachusetts, should the result in the principal case have been different?

5. Edwardsville Nat. Bank v. Marion Laboratories, Inc., 808 F.2d 648 (7th Cir. 1987), was a wrongful death action based on a claim of medical malpractice. Death to a young boy resulted after allegedly harmful drug applications were given to him for an ear infection. The boy had lived with his parents in Illinois, which unlike Indiana, did not require medical malpractice claims to be reviewed by a panel before suit is filed. The court rejected the plaintiff's position that Illinois' pro-recovery rule should apply, despite the fact that telephone calls relating to the boy's treatment were made from Illinois and the defendant hospital advertised in Illinois.

6. La Plante v. American Honda Motor Co., 27 F.3d 731 (1st Cir.1994). The plaintiff resided in Rhode Island before enlisting in the Army. Eight years after enlisting, plaintiff was stationed in Colorado. He was rendered quadriplegic by an off-duty accident in Colorado while driving an all-terrain vehicle designed, manufactured, and distributed by defendants. He retained his Rhode Island domicile while in the service and returned to Rhode Island after the accident, where he brought suit against Honda Japan and its United States subsidiary. The jury awarded plaintiff $6,000,000 for pain and suffering. This amount was recoverable under Rhode Island law, but Colorado law placed a $250,000 ceiling on damages for pain and suffering. Held that although there was reversible error requiring a new trial on liability, Rhode Island law was properly applied to damages for pain and suffering. Rhode Island has an interest in full compensation of plaintiff for pain and suffering. Because "there is not the slightest hint of forum shopping, plaintiff's return to Rhode Island should not be ignored." The court "can see no reason why the Colorado legislature would be concerned with the affordability of insurance to a multinational Japanese corporation or its wholly-owned subsidiary, a California corporation."

See also Tjepkema v. Kenney, 31 A.D.2d 908, 298 N.Y.S.2d 175, motion to appeal dism'd, 24 N.Y.2d 740, 302 N.Y.S.2d 1025, 250 N.E.2d 68 (1969), which held that the Missouri statutory limit on damages did not apply to a suit for death of a New Yorker killed in an automobile accident in Missouri by a Missouri driver. Jurisdiction was obtained under Seider v. Roth, p. 150, supra.

Compare Rice v. Dow Chem. Co., 124 Wn.2d 205, 875 P.2d 1213 (1994). After extensive exposure to defendant's chemicals in Oregon, the plaintiff moved to Washington. The Oregon statute of repose barred his suit for damage resulting from the exposure, but the action was timely under Washington law. The court held the action barred. "Although [the interest in compensating residents] is a real interest, recognizing this as an overriding concern, despite the lack of contacts, would mean that Washington law would be applied in all tort cases involving any Washington resident, regardless of where all the activity relating to the tort occurred." Id. at 1219.

Brilmayer, Conflict of Laws: Foundations and Future Directions 107 (1991), states that an individual has a right "to be left alone by a state [if] he or she has not come within the state's legitimate sphere of regulation." Is this "right" protected by the Constitution?

Some scholars have attacked interest analysis on constitutional bases. Professor Ely, in Choice of Law and the State's Interest in Protecting Its Own, 23 Wm. & Mary L.Rev. 173, 187–88 (1981), states that under the Privileges and Immunities Clauses of Article IV, "whenever a state would claim an interest in enforcing its protective policy on the ground that the party its law would protect is a local resident ... it is obligated ... to claim a similar interest in protecting out-of-staters, irrespective of what their home states' law provides." Professor Laycock, in Equal Citizens of Equal and Territorial States: The Constitutional Foundations of Choice of Law, 92 Colum.L.Rev. 249 (1992), states that the Full Faith and Credit Clause forbids preference for forum law or an approach that applies the "better law." Id. at 310, 312. He also states that if a Wisconsin driver and passenger are injured in an accident in Minnesota, Wisconsin law may be applied based on the location of their relationship in Wisconsin, but that if "two strangers from Wisconsin collide on a Minnesota highway ... there is no basis to apply any law but Minnesota's." Id. at 324. Is it likely that, in the light of the materials in Chapter 6 and Sun Oil Co. v. Wortman, 486 U.S. 717 (1988), page 434, supra, a majority of the Supreme Court of the United States would agree with these statements? Should it agree?

5. "NO INTEREST" CASES

Reyno v. Piper Aircraft Co.
United States Circuit Court of Appeals, Third Circuit, 1980.
630 F.2d 149, reversed, 454 U.S. 235, 102 S.Ct. 252, 70 L.Ed.2d 419 (1981).

[Wrongful death action, stemming from airplane crash in Scotland against Pennsylvania plane manufacturer. The plane was owned by a Scottish air taxi service and all the passengers and crew were Scottish. The action was originally brought in California and then was transferred to the federal court in Pennsylvania under 28 U.S.C. § 1404(a). The Court of Appeals first held that under Van Dusen v. Barrack (p. 196, supra), the California choice-of-law rules should be applied in the suit against Piper, the plane manufacturer. The court then continued:]

■ ADAMS, CIRCUIT JUDGE.

. . .

a. *California Conflicts Law Applied to Piper*

California was a pioneering state in the governmental interest analysis approach to choice of law that was developed by Professor Currie.....

Any asserted conflict between American strict liability and Scottish negligence law is, we believe, a false one. Two basic policies underlie theories of tort liability: deterrence of harm-causing conduct and compensation of persons injured by that conduct. In private tort law, in which civil rather than criminal liability is imposed, the deterrence function is accomplished by compensation of the plaintiff. The choice between holding a manufacturer liable only for negligence and holding it strictly liable for any dangerous products or design is, practically speaking, a matter both of searching for optimal deterrence of harmful conduct and of allocating the costs of injuries either to producers or consumers. A negligence standard is, broadly speaking, more protective of producers, while strict liability is more solicitous of consumers.

The perceived conflict in this case is between Scotland's interest in encouraging industry by protecting manufacturers and making it relatively more difficult for consumers to recover. Pennsylvania, by contrast, in adopting strict liability, has shifted some of the burdens of injuries from consumers to producers. By adopting this policy of increased deterrence, it seeks to make manufacturers more careful in production and design than they would be if held to a negligence standard.

Applying Pennsylvania's strict liability standard to its resident manufacturer would serve that state's interest in the regulation of manufacturing. Scotland's interest in encouraging industry within its borders would not be impaired, however, by applying a stricter standard of care on a foreign corporation which has no industrial operations in Scotland. Furthermore, Scotland would have no interest in *denying* compensation to its residents for the purpose of benefiting a foreign corporation. Finally, imposition of strict liability on Piper cannot be said to be unfair to it. Inasmuch as Pennsylvania, the state in which Piper makes its product, and the vast majority of American jurisdictions in which most of Piper's aircraft are sold and fly, have strict liability, that is the legal standard under which it plans its operations.

Pennsylvania's interest in deterring defects in products can be served without impairing any significant interest in Scotland. Application of Scotland's negligence law would only harm resident beneficiaries without any countervailing benefit to its industrial economy. We therefore conclude that, as between Pennsylvania and Scottish law on this issue, a California court would apply Pennsylvania's strict liability analysis....

. . .

[This case was subsequently reversed by the Supreme Court [Piper Aircraft Co. v. Reyno, 454 U.S. 235 (1981), page 184, supra] on the ground that the suit should have been dismissed for forum non conveniens reasons.]

NOTES

1. The "no interest" in the title of this section is taken from the notion that when the plaintiff's law favors the defendant and the defendant's law favors the plaintiff, neither state has an "interest" in applying its law. See B. Currie, Selected Essays on the Conflict of Laws 184 (1963) ("neither state has an interest in the application of its law and policy"). A few courts have used this language. In Erwin v. Thomas, 264 Or. 454, 506 P.2d 494 (1973), an Oregon resident, while driving in Washington in the course of his employment, injured a Washington resident. The victim's wife sued for loss of consortium, a remedy permitted under Oregon law, but not under Washington law. Concluding that "neither state has a vital interest in the outcome of this litigation," (id. at 496), the court applied Oregon law as the law of the forum on the ground that this was the natural result in an Oregon court and would not offend any Washington policy. Kramer, The Myth of the "Unprovided–For" Case, 75 Va.L.Rev. 1045 (1989) disagrees with the result in *Erwin* on the ground that under Washington law the plaintiff has "suffered no legally cognizable injury." Id. at 1062. Under his analysis, "there is no such thing as an unprovided-for case." Id. at 1047.

Most courts have not used the "no interest" or "unprovided-for" language, but, as in the principal case, have analyzed the problem so that one state has an applicable policy and the other does not. In the principal case, the court finds that Pennsylvania's deterrence policy is advanced and that Scotland would not object to making recovery easier for its citizens. For approval of this deterrence reasoning, see Singer, A Pragmatic Guide to Conflicts, 70 B.U.L.Rev. 731, 773 (1990).

Deemer v. Silk City Textile Mach. Co., 193 N.J.Super. 643, 475 A.2d 648 (1984), reached the opposite result. A North Carolina worker was fatally injured in North Carolina while working with a machine manufactured in New Jersey by a New Jersey company. New Jersey, but not North Carolina, had adopted strict tort liability. The court held North Carolina law applicable: "Furthermore, the effect of holding New Jersey law applicable in a matter of this kind is to subject any corporation conducting manufacturing activities in this state against whom a product liability claim is asserted to suit in New Jersey under New Jersey law.

Such a holding would have the undesirable consequence of deterring the conduct of manufacturing operations in this state and would likely result in an unreasonable increase in litigation and thereby unduly burden our courts." Id. at 652.

In international product liability cases, the concern has been expressed that applying United States law more favorable to a foreign user than the law of the user's own country would place United States manufacturers at a competitive disadvantage. See Harrison v. Wyeth Laboratories, 510 F.Supp. 1, 5 (E.D.Pa.1980), aff'd w.o. opinion, 676 F.2d 685 (3d Cir.1982). Moreover, *Harrison* found that applying United States law might sometimes interfere with policies of the foreign country: "Faced with different needs, problems and resources ... India may, in balancing the pros and cons of a drug's use, give different weight to various factors than would our society, and more easily conclude that any risks associated with use of a particular oral contraceptive are far outweighed by its overall benefits to India and its people." Id. at 4–5. Does the cogency of these arguments depend upon whether the manufacturer's liability is based on strict liability, negligence, gross negligence, or intentional misconduct?

The result in the *Harrison* case supra, after deciding that United Kingdom rather than Pennsylvania law applied (the reference to India in the quotation above is a hypothetical illustration), was to order a forum non conveniens dismissal. This is frequently the result in such cases once the decision is made that foreign law applies. In the principal case, the district court's forum non conveniens dismissal was upheld by the United States Supreme Court even after the Third Circuit had decided that United States law applied.

One effect of permitting suit here, even if foreign law is applied, is that the damages under the foreign damages categories will be determined by a United States jury and will probably be in an amount greater than could be recovered in the foreign country. General levels of damages awarded in the foreign country are not relevant even though the United States court is applying foreign damages law, unless the foreign law places either a statutory cap on recovery, or perhaps the judge-made equivalent of a statutory cap. See Weintraub, International Litigation and Forum Non Conveniens, 29 Texas Int'l L.J. 321, 323–24 (1994) (suggesting that this practice be changed by informing the trial judge of typical recoveries in the foreign country and giving the judge power to order remittitur if the jury award is clearly excessive under foreign standards).

2. The pattern of defendant's law favorable to plaintiff and plaintiff's law favorable to defendant, also appears in automobile accident cases. Neumeier v. Kuehner, 31 N.Y.2d 121, 335 N.Y.S.2d 64, 286 N.E.2d 454 (1972), page 525, supra, applied Ontario law to prevent recovery against the New York host for the death of the Ontario guest, finding that New York had "no legitimate interest in ignoring the public policy" underlying the Ontario guest statute, which was to deter "ungrateful guests." Labree v. Major, 111 R.I. 657, 306 A.2d 808 (1973) rejected the *Neumeier* "rules" and result, applied Rhode Island law to facilitate recovery by a Massachusetts passenger injured in Massachusetts, and magnanimously declared: "where a driver is from a state which allows a passenger to recover for ordinary negligence, the plaintiff should recover, no matter what the law of his residence or the place of accident." Id. at 818. Hurtado v. Superior Court, 11 Cal.3d 574, 114 Cal.Rptr. 106, 522 P.2d 666 (1974), applied California law to permit much greater recovery for the wrongful death of a Mexican killed in a traffic accident in California than would have been recovered under Mexican law. *Hurtado* differed from *Neumeier* and *Labree* in that the injury was in the defendant's state. The court utilized this factor to find that California had an interest in deterring negligent conduct on its highways, whereas Mexico had no interest in limiting the recovery of its citizens against California defendants. Do you agree with the reasoning of any of these cases?

6. COMPLEX LITIGATION

The most difficult choice-of-law problem for modern methods to resolve occurs when plaintiffs from many different jurisdictions sue defendants from many different jurisdictions. This problem occurs in two contexts. The first is the mass disaster at a single location, such the crash of a commercial airplane. Hundreds of claimants from dozens of states and countries then sue the airline and various other defendants, such as the airplane manufacturer, the manufacturers of component parts, and air traffic controllers. At least the traditional place-of-wrong rule simplified the choice of law in tort, but complications could arise if claims were based on contract theories. The second form of the problem is difficult for either traditional or modern methods—many plaintiffs injured at different locations by a defective product produced by many defendants. Can modern methods of choosing law be adapted to these situations so as to encourage rather than prevent consolidation of the cases for timely disposition?

Some courts have found that the need to apply different law to different claims is inconsistent with the class-action requirement that common questions of law predominate. See Zandman v. Joseph, 102 F.R.D. 924, 929 (N.D.Ind.1984); In re United States Fin. Sec. Litig., 64 F.R.D. 443, 455 (S.D.Cal.1974). Other courts have found that the need for differential choice-of-law treatment of plaintiffs' claims did not prevent class certification if the parties and applicable laws could be grouped into a manageable number of subclasses. Miner v. Gillette Co., 87 Ill.2d 7, 56 Ill.Dec. 886, 428 N.E.2d 478, 484 (1981), cert. dism'd, 459 U.S. 86 (1982).

Some courts and commentators have stated that the law applicable to compensatory damages does not necessarily apply to punitive damages. This is because the law of plaintiff's state is "interested" in compensation, but the places where the defendant acted are "interested" in deterring and punishing outrageous conduct. See In re Air Crash Disaster Near Chicago, 644 F.2d 594, 612–13 (7th Cir.), cert. denied, 454 U.S. 878 (1981); Reese, The Law Governing Airplane Accidents, 39 Wash. & Lee L.Rev. 1303, 1313 (1982). Do higher compensatory damages also punish and deter?

A case that gives a glimpse of some of the choice-of-law problems that may bedevil the courts is In re Paris Air Crash of March 3, 1974, 399 F.Supp. 732 (C.D.Cal.1975). That case involved the crash in France of a Turkish Air Lines plane, in which all 346 occupants were killed. Of these, 23 were Americans from 12 different states; the remainder came from 24 foreign countries. In all, some 203 suits were filed against McDonnell Douglas Corporation, the manufacturer of the plane, and General Dynamics, a subcontractor. Both defendants are incorporated in California, which was also the state where the plane had been manufactured. Most of the suits were originally brought in the federal district court in California and others were transferred there under 28 U.S.C.A. § 1407 by the Judicial Panel on Multidistrict Litigation. One of the principal issues involved the basis of liability. Under California law, the defendants would be strictly liable for injuries resulting from an original defect in the plane. Under the laws of most of the foreign countries involved, proof of negligence, would be required to hold them liable. Also, the amount of damages recoverable varied widely from law to law. Recovery would be most restricted under the law of England where most of the passengers had been domiciled. It would be considerably larger under the laws of France, Turkey, Japan and California.* After lengthy discussion, the judge determined that California law should be applied to determine both the basis of liability and the measure of recovery. To be sure, California "has no interest in the distribution of proceeds to foreign beneficiaries." But application of California law was required because of that state's interest in "(1) deterring conduct of its defendants, (2) avoiding the imposition of excessive financial burdens on its resident defendants, and ... (3) providing a uniform rule of liability and damages so that those who come under the ambit of California strict product liability law and market their product outside of California and/or in foreign countries may know what risks they are subject to when they make and sell their products."

The American Law Institute has completed a major project designed to produce a workable method of dealing with complex cases involving many parties and many places of suit. The general scheme of the institute's proposal is to consolidate related multi-forum, multi-party litigation in one court, federal or state, by providing legislative authority for the consolidation procedures. The thorniest question facing the Institute was to devise a choice-of-law scheme that would be sensitive to substantive considerations, while at the same time achieving a measure of predictability and uniformity in operation. The tort choice of law provisions are contained in § 6.01 of the Institute's project.

In an introductory note, the Institute's reporters acknowledged that "certainly, the most direct way to attempt to solve the issues posed [by complex litigation] would be to adopt national standards to govern the conduct of individuals or entities who are engaging in activities having interstate effects and who now are controlled by multiple, sometimes conflicting, state laws." Introductory Note, p. 375. However, the possibility of reaching a political consensus on the appropriate federal substantive standards was deemed infeasible.

Accordingly, the choice-of-law system was chosen to be the "most compatible with the objectives of fostering a fair, just and efficient resolution of the cases embraced by this Complex Litigation Project." Ibid. The Mass Torts provision is contained in § 6.01, which provides:

A. Choice of Law Rules in State Created Actions

§ 6.01. Mass Torts

    (a) Except as provided in § 6.04 through § 6.06, in actions consolidated under § 3.01 or removed under § 5.01 in which the

---

* The statements with respect to the relevant local law rules of the states and countries involved are based on Speiser, Conflict of Laws in Wrongful Death Cases, 81 Case & Comment 49 (1975).

parties assert the application of laws that are in material conflict, the transferee court shall choose the law governing the rights, liabilities, and defenses of the parties with respect to a tort claim by applying the criteria set forth in subsections (c)–(e) with the objective of applying, to the extent feasible, a single state's law to all similar tort claims being asserted against a defendant.

(b) If the court determines that the application of a single state's law to all elements of the claims pending against a defendant would be inappropriate, it may divide the actions into subgroups of claims, issues, or parties to foster consolidated treatment under § 3.01, and allow more than one state's law to be applied. The court also may determine that only certain claims or issues involving one or more of the parties should be governed by the law chosen by the application of the rules in subsections (d)–(e), and that other claims or parties should be remanded to the transferor courts for individual treatment under the laws normally applicable in those courts. In either instance, the court may exercise its authority under § 3.06(c) to sever, transfer, or remand issues or claims for treatment consistent with its determination.

(c) In determining the governing law under subsection (a), the court shall consider the following factors for purposes of identifying each state having a policy that would be furthered by the application of its laws:

(1) the place or places of injury;

(2) the place or places of the conduct causing the injury; and

(3) the primary places of business or habitual residences of the plaintiffs and defendants.

(d) If, in analyzing the factors set forth in subsection (c), the court finds that only one state has a policy that would be furthered by the application of its law, that state's law shall govern. If more than one state has a policy that would be furthered by the application of its law, the court shall choose the applicable law from among the laws of the interested states under the following rules:

(1) If the place of injury and the place of the conduct causing the injury are in the same state, that state's law governs.

(2) If subsection (d)(1) does not apply, but all of the plaintiffs habitually reside or have their primary places of business in the same state, and a defendant has its primary place of business or habitually resides in that state, that state's law governs the claims with respect to that defendant. Plaintiffs shall be considered as sharing a common habitual residence or primary place of business if they are located in states whose laws are not in material conflict.

(3) If neither subsection (d)(1) nor (d)(2) applies, but all of the plaintiffs habitually reside or have their primary places of business in the same state, and that state also is the place of

injury, then that state's law governs. Plaintiffs shall be considered as sharing a common habitual residence or primary place of business if they are located in states whose laws are not in material conflict.

(4) In all other cases, the law of the state where the conduct causing the injury occurred governs. When conduct occurred in more than one state, the court shall choose the law of the conduct state that has the most significant relationship to the occurrence.

(e) To avoid unfair surprise or arbitrary results, the transferee court may choose the applicable law on the basis of other factors that reflect the regulatory policies and legitimate interests of a particular state not otherwise identified under subsection (c), or it may depart from the order of preferences for selecting the governing law prescribed by subsection (d).

§ 6.03. Mass Contracts: Law Governing in the Absence of Effective Party Choice

(a) Except as provided in § 6.02, in actions consolidated under § 3.01 or removed under § 5.01, in which the parties assert the application of laws that are in material conflict, the transferee court shall choose the law governing the rights, liabilities, and defenses of the parties with respect to a contract claim by applying the criteria set forth in subsections (c) and (d) with the objective of applying a single state's law to every claim being asserted under the same or similar contracts with a common party.

(b) If the court determines that the application of a single state's law to all the claims being asserted under similar contracts with a common party would be inappropriate, it may divide the actions into subgroups of claims, issues, or parties to foster consolidated treatment under § 3.01, and allow more than one state's law to be applied. The court also may determine that only certain claims involving one or more of the parties should be governed by the law chosen by the application of the rules in subsection (d), and that other claims or parties should be remanded to the transferor courts for individual treatment under the laws normally applicable there. In either instance, the transferee court may retain all the claims, treating them under the appropriately designated laws, or it may exercise its authority under § 3.06(c) to sever, transfer, or remand the claims to the transferor courts for individual treatment there consistent with its determination.

(c) In determining the governing law under subsection (a), the court shall consider the following factors for purposes of identifying each state having a policy that would be furthered by the application of its law:

(1) the place or places of contracting;

(2) the place or places of performance;

(3) the location of the subject matter of the contract; and

(4) the primary places of business or habitual residences of the plaintiffs and defendants.

(d) If, in analyzing the factors set forth in subsection (c), the court finds that only one state has a policy that would be furthered by the application of its law, that state's law shall govern. If more than one state has a policy that would be furthered by the application of its law, the court shall apply the law of the state in which the common contracting party has its primary place of business, unless the court finds that that law is in material conflict with the regulatory objectives of the state law in the place of performance or where the other contracting parties habitually reside. In that event, the court shall apply those state laws to the contracts legitimately within their scope.

A Symposium on the Complex Litigation Project appears in 54 La. L.Rev. (March 1994) with articles by Cooper, Juenger, Kalis, Kozyris, Mullenix, Nafziger, Sedler, Segerdahl, Seidelson, Shreve, Symeonides, Donald Trautman, Waldron, and, Wilkins. See also Weinberg, Mass Torts and the Neutral Forum: A Critical Analysis of the ALI's Proposed Choice Rule, 56 Alb.L.Rev. 807 (1993). A symposium on Conflict of Laws and Complex Litigation Issues in Mass Tort Litigation appears in 1989 U.Ill.L.Rev. (No. 1) with an introduction by Hay and Marcus, and articles by Hensler, Juenger, Lowenfeld, Trangsrud, Weintraub, and Yeazell.

How would the ALI choice-of-law provision for mass torts apply to a product liability action in which many plaintiffs have been injured in many jurisdictions by the same defectively manufactured product? Is it likely that rules 6.01(d)(1), (2), or (3) will apply? Will 6.01(d)(4) lead to a "race to the bottom" with states vying to provide an attractive haven for manufacturers?

New Approaches; An Epilogue

From the welter of latter-day decisions, commentary and occasional legislative proposals concerning choice of law, it is possible to discern at least a half-dozen approaches to the problem of bringing the chaos under control.

(1) *Jurisdiction-selecting rules.* The orthodox rules of this type, general in sweep, intent on the search for the goals of uniformity, simplicity and certainty, have failed in substantial part. Broad choice-of-law rules in the fields of torts and contracts such as that "The law of the place of wrong determines whether a person has sustained a legal injury", (Restatement, Conflict of Laws § 378 (1934)), have few champions today. The old rules were blind to the content of the law whose selection they compelled and were prone to lead to unfortunate results. However, narrow choice-of-law rules, based on an appreciation of the underlying purposes and policies at stake, can be useful. An example is Restatement, Second, Conflict of Laws § 217, referring details of presentment, payment, protest and notice of dishonor of negotiable instruments to the local law of the state where the activity in question occurs.

(2) *Rules that presumptively select the law of a determinate state, subject to displacement,* are another possibility. An example is Restatement, Second, Conflict of Laws § 146, dealing with personal injuries. It provides that in an action of that type, the local law of the state where the injury occurred determines the rights and liabilities of the parties *unless*, having regard for the particular *issue* involved, there is a state that has a more significant relationship to the elements of the dispute, as more fully spelled out. This sort of rule creates a defeasible presumption that points at the start to a selected state as the source of the rule of decision, but is not contents-blind in its formulation. The presumption it creates is based upon a conscious choice of applicable policy; and flexibility is built in to take care of exotic or merely unexpected patterns of fact, law and policy.

(3) *Principles of preference.* These are the creation of Professor David F. Cavers and set guidelines for courts and lawyers dealing with multistate choice of law problems in common contexts. Their basic design is to create presumptions favoring choices of rules of particular content when the underlying fact pattern is of a carefully defined type. A distinctive feature of these principles is that they nominate a key connecting factor, based upon the nature of the issue and an awareness of underlying policies that are deemed decisive. In common with the rules mentioned above, they would presumably apply in whatever forum the particular issue is presented.

(4) *Alternative reference rules.* Rules of this type combine an effort to select a certain state with an effort to favor a particular resolution of the substantive issue presented. Thus Restatement, Second, Conflict of Laws § 203(2) says that when usury is raised as a defense to the validity of an interest-bearing contract, the contract will be upheld if the rate charged is valid in a state with a substantial relationship to the contract and if the rate is not greatly in excess of that permitted by the state of most significant relationship as determined by the Restatement's approach in Section 188. This alternative reference rule is a contents-conscious rule, with a bias in favor of validating a contract of the type described. Other validation-favoring alternative reference rules are to be found in the areas of trusts and wills.

(5) *Special substantive rules for multistate cases.* Professor Arthur von Mehren has suggested that when two or more concerned states have domestic decisional rules that point to opposed results in the case, the proper resolution is to fashion a "special substantive rule" for the problem. The special rule would be different from the domestic rule of any concerned state. See von Mehren, Special Substantive Rules for Multi-State Problems: Their Role and Significance in Contemporary Choice of Law Methodology, 88 Harv.L.Rev. 347 (1974). For the Neumeier case, p. 525, supra, the author suggests that a compromise between New York's full-recovery and Ontario's no-recovery rules should be effected, in "the form of allowing partial recovery by permitting the guest to recover one-half of the damage suffered." (Id., at p. 369.)

(6) *Result selective approach.* Here, there is no "rule" as such except that the validity of a marriage or of a contract or trust is to be upheld in the absence of strong reasons to the contrary, or that higher standards of liability are to be applied whenever constitutionally possible, or that the court is to apply what it conceives to be the "better" rule, or the decisional norm that is on the upswing rather than regressing, or a combination of such approaches. This view of the choice-of-law process is entirely contents conscious. It is not concerned with preventing forum shopping or variations in outcome depending on the court in which the issue is presented. Presumably, its proponents assume that most courts and judges will be prone to select the same result and that this will keep subjectivity from becoming too rampant.

(7) *Narrow choice-of-law rules based upon experience with a recurrent problem.* An example, in the field of automobile-caused wrongful death cases involving the applicability of a ceiling on collectible damages, has been proposed by one of the editors of this volume. Rosenberg, Comments on *Reich v. Purcell*, 15 U.C.L.A.L.Rev. 551, 641, 646–7:

Group 1. Death damage limit not applicable.

Rule 1.1. A limit upon damages for wrongful death that is prescribed by the state in which the harm occurred will not be applied if no similar limit is prescribed by the law of any domiciliary state.

Rule 1.2. A limit upon damages for wrongful death that is prescribed by the state of the defendant's domicile will not be applied if no similar limit is prescribed either by the state in which the accident occurred or in which the decedent was domiciled.

Rule 1.3. A limit upon damages for wrongful death that is prescribed by the state in which the decedent was domiciled will not be applied if no similar limit is prescribed either by the state in which the accident occurred or in which the defendant was domiciled.

Group 2. Death damage limit applicable.

Rule 2.1. A limit upon damages for wrongful death that is prescribed by the state in which the accident occurred will be applied if either

(a) defendant is domiciled there, *or*

(b) defendant is domiciled in a state that similarly limits damages, *or*

(c) the decedent was domiciled in a state that similarly limits damages.

The premise of drafting such narrowly specific rules is to avoid litigation whenever possible in the all too common circumstances of multistate highway fatalities.

The strategy of efforts to draft rules of whatever kind, for situations where rules can function effectively, is to prevent choice of law from becoming an over-sophisticated game that leaves judges and lawyers, bewildered and confused; and that adds complex multistate litigations to the crushing caseload of busy courts.

NOTES

1. Professor Friedrich K. Juenger has argued that applying the "simple and straightforward" German choice-of-law rules for torts would improve the decisional process in the group of well known New York cases on guest statutes and wrongful death damage limits. See Juenger, Lessons Comparison Might Teach, 23 Am. J.Comp.L. 742, 747–748 (1975):

"To illustrate, I propose to apply German tort choice-of-law rules to several New York decisions. The rules—in part statutory, in part judge-made—are simple and straightforward:

"(1) If both parties have the same nationality the law of the country whose nationals they are governs;

"(2) If the parties have different nationalities the law of the place of wrong governs;

"(a) The term 'place of wrong' refers to all jurisdictions in which any tortious conduct or any injuries occur;

"(b) If there is more than one 'place of wrong,' the law most favorable to the injured party will prevail.

"[I shall leave aside one further statutory provision of a somewhat chauvinistic nature which the German courts have, with laudable urbanity, construed rather narrowly. It establishes the rule that German parties cannot be held liable for torts committed abroad in excess of the liability provided by German law.] ..."

2. For a further elaboration of the suggestion that special substantive rules should be fashioned for cases involving collisions in substantive policies in multistate situations, see von Mehren, Choice of Law and the Problem of Justice, 41 Law and Contemp. Problems 27 (1977); Twerski and Mayer, Toward a Pragmatic Solution of Choice-of-Law Problems—at the Interface of Substance and Procedure, 74 N.W.U.L.Rev. 781 (1979).

D. Additional Problems

Other chapters cover choice-of-law problems in particular areas. See Chapter 11 Property, Chapter 12 Family Law, Chapter 13 Administration of Estates, and Chapter 14 Agency, Partnerships and Corporations. This final section of this chapter covers topics important to understanding the choice-of-law process.

1. MULTISTATE DEFAMATION

Dale System, Inc. v. Time, Inc.

United States District Court, District of Connecticut, 1953.
116 F.Supp. 527.

■ HINCKS, CHIEF JUDGE. This is an action in tort. Plaintiff is a Connecticut corporation which furnishes to clients, most of which are retail stores, in Connecticut, New York, Massachusetts, Rhode Island and New Jersey, a service for testing the efficiency and honesty of the clients' employees. This is done by reports recording the experiences of plaintiff's employees, posing as ordinary customers, in making purchases at the clients' stores.

Defendant Willmark is engaged in the same line of business. Both Willmark and Time are New York corporations.

The complaint alleges that the defendants caused to be published an article in Life magazine describing in detail Willmark's business and asserting falsely and maliciously that Willmark was "unique" and "the only company of its kind." The complaint also alleges that the defendants caused the Life article to be digested in the Readers Digest of September 1951, in which it was falsely and maliciously stated that Willmark is "the only company of its kind in the world"; and that the defendants caused to be broadcast over radio Station WOR a summary of the Readers Digest article with the statement that "Willmark is the only company of its kind."

The parties have stipulated as follows. The text of the Life article was prepared in New York, the plates were made in Illinois, and printing first commenced in Illinois which was followed by printing in Philadelphia and Los Angeles. The broadcast took place from a studio in New York City, but was accomplished through a transmitter located in New Jersey. The broadcast could be heard from Massachusetts to Georgia. The Readers Digest article was edited in New York; its plates were made in New Hampshire; the printing for the domestic issue was done in New Hampshire and Ohio; and foreign editions were printed in many foreign countries. And it was in New York that Willmark gave Time the information upon which the alleged publications were made.

The defendants have moved to dismiss the complaint for failure to state a claim upon which relief can be granted....

Although the Connecticut courts as yet have had no occasion to discuss and pass upon the "single publication" rule which has been adopted in New York as recently restated in Gregoire v. G. P. Putnam's Sons, 298 N.Y. 119, 81 N.E.2d 45, 50, ... the general policy of the Connecticut courts to shape the law of the State to harmonize with the realities of contemporary life, convince me that a Connecticut court if confronted with this case would adopt the "single publication rule". It would hold, I think, that the complaint purported to state at most three torts: one growing out of the publication in Life, one out of that in Readers Digest and the other out of the WOR broadcast; and that on each the Statute of Limitations began to run "when the finished product (was) released by the publisher for sale in accord with trade practice", as stated in the Gregoire opinion....

But when it comes to determine the State, the law of which shall govern a case such as this of libel published in many states, there appear to be no cases in Connecticut, or New York, or indeed in other jurisdictions where the single publication rule prevails, which lay down an authoritative conflict of laws rule of general application or which even discuss the underlying problem. However, ... the "single publication" rule fails to achieve its major objective as a needed development of the substantive law if in practice it is tied to a multiple-publication, conflict-of-laws rule. The terrifying babel of media having publications of nation-wide and international scope urgently requires the development of a conflict of laws rule which shall provide the certainty so essential for the protection of the public, an ease of application which is so helpful to judicial administration and without which justice through litigation becomes for many an unattainable luxury, and an intrinsic realism whereby the existence and incidents of a libel may be determined by the law of the place in which generally, more often than not, the libel will have done the most harm. The law of the plaintiff's domicil, I think, best meets these and any other pertinent requirements. Acting vicariously, as it were, for the Connecticut Courts I hold the Connecticut conflict of laws rule to be that the law of plaintiff's domicil is the law to be applied to a multi-state libel which has been communicated in the state of plaintiff's domicil as well as in other jurisdictions....

After all, a plaintiff's repute is his character and personality in the eyes of others. It thus comprises myriad relationships in all of which the plaintiff's individuality is the focus. Thus viewed, the concept of repute, even though not involving legal relationships, is akin to the concept of status which traditionally is determined by the law of the domicil. The same compelling reasons for applying the law of the domicil to the determination of one's status require that the law of the domicil should determine one's right to his good repute: in cases of multi-state libel generally the greatest harm to repute will occur in the state of domicil.

Of course the artificial rule whereby a corporation is deemed to be domiciled in the state of its incorporation irrespective of the places of its greater activities may at times create situations in which there is substantially less harm to the corporate business by libelous publication in the state of incorporation than by publications occurring where it is more active. For this reason perhaps something could be said for a rule fixing the location of the harm to a corporation in the state of its principal office rather than its domicil. If such were the rule here, the same result would obtain: the plaintiff here is a Connecticut corporation having its principal place of business in Connecticut. However, in my opinion the certainty of domicil and its use generally to locate the law which governs many corporate relationships, commends a rule whereby the law of plaintiff's corporate domicil shall govern also questions relating to harm to its repute....

If it should seem at first glance that the rule is without reasonable relation to the subject-matter, reflection will demonstrate that no other rule—at least no other *uniform* rule—more reasonably related could be devised.... If we were to adopt the rule that the *place of wrong* is the place where the product was released, etc., as likely as not it might be that the place of release was not only difficult to determine but also some place completely unrelated to plaintiff's injury. For example, under the stipulation here, the "release" of the Life issue might be found to have occurred in Illinois or California where plaintiff was not known at all.

In addition to its simplicity, certainty and ease of application the rule of plaintiff's domicil has some merit for its tendency to prevent plaintiff from shopping for the most favorable out of a plurality of jurisdictions: wherever it sues the same law will apply. And surely one would not expect that future libel litigation as a plaintiff would influence the choice of the state in which to incorporate. On the other hand, somewhat less remote is the possibility that a corporation engaging in publishing as its principal business and hence peculiarly liable to libel actions, might be influenced to incorporate in a state the law of which was deemed favorable to defendants in libel suits, if the *defendant's domicil*, were deemed to be a factor in determining the choice of law.

[The court held the article was not defamatory under Connecticut law, but it stated a cause of action against Willmark for unfair competition by means of injurious falsehood.]

RESTATEMENT, SECOND, CONFLICT OF LAWS *

§ 149. Defamation

In an action for defamation, the local law of the state where the publication occurs determines the rights and liabilities of the parties, except as stated in § 150, unless, with respect to the particular issue, some other state under the principles stated in § 6 has a more significant relationship to the occurrence and the parties, in which event the local law of the other state will be applied.

§ 150. Multistate Defamation

(1) The rights and liabilities that arise from defamatory matter in any one edition of a book or newspaper, or any one broadcast over radio or television, exhibition of a motion picture, or similar aggregate communication are determined by the local law of the state which, with respect to the particular issue, has the most significant relationship to the occurrence and the parties under the principles stated in § 6.

(2) When a natural person claims that he has been defamed by an aggregate communication, the state of most significant relationship will usually be the state where the person was domiciled at the time, if the matter complained of was published in that state.

(3) When a corporation, or other legal person, claims that it has been defamed by an aggregate communication, the state of most significant relationship will usually be the state where the corporation, or other legal person, had its principal place of business at the time, if the matter complained of was published in that state.

NOTES

1. Is the interest analysis desirable or feasible in deciding the applicable rule for issues in multistate defamation cases where there are aggregate communications? If the forum has the single publication rule (Restatement, Second, Torts § 577A), (cf. Zuck v. Interstate Pub. Corp., 317 F.2d 727 (2d Cir. 1963)), the possibility of

---

* Quoted with the permission of the copyright owner, The American Law Institute.

effectively applying the interest methodology theoretically exists, but problems remain.

2. Palmisano v. News Syndicate Co., 130 F.Supp. 17 (S.D.N.Y.1955), identifies nine proffered solutions to the choice of law problem: the state of plaintiff's domicile; of plaintiff's principal activity to which the defamation relates; where plaintiff in fact suffered the greatest harm; the publisher's domicile (or state of incorporation); where defendant's main publishing office is located; the state of principal circulation; of emanation; where the defamation was first published; and the law of the forum.

In Prosser, Interstate Publication, 51 Mich.L.Rev. 959 (1953), there is a similar list identifying 10 choices. See, also, Warner, Multistate Publication in Radio and Television, 23 Law & Contemp.Prob. 14 (1958); Note, 77 Harv.L.Rev. 1463 (1964).

3. Hartmann v. Time, Inc., 166 F.2d 127 (3d Cir. 1947), cert. den. 334 U.S. 838 (1948). Plaintiff alleged that he was libeled by an issue of Life magazine which was distributed first in Illinois and later throughout the world. The court held that Pennsylvania, the situs of the court, would follow the single publication rule as a matter of internal law. However, as to injury in other states, also covered by the complaint, it was bound by Pennsylvania conflicts rules to refer to the law of each jurisdiction where the magazine was distributed. In determining the applicable statute of limitations the cause of action was held barred as to publication in all single publication jurisdictions since it was barred in Illinois, the place of first distribution. As to all common law jurisdictions, the statute of limitations of each state applied and the period ran from the last publication in that state. The rule of the Hartmann case was disapproved in Tocco v. Time, Inc., 195 F.Supp. 410 (E.D.Mich.1961) where the court held that a libel action instituted more than one year after the first public release of the offending issue of Life magazine was barred by the Michigan one-year statute of limitations.

2. DÉPEÇAGE

Dépeçage, as the term is used in this book, is the application by a court of the law of different states to govern different issues in a case. As seen from the cases in Chapter 7, it has long been customary for the courts to apply their own law to issues of procedure and the applicable foreign law to issues of substance. More recently, it has come to be recognized that there are situations where it is appropriate to apply the law of different states to different issues of substance. It can be expected that the trend in this direction will accelerate in view of the prevalence of the doctrine that choice of the applicable law should depend upon the precise issue to be determined.

There are, however, countervailing considerations. Application of the law of a number of states obviously places a greater burden upon the courts and the lawyers involved than does application of the law of a single state. There is also the question whether it is appropriate for a court to apply the law of different states to arrive at a result that could not be obtained in a local case based on identical facts by applying the decisional rules of any one of these states. Finally, and most important, application of the law of different states will sometimes result in frustrating the policy underlying one or more of the laws involved. Clearly, there will come a point where such application would be unsound. The general problem is explored in the cases that follow. The Inter–American Convention on General Rules of

Private International Law, Article 9, states: "The different laws that may be applicable to various aspects of one and the same juridical relationship shall be applied harmoniously in order to attain the purposes pursued by each of such laws. Any difficulties that may be caused by their simultaneous application shall be resolved in the light of the requirements of justice in each specific case." Reprinted in I–I Garcia–Amador, The Inter–American System: Treaties, Conventions & Other Documents 486, 487 (1983).

Lillegraven v. Tengs
Supreme Court of Alaska, 1962.
375 P.2d 139.

[Plaintiff was a passenger in a "share-the-expense" auto trip from Seattle to Alaska and sustained injuries when the nonowner-driven car met with an accident en route in British Columbia on October 8, 1958. She commenced an action against the owner on September 26, 1960, within Alaska's two-year statute of limitations, but beyond the one-year period prescribed by Section 80(1) of the Motor Vehicle Act of British Columbia.

Unlike Alaska, which did not hold an owner liable in these circumstances, British Columbia's Motor Vehicle Act imposed liability on the consenting owner. This statute was used as the basis of plaintiff's suit against the owner. The Supreme Court reversed a summary judgment for defendant based on the British Columbia one-year statute.]

■ DIMOND, J.

There is nothing in the law showing that the legislative body of the province of British Columbia gave special consideration to the impact of Section 80 upon the particular right sought to be enforced in this case, as distinguished from other rights to which the act was also applicable. Because of this, we look upon Section 80 as a broad limitation on all tort actions growing out of the operation of motor vehicles, having as its purpose that of all general statutes of limitation, which is to encourage promptness in the prosecution of actions and thus avoid injustice that would result from the assertion of claims after evidence has been lost, memories have faded, and witnesses have disappeared. What minimum period of time for commencing actions would best effect that purpose is a matter of policy of government. British Columbia has declared it to be one year. But Alaska has chosen a longer period of two years, and it is the forum in which the rights of the parties are being determined. In these circumstances, we can see no good reason why this state's policy as to limitation of tort actions should give way to the differing view of a foreign country. The trial court erred in applying the British Columbia one-year period of limitation to plaintiff's claim. . . .

NOTE

Professor Currie disapproved of the result reached in the Lillegraven case on the ground that the British Columbia limitations' period should have been considered to be a substantive limitation on the right. Cavers, The Choice-of-Law Process 38–39 (1965). On the other hand, the decision is approved in Reese, Dépeçage: A Common Phenomenon in Choice of Law, 73 Colum.L.Rev. 58, 69 (1973).

FELLS v. BOWMAN, 274 So.2d 109 (Miss.1973): Action to recover for personal injuries suffered in a collision between a truck and an automobile in Louisiana. All of the parties involved were domiciled in Mississippi. Held: The Mississippi comparative negligence rule, rather than the contributory negligence rule of Louisiana, should be applied since this issue was of interest to Mississippi but of no "legitimate concern" to Louisiana. On the other hand, Louisiana law governed with respect to the proper placement of tail lights since "the primary concern of Louisiana was with the safety of its highways." Was the result correct even though it probably could not have been obtained by the exclusive application of either Mississippi or Louisiana law?

It will be recalled that in Kilberg v. Northeast Airlines, Inc., p. 503, supra, the New York Court of Appeals applied the Massachusetts wrongful death statute except that it disregarded the statute's provision with respect to the limitation of damages and applied the law of New York instead. Was the decision nevertheless correct? Would the answer be different if New York law had not had a wrongful death statute of its own?

MARYLAND CASUALTY CO. v. JACEK, 156 F.Supp. 43 (D.N.J.1957): A New Jersey couple was involved in an automobile accident in New York as a result of the husband's negligence. New Jersey law does not permit spouses to sue each other, while New York law (by amendment of the Domestic Relations Law, sec. 57, after Mertz v. Mertz, p. 379, supra) does. But at the time of the removal of interspousal immunity, the New York Insurance Law, c. 28, § 167, was amended to provide: "No policy or contract shall be deemed to insure against any liability of an insured because of death or injuries to his or her spouse ... unless express provision ... is included in the policy." The insurer brought a diversity action for a declaratory judgment that its policy did not cover liability for the wife's injuries. Applying New Jersey conflicts law, the court granted judgment against the insurer: New York law permits the tort liability; New Jersey law, as the place of making the insurance contract, provides the coverage.

NOTE

Would the appropriateness of this result depend upon whether the purpose of the New Jersey rule of interspousal immunity was to preserve marital harmony or to protect insurance companies against fraud? Did the court promote the purpose of either state's legislative plan?

BRANIFF AIRWAYS, INC. v. CURTISS-WRIGHT CORP., 424 F.2d 427 (2d Cir. 1970): Suit was brought in New York by two passengers against Curtiss-Wright, the manufacturer of the airplane, to recover for personal injuries suffered in a Florida airplane accident. The suit was brought more than three years, but less than six years, after the accident. The suit was barred by the 6-year New York statute of limitations, which started to run at the time of the sale of the engine. The suit was also barred by the 3-year Florida statute which began to run only when the party seeking recovery had discovered, or should have discovered, the defect. The plaintiffs urged, however, that the court should apply the New York 6-year statute, but hold, in accordance with Florida law, that the statutory period began to run only from the date of the accident. A majority of the court rejected this argument and found for the defendant, Curtiss-Wright. There was a dissent. Who was right?

Marie v. Garrison

13 Abb.N.C. 210 (N.Y.1883).

[The plaintiffs alleged that the defendant, Garrison, a large bondholder of a railroad in Missouri, had instituted a suit in Missouri to foreclose the mortgage. To induce the plaintiffs not to defend the foreclosure action, Garrison had written a letter in Missouri in which he proposed that if he bought in the property at the foreclosure sale and if they would organize a successor corporation which would reimburse him for his expenditures, he would convey the property to the successor corporation. On the faith of the letter, the plaintiffs had withdrawn their opposition to the foreclosure. The plaintiffs further alleged that after the decree of foreclosure but before the foreclosure sale they had surrendered the letter to the defendant in New York because of a modification of the agreement. Under the new agreement, the defendant had orally promised that if he were the purchaser at the foreclosure sale *he* would organize the successor company and convey the property to it. The defendant purchased at the foreclosure but refused to carry out the agreement. The defendant moved to exclude the evidence of the alleged contract. The cause was referred to Dwight, Referee, who denied the motion, saying:]

"The introduction of the letter in evidence is objected to by the defendant as not complying with the New York Statute of Frauds, on the ground that it does not 'express the consideration' . . . in the New York statute an agreement in contravention of its provisions is declared to be 'void'.* . . .

"Can it fairly be said that a contract declared 'void' by statute still subsists *as a contract*, and that the only effect of the statute is to deprive a party of a remedy? Is such a word as 'void' a mere word of *evidence?*

---

* The New York statute provided: "Every contract for the leasing for a longer period than one year, or for the sale of any lands or any interest in lands, shall be void unless the contract, or some note or memorandum thereof, expressing the consideration, be in writing and be subscribed by the party by whom the lease or sale is to be made."—Eds.

"I think not. I regard the word 'void' as a word of substance, and not as a mere word of procedure. In that view, the statute cannot, by accepted rules under the Conflict of Laws, be applied to contracts made in other States, and accordingly not to the present case. . . .

"I now propose to examine the point whether the Statute of Frauds of Missouri has been violated so as to affect the validity of the contract or its provability in this court.

"Considering still the subject of the real estate embraced within the letter, I find that the statute of Missouri differs from our own in important respects. . . .

"The contract for the sale of land is not made *void* in Missouri, if the statute is not complied with. It is only enacted that no 'action shall be brought,' in that case. Under the rule in Leroux v. Brown, [1852] 12 C.B. 801, 138 E.R. 1119, the remedy *in Missouri only* is affected by these words. . . .

"The conclusion then is that this letter, whether tested by the law of New York or Missouri, does not trench upon any provision of the Statute of Frauds. . . ."

NOTE

See Reese, Dépeçage: A Common Phenomenon in Choice of Law, 73 Colum.L.Rev. 58 (1973); Weintraub, Beyond Dépeçage: A "New Rule" Approach to Choice of Law in Consumer Credit Transactions and a Critique of the Territorial Application of the Uniform Consumer Credit Code, 25 Case Western Res.L.Rev. 16 (1974); Wilde, Dépeçage in the Choice of Tort Law, 41 S.Calif.L.Rev. 329 (1968).

European conflicts law has traditionally disfavored dépeçage. Modern law, however, permits law-splitting by the parties and, exceptionally, also when the applicable law is determined by the court. Art. 3(1) of the Rome Convention on the Law Applicable to Contractual Obligations, supra p. 547, provides that "the parties can select the law applicable to the whole or a part only of the contract." Art. 4(1), which provides for the application of the law with the "closest connection" to the contract when the parties have not stipulated the applicable law, states that if a part of the contract is severable and if it has a closer connection to the law of a different state (than to the state principally identified), that law may be applied by way of "exception." Commenting on the German version of Art. 3(1) (Art. 27 German EGBGB), Martiny states: "Application of different laws to a contract carries with it the danger of inconsistencies and gaps: the splitting leads to legal insecurity. On the other hand, it may comport with party interests and economic needs and circumstances to apply the law of different legal systems." Martiny, in 7 Münchener Kommentar, EGBGB anno. 33 preceding Art. 33 (2d ed. 1990) (translation by eds.). From among the contributions in the Continental literature, see Jayme, Betrachtungen zur "dépeçage" im internationalen Privatrecht, Festschrift für Kegel 253 (1987); Patocchi, Règles de rattachement localisatrices et règles de rattachement de caractère substantiel (1985).

3. NO FAULT

No-fault statutes do essentially two things: (1) they provide that the insured and some designated classes of persons can claim reimbursement without regard to fault from the insured's own insurance company for certain losses resulting from injuries sustained in a motor vehicle accident and (2) they eliminate certain negligence claims in tort unless the injuries sustained are of a defined type or result in financial loss in excess of a prescribed amount. See Keeton and O'Connell, Basic Protection for the Traffic Victim (1965); Symposium on No-Fault Automobile Insurance, 71 Colum.L.Rev. 189 et seq. (1971). Most no-fault statutes contain provisions directed to their territorial application. The relevant provisions of a typical statute appear below.

Usually choice-of-law problems in this area will concern the extent to which the no-fault statute of one state will be given effect in another state. Suppose that persons domiciled in a state that would allow an action in tort are involved in an automobile accident in a state which has enacted a no-fault statute, and that subsequently one of these persons brings suit against the other in tort in the home state. Will the court give effect to the statute by dismissing the suit? A similar problem can arise as between the two no-fault states in a situation where the injured party is precluded from suing in tort under the no-fault statute of the state of injury but not under that of his home state where he brings suit.

Provisions in no-fault statutes that are directed to their territorial application involve two important questions. One relates to the scope of applicability of their benefits: To whom do these apply in cases that involve multi-state elements? The other relates to exemptions from tort liability: When, if ever, are non-residents given exemption from tort liability by force of a no-fault statute? Do residents retain statutory exemptions when they travel outside the state? These questions raise issues of constitutionality as well as sound policy. See Pierce, Institutional Aspects of Tort Reform, 73 Calif.L.Rev. 917 (1985).

NOTES

1. The New York no-fault statute's limitation of personal injury suits to "serious injury" was held inapplicable to an accident outside New York (*i.e.*, New Jersey) involving solely New York residents. Hence, it was improper to charge the jury that to recover plaintiff must prove a serious injury. Morgan v. Bisorni, 100 A.D.2d 956, 475 N.Y.S.2d 98 (2d Dep't 1984).

2. In O'Connor v. O'Connor, 201 Conn. 632, 519 A.2d 13 (1986), the parties were passenger and driver in a one-car accident in Quebec, where the no-fault statute barred a common-law recovery. The no-fault statute in Connecticut, where the parties were resident, would allow a tort suit. Employing the approach of the Restatement, Second, and an interest analysis, the court allowed the action to go forward.

3. In Thomas v. Hanmer, 109 A.D.2d 80, 489 N.Y.S.2d 802 (4th Dep't 1985), the issue was whether the Quebec no-fault statute applied to New York occupants of two New York cars that collided in Quebec. Using a Babcock-type analysis the court held that New York law applied and permitted the suit. In Blais v. Deyo, 92 A.D.2d 998, 1000, 461 N.Y.S.2d 471, 473 (3d Dep't 1983), affirmed 60 N.Y.2d 679, 468 N.Y.S.2d 103, 455 N.E.2d 662 (1983), the defendant was a New York resident,

but the plaintiffs were not. The court dismissed the action on *forum non conveniens* grounds, saying in its opinion: "Quebec has a more substantial interest than New York in the compensation of plaintiffs, residents of Quebec, when the accident occurred in Quebec."

4. In Wierbinski v. State Farm Mutual Automobile Insurance Co., 477 F.Supp. 659 (W.D.Pa.1979), the plaintiff, a New York domiciliary, was injured in a one-car accident in Pennsylvania. Plaintiff's medical and rehabilitative expenses were far in excess of the basic loss coverage available under the New York No–Fault Act. The court found that Pennsylvania was the state of most significant relationship and that, accordingly, Pennsylvania law governed. The Pennsylvania no-fault statute, however, provides that the basic loss benefits shall be determined by the no-fault law of the state of the victim's domicile, in this case New York. Ultimately, however, the plaintiff was permitted to recover the larger amount provided by Pennsylvania law, since, under the New York statute, the insurance company was required to provide coverage in the amount required by the law of any state in which the covered vehicle was involved in an accident.

Uniform Motor Vehicle Accident Reparations Act (1972)

14 U.L.A. 35

SECTION 1. [Definitions]

(a) In this Act:

(1) . . .

(2) "Basic reparation benefits" mean benefits providing reimbursement for net loss suffered through injury arising out of the maintenance or use of a motor vehicle. . . .

(3) "Basic reparation insured" means:

(i) a person identified by name as an insured in a contract of basic reparation insurance complying with this Act . . . ; and

(ii) while residing in the same household with a named insured, the following persons not identified by name as an insured in any other contract of basic reparation insurance complying with this Act: a spouse or other relative of a named insured; and a minor in the custody of a named insured or of a relative residing in the same household with a named insured. A person resides in the same household if he usually makes his home in the same family unit, even though he temporarily lives elsewhere.

SECTION 2. [Right to Basic Reparation Benefits]

(a) If the accident causing injury occurs in this State, every person suffering loss from injury arising out of maintenance or use of a motor vehicle has a right to basic reparation benefits.

(b) If the accident causing injury occurs outside this State, the following persons and their survivors suffering loss from injury arising out of maintenance or use of a motor vehicle have a right to basic reparation benefits:

(1) basic reparation insureds; and

(2) the driver and other occupants of a secured vehicle....

COMMENT

All persons injured in motor vehicle accidents within this State are entitled to receive basic reparation benefits for the loss suffered, with two limited exceptions. Limited disqualifications are provided for some converters of motor vehicles (Section 21) and those intentionally causing injury to themselves or other persons (Section 22).... As to accidents occurring outside this State, basic reparation insureds and persons occupying the secured vehicle are entitled to basic reparation benefits. Non-occupants, such as pedestrians who are not basic reparation insureds, are not entitled to basic reparation benefits solely because they have been injured in an out-of-State accident involving a secured vehicle....

SECTION 5. [Partial Abolition of Tort Liability]

[This section provides that tort liability for automobile accidents occurring "in this state" is abolished except if the vehicle involved is not covered by required insurance; or the harm caused is the result of a failure by a repair business; is intentional; exceeds amounts recoverable as basic reparation benefits; or if the accident causes death or severe injuries of specified kinds.]

SECTION 9. [Included Coverages]

(a) An insurance contract which purports to provide coverage for basic reparation benefits ... has the legal effect of including all coverages required by this Act.

(b) Notwithstanding any contrary provision in it, every contract of liability insurance for injury, wherever issued, covering ownership, maintenance, or use of a motor vehicle ... includes basic reparation benefit coverages and minimum security for tort liabilities required by this Act, while it is in this State, and qualifies as security covering the vehicle.

(c) An insurer authorized to transact or transacting business in this State may not exclude, in any contract of liability insurance for injury, wherever issued, covering ownership, maintenance, or use of a motor vehicle ... the basic reparation benefit coverages and required minimum security for tort liabilities required by this Act, while the vehicle is in this State.

COMMENT

Subsection (a) assures that every contract purporting to do so contains the mandated basic reparation and liability coverages regardless of the language actually used in the contract.

Subsection (b) explicitly applies to an insurer even though the insured is a nonresident of this State, the insurer is not qualified to do business in this State, and the only contact of the insurer with this State is that its insured permitted operation of the insured vehicle in this State. The effect of this provision is to convert a foreign insurer's automobile or motor vehicle liability policy or contract to the coverages required under this Act if the insured vehicle is registered in this State or operated in this State with the owner's permission. Since only "liability" insurance contracts are converted, an insurance contract limited to collision and comprehensive coverages is unaffected by this provision. Given the ready ability of the owner of a motor vehicle to drive his vehicle from state to state within a few days over an interstate highway system, it is unreasonable for an insurer to argue that it could not contemplate out-of-state use of the motor vehicle, or that it could only contemplate or foresee use within a limited geographic area. Accordingly, operation of the insured vehicle within the State, standing alone, should be a sufficient contact allowing the State to impose its substantive laws upon the out-of-State insurer of an out-of-State vehicle. Cf. Clay v. Sun Insurance Office, 377 U.S. 179 (1964) [p. 346, supra].

Subsection (c) is, in part, a safety valve in the event subsection (b) were held to be unconstitutional. Without reference to where the contract is written, it requires, if the insurer is authorized to transact or is transacting business in this State, that the coverages required by this Act be included in any automobile or motor vehicle liability insurance contract if the insured vehicle is registered or operated in this State. . . .

NOTES

1. Is there justification for having the no-fault provisions of the Act apply to accidents within the state which involve only out-of-state automobiles and in which only nonresidents are injured? Conversely, is there good reason for making these provisions inapplicable to the claims of a resident of the state who, although not himself a "basic reparation insured," is injured outside the state by an automobile that is licensed and insured in the state?

2. Is there justification for giving some extraterritorial application to the no-fault benefits of the Act (Section 2) and for restricting exemption from tort liability to accidents within the state (Section 5)? Would it be better to have the victim recover under the no-fault plan of the victim's domicile, or if there was no such plan available there, the no-fault plan of the place of accident?

KOZYRIS, NO-FAULT AUTOMOBILE INSURANCE AND THE CONFLICT OF LAWS—CUTTING THE GORDIAN KNOT HOME-STYLE, 1972 Duke L.J. 331, 335–336.

It is too early to predict the outcome of the no-fault versus negligence liability battle. . . . If opposition to no-fault remains strong, however, a permanent stalemate may result, with some states switching to no-fault while others retain negligence liability. In either case, a "crazy-quilt" pattern lasting for many years is quite likely to develop, and the problems of choice of law will be multiplied to an unprecedented degree.

"Conflict of laws controversies have not reached the proportions that one might have expected in the early 1970s when the no fault tide was gaining momentum. Now with the country split evenly into states which have some system of reparations for economic loss without regard to fault, and another camp of about equal size adhering to the traditional torts system, it is still possible that there might be growth in the volume of conflicts cases in this area of the law.... J. King, No Fault Automobile Law 381 (1987)."

NOTES

1. In the above-quoted article, Professor Kozyris examined a number of no-fault laws and concluded (at page 405):

> "A personal system of choice of law incorporating explicit directives based on domicil or habitual residence, adequately defined, giving to all parties the benefits of, and imposing on them the obligations under, their own home state law, with certain minor territorial exceptions for special problems, is clearly more consistent with the goals of no-fault automobile reparations than a territorial or any other presently known system."

2. In a follow-up article, "An Interim Update," 1973 Duke L.J. 1009, Professor Kozyris defended his thesis by comparing the operation of his proposed principles in a modified hypothetical version of Tooker v. Lopez (Note 5, p. 525, supra). He found that his proposed approach worked much better than choice-of-law provisions of various no-fault statutes.

3. There have been proposals for the enactment of a federal No-Fault Motor Vehicle Insurance Act. See, e.g., S. 354 and H.R. 19000 (94th Congress). This Act would provide for a federal system of no-fault that would take effect in states which either have enacted no legislation of this sort or whose legislation does not meet federal standards. Under § 110(c) of the Act, no-fault benefits would be determined in accordance with the law of the state of the victim's domicile provided that this law satisfies federal standards. The proposed Act was considered by a number of sessions of Congress, but has not been enacted.

4. WORKERS' COMPENSATION

Workers' compensation statutes generally impose liability upon employers for work-related injuries to employees regardless of fault. As a quid pro quo, employers are relieved of ordinary liability in tort and wrongful death. Awards recoverable by injured employees under the compensation systems are usually limited by fixed schedules, and in each state the program is ordinarily administered by special tribunals of prescribed powers and procedures. In consequence, relief under a particular state's workers' compensation system is usually obtainable only in that state, in the manner and amounts prescribed. While this inhibition on other states is not constitutionally mandated, Crider v. Zurich Insurance Co., 380 U.S. 39 (1965) (set forth at Note 3, p. 211, supra), it is so common that when suit is brought in State F for workers' compensation benefits, choice-of-law analysis is limited to the territorial scope of the F Statute. F uses its own special administrative tribunals and award system even though other states could properly have applied their compensation machinery had the employee chosen to assert his claim in one of them. Thus, Restatement, Second, Conflict of Laws declares in Section 182: "Relief may be awarded under the workmen's compensation statute of a State of the United States, although the statute of a sister State is also applicable."

Yet, significant choice-of-law problems arise when multistate industrial accidents occur because of the interaction of the workers' compensation and tort law regimes. For instance, a statute of the state where the employee was hired, or of the state where he was injured, may explicitly provide that the employee's remedies under the particular workers' compensation system of the particular state are exclusive of any rights he might otherwise have under the local law of another state.

The manifold possibilities of choice-of-law problems that flow from the circumstance that many states have a sufficient relationship to apply their tort or compensation laws to industrial injuries become apparent when we consider how many of these there may be in a given case: the state where the employee was injured; where he contracted to be employed; where he lives; where he usually works; where the employer supervises his activities; where the parties have agreed he will look for compensation in the event of injury, etc. See Restatement, Second, Conflict of Laws § 181. The Reporter's Note to Section 181 collects numerous illustrative cases.

These numerous possibilities are compounded when the employment and accident circumstances are not in the simple pattern of an employee sustaining an on-the-job injury in which only his own employer is a potential source of damage benefits. The following case, Wilson v. Faull, suggests a few of the ramifications.

Wilson v. Faull

Supreme Court of New Jersey, 1958.
27 N.J. 105, 141 A.2d 768.

[Action in tort by an employee of a subcontractor against the general contractor. The defendant, Faull, who resided and maintained his regular place of business in New Jersey, made a contract in Pennsylvania to repair a building there. In New Jersey he made a subcontract with Tragle for part of the repairs, and he agreed to erect a scaffold on which Tragle's employees would work. The plaintiff, Wilson, who resided in New Jersey as did Faull and Tragle, was hired in New Jersey by Tragle and was sent to the Pennsylvania job. While at work in Pennsylvania, Wilson fell from the scaffold that the general contractor, Faull, had erected. For the resulting injuries he obtained workers' compensation in New Jersey from Tragle, his employer. He then brought the present common law negligence action in New Jersey against the general contractor, Faull.

Faull, the general contractor, carried workers' compensation insurance for plaintiff's benefit under the Pennsylvania compensation law. The subcontractor, Tragle, carried workers' compensation insurance for plaintiff's benefit under the New Jersey act. The laws of the two states differed as to the liability of the general contractor to the employees of the subcontractor. Under the Pennsylvania statute, the general contractor was liable for the payment of compensation to the subcontractor's employees; but the general contractor was granted immunity from common law liability for negligence. Under the New Jersey law a general contractor was liable for compensation to an employee of a subcontractor only if the subcontractor had not secured workers' compensation insurance. Where the subcontractor had procured compensation insurance, as he had in the present case, the general contractor was not granted immunity from liability in negligence to the subcontractor's employee.

The trial court granted the defendant's motion for summary judgment on the ground the law of the place of injury controlled the right of action in tort. On appeal, the Appellate Division reversed, since in its view the choice-of-law problem was concerned not with tort law but with "the regulation of employment relations" and the law of New Jersey should be applied as that state had "the preponderance of significant contacts with the employment relationship involved".]

■ PROCTOR, J. ... Workmen's compensation laws were designed to provide an expeditious and certain remedy for employees who sustain work injuries by the statutory imposition of absolute but limited and determinate liability upon the employer.... These laws generally provide that the compensation remedy is exclusive. The theory behind this exclusiveness is that the laws provide predictable compensation for any on the job injury. They represent a compromise that inures to the ultimate benefit of both employer and employee. The employee surrenders his right to seek damages in an action at law in return for swift recovery independent of proof of fault. The employer gives up common law defenses to negligence suits and assumes an absolute liability to provide compensation; in return he is granted immunity from common law negligence suits by his employees....

... If the injured employee is seeking a compensation remedy, application by the forum of its compensation law, whether it be the state of the injury or the state of the contract or the state of the employment relation, does no violence to the basic principles of workmen's compensation. The employee is provided a prompt and certain recovery and the employer's liability is limited to that provided by the compensation law of the forum, which has a sufficient interest in the work-injury to justify the application of its own law. Nor is there any constitutional impediment to the forum's application of its own compensation law, whether the forum be the state of the injury ... or the state of contract or employment relation ... notwithstanding that the compensation law of another interested state purports to provide an exclusive remedy....

However, where the injured employee seeks to maintain a common law tort action against his employer in one of two or more states having a legitimate interest in the work-injury, the forum has almost invariably applied the law of the state in which the employer has provided compensation insurance and whose law granted such employer immunity from common law negligence actions by the employee, and dismissed the suit.... This choice of law has been made by ... the forum, whether it was the state of the injury, ... or the state of employment relation, ...

This almost universal recognition by the forum of the compensation law of a sister state which grants immunity to an employer who has provided compensation insurance for an employee, irrespective of the interest of the state of the forum, cannot be said to be the result of an inflexible or mechanical application by the forum of "tort," "contract" or "employment relation" conflict of laws principles. Instead, the recognition of the law of a sister state in this situation reflects the basic philosophy underlying the adoption of workmen's compensation acts by the several states as the exclusive remedy for industrial accidents....

The question remains whether this reasoning applies with equal force when an injured employee of a subcontractor brings a common law negligence action in the state of contract or employment relation against a general contractor, who under the compensation law of the state of the injury is substituted for the immediate employer for compensation purposes....

We think ... there is no substantial difference between an immediate employer-subcontractor who is obligated to provide compensation coverage for his employees, and a general contractor, who, under the law of the state of the injury, is substituted in the employment relation for the immediate employer and becomes primarily liable for workmen's compensation to the employees of the immediate employer....

Choice of law in the situation presented here should not be governed by wholly fortuitous circumstances such as where the injury occurred, or where the contract of employment was executed, or where the parties resided or maintained their places of business, or any combination of these "contacts." Rather, it should be founded on broader considerations of basic compensation policy which the conflicting laws call into play, with a view toward achieving a certainty of result and effecting fairness between the parties within the framework of that policy. The injured workman has a prompt and practical compensation remedy in any state having a legitimate interest in his welfare. The person who provides that compensation in an interested state has a definitive liability which is predictable with some degree of accuracy and is granted an immunity from an employee's suit for damages which does not disappear whenever his enterprise chances to cross state lines and the suit is brought in another state....

The judgment of the Appellate Division is reversed and the judgment of the trial court is reinstated.

[The concurring opinion of WEINTRAUB, C.J. is omitted.]

NOTES

1. It is clear that on the facts of the principal case, New Jersey would have been constitutionally privileged to apply its own local law to hold Faull liable in tort. Carroll v. Lanza, 349 U.S. 408 (1955), set forth at p. 339, supra.

2. Restatement, Second, Conflict of Laws § 184 provides that a defendant should not be exposed to liability in tort or wrongful death at the suit of an employee when the defendant has been declared immune from such liability by the workers'

compensation statute of any state under which the employee has already obtained an award for the injury or under the statute of any one of a number of enumerated states under which the employee could obtain such an award.

3. Approving the Restatement's position and reasoning is Elston v. Industrial Lift Truck Co., 420 Pa. 97, 216 A.2d 318 (1966). The Pennsylvania supplier of a forklift truck which had allegedly injured a Pennsylvanian on the job in New Jersey was sued at common law for tort damages. The supplier tried to join Elston's New Jersey employer, but failed. The court held that even though partial contribution from the employer was allowed by the Pennsylvania rule, in the interests of equitable distribution of loss from industrial accidents, the immunity given the employer by New Jersey's compensation system should prevail: "The extent to which the New Jersey program of workmen's compensation should assimilate the equities underlying contribution is a determination more appropriately to be made by that state."

For a case permitting recovery in tort in situations where such recovery would not be permitted by § 184 of the Restatement, see O'Connor v. Lee-Hy Paving Corp., 579 F.2d 194 (2d Cir. 1978).

4. Are Wilson v. Faull and Elston v. Industrial Lift Truck Co. examples of cases where the forum subordinates its own policies and interests to what it deems to be the basic policy underlying the substantive field involved?

5. In Gentry v. Jett, 235 Ark. 20, 356 S.W.2d 736 (1962), an Arkansas employee, who had been injured in Oklahoma, obtained recovery in tort in an Arkansas court against the tortfeasor by application of Oklahoma law. When the employee subsequently sought workers' compensation against his employer in Arkansas, he was met with the defense that under Oklahoma law a workers' compensation award is barred after there has been recovery in tort from a third-party tortfeasor. Held for the employee. Full faith and credit does not prevent Arkansas from giving relief under its own workers' compensation act in these circumstances.

6. To what extent, if any, does full faith and credit preclude an employee who has obtained a workers' compensation award in one state from obtaining a second award for the same injury in another state? Thomas v. Washington Gas Light Co., p. 273, supra.

5. ADMIRALTY

Lauritzen v. Larsen
Supreme Court of the United States, 1953.
345 U.S. 571, 73 S.Ct. 921, 97 L.Ed. 1254.

■ MR. JUSTICE JACKSON delivered the opinion of the Court.

The key issue in this case is whether statutes of the United States should be applied to this claim of maritime tort. Larsen, a Danish seaman, while temporarily in New York joined the crew of the *Randa*, a ship of Danish flag and registry, owned by petitioner, a Danish citizen. Larsen signed ship's articles, written in Danish, providing that the rights of crew members would be governed by Danish law and by the employer's contract with the Danish Seamen's Union, of which Larsen was a member. He was negligently injured aboard the *Randa* in the course of employment, while in Havana harbor.

Respondent brought suit under the Jones Act on the law side of the District Court for the Southern District of New York and demanded a jury. Petitioner contended that Danish law was applicable and that, under it, respondent had received all of the compensation to which he was entitled. [The district court ruled that American rather than Danish law applied and gave judgment for the plaintiff.] The Court of Appeals, Second Circuit, affirmed.

[The Supreme Court first conceded that taken literally the Jones Act applied, but]

... [I]t has long been accepted in maritime jurisprudence that " ... if any construction otherwise be possible, an Act will not be construed as applying to foreigners in respect to acts done by them outside the dominions of the sovereign power enacting. That is a rule based on international law, by which one sovereign power is bound to respect the subjects and the rights of all other sovereign powers outside its own territory." Lord Russell of Killowen in The Queen v. Jameson [1896], 2 Q.B. 425, 430....

Congress could not have been unaware of the necessity of construction imposed upon courts by such generality of language and ... that in the absence of more definite directions than are contained in the Jones Act it would be applied by the courts to foreign events, foreign ships and foreign seamen only in accordance with the usual doctrine and practices of maritime law.

Respondent places great stress upon the assertion that petitioner's commerce and contacts with the ports of the United States are frequent and regular ... But the virtue and utility of sea-borne commerce lies in its frequent and important contacts with more than one country. If, to serve some immediate interest, the courts of each were to exploit every such contact to the limit of its power, it is not difficult to see that a multiplicity of conflicting and overlapping burdens would blight international carriage by sea....

Maritime law, like our municipal law, has attempted to avoid or resolve conflicts between competing laws by ascertaining and valuing points of contact between the transaction and the states or governments whose competing laws are involved. The criteria, in general, appear to be arrived at from weighing of the significance of one or more connecting factors between the shipping transaction regulated and the national interest served by the assertion of authority....

... [I]n dealing with international commerce we cannot be unmindful of the necessity for mutual forbearance if retaliations are to be avoided; nor should we forget that any contact which we hold sufficient to warrant application of our law to a foreign transaction will logically be as strong a warrant for a foreign country to apply its law to an American transaction.

In the case before us, two foreign nations can claim some connecting factor with this tort—Denmark, because, among other reasons, the ship and the seaman were Danish nationals; Cuba, because the tortious conduct occurred and caused injury in Cuban waters. The United States may also claim contacts because the seaman had been hired in and was returned to the United States, which also is the state of the forum. We therefore review the several factors which, alone or in combination, are generally conceded to influence choice of law to govern a tort claim, particularly a maritime tort claim, and the weight and significance accorded them.

1. *Place of the Wrongful Act.*—The solution most commonly accepted as to torts in our municipal and in international law is to supply the law of the place where the acts giving rise to the liability occurred, the *lex loci delicti commissi.* This rule ... would indicate application of the law of Cuba, in whose domain the actionable wrong took place. The test of location of the wrongful act or omission, however sufficient for torts ashore, is of limited application to shipboard torts, because of the varieties of legal authority over waters she may navigate....

2. *Law of the Flag.*—Perhaps the most venerable and universal rule of maritime law relevant to our problem is that which gives cardinal importance to the law of the flag....

3. *Allegiance or Domicile of the Injured....* the longstanding rule ... was that the nationality of the vessel for jurisdictional purposes was attributed to all her crew.... Surely during service under a foreign flag some duty of allegiance is due. But, also, each nation has a legitimate interest that its nationals and permanent inhabitants be not maimed or disabled from self-support.... We need not, however, weigh the seaman's nationality against that of the ship, for here the two coincide without resort to fiction....

4. *Allegiance of the Defendant Shipowner.*—... in recent years a practice has grown, particularly among American shipowners, to avoid stringent shipping laws by seeking foreign registration ... Confronted with such operations, our courts on occasion have pressed beyond the formalities of more or less nominal foreign registration to enforce against American shipowners the obligations which our law places upon them. But here ... it appears beyond doubt that this owner is a Dane by nationality and domicile.

5. *Place of Contract.*—Place of contract, which was New York, is the factor on which respondent chiefly relies to invoke American law....

The place of contracting in this instance ... was fortuitous.... The practical effect of making the *lex loci contractus* govern all tort claims during the service would be to subject a ship to a multitude of systems of law, to put some of the crew in a more advantageous position than others, and not unlikely in the long run to diminish hirings in ports of countries that take best care of their seamen.

But if contract law is nonetheless to be considered, we face the fact that this contract was explicit that the Danish law and the contract with the Danish union were to control....

6. *Inaccessibility of Foreign Forum.*—It is argued ... that justice requires adjudication under American law to save seamen expense and loss of time in returning to a foreign forum. This might be a persuasive

argument for exercising a discretionary jurisdiction to adjudge a controversy; but it is not persuasive as to the law by which it shall be judged....

7. *The Law of the Forum.*—It is urged that, since an American forum has perfected its jurisdiction over the parties and defendant does more or less frequent and regular business within the forum state, it should apply its own law to the controversy between them.... The purpose of a conflict-of-laws doctrine is to assure that a case will be treated in the same way under the appropriate law regardless of the fortuitous circumstances which often determine the forum. Jurisdiction of maritime cases in all countries is so wide and the nature of its subject matter so far-flung that there would be no justification for altering the law of a controversy just because local jurisdiction of the parties is obtainable....

This review of the connecting factors which either maritime law or our municipal law of conflicts regards as significant in determining the law applicable to a claim of actionable wrong shows an overwhelming preponderance in favor of Danish law.... [The decision below was reversed on the theory that Danish, not American, law applied. Justice Black dissented.]

NOTE

Romero v. International Terminal Operating Co., 358 U.S. 354 (1959) applied the seven *Lauritzen* factors to deny coverage under the Jones Act or general maritime law of the United States to a Spanish seaman injured in United States territorial waters off Hoboken, New Jersey. Hellenic Lines Ltd. v. Rhoditis, added "base of operations" to the seven *Lauritzen* factors to permit Jones Act recovery for a Greek seaman injured in American territorial waters on a Greek ship based in the United States and operated by a Greek corporation, which had its main office in New York.

Does *Lauritzen* analyze the seven factors it enumerated in the manner a modern court would under a "most significant relationship" approach? When the Court's analysis is complete, the seven factors are reduced to only three that are relevant when suit is by a seaman against the shipowner: the law of the flag which "must prevail unless some heavy counterweight appears"; the allegiance or domicile of the seaman; and the allegiance of the shipowner. Are these the only contacts that are likely to be related to some policy of compensating injured seamen? *Rhoditis* seems even closer to a most-significant-relationship approach: "The significance of one or more factors must be considered in light of the national interest served by the assertion of Jones Act jurisdiction. Moreover, the list of seven factors in *Lauritzen* was not intended as exhaustive." 398 U.S. at 309.

State law applies in admiralty cases if there is no established admiralty rule and if there is no need to fashion one, because there is no pressing need for a uniform federal rule governing the particular issue. Wilburn Boat Co. v. Fireman's Fund Ins. Co., 348 U.S. 310, 314 (1955). When federal courts use admiralty choice-of-law rules to select state law, they expressly utilize a most significant relationship approach. Albany Ins. Co. v. Anh Thi Kieu, 927 F.2d 882 (5th Cir.), cert. denied, 502 U.S. 901 (1991), held that state law on the effect of misrepresentations by the insured is not pre-empted by federal admiralty law and stated: "Modern choice of law analysis, whether maritime or not, generally requires the application of the law of the state with the 'most significant relationship' to the substantive issue in question." Id. at 891. See also Lien Ho Hsing Steel Enterprise Co. v. Weihtag, 738 F.2d 1455, 1458 (9th Cir.1984) (whether a maritime insurance broker is the insurer's agent is determined by "the law of the state with the greatest interest in the issue"); Edinburgh Assur. Co. v. R.L. Burns Corp., 479 F.Supp. 138, 152–53 (C.D.Cal.1979), aff'd in part and rev'd in part on other grounds, 669 F.2d 1259 (9th Cir.1982) (applying "the points of contact analysis of *Lauritzen* and *Romero*" and holding that English law determines the meaning of "actual total loss," because England has "the most significant relationship to the transaction," citing Restatement (Second) of Conflict of Laws §§ 188 and 193).

---

6. ASSIGNMENT OF CONTRACTUAL RIGHTS

Assignment of legal interests not embodied in negotiable instruments may raise choice-of-law problems. One question is whether the right is assignable. If so, other questions concern the legal effect of the assignment on the assignor and assignee and on the obligor of the underlying obligation as well as questions of priority among successive assignees.

To a large degree the importance of formulating common law conflicts rules about assignments has been eclipsed by the nearly universal enactment of the Uniform Commercial Code, which has all but eliminated prospects of serious conflicts in this area. Assignments of future wages and of life insurance benefits have accounted for a large fraction of the cases that have come to the courts in recent years.

DOWNS v. AMERICAN MUTUAL LIABILITY INSURANCE CO., 14 N.Y.2d 266, 251 N.Y.S.2d 19, 200 N.E.2d 204 (1964): H and W, New York residents, entered into a separation agreement by which H assigned validly, under New York, one-half his future wages to W. He moved to Massachusetts and was employed as a salesman by the Insurance Company. In New York, W sued to compel the Insurance Company to pay her half of H's wages and was met by the defense that they were not assignable under a Massachusetts statute. Even on the assumption the Massachusetts statute barred an assignment for family support, the Court of Appeals (per Fuld, J.) said:

> "... Since New York undoubtedly has the most significant relationship and contacts with the assignment and a predominant interest and concern in assuring support to a New York wife and New York children, its law is applicable. (Cf. Auten v. Auten, 308 N.Y. 155, 124 N.E.2d 99, 50 A.L.R.2d 246; Morris Plan Industrial Bank of N.Y. v. Gunning, 295 N.Y. 324, 329–330, 67 N.E.2d 510, 511–512.) The assignment of wages was made in New York by a New York husband and, quite obviously, without regard as to where he would be employed, for the protection of his family. The marital domicile of the parties was New York, the separation agreement recited that the law applicable was that of New York and the agreement and the obligations of the parties are embodied in a New York judgment...."

On the ground of the manifest "paramount interest" of New York, the Court affirmed a judgment for W. How could New York law properly be applied to determine the assignability of wages paid in Massachusetts by a Massachusetts employer?

A contrary result was reached on similar facts in Freedom Finance Co., Inc. v. New Jersey Bell Telephone Co., 123 N.J.Super. 255, 302 A.2d 184 (1973), affirmed 126 N.J.Super. 375, 314 A.2d 614 (1974).

NOTES

1. As to assignability of a contractual right, Section 208, Restatement, Second, Conflict of Laws uses its familiar formula, referring the dispute to the local law of the state with the most significant relationship to the contract and the parties with respect to the issue.

The European Convention (Art. 12) calls for the application of the law applicable to the assignment "under this Convention" for the determination of the rights and obligations of assignor and assignee. This will be either the law of the state with the "closest connection," above at p. 544 or the law chosen by the parties. The law governing the right assigned determines assignability of the right, the relationship between assignee and debtor, and the discharge of the debtor's obligations. Do these rules track the Restatement (Second) approach?

2. Section 209 of the Restatement, Second, uses the same formula (making allowance for the change in issue) to determine whether the assignor had capacity, observed the required formalities, needed to receive consideration, was subjected to duress, etc., and the nature of interests transferred as a result of the assignment. Thus, whether a life insurance policy is assignable is determined under Section 208; whether the assignee must have an insurable interest, by Section 209. (Id., *Comment a.*) Sections 210 and 211 treat, respectively, the law governing the effect of the assignment on the obligor of the underlying obligation and questions of priority as between two or more assignees.

3. New England Mut. Life Insurance Co. v. Spence, 104 F.2d 665 (2d Cir. 1939). The insured took out a life insurance policy in New York, payable to his wife, at a time when the parties resided in New York. Subsequently they became domiciled in Texas, where the wife obtained a divorce. Under Texas law the divorce decree operated to pass the wife's interest in the policy to the husband. L. Hand, J.: "The question before us is whether the law of conflict of laws of New York will treat as valid an involuntary transfer of the wife's chose in action, valid by the law of the place where both parties resided. There can be no doubt that if the transfer had been voluntary, i.e. by assignment, the courts of New York would follow the law of the place where the assignment took place . . . We can see no reason to distinguish an involuntary transfer, when both parties are present within the state, where the transaction occurs; a fortiori, when they are both domiciled there. There is no magic in consent . . . this part of the law of Texas is not so repugnant to notions of justice prevalent in New York that we must reject it." Judge Clark, dissenting, stated that the Texas decree did not operate as a transfer, and that the case was not one of assignment. The peculiar Texas law was in effect merely a rule under which a divorced wife could not prove in a Texas court that she had an insurable interest under the policy. The question was solely the identity of the beneficiary under the terms of the policy, a contract question to be determined by the law of New York as the place of contracting.

For a more recent case reaching a similar result on similar reasoning, see Travelers Insurance Co. v. Fields, 451 F.2d 1292 (6th Cir. 1971).

7. ARBITRATION

Commercial Arbitration—An Atypical Conflicts Problem

A multistate contract containing a provision for submission of disputes arising under it to arbitration presents an atypical choice-of-law question if one side breaks the promise to arbitrate. Usually the problem in such cases is whether one side can compel arbitration over the objection of the other, or compel it to be conducted in a certain way, or insist that the arbitrators have or have nor particular powers.

In bygone days, the courts viewed agreements to arbitrate with hostility. As a result, they would usually entertain a suit brought in violation of an arbitration provision. This result would be justified either on the ground that it was dictated by forum public policy or on the theory that since arbitration is a procedural device, a matter of remedy, the law of the forum should control. See Leflar, McDougal and Felix, American Conflicts Law 439 (4th ed. 1986). Today the situation is almost the exact reverse of what it formerly was. The great majority of states have enacted statutes which make arbitration agreements enforceable. Also, according to § 219 of the Restatement, Second, Conflict of Laws, the courts will refuse to entertain a suit brought in violation of an arbitration agreement unless such a suit could be maintained under the law which governs the agreement as a contract.

NOTES

1. Most American states provide statutory procedures for reducing awards to judgments, after which they become entitled to full faith and credit. Foreign country and sister state awards not reduced to judgment will nevertheless often be enforced. Restatement, Second, Conflict of Laws, Section 220 indicates prerequisites for enforcement of awards in the latter categories if the forum possesses jurisdiction and competence: that the award be enforceable in the state of rendition, has been rendered with due process, and does not violate the forum's strong public policy.

2. When enforcement is sought of a sister-state arbitration award, the validity of the award is determined under the law of the state where it was rendered. Moyer v. Van-Dye-Way Corp., 126 F.2d 339 (3d Cir. 1942); Maxwell Shapiro Woolen Co., Inc. v. Amerotron Corp., 339 Mass. 252, 158 N.E.2d 875 (1959).

3. The forum's procedures will govern the mode of enforcing an arbitration agreement, including ordering arbitration to proceed in another state. See Domke, The Law and Practice of Commercial Arbitration 256–259 (1968).

AMTORG TRADING CORP. v. CAMDEN FIBRE MILLS, INC., 304 N.Y. 519, 109 N.E.2d 606 (1952): Camden Fibre Mills, a Pennsylvania corporation, made a contract of purchase and sale with Amtorg Trading Corporation. Amtorg is a New York corporation which is in effect an agency of the Soviet

Government in carrying on trade in this country. The contract provided for the arbitration of disputes before the U.S.S.R. Chamber of Commerce Foreign Trade Arbitration Commission in Moscow, U.S.S.R. The designated arbitrator was a juridical person but it was also a public organization subject to the general supervision of the People's Commissariat for Foreign Trade. Camden brought suit in New York against Amtorg on the contract. Amtorg moved for a stay of the suit until arbitration was had before the arbitrator and at the place designated. Held, the suit should be stayed.

■ PER CURIAM. "Camden chose to do business with Amtorg and to accept, as one of the conditions imposed, arbitration in Russia; it may not now ask the courts to relieve it of the contractual obligation it assumed.

"It may be noted that the order of the Appellate Division does not preclude Camden from taking appropriate action should the arbitration in fact deprive it of its fundamental right to a fair and impartial determination."

NOTES

1. The United States Arbitration Act makes "valid, irrevocable, and enforceable", subject to the defenses usually available in contracts, a written provision for arbitration "in any maritime transaction or a contract evidencing a transaction involving commerce." 43 Stat. 883 (1925), 9 U.S.C.A. § 1 (1926). The statute, being confined to "any maritime transaction" and "a transaction involving [interstate or foreign] commerce," does not settle the matter where a case is in the federal courts under the diversity of citizenship clause. Such a case was Bernhardt v. Polygraphic Co. of America, Inc., 350 U.S. 198 (1956), where a suit for damages for the discharge of plaintiff under an employment contract was removed from a Vermont state court to the federal court sitting in that state. The contract, which was made in New York between New York parties, contained a provision that in case of dispute the parties would submit the matter to arbitration under New York law by the American Arbitration Association. The defendant moved in the federal court for a stay of the proceedings so the controversy could go to arbitration in New York. A question was whether the effectiveness of the arbitration provision should be determined by the law of the federal courts or by the law of one of the states, Vermont or New York. The Supreme Court held that state law, not federal courts law, should be applied, saying: "For the remedy by arbitration, whatever its merits or shortcomings, substantially affects the cause of action created by the State". Conversely, in Southland Corp. v. Keating, 465 U.S. 1 (1984), the Supreme Court held that the Federal Arbitration Act forecloses states from creating exceptions to the enforcement of arbitration agreements entered into by the disputing parties. See also Chapter 9, Section 1, infra and Note 2, page 576, supra, discussing the effects of choice-of-law clauses in arbitration agreements.

2. In international business dealings, arbitration has become the favored mode of resolving disputes. An arbitration agreement allows the parties to the contract great flexibility in choosing their forum, arranging for the composition of the tribunal, the applicable procedures, and—within limits—the rules of law that will be applicable to disputes that may arise. For a treatment of a variety of legal problems in this context, see International Trade Arbitration (Domke ed. 1958).

3. The United States has acceded to the United Nations-developed Convention on the Recognition and Enforcement of Foreign Arbitral Awards. See Aksen, American Arbitration Accession Arrives in the Age of Aquarius, 3 Sw.U.L.Rev. 1 (1971); Quigley, Convention on Foreign Arbitral Awards, 58 A.B.A.J. 821 (1972). The Convention facilitates enforcement of foreign arbitration awards in American courts. The permissible grounds for refusing enforcement of an award that is covered by the Convention are quite narrow. Section 207 of the Federal Arbitration Act provides that federal courts will confirm an award within three years after it is made, unless one of the grounds for refusing or deferring recognition or enforcement specified in the Convention exists.

4. Foreign law similarly favors arbitration. E.g., Art. 178 of the Swiss Conflicts Statute of 1988 requires that there be some kind of writing evidencing the agreement to arbitrate but, beyond that, validates agreements which conform to the law chosen by the parties, the law applicable to the claim, or to Swiss law. See generally Scoles and Hay, Conflict of Laws 1018–1024 (2d ed. 1992); Note, 47 Wash.L.Rev. 441 (1972).

Parsons & Whittemore Overseas Co., Inc. v. Societe Generale de L'Industrie Du Papier (RAKTA)

United States Court of Appeals, Second Circuit, 1974.
508 F.2d 969.

■ J. JOSEPH SMITH, CIRCUIT JUDGE:

Parsons & Whittemore Overseas Co., Inc., (Overseas), an American corporation, appeals from the entry of summary judgment ... on the counterclaim by Societe Generale de L'Industrie du Papier (RAKTA), an Egyptian corporation, to confirm a foreign arbitral award holding Overseas liable to RAKTA for breach of contract.... Jurisdiction is based on 9 U.S.C. § 203, which empowers federal district courts to hear cases to recognize and enforce foreign arbitral awards, and 9 U.S.C. § 205, which authorizes the removal of such cases from state courts, as was accomplished in this instance. We affirm the district court's confirmation of the foreign award. ....

In November 1962, Overseas consented by written agreement with RAKTA to construct, start up and, for one year, manage and supervise a paperboard mill in Alexandria, Egypt. The Agency for International Development (AID), a branch of the United States State Department, would finance the project.... Among the contract's terms was an arbitration clause, which provided a means to settle differences arising in the course of performance, and a "force majeure" clause, which excused delay in performance due to causes beyond Overseas' reasonable capacity to control.

Work proceeded as planned until May, 1967. Then, with the Arab-Israeli Six Day War on the horizon, recurrent expressions of Egyptian hostility to Americans—nationals of the principal ally of the Israeli enemy—caused the majority of the Overseas work crew to leave Egypt. On June 6, the Egyptian government broke diplomatic ties with the United

States and ordered all Americans expelled from Egypt except those who would apply and qualify for a special visa.

Having abandoned the project for the present with the construction phase near completion, Overseas notified RAKTA that it regarded this postponement as excused by the force majeure clause. RAKTA disagreed and sought damages for breach of contract. Overseas refused to settle and RAKTA, already at work on completing the performance promised by Overseas, invoked the arbitration clause. Overseas responded by calling into play the clause's option to bring a dispute directly to a three-man arbitral board governed by the rules of the International Chamber of Commerce. After several sessions in 1970, the tribunal issued a preliminary award, which recognized Overseas' force majeure defense as good only during the period from May 28 to June 30, 1967. In so limiting Overseas' defense, the arbitration court emphasized that Overseas had made no more than a perfunctory effort to secure special visas and that AID's notification that it was withdrawing financial backing did not justify Overseas' unilateral decision to abandon the project....

... The principal issues [raised by Overseas] on this appeal are derived from the express language of the applicable United Nations Convention on the Recognition and Enforcement of Foreign Arbitral Awards (Convention), 330 U.N.Treaty Ser. 38.... These include: enforcement of the award would violate the public policy of the United States, the award represents an arbitration of matters not appropriately decided by arbitration; the tribunal denied Overseas an adequate opportunity to present its case; the award is predicated upon a resolution of issues outside the scope of the contractual agreement to submit to arbitration; and the award is in manifest disregard of law....

In 1958 the Convention was adopted by 26 of the 45 states participating in the United Nations Conference on Commercial Arbitration held in New York. For the signatory states, the New York Convention superseded the Geneva Convention of 1927, 92 League of Nations Treaty Ser. 302. The 1958 Convention's basic thrust was to liberalize procedures for enforcing foreign arbitral awards: While the Geneva Convention placed the burden of proof on the party seeking enforcement of a foreign arbitral award and did not circumscribe the range of available defenses to those enumerated in the convention, the 1958 Convention clearly shifted the burden of proof to the party defending against enforcement and limited his defenses to seven set forth in Article V.... Not a signatory to any prior multilateral agreement on enforcement of arbitral awards, the United States declined to sign the 1958 Convention at the outset. The United States ultimately acceded to the Convention, however, in 1970, [1970], 3 U.S.T. 2517, T.I.A.S. No. 6997, and implemented its accession with 9 U.S.C. §§ 201–208. Under 9 U.S.C. § 208, the existing Federal Arbitration Act, 9 U.S.C. §§ 1–14, applies to the enforcement of foreign awards except to the extent to which the latter may conflict with the Convention....

A. *Public Policy*

Article V(2)(b) of the Convention allows the court in which enforcement of a foreign arbitral award is sought to refuse enforcement, on the defendant's motion or *sua sponte*, if "enforcement of the award would be contrary to the public policy of [the forum] country." The legislative history of the provision offers no certain guidelines to its construction....

Perhaps more probative ... are the inferences to be drawn from the history of the Convention as a whole. The general pro-enforcement bias informing the Convention and explaining its supersession of the Geneva Convention points toward a narrow reading of the public policy defense. An expansive construction of this defense would vitiate the Convention's basic effort to remove preexisting obstacles to enforcement.... Additionally, considerations of reciprocity—considerations given express recognition in the Convention itself[4] —counsel courts to invoke the public policy defense with caution lest foreign courts frequently accept it as a defense to enforcement of arbitral awards rendered in the United States.

We conclude, therefore, that the Convention's public policy defense should be construed narrowly. Enforcement of foreign arbitral awards may be denied on this basis only where enforcement would violate the forum state's most basic notions of morality and justice....

Under this view of the public policy provision in the Convention, Overseas' public policy defense may easily be dismissed. Overseas argues that various actions by United States officials subsequent to the severance of American-Egyptian relations—most particularly, AID's withdrawal of financial support for the Overseas-RAKTA contract—required Overseas, as a loyal American citizen, to abandon the project. Enforcement of an award predicated on the feasibility of Overseas' returning to work in defiance of these expressions of national policy would therefore allegedly contravene United States public policy. In equating "national" policy with United States "public" policy, the appellant quite plainly misses the mark. To read the public policy defense as a parochial device protective of national political interests would seriously undermine the Convention's utility. This provision was not meant to enshrine the vagaries of international politics under the rubric of "public policy." Rather, a circumscribed public policy doctrine was contemplated by the Convention's framers and every indication is that the United States, in acceding to the Convention, meant to subscribe to this supranational emphasis....

To deny enforcement of this award largely because of the United States' falling out with Egypt in recent years would mean converting a defense intended to be of narrow scope into a major loophole in the Convention's mechanism for enforcement. We have little hesitation, therefore, in disallowing Overseas' proposed public policy defense.

---

4. A Contracting State shall not be entitled to avail itself of the present Convention against other Contracting States except to the extent that it is itself bound to apply the Convention.

Article XIV....

B. *Non-arbitrability*

Article V(2)(a) authorizes a court to deny enforcement, on a defendant's or its own motion, of a foreign arbitral award when "[t]he subject matter of the difference is not capable of settlement by arbitration under the law of that [the forum] country." Under this provision, a court sitting in the United States might, for example, be expected to decline enforcement of an award involving arbitration of an antitrust claim in view of domestic arbitration cases which have held that antitrust matters are entrusted to the exclusive competence of the judiciary.... On the other hand, it may well be that the special considerations and policies underlying a "truly international agreement," Scherk v. Alberto-Culver Co., 417 U.S. 506, at 515, 94 S.Ct. 2449 (see p. 172, n. 2, supra) call for a narrower view of non-arbitrability in the international than the domestic context. Compare id. with Wilko v. Swan, 346 U.S. 427, 74 S.Ct. 182, 98 L.Ed. 168 (1953) (enforcement of international, but not domestic, agreement to arbitrate claim based on alleged Securities Act violations.)

Resolution of Overseas' non-arbitrability argument, however, does not require us to reach such difficult distinctions between domestic and foreign awards. For Overseas' argument, that "United States foreign policy issues can hardly be placed at the mercy of foreign arbitrators 'who are charged with the execution of no public trust' and whose loyalties are to foreign interests," ... plainly fails to raise so substantial an issue of arbitrability. The mere fact that an issue of national interest may incidentally figure into the resolution of a breach of contract claim does not make the dispute not arbitrable. Rather, certain *categories* of claims may be non-arbitrable because of the special national interest vested in their resolution.... Furthermore, even were the test for non-arbitrability of an ad hoc nature, Overseas' situation would almost certainly not meet the standard, for Overseas grossly exaggerates the magnitude of the national interest involved in the resolution of its particular claim. Simply because acts of the United States are somehow implicated in a case one cannot conclude that the United States is vitally interested in its outcome. Finally, the Supreme Court's decision in favor of arbitrability in a case far more prominently displaying public features than the instant one, Scherk v. Alberto-Culver, Co., supra, compels by analogy the conclusion that the foreign award against Overseas dealt with a subject arbitrable under United States law....

[The court then proceeded to reject Overseas' other defenses.]

NOTE

The Supreme Court has held a contract to arbitrate to be enforceable despite an antitrust claim in an international setting. There was a vigorous dissent by Justice Stevens. Mitsubishi Motors Corp. v. Soler Chrysler–Plymouth Inc., 473 U.S. 614 (1985). For further discussion see Carbonneau, The Exuberant Pathway to Quixotic Internationalism: Assessing the Folly of Mitsubishi, 19 Vand.J.Transnat'l.Law 265 (1986).

8. NEGOTIABLE INSTRUMENTS

RESTATEMENT, SECOND, CONFLICT OF LAWS 357–58 *

CHAPTER 8. CONTRACTS

TOPIC 4. NEGOTIABLE INSTRUMENTS

INTRODUCTORY NOTE

This Topic is directed to choice of law questions relating to negotiable drafts (bills of exchange), including checks, and notes and certificates of deposit. These instruments are covered by Article 3 of the Uniform Commercial Code. Attention is not here given to negotiable documents embodying title to a chattel, as bills of lading and warehouse receipts (see Article 7 of the Uniform Commercial Code). Cases of multistate transactions involving the contractual aspects of such documents have not yet come before the courts with sufficient frequency to make appropriate the statement of choice of law rules respecting them. Nor is consideration here given to negotiable debt securities (see Article 8 of the Uniform Commercial Code)....

On account of the previous widespread enactment by States of the United States of the Uniform Negotiable Instrument Law, choice of law problems relating to negotiable instruments have arisen infrequently in the interstate area. They have done so on occasion, however, because of minor differences in the statutes of certain States and because of the different judicial interpretations that a given provision has sometimes received.... This country's foreign commerce provides an area where choice of law problems of this sort have arisen and will continue to arise.

Negotiable instruments have both contractual and property aspects. Each of these instruments upon its effective delivery imposes contractual obligations on one or more of the original parties thereto. Furthermore, each of these instruments may give rise to a series of obligations, as those from the drawer and the acceptor to the payee of a draft, from the maker to the payee of a note, and from an indorser to an indorsee of either a draft or a note. The question therefore arises whether one law regulates all the obligations arising from a single instrument or whether each of these obligations may be governed by a separate law. By and large, the latter alternative is the one adopted by the courts. In general, the validity of each individual obligation and the rights created thereby are determined by the proper law of that obligation....

. . .

§ 214. Obligations of Makers and Acceptors

(1) The obligations of the maker of a note and of the acceptor of a draft are determined, except as stated in §§ 216–217, by the local law of the state designated in the instrument as the place of payment.

---

* Quoted with the permission of the copyright owner, The American Law Institute.

(2) In the absence of a designated place of payment, the obligations of a maker or acceptor are determined, except as stated in §§ 216–217, by the local law of the state where he delivered the instrument. That state is presumptively the state where the instrument is dated, if such a state is indicated, and this presumption is conclusive with respect to a holder in due course.

NOTES

1. (1) See, e.g., Youngstown Sheet and Tube Co. v. Westcott, 147 F.Supp. 829 (W.D.Okl.1957); McCornick & Co. v. Tolmie Bros., 46 Idaho 544, 269 P. 96 (1928).

2. See generally Bailey, Conflict of Laws in the Law of Bank Checks, 80 Banking L.J. 404 (1963); Johnson and Parachini, Forged Indorsements and Conflict of Laws, 82 Banking L.J. 95 (1965).

3. As to the duties of a bank in this context, the Uniform Commercial Code provides in Section 4–102(2) that the law of the place where the bank is located determines its liability "for action or non-action with respect to any item handled by it for purposes of presentment, payment or collection."

Koechlin Et CIE. v. Kestenbaum Brothers

Court of Appeal, 1927.
[1927] 1 K.B. 889.

The plaintiffs as indorsees of a bill of exchange for 60,000 francs, dated December 14, 1925, drawn payable to the order of M. Vigderhaus, claimed to recover 461*l*. 10*s*. thereon from the defendants as acceptors.

The bill was drawn in France by E. Vigderhaus upon the defendants in London to the order of M. Vigderhaus. It was sent to London, was accepted by the defendants payable at a London bank, returned to Paris, indorsed there by E. Vigderhaus, and discounted by the plaintiffs. On presentation for payment the defendants refused to meet it on the ground that it did not bear the indorsement of M. Vigderhaus, but merely the indorsement of E. Vigderhaus in his own name....

The plaintiffs appealed.

■ BANKES, L.J. . . . The defence is that the indorsement is not in order, because the bill being drawn in favour of the father, M. Vigderhaus, should have been indorsed by him. The appellants' answer to that is that by French law if the son E. Vigderhaus was duly authorized, as he was, he was entitled to indorse the bill in his own name simpliciter, without adding the words "per pro"; and that being a French bill and the indorsement being good by French law the appellants are entitled to sue the acceptors in this country upon their contract of acceptance.

. . . At the trial one witness only was called on the subject, and he was called for the appellants. He said that the indorsement in question was good by French law, assuming that the son had his father's authority to indorse the bill.... In my opinion, the judge was justified in coming to the conclusion he did, that the witness correctly informed him as to French law. That being so we have to deal with the case on the footing that the indorsement is good according to French law.

... This at any rate is clear, because it was so decided by the Court of Appeal in Embiricos v. Anglo-Austrian Bank, [1905] 1 K.B. 677, long after the Bills of Exchange Act was passed, that "the rule of international law, that the validity of a transfer of movable chattels must be governed by the law of the country in which the transfer takes place, applies to the transfer of bills of exchange or cheques by indorsement." That is clear authority, if authority were required, that the ordinary rule of international law applies to this particular indorsement, and as the law applicable is French law, the appellants as indorsees have, according to French law, a perfectly good title to the bill. . . . Sect. 72 of the Bills of Exchange Act appears to me for this purpose to be exhaustive, because it provides that "where a bill drawn in one country is negotiated, accepted, or payable in another, the rights, duties and liabilities of the parties thereto"—that includes this acceptance—"are determined as follows: (1) The validity of a bill as regards requisites in form is determined by the law of the place of issue"—this bill is in form according to the law of France—"and the validity as regards requisites in form of the supervening contracts, such as acceptance, or indorsement, or acceptance supra protest, is determined by the law of the place where such contract was made."

In my opinion this appeal must be allowed.

■ [The concurring opinions of SARGANT, L.J., and AVORY, J., are omitted.]

NOTES

1. Sections 216 and 217 of the Restatement, Second, Conflict of Laws, are couched in hard-and-fast terms to provide, respectively, that the local law of the state where a negotiable instrument actually was when transferred determines, in the commonest situations, whether the transferee holds the instrument in due course and has title; and that details of presentment, payment, protest and dishonor are determined by the local law of the state where these actions occur. For leading cases involving international transactions and the title problem, see United States v. Guaranty Trust Co., 293 U.S. 340 (1934); Weissman v. Banque de Bruxelles, 254 N.Y. 488, 173 N.E. 835 (1930).

2. Duties of indorsers and drawers are dealt with in Section 215 of Restatement, Second, Conflict of Laws, which, in general, provides that their obligations are determined by the local law of the state where the indorser or drawer delivered the instrument. The state where the paper was dated, if indicated, is presumptively the state of delivery. The designated place of payment is the source of the law as to where presentment may be made.

CHAPTER 9

CONFLICTS PROBLEMS IN FEDERAL AND INTERNATIONAL SETTINGS

SECTION 1. SPECIAL PROBLEMS IN FEDERAL COURTS

A. THE CONSTRAINTS AND TOLERANCES OF THE ERIE PRINCIPLE

INTRODUCTORY NOTE

This section brings together a group of issues that have appeared episodically in earlier chapters. Their theme is a broad question: how completely are federal courts bound to follow state conflicts principles in diversity cases? As examples: May the federal diversity court entertain a suit based on state-created rights that would not be entertained in a state court of the forum? Does the *Erie* doctrine compel a diversity court to follow the choice-of-law rules or methods of the forum's state courts and to apply at the end the same decisional rule the state judges would? As the *Erie* principle has changed shape over the years, has comparable change occurred in its influence on conflicts methodology?

This chapter also focuses on the issue of federal common law. When the Constitution of the United States, a treaty, or federal statute supplies the rule of decision, state law is superseded. When interstices appear in those sources of law, two issues arise. First, should a uniform federal judge-made rule fill the gap? Second, if state law governs, should state or federal choice-of-law rules select that law? Previously, discussion of choice-of-law in admiralty touched on these issues. See Note, page 651, supra.

We shall take up the problem of state law in the federal courts in a broad context, tracing the movements and counter-movements in state law-federal law relations that bear on the conflicts problems that are the focus of our interest. Two of the important movements concern only the federal courts. The third applies also to the state courts.

(1) Erie Railroad Co. v. Tompkins, infra, p. 665, sharply curtailed the growth of a general and independent body of common law rules in the federal courts. For in overruling Swift v. Tyson, 41 U.S. (16 Pet.) 1 (1842), it obliterated the century old doctrine of a separate substantive common law as to commercial matters in the federal courts. It thereby sharpened the question: from what source can the federal courts get separate rules of conflict of laws?

(2) In the same year Erie Railroad Co. v. Tompkins was decided the area of federal courts law was much expanded by occupying the entire field

of federal "procedure". For many years the Conformity Act had directed the federal district courts hearing actions at law to follow the procedure of the states in which the federal courts were sitting. But in 1938 the Federal Rules of Civil Procedure, went into effect as a uniform set of rules for litigation in the federal district courts throughout the country. By coincidence the Rules created a special law of procedure for the federal district courts at almost the same time the Erie case was ending the special body of general common law on substantive matters lying outside the ordinary sphere of national law.

(3) A third movement, affecting state and federal courts alike but more conspicuous in the federal courts, is concerned with federal law. The increasing regulation of interstate and foreign commerce and the growing activities of the federal government have brought the realization that there are areas of substantive law which are not explicitly dealt with by the federal statutes but which are nevertheless covered by a single national law. This corpus is a part of the law of the land to be applied by all courts, state or federal. Its importance for lawyers with private interstate or international cases is manifest, for in so far as the national law comes into play there is no conflict of laws.

TWO FEDERAL STATUTES

Judiciary Act of 1789, ch. 20, § 34, 1 Stat. 92: "[T]he laws of the several states, except where the constitution, treaties or statutes of the United States shall otherwise require or provide, shall be regarded as rules of decision in trials at common law in the courts of the United States in cases where they apply."

In the 1948 recodification, after the merger in federal courts of law and equity proceedings, the words "civil actions" were substituted for "trials at common law." As so amended, and with the words "Acts of Congress" substituted for "statutes," this Act is codified as 28 U.S.C.A. § 1652 (1988).

Rules Enabling Act of June 19, 1934, 48 Stat. 1064: "Sec. 1. [T]he Supreme Court of the United States shall have the power to prescribe by general rules, for the district courts of the United States ... the forms of process, writs, pleadings, and motions, and the practice and procedure in civil actions at law. Said rules shall neither abridge, enlarge, nor modify the substantive rights of any litigant. They shall take effect six months after their promulgation, and thereafter all laws in conflict therewith shall be of no force or effect.

"Sec. 2. The court may at any time unite the general rules prescribed by it for cases in equity with those at law so as to secure one form of civil action and procedure for both: Provided, however, That in such union of rules the right of trial by jury as at common law and declared by the seventh amendment to the Constitution shall be preserved to the parties inviolate. Such unified rules shall not take effect until they shall have been reported to Congress by the Attorney General at the beginning of a regular session thereof and until after the close of such session."

In the 1948 recodification, the provision for uniting of rules for suits in equity and actions at law was deleted because unification had been accomplished. The Act is codified in the following provisions:

28 U.S.C.A. § 2072 (1988): "(a) The Supreme Court shall have the power to prescribe the general rules of practice and procedure and rules of evidence for cases in the United States district courts ... and courts of appeals.

"(b) Such rules shall not abridge, enlarge or modify any substantive right. All laws in conflict with such rules shall be of no further force or effect after such rules have taken effect...."

The procedure for prescribing rules of evidence and procedure is codified in 28 U.S.C.A. §§ 2073–74 (1988). Section 2074(b) provides: "Any such rule creating, abolishing, or modifying an evidentiary privilege shall have no force or effect unless approved by Act of Congress."

Erie Railroad Co. v. Tompkins

Supreme Court of the United States, 1938.
304 U.S. 64, 58 S.Ct. 817, 82 L.Ed. 1188, 114 A.L.R. 1487.

Certiorari to the United States Circuit Court of Appeals for the Second Circuit.

■ JUSTICE BRANDEIS delivered the opinion of the Court.

The question for decision is whether the oft-challenged doctrine of Swift v. Tyson [, 16 Pet. 1 (1842),] shall now be disapproved.

Tompkins, a citizen of Pennsylvania, was injured on a dark night by a passing freight train of the Erie Railroad Company while walking along its right of way at Hughestown in that state. He claimed that the accident occurred through negligence in the operation, or maintenance, of the train; that he was rightfully on the premises as licensee because on a commonly used beaten footpath which ran for a short distance alongside the tracks; and that he was struck by something which looked like a door projecting from one of the moving cars. To enforce that claim he brought an action in the federal court for Southern New York, which had jurisdiction because the company is a corporation of that state. It denied liability; and the case was tried by a jury.

The Erie insisted that its duty to Tompkins was no greater than that owed to a trespasser. It contended, among other things, that its duty to Tompkins, and hence its liability, should be determined in accordance with the Pennsylvania law; that under the law of Pennsylvania, as declared by its highest court, persons who use pathways along the railroad right of way—that is, a longitudinal pathway as distinguished from a crossing—are to be deemed trespassers; and that the railroad is not liable for injuries to undiscovered trespassers resulting from its negligence, unless it be wanton or willful. Tompkins denied that any such rule had been established by the decisions of the Pennsylvania courts; and contended that, since there was no statute of the state on the subject, the railroad's duty and liability is to be determined in federal courts as a matter of general law.

The trial judge refused to rule that the applicable law precluded recovery. The jury brought in a verdict of $30,000; and the judgment entered thereon was affirmed by the Circuit Court of Appeals, which held (2 Cir., 90 F.2d 603, 604), that it was unnecessary to consider whether the law of Pennsylvania was as contended, because the question was one not of local, but of general, law, and that "upon questions of general law the federal courts are free, in absence of a local statute, to exercise their independent judgment as to what the law is...."

Because of the importance of the question whether the federal court was free to disregard the alleged rule of the Pennsylvania common law, we granted certiorari. 302 U.S. 671.

First. Swift v. Tyson, 16 Pet. 1, 18, held that federal courts exercising jurisdiction on the ground of diversity of citizenship need not, in matters of general jurisprudence, apply the unwritten law of the state as declared by its highest court; that they are free to exercise an independent judgment as to what the common law of the state is—or should be; and that, as there stated by Mr. Justice Story: "the true interpretation of the 34th section [of the Judiciary Act of 1789] limited its application to state laws, strictly local, that is to say, to the positive statutes of the state, and the construction thereof adopted by the local tribunals, and to rights and titles to things having a permanent locality, such as the rights and titles to real estate, and other matters immovable and intraterritorial in their nature and character. It never has been supposed by us, that the section did apply, or was designed to apply, to questions of a more general nature, not at all dependent upon local statutes or local usages of a fixed and permanent operation, as, for example, to the construction of ordinary contracts or other written instruments, and especially to questions of general commercial law, where the state tribunals are called upon to perform the like functions as ourselves, that is, to ascertain, upon general reasoning and legal analogies, what is the true exposition of the contract or instrument, or what is the just rule furnished by the principles of commercial law to govern the case."

... The federal courts assumed, in the broad field of "general law," the power to declare rules of decision which Congress was confessedly without power to enact as statutes. Doubt was repeatedly expressed as to the correctness of the construction given section 34, and as to the soundness of the rule which it introduced. But it was the more recent research of a competent scholar, who examined the original document, which established that the construction given to it by the Court was erroneous; and that the purpose of the section was merely to make certain that, in all matters except those in which some federal law is controlling, the federal courts exercising jurisdiction in diversity of citizenship cases would apply as their rules of decision the law of the state, unwritten as well as written.[5]

Criticism of the doctrine became widespread after the decision of Black & White Taxicab & Transfer Co. v. Brown & Yellow Taxicab & Transfer Co., 276 U.S. 518 [(1928). In this case, a Kentucky corporation, by the device of dissolving and re-incorporating in Tennessee, was permitted to manufacture diversity of citizenship jurisdiction and to enforce in a federal court, sitting in Kentucky, a contract that no Kentucky court would have enforced.]

Second. Experience in applying the doctrine of Swift v. Tyson, had revealed its defects, political and social; and the benefits expected to flow from the rule did not accrue. Persistence of state courts in their own opinions on questions of common law prevented uniformity; and the impossibility of discovering a satisfactory line of demarcation between the province of general law and that of local law developed a new well of uncertainties.

On the other hand, the mischievous results of the doctrine had become apparent. Diversity of citizenship jurisdiction was conferred in order to prevent apprehended discrimination in state courts against those not citizens of the state. Swift v. Tyson introduced grave discrimination by noncitizens against citizens. It made rights enjoyed under the unwritten "general law" vary according to whether enforcement was sought in the state or in the federal court; and the privilege of selecting the court in which the right should be determined was conferred upon the noncitizen. Thus, the doctrine rendered impossible equal protection of the law. In attempting to promote uniformity of law throughout the United States, the doctrine had prevented uniformity in the administration of the law of the state.

The discrimination resulting became in practice far-reaching. This resulted in part from the broad province accorded to the so-called "general law" as to which federal courts exercised an independent judgment....

. . .

The injustice and confusion incident to the doctrine of Swift v. Tyson have been repeatedly urged as reasons for abolishing or limiting diversity of citizenship jurisdiction. Other legislative relief has been proposed. If only a question of statutory construction were involved, we should not be prepared to abandon a doctrine so widely applied throughout nearly a century. But the unconstitutionality of the course pursued has now been made clear, and compels us to do so.

Third. Except in matters governed by the Federal Constitution or by acts of Congress, the law to be applied in any case is the law of the state. And whether the law of the state shall be declared by its Legislature in a statute or by its highest court in a decision is not a matter of federal

---

5. Charles Warren, New Light on the History of the Federal Judiciary Act of 1789 (1923) 37 Harv.L.Rev. 49, 51–52, 81–88, 108.

concern. There is no federal general common law. Congress has no power to declare substantive rules of common law applicable in a state whether they be local in their nature or "general," be they commercial law or a part of the law of torts. And no clause in the Constitution purports to confer such a power upon the federal courts....

The fallacy underlying the rule declared in Swift v. Tyson is made clear by Mr. Justice Holmes.[23] The doctrine rests upon the assumption that there is "a transcendental body of law outside of any particular State but obligatory within it unless and until changed by statute," that federal courts have the power to use their judgment as to what the rules of common law are; and that in the federal courts "the parties are entitled to an independent judgment on matters of general law":

"but law in the sense in which courts speak of it today does not exist without some definite authority behind it. The common law so far as it is enforced in a State, whether called common law or not, is not the common law generally but the law of that State existing by the authority of that State without regard to what it may have been in England or anywhere else. ...

"the authority and only authority is the State, and if that be so, the voice adopted by the State as its own [whether it be of its Legislature or of its Supreme Court] should utter the last word."

Thus, the doctrine of Swift v. Tyson is, as Mr. Justice Holmes said, "an unconstitutional assumption of powers by the Courts of the United States which no lapse of time or respectable array of opinion should make us hesitate to correct." In disapproving that doctrine we do not hold unconstitutional section 34 of the Federal Judiciary Act of 1789 or any other act of Congress. We merely declare that in applying the doctrine this Court and the lower courts have invaded rights which in our opinion are reserved by the Constitution to the several states.

... The Circuit Court of Appeals ruled that the question of liability is one of general law; and on that ground declined to decide the issue of state law. As we hold this was error, the judgment is reversed and the case remanded to it for further proceedings in conformity with our opinion.

Reversed.

■ JUSTICE CARDOZO took no part in the consideration or decision of this case.

■ [JUSTICE BUTLER dissented in an opinion in which JUSTICE MCREYNOLDS concurred. The dissent urged (a) that the doctrine of Swift v. Tyson be adhered to and applied; and (b) that otherwise the case be set down for reargument, for counsel on both sides had assumed in their briefs the validity of Swift v. Tyson; so important a question as the constitutional overruling of that case should not be decided without argument.]

---

23. Kuhn v. Fairmont Coal Co., 215 U.S. 349, 370–372; Black & White Taxicab, etc., Co. v. Brown & Yellow Taxicab, etc., Co., 276 U.S. 518, 532–536.

■ JUSTICE REED (concurring in part).

. . .

To decide the case now before us and to "disapprove" the doctrine of Swift v. Tyson requires only that we say that the words "the laws" include in their meaning the decisions of the local tribunals.... It is unnecessary to go further and declare that the "course pursued" was "unconstitutional," instead of merely erroneous.

The "unconstitutional" course referred to in the majority opinion is apparently the ruling in Swift v. Tyson that the supposed omission of Congress to legislate as to the effect of decisions leaves federal courts free to interpret general law for themselves. I am not at all sure whether, in the absence of federal statutory direction, federal courts would be compelled to follow state decisions. There was sufficient doubt about the matter in 1789 to induce the first Congress to legislate. No former opinions of this Court have passed upon it.... If the opinion commits this Court to the position that the Congress is without power to declare what rules of substantive law shall govern the federal courts, that conclusion also seems questionable....

... It seems preferable to overturn an established construction of an act of Congress, rather than, in the circumstances of this case, to interpret the Constitution.

NOTES

1. A continuing debate broke out over whether the Erie doctrine is constitutionally compelled. In the affirmative, Judge Henry J. Friendly wrote In Praise of Erie—and of the New Federal Common Law, 39 N.Y.U.L.Rev. 383, 385–386 (1964). On the other side Judge Charles E. Clark wrote State Law in the Federal Courts: The Brooding Omnipresence of Erie v. Tompkins, 55 Yale L.J. 267–278 (1946). See Wright, Law of Federal Courts 381–386 (5th Ed.1994).

2. On remand, the district court was required by the majority's opinion to "decide the issue of state law." Did the Supreme Court's decision intend that the federal district court in New York would apply Pennsylvania law? If so, why? Is it because there is a federal choice-of-law rule that applies the law of the place of the tort? Or because the New York courts do so? Or because the Court assumed that "place-of-the-tort" was the uniform conflicts rule in tort? See also Klaxon Co. v. Stentor Electric Manufacturing Co., 313 U.S. 487 (1941), p. 688, infra.

3. For examples of the "new federal common law" or "national common law," see the D'Oench, Duhme and Bank of America cases, pp. 713, 723, infra. Under the interstate commerce power, could not Congress enact rules determining the measure of an interstate railroad's duty to persons walking along the railroad's right of way? See Louise Weinberg, Federal Common Law, 83 Nw.U.L.Rev. 805 (1989), urging expanded use of federal common law for matters of national concern, such as aviation and environmental disasters.

For nearly two decades the sway of the Erie doctrine expanded, requiring federal courts to apply one state rule after another as "substantive." Strong impetus to the spread of substantive characterization came from Guaranty Trust v. York, which propounded a deceptively attractive test, the first of several recastings of the doctrine by the Supreme Court.

Guaranty Trust Co. v. York
Supreme Court of the United States, 1945.
326 U.S. 99, 65 S.Ct. 1464, 89 L.Ed. 2079.

[In 1942 York filed a class suit in a Federal district court in New York, charging defendant with breach of trust in connection with transactions in 1931. Defendant obtained a summary judgment on the ground the suit was time-barred under the New York rule, but this was reversed, the Court of Appeals ruling that in a diversity action brought on its equity side the district court was not bound to apply the statute of limitations as it would have been applied by a New York court. The Supreme Court granted certiorari.]

■ JUSTICE FRANKFURTER delivered the opinion of the Court....

Our starting point must be the policy of federal jurisdiction which Erie R. Co. v. Tompkins, 304 U.S. 64, embodies....

. . .

In relation to the problem now here, the real significance of Swift v. Tyson lies in the fact that it did not enunciate novel doctrine. Nor was it restricted to its particular situation. It summed up prior attitudes and expressions in cases that had come before this Court and lower federal courts for at least thirty years, at law as well as in equity....

. . .

And so this case reduces itself to the narrow question whether, when no recovery could be had in a State court because the action is barred by the statute of limitations, a federal court in equity can take cognizance of the suit because there is diversity of citizenship between the parties. Is the outlawry, according to State law, of a claim created by the States a matter of "substantive rights" to be respected by a federal court of equity when that court's jurisdiction is dependent on the fact that there is a State-created right, or is such statute of "a mere remedial character" ... which a federal court may disregard?

Matters of "substance" and matters of "procedure" are much talked about in the books as though they defined a great divide cutting across the whole domain of law. But, of course, "substance" and "procedure" are the same key-words to very different problems. Neither "substance" nor "procedure" represents the same invariants. Each implies different variables depending upon the particular problem for which it is used. See Home Ins. Co. v. Dick, 281 U.S. 397, 409. And the different problems are only distantly related at best, for the terms are in common use in connection with situations turning on such different considerations as those that are relevant to questions pertaining to ex post facto legislation, the impairment of the obligations of contract, the enforcement of federal rights in the State courts and the multitudinous phases of the conflict of laws.

Here we are dealing with a right to recover derived not from the United States but from one of the States. When, because the plaintiff happens to be a non-resident, such a right is enforceable in a federal as well as in a State court, the forms and mode of enforcing the right may at times, naturally enough, vary because the two judicial systems are not identic. But since a federal court adjudicating a state-created right solely because of the diversity of citizenship of the parties is for that purpose, in effect, only another court of the State, it cannot afford recovery if the right to recover is made unavailable by the State nor can it substantially affect the enforcement of the right as given by the State.

And so the question is not whether a statute of limitations is deemed a matter of "procedure" in some sense. The question is whether such a statute concerns merely the manner and the means by which a right to recover, as recognized by the State, is enforced, or whether such statutory limitation is a matter of substance in the aspect that alone is relevant to our problem, namely does it significantly affect the result of a litigation for a federal court to disregard a law of a State that would be controlling in an action upon the same claim by the same parties in a State court?

It is therefore immaterial whether statutes of limitation are characterized either as "substantive" or "procedural" in State court opinions in any use of those terms unrelated to the specific issue before us. Erie R. Co. v. Tompkins was not an endeavor to formulate scientific legal terminology. It expressed a policy that touches vitally the proper distribution of judicial power between State and federal courts. In essence, the intent of that decision was to insure that, in all cases where a federal court is exercising jurisdiction solely because of the diversity of citizenship of the parties, the outcome of the litigation in the federal court should be substantially the same, so far as legal rules determine the outcome of a litigation, as it would be if tried in a State court. The nub of the policy that underlies Erie R. Co. v. Tompkins is that for the same transaction the accident of a suit by a nonresident litigant in a federal court instead of in a State court a block away, should not lead to a substantially different result. And so, putting to one side abstractions regarding "substance" and "procedure," we have held that in diversity cases the federal courts must follow the law of the State as to burden of proof, Cities Service Oil Co. v. Dunlap, 308 U.S. 208, as to conflict of laws, Klaxon Co. v. Stentor Co., 313 U.S. 487, as to contributory negligence, Palmer v. Hoffman, 318 U.S. 109, 117. And see Sampson v. Channell, 1 Cir., 110 F.2d 754. Erie R. Co. v. Tompkins has been applied with an eye alert to essentials in avoiding disregard of State law in diversity cases in the federal courts. A policy so important to our federalism must be kept free from entanglements with analytical or terminological niceties.

Plainly enough, a statute that would completely bar recovery in a suit if brought in a State court bears on a State-created right vitally and not merely formally or negligibly. As to consequences that so intimately affect recovery or nonrecovery a federal court in a diversity case should follow State law. See Morgan, Choice of Law Governing Proof (1944) 58 Harv. L.Rev. 153, 155–158. . . .

. . .

Diversity jurisdiction is founded on assurance to non-resident litigants of courts free from susceptibility to potential local bias. The Framers of the Constitution, according to Marshall, entertained "apprehensions" lest distant suitors be subjected to local bias in State courts, or, at least, viewed with "indulgence the possible fears and apprehensions" of such suitors. Bank of the United States v. Deveaux, 5 Cranch 61, 87. And so Congress afforded out-of-State litigants another tribunal, not another body of law. The operation of a double system of conflicting laws in the same State is plainly hostile to the reign of law. Certainly, the fortuitous circumstance of residence out of a State of one of the parties to a litigation ought not to give rise to a discrimination against others equally concerned but locally resident. The source of substantive rights enforced by a federal court under diversity jurisdiction, it cannot be said too often, is the law of the States. Whenever that law is authoritatively declared by a State, whether its voice be the legislature or its highest court, such law ought to govern in litigation founded on that law, whether the forum of application is a State or a federal court and whether the remedies be sought at law or may be had in equity.

. . .

The judgment is reversed and the case is remanded for proceedings not inconsistent with this opinion . . . .

■ JUSTICE ROBERTS and JUSTICE DOUGLAS took no part in the consideration or decision of this case.

■ [JUSTICE RUTLEDGE dissented in an opinion, in which JUSTICE MURPHY joined, which argued that "this case arises from what are in fact if not in law interstate transactions," involving "the rights of security holders in relation to securities which were distributed not in New York or Ohio alone but widely throughout the country."]

NOTES

1. Since the limitations issue in the Guaranty Trust case was statutory, why was Erie apposite at all? Does the outcome-determinative test mean that even state rules undoubtedly regulating the conduct of the litigation are subject to the Erie command if they can affect the result of the action?

2. In Sun Oil Co. v. Wortman, 486 U.S. 717 (1988), p. 434, supra, the Supreme Court held that statutes of limitation are traditionally procedural and that the forum did not violate the Due Process and Full Faith and Credit Clauses by applying its own longer statute to a claim governed by the substantive law of

another jurisdiction. A statute of limitations may therefore be "substantive" for *Erie* purposes (since it "substantially affect[s] the enforcement" of a state-law based claim) and, at the same time, "procedural" for due process purposes. Justice O'Connor, in her partial concurrence, left open the question whether *Wortman* should be decided differently if the state whose substantive law applies to the claim also considers its statute of limitations to be "substantive." Why should this make a difference? While Guaranty Trust v. York, supra, and Phillips Petroleum Co. v. Shutts, p. 362, supra, address different concerns (the *Erie* problem and Due Process, respectively), does either decision turn on the characterization of the issue as "procedural" or as "substantive?"

3. Substance-procedure characterization has been a pervasive issue in state-state conflicts cases as Chapter 7, supra, demonstrates. It is also a recurring issue in federal court diversity suits, where a federal rule that is arguably procedural may differ significantly from a forum state rule addressed to the same problem. To what extent are similar considerations and criteria at work in the federal diversity area? See Meador, State Law and the Federal Judicial Power, 49 Va.L.Rev. 1082 (1963).

4. In 1949 a trio of important cases accepted the broad view of Erie and made major inroads on the independence of federal diversity courts in their conduct of state-law-based litigation. In Ragan v. Merchants Transfer and Warehouse Co., 337 U.S. 530 (1949), a state rule was held to be dispositive of whether a suit had been started in time to avoid being barred by limitations. In Cohen v. Beneficial Industrial Loan Corp., 337 U.S. 541 (1949), the state security-for-costs rule was held applicable in the diversity suit. Both cases are discussed in the concurring opinion of Harlan, J., in Hanna v. Plumer, p. 678, infra. *Ragan* was confirmed by Walker v. Armco Steel Corp., p. 683, infra. Woods v. Interstate Realty Co., 337 U.S. 535 (1949), held that a corporation barred from state courts because not certified to do business in the state, could not bring a diversity suit in a federal court in that state.

5. "The question of the burden of [proof in] establishing contributory negligence is a question of local law which federal courts in diversity of citizenship cases ... must apply." See Palmer v. Hoffman, 318 U.S. 109, 117 (1943). In direct contrast is Garrett v. Moore-McCormack Co., 317 U.S. 239 (1942), involving the burden of proof as to the validity of a release in an admiralty case tried in a state court, with a federal statute governing the major rights of the parties. The court held that the federal law must be used by the state court.

BERNHARDT V. POLYGRAPHIC CO., 350 U.S. 198 (1956): Plaintiff sued in a Vermont court for damages for breach of a contract of employment. Defendant removed the action to the federal district court and moved for a stay pending arbitration, invoking a provision of the contract. The district judge refused the stay for the reason that under Vermont law an arbitration agreement is revocable at any time before award and therefore could not be enforced in a federal court. The Supreme Court agreed declaring:

"... [The] right to recover ... owes its existence to one of the States, not to the United States. The federal court enforces the state-created right by rules of procedure which it has acquired from the Federal Government and which therefore are not identical with those of the state courts. Yet, in spite of that difference in procedure, the federal court ... may not 'substantially affect the enforcement of the right as given by the State.' [Guaranty Trust Co. v. York, 326 U.S. 99, 109.] If the federal court allows arbitration where the state court would disallow it, the outcome of litigation might depend on the courthouse where suit is brought. For the remedy by arbitration, whatever its merits or shortcomings, substantially affects the cause of action created by the State. The nature of the tribunal where suits are tried is an important part of the parcel of rights behind a cause of action. The change from a court of law to an arbitration panel may make a radical difference in ultimate result. Arbitration carries no right to trial by jury that is guaranteed both by the Seventh Amendment and by Ch. 1, Art. 12th, of the Vermont Constitution. Arbitrators do not have the benefit of judicial instruction on the law; they need not give their reasons for their results; the record of their proceedings is not as complete as it is in a court trial; and judicial review of an award is more limited than judicial review of a trial—all as discussed in Wilko v. Swan, 346 U.S. 427, 435–438.... There would in our judgment be a resultant discrimination if the parties suing on a Vermont cause of action in the federal court were remitted to arbitration, while those suing in the Vermont court could not be."

9 U.S.C.A. § 2 (1988) provides that arbitration agreements in "a contract evidencing a transaction involving commerce ... shall be valid, irrevocable, and enforceable." 9 U.S.C.A. § 3 (1988) provides that United States courts shall stay suits brought in violation of such an arbitration agreement. These provisions were held not applicable in Bernhardt because there was no showing that the contract in that case involved interstate commerce. 350 U.S. at 200–201. Wilko v. Swan, cited in the quotation from Bernhardt, held that an agreement to arbitrate could not preclude a buyer of a security from seeking a judicial remedy under the Securities Act of 1933, in view of the language of that Act barring a "provision ... to waive compliance" with the Act. Wilko v. Swan was overruled by Rodriguez De Quijas v. Shearson/American Exp., Inc., 490 U.S. 477 (1989).

Byrd v. Blue Ridge Rural Electric Cooperative, Inc.

Supreme Court of the United States, 1958.
356 U.S. 525, 78 S.Ct. 893, 2 L.Ed.2d 953.

[Petitioner was injured in South Carolina while working as a lineman for a firm which had a contract to erect electrical power lines for respondent. As a defense to his diversity action for damages resulting from its negligence, respondent asserted that petitioner was a statutory employee and could recover only the statutory compensation benefits. Respondent claimed further that the defense was to be decided by the court and not the jury because of a controlling South Carolina decision. The Court of Appeals reversed a judgment for petitioner entered on a jury verdict.]

■ JUSTICE BRENNAN delivered the opinion of the Court....

... The respondent argues on the basis of the decision of the Supreme Court of South Carolina in Adams v. Davison-Paxon Co., 230 S.C. 532, 96 S.E.2d 566, that the issue of immunity should be decided by the judge and not by the jury. That was a negligence action brought in the state trial court against a store owner by an employee of an independent contractor who operated the store's millinery department. The trial judge denied the store owner's motion for a directed verdict made upon the ground that § 72–111 [of the South Carolina Workmen's Compensation Act] barred the plaintiff's action. The jury returned a verdict for the plaintiff. The South Carolina Supreme Court reversed, holding that it was for the judge and not the jury to decide on the evidence whether the owner was a statutory employer, and that the store owner had sustained his defense. . . .

The respondent argues that this state-court decision governs the present diversity case and "divests the jury of its normal function" to decide the disputed fact question of the respondent's immunity under § 72–111. This is to contend that the federal court is bound under Erie R. Co. v. Tompkins, 304 U.S. 64, to follow the state court's holding to secure uniform enforcement of the immunity created by the State.

First. It was decided in Erie R. Co. v. Tompkins that the federal courts in diversity cases must respect the definition of state-created rights and obligations by the state courts. We must, therefore, first examine the rule in Adams v. Davison-Paxon Co. to determine whether it is bound up with these rights and obligations in such a way that its application in the federal court is required. Cities Service Oil Co. v. Dunlap, 308 U.S. 208.

The Workmen's Compensation Act is administered in South Carolina by its Industrial Commission. The South Carolina courts hold that, on judicial review of actions of the Commission under § 72–111, the question whether the claim of an injured workman is within the Commission's jurisdiction is a matter of law for decision by the court, which makes its own findings of fact relating to that jurisdiction. The South Carolina Supreme Court states no reasons in Adams v. Davison-Paxon Co. why, although the jury decides all other factual issues raised by the cause of action and defenses, the jury is displaced as to the factual issue raised by the affirmative defense under § 72–111. The decisions cited to support the holding ... are concerned solely with defining the scope and method of judicial review of the Industrial Commission. A State may, of course, distribute the functions of its judicial machinery as it sees fit. The decisions relied upon, however, furnish no reason for selecting the judge rather than the jury to decide this single affirmative defense in the negligence action. They simply reflect a policy, cf. Crowell v. Benson, 285 U.S. 22, that administrative determination of "jurisdictional facts" should not be final but subject to judicial review. The conclusion is inescapable that the Adams holding is grounded in the practical consideration that the question had theretofore come before the South Carolina courts from the Industrial Commission and the courts had become accustomed to deciding the factual issue of immunity without the aid of juries. We find nothing to suggest that this rule was announced as an integral part of the special relationship created by the statute. Thus the requirement appears to be merely a form and mode of enforcing the immunity, Guaranty Trust Co. v. York, 326 U.S. 99, 108, and not a rule intended to be bound up with the definition of the rights and obligations of the parties. The situation is therefore not analogous to that in Dice v. Akron, C. & Y. R. Co., 342 U.S. 359, where this Court held that the right to trial by jury is so substantial a part of the cause of action created by the Federal Employers' Liability Act that the Ohio courts could not apply, in an action under that statute, the Ohio rule that the question of fraudulent release was for determination by a judge rather than by a jury.

Second. But cases following Erie have evinced a broader policy to the effect that the federal courts should conform as near as may be—in the absence of other considerations—to state rules even of form and mode where the state rules may bear substantially on the question whether the litigation would come out one way in the federal court and another way in the state court if the federal court failed to apply a particular local rule. E.g., Guaranty Trust Co. v. York, supra; Bernhardt v. Polygraphic Co., 350 U.S. 198. Concededly the nature of the tribunal which tries issues may be important in the enforcement of the parcel of rights making up a cause of action or defense, and bear significantly upon achievement of uniform enforcement of the right. It may well be that in the instant personal-injury case the outcome would be substantially affected by whether the issue of immunity is decided by a judge or a jury. Therefore, were "outcome" the only consideration, a strong case might appear for saying that the federal court should follow the state practice.

But there are affirmative countervailing considerations at work here. The federal system is an independent system for administering justice to litigants who properly invoke its jurisdiction. An essential characteristic of that system is the manner in which, in civil common-law actions, it distributes trial functions between judge and jury and, under the influence—if not the command—of the Seventh Amendment, assigns the decisions of disputed questions of fact to the jury. Jacob v. New York, 315 U.S. 752. The policy of uniform enforcement of state-created rights and obligations, see, e.g., Guaranty Trust Co. v. York, supra, cannot in every case exact compliance with a state rule—not bound up with rights and obligations—which disrupts the federal system of allocating functions between judge and jury. Herron v. Southern Pacific Co., 283 U.S. 91. Thus the inquiry here is whether the federal policy favoring jury decisions of disputed fact questions should yield to the state rule in the interest of furthering the objective that the litigation should not come out one way in the federal court and another way in the state court.

We think that in the circumstances of this case the federal court should not follow the state rule. It cannot be gainsaid that there is a strong federal policy against allowing state rules to disrupt the judge-jury relationship in the federal courts. In Herron v. Southern Pacific Co., supra, the trial judge in a personal-injury negligence action brought in the District Court for Arizona on diversity grounds directed a verdict for the defendant when it appeared as a matter of law that the plaintiff was guilty of contributory negligence. The federal judge refused to be bound by a provision of the Arizona Constitution which made the jury the sole arbiter of the question of contributory negligence. This Court sustained the action of the trial judge, holding that "state laws cannot alter the essential character or function of a federal court" because that function "is not in any sense a local matter, and state statutes which would interfere with the appropriate performance of that function are not binding upon the federal court under either the Conformity Act or the 'rules of decision' Act." Id., at 94. Perhaps even more clearly in light of the influence of the Seventh Amendment, the function assigned to the jury "is an essential factor in the process for which the Federal Constitution provides." Id., at 95. Concededly the Herron case was decided before Erie R. Co. v. Tompkins, but even when Swift v. Tyson, 16 Pet. 1, was governing law and allowed federal courts sitting in diversity cases to disregard state decisional law, it was never thought that state statutes or constitutions were similarly to be disregarded. Green v. Neal's Lessee, 6 Pet. 291. Yet Herron held that state statutes and constitutional provisions could not disrupt or alter the essential character or function of a federal court.

Third. We have discussed the problem upon the assumption that the outcome of the litigation may be substantially affected by whether the issue of immunity is decided by a judge or a jury. But clearly there is not present here the certainty that a different result would follow, cf. Guaranty Trust Co. v. York, supra, or even the strong possibility that this would be the case, cf. Bernhardt v. Polygraphic Co., supra. There are factors present here which might reduce that possibility. The trial judge in the federal system has powers denied the judges of many States to comment on the weight of evidence and credibility of witnesses, and discretion to grant a new trial if the verdict appears to him to be against the weight of the evidence. We do not think the likelihood of a different result is so strong as to require the federal practice of jury determination of disputed factual issues to yield to the state rule in the interest of uniformity of outcome.

The Court of Appeals did not consider other grounds of appeal raised by the respondent because the ground taken disposed of the case. We accordingly remand the case to the Court of Appeals for the decision of the other questions, with instructions that, if not made unnecessary by the decision of such questions, the Court of Appeals shall remand the case to the District Court for a new trial of such issues as the Court of Appeals may direct.

Reversed and remanded.*

NOTES

1. The principal case signalled a changed approach to the Erie doctrine: a state law need not be applied if it alters the "essential character or function of a Federal

---

* Mr. Justice Whittaker dissented on the issue of how integral it was to the South Carolina rule that the question of statutory immunity be decided by the judge. Justices Harlan and Frankfurter also dissented. [Eds.]

court." See Smith, Blue Ridge and Beyond: A Byrd's-Eye View of Federalism in Diversity Litigation, 36 Tul.L.Rev. 443 (1962).

2. Since Byrd, to what extent must the forum state's rules be followed as to: availability of a jury; power to remove cases from its determination; review of sufficiency of evidence for directed verdict or new trial purposes, and similar issues?

(a) As to the grant of trial by jury, the diversity court is not bound to follow the state view, because of the heavy involvement of the Seventh Amendment. See Simler v. Conner, 372 U.S. 221 (1963), rejecting the state view that trial by jury was not available on the ground the suit was in "equity."

(b) As to tests for a directed verdict and sufficiency of evidence, in pre-Byrd days, Stoner v. New York Life Insurance Co., 311 U.S. 464 (1940) was read by some courts to mean that a diversity court is bound by state rules as to the sufficiency of the evidence to go to the jury. The question was explicitly left open in Dick v. New York Life Insurance Co., 359 U.S. 437, 444–445 (1959). Wratchford v. S. J. Groves & Sons Co., 405 F.2d 1061 (4th Cir. 1969) and Planters Manufacturing Co. v. Protection Mutual Insurance Co., 380 F.2d 869 (5th Cir. 1967) held that federal, not state, law determines when the judge takes an issue from the jury for insufficiency of opposing evidence. See Wright, Law of Federal Courts 649–662 (5th Ed.1994). Federal law also governs the admissibility of evidence, including admissibility of evidence of insurance. Reed v. General Motors Corp., 773 F.2d 660 (5th Cir. 1985).

(c) As to size of the jury in civil cases, Wilson v. Nooter Corp., 475 F.2d 497 (1st Cir. 1973) ruled that having 12 jurors is not an "integral" part of the state-created right in a diversity action, so that a six-member jury suffices even when the state forum requires 12. See also Palmer v. Ford Motor Co., 498 F.2d 952 (10th Cir. 1974). See Moore & Bendix, Congress, Evidence and Rulemaking, 84 Yale L.J. 9 (1974); Note, The Law Applied in Diversity Cases: The Rules of Decision and the *Erie* Doctrine, 85 Yale L.J. 678 (1976).

(d) Kamen v. Kemper Financial Services, Inc., 500 U.S. 90 (1991) held that state law determines whether the plaintiff in a stockholder's derivative suit is excused from making a futile demand that the company's board of directors take action. The Court held that Federal Rule of Civil Procedure 23.1, which requires the complaint in such an action to "allege with particularity the efforts, if any, made by the plaintiff to obtain the action the plaintiff desires from the directors," did not require displacement of state law on the "futility" exception.

Hanna v. Plumer

Supreme Court of the United States, 1965.
380 U.S. 460, 85 S.Ct. 1136, 14 L.Ed.2d 8.

■ CHIEF JUSTICE WARREN delivered the opinion of the Court.

The question to be decided is whether, in a civil action where the jurisdiction of the United States district court is based upon diversity of citizenship between the parties, service of process shall be made in the manner prescribed by state law or that set forth in Rule 4(d)(1) of the Federal Rules of Civil Procedure.

On February 6, 1963, petitioner, a citizen of Ohio, filed her complaint in the District Court for the District of Massachusetts, claiming damages in excess of $10,000 for personal injuries resulting from an automobile accident in South Carolina, allegedly caused by the negligence of one Louise Plumer Osgood, a Massachusetts citizen deceased at the time of the filing of the complaint. Respondent, Mrs. Osgood's executor and also a Massachusetts citizen, was named as defendant. On February 8, service was made by leaving copies of the summons and the complaint with respondent's wife at his residence, concededly in compliance with Rule 4(d)(1), which provides: "The summons and complaint shall be served together . . . . as follows: (1) Upon an individual . . . by delivering a copy . . . to him personally or by leaving copies thereof at his . . . usual place of abode with some person of suitable age and discretion then residing therein. . . ." Respondent filed his answer . . . alleging, *inter alia*, that the action could not be maintained because [service had not been made in accordance with the "delivery in hand"] provisions of Massachusetts General Laws (Ter. Ed.) Chapter 197, Section 9. . . . On October 17, 1963, the District Court granted respondent's motion for summary judgment, citing Ragan v. Merchants Transfer & Warehouse Co., 337 U.S. 530, and Guaranty Trust Co. of New York v. York, 326 U.S. 99, . . . The Court of Appeals for the First Circuit, . . . unanimously affirmed. . . .

We conclude that the adoption of Rule 4(d)(1), designed to control service of process in diversity actions, neither exceeded the congressional mandate embodied in the Rules Enabling Act [quoted on pages 664–665 of the Casebook] nor transgressed constitutional bounds, and that the Rule is therefore the standard against which the District Court should have measured the adequacy of the service. Accordingly, we reverse the decision of the Court of Appeals. . . .

Respondent suggests that the Erie doctrine acts as a check on the Federal Rules of Civil Procedure . . . Reduced to essentials, the argument is: (1) Erie, as refined in York, demands that federal courts apply state law whenever application of federal law in its stead will alter the outcome of the case. (2) In this case a determination that the Massachusetts service requirements obtained will result in immediate victory for respondent. If, on the other hand, it should be held that Rule 4(d)(1) is applicable, the litigation will continue, with possible victory for petitioner. (3) Therefore, Erie demands application of the Massachusetts rule. The syllogism possesses an appealing simplicity, but is for several reasons invalid.

In the first place, it is doubtful that, even if there were no Federal Rule making it clear that in-hand service is not required in diversity actions, the Erie rule would have obligated the District Court to follow the Massachusetts procedure. "Outcome-determination" analysis was never intended to serve as a talisman. . . . Indeed, the message of *York* itself is that choices between state and federal law are to be made not by the application of any automatic, "litmus paper" criterion, but rather by reference to the policies underlying the *Erie* rule. Guaranty Trust Co. v. York, supra, at 108–112.

The Erie rule is rooted in part in a realization that it would be unfair for the character or result of a litigation materially to differ because the suit had been brought in a federal court. . . . The decision was also in part a reaction to the practice of "forum-shopping" which had grown up in response to the rule of Swift v. Tyson.... Not only are nonsubstantial, or trivial, variations not likely to raise the sort of equal protection problems which troubled the Court in Erie; they are also unlikely to influence the choice of a forum. The "outcome-determination" test therefore cannot be read without reference to the twin aims of the Erie rule: discouragement of forum-shopping and avoidance of inequitable administration of the laws.

The difference between the conclusion that the Massachusetts rule is applicable, and the conclusion that it is not, is of course at this point "outcome-determinative" in the sense that if we hold the state rule to apply, respondent prevails, whereas if we hold that Rule 4(d)(1) governs, the litigation will continue. But in this sense *every* procedural variation is "outcome-determinative." For example, having brought suit in a federal court, a plaintiff cannot then insist on the right to file subsequent pleadings in accord with the time limits applicable in state courts, even though enforcement of the federal timetable will, if he continues to insist that he must meet only the state time limit, result in determination of the controversy against him. So it is here. Though choice of the federal or state rule will at this point have a marked effect upon the outcome of the litigation, the difference between the two rules would be of scant, if any, relevance to the choice of a forum. Petitioner, in choosing her forum, was not presented with a situation where application of the state rule would wholly bar recovery; rather, adherence to the state rule would have resulted only in altering the way in which process was served....

There is, however, a more fundamental flaw in respondent's syllogism: the incorrect assumption that the rule of Erie R. Co. v. Tompkins constitutes the appropriate test of the validity and therefore the applicability of a Federal Rule of Civil Procedure. The Erie rule has never been invoked to void a Federal Rule....

... It is true that both the Enabling Act and the Erie rule say, roughly, that federal courts are to apply state "substantive" law and federal "procedural" law, but from that it need not follow that the tests are identical. For they were designed to control very different sorts of decisions. When a situation is covered by one of the Federal Rules, the question facing the court is a far cry from the typical, relatively unguided Erie choice: the court has been instructed to apply the Federal Rule, and can refuse to do so only if the Advisory Committee, this Court, and Congress erred in their prima facie judgment that the Rule in question transgresses neither the terms of the Enabling Act nor constitutional restrictions.

... [T]he opinion in Erie, which involved no Federal Rule and dealt with a question which was "substantive" in every traditional sense (whether the railroad owed a duty of care to Tompkins as a trespasser or a licensee), surely neither said nor implied that measures like Rule 4(d)(1) are unconstitutional. For the constitutional provision for a federal court system (augmented by the Necessary and Proper Clause) carries with it congressional power to make rules governing the practice and pleading in those courts, which in turn includes a power to regulate matters which, though falling within the uncertain area between substance and procedure, are rationally capable of classification as either....

Erie and its offspring cast no doubt on the long-recognized power of Congress to prescribe housekeeping rules for federal courts even though some of those rules will inevitably differ from comparable state rules.... To hold that a Federal Rule of Civil Procedure must cease to function whenever it alters the mode of enforcing state-created rights would be to disembowel either the Constitution's grant of power over federal procedure or Congress' attempt to exercise that power in the Enabling Act. Rule 4(d)(1) is valid and controls the instant case.

Reversed.

■ JUSTICE HARLAN, concurring.

It is unquestionably true that up to now Erie and the cases following it have not succeeded in articulating a workable doctrine governing choice of law in diversity actions. I respect the Court's effort to clarify the situation in today's opinion. However, in doing so I think it has misconceived the constitutional premises of Erie and has failed to deal adequately with those past decisions upon which the courts below relied.

Erie was something more than an opinion which worried about "forum-shopping and avoidance of inequitable administration of the laws," ... although to be sure these were important elements of the decision. I have always regarded that decision as one of the modern cornerstones of our federalism, expressing policies that profoundly touch the allocation of judicial power between the state and federal systems. Erie recognized that there should not be two conflicting systems of law controlling the primary activity of citizens, for such alternative governing authority must necessarily give rise to a debilitating uncertainty in the planning of everyday affairs. And it recognized that the scheme of our Constitution envisions an allocation of law-making functions between state and federal legislative processes which is undercut if the federal judiciary can make substantive law affecting state affairs beyond the bounds of congressional legislative powers in this regard. Thus, in diversity cases Erie commands that it be the state law governing primary private activity which prevails.

The shorthand formulations which have appeared in some past decisions are prone to carry untoward results that frequently arise from oversimplification. The Court is quite right in stating that the "outcome-determinative" test of Guaranty Trust Co. of New York v. York, 326 U.S. 99, if taken literally, proves too much, for any rule, no matter how clearly "procedural," can affect the outcome of litigation if it is not obeyed. In turning from the "outcome" test of York back to the unadorned forum-shopping rationale of Erie, however, the Court falls prey to like oversimplification, for a simple forum-shopping rule also proves too much; litigants often choose a federal forum merely to obtain what they consider the advantages of the Federal Rules of Civil Procedure or to try their cases before a supposedly more favorable judge. To my mind the proper line of approach in determining whether to apply a state or a federal rule, whether "substantive" or "procedural," is to stay close to basic principles by inquiring if the choice of rule would substantially affect those primary decisions respecting human conduct which our constitutional system leaves to state regulation. If so, Erie and the Constitution require that the state rule prevail, even in the face of a conflicting federal rule.

The Court weakens, if indeed it does not submerge, this basic principle by finding, in effect, a grant of substantive legislative power in the constitutional provision for a federal court system ..., and through it, setting up the Federal Rules as a body of law inviolate. So long as a reasonable man could characterize any duly adopted federal rule as "procedural," the Court, unless I misapprehend what is said, would have it apply no matter how seriously it frustrated a State's substantive regulation of the primary conduct and affairs of its citizens. Since the members of the Advisory Committee, the Judicial Conference, and this Court who formulated the Federal Rules are presumably reasonable men, it follows that the integrity of the Federal Rules is absolute. Whereas the unadulterated outcome and forum-shopping tests may err too far toward honoring state rules, I submit that the Court's "arguably procedural, *ergo* constitutional" test moves too fast and far in the other direction.

The courts below relied upon this Court's decisions in Ragan v. Merchants Transfer & Warehouse Co., 337 U.S. 530, and Cohen v. Beneficial Indus. Loan Corp., 337 U.S. 541. Those cases deserve more attention than this Court has given them, particularly Ragan which, if still good law, would in my opinion call for affirmance of the result reached by the Court of Appeals. Further, a discussion of these two cases will serve to illuminate the "diversity" thesis I am advocating.

In Ragan a Kansas statute of limitations provided that an action was deemed commenced when service was made on the defendant. Despite Federal Rule 3 which provides that an action commences with the filing of the complaint, the Court held that for purposes of the Kansas statute of limitations a diversity tort action commenced only when service was made upon the defendant. The effect of this holding was that although the plaintiff had filed his federal complaint within the state period of limitations, his action was barred because the federal marshal did not serve a summons on the defendant until after the limitations period had run. I think that the decision was wrong. At most, application of the Federal Rule would have meant that potential Kansas tort defendants would have to defer for a few days the satisfaction of knowing that they had not been sued within the limitations period. The choice of the Federal Rule would have had no effect on the primary stages of private activity from which torts arise, and only the most minimal effect on behavior following the commission of the tort. In such circumstances the interest of the federal system in proceeding under its own rules should have prevailed.

Cohen v. Beneficial Indus. Loan Corp. held that a federal diversity court must apply a state statute requiring a small stockholder in a stockholder derivative suit to post a bond securing payment of defense costs as a condition to prosecuting an action. Such a statute is not "outcome determinative"; the plaintiff can win with or without it.... The proper view of Cohen is, in my opinion, that the statute was meant to inhibit small stockholders from instituting "strike suits," and thus it was designed and could be expected to have a substantial impact on private primary activity. Anyone who was at the trial bar during the period when Cohen arose can appreciate the strong state policy reflected in the statute. I think it wholly legitimate to view Federal Rule 23 as not purporting to deal with the problem. But even had the Federal Rules purported to do so, and in so doing provided a substantially less effective deterrent to strike suits, I think the state rule should still have prevailed. That is where I believe the Court's view differs from mine; for the Court attributes such overriding force to the Federal Rules that it is hard to think of a case where a conflicting state rule would be allowed to operate, even though the state rule reflected policy considerations which, under Erie, would lie within the realm of state legislative authority.

It remains to apply what has been said to the present case. The Massachusetts rule provides that an executor need not answer suits unless in-hand service was made upon him or notice of the action was filed in the proper registry of probate within one year of his giving bond. The evident intent of this statute is to permit an executor to distribute the estate which he is administering without fear that further liabilities may be outstanding for which he could be held personally liable. If the Federal District Court in Massachusetts applies Rule 4(d)(1) of the Federal Rules of Civil Procedure instead of the Massachusetts service rule, what effect would that have on the speed and assurance with which estates are distributed? As I see it, the effect would not be substantial. It would mean simply that an executor would have to check at his own house or the federal courthouse as well as the registry of probate before he could distribute the estate with impunity. As this does not seem enough to give rise to any real impingement on the vitality of the state policy which the Massachusetts rule is intended to serve, I concur in the judgment of the Court.

WALKER V. ARMCO STEEL CORP., 446 U.S. 740 (1980): In a diversity action the complaint was filed within the two year statute of limitations of the forum state, but defendant was not served with process until after the statutory period had run. The Court found these facts "indistinguishable" from those in Ragan v. Merchants Transfer & Warehouse Co., 337 U.S. 530 (1949), Note 4, p. 673, supra. Contrary to petitioner's claim, Ragan was not weakened by Hanna v. Plumer because Rule 3 did not come into "direct collision" with state law by affecting the running of state statutes of limitation. The Court said, 446 U.S., at pp. 751–52:

"In contrast to Rule 3, the Oklahoma statute is a statement of a substantive decision by that State that actual service on, and accordingly actual notice by, the defendant is an integral part of the several policies served by the statute of limitations. See C & C Tile Co. v. Independent

School District No. 7 of Tulsa County, 503 P.2d 554, 559 (Okl.1972). The statute of limitations establishes a deadline after which the defendant may legitimately have peace of mind; it also recognizes that after a certain period of time it is unfair to require the defendant to attempt to piece together his defense to an old claim. A requirement of actual service promotes both of those functions of the statute. See generally ibid.; Seitz v. Jones, 370 P.2d 300, 302 (Okl.1961). See also Ely, The Irrepressible Myth of Erie, 87 Harv.L.Rev. 693, 730–731 (1974).[12] It is these policy aspects which make the service requirement an 'integral' part of the statute of limitations both in this case and in *Ragan*. As such, the service rule must be considered part and parcel of the statute of limitations."

NOTES

1. For a treatment of Hanna and the problems it addresses, see Ely, The Irrepressible Myth of Erie, 87 Harv.L.Rev. 693 (1974). Commenting *dubitante* on Professor Ely's view that the Enabling Act furnishes a useful standard in determining whether federal law is applicable whenever the issue is covered by a Federal Rule, see Chayes, The Bead Game, 87 Harv.L.Rev. 741 (1974). After *Hanna* and *Walker* if the Federal Rules of Civil Procedure adopt provisions fixing time limitations for diversity actions in the federal courts, will they be constitutional? If so, is Guaranty Trust Co. v. York overruled?

2. Byrnes v. Kirby, 453 F.Supp. 1014 (D.Mass.1978). Diversity action in a federal district court in Massachusetts to recover for injuries suffered in this state as the result of alleged malpractice. Upon motion of the defendant, the court referred the case to a medical malpractice tribunal pursuant to a Massachusetts statute which provided that if the tribunal were to find that the case involved "merely an unfortunate medical result" the plaintiff could maintain the action only after filing a bond. The court said that

> reference to a medical malpractice tribunal ... would fulfill the "twin aims of Erie," expressed in the *Hanna* case, of preventing forum shopping and avoiding unfairness in the administration of the laws.... It would ... be inequitable to permit [diversity] litigants to bypass the procedure of a tribunal hearing.... There appears to be no federal policy, such as that favoring jury determination of factual issues ... that would be contravened by [this] reference to a state medical malpractice tribunal.

12. The importance of actual service, with corresponding actual notice, to the statute of limitations scheme in Oklahoma is further demonstrated by the fact that under Okla.Stat., Tit. 12, § 97 (1971) the statute of limitations must be tolled as to each defendant through individual service, unless a codefendant who is served is "united in interest" with the unserved defendant. That requirement, like the service requirement itself, does nothing to promote the general policy behind all statutes of limitations of keeping stale claims out of court. Instead, the service requirement furthers a different but related policy decision: that each defendant has a legitimate right not to be surprised by notice of a lawsuit after the period of liability has run. If the defendant is "united in interest" with a codefendant who has been served, then presumably the defendant will receive actual notice of the lawsuit through the codefendant and will not have his peace of mind disturbed when he receives official service of process. Similarly, the defendant will know that he must begin gathering his evidence while that task is still deemed by the State to be feasible.

For a discussion of the factors that should be considered by a federal court in determining whether to apply federal or state law in a situation not covered by a federal rule, see Redish and Phillips, *Erie* and the Rules of Decision Act: In Search of the Appropriate Dilemma, 91 Harv.L.Rev. 356 (1977). See also Wellborn, The Federal Rules of Evidence and The Application of State Law in The Federal Courts, 55 Tex.L.Rev. 371 (1977).

That federal, not state, standards determine whether a preliminary injunction should issue, see Southern Milk Sales, Inc. v. Martin, 924 F.2d 98 (6th Cir.1991); Equifax Services, Inc. v. Hitz, 905 F.2d 1355 (10th Cir.1990).

3. Burlington Northern R. Co. v. Woods, 480 U.S. 1 (1987): Federal Rule of Appellate Procedure 38, giving the Court of Appeals discretion to assess "just damages" in order to penalize an appellant for filing a frivolous appeal, applied over conflicting rule of state law providing for mandatory affirmance as the penalty.

But see Simmons v. City of Philadelphia, 947 F.2d 1042 (3d Cir.1991), cert. denied, 503 U.S. 985 (1992) (sovereign immunity defense which was not raised during the trial but which is non-waivable under state law given preference over Federal Rule 50(b), requiring motions for judgments "as a matter of law" to be made before submission to the jury).

In Johnson v. Hugo's Skateway, 974 F.2d 1408 (4th Cir.1992, en banc), the appellate court accommodated the forum state's practice of allowing the trial judge to adjust jury verdicts, including punitive damage awards, as against the more restrictive Federal Rules 50(b) and 59, by directing the incorporation of the relevant state standards for the award of punitive damages in the initial jury instructions. Other examples of accommodation of federal and state practice include: Nereson v. Zurich Insurance Co., 1992 WL 212233 (D.N.D.1992); Connolly v. Foudree, 141 F.R.D. 124 (S.D.Iowa 1992).

4. To what extent do state rules of res judicata prevail over federal in determining the effect of the decision in later litigation? See Vestal, Res Judicata/Preclusion by Judgment: The Law Applied in Federal Courts, 66 Mich.L.Rev. 1723 (1968). Cf. Vestal, Res Judicata Preclusion: Expansion, 47 So.Cal.L.Rev. 357, 359 (1974); Vestal, Preclusion/Res Judicata Variables: Parties, 50 Iowa L.Rev. 27 (1964). See Chapter 5, pp. 246–250, supra; Angel v. Bullington, p. 705. Havoco of America, Ltd. v. Freeman, Atkins & Coleman, Ltd., 58 F.3d 303 (7th Cir.1995), holds that federal principles of issue preclusion apply when the first judgment is that of a federal court sitting in diversity and collects authority.

5. When it appears to a federal court that there is no controlling precedent in state supreme court or intermediate appellate court decisions, determination of state law is made easier in all but seven states by state statutes permitting a federal court to certify the question to the highest state court. Nine states limit certification to federal appellate courts. See Hogue, Law in a Parallel Universe: Erie's Betrayal, Diversity Jurisdiction, Georgia Conflict of Laws Questions in Contracts Cases in the Eleventh Circuit, and Certification Reform, 11 Ga.State U.L.Rev. 531, 536 (1995) (citing statutes). For discussion of the precedential value of intermediate appellate decisions and of plurality decisions of a state supreme court see Klippel v. U–Haul Co. of Northeastern Michigan, 759 F.2d 1176, 1181 (4th Cir.1985) (stating that "we are free to disregard [a decision of a state intermediate appellate court] when it appears to be an aberration and we are reasonably convinced that the [state's highest court] would not embrace it"); McGowan v. University of Scranton, 759 F.2d 287, 291–93 (3d Cir.1985) (discussing precedential value of both state intermediate appellate and state supreme court plurality decisions). See also Factors Etc., Inc. v. Pro Arts, Inc., 701 F.2d 11 (2d Cir.1983), p. 702 infra.

Salve Regina College v. Russell, 499 U.S. 225 (1991) holds that federal courts of appeal must review de novo district courts' determinations of state law, overruling cases from a majority of the circuits that had deferred to district court determinations.

6. One issue affecting the relationship between federal and state courts is whether a federal court should dismiss or stay a suit when the same action is pending in a state court. Colorado River Water Conservation District v. United States, 424 U.S. 800 (1976), held that a federal district court properly dismissed an action brought by the United States to determine water rights that it asserted in Colorado. The same rights were being adjudicated in state proceedings. The Court, however, indicated that circumstances were rare in which a federal district court should dismiss because of parallel state litigation and referred to the "virtually unflagging obligation of the federal courts to exercise the jurisdiction given them." Id. at 817. The Court stated that there were only three general categories of cases in which abstention in favor of state litigation was proper: (1) "cases presenting a federal constitutional issue which might be mooted or presented in a different posture by a state court determination of pertinent state law"; (2) "there have been presented difficult questions of state law bearing on policy problems of substantial public import whose importance transcends the result in the case then at bar"; (3) "absent bad faith, harassment or a patently invalid state statute, federal jurisdiction has been invoked for the purpose of restraining state criminal proceedings." Id. at 814. Outside of these three categories, "[o]nly the clearest of justifications will warrant dismissal." Id. at 819. Factors indicating whether such a justification is present include whether the state has first assumed jurisdiction over property in which interests are being adjudicated, forum convenience, the desirability of avoiding piecemeal adjudication, and the order in which jurisdiction was obtained. Id. at 818. In this case, the most important factor justifying dismissal was the enactment of 43 U.S.C.A. § 666 consenting to jurisdiction over the United States in any suit adjudicating water rights, thus evidencing a federal policy of avoiding piecemeal adjudication of water rights.

Moses H. Cone Memorial Hospital v. Mercury Construction Corp., 460 U.S. 1 (1983), held it improper for a district court to stay an action to compel arbitration pursuant to § 4 of the United States Arbitration Act pending resolution of a state-court suit that also involved the arbitrability of the claims in issue. The Court stated that none of the exceptional circumstances discussed in Colorado River were present.

Wilton v. Seven Falls Co., 115 S.Ct. 2137 (1995), held it proper for a federal district court to stay an action for a declaratory judgment brought by insurers. The federal action was brought after the insureds had notified the insurers that the insureds intended to sue on the policies in state court. The state action was then brought. The Court stated that the Colorado River and Moses H. Cone restrictions on federal abstention in favor of parallel state proceedings do not apply to declaratory judgment actions, noting that the Declaratory Judgment Act, 28 U.S.C.A. § 2201(a) (1988), stated that a federal court "may" declare litigants' rights. A district court's stay or dismissal of a declaratory judgment action should be reversed only for abuse of discretion.

7. Piper Aircraft Co. v. Reyno, 454 U.S. 235 (1981), supra page 184, left open the question of whether in diversity cases a federal court must apply the forum non conveniens doctrine of the state in which it sits or whether it should apply a federal standard. Id. at 248 n. 13. Forum non conveniens has not been displaced in federal courts by 28 U.S.C.A. § 1404(a) transfers when the alternative forum is not another federal district court. The Erie question is of great tactical importance in states that do not grant forum non conveniens dismissals or do so in much more limited circumstances than permitted by the federal doctrine. If federal courts are free to dismiss when a state court would not, plaintiffs will sue in states with no or limited conveniens doctrines and will take steps to prevent removal to federal court, such as joining a local defendant. See 28 U.S.C.A. § 1441(b) (1988), providing that a case cannot be removed if any defendant is a citizen of the state in which suit is brought. The defendant may counter such tactics by claiming that the joinder of the local defendant was fraudulent. See Cabalceta v. Standard Fruit Co., 883 F.2d 1553 (11th Cir.1989) (reversing the district court's forum non conveniens dismissal, which was based on a finding of fraudulent joinder under Florida law, and remanding for determination of the fraudulent joinder claim under the applicable Costa Rican law).

The First, Fifth, and Eleventh circuits have decided that a federal court may grant a forum non conveniens dismissal even though a court of the state in which it is sitting would not. Royal Bed & Spring Co. v. Famossul Industria e Comercio de Moveis Ltda., 906 F.2d 45, 50 (1st Cir.1990); In re Air Crash Disaster Near New Orleans, La., 821 F.2d 1147, 1153–59 (5th Cir.1987), judgment vacated for further consideration of another issue, 490 U.S. 1032 (1989), remanded for reconsideration of damages, otherwise reinstated, 883 F.2d 17 (5th Cir.1989); Sibaja v. Dow Chem. Co., 757 F.2d 1215, 1219 (11th Cir.1985), cert. denied, 474 U.S. 948 (1985). Accord 15 Wright, Federal Practice & Procedure § 3828, at 293–94 (2d ed. 1986). It is doubtful that Learned Hand's statement in Weiss v. Routh, 149 F.2d 193, 195 (2d Cir.1945), that "we should follow the New York decisions" extends beyond the special rule denying jurisdiction over the "internal affairs" of a foreign corporation, or whether, if it does, the decision is viable. Gilbert v. Gulf Oil Corp., 153 F.2d 883, 885 (2d Cir.1946), rev'd on other grounds, 330 U.S. 501 (1947), explains Weiss as dealing with the internal affairs rule and states that "New York law should not control" with regard to the application of forum non conveniens.

American Dredging Co. v. Miller, 114 S.Ct. 981 (1994), held that a Louisiana statute preventing forum non conveniens dismissals in federal maritime actions in state court, including actions under the Jones Act for injuries to seamen, is not preempted by federal maritime law. The opinion stated that the doctrine of forum non conveniens is not "either a 'characteristic feature' of admiralty or a doctrine whose uniform application is necessary to maintain the 'proper harmony' of maritime law." Id. at 985.

B. THE ERIE DOCTRINE AND CONFLICT OF LAWS IN DIVERSITY CASES

In Sampson v. Channell, 110 F.2d 754 (1st Cir. 1940), cert. denied 310 U.S. 650, the issue was whether a federal diversity court in Massachusetts was bound to follow state or federal law as to burden of proof of contributory negligence by plaintiff in a Maine auto accident case; and if state law, that of Maine or Massachusetts. In the view of the Court of Appeals, the questions turned on whether the burden of proof question should be classified as an issue of federal procedure, in order to implement the underlying policy of the Erie doctrine, or whether it should be viewed as substantive under a fair reading of that doctrine's criteria. In a superb opinion Judge Magruder ruled that the issue was substantive by Erie criteria and, hence, that state law was determinative; that Massachusetts would have applied its own burden rule, classifying the issue as procedural for state-state choice-of-law purposes; that this would be a constitutionally valid approach; and that consistent with the "implications" of Erie, the federal court must follow the Massachusetts conflict of laws approach, in order to promote uniformity between the federal and state courts of the forum.

Does not the Sampson decision pose the prospect of a lack of uniformity among federal courts, not only on any given issue, but even on a single issue in a single case? Thus, if suit is brought in one federal court (i.e., Maine, the site of the accident) rather than in another possible forum (i.e., Massachusetts, where one side was domiciled), the outcome changes.

In non-diversity cases, such as admiralty or other federal specialities, the federal courts are, of course, free to fashion independent choice-of-law rules. See e.g., Scott v. Eastern Air Lines, 399 F.2d 14 (3d Cir. 1967), cert. denied 393 U.S. 979 (1968); Cohen v. Hathaway, 595 F.Supp. 579 (D.Mass. 1984) (suits in admiralty are governed by federal substantive and procedural law). For a discussion of choice of law in admiralty, see Note, supra page 651.

Klaxon Co. v. Stentor Electric Manufacturing Co.

Supreme Court of the United States, 1941.
313 U.S. 487, 61 S.Ct. 1020, 85 L.Ed. 1477.

■ JUSTICE REED delivered the opinion of the Court.

The principal question in this case is whether in diversity cases the federal courts must follow conflict of laws rules prevailing in the states in which they sit. We left this open in Ruhlin v. New York Life Insurance Company, 304 U.S. 202, 208, note 2. The frequent recurrence of the problem, as well as the conflict of approach to the problem between the Third Circuit's opinion here and that of the First Circuit in Sampson v. Channell, 110 F.2d 754, 759–762, 128 A.L.R. 394, led us to grant certiorari.

In 1918 respondent, a New York corporation, transferred its entire business to petitioner, a Delaware corporation. Petitioner contracted to use its best efforts to further the manufacture and sale of certain patented devices covered by the agreement, and respondent was to have a share of petitioner's profits. The agreement was executed in New York, the assets were transferred there, and petitioner began performance there although later it moved its operations to other states. Respondent was voluntarily dissolved under New York law in 1919. Ten years later it instituted this action in the United States District Court for the District of Delaware, alleging that petitioner had failed to perform its agreement to use its best efforts. Jurisdiction rested on diversity of citizenship. In 1939 respondent recovered a jury verdict of $100,000, upon which judgment was entered. Respondent then moved to correct the judgment by adding interest at the rate of six percent from June 1, 1929, the date the action had been brought.

The basis of the motion was the provision in section 480 of the New York Civil Practice Act directing that in contract actions interest be added to the principal sum "whether theretofore liquidated or unliquidated." The District Court granted the motion, taking the view that the rights of the parties were governed by New York law and that under New York law the addition of such interest was mandatory. 30 F.Supp. 425, 431. The Circuit Court of Appeals affirmed, 3 Cir., 115 F.2d 268, 275, and we granted certiorari, limited to the question whether section 480 of the New York Civil Practice Act is applicable to an action in the federal court in Delaware, 312 U.S. 674.

The Circuit Court of Appeals was of the view that under New York law the right to interest before verdict under section 480 went to the substance of the obligation, and that proper construction of the contract in suit fixed New York as the place of performance. It then concluded that section 480 was applicable to the case because "it is clear by what we think is undoubtedly the better view of the law that the rules for ascertaining the measure of damages are not a matter of procedure at all, but are matters of substance which should be settled by reference to the law of the appropriate state according to the type of case being tried in the forum. The measure of damages for breach of a contract is determined by the law of the place of performance; Restatement, Conflict of Laws, sec. 413." The court referred also to section 418 of the Restatement, which makes interest part of the damages to be determined by the law of the place of performance. Application of the New York statute apparently followed from the court's independent determination of the "better view" without regard to Delaware law, for no Delaware decision or statute was cited or discussed.

We are of opinion that the prohibition declared in Erie Railroad v. Tompkins, 304 U.S. 64, against such independent determinations by the federal courts extends to the field of conflict of laws. The conflict of laws rules to be applied by the federal court in Delaware must conform to those prevailing in Delaware's state courts. Otherwise the accident of diversity of citizenship would constantly disturb equal administration of justice in coordinate state and federal courts sitting side by side. ... Any other ruling would do violence to the principle of uniformity within a state upon which the Tompkins decision is based. Whatever lack of uniformity this may produce between federal courts in different states is attributable to our federal system, which leaves to a state, within the limits permitted by the Constitution, the right to pursue local policies diverging from those of its neighbors. It is not for the federal courts to thwart such local policies by enforcing an independent "general law" of conflict of laws. Subject only to review by this Court on any federal question that may arise, Delaware is free to determine whether a given matter is to be governed by the law of the forum or some other law. Cf. Milwaukee County v. White Co., 296 U.S. 268, 272. This Court's views are not the decisive factor in determining the applicable conflicts rule. Cf. Funkhouser v. J.B. Preston Co., 290 U.S. 163. And the proper function of the Delaware federal court is to ascertain what the state law is, not what it ought to be.... [The opinion states it would be constitutional for Delaware to apply its local law in this case.]

Accordingly, the judgment is reversed and the case remanded to the Circuit Court of Appeals for decision in conformity with the law of Delaware.

NOTES

1. On remand of the principal case the Court of Appeals found there was no Delaware statute or decision directly on the conflict of laws point. It adhered to its earlier conclusion that the Delaware conflict of laws rule was that the New York local law would govern. 125 F.2d 820 (1942). The Supreme Court denied certiorari. 316 U.S. 685 (1942).

Yohannon v. Keene Corp., 924 F.2d 1255 (3d Cir.1991) held that because a Pennsylvania state court would regard pre-judgment interest as procedural, a federal court sitting in Pennsylvania should apply the Pennsylvania rule even though New Jersey law was applicable to all other aspects of the case.

2. Is Klaxon v. Stentor an inevitable deduction from the logic of Erie? Should a federal court in a diversity action be any less able to prescribe its own choice of law rules than a court of State Z in a transaction solely connected with states X and Y? Cf. Cheatham, Federal Control of Conflict of Laws, 6 Vand.L.Rev. 581 (1953). For a penetrating and comprehensive discussion of the subject, see Cavers, Change in Choice-of-Law Thinking and Its Bearing on the Klaxon Problem, in the American Law Institute's Study of the Division of Jurisdiction Between State and Federal Courts (Official Draft 1969). See also Baxter, Choice of Law and the Federal System, 16 Stan.L.Rev. 1 (1963); Meador, State Law and the Federal Judicial Power, 49 Va.L.Rev. 1082 (1963); Weintraub, Commentary on the Conflict of Laws 587–614 (3d Ed.1986).

3. The Supreme Court went out of its way in Day and Zimmerman v. Challoner, 423 U.S. 3 (1975), to reaffirm Klaxon. In a tort action, the Fifth Circuit had held that Cambodia, the country where an artillery round had prematurely exploded and had caused injury to American service personnel, had no interest in having its law applied in an action by American claimants against the American manufacturer. In the absence of a conflict among interested states, the court had applied the law of the forum (Texas). The Supreme Court reversed:

> "... A federal court in a diversity case is not free to engraft onto ... state rules [of choice of law] exceptions or modifications which may commend themselves to the federal court, but which have not commended themselves to the State in which the federal court sits."

4. In re Holiday Airlines Corp., 620 F.2d 731 (9th Cir. 1980). The question involved the effect that should be given in a California bankruptcy proceeding to an artisan's lien for work done in the State of Washington on a propeller assembly. The Court held that the lien was effective under the law of Washington which, being the state of most significant relationship, was the state whose law should be applied. The Court said that "the rule in diversity of citizenship cases, i.e., a mechanical application of the conflicts law of the forum State, should not be required in bankruptcy proceedings, at least in Federal Aviation Act cases."

Wood v. Mid–Valley Inc., 942 F.2d 425 (7th Cir.1991) held that if the parties agree at trial that forum law applies, a federal court will apply that law and need not follow state "procedure" that might require the court to raise the issue on its own motion. The court distinguished choice-of-law clauses in contracts. The validity of such clauses must be determined by state law.

GRIFFIN V. MCCOACH, 313 U.S. 498 (1941): A policy of insurance on the life of a syndicate promoter named the members of the syndicate, who were to pay the premiums as the principal beneficiaries. The promoter was a citizen of Texas, but the policy was applied for and delivered in New York. The application was acted on in New Jersey at the home office of the Insurance company. Years later an agreement not to change beneficiaries was executed. All elements of this latter transaction occurred in either New York or New Jersey, except that the promoter insured signed the insurance forms in Texas. On the death of the insured his personal representative contended that the syndicate members could not take under the policy, for according to Texas law they had no insurable interest. The insurance company filed a bill of interpleader in the federal court in Texas to have it determined who was entitled to the proceeds of the policy. Federal interpleader permits nationwide service of process. The personal representative of the insured urged that Texas law should be held to govern the transaction, but that even if the law of another state applied it was against the public policy of Texas for the syndicate members to collect the proceeds.

■ JUSTICE REED....

For the reasons given in Klaxon Co. v. Stentor Electric Manufacturing Co., 313 U.S. 487, decided today, we are of the view that the federal courts in diversity of citizenship cases are governed by the conflict of laws rules of the courts of the states in which they sit. In deciding that the changes made in the insurance contract left its governing law unaffected and that the laws of Texas could not be applied to a foreign contract in Texas courts, the federal courts were applying rules of law in a way which may or may not have been consistent with Texas decisions. Likewise it is for Texas to say whether its public policy permits a beneficiary of an insurance policy on the life of a Texas citizen to recover where no insurable interest in the decedent exists in the beneficiary.... The decision must be reversed and remanded to the Circuit Court of Appeals for determination of the law of Texas as applied to the circumstances of this case.

. . .

If upon examination of the Texas law it appears that the courts of Texas would refuse enforcement of an insurance contract where the beneficiaries have no insurable interest on the ground of its interference with local law, such refusal would be, in our opinion, within the constitutional power of the Texas courts.... [T]his Court affirmed the federal court in following Texas' decisions which refused to enforce a valid foreign contract of guarantyship against a married woman. Union Trust Co. v. Grosman, 245 U.S. 412.... Where this Court has required the state of the forum to apply the foreign law under the full faith and credit clause or under the

Fourteenth Amendment it has recognized that a state is not required to enforce a law obnoxious to its public policy. . . .

. . . It is for the state to say whether a contract contrary to such a statute or rule of law is so offensive to its view of public welfare as to require its courts to close their doors to its enforcement.

Reversed.

■ JUSTICE FRANKFURTER concurs in the result.

NOTES

1. Is the Griffin case "unreasonable" in applying the law of Texas to a person from outside the state considering that a Texas state court could not have exercised judicial jurisdiction over him? See Vestal, Erie R.R. v. Tompkins: A Projection, 48 Iowa L.Rev. 248, 269 (1963). See Whirlpool Corp. v. Ritter, 929 F.2d 1318, 1321 (8th Cir.1991), which, in dictum, rejects the argument that *Klaxon* should not apply to federal interpleader proceedings in which the stakeholder filing the action has no interest in the outcome and jurisdiction is exercised over parties beyond the reach of state courts.

2. Are the federal courts to have any share in the development of conflict of laws? See Freund, Chief Justice Stone and the Conflict of Laws, 59 Harv.L.Rev. 1210, 1236 (1946). Did the summary rejection of federally fashioned choice-of-law rules and reaffirmation of Klaxon in Day and Zimmerman, Inc. v. Challoner, 423 U.S. 3 (1975), end that speculation?

The Impact of Interest Analysis Upon Klaxon and Griffin

Was Klaxon correct to fear that freeing a federal diversity court from the choice-of-law rules of the state forum "would do violence" to Erie's principle? Many commentators believe not. Professor Alfred Hill argued that local bias—the very evil federal diversity jurisdiction was to combat—can make itself felt "particularly through arbitrary choice of law rules" which bear unevenly on out-of-state litigants. Hill, The Erie Doctrine and The Constitution, 53 Nw.U.L.Rev. 427, 544 (1958). This was true even in the days when the vested rights approach to choice of law was the norm. It may be even more true in modern times, with the rise of the interest analysis, which some commentators claim has strong forum-favoring tendencies.

In Hart and Wechsler, The Federal Courts and The Federal System 634–35 (1953), the argument was made that the Klaxon doctrine is directly opposed to Erie's purpose of avoiding uncertainty for persons conducting primary activities, because when the doctrine is applied results will shift with the happenstance of the forum's choice-of-law rules; and the unpredictability will apply in federal courts as much as in state courts.

Is the Erie doctrine not misapplied here for yet another reason? When multistate "interests" collide, why should the United States courts not function as federal system umpires, rather than as "ventriloquists' dummies" for the state courts of the forum? See Hart, The Relations Between State and Federal Law, 54 Colum.L.Rev. 489 (1954); Baxter, Choice of Law and The Federal System, 16 Stan.L.Rev. 1 (1963); Horowitz, Toward a Federal Common Law of Choice of Law, 14 U.C.L.A.L.Rev. 1191 (1967).

Taking the other side of the argument, Professor Cavers, p. 690, n. 2, supra, favors the Klaxon doctrine for several reasons already noted and also on the pragmatic ground that forum-shopping as between state and federal courts in a given state is a more serious risk than the possibility of shopping across state lines. This is so because the person in control of the choice of forum is the plaintiff's lawyer, who may not want to send the case to an attorney in another state, thus losing or reducing the fee.

Ferens v. John Deere Company
Supreme Court of the United States, 1990.
494 U.S. 516, 110 S.Ct. 1274, 108 L.Ed.2d 443.

■ KENNEDY, J.

I

Albert Ferens lost his right hand when, the allegation is, it became caught in his combine harvester, manufactured by Deere & Company. The accident occurred while Ferens was working with the combine on his farm in Pennsylvania. For reasons not explained in the record, Ferens delayed filing a tort suit and Pennsylvania's 2-year limitations period expired. In the third year, he and his wife sued Deere in the United States District Court for the Western District of Pennsylvania, raising contract and warranty claims as to which the Pennsylvania limitations period had not yet run. The District Court had diversity jurisdiction, as Ferens and his wife are Pennsylvania residents, and Deere is incorporated in Delaware with its principal place of business in Illinois.

Not to be deprived of a tort action, the Ferenses in the same year filed a second diversity suit against Deere in the United States District Court for the Southern District of Mississippi, alleging negligence and products liability. Diversity jurisdiction and venue were proper. The Ferenses sued Deere in the District Court in Mississippi because they knew that, under Klaxon Co. v. Stentor Electric Mfg. Co. [supra p. 688], the federal court in the exercise of diversity jurisdiction must apply the same choice of law rules that Mississippi state courts would apply if they were deciding the case.

The Mississippi courts ... would apply Mississippi's 6-year statute of limitations to the tort claim arising under Pennsylvania law and the tort action would not be time-barred under the Mississippi statute.

The issue now before us arose when the Ferenses took their forum shopping a step further: having chosen the federal court in Mississippi to take advantage of the State's limitations period, they next moved, under § 1404(a), to transfer the action to the federal court in Pennsylvania on the ground that Pennsylvania was a more convenient forum. The Ferenses acted on the assumption that, after the transfer, the choice of law rules in the Mississippi forum, including a rule requiring application of the Mississippi statute of limitations, would continue to govern the suit.

[The case was transferred to Pennsylvania. The federal district court applied the Pennsylvania limitation on the ground that *Van Dusen,* supra p. 196, does not apply when plaintiff seeks the transfer. The Third Circuit affirmed, but on the ground that the application of the Mississippi limitation would violate due process because Mississippi had no legitimate interest in the case. The U.S. Supreme Court remanded for further consideration in light of *Sun Oil,* supra p. 434. On remand, the Third Circuit again applied the Pennsylvania limitation, this time for the reason given by the trial court.]

II

Section 1404(a) states only that a district court may transfer venue for the convenience of the parties and witnesses when in the interest of justice. It says nothing about choice of law, and nothing about affording plaintiffs different treatment from defendants. We touched upon these issues in *Van Dusen,* but left open the question presented in this case.... We said:

> "This legislative background supports the view that § 1404(a) was not designed to narrow the plaintiff's venue privilege or to defeat the state-law advantages that might accrue from the exercise of this venue privilege but rather the provision was simply to counteract the inconveniences that flowed from the venue statutes by permitting transfer to a convenient federal court. The legislative history of § 1404(a) certainly does not justify the rather startling conclusion that one might 'get a change of a law as a bonus for a change of venue.' Indeed, an interpretation accepting such a rule would go far to frustrate the remedial purposes of § 1404(a). If a change in the law were in the offing, the parties might well regard the section primarily as a forum-shopping instrument. And, more importantly, courts would at least be reluctant to grant transfers, despite considerations of convenience, if to do so might conceivably prejudice the claim of a plaintiff who initially selected a permissible forum. We believe, therefore, that both the history and purposes of § 1404(a) indicate that it should be regarded as a federal judicial housekeeping measure, dealing with the placement of litigation in the federal courts and generally intended, on the basis of convenience and fairness, simply to authorize a change of courtrooms." ...

We thus held that the law applicable to a diversity case does not change upon a transfer initiated by a defendant.

III

The quoted part of *Van Dusen* reveals three independent reasons for our decision. First, § 1404(a) should not deprive parties of state law advantages that exist absent diversity jurisdiction. Second, § 1404(a) should not create or multiply opportunities for forum shopping. Third, the decision to transfer venue under § 1404(a) should turn on considerations of convenience and the interest of justice rather than on the possible prejudice resulting from a change of law.

A

The policy that § 1404(a) should not deprive parties of state law advantages, although perhaps discernible in the legislative history, has its real foundation in Erie R. Co. v. Tompkins. See *Van Dusen,* 376 U.S. at 637. The *Erie* rule remains a vital expression of the federal system and the concomitant integrity of the separate States.

The *Erie* policy had a clear implication for *Van Dusen.* The existence of diversity jurisdiction gave the defendants the opportunity to make a motion to transfer venue under § 1404(a), and if the applicable law were to change after transfer, the plaintiff's venue privilege and resulting state-law advantages could be defeated at the defendant's option. To allow the transfer and at the same time preserve the plaintiff's state-law advantages, we held that the choice of law rules should not change following a transfer initiated by a defendant.

Transfers initiated by a plaintiff involve some different considerations, but lead to the same result. Applying the transferor law, of course, will not deprive the plaintiff of any state law advantages. A defendant, in one sense, also will lose no legal advantage if the transferor law controls after a transfer initiated by the plaintiff; the same law, after all, would have applied if the plaintiff had not made the motion.

Applying the transferee law, by contrast, would undermine the *Erie* rule in a serious way. It would mean that initiating a transfer under § 1404(a) changes the state law applicable to a diversity case. We have held, in an isolated circumstance, that § 1404(a) may pre-empt state law. See Stewart Organization, Inc. v. Ricoh Corp. [supra Note 4, p. 176], (holding that federal law determines the validity of a forum selection clause). In general, however, we have seen § 1404(a) as a housekeeping measure that should not alter the state law governing a case under *Erie.*

B

Van Dusen also sought to fashion a rule that would not create opportunities for forum shopping.... No interpretation of § 1404(a), however, will create comparable opportunities for forum shopping by a plaintiff because, even without § 1404(a), a plaintiff already has the option of shopping for a forum with the most favorable law.... Diversity jurisdiction did not eliminate these forum shopping opportunities; instead, under *Erie,* the federal courts had to replicate them....

Applying the transferee law, by contrast, might create opportunities for forum shopping in an indirect way. The advantage to Mississippi's personal injury lawyers that resulted from the State's then applicable 6–year statute of limitations has not escaped us; Mississippi's long limitation period no doubt drew plaintiffs to the State. Although *Sun Oil* held that the federal courts have little interest in a State's decision to create a long statute of limitations or to apply its statute of limitations to claims governed by foreign law, we should recognize the consequences of our interpretation of § 1404(a). Applying the transferee law, to the extent that it discourages plaintiff-initiated transfers, might give States incentives to enact similar laws to bring in out-of-state business that would not be moved at the instance of the plaintiff.

C

Van Dusen also made clear that the decision to transfer venue under § 1404(a) should turn on considerations of convenience rather than on the possibility of prejudice resulting from a change in the applicable law....

Some might think that a plaintiff should pay the price for choosing an inconvenient forum by being put to a choice of law versus forum. But this assumes that § 1404(a) is for the benefit only of the moving party. By the statute's own terms, it is not. Section 1404(a) also exists for the benefit of the witnesses and the interest of justice, which must include the convenience of the court. Litigation in an inconvenient forum does not harm the plaintiff alone.... The desire to take a punitive view of the plaintiff's actions should not obscure the systemic costs of litigating in an inconvenient place.

D

... If we were to hold that the transferee law applies following a § 1404(a) motion by a plaintiff, cases such as this would not arise in the future.... The rule would leave unclear which law should apply when both a defendant and a plaintiff move for a transfer of venue or when the court transfers venue on its own motion. The rule also might require variation in certain situations, such as when the plaintiff moves for a transfer following a removal from state court by the defendant, or when only one of several plaintiffs requests the transfer, or when circumstances change through no fault of the plaintiff making a once convenient forum inconvenient. True, we could reserve any consideration of these questions for a later day. But we have a duty, in deciding this case, to consider whether our decision will create litigation and uncertainty. On the basis of these considerations, we again conclude that the transferor law should apply regardless who makes the § 1404(a) motion.

IV

[O]ne might contend that, because no *per se* rule requiring a court to apply either the transferor law or the transferee law will seem appropriate in all circumstances, we should develop more sophisticated federal choice of law rules for diversity actions involving transfers. To a large extent, however, state conflicts of law rules already ensure that appropriate laws will apply to diversity cases. Federal law, as a general matter, does not interfere with these rules. See *Sun Oil,* [supra p. 434]. Even if more elaborate federal choice of law rules would not run afoul of *Klaxon* and *Erie,* we believe that applying the law of the transferor forum effects the appropriate balance between fairness and simplicity.

For the foregoing reasons, we conclude that Mississippi's statute of limitations should govern the Ferenses' action. We reverse and remand for proceedings consistent with this opinion.

■ JUSTICE SCALIA, with whom JUSTICE BRENNAN, JUSTICE MARSHALL, and JUSTICE BLACKMUN join, dissenting.

[J]ust as it is unlikely that Congress, in enacting § 1404(a), meant to provide the defendant with a vehicle by which to manipulate in his favor the substantive law to be applied in a diversity case, so too is it unlikely that Congress meant to provide the *plaintiff* with a vehicle by which to appropriate the law of a distant and inconvenient forum in which he does not intend to litigate, and to carry that prize back to the State in which he wishes to try the case. [Further], application of the transferor court's law in this context would encourage forum-shopping between federal and state courts in the same jurisdiction on the basis of differential substantive law. It is true, of course, that the plaintiffs here did not select the *Mississippi* federal court in preference to the Mississippi state courts because of any differential substantive law; the former, like the latter, would have applied Mississippi choice-of-law rules, and thus the Mississippi statute of limitations. But one must be blind to reality to say that it is the *Mississippi* federal court in which these plaintiffs have chosen to sue. That was merely a way station en route to suit in the *Pennsylvania* federal court. The plaintiffs were seeking to achieve exactly what *Klaxon* was designed to prevent: the use of a Pennsylvania federal court instead of a Pennsylvania state court in order to obtain application of a different substantive law. Our decision in *Van Dusen* compromised "the principle of uniformity within a state," [citing to *Klaxon*], only in the abstract, but today's decision compromises it precisely in the respect that matters—i.e., insofar as it bears upon the plaintiff's choice between a state and a federal forum. The significant federal judicial policy expressed in *Erie* and *Klaxon* is reduced to a laughingstock if it can so readily be evaded through filing-and-transfer.

The Court is undoubtedly correct that applying the Klaxon rule after a plaintiff-initiated transfer would deter a plaintiff in a situation such as exists here from seeking a transfer, since that would deprive him of the favorable substantive law. But that proves only that this disposition achieves what *Erie* and *Klaxon* are designed to achieve: preventing the plaintiff from using "the accident of diversity of citizenship," *Klaxon*, ... to obtain the application of a different law within the State where he wishes to litigate. In the context of the present case, he must either litigate in the State of Mississippi under Mississippi law, or in the Commonwealth of Pennsylvania under Pennsylvania law.

The Court suggests that applying the choice-of-law rules of the forum court to a transferred case ignores the interest of the federal courts themselves in avoiding the "systemic costs of litigating in an inconvenient place," quoting Justice Jackson's eloquent remarks on that subject in Gulf Oil Corp. v. Gilbert, [supra p. 182] ... The point, apparently, is that these systemic costs will increase because the change in law attendant to transfer will not only deter the plaintiff from moving to transfer but will also deter the court from ordering *sua sponte* a transfer that will harm the plaintiff's case. Justice Jackson's remarks were addressed, however, not to the operation of § 1404(a), but to "those rather rare cases where the doctrine [of *forum non conveniens*] should be applied." Where the systemic costs are that severe, transfer ordinarily will occur whether the plaintiff moves for it or not; the district judge can be expected to order it *sua sponte*. I do not think that the prospect of depriving the plaintiff of favorable law will any more deter a district judge from transferring than it would have deterred a district judge, under the prior regime, from ordering a dismissal *sua sponte* pursuant to the doctrine of *forum non conveniens*.

The Court and I reach different results largely because we approach the question from different directions. For the Court, this case involves an "interpretation of § 1404(a)," and the central issue is whether *Klaxon* stands in the way of the policies of that statute. For me, the case involves an interpretation of the Rules of Decision Act, and the central issue is whether § 1404(a) alters the "principle of uniformity within a state" which *Klaxon* says that Act embodies. I think my approach preferable, not only because the Rules of Decision Act does, and § 1404(a) does not, address the specific subject of which law to apply, but also because, as the Court acknowledges, our jurisprudence under that statute is "a vital expression of the federal system and the concomitant integrity of the separate States." To ask, as in effect the Court does, whether *Erie* gets in the way of § 1404(a), rather than whether § 1404(a) requires adjustment of *Erie,* seems to me the expression of a mistaken sense of priorities.

NOTES AND QUESTIONS

1. What are the systemic costs and savings of the decision in *Ferens?* Will fewer cases be *tried* in really inconvenient forums, will more be *filed* in forums where no trial is intended, and will a transferee court face an additional burden as a result of the decision (by having to determine the law of the transferor)? For arguments against *Ferens,* see Maltz, Choice of Forum and Choice of Law in the Federal Courts: A Reconsideration of Erie Principles, 79 Ky.L.J. 231 (1991). Spar Inc. v. Information Resources Inc., 956 F.2d 392 (2d Cir.1992), affirmed a district court that dismissed the case on the ground that the forum's statute of limitations had run and refused to transfer the case to a forum whose period had not expired. The court stated "that allowing a transfer in this case would reward plaintiffs for their lack of diligence in choosing a proper forum and this would not be in the interests of justice," disagreeing with Porter v. Groat, 840 F.2d 255 (4th Cir.1988).

Since its law was applied in *Ferens,* Mississippi has shortened its tort limitations to three years (Miss.Code.Ann. § 15–1–49 (Supp.1994)) and has enacted a statute that applies the shorter limitations period of the place where the cause of action "accrued" if the plaintiff is not a Mississippi resident (Miss.Code Ann. § 15–1–65 (Supp.1994)).

2. LaVay Corp. v. Dominion Federal Savings & Loan Ass'n, 830 F.2d 522, 526 (4th Cir.1987), cert. denied, 484 U.S. 1065 (1988) holds that "a district court receiving a case under the mandatory transfer provisions of § 1406(a) must apply the law of the state in which it is held rather than the law of the transferor district court."

Section 1406(a) provides that "[t]he district court of a district in which is filed a case laying venue in the wrong ... district shall dismiss, or if it be in the interest of justice, transfer such case to any district ... in which it could have been brought." See also Tel–Phonic Services, Inc. v. TBS Int'l, Inc., 975 F.2d 1134 (5th Cir.1992) (after transfer under 1406(a), the law of the transferee state applies to state-law claims and the law of the transferee circuit applies on matters of federal law).

If transfer is ordered by a district court without personal jurisdiction over the defendant, the law of the transferee forum applies. See Ross v. Colorado Outward Bound School, Inc., 822 F.2d 1524 (10th Cir.1987) (transfer for lack of personal jurisdiction is under 28 U.S.C.A. § 1631, which makes Van Dusen inapplicable); Levy v. Pyramid Co. of Ithaca, 687 F.Supp. 48, 51 (N.D.N.Y.1988), affirmed, adopting district court opinion, 871 F.2d 9 (2d Cir.1989) (§ 1631 applies to lack of subject matter, not personal, jurisdiction, but though transfer for lack of personal jurisdiction is under § 1404 or § 1406, the law of the transferee state applies).

3. Intrastate forum-shopping, i.e., between the state and federal court in the same state, may also result when a federal court exercises pendent jurisdiction or when it exercises personal jurisdiction pursuant to the 100–mile bulge rule. Pendent jurisdiction may permit the federal court in a federal-question case—not a diversity case—to adjudicate a related state-law claim even when the federal claim fails. The 1993 amendments to Federal Rules of Civil Procedure now give nationwide jurisdiction (consistent with Due Process) to federal courts when the claim arises under federal law; as a result, federal courts may exercise more far-reaching jurisdiction on pendent state claims than the state courts of the forum could have done. FRCP 4(k)(2). If *Klaxon* then requires applying the law of the forum, the result will run counter to the *Erie* policy of intrastate decisional harmony and may encourage forum-shopping. See Comment, Pendent Personal Jurisdiction and Nationwide Service of Process, 64 N.Y.U.L.Rev. 113 (1989).

Similarly, Federal Rule of Civil Procedure 4(k)(1)(B) permits service on third-party defendants and specified additional third parties to a pending claim or counterclaim within a 100–mile radius of the place of suit. Thus, it is quite possible that "the federal court will be able to reach vast population centers outside the state." Vestal, Expanding the Jurisdictional Reach of the Federal Courts: The 1973 Change in Federal Rule 4, 38 N.Y.U.L.Rev. 1053, 1065 (1963). Here too, under Klaxon, the plaintiff may gain the benefit of forum law even though the state courts of the forum could not have applied it for lack of personal jurisdiction over the defendant.

Do the Supreme Court's decisions in Allstate Ins. Co. v. Hague, p. 349, supra, and Phillips Petroleum Co. v. Shutts, p. 362, supra, have any relevance to the foregoing?

4. The multi-district consolidation statute, 28 U.S.C.A. § 1407, lacks a choice-of-law provision and the rule that the transferee court applies the law that the transferor court would have applied has been traditionally followed. For an application, see In re San Juan Dupont Plaza Hotel Fire Litigation, 745 F.Supp. 79, 81 (D.Puerto Rico 1990), which involved consolidated actions originally instituted in California, Connecticut, New York, and Puerto Rico. "The simplicity of this general principle is deceptive, to say the least, in 'mass tort' cases which involve large numbers of victims and defendants from multiple fora as well as a myriad of claims based on conduct which may have touched upon several states. In this type of litigation, the application of choice of law standards turns into a colossal struggle for the transferee court in attempting to ascertain relevant contacts between the parties and the multiple states and in struggling to understand, evaluate and weigh the particular policies behind the different statutes allowing or disallowing claims and/or remedies. In suits arising from product liability claims against manufacturers or distributors, the problem is further compounded by the very nature of corporations which are not 'domiciled' in a particular forum but instead have contacts with numerous jurisdictions since they may be 'incorporated in one state, headquartered in another, have their principal place of business in a third, manufacture products in several others, and do business in many more states.' Note, *Interest Analysis Applied to Corporations: The Unprincipled Use of A Choice of Law Method,* 98 Yale L.J. 597, 603 (1989).... Choice of law rules have been designed and developed with the two-party case in mind, where the relevant contacts or interests at stake between the parties and the statutes in conflict are more easily ascertainable and not so difficult in application." See also In re United Mine Workers of America Employee Benefit Plans Litigation, 854 F.Supp. 914 (D.D.C. 1994) (transferor forum's statute of limitations applies in multidistrict litigation case transferred pursuant to 28 U.S.C.A. § 1407). For further discussion of "mass torts," and H.R. 2450, see infra pp. 720–722, Notes (5)–(7).

5. In intercircuit transfers involving questions of federal law, the transferee court applies the interpretation adopted by its own circuit, not the view of the transferor circuit. See Marcus, Conflicts Among Circuits and Transfers Within the Federal Judicial System, 93 Yale L.J. 677 (1984). This allows the defendant to forum-shop. But see Ragazzo, Transfer and Choice of Federal Law: The Appellate Model, 93 Mich.L.Rev. 703 (1995), contending that federal precedent of the transferee circuit should apply after permanent but not multi-district consolidation transfers. See also Norwood, Double Forum Shopping and the Extension of Ferens to Federal Claims that Borrow State Limitations Periods, 44 Emory L.J. 501, 508–09 (1995) (when a claim under federal law borrows the limitations period from state law, the law of transferor forum should apply to all defendant-initiated transfers, but the law of the transferee forum should apply to all other transfers).

However, the rule is important and desirable when circuits are split on a question of federal law and the case involves a multidistrict consolidation. Adherence to *Van Dusen* in these circumstances would have the court apply not only different state laws but also possibly different interpretations of federal law to different parties in the same case. A recent decision applying the transferee circuit's interpretation of federal law is In re Air Crash at Detroit Metropolitan Airport, Detroit, Michigan on August 16, 1987, 791 F.Supp. 1204 (E.D.Mich.1992).

Samuelson v. Susen

United States Court of Appeals, Third Circuit, 1978.
576 F.2d 546.

[A portion of the opinion in this case appears in Chapter 7, supra, starting at p. 412.]

. . .

Prior to the enactment of Rule 501, federal court decisions had determined that in civil actions and proceedings governed by Erie R. Co. v. Tompkins, 304 U.S. 64 (1938), state created privileges conferred substantive rights beyond regulation by federal procedural rules. See Republic Gear Co. v. Borg-Warner Corp., 381 F.2d 551, 555–556 n. 2 (2d Cir. 1967). In the form originally prepared, the Federal Rules of Evidence would not have required federal courts to recognize privileges created by state law in civil actions and proceedings governed by *Erie*. Preliminary Draft of Proposed Rules of Evidence for the United States Courts and Magistrates, 46 F.R.D. 161 (1969).

The House of Representatives amended the proposed rules to require the application of state privilege law in cases governed by *Erie*. (It was the House amendment that was eventually enacted into law as Rule 501). The House supported its position with the following contentions: (1) privilege rules are and should continue to be considered substantive for *Erie* purposes; (2) privilege rules are outcome determinative; (3) where state law supplies the rule of decision, state rules of privilege should be applied because there is no federal interest substantial enough to justify departure from state policy; and (4) state policy regarding privilege should not be thwarted merely because of diversity jurisdiction, a situation which, if allowed, would encourage forum shopping. H.R.Rep.No.650, 93rd Cong., 1st Sess. 9 (1973).

A federal court's application of the law of privilege which the forum states' courts would apply in cases like the instant one, seems to us to be consistent with Congress' goal of effectuating state substantive rights, laws and policies in controversies where there is no substantial federal interest. Such an approach furthers Congress' goal of preserving the domain of state privilege law in diversity cases by achieving outcome identity between state and federal courts of the forum state on choice of law, thus discouraging forum shopping. Such an approach also takes cognizance of the fact that a forum state's choice-of-law rules may reflect important policy underpinnings of its own law and are an integral part of it. . . .

We are mindful of the fact that in *Klaxon* the Supreme Court was in effect interpreting the reference in the Rules of Decision Act to "the laws of the several states . . . in cases where they 'apply' to include a forum state's choice-of-law rules." As one commentator has pointed out, "[t]he reference in that Act to the laws of the several states . . . in cases where they apply is no less ambiguous in terms of horizontal choice of law than the references to 'State law' in the Federal Rules of Evidence." Wellborn, The Federal Rules of Evidence and the Application of State Law in Federal Courts, 55 Texas L.Rev. 371, 446 (1977).

The interpretation of "State law" urged upon us by plaintiff would prevent the application of all of a forum state's law, including its choice-of-law rules. Such a denial would be antithetical to one of the primary goals of Rule 501, the recognition that where states have created rights, the federal courts should apply the same rules of law to those rights which the states themselves would apply. Moreover, to require a federal court to ignore some of a state's choice-of-law rules, as plaintiff's interpretation of "State law" in Rule 501 would do, would obviously invite forum shopping in direct contradiction of one of the aims of Rule 501.

We believe our interpretation of the meaning of "State law" in the second sentence of Rule 501 to be the most consistent with the prevailing view of federalism on the allocation of lawmaking authority in diversity cases—a view Congress seemed intent upon preserving when it enacted the measure. . . .

FACTORS, ETC., INC. v. PRO ARTS, INC., 652 F.2d 278 (2d Cir. 1981), cert. denied 456 U.S. 927 (1982): The Memphis Development Foundation was formed to erect a bronze statue of Elvis Presley in downtown Memphis. The Foundation sought to raise money by selling eight-inch pewter replicas of the proposed statue at $25 each. It sued in a federal court in Tennessee to prevent Factors from interfering with the Foundation's efforts to market the Presley statuettes. Factors claimed under an exclusive license to use Presley's name and likeness for the manufacture and sale of merchandise of all kinds. The Sixth Circuit Court of Appeals decided in favor of the Foundation, holding that under Tennessee law Presley's right of publicity did not survive his death. Memphis Development Foundation v. Factors Etc., Inc., 616 F.2d 956 (6th Cir.), cert. denied 449 U.S. 953 (1980).

Contemporaneously, Factors started a diversity action in New York to enforce its exclusive license against Pro Arts, Inc. On the question of Factors' right to enforce its license on the basis of Tennessee law, the Court of Appeals for the Second Circuit decided in the negative because it felt it was obliged to follow the holding to that effect by Tennessee's "home" circuit, the Sixth:

> . . . Where, as here, the pertinent court of appeals has essayed its own prediction of the course of state law on a question of first impression within that state, the federal courts of other circuits should defer to that holding, perhaps always, and at least in all situations except the rare instance when it can be said with conviction that the pertinent court of appeals has disregarded clear signals emanating from the state's highest court pointing toward a different rule. . . .

A few months after this decision, a Tennessee Chancery judge held that the right of publicity did survive. The plaintiffs were allowed to petition the Second Circuit to recall its mandate and rehear the case in the light of the Tennessee decision. The Second Circuit then denied the petition following a contrary decision by another Tennessee Chancery judge, stating that "the appearance of two conflicting decisions of the Chancery Court" did not afford a basis for concluding that the law of Tennessee had authoritatively changed since the Second Circuit's previous decision. Factors, Etc., Inc. v. Pro Arts, Inc., 541 F.Supp. 231 (S.D.N.Y. 1982), rehearing denied, 701 F.2d 11, 12 (2d Cir.1983).

Doggrell v. Southern Box Co.
Court of Appeals of the United States, Sixth Circuit, 1953.
208 F.2d 310.

[An Arkansas corporation was formed with three men as the incorporators and stockholders, two of whom were residents of Tennessee and the third a resident of Arkansas. The statutes of Arkansas called for the articles of incorporation to be filed with the Secretary of State and also with the County Clerk of the county in which the corporation had its principal place of business. Through the inadvertence of the Arkansas stockholder the articles were not filed with the County Clerk until after the corporate purchase mentioned below, though the Tennessee stockholders did not know of the failure. Under the Arkansas law the stockholders of a corporation were liable as partners when the articles of incorporation were not filed with the County Clerk. The Arkansas stockholder, who managed the business of the corporation, purchased goods in Arkansas in the name of the corporation. When the goods were not paid for, the creditor brought suit for the purchase price against the Tennessee stockholders in the Federal district court in Tennessee. The defense was made that the Arkansas statute was a penal one, but the District Court rejected the defense and gave judgment for the plaintiff. The Court of Appeals, with the judges divided two to one, affirmed the judgment for the plaintiff. (206 F.2d 671.) The defendant filed a petition for rehearing. During the pendency of the petition for rehearing, the Supreme Court of Tennessee held in another case that the Arkansas statute was a penal one and would not be enforced by the Tennessee state courts.

Thereupon the Court of Appeals, with the same three judges sitting, withdrew their earlier ruling and reversed the judgment for the plaintiff, again by a vote of two to one.]

■ McALLISTER, CIRCUIT JUDGE. For the reasons stated in the dissenting opinion heretofore filed,* and because of the decisions of the Supreme Court of Tennessee in the cases of Paper Products Co. v. Doggrell, 261 S.W.2d 127 [195 Tenn. 581] as well as the decision and opinion of the Supreme Court of Tennessee on the petition for rehearing of Paper Products Co. v. Doggrell, 261 S.W.2d 130 [195 Tenn. 581, 588], all filed during the pendency of a motion for rehearing in the above entitled cause, in which it was held that the provision of the Arkansas statute in question was a penal statute and would not be enforced by the courts of Tennessee, and that appellant was a stockholder in a *de facto* corporation and, according to the law of Tennessee, would not be individually liable for the payment of the debts of the Arkansas corporation, I am of the opinion that the petition for rehearing should be granted; that the opinion heretofore filed should be set aside; and that a judgment should be entered in favor of appellant.

■ MILLER, CIRCUIT JUDGE. Although I am not in agreement with the recent opinion of the Supreme Court of Tennessee in the case of Paper Products Co. v. Doggrell, Tenn.Sup., 261 S.W.2d 127, rehearing denied, October 9, 1953, Tenn.Sup., 261 S.W.2d 130, I am of the opinion that under the authority of Erie R. Co. v. Tompkins, 304 U.S. 64; Vandenbark v. Owens-Illinois Glass Co., 311 U.S. 538; Klaxon Co. v. Stentor Co., 313 U.S. 487, and Guaranty Trust Co. v. York, 326 U.S. 99, 109–110, the ruling in that case is controlling in this case, with the result that the petition for

---

* Doggrell v. Great Southern Box Co., 206 F.2d 671, 679 (1953)—Eds.

rehearing should be granted and the judgment of the District Court be reversed.

■ MARTIN, CIRCUIT JUDGE (dissenting).

Appellant presents on petition for rehearing the opinion of the Supreme Court of Tennessee in Paper Products Co. v. Doggrell, Tenn.Sup., 261 S.W.2d 130, wherein the state court adheres to its previous decision and cites and discusses with approval the dissenting opinion of Judge McAllister in the instant case. Judge McAllister adheres to his previous views and Judge Miller, who concurred in the opinion which I wrote, while not in agreement with the conclusion reached by the Supreme Court of Tennessee, is of the opinion that the petition to rehear should be sustained, the former ruling of this court set aside, and the judgment of the district court reversed. He bases this conclusion upon what he considers to be the compelling effect of the following authorities: . . . if we had before us a simple issue of conflict in the common law between states, the Klaxon case would be controlling. . . .

But, in my judgment, we confront no such situations here. I think that, in the instant matter, the Supreme Court of Tennessee, contrary to the Constitution of the United States, has failed to give full faith and credit as required by the Constitution to the judgment of the highest court of Arkansas, based upon the latter court's interpretation of an Arkansas statute. The appellant in the case at bar occupies the exact status which the Supreme Court of Arkansas, in an identical case, Whitaker v. Mitchell Mfg. Co., 219 Ark. 779, 244 S.W.2d 965, held imposed liability upon a stockholder of an Arkansas corporation which had failed to conform to the corporate organization laws of that state.

Long before the revolutionary doctrine of Erie R. Co. v. Tompkins was promulgated, it had been recognized that the interpretation of a state statute by its highest court becomes in effect a part of the statute, unless in contravention of the federal Constitution or of federal law. As pointed out in my previous writing in this case, Huntington v. Attrill, 146 U.S. 657, held that whether a state statute is penal in the sense that it cannot be enforced in another state depends upon whether the purpose of the statute is to punish an offense against the public justice or to afford a private remedy to a person injured by wrongful act; and that the Supreme Court of the United States would decide for itself whether or not a state statute is penal in the international sense. The Supreme Court of Tennessee has ignored this long-established doctrine. . . . I read nothing in Erie R. Co. v. Tompkins, or in any other Supreme Court opinion, which permits the Supreme Court of Tennessee to exercise any such authority. I refer again to the authorities cited in my original opinion for the then-majority of our court to the point that the courts of a forum state, including a federal court sitting therein, are bound to apply the pertinent statutes of a sister state as construed by the highest court of that state. Broderick v. Rosner, 294 U.S. 629, 643; Converse v. Hamilton, 224 U.S. 243, 260, 261; Hughes v. Fetter, 341 U.S. 609, 613. . . .

For the foregoing reasons, I would adhere to the former decision of this court and deny appellant's petition for rehearing.

NOTES

1. Judge Martin cited Huntington v. Attrill, p. 297, supra (cf. Milwaukee County v. White, p. 308, supra) to support his view that "penal" characterization is a federal question, not controlled by state views. Is Huntington authority for closing federal court doors in order to vindicate state door-closing policies?

2. Does full faith and credit receive shorter shrift in this case than it deserves?

Angel v. Bullington

Supreme Court of the United States, 1947.
330 U.S. 183, 67 S.Ct. 657, 91 L.Ed. 832.

■ JUSTICE FRANKFURTER delivered the opinion of the Court.

In 1940, Bullington, a citizen of Virginia, sold land in Virginia to Angel, a citizen of North Carolina. Only part of the purchase price was paid. For the balance, Angel executed a series of notes secured by a deed of trust on the land. Upon default on one of the notes, Bullington, acting upon an acceleration clause in the deed, caused all other notes to become due and called upon the trustees to sell the land. The sale was duly made in Virginia and the proceeds of the sale applied to the payment of the notes. This controversy concerns attempts to collect the deficiency.

Bullington began suit for the deficiency in the Superior Court of Macon County, North Carolina. Angel countered with a demurrer, the substance of which was that a statute of North Carolina (c. 36, Public Laws 1933, Michie's Code § 2593(f)) precluded recovery of such a deficiency judgment. This is the relevant portion of that enactment:

"In all sales of real property by mortgagees and/or trustees under powers of sale contained in any mortgage or deed of trust hereafter executed, ... the mortgagee or trustee or holder of the notes secured by such mortgage or deed of trust shall not be entitled to a deficiency judgment on account of such mortgage, deed of trust or obligation secured by the same. ..." The Superior Court overruled the demurrer, and an appeal to the Supreme Court of North Carolina followed. Bullington supported his Superior Court judgment on the ground that the United States Constitution precluded North Carolina from shutting the doors of its courts to him. The North Carolina Supreme Court, holding that the North Carolina Act of 1933 barred Bullington's suit against Angel, reversed the Superior Court and dismissed the action. 220 N.C. 18. Bullington did not seek to review this judgment here. Instead, he sued Angel for the deficiency in the United States District Court for the Western District of North Carolina. Angel pleaded in bar the judgment in the North Carolina action. The District Court gave judgment for Bullington and the Circuit Court of Appeals for the Fourth Circuit affirmed. 150 F.2d 679. We granted certiorari, 326 U.S. 713, because the failure to dismiss this action, on the ground that the judgment in the North Carolina court precluded the right thereafter to recover on the same cause of action in the federal court, presented an important question in the administration of justice.

1. We start with the fact that the prevailing rule as to res judicata is settled law in North Carolina. An adjudication bars future litigation between the same parties not only as to all issues actually raised and decided but also as to those which could have been raised.... It is indisputable that the parties, the nature of the claim and the desired relief were precisely the same in the two actions successively brought by Bullington against Angel, first in the Superior Court of Macon County and then in the federal district court. For all practical purposes, the complaint in the present action was a carbon copy of the complaint in the State court action....

2. The judgment of the Supreme Court of North Carolina would clearly bar this suit had it been brought anew in a state court. For purposes of diversity jurisdiction a federal court is "in effect, only another court of the State" [Citing cases.] Of course, Bullington could not have succeeded in the District Court for the Western District of North Carolina after an adverse judgment in the State courts, had the decision in this case involved no federal ground. That is equally true where a federal question was decided in the State courts. That the adjudication of federal questions by the North Carolina Supreme Court may have been erroneous is immaterial for purposes of res judicata. Baltimore S. S. Co. v. Phillips, 274 U.S. 316, 325. A higher court was available for an authoritative adjudication of the federal questions involved. And so the question is whether federal rights were necessarily involved and adjudicated in the litigation in the State courts.

3. For purposes of res judicata, the significance of what a court says it decides is controlled by the issues that were open for decision. What were the issues in the North Carolina litigation? Bullington sought a deficiency judgment. Angel, by demurrer, resisted on the ground that a North Carolina statute precluded a deficiency judgment. The North Carolina Supreme Court, reversing the trial court, found the North Carolina statute a bar to such a suit. It said that "the limitation created by the statute is upon the jurisdiction of the court in that it is declared that the holder of notes given to secure the purchase price of real property 'shall not be entitled to a deficiency judgment on account' thereof. This closes the courts of this state to one who seeks a deficiency judgment on a note given for the purchase price of real property. The statute operates upon the adjective law of the state, which pertains to the practice and procedure, or legal machinery by which the substantive law is made effective, and not upon the substantive law itself. It is a limitation of the jurisdiction of the courts of this state." 220 N.C. 18, 20, 16 S.E.2d 411, 412.

But the allowable "limitation of the jurisdiction of the courts" of North Carolina presents more than a question of local law for determination by the North Carolina Supreme Court. Speaking for a unanimous Court, Mr. Justice Brandeis thus expressed the subordination to the requirements of the Constitution of the power of a State to withdraw jurisdiction from its courts: "The power of a state to determine the limits of the jurisdiction of its courts and the character of the controversies which shall be heard in them is, of course, subject to the restrictions imposed by the Federal Constitution." McKnett v. St. Louis & S. F. R. Co., 292 U.S. 230, 233....

4. Here, claims based on the United States Constitution were plainly and reasonably made in the North Carolina suit. The North Carolina Supreme Court met these claims. It met them by saying that the North Carolina statute did not deal with substantive matters but merely with matters regulating local procedure. But whether the claims are based on a federal right or are merely of local concern is itself a federal question on which this Court, and not the Supreme Court of North Carolina, has the last say. That Court could not put a federal claim aside, as though it were not in litigation, by the talismanic word "jurisdiction." When an asserted federal right is denied, the sufficiency of the grounds of denial is for this Court to decide.... Since it was open for Bullington to come here to seek reversal of the decision of the North Carolina Supreme Court shutting him out of the North Carolina courts and he chose not to do so, the decision of the North Carolina Supreme Court concluded an adjudication of a federal question even though it was not couched in those terms. For purposes of litigating the issues in controversy in the North Carolina action, the North Carolina Supreme Court was an intermediate tribunal....

5. It is suggested that the North Carolina Supreme Court did not adjudicate the "merits" of the controversy. It is a misconception of res judicata to assume that the doctrine does not come into operation if a court has not passed on the "merits" in the sense of the ultimate substantive issues of a litigation. An adjudication declining to reach such ultimate substantive issues may bar a second attempt to reach them in another court of the State. Such a situation is presented when the first decision is based not on the ground that the distribution of judicial power among the various courts of the State requires the suit to be brought in another court in the State, but on the inaccessibility of all the courts of the State to such litigation. And that is the essence of the present case....

The "merits" of a claim are disposed of when they are refused enforcement. If an asserted federal claim is denied enforcement on a professed local ground, but a so-called local ground which is subject to review here because it is in fact the adjudication of a federal question, then the "merits" of that claim were adjudicated in the only sense that adjudication of the "merits" is relevant to the principles of res judicata. A State court cannot sterilize federal claims by putting on the adjudication a local label.

6. The merits of this controversy were adjudicated by the North Carolina Supreme Court since that court, or this Court on appeal, might have decided that the North Carolina statute did not bar Bullington's first action. The North Carolina statute might have been found unconstitutional. Federal issues were thus involved in the adjudication by the North Carolina Supreme Court. Bullington knew that there were federal issues

in the State suit because he raised them. He was then content to drop them and let the intermediate adjudication stand. Now he wants an encore.

7. It is suggested that the North Carolina Supreme Court construed the North Carolina statute to close only the North Carolina state courts but not the federal court sitting in North Carolina. In the first place, the North Carolina Supreme Court said no such thing. It construed the statute expressive of state policy and spoke only of the jurisdiction of the state courts because it was concerned only with the state courts. Secondly, it is most incongruous to attribute to the legislature and judiciary of North Carolina the imposition of a restriction against all its citizens from suing for a deficiency judgment, while impliedly authorizing citizens of other states to secure such deficiency judgments against North Carolinians. Thirdly, a North Carolina statute, upheld by the highest court of North Carolina, is of course expressive of North Carolina policy. The essence of diversity jurisdiction is that a federal court enforces state law and state policy. If North Carolina has authoritatively announced that deficiency judgments cannot be secured within its borders, it contradicts the presuppositions of diversity jurisdiction for a federal court in that state to give such a deficiency judgment. North Carolina would hardly allow defeat of a state-wide policy through occasional suits in a federal court. What is more important, diversity jurisdiction must follow state law and policy.... A federal court in North Carolina, when invoked on grounds of diversity of citizenship, cannot give that which North Carolina has withheld. Availability of diversity jurisdiction which was put into the Constitution so as to prevent discrimination against outsiders is not to effect discrimination against the great body of local citizens....

8. After an adverse decision against Bullington on a cause of action created by State law, Bullington wants to start all over again in another North Carolina court, albeit a federal court. The first litigation raised and adjudicated federal issues every one of which is again involved in the second suit....

Judgment reversed.

■ JUSTICE REED, dissenting.

My understanding of the Court's decision is that the doctrine of res judicata, that is a former adjudication, defeats Bullington's claim against Angel....

. . .

In my view, the North Carolina court merely decided that it had no power to adjudicate the cause of action. Certainly the state court had the power to interpret its own statute. [Citing cases.] The withdrawal of jurisdiction surely does not make a judgment one upon the merits....

. . .

The pith of the problem ... consists of the question whether the North Carolina decision establishes a controlling rule of law upon the constitutionality of the state statute as tested by the federal Constitution or adjudicates that the statute merely withdraws jurisdiction from state courts over a type of action....

. . .

... [T]his Court's present determination that the statute is substantive for our purposes cannot change the effect in this litigation of the state's decision to the contrary. When the state court held that for its purposes the statute was remedial, it was remedial in that court. If remedial, the state judgment was not upon the merits and could not be res judicata in any court as to the right to recover on the cause of action.

If the plea of res judicata is not good and this Court should decide that the state statute is substantive law, i.e., a declaration of the policy of North Carolina against claims on deficiencies after sales of incumbered property, it would be necessary to determine the constitutionality of the North Carolina statute that declares uncollectible in North Carolina a claim on a contract that was good in Virginia. In view of this Court's present decision, I express no opinion upon this issue.

■ JUSTICE JACKSON and JUSTICE RUTLEDGE join in this opinion.

■ JUSTICE RUTLEDGE, dissenting.

This is a hard case making, I think, proverbially bad law. On the surface what seems to be decided is simply a question of res judicata. Actually the decision rests on an "and/or" hodgepodge of res judicata and Erie doctrines. In my judgment the admixture not only is unnecessary but distorts and misapplies both doctrines....

. . .

Res judicata is a generally sound but by no means unlimited policy of judicial action. The doctrine is grounded in the need for putting an end to litigation. It does this by precluding the parties from showing what is or may be the truth. The sound core of the policy is that ordinarily one suit which determines or gives a full and fair chance for determining causes of action and issues between litigants should be enough....

. . .

Upon the law as well as the policy, the question has been one of balancing considerations of justice and convenience between stopping litigation and stopping the showing of the truth. That balance has never been so one-sided in favor of the former that the matter is ended simply by showing that a party has had some chance however slight, in a previous litigation to secure a favorable decision....

. . .

Bullington has not had such an opportunity. He has never received, and now never can receive a decision on the substantive merits of his claim, unless possibly he can catch and serve Angel in another state and after prolonged further litigation succeed in inducing this Court to hold the North Carolina bar and res judicata not operative there....

. . .

The real trouble here is not with the law of res judicata, for that law has no valid application to these facts. It is that the doctrine is used as an escape from facing squarely the real question presented. This is whether North Carolina's decision made the Erie doctrine applicable....

That issue is inescapable here. The Erie rule did not purport to change the law of federal jurisdiction in diversity cases, taking it out of the hands of Congress and the federal courts and putting it within the states' power to determine. It purported only to prescribe the rule federal courts should follow in applying the substantive law. If the North Carolina decision was exclusively a jurisdictional one, it had no effect on the power of the federal courts in that state to hear controversies excluded by it from the state courts ...

From the Court's opinion I cannot say whether the question has been resolved.... But, if so, why speak also of res judicata? The law should not be made into such a merry-go-round. Bullington is entitled to one full day in court on the substance of his claim. This he has not had.

■ I hardly need add that I agree with the views expressed by JUSTICE REED.

■ JUSTICE JACKSON joins in this opinion.

NOTES

1. Does the North Carolina statute read as if it is intended to be door-closing, rather than to define substantive entitlements? Can any other interpretation prevail after the Supreme Court of North Carolina has construed it as a "limitation ... upon the jurisdiction of the court"?

2. Does Justice Frankfurter tell us whether the res judicata law of North Carolina would regard the first decision as an adjudication on the merits for purposes of precluding all issues that might have been raised? Without knowing the answer to that question, can we know what the outcome would be if, as Justice Rutledge speculated, Bullington were able to "catch and serve Angel in another state"? For example, in Virginia, would Bullington be precluded from challenging the constitutionality of the North Carolina ban on deficiency judgments as applied to a Virginian who sold Virginia land and was left with a deficiency claim after a foreclosure sale?

3. If prior to the instant action, another creditor in Bullington's position had sued and then met with the North Carolina Supreme Court's interpretation of its statute, would the outcome in the instant case have been the same? If so, as a consequence of res judicata or of Erie? If the first judgment had been rendered by a federal district court, would the res judicata effect be determined under North Carolina law, Federal law, or would the answer depend on which forum was the locus for the succeeding action?

4. A different situation would be presented, of course, if North Carolina closed its courts' doors to deficiency suits by non-residents while opening them to residents. See Szantay v. Beech Aircraft Corp., 349 F.2d 60 (4th Cir. 1965), in which a federal

diversity court was held not bound by a South Carolina statute barring suits by non-residents against foreign corporations on foreign causes of action. The court was unimpressed with the argument that the statute implemented the forum state's doctrine of forum non conveniens; it spoke favorably of the full faith and credit clause's policy of abetting enforcement of rights created by sister states. Angel v. Bullington was distinguished. Should it have been? See Note, 66 Colum.L.Rev. 377 (1966).

5. Compare Poitra v. Demarrias, 502 F.2d 23 (8th Cir. 1974), cert. denied 421 U.S. 934 (1975). The diversity litigants in a wrongful death action based on state-created rights were Indians who lived on opposite sides of the state line running through their reservation. The federal district court in North Dakota dismissed the action on the ground that in the absence of the tribe's consent, the doors of the North Dakota state courts were closed to the plaintiff; and this required the same result, according to the district judge, when federal diversity jurisdiction was invoked in that state.

Reversing, the court of appeals held that the closing of the state courts in this case was not a result of any underlying state policy, but a consequence of the Indian tribe's declining to give consent to state court jurisdiction. Accordingly, the court of appeals held, the state-created right was enforceable in the federal diversity court. Distinguished were Hot Oil Service, Inc. v. Hall, 366 F.2d 295 (9th Cir. 1966) and Littell v. Nakai, 344 F.2d 486 (9th Cir. 1965), cert. denied 382 U.S. 986, holding federal courts could not assume diversity jurisdiction in disputes arising on an Indian Reservation unless the state courts would have had subject matter jurisdiction.

C. Federal Questions in Relation to State Law

INTRODUCTORY NOTE

Even in areas where the national power clearly reaches and the Erie doctrine clearly does not, there can be problems of interplay between federal and state law. First, in national spheres Congress may if it chooses specify the rules of decision, entirely supplanting any contrary state rules and indirectly eradicating interstate choice of law problems, as the Federal Employers Liability Act did with reference to the fellow-servant issue illustrated in Alabama Great Southern Railway Co. v. Carroll, supra, p. 453. Second, Congress may see fit to legislate directly and explicitly on the conflict of laws problem, as it did in the Federal Tort Claims Act provision making the government liable in certain circumstances "in accordance with the law of the place where the act or omission occurred" (28 U.S.C.A. § 1346(b)). See Richards v. United States, 369 U.S. 1 (1962), supra p. 446, n. 3; cf. Meisenhelder v. Chicago & Northwestern Railway Co., 170 Minn. 317, 213 N.W. 32 (1927), infra, p. 832, n. 2. Third, Congress may choose to incorporate state definitions of legal rights by using terms and referring to subjects as to which the states alone have well developed bodies of law. For instance, in a copyright case the question was whether the deceased author's illegitimate son came within the federal copyright statute's term "children" for the purpose of sharing in renewal rights. While the "scope of a federal right is, of course, a federal question," the Court declared, "that does not mean that its content is not to be determined by state, rather than federal law." De Sylva v. Ballentine, 351 U.S. 570, 580 (1956). See also Roecker v. United States, 379 F.2d 400 (5th Cir. 1967), cert. denied 389 U.S. 1005 (1967) (power of guardian to affect a change of beneficiary in national service life insurance policy governed by state law); Marathon Enterprises, Inc. v. Feinberg, 595 F.Supp. 368 (S.D.N.Y.1984) (when federally-created right of action has no accompanying statute of limitations, state law applies); United States v. Kimbell Foods, Inc., p. 717, infra.

In each case not obviously ruled entirely by federal law, a federal court must decide first whether it is *bound* to apply state rules, or whether it is free to apply rules from whichever source, federal or state, the federal choice of law rule makes appropriate. Then, having decided for the federal source, the court may still have to look to state law to give content or add meaning to some terms of the federal law.

CLEARFIELD TRUST CO. v. UNITED STATES, 318 U.S. 363 (1943): Action by the United States to recover the amount of a check on which the payee's name had been forged. The check was drawn on the Treasurer of the United States for services rendered to the Works Progress Administration. It was cashed under the forged endorsement and then endorsed over to the defendant bank, which as agent for collection guaranteed all prior endorsements. Fifteen months after notification of the United States agents of payee's non-receipt of her check, notice of the forgery was communicated to the defendant bank in a demand for reimbursement of the Treasurer who had paid for payee's services a second time. Suit followed upon the express guaranty. The District Court held the rights of the parties to be governed by Pennsylvania law and that since the United States had delayed unreasonably in giving notice of the forgery to defendant, it was barred from recovery. On appeal from a reversal by the Circuit Court of Appeals, affirmed.

■ DOUGLAS, J. . . . We agree with the Circuit Court of Appeals that the rule of Erie Railroad Co. v. Tompkins, 304 U.S. 64, does not apply to this action. The rights and duties of the United States on commercial paper which it issues are governed by federal rather than local law. When the United States disburses its funds or pays its debts, it is exercising a constitutional function or power.... The authority to issue the check had its origin in the Constitution and the statutes of the United States and was in no way dependent on the laws of Pennsylvania or of any other state. Cf. Board of Commissioners v. United States, 308 U.S. 343; Royal Indemnity Co. v. United States, 313 U.S. 289. The duties imposed upon the United States and the rights acquired by it as a result of the issuance find their roots in the same federal sources.... In absence of an applicable Act of Congress it is for the federal courts to fashion the governing rule of law according to their own standards. United States v. Guaranty Trust Co., 293 U.S. 340, is not opposed to this result. That case was concerned with a conflict of laws rule as to the title acquired by a transferee in Yugoslavia under a forged endorsement. Since the payee's address was Yugoslavia, the check had "something of the quality of a foreign bill" and the law of Yugoslavia was applied to determine what title the transferee acquired.

In our choice of the applicable federal rule we have occasionally selected state law.... But reasons which may make state law at times the appropriate federal rule are singularly inappropriate here. The issuance of commercial paper by the United States is on a vast scale and transactions in that paper from issuance to payment will commonly occur in several states. The application of state law, even without the conflict of laws rules of the forum, would subject the rights and duties of the United States to exceptional uncertainty. It would lead to great diversity in results by making identical transactions subject to the vagaries of the laws of the several states. The desirability of a uniform rule is plain. And while the federal law merchant, developed for about a century under the regime of Swift v. Tyson, 16 Pet. 1, represented general commercial law rather than a choice of a federal rule designed to protect a federal right, it nevertheless stands as a convenient source of reference for fashioning federal rules applicable to these federal questions....

D'Oench, Duhme & Co. v. Federal Deposit Insurance Corp.

Supreme Court of the United States, 1942.
315 U.S. 447, 62 S.Ct. 676, 86 L.Ed. 956.

■ JUSTICE DOUGLAS delivered the opinion of the Court.

Respondent instituted this suit in the United States District Court for the Eastern Division of the Eastern District of Missouri on a demand note for $5000 executed by petitioner in 1933 and payable to the Belleville Bank & Trust Co., Belleville, Illinois. Respondent insured that bank January 1, 1934; and it acquired the note in 1938 as part of the collateral securing a loan of over $1,000,000 to the bank, made in connection with the assumption of the latter's deposit liabilities by another bank. Since 1935 the note had been among the charged off assets of the bank. The note was executed by petitioner in renewal of notes which it had executed in 1926. Petitioner who was engaged in the securities business at St. Louis, Missouri, had sold the bank certain bonds which later defaulted. The original notes were executed to enable the bank to carry the notes and not show any past due bonds. Proceeds of the bonds were to be credited on the notes. The receipts for the notes contained the statement, "This note is given with the understanding it will not be called for payment. All interest payments to be repaid." Respondent had no knowledge of the existence of the receipts until after demand for payment on the renewal note was made in 1938. Certain interest payments on the notes were made prior to renewal for the purpose of keeping them "as live paper." Petitioner's president who signed the original notes knew that they were executed so that the past due bonds would not appear among the assets of the bank, and that the purpose of the interest payments was "to keep the notes alive." The original notes were signed in St. Louis, Missouri, were payable at petitioner's office there, and were delivered to the payee in Illinois. The evidence does not disclose where the note sued upon was signed, though it was dated at Belleville, Illinois, and payable to the bank there.

The main point of controversy here revolves around the question as to what law is applicable. The District Court held that Illinois law was applicable and that petitioner was liable. The Circuit Court of Appeals applied "general law" to determine that the note was an Illinois rather than a Missouri contract; and it decided that under Illinois law respondent was the equivalent of a holder in due course and entitled to recover. 117 F.2d 491. Petitioner contends that under the rule of Klaxon Company v. Stentor Electric Mfg. Co., 313 U.S. 487, a federal court sitting in Missouri must apply Missouri's conflict of law rules; that if, as was the case here, Illinois law was not pleaded or proved, a Missouri court would have ascertained Illinois law from Missouri decisions since in such a case Illinois law would be presumed to be the same as the Missouri law; and that the District Court was bound to follow that same course. We granted the petition for certiorari, because of the asserted conflict between the decision below and Klaxon Company v. Stentor Electric Mfg. Co., supra.

. . .

The jurisdiction of the District Court in this case, however, is not based on diversity of citizenship. Respondent, a federal corporation, brings this suit under an Act of Congress authorizing it to sue or be sued "in any court of law or equity, State or Federal." Sec. 12B, Federal Reserve Act, 12 U.S.C. § 264(j), 48 Stat. 162, 168, 172, 49 Stat. 684, 692. And see 28 U.S.C. § 42, 43 Stat. 941. Whether the rule of the Klaxon case applies where federal jurisdiction is not based on diversity of citizenship, we need not decide. For we are of the view that the liability of petitioner on the note involves decision of a federal not a state question under the rule of Deitrick v. Greaney, 309 U.S. 190. . . .

Sec. 12B(s) of the Federal Reserve Act, 12 U.S.C. § 264(s), provides that "Whoever, for the purpose of obtaining any loan from the Corporation . . . or for the purpose of influencing in any way the action of the Corporation under this section, makes any statement, knowing it to be false, or willfully overvalues any security, shall be punished by a fine of not more than $5,000, or by imprisonment for not more than two years or both." Subdivision (y) of the same section provided, at the time respondent insured the Belleville bank, that such a state bank "with the approval of the authority having supervision" of the bank and on "certification" to respondent "by such authority" that the bank "is in solvent condition" shall "after examination by, and with the approval of" the respondent be entitled to insurance.

These provisions reveal a federal policy to protect respondent and the public funds which it administers against misrepresentations as to the securities or other assets in the portfolios of the banks which respondent insures or to which it makes loans. If petitioner and the bank had arranged to use the note for the express purpose of deceiving respondent on insurance of the bank or on the making of the loan, the case would be on all fours with Deitrick v. Greaney, supra.... But the reach of the rule which prevents an accommodation maker of a note from setting up the defense of no consideration against a bank or its receiver or creditors is not delimited to those instances where he has committed a statutory offense....

. . .

Those principles are applicable here because of the federal policy evidenced in this Act to protect respondent, a federal corporation, from misrepresentations made to induce or influence the action of respondent, including misstatements as to the genuineness or integrity of securities in the portfolios of banks which it insures or to which it makes loans....

. . .

Affirmed.

■ [JUSTICE FRANKFURTER and THE CHIEF JUSTICE concurred on the ground that the result reached by the majority would also follow under Missouri or Illinois law and that it was unnecessary to stretch the federal statute to fit the case.]

■ JUSTICE JACKSON, concurring:

I think we should attempt a more explicit answer to the question whether federal or state law governs our decision in this sort of case than is found either in the opinion of the Court or in the concurring opinion of Mr. Justice Frankfurter. That question, as old as the federal judiciary, is met inescapably at the threshold of this case....

. . .

Although by Congressional command this case is to be deemed one arising under the laws of the United States, no federal statute purports to define the Corporation's rights as a holder of the note in suit or the liability of the maker thereof. There arises, therefore, the question whether in deciding the case we are bound to apply the law of some particular state or whether, to put it bluntly, we may make our own law from materials found in common-law sources.

This issue has a long historical background of legal and political controversy as to the place of the common law in federal jurisprudence....

I do not understand Justice Brandeis's statement in Erie R. Co. v. Tompkins, 304 U.S. 64, at 78, that "There is no federal general common law," to deny that the common law may in proper cases be an aid to or the basis of decision of federal questions. In its context it means to me only that federal courts may not apply their own notions of the common law at variance with applicable state decisions except "where the Constitution, treaties, or statutes of the United States [so] require or provide." Indeed, in a case decided on the same day as Erie R. Co. v. Tompkins, Justice Brandeis said that "whether the water of an interstate stream must be apportioned between the two States is a question of 'federal common law' upon which neither the statutes nor the decisions of either State can be conclusive." Hinderlider v. La Plata Co., 304 U.S. 92, 110.

Were we bereft of the common law, our federal system would be impotent. This follows from the recognized futility of attempting all-complete statutory codes, and is apparent from the terms of the Constitution itself.

. . .

... Federal law is no juridical chameleon, changing complexion to match that of each state wherein lawsuits happen to be commenced because of the accidents of service of process and of the application of the venue statutes. It is found in the federal Constitution, statutes, or common law. Federal common law implements the federal Constitution and statutes, and is conditioned by them.[10] Within these limits, federal courts are free to apply the additional common-law technique of decision and to draw upon all the sources of the common law in cases such as the present. Board of Commissioners v. United States, 308 U.S. 343, 350.

The law which we apply to this case consists of principles of established credit in jurisprudence selected by us because they are appropriate to effectuate the policy of the governing Act.... That a particular state happened to have the greatest connection in the conflict of laws sense with the making of the note involved or that the subsequent conduct happened to be chiefly centered there is not enough to make us subservient to the legislative policy or the judicial views of that state.

I concur in the Court's holding because I think that the defense asserted is nowhere admissible against the Corporation and that we need not go to the law of any particular state as our authority for so holding.

. . .

O'MELVENY & MYERS V. FEDERAL DEPOSIT INSURANCE CORP., 114 S.Ct. 2048 (1994): The FDIC became receiver for an insolvent California savings and loan (S & L) and ordered the S & L to make refunds to investors in fraudulent real estate ventures in which the S & L had been represented by O'Melveny & Myers, a law firm. The FDIC filed suit against the law firm in federal court and alleged state causes of action for professional negligence and breach of fiduciary duty. The law firm moved for summary judgment on the ground that the knowledge of the fraudulent conduct of the S & L's officers must be imputed to the S & L and to the FDIC, which, as receiver, stood in the shoes of the S & L. The district court granted the motion, but the Ninth Circuit reversed, holding that a federal common-law

---

10. For example, the common-law doctrines of conflict of laws worked out in a unitary system to deal with conflicts between domestic and truly foreign law may not apply unmodified in conflicts between the laws of states within our federal system which are affected by the full faith and credit or other relevant clause of the Constitution.

rule applied. The Supreme Court reversed the Ninth Circuit, holding that California law rather than federal law governed the issue of whether a corporate officer's knowledge of fraud would be imputed to a corporation asserting a cause of action created by state law, and whether this knowledge would be imputed to the FDIC as receiver. The Court remanded for determination of California law on this issue. The Supreme Court did not cite *D'Oenche*. The Court held that state law applied whether or not the Financial Institutions Reform, Recovery, and Enforcement Act of 1989 (FIRREA) applied retroactively to this case, in which the FDIC had taken over as receiver of the S & L in 1986. 12 U.S.C.A. § 1821(d)(2)(A)(i) (1988 ed., Supp. IV), part of this Act, provides that the FDIC shall "succeed to all rights, titles, powers and privileges of the insured depository institution." The Court states that this provision "places the FDIC in the shoes of the insolvent S & L, to work out its claims under state law, except where some provision in the extensive framework of the FIRREA provides otherwise." Id. at 2054.

On remand, the Ninth Circuit held that under California law, the FDIC was not barred by equitable defenses that could have been raised against the S & L, and declared that D'Oench has "now been overruled by the Supreme Court." F.D.I.C. v. O'Melveny & Myers, 61 F.3d 17, 19 (9th Cir.1995).

See also Murphy v. Federal Deposit Ins. Corp., 61 F.3d 34 (D.C.Cir. 1995). An investor in a failed real estate development sought damages from the FDIC on the theory that a failed bank that financed the venture was responsible for his loss and that the FDIC, as receiver, stood in the shoes of the bank. The district court granted summary judgment for the FDIC on both D'Oench and statutory grounds. 12 U.S.C.A. § 1823(e), part of FIRREA, provides that "[n]o agreement which tends to diminish or defeat the interest of the [FDIC] in any asset acquired by it ... shall be valid against the [FDIC] unless that agreement "has been, continuously, from the time of its execution an official [written] record of the depository institution." The D.C. Circuit reversed and remanded for further proceedings, holding that § 1823(e) did not bar the claim "because the FDIC has not demonstrated ... that the FDIC's interest in a specific asset would be diminished if the claims were upheld" and that "the Supreme Court's recent decision in O'Melveny & Myers v. FDIC ... removes the federal common law D'Oench doctrine as a separate bar to such claims." Id. at 35.

United States v. Kimbell Foods, Inc.
Supreme Court of the United States, 1979.
440 U.S. 715, 99 S.Ct. 1448, 59 L.Ed.2d 711.

■ JUSTICE MARSHALL delivered the opinion of the Court.

We granted certiorari in these cases to determine whether contractual liens arising from certain federal loan programs take precedence over private liens, in the absence of a federal statute setting priorities. To resolve this question, we must decide first whether federal or state law governs the controversies; and second, if federal law applies, whether this Court should fashion a uniform priority rule or incorporate state commercial law. We conclude that the source of law is federal, but that a national rule is unnecessary to protect the federal interests underlying the loan programs. Accordingly, we adopt state law as the appropriate federal rule for establishing the relative priority of these competing federal and private liens....

This Court has consistently held that federal law governs questions involving the rights of the United States arising under nationwide federal programs....

... [W]e think it clear that the priority of liens stemming from federal lending programs must be determined with reference to federal law. The SBA [Small Business Authority] and FHA [Farmers Home Administration] unquestionably perform federal functions within the meaning of *Clearfield* [p. 712, supra].

... [W]hen there is little need for a nationally uniform body of law, state law may be incorporated as the federal rule of decision. Apart from considerations of uniformity, we must also determine whether application of state law would frustrate specific objectives of the federal programs. If so, we must fashion special rules solicitous of those federal interests. Finally, our choice of law inquiry must consider the extent to which application of a federal rule would disrupt commercial relationships predicated on state law.

... We are unpersuaded that in the circumstances presented here, nationwide standards favoring claims of the United States are necessary to ease program administration or to safeguard the federal treasury from defaulting debtors. Because the state commercial codes "furnish convenient solutions in no way inconsistent with adequate protection of the federal interest[s]," United States v. Standard Oil Co., ..., 332 U.S., at 309, we decline to override intricate state laws of general applicability on which private creditors base their daily commercial transactions.

. . .

... [T]he agencies' own operating practices belie their assertion that a federal rule of priority is needed to avoid the administrative burdens created by disparate state commercial rules. The programs already conform to each State's commercial standards. By using local lending offices and employees who are familiar with the law of their respective localities, the agencies function effectively without uniform procedures and legal rules.

... The importance of securing adequate revenues to discharge national obligations justifies the extraordinary priority accorded federal tax liens through the choateness and first in time doctrines. By contrast, when the United States operates as a money-lending institution under carefully circumscribed programs, its interest in recouping the limited sums advanced is of a different order. Thus, there is less need here than in the tax lien area to invoke protective measures against defaulting debtors in a manner disruptive of existing credit markets.

... The overriding purpose of the tax lien statute obviously is to ensure prompt revenue collection. The same cannot be said of the SBA and FHA lending programs. They are a form of social welfare legislation, primarily designed to assist farmers and businesses that cannot obtain funds from private lenders on reasonable terms. We believe that had Congress intended the private commercial sector, rather than taxpayers in general, to bear the risks of default entailed by these public welfare programs, it would have established a priority scheme displacing state law....

. . .

In structuring financial transactions, businessmen depend on state commercial law to provide the stability essential for reliable evaluation of the risks involved. Cf. National Bank of Genesee v. Whitney, 103 U.S. 99, 102 (1881). However, subjecting federal contractual liens to the doctrines developed in the tax lien area could undermine that stability. Creditors who justifiably rely on state law to obtain superior liens would have their expectations thwarted whenever a federal contractual security interest suddenly appeared and took precedence.

Because the ultimate consequences of altering settled commercial practices are so difficult to foresee, we hesitate to create new uncertainties, in the absence of careful legislative deliberation. Of course, formulating special rules to govern the priority of the federal consensual liens in issue here would be justified if necessary to vindicate important national interests. But neither the Government nor the Court of Appeals advanced any concrete reasons for rejecting well-established commercial rules which have proven workable over time. Thus, the prudent course is to adopt the readymade body of state law as the federal rule of decision until Congress strikes a different accommodation.

. . .

[In disposing of the two decisions under review, the court affirmed the judgment which had applied Texas law giving preference to the respondent's lien and remanded the other case for determination of lien priorities under applicable Georgia law.]

NOTES

1. Is this decision inconsistent with Clearfield Trust Co. v. United States, p. 712, supra? See Note, Formulating a Federal Rule of Decision in Commercial Transactions after Kimbell, 66 Iowa L.Rev. 391 (1981).

2. Federal precedent generally supplants the provisions of the UCC, according to Comment, Application of the Uniform Commercial Code to Federal Government Contracts: Doing Business on Business Terms, 16 Wm. & Mary L.Rev. 395 (1974). See also the dictum in Woods-Tucker Leasing Corp. v. Hutcheson-Ingram, 642 F.2d 744, 749 (5th Cir. 1981): "If we *were* required to exercise independent federal judgment in choosing whether to apply Texas or Mississippi law to this UCC–

regulated transaction ..., we would likewise look to UCC § 1–105 (1) [validating the parties' contractual choice of law] ... as part of a national effort to establish a nationally uniform law to govern the validity and effect of commercial transactions.... [The UCC] 'should generally be considered as the federal law of commerce—including secured transactions,' " quoting from In re King-Porter, 446 F.2d 722, 732 (5th Cir. 1971), original emphasis.

3. Vanston Bondholders Protective Committee v. Green, 329 U.S. 156 (1946) concerned a Delaware corporation with its principal place of business in Kentucky which mortgaged Kentucky property under an indenture. The indenture, executed in New York with a New York bank as trustee, provided the bonds secured by it would be paid in New York or Illinois at the option of the holder. The corporation went into an equity receivership and then into reorganization under the Bankruptcy Act, in a federal court in Kentucky. The indenture and the bonds provided for payment of interest on unpaid interest, and the validity of this provision was in issue. The district court and the circuit court of appeals treated the matter as one of conflict of laws to be governed by the law of New York. The Supreme Court in an opinion by Black, J., stated: "In determining what claims are allowable and how a debtor's assets shall be distributed, a bankruptcy court does not apply the law of the state where it sits. Erie R.R. v. Tompkins, 304 U.S. 64, has no such implication.... [B]ankruptcy courts must administer and enforce the Bankruptcy Act as interpreted by this Court in accordance with authority granted by Congress to determine how and what claims shall be allowed under equitable principles. And we think an allowance of interest on interest under the circumstances shown by this case would not be in accord with the equitable principles governing bankruptcy distributions."

4. Federal law may also determine common law tort issues. In United States v. Standard Oil Co., 332 U.S. 301 (1947), it was held that federal law determined whether the United States could obtain reimbursement from one who had negligently injured a soldier, for hospital care and pay during his disablement. The defendant was held not liable. See also Kohr v. Allegheny Airlines, Inc., 504 F.2d 400 (7th Cir. 1974), holding that federal common law determines rights of indemnity and contribution in airplane crash litigation. The argument suggested by its title is advanced in Note, The Case for a Federal Common Law of Aircraft Disaster Litigation, 51 N.Y.U.L.Rev. 232 (1976). The note writer asserts that federal courts should exercise their power to imply a federal cause of action for victims of air crashes, borrowing from the Supreme Court's decision in Cort v. Ash, 422 U.S. 66 (1975), where four factors were listed as determinative of when a federal right of action should be implied from a statute not expressly creating one. See Lowenfeld, Mass Torts and the Conflict of Laws: The Airline Disaster, 1989 U.Ill.L.Rev. 157 (1989).

5. In re "Agent Orange" Product Liab. Litigation, 635 F.2d 987 (2d Cir. 1980) was a class action by Army veterans asserting a right under federal common law to recover against corporations that supplied the United States government with chemicals that were alleged to have been contaminated and to have injured the veterans. Held that veterans had no claim under federal common law. The court found that there was "no federal interest in uniformity for its own sake" since the litigation was between private parties and "no substantial rights or duties of the government hinged on its outcome." Also, the interests of the federal government were conflicting since it had an interest both in the welfare of its veterans and in that of the suppliers of its material. "The extent to which either group should be favored ... is preeminently a policy determination of the sort reserved in the first instance for Congress." Congress has not yet determined how these two competing interests should be reconciled. "... before common law rules should be fashioned, the use of state law must pose a threat to an 'identifiable' federal policy.... In the present litigation the federal policy is not yet identifiable." The dissent emphasized that it would be unfortunate if veterans' recoveries for Agent Orange injuries were to vary from state to state "despite the fact that these soldiers fought shoulder to shoulder, without regard to state citizenship, in a national endeavor abroad." Likewise "the conclusion seems inescapable" that the United States has a greater interest in the welfare of its veterans than in that of its suppliers.

The case was then continued on the basis of the federal court's diversity jurisdiction. Now required to apply state law, the trial court concluded that all of the states involved would apply "a form of national consensus law or of federal law itself" because of the need for a uniform result. In re Agent Orange Product Liability Litigation, 580 F.Supp. 690, 698 (E.D.N.Y.1984). A settlement was reached and ordered. 597 F.Supp. 740, 755 (E.D.N.Y.1984), decision affirmed 818 F.2d 145 (2d Cir.1987).

6. Litigation over asbestos-caused diseases has surpassed the other important products liability cases, including Agent Orange, DES, Dalkon–Shield, and automobile defects. By 1983, suits had been filed on behalf of 24,000 claimants and in 1984 new suits were filed at the rate of 500 per month. One prospect in multiple litigation of this magnitude is that the financial resources of defendant manufacturers will be exhausted before the claims of all victims have progressed to judgment or settlement. In Jackson v. Johns–Manville Sales Corp., 750 F.2d 1314 (5th Cir. 1985), the defendants sought a nationwide solution through the development of federal common law. However, the Fifth Circuit held, over strong dissent, "that this case is not an appropriate one for the creation of federal common law because of the absence of a uniquely federal interest and the practical problems that would attend the displacement of state law." 750 F.2d at 1327.

For discussion of the jurisdictional and choice-of-law aspects of mass torts see Symposium: Conflict of Laws and Complex Litigation Issues in Mass Tort Litigation, 1989 University of Illinois Law Review 35. For Professor Weintraub's proposed choice-of-law rules to govern products liability, see supra pp. 517–518.

7. On November 6, 1991, the Subcommittee on Intellectual Property and Judicial Administration, House Judiciary Committee, approved H.R. 2450, the Multiparty, Multiforum Jurisdiction Act of 1991. The bill provides for consolidation in a central federal forum, by transfer from state courts, as well as from other federal district courts, of actions arising from a "single-event" mass tort such as a hotel fire, bridge collapse or plane crash. The forum court would determine applicable law, liability and punitive damages, then retransfer cases to their courts of origin to assess compensatory damages. The most difficult challenge in writing this legislation is the choice-of-law problem, which H.R. 2450 attacks as follows:

SEC. 6. CHOICE OF LAW

(a) DETERMINATION BY THE COURT.—Chapter 111 of title 28, United States Code, is amended by adding at the end the following new section:

§ 1659. Choice of Law in multiparty, multiforum actions

(a) In an action which is or could have been brought, in whole or in part, under section 1368 of this title, the district court in which the action is brought or to which it is removed shall determine the source of the applicable substantive law, except that if an action is transferred to another district court, the transferee court shall determine the source of the applicable substantive law. In making this determination, a district court shall not be bound by the choice of law rules of any State, and the factors that the court may consider in choosing the applicable law include—

(1) the place of the injury;

(2) the place of the conduct causing the injury;

(3) the principal places of business or domiciles of the parties;

(4) the danger of creating unnecessary incentives for forum shopping; and

(5) whether the choice of law would be reasonably foreseeable to the parties.

The factors set forth in paragraphs (1) through (5) shall be evaluated according to their relative importance with respect to the particular action. If good cause is shown in exceptional cases, including constitutional reasons, the court may allow the law of more than one State to be applied with respect to a party, claim, or other element of an action.

(b) The district court making the determination under subsection (a) shall enter an order designating the single jurisdiction whose substantive law is to be applied in all other actions under the statute arising from the same accident as that giving rise to the action in which the determination is made. The substantive law of the designated jurisdiction shall be applied to the parties and claims in all such actions before the court, and to all other elements of each action, except where Federal law applies or the order specifically provides for the application of the law of another jurisdiction with respect to a party, claim, or other element of an action. . . .

GREENBERG V. PANAMA TRANSPORT CO., 185 F.Supp. 320 (D.Mass.1960): Suit by an attorney against two corporations for interference with advantageous contractual relations. Plaintiff claimed that his client, a seaman, had been induced to discharge plaintiff as his proctor in admiralty in a Jones Act suit for personal injury.

■ WYZANSKI, J. . . . Despite the fact that this case is presented as one within the diversity jurisdiction, it does not automatically follow that, in considering the validity of Greenberg's retainer, this Court must turn to the state law of Massachusetts for guidance as to the appropriate conflict of laws rules or the appropriate substantive rules. . . . The claims for which Vazquez retained Greenberg arose out of the general maritime law and out of an Act of Congress, the Jones Act. Such claims, while theoretically presentable in either a state court or a federal court, are usually presented in a federal court. And, in fact, presentation before the federal court in the Southern District of New York did occur in the case at bar.

To hold that the validity of a retainer to perform services in a federal court with respect to a federal cause of action should be determined by state law would seem highly artificial. Every policy consideration dictates that the federal courts should enunciate uniform national rules to determine the validity of contracts made by proctors in admiralty, who are officers of federal courts, to present claims to federal courts. That is, there should be "a uniform national rule of law, binding on state and federal courts alike, where the operative legal policies are federal in origin." Paul A. Freund, Federal-State Relations In The Opinions of Judge Magruder, 72 Harv.L.Rev. 1204, 1213.

Applying a national rule of law this Court concludes that the contract under which Vazquez retained Greenberg was valid. The contract was an entirely normal arrangement. It did not in the technical sense provide for a contingent fee. And the terms of compensation fall within the zone of reasonableness.

Having determined that the retainer contract is governed by federal law, and that under such law the contract is valid, the Court must next consider what law governs a claim that defendants have tortiously interfered with the contract. It is usually assumed that in connection with the tort of interfering with advantageous contract relations, as in connection with torts generally, the governing rule is supplied by the law of the place where the tort occurs.... But the grounds of logic, history, convenience, and policy which support this doctrine in many cases, particularly cases of physical injury, are not appropriately invoked in every type of case. Different torts may be governed by different principles of conflict of laws. Cf. Gordon v. Parker, D.C.D.Mass., 83 F.Supp. 40, affirmed sub nom. Parker v. Gordon, 1 Cir., 178 F.2d 888. [p. 460, supra.] See A.A. Ehrenzweig, Alienation of Affections In the Conflict of Laws, 45 Cornell Law Qu. 514, 515. And the conflict of laws rules governing even the particular tort of interference with advantageous contractual relations may depend upon what type of contract relationship is said to have been impeded.

Here we have a claim that when sued in a federal court defendants interfered with the contractual relationship between the then plaintiff who was suing them and his attorney, the present plaintiff. In determining the applicable law to decide this claim, it does not seem of the greatest importance where that interference occurred. Nor does it seem of decisive importance in what forum the claim of alleged interference is made. The controlling principles of substantive law should be enunciated on a national basis applicable to anyone who is said to have interfered with a professional relation between an officer of a national court and his client....

The federal courts being free to apply a national rather than a state standard to claims that defendants have interfered with relations between federal lawyers and their clients, the federal courts would probably mould the national standard with appropriate references to Restatement, Torts, §§ 766–774. Drawing upon those sections as well as the general case law this Court concludes that in the case at bar defendants, without a privilege so to do, have induced Vazquez not to continue his professional relations with Greenberg and are therefore liable to Greenberg for the damages thereby caused to Greenberg.

Bank of America National Trust & Savings Association v. Parnell

Supreme Court of the United States, 1956.
352 U.S. 29, 77 S.Ct. 119, 1 L.Ed.2d 93.

[An action was brought in a federal court in Pennsylvania for the conversion of bonds which had been owned by the plaintiff. The bonds were bearer bonds of Home Owners' Loan Corporation, with payment guaranteed by the United States. The bonds were originally due to mature in 1952, but pursuant to their terms they had been called for payment on or about May 1, 1944. On May 2, 1944, they disappeared, apparently having been stolen from plaintiff. In 1948 they were cashed by the defendant bank in Pennsylvania when presented to it by the individual defendant. At the trial the principal issue was the burden of establishing that the defendants took the bonds in good faith, without knowledge or notice of the defect in title. The jury brought in verdicts against both defendants and judgment was entered against them.]

■ JUSTICE FRANKFURTER delivered the opinion of the court.

. . .

The District Court in this suit, based on diversity jurisdiction, for the conversion in Pennsylvania of pieces of paper of defined value, deemed itself a court of Pennsylvania in which, in view of the nature of the claim, Pennsylvania law would govern. See Guaranty Trust Co. of New York v. York, 326 U.S. 99, 108. But respondents claim, and the Court of Appeals sustained them, that the decision in Clearfield Trust Co. v. United States, 318 U.S. 363, 63 S.Ct. 573, 87 L.Ed. 838, [p. 712, supra] compels the application of federal law to the entire case. The Court of Appeals misconceived the nature of this litigation in holding that the Clearfield Trust case controlled. . . .

Securities issued by the Government generate immediate interests of the Government. These were dealt with in Clearfield Trust and in National Metropolitan Bank v. United States, 323 U.S. 454. But they also radiate interests in transactions between private parties. The present litigation is purely between private parties and does not touch the rights and duties of the United States. The only possible interest of the United States in a situation like the one here, exclusively involving the transfer of Government paper between private persons, is that the floating of securities of the United States might somehow or other be adversely affected by the local rule of a particular State regarding the liability of a converter. This is far too speculative, far too remote a possibility to justify the application of federal law to transactions essentially of local concern.

We do not mean to imply that litigation with respect to Government paper necessarily precludes the presence of a federal interest to be governed by federal law, in all situations merely because it is a suit between private parties, or that it is beyond the range of federal legislation to deal comprehensively with Government paper. We do not of course foreclose such judicial or legislative action in appropriate situations by concluding that this controversy over burden of proof and good faith represents too essentially a private transaction not to be dealt with by the local law of Pennsylvania where the transaction took place. Federal law of course governs the interpretation of the nature of the rights and obligations created by the Government bonds themselves. A decision with respect to the "overdueness" of the bonds is therefore a matter of federal law, which, in view of our holding, we need not elucidate. . . .

Reversed and remanded.

■ JUSTICE BLACK and JUSTICE DOUGLAS, dissenting.

We believe that the "federal law merchant" which Clearfield Trust Co. v. United States, 318 U.S. 363, 367, held applicable to transactions in the commercial paper of the United States should be applicable to all transactions in that paper.... Not until today has a distinction been drawn between suits by the United States on that paper and suits by other parties. But the Court does not stop there. Because this is "essentially a private transaction", it is to be governed by local law. Yet the nature of the rights and obligations created by commercial paper of the United States Government is said to be controlled by federal law. Thus, federal law is to govern some portion of a dispute between private parties, while that portion of the dispute which is "essentially of local concern" is to be governed by local law. The uncertainties which inhere in such a dichotomy are obvious.

The virtue of a uniform law governing bonds, notes, and other paper issued by the United States is that it provides a certain and definite guide to the rights of all parties rather than subjecting them to the vagaries of the law of many States.... If the rule of the Clearfield Trust case is to be abandoned as to some parties, it should be abandoned as to all and we should start afresh on this problem.

NOTES

1. Professor Mishkin has urged that "a decision to apply state law as a matter of federal incorporation does not necessarily carry with it the obligation to adhere to the range and techniques which have been held to govern under Erie; there remains a freedom ... to control the extent and methods of that adoption ..." State law may be applied to issues singly, having regard for the content of the state rule, without the need to follow state choice of law rules, and with little fear of disparity between federal and state decisions in a single forum. Mishkin, The Variousness of "Federal Law": Competence and Discretion in the Choice of National and State Rules for Decision, 105 U.Pa.L.Rev. 797, 804–10 (1957).

2. Does the Parnell case imply that federal courts lack authority to fashion rules governing private parties' interests in government securities? See Friendly, In Praise of Erie—and of the New Federal Common Law, 19 Record of N.Y.C.B.A. 64 (1964); 39 N.Y.U.L.Rev. 383 (1964).

See also Miree v. DeKalb County, 433 U.S. 25 (1977). Petitioners sought to recover for the death of airline passengers asserting a right of recovery as third-party beneficiaries under a government grant contract requiring the county to maintain the airport in a manner permitting normal operations. The Supreme Court concluded that, unlike the situation in *Clearfield Trust,* "petitioners' breach-of-contract claim will have no direct effect upon the United States or its Treasury.... The parallel between *Parnell* and [this case] is obvious ... [N]o substantial rights or duties of the United States hinge on its outcome ... [and any federal interest, e.g., promoting compliance with air safety regulations is] far too speculative ... to justify the application of federal law to transactions essentially of local concern." 433 U.S. at 29–32 passim. Chief Justice Burger said in his concurrence that *Clearfield Trust* does not preclude "... the application of 'federal common law' to all matters involving only the rights of private citizens.... I am not prepared to foreclose ... the possibility that there may be situations where the rights and obligations of private parties are ... dependent on a specific exercise of congressional regulatory power.... [If Congress has not exercised that power, then] 'the inevitable incompleteness presented by all legislation means that interstitial federal law making is a basic responsibility of the federal courts.'" 433 U.S. at 34–35, quoting from United States v. Little Lake Misere Land Co., 412 U.S. 580, 593 (1973). Are the mass tort cases, pp. 720–721, Notes (5) and (6), an appropriate area for federal law-making by the federal courts?

See Field, Sources of Law: The Scope of Federal Common Law, 99 Harv.L.Rev. 881 (1986); Jay, Origins of Federal Common Law, 133 U.Pa.L.Rev. 1003 (1983); Merrill, The Common Law Powers of Federal Courts, 52 U.Chi.L.Rev. 1 (1985); Weinberg, Federal Common Law, 83 Nw.U.L.Rev. 805 (1989).

3. Assuming that an area is appropriate for federal common law, what is the relation between it and prior or subsequent legislation? Chief Justice Burger wrote of "interstitial federal law making" in *Miree,* Note (2) supra. In dealing with the pollution of an interstate stream, one court of appeals stated that "until the field has been the subject of comprehensive legislation or authorized administrative standards, only a federal common law basis can provide an adequate means for dealing with such claims...." Texas v. Pankey, 441 F.2d 236, 241 (10th Cir.1971). In Illinois v. City of Milwaukee, 406 U.S. 91 (1972), the Supreme Court initially agreed. But, in a second case, the Court stated that, "when Congress addresses a question previously governed by a decision rested on federal common law the need for such unusual exercise of lawmaking by the federal courts disappears." City of Milwaukee v. Illinois and Michigan, 451 U.S. 304, 314 (1981). Justice Blackmun argued in dissent that the "automatic displacement" approach is inadequate in two respects: failing to reflect the unique role federal common law plays in resolving disputes between a State and the citizens or government of another; and ignoring the "Court's frequent recognition that federal common law may complement congressional action in the fulfillment of federal policies." 451 U.S. at 334. In O'Melveny & Myers v. FDIC, p. 716, supra, the Court stated: "In answering the central question of displacement of [state law], we of course would not contradict an explicit federal statutory provision. Nor would we adopt a court-made rule to supplement federal statutory regulation that is comprehensive and detailed; matters left unaddressed in such a scheme are presumably left subject to the disposition provided by state law." 114 S.Ct. at 2054.

International Paper Co. v. Ouellette et al., 479 U.S. 481 (1987) was an action for common law nuisance (water pollution). Held: the state of injury (Vermont) has jurisdiction over the New York defendant; however, the federal Clean Water Act preempts all federal common law (in application of *City of Milwaukee* (1981), supra). In addition, application by Vermont of its own law was also preempted lest the federal scheme for uniform regulation through administrative agencies be frustrated. Since there were no federal standards extant at the time, the only law that could be applied was that of New York, the point source of the pollution. Why should federal common law not continue as interstitial law unless actually displaced? Or, in the absence of applicable federal administrative or common law standards, why does not *Klaxon* require resort to Vermont conflicts law? If Vermont conflicts law calls for the application of Vermont law would that lead to an unconstitutional result in light of Allstate Ins. Co. v. Hague and Phillips Petroleum Co. v. Shutts, pp. 349, 362, supra?

Section 2. Conflicts Problems in International Settings

With international travel, commerce and private transactions increasing by quantum leaps, the subject of "private international law" in its literal sense has grown in importance for American lawyers. All through the book we have encountered conflicts cases that cut across international boundaries. They were sprinkled, almost interchangeably, among the cases involving states of the Union. In re Annesley, Matter of Schneider, Gilbert v. Burnstine, Hilton v. Guyot, Holzer v. Deutsche-Reichsbahn Gesellschaft, Slater v. Mexican Nat'l Ry. Co., Walton v. Arabian American Oil Co., Babcock v. Jackson, Home Insurance Co. v. Dick and many others made their appearance. From time to time, it was observed that international judgments, statutes and other legal affirmations differ from sister-state judgments and statutes at least in the respect that amorphous principles of comity rather than pointed commands of full faith and credit are involved in their recognition.

In Hilton v. Guyot, another type of question was raised: May the several states impose diverse, individual tests for recognition of foreign judgments, or is the problem one committed to the national government? In somewhat more dilute form, the same sort of issue lurked in the Holzer case, where the New York Court of Appeals was asked to refuse to countenance a defense based upon the Nazi government's anti-Jewish laws. In the materials that follow in the first subsection, questions of the effective scope of state law in the international arena are considered against the backdrop of the accepted principle that the United States, in its relations with foreign nations, should speak with a single voice, not with more than fifty voices; and that traditionally and constitutionally, for the most part, the spokesman has been the chief executive and his delegates.

A second subsection explores the growing participation by the United States in international conventions that provide uniform procedural, conflicts and even substantive rules of law. As federal law, these conventions displace inconsistent state law under the Supremacy Clause as well as inconsistent prior federal law. Their application often raises important questions of interpretation—for instance, whether a particular state rule is indeed incompatible with the convention.

Even when the federal control over foreign affairs does not set limits on the states in international conflicts cases and even when no federal law expressly displaces state law, the question remains: Should international conflicts cases be treated differently from interstate cases and, if so, in what circumstances? The third subsection touches upon these issues.

A. INTERNATIONAL CONFLICTS CASES AND THE FEDERAL CONTROL OF FOREIGN AFFAIRS

Zschernig v. Miller

Supreme Court of the United States, 1968.
389 U.S. 429, 88 S.Ct. 664, 19 L.Ed.2d 683.

[An American citizen died in Oregon, leaving property to relatives in the Soviet Zone of Germany. An Oregon statute conditioned a nonresident alien's right to inherit property in Oregon upon the existence of a reciprocal right of American citizens to inherit in the alien's country upon the same terms as citizens of that country; upon the right of American citizens to receive payment within the United States from the estates of decedents dying in that country; and upon proof that the alien heirs of the American decedent would receive the benefit, use, and control of their inheritance without confiscation. The Oregon Supreme Court affirmed the finding of the trial court that the evidence did not establish that American citizens were accorded reciprocal rights to take property from or to receive the proceeds of East German estates. However, it found that a 1923 treaty was still effective with respect to East Germany, and consequently held that under Clark v. Allen, 331 U.S. 503, the East German heirs must be permitted to take the real property despite the Oregon statute. They were not permitted to take the personal property.] *

■ JUSTICE DOUGLAS delivered the opinion of the Court.

This case concerns the disposition of the estate of a resident of Oregon who died there intestate in 1962. Appellants are decedent's sole heirs and they are residents of East Germany. Appellees include members of the State Land Board that petitioned the Oregon probate court for the escheat of the net proceeds of the estate under the provisions of Ore.Rev.Stat. § 111.070 (1957), which provides for escheat in cases where a nonresident alien claims real or personal property unless three requirements are satisfied:

(1) the existence of a reciprocal right of a United States citizen to take property on the same terms as a citizen or inhabitant of the foreign country;

(2) the right of United States citizens to receive payment here of funds from estates in the foreign country; and

(3) the right of the foreign heirs to receive the proceeds of Oregon estates "without confiscation."

The Oregon Supreme Court held that the appellants could take the Oregon realty involved in the present case by reason of Article IV of the 1923 Treaty of Friendship, Commerce and Consular Rights with Germany (44 Stat. 2135) but that by reason of the same Article, as construed in Clark v. Allen, 331 U.S. 503, 67 S.Ct. 1431, 91 L.Ed. 1633, they could not take the personalty....

. . .

We do not accept the invitation to re-examine our ruling in Clark v. Allen. For we conclude that the history and operation of this Oregon statute make clear that § 111.070 is an intrusion by the State into the field of foreign affairs which the Constitution entrusts to the President and the Congress. See Hines v. Davidowitz, 312 U.S. 52, 63....

* The statement of facts is taken from the concurring opinion of Justice Harlan.

.... It has never been seriously suggested that state courts are precluded from performing [the probate] function, although there is a possibility, albeit remote, that any holding may disturb a foreign nation—whether the matter involves commercial cases, tort cases, or some other type of controversy. At the time Clark v. Allen was decided, the case seemed to involve no more than a routine reading of foreign laws. It now appears that in this reciprocity area under inheritance statutes, the probate courts of various States have launched inquiries into the type of governments that obtain in a particular foreign nation—whether aliens under their law have enforceable rights, whether the so-called "rights" are merely dispensations turning upon the whim or caprice of government officials, whether the representation of consuls, ambassadors, and other representatives of foreign nations are credible or made in good faith, whether there is in the actual administration in the particular foreign system of law any element of confiscation.

. . .

As we read the decisions that followed in the wake of Clark v. Allen, we find that they radiate some of the attitudes of the "cold war," where the search is for the "democracy quotient" of a foreign regime as opposed to the Marxist theory. The Oregon statute introduces the concept of "confiscation," which is of course opposed to the Just Compensation Clause of the Fifth Amendment. And this has led into minute inquiries concerning the actual administration of foreign law, into the credibility of foreign diplomatic statements, and into speculation whether the fact that some received delivery of funds should "not preclude wonderment as to how many may have been denied 'the right to receive'...." See State Land Board v. Kolovrat, 220 Or. 448, 461–462, 349 P.2d 255, 262, rev'd sub nom. Kolovrat v. Oregon, 366 U.S. 187 on other grounds.

That kind of state involvement in foreign affairs and international developments—matters which the Constitution entrusts solely to the Federal Government—is not sanctioned by Clark v. Allen. Yet such forbidden state activity has infected each of the three provisions of § 111.070, as applied by Oregon.

. . .

It seems inescapable that the type of probate law that Oregon enforces affects international relations in a persistent and subtle way.... Reversed.

NOTE

In Clark v. Allen, 331 U.S. 503 (1947), Justice Douglas wrote for the Court that a California reciprocal inheritance statute was constitutional and permitted German nationals to take as legatees of a California resident decedent's personal property in that state. (The United States Alien Property Custodian had vested in himself all interest of the German nationals in the decedent's estate, but the question of the validity of the attempted testamentary disposition remained because a California statute provided that nonresident aliens could not inherit real or personal property in the state unless United States citizens had reciprocal rights in property in the aliens' country, but unlike the Oregon statute in Zschernig, the California act did not refer to the right of foreign heirs to receive the proceeds of California property "without confiscation.") The opinion said in part:

"... Rights of succession to property are determined by local law.... Those rights may be affected by an overriding federal policy, as where a treaty makes different or conflicting arrangements.... Then the state policy must give way.... But here there is no treaty governing the rights of succession to the personal property. Nor has California entered the forbidden domain of negotiating with a foreign country, United States v. Curtiss-Wright Export Corp., 299 U.S. 304, 316, 317, or making a compact with it contrary to the prohibition of Article I, Section 10 of the Constitution. What California has done will have some incidental or indirect effect in foreign countries. But that is true of many state laws which none would claim cross the forbidden line."

Was Justice Douglas consistent in the two cases?

Dougherty v. Equitable Life Assurance Society

Court of Appeals of New York, 1934.
266 N.Y. 71, 193 N.E. 897.

[Actions against the Equitable Life Assurance Society, a New York corporation, growing out of life insurance policies issued by the Society to Russian citizens in Russia before the Russian Revolution of 1917. The defendant had been licensed to do business in Russia and the policies issued by it contained the following provisions of Russian law: Russian law should govern all disputes; the Russian government could at any time cancel the defendant's right to do business in Russia, whereupon the defendant must immediately liquidate and settle its accounts with the assured in the manner that should be indicated by the Russian government; the Society was obliged to keep on deposit with the government or the state bank assets sufficient to more than meet the liabilities incurred by the policies issued; and, further, "the exact fulfillment of the obligations entered into by the Society regarding the Russian assured shall be guaranteed, besides its sums and security found in Russia, by all the property belonging to the Society."

After the Revolution the Soviet government by its decrees declared that the business of insurance should be a state monopoly; that all private companies be liquidated immediately; and that the state assumed all obligations of the Society under its Russian policies. By a later decree all existing life insurance policies were cancelled and the government established a system of social protection. The Soviet government seized and confiscated the Society's assets in Russia.

The policies were payable according to their terms in rubles. Some of the present actions were brought to recover the premiums paid, on the theory of rescission; others were brought for the face value of the matured policies. From judgment of the appellate division affirming judgments in favor of certain plaintiffs and reversing judgments in favor of defendant (238 App.Div. 696, 265 N.Y.S. 714), all the parties appeal.]

■ CRANE, J. ... The question now for us to determine is, What effect these laws and decrees of an established government, binding upon the citizens of Russia in Russia, have upon this defendant's contracts, made in Russia with Russian citizens, to be determined and interpreted and given effect, if any, according to Russian law....

... Soviet Russia, as to all the insurance policies here in question, stands in the same position as if the government of Russia had never been interrupted by revolution; its decrees have the same force and effect as if they had been issued by the imperial government....

. . .

The plaintiffs seek to make a distinction between the seizure of tangible property ... and the disposition and canceling of rights to intangible property. We can see no distinction in this instance. The right to collect money by a Russian citizen on a contract to be interpreted according to Russian law is no different in this respect than the right to tangible property in Russia or the possession thereof. Both rights are dependent upon the law of Russia....

. . .

... [I]t cannot be against the public policy of this state to hold nationals to the contracts which they have made in their own country to be performed there according to the laws of that country. When they have specifically stipulated that the laws of their native land shall govern their acts, we give effect to those laws after recognition by this country the same as we would give effect to the laws of any nation which had not developed out of revolution.

Our conclusion, therefore, is that, since recognition, the Soviet decree became the laws of Russia, governing the policies here in question, and that obligations thereunder were at an end.

Assuming, however, that these contracts of insurance were not terminated by these Soviet decrees, and that the plaintiffs may recover the premiums paid prior to 1918, upon the theory of repudiation by the company in 1920, we also find that the plaintiffs cannot maintain this action, for the reason that the rubles in which payment is to be made are valueless....

. . .

The Soviets, in order to give to their money an exchange value, created the chervonetz bank notes, taking the chervonetz as a standard, worth ten rubles. Having placed its notes or currency on a supposed gold basis, with a reserve of gold to meet them, the ruble became worth 51 cents of our money. On the withdrawal of all other paper money, by 1924 the chervonetz bank notes and the state treasury notes became the only circulating medium or legal tender. The plaintiffs' claim, sustained by the referee, is, that all previous obligations, even those created in 1918 and before, were payable "ruble for ruble" in this new gold currency, whereas the day before its creation their obligations were worthless.

. . .

... The plaintiffs can only recover when they show that by the law of Soviet Russia pre-existing obligations are to be paid "ruble for ruble" in the new chervonetz gold note, or, that there is an established ratio between such gold standard and the pre-existing ruble of the obligation. It is the ruble recovery in Russia—what would they get there—which is sued for here. When established, it is translated into our money.

. . .

The judgments of the lower courts should, therefore, be reversed, and the complaints dismissed, with costs in all courts.

■ LEHMAN, JUDGE (concurring).... The primary question presented upon this appeal is whether under the law of this jurisdiction the defendant's contractual obligation has been canceled or discharged.

. . .

... We may assume, as the defendant contends, that the intended effect of the decree was cancellation of the obligation, so far as the Soviet government had power to cancel. Even so, the Russian government could not decree cancellation which would be effective beyond its borders, except in so far as the courts of other jurisdictions choose to give effect to such a decree.

The problem now presented would be simple if the sole situs of the defendant's obligation had been in Russia and resort was had to our courts for remedy of a wrong arising in Russia, or for vindication of property or contractual rights there. Cf. Salimoff & Co. v. Standard Oil Co. of New York, supra [262 N.Y. 220, 223, 186 N.E. 679, 681, 89 A.L.R. 345]. For some purposes the situs of the defendant's obligation was in Russia; not for all. The defendant is a domestic corporation. Seizure of its assets and termination of its privilege of doing business did not end its contractual obligations. Though with one exception, all the assured were residents or subjects of Russia at the time the policies were issued, many of them had ceased to be subjects or residents of that country at the time the Soviet government decreed cancellation of the obligations due to them. We have said in similar circumstances, "The intangible chose in action, at least when it is the result of a deposit in a bank, has for some purposes a situs at the residence or place of business of the debtor, though the creditor be far away." Sokoloff v. National City Bank of New York, 239 N.Y. 158, 169, 145 N.E. 917, 920, 37 A.L.R. 712. That is true, to at least the same degree, where the intangible chose in action is a promise to pay insurance in a foreign jurisdiction. In this case, indeed, that legal principle is fortified by the express agreement of the defendant that its assets everywhere should constitute a guaranty of the "exact fulfillment," of its obligations in Russia.

... We cannot hold that Russian law can relieve the defendant of an obligation for which it has received payment unless we give Russian law an extraterritorial effect which under our own law we are not required to accord to foreign law. The obligation of exact fulfillment remains in force. That obligation has been repudiated or breached. Right to restitution or damages still remains. It has not been discharged by confiscation of the obligation due to the assured, for a confiscatory foreign law offends our public policy and cannot constitute excuse for restitution or performance here. It has not been discharged by confiscation of the assets of the defendant in Russia, for the assured have the right under the policies to look to the assets of the defendant here for fulfillment of the obligation.

Judge Crane's conclusion rests, in my opinion, upon premises which are entirely fallacious. A majority of the assured, even though Russian citizens at the time the policies were issued, were not subjects of Russia domiciled there when the decrees were made. The insurer was not a Russian corporation. The obligation of the insurer followed it wherever the insurer could be found. It was, therefore, not intangible property within Russia and the Russian government did not have the same dominion over it as it had over tangible property situated there....

. . .

Assuming that the plaintiff has a cause of action, the question of how recovery shall be measured still remains....

The obligation of the defendant at its inception could be discharged by payment of imperial rubles. When new issues of rubles were made, the defendant's debt was payable either in imperial rubles or in rubles of the new issues. All these rubles depreciated until they were without value. The result was that the obligation to the assured by the insurer, payable in valueless rubles, was also valueless ...

... That was not the result of a confiscatory decree, but of unrestrained inflation. For loss so sustained, our law furnishes no remedy. That was true before the Soviet government was recognized; it is true now.

We can measure the value of the defendant's obligation only upon the basis of the value of the currency in which it was payable.... Here the defendant was required to leave such equitable value [of the policy] in Russia. It has been confiscated by the Russian government, but even if it had not been confiscated, it would itself have become valueless by reason of the depreciation of the ruble. Thus, even though events have rendered performance of the defendant's obligation valueless, the same events have rendered valueless the consideration received by the defendant.

For these reasons, I concur in the reversal of the judgment.

Johansen v. Confederation Life Association

United States Court of Appeals, Second Circuit, 1971.
447 F.2d 175.

■ LUMBARD, CHIEF JUDGE: ...

I

Defendant is a Canadian life insurance company with its head office in Toronto. It does business not only in Canada and in the United States, but also in twenty-two other countries including Cuba. Since 1909 it has had a branch office in Cuba; and from 1909 to 1959, when Castro took over, it issued policies to residents of Cuba. Its operations in that country have always been subject to Cuban laws and to the supervision of the Cuban government.

Turull, who was the insured of the two policies upon which plaintiffs now seek to recover, moved from his birthplace, Brooklyn, New York, to Cuba when he was a young man. He married a Cuban and had a substantial export-import business in Havana. In 1937 and 1939, he took out the two policies in question here with the defendant's Cuban office, his wife being the beneficiary of the first and his daughter the beneficiary of the second. He moved back to New York only after Castro came into power and died in New York in 1961.

Johansen, also a United States citizen born in New York, married Turull's daughter in New York in 1941 and thereafter went to work for his father-in-law in Cuba. In 1946, he took out a policy with defendant's Cuban office, and he remained in Cuba until Castro took over. Afterwards, he moved back to New York where he now resides. He seeks a declaration that defendant is obligated to accept premium payments from him in United States dollars, to make policy loans in United States dollars, and to pay proceeds upon his death in United States dollars.

Each of the three policies stated that "[a]ll sums payable or [receivable] under the policy shall be paid at ... Havana, Republic of Cuba." Further, with respect to currency, each provided that "[a]ll sums payable or [receivable] under this policy shall be paid in lawful currency of the United States of America."

Although the latter provision might seem at first glance to solve the problem of this case, it does not do so because of the effect of the Cuban currency laws throughout the years. From 1914 to 1939, two currencies were legal tender in Cuba, the peso and the United States dollar. Theoretically they were of equal value and creditors could demand payment in whichever currency they chose. By 1939, however, the peso was actually worth less than the dollar. In an effort to bolster the peso, the Cuban government enacted a law in 1939 making the dollar and the peso interchangeable on a one-for-one basis. Each continued to be legal tender, but they could be used interchangeably, and debtors were now given the option as to which currency they wished to use in payment of their debts. Creditors were required to accept pesos in extinguishment of an obligation expressed in dollars and vice versa. Thus, it is evident that when the policies in question here stated that United States currency was to be paid, it was referring to a legal Cuban tender which after 1939 could be paid in either dollars or pesos.

In 1951, however, there was a significant change in the Cuban law. The new decree provided that henceforth pesos would be the only legal tender. United States dollars ceased to be legal tender and all obligations had to be expressed and paid in pesos. Obligations previously contracted in dollars had to be discharged in pesos at the rate of one peso for one dollar. Although a person could still own dollars in Cuba, he could not use them to pay debts. Thus, this Cuban law in effect changed the insurance contracts in question here from dollar contracts to peso contracts. The 1951 law was widely published in Cuba and defendant notified all its Cuban policyholders that all payments under policies which referred to United States currency would henceforth by payable in pesos. Neither Turull nor Johansen objected to this and both paid their premiums in pesos after 1951 as they were required to do. Indeed, even before 1951 Johansen had paid in pesos, although Turull had paid in dollars.

In 1959, when Castro took over, a new Cuban law made it a criminal offense to hold dollars and required owners of dollars to turn them in for pesos on a one-for-one basis. Since that time the peso has diminished in value in relation to dollars and today is substantially worthless in terms of dollars. This fact causes the dilemma of the instant case.

Although defendant is willing to pay plaintiffs the amounts due them in pesos and in Havana, plaintiffs seek payment of dollars in New York, because pesos are worthless to them here and they are forbidden by United States law to travel to Cuba. Defendant wants to pay in pesos because throughout the years it has invested the insurance proceeds from its Cuban policyholders in Cuban assets precisely in order to meet the obligations in pesos to those policyholders. Now, since it is forbidden by Cuban law to transfer those funds out of Cuba and since pesos are as worthless to it as to plaintiffs in terms of dollars, it has no present use for the funds which it invested in Cuba other than to pay off the Cuban policies. Hence, to require defendant to pay plaintiffs in New York dollars out of its general assets would leave it with worthless reserves of pesos on its hands.

II

The first question arising here is one of conflict of laws, i.e., whether the applicable law governing the disposition of this case is Cuban law, New York law, or Canadian law....

... According to plaintiffs, New York has a vital interest in determining whether or not its citizens who have fully performed insurance contracts in hard currency will receive hard currency back from the insurance company. On the other hand, they contend, Cuba has no legitimate interest in having its internal currency regulations applied to determine the outcome of this litigation.

Plaintiffs argue further that under this "greatest interest" rationale now used by New York courts, the present domicile of the parties seeking to recover is generally decisive....

Finally, plaintiffs argue, Canada also has an important interest in this case—that of having insurance companies domiciled there perform their contracts according to their express terms. In plaintiffs' view, the district court's decision here frustrates that policy....

... The cases cited by plaintiffs in this regard were either wrongful death actions where New York domiciliaries were killed in out-of-state automobile accidents ... or actions involving property rights.... This case, however, is an insurance contract matter; and if domicile is to be determinative in such a case, it seems more logical to look to the domicile of the insureds themselves at the time they entered into the contracts, rather than to the domicile of the plaintiffs at the time of bringing suit. For the rights and obligations of the parties under such contracts are determined by the law of the place where the insureds lived when the contracts were made and can hardly be changed solely because the insureds or the beneficiaries subsequently changed domiciles.

. . .

In addition, the large number of contacts between the insurance contracts and Cuba cannot be ignored.... Judge McLean found those contacts to be overwhelming and decisive. Moreover, Turull and Johansen did not object to the 1951 notice that payments on the policies would henceforth be made in pesos; and indeed until Castro, they were clearly willing to accept Cuban law as governing those policies.

Thus, we hold that under either the "grouping of contacts" test or the test propounded by plaintiffs, Cuban law governs the disposition of this case; and under Cuban law, defendant's obligation on these policies is to pay in pesos, since the 1951 Cuban law forbade defendant to pay in dollars and changed the contracts in question here from dollar contracts to peso contracts.

III

. . .

Plaintiffs argue that ... there is no reason to give the Cuban law effect in New York, when both New York and Canada have stronger interests in the outcome of this case than Cuba has. According to plaintiffs, the insurance contracts imposed upon the company a general obligation to pay plaintiffs when the insureds died.... [H]ence the company has no right to convert its general obligation into a limited one to pay only from the assets which it had elected to invest in Cuba. This is especially true, plaintiffs contend, since the company failed to inform the insureds of the limitation which it now asserts. Thus, in plaintiffs' view, the defendant must pay its debts out of its general assets, not out of the limited reserves in Cuba.

We do not agree. As shown above, Cuban law governed these policies when they were made; that law in 1951 converted the currency of these policies to pesos; and until Castro, Turull and Johansen accepted the applicability of Cuban law and acquiesced in the shift in premiums from dollars to pesos. Neither objected to the 1951 change or to the contractual provision that all payments were to be made in Cuba until after Castro came into power—which in our view was too late. Thus ... there is no reason or policy for a New York court not to give effect to the Cuban law, under which defendant's obligation is to pay in pesos.

. . .

IV

Looking finally to the "equities" of the situation, they seem to us to tip the scale slightly in the defendant's favor. On the one hand, plaintiffs would have no use for pesos; and, according to them, they are entitled to payment on their policies in valuable currency since they paid their premiums in hard valuable currency. On the other hand, defendant accumulated reserves of pesos and invested in Cuba in order to meet its obligations on the Cuban policies, and those pesos are now worthless to it except to pay off the Cuban policies. . . .

Plaintiffs rely on the fact that the company was not compelled by any law to invest in Cuban assets in order to meet its obligations on the Cuban policies, but rather did so voluntarily and as part of its general policy; and they argue that therefore the company should now have to meet its obligations in currency valuable to plaintiffs. It seems to us, however, that the company's policy of investing in the country where the insured lived was a reasonable and almost necessary business decision, especially where, as here, the policy expressly provided for payment in that country. Thus, the company would not be unjustly enriched by being allowed to pay in pesos, whereas requiring it to pay in dollars would in effect be compelling it to pay twice and thereby put a burden on its general uncommitted reserves.

Affirmed.

■ [The concurring opinion of JUDGE SMITH is omitted.]

■ FEINBERG, CIRCUIT JUDGE (dissenting):

The basic issue in this case is whether the promise of an insurance company to an American citizen to pay death benefits "in lawful currency of the United States of America" should be enforced. The case would have been far different had the insurer's obligation been to pay benefits in "lawful currency" or in "legal tender" or in "lawful currency of Cuba." The first two phrases are capable of the construction defendant seeks, which the third embodies. But that is not what the policy said. The obligation instead was to pay benefits in "lawful currency of the United States." The majority concludes that this unmistakably clear promise of defendant insurance company is unenforceable even though that conclusion is inconsistent with the insurer's own selling practices and the insured's justified expectations and is contrary to the most relevant precedents. I emphatically dissent from such an inequitable and unjustified result. . . .

. . .

... It is true that ordinarily the rights created by a life insurance contract are determined by the local law of the jurisdiction (here Cuba) where the insured was domiciled at the time of application for the policy. See Restatement (Second) of Conflict of Laws § 192 (P.O.D.1969). But that rule is by no means ironclad, particularly in international cases. See Rossano v. Manufacturers' Life Insurance Co. [1963] 2 QB 352, and other cases cited in Restatement, supra, Reporter's Note § 192 at 10. When the insured changes his domicile after the policy is issued, as concededly occurred here in 1959, the jurisdiction to which he has moved has "the dominant interest in him." Restatement, supra, Explanatory Notes § 192, comment d at 3. Moreover, in view of defendant's selling practices ... such a move was clearly foreseeable to it. Cf. Clay v. Sun Insurance Office, Ltd., 377 U.S. 179 (1964). These practices gave rise to a justified expectation by the insured that he could count on payment of benefits in American dollars when he went back to his domicile of origin where American dollars, rather than pesos, were used.... When to these considerations is added the fact that the beneficiaries here are New York domiciliaries and that New York's choice of law would be influenced by its strong policy of construing insurance contracts to protect the insured.... I do not think that New York would apply the Cuban law in this case and render worthless the benefits under the contracts.

Defendant argues that a New York court would look to the law of the place of payment as specified in the contract to decide in which currency payment of the obligation is to be made. That may correctly state a New York conflicts principle, but it only governs "details of performance and not ... matters which substantially affect the nature and extent of the obligations imposed by the contract." See Restatement (Second) of Conflict of Laws, Explanatory Notes § 206, comment b at 319 (P.O.D.1968). In any event, application of that rule is doubtful where the contract itself makes provision, as do the policies in this case, for the type of currency to be used. Liebeskind v. Mexican Light & Power Co., 116 F.2d 971, 974 (2d Cir. 1941). Without deciding which law applies as to where performance is to be had, it seems reasonably clear that under New York or Cuban law the duty of defendant to pay benefits should not be narrowly construed as a duty to pay only in Havana. Defendant points to no Cuban law that limits the obligation to pay money under a contract to the place named in a place of payment clause. As the district court found, it would not be illegal under Cuban law for defendant to pay dollars in New York. 312 F.Supp. at 1056. The policies themselves contemplated that payment might be made elsewhere.... It seems clear that the place of payment clause was inserted into the policies as a matter of convenience and not as an essential part of the bargain. In light of this and the other conflicts considerations discussed in this opinion, I do not believe that under New York law the naming of Havana as the place of payment requires that Cuban law be applied to these policies.

There are only two jurisdictions, other than New York, with any arguable interest in the outcome of this case, Cuba and Canada. I agree that Cuba has numerous contacts with the transaction, but on analysis it is apparent that Cuba has no interest in the outcome of this case. Whether or not defendant has to pay plaintiffs, neither defendant's nor plaintiffs' assets in Cuba will be removed from that country. On the other hand, insurance is a highly regulated business and Canada has a strong interest in the practices of an insurance company domiciled there. Therefore, New York courts would be influenced by a recent ruling of the Canadian Supreme Court, Imperial Life Assurance Co. v. Casteleiro y Colemnares [1967] Can.S.Ct. 443, 62 D.L.R.2d 138, which refused to apply Cuban law in a situation not fairly distinguishable from this case.

In *Imperial Life*, defendant, a Canadian insurance company, had issued life insurance to plaintiff, a Cuban national. The policies were written in Spanish, were delivered in Cuba, and were payable in United States dollars. The Canadian court reasoned that a contract is governed by the law "with which it appears to have the closest and most substantial connection." 62 D.L.R.2d at 143. Finding that the decision to "go on the risk" was made at defendant's head office in Toronto, that the policies, although in Spanish, were a standard form that complied with the law of Ontario, that the place of contracting was Ontario, and that the insured would reasonably anticipate that the law of Ontario would govern the contracts, the court held that Ontario law applied to the policies. Accordingly, defendant was required to pay in Canadian currency the equivalent of the United States dollar value of the policies.

The decision below reaches a result, therefore, that defendant could not have obtained in its home jurisdiction of Canada. When the local law of the jurisdictions with the most interest in the insured, the beneficiaries, and the insurer would allow plaintiffs to recover, a New York court would not choose Cuban law. As between the law of Canada and that of the forum, there is no conflict and New York would apply its own local law.

That defendant can no longer transfer its assets out of Cuba does not require affirmance of the district court order. Defendant's obligation to plaintiffs is a general one, payable from defendant's general assets. Defendant's unannounced policy of investing in Cuban assets enough funds to cover payment of its Cuban policies is irrelevant to its obligation to plaintiffs. On their face, there is no indication that the policies are restricted to assets held in Cuba. While perhaps it was a reasonable business practice to invest in Cuban assets, no Cuban law required defendant to do so....

Finally, a word on the equities. The district court regarded as inequitable the allocation to defendant of the loss resulting, in truth, from its decision to invest in Cuban pesos its net premium income from policies issued to American citizens who resided in Cuba.... I fail to see how this makes great sense. It places the loss resulting directly from defendant's voluntary, if now proved to be unfortunate, decision to invest in Cuba on those who had no part in making, nor notice of, that decision and who can clearly less afford to bear it than defendant....

NOTES

1. The Castro government of Cuba adopted a series of financial measures involving Cuban holders of policies in life insurance companies in the United States. The measures included the expropriation of the Cuban property of the companies, the substitution of the Cuban state as the obligor under the policies, and a prohibition of payment of monies to Cuban nationals anywhere except in Cuba. Several Cuban holders of policies with an American company, who had escaped from Cuba after the Castro regime came to power, brought suit on the policies in the United States. The insurance companies set up the Cuban laws as a defense. This defense was rejected in Pan-American Life Insurance Co. v. Recio, 154 So.2d 197 (Fla.App.1963) largely on the ground that the policy provided for payments in New Orleans. In de Lara v. Confederation Life Insurance Co., 257 So.2d 42 (Fla.1971), cert. denied 409 U.S. 953 (1972), the state courts applied Florida law which called for payment in dollars rather than Cuban pesos. Two dissenting United States Supreme Court Justices would have granted certiorari to determine whether the choice of law was consistent with the Fourteenth Amendment due process protection as outlined in Home Insurance Co. v. Dick, p. 325, supra.

2. Santovenia v. Confederation Life Association, 460 F.2d 805 (5th Cir.1972), involved a policy which was issued in Cuba and called for payment in Cuba in Cuban pesos. By a provision in the policy the parties agreed to be bound by any change in the Cuban currency laws. It was held that the insurance company would not be ordered to make payment in dollars in the United States. In another case the defense was upheld on the ground, among others, that respect for the Cuban decrees was required by the International Monetary Fund to which Cuba and the United States had adhered. Theye Y Ajuria v. Pan American Life Insurance Co., 154 So.2d 450 (La.1963). The extent to which the exchange systems of the two countries accord with the purposes of the Fund appear from brief surveys of the two systems in International Monetary Fund, Thirteenth Annual Report on Exchange Restrictions 89, 355 (1962).

3. Although Restatement, Second, Conflict of Laws § 192 refers the validity of a life insurance contract and the rights it creates prima facie to the law of the state of the insured's domicil at the time of issue, in international cases, where confiscation is a factor, the courts have shied away from that result. Thus, in Blanco v. Pan-American Life Ins. Co., 221 F.Supp. 219 (S.D.Fla.1963), affirmed 362 F.2d 167 (5th Cir.1966), the court decided the effect of Cuban decrees under the law of the place of payment, which was the insurer's place of incorporation. Accord: Rossano v. Manufacturers' Life Assurance Co. [1963], 2 Q.B. 352.

Banco Nacional de Cuba v. Sabbatino

Supreme Court of the United States, 1964.
376 U.S. 398, 84 S.Ct. 923, 11 L.Ed.2d 804.

[This was a dispute over who was entitled to the proceeds of the sale of sugar. The sugar had been the property of a Cuban corporation whose stock was owned principally by United States residents. Before the sugar was shipped from a Cuban port, it was expropriated without adequate compensation by the Cuban government. The expropriation was in retaliation for a reduction by the United States of the sugar quota for Cuba. An American commodity broker, contrary to its agreement with an instrumentality of the Cuban government, obtained possession of the sugar without paying for it. The broker received payment for the sugar from its customer and deposited the funds with a court-appointed receiver pending judicial determination as to whether Cuba or the former owners were entitled to the money.

Cuba relied on the "act of state doctrine," contending that the legality of Cuba's actions on its own territory could not be questioned by a United States court. The courts below held for the former owners, deciding that the act of state doctrine did not apply because Cuba's action violated international law. The Supreme Court of the United States granted certiorari and reversed.]

■ JUSTICE HARLAN.... Preliminarily, we discuss the foundations on which we deem the act of state doctrine to rest, and more particularly the question of whether state or federal law governs its application in a federal diversity case.

We do not believe that this doctrine is compelled either by the inherent nature of sovereign authority ... or by some principle of international law.... While historic notions of sovereign authority do bear upon the wisdom of employing the act of state doctrine, they do not dictate its existence....

. . .

... The text of the Constitution does not require the act of state doctrine; it does not irrevocably remove from the judiciary the capacity to review the validity of foreign acts of state.

The act of state doctrine does, however, have "constitutional" underpinnings. It arises out of the basic relationship between branches of government in a system of separation of powers. It concerns the competency of dissimilar institutions to make and implement particular kinds of decisions in the area of international relations. The doctrine as formulated in past decisions expresses the strong sense of the Judicial Branch that its engagement in the task of passing on the validity of foreign acts of state may hinder rather than further this country's pursuit of goals both for itself and for the community of nations as a whole in the international sphere. Many commentators disagree with this view.... Whatever considerations are thought to predominate, it is plain that the problems involved are uniquely federal in nature. If federal authority, in this instance this Court, orders the field of judicial competence in this area for the federal courts, and the state courts are left free to formulate their own rules, the purposes behind the doctrine would be as effectively undermined as if there had been no federal pronouncement on the subject.

. . .

... [W]e are constrained to make it clear that an issue concerned with a basic choice regarding the competence and function of the Judiciary and the National Executive in ordering our relationships with other members of the international community must be treated exclusively as an aspect of federal law.[23] It seems fair to assume that the Court did not have rules like the act of state doctrine in mind when it decided Erie R. Co. v. Tompkins. Soon thereafter, Professor Philip C. Jessup, now a judge of the International Court of Justice, recognized the potential dangers were Erie extended to legal problems affecting international relations.[24] He cautioned that rules of international law should not be left to divergent and perhaps parochial state interpretations. His basic rationale is equally applicable to the act of state doctrine.

. . .

... We conclude that the scope of the act of state doctrine must be determined according to federal law.

If the act of state doctrine is a principle of decision binding on federal and state courts alike but compelled by neither international law nor the Constitution, its continuing vitality depends on its capacity to reflect the proper distribution of functions between the judicial and political branches of the Government on matters bearing upon foreign affairs. It should be apparent that the greater the degree of codification or consensus concerning a particular area of international law, the more appropriate it is for the judiciary to render decisions regarding it, since the courts can then focus on the application of an agreed principle to circumstances of fact rather than on the sensitive task of establishing a principle not inconsistent with the national interest or with international justice. It is also evident that some aspects of international law touch much more sharply on national nerves than do others; the less important the implications of an issue are for our foreign relations, the weaker the justification for exclusivity in the political branches. The balance of relevant considerations may also be shifted if the government which perpetrated the challenged act of state is no longer in existence as in the *Bernstein* case [Bernstein v. N.V. Nederlandsche–Amerikaansche Stoomvaart–Maatschappij, 173 F.2d 71 (2d Cir.1949), dealing with Nazi decrees], for the political interest of this country may, as a result, be measurably altered. Therefore, rather than laying down or reaffirming an inflexible and all-encompassing rule in this case, we decide only that the Judicial Branch will not examine the validity of a taking of property within its own territory by a foreign sovereign government, extant and recognized by this country at the time of suit, in the absence of a treaty or other unambiguous agreement regarding controlling legal principles, even if the complaint alleges that the taking violates customary international law.

. . .

23. At least this is true when the Court limits the scope of judicial inquiry. We need not consider whether a state court might, in certain circumstances, adhere to a more restrictive view concerning the scope of examination of foreign acts than that required by the Court.

24. The Doctrine of Erie Railroad v. Tompkins Applied to International Law, 33 Am.J.Int'l.L. 740 (1939).

... [W]hatever way the matter is cut the possibility of conflict between the Judicial and Executive Branches could hardly be avoided.

■ [JUSTICE WHITE dissented.]

NOTES

1. An important sequel to the Sabbatino decision is First National City Bank v. Banco Nacional de Cuba, 406 U.S. 759 (1972), in which a plurality agreed that Banco, an instrumentality of the Cuban government, could not sue for funds due to it without submitting to a decision on the merits of a counterclaim. City Bank had made a loan to Banco's predecessor. City Bank sold the collateral when the loan was in default and retained a surplus from this sale. When Banco sued for this surplus, City Bank counterclaimed to offset against Banco's claim, the value of City Bank's Cuban properties that had been expropriated. For an enlightening treatment of the main decision, see Henkin, The Foreign Affairs Power of the Federal Courts: *Sabbatino*, 64 Colum.L.Rev. 805 (1964).

2. Following the Sabbatino decision, Congress enacted, and the President signed, the so-called Hickenlooper Amendment, (22 U.S.C.A. § 2370(e)(2)), which provides that "... no court in the United States shall decline on the ground of the federal act of state doctrine to make a determination on the merits giving effect to the principles of international law in a case in which a claim ... is asserted ... based upon ... a confiscation or other taking after January 1, 1959 ... [unless] the President determines that application of the act of state doctrine is required in that particular case by the foreign policy interests of the United States...."

After remand, it was held that the Sabbatino case itself came under the scope of the Hickenlooper Amendment and the complaint was dismissed. Banco Nacional de Cuba v. Farr, 383 F.2d 166 (2d Cir. 1967), cert. denied 390 U.S. 956. See Paul, The Act of State Doctrine: Revived but Suspended, 113 U.Pa.L.Rev. 691 (1965).

3. A Turkish bank raised the act-of-state doctrine unsuccessfully in trying to avoid a commitment to pay the plaintiff bank in Swiss francs in New York. The payment was due on a note executed in Turkey. The court rejected the defense that a Turkish currency regulation barred payment by the defendant in non-Turkish currency. Weston Banking Corp. v. Turkiye Garanti Bankasi A.S., 57 N.Y.2d 315, 456 N.Y.S.2d 684, 442 N.E.2d 1195 (1982). Could the Sabbatino doctrine have been applied in Holzer v. Deutsche-Reichsbahn Gesellschaft, p. 390, supra?

4. For a helpful discussion of the act-of-state doctrine in the Sabbatino context, see Cheatham and Maier, Private International Law and Its Sources, 22 Vand. L.Rev. 27, 88 (1968). Its history in relation to sovereign immunity is summarized:

"The act-of-state doctrine in American law is closely related to the principle of sovereign immunity. Both stemmed, initially, from conceptions of absolute territorial sovereignty and the relationship between those conceptions and a power-oriented theory of jurisdiction which equated physical power over parties with a right to decide their disputes and lack of such power with a lack of jurisdiction. Thus, the adjudication of disputes concerning either the person or the acts of a foreign sovereign was conceived as the application of physical force against the sovereign personality. But the decision to apply force to a foreign sovereign is essentially political in nature. It is not to be made upon the accident of the presence of the sovereign, or of one claiming legal rights based upon the validity of the sovereign's acts, before a court whose even-handed justice could be enforced only by the exercise of its own sovereign's power...."

See also Williams v. Curtiss–Wright Corp., 694 F.2d 300, 303 (3d Cir.1982): "The Act of State doctrine is a policy of judicial abstention from inquiry into the validity of an act by a foreign state *within its own sovereignty....*" (Emphasis added). The territorial limitation of the Act-of-State doctrine—"within its own sovereignty"—has been recognized in many decisions. How should the doctrine be applied when the asset cannot be located physically, when it is an intangible? Allied Bank International v. Banco Credito Agricola de Cartago, 757 F.2d 516 (2d Cir.1985), cert. dismissed 473 U.S. 934 (1985), held the act of state doctrine to be inapplicable with respect to Costa Rican decrees purporting to defer payments on foreign debts because the situs of the debts in issue was determined to be in the United States. The Restatement, Third, Foreign Relations Law of the United States § 443, Reporters' Note 4 (1987), suggests that there should not be a search "for an imaginary situs for property that has no real situs, but [a determination] how the act of the foreign state in the particular circumstances fits within the reasons for the act of state doctrine and for the territorial limitation."

B. Treaties

Foreign countries have long used conventions (treaties) to bring about uniform rules of substantive law or, at least, of choice of law. In addition, a number of treaties deal with the way international cases are handled procedurally. With notable exceptions such as the Warsaw Convention, which contains rules and limitations with respect to a carrier's liability in international air traffic, the United States has been slow to participate. It does not belong to the Geneva Convention on bills of exchange and checks, and it does not have any treaties with other countries on the recognition of judgments.

However, in 1964 the United States joined the Hague Conference on Private International Law which sponsors conventions on conflicts and procedural issues and the Rome Institute on the Unification of Private Law (i.e., dealing with substantive law). One substantive convention—drafted under United Nations auspices—was adopted by the United States and became law in 1988: the Convention on the International Sale of Goods. 15 U.S.C.A. App..

The United States has ratified a number of Hague Conventions. The most important of these are the Convention on the Service of Documents Abroad, the Convention on the Taking of Evidence Abroad, and the Convention on the Civil Aspects of International Child Abduction. The last of these, in force since 1988, seeks to counteract parental kidnapping in the international arena in a fashion similar to the domestic Uniform Child Custody Jurisdiction Act and the federal Parental Kidnapping Prevention Act, p. 893, infra. For a decision involving the Hague Documents Convention see Volkswagenwerk Aktiengesellschaft v. Schlunk, supra p. 105. Société Nationale Industrielle Aerospatiale v. United States District Court for the Southern District of Iowa, 482 U.S. 522 (1987), involved the Convention on the Taking of Evidence Abroad. The plaintiffs had brought a personal injury action against a French airplane manufacturer in federal court in Iowa. They served a number of discovery requests under the Federal Rules of Civil Procedure. The defendant sought a protective order on the twin grounds that (1) a French "blocking statute" forbids the production of documents located in France in response to foreign judicial orders or requests and that (2) the Hague Convention represents the exclusive means for obtaining evidence located abroad. The District Court denied the motion and the Court of Appeals denied a petition for mandamus.

Upon review of the drafting history of the Convention, the Supreme Court concluded, contrary to some lower court decisions, that the Convention does apply to litigants and third parties who are subject to the U.S. court's jurisdiction. However, its procedures are not exclusive and do not displace American procedural law. Instead, it provides an optional, parallel means for obtaining evidence located abroad. Nor does comity, the respect for other countries' judicial sovereignty, or even the existence of a blocking statute require a rule of first resort to Convention procedures. "[T]he concept of international comity requires in this context a more particularized analysis than petitioners' proposed general rule would generate.... [There must be] prior scrutiny in each case of the particular facts, sovereign interests, and likelihood that resort to ... [the Convention] procedures will prove effective." 482 U.S. at 543–44. "The French 'blocking statute' ... does not alter our conclusion. It is well-settled that such statutes do not deprive an American court of the power to order a party subject to its jurisdiction to produce evidence even though the act of production may violate that statute.... Extraterritorial assertions of jurisdiction are not one-sided. While the District Court's discovery orders arguably have some impact in France, the French blocking statute asserts similar authority over acts to take place in this country. The lesson of comity is that neither the discovery order nor the blocking statute can have the same omnipresent effect that it would have in a world of only one sovereign. The blocking statute thus is relevant to the court's particularized comity analysis only to the extent that its terms and its enforcement identify the nature of the sovereign interests in nondisclosure...." 482 U.S. at 544 n. 29. The majority concluded by emphasizing the importance of foreign interests and by admonishing trial courts to "exercise special vigilance to protect foreign litigants from the danger that unnecessary, or unduly burdensome, discovery may place them in a disadvantageous position." 482 U.S. at 546.

Justice Blackmun, joined by Justices Brennan, Marshall, and O'Connor, filed a partial dissent. "When there is a conflict, a court ... should perform a tripartite analysis that considers the foreign interests, the interests of the United States, and the mutual interests of all nations in a smoothly functioning international legal regime." 482 U.S. at 555. This view of comity, of accommodating conflicting interests for the smooth functioning of the international system, led him to favor the adoption of a rule requiring first resort to Convention procedures unless there are "strong indications that no evidence would be forthcoming." 482 U.S. at 566–67. His view was adopted in Hudson v. Hermann Pfauter GmbH & Co., 117 F.R.D. 33 (N.D.N.Y.1987): service of interrogatories in accordance with the Convention ordered, despite plaintiff's objections on the grounds of cost, delay, and unfamiliar procedures. A long line of subsequent cases, however, places the burden of proof on the proponent of Convention procedures. See, e.g., Doster v. Carl Schenk A.G., 141 F.R.D. 50, 51 (M.D.N.C.1991).

NOTES

1. The Hague Convention on the Law Applicable to Trusts and on Their Recognition, the "Washington" Convention Providing a Uniform Law on the Form of an International Will, and the Inter–American Convention on International Commercial Arbitration have been submitted for Congressional action. In 1989, the Hague Conference proposed a new convention on decedents' estates.

2. See Gaillard and Trautman, Trusts in Non–Trust Countries: Conflict of Laws and the Hague Convention on Trusts, 35 Am.J.Comp.L. 307 (1987). The area of American conflicts law controlled by treaties is discussed generally in Scoles and Hay, Conflict of Laws § 3.56 (2d Ed.1992).

C. International Conflicts Cases in the Absence of Federal Limitations or Preemption

In the absence of federal limitations or inconsistent federal law, conflicts law is state law, in international cases as well as in interstate cases. Should state conflicts rules affecting international cases be "segregated" from those applicable to sister-state situations? Professor Cheatham doubted the desirability of making such a distinction. He pointed out that the question of which foreign nation is involved and which underlying policies are in issue may be more significant than the simple issue of whether the case is international rather than interstate. Consider three parallel San Francisco cases on judgments or contracts, one with Seattle, another with Vancouver, and a third with Beijing. Surely, it would be unusual for the California court to treat the Vancouver case differently from the Seattle case. Almost certainly, it would find the Vancouver case closer to the Seattle case than to the other international case, the Beijing case. Cheatham, Book Review, 45 A.B.A.J. 1190 (1959).

There is no ipso facto warrant for treating a case differently merely because it is an international instead of an interstate one, or merely because it involves an alien instead of a citizen. The purpose of conflict of laws is to aid in making the international and the interstate systems work well when they affect multistate legal affairs of private persons. Principles must be developed to advance that fundamental purpose. Whenever there is a difference in the treatment of international and interstate cases, it should be justified by differences in the circumstances that call for differences in treatment. See Leflar, McDougal & Felix, American Conflicts Law 9–11 (4th ed. 1986).

An example is the Uniform Foreign Money Judgments Recognition Act, on January 1, 1995, in force in 25 states and the Virgin Islands, which, subject to enumerated exceptions, provides for the recognition and enforcement "in the same manner as the judgment of a sister state which is entitled to full faith and credit" of foreign-country judgments which grant or deny the recovery of a sum of money. One of the exceptions, not available for sister-state judgments, is that "the cause of action on which the judgment is based is repugnant to the public policy of this state." Lack of jurisdiction of the F–1 court is a defense, as it would be in the interstate setting. The circumstance that the judgment was rendered in a foreign country rather than in a sister state is reflected in the condition that the judgment must have been rendered in a legal system providing impartial tribunals "or procedures compatible with the requirements of due process...." The versions of the Uniform Act in force in some states require in addition that the foreign country accord reciprocity to American judgments. What policy considerations support or speak against such a requirement?

NOTES

1. With respect to foreign-country judgments, the traditional view was that the successful plaintiff's judgment did not merge the underlying claim, thus leaving the plaintiff free to seek either recognition of the judgment or to relitigate the original claim in the United States. See Restatement, Second, Conflict of Laws § 95 (1988 Revision). This view reflected the fact that common law notions of res judicata and collateral estoppel are not part of many foreign legal systems, especially civil law systems. See Schlesinger, Baade, Damaska, & Herzog, Comparative Law 454 (5th ed. 1988). German law, for instance, attaches res judicata effect only to the claim between the same parties and defines "claim" to include both the facts giving rise to the claim *and* the remedy sought. If there are different facts or if the plaintiff seeks another remedy, even an additional recovery upon the same facts, a further action may not be precluded. Accordingly, collateral estoppel is unknown in the German system.

Should the fact that notions of res judicata are not the same—for instance, that the plaintiff may be entitled to additional relief under the foreign law—mean that the judgment should not receive the same recognition as a judgment rendered by a sister state? The modern answer is reflected in the Uniform Foreign Money-Judgments Recognition Act, p. 312, supra. See Scoles & Hay, Conflict of Laws 957 (2d ed. 1992) ("non-merger rule ... makes little sense today"). See also Restatement, Second, Conflict of Laws § 98 (1971), which states that valid foreign-country judgments will be recognized "after a fair trial in a contested proceeding ... so far as the immediate parties and the underlying cause of action are concerned." Even foreign default judgments "will usually be recognized provided that the foreign court had jurisdiction" and the defendant was given notice and opportunity to be heard. Id. comment d. Assume that an American plaintiff seeks and obtains a recovery upon part of her claim in Germany, as permitted by German law. Should German notions of res judicata govern the question of whether the plaintiff may subsequently seek an additional recovery in the United States?

2. A foreign money judgment presumably will be expressed in the foreign currency. May the judgment creditor seek recognition and enforcement in the United States in the foreign currency? If the foreign judgment is to be converted into dollars, is the relevant time for the conversion the time of breach, the time the foreign judgment was rendered, the time of recognition, or some other time? Section 823 of the Restatement, Third, Foreign Relations Law of the United States

(1988), states that United States courts will ordinarily express judgments enforcing foreign judgments in United States dollars "but they are not precluded from giving judgment in the currency in which the obligation is denominated...." See Waterside Ocean Navigation Co., Inc. v. International Navigation Ltd., 737 F.2d 150 (2d Cir.1984) (enforcing foreign arbitral award partly in dollars and partly in English pounds).

When enforcement of the judgment is not sought or granted in the foreign currency, the rule with respect to the time for conversion, as stated in Restatement, Second, Conflict of Laws (1971) § 144, comment g: conversion into dollars is of the date of the award. This rule may disadvantage a judgment creditor if, since the award, the dollar has depreciated relative to the foreign currency. As a result, there are substantial variations in the case law. See Competex v. LaBow, 783 F.2d 333 (2d Cir.1986). The Uniform Foreign–Money Claims Act, on January 1, 1995, in force in eighteen states and the Virgin Islands, permits the parties to stipulate the currency which is to be used to satisfy claims arising out of their transaction. In the absence of a stipulation, foreign money claims as well as foreign judgments expressed in foreign money are to be stated in the foreign currency, but the judgment debtor may effect payment in dollars at the conversion rate in effect at the time of payment. "The principle of the Act is to restore the aggrieved party to the economic position it would have been in had the wrong not occurred." Id., Prefatory Note. Will the plaintiff really have been restored by receiving today's equivalent of a currency which may depreciated severely during the course of litigation? Does not the successful plaintiff in a domestic action face the same problem? Is there a difference between domestic plaintiffs and foreign judgment creditors that justifies greater protection of the foreign creditors? Restatement (Third) Foreign Relations Law of the United States § 823, comment c, provides that a court should convert the foreign currency to United States dollars as of the breach day if, compared with the foreign currency in which the debt is owed, the dollar has since appreciated, and should choose judgment-day conversion if the dollar has depreciated.

For the view that such a rule "introduces into a purely procedural rule an element of substantive justice" and that compensation for delay and ensuing loss due to currency fluctuations should therefore be left to the law applicable to the claim or judgment, see F.A. Mann, The Legal Aspect of Money 351 (5th ed. 1992); Hay, Fremdwährungsanprüche und -urteile nach dem US-amerikanischen Uniform Act, [1995] Recht der Internationalen Wirtschaft 113, 115 n. 35, 118 n. 66.

International conflicts cases once again raise the question of the extent to which one state may infringe upon the interests of another, even if the issue has been litigated by the parties. Recall Justice Stone's dissent in Yarborough v. Yarborough, p. 261, supra: that "There is often an inescapable conflict of interest of the two states, and there comes a point beyond which the imposition of the will of one state beyond its own borders involves a forbidden infringement of some legitimate domestic interest of the other." Justice Stone's dissent focussed on state interest, not due process to the parties. His views derived from full faith and credit considerations. They were echoed in the position of the New York Times in opposing the exercise of jurisdiction by Alabama in a defamation action against it: "The need for such restraint is emphasized in our system by the full faith and credit clause.... If Alabama stood alone it would be impotent ... to render any judgment that would be of practical importance [but the Full Faith and Credit Clause will give it force throughout the country]. Thus jurisdictional delineations must be based on grounds that command general assent throughout the Union; otherwise full faith and credit will become a burden that the system cannot bear." Petitioner's Brief, at 86, in New York Times Co. v. Sullivan, 376 U.S. 254 (1964). The Supreme Court held for the petitioner but did not address this issue. To what extent do the full faith and credit cases, pp. 227–311, supra, respond to Justice Stone and the petitioner in New York Times?

The Full Faith and Credit clause, does not apply, of course, to international cases. Instead, we use the act of state doctrine, invoke notions of comity, and, as the introductory comments stated, treat international cases like domestic ones unless the facts warrant differently. Is "infringement" upon policies of another state such a distinguishing circumstance?

Hartford Fire Insurance Co. v. California

Supreme Court of the United States, 1993.
___ U.S. ___, 113 S.Ct. 2891, 125 L.Ed.2d 612.

[Nineteen states and many private plaintiffs sued domestic insurance companies, domestic reinsurance companies, and London-based reinsurance companies for conspiring in violation of § 1 the Sherman Antitrust Act (15 U.S.C. § 1) to change the form of commercial general liability insurance (CGL) available in the United States. The alleged conspiracy was to refuse to insure or reinsure risks unless four changes were made in the standard forms prepared by the Insurance Services Office, an organization that provided this and other important services to United States insurance companies. The four changes were: (1) Provide coverage on a "claims made" basis rather than "occurrence" basis. This meant that liability for damage would be covered only if the claim was made during the policy period. This would make it less likely that an insurer would have to defend and indemnify an insured for harm caused while the policy was in force, but not discovered until many years later when the claim was made. (2) Limit the time after an occurrence when a claim would be covered. This would further limit the insurer's exposure for harm occurring in the past. (3) Eliminate coverage for "sudden and accidental" pollution. (4) Charge legal defense costs against the limits of the policy.

The United States defendants asserted a defense under the McCarran–Ferguson Act, which exempted from Sherman Act liability, a defendant engaged in "the business of insurance" that is "regulated by State law." (15 U.S.C. § 1012(b)). This exemption was removed if the defendant engaged in acts of "boycott, coercion, or intimidation." (Id. § 1013(b)). The London-based defendants contended that "international comity" prevented application of the Sherman Act to them.

The federal district court in which suit was brought dismissed the claims against all defendants. It found the United States defendants exempted by the McCarran–Ferguson Act and that they were not engaged in a "boycott." It agreed with the comity defense asserted by the London-based defendants. The Ninth Circuit reversed, finding that the United States defendants lost their exemption by conspiring with nonexempt foreign defendants and, in any event, that the complaints sufficiently alleged a boycott. The circuit court further found that international comity did not bar application of the Sherman Act to the London-based defendants.

The Supreme Court granted certiorari, reversed in part, affirmed in part, and remanded. Justice Souter, in an opinion joined by Rehnquist, C.J., and White, Blackmun, and Stevens, JJ., wrote the opinion for the court rejecting the comity defense of the London-based insurers. Justice Scalia dissented in an opinion joined by O'Connor, Kennedy, and Thomas, JJ. On the boycott issue, Justice Scalia, in an opinion joined by Rehnquist, C.J. and O'Connor, Kennedy, and Thomas, JJ., wrote the opinion for the court holding that on remand, in order to prevail under the "boycott" exception to McCarran–Ferguson, the plaintiffs would have to show that the defendants' refusal to deal involved refusal to reinsure forms of insurance other than CGL unless changes were made in the CGL forms. Justice Souter, in an opinion joined by White, Blackmun, and Stevens, JJ., would permit a finding of "boycott" if the United States insurers solicited refusals to deal from reinsurers, thereby to compel agreement from other insurers, even though the refusals to deal concerned only the CGL forms. The Court unanimously agreed that the United States defendants did not lose their McCarran–Ferguson defense by conspiring with foreign reinsurers. Only the opinions dealing with the extraterritorial application of the Sherman Act and comity follow.]

■ JUSTICE SOUTER: . . .

III

Finally, we take up the question whether certain claims against the London reinsurers should have been dismissed as improper applications of the Sherman Act to foreign conduct. . . .

At the outset, we note that the District Court undoubtedly had jurisdiction of these Sherman Act claims, as the London reinsurers apparently concede. See Tr. of Oral Arg. 37 ("Our position is not that the Sherman Act does not apply in the sense that a minimal basis for the exercise of jurisdiction doesn't exist here. Our position is that there are certain circumstances, and that this is one of them, in which the interests of another State are sufficient that the exercise of that jurisdiction should be restrained"). Although the proposition was perhaps not always free from doubt, see American Banana Co. v. United Fruit Co., 213 U.S. 347 (1909), it is well established by now that the Sherman Act applies to foreign conduct that was meant to produce and did in fact produce some substantial effect in the United States. Such is the conduct alleged here: that the

London reinsurers engaged in unlawful conspiracies to affect the market for insurance in the United States and that their conduct in fact produced substantial effect.

According to the London reinsurers, the District Court should have declined to exercise such jurisdiction under the principle of international comity. The Court of Appeals agreed that courts should look to that principle in deciding whether to exercise jurisdiction under the Sherman Act. This availed the London reinsurers nothing, however. To be sure, the Court of Appeals believed that "application of [American] antitrust laws to the London reinsurance market 'would lead to significant conflict with English law and policy,'" and that "[s]uch a conflict, unless outweighed by other factors, would by itself be reason to decline exercise of jurisdiction." [938 F.2d] at 933 (citation omitted). But other factors, in the court's view, including the London reinsurers' express purpose to affect United States commerce and the substantial nature of the effect produced, outweighed the supposed conflict and required the exercise of jurisdiction in this case. Id., at 934....

The only substantial question in this case is whether "there is in fact a true conflict between domestic and foreign law." Societe Nationale Industrielle Aerospatiale v. United States District Court, 482 U.S. 522, 555 (1987) (Blackmun, J., concurring in part and dissenting in part). The London reinsurers contend that applying the Act to their conduct would conflict significantly with British law, and the British Government, appearing before us as amicus curiae, concurs. They assert that Parliament has established a comprehensive regulatory regime over the London reinsurance market and that the conduct alleged here was perfectly consistent with British law and policy. But this is not to state a conflict. "[T]he fact that conduct is lawful in the state in which it took place will not, of itself, bar application of the United States antitrust laws," even where the foreign state has a strong policy to permit or encourage such conduct. Restatement (Third) Foreign Relations Law § 415, Comment j. No conflict exists, for these purposes, "where a person subject to regulation by two states can comply with the laws of both." Restatement (Third) Foreign Relations Law § 403, Comment e. Since the London reinsurers do not argue that British law requires them to act in some fashion prohibited by the law of the United States, or claim that their compliance with the laws of both countries is otherwise impossible, we see no conflict with British law. We have no need in this case to address other considerations that might inform a decision to refrain from the exercise of jurisdiction on grounds of international comity....

■ JUSTICE SCALIA:...

II

The petitioners, various British corporations and other British subjects, argue that certain of the claims against them constitute an inappropriate extraterritorial application of the Sherman Act. It is important to distinguish two distinct questions raised by this petition: whether the

District Court had jurisdiction, and whether the Sherman Act reaches the extraterritorial conduct alleged here. On the first question, I believe that the District Court had subject-matter jurisdiction over the Sherman Act claims against all the defendants (personal jurisdiction is not contested). The respondents asserted nonfrivolous claims under the Sherman Act, and 28 U.S.C. § 1331 vests district courts with subject-matter jurisdiction over cases "arising under" federal statutes. As precedents such as Lauritzen v. Larsen, 345 U.S. 571 (1953), make clear, that is sufficient to establish the District Court's jurisdiction over these claims. *Lauritzen* involved a Jones Act claim brought by a foreign sailor against a foreign shipowner. The shipowner contested the District Court's jurisdiction, apparently on the grounds that the Jones Act did not govern the dispute between the foreign parties to the action. Though ultimately agreeing with the shipowner that the Jones Act did not apply, the Court held that the District Court had jurisdiction....

The second question—the extraterritorial reach of the Sherman Act—has nothing to do with the jurisdiction of the courts. It is a question of substantive law turning on whether, in enacting the Sherman Act, Congress asserted regulatory power over the challenged conduct. If a plaintiff fails to prevail on this issue, the court does not dismiss the claim for want of subject-matter jurisdiction—want of power to adjudicate; rather, it decides the claim, ruling on the merits that the plaintiff has failed to state a cause of action under the relevant statute.

There is, however, a type of "jurisdiction" relevant to determining the extraterritorial reach of a statute; it is known as "legislative jurisdiction," or "jurisdiction to prescribe," 1 Restatement (Third) of Foreign Relations Law of the United States 235 (1987) (hereinafter Restatement (Third)). This refers to "the authority of a state to make its law applicable to persons or activities," and is quite a separate matter from "jurisdiction to adjudicate," see id., at 231. There is no doubt, of course, that Congress possesses legislative jurisdiction over the acts alleged in this complaint: Congress has broad power under Article I, § 8, cl. 3 "[t]o regulate Commerce with foreign Nations," and this Court has repeatedly upheld its power to make laws applicable to persons or activities beyond our territorial boundaries where United States interests are affected. But the question in this case is whether, and to what extent, Congress has exercised that undoubted legislative jurisdiction in enacting the Sherman Act.

Two canons of statutory construction are relevant in this inquiry. The first is the "long-standing principle of American law 'that legislation of Congress, unless a contrary intent appears, is meant to apply only within the territorial jurisdiction of the United States.'" [EEOC v. Arabian American Oil Co. (Aramco)], 111 S.Ct. [1227] at 1230 (quoting Foley Bros., Inc. v. Filardo, 336 U.S. 281, 285 (1949)). Applying that canon in Aramco, we held that the version of Title VII of the Civil Rights Act of 1964 then in force, 42 U.S.C. §§ 2000e–2000e–17 (1988 ed.), did not extend outside the territory of the United States even though the statute contained broad provisions extending its prohibitions to, for example, "'any activity, business, or industry in commerce.'" 111 S.Ct., at 1231 (quoting 42 U.S.C. § 2000e(h)). We held such "boilerplate language" to be an insufficient indication to override the presumption against extraterritoriality. 111 S.Ct., at 1232. The Sherman Act contains similar "boilerplate language," and if the question were not governed by precedent, it would be worth considering whether that presumption controls the outcome here. We have, however, found the presumption to be overcome with respect to our antitrust laws; it is now well established that the Sherman Act applies extraterritorially.

But if the presumption against extraterritoriality has been overcome or is otherwise inapplicable, a second canon of statutory construction becomes relevant: "[A]n act of congress ought never to be construed to violate the law of nations if any other possible construction remains." Murray v. The Charming Betsy, 2 Cranch 64, 118 (1804) (Marshall, C.J.). This canon is "wholly independent" of the presumption against extraterritoriality. Aramco, 111 S.Ct., at 1239. It is relevant to determining the substantive reach of a statute because "the law of nations," or customary international law, includes limitations on a nation's exercise of its jurisdiction to prescribe. Though it clearly has constitutional authority to do so, Congress is generally presumed not to have exceeded those customary international-law limits on jurisdiction to prescribe....

In sum, the practice of using international law to limit the extraterritorial reach of statutes is firmly established in our jurisprudence. In proceeding to apply that practice to the present case, I shall rely on the Restatement (Third) of Foreign Relations Law for the relevant principles of international law. Its standards appear fairly supported in the decisions of this Court construing international choice-of-law principles and in the decisions of other federal courts.... Whether the Restatement precisely reflects international law in every detail matters little here, as I believe this case would be resolved the same way under virtually any conceivable test that takes account of foreign regulatory interests.

Under the Restatement, a nation having some "basis" for jurisdiction to prescribe law should nonetheless refrain from exercising that jurisdiction "with respect to a person or activity having connections with another state when the exercise of such jurisdiction is unreasonable." Restatement (Third) § 403(1). The "reasonableness" inquiry turns on a number of factors including, but not limited to: "the extent to which the activity takes place within the territory [of the regulating state] *," id., § 403(2)(a); "the connections, such as nationality, residence, or economic activity, between the regulating state and the person principally responsible for the activity to be regulated," id., § 403(2)(b); "the character of the activity to be regulated, the importance of regulation to the regulating state, the extent to which other states regulate such activities, and the degree to which the desirability of such regulation is generally accepted," id., § 403(2)(c); "the extent to which another state may have an interest in

---

* Brackets in original.—Eds.

regulating the activity," id., § 403(2)(g); and "the likelihood of conflict with regulation by another state," id., § 403(2)(h). Rarely would these factors point more clearly against application of United States law. The activity relevant to the counts at issue here took place primarily in the United Kingdom, and the defendants in these counts are British corporations and British subjects having their principal place of business or residence outside the United States. Great Britain has established a comprehensive regulatory scheme governing the London reinsurance markets, and clearly has a heavy "interest in regulating the activity," id., § 403(2)(g). Finally, § 2(b) of the McCarran–Ferguson Act allows state regulatory statutes to override the Sherman Act in the insurance field, subject only to the narrow "boycott" exception set forth in § 3(b)—suggesting that "the importance of regulation to the [United States]," id., § 403(2)(c), is slight. Considering these factors, I think it unimaginable that an assertion of legislative jurisdiction by the United States would be considered reasonable, and therefore it is inappropriate to assume, in the absence of statutory indication to the contrary, that Congress has made such an assertion.

It is evident from what I have said that the Court's comity analysis ... is simply misdirected.... It concludes that no "true conflict" counseling nonapplication of United States law (or rather, as it thinks, United States judicial jurisdiction) exists unless compliance with United States law would constitute a violation of another country's law. That breathtakingly broad proposition, which contradicts the many cases discussed earlier, will bring the Sherman Act and other laws into sharp and unnecessary conflict with the legitimate interests of other countries—particularly our closest trading partners.

In the sense in which the term "conflic[t]" was used in *Lauritzen,* 345 U.S., at 582, 592 and is generally understood in the field of conflicts of laws, there is clearly a conflict in this case. The petitioners here, like the defendant in *Lauritzen,* were not compelled by any foreign law to take their allegedly wrongful actions, but that no more precludes a conflict-of-laws analysis here than it did there. Where applicable foreign and domestic law provide different substantive rules of decision to govern the parties' dispute, a conflict-of-laws analysis is necessary. See generally R. Weintraub, Commentary on Conflict of Laws 2–3 (1980); Restatement (First) of Conflict of Laws § 1, Comment c and Illustrations (1934).

Literally the only support that the Court adduces for its position is § 403 of the Restatement (Third) of Foreign Relations Law—or more precisely Comment e to that provision, which states: "Subsection (3) [which says that a state should defer to another state if that state's interest is clearly greater] applies only when one state requires what another prohibits, or where compliance with the regulations of two states exercising jurisdiction consistently with this section is otherwise impossible. It does not apply where a person subject to regulation by two states can comply with the laws of both...." The Court has completely misinterpreted this provision. Subsection (3) of § 403 (requiring one State to defer to another in the limited circumstances just described) comes into play only after subsection (1) of § 403 has been complied with—i.e., after it has been determined that the exercise of jurisdiction by both of the two states is not "unreasonable." That prior question is answered by applying the factors (inter alia) set forth in subsection (2) of § 403, that is, precisely the factors that I have discussed in text and that the Court rejects....

I would reverse the judgment of the Court of Appeals on this issue, and remand to the District Court with instructions to dismiss for failure to state a claim [against the London-based defendants].

NOTES

1. Justice Scalia is correct that according to the Restatement (Third) of The Foreign Relations Law of the United States, the factors set out in § 403(2) are applied to determine whether application of law under the "effects" doctrine is reasonable, even though different sovereigns do not compel inconsistent conduct. Is Justice Souter misreading § 403 or is the following a proper interpretation of his opinion? Under any comity analysis, including that of § 403(2), it is clear that the Sherman Act properly applies to the foreign defendants' conduct, which was intended to and did cause effects in the United States that the Sherman Act forbids. Therefore the only defense available to the English defendants would be that their conduct was compelled by a foreign sovereign, and such a defense is not available on the facts of this case.

2. In quoting from § 403(2)(a), Justice Scalia omits the following words: "or has substantial, direct, and foreseeable effect upon or in the territory." Considering these words, is Justice Scalia correct in stating "[r]arely would [the § 403(2)] factors point more clearly against application of United States law."

3. Justice Scalia states that the McCarran–Ferguson Act exemption from the Sherman Act of the business of insurance "regulated by State law" indicates that the importance to the United States of regulating the conduct of the English defendants "is slight." Is this true if English regulation, unlike state regulation, does not protect the American public from anticompetitive conduct by insurers?

4. Does the decision whether to apply United States public law, such as the Sherman Act, to conduct outside the United States, differ from the typical choice-of-law problem involving private law rules such as tort and contract? A wide diversity of opinion has been expressed on this question. (1) There is a presumption against extraterritorial application of United States public law, which can be rebutted only by express statutory language. This is the position taken by Justice Holmes in a Sherman Act decision, American Banana Co. v. United Fruit Co., 213 U.S. 347 (1909). Justice Scalia says that this approach would be "worth considering" if it were not foreclosed by subsequent precedent. (2) The application of United States public law should be treated as other choice-of-law problems, and United States law applied only if our country has the "most significant relationship" to the parties and the transaction. For this position, see Born, A Reappraisal of the Extraterritorial Reach of U.S. Law, 24 Law & Policy in Int'l Business 1, 88 (1992). (3) Even though conduct abroad causes effects in the United States, United States public law should be applied to that conduct only if this is reasonable under considerations of international comity. This is the position of Restatement (Third) of Foreign Relations Law § 403. See also Lowenfeld, Public Law in the International Arena: Conflict of Laws, International Law, and Some Suggestions for Their Interaction,

163 Collected Courses [Recueil des cours] Academy of International Law 311 (1979). Professor Lowenfeld was Associate Reporter for the Restatement (Third). (4) Presume that United States public law applies whenever conduct abroad produces substantial and foreseeable effects here that it is the purpose of our law to prevent. This presumption is rebutted if the effects in the United States are slight when compared with the reasonable interest of the foreign country in permitting the conduct centered there. For this position, see Weintraub, The Extraterritorial Application of Antitrust and Security Laws: An Inquiry into the Utility of a "Choice-of-Law" Approach, 70 Texas L.Rev. 1799 (1992). Consolidated Gold Fields PLC v. Minorco, S.A. 871 F.2d 252, modified, 890 F.2d 569 (2d Cir.), cert. dismissed, 492 U.S. 939 (1989) is an example of a case in which it is arguable that the presumption in favor of application of United States public law should have been rebutted. The Second Circuit enjoined worldwide the hostile takeover of one foreign corporation by another even though only 2.5% of the target's shareholders resided in the United States. The tender offer did not meet United States disclosure standards, although it met all foreign requirements. (5) Make a purely unilateral analysis of the relevant United States public law and apply it to conduct abroad whenever the policies underlying the law will be advanced. Under this approach, United States law would be applied whenever conduct abroad causes substantial and foreseeable effects here that it is the purpose of the law to prevent. For this position, see Scharf, Case 2, Conference on Jurisdiction, Justice and Choice of Law for the 21st Century, 29 New Eng.L.Rev. 618 (May 1995).

CHAPTER 10

Property

INTRODUCTORY NOTE

Cook, The Jurisdiction of Sovereign States and The Conflict of Laws, 31 Colum.L.Rev. 368, 381 (1931): "Since all legislation, all judicial action, creates (and destroys) the rights of persons, even though these have relation to things, there is no logical basis upon which to classify laws into those which affect persons and those which affect things."

Section 1. Land *

Introuctory Note

Restatement, Second, Conflict of Laws **

§ 223. Validity and Effect of Conveyance of Interest in Land

(1) Whether a conveyance transfers an interest in land and the nature of the interest transferred are determined by the law that would be applied by the courts of the situs.

(2) These courts would usually apply their own local law in determining such questions.

Thus the Second Restatement of Conflict of Laws refers almost [1] every question concerning land, whether arising from inter vivos transactions or on testate or intestate succession, to the whole law of the situs of the realty, including the conflicts rules of the situs. This is not a typical choice-of-law rule, for it provides no guidance to a court at the situs, except to state that situs courts "would usually apply their own local law in determining such questions." See § 223(2), supra.

---

* See Restatement, Second, Conflict of Laws §§ 223–243.

** Quoted with the permission of the copyright owner, The American Law Institute.

1. Construction of an instrument of conveyance is "in accordance with the rules of construction of the state designated for this purpose in the instrument." Restatement, Second § 224(1). "A will insofar as it devises an interest in land is construed in accordance with the rules of construction of the state designated for this purpose in the will." Id. § 240(1).

The Second Restatement bases its adherence to the traditional situs rule on "principles looking to further the needs of the interstate and international systems, application of the law of the state of dominant interest, protection of justified expectations, certainty, predictability and uniformity of result and ease in the determination and application of the law to be applied." Id. § 223, comment a. If none of the parties to the transaction is domiciled or headquartered at the situs, what policy of the situs is furthered by application of its law to determine the interest of those parties in the land? Perhaps one of the parties will rely on situs law for some purpose, such as the method of foreclosing a security interest in the land. Title searchers will rely on records at the situs and interpret these records under situs law. Are these reasons sufficient for application of situs law when none of the parties has relied on that law and the interests of innocent third parties are not affected? Can the title search problem be resolved by requiring a party whose interest in the land is determined by the law of a jurisdiction other than the situs, to record that determination in records at the situs or lose protection against innocent parties who rely on situs records and law? In how many of the cases in this section is the application of situs law justified by any of the reasons listed in the Restatement?

See Hay, The Situs Rule in European and American Conflicts Law—Comparative Notes, in Hay & Hoeflich, eds., Property Law & Legal Education 109 (1988). For an extensive criticism of the rule that the law of the situs should be applied to determine questions involving transfers of interests in land, see Weintraub, Commentary on the Conflict of Laws 421–60 (3d ed. 1986); see, also, Note, Modernizing the Situs Rule for Real Property Conflicts, 65 Tex.L.Rev. 585 (1987).

Succession Under Civil Law Concepts

As indicated in Note 2, p. 19 supra, most civil law countries take a unitary approach to succession: the same law applies to succession to movable and immovable property. Traditionally, the law selected for that purpose was that of the decedent's nationality. See, e.g. § 28, Austrian Conflicts Statute of 1978; Art. 25, German Conflicts Statute of 1986. To bridge the differences between civil law and common law countries, the Hague Conference on Private International Law in 1988 proposed a Convention on the Law Applicable to Decedents' Estates. The Convention adopts the unitary approach. The applicable law is that of the state where the decedent had his habitual residence for five years prior to death or the law of the state of his habitual residence and nationality, if the same, or— in order to protect recent immigrants in their expectations—the law of the country with which the decedent had the closest connection at the time of death. A testator may also designate the law of any country to govern succession to particular assets (for instance, situs law) but, with respect to statutory interests of family members, is restricted to the choice of the law of the state of his habitual residence or nationality at the time of designation or death. Many United States probate codes also recognize the interest of the decedent's domicile at death in protecting a surviving spouse against disinheritance. See, e.g., Uniform Probate Code § 2–201 (referring to the elective share of the surviving spouse of a person who dies domiciled in the state) and N.Y.E.P.T. Law § 5–1.1(d)8 (1986 amendment) (providing that for purposes of a surviving spouse's elective share, the estate includes "all property of the decedent, wherever situated"). But see N.Y.E.P.T. Law § 3–5.1, Note 4, infra p. 780.

Illustrations: Mary, an American citizen originally from Connecticut, has made her home in Austria for the last twenty years. She dies intestate there, leaving land in Connecticut, Michigan, and England as well as personal property in all of those places. Under existing law, Austria would distribute her Austrian property, both movable and immovable, according to the law of her nationality. Since there is no "American succession law," the Austrian court would particularize further and apply the law of Connecticut, her last American domicile (see § 5(3) of the Austrian Conflicts Statute). Connecticut law presumably refers to Austria because it is the situs of the immovable property and, as to the movable property, was the decedent's domicile at death. Austria accepts the reference (§ 5(2)) and thus will apply Austrian law to all of Mary's Austrian property. Common law jurisdictions—England and the two U.S. states—will apply their respective internal rules to local immovable property and Austrian domiciliary law to local movable property. Under the Convention, *Austrian law would apply to all property* in states adhering to the Convention, since Mary has satisfied the Convention's durational residence requirement. Note that, in her will Mary could have selected another law for application. However, she could have affected rights of a surviving spouse only by selecting U.S. law (that is, the law of her last U.S. domicile) as an alternative to Austrian law. In countries adopting it, the Convention thus displaces prior succession law for the estates of decedents meeting its test for application. It is not required that the decedent's foreign country of nationality or habitual residence also adhere to the Convention. The Convention does not apply to the formal requirements of a will nor to matrimonial or community property.

A. SUCCESSION ON DEATH

In Re Estate of Barrie
Supreme Court of Iowa, 1949.
240 Iowa 431, 35 N.W.2d 658.

■ HAYS, J.—Appeal from an order overruling a motion to strike objections to petition for probate of the alleged last will and testament of Mary E. Barrie, deceased.

Mary E. Barrie, domiciled in Whiteside County, Illinois, died owning real and personal property in Illinois and real property in Tama County, Iowa. The instrument in question was offered for probate in Whiteside County, Illinois. Although first admitted to probate, it was later denied probate after the Illinois Supreme Court had ruled that said instrument had been revoked by cancellation and that decedent died intestate.

Thereafter the instrument was offered for probate in Tama County, Iowa, by one of the beneficiaries named therein. To the petition for probate, decedent's heirs at law filed objections based upon the judgment of the Illinois Supreme Court, to the effect that the said last will and testament had been revoked. Objectors assert that this judgment is conclusive upon the Iowa courts. Proponent's motion to strike said objections for the reason that they do not constitute a valid basis for denying probate, being overruled by the trial court, this appeal was taken.

The instrument offered for probate was duly signed by decedent and witnessed by two witnesses.... When found, after the death of decedent, the instrument had the word "void" written across its face in at least five places, including the attestation clause. Also, upon the cover and upon the envelope containing same appears the word "void" written with the name "M. E. Barrie" and "Mary E. Barrie." The Illinois court found that the writing of the word "void" on the instrument, as above related, constituted a revocation by cancellation within the purview of the Illinois Revised Statutes, 1945, chapter 3, section 197. This statute provides for the revocation of a will " ... (a) by burning, cancelling, tearing, or obliterating it by the testator."

No question is raised as to the due execution of the instrument either under the Illinois or the Iowa statutes. No question is raised as to the testamentary capacity of decedent, nor is it claimed by the objectors that there has been a revocation under the Iowa statute, section 633.10, Code of 1946. The question before this court for determination may be stated thus, "Is the judgment of the Illinois court, holding that said instrument had been revoked and that decedent died intestate, conclusive and binding upon the Iowa courts?" ...

Decedent was a nonresident of the state and died owning property in Tama county which was subject to administration. Clearly the district court of Tama county has original jurisdiction to probate this instrument unless the Illinois judgment has the effect of nullifying or modifying said statute.... That this is in accordance with the recognized rule, see Restatement of the Law, Conflict of Laws, section 469, which states: "The will of a deceased person can be admitted to probate in a competent court of any state in which an administrator could have been appointed had the decedent died intestate", and under comment c of said provision: "Probate in a state other than at the domicil can be had although the will has not been admitted to probate in the state of the decedent's domicil." ...

Section 633.33, Code of 1946, provides: "A will probated in any other state or country shall be admitted to probate in this state, without the notice required in the case of domestic wills, on the production of a copy thereof and of the original record of probate."

Upon the general question as to the validity, operation, effect, etc. of a will by which property is devised, there are certain well-established and generally recognized rules, and which definitely differentiate between movable (personal) and immovable (real) property. We are only concerned with immovables in the instant case.

The general rule as stated in Story on Conflict of Laws, Eighth Ed., page 651, is, "the doctrine is clearly established at the common law, that the law of the place where the property [speaking of real (immovable) property] is locally situate is to govern as to the capacity or the incapacity of the testator ... the forms and solemnities to give the will or testament its due attestation and effect." ... Restatement of the Law, Conflict of Laws, section 249, states: "The validity and effect of a will of an interest in land are determined by the law of the state where the land is." Upon the specific question as to revocation of a will, ... Restatement of the Law, Conflict of Laws, section 250, says: "The effectiveness of an intended revocation of a will of an interest in land is determined by the law of the state where the land is." ...

. . .

Under the above-stated rule Iowa courts are free to place their construction, interpretation and sanction upon the will of a nonresident of the state who dies owning real property within the state whether the will be admitted to probate under section 604.3 or section 633.33, Code of 1946, both supra, although it has been admitted to probate in the state of the domicile of testator....

Does a different rule pertain where instead of being admitted to probate in the domicile state probate is denied? We think not. It is generally held that the full faith and credit provision of the Constitution of the United States, Article IV, section 1, does not render foreign decrees of probate conclusive as to the validity of a will as respects real property situated in a state other than the one in which the decree was rendered, nor does the doctrine of res adjudicata or estoppel by judgment apply....

. . .

... To hold that an act which constitutes a revocation in one state is a revocation in another state where under the law the act does not constitute a revocation is contrary to the general rule, which is stated in 57 Am.Jur., Wills, section 493, to be, "where a statute prescribes the method and acts by which a will may be revoked, no acts other than those mentioned in the statute are to operate as a revocation, no matter how clearly appears the purpose of the testator to revoke his will and his belief that such purpose has been accomplished." ... That the acts held to be a revocation in Illinois do not constitute such in Iowa, see section 633.10, Code of 1946. ...

Section 633.49, Code of 1946 provides:

"A last will and testament executed without this state, in the mode prescribed by the law either of the place where executed or of the testator's domicile, shall be deemed to be legally executed, and shall be of the same force and effect as if executed in the mode prescribed by the laws of this state, provided said last will and testament is in writing and subscribed by the testator."

This statute has not been before this court, so far as the writer of this opinion can find. It is clearly a modification of the common law and should not be extended to include matters not clearly included therein. It specifically deals with the formalities in the execution of the will, and nothing more. No question of execution is here involved. That the legislature might have waived the common-law rule as applicable to revocations as well as to the formal execution, as it has done, cannot be denied. However, the legislature has not seen fit to do so.... The statute is not applicable.

We hold that the Illinois judgment denying probate to the will in question is not conclusive and binding upon the courts of this state in so far as the disposition of the Iowa real estate is concerned; that the objections filed to the petition do not constitute a basis for denying probate of the will and the appellant's motion to strike should have been sustained. Reversed and remanded for an order in accordance herewith.—Reversed and remanded.

■ SMITH, J. (dissenting)

. . .

III. It is true of course that Code section 633.49 refers to *execution* and not directly to *revocation*; and we have here a document, held in Illinois to be nontestamentary, because of *revocation* and not because of any defect in original *execution*. In other words, we have an instrument not merely "executed" but also *revoked* "without this state, in the mode prescribed by the law ... of the testator's domicile."

But revocation is merely the converse of execution. The power to execute implies the power to revoke. A will can no longer be said to be *executed* after it has been *revoked*. Whether an instrument is a will is determined not only by the manner of its execution but also by the manner of its attempted revocation. Both acts are a part of the testamentary process. It is unthinkable that our legislature intended to require recognition of the laws of another jurisdiction in the matter of one and not of the other.

. . .

The purpose of both Code sections 633.33 and 633.49 must have been to abolish or minimize confusion and conflict between states in the matter of handling wills. Foreign ownership of property has become common. Owners of property in different jurisdictions should not be required in making and revoking their wills to do more than comply with the law of their own domiciles, or with the law of the jurisdiction where the instrument is drawn or revoked....

. . .

The fundamental error in the majority opinion is in assuming that the validity of an instrument offered as a *foreign* will is to be determined by the same standard that would determine its status if offered as a *domestic* will. But the Iowa statutes establish a different standard without any differentiation between real and personal property. The lex loci rei sitae is in that respect changed. Code section 633.49 is just as effective in its field as are our general statutes prescribing the forms and solemnities for the execution and revocation of domestic wills.

NOTE

1. Does the decision protect the reasonable expectations of the testatrix? Suppose that the Illinois decision had exercised in personam jurisdiction over persons before it in order to determine their interests in the Iowa land. Would the Iowa court have had to give this decision full faith and credit insofar as the interests of these persons were concerned? See pp. 254–259, supra.

2. Statutes in more than thirty states provide for alternative places of reference to determine whether a will has been executed in proper form. In the majority of these states a will executed elsewhere, when in writing and subscribed by the testator, is legally effective if executed in the mode prescribed by the law of the forum, or by the law of the place of execution or by the law of the testator's domicile. There are differences among the states as to whether the reference is to the testator's domicile at the time of execution of the will or at the time of death. See, for example, Uniform Probate Code § 2–506 (domicile at time of execution of the will or at time of death). See also Rees, American Wills Statutes: II, 46 Va.L.Rev. 856, 905 (1960).

A liberal provision, recognizing numerous places of alternative reference to determine issues of testamentary formalities, is The English Wills Act 1963, 11 & 12 Eliz. 2, Chapter 44. This provision is based upon the Hague Convention of 1960, which is reprinted in 9 Am.J.Comp.Law 705 (1960).

3. Craig v. Craig, 140 Md. 322, 117 A. 756 (1922). The intestate died domiciled in Pennsylvania leaving a leasehold interest in Maryland land. The Maryland courts characterized this interest as one in a movable and held that it should be distributed in accordance with the Pennsylvania rules of intestacy.

IN RE ESTATE OF HANNAN, 246 Neb. 828, 523 N.W.2d 672 (1994): Before his death, James Hannan adopted Glover, his wife's daughter from a previous marriage. First James and then his mother died. His mother's will left her estate to her surviving children and to the "issue" of her deceased children. Her will was probated in a court of her domicile at death, Virginia. The Virginia court held that "issue" did not include adopted children. In ancillary probate proceedings of real estate in Nebraska, the court held that Nebraska law applied to determine the construction of the will as it affected Nebraska real estate. Under Nebraska law "issue" includes adopted children and Glover was awarded 20 percent of the proceeds of the sale of the Nebraska land. The court rejected the argument that the testatrix had relied on Virginia law in drafting her will and stated: "Although Nebraska does grant reciprocal recognition to the final orders of other states as to the validity or construction of a will ..., Virginia has no such reciprocal statutory provision. In fact, Virginia has indicated that its policy is to apply its own law to the devise of real property located in Virginia."

UNIFORM PROBATE CODE, 8 U.L.A. § 2–602:

The meaning and legal effect of a disposition in a will shall be determined by the local law of a particular state selected by the testator in his instrument unless the application of that law is contrary to ... any ... public policy of this State ... applicable to the disposition.

COMMENT

... This provision ... enables a testator to select the law of a particular state for purposes of interpreting his will without regard to the location of property covered thereby. So long as local public policy is accommodated, the section should be accepted as necessary and desirable to add to the utility of wills....

DUCKWALL V. LEASE, 106 Ind.App. 664, 20 N.E.2d 204 (1939): Testatrix died domiciled in Ohio owning a farm in Indiana. In her will she gave her husband a life estate in the farm and directed that at his death the farm should be sold and the proceeds divided equally between a brother and a sister. The brother and sister predeceased the testatrix and the question was whether their legacies had lapsed. This would be so under the law of Indiana but not under the law of Ohio. The court held that Ohio law was applicable and that the legacies had not lapsed. The law of Indiana, the state of the situs was said to determine whether an equitable conversion had taken place. Under this law, the effect of the provision in the will for the sale of the farm was equitably to convert the farm into personalty. Hence the farm was treated as personal property, and its distribution and disposition held to be governed by the law of Ohio. For a more recent and similar holding by the same court, see Moore v. Livingston, 148 Ind.App. 275, 265 N.E.2d 251 (1970).

IN RE McDOUGAL'S WILL, 49 N.J.Super. 485, 140 A.2d 249 (1958), affirmed 55 N.J.Super. 36, 149 A.2d 801 (1959): The testatrix died domiciled in California leaving land in New Jersey. By a holographic will valid under the law of California but not under the law of New Jersey, she provided that this land should be sold and the proceeds divided among her brother's children. The court held that the will failed with respect to the New Jersey land but not as to any personal property held by the testatrix in New Jersey. In dissent Justice Schettino contended that under New Jersey law the land should be deemed to have been equitably converted into personal property with the result that it passed under the will. He emphasized the "value of upholding the will and the testator's intent" and stated that the current "trend ... is to minimize the importance of formalities."

NOTE

For a discussion of "equitable conversion" as a device for avoiding the law of the situs, see Note 3, supra p. 492.

In re Schneider's Estate

Surrogate's Court of New York, New York County, 1950.
198 Misc. 1017, 96 N.Y.S.2d 652.

■ FRANKENTHALER, SURROGATE. This case presents a novel question in this State in the realm of the conflict of laws. Deceased, a naturalized American citizen of Swiss origin, died domiciled in New York County, leaving as an asset of his estate certain real property located in Switzerland. In his will he attempted to dispose of his property, including the parcel of Swiss realty, in a manner which is said to be contrary to the provisions of Swiss internal law. That law confers upon one's legitimate heirs a so-called *legitime*, i.e., a right to specified fractions of a decedent's property, which right cannot be divested by testamentary act. The precise issue, therefore, is whether this deceased had the power to dispose of the realty in the manner here attempted.

Ordinarily, the courts of a country not the situs of an immovable are without jurisdiction to adjudicate questions pertaining to the ownership of that property.... However, in this case the administratrix appointed prior to the probate of the will has liquidated the foreign realty and transmitted the proceeds to this State. She is now accounting for the assets of the estate including the fund representing that realty. As a consequence this court is called upon to direct the administration and distribution of the substituted fund and to determine the property rights therein.... In doing so, however, reference must be made to the law of the situs, as the question of whether the fund shall be distributed to the devisee of the realty under the terms of the will is dependent upon the validity of the original devise thereof....

The court is confronted at the outset with a preliminary question as to the meaning of the term "law of the situs"—whether it means only the internal or municipal law of the country in which the property is situated or whether it also includes the conflict of laws rules to which the courts of that jurisdiction would resort in making the same determination. If the latter is the proper construction to be placed upon that term, then this court must, in effect, place itself in the position of the foreign court and decide the matter as would that court in an identical case.

The meaning of the term "law of the situs" can be ascertained best from a consideration of the reasons underlying the existence of the rule which requires the application thereof. The primary reason for its existence lies in the fact that the law-making and law-enforcing agencies of the country in which land is situated have exclusive control over such land. ... As only the courts of that country are ultimately capable of rendering enforceable judgments affecting the land, the legislative authorities thereof have the exclusive power to promulgate the law which shall regulate its ownership and transfer....

Hence, the rights which were created in that land are those which existed under the whole law of the situs and as would be enforced by those courts which normally would possess exclusive judicial jurisdiction. Griswold, Renvoi Revisited, 51 Harvard L.R. 1165, 1186.... The purely fortuitous transfer of the problem to the courts of another state by virtue of a postmortuary conversion of the land, effected for the purpose of administering the entire estate in the country of domicile, ought not to alter the character of the legal relations which existed with respect to the land at the date of death and which continued to exist until its sale. Consequently, this court in making a determination of ownership, must ascertain the body of local law to which the courts of the situs would refer if the matter were brought before them.

It has been urged, however, that a reference to the conflict of laws rules of the situs may involve an application of the principle of *renvoi,* and if so it would place the court in a perpetually-enclosed circle from which it could never emerge and that it would never find a suitable body of substantive rules to apply to the particular case.... This objection is based upon the assumption that if the forum must look to the whole law of the situs, and that law refers the matter to the law of the domicile, this latter reference must be considered to be the whole law of the latter country also, which would refer the matter back to the law of the situs, which process would continue without end. That reasoning is based upon a false premise, for as has been said by Dean Griswold, Renvoi Revisited, op. cit. supra, p. 1190: "Recognition of the foreign conflict of laws rule will not lead us into an endless chain of references if it is clear for any reason that the particular foreign conflicts rule (or any rule along the line of reference) is one which refers to the internal law alone...." ...

The precise question here considered, namely whether there shall be a reference to the entire law of the situs to determine the ownership of the proceeds of foreign realty, is one of first impression in this State. Nevertheless, the above stated principles, together with the rule enunciated in ... the English authorities on the subject and in analogous cases in courts of this State and others, require us to accept it as a part of our law and to hold that a reference to the law of the situs necessarily entails a reference to the whole law of that country, including its conflict of laws rule.

The rule as formulated in the Restatement is as follows: "Section 8. Rule in questions of title to land or divorce. (1) All questions of title to land are decided in accordance with the law of the state where the land is, including the Conflict of Laws rules of that State. (2) All questions concerning the validity of a decree of divorce are decided in accordance with the law of the domicile of the parties, including the Conflict of Laws rules of that State." In all other cases the Restatement rejects the *renvoi* principle and provides that where a reference is made to foreign law that law should be held to mean only the internal law of the foreign country. Section 7....

The decisions in this State also indicate the applicability of the doctrine of *renvoi* in this field. In the early case of Dupuy v. Wurtz, 53 N.Y. 556, which involved personal property, there appears the first reference to the doctrine. The Court there said by way of dictum, 53 N.Y. at page 573: "[W]hen we speak of the law of domicile as applied to the law of succession, we mean not the general law, but the law which the country of the domicile applies to the particular case under consideration...."

The implications of that dictum were disregarded in the celebrated Matter of Tallmadge, Surr.Ct., New York County, 109 Misc. 696, 181 N.Y.S. 336 per Winthrop, R., where the Referee, rejecting the *renvoi* principle completely, asserted that it "is no part of New York law."

The broad assertion in Matter of Tallmadge, supra, that the *renvoi* principle is not applicable in New York is not in accord with the earlier or later cases. The precise limits of its applicability are as yet undefined....

Thus it is now necessary to ascertain the whole of the applicable Swiss law and apply it to this case....

Concerning the actual content of Swiss law, the expert witnesses summoned by the respective parties are in agreement that the Swiss internal law would apply to the real and personal estate of a Swiss citizen domiciled in Switzerland, and that the laws of the country of domicile would, under the Swiss theory of unity of succession, apply to all of the Swiss property belonging to a foreign national....

Consequently, the court holds that the testamentary plan envisaged by the testator and set out in his will is valid, even in its application to the Swiss realty. The proceeds of that realty must therefore be distributed pursuant to the directions contained in the will....

Submit, on notice, decree settling the account accordingly.[1]

NOTE

If Switzerland would have applied its own law, would the decision of the court have been different? Is deference to the whole law of Switzerland, including its choice-of-law rules, more desirable because Switzerland is a foreign country and not a sister state? Should the New York court have determined whether a Swiss court, as a matter of comity, would recognize the New York court's determination of interests in Swiss land? Is the result, in any event, better than if the court had not referred to the Swiss conflicts rules?

B. SECURITY TRANSACTIONS

Swank v. Hufnagle

Supreme Court of Judicature of Indiana, 1887.
111 Ind. 453, 12 N.E. 303.

■ ELLIOTT, J. The appellant sued the appellee, Melissa Hufnagle, and her husband, upon a note and mortgage executed in Darke county, Ohio, on land situate in this State. The appellee, Melissa Hufnagle, answered that

---

1. There is a subsequent opinion, further discussing the Swiss law, in In re Schneider's Estate, 198 Misc. 1017, 100 N.Y.S.2d 371 (1950). The decision has been criticized on the ground the Surrogate misunderstood the Swiss law. See Falconbridge, The Renvoi in New York and Elsewhere, 6 Vanderbilt L.Rev. 708, 725–31 (1953)—Eds.

she was a married woman, and that the mortgage was executed by her as the surety of her husband, and assumed to convey land in this State owned by her. The appellant replied that the contract was made in Ohio, and that by a statute of that State a married woman had power to execute such a mortgage, but the statute of Ohio is not set forth.

The trial court did right in adjudging the reply bad. The validity of the mortgage of real property is to be determined by the law of the place where the property is situated....

Under the act of 1881 a mortgage executed by a married woman as surety on land owned by her in this State is void....

Judgment affirmed.

NOTES

1. In Thomson v. Kyle, 39 Fla. 582, 23 So. 12 (1897), the defendant, a married woman, had executed in Alabama a promissory note together with her husband, and also had given a mortgage on Florida land. The note and mortgage were executed by her to secure a debt of the husband. The court enforced the mortgage against the Florida land, even though the note was void as to the defendant under the law of Alabama. "Notwithstanding Mrs. Thomson's incapacity by the laws of Alabama to execute the mortgage sought to be foreclosed here, she was capable under our laws of executing in Alabama, a mortgage upon her separate statutory real property in this State to secure her husband's debt."

2. In Burr v. Beckler, 264 Ill. 230, 106 N.E. 206, L.R.A.1916A, 1049, Ann.Cas. 1915D, 1132 (1914), a married woman domiciled in Illinois, executed and delivered in Florida a note and as security therefor a trust deed to Illinois land. Although the note would have been good if executed and delivered in Illinois, the court held that the note was void since the woman lacked capacity under Florida law. The court held that since the note was void, "the trust deed, which was incidental and intended to secure a performance of the obligation created by the note, could not be enforced." The Burr case is discussed in University of Chicago v. Dater, Note 2, p. 502, supra.

PROCTOR V. FROST, 89 N.H. 304, 197 A. 813 (1938): A married woman executed and delivered at her home in Massachusetts a mortgage on New Hampshire land to secure her husband's debt. The mortgage was enforceable under Massachusetts law, but a New Hampshire statute provided, "No contract or conveyance by a married woman, as surety or guarantor for her husband ... shall be binding on her ..." The court held that the effect of the mortgage was to be determined by New Hampshire law, but that the statute was not meant to apply to mortgages executed outside of New Hampshire. The court stated that New Hampshire had no power to regulate contracts executed elsewhere and that "The primary purpose of the statute ... was not to regulate the transfer of New Hampshire real estate, but to protect married women in New Hampshire. ..."

KEY BANK OF ALASKA V. DONNELS, 106 Nev. 49, 787 P.2d 382 (1990). A Nevada corporation borrowed money from an Alaska bank. The note was secured by a deed of trust on Nevada real estate and guaranteed by defendant, the president of the Nevada corporation. The note and guarantee contained provisions choosing Alaska law, but the deed of trust referred to Nevada foreclosure procedures. When the corporate borrower defaulted, the bank sold the Nevada property pursuant to the terms of the deed of trust, effecting a non-judicial foreclosure. The bank then sued the guarantor in Nevada to recover a deficiency between the proceeds of the sale and the loan. The guarantor defended on the ground that under Alaska law there was no right to a deficiency judgment after a non-judicial foreclosure. Nevada law would permit the deficiency judgment. Held: for the bank. Alaska law applied pursuant to the choice-of-law clauses in the note and mortgage, but the Alaska statute precluding a deficiency judgment only applied to foreclosures in Alaska. The Alaska statute provided: "When a sale is made by a trustee under a deed of trust, as authorized by AS 34.20.070–34.20.130, [a deficiency judgment is precluded]." The court stated: "we read the offsetting commas as indicating a clear intent to limit the effect of the statute to foreclosures under those sections, especially because AS 34.20.070 refers to deed of trust conveyances of property *located in Alaska*. Furthermore, because anti-deficiency statutes derogate from the common law, they should be narrowly construed."

NOTE

In the light of Proctor v. Frost, the decision in Thomson v. Kyle is easier to justify than the decision in Swank v. Hufnagle. Why? Should it have made a difference in Thomson v. Kyle that all of the parties were domiciled in Alabama? Cf. Resolution Trust Corp. v. Northpark Joint Venture, 958 F.2d 1313 (5th Cir.1992), cert. denied, 113 S.Ct. 963 (1993), in which a loan by a Texas lender to a Texas joint venture was guaranteed by Texans and secured by a deed of trust on Mississippi land. The loan was not repaid. The lender foreclosed by selling the Mississippi land, but did not recover the full amount of the loan. Under Texas law, the lender was entitled to summary judgment against the guarantors for the deficiency. Under Mississippi law, the lender had the burden of proving that the foreclosure sale was conducted in such a manner that a deficiency judgment would be equitable. Held: Texas law applied and the lender was entitled to summary judgment. "Texas has a direct interest in ensuring that Texas debts are handled properly and that Texas debtors and creditors are treated fairly. By contrast, Mississippi has little interest in this case. In enacting their guaranty laws, Mississippi legislators and judges intended to protect Mississippi citizens. There is no reason why Mississippi would have an interest in the application of its laws to resolve the claims of foreign creditors against foreign debtors." 958 F.2d at 1319.

C. CONVEYANCES AND CONTRACTS

SMITH V. INGRAM, 130 N.C. 100, 40 S.E. 984 (1902): In 1878, the plaintiff, who was then a married woman, sold land located in North Carolina for the sum of $130. Thereafter, the town of Star was built on the land and its value increased to at least $40,000. In this action, the plaintiff claimed the right to recover the land from its present owners on the ground that her deed to the original purchaser was void under North

Carolina law since she had not been given a "privy examination", as required by North Carolina law, to ascertain whether she was selling the land of her own free will. No such privy examination was required by the law of South Carolina where the plaintiff was at all times domiciled. The court held, nevertheless, for the plaintiff on the ground that the validity of a conveyance of an interest in land is determined by the law of the situs. In denying a petition for rehearing (132 N.C. 959, 44 S.E. 643 (1903)), the court left open the possibility that the dispossessed bona fide purchasers might have an equitable remedy for the value of the improvements.

NOTE

The law of the situs is commonly said to determine the validity and effect of a conveyance of an interest in land including the question of formalities and of the capacity of the respective parties to convey and to receive title. Restatement, Second, Conflict of Laws § 223.

Polson v. Stewart

Supreme Judicial Court of Massachusetts, 1897.
167 Mass. 211, 45 N.E. 737, 36 L.R.A. 771, 57 Am.St.Rep. 452.

Bill in Equity, filed June 6, 1895, to enforce specific performance of a covenant executed by the defendant to his wife, Kitty T.P. Stewart, who died on December 26, 1893, intestate, and of whose estate the plaintiff, who was her brother, was appointed administrator, he having also acquired the rights of the other heirs in her estate....

The defendant demurred to the bill, assigning several grounds therefor. Hearing before Knowlton, J., who, at the request of the parties, reserved the case upon the bill and demurrer for the consideration of the full court.

■ HOLMES, J. This is a bill to enforce a covenant made by the defendant to his wife, the plaintiff's intestate, in North Carolina, to surrender all his marital rights in certain land of hers. The land is in Massachusetts. The parties to the covenant were domiciled in North Carolina. According to the bill, the wife took steps which under the North Carolina statutes gave her the right to contract as a feme sole with her husband as well as with others, and afterwards released her dower in the defendant's lands. In consideration of this release, and to induce his wife to forbear suing for divorce, for which she had just cause, and for other adequate considerations, the defendant executed the covenant. The defendant demurs....

But it is said that the laws of the parties' domicil could not authorize a contract between them as to lands in Massachusetts. Obviously this is not true. It is true that the laws of other States cannot render valid conveyances of property within our borders which our laws say are void, for the plain reason that we have exclusive power over the res.... But the same reason inverted establishes that the lex rei sitae cannot control personal covenants, not purporting to be conveyances, between persons outside the jurisdiction, although concerning a thing within it. Whatever the covenant, the laws of North Carolina could subject the defendant's property to seizure on execution, and his person to imprisonment, for a failure to perform it. Therefore, on principle, the law of North Carolina determines the validity of the contract. Such precedents as there are, are on the same side.... Lord Cottenham stated and enforced the rule in the clearest way in Ex parte Pollard, 4 Deac. 27, 40 et seq.; S.C.Mont. & Ch. 239, 250....

If valid by the law of North Carolina there is no reason why the contract should not be enforced here. The general principle is familiar. Without considering the argument addressed to us that such a contract would have been good in equity if made here ... we see no ground of policy for an exception. The statutory limits which have been found to the power of a wife to release dower ... do not prevent a husband from making a valid covenant that he will not claim marital rights with any person competent to receive a covenant from him.... The competency of the wife to receive the covenant is established by the law of her domicil and of the place of the contract. The laws of Massachusetts do not make it impossible for him specifically to perform his undertaking. He can give a release which will be good by Massachusetts law. If it be said that the rights of the administrator are only derivative from the wife, we agree, and we do not for a moment regard anyone as privy to the contract except as representing the wife. But if then it be asked whether she could have enforced the contract during her life, an answer in the affirmative is made easy by considering exactly what the defendant undertook to do. So far as occurs to us, he undertook three things: first, not to disturb his wife's enjoyment while she kept her property; secondly, to execute whatever instrument was necessary in order to release his rights if she conveyed; and thirdly, to claim no rights on her death, but to do whatever was necessary to clear the title from such rights then. All these things were as capable of performance in Massachusetts as they would have been in North Carolina. Indeed, all the purposes of the covenant could have been secured at once in the lifetime of the wife by a joint conveyance of the property to a trustee upon trusts properly limited. It will be seen that the case does not raise the question as to what the common law and the presumed law of North Carolina would be as to a North Carolina contract calling for acts in Massachusetts, or concerning property in Massachusetts, which could not be done consistently with Massachusetts law....

Demurrer overruled.

■ FIELD, C.J. I cannot assent to the opinion of a majority of the court.... By our law husband and wife are under a general disability or incapacity to make contracts with each other.... It seems to me illogical to say that we will not permit a conveyance of Massachusetts land directly between husband and wife, wherever they may have their domicil, and yet say that they may make a contract to convey such land from one to the other which our courts will specifically enforce. It is possible to abandon the rule of lex rei sitae, but to keep it for conveyances of land and to abandon it for contracts to convey land seems to me unwarrantable....

It is only on the ground that the contract conveyed an equitable title that the plaintiff as heir has any standing in court. His counsel founds his argument on the distinction between a conveyance of the legal title to land and a contract to convey it.... On reason and authority I think it cannot be held that, although a deed between a husband and his wife, domiciled in North Carolina, of the rights of each in the lands of the other in Massachusetts, is void as a conveyance by reason of the incapacity of the parties under the law of Massachusetts to make and receive such a conveyance to and from each other, yet, if there are covenants in the deed to make a good title, the covenants can be specifically enforced by our courts, and a conveyance compelled, which, if voluntarily made between the parties, would be void.

... Whatever may be true of contracts between husband and wife made in or when they are domiciled in other jurisdictions, so far as personal property or personal liability is concerned, I think that contracts affecting the title to real property situate within the Commonwealth should be such as are authorized by our laws. I am of opinion that the bill should be dismissed.

NOTES

1. The principal case is often cited as an example of the contract-conveyance distinction, which was sometimes used to avoid applying the law of the situs to issues affecting real property. Courts have drawn distinctions between the contract to convey and the conveyance itself (Polson), and between a promissory note and the mortgage securing the note (Thomson v. Kyle, note 1, supra p. 768, and Burr v. Beckler, note 2, supra p. 768). The conveyance and the mortgage are analyzed as a "land" problem to which the law of the situs is applicable. The contract to convey and the promissory note are treated as a "contract" problem to be resolved by a choice-of-law rule appropriate to contracts—typically, in the old cases, the law of the place of making of the contract. The contract-conveyance distinction may, like the equitable conversion fiction (see p. 505, supra), be more likely than the situs rule to give effect to the policies of the state that will experience the consequences of the decision. In Burr v. Beckler (note 2, p. 768), however, the application of the law of the place of contracting resulted in invalidating a wife's note and the trust deed securing it, though the instruments were valid at her marital domicile, which was also the situs of the land. She executed the note while on a visit in Florida, which denied married women capacity to make the contract in issue.

2. In Ex parte Pollard, Mont. & C. 239 (1840), relied on by Justice Holmes in the Polson case, a borrower had deposited with an English lender title deeds to land in Scotland and a memorandum assuming to give a lien on the land. Under the law of England, an equitable security interest was thereby created, but under the law of Scotland no such interest arose. After the borrower became insolvent, the lender claimed in the English bankruptcy proceedings that his debt should be paid out of the Scottish land in preference to the claims of general creditors. The English court found for the lender and ordered execution by the borrower in the proper Scottish form of an instrument giving the creditor the requisite security interest in the land. In the course of his opinion, the Lord Chancellor said that in cases involving foreign land the English courts "act upon their own rules" in "administering equities between parties residing here" and then continued: "Bills for specific performance of contracts for the sale of lands, or respecting mortgages of estates, in the colonies and elsewhere out of the jurisdiction of this Court, are of familiar occurrence. Why then, consistently with these principles and these authorities, should the fact, that by the law of Scotland no lien or equitable mortgage was created by the deposit and memorandum in this case, prevent the courts of this country from giving such effect to the transactions between the parties as it would have given if the land had been in England? If the contract had been to sell the lands a specific performance would have been decreed; and why is all relief to be refused because the contract is to sell, subject to a condition for redemption?"

Is this an early example of a governmental interest analysis approach?

3. Mallory Associates, Inc. v. Barving Realty Co., 300 N.Y. 297, 90 N.E.2d 468 (1949). Lessor and lessee, both of New York, there executed a lease on Virginia property. The lessee sued to recover a deposit given pursuant to the lease as security for performance. He claimed that the lessor had converted this deposit by mingling it with other funds in violation of a New York statute providing that lessees' deposits should be held in trust. The court held the statute to be applicable although the land was in another state. The court first wrote in terms reminiscent of the contract-conveyance distinction, discussed in Note (1), supra: "The provision in the lease for the deposit of security is a personal covenant between the contracting parties, creating rights in personam.... The question presented ... relates solely to the rights and liabilities of the parties as a matter of contractual obligation. Accordingly, it is to be determined by the law governing the contract, even though the subject matter of the contract may be land in another State." The court then, however, focused on the purpose of the statute: "[T]he Legislature was attempting to prevent the depletion of funds deposited with the lessor.... The lessee, resident in this State, was the person to be protected. The need for protection is obviously no less, but rather more, when the land to which the lease relates is situated outside of this State."

SELOVER, BATES & CO. V. WALSH, 226 U.S. 112 (1912): Action in a state court in Minnesota for damages for breach of an executory contract for the sale by the defendant to the plaintiff's assignor of land in Colorado. The contract was made and the instalments on the purchase price were to be paid in Minnesota. The contract provided time was of the essence of the contract, and upon failure to make payments punctually or to perform literally any covenant in the contract, at the option of the vendor, the contract should be terminated, the sums paid being forfeited. The vendee having defaulted in the payment of taxes, the defendant elected to exercise his option and resold the land to a third party. Plaintiff relied on a Minnesota statute which provided that a vendor could not cancel a contract for the sale of land except upon thirty days' written notice to the vendee, who would then have thirty days in which to remedy the default. The Supreme Court of Minnesota, in affirming a judgment for the plaintiff, held the Minnesota statute applicable. The defendant, contending that the application of the statute to this contract involving land in Colorado deprived it of its property without due process of law, carried the case to the Supreme Court of the United States. In overruling the defendant's contention, the Supreme Court said: "The argument to support the contention is somewhat confused, as it mingles with the right of contract simply a consideration of the state's jurisdiction over the land which was the subject of the contract. As to the contract simply, we have no doubt of the state's power over it, and the law of the state, therefore, constituted part of it.... Whether it had extraterritorial effect is another question ... Courts, in many ways, through action upon or constraint of the person, affect property in other states ..., and in the case at bar the action is strictly personal.... The case at bar is certainly within the principle expressed in Polson v. Stewart. The Minnesota supreme court followed the prior decision in Finnes v. Selover, Bates & Co., 102 Minn. 334, 113 N.W. 883, in which it said that, upon repudiation of a contract by the seller of land, two courses were open to the purchaser: 'He might stand by the contract, and seek to recover the land, or he could declare upon a breach of the contract, and recover the amount of his damages.' If he elected the former, it was further said, the courts of Colorado alone could give him relief; if he sought redress in damages, the courts of Minnesota were open to him. And this, it was observed, was in accordance with the principle that the law of the situs governs as to the land, and the law of contract as to the rights of the parties in the contract."

NOTES

1. In comparing the instant case with Polson v. Stewart, p. 770, supra, consider the difference in the relief prayed for—in Polson v. Stewart, there was a suit for specific performance, while in the instant case the plaintiff was suing for damages.

2. Kryger v. Wilson, 242 U.S. 171 (1916). By contract "made and to be performed in Minnesota," the plaintiff agreed to sell North Dakota land to the defendant. Upon the latter's default, plaintiff caused notice of cancellation to be served in accordance with the requirements of North Dakota law and then brought suit in a North Dakota court to quiet title to the land. Defendant appeared in the action and requested the court to find that the contract was still valid and subsisting since plaintiff had not taken the action prescribed by Minnesota law to entitle a vendor to cancel a contract for the sale of land. From a decree of the North Dakota courts finding that the contract had been legally cancelled and quieting title in plaintiff, defendant appealed to the Supreme Court on the ground that he had been deprived of his property without due process of law. Held: Affirmed. "The most that the plaintiff in error can say is that the state court made a mistaken application of doctrines of the conflict of laws in deciding that the cancellation of a land contract is governed by the law of the situs instead of the place of making and performance. But that, being purely a question of local common law, is a matter with which this court is not concerned...."

"If the contract properly interpreted or the law properly applied required that this condition [the notice of cancellation] be performed in Minnesota, steps taken by him [the defendant in error] under the North Dakota statute would be ineffective. Whether or not proper proceedings had been taken to secure cancellation could be determined only by a court having jurisdiction; and the North Dakota court had jurisdiction not only over the land but through the voluntary appearance of plaintiff in error, also over him.... If the plaintiff in error had not submitted himself to the jurisdiction of the court, the decree could have determined only the title to the land ... But having come into court ... he cannot now complain if he has been concluded altogether in the premises. The plaintiff in error relies upon Selover,

Bates & Co. v. Walsh, 226 U.S. 112. That was a personal action for breach of contract and not, like the present case, an action merely to determine the title to land...."

BEAUCHAMP v. BERTIG, 90 Ark. 351, 119 S.W. 75 (1909): Action for Arkansas land. An Oklahoma court had rendered a judgment removing the disabilities of nonage of the two minor owners of the land and had specifically authorized them to sell the land. The minors had then executed in Oklahoma a deed of the land to the defendant in which they covenanted to warrant and defend the title against all lawful claims. The deed was recorded in Arkansas. Immediately after the younger had reached his majority, the two executed a deed to the plaintiff of "all their right, title and interest in and to" the land but gave no covenants of title. Plaintiff then brought the present action to determine his interest in the land. The defendant relied on the Oklahoma judgment and the deed pursuant to it.

Held for the plaintiff: "Since immovable property is fixed forever in the State where it lies, and since no other State can have any jurisdiction over it, it follows necessarily that no right, title or interest can be finally acquired therein, unless assented to by the courts of that State, in accordance with its laws." Minor on Conflict of Laws, sec. II....

It has long been the rule in this State that an infant's deed conveys title to his real estate subject to his right to disaffirm when he becomes of age. Bagley v. Fletcher, 44 Ark. 153; ...

But appellees argue that the covenants for title are separate contracts, creating personal obligations and therefore governed by the lex loci contractus.... even if these covenants create obligations that would, generally speaking, be governed by the lex loci contractus, still that law would have to give way to the local policy as declared by this court.

The covenants under consideration, however, are not personal in the sense that the obligations incurred under them are governed by the law concerning movables. There are many contracts relating to real estate that are so governed. For example, covenants of seisin, of right to convey and against incumbrances, and executory contracts for deeds or other instruments containing covenants that do not run with the land. All these contracts, in the absence of statutory law or an expressed intention to the contrary, are usually governed by the law of the place where such contracts are made. Such is not the case, however, with contracts containing covenants that run with the land—as, for instance, covenants of warranty and for quiet enjoyment; or covenants that can only be performed where the land lies, as, for instance, to defend title, to pay taxes, to repair, etc. These are governed by the law of the place where the land is situated....

... It is unnecessary to determine whether the district court of Oklahoma had jurisdiction to render judgment removing the disabilities of the Sitterdings, for it follows from what we have said that they had the right to disaffirm, even if such judgment be valid....

NOTES

1. If, because of the Oklahoma judgment, the owners could not have disaffirmed their deed in Oklahoma on reaching majority, was the Arkansas court's decision a denial of full faith and credit?

2. Suppose that in State X, A executes and delivers to B a deed to land situated in State Y. The deed contains no express covenants and for this reason A would not be liable to B under the law of X for any defects in his title. By the law of State Y, however, the usual covenants of title would be implied by the use of the terms of bargain and sale contained in the deed. What law governs B's right to damages against A in the event of a defective title? Should the answer depend upon whether under the law of State Y the covenants are personal to the parties or run with the land in the sense that they impose duties upon the grantor in favor of a remote grantee? See Scoles and Hay, Conflict of Laws 753 (2d ed. 1992): "That a distinction should be made between those covenants for title that run with the land and those which are called purely personal, such as a covenant of seisin, seems doubtful."

3. Sun Oil Co. v. Guidry, 99 So.2d 424 (La.App.1957). Proceeding to determine ownership of mineral interests in Louisiana land. The question was whether the interest of one of the parties was barred on account of non-user. This would be so if the prescriptive period commenced running from the date when he was judicially emancipated in Texas, the state of his domicile. Held claimant's interest is barred by non-user. "The general rule is that the law of the individual's domicile determines his status of majority or minority ..., but the law of the place where the immovable property is situated determines the effect of such status.... [Under] Louisiana law ... prescription runs against the minor over the age of eighteen fully emancipated by marriage ... or judicially.... Thus, in our opinion, prescription commenced running in Louisiana ... as soon as [the minor] attained the personal status of an emancipated minor under the law of his domicile...." The court distinguished Beauchamp v. Bertig on the ground that under the law of Arkansas, the situs of the land, "even a local decree removing the disability of minority" would not prevent the minor from disavowing the sale after he had reached the age of twenty-one years.

Irving Trust Co. v. Maryland Casualty Co.

United States Circuit Court of Appeals, Second Circuit, 1936.
83 F.2d 168.*

[Suit by a trustee in bankruptcy against transferees of the bankrupt, a Delaware corporation doing business in New York, to avoid preferential transfers of land and personal property made in violation of New York law. Some of the land was in states other than New York.]

■ L. HAND, CIRCUIT JUDGE. ... A more troublesome question concerns the property outside New York. Although the bill does not say where the

---

* Certiorari denied 299 U.S. 571 (1936).

transfers were made, the contracts required them to be delivered in [New York], and we are to assume that the parties performed as stipulated. The receipt of the deeds by the defendants was therefore a wrong, and any liabilities imposed as a remedy would be recognized and enforced elsewhere, for the law of the place where acts occur normally fixes their jural character.... The question here is whether it makes a difference that the wrong consisted in the conveyance of property in another state, under whose laws the conveyance might perhaps have been valid. It is in general no objection to a liability arising out of a consensual transaction that it may be determined by events happening in another jurisdiction.... A fortiori it is none that it may have indirect effects upon extraterritorial rights. But it might nevertheless be true that when the transaction consisted in the transfer of property situated elsewhere and would be valid by the lex rei sitae, the act of conveyance would not be a wrong where executed, though the law of that place forbade it as respects property within its own borders. The local doctrine of conflict of laws might impose that exception upon the general language of the statute. The doctrine is of course well settled, certainly as to real property, and, as we shall assume arguendo, equally at the present time as to personal, that the law of the situs absolutely determines the validity of conveyances wherever made. No title will pass and no interest will arise, save as that law prescribes....

We have no doubt therefore that title passed by the deeds delivered in New York to property situated in those of the three states whose laws did not forbid such transfers; yet the law of New York might still make receipt of the deed a wrong and impose a liability upon the grantee though he got a good title. That would not trench upon the sovereignty of the state of the situs whose power over the res would remain wholly unimpaired. Nobody would question this so far as concerned the grantee's liability in damages; it would be but reasonable that he should become liable to the grantor's creditors just because his title was unimpeachable. In the case of contracts for the sale of land the lex loci contractus certainly controls.... True, the same doctrine might not apply to the remedy of specific restitution, or specific performance; English speaking courts have always been sensitive about land and in recent years the doctrine of the lex rei sitae has been extended to chattels. Yet in principle there ought to be no distinction between the remedies, for, as we have said, one would invade as little as the other the sovereignty of the state of the situs, which would be free to refuse any effect to the enforced conveyance, if it chose. The result of such a refusal upon a suit elsewhere might indeed be crucial, but only because, seeing that its remedy would be futile if granted, the court would decline to act at all, when, as here, there is no reason to suspect that the lex rei sitae would not recognize such conveyances as valid though made under the duress of a decree, there is no reason to hesitate.

The authorities are not indeed many ... There are a few cases which do raise the point and they support our view. The first is Lord Cranstown v. Johnson, 3 Ves.Jr. 170, where the defendant in England beguiled the plaintiff into letting him pursue his remedies against land in St. Kitt's. The law of St. Kitt's gave the plaintiff no remedy either in equity, or at law.

Yet Lord Alvanley held that the defendant's conduct in England raised a liability for which he could award specific restitution. In Ex parte Pollard, Mont. & C. 239, the defendant in England pledged to the plaintiff his title papers to land in Scotland, which would have created a valid equitable lien upon English land, but did not upon Scotch. Lord Cottenham held the defendant to be subject to an equitable obligation which could be enforced specifically in personam.... Some of the relief asked by the bill cannot therefore be granted; the court cannot adjudge the transfers void as to land and chattels outside the state, except as the lex rei sitae is the same as [the law of New York]. But under his general prayer the plaintiff, if he proves his case, may have a decree as to any of the property transferred directing the defendants to reconvey it, and this he can enforce in personam. Of course he may also recover damages as a substitute if he so elects.

Decree reversed; defendants to answer over.

NOTES

1. See First Commerce Realty Investors v. K–F Land Co., 617 S.W.2d 806, 809 (Tex.Civ.App.1981) in which the court applied the Louisiana Deficiency Judgment Act in a foreclosure proceeding with respect to Texas land. The secured party's principal place of business had been in Louisiana, the loan was negotiated and to be performed there, the promissory note and the deed of trust selected Louisiana law, and all documents were executed in Louisiana. "It is difficult to conceive of other steps that could have been taken by the parties to imprint this transaction with Louisiana law ... [T]he parties clearly bargained in the most specific terms for the applicability of Louisiana law. We see no reason to frustrate such intention so clearly expressed."

2. In view of how frequently it is uncertain whether a court will apply the law governing the contract or the law of the situs, what precautions can a lawyer take in planning a transaction to insure so far as possible the application of a particular law?

3. See generally Hancock, "In the Parish of St. Mary le Bow, in the Ward of Cheap," 16 Stan.L.Rev. 561 (1964); Hancock, Equitable Conversion and the Land Taboo in Conflict of Laws, 17 Stan.L.Rev. 1095 (1965); Hancock, Full Faith and Credit to Foreign Laws and Judgments in Real Property Litigation, 18 Stan.L.Rev. 1299 (1966); Hancock, Conceptual Devices for Avoiding the Land Taboo in Conflict of Laws, 20 Stan.L.Rev. 1 (1967); Weintraub, Commentary on the Conflict of Laws §§ 8.1–8.22 (3d ed. 1986).

SECTION 2. MOVABLES, IN GENERAL *

A. SUCCESSION ON DEATH

RESTATEMENT, SECOND, CONFLICT OF LAWS **

§ 260. Intestate Succession to Movables

The devolution of interests in movables upon intestacy is determined by the law that would be applied by the courts of the state where the decedent was domiciled at the time of his death.

---

* See Restatement, Second, Conflict of Laws §§ 244–266.

Comment:

a. Scope of section. The rule of this Section applies to a decedent's interests in chattels, in rights embodied in a document and in rights that are not embodied in a document.

b. Rationale....

It is desirable that insofar as possible an estate should be treated as a unit and, to this end, that questions of intestate succession to movables should be governed by a single law. This is the law that would be applied by the courts of the state where the decedent was domiciled at the time of his death. This state would usually have the dominant interest in the decedent at the time.

Provided that they apply the common law rules of choice of law, the courts of the state where the decedent was domiciled at the time of his death would look to their own local law to determine what categories of persons are entitled to inherit upon intestacy....

§ 263. Validity and Effect of Will of Movables

(1) Whether a will transfers an interest in movables and the nature of the interest transferred are determined by the law that would be applied by the courts of the state where the testator was domiciled at the time of his death.

(2) These courts would usually apply their own local law in determining such questions.

Comment:

a. Scope of section. The ... law selected by application of the present rule determines the capacity of a person to make a will or to accept a legacy, the validity of a particular provision in the will, such as whether it violates the rule against perpetuities or constitutes a forbidden gift to a charity, and the nature of the estate created. Questions concerning the required form of the will and the manner of its execution also fall within the scope of the present rule. The rule applies to a decedent's interests in chattels, in rights embodied in a document and in rights that are not embodied in a document.

b. Rationale. For reasons stated in § 260, Comment *b*, questions relating to the validity of a will of movables and the rights created thereby

---

** Quoted with the permission of the copyright owner, The American Law Institute.

are determined by the law that would be applied by the courts of the state where the decedent was domiciled at the time of his death. These courts would usually apply their own local law to determine such questions as the testator's capacity to make a will, the nature of the estates that can validly be created and the categories of legatees to whom the testator may leave his movables. These courts would also usually apply their own local law in determining whether a legacy for charitable purposes is invalid, in whole or in part, because of statutory restrictions on the power of a testator to make charitable dispositions by will. ...

NOTES

1. Restatement Second § 260 comment b provides the rationale for applying the law of the decedent's domicile at death to testate and intestate succession: "This state would usually have the dominant interest the decedent at the time." Was this true for intestate succession in Estate of Jones, supra p. 7, or White v. Tennant, supra p. 11; for testate succession in In re Annesley, supra p. 441. Is a preferable rule that of Article 3(2) of the Hague Convention on the Law Applicable to Succession to the Estates of Deceased Persons, referring to the country in which the decedent was "habitually resident ... for ... five years [at] death.... [unless] in exceptional circumstances ... at the time of his death he was manifestly more closely connected with the State of which he was then a national"? See note, Succession Under Civil Law Concepts, p. 758, supra, and Note (2), p. 19, supra.

If as stated in Restatement Second § 260, comment b, "[i]t is desirable that insofar as possible an estate should be treated as a unit," should the law of the situs apply if the property is land and not movables? As indicated in the notes referred to in the preceding paragraph, both the Convention and most civil law countries apply the same law to personalty and realty in the estate.

2. More than thirty states provide for alternative places of reference to determine whether a will has been executed in proper form. Ester and Scoles, Estate Planning and the Conflict of Laws, 24 Ohio St.L.J. 270 (1963). The English Wills Act 1963 (11 and 12 Eliz. 2, chapter 44) provides numerous places of alternative reference. See p. 763, Note 2, supra.

3. The law of the testator's domicile at death determines whether certain events, such as divorce or the birth of a child to the testator after execution of a will involving movables, operate to revoke the will. Restatement, Second, Conflict of Laws § 263, Comment *i*. On the other hand, the law of the situs determines whether similar circumstances operate to revoke a will involving land. In re Estate of Barrie, 240 Iowa 431, 35 N.W.2d 658 (1949), p. 759, supra.

4. Some states provide by statute that their own local law shall be applied to govern the validity and effect of the will of a non-resident testator on local movables if the testator has expressed a desire in his will to have this law applied. See, e.g. Ill.Comp.Stat.Ann. ch. 755 § 5/7–6; N.Y.E.P.T. Law § 3–5.1; Uniform Probate Code § 2–602. Are these provisions sound policy if, as in the case of the Illinois and New York statutes, they permit the testator to disinherit family members in a manner not permitted by the testator's domicile? Uniform Probate Code § 2–602 does not permit the testator or testatrix to choose law to evade the rules of the decedent's domicile concerning a surviving spouse's elective share. See In re Estate of Clark, p. 17, supra, In re Estate of Renard, Note (1), p. 19, supra. See generally Bright, Permitting a Non-Resident to Choose a Place of Probate, 95 Trusts and

Estates 865 (1956); Lowenfeld, "Tempora Mutantur"—Wills and Trusts and the Conflicts Restatement, 72 Colum.L.Rev. 382 (1972).

B. INTER VIVOS TRANSACTIONS

Although the Uniform Commercial Code, by unifying substantive law, decreases the frequency of conflicts problems in commercial property transactions, there are reasons why there remain a substantial number of cases in which the need to choose law arises. (1) The various state versions of the Code are not uniformly enacted or interpreted. (2) The frequent official revisions of the code, even if eventually adopted by all states, go into effect at different times in each state. For example, in 1986, there were three different "official" versions of § 9–103, the primary choice-of-law provision for secured transactions, in force in different states—the 1962, 1972, and 1977 revisions. Because all articles of the Code have again been recently revised or are in the process of revision, states are increasingly likely to have different versions of the Code in force. (3) The Code leaves in force various nonuniform state enactments, such as those concerning usury, small loans, and retail installment sales. (4) Even if all states eventually enact the same Code and construe it in the same manner, international transactions will continue to present conflicts problems.

RESTATEMENT, SECOND, CONFLICT OF LAWS *

TOPIC 3. MOVABLES

§ 244. Validity and Effect of Conveyance of Interest in Chattel

(1) The validity and effect of a conveyance of an interest in a chattel as between the parties to the conveyance are determined by the local law of the state which, with respect to the particular issue, has the most significant relationship to the parties, the chattel and the conveyance under the principles stated in § 6.

§ 245. Effect of Conveyance on Pre-Existing Interests in Chattel

(1) The effect of a conveyance upon a pre-existing interest in a chattel of a person who was not a party to the conveyance will usually be determined by the law that would be applied by the courts of the state where the chattel was at the time of the conveyance.

(2) These courts would usually apply their own local law in determining such questions.

Youssoupoff v. Widener

Court of Appeals of New York, 1927.
246 N.Y. 174, 158 N.E. 64.

[In 1921, the plaintiff, Prince Youssoupoff, a Russian refugee in dire need of funds, entered into an arrangement for the sale or transfer of two

---

* Quoted with the permission of the copyright owner, The American Law Institute.

Rembrandt portraits to the defendant, Mr. Widener of Pennsylvania, for one hundred thousand pounds. The negotiations were entered into in England. The writing evidencing the transaction was executed by the defendant in Pennsylvania and was sent to his agent in London, where it was executed by the plaintiff and duly delivered. Thereupon the portraits were delivered to the defendant's representative in London and were removed to the defendant's residence in Pennsylvania.

The writing evidencing the transaction provided: "... Mr. Widener grants to Prince Youssoupoff the right and privilege to be exercised on or before January 1, 1924 and not thereafter, of repurchasing these pictures at the purchase price, one hundred thousand pounds (£ 100,000) plus eight per cent. (8%) interest from this date to the date of repurchase; the repurchase to be made in the City of Philadelphia and the pictures to be redelivered to Prince Youssoupoff upon payment of the full purchase money.

"This privilege is a purely personal one granted to Prince Youssoupoff in recognition of his love and appreciation of these wonderful pictures. It is not assignable nor will it inure to the benefit of his heirs, assigns or representatives and Prince Youssoupoff represents that this privilege of repurchase will be exercised only in case he finds himself in the position again to keep and personally enjoy these wonderful works of art. ..."

In 1923, the plaintiff tendered to the defendant in Pennsylvania in money of the United States the equivalent of the stipulated one hundred thousand pounds plus interest at eight per cent., and demanded the return of the portraits; but the money so tendered was borrowed by the plaintiff from a lender with whom the portraits if returned by the defendant were to be pledged as security.]

■ LEHMAN, J. ... The defendant declined the tender and refused to transfer the pictures to the plaintiff. In effect the defendant's reply to the plaintiff's demand is that the defendant is the absolute owner of the pictures under the contract of sale, subject only to the right of the plaintiff to repurchase the pictures in accordance with the terms contained in the contract. That right is, by its terms, to be exercised only in case the plaintiff "finds himself in the position again to keep and personally enjoy these wonderful works of art." It may not be exercised for the purpose of enabling the plaintiff to transfer the pictures to another....

The plaintiff has brought this action in equity to compel the defendant to accept the money tendered to him, and to transfer the pictures.

It is said ... that under the law of Pennsylvania, where Mr. Widener resided, where he kept his collection of paintings and where any option to repurchase must be exercised, the contract between the parties hereto would be conclusively presumed to be a mortgage, regardless of the actual intention of the parties, and enforced only as a mortgage. The courts below have made no finding to that effect. We have not analyzed the testimony or the Pennsylvania decisions introduced in evidence to determine whether they would support such a finding. We hold that the law of England and not the law of Pennsylvania governs this transaction.

The general rule is well established that the construction and legal effect of a contract for the transfer of, or the creation of a lien upon, property situated in the jurisdiction where the contract is made is governed by the law of that jurisdiction. (Goetschius v. Brightman, 245 N.Y. 186, 156 N.E. 360.) Various grounds, however, are urged upon which it is said that this case presents an exception to the general rule. We dispose of them briefly....

The fact that Mr. Widener obtained the pictures with the intention of removing them to his home, does not change the general rule. It is true that it has been held in some States that where property, transferred by contract in one jurisdiction, must be removed to another jurisdiction in order to carry out the purpose of the contract, the construction and effect of the contract may be governed, in accordance with the intention of the parties, not by the law of the jurisdiction where the contract was made and where the property was then situated, but by the law of the jurisdiction to which the property was removed thereafter and where the parties intended that it should be permanently located. (Beggs v. Bartels, 73 Conn. 132, 46 A. 874.) We need not now consider whether upon a similar state of facts we should reach a similar conclusion. If under such circumstances exception to the general rule may be created, that may be done only for the purpose of carrying out a presumed intention of the parties. Here the parties have given convincing evidence that the parties intended that the law of England should apply....

Finally, it is said that since the provisions for the repurchase of the paintings in Pennsylvania were the only executory provisions of the contract, we should construe the contract according to the law of Pennsylvania where performance was to be made. (International Text Book Co. v. Connelly, 206 N.Y. 188, 99 N.E. 722.) The contract in effect is primarily a bill of sale of the paintings, and was so intended. The right to repurchase was merely an incident to the transfer. The transfer of title was completed simultaneously with the signing of the contract. The parties certainly did not intend the law of Pennsylvania should apply to the transfer of property completed in England by contract made and dated there and by delivery accepted there. Under the law of England, full ownership was then transferred to the defendant, subject only to a condition that plaintiff should have a limited right to repurchase in Pennsylvania. Since full ownership had then been transferred to the defendant, and the plaintiff no longer held an equity of redemption, he might regain the pictures only by exercising his option of repurchase in accordance with the provisions of the contract. If we assume that the parties intended that the law of Pennsylvania should apply to the provisions giving an option of repurchase, and construe those provisions accordingly (Hamlyn & Co. v. Talisker Distillery, [1894] Appeal Cases 202), we must begin construction upon the basis, fatal to plaintiff's claim, that these provisions apply to property of which the defendant is the full owner and in which the plaintiff has no equity of redemption....

Judgment affirmed, etc.

NOTES

1. When faced with the question of what law governs a consensual transaction involving movables, should a court adopt the approach ordinarily used in contracts cases, i.e., "place of making," "place of performance," or an approach based on property concepts, i.e., "title," "situs"? Which approach was used in the principal case?

2. See Cavers, The Conditional Seller's Remedies and the Choice-of-Law Process, 35 N.Y.U.L.Rev. 1126 (1960).

Cammell v. Sewell
Court of Exchequer Chamber, 1860.
5 Hurl. & N. 728.

[Action of trover for lumber, with a count for money had and received. The plaintiffs were English underwriters and the defendants were London merchants.

The lumber had been part of a cargo shipped on board a Prussian vessel from a Russian port to a firm in Hull, England, and insured with the plaintiffs.

The Prussian ship put into Norwegian waters in consequence of the shifting of the deck cargo, and was driven on rocks off the Norwegian coast. The cargo was unloaded, and the master of the ship applied to a Norwegian official to fix a day for the sale of the cargo at auction. This was done and the cargo was sold to one Clausen. The plaintiffs, having paid the Hull firm as for a total loss, instituted proceedings in Norway against the master and the purchaser of the cargo to have the action disavowed, but the court confirmed it. After the auction sale but before the judicial confirmation, the purchaser at the auction sale forwarded the lumber to the defendants in London, who refused to deliver it to the plaintiffs on demand.

The present action was thereupon instituted. After a verdict for the plaintiffs, subject to a special case, in the Court of Exchequer, the verdict for the plaintiffs was set aside and a verdict entered for the defendants. (3 Hurl. & N. 617.)

Proceedings in error were instituted in the Exchequer Chamber.]

■ CROMPTON, J. In this case the majority of the Court are of opinion that the judgment of the Court of Exchequer should be affirmed. At the same time we are by no means prepared to agree with the Court of Exchequer in thinking the judgment of the Diocesan Court in Norway conclusive as a judgment in rem, nor are we satisfied that the defendants in the present action were estopped by the judgment of that Court or what was relied on as a judicial proceeding at the auction. It is not, however, necessary for us to express any decided opinion on these questions, as we think that the case should be determined on the real merits as to the passing of the property.

If we are to recognize the Norwegian law, and if according to that law the property passed by the sale in Norway to Clausen as an innocent purchaser, we do not think that the subsequent bringing the property to England can alter the position of the parties.... [I]t appears to us that the questions are—did the property by the law of Norway vest in him as an innocent purchaser? and are we to recognize that law? ... The conclusion which we draw from the evidence is, that by the law of Norway the captain, under circumstances such as existed in this case, could not, as between himself and his owners, or the owners of the cargo, justify the sale, but that he remained liable and responsible to them for a sale not justified under the circumstances; whilst, on the other hand, an innocent purchaser would have a good title to the property bought by him from the agent of the owners.

It does not appear to us that there is anything so barbarous or monstrous in this state of the law as that we can say that it should not be recognized by us.... We think that the law on this subject was correctly stated by the Lord Chief Baron in the course of the argument in the Court below, where he says "If personal property is disposed of in a manner binding according to the law of the country where it is, that disposition is binding everywhere." And we do not think that it makes any difference that the goods were wrecked, and not intended to be sent to the country where they were sold. We do not think that the goods which were wrecked here would on that account be the less liable to our laws as to market overt, or as to the landlord's right of distress, because the owner did not foresee that they would come to England....

... [A]s, on the evidence before us, we cannot treat Clausen otherwise than as an innocent purchaser, and as the law of Norway appears to us, on the evidence, to give a title to an innocent purchaser, we think that the property vested in him, and in the defendants as subpurchasers from him, and that, having once so vested, it did not become devested by its being subsequently brought to this country, and, therefore, that the judgment of the Court of Exchequer should be affirmed.

■ BYLES, J. This alleged law of Norway ... placing the cargo at the caprice of the master, seems to me to be a law not only of an alarming nature, but so far as I can perceive without precedent, without necessity and at variance with the general maritime law of the world, at least as understood in this country. I think the comity of nations would not recognize a law of this character ...

I admit, if there be a judgment in rem founded on a recognized law, and pronounced by a competent tribunal of the country where a movable chattel then is, that that judgment determines and changes the property everywhere and between all persons, as in the cases of a condemnation of goods in the Exchequer, or of a ship in a lawful prize Court.

... I collect that the opinion of the rest of the Court is that there has been no judgment in rem, and I entirely agree with them.... At the time of that judgment the goods in question were not within the jurisdiction of the Diocesan Court, for they had long before arrived in England.

As to the effect of the same judgment as a judgment *inter partes,* I collect that both the parties to this action are not in privity with that judgment, because the defendant's title to the deals had accrued before the judgment. This is not a mere objection of form against the justice of the case. For that judgment is contended to be an estoppel, and not examinable....

But as the rest of the Court are of a different opinion on the first point, the judgment of the Court of Exchequer will be affirmed.

Judgment affirmed.

NOTES

1. Is the problem presented by the principal case essentially different from that in Youssoupoff v. Widener? If so, does it call for the application of a different choice of law rule?

2. The principal case was not an action to determine title but a suit in trover for conversion. Where did the defendant commit the alleged exercise of dominion or refusal to return on demand? What is normally the controlling law in tort cases?

3. For a modern case citing Cammell v. Sewell and reaching the same result, see Winkworth v. Christie, Manson and Woods, Ltd. [1980] 2 W.L.R. 937.

4. The Hague Convention on the Law Applicable to the Estates of Deceased Persons, approved in 1988 by the Hague Conference on Private International Law, makes no distinction between interests in real and personal property. A similar approach has been taken in the Uniform Probate Code § 2–201.

C. SECURITY TRANSACTIONS

Green v. Van Buskirk

Supreme Court of the United States, 1866, 1868.
72 U.S. (5 Wall.) 307, 18 L.Ed. 599; 74 U.S. (7 Wall.) 139, 19 L.Ed. 109.

[Bates, who lived in New York, executed and delivered to Van Buskirk, who lived in the same State, a chattel mortgage on certain iron safes which were then in the City of Chicago. Two days after this, Green, who was also a citizen of New York, being ignorant of the existence of the mortgage, sued out a writ of attachment in the courts of Illinois, levied on the safes, and subsequently had them sold in satisfaction of the judgment obtained in the attachment suit. There was no appearance or contest in this attachment suit, and Van Buskirk was not a party to it, although he could have made himself such party and contested the right of Green to levy on the safes, being expressly authorized by the laws of Illinois so to do. It was conceded that by the law of Illinois mortgages of personal property, until acknowledged and recorded, were void as against third persons. Subsequently Van

Buskirk sued Green in New York for the value of the safes mortgaged to him by Bates, of which Green had thus received the proceeds. The courts of New York gave judgment in favor of Van Buskirk, holding that the law of New York was to govern and not the law of Illinois, although the property was situated in the latter State, and that the title passed to Van Buskirk by the execution of the mortgage. The cause was then brought to this court and first considered upon a motion to dismiss for want of jurisdiction.*]

JUSTICE MILLER delivered the opinion of the Court:

... It is claimed by the plaintiff in error that the faith and credit which these proceedings have by law and usage in the state of Illinois, were denied to them by the decision of the courts of New York, and that in doing so, they decided against a right claimed by him under section 1, article IV of the Constitution and the act of Congress of May 26, 1790, on that subject....

The record before us contains the pleadings in the case, the facts found by the court, and the conclusions of law arising thereon.

Among the latter, the court decides "that, by the law of the state of New York, the title to the property passed on the execution and delivery of the instrument under the facts found in the case, and overreached the subsequent attachment of the state of Illinois and actual prior possession under it at the suit of defendant, although he was a creditor having a valid and fair debt against Bates, and had no notice of the previous assignment and sale. And that the law of the state of New York was to govern the transaction and not the law of the state of Illinois, where the property was situated." ...

It is said that Van Buskirk, being no party to the proceedings in Illinois, was not bound by them, but was at liberty to assert his claim to the property in any forum that might be open to him; and, strictly speaking, this is true. He was not bound by way of estoppel, as he would have been if he had appeared and submitted his claim, and contested the proceedings in attachment. He has a right to set up any title to the property which is superior to that conferred by the attachment proceedings; and he has the further right to show that the property was not liable to the attachment—a right from which he would have been barred if he had been a party to that suit. And this question of the liability of the property in controversy to that attachment is the question which was raised by the suit in New York, and which was there decided. That court said that this question must be decided by the laws of the state of New York, because that was the domicil of the owner at the time the conflicting claims to the property originated.

We are of opinion that the question is to be decided by the effect given by the laws of Illinois, where the property was situated, to the proceedings in the courts of that state, under which it was sold.

* The statement of facts is taken from the outline of the principal case given in Cole v. Cunningham, 133 U.S. 107, 132.

There is no little conflict of authority on the general question as to how far the transfer of personal property by assignment or sale, made in the country of the domicil of the owner, will be held to be valid in the courts of the country where the property is situated, when these are in different sovereignties.... And it may be conceded that as a question of comity, the weight of ... authority is in favor of the proposition that such transfers will, generally, be respected by the courts of the country where the property is located, although the mode of transfer may be different from that prescribed by the local law....

But, after all, this is a mere principle of comity between the courts, which must give way when the statutes of the country where property is situated, or the established policy of its laws prescribe to its courts a different rule....

We do not here decide that the proceedings in the state of Illinois have there the effect which plaintiff claims for them; because that must remain to be decided after argument on the merits of the case. But we hold that the effect which these proceedings have there, by the law and usage of that state was a question necessarily decided by the New York courts, and that it was decided against the claim set up by plaintiff in error under the constitutional provision and statute referred to, and that the case is, therefore, properly here for review.

The motion to dismiss the writ of error is overruled....

■ JUSTICE NELSON, dissenting.... The court below decided that the instrument was to be governed by the law of the state of New York, where it was made, and which was the domicil of the parties.... The question here is whether, in so deciding, the court denied full faith, credit, and effect to the judgment in Illinois. In other words, did the court, in holding that the prior assignment was not fraudulent and void but valid and effectual to transfer the title, thereby discredit the Illinois judgment? The answer to the question, I think, is obvious. These assignees were not parties to the judgment. It could not bind them. They were free, therefore, to set up and insist upon this prior title to the property; and, if there was nothing else in the case, it is clear the junior attachment could not hold it....

I agree, if the attachment had been levied before the assignment, and the court had given effect to this instrument over the levy, it might be said that full faith and credit had not been given to it; but, being posterior, these proceedings could not have the effect, per se, to displace the assignment as against a stranger. Another element must first be shown, namely; fraud or other defect in the instrument, to render it inoperative.

My conclusion is that the regularity of the attachment proceedings was not called in question in the court below; but, on the contrary, full force and credit were given to them, and the case should be dismissed for want of jurisdiction.

■ JUSTICE SWAYNE concurs in this opinion.

[The case then came up for final adjudication. 7 Wall. 139 (1868).]

■ JUSTICE DAVIS delivered the opinion of the Court:

That the controversy in this case was substantially ended when this court refused, 5 Wall. 312, to dismiss the writ of error for want of jurisdiction, is quite manifest, by the effort which the learned counsel for the defendants in error now made, to escape the force of that decision....

This decision, supported as it was by reason and authority, left for consideration on the hearing of the case, the inquiry, whether the Supreme Court of New York did give to the attachment proceedings in Illinois the same effect they would have received in the courts of that State....

[The court here stated the law of Illinois, and showed that under that law the purchaser at the attachment sale would prevail over the New York mortgagee.]

... And as the effect of the levy, judgment and sale is to protect Green if sued in the courts of Illinois, and these proceedings are produced for his own justification, it ought to require no argument to show that when sued in the court of another State for the same transaction, and he justifies in the same manner, that he is also protected. Any other rule would destroy all safety in derivative titles, and deny to a State the power to regulate the transfer of personal property within its limits and to subject such property to legal proceedings....

The judgment of the Supreme Court of the State of New York is reversed, and the cause remitted to that court, with instructions to enter judgment for the plaintiff in error.

NOTES

1. In the principal case, was full faith and credit denied to a judgment of the courts of Illinois or to that state's law? Would the decision be followed today?

2. Does the decision in the principal case require, as a compliance with full faith and credit, that in a case involving tangible things the reference to the law of the state of the situs be to that state's conflict of laws rules?

Choice-of-law questions involving secured transactions in movables fall into two broad categories: those arising between the secured creditor and his immediate debtor and those involving the rights of the creditor against some third person, such as an attaching creditor or a transferee of the immediate debtor.

Today, such questions are governed in large measure by the Uniform Commercial Code, which has obtained almost universal enactment throughout the United States. Initially, there was some question whether the rights inter se of the secured creditor and his immediate debtor were governed exclusively by Section 1–105 (which is set forth at p. 543, supra) or also by Sections 9–102 and 9–103. This uncertainty was removed by a 1972 revision of the Code which removes all references to choice of law in Section 9–102 and amends Section 9–103 to deal exclusively with problems of perfection of security interests and the effect of perfection or non-perfection. As a result, it is now clear that choice-of-law questions arising between the secured creditor and his immediate debtor are governed by Section 1–105.

John J. Shanahan v. George B. Landers Construction Co.

United States Court of Appeals, First Circuit, 1959.
266 F.2d 400.

[The plaintiff, a construction corporation of New Hampshire with its principal office there, entered a conditional sale contract for the purchase of a trench hoe for about $25,000 plus a finance charge f.o.b. Burlington, Vermont. The seller was John J. Shanahan, Inc., a Massachusetts corporation with its principal place of business in that state. The conditional sale contract and the accompanying promissory note were executed by the plaintiff in New Hampshire in 1953, and the conditional sale contract was signed by the seller at its place of business in Massachusetts where the note and the conditional sale contract were assigned with recourse to a finance company.

The hoe was delivered to the plaintiff in Vermont. On the completion of the construction job there, the plaintiff shipped it to New Hampshire for use on a job in that state, where it remained until it was repossessed.

The plaintiff never met any installments when they fell due, but on December 20, 1954 it paid all accrued installments, which amounted to about $17,000. The next installment due on December 28th was not met, and on January 6, 1955, an agent of the finance company repossessed the hoe in New Hampshire without the knowledge of the plaintiff and removed it to Massachusetts. There, after payment to the finance company of the balance due, the seller, Shanahan, Inc., without notice to the plaintiff, sold the hoe to Shanahan, the individual, for the balance due by plaintiff of about $8,300, and after making repairs and changes Shanahan sold it to a third party for about $15,000.

The plaintiff, the purchaser under the conditional sale contract, brought this action for the conversion of the hoe in the federal court in Massachusetts. The defendants were the seller, Shanahan, Inc., as well as Shanahan, the individual and the finance company. The District Court gave judgment for the plaintiff, and the defendants appeal.]

■ WOODBURY, CIRCUIT JUDGE. ... The court below ruled and the parties concede that if the law of Massachusetts applies the plaintiff has no claim for the reason that the defendants in repossessing the hoe as they did acted in full compliance with the provisions of the Massachusetts Conditional Sales Act, Mass.G.L., c. 255 §§ 11–13H, and thus extinguished the plaintiff's right of redemption. On the other hand, it was ruled by the court below and is likewise conceded by the parties, that the opposite result would have to be reached if the law of New Hampshire applies. The reason for this is that repossession by a conditional vendor without prior notice in writing to the conditional vendee, plus immediate removal of the repossessed property from the state, violates the provisions of N.H.Rev.Stat. c. 361 §§ 18, 19 which require a conditional vendor either to give written notice to the conditional vendee not more than forty nor less than twenty days prior to retaking, or else, after retaking without such notice, to retain the property within the state for ten days after repossession, during which time on tender of the amount in default under the contract, with interest, expenses of retaking and costs of keeping and storage, the conditional vendee "may redeem the goods and become entitled to take possession of them and to continue in the performance of the contract as if no default had occurred." The District Court ruled that the law of New Hampshire applied and we agree.

The court below quite rightly recognized that it must follow the choice of law rules of the forum, Massachusetts, in deciding what law to apply.... Also the court below very appropriately began its study of the problem presented by the case at bar with consideration of Jewett, Inc. v. Keystone Driller Co., 1933, 282 Mass. 469, 185 N.E. 369, 371, 87 A.L.R. 1298, a case in some respects like the present, on which the appellants heavily rely.

The Jewett case, like the one at bar, was an action for conversion of ... a gasoline powered shovel brought by a conditional vendee against a repossessing conditional vendor. The plaintiff-vendee ... was a Massachusetts corporation with its principal office in that Commonwealth and the defendant-vendor was a Pennsylvania corporation with its principal place of business in that Commonwealth but with a sales agent in Massachusetts. The contract of conditional sale of the gasoline powered shovel was executed in Massachusetts and the purchase price was payable at a Massachusetts bank. It does not appear where the shovel actually was when the contract was signed but it was delivered as the contract required F.O.B. Manchester, New Hampshire. It was used for a short time in New Hampshire and then remained in storage in that state until, the buyer being in default, the defendant-vendor took possession of the shovel, immediately removed it to Connecticut, and there sold it, without giving notice to the plaintiff-vendee as the New Hampshire statute required.

On these basic facts a divided court held that the law of Massachusetts, rather than the law of New Hampshire, applied. Mr. Justice Crosby writing for the majority rested the conclusion that the law of Massachusetts governed on the [ground that this law governed the contract between the parties].

Justice Lummus in dissent rejected characterization of the problem as one of contract. He treated the problem instead as one of property, saying: ... "that the right of redemption given by the New Hampshire statute applied to the shovel, either because the shovel was in New Hampshire when the interests of the parties under the conditional sale became vested ... or on the ... ground ... that the law of the state in which the chattel is situated when foreclosure or redemption proceedings are begun shall govern...."

From the decision in the Jewett case we may infer that the Supreme Judicial Court of the Commonwealth of Massachusetts, were it deciding the case at bar, would treat the fact that the power hoe was delivered in Vermont as "immaterial." For here, as in Jewett, the evidence warrants the inference that delivery in Vermont was only for the convenience of the purchaser in performing a single contract in that state and on completion of its work there the plaintiff-purchaser intended to remove the shovel to its headquarters in New Hampshire or to some other place, in New Hampshire or elsewhere, where it might obtain another contract. This eliminates the law of Vermont from our consideration. Furthermore, we may also infer from the Jewett case that under circumstances like the present the Massachusetts court would not concern itself with the law of the state where the shovel was when the contract for its conditional sale arose and the rights of the parties with respect to it were created. We say this because there is no reference in the majority opinion in the Jewett case to the place where the shovel was when the contract for its conditional sale was entered into. In choosing Massachusetts law as the law to apply, the majority gave controlling consideration to the place where the contract of conditional sale was entered into, and did not even mention the place where the shovel was when that contract was made.... Indeed, under circumstances like the present, to apply the law of the place where the chattel is at the time of contracting might well produce the incongruous result of applying the law of some state with which neither the parties nor the transaction had any substantial contacts whatever. That is to say, it might require application of the law of the state where the chattel was manufactured (we were given to understand at oral argument that the power hoe involved herein was manufactured in a middle western state), and where after shipment that chattel might never be again and where the parties neither contracted nor resided. It might even require application of the law of a state through which the chattel was only in transit from the state of its manufacture to the state of its delivery. Thus ... it would seem that under Massachusetts law as expounded in the Jewett case there is no occasion for us to send this case back to the court below to find out where the power hoe actually was on the date of its conditional sale—whether it was still in the state of its manufacture, wherever that was, or in some other state on its way to its place of delivery in Vermont.

As we understand the law of Massachusetts our choice lies between the law of Massachusetts and the law of New Hampshire. The appellants strongly urge that the Jewett case requires us to choose the law of Massachusetts. We do not think so.

The court below distinguished Jewett on the ground that the majority of the court in that case placed emphasis on the fact that the shovel was not permanently located in New Hampshire but was only delivered in that state for the convenience of the purchaser, who was a citizen of Massachusetts, whereas in the instant case the purchaser was a New Hampshire corporation with its principal place of business in that state. On these facts the District Court thought the majority in the Jewett case might well have reached the result advocated by the dissenting justice.... it does seem to us ... that the Supreme Judicial Court of Massachusetts ... would not be disposed to extend the rule of the Jewett case to facts like those in the case at bar, where the purchaser of the chattel was not a Massachusetts corporation but a New Hampshire corporation with its headquarters in that state and where in addition the shovel was not only located in New Hampshire when it was repossessed, but also where the shovel would presumably be kept when not in use on out-of-state jobs....

[The Court of Appeals concluded that the New Hampshire law governed and the statute of that state relating to conditional sales had not been complied with. But it found the District Court had erred in the amount of the award to the plaintiff, $12,500, so it remanded the case.]

NOTES

1. The Shanahan opinion provides a good example of the reasoning that was employed by the courts prior to the adoption of the Uniform Commercial Code. Was not the result reached sensible and desirable? Could the court arrive at the same result now that Massachusetts has adopted the Code? Choice of law between vendor and vendee would be governed by § 1–105, which is in the process of being revised. See p. 543, supra, and Notes (1) and (2), p. 543, supra.

2. For discussion of the Shanahan case, see Cavers, The Conditional Seller's Remedies and the Choice-of-Law Process, 35 N.Y.U.L.Rev. 1126 (1960).

We turn now to a consideration of the law governing the rights of the secured creditor against persons other than the immediate debtor. We are concerned with a situation where a chattel has first been subjected to a security interest in state X and then is taken to state Y where it becomes involved in a transaction with a third person who is unaware of the existence of the security interest. Typically, the secured creditor is a conditional vendor or a chattel mortgagee and the third person a purchaser of the chattel or an attaching creditor. The question is whether the interests of the secured creditor or of the third person should be preferred. This question is now governed by § 9–103 of the Uniform Commercial Code.

Prior to the nearly universal adoption of the Uniform Commercial Code, the usual position of the courts was that the secured creditor would be preferred over the third person if (a) the security interest had been perfected under the law of the state (X) where the chattel was situated at the time and (b) the chattel was taken to another state (Y) without the creditor's knowledge or consent and was there dealt with by the third person before the secured creditor had become aware of the chattel's presence in the state. On the other hand, the third person would usually be preferred over the secured creditor if the security interest had not been perfected in state Y and either the chattel had been taken to Y with the creditor's knowledge and consent or the creditor had become aware of the chattel's presence in Y prior to the time that it was there dealt with by the third person.

For automobiles the rule may have been somewhat different. There was at least a tendency to prefer the interests of the third person over those of the secured creditor in all situations where a title certificate which did not show the existence of the security interest had been issued for the automobile in Y prior to the time that it was there dealt with by the third person. Restatement, Second, Conflict of Laws, §§ 252–253, 1 Gilmore, Security Interests in Personal Property 551–552, 595–632 (1965); Leary, Horse and Buggy Lien Law and Migratory Automobiles, 96 U. of Pa.L.Rev. 455 (1948); Vernon, Recorded Chattel Security Interests in the Conflicts of Laws, 47 Iowa L.Rev. 346 (1962).

Significant portions of § 9–103 of the 1972 version of the Uniform Commercial Code are set forth below:

§ 9–103. Perfection of Security Interests in Multiple State Transactions

(1) Documents, instruments and ordinary goods.

(a) This subsection applies to documents and instruments and to goods other than those covered by a certificate of title described in subsection (2)....

(b) Except as otherwise provided in this subsection, perfection and the effect of perfection or non-perfection of a security interest in collateral are governed by the law of the jurisdiction where the collateral is when the last event occurs on which is based the assertion that the security interest is perfected or unperfected.

(c) If the parties to a transaction creating a purchase money security interest in goods in one jurisdiction understand at the time that the security interest attaches that the goods will be kept in another jurisdiction, then the law of the other jurisdiction governs the perfection and the effect of perfection or non-perfection of the security interest from the time it attaches until thirty days after the debtor receives possession of the goods and thereafter if the goods are taken to the other jurisdiction before the end of the thirty-day period.

(d) When collateral is brought into and kept in this state while subject to a security interest perfected under the law of the jurisdiction from which the collateral was removed, the security interest remains perfected, but if action is required by Part 3 of this Article to perfect the security interest,

(i) if the action is not taken before the expiration of the period of perfection in the other jurisdiction or the end of four months after the collateral is brought into this state, whichever period first expires, the security interest becomes unperfected at the end of that period and is thereafter deemed to have been unperfected as against a person who became a purchaser after removal;

(ii) if the action is taken before the expiration of the period specified in subparagraph (i), the security interest continues perfected thereafter....

(2) Certificate of title.

(a) This subsection applies to goods covered by a certificate of title issued under a statute of this state or of another jurisdiction under the law of which indication of a security interest on the certificate is required as a condition of perfection.

(b) Except as otherwise provided in this subsection, perfection and the effect of perfection or non-perfection of the security interest are governed by the law (including the conflict of laws rules) of the jurisdiction issuing the certificate until four months after the goods are removed from that jurisdiction and thereafter until the goods are registered in another jurisdiction, but in any event not beyond surrender of the certificate. After the expiration of that period, the goods are not covered by the certificate of title within the meaning of this section.

(c) Except with respect to the rights of a buyer described in the next paragraph, a security interest, perfected in another jurisdiction otherwise than by notation on a certificate of title, in goods brought into this state and thereafter covered by a certificate of title issued by this state is subject to the rules stated in paragraph (d) of subsection (1).

(d) If goods are brought into this state while a security interest therein is perfected in any manner under the law of the jurisdiction from which the goods are removed and a certificate of title is issued by this state and the certificate does not show that the goods are subject to the security interest or that they may be subject to security interests not shown on the certificate, the security interest is subordinate to the rights of a buyer of the goods who is not in the business of selling goods of that kind to the extent that he gives value and receives delivery of the goods after issuance of the certificate and without knowledge of the security interest. ...

NOTES

1. For an extensive discussion of the original and amended versions of §§ 9–102 and 9–103 and of many of the leading cases, see Weintraub, Commentary on the Conflict of Laws 468–510 (3d ed. 1986). See also Adams, The 1972 Official Text of the Uniform Commercial Code: Analysis of Conflict of Laws Provision, 45 Miss.L.J. 281 (1974).

2. The movement of motor vehicles from state to state gives rise to difficult problems involving the conflicting interests of a secured creditor and a bona fide purchaser. At the present time all, or nearly all, of the states have adopted certificate-of-title laws which provide for the notation of the security interests on the certificate. There are, however, significant differences among these laws. In some states, perfection of the security interest is completed by the notation of the interest on the certificate of title or by the issuance of a new certificate after such notation. Other states provide that perfection is complete as soon as delivery of the appropriate papers has been made by the secured creditor to the proper official, even though the interest is not noted on the certificate of title or indeed even though no certificate is ever issued.

3. Section 9–103 was further amended in 1977 and 1994, but these amendments did not affect the provisions quoted above. A major revision of § 9–103 is now underway. For documents, instruments and ordinary goods, the current draft proposes eliminating reference to the situs of the collateral in § 9–103(1)(b) and instead referring to the law of the state where the debtor is located, which present § 9–103(3) uses for accounts, general intangibles, and mobile goods. The draft revision also proposes changing the definition of the debtor's location from its "chief executive office" (§ 9–103(3)(d)) to "its jurisdiction of organization."

Gordon v. Clifford Metal Sales Co.
Supreme Court of Rhode Island, 1992.
602 A.2d. 535.

[Fleet National Bank loaned money to Clifford Metal Sales, a Rhode Island Company, and perfected a security interest in all Clifford's assets, then owned for thereafter acquired, by filing a financing statement with the Rhode Island Secretary of State. Maksteel, a Canadian corporation, then sold steel to Clifford. The steel was delivered to Clifford's place of business in Rhode Island. Each bill of lading stated that "this material remains the property of Maksteel . . . until full payment." Clifford was placed in receivership. Maksteel was not paid for the steel. Under Canadian law, Maksteel would be entitled to reclaim the steel or its proceeds. The court affirmed a judgment in favor of Fleet National Bank, ruling that its rights as a creditor with a perfected security interest in the steel prevailed over those of Maksteel.]

■ MURRAY, J. . . . [The court quotes Uniform Commercial Code § 9–103(1)(b).] Maksteel asserts, and we agree, that the most important function of the choice-of-law rules is to make the interstate and international systems work well. Maksteel's argument relating to the needs of the interstate and international system, however, mistakenly concerns only the original parties to the contract, Maksteel and Clifford. A critical aspect of this dispute that simply cannot be ignored is the fact that this dispute no longer involves only the original parties to the contract. There now exist other interests to be considered, those of the receiver and of Fleet, as well as other potential creditors of Clifford. . . .

Creditors or potential buyers of a Rhode Island corporation's assets rely upon the filing requirements established under the code for knowledge of the existence of a security interest or lien with respect to the assets of that corporation. As provided under the code provisions, such records are required to be filed in the state in which the goods are located. Thus, in a situation wherein third parties such as Fleet and the receiver have relied on the provisions of such filing requirements, the needs of a uniform and consistent international system can only be served by application of the code. To conclude otherwise would leave third parties, whether from Rhode Island, a neighboring state, or Canada, without the ability to verify the existence or nonexistence of other interests in a corporation's assets. Such a result would only serve to destroy the "certainty, predictability and uniformity of result" so successfully created by the code with respect to secured transactions. Restatement (Second) Conflict of Laws § 6(f).

NOTE

Maksteel would have prevailed over Fleet National Bank if, before Clifford received the steel, Maksteel had filed a financing statement in Rhode Island and had notified Fleet that Maksteel has a purchase money security interest in the steel. Uniform Commercial Code § 9–312(3).

ISTIM, INC. v. CHEMICAL BANK, 78 N.Y.2d 342, 575 N.Y.S.2d 796, 581 N.E.2d 1042 (1991). Istim loaned money to Coronet Enterprises, a Utah mining company. The loan was not repaid and Istim obtained a default judgment in New York against Coronet. Previously Coronet had sued a third party in Illinois. This suit was settled favorably to Coronet. Coronet was represented in the Illinois suit by Willkie Farr & Gallagher, a New York law firm. Willkie Farr claims a statutory attorney's lien in the settlement fund, which would take priority over Istim's right to the funds. Under New York law, Willkie Farr's lien would be valid, but under Illinois law Willkie Farr would have waived its lien because it did not notify the defendant in the Illinois action that Willkie Farr claimed an attorney's lien in any money recovered in the action. The court ruled for Willkie Farr, applying New York law. "The purpose of the New York attorney's lien statute is to ensure that attorneys have the means to enforce the right to their fees. The basic purpose of the Illinois statute is the same, but its provision for notice to the judgment debtor in the action in which the lien was obtained is intended to benefit the judgment debtor.... [T]he judgment debtor in the Illinois lawsuit [is] not a party to the instant dispute [and] has nothing to do with Willkie's enforcement of its attorney's lien. Therefore, whatever interest Illinois might have in requiring Willkie to give notice to [the judgment debtor] is not now applicable.... Because Illinois' policy of requiring notice to judgment debtors is irrelevant, the only relevant policy interest is that of New York in having its attorneys fairly compensated.... We also reject Istim's contention that section 251 of the Restatement (Second) of Conflict of Laws requires the application of Illinois law. New York has not adopted that rule."

NOTE

Restatement Second of Conflict of Laws, § 251, "Validity and Effect of Security Interest in Chattel," referred to by the court, provides in subsection (2): "In the absence of an effective choice of law by the parties, greater weight will usually be given to the location of the chattel at the time that the security interest attached than to any other contact in determining the state of the applicable law."

OIL SHIPPING (BUNKERING) B.V. v. SONMEZ DENIZCILIK VE TICARET A.S., 10 F.3d 1015 (3d Cir.1993). Oil Shipping and Bayutur Trading supplied fuel oil to a ship of Turkish registry. Royal Bank of Scotland loaned money to the owners of the vessel and this loan was secured by a ship mortgage. Neither Oil Shipping nor Bayutur were paid for the oil and the loan from Royal Bank was in default. To recover payment for the fuel, Oil Shipping had the vessel seized when it arrived in Philadelphia. Bayutur intervened to enforce a maritime lien for the oil it had supplied in Turkey. Royal Bank intervened to enforce its mortgage. Under Turkish law, Bayutur would have prevailed, but under The United States Ship Mortgage Act, 46 U.S.C.A. § 31326(b), Royal Bank would prevail. Summary judgment for Royal Bank was affirmed. The court noted a split between the circuits on the proper choice-of-law approach in these circumstances. The First Circuit, in Payne v. SS Tropic Breeze, 423 F.2d 236 (1st Cir.1970), declared that Congress has the power "to condition access to our ports by foreign-owned vessels upon submission to our law" and held that the United States Ship Mortgage Act applied "to all foreclosures of foreign ship mortgages in American courts." 423 F.2d at 238–239. The Ninth Circuit, in Gulf Trading & Transportation, Co. v. M/V Tento, 694 F.2d 1191 (9th Cir.1982), cert. denied, 461 U.S. 929 (1983), however, chose United States law only after "weighing and evaluating the points of contacts between the transaction and the sovereign legal systems touched and affected by it." 694 F.2d at 1195. In *Oil Shipping,* the Third Circuit agreed with the First Circuit and applied the priority provision of the United States Ship Mortgage Act without a preliminary choice-of-law analysis. "Of controlling importance ... is the language of the statute itself. That too is in accord with our holding that Congress intended the Ship Mortgage Act to govern priorities among maritime liens in United States courts. [The Act] expressly applies to both domestic and foreign mortgage and lien transactions.... Indeed, the Ship Mortgage Act specifically speaks to a limited role for foreign law by making the preferred status of foreign mortgages dependent only on their compliance with the execution and registration requirements of the applicable foreign law.... To require any further choice or conflicts of law analysis in light of the limited express reference to the role of foreign law in the determination of maritime mortgages and liens and priority among them seems to us inconsistent with the intent of the Ship Mortgage Act as evidenced by its language and history."

NOTES

1. The First Circuit decision, with which the court agreed, justified applying the United States Ship Mortgage Act on the ground that Congress has the power "to condition access to our ports by foreign-owned vessels upon submission to our law." Does this justify applying United States law to a company that supplied fuel oil to the vessel in Turkey?

2. Macmillan Inc. v. Bishopsgate Investment Trust PLC, [1995] 1 W.L.R. 978 (Ch.), adjudicated the rights of several claimants to stock that the late Robert Maxwell had withdrawn from his companies' pension funds and had used as collateral for loans. In part, the result turned on the location of the stock at the time the loans were made. Under New York law, where the share register was maintained, the stock was considered to have its situs where the share certificates were located when the loans were made, which was England. Under English law, the shares were considered located where the share register was maintained, which was New York. The court held that the shares had their situs in New York: "For the purpose of English conflict of laws, however, the domestic rule must prevail, for the situs of a thing, like any other connecting factor, must be ascertained by reference to the lex fori." Id. at 991.

D. FUTURE INTERESTS AND TRUSTS *

Validity—Inter Vivos Trusts

Hutchison v. Ross
Court of Appeals of New York, 1933.
262 N.Y. 381, 187 N.E. 65, 89 A.L.R. 1007.

[Under an antenuptial agreement executed in 1902 in Quebec, where the parties to it were both domiciled, John Ross promised to establish by deed or will a trust fund of $125,000 for the benefit of his prospective wife. In 1916, after inheriting $10,000,000 from his father, Ross decided to set up a trust of $1,000,000 for the benefit of his wife and children, and he directed that some securities then in New York City be used for that purpose. The trust instrument was drawn in New York and was signed in Quebec by Ross and his wife. It was then sent back to New York City where the trustee, the Equitable Trust Company of New York, signed it and where the securities constituting the corpus of the trust were thereupon delivered to it. The trust instrument contained a clause to the effect that the $1,000,000 trust was in lieu of the $125,000 trust.

Ross had lost almost the entire fortune by 1926 when he discovered that under the law of Quebec an antenuptial agreement cannot be modified in any way and under that law the trust of $1,000,000 with respect to the wife was invalid. In consideration for a further loan, Ross promised a creditor to institute proceedings to have the trust set aside and to deliver the trust res to the creditor as collateral. Ross commenced the action and, upon his involuntary bankruptcy, his trustee in bankruptcy was substituted as party plaintiff. The trial court held that the attempted modification of the antenuptial agreement was governed by the law of Quebec, the matrimonial domicile, and, therefore, that the $1,000,000 trust was invalid. The Appellate Division reversed the trial court, and the plaintiff appealed.]

■ LEHMAN, J. ... With possible limitations, not relevant to the question here presented ... the rule is well established that the essential validity of a testamentary trust must be determined by the law of the decedent's domicile.... The plaintiff urges that the same rule should be applied to a conveyance in trust inter vivos, especially where such trust is established for the benefit of the wife and children of the settlor.

It cannot be gainsaid that there are expressions in the opinions of the courts of this State which support the plaintiff's contentions. In considering the effect of these expressions, we must give due weight to the circumstances under which they were made. The paucity of old judicial decisions upon conveyances in trust inter vivos, compared with the number of decisions upon testamentary trusts, shows that conveyances in trust inter vivos were comparatively rare. Thus the possible importance of drawing distinctions between the rules applicable to testamentary trusts

---

* See Restatement, Second, Conflict of Laws §§ 267–282.

and trusts inter vivos, was not apparent or brought to the attention of the courts.... Today the courts cannot close their eyes to the fact that trusts of personal property and securities are created by settlors during their lifetime for many purposes, and for the first time our court is called upon to decide directly the question whether conveyances in trust of securities made inter vivos shall be governed by the same rules as testamentary trusts or by the same rules as other conveyances inter vivos....

... [N]ow that we are called upon to decide that question, we must weigh other considerations not then apparent to the courts which seem to point logically to the need for differentiation between the rule to be applied to testamentary trusts and the rule to be applied to trusts inter vivos.

In all the affairs of life there has been a vast increase of mobility. Residence is growing less and less the focal point of existence and its practical effect is steadily diminishing. Men living in one jurisdiction often conduct their affairs in other jurisdictions, and keep their securities there. Trusts are created in business and financial centers by settlors residing elsewhere. A settlor, regardless of residence, cannot establish a trust to be administered here which offends our public policy. If we hold that a nonresident settlor may also not establish a trust of personal property here which offends the public policy of his domicile, we shackle both the nonresident settlor and the resident trustee.

Our courts have sought whenever possible to sustain the validity even of testamentary trusts to be administered in a jurisdiction other than the domicile of the testator.... In regard to other conveyances or alienations of personal property situated here, they have steadfastly applied the law of the jurisdiction where the personal property is situated.... Where a nonresident settlor establishes here a trust of personal property intending that the trust should be governed by the law of this jurisdiction, there is little reason why the courts should defeat his intention by applying the law of another jurisdiction....

... We may throw in the balance also expressions of public policy by the Legislature of this State. It has provided that: "Whenever a person being a citizen of the United States, or a citizen or a subject of a foreign country, wherever resident, creates a trust of personal property situated within this State at the time of the creation thereof, and declares in the instrument creating such trust that it shall be construed and regulated by the laws of this State, the validity and effect of such trust shall be determined by such laws." (Pers.Prop.Law; Const. Laws, ch. 41, sec. 12-a). It is true that the statute was enacted long after the creation of the trust now the subject of this litigation and the validity of the trust must, probably, be determined by the law as it then existed. The statute does not change retroactively a well-established rule of law. It merely establishes a definite public policy in a field where the rules of law were still fluid and undefined. When the courts are called upon to define these rules even as of an earlier date, they cannot entirely disregard this public policy....

It is said that the statute establishes a public policy only where there is an express declaration of intention in the instrument that it shall be construed and regulated by the laws of this State. Here there is no express declaration of intention, but the intention is implied in every act and word of the parties. The statute makes express declaration of intention conclusive, but a construction which would deny effect to intention appearing by implication would be unreasonable.... It follows that the validity of a trust of personal property must be determined by the law of this State, when the property is situated here and the parties intended that it should be administered here in accordance with the laws of this State....

The judgment in each action should be affirmed, with costs....

[Two judges dissented.]

Shannon v. Irving Trust Co.

Court of Appeals of New York, 1937.
275 N.Y. 95, 9 N.E.2d 792.

■ RIPPEY, JUDGE. ... a trust indenture was duly executed in the city of New York between Joseph G. Shannon, who was ... domiciled within the State of New Jersey, and the Irving Trust Company, a corporation organized and existing under the laws of the State of New York ... as trustee, whereby an irrevocable trust was created for the benefit, among others, of Goewey F. Shannon, wife of the settlor, and plaintiff herein, John Shannon, the son of the settlor, both of which beneficiaries were then ... domiciled within the State of New Jersey.... The trust created for the wife consisted of fixed items of income with the provision that all income in excess of the amount named should accumulate and become part of the principal of the trust. Up to December 26, 1933, when Goewey F. Shannon died, she continued to be ... domiciled within the State of New Jersey.... The trust instrument provided that upon her death the trustee should thereafter pay to the son, John Shannon, monthly, an aggregate annual income of $3,000 until the son should arrive at twenty-five years of age; that thereafter the income to the son, payable in monthly installments, should aggregate $5,000 per year until the son arrived at the age of thirty years; that thereafter the income to the son should be increased to $10,000 per year until he should arrive at the age of thirty-five years, after which time he should receive the full income from the trust estate for the balance of his life. All income in excess of the amounts thus payable to the son was directed to become a part of the trust estate. The trust instrument provided that, at the death of the son, the principal and accumulated income should pass to the issue of the son, or, if the son should die without issue surviving, to the Hill School of Pottstown, Pa. At the time the trust was created, the plaintiff was a resident of and domiciled within the State of New Jersey and his domicile has continued in that state to the time of the commencement of the action.... the trust instrument [provided] "The Trustee shall receive for its services, its necessary expenses and the commissions allowed testamentary trustees by the laws of the State of New

York instead of the laws of the State of New Jersey, but otherwise the laws of the State of New Jersey shall govern this trust indenture and any construction to be placed thereupon or interpretation thereof."

... [T]he plaintiff contended that the validity of the trust is to be determined by the laws of the State of New York and, inasmuch as the provisions for accumulations of income are void under section 16 of the Personal Property Law (Consol.Laws, c. 41) of the State of New York (Laws 1909, c. 45), the accumulations should be paid over to him as the person presumptively entitled to the next eventual estate ... while the defendants assert that the validity of the trust provisions is to be determined by the laws of the State of New Jersey, where the accumulations are valid.... The Appellate Division found that the trust was valid and certified to this court that a question of law was involved which ought to be here reviewed.

... Where the domicile of the owner of the res and the actual and business situs of the trust do not coincide, the law applicable to the interpretation, construction, and validity of the trust and the legal obligations arising out of it ... depend upon facts involved in and circumstances surrounding the particular case. In such a situation, the express or clearly implied intent of the settlor may control....

In the case at bar the execution of the trust instrument, the location of the res, the domicile of the trustee, and the place of administration of the trust are in the city of New York. The intent of the settlor that in all matters affecting the trust except remuneration of the trustee his domiciliary law shall govern is expressly stated in the body of the trust instrument.... The instrument should be construed and a determination of its validity made according to the law chosen by the settlor unless so to do is contrary to the public policy of this state....

Consideration of the New Jersey law and our own relating to perpetuities and accumulations of income will indicate that our policy in that connection is substantially the same as that of New Jersey.... The general policy of New Jersey and New York to put some limitation on the absolute suspension of the power of alienation of property and the accumulation of income from trusts is the same. Difference arises only as to the ending of the period during which such power to suspend alienation and to provide for accumulation of income may be permitted.

Under the facts existing in the case at bar, ... we find nothing in our public policy which forbids extending comity and applying the New Jersey law so as to carry out the wish of the settlor and sustain the trust. The positive direction contained in the trust instrument that the validity of the trust should be determined by the law of the settlor's domicile must prevail. Our decision here does not extend, however, beyond instances where conflict arises between the domiciliary law of the settlor and the law of the situs of the trust where the construction and validity of trusts inter vivos are involved.

Judgment affirmed.

NOTES

1. What common principle reconciles the Hutchison and Shannon decisions?

2. Would Shannon be differently decided if an interests analysis were applied? To what extent is the settlor's expressed choice of one applicable law to determine the trustee's reimbursement for expenses and commissions, and another to determine other aspects of the trust analogous to the problem of autonomy in contract choice of law? Is there anything wrong with the dépeçage employed here?

3. National Shawmut Bank v. Cumming, 325 Mass. 457, 91 N.E.2d 337 (1950). S, a Vermont resident, transferred a fund to a Massachusetts trustee to pay the income to himself for life and after his death to distribute it in equal shares among his widow, mother, brothers and sister; upon the death of the life beneficiaries, the corpus was to go to the settlor's nephews and nieces. After S's death, his widow claimed the principal of the trust contending that the trust was invalid under Vermont law since it was made for the purpose of depriving her of her inheritance rights. Held: Massachusetts law governs and under that law the trust is valid. "The general tendency of authorities ... is away from the adoption of the law of the settlor's domicil where the property, the domicil and place of business of the trustee and the place of administration intended by the settlor are in another State."

Did not Vermont have a greater interest than Massachusetts in the decision of the particular issue? Did the court place too much weight upon the policy in favor of upholding the validity of a trust? Was the issue one where the respective policies of Massachusetts and Vermont differed markedly?

4. See generally 5A Scott and Fratcher, The Law of Trusts ch. 14 (4th ed. 1989); Leflar et al., American Conflicts Law § 188 (4th ed. 1986); Scoles and Hay, Conflict of Laws 831–852 (2d ed. 1992).

RESTATEMENT, SECOND, CONFLICT OF LAWS: *

§ 270. Validity of Trust of Movables Created Inter Vivos

An inter vivos trust of interests in movables is valid if valid

(a) under the local law of the state designated by the settlor to govern the validity of the trust, provided that this state has a substantial relation to the trust and that the application of its law does not violate a strong public policy of the state with which, as to the matter at issue, the trust has its most significant relationship under the principles stated in § 6, or

(b) if there is no such effective designation, under the local law of the state with which, as to the matter at issue, the trust has its most significant relationship under the principles stated in § 6.

Comment:

a. The general principle. It is desirable that a trust should be treated as a unit and, to this end, that the trust as to all of the movables included therein, no matter where they happen to be at the time of the creation of the trust, should be governed by a single law. The creation of a trust is

---

* Quoted with the permission of the copyright owner, The American Law Institute.

different from an outright conveyance, which is either valid or invalid at the outset. In the case of a trust there is something more. In the first place, the creation of a trust establishes a continuing relationship between the trustee and the beneficiaries, and the state in which the trust is to be administered or which is otherwise connected with the trust may be different from the state in which the trust property is situated when the trust is created. In the second place, the trust property is ordinarily not a single movable but includes a group of movables which may be situated in different states at the time of the creation of the trust. The validity of a trust of movables, therefore, should be governed by a single law and not held valid as to some of the movables included in the trust and invalid as to others. This is true whether the movables consist of chattels, rights embodied in a document or intangibles. The rule of this Section is applicable to all these types of movables, no matter where they are situated at the time of the creation of the trust. It does not follow, however, that all questions of validity are determined by the same law. See Comment *e*.

Wilmington Trust Co. v. Wilmington Trust Co.

Supreme Court of Delaware, 1942.
26 Del.Ch. 397, 24 A.2d 309, 139 A.L.R. 1117.

[In 1920, William Donner as settlor created a trust through the deposit of personal property with the trustee, Dora Donner. The trust instrument provided that the income was to be paid to members of the settlor's family, and gave to each of his children a power of appointment over a part of the trust property. The settlor and the trustee were domiciled in New York and the trust was created there.

Subsequent to 1920, a successor trustee was named under a power given by the trust instrument. The new trustee was a trust company of Delaware.

In 1929, Joseph W. Donner, one of the settlor's children assumed to exercise the power of appointment given him. In doing so he set up trusts which were invalid under the New York rules against perpetuities but were valid under the law of Delaware.

From a decree of the Court of Chancery upholding the validity of the exercise of the power, an appeal was taken to the Supreme Court of Delaware.] *

■ LAYTON, CHIEF JUSTICE. ... The power of appointment exercised by Joseph W. Donner for the benefit of his two children had its origin in the donor's deed of trust; the provisions of the deed of appointment are viewed in law as though they had been embodied in that instrument.... The validity of the deed of appointment and of the rights and interests assigned thereunder depend upon the law of the jurisdiction in which the trust had its seat when the power of appointment was exercised.

---

* The statement of facts is taken in part from the report of the case on the original hearing in the Court of Chancery, 21 Del.Ch. 102, 180 A. 597.

The diversity of judicial opinion with respect to the discovery of the jurisdiction under whose law the validity of a trust inter vivos of intangible personal property is to be determined is such that no useful purpose will be served by an attempted analysis of the decisions. Courts have variously looked to the domicile of the donor, the place of execution of the trust instrument, the situs of the trust property, the place of administration of the trust, the domicile of the trustee, the domicile of the beneficiaries, and to the intent or desire of the donor, or to a combination of some of these denominators, in deciding the troublesome question of conflict of law.... The place of one's residence no longer is a sure indication of one's place of business; nor is ownership of property closely tied to residence. The domicile of the donor is, of course, a circumstance to be considered in the ascertainment of the seat of the trust; but courts, today, ... are disposed to take a more realistic and practical view of the problem; and the donor's domicile is no longer regarded as the decisive factor. The place of execution of the trust instrument and the domicile of the beneficiaries are not important indicia. The domicile of the trustee and the place of administration of the trust—quite generally the same place—are important factors; and the intent of the donor, if that can be ascertained, has been increasingly emphasized....

Where the donor in a trust agreement has expressed his desire, or if it pleases, his intent to have his trust controlled by the law of a certain state, there seems to be no good reason why his intent should not be respected by the courts, if the selected jurisdiction has a material connection with the transaction. More frequently, perhaps, the trust instrument contains no expression of choice of jurisdiction; but, again, there is no sufficient reason why the donor's choice should be disregarded if his intention in this respect can be ascertained ... provided that the same substantial connection between the transaction and the intended jurisdiction shall be found to exist....

The donor was careful to provide for a change of trustee subject to his approval in his lifetime. In the event of such change he declared that the successor trustee should "hold the said trust estate subject to all the conditions herein *to the same effect as though now named herein*". The italicized language either has a significance of its own or it is to be considered as no more than a superfluous or redundant phrase.... We are of opinion that the phrase "to the same effect as though now named herein", as applied to the power to appoint a successor trustee in another state, must be accepted as authorizing a removal of the seat of the trust from its original location, and its re-establishment under the law of another jurisdiction....

There is no substantial reason why a donor, in dealing with that which is his own, may not provide for a change in the location of his trust with a consequent shifting of the controlling law. In an era of economic uncertainty, with vanishing returns from investments and with tax laws approaching confiscation, such a provision would seem to amount to no more than common foresight and prudence. The rights of beneficiaries may, it is true, be disturbed by a shift of jurisdiction, but if such change has been provided for, they have no more cause to complain that other persons who are the recipients of bounty under some condition or limitation.

The adult beneficiaries, with the donor's approval, transferred the seat of the trust from New York to Delaware. On October 9, 1929, when Joseph W. Donner availed himself of the power of appointment conferred on him by the trust agreement, the home of the trust was in this State, and, being subject then to local law, the validity and effect of his deed of appointment and of the rights and interests of the appointees thereunder are to be adjudged and determined by the law of Delaware....

[Affirmed.]

NOTE

1. See Cavers, Trusts Inter Vivos and the Conflict of Laws, 44 Harv.L.Rev. 161 (1930); Ester and Scoles, Estate Planning and Choice of Law, 24 Ohio St.L.J. 270 (1963); Scott, What Law Governs Trusts? 99 Trusts and Estates, 186 (1960); Scott, Spendthrift Trusts and the Conflict of Laws, 77 Harv.L.Rev. 845 (1964); Comment, Choice of Law: The Validity of Trusts of Movables—Intention and Validation, 64 Nw.L.Rev. 388 (1969).

2. For the Hague Convention on the Law Applicable to Trusts and Their Recognition, see infra at p. 811, Note (3).

In Re Bauer's Trust

New York Court of Appeals, 1964.
14 N.Y.2d 272, 251 N.Y.S.2d 23, 200 N.E.2d 207.

■ DESMOND, CHIEF JUDGE. In 1917 Dagmar Bauer, then a resident of New York, executed in New York City an irrevocable trust indenture which stipulated that she should receive the life income and that the remainder should go to her husband. In the event her husband predeceased her, the principal was to be distributed to such person or persons as she appointed by her will and, failing a valid disposition in her will, to the settlor's next of kin pursuant to the statutes of the State of New York. Settlor's husband predeceased her. She died a resident of London, England, in 1956. A codicil [to her will probated in England] left the trust fund to Midland Bank for the benefit of two nieces for life with the remainder to Dr. Barnardo's Homes, etc., a charitable corporation of the United Kingdom and Northern Ireland....

We ... summarize our holdings as follows:

(1) The law to be applied here is the law of New York which was the donor's domicile and where there was executed the trust agreement containing the power of appointment.... This rule applies where the same person is donor and donee....

(2) The trust was irrevocable and created a remainder interest but no reversionary interest in Mrs. Bauer. She retained no more than a testa-

mentary power of appointment and hers was, therefore, one of the "measuring lives"....

(3) The original trust plus the codicil trust thus involved three lives in being, resulting in unenforceability under the applicable former New York law ... and thus the attempt in the will and codicil to exercise the power of appointment was ineffective....

(5) Since ... there has been no valid testamentary disposition of the trust principal it must, as directed by the indenture itself, be distributed to the settlor's next of kin pursuant to the statutes of New York.

The order appealed from should be modified accordingly, with costs to parties filing separate briefs.

[The dissenting opinion of Judge Dye is omitted.]

■ FULD, JUDGE (dissenting)....

We deal here with a testatrix (Dagmar Bauer) who died in England, where she had long been domiciled, after there executing a will in which she exercised a general power of appointment, of which she was donor as well as donee, pursuant to a trust indenture executed in New York almost 40 years earlier. The court's decision to apply New York law to test the validity of Mrs. Bauer's exercise in England (in 1954) of the power of appointment which she had reserved to herself (in 1917) strikes me as an unfortunate example of adherence to mechanical and arbitrary formulae. The same considerations which prompted a departure from the inflexible and traditional choice-of-law rules in other cases (see, e.g., Auten v. Auten, 308 N.Y. 155, 124 N.E.2d 99, 50 A.L.R.2d 246; Babcock v. Jackson, 12 N.Y.2d 473, 240 N.Y.S.2d 743, 191 N.E.2d 279), it seems to me, should move the court to re-examine the wisdom and justice of continuing to apply similarly inflexible rules, with regard to significant underlying factors, in disposing of cases such as the present one.

The traditional rule which identifies the instrument exercising the power with the instrument creating it, for the purpose of testing the validity of the exercise of the power ... assumes that ownership of the appointive property remains at all times in the donor of the power and that the donee of the power serves merely as a conduit or agency through which the donor's intention with respect to the appointive property is realized.... Such an assumption is, perhaps, justified where the power created is "special" and confines the donee's exercise of the power within the limits prescribed by the instrument creating the power. However, the assumption is certainly not justified when the power created is "general" or "beneficial", whether exercisable by deed or will or by will alone, and no restrictions of any other kind are imposed on its exercise by the donee. In the latter case—and in the one before us upon the death of Mrs. Bauer's husband—it is evident that the donee is vested with the equivalence of ownership as to the appointive property.... And this is particularly true where the donor and donee of the general power are the same person. This being so, it runs counter to reason to assume that the donor in such a case becomes his own agent to preserve an attachment to the place where the original trust agreement was executed, even though he has abandoned that place as his residence and acquired a new domicile in another jurisdiction, to the laws of which he voluntarily subjected himself.

In exercising the general power of appointment in England 37 years after she had conferred such power upon herself, Mrs. Bauer was justified in treating the appointive property as her own, and it is reasonable to suppose that, in disposing of such property under a will executed in England by an English solicitor, designating an English institutional executor and trustee to administer the trust and conferring benefits, at least in part, upon an English charity, Mrs. Bauer (through her English solicitor) had exercised the power in the light of English, rather than New York, law. The inference is inescapable that she intended the disposition of the appointive property to be governed by the same law which would govern the disposition of her personal estate, namely, the law of her last domicile. Since no discernible New York policy or interest dictates the application of its law to invalidate the disposition by the English testatrix valid under her personal law—and, indeed, now valid under present New York law—such intention should be given effect.

I do not, of course, mean to suggest that New York law would not govern the validity and effect of the provisions of the *trust indenture*. That instrument was executed in 1917 against the background of New York law, which Mrs. Bauer at that time undoubtedly intended would control.... However, I reject as insupportable any suggestion ... that the law governing the trust conclusively governs the exercise of the power of appointment in every case, even to the extent of overriding the manifest intent of the donor-donee to have the law of his last domicile apply so as to effect a valid exercise of the general power....

In sum, then, I would disavow the rule requiring the inexorable application of the law governing the instrument creating the power and I would apply the law of the jurisdiction intended by the donor-donee to control—in the case before us, England which, quite obviously, has the principal, if not the sole, interest and concern with " 'the outcome of ... [this] litigation' "....

Validity—Testamentary Trusts

Farmers and Merchants Bank v. Woolf

Supreme Court of New Mexico, 1974.
86 N.M. 320, 523 P.2d 1346.

■ MONTOYA, JUSTICE.

The plaintiff-trustee (trustee), Farmers and Merchants Bank of Las Cruces, New Mexico, filed this action for declaratory judgment to determine the rights of the parties involved in a trust estate. From a judgment awarding the balance of the trust estate of Mabel Evelyn Jones (testatrix) to the Alcoholics Foundation of San Antonio, Texas (Foundation), Dale

Woolf (Woolf), the administrator with will annexed of the estate of Gordon Vance Jones brings this appeal....

[By will the testatrix, who died domiciled in Arizona, left her residuary estate in trust to the Farmers and Merchants Bank with the provision that following the death of her brother, the corpus of the trust should be paid to Alcoholics Anonymous of San Antonio, Texas. The trial court upheld the provision for Alcoholics Anonymous under Texas law although it would have been invalid under the law of Arizona. Woolf, the administrator of the deceased brother's estate appealed on the ground, among others, that the trial court had erred in not applying the law of Arizona, the state of the testatrix' domicil, since her estate consisted entirely of personal property.]

We first consider which law governs the disposition of the trust property. The testatrix was domiciled in Arizona and the main probate proceeding was held there. Ancillary probate proceedings were completed by the Dona Ana County Probate Court, since the funds involved in the trust were in the custody of the trustee in New Mexico. The legatee of the trust property is organized under the laws of the State of Texas, and the administration of the trust will also be in the State of Texas.

Under Restatement, Second, Conflict of Laws, Ch. 10 Trusts, § 269, at 152–153, it is stated:

"§ 269. Validity of Trust of Movables Created by Will

"The validity of a trust of interests in movables created by will is determined

"(a) as to matters that affect the validity of the will as a testamentary disposition, by the law that would be applied by the courts of the state of the testator's domicil at death, and

"(b) as to matters that affect only the validity of the trust provisions, except when the provision is invalid under the strong public policy of the state of the testator's domicil at death,

"(i) by the local law of the state designated by the testator to govern the validity of the trust, provided that this state has a substantial relation to the trust, or

"(ii) if there is no such effective designation, by the local law of the state of the testator's domicil at death, except that the local law of the state where the trust is to be administered will be applied if application of this law is necessary to sustain the validity of the trust."

Since the testatrix did not designate what law was to govern the validity of the trust, the provisions of § 269(b)(ii), supra, would apply. In the commentary to the foregoing section in Restatement, supra, the following appears in comment (h) at 157:

"h. Charitable trusts. In the case of charitable trusts, the courts have been even more ready than in the case of private trusts to uphold the trust if valid under the local law of the state of administration, even though the trust would be invalid under the local law of the testator's domicil...."

"When a testator bequeaths movables to be administered for charitable purposes in a state other than that of his domicil, the disposition is valid if valid under the local law of the state of administration, even though it would be invalid under the local law of the state of the testator's domicil...."

In Fletcher v. Safe Deposit & Trust Co., 193 Md. 400, 410–411, 67 A.2d 386, 390 (Ct.App.1949), in considering the question of the applicable law to determine the validity of a trust estate, the court stated:

"The general rule is that the validity of a will of movables, or of a trust of movables created by will, is determined by the law of the testator's domicile.... 'However, where a trust is to be administered in a state other than that of the domicile, but is by the domiciliary law invalid from the outset under a rule grounded in a feeling that the administration of such a trust would be difficult or against the policy of the domicile, if such objections do not prevail at the place of administration the courts of the domicile will hold the trust valid.' [Citations omitted.]" ...

Accordingly, we hold that the trial court did not err as claimed by Woolf under his first point....

NOTES

1. Cross v. United States Trust Co., 131 N.Y. 330, 30 N.E. 125 (1892). The will of testatrix who died domiciled in Rhode Island was admitted to probate in that state. The will created a trust of personal property to be administered in New York by a New York trust company. The provisions of the trust violated the New York rule against perpetuities but were valid under the law of Rhode Island. The court applied Rhode Island law and held the trust valid. It stated that application of Rhode Island law would not be contrary to New York public policy. "The only material difference in the law of the two states on this subject [rule against perpetuities] is that in each a different rule is adopted for measuring the period within which absolute ownership may lawfully be suspended.... If ... a person desiring to make a will must not only know the law of his domicile, but also the law of every country in which his personal estate may happen to be at his death, ... our courts would become the resort of dissatisfied heirs, or legatees, seeking to nullify wills, valid by the laws of the state where the persons who made them were domiciled. The question is not changed by the circumstance that the trustee and the trust fund is within our jurisdiction and all the beneficiaries but one are now residents of this state."

Matter of Chappell, 124 Wash. 128, 213 P. 684 (1923). By will, the testator, who died domiciled in California, established a trust covering personal property situated in Washington. The trust provisions were valid under Washington law; they were invalid under the California rule against perpetuities. Held that the validity of the trust should be sustained by application of Washington law. The trust did not contain any choice-of-law provision. But the court reasoned that the testator had obviously intended that the trust should be valid and that his intentions should be given effect "if that be possible and lawful."

2. Hope v. Brewer, 136 N.Y. 126, 32 N.E. 558 (1892). The will of testator, a domiciliary of New York, directed his executors to convert his New York real estate into money and to pay over the proceeds to three named Scottish trustees, in trust, for the purpose of founding and endowing an infirmary "for the care and relief of

the sick and infirm of Langholm, in Dunfrieshire, Scotland." This disposition was void under New York law on the ground of indefiniteness of beneficiaries; under the law of Scotland it was valid. On appeal from a judgment, upholding the validity of the trust against attack by a legatee, held, affirmed. "I have not been able to find any well-considered case ... where a gift to a foreign charity in trust, contained in a valid testamentary instrument, has been held void, where there was a trustee competent to take and hold, and the trust was capable of being executed and enforced, according to the law of the place to which the property was to be transmitted under the will of the donor.... Our law with respect to the creation and validity of trusts ... was designed only to regulate the holding of property under our laws, and in our state, and a trust intended to take effect in another state, or in a foreign country, would not seem to be within either its letter or spirit."

3. Trusts have no exact counterpart in the legal systems of civil law countries. Their recognition and enforcement in those countries has therefore been uncertain. Since trusts increasingly contain assets located abroad, common law countries have pressed for a resolution of these uncertainties. The 1984 Hague Convention on the Law Applicable to Trusts and Their Recognition (not yet in force, but ratification by the United States is pending) provides that a trust shall be governed by the law chosen by the settlor or, in the absence of a choice, by the law of the country with which it is most closely connected. The governing law applies to validity, construction, and effect of the trust. The same law, or another, may apply to administration. See Gaillard & Trautman, Trust in Non–Trust Countries: The Hague Trust Convention, 35 AM.J.Comp.L. 307 (1987).

4. As to the law governing the validity of testamentary trusts of movables, see 5A Scott & Fratcher, Trusts §§ 588–596A (4th ed. 1989). As to the law governing powers of appointment of movables, see id. §§ 629–642.

Administration of Trusts

RESTATEMENT, SECOND, CONFLICT OF LAWS: *

§ 271. Administration of Trust of Movables Created by Will

The administration of a trust of interests in movables created by will is governed as to matters which can be controlled by the terms of the trust

(a) by the local law of the state designated by the testator to govern the administration of the trust, or

(b) if there is no such designation, by the local law of the state of the testator's domicil at death, unless the trust is to be administered in some other state, in which case the local law of the latter state will govern.

Comment:

a. What are matters of administration. The term "administration of a trust," as it is used in the Restatement of this Subject, includes those matters which relate to the management of the trust. Matters of administration include those relating to the duties owed by the trustee to the beneficiaries.... They include the powers of a trustee, such as the power

---

* Quoted with the permission of the copyright owner, The American Law Institute.

to lease, to sell and to pledge, the exercise of discretionary powers, the requirement of unanimity of the trustees in the exercise of powers, and the survival of powers.... They include the liabilities which may be incurred by the trustee for breach of trust.... They include questions as to what are proper trust investments.... They include the trustee's right to compensation.... They include the trustee's right to indemnity for expenses incurred by him in the administration of the trust.... They include the removal of the trustee and the appointment of successor trustees.... They include the terminability of the trust....

On the other hand, where the question is as to who are beneficiaries of the trust and as to the extent of their interests, the question is one of construction rather than of administration....

c. Law designated by the testator to govern administration of the trust. The testator may designate in the will a state whose local law is to govern the administration of the trust. As to the effectiveness of such designation, a distinction must be made between those matters of administration which the testator can control by provisions in the will and those which he cannot control.

As to those matters which are subject to his control, he may designate a state which has no relation to the trust. The testator can freely regulate most matters of administration....

The testator may provide that different matters of administration shall be governed by different laws. Thus, he may provide that the local law of one state shall govern the compensation of the trustee, and that the local law of another state shall govern investments....

h. Matters which cannot be controlled by the terms of the trust. Certain matters of administration may be such that the testator cannot regulate them by any provision in the terms of the trust. Thus, ... under the local law of the state of the testator's domicil there may be unusually strict rules as to self-dealing. If a testator fixes the administration of a trust in a state other than that of his domicil, it is not certain whether the courts will apply the rule of the domicil or the rule of the place of administration.

§ 272. Administration of Trust of Movables Created Inter Vivos

The administration of an inter vivos trust of interests in movables is governed as to matters which can be controlled by the terms of the trust

(a) by the local law of the state designated by the settlor to govern the administration of the trust, or

(b) if there is no such designation, by the local law of the state to which the administration of the trust is most substantially related.

NOTES

1. Appointment of a trust company as trustee provides persuasive evidence that the settlor of either an inter vivos or a testamentary trust intended that the trust should be administered in the state where the trust company is incorporated. Restatement, Second, Conflict of Laws §§ 271–272; see also Boston Safe Deposit & Trust Co. v. Alfred University, 339 Mass. 82, 157 N.E.2d 662 (1959).

2. Application of New York Trust Co., 195 Misc. 598, 87 N.Y.S.2d 787 (1949). The case involved the question whether the situs of an inter vivos trust created in New York by a resident of that state with a New York trust company as trustee could be removed to California. The trust deed appointed two trustees, an individual and a corporation, and provided that the individual trustee, who was also the life beneficiary, could "request in writing the resignation of the corporate trustee, and upon receiving such request such corporate trustee shall forthwith resign...." Acting under this provision, the individual trustee, who was a resident of California, requested the resignation of the New York corporate trustee and appointed a California trust company in its stead. Held, in a proceeding brought by the New York trust company, that the situs of the trust could be removed to California and that the California trust company was qualified to act as trustee. "... the express provision in the clause under discussion ... makes it perfectly clear that the grantor contemplated the substitution when she executed the trust agreement.... The grantor must have realized that her son might find it more convenient to have the trust administered in a place readily accessible to him and that he might request the resignation of the corporate trustee for the very purpose of bringing about this result." Neither the law nor the public policy of New York were found to be offended by such a transfer.

Would the change in the place of administration in the New York Trust Co. case result in a change in the law governing the administration of the trust?

Does a provision of the type found in this case afford a convenient and effective way of giving a beneficiary power to change the law governing the validity of a trust?

3. The authorities are divided on the question whether allocation of the federal estate tax as between life tenant and remainderman of an inter vivos trust, which has been included in the settlor's gross estate for tax purposes, should be determined by the law governing the administration of the trust or by the law of the settlor's domicile at death. See Scoles, Apportionment of Federal Estate Taxes and Conflict of Laws, 55 Colum.L.Rev. 261 (1955); Doetsch v. Doetsch, 312 F.2d 323 (7th Cir. 1963).

Mullane v. Central Hanover Bank & Trust Co.

Supreme Court of the United States, 1950.
339 U.S. 306, 70 S.Ct. 652, 94 L.Ed. 865.

[The case appears p. 160, supra.]

NOTE

Jurisdiction to supervise the administration of a trust of interests in movables and, if necessary, to remove a trustee and to appoint a successor trustee is usually exercised by the court in which the trustee has qualified as trustee or by the courts of the state in which the trust is to be administered. Restatement, Second, Conflict of Laws § 267.

SECTION 3. INTANGIBLES

Morson v. Second National Bank of Boston

Supreme Court of Massachusetts, 1940.
306 Mass. 588, 29 N.E.2d 19, 131 A.L.R. 189.

■ QUA, JUSTICE. This is a bill in equity by the administrator of the estate of Herbert B. Turner ... alleging ... that a certificate for one hundred and fifty shares of the stock of the defendant Massachusetts Mohair Plush Company, a Massachusetts corporation, had been originally issued to Herbert B. Turner, but had been delivered to the defendant bank as "transfer agent" of the Plush company by the defendant Mildred Turner Copperman for transfer to her on the ground that Herbert B. Turner in his lifetime had made her a gift of the stock. The prayers are for injunctions against the transfer of the stock and for recovery of the certificate.

The judge ... entered a decree for the plaintiff. The issue is whether the facts found show a valid gift of the stock, which should now be recognized by a transfer on the books of the corporation and the issuance of a new certificate to Mildred Turner Copperman. We think that they do.

Among the facts found are these: About September 20, 1937, while Turner and Mildred Turner Copperman were travelling together in Italy, Turner handed to Mildred Turner Copperman a sealed envelope previously marked by him "Property of Mildred Turner Copperman." As he did so he said, "These are yours." The certificate in his name, dated October 6, 1933, was in the envelope. He also said that he would have to sign the back of the certificate. Two days later a notary and two witnesses came to the hotel where the parties were staying. Mildred Turner Copperman produced the certificate, and "Turner signed his name on the back ... and then he filled in the name of Miss Copperman and her address" and delivered the certificate to Mildred Turner Copperman, who "accepted it." Turner's intention at that time was "to make an absolute gift to Mildred Copperman to take effect at once."

It is provided by G.L.(Ter.Ed.) c. 155, sec. 27 (Uniform Stock Transfer Act sec. 1), that title "to a certificate and to the shares represented thereby shall be transferred only—(a) By delivery of the certificate endorsed either in blank or to a specified person by the person appearing by the certificate to be the owner of the shares represented thereby; or (b) By delivery of the certificate and a separate document containing a written assignment of the certificate or a power of attorney to sell, assign or transfer the same or the shares represented thereby, signed by the person appearing by the certificate to be the owner of the shares represented thereby...." Plainly that which was done in Italy would have been sufficient, if it had been done in Massachusetts, to effect a transfer of legal title to the shares.

But it is argued that the validity of the transfer is to be judged by the law of Italy, and that certain formalities required by that law for the making of gifts in general were not observed. Doubtless it is true that whether or not there is a completed gift of an ordinary tangible chattel is to be determined by the law of the situs of the chattel.... Shares of stock, however, are not ordinary tangible chattels. A distinction has been taken between the shares and the certificate, regarded as a piece of paper which can be seen and felt, the former being said to be subject to the jurisdiction of the state of incorporation and the latter subject to the jurisdiction of the state in which it is located.... The shares are part of the structure of the corporation, all of which was erected and stands by virtue of the law of the state of incorporation. The law of that state determines the nature and attributes of the shares. If by the law of that state the shares devolve upon one who obtains ownership of the certificate it may be that the law of the state of a purported transfer of the certificate will indirectly determine share ownership.... But at the least when the state of incorporation has seen fit in creating the shares to insert in them the intrinsic attribute or quality of being assignable in a particular manner it would seem that that state, and other states as well, should recognize assignments made in the specified manner wherever they are made, even though that manner involves dealing in some way with the certificate....

The final decree is reversed, and a final decree is to be entered dismissing the bill with costs to the defendant Mildred Turner Copperman.

NOTES

1. Does the principal case establish an alternative reference rule to determine the effect of a voluntary transfer of a stock certificate which embodies the underlying share—i. e., such a transfer will be held effective so long as this result would follow by applying either the law of the state of incorporation or that of the situs of the certificate?

2. Travelers Insurance Co. v. Fields, 451 F.2d 1292 (6th Cir. 1971). While domiciled in Kentucky with his first wife, the decedent obtained employment in Ohio. He designated his first wife as beneficiary of group insurance policies issued by Travelers and which insured the employees of the Ohio employer against accidental death. The policies expressly provided that they should be governed by Ohio law. Thereafter, the decedent was divorced by his first wife in Kentucky. In due course, the decedent remarried but did not amend the provision in the policies which designated his first wife as beneficiary. He later changed his domicile to Ohio and there met an accidental death. Both the first and second wives claimed the proceeds of the policies. Held for the second wife. The divorce took place in Kentucky where the decedent and his first wife were domiciled at the time. Hence Kentucky law, under which the divorce extinguished the first wife's rights under the policy, was applicable. The first wife would have won if Ohio law had been held applicable.

3. The 1962 version of the UCC contained difficult and confusing provisions for the perfection of security interests in accounts receivable. The 1972 revision of

Section 9–103(3) removes these difficulties and refers generally to the law where the debtor is "located." The debtor's location is (1) his place of business; (2) his chief executive office if there is more than one place of business; otherwise, (3) his residence. If the debtor is located outside the United States, the reference is to his chief executive place of business in the United States. If he is located both outside the United States and Canada and the collateral consists of accounts or general intangibles for money, the security interest can be perfected by notice to the account debtor. The purpose of these rules is to "allow subsequent creditors of the debtor-assignor to determine the true state of his affairs." UCC § 9–103, comment 5(a) (1978). For the "chief place of business" test, see In re J.A. Thompson & Son, Inc., 665 F.2d 941 (9th Cir.1982). For a comparative perspective see Schilling, Some European Decisions on Non–Possessory Security Rights in Private International Law, 34 Int'l & Comp.L.Q. 87 (1985).

SECTION 4. INTERPRETATION AND CONSTRUCTION OF DOCUMENTS

The meaning and effect of words contained in wills, trusts, deeds and other instruments of transfer may be determined in any one of three ways:

(1) *Interpretation.* This is the process used most frequently. It involves the attempt to determine the meaning which the words in question were actually intended to bear. In ascertaining the intentions of the party or parties, the court will consider the ordinary meaning of the words, the context in which they appear in the instrument, and the circumstances in which the instrument was drafted. It will consider who drafted the instrument (whether the party or parties or some third person) and whether the draftsman was probably using the language of his domicile or of the place of execution or of the situs of the land or chattel. The tribunal will also consider any other properly admissible evidence that casts light on the actual intentions of the party or parties. The question to be determined is one of fact rather than one of law. The forum will apply its own rules in determining the admissibility of evidence, and it will use its own standards in drawing conclusions from the evidence. Accordingly, interpretation does not involve choice-of-law problems.

(2) *Construction.* Sometimes it proves impossible to determine the meaning the words in an instrument were intended to bear, either because the party or parties did not give thought to the question or left no evidence of their thinking. In such cases, a rule of construction must be employed to fill what would otherwise be a gap in the instrument.

A typical problem of this sort arises when the question is whether an adopted child should be included within the scope of the word "heirs," as used in an instrument of conveyance, and there is no satisfactory evidence of what was actually intended. Here a rule of construction must be employed to provide an answer to this question.

(3) *Legal effect.* Sometimes the law ascribes definite legal consequences, irrespective of the parties' actual intent, to the use of certain words in an instrument of transfer. Here the sole inquiry is as to the legal

effect of the language, and so the term "legal effect" is used to describe the process. Instances of this sort are comparatively rare and, generally speaking, are confined to transfers of interests in land. One example is the common law rule that, in order to convey a fee simple interest in land by transfer inter vivos, the words "his heirs" must appear in the deed following the name of the grantee. Another is the rule in Shelley's Case, that when an owner of land made a conveyance to a person for life and limited a remainder to the heirs of the same person, he created an estate in fee simple in that person and not a life estate in him with a remainder to his heirs.

Where the contacts are divided among two or more states, determination of the meaning and effect of the language contained in an instrument of transfer may involve the preliminary inquiry: what law governs questions of construction and legal effect, and, assuming a change in this law during the period involved, at what time did the meaning and effect of the language become fixed? The necessity of making a selection among two or more competing laws is obvious when the problem at hand relates to the "legal effect" of words, an area where the actual intention of the parties is irrelevant and hard-and-fast rules of law supreme. As has already been stated, questions of this sort are usually confined to transfers of interests in land, and as to them it is agreed that the law of the situs governs. Restatement, Second, Conflict of Laws §§ 224, 240.

"Construction" is likewise a fertile field for choice-of-law questions. Canons of construction are actual rules of law, and where the laws of the interested states differ in this regard, the problem of making a selection between them is essentially the same as that arising in any other field of choice of law.

Typical of the conflicts problems which may arise in this field is what law determines (1) the meaning of a term, such as "heirs," "issue" or "next of kin," contained in a will or conveyance inter vivos, (2) whether covenants for title will be implied from ordinary words of grant (e.g., "bargain, sell and convey") in a deed of land, (3) whether, in the absence of any provision on the point in her husband's will, a wife can take under the will and claim dower as well or whether she must make an election between the two and (4) assuming again that the will is silent, whether a devisee of land that is encumbered by a mortgage receives only the remaining equity or whether the mortgage must be paid from the personal property in the estate.

Effect will be given to a provision in an instrument that the instrument should be construed in accordance with the rules of construction of a particular state. It is not necessary that this state have a substantial connection with the parties or the subject-matter of the transfer. This is because construction is a process for giving meaning to an instrument in areas where the intentions of the parties would have been followed if these intentions had been made clear. Restatement, Second, Conflict of Laws § 224, Comment *e*.

In the absence of a choice-of-law provision, the cases are agreed that instruments of transfer of interests of land will be construed in accordance with the law that would be applied by the courts of the situs. When the transfer is gratuitous, as in the case of a will or trust, the transferor's intentions are particularly important. Here authority is divided as to whether the situs courts would apply the rules of construction of the situs or the rules of the state where the transferor was domiciled at the time that he made the conveyance or executed the will or trust. When the transfer is based on consideration, as in the case of a sale or lease, the intentions of both the transferor and transferee are important. Here the situs courts would presumably construe the words in accordance with their own local rules unless perhaps the transferor and transferee were both domiciled in another state or, although they were domiciled in different states, the words happened to bear the same meaning in each state of domicile. In any event, all courts will construe the words in accordance with the rules which the situs courts would have applied. Restatement, Second, Conflict of Laws §§ 224, 240.

In the absence of a choice-of-law provision, words in a will of movables will be construed in accordance with the rules of construction that would be applied by the courts of the state where the testator was domiciled at the time of his death. These courts, in the absence of controlling circumstances to the contrary, would usually construe the words in accordance with the rules of construction prevailing in the state where the testator was domiciled at the time the will was executed. Restatement, Second, Conflict of Laws § 264; White v. United States, 511 F.Supp. 570 (S.D.Ind.1981), affirmed 680 F.2d 1156 (7th Cir. 1982); Hamilton National Bank of Chattanooga v. Hutcheson, 357 F.Supp. 114 (E.D.Tenn.1973); In re Sewart, 342 Mich. 491, 70 N.W.2d 732, 52 A.L.R.2d 482 (1955) (law of testator's domicile at time of death applies to interpretation of the will for all purposes).

On occasion, the meaning of a term, such as "heirs" or "next of kin," has been determined by applying the law of the testator's domicile as of the time of the death of the person to whose heirs or next of kin the remainder was given. Second Bank-State Street Trust Co. v. Weston, 342 Mass. 630, 174 N.E.2d 763 (1961); Matter of Battell, 286 N.Y. 97, 35 N.E.2d 913 (1941); cf. Carnegie v. First National Bank of Brunswick, 218 Ga. 585, 129 S.E.2d 780 (1963). It may be suspected that in such cases the courts frequently apply that law which they believe will achieve the fairest and most desirable result for all concerned.

Words in a trust of movables, in the absence of a choice-of-law provision, will be construed, as to matters pertaining to administration, in accordance with the rules of construction of the state whose law governs the administration of the trust and, as to other matters, in accordance with the rules of construction of the state which the testator or settlor would probably have wished to be applied. Restatement, Second, Conflict of Laws § 268.

NOTES

1. See generally 5A Scott and Fratcher, The Law of Trusts §§ 575, 576, 579, 641, 648 (4th ed. 1989); Scoles and Hay, Conflict of Laws 840–843, 845–849 (2d ed. 1992).

2. For discussion of the choice-of-law rules applicable to the interpretation of contracts, see Restatement, Second, Conflict of Laws § 204; Weintraub, Commentary on the Conflict of Laws 409–411 (3d ed. 1986).

CHAPTER 11

FAMILY LAW

RESTATEMENT, SECOND, CONFLICT OF LAWS *

Chapter 11

Status

INTRODUCTORY NOTE

In law, a status can be viewed from two standpoints. It can be viewed as a relationship which continues as the parties move from state to state, or it can be viewed from the standpoint of the incidents that arise from it. So marriage can be viewed as a relationship, namely solely from the point of view of whether a given man and woman are husband and wife. On the other hand, marriage can be viewed from the standpoint of its incidents, such as whether the man and woman may lawfully cohabit as husband and wife, the interests which the one has in the other's assets and the right of each to inherit, or to take a forced share in, the other's estate....

On occasion, the courts are faced with a question of pure status—[whether there exists a marital, or a legitimate, or an adoptive relationship between the parties.] For example, in the case of marriage, a question of pure status may arise in an action for an annulment, in an action for a declaratory judgment that a marriage does or does not exist or in a criminal prosecution for bigamy. It is clear, however, that questions involving the incidents of a status arise more frequently than do questions which purely involve the status as such. One problem is whether a question involving the incidents of a status can properly be decided without having made a preliminary determination of whether the status does, or does not, exist. For example, can a court properly determine that a woman may inherit from the deceased as a "surviving spouse" within the meaning of its intestacy statute without having first determined that she was validly married to him ...? Or can a court properly determine that a child born before the marriage of his parents may inherit from his father under its intestacy statute without having first determined that the child is legitimate ...? By and large, the courts have acted on the assumption that a decision of questions involving the incidents of a marriage should be preceded by a determination of the validity of the marriage. On the other hand, the courts have been more inclined to decide questions of incidents

---

* Quoted with the permission of the copyright owner, The American Law Institute.

involving legitimacy and adoption without having first determined whether legitimacy or adoption existed as a status.

It is increasingly common for persons to live together without entering a marriage relationship. Presumably some of these relationships are intended to be permanent while others are not. Increasingly, the law attaches rights and duties to these relationships. These developments in local law can be expected to have repercussions in the conflicts area.

NOTE

As the excerpt from the Restatement, Second, points out, the issue usually arises out of a claim for support, an interest in property, compensation in tort, and so forth, so that the status issue is only an "incidental" or "preliminary" question. See Gottlieb, The Incidental Question Revisited, 26 Int'l & Comp.L.Q. 734 (1977); Lipstein, Recognition of Divorces, Capacity to Marry, Preliminary Questions and Dépeçage, 35 Int'l & Comp.L.Q. 178 (1986). In modern American case law, incidental questions are not automatically decided under the law applicable to the principal claim. Cf. Reese, Dépeçage: A Common Phenomenon in Choice of Law, 73 Colum.L.Rev. 58 (1973).

Section 1. Marriage *

In Re May's Estate
Court of Appeals of New York, 1953.
305 N.Y. 486, 114 N.E.2d 4.

■ Lewis, Chief Judge. In this proceeding, involving the administration of the estate of Fannie May, deceased, we are to determine whether the marriage in 1913 between the respondent Sam May and the decedent, who was his niece by the half blood—which marriage was celebrated in Rhode Island, where concededly such marriage is valid—is to be given legal effect in New York where statute law declares incestuous and void a marriage between uncle and niece. Domestic Relations Law, § 5, subd. 3, McK.Consol.Laws.

The question thus presented arises from proof of the following facts: The petitioner Alice May Greenberg, one of six children born of the Rhode Island marriage of Sam and Fannie May, petitioned in 1951 for letters of administration of the estate of her mother Fannie May, who had died in 1945. Thereupon, the respondent Sam May, who asserts the validity of his marriage to the decedent, filed an objection to the issuance to petitioner of such letters of administration upon the ground that he is the surviving

---

* See Restatement, Second, Conflict of Laws §§ 283–284.

husband of the decedent and accordingly under section 118 of the Surrogate's Court Act, he has the paramount right to administer her estate. . . .

The record shows that for a period of more than five years prior to his marriage to decedent the respondent Sam May had resided in Portage, Wisconsin; that he came to New York in December, 1912, and within a month thereafter he and the decedent—both of whom were adherents of the Jewish faith—went to Providence, Rhode Island, where, on January 21, 1913, they entered into a ceremonial marriage performed by and at the home of a Jewish rabbi. The certificate issued upon that marriage gave the age of each party as twenty-six years and the residence of each as "New York, N.Y." Two weeks after their marriage in Rhode Island the respondent May and the decedent returned to Ulster County, New York, where they lived as man and wife for thirty-two years until the decedent's death in 1945. Meantime the six children were born who are parties to this proceeding. . . .

In Surrogate's Court, where letters of administration were granted to the petitioner, the Surrogate ruled that although the marriage of Sam May and the decedent in Rhode Island in 1913 was valid in that State, such marriage was not only void in New York as opposed to natural law but is contrary to the provisions of subdivision 3 of section 5 of the Domestic Relations Law. . . .

At the Appellate Division the order of the Surrogate was reversed on the law and the proceeding was remitted to Surrogate's Court with direction that letters of administration upon decedent's estate be granted to Sam May who was held to be the surviving spouse of the decedent. . . .

We regard the law as settled that, subject to two exceptions presently to be considered and in the absence of a statute expressly regulating within the domiciliary State marriages solemnized abroad, the legality of a marriage between persons *sui juris* is to be determined by the law of the place where it is celebrated. . . .

The statute of New York upon which the appellants rely is subdivision 3 of section 5 of the Domestic Relations Law which, insofar as relevant to our problem, provides:

"§ 5. *Incestuous and void marriages*

"A marriage is incestuous and void whether the relatives are legitimate or illegitimate between either: . . .

"3. An uncle and niece or an aunt and nephew.

"If a marriage prohibited by the foregoing provisions of this section be solemnized it shall be void, and the parties thereto shall each be fined not less than fifty nor more than one hundred dollars and may, in the discretion of the court in addition to said fine, be imprisoned for a term not exceeding six months. Any person who shall knowingly and wilfully solemnize such marriage, or procure or aid in the solemnization of the same, shall be deemed guilty of a misdemeanor and shall be fined or imprisoned in like manner."

Although the New York statute quoted above declares to be incestuous and void a marriage between an uncle and a niece and imposes penal measures upon the parties thereto, it is important to note that the statute does not by express terms regulate a marriage solemnized in another State where, as in our present case, the marriage was concededly legal ....

[T]he statute's scope should not be extended by judicial construction. ... Accordingly, as to the first exception to the general rule that a marriage valid where performed is valid everywhere, we conclude that, absent any New York statute expressing clearly the Legislature's intent to regulate within this State marriages of its domiciliaries solemnized abroad, there is no "positive law" in this jurisdiction which serves to interdict the 1913 marriage in Rhode Island of the respondent Sam May and the decedent.

As to the application of the second exception to the marriage here involved—between persons of the Jewish faith whose kinship was not in the direct ascending or descending line of consanguinity and who were not brother and sister—we conclude that such marriage, solemnized, as it was, in accord with the ritual of the Jewish faith in a State whose legislative body has declared such a marriage to be "good and valid in law", was not offensive to the public sense of morality to a degree regarded generally with abhorrence and thus was not within the inhibitions of natural law. ...

■ DESMOND, JUDGE (dissenting). It is fundamental that every State has the right to determine the marital status of its own citizens [citing cases]. Exercising that right, New York has declared in section 5 of the Domestic Relations Law that a marriage between uncle and niece is incestuous, void and criminal. Such marriages, while not within the Levitical forbidden degrees of the Old Testament, have been condemned by public opinion for centuries (see 1 Bishop on Marriage, Divorce and Separation, § 738), and are void, by statute in (it would seem) forty-seven of the States of the Union (all except Georgia, see Martindale–Hubbell, Law Digests, and except, also, that Rhode Island, one of the forty-seven, exempts from its local statute "any marriage which shall be solemnized among the Jews, within the degrees of affinity or consanguinity allowed by their religion", Gen.L. of R.I., ch. 415, § 4). It is undisputed here that this uncle and niece were both domiciled in New York in 1913, when they left New York for the sole purpose of going to Rhode Island to be married there, and that they were married in that State conformably to its laws (see above) and immediately returned to New York and ever afterwards resided in this State. That Rhode Island marriage, between two New York residents, was in New York, absolutely void for any and all purposes, by positive New York law which declares a strong public policy of this State. See Penal Law, § 1110.

The general rule that "a marriage valid where solemnized is valid everywhere" (see Restatement, Conflict of Laws, § 121) does not apply. To that rule there is a proviso or exception, recognized, it would seem, by all the States, as follows: "unless contrary to the prohibitions of natural law or the express prohibitions of a statute". See Thorp v. Thorp, 90 N.Y. 602, 605. Section 132 of the Restatement of Conflict of Laws states the rule apparently followed throughout America: "A marriage which is against the law of the state of domicil of either party, though the requirements of the law of the state of celebration have been complied with, will be invalid everywhere in the following cases: ... (b) incestuous marriage between persons so closely related that their marriage is contrary to a strong public policy of the domicil". ...

... Section 5 of the Domestic Relations Law, the one we are concerned with here, lists the marriages which are "incestuous and void" in New York, as being those between parent and child, brother and sister, uncle and niece, and aunt and nephew. All such misalliances are incestuous, and all, equally, are void. The policy, language, meaning and validity of the statute are beyond dispute. It should be enforced by the courts.

. . .

Decree affirmed.

NOTES

1. As indicated by In re May's Estate, a marriage will usually be held valid everywhere if it is good under the law of the state of celebration. This state has an obvious interest in the manner in which the marriage is celebrated. On the other hand, this state will not, simply by reason of the fact that it is the state of celebration, be the state of most significant relationship for purposes of questions that do not relate to formalities, e.g., whether the parties have the capacity to marry or are within one of the forbidden degrees of relationship. Application of the law of the state of celebration to uphold the validity of the marriage with respect to questions of the latter sort must therefore rest on other grounds. See Restatement, Second, Conflict of Laws § 283, Comments *f-h;* Baade, Marriage and Divorce in American Conflicts of Law, 72 Colum.L.Rev. 329 (1972); Fine, The Application of Issue–Analysis to Choice of Law Involving Family Law Matters in the United States, 26 Loyola L.Rev. 31, 295 (1980); Reese, Marriage in American Conflicts Law, 26 Int'l & Comp.L.Q. 952 (1977); Scoles and Hay, Conflict of Laws 430–463 (2d ed. 1992).

2. Does it follow that a marriage which is invalid under the law of the state of celebration must necessarily be invalid everywhere? In this connection, should a distinction be drawn between questions of formalities and questions of substance? See Restatement, Second, Conflict of Laws § 283, Comment *i.* In re Estate of Shippy, 37 Wn.App. 164, 678 P.2d 848 (1984), involved the question whether the claimant was the deceased putative husband's spouse. In selecting the applicable law, the court held: "There are, however, exceptions to applying the traditional rule that the validity of a marriage is governed by the law of the state where the marriage was contracted. ... One of the exceptions ... is that a marriage should not necessarily be invalid in other states if it would be valid under the law of some other state having a substantial relation to the parties and the marriage. ... [In] light of this state's strong present interest [as the parties' last domicile], and to protect the expectations of James and Inge, we will ... validate Inge's otherwise void marriage [entitling her to be treated] as the 'surviving spouse' ... for all purposes in the administration and distribution of [James'] estate." But see Randall v. Randall, 216 Neb. 541, 345 N.W.2d 319 (1984), confirming older decisions that strictly follow the place-of-celebration rule: "... [I]f valid there, [the marriage]

will be held valid everywhere, and conversely if invalid by the [law of the place where it was celebrated], it will be invalid wherever the question may arise."

3. The general rule is that the validity of a marriage celebrated on board a vessel on the high seas is governed by the law of the vessel's flag. When the flag is that of the United States, this rule alone is insufficient to determine the applicable law since there is no federal law of marriage. In Fisher v. Fisher, 250 N.Y. 313, 165 N.E. 460 (1929) (an action for separation and support), the law of the shipowner's domicile was applied to validate the marriage in preference to that of the ship's registry, which would have invalidated the marriage.

4. See Starkowski v. Attorney General (1953) 2 All E.R. 1272 (H.L.), which upheld a marriage celebrated in Austria by application of an Austrian statute enacted subsequent to the marriage at a time when the spouses were no longer living in Austria. The marriage was originally invalid under Austrian law because it had been celebrated by a priest rather than by the civil authorities. The validating act was held to relate to formalities. See Da Costa, The Formalities of Marriage in the Conflict of Laws, 7 Int'l & Comp.L.Q. 217 (1958).

5. Under the place-of-celebration rule, states that do not permit informal methods of creating the matrimonial status ("common law" marriage) usually will recognize a marriage of that kind when it was contracted in a state permitting such a method. See, e.g., Enis v. State, 408 So.2d 486 (Miss.1981); Mott v. Duncan Petroleum Trans., 51 N.Y.2d 289, 434 N.Y.S.2d 155, 414 N.E.2d 657 (1980). The same is generally true with respect to marriages by proxy. See In re Marriage of Holemar, 27 Or.App. 613, 557 P.2d 38 (1976). However, the courts in the state of the parties' domicile have refused recognition to out-of-state common law marriages when the link with the state of celebration was insubstantial. See, e.g., Matter of Estate of Brack, 121 Mich.App. 585, 329 N.W.2d 432 (1982) (one night in a Georgia motel while en route to Florida was insufficient to establish a Georgia common law marriage).

6. Problems arise when the validity of a second marriage depends upon the dissolution or invalidity of the first marriage. It has been said that the "generally accepted American view is that the presumption of the validity of the second marriage is 'stronger' than the presumption of the continuance of the first marriage." Headen v. Pope & Talbot, Inc., 252 F.2d 739 (3d Cir.1958); cf. Woolery v. Metropolitan Life Insurance Co., 406 F.Supp. 641 (E.D.Va.1976).

Wilkins v. Zelichowski

Supreme Court of New Jersey, 1958.
26 N.J. 370, 140 A.2d 65.

■ JACOBS, J. ... The plaintiff and the defendant were domiciled in New Jersey as were their respective parents. They ran away from New Jersey to marry and they chose Indiana because they believed "it was the quickest place." The Indiana statutes provide that "females of the age of sixteen" are capable of marriage although they also provide that where the female is within the age of 18 the required marriage license shall not be issued without the consent of her parents. See Burns, Indiana Statutes Annotated, §§ 44–101, 44–202. After their marriage in Indiana on April 23, 1954, the plaintiff and defendant returned immediately to New Jersey where they set up their home. On February 22, 1955 the plaintiff bore the defendant's child. . . . On January 4, 1956 the plaintiff filed her annulment complaint under N.J.S. 2A:34–1(e), N.J.S.A., which provides that a judgment of nullity may be rendered on the wife's application upon a showing that she was under the age of 18 years at the time of her marriage and that the marriage has not been "confirmed by her after arriving at such age"; the statute also provides that where a child has been born there shall be no judgment of nullity unless the court is of the opinion that the judgment "will not be against the best interests of the child." . . .

The plaintiff's evidence adequately established that she was 16 years of age when she was married and that she did not confirm her marriage after she had reached 18 years of age and the Chancery Division expressly found that an annulment would be "for the best interests of the child"; nevertheless it declined to grant the relief sought by the plaintiff on the ground that the marriage was valid in Indiana and should therefore, under principles of the conflict of laws, not be nullified by a New Jersey court because of the plaintiff's nonage. In reaching the same result the Appellate Division recognized that the Chancery Division had ample power to nullify the Indiana marriage of the New Jersey domiciliaries . . . but expressed the view that comity dictated that it should not take such action unless there was an imperative New Jersey policy (which it did not find) against marriages of 16–year–old females. . . .

In 1905 the Court of Chancery had occasion to deal with an application by a New Jersey resident for annulment of an English marriage entered into when she was 14 years of age; the court expressed the view that there could be "no doubt" as to its jurisdiction. After reviewing the plaintiff's evidence of fraud and duress and pointing out that while our law is interested in the permanency and inviolability of the marriage contract "it is equally interested in having it entered into by persons of competent age and judgment," it awarded a decree of annulment. See Avakian v. Avakian, 69 N.J.Eq. 89, 100, 60 A. 521, 525 (Ch.1905, per Pitney, V.C.), affirmed 69 N.J.Eq. 834, 66 A. 1133 (E. & A.1906). In 1907 the Legislature revised the statutory provisions relating to annulments (L.1907, c. 216, p. 474); it directed that a decree of nullity could be rendered not only in the case of a bigamous or incestuous marriage (see L.1902, c. 157, p. 502) but also in any case, among others, where the wife sought the decree and established that she was under 16 at the time of the marriage and had not confirmed it after attaining such age. . . . In 1928 the Legislature strengthened its policy by increasing the wife's age requirement and providing that the wife could obtain a decree of nullification "when she was under the age of eighteen years at the time of the marriage, unless such marriage be confirmed by her after arriving at such age." See L.1928, c. 65, p. 139. ==The vigor of New Jersey's policy against marriages by persons under the prescribed age is evidenced not only by the breadth of the statutory language but also by the judicial decisions.== [The court discussed at this point a number of New Jersey decisions.]

It is undisputed that if the marriage between the plaintiff and the defendant had taken place here, the public policy of New Jersey would be applicable and the plaintiff would be entitled to the annulment; and it seems clear to us that if New Jersey's public policy is to remain at all meaningful it must be considered equally applicable though their marriage took place in Indiana. While that State was interested in the formal ceremonial requirements of the marriage it had no interest whatever in that marital status of the parties. Indeed, New Jersey was the only State having any interest in that status, for both parties were domiciled in New Jersey before and after the marriage and their matrimonial domicile was established here. The purpose in having the ceremony take place in Indiana was to evade New Jersey's marriage policy and we see no just or compelling reason for permitting it to succeed....

... We are not here concerned with a collateral attack on an Indiana marriage or with a direct attack on an Indiana marriage between domiciliaries of Indiana or some state other than New Jersey. We are concerned only with a direct and timely proceeding, authorized by the New Jersey statute (N.J.S. 2A:34–1(e), N.J.S.A.), by an underage wife for annulment of an Indiana marriage between parties who have at all times been domiciled in New Jersey. We are satisfied that at least in this situation the strong public policy of New Jersey (see Restatement, Conflict of Laws § 132(b), comment b) requires that the annulment be granted. The annulment will not render the plaintiff's child illegitimate (N.J.S. 2A:34–20, N.J.S.A.) and, as the Chancery Division found, it will be for his best interests. The annulment will also serve the plaintiff's best interests for it will tend to reduce the tragic consequences of her immature conduct and unfortunate marriage. The Legislature has clearly fixed the State's policy in her favor and has granted her the right to apply for a judgment nullifying her marriage; we know of no considerations of equity or justice or overriding principles of the law which would lead us to deprive her of the relief she seeks under the circumstances she presents....

Reversed.

NOTES

1. Statutes in a number of states expressly declare that a marriage, valid where contracted, is valid within the state. See, e.g., Cal.Civ.Code Ann. § 4104; Idaho Code Ann. § 32–209; Kan.Gen.Stat.Ann. § 23–115; Ky.Rev.Stat. § 402.040; Neb. Rev.Stat. § 42–117; N.M.Stat.Ann. § 40–1–4; N.D.Code 14–03–08 (but note exception as to its residents' contracting a marriage prohibited by North Dakota); S.D.C.L. 25–1–38; Utah Code Ann. § 30–1–4.

Section 210 of the Uniform Marriage and Divorce Act (currently in effect in eight states) carries the validation urge even further. It provides:

All marriages contracted within this State prior to the effective date of this Act, or outside this State, that were valid at the time of the contract or subsequently validated by the laws of the place in which they were contracted or by the domicil of the parties, are valid in this State.

Are general provisions of this sort desirable? Would Section 210 have required the court to reach a different result in the Wilkins case? Would it be possible to frame a general choice-of-law rule on the subject of marriage that would permit the court to give consideration to the particular issue?

2. The Wilkins case demonstrates that a marriage which meets the requirements of the place of celebration will occasionally be held invalid under the law of another jurisdiction. With rare exceptions (see, e.g., Catalano v. Catalano, 148 Conn. 288, 170 A.2d 726 (1961)), such a marriage will be invalidated only by application of the law of the state which was the domicile of either one or both parties at the time of marriage and which was also the place where they intended to live thereafter. Restatement, Second, Conflict of Laws § 283; Taintor, Marriage to a Paramour after Divorce: The Conflict of Laws, 43 Minn.L.Rev. 889 (1959). It has been suggested that the law of the state where the parties intend to make their home should have the ultimate voice in determining the validity of their marriage. See Cook, The Logical and Legal Bases of the Conflict of Laws 452–56 (1942). What objections could be advanced to the adoption of such a rule?

3. Did the marriage in the Wilkins case represent a more objectionable union than the one upheld in In re May's Estate, p. 821 supra? In the absence of a statute expressly dealing with the problem, what criteria should guide the courts in determining whether to invalidate a marriage that meets the requirements of the state of celebration? Should the decision depend upon the particular issue involved? In Leszinske v. Poole, 110 N.M. 663, 798 P.2d 1049 (App.1990), cert. denied, 110 N.M. 533, 797 P.2d 983 (1990), a father appealed a lower court decision to permit the mother to retain primary physical custody of the three minor children only if the mother and her uncle, who wished to marry, entered into a valid marriage. A marriage between uncle and niece was prohibited by the laws of New Mexico and California (where the mother wished to reside). Soon thereafter, niece and uncle were married in Costa Rica, which permits such marriages. The lower court recognized the marriage because it was valid where celebrated and awarded physical custody of the children to the mother. On appeal, the father argued that the lower court had encouraged the mother to violate New Mexico public policy. The court of appeals affirmed. The lower court had properly recognized the strong probability of the mother seeking such a marriage, considered the possible impact of any attack on the validity of such a marriage upon the best interests of the children, and concluded that the children should remain with the mother. See also Notes 2 and 3, pp. 824–825, supra.

4. A statute directed explicitly to out-of-state marriages is the Uniform Marriage Evasion Act.[1]

Sec. 1. If any person residing and intending to continue to reside in this state who is disabled or prohibited from contracting marriage under the laws of this state shall go into another state or country and there contract a marriage prohibited and declared void by the laws of this state, such marriage shall be null and void for all purposes in this state with the same effect as though such prohibited marriage had been entered into in this state.

Sec. 2. No marriage shall be contracted in this state by a party residing and intending to continue to reside in another state or jurisdiction if such marriage

---

1. The Act is currently in force in four states, Ill.Ann.Stat. ch. 40, §§ 216–219 (Smith–Hurd 1980); Mass.Ann.Laws ch. 207, §§ 10–13, 50 (Michie/Law Coop.1981) (with modifications); Vt.Stat.Ann. tit. 15, §§ 5–6 (1974); Wis.Stat.Ann. § 765–04 (West 1981). For somewhat similar statutes, see La.Civ. Code Ann. art. 95 (West 1952); N.D.Cent. Code § 14–03–08 (1981).

would be void if contracted in such other state or jurisdiction and every marriage celebrated in this state in violation of this provision shall be null and void.

The Commissioners on Uniform State Laws withdrew the Act in 1943 stating that it tended to produce confusion in the law because so few states had adopted it.[2]

5. At one time, statutes in the divorce states commonly imposed restrictions upon the further marriage of divorced persons. Most of these statutes have now been repealed. Even in their heyday, they were usually denied extraterritorial effect. When directed against the guilty party alone, they would frequently be denied effect in other states on the ground that they were penal in nature. When directed against both parties (e.g., by prohibiting remarriage for a certain period after divorce), they would usually be refused application against parties who did not seek to remarry until after they had acquired a domicile in another state. Even courts in the divorce state itself were reluctant to apply their local prohibitions to invalidate out-of-state marriages of local domiciliaries. Scoles and Hay, Conflict of Laws 445–450 (2d ed. 1992); Restatement, Second, Conflict of Laws § 283, Comment *l*.

6. If a divorce does not become final until the termination of the period within which remarriage is prohibited, a new marriage within this period in a second state will usually be invalid under the law of the second state and, if so, will be held invalid everywhere. Randall v. Randall, 216 Neb. 541, 345 N.W.2d 319 (1984); Marek v. Flemming, 192 F.Supp. 528 (S.D.Tex.1961), judgment vacated, 295 F.2d 691 (5th Cir.1961).

In Re Ommang's Estate
Supreme Court of Minnesota, 1931.
183 Minn. 92, 235 N.W. 529.

■ OLSEN, J. ...

This is a contest ... as to who is entitled to administer the estate of one Nick Ommang, a resident of St. Louis county, in this state, who died

2. The District of Columbia, Maine, Mississippi, Virginia and West Virginia have evasion statutes similar in effect to section 1 of the Uniform Marriage Evasion Act. D.C.Code Ann. § 30–105 (1981); Me.Rev. Stat.Ann. tit. 19 § 91 (1981) (requires an "intent to evade" the local law); Miss.Code Ann. § 93–1–3 (1973) ("any attempt to evade"); Va.Code § 20–40 (1983); W.Va. Code § 48–1–17 (1980) ("in order to evade"). The Connecticut statute states that marriages celebrated outside of the state shall be valid provided "each party would have legal capacity to contract such marriage in this state." Conn.Gen.Stat.Ann. § 46(b)–28 (West 1986). The Arizona statute provides that marriages celebrated outside of the state by parties intending to reside at the time in Arizona shall have the same legal consequences as if solemnized in Arizona. Ariz. Rev.Stat.Ann. § 25–112 (1976). The Georgia statute is substantially the same as the Arizona statute. Ga.Code Ann. § 53–214 (1982). The Wyoming statute makes it the duty of the clerk to inquire whether the parties have capacity to contract by the law of the domicile, and provides that a license shall be refused if it appears that there be an impediment to marriage by that law. Wyo. Stat. § 20–1–103 (1987).

Some states make it unlawful for their residents to cohabit within the state if they have elsewhere contracted a marriage which is prohibited by the law of the state. See, e.g., Del.Code Ann. tit. 13 § 104 (1975); Miss.Code Ann. § 97–29–9 (1973); Va.Code § 20–40 (1983); W.Va.Code § 48–1–18 (1980). But see State v. Austin, 160 W.Va. 337, 234 S.E.2d 657 (1977), involving a charge of contributing to the delinquency of a 15-year old by marrying her out of state. The court said that although the marriage was voidable (by or on behalf of the minor) it was valid until then, hence no crime had been committed.

intestate at Duluth in said county on March 13, 1929. Appellant is a half-sister of the decedent, and claims to be one of his heirs at law entitled to the estate, and to be entitled to have an administrator appointed. Respondent claims she is the widow of the deceased and his sole heir, and entitled to have an administrator appointed. The probate court of St. Louis county found against the respondent, and held she was not the lawful wife of the deceased prior and up to the time of his death. On appeal to the district court, that court reversed the probate court and held that respondent was the lawful wife of the deceased prior to and at the time of his death, his sole heir at law, and entitled to have an administrator appointed.

. . .

1. In 1907, Nick Ommang and respondent, whose name was then Mrs. Seligman, were residents of Superior, Wis. Respondent had secured a divorce from her husband on January 2, 1907. On August 7, 1907, respondent and Nick Ommang went to Duluth and were there lawfully married. They returned to Superior immediately after the marriage, and lived there together as husband and wife for about two years. They then separated, and decedent moved to Duluth late in 1909, and there resided until his death. Respondent remained in Superior for about two more years, then moved to Duluth, and resided there for three or more years. She then came to St. Paul to live with a daughter of her prior marriage, and has since resided there. After their separation, decedent met and visited the respondent from time to time, but they did not thereafter live together. After respondent moved to St. Paul, decedent visited her there many times. At one time he took her out to entertainments there. He gave her money at times. He asked her to come back and live with him. One time, at his request, respondent came to Duluth and stayed with decedent in his room overnight. He wanted her to remain, but she did not like the place or surroundings where he was living, and left the next day. This evidence, while it does not clearly prove cohabitation by the parties in this state, does show that decedent recognized the marriage relation existing between them and acknowledged respondent as his wife after both parties had become residents of this state. We do not hold that actual cohabitation in this state, under the circumstances shown, was necessary.

The marriage of the parties in this state, more than six months after respondent had obtained a divorce from her former husband, was a valid marriage under our laws. Its validity, at the time of the death of one of the parties in this state, after both parties were and had been residents of this state for many years, is now attacked. The marriage has never been set aside or adjudged invalid.

2. The general rule, that the validity of a marriage must be tested by the laws of the state or country where the marriage ceremony was performed and that a marriage valid where performed is valid everywhere, as well as the exceptions to the general rule, has been argued. The general rule is followed in this state.... This general rule has application when the

marriage was performed in one state or country and the question of its validity arises in the courts of another state or country. The rule and the exceptions thereto would seem to have but incidental bearing upon the present case, where the marriage was performed in this state and was valid under our laws; the parties thereto were residents of this state at the time one of them died; the survivor remains a resident here; and the validity of the marriage is challenged in a court of this state.

3. The ground urged by appellant for holding the marriage invalid is that the law of Wisconsin, wherein the parties resided at the time of the marriage, provides that it shall not be lawful for a divorced person to remarry within one year after the judgment of divorce was entered, and declares any such marriage, within the year, null and void. The Wisconsin court, in Lanham v. Lanham, 136 Wis. 360, 117 N.W. 787, 17 L.R.A. (N.S.) 804, 128 Am.St.Rep. 1085, held that this statute invalidated a marriage performed in Michigan, where the parties were residents of Wisconsin, and, for the purpose of evading the law, went to Michigan, were there married, and returned to Wisconsin to live....

4. This court, as stated, has consistently followed the rule that the validity of a marriage is to be tested by the laws of the state or country where it was performed....

The Meisenhelder Case [note 2, infra] was an action to recover for the death of one D'Albani, under the Federal Employers' Liability Act (45 USCA §§ 51–59). Louise D'Albani claimed to be his widow and beneficiary. The parties resided in Illinois, and decedent was there killed. The cause of action arose in that state. If Louise D'Albani was not the lawful wife of decedent, under the Illinois law, she was not a beneficiary under the act, and no cause of action existed in her favor. In other words, her status as the wife of decedent in Illinois was an essential link in the cause of action. The general rule, that a marriage valid where performed is valid everywhere, is not departed from in this case, except to the extent of holding that, where a marriage between residents of Illinois is by the laws of that state declared invalid although performed in another state where it is not invalid, the laws and decisions of Illinois, where the cause of action arose, govern the cause of action here. Had the marriage been a valid marriage performed in Illinois, it could not have been questioned here.

. . .

6. Counsel urge that the parties came to Minnesota to be married with the intention of avoiding the Wisconsin law, and therefore the marriage should be held invalid here. We are not prepared to so hold. The marriage was legal in this state, and the parties did not evade, or seek to evade, any of our laws....

Order affirmed.

NOTES

1. Would the decision have been the same if the parties had remained domiciled in Wisconsin? If not, did the originally invalid marriage become valid when the parties moved to Minnesota? Or is there some other explanation for the decision?

2. Did the court in the principal case satisfactorily distinguish its earlier decision in Meisenhelder v. Chicago & N.W. Ry. Co., 170 Minn. 317, 213 N.W. 32 (1927)? In that case, first cousins, who were domiciled in Illinois and were prohibited by Illinois law from marrying, went to Kentucky to be married and then returned to Illinois. This marriage was void in Illinois, which had enacted the Uniform Marriage Evasion Act. Thereafter, the man was killed in Illinois in the course of his employment and the woman brought suit against his employer in Minnesota under the Federal Employees' Liability Act. Recovery was denied on the ground that she was not a "surviving widow" within the meaning of the Act. The court said that since the term "surviving widow" was not defined in the Act, its meaning must be sought in state law, "in this case the law of Illinois." The Illinois statute

> "modifies the rule that marriages valid where the ceremony is performed are valid anywhere. . . .
>
> "There is no real question but that the purpose of the decedent and Louise D'Albani in going to Kentucky and marrying was to evade the Illinois law. There is evidence that they intended moving later to Minnesota, but it is indefinite, and their removal was entirely contingent. When married they gave their residence as Illinois, they were under oath, they were in Kentucky not more than four or five days, and they returned to Illinois to live and lived there until the decedent's death in December, 1924.
>
> "The result, following the Illinois law, is that Louise D'Albani is not the widow of the deceased and cannot take as beneficiary under the Federal Employers' Liability Act."

3. Section 210 of the Uniform Marriage and Divorce Act [set forth at p. 827, Note 1, supra] provides that a marriage celebrated outside of the state shall be held valid if it was valid or was "subsequently validated" by the law of the state in which the marriage was contracted or where the parties were domiciled.

In re Estate of Lenherr

Supreme Court of Pennsylvania, 1974.
455 Pa. 225, 314 A.2d 255.

■ NIX, JUSTICE. The sole issue involved in this appeal is whether or not the West Virginia marriage of Sarah T. Lenherr to Leo A. Lenherr, the decedent, will be recognized in this Commonwealth for purposes of the marital exemption to the Transfer Inheritance Tax. See, Act of June 15, 1961, P.L. 373, Art. III, § 311, 72 P.S. § 2485–311. If their marriage is so recognized, property held in their joint names will pass from the decedent to Sarah Lenherr without the imposition of a Pennsylvania inheritance tax. . . .

The pertinent facts are as follows. On October 23, 1930, the deceased, Leo A. Lenherr was divorced on the grounds of adultery from his then wife Anna Kelly Lenherr and Sarah Barney [Lenherr] was named as the co-respondent. On December 27, 1930, Sarah was divorced from her then husband William K. Barney on the grounds of adultery and Leo Lenherr was named as co-respondent.

On March 12, 1932, after the two divorce decrees were entered and while William Barney and Anna Lenherr were living, Leo Lenherr and

Sarah Gillespie Barney were married in West Virginia. They returned to Pennsylvania where they lived as husband and wife until the death of Leo Lenherr in August of 1971.

At the outset, it should be noted that all parties agree that Leo and Sarah's marriage was valid under the applicable laws of West Virginia. This dispute arises because of the Act of June 17, 1971, P.L. ___, No. 16, § 1, amending, Act of March 13, 1815, P.L. 150, § 9, 48 P.S. § 169 (Supp.1973–74), which provides:

> "The husband or wife, who shall have been guilty of the crime of adultery, shall not marry the person with whom the said crime was committed during the life of the former wife or husband...." ...

[Since] the laws of Pennsylvania and West Virginia are in conflict with regard to the validity of this marriage, we must next determine which law should be applied in this case....

Since both Leo and Sarah were residents of Pennsylvania before and after their West Virginia marriage, we have no trouble concluding that Pennsylvania has the most significant relationship to the spouses and the marriage. It remains for us to determine whether the policy behind section 169 is so strong that it must be given extraterritorial effect in this case, thereby destroying the uniformity of result which is so desirable in a case concerning the recognition of a marriage that is valid in the state where it was contracted.

In resolving that conflict, we must realize that the strength of the policy behind section 169 depends to a significant degree upon the incident of marriage under consideration. For example, the legislature has determined that at least one incident of marriage—the legitimacy of the children—is not to be denied despite the prior adjudication of adultery. See, Act of June 17, 1971, supra. Our task therefore is to balance on the one hand the policy behind section 169, *as it relates to the marital exemption to the inheritance tax*, against the need for uniformity and predictability of result on the other.

It is apparent from the terms of section 169 that the provision is intended not so much as a penalty upon the parties who failed to recognize the sanctity of the former marriage vow as it is intended to protect the sensibilities of the injured spouse. Were it otherwise, the prohibition would not be limited to the lifetime of that spouse....

While that policy may yet be quite strong with respect to cohabitation and many other incidents of marriage, ... we are concerned here only with the marital exemption to the inheritance tax. We are not convinced that the denial of that exemption will foster the policy of section 169 to any significant extent. Such denial could do so only if it: (1) could deter either the adulterous conduct during the valid marriage or the subsequent marriage of the guilty spouse and his or her paramour; or (2) could in any way spare the aggrieved former spouse the affront caused by such marriage.

We are convinced that denying the marital exemption would be all but fruitless in achieving the above goals. Moreover, we must balance any illusory gain from such denial against the need for uniformity of result in this area and against the statutory policy that the property of two persons living as man and wife and held in their joint names with right of survivorship is in reality the product of their joint efforts and should pass to the survivor without the imposition of a tax. Both of those policies would be frustrated by applying section 169 to this marriage. On balance, we find that the degree to which the policy behind section 169 will be fostered by application in this case is significantly outweighed by countervailing policies. We therefore decline to apply Pennsylvania law to invalidate this marriage for this purpose....

NOTES

1. Does the Lenherr case suggest that marriage is not an all-purpose concept and that in effect a marriage may be valid for one purpose and yet invalid for another?

2. The courts are frequently called upon to determine the meaning of such terms as "wife," "widow" or "surviving spouse" in local statutes. Usually, such inquiry has been held to require an investigation of whether there was a valid marriage under choice-of-law principles. See, e.g., In re May's Estate, p. 821, supra. Sometimes, however, this approach has not been followed. For example, in Borax v. Commissioner, 349 F.2d 666 (2d Cir.1965), a man and a woman with whom he had gone through a wedding ceremony following a Mexican divorce were held entitled to file joint income tax returns and deduct alimony paid to the first wife even after the first wife had obtained a New York judgment that the Mexican divorce was invalid and that she and the man were still married. In Toler v. Oakwood Smokeless Coal Corp., 173 Va. 425, 4 S.E.2d 364 (1939), W, erroneously believing her first husband dead, married H in West Virginia where a bigamous marriage is void only from the time it is so judicially decreed. A few weeks later H and W moved to Virginia where H was killed in the course of his employment. By Virginia law a bigamous marriage is void ab initio. Compensation was denied W on the ground that the marriage was void, and therefore W was not H's widow.

See D. Currie, Suitcase Divorce in the Conflict of Laws, 34 U.Chi.L.Rev. 26, 64–77 (1967); Engdahl, Proposal for a Benign Revolution in Marriage Law and Marriage Conflicts Law, 55 Iowa L.Rev. 56 (1969); Fine, The Application of Issue–Analysis to the Choice of Law Involving Family Matters in the United States, 26 Loyola L.Rev. 31, 295 (1980); Reese, Marriage in American Conflict of Laws, 26 Int. & Comp.L.Q. 952 (1977). See also Hovermill, A Conflict of Laws and Morals: The Choice of Law Implications of Hawaii's Recognition of Same–Sex Marriages, 53 Md.L.Rev. 450 (1994); Note, 'Til Death Do Us Part: Granting Full Faith and Credit to Marital Status, 68 S.Cal.L.Rev. 397 (1995).

IN RE DALIP SINGH BIR'S ESTATE, 83 Cal.App.2d 256, 188 P.2d 499 (1948): While domiciled in the Punjab Province of India, the decedent legally married two wives. Thereafter, he moved to California where he died intestate. The question was whether both women could inherit as "wives" of the decedent. Held that they could so inherit. The conclusion might be different "if the decedent had attempted to cohabit with his two wives in California." But the "public policy" of California would not be violated by dividing money equally between them.

NOTES

1. A state will usually afford the same incidents—in the sense of resulting legal interests—to a valid foreign marriage that it gives to a marriage contracted within its territory. Restatement, Second, Conflict of Laws § 284. It will not do so, however, when it believes that doing so would be contrary to its strong public policy in the sense discussed by Judge Cardozo in Loucks v. Standard Oil Co., p. 375, supra. People v. Ezeonu, 155 Misc.2d 344, 588 N.Y.S.2d 116 (1992); In re Takahashi's Estate, 113 Mont. 490, 129 P.2d 217 (1942) (inheritance); State v. Bell, 7 Baxt. (Tenn.) 9 (1872) (cohabitation). To be effectively invoked the "public policy" reason must, of course, be a constitutional one. Before the Supreme Court declared miscegenation statutes unconstitutional as violative of the due process and equal protection clauses of the Constitution. (Loving v. Virginia, 388 U.S. 1 (1967)), marriages between persons of different races were sometimes denied recognition.

2. Sec. 47 of the English Matrimonial Causes Act of 1973 provides that a court in England or Wales may grant (a) "matrimonial relief" and (b) make "a declaration concerning the validity of a marriage" even though "the marriage in question was entered into under a law which permits polygamy." The first of these provisions addresses the incidents of an actually or potentially polygamous marriage, as in *Dalip Singh Bir's Estate,* supra. The second addresses the validity of a persisting marriage, between actually *monogamous* spouses, contracted in a legal system in which a polygamous marriage would also be valid. Sec. 5(1) of the Private International Law (Miscellaneous Provisions) Act 1995 (c 42) now specifies more generally that a marriage contracted by parties not already married is "not void under the law of England and Wales" on the ground that it was entered into in a legal system permitting polygamous marriages. Sec. 7(2), making essentially the same provision with respect to Scots law, specifies further: "so long as neither party marries a second spouse during the subsistence of the marriage." See also Hussain v. Hussain, [1982] 3 All E.R. 369 (C.A.); R. v. Secretary of State for the Home Dep't ex parte Rahman, Court of Appeal, Nov. 20, 1985, *unpublished available in* LEXIS, UK library, ALLCAS file; Fentiman, The Validity of Marriage and the Proper Law, 44 Camb.L.J. 256, 273 (1985).

3. Marriage among the American Indians according to their laws and customs, where tribal regulations and government exist, has been almost universally recognized in the United States, even though both polygamy and termination by mutual consent may be permitted. See, e.g., In re Marriage of Red Fox, 23 Or.App. 393, 542 P.2d 918 (1975); Scoles and Hay, Conflict of Laws 459–461 (2d ed. 1992).

4. A difficult problem may arise when a court is required to determine what incidents should be attached to a relationship or status that is unknown to its law. A case in point is Nevarez v. Bailon, 287 S.W.2d 521 (Tex.Civ.App.1956). Appellant and the deceased had lived together in Mexico in a relationship termed "concubinage" by Mexican law but which would have constituted a common-law marriage had they lived in Texas. Her petition for a widow's allowance and to be appointed administratrix of the deceased's Texas estate was denied. "It should be said in passing that the term 'concubine' as used in Mexico does not carry with it the stigma ordinarily attached to it by the English language. It is an institution recognized by the law of Mexico, and ... the relationship of more than half a million Mexican couples.... [B]ecause the relationship between appellant and deceased was entered into and existed wholly within [Mexico], it must be regulated and defined by the Code Law of that state. This Code Law ... defines appellant as a concubine, and grants her certain rights of inheritance as such, but does not recognize her relationship as a valid, provable marriage in ... Mexico. The Courts of Texas must therefore recognize her as do the courts of her residence, viz., as a concubine, and there is no provision in the Texas law for her to inherit as such.... [S]he could not claim as a common-law wife in Texas for such a relationship is nonexistent in the jurisdiction of her residence." How could that result have been avoided by the court?

5. See Fine, Choice of Law for Putative Spouses, 32 Int'l & Comp.L.Q. 708 (1983).

Section 2. Divorce *

A. Conditions for Decreeing Divorce

Alton v. Alton

United States Court of Appeals, Third Circuit, 1953.
207 F.2d 667.

■ GOODRICH, CIRCUIT JUDGE. This case involves an important and novel question with regard to jurisdiction for divorce. The plaintiff, Sonia Alton, left her home in West Hartford, Connecticut, and went to the Virgin Islands, where she arrived February 10, 1953. After six weeks and one day continuous presence there she filed a suit for divorce on March 25, 1953. Her husband, David Alton, defendant, entered an appearance and waived service of summons. He did not contest the allegations of the complaint.... When the case came to the judge of the district court he asked for further proof on the question of domicile. This was not furnished. He thereupon denied the plaintiff the relief sought, and the case comes here on her appeal. The defendant has filed no brief and made no argument.

The core of our question is found in two acts of the Legislative Assembly of the Virgin Islands. The first is the Divorce Law of 1944, section 9 of which requires six weeks' residence in the Islands prior to commencement of a suit for divorce. In Burch v. Burch, 3 Cir., 1952, 195 F.2d 799, this court construed the words "inhabitant" and "residence" in that statute to mean "domiciliary" and "domicile." In 1953 the Legislative Assembly passed another act which must be stated in full in order to understand the specific problem involved in this case. It amends section 9 of the Divorce Law of 1944 by adding to it an additional subsection (a) which reads:

"Notwithstanding the provisions of sections 8 and 9 hereof, if the plaintiff is within the district at the time of the filing of the complaint and has been continuously for six weeks immediately prior thereto, this shall be prima facie evidence of domicile, and where the defendant has been personally served within the district or enters a general appearance in the action, then the Court shall have jurisdiction of the action and of the

---

* See Restatement, Second, Conflict of Laws §§ 70–74.

parties thereto without further reference to domicile or to the place where the marriage was solemnized or the cause of action arose."

[W]e think it pretty clear as a matter of construction of the English language that there are here two separable provisions. There are two rules provided and they are connected with a conjunctive "and." We think, therefore, that we must give attention to the two clauses independently.

[The Court struck down the first clause of the statute on the ground that "If domicile is really the basis for divorce jurisdiction ... six weeks' physical presence without more is not a reasonable way to prove it."]

... The second part of the statute goes on to provide that the court shall have jurisdiction, after six weeks' residence by the plaintiff, where the defendant has been personally served or appeared, "without further reference to domicile." ... The action, in other words, is to become a simple transitory action like a suit for tort or breach of contract.... Can divorce be turned into a simple, transitory action at the will of any legislature?

The background of divorce legislation and litigation shows that it has not been considered a simple transitory personal action. The principle said to govern is that marriage is a matter of public concern, as well as a matter of interest to the parties involved. Because it is a matter of public concern, the public, through the state, has an interest both in its formation and in its dissolution, and the state which has that interest is the state of domicile, because that is where the party "dwelleth and hath his home."

. . .

So deeply has it been thought that the responsibility for divorce was that of the domicile, that divorce litigation has been called an action in rem, the res being the marital relationship between the parties. One may question whether the analogy has not caused more confusion than clarity, but at any rate it shows the way in which the matter has been regarded in the law. It is of significance upon the importance of domicile as the foundation for jurisdiction that the Supreme Court has recently held that a divorce action at the domicile of one of the parties is entitled to full faith and credit as a matter of constitutional compulsion even without the presence of the defending spouse.[20] On the other hand, a divorce not at the domicile gives no protection against a prosecution for bigamy in the state of the domicile,[21] although if the defendant is in court he, himself, may be precluded from questioning the decree on the grounds of res judicata.[22]

We now go out beyond the place where legal trails end. The Supreme Court has never had occasion to say what would happen in a case where two parties, being personally before the court, are purportedly divorced by a state which has no domiciliary jurisdiction, and the question of the validity of the decree comes up in a second state in a prosecution for

20. Williams v. North Carolina (I), 1942, 317 U.S. 287.

21. Williams v. North Carolina (II), 1945, 325 U.S. 226.

22. Sherrer v. Sherrer, 1948, 334 U.S. 343; Coe v. Coe, 1948, 334 U.S. 378.

bigamy, or in a suit for necessaries by a creditor, or in some other such fashion. Granted that the parties are precluded from attacking the decree, does that immunity extend only to attacks by them or by those in privity with them? [23] Here is an unanswered question....

But assume that the Virgin Islands cannot grant to a nondomiciliary a decree which will be impregnable elsewhere by the shield of full faith and credit. Can it not, if it pleases, provide for the granting of a divorce decree to any plaintiff who has a defendant in court in the Virgin Islands? If the decree is good by the law of the Islands and the parties thereto and those in privity with them cannot attack it, it may well be good enough for practical purposes in a world where divorce decrees as well as everything else may fall short of perfection. But is such a decree, which the parties might regard as good enough, one which a nondomiciliary court may grant?

. . .

Before the days of the Fourteenth Amendment, a state could and some states did, pass rules for the exercise of jurisdiction against nonconsenting, nonresident absentee defendants. These rules were not based upon what are now considered the fundamental requisites for such jurisdiction. The judgments were not recognized in other states under the full faith and credit clause, but there was no foundation for testing their validity in the state where they were rendered. After the Fourteenth Amendment provided a way for testing the validity of these judgments in the rendering state under the due process clause, it became well settled that an attempt to give a personal judgment for money against one not subject to the state's jurisdiction was invalid at home under due process, as well as invalid abroad under full faith and credit. With regard to this type of case one can generalize and say that due process at home and full faith and credit in another state are correlative.

. . .

We think that adherence to the domiciliary requirement is necessary if our states are really to have control over the domestic relations of their citizens. The instant case would be typical. In the Virgin Islands incompatibility of temperament constitutes grounds for divorce. In Connecticut it does not. We take it that it is all very well for the Virgin Islands to provide for whatever matrimonial regime it pleases for people who live there. But the same privilege should be afforded to those who control affairs in Connecticut.

Our conclusion is that the second part of this statute conflicts with the due process clause of the Fifth Amendment.... Domestic relations are a matter of concern to the state where a person is domiciled. An attempt by another jurisdiction to affect the relation of a foreign domiciliary is uncon-

---

23. Following the Sherrer and Coe cases, supra, note 22, the Supreme Court has held that if a person cannot collaterally attack the decree by the law of the state which rendered it, he cannot do so in the second state. Johnson v. Muelberger, 1951, 340 U.S. 581. See also Cook v. Cook, 1951, 342 U.S. 126.

stitutional even though both parties are in court and neither one raises the question. The question may well be asked as to what the lack of due process is. The defendant is not complaining. Nevertheless, if the jurisdiction for divorce continues to be based on domicile, as we think it does, we believe it to be lack of due process for one state to take to itself the readjustment of domestic relations between those domiciled elsewhere....

The judgment of the district court will be affirmed.

■ HASTIE, CIRCUIT JUDGE (dissenting). The majority of the court think that both ... changes [in the Virgin Islands statute] violate the Constitution of the United States. Dissenting, I think both changes are within legislative competency....

[That part of Judge Hastie's opinion dealing with the first clause of the statute is omitted.]

In striking down the second amendment of the statute ... this court now says that the Fifth Amendment requires the exercise of legal power to grant divorce be restricted to those cases where one party at least is a local domiciliary. The agreed starting point in this phase of the case is the fact that English and American judges in recent times have refrained, in the absence of statute, from exercising their divorce power except in cases involving local domiciliaries. But what is it that raises this judicial rule of self-restraint to the status of an invariable Constitutional principle? ...

I can find nothing in the history of the present judge-made rule which entitles it to Constitutional sanction. Certainly it is no ancient landmark of the common law....

[T]he rule ... is a creation of nineteenth century American judges. It is also clear that the rule did not become settled in England ... until the 1895 decision of the Privy Council in Le Mesurier v. Le Mesurier, [1895] A.C. 517....

I do not mean to suggest that pre-revolutionary existence is essential to Constitutional protection of a doctrine.... I think our real question on this phase of the case is whether it is clearly arbitrary or unfair for a legislature to adopt an alternative for domicil as an appropriate foundation for divorce power.

When I get to this point I am impressed that a number of states in the British Commonwealth have by legislation made domicil unnecessary to divorce jurisdiction in various situations. See Griswold, Divorce Jurisdiction and Recognition of Divorce Decrees—A Comparative Study, 1951, 65 Harv.L.Rev. 193, 197–208. I find it difficult to see in what respect these abandonments of domicil as a fundamental basis of divorce are patently unfair and arbitrary, even though a particular legislature may not have been restrained by a written Constitution....

Actually, the concept of domicil as a basis of jurisdiction is in practice elusive and very unsatisfactory for several reasons. It is a highly technical concept depending upon the proof of the mental attitude of a person toward a place. Whether in taxation or in divorce, the use of domicil as a jurisdictional base gives trouble when it is applied to people who really have no "home feeling" toward any place or, at the other end of the scale, to those who have more than one home. And ... in the divorce field difficulties are multiplied because the estranged spouses so often establish separate homes. Thus, when a court is asked to grant a divorce it very often finds that not one domicil but at least two—potentially more through refinements of the "marital domicil" concept—may be interested in the parties and their relationship. In these all too familiar situations of divided domicil, the jurisdictional requirement which the majority regards as so essential to fairness that it can not be changed is a troublemaker and a potential source of injustice.

[I]t seems to me that a reasonable person can say that the domiciliary rule does not accomplish what its proponents, including the majority here, claim for it. If it is socially justified in some circumstances, it works unfairly without social justification in others. Perhaps the trouble is that it exaggerates the theoretical interest of the technical domicil of a plaintiff at the time of suit for divorce at the expense of personal and community interests on the defendant's side....

In the Virgin Islands it has seemed to the legislature that an alternative to the domiciliary rule is worth a trial. And in selecting the alternative of personal jurisdiction over both parties, the legislature has obviated that very disregard of interests on the defendant's side which is the great weakness of the domiciliary rule. In this action I can find nothing arbitrary or unfair; hence, nothing inconsistent with the Fifth Amendment.

One other matter should be mentioned. Although the court recognizes that, as concerns authoritative precedents, this case requires us to travel beyond the place "where legal trails end", the majority opinion places some reliance upon the less than pellucid body of case law which is concerned with various aspects of the problem of recognition of divorce granted in one state of the union by a sister state. For present purposes I do not find these cases very helpful. The due process question in divorce jurisdiction which we have to decide is whether it is fair for a state and its courts to adjudicate the merits of a petition for the dissolution of a particular marriage. The problem of the full faith and credit cases is to what extent a second state must subordinate its notions of policy about a marital matter in which it wants to have a voice to what a sister state has already decided. Perhaps full faith should be given to every American divorce decree which satisfies due process. But until the Supreme Court makes it clear that in this area due process and full faith are of the same dimensions, I mistrust any inversion of reasoning which would extract from the not invariant line of decisions on full faith and credit the essentials of due process in the original exercise of divorce power.

[I]t seems proper to point out that if a state proceeds upon this new basis of divorce jurisdiction another conflict of laws difficulty must be faced before the merits of the claim can be decided. That difficulty is the proper choice of the law to govern the controversy.

So long as one of the spouses has had a domiciliary relationship to the forum it has been conventional theory that the forum has sufficient connection with the domestic relation which is the subject matter of suit to justify not only the exercise of its judicial power to decide the controversy but also the application of its own substantive law of divorce as well. Stewart v. Stewart, 1919, 32 Idaho 180, 180 P. 165. It is quite possible that some of the difficulties which have arisen in this field are the result of failure to keep in view that these are distinct problems although the existence of a domiciliary relationship is thought to solve both.

But once the power to decide the case is based merely upon personal jurisdiction a court must decide as a separate question upon what basis, if any, the local substantive law of divorce can properly be applied to determine whether the plaintiff is entitled to the relief sought. In this case, if it should appear that Mr. and Mrs. Alton were both domiciled in Connecticut at the time of suit in the Virgin Islands and that their estrangement had resulted from conduct in the matrimonial home state, it may well be that under correct application of conflict of laws doctrine, and even under the due process clause, it is encumbent upon the Virgin Islands, lacking connection with the subject matter, to apply the divorce law of some state that has such connection, here Connecticut....

Of course such a solution would be a novelty in divorce procedure. But the entire situation presented by this statute is very unusual. And the legislation is an innovation in a very important area. I think, therefore, that we should try to answer no more questions than the exigencies of this litigation require.... Accordingly, I do no more than point out that this choice of law question would have to be considered if the court's power to decide this case depended upon personal jurisdiction and that basis of jurisdiction were sustained, as I believe it should be.

. . .

■ I am authorized to state that CHIEF JUDGE BIGGS and CIRCUIT JUDGE KALODNER concur in the views stated in this opinion.

NOTES

1. The Supreme Court granted certiorari in the Alton case, but then dismissed the proceeding as moot upon learning that in the meantime one of the spouses had procured a second divorce in another jurisdiction, 347 U.S. 911 (1954). In Granville–Smith v. Granville–Smith, 349 U.S. 1 (1955), the Supreme Court invalidated the Virgin Islands statute, however, without passing upon the constitutionality of the statute under the due process clause. The decision was based on the ground that in enacting the statute the Virgin Islands Legislative Assembly had exceeded the power granted it by Congress. This power was to legislate on "all subjects of local application," and this language was held not to include the granting of a divorce to non-residents.

2. How can a state violate due process by giving spouses a divorce which both desire? Apart from considerations of fairness to the individual parties, should there be some restrictions upon the power of a member state of a federal union to hear and adjudicate issues which are of far greater concern to a sister state? See Rheinstein, The Constitutional Bases of Jurisdiction, 22 U.Chi.L.Rev. 775 (1955).

3. The Supreme Court has never had occasion to determine whether domicile of one of the spouses in the divorce state is an essential jurisdictional basis for the granting of a divorce. The *Williams* case, pp. 847–855, infra, have been cited for the proposition that domicile is a required jurisdictional basis for divorce. However, the Nevada statute in *Williams,* as interpreted by the Nevada courts, required the petitioner to be a domiciliary. The issue in *Williams,* therefore, was whether domicile of the petitioning spouse was a sufficient jurisdictional basis, not whether it was the only one.

Statutes in an increasing number of states permit the rendering of a divorce on some basis other than domicile. The most common type of statute is one which authorizes the granting of a divorce to military personnel who have been stationed in the state for a given period, which is frequently a year but is only 90 days under § 302 of the Uniform Marriage and Divorce Act.

An Arkansas statute (Ark.Stats.Ann. §§ 34–1208, 34–1208.1 (1947)) empowers the Arkansas courts to grant a divorce to one who alleges and proves "actual presence" within the state for a three-month period. The constitutionality of this statute was upheld in Wheat v. Wheat, 229 Ark. 842, 318 S.W.2d 793 (1958).

4. Comment *b* of § 72 of Restatement, Second, Conflict of Laws reads as follows:

b. Relationships other than domicil. If one or both of the spouses are domiciled in the state, the state has a sufficient interest in the marriage status to give it judicial jurisdiction to dissolve the marriage (see §§ 70–71). The domicil of one or of both of the spouses in the state is not, however, the only possible basis of jurisdiction. A state may have a sufficient interest in a spouse by reason of some relationship other than domicil, to give the state judicial jurisdiction to dissolve the marriage. In the present state of the authorities, few definite statements can be made as to what relationships with a state, other than domicil, will suffice. Residence, as distinguished from domicil, by one of the spouses in the state for a substantial period, such as a year, is an adequate jurisdictional basis for the rendition of a divorce. On the other hand, the fact that the spouses were married in the state should not of itself provide an adequate jurisdictional basis. A distinction may ultimately be drawn between situations where both spouses are subject to the personal jurisdiction of the divorce court and where there is jurisdiction over only one spouse. One or more jurisdictional bases may be found adequate for the granting of a divorce in the first situation and inadequate in the second.*

5. Indyka v. Indyka, [1967] 3 W.L.R. 510. The case involved the status in England of a divorce granted in Czechoslovakia. H and W were Czech nationals who had married in Czechoslovakia. After the start of World War II, H acquired a domicile in England. Thereafter W, who had remained in Czechoslovakia, obtained there an ex parte divorce. H remarried in England and, when his second wife sought a divorce, defended on the ground that their marriage was void for bigamy, attacking the Czech divorce as invalid. The House of Lords unanimously held that the Czech divorce was valid and that domicile of at least one of the spouses is not the only jurisdictional basis for divorce. Among other jurisdictional bases suggested in the five opinions were nationality and residence. The case probably stands for

---

* Quoted with the permission of the copyright owner, The American Law Institute.

no more precise a proposition than that a state will be recognized as having jurisdiction to grant a divorce if it has a "real and substantial connection" with the plaintiff spouse. See 2 Dicey and Morris, The Conflict of Laws 731–733 (12th ed. by Collins 1993). Indyka's common law standard was abolished by the Family Law Act 1986, which implements the 1968 Hague Convention and provides that a foreign divorce decree will be recognized only if it comports with the standards of the Act or other statutes. Id. at 733.

6. As made clear by both opinions in the *Alton* case, one of the most peculiar aspects of American divorce litigation is that the law of the forum is usually applied to determine whether there are adequate grounds for a divorce. So if the action is brought in state X, the law of X will usually be applied even though the complained-of conduct took place in state Y. Restatement, Second, Conflict of Laws § 285.

Would adoption of Judge Hastie's suggestion in Alton with respect to the choice of law for divorce place as serious a road block in the way of a nonresident seeking a divorce as the majority decision? Continental countries traditionally applied the law of the parties' nationality or forum law if one of the parties was a national of the forum. As a result of conflicts law reform in Austria and Germany, those countries now use a series of references (in order of priority) to the law of the parties' common nationality, last common nationality, common habitual residence or, if all else fails, the law of the country with the closest connection to the spouses. Would such an approach adequately address the concerns?

7. The Supreme Court has not yet squarely passed upon the question of what sort of notice of the divorce proceedings must be given the defendant spouse. State statutes sometimes authorize the giving of notice to a nonresident spouse by some form of publication. If the respondent spouse's address is known to petitioner would such statutes be upheld today by the Supreme Court? See Mullane v. Central Hanover Bank & Trust Co., p. 160, supra; p. 166, Note (1), supra.

8. Compare Hartford v. Superior Court, 47 Cal.2d 447, 304 P.2d 1 (1956). Plaintiff, domiciled in California, brought an action to have it determined that defendant was his father. Defendant was not domiciled in California and was served with process outside the state. Plaintiff contended that the California courts had jurisdiction on the ground that the proceeding to establish paternity was a proceeding in rem by analogy to ex parte divorce proceedings. Held, (Traynor, J.) California has no judicial jurisdiction over the defendant. Plaintiff's action against the defendant is in personam. "Basically the difference [between this action and an ex parte divorce action] is between the state's power to insulate its domiciliary from a relationship with one not within its jurisdiction and its lack of power to reach out and fasten a relationship upon a person over whom it has no jurisdiction." See, also, Conlon by Conlon v. Heckler, 719 F.2d 788 (5th Cir.1983): the court at the plaintiff's domicile had divorce jurisdiction but lacked jurisdiction for a declaration of paternity in the absence of personal jurisdiction over the putative father. The petitioner therefore could not claim social security benefits as the deceased putative father's "child." Is the distinction sound? See also p. 878, infra, with respect to annulment jurisdiction.

SOSNA v. IOWA, 419 U.S. 393 (1975): In recent years, a frequently litigated question has been whether a state may constitutionally impose a durational residence requirement for obtaining a divorce. The cases were divided. In the principal case, the Supreme Court upheld the constitutionality of the Iowa one-year residence requirement. The suit was a class action on behalf of all Iowa residents who had resided in the state for less than one year but wished to institute divorce proceedings there. For the majority, Justice Rehnquist said:

> "The imposition of a durational residency requirement for divorce is scarcely unique to Iowa, since 48 States impose such a requirement as a condition for maintaining an action for divorce.[15] As might be expected, the periods vary among the States and range from six weeks[16] to two years.[17] The one-year period selected by Iowa is the most common length of time prescribed.[18]
>
> "Appellant contends that the Iowa requirement of one year's residence is unconstitutional for two separate reasons: first, because it establishes two classes of persons and discriminates against those who have recently exercised their right to travel to Iowa ... and, second, because it denies a litigant the opportunity to make an individualized showing of bona fide residence and therefore denies such residents access to the only method of legally dissolving their marriage....
>
> "Iowa's residency requirement may reasonably be justified on grounds other than purely budgetary considerations or administrative convenience. Cf. Kahn v. Shevin, 416 U.S. 351 (1974).... Both spouses are obviously interested in the proceedings, since it will affect their marital status and very likely their property rights. Where a married couple has minor children, a decree of divorce would usually include provisions for their custody and support. With consequences of such moment riding on a divorce decree issued by its courts, Iowa may insist that one seeking to initiate such a proceeding have the modicum of attachment to the State required here.
>
> "Such a requirement additionally furthers the State's parallel interests in both avoiding officious intermeddling in matters in which another State has a paramount interest, and in minimizing the susceptibility of its own divorce decrees to collateral attack. A State such as Iowa may quite reasonably decide that it does not wish to become a divorce mill for unhappy spouses who have lived there as short a time as appellant had when she commenced her action in the state court after having long resided elsewhere.... Perhaps even more importantly, Iowa's interests extend beyond its borders and include the recognition of its divorce decrees by other States under the Full Faith and Credit Clause of the Constitution,

---

15. Louisiana and Washington are the exceptions. La.Civ.Code, Art. 10A(7) (Supp. 1974). But see Art. 10B providing that "if a spouse has established and maintained a residence in a parish of this state for a period of twelve months, there shall be a rebuttable presumption that he has a domicile in this state in the parish of such residence." Wash. Laws 1973, 1st Ex.Sess., c. 157. Among the other 48 States, the durational residency requirements are of many varieties, with some applicable to all divorce actions, others only when the respondent is not domiciled in the State, and still others applicable depending on where the grounds for divorce accrued. See the 50–State compilation issued by the National Legal Aid and Defenders Association, Divorce, Annulment and Separation in the United States (1973). [Some of the Court's footnotes have been omitted.]

16. See, e.g., Idaho Code § 32–701 (1963); Nev.Rev.Stat. § 125.020 (1973).

17. See, e.g., R.I.Gen.Laws Ann. § 15–2–2 (1970); Mass.Gen.Laws Ann., c. 208, §§ 4–5 (Supp.1974).

18. More than a majority of the States impose a one-year residency requirement of some kind. Divorce, Annulment and Separation in the United States, supra, n. 15.

Art. IV, § 1.... For that reason, the State asked to enter such a decree is entitled to insist that the putative divorce plaintiff satisfy something more than the bare minimum of constitutional requirements before a divorce may be granted. The State's decision to exact a one-year residency requirement as a matter of policy is therefore buttressed by a quite permissible inference that this requirement not only effectuate[s] state substantive policy but likewise provides a greater safeguard against successful collateral attack than would a requirement of bona fide residence alone.[21] ...."

■ In his dissenting opinion, JUSTICE MARSHALL said:

"The Court omits altogether what should be the first inquiry: whether the right to obtain a divorce is of sufficient importance that its denial to recent immigrants constitutes a penalty on interstate travel. In my view, it clearly meets that standard....

"Having determined that the interest in obtaining a divorce is of substantial social importance, I would scrutinize Iowa's durational residency requirement to determine whether it constitutes a reasonable means of furthering important interests asserted by the State. The Court, however, has not only declined to apply the 'compelling interest' test to this case, it has conjured up possible justifications for the State's restriction in a manner much more akin to the lenient standard we have in the past applied in analyzing equal protection challenges to business regulations.... I continue to be of the view that the 'rational basis' test has no place in equal protection analysis when important individual interests with constitutional implications are at stake....

"... Certainly the stakes in a divorce are weighty both for the individuals directly involved in the adjudication and for others immediately affected by it. The critical importance of the divorce process, however, weakens the argument for a long residence requirement rather than strengthening it. The impact of the divorce decree only underscores the necessity that the State's regulation be evenhanded.

"It is not enough to recite the State's traditionally exclusive responsibility for regulating family law matters; some tangible interference with the State's regulatory scheme must be shown. Yet in this case, I fail to see how any legitimate objective of Iowa's divorce regulations would be frustrated by granting equal access to new state residents....

"... Iowa has a legitimate interest in protecting itself against invasion by those seeking quick divorces in a forum with relatively lax divorce laws, and it may have some interest in avoiding collateral attacks on its decree in other States. These interests, however, would adequately be protected by

---

21. Since the majority of States require residence for at least a year, see n. 18, supra, it is reasonable to assume that Iowa's one-year "floor" makes its decrees less susceptible to successful collateral attack in other States. As the Court of Appeals for the Fifth Circuit observed in upholding a six-month durational residency requirement imposed by Florida, an objective test may impart to a State's divorce decrees "a verity that tends to safeguard them against the suspicious eyes of other states' prosecutorial authorities, the suspicions of private counsel in other states, and the post-decree dissatisfaction of parties to the divorce who wish a second bite. Such a reputation for validity of divorce decrees is not, then, merely cosmetic."

Makres v. Askew, 500 F.2d 577, 579 (CA5 1974), aff'g 359 F.Supp. 1225 (M.D.Fla. 1973).

a simple requirement of domicile—physical presence plus intent to remain—which would remove the rigid one-year barrier while permitting the State to restrict the availability of its divorce process to citizens who are genuinely its own.[6] ... If, as the majority assumes, Iowa is interested in assuring itself that its divorce petitioners are legitimately Iowa citizens, requiring petitioners to provide convincing evidence of bona fide domicile should be more than adequate to the task.[9]"

B. EXTRATERRITORIAL RECOGNITION

Three principal different situations should be distinguished. In the first the divorce is handed down in a state where both spouses are domiciled. In the second the divorce state is the domicile of only one spouse, and in the third this state is the domicile of neither spouse. Foreign-country divorces and non-judicial (e.g., religious) divorces raise additional problems and are treated briefly at pp. 874–877, infra.

Prior to the Williams decisions, the situation which gave rise to most litigation was the second one, in which a divorce had been rendered in State F–1 where one spouse was domiciled, and its effect was questioned in State F–2. Many states recognized such a divorce under their rules of conflict of laws. But some states refused to do so except as compelled by the full faith and credit requirement.

The two leading decisions on full faith and credit were Atherton v. Atherton, 181 U.S. 155 (1901) and Haddock v. Haddock, 201 U.S. 562 (1906). Both involved the second situation. In the Atherton case, a divorce granted to the husband in the state of matrimonial domicile was held entitled to full faith and credit and thus to constitute a bar to an action for separation brought by the wife in a second state. But in the Haddock case a divorce granted to the husband in a state where he was then domiciled, but which was not the state of matrimonial domicile, was denied constitutional protection in the second state where the wife brought a suit for separation and alimony. In neither case did State F–1 have

---

6. The availability of a less restrictive alternative such as a domicile requirement weighs heavily in testing a challenged state regulation against the "compelling interest" standard. See Shapiro v. Thompson, 394 U.S., at 638; Dunn v. Blumstein, 405 U.S., at 342, 350–352; Memorial Hospital v. Maricopa County, 415 U.S., at 267; Shelton v. Tucker, 364 U.S. 479, 488 (1960). Since the Iowa courts have in effect interpreted the residence statute to require proof of domicile as well as one year's residence, see Korsrud v. Korsrud, 242 Iowa 178, 45 N.W.2d 848 (1951); Julson v. Julson, 255 Iowa 301, 122 N.W.2d 329 (1963), a shift to a "pure" domicile test would impose no new burden on the State's fact-finding process.

9. The majority argues that since most States require a year's residence for divorce, Iowa gains refuge from the risk of collateral attack in the understanding solicitude of States with similar laws. Of course, absent unusual circumstances, a judgment by this Court striking down the Iowa statute would similarly affect the other states with one- and two-year residency requirements. For the same reason, the risk of subjecting Iowa to an invasion of divorce-seekers seems minimal. If long residency requirements are held unconstitutional, Iowa will not stand conspicuously alone without a residency requirement "defense." Moreover, its 90–day conciliation period, required of all divorce petitioners in the State, would still serve to discourage peripatetic divorce-seekers who are looking for the quickest possible adjudication.

personal jurisdiction over the respondent. These decisions led to the belief that a divorce at the domicile of one spouse was not entitled to full faith and credit, unless there was some additional strengthening factor, e.g., that F–1 was the matrimonial domicile or had personal jurisdiction over the respondent.

Williams v. North Carolina

Supreme Court of the United States, 1942.
317 U.S. 287, 63 S.Ct. 207, 87 L.Ed. 279, 143 A.L.R. 1273.

Certiorari to the Supreme Court of North Carolina.

■ JUSTICE DOUGLAS delivered the opinion of the Court.

Petitioners were tried and convicted of bigamous cohabitation under § 4342 of the North Carolina Code, 1939, and each was sentenced for a term of years to a state prison. The judgment of conviction was affirmed by the Supreme Court of North Carolina. 220 N.C. 445, 17 S.E.2d 769. The case is here on certiorari.

Petitioner Williams was married to Carrie Wyke in 1916 in North Carolina and lived with her there until May, 1940. Petitioner Hendrix was married to Thomas Hendrix in 1920 in North Carolina and lived with him there until May, 1940. At that time petitioners went to Las Vegas, Nevada, and on June 26, 1940, each filed a divorce action in the Nevada court. The defendants in those divorce actions entered no appearance nor were they served with process in Nevada. In the case of defendant Thomas Hendrix, service by publication was had by publication of the summons in a Las Vegas newspaper and by mailing a copy of the summons and complaint to his last post-office address. In the case of defendant Carrie Williams, a North Carolina sheriff delivered to her in North Carolina a copy of the summons and complaint. A decree of divorce was granted petitioner Williams by the Nevada court on August 26, 1940, ... the court finding that "the plaintiff has been and now is a *bona fide* and continuous resident of the County of Clark, State of Nevada, and had been such resident for more than six weeks immediately preceding the commencement of this action in the manner prescribed by law." The Nevada court granted petitioner Hendrix a divorce on October 4, 1940 ... and made the same finding as to this petitioner's *bona fide* residence in Nevada as it made in the case of Williams. Petitioners were married to each other in Nevada on October 4, 1940. Thereafter they returned to North Carolina where they lived together until the indictment was returned.... The Supreme Court of North Carolina in affirming the judgment held that North Carolina was not required to recognize the Nevada decrees under the full faith and credit clause of the Constitution (Art. IV, § 1) by reason of Haddock v. Haddock, 201 U.S. 562. The intimation in the majority opinion (220 N.C. pp. 460–464) that the Nevada divorces were collusive suggests that the second theory on which the State tried the case may have been an alternative ground for the decision below, adequate to sustain the judgment under the rule of Bell v. Bell, 181 U.S. 175—a case in which this Court held that a decree of divorce was not entitled to full faith and credit when it had been granted on constructive service by the courts of a state in which neither spouse was domiciled. But ... North Carolina does not seek to sustain the judgment below on that ground. Moreover it admits that there probably is enough evidence in the record to require that petitioners be considered "to have been actually domiciled in Nevada...." Accordingly, we cannot avoid meeting the Haddock v. Haddock issue in this case ... on the easy assumption that petitioners' domicil in Nevada was a sham and a fraud. Rather, we must treat the present case for the purpose of the limited issue before us precisely the same as if petitioners had resided in Nevada for a term of years and had long ago acquired a permanent abode there....

The Haddock case involved a suit for separation and alimony, brought in New York by the wife on personal service of the husband. The husband pleaded in defense a divorce decree obtained by him in Connecticut where he had established a separate domicil. This Court held that New York, the matrimonial domicil where the wife still resided, need not give full faith and credit to the Connecticut decree, since it was obtained by the husband who wrongfully left his wife in the matrimonial domicil, service on her having been obtained by publication and she not having entered an appearance in the action. But we do not agree with the theory of the Haddock case that so far as the marital status of the parties is concerned, a decree of divorce granted under such circumstances by one state need not be given full faith and credit in another....

Haddock v. Haddock is not based on the ... theory ... that a decree of divorce granted by the courts of one state need not be given full faith and credit in another if the grounds for the divorce would not be recognized by the courts of the forum. It does not purport to challenge or disturb the rule, earlier established by Christmas v. Russell [5 Wall. 290], and subsequently fortified by Fauntleroy v. Lum [210 U.S. 230] that, even though the cause of action could not have been entertained in the state of the forum, a judgment obtained thereon in a sister state is entitled to full faith and credit.... [Haddock was based on the theory that] the state granting the divorce had no jurisdiction over the absent spouse, since it was not the state of the matrimonial domicil, but the place where the husband had acquired a separate domicil after having wrongfully left his wife....

The historical view that a proceeding for a divorce was a proceeding *in rem* (2 Bishop, Marriage & Divorce, 4th ed., § 164) was rejected by the Haddock case. We likewise agree that it does not aid in the solution of the problem presented by this case to label these proceedings as proceedings *in rem*. Such a suit, however, is not a mere *in personam* action. Domicil of the plaintiff, immaterial to jurisdiction in a personal action, is recognized in the Haddock case and elsewhere (Beale, Conflict of Laws, § 110.1) as essential in order to give the court jurisdiction which will entitle the divorce decree to extraterritorial effect, at least when the defendant has neither been personally served nor entered an appearance. The findings made in the divorce decrees in the instant case must be treated on the issue before us as meeting those requirements. For it seems clear that the provision of the Nevada statute that a plaintiff in this type of case must "reside" in the State for the required period requires him to have a domicil, as distinguished from a mere residence, in the state.... Hence, the decrees in this case, like other divorce decrees, are more than *in personam* judgments. They involve the marital status of the parties. Domicil creates a relationship to the state which is adequate for numerous exercises of state power.... Each state as a sovereign has a rightful and legitimate concern in the marital status of persons domiciled within its borders. The marriage relation creates problems of large social importance. Protection of offspring, property interests, and the enforcement of marital responsibilities are but a few of commanding problems in the field of domestic relations with which the state must deal. Thus it is plain that each state, by virtue of its command over its domiciliaries and its large interest in the institution of marriage, can alter within its own borders the marriage status of the spouse domiciled there, even though the other spouse is absent. There is no constitutional barrier if the form and nature of the substituted service ... meet the requirements of due process....

[I]f one is lawfully divorced and remarried in Nevada and still married to the first spouse in North Carolina, [a] ... complicated and serious condition would be realized.... Under the circumstances of this case, a man would have two wives, a wife two husbands. The reality of a sentence to prison proves that that is no mere play on words. Each would be a bigamist for living in one state with the only one with whom the other state would permit him lawfully to live. Children of the second marriage would be bastards in one state but legitimate in the other. And all that would flow from the legalistic notion that where one spouse is wrongfully deserted he retains power over the matrimonial domicil so that the domicil of the other spouse follows him wherever he may go, while, if he is to blame, he retains no such power. But such considerations are inapposite. As stated by Mr. Justice Holmes in his dissent in the Haddock case (201 U.S. p. 630), they constitute a "pure fiction, and fiction always is a poor ground for changing substantial rights." Furthermore, the fault or wrong of one spouse in leaving the other becomes under that view a jurisdictional fact on which this Court would ultimately have to pass. Whatever may be said as to the practical effect which such a rule would have in clouding divorce decrees, the question as to where the fault lies has no relevancy to the existence of state power in such circumstances. See Bingham, In the Matter of Haddock v. Haddock, 21 Corn.L.Q. 393, 426. The existence of the power of a state to alter the marital status of its domiciliaries, as distinguished from the wisdom of its exercise, is not dependent on the underlying causes of the domestic rift.... Moreover, so far as state power is concerned, no distinction between a matrimonial domicil and a domicil later acquired has been suggested or is apparent.... It is one thing to say as a matter of state law that jurisdiction to grant a divorce from an absent spouse should depend on whether by consent or by conduct the latter has subjected his interest in the marriage status to the law of the separate domicil acquired by the other spouse.... But where a state adopts, as it has the power to do, a less strict rule, it is quite another thing to say that its decrees affecting the marital status of its domiciliaries are not entitled to full faith and credit in sister states. Certainly if decrees of a state altering the marital status of its domiciliaries are not valid throughout the Union even though the requirements of procedural due process are wholly met, a rule would be fostered which could not help but bring "considerable disaster to innocent persons" and "bastardize children hitherto supposed to be the offspring of lawful marriage" (Mr. Justice Holmes dissenting in Haddock v. Haddock, supra, p. 628), or else encourage collusive divorces. Beale, Constitutional Protection of Decrees for Divorce, 19 Harv.L.Rev. 586, 596. These intensely practical considerations emphasize for us the essential function of the full faith and credit clause in substituting a command for the former principles of comity [Broderick v. Rosner, 294 U.S. 629 at p. 643] and in altering the "status of the several states as independent foreign sovereignties" by making them "integral parts of a single nation." Milwaukee County v. White Co. [296 U.S. 268 at p. 277].

It is objected, however, that if such divorce decrees must be given full faith and credit, a substantial dilution of the sovereignty of other states will be effected. For it is pointed out that under such a rule one state's policy of strict control over the institution of marriage could be thwarted by the decree of a more lax state. But such an objection goes to the application of the full faith and credit clause to many situations. It is an objection in varying degrees of intensity to the enforcement of a judgment of a sister state based on a cause of action which could not be enforced in the state of the forum. Mississippi's policy against gambling transactions was overridden in Fauntleroy v. Lum [210 U.S. 230], when a Missouri judgment based on such a Mississippi contract was enforced by this Court. Such is part of the price of our federal system.

This Court, of course, is the final arbiter when the question is raised as to what is a permissible limitation on the full faith and credit clause.... But the question ... as to what is a permissible limitation on the full faith and credit clause does not involve a decision on our part as to which state policy on divorce is the most desirable one.... It is a Constitution which we are expounding—a Constitution which in no small measure brings separate sovereign states into an integrated whole through the medium of the full faith and credit clause. Within the limits of her political power North Carolina may, of course, enforce her own policy regarding the marriage relation—an institution more basic in our civilization than any other. But society also has an interest in the avoidance of polygamous marriages ... and in the protection of innocent offspring of marriages deemed legitimate in other jurisdictions. And other states have an equally legitimate concern in the status of persons domiciled there as respects the institution of marriage. So, when a court of one state acting in accord with the requirements of procedural due process alters the marital status of one domiciled in that state by granting him a divorce from his absent spouse, we cannot say its decree should be excepted from the full faith and credit clause merely because its enforcement or recognition in another state would conflict with the policy of the latter....

Haddock v. Haddock is overruled. The judgment is reversed and the cause is remanded to the Supreme Court of North Carolina for proceedings not inconsistent with this opinion.

Reversed.

■ JUSTICE FRANKFURTER concurred in a separate opinion and JUSTICE MURPHY and JUSTICE JACKSON dissented in separate opinions.

NOTE

Was attention given in the principal case to the value of fairness to the defendant that was stressed so heavily in International Shoe Co. v. State of Washington, p. 47, supra? What about the admonition, in Shaffer v. Heitner, supra p. 136, that "all" assertion of state court jurisdiction must be evaluated in light of the standards of *International Shoe?* Does *Shaffer* affect the decision in *Williams?* See supra p. 138, footnote 30.

Was the application in the principal case of Nevada law to determine the plaintiff spouse's right to a divorce consistent with the rule of Home Insurance Co. v. Dick, p. 325, supra?

Williams v. North Carolina

Supreme Court of the United States, 1945.
325 U.S. 226, 65 S.Ct. 1092, 89 L.Ed. 1577, 157 A.L.R. 1366.

Certiorari to the Supreme Court of North Carolina.

■ JUSTICE FRANKFURTER delivered the opinion of the Court.

This case is here to review judgments of the Supreme Court of North Carolina, affirming convictions for bigamous cohabitation, assailed on the ground that full faith and credit, as required by the Constitution of the United States, was not accorded divorces decreed by one of the courts of Nevada. Williams v. North Carolina, 317 U.S. 287, decided an earlier aspect of the controversy.... The record then before us did not present the question whether North Carolina had the power "to refuse full faith and credit to Nevada divorce decrees because, contrary to the findings of the Nevada court, North Carolina finds that no *bona fide* domicil was acquired in Nevada." Williams v. North Carolina, supra, at 302. This is the precise issue which has emerged after retrial of the cause following our reversal. Its obvious importance brought the case here. 322 U.S. 725.

. . .

Under our system of law, judicial power to grant a divorce—jurisdiction, strictly speaking—is founded on domicil. Bell v. Bell, 181 U.S. 175; Andrews v. Andrews, 188 U.S. 14. The framers of the Constitution were familiar with this jurisdictional prerequisite, and since 1789, neither this Court nor any other court in the English-speaking world has questioned it. Domicil implies a nexus between person and place of such permanence as to control the creation of legal relations and responsibilities of the utmost significance. The domicil of one spouse within a State gives power to that

State, we have held, to dissolve a marriage wheresoever contracted.... Williams v. North Carolina, supra ...

It is one thing to reopen an issue that has been settled after appropriate opportunity to present their contentions has been afforded to all who had an interest in its adjudication. This applies also to jurisdictional questions. After a contest these cannot be relitigated as between the parties.... But those not parties to a litigation ought not to be foreclosed by the interested actions of others; especially not a State which is concerned with the vindication of its own social policy and has no means, certainly no effective means, to protect that interest against the selfish action of those outside its borders. The State of domiciliary origin should not be bound by an unfounded, even if not collusive, recital in the record of a court of another State. As to the truth or existence of a fact, like that of domicil, upon which depends the power to exert judicial authority, a State not a party to the exertion of such judicial authority in another State but seriously affected by it has a right, when asserting its own unquestioned authority, to ascertain the truth or existence of that crucial fact.

These considerations of policy are equally applicable whether power was assumed by the court of the first State or claimed after inquiry. This may lead, no doubt, to conflicting determinations of what judicial power is founded upon. Such conflict is inherent in the practical application of the concept of domicil in the context of our federal system.... What was said in Worcester County Trust Co. v. Riley ... is pertinent here. "Neither the Fourteenth Amendment nor the full faith and credit clause requires uniformity in the decisions of the courts of different states as to the place of domicil, where the exertion of state power is dependent upon domicil within its boundaries." 302 U.S. 292, 299. If a finding by the court of one State that domicil in another State has been abandoned were conclusive upon the old domiciliary State, the policy of each State in matters of most intimate concern could be subverted by the policy of every other State....

Although it is now settled that a suit for divorce is not an ordinary adversary proceeding, it does not promote analysis, as was recently pointed out, to label divorce proceedings as actions *in rem*. Williams v. North Carolina, supra, at 297. But insofar as a divorce decree partakes of some of the characteristics of a decree *in rem*, it is misleading to say that all the world is party to a proceeding *in rem*.... All the world is not party to a divorce proceeding. What is true is that all the world need not be present before a court granting the decree and yet it must be respected by the other ... States provided—and it is a big proviso—the conditions for the exercise of power by the divorce-decreeing court are validly established whenever that judgment is elsewhere called into question. In short, the decree of divorce is a conclusive adjudication of everything except the jurisdictional facts upon which it is founded, and domicil is a jurisdictional fact. To permit the necessary finding of domicil by one State to foreclose all States in the protection of their social institutions would be intolerable.

But to endow each State with controlling authority to nullify the power of a sister State to grant a divorce based upon a finding that one spouse had acquired a new domicil within the divorcing State would, in the proper functioning of our federal system, be equally indefensible.... The necessary accommodation between the right of one State to safeguard its interest in the family relation of its own people and the power of another State to grant divorces can be left to neither State.

The problem is to reconcile the reciprocal respect to be accorded by the members of the Union to their adjudications with due regard for another most important aspect of our federalism whereby "the domestic relations of husband and wife ... were matters reserved to the States," Popovici v. Agler, 280 U.S. 379, 383–84 ... The rights that belong to all the States and the obligations which membership in the Union imposes upon all, are made effective because this Court is open to consider claims ... that the courts of one State have not given the full faith and credit of a sister State that is required by Art. IV, § 1 of the Constitution.

But the discharge of this duty does not make of this Court a court of probate and divorce. Neither a rational system of law nor hard practicality calls for our independent determination, in reviewing the judgment of a State court, of that rather elusive relation between person and place which establishes domicil.... The challenged judgment must, however, satisfy our scrutiny that the reciprocal duty of respect owed by the States to one another's adjudications has been fairly discharged, and has not been evaded under the guise of finding an absence of domicil and therefore a want of power in the court rendering the judgment.

What is immediately before us is the judgment of the Supreme Court of North Carolina. We have authority to upset it only if there is want of foundation for the conclusion that that Court reached. The conclusion it reached turns on its findings that the spouses who obtained the Nevada decrees were not domiciled there. The fact that the Nevada court found that they were domiciled there is entitled to respect, and more. The burden of undermining the verity which the Nevada decrees import rests heavily upon the assailant. But simply because the Nevada court found that it had power to award a divorce decree cannot, we have seen, foreclose reexamination by another State.... If this Court finds that proper weight was accorded to the claims of power by the court of one State in rendering a judgment the validity of which is pleaded in defense in another State, that the burden of overcoming such respect by disproof of the substratum of fact—here domicil—on which such power alone can rest was properly charged against the party challenging the legitimacy of the judgment, that such issue of fact was left for fair determination by appropriate procedure, and that a finding adverse to the necessary foundation for any valid sister-State judgment was amply supported in evidence, we cannot upset the judgment before us. And we cannot do so even if we also found in the record of the court of original judgment warrant for its finding that it had jurisdiction. If it is a matter turning on local law, great deference is owed by the courts of one State to what a court of another State has done.... But when we are dealing as here with an historic notion common to all English-speaking courts, that of domicil, we should not find a want of deference to a sister State on the part of a court of another State which finds an absence of domicil where such a conclusion is warranted by the record....

... The trial judge charged that the State had the burden of proving beyond a reasonable doubt that (1) each petitioner was lawfully married to one person; (2) thereafter each petitioner contracted a second marriage with another person outside North Carolina; (3) the spouses of petitioners were living at the time of this second marriage; (4) petitioners cohabited with one another in North Carolina after the second marriage. The burden, it was charged, then devolved upon petitioners "to satisfy the trial jury, not beyond a reasonable doubt nor by the greater weight of the evidence, but simply to satisfy" the jury from all the evidence, that petitioners were domiciled in Nevada at the time they obtained their divorces. The court further charged that "the recitation" of *bona fide* domicil in the Nevada decree was "prima facie evidence" sufficient to warrant a finding of domicil in Nevada but not compelling "such an inference." If the jury found ... that petitioners had been domiciled in North Carolina and went to Nevada "simply and solely for the purpose of obtaining divorces, intending to return to North Carolina on obtaining" them, they never lost their North Carolina domicils nor acquired new domicils in Nevada....

The scales of justice must not be unfairly weighted by a State when full faith and credit is claimed for a sister-State judgment. But North Carolina has not so dealt with the Nevada decrees. She has not raised unfair barriers to their recognition. North Carolina did not fail in appreciation or application of federal standards of full faith and credit. Appropriate weight was given to the finding of domicil in the Nevada decrees, and that finding was allowed to be overturned only by relevant standards of proof. There is nothing to suggest that the issue was not fairly submitted to the jury and that it was not fairly assessed on cogent evidence....

We conclude that North Carolina was not required to yield her State policy because a Nevada court found that petitioners were domiciled in Nevada when it granted them decrees of divorce. North Carolina was entitled to find, as she did, that they did not acquire domicils in Nevada and that the Nevada court was therefore without power to liberate the petitioners from amenability to the laws of North Carolina governing domestic relations. And, as was said in connection with another aspect of the Full Faith and Credit Clause, our conclusion "is not a matter to arouse the susceptibilities of the States, all of which are equally concerned in the question and equally on both sides." Fauntleroy v. Lum, 210 U.S. 230, 238.

Affirmed.

■ JUSTICE MURPHY wrote a concurring opinion, joined in by CHIEF JUSTICE STONE and JUSTICE JACKSON, which reemphasizes the jurisdictional fact rationale of the majority opinion.

■ JUSTICE RUTLEDGE wrote a dissenting opinion questioning the entire domiciliary concept, reasoning that "jurisdictional fact" has been used to cloak "unitary domicil" so that divorce is back to the era of Haddock with respect to effects.

■ JUSTICE BLACK wrote a dissenting opinion, joined in by JUSTICE DOUGLAS, which reasons that civil liberties are endangered when a criminal offense is grounded on refusal to recognize what another state has apparently regarded as sufficient domicil, and on the further reasoning that the Constitution does not "measure the power of state courts to pass upon petitions for divorce".]

NOTES

1. What law should the F–2 court apply in determining whether the plaintiff spouse acquired a bona fide domicile in F–1? Specifically, is it Supreme Court law, F–1 law or that of F–2? In note 7, on page 231 of the opinion in Williams II, it is said: "Since an appeal to the Full Faith and Credit Clause raises questions arising under the Constitution of the United States, the proper criteria for ascertaining domicil, should these be in dispute, become matters for federal determination...." See Rice v. Rice, 336 U.S. 674 (1949), where the Supreme Court sustained the finding of a Connecticut court that a Nevada divorce was not supported by a bona fide domicile. This case is commented upon in Freund, Rice v. Rice—A Comment, 23 Conn.Bar J. 182 (1949); Rheinstein, Domicile as Jurisdictional Basis of Divorce Decrees, 23 Conn.Bar J. 280 (1949).

2. A helpful article on the problems presented by the Williams cases is D. Currie, Suitcase Divorce in the Conflict of Laws, 34 U.Chi.L.Rev. 26 (1967).

3. For a discussion of professional ethics problems which may arise in connection with matrimonial litigation, see Adams and Adams, Ethical Problems in Advising Migratory Divorce, 16 Hastings L.J. 60 (1964); Drinker, Problems of Professional Ethics in Matrimonial Litigation, 66 Harv.L.Rev. 443 (1953); Drinker, Legal Ethics 80, 122–128 (1953); Neuman, Legal Advice Toward Illegal Ends, 28 U.Rich.L.Rev. 287, 304–308 (1994).

4. The effect given U.S. divorces in foreign countries may depend on whether the particular country has adopted the Hague Convention on the Recognition of Divorces and Legal Separations of 1970. The Convention provides for recognition of divorces decreed in observance of its jurisdictional standards (including either party's domicile). When the Convention applies, the divorce has the same effect in F–2 as where rendered. See, e.g., Lawrence v. Lawrence, [1985] 3 W.L.R. 125, 2 All E.R. 733 (C.A.): a Brazilian woman obtained a Nevada divorce, remarried in Nevada, and subsequently contested the validity of her remarriage in England on the ground that Brazil would not have recognized the Nevada divorce so that she lacked capacity to remarry. Held: the Nevada divorce met the Convention's jurisdictional requirements and was valid; its effect, including capacity to remarry, was determined by Nevada law. See contributions by Downes and Lipstein in 35 Int'l & Comp.L.Q. 170, 178 respectively (1986). The matter may be different in civil law countries which have not adopted the Hague Convention and which combine jurisdiction and choice-of-law considerations. For instance, if validity of a divorce depends, in addition to jurisdiction of the F–1 court, on a requirement that the divorcing court apply the right substantive law (e.g., the law of nationality), then a U.S. divorce of a foreign national by application of the local law of F–1 may prevent recognition of the decree in F–2. An illustration is the fact situation in *Lawrence,* supra, in circumstances where the validity of the Nevada decree was placed in issue in Brazil.

C. Extraterritorial Recognition: Limits on Attack for Jurisdictional Defects

DAVIS v. DAVIS, 305 U.S. 32 (1938): Husband, alleging he was a Virginia domiciliary, instituted divorce action there. Wife was served personally in the District of Columbia, her domicile, and appeared in the Virginia action to contest husband's allegations as to his domicile. The court found that husband was domiciled in Virginia and granted the divorce. Husband thereafter brought suit in the District of Columbia to have a prior separation decree modified as a result of the Virginia divorce. The District of Columbia court refused to recognize the Virginia divorce on the grounds of lack of jurisdiction. Held, reversed. Both parties having appeared, and the domicile question having been fully argued, the Virginia decision is res judicata.

Sherrer v. Sherrer

Supreme Court of the United States, 1948.
334 U.S. 343, 68 S.Ct. 1087, 92 L.Ed. 1429, 1 A.L.R.2d 1355.

Certiorari to the Probate Court for Berkshire County, Massachusetts.

■ CHIEF JUSTICE VINSON delivered the opinion of the Court.

We granted certiorari in this case and in Coe v. Coe ... to consider the contention of petitioners that Massachusetts has failed to accord full faith and credit to decrees of divorce rendered by courts of sister States.

Petitioner Margaret E. Sherrer and the respondent, Edward C. Sherrer, were married in New Jersey in 1930, and from 1932 until April 3, 1944, lived together in Monterey, Massachusetts. Following a long period of marital discord, petitioner, accompanied by the two children of the marriage, left Massachusetts on the latter date, ostensibly for the purpose of spending a vacation in the State of Florida. Shortly after her arrival in Florida, however, petitioner informed her husband that she did not intend to return to him. . . .

On July 6, 1944, a bill of complaint for divorce was filed at petitioner's direction in the Circuit Court of the Sixth Judicial Circuit of the State of Florida. The bill alleged extreme cruelty as grounds for divorce and also alleged that petitioner was a "bona fide legal resident of the State of Florida." The respondent received notice by mail of the pendency of the divorce proceedings. He retained Florida counsel who entered a general appearance and filed an answer denying the allegations of petitioner's complaint, including the allegation as to petitioner's Florida residence.

On November 14, 1944, hearings were held in the divorce proceedings. Respondent appeared personally to testify with respect to a stipulation entered into by the parties relating to the custody of the children.

Throughout the entire proceedings respondent was represented by counsel. Petitioner introduced evidence to establish her Florida residence and testified generally to the allegations of her complaint. Counsel for respondent failed to cross-examine or to introduce evidence in rebuttal.

The Florida court on November 29, 1944, entered a decree of divorce after specifically finding that petitioner "is a bona fide resident of the State of Florida, and that this court has jurisdiction of the parties and the subject matter in said cause ..." Respondent failed to challenge the decree by appeal to the Florida Supreme Court.

On December 1, 1944, petitioner was married in Florida to one Henry A. Phelps, whom petitioner had known while both were residing in Massachusetts and who had come to Florida shortly after petitioner's arrival in that State. Phelps and petitioner lived together as husband and wife in Florida, where they were both employed, until February 5, 1945, when they returned to Massachusetts.

In June, 1945, respondent instituted an action in the Probate Court of Berkshire County, Massachusetts, which has given rise to the issues of this case. Respondent alleged that he is the lawful husband of petitioner, that the Florida decree of divorce is invalid, and that petitioner's subsequent marriage is void. Respondent prayed that he might be permitted to convey his real estate as if he were sole and that the court declare that he was living apart from his wife for justifiable cause. Petitioner joined issue on respondent's allegations.

In the proceedings which followed, petitioner gave testimony in defense of the validity of the Florida divorce decree. The Probate Court, however, resolved the issues of fact adversely to petitioner's contentions, found that she was never domiciled in Florida, and granted respondent the relief he had requested. The Supreme Judicial Court of Massachusetts affirmed the decree on the grounds that it was supported by the evidence and that the requirements of full faith and credit did not preclude the Massachusetts courts from reexamining the finding of domicile made by the Florida court. . . .

That the jurisdiction of the Florida court to enter a valid decree of divorce was dependent upon petitioner's domicile in that State is not disputed. This requirement was recognized by the Florida court which rendered the divorce decree, and the principle has been given frequent application in decisions of the State Supreme Court. But whether or not petitioner was domiciled in Florida at the time the divorce was granted was a matter to be resolved by judicial determination. Here, unlike the situation presented in Williams v. North Carolina, 325 U.S. 226 (1945), the finding of the requisite jurisdictional facts was made in proceedings in which the defendant appeared and participated. The question with which we are confronted, therefore, is whether such a finding made under the circumstances presented by this case may, consistent with the requirements of full faith and credit, be subjected to collateral attack in the courts of a sister State in a suit brought by the defendant in the original proceedings.

The question of what effect is to be given to an adjudication by a court that it possesses requisite jurisdiction in a case, where the judgment of that court is subsequently subjected to collateral attack on jurisdictional grounds has been given frequent consideration by this Court over a period of many years. Insofar as cases originating in the federal courts are concerned, the rule has evolved that the doctrine of *res judicata* applies to adjudications relating either to jurisdiction of the person or of the subject matter where such adjudications have been made in proceedings in which those questions were in issue and in which the parties were given full opportunity to litigate....

We believe that the decision of this Court in the Davis case [p. 856, supra] and those in related situations are clearly indicative of the result to be reached here. Those cases stand for the proposition that the requirements of full faith and credit bar a defendant from collaterally attacking a divorce decree on jurisdictional grounds in the courts of a sister State where there has been participation by the defendant in the divorce proceedings, where the defendant has been accorded full opportunity to contest the jurisdictional issues, and where the decree is not susceptible to such collateral attack in the courts of the State which rendered the decree.

Applying these principles to this case, we hold that the Massachusetts courts erred in permitting the Florida divorce decree to be subjected to attack on the ground that petitioner was not domiciled in Florida at the time the decree was entered....

It is urged further, however, that because we are dealing with litigation involving the dissolution of the marital relation, a different result is demanded from that which might properly be reached if this case were concerned with other types of litigation. It is pointed out that under the Constitution the regulation and control of marital and family relationships are reserved to the States. It is urged, and properly so, that the regulation of the incidents of the marital relation involves the exercise by the States of powers of the most vital importance. Finally, it is contended that a recognition of the importance to the States of such powers demands that the requirements of full faith and credit be viewed in such a light as to permit an attack upon a divorce decree granted by a court of a sister State under the circumstances of this case even where the attack is initiated in a suit brought by the defendant in the original proceedings.

But the recognition of the importance of a State's power to determine the incidents of basic social relationships into which its domiciliaries enter does not resolve the issues of this case. This is not a situation in which a State has merely sought to exert such power over a domiciliary. This is, rather, a case involving inconsistent assertions of power by courts of two States of the Federal Union and thus presents considerations which go beyond the interests of local policy, however vital. In resolving the issues here presented, we do not conceive it to be a part of our function to weigh the relative merits of the policies of Florida and Massachusetts with respect to divorce and related matters. Nor do we understand the decisions of this Court to support the proposition that the obligation imposed by Article IV,

§ 1 of the Constitution and the Act of Congress passed thereunder amounts to something less than the duty to accord *full* faith and credit to decrees of divorce entered by courts of sister States. The full faith and credit clause is one of the provisions incorporated into the Constitution by its framers for the purpose of transforming an aggregation of independent, sovereign States into a nation. If in its application local policy must at times be required to give way, such "is part of the price of our federal system." Williams v. North Carolina, 317 U.S. 287, 302 (1942).

This is not to say that in no case may an area be recognized in which reasonable accommodations of interest may properly be made. But as this Court has heretofore made clear, that area is of limited extent. We believe that in permitting an attack on the Florida divorce decree which again put in issue petitioner's Florida domicile and in refusing to recognize the validity of that decree, the Massachusetts courts have asserted a power which cannot be reconciled with the requirements of due faith and credit. We believe that assurances that such a power will be exercised sparingly and wisely render it no less repugnant to the constitutional commands.

It is one thing to recognize as permissible the judicial reexamination of findings of jurisdictional fact where such findings have been made by a court of a sister State which has entered a divorce decree in *ex parte* proceedings. It is quite another thing to hold that the vital rights and interests involved in divorce litigation may be held in suspense pending the scrutiny by courts of sister States of findings of jurisdictional fact made by a competent court in proceedings conducted in a manner consistent with the highest requirements of due process and in which the defendant has participated. We do not conceive it to be in accord with the purposes of the full faith and credit requirement to hold that a judgment rendered under the circumstances of this case may be required to run the gauntlet of such collateral attack in the courts of sister States before its validity outside of the State which rendered it is established or rejected. That vital interests are involved in divorce litigation indicates to us that it is a matter of greater rather than lesser importance that there should be a place to end such litigation. And where a decree of divorce is rendered by a competent court under the circumstances of this case, the obligation of full faith and credit requires that such litigation should end in the courts of the State in which the judgment was rendered.

Reversed.

■ JUSTICE FRANKFURTER, with whom JUSTICE MURPHY concurs, dissented. In the course of the dissenting opinion, he said (334 U.S. at 368) "A divorce may satisfy due process requirements, and be valid where rendered, and still lack the jurisdictional requisites for full faith and credit to be mandatory."

NOTES

1. In Coe v. Coe, 334 U.S. 378 (1948), decided the same day as Sherrer v. Sherrer, H after residing for six weeks in Nevada sued W for divorce. W appeared

personally and through her attorney filed an answer admitting H's residence in Nevada and a cross-complaint for divorce. The Nevada court found it had jurisdiction of the parties and subject matter and entered a decree granting W a divorce. H remarried and returned to Massachusetts where W brought proceedings against him under a decree for support rendered in Massachusetts before the Nevada divorce. The Massachusetts court disregarded the Nevada divorce as void for lack of jurisdiction. Held, that Massachusetts could not under the requirements of full faith and credit subject the Nevada decree to collateral attack by readjudicating the existence of jurisdictional facts. The dissent in Sherrer v. Sherrer also encompassed Coe v. Coe. For discussion of the Sherrer and Coe cases, see Carey and MacChesney, Divorces by the Consent of the Parties and Divisible Divorce Decrees, 43 Ill.L.Rev. 608 (1948); Paulsen, Migratory Divorce: Chapters III and IV, 24 Ind.L.J. 25 (1948).

2. There are differences among the state courts as to whether the rule of the Sherrer case applies in a situation where the defendant enters an appearance through an attorney in the divorce proceedings but is not physically present and does not contest any issues. In Boxer v. Boxer, 12 Misc.2d 205, 177 N.Y.S.2d 85 (1958), affirmed without opinion, 7 N.Y.2d 781, 194 N.Y.S.2d 47, 163 N.E.2d 149 (1959), H obtained a divorce in Alabama after having been in that state only one day. W appeared through an Alabama attorney whom she had appointed by an instrument mailed from New York. The decree was held entitled to full faith and credit. A similar result was reached in Boudreaux v. Welch, 249 La. 983, 192 So.2d 356 (1966).

On the other hand a divorce has been held subject to collateral attack when the defendant spouse did not appear personally in the divorce proceedings and (a) was represented by an attorney employed and controlled by the plaintiff spouse (Pelle v. Pelle, 229 Md. 160, 182 A.2d 37 (1962); Staedler v. Staedler, 6 N.J. 380, 78 A.2d 896 (1951)) or (b) filed in the divorce proceedings an answer admitting that plaintiff spouse was domiciled in the divorce state. Donnell v. Howell, 257 N.C. 175, 125 S.E.2d 448 (1962). Can these decisions be reconciled with Johnson v. Muelberger, which appears immediately below, and Cook v. Cook, p. 862, infra?

Johnson v. Muelberger

Supreme Court of the United States, 1951.
340 U.S. 581, 71 S.Ct. 474, 95 L.Ed. 552.

■ JUSTICE REED delivered the opinion of the Court.

The right of a daughter to attack in New York the validity of her deceased father's Florida divorce is before us. She was his legatee. The divorce was granted in Florida after the father appeared there and contested the merits. The issue turns on the effect in New York under these circumstances of the Full Faith and Credit Clause of the Federal Constitution.

Eleanor Johnson Muelberger, respondent, is the child of decedent E. Bruce Johnson's first marriage. After the death of Johnson's first wife in 1939, he married one Madoline Ham, and they established their residence in New York. In August 1942, Madoline obtained a divorce from him in a Florida proceeding, although the undisputed facts as developed in the New York Surrogate's hearing show that she did not comply with the jurisdictional ninety-day residence requirement. The New York Surrogate found that

> "In the Florida court, the decedent appeared by attorney and interposed an answer denying the wrongful acts but not questioning the allegations as to residence in Florida. The record discloses that testimony was taken by the Florida court and the divorce granted Madoline Johnson. Both parties had full opportunity to contest the jurisdictional issues in that court and the decree is not subject to attack on the ground that petitioner was not domiciled in Florida."

In 1944 Mr. Johnson entered into a marriage, his third, with petitioner, Genevieve Johnson, and in 1945 he died, leaving a will in which he gave his entire estate to his daughter, Eleanor. After probate of the will, the third wife filed notice of her election to take the statutory one-third share of the estate, under § 18 of the New York Decedent's Estate Law. This election was contested by respondent daughter, and a trial was had before the Surrogate, who determined that she could not attack the third wife's status as surviving spouse, on the basis of the alleged invalidity of Madoline's divorce, because the divorce proceeding had been a contested one, and "[s]ince the decree is valid and final in the State of Florida, it is not subject to collateral attack in the courts of this state."

The Appellate Division affirmed the Surrogate's decree *per curiam,* but the New York Court of Appeals reversed. 301 N.Y. 13, 92 N.E.2d 44.... The Court ... held that the Florida judgment finding jurisdiction to decree the divorce bound only the parties themselves. This followed from their previous opportunity to contest the jurisdictional issue. As the court read the Florida cases to allow Eleanor to attack the decree collaterally in Florida, it decided she should be equally free to do so in New York. The Court of Appeals reached this decision after consideration of the Full Faith and Credit Clause. Because the case involves important issues in the adjustment of the domestic-relations laws of the several states, we granted certiorari, 340 U.S. 874.

... There is substantially no legislative history to explain the purpose and meaning of the [full faith and credit] clause and of the [implementing] statute. From judicial experience with and interpretation of the clause, there has emerged the succinct conclusion that the Framers intended it to help weld the independent states into a nation by giving judgments within the jurisdiction of the rendering state the same faith and credit in sister states as they have in the state of the original forum. The faith and credit given is not to be niggardly but generous, full....

This constitutional purpose promotes unification, not centralization. It leaves each state with power over its own courts but binds litigants, wherever they may be in the Nation, by prior orders of other courts with jurisdiction....

[At this point, the Court discussed the Davis, Williams, Sherrer and Coe cases.]

It is clear from the foregoing that, under our decisions, a state by virtue of the clause must give full faith and credit to an out-of-state divorce by barring either party to that divorce who has been personally served or who has entered a personal appearance from collaterally attacking the decree. Such an attack is barred where the party attacking would not be permitted to make a collateral attack in the courts of the granting state. This rule the Court of Appeals recognized. 301 N.Y. 13, 17, 92 N.E.2d 44. It determined, however, that a "stranger to the divorce action," as the daughter was held to be in New York, may collaterally attack her father's Florida divorce in New York if she could have attacked it in Florida.

No Florida case has come to our attention holding that a child may contest in Florida its parent's divorce where the parent was barred from contesting, as here, by *res judicata*.... If the laws of Florida should be that a surviving child is in privity with its parent as to that parent's estate, surely the Florida doctrine of res judicata would apply to the child's collateral attack as it would to the father's. If, on the other hand, Florida holds ... that the child of a former marriage is a stranger to the divorce proceedings, late opinions of Florida indicate that the child would not be permitted to attack the divorce, since the child had a mere expectancy at the time of the divorce. [At this point, the Court discussed certain Florida cases.]

We conclude that Florida would not permit Mrs. Muelberger to attack the Florida decree of divorce between her father and his second wife as beyond the jurisdiction of the rendering court. In that case New York cannot permit such an attack by reason of the Full Faith and Credit Clause. When a divorce cannot be attacked for lack of jurisdiction by parties actually before the court or strangers in the rendering state, it cannot be attacked by them anywhere in the Union. The Full Faith and Credit Clause forbids.

Reversed.

■ JUSTICE FRANKFURTER dissents, substantially for the reasons given in the opinion of the New York Court of Appeals, 301 N.Y. 13, 92 N.E.2d 44, in light of the views expressed by him in Sherrer v. Sherrer and Coe v. Coe, 334 U.S. 343, 356.

■ JUSTICE MINTON took no part in the consideration or decision of this case.

Cook v. Cook

Supreme Court of the United States, 1951.
342 U.S. 126, 72 S.Ct. 157, 96 L.Ed. 146.

[Shortly after he had gone through a marriage ceremony with W, H discovered that she was still the lawful wife of one Mann. H and W thereupon agreed to remarry after W had procured a Florida divorce from Mann. This course was followed, but after the remarriage marital difficulties developed and eventually H brought suit in Vermont to have the marriage annulled. This relief was granted by the Vermont courts on the ground that the divorce, and hence the remarriage, were void since W had never acquired a Florida domicile. The case was then taken on certiorari to the Supreme Court.]

■ JUSTICE DOUGLAS delivered the opinion of the Court.

. . .

On this record we do not know what happened in the Florida divorce proceedings except that the Florida court entered a divorce decree in favor of petitioner and against Mann. So far as we know, Mann was a party to the proceedings. So far as we know, the issue of domicile was contested, litigated and resolved in petitioner's favor. If the defendant spouse appeared in the Florida proceedings and contested the issue of the wife's domicile, Sherrer v. Sherrer, 334 U.S. 343, or appeared and admitted her Florida domicile, Coe v. Coe, 334 U.S. 378, 340 U.S. 581, 587, he would be barred from attacking the decree collaterally; and so would a stranger to the Florida proceedings, such as respondent, unless Florida applies a less strict rule of res judicata to the second husband than it does to the first. See Johnson v. Muelberger, supra. On the other hand, if the defendant spouse had neither appeared nor been served in Florida, the Vermont court, under the ruling in Williams v. State of North Carolina, 325 U.S. 226, could reopen the issue of domicile.

. . . The Vermont Supreme Court recognized that there were no findings on those issues in the present record. The Court in referring to the case of Williams v. State of North Carolina, 325 U.S. 226, said, "It was there held that the question of bona fide domicile was open to attack, notwithstanding the full faith and credit clause when the other spouse neither had appeared nor been served with process in the state. The findings here do not show either of these criteria." 116 Vt. 374, 378, 76 A.2d 593, 595. Yet it is essential that the court know what transpired in Florida before this collateral attack on the Florida decree can be resolved. For until Florida's jurisdiction is shown to be vulnerable, Vermont may not relitigate the issue of domicile on which the Florida decree rests. . . .

Reversed.

■ JUSTICE FRANKFURTER dissented in a separate opinion.

NOTES

1. A Nevada statute bars all third-party attacks on Nevada divorce decrees that are binding on the parties to the action. Nev.Rev.Stat. § 125.185 (1967). Would this statute also have the effect of barring third-party attacks in sister states?

2. In the *Williams* cases, pp. 847–855, supra, the absent spouses had not questioned the validity of the Nevada divorces obtained by Mr. Williams and Ms. Hendrix. It was the State of North Carolina that asserted the invalidity of the divorces and prosecuted Williams and Hendrix for bigamy. Does the state of the ex-spouses' last matrimonial domicile have an independent interest in the validity of the out-of-state divorce which it may assert when (a) the divorce was ex parte (as in *Williams*) and (b) even when both parties participated? Does Johnson v. Muelberger answer this question? See Weber v. Weber, 200 Neb. 659, 265 N.W.2d 436, 440 (1978), refusing to recognize a Dominican Republic bilateral divorce: "The state is impliedly a party to the marriage contract and has an interest in the continuance and dissolution of the marital relation."

Krause v. Krause

Court of Appeals of New York, 1940.
282 N.Y. 355, 26 N.E.2d 290.

■ FINCH, JUDGE. This is an action for separation brought by a wife in which she seeks support. The husband seeks to avoid liability to plaintiff by alleging the invalidity of a Nevada divorce which he obtained from his first wife. May he avail himself of such a defense?

. . .

The facts presented by the defense are as follows: Defendant and his first wife domiciled in this State, were married here in 1905. There are two children by that marriage. In 1932 the present defendant, while retaining his residence in this State, made a visit to Reno, Nev., where he invoked the jurisdiction of the courts of that State and obtained a decree of divorce from his first wife, who neither entered an appearance nor was personally served in that action, and who at all times has remained a resident of this State.... Consequently this divorce against the first wife is not recognized by the courts of this State.... The subsequent marriage between plaintiff and defendant, therefore, was void for the incapacity of the defendant to marry. But none the less plaintiff and defendant participated in a complete marriage ceremony and did live together as man and wife for six years pursuant thereto, after which time defendant abandoned plaintiff, who now brings this action. Defendant entered the defense already noted, viz., that he lacked capacity to marry plaintiff because the court, which upon his petition purported to accord him a divorce from his first wife, lacked jurisdiction to act in the premises. Upon motion of plaintiff Special Term struck out the defense as insufficient in law ... The Appellate Division affirmed by a divided court ...

The question upon this appeal, therefore, depends upon whether defendant husband may now be heard to assert in this action, brought by his second "wife," that the judgment of divorce which he sought and obtained failed of its purpose and thereby did not give to the defendant that freedom to remarry which he appeared to possess by virtue of said judgment.

In general, a person who invokes the jurisdiction of a court will not be heard to repudiate the judgment which that court entered upon his seeking and in his favor.... The rule has been applied in this State in cases where property rights arising out of the marriage have been involved.... It is said, however, that in Stevens v. Stevens [273 N.Y. 157, 7 N.E.2d 26] we have answered the question upon which the case at bar turns. But in the Stevens case an action for separation was brought in this State by a wife against her husband who had previously secured a divorce in a Nevada court which was admittedly without jurisdiction. The husband counterclaimed for a divorce. At the trial the wife sought to defeat the counterclaim by introducing in evidence the Nevada divorce obtained by the husband in order to put him in a position where he could not maintain his claim for divorce because he was no longer the husband of the wife. Upon the facts of that case this court held that the husband was not prevented from maintaining the action for divorce despite the prior Nevada decree which he had obtained.... In the Stevens case the position which the husband assumed in the proceedings in this State was inconsistent with the decree which he had obtained in Nevada only in the sense that as part of a cause of action for divorce it is necessary to prove the marriage.... But the action which he sought to take was parallel with that which he had previously undertaken in the Nevada proceedings in that the object of both was the same, to wit, termination of the marriage with his wife. Such is not the situation in the case at bar where the action which defendant seeks to take is inconsistent with the result purportedly achieved by the invalid Nevada decree....

We come, then, to a consideration of the principle applicable in the case at bar. We cannot lose sight of the fact that the present defendant was himself the party who had obtained the decree of divorce which he now asserts to be invalid and repudiates in order that he may now disown any legal obligation to support the plaintiff, whom he purported to marry. To refuse to permit this defendant to escape his obligation to support plaintiff does not mean that the courts of this State recognize as valid a judgment of divorce which necessarily is assumed to be invalid in the case at bar, but only that it is not open to defendant in these proceedings to avoid the responsibility which he voluntarily incurred.

It is conceded that the estoppel which is invoked against the present defendant is not a true estoppel as that term is ordinarily understood, although the effect is the same in the case at bar.

But it is urged that even though the prior authorities in this State do not compel a contrary result, a different conclusion should be reached as a matter of principle. It is said that public policy requires that the interest of the State in the first marriage be protected even though that may also give to the individual defendant an incidental advantage to which he is not entitled in his private right. Thus defendant seeks to avoid the obligation which he has purported to undertake to support his second wife, upon the pretext that such is inconsistent with his obligations toward his first wife. Objection upon this score is fully met by the fact that the needs of the first wife are to be taken into account in arriving at the ability of defendant to support plaintiff in the case at bar. Defendant would altogether disavow any obligation toward this plaintiff because of his obligation to his first wife. The result which we reach here is the only one which awards justice to this plaintiff, prevents her from becoming a public charge if she should be impecunious and at the same time protects the first wife in adequate degree. Thus there is complete observance of not only the interest of the

State in the protection of the first marriage, but also of the other interest of the State that marriage obligations shall not be lightly undertaken and lightly discarded.

Nothing in this decision should be taken to mean that because the defendant may not in these proceedings avail himself of the invalidity of his Nevada decree he is not the husband of his first wife. On the contrary, the very theory that defendant is precluded in these proceedings presupposes that the true situation is the contrary of that which he may show in the case at bar.

It follows, therefore, that the order appealed from should be affirmed, with costs, and the question certified answered in the negative.

Order affirmed, etc.

[The dissenting opinion is omitted.]

NOTES

1. Suppose that a spouse would be estopped from attacking the divorce in F–1. Does the Constitution require in such a case that he likewise be estopped in F–2? Will the Sherrer, Coe, Johnson and Cook cases result in a narrower application of the estoppel doctrine?

2. The estoppel principle is frequently applied to a spouse who did not obtain the divorce but who took advantage of it by remarrying. Carbulon v. Carbulon, 293 N.Y. 375, 57 N.E.2d 59 (1944). Cf. Hewett v. Zegarzewski, 90 N.C.App. 443, 368 S.E.2d 877 (1988). On the other hand, the principle has not been applied to the children of a spouse who would himself be estopped. So in Matter of Lindgren, 293 N.Y. 18, 55 N.E.2d 849 (1944), W–2 could not prevail over a child of H by his first marriage, H having secured a "divorce" from W–1.

D. EXTRATERRITORIAL RECOGNITION: DIVISIBLE DIVORCE

Estin v. Estin

Supreme Court of the United States, 1948.
334 U.S. 541, 68 S.Ct. 1213, 92 L.Ed. 1561, 1 A.L.R.2d 1412.

Certiorari to the Court of Appeals of New York.

■ Opinion of the Court by JUSTICE DOUGLAS, announced by JUSTICE REED.

This case, here on certiorari to the Court of Appeals of New York, presents an important question under the Full Faith and Credit Clause of the Constitution. Article IV, § 1. It is whether a New York decree awarding respondent $180 per month for her maintenance and support in a separation proceeding survived a Nevada divorce decree which subsequently was granted petitioner.

The parties were married in 1937 and lived together in New York until 1942 when the husband left the wife. There was no issue of the marriage. In 1943 she brought an action against him for a separation. He entered a general appearance. The court, finding that he had abandoned her, granted her a decree of separation and awarded her $180 per month as permanent alimony. In January 1944 he went to Nevada where in 1945 he instituted an action for divorce. She was notified of the action by constructive service but entered no appearance in it. In May, 1945, the Nevada court, finding that petitioner had been a bona fide resident of Nevada since January 30, 1944, granted him an absolute divorce "on the ground of three years continual separation, without cohabitation." The Nevada decree made no provision for alimony, though the Nevada court had been advised of the New York decree.

Prior to that time petitioner had made payments of alimony under the New York decree. After entry of the Nevada decree he ceased paying. Thereupon respondent sued in New York for a supplementary judgment for the amount of the arrears. Petitioner appeared in the action and moved to eliminate the alimony provisions of the separation decree by reason of the Nevada decree. The Supreme Court denied the motion and granted respondent judgment for the arrears. 63 N.Y.S.2d 476. The judgment was affirmed by the Appellate Division, 271 App.Div. 829, 66 N.Y.S.2d 421, and then by the Court of Appeals, 296 N.Y. 308, 73 N.E.2d 113.

We held in Williams v. North Carolina, 317 U.S. 287; 325 U.S. 226 (1) that a divorce decree granted by a State to one of its domiciliaries is entitled to full faith and credit in a bigamy prosecution brought in another State, even though the other spouse was given notice of the divorce proceeding only through constructive service; and (2) that while the finding of domicile by the court that granted the decree is entitled to *prima facie* weight, it is not conclusive in a sister State but might be relitigated there. And see Esenwein v. Esenwein, 325 U.S. 279. The latter course was followed in this case, as a consequence of which the Supreme Court of New York found, in accord with the Nevada court, that petitioner "is now and since January, 1944, has been a bona fide resident of the State of Nevada."

Petitioner's argument therefore is that the tail must go with the hide—that since by the Nevada decree, recognized in New York, he and respondent are no longer husband and wife, no legal incidence of the marriage remains.

[T]he highest court in New York has held in this case that a support order can survive divorce and that this one has survived petitioner's divorce. That conclusion is binding on us, except as it conflicts with the Full Faith and Credit Clause.... The only question for us is whether New York is powerless to make such a ruling in view of the Nevada decree.

We can put to one side the case where the wife was personally served or where she appeared in the divorce proceedings.... The only service on her in this case was by publication and she made no appearance in the Nevada proceeding. The requirements of procedural due process were satisfied and the domicile of the husband in Nevada was foundation for a decree effecting a change in the marital capacity of both parties in all the other States of the Union, as well as in Nevada. Williams v. North Carolina, 317 U.S. 287. But the fact that marital capacity was changed does not mean that every other legal incidence of the marriage was necessarily affected.

Although the point was not adjudicated in Barber v. Barber, 21 How. 582, 588, the Court in that case recognized that while a divorce decree obtained in Wisconsin by a husband from his absent wife might dissolve the *vinculum* of the marriage, it did not mean that he was freed from payment of alimony under an earlier separation decree granted by New York. An absolutist might quarrel with the result and demand a rule that once a divorce is granted, the whole of the marriage relation is dissolved, leaving no roots or tendrils of any kind. But there are few areas of the law in black and white. The greys are dominant and even among them the shades are innumerable. For the eternal problem of the law is one of making accommodations between conflicting interests. This is why most legal problems end as questions of degree. That is true of the present problem under the Full Faith and Credit Clause....

Marital status involves the regularity and integrity of the marriage relation. It affects the legitimacy of the offspring of marriage. It is the basis of criminal laws, as the bigamy prosecution in Williams v. North Carolina dramatically illustrates. The State has a considerable interest in preventing bigamous marriages and in protecting the offspring of marriages from being bastardized. The interest of the State extends to its domiciliaries. The State should have the power to guard its interest in them by changing or altering their marital status and by protecting them in that changed status throughout the farthest reaches of the nation. For a person domiciled in one State should not be allowed to suffer the penalties of bigamy for living outside the State with the only one which the State of his domicile recognizes as his lawful wife. And children born of the only marriage which is lawful in the State of his domicile should not carry the stigma of bastardy when they move elsewhere. These are matters of legitimate concern to the State of the domicile. They entitle the State of the domicile to bring in the absent spouse through constructive service. In no other way could the State of the domicile have and maintain effective control of the marital status of its domiciliaries.

Those are the considerations that have long permitted the State of the matrimonial domicile to change the marital status of the parties by an *ex parte* divorce proceeding ... considerations which in the Williams case we thought were equally applicable to any State in which one spouse had established a bona fide domicile. See 817 U.S. pp. 300–301. But those considerations have little relevancy here. In this case New York evinced a concern with this broken marriage when both parties were domiciled in New York and before Nevada had any concern with it. New York was rightly concerned lest the abandoned spouse be left impoverished and perhaps become a public charge. The problem of her livelihood and support is plainly a matter in which her community had a legitimate interest. The New York court, having jurisdiction over both parties, undertook to protect her by granting her a judgment of permanent alimony. Nevada, however, apparently follows the rule that dissolution of the marriage puts an end to a support order.... But the question is whether Nevada could under any circumstances adjudicate rights of respondent under the New York judgment when she was not personally served or did not appear in the proceeding.

Bassett v. Bassett, 141 F.2d 954, held that Nevada could not. We agree with that view.

The New York judgment is a property interest of respondent, created by New York in a proceeding in which both parties were present.... The property interest which it created was an intangible, jurisdiction over which cannot be exerted through control over a physical thing. Jurisdiction over an intangible can indeed only arise from control of power over the persons whose relationships are the source of the rights and obligations....

Jurisdiction over a debtor is sufficient to give the State of his domicile some control over the debt which he owes.... But we are aware of no power which the State of domicile of the debtor has to determine the personal rights of the creditor in the intangible unless the creditor has been personally served or appears in the proceeding....

We know of no source of power which would take the present case out of that category. The Nevada decree that is said to wipe out respondent's claim for alimony under the New York judgment is nothing less than an attempt by Nevada ... to exercise an *in personam* jurisdiction over a person not before the court. That may not be done. Since Nevada had no power to adjudicate respondent's rights in the New York judgment, New York need not give full faith and credit to that phase of Nevada's judgment. A judgment of a court having no jurisdiction to render it is not entitled to the full faith and credit which the Constitution and statute of the United States demand....

The result in this situation is to make the divorce divisible—to give effect to the Nevada decree insofar as it affects marital status and to make it ineffective on the issue of alimony. It accommodates the interests of both Nevada and New York in this broken marriage by restricting each State to the matters of her dominant concern.

Since Nevada had no jurisdiction to alter respondent's rights in the New York judgment, we do not reach the further question whether in any event that judgment would be entitled to full faith and credit in Nevada.... And it will be time enough to consider the effect of any discrimination shown to out-of-state *ex parte* divorces when a State makes that its policy.

Affirmed.

■ JUSTICE FRANKFURTER and JUSTICE JACKSON dissent in separate opinions.

NOTES

1. Carey and MacChesney, Divorces by the Consent of the Parties and Divisible Divorce Decrees, 43 Ill.L.Rev. 608 (1948); Krauskopf, Divisible Divorce and Rights to Support, Property and Custody, 24 Ohio St.L.J. 346 (1963).

2. Lynn v. Lynn, 302 N.Y. 193, 97 N.E.2d 748 (1951). The case involved exactly the same facts as Estin v. Estin except that the wife appeared in the Nevada divorce proceedings. The decree made no provision for alimony and recited that the wife had made no claim therefor. It was held that an earlier New York support order did not survive the divorce decree since "the Nevada court had jurisdiction of the wife's person by reason of her appearance."

3. Vanderbilt v. Vanderbilt, 354 U.S. 416 (1957), affirming, 1 N.Y.2d 342, 135 N.E.2d 553 (1956). The spouses separated in 1952 while living in California. Thereafter, the husband became domiciled in Nevada and obtained there an ex parte divorce whose effect under Nevada law was to put an end to his duty to support the wife. The wife had moved to New York prior to the institution of the Nevada action, and, after the handing down of the decree, she sued the husband for alimony in New York under a New York statute (now Dom.Rel.L. § 236) which in terms authorizes such an action. The New York courts found for the wife and the Supreme Court affirmed on the ground that "[s]ince the wife was not subject to its jurisdiction, the Nevada divorce court had no power to extinguish any right which [the wife] had under the law of New York to financial support from her husband." There were dissents by Justices Frankfurter and Harlan. Justice Frankfurter believed that Nevada had as much power under due process to affect support rights ex parte as it had to dissolve the marriage. Justice Harlan summarized the grounds of his dissent in his concurring opinion in Simons v. Miami Beach First Nat. Bank, p. 871, infra.

In *Vanderbilt,* the former wife proceeded against the ex-husband by sequestering his property in New York. "Applying *Shaffer* [p. 136, supra] to support-alimony cases would limit what appears to have been the goal of the *Estin* line of cases—to protect the dependent spouse—in that such a spouse would be denied the power to select the forum to determine property rights." Vernon, State–Court Jurisdiction: A Preliminary Inquiry Into the Impact of Shaffer v. Heitner, 63 Iowa L.Rev. 997, 1017 (1978). Consider also the impact of Rush v. Savchuk, p. 148, supra. In what forum may the claimant seek a determination of property rights following an ex parte divorce?

Loeb v. Loeb, 4 N.Y.2d 542, 176 N.Y.S.2d 590, 152 N.E.2d 36 (1958). The spouses originally were domiciled in Vermont. After the husband had obtained an ex parte divorce in Nevada, the wife sought alimony in Vermont but was denied this relief on the ground that the Vermont courts could not grant alimony after a valid divorce. The wife moved to New York and there sought alimony from the husband under the New York statute (now Dom.Rel.L. § 236). Relief was denied on the ground that the New York statute should not be applied to give relief to a wife who was not domiciled in New York when the husband obtained the ex parte divorce. Could the New York statute have been constitutionally applied in this case to award support to the wife? Must a state have had some contact with the spouses prior to the divorce in order to have the power to grant support to one of them? If so, what sort of contact is required?

4. Suppose that the forum does not have an available remedy at all. In some states, alimony can only be given in connection with a divorce, and the action for separate maintenance and support will lie only between parties who are married. Coleman v. Coleman, 361 Pa.Super. 446, 522 A.2d 1115 (1987). Stambaugh v. Stambaugh, 458 Pa. 147, 329 A.2d 483 (1974). Paulsen, Support Rights and an Out-of-State Divorce, 38 Minn.L.Rev. 709 (1954). By common law rule, the California courts may require a husband to pay alimony to his wife following the entry of an ex parte divorce. Hudson v. Hudson, 52 Cal.2d 735, 344 P.2d 295

(1959); Weber v. Superior Court of Los Angeles County, 53 Cal.2d 403, 2 Cal.Rptr. 9, 348 P.2d 572 (1960). Suppose that the claimant in the support action was the defendant in the ex parte divorce and that support can be granted under the law of the divorce state either as part of the divorce or afterwards. Should the fact that the present defendant (petitioner in the divorce) chose that forum prompt F–2 to grant the remedy available in F–1?

5. Suppose that after a Nevada ex parte divorce the non-appearing spouse brings an original suit for alimony and support against the other spouse in the Nevada courts. May these courts refuse to entertain the action on the ground that, so far as Nevada is concerned, plaintiff's right to such relief was terminated by the divorce decree? This question was answered in the affirmative, with one judge dissenting, in Cavell v. Cavell, 90 Nev. 334, 526 P.2d 330 (1974). Is this result consistent with or does it go beyond the *Simons* case, immediately following?

6. A result similar to that of the *Estin* case has been reached in England. Wood v. Wood, [1957] 2 All E.R. 14 (C.A.).

Simons v. Miami Beach First National Bank

Supreme Court of the United States, 1965.
381 U.S. 81, 85 S.Ct. 1315, 14 L.Ed.2d 232.

■ JUSTICE BRENNAN delivered the opinion of the Court.

The question to be decided in this case is whether a husband's valid Florida divorce, obtained in a proceeding wherein his nonresident wife was served by publication only and did not make a personal appearance, unconstitutionally extinguished her dower right in his Florida estate.

The petitioner and Sol Simons were domiciled in New York when, in 1946, she obtained a New York separation decree that included an award of monthly alimony. Sol Simons moved to Florida in 1951 and, a year later, obtained there a divorce in an action of which petitioner had valid constructive notice but in which she did not enter a personal appearance. After Sol Simons' death in Florida in 1960, respondent, the executor of his estate, offered his will for probate in the Probate Court of Dade County, Florida. Petitioner appeared in the proceeding and filed an election to take dower under Florida law, rather than have her rights in the estate governed by the terms of the will, which made no provision for her. The respondent opposed the dower claim, asserting that since Sol Simons had divorced petitioner she had not been his wife at his death, and consequently was not entitled to dower under Florida law. Petitioner thereupon brought the instant action in the Circuit Court for Dade County in order to set aside the divorce decree and to obtain a declaration that the divorce, even if valid to alter her marital status, did not destroy or impair her claim to dower. The action was dismissed after trial, and the Florida District Court of Appeal for the Third District affirmed. 157 So.2d 199. The Supreme Court of Florida declined to review the case, 166 So.2d 151. We granted certiorari, 379 U.S. 877. We affirm.

Petitioner's counsel advised us during oral argument that he no longer challenged the judgment below insofar as it embodied a holding that the

1952 Florida divorce was valid and terminated the marital status of the parties. We therefore proceed to the decision of the question whether the Florida courts unconstitutionally denied petitioner's dower claim.

Petitioner argues that since she had not appeared in the Florida divorce action the Florida divorce court had no power to extinguish any right which she had acquired under the New York decree. She invokes the principle of Estin v. Estin, 334 U.S. 541, where this Court decided that a Nevada divorce court, which had no personal jurisdiction over the wife, had no power to terminate a husband's obligation to provide the wife support as required by a pre-existing New York separation decree....

The short answer to this contention is that the only obligation imposed on Sol Simons by the New York decree, and the only rights granted petitioner under it, concerned monthly alimony for petitioner's support. Unlike the ex-husband in Estin, Sol Simons made the support payments called for by the separate maintenance decree notwithstanding his *ex parte* divorce.... when he died there was consequently nothing left of the New York decree for Florida to dishonor....

Insofar as petitioner argues that since she was not subject to the jurisdiction of the Florida divorce court its decree could not extinguish any dower right existing under Florida law, Vanderbilt v. Vanderbilt, 354 U.S. 416, 418, the answer is that under Florida law no dower right survived the decree. The Supreme Court of Florida has said that dower rights in Florida property, being inchoate, are extinguished by a divorce decree predicated upon substituted or constructive service. Pawley v. Pawley, 46 So.2d 464.[6]

It follows that the Florida courts transgressed no constitutional bounds in denying petitioner dower in her ex-husband's Florida estate.

Affirmed.

---

6. In Pawley the Supreme Court of Florida distinguished the dower right from the right to support saying at 46 So.2d 464, 472–473, n. 2:

"In this, if not in every jurisdiction, right of dower can never be made the subject of a wholly independent issue in any divorce suit. It stands or falls as a result of the decree which denies or grants divorce. It arises upon marriage, as an institution of the law. The inchoate right of dower has some of the incidents of property. It partakes of the nature of a lien or encumbrance. It is not a right which is originated by or is derived from the husband; nor is it a personal obligation to be met or fulfilled by him, but it is a creature of the law, is born at the marriage altar, cradled in the bosom of the marital status as an integral and component part thereof, survives during the life of the wife as such and finds its sepulcher in divorce. Alimony too is an institution of the law but it is a personal obligation of the husband which is based upon the duty imposed upon him by the common law to support his wife and gives rise to a personal right of the wife to insist upon, if she be entitled to, it. It has none of the incidents of, and is in no sense a lien upon or interest in, property. Consequently, the right of the wife to be heard on the question of alimony should not, indeed lawfully it cannot, be destroyed by a divorce decree sought and secured by the husband in an action wherein only constructive service of process was effected."

...

■ JUSTICE HARLAN, concurring.

I am happy to join the opinion of the Court because it makes a partial retreat from Vanderbilt v. Vanderbilt, 354 U.S. 416, a decision which I believe must eventually be rerationalized, if not entirely overruled.

The Vanderbilt case was this. The Vanderbilt couple was domiciled in California. Mr. Vanderbilt went to Nevada, established a new domicile, and obtained an *ex parte* divorce decree which did not provide for alimony payments to Mrs. Vanderbilt. In the meantime Mrs. Vanderbilt went to New York. After the Nevada decree had become final, she sued in New York for support under New York law, sequestering Mr. Vanderbilt's property located there. New York ordered support payments, rejecting full-faith-and-credit arguments based on the Nevada decree....

Two rules emerged from the case, neither of which, I suggest with deference, commends itself: (1) an *ex parte* divorce can have no effect on property rights; (2) a State in which a wife subsequently establishes domicile can award support to her regardless of her connection with that State at the time of the *ex parte* divorce and regardless of the law in her former State of domicile.[2]

The first rule slips unobtrusively into oblivion in today's decision, for Florida is allowed to turn property rights on its *ex parte* decree....

Because New York was petitioner's State of domicile at all times relevant to this case and did not purport to invest her with any rights to property beyond those she received from her husband, the second rule is not involved here. My hope is that its time will come too....

■ JUSTICE BLACK, with whom JUSTICE DOUGLAS joins, concurring....

I do not think that today's decision marks any "retreat" at all from the opinion or holding in Vanderbilt, ... Vanderbilt held that a wife's right to support could not be cut off by an *ex parte* divorce. In the case before us, Mrs. Simons' Florida dower was not terminated by the *ex parte* divorce. It simply never came into existence. No one disputes that the *ex parte* divorce was effective to end the marriage, so that after it Mrs. Simons was no longer Mr. Simons' wife. Florida law, as the Court's opinion shows, grants dower only to a woman who is the legal wife of the husband when he dies. Mrs. Simons therefore had no property rights cut off by the divorce. She simply had her marriage ended by it, and for that reason was not a

---

2. The Vanderbilt result might have been proper on any of three grounds. (1) If New York was Mrs. Vanderbilt's State of domicile at the time of the *ex parte* Nevada divorce, New York law investing a wife with support rights should not be overborne by an *ex parte* decree in another State. (2) If California was Mrs. Vanderbilt's domicile at the time of the Nevada divorce and under California law support could have been awarded, New York should also be free (though not bound) to award support. (3) If Mr. Vanderbilt owned property in New York at the time of the *ex parte* divorce, New York might arguably be free to hold that ownership of New York property carries with it the obligation to support one's wife, at least to the extent of the value of that property.

The Court did not concern itself with the location of Mrs. Vanderbilt's domicile or Mr. Vanderbilt's property at the time of the Nevada divorce.

"widow" within the meaning of the Florida law. Unless this Court were to make the novel declaration that Florida cannot limit dower rights to widows, I see no possible way in which the Vanderbilt case, which dealt with rights which a State did give to divorced wives, could be thought to apply.

■ [A dissenting opinion by JUSTICE STEWART, joined in by JUSTICE GOLDBERG, is omitted.]

NOTES

1. The Simons case makes clear that an absent spouse can constitutionally lose "inchoate" property interests as a result of an ex parte divorce decree. Can this case be reconciled with Estin v. Estin? See D. Currie, Suitcase Divorce in the Conflict of Laws, 34 U.Chi.L.Rev. 26 (1967).

2. Carr v. Carr, 46 N.Y.2d 370, 413 N.Y.S.2d 305, 385 N.E.2d 1234 (1978). The issue was which of two wives was entitled to certain survivor benefits. After having become separated from her husband, the first wife settled in New York. He subsequently obtained an ex parte divorce and remarried. Then, following his death, the first wife brought an action in New York seeking a declaration that her husband's divorce was invalid and that accordingly she was his lawful wife. Held: The action must be dismissed for lack of personal jurisdiction over the second wife. The dissenting judges argued that "when the first wife came to New York, she brought with her the 'res' of the marriage" and that accordingly New York had in rem jurisdiction to determine the validity of this marriage. "The majority's analysis would presumably prevent even a woman married in New York and a lifelong resident from seeking in New York a declaration, for estate purposes, that her husband's out-of-state divorce was invalid."

NOTE ON FOREIGN COUNTRY DIVORCES

Domicile in the state by at least one of the parties is not the only jurisdictional basis for divorce under the law of most foreign countries. Indeed, "most countries do not even have a concept equivalent to our notion of domicile." Juenger, Recognition of Foreign Divorces, 20 Am.J. Comp.L. 1, 19 (1972). To the extent that ties other than domicile in the state suffice as a jurisdictional basis for divorce in the forum state, some foreign country divorces will be entitled to recognition in the United States. Juenger, supra. On the other hand, many of the divorces that were denied recognition in this country involved situations where the divorce had been sought abroad by an American citizen in order to escape the restrictions of his state of domicile. Mexican divorces provide striking examples. In some Mexican states, a divorce could be granted for practically any reason. Sometimes there was no residence requirement, and in certain states a petitioning spouse did not even have to appear in person but could arrange by mail to have an appearance entered on his or her behalf. For these reasons, thousands of Americans sought Mexican divorces, and the question of what extraterritorial effect should be given these divorces has frequently come before American courts. Mexican "mail-order divorces"—i.e. those where neither spouse personally appears before the divorce court—have almost invariably been denied legal effect. Divorces granted upon the personal appearance of one or both spouses have also been denied recognition in most states on the ground that neither spouse had a bona fide domicile in Mexico. The New York courts, on the other hand, have given effect to Mexican divorces if one spouse was before the divorce court and the other appeared either personally or by attorney.

ROSENSTIEL V. ROSENSTIEL, WOOD V. WOOD, 16 N.Y.2d 64, 73, 262 N.Y.S.2d 86, 90, 209 N.E.2d 709, 712 (1965): Both of these cases involved divorces obtained in Chihuahua, Mexico, by New Yorkers. In both cases the plaintiff spouse was in Mexico for less than twenty-four hours during which time he appeared personally before the divorce court. The defendant spouse in both cases entered an appearance by an attorney but did not personally go to Mexico. Held, the divorces should be recognized in New York. "The State or county of true domicile has the closest real public interest in a marriage but, when a New York spouse goes elsewhere to establish a synthetic domicile to meet technical acceptance of a matrimonial suit, our public interest is not affected differently by a formality of one day than by a formality of six weeks. Nevada gets no closer to the real public concern with the marriage than Chihuahua."

In 1971, the Federal Government of Mexico issued a decree stating that an alien may not obtain a divorce in any Mexican state without having been present in Mexico for a period of not less than six months. See Diario Oficial (Mexico) 18, Feb. 20, 1971. As a result, "quickie" divorces are no longer obtainable in Mexico. Haiti and the Dominican Republic then entered the lists by enacting legislation similar to that of the Mexican states referred to above. A whole new industry sprang up, with tour packages complete with 24–hour divorces. It seems probable that such Haitian and Dominican Republic divorces will be recognized as freely in New York as were those of Mexico. Greschler v. Greschler, 51 N.Y.2d 368, 434 N.Y.S.2d 194, 414 N.E.2d 694 (1980).

NOTES

1. On the subject of Mexican divorces, see D. Currie, Suitcase Divorce in the Conflict of Laws, 34 U.Chi.L.Rev. 26 (1967), Caballero, A Reexamination of Mexican "Quickie" Divorces, 4 Int.Lawyer 871 (1970).

In addition to New York, it seems that Connecticut, Indiana, Massachusetts, New Jersey, Tennessee, and the Virgin Islands will either recognize Haitian and Dominican Republic divorces or estop a party who participated in or earlier invoked the benefits of such a divorce from attacking its validity. Scoles and Hay, Conflict of Laws 518–519 (2d ed. 1992); see Perrin v. Perrin, 408 F.2d 107 (3d Cir.1969). See also Swisher, Foreign Migratory Divorces—A Reappraisal, 21 J.Fam.Law 9

(1982/83); Guilford, Guam Divorces: Fast, Easy, and Dangerous, M.A.R. Army Law 20 (1990).

2. Suppose that parties previously domiciled in a state that does not recognize Rosenstiel-type divorces have obtained one in a foreign country. They subsequently engage in litigation in New York with both parties participating to determine rights to property there. The New York court recognizes the foreign divorce (i.e., it decides the "preliminary question," p. 821, supra) before then turning to the property determination. Would a subsequent collateral attack by one of the parties or by a third party on the foreign-country divorce (e.g., in the state of the parties' original domicile) be successful? Does Sherrer v. Sherrer, p. 856, supra, apply?

Suppose the following variation:

In a foreign country a New Yorker gets a Rosenstiel-type divorce that New York would recognize as valid. He then returns to New York and eventually moves to a sister state where he marries for a second time. Should the second state recognize the divorce and the remarriage as valid even though it would have held invalid a similar divorce obtained by one of its own domiciliaries? See Note, 114 U.Pa.L.Rev. 771 (1966).

3. In Caldwell v. Caldwell, 298 N.Y. 146, 81 N.E.2d 60 (1948), a spouse who procured a "mail order" Mexican divorce was held not estopped from attacking it because "there is not even the slightest color of jurisdiction." The rule of the Caldwell case was extended somewhat in Alfaro v. Alfaro, 5 A.D.2d 770, 169 N.Y.S.2d 943 (2d Dep't 1958), affirmed without opinion, 7 N.Y.2d 949, 198 N.Y.S.2d 318, 165 N.E.2d 880 (1960). In that case a spouse was permitted collaterally to attack an ex parte Mexican divorce which he had procured even though the decree recited that he had appeared before the court and he had testified that he had visited the court and "picked up" the decree.

On the other hand, it has been held more recently that a spouse would be held estopped if his purpose in attacking the "mail order" Mexican divorce he had procured was "primarily for the purpose of obtaining financial gain" rather than to re-establish his former marital status. Considine v. Rawl, 39 Misc.2d 1021, 242 N.Y.S.2d 456 (Sup.Ct.1963). In England, the House of Lords refused to recognize a Belgian annulment of a prostitute's sham marriage which she sought to avoid in order to claim, as the surviving spouse, the substantial English estate of her employer whom she had married in Italy and who died at the wedding reception. Vervaeke v. Smith, [1982] 2 All E.R. 144 (H.L.).

NON-JUDICIAL DIVORCES

Under Islamic law, a husband of Muslim faith may divorce a wife by issuing the *talaq,* the triple repetition of words of divorce before witnesses. In a number of Islamic countries, some public act—notice, registration, or confirmation of the talaq—is now required. Judaic law permits divorce by delivery to the wife of a bill of divorcement, the *get.* Non-judicial divorces, by unilateral act or by contract of the parties, are also possible under Chinese, Japanese, and Korean law. According to American Indian tribal custom, a divorce may also be effected by agreement on an Indian reservation. The effect of non-judicial divorces has been a question of considerable difficulty, especially in countries of immigration from Muslim countries (e.g., in England with respect to immigrants from Arab and Asian countries).

In both the United States and in England, religious divorces will be recognized if they were obtained by foreign domiciliaries abroad and are valid where obtained. In contrast, a valid domestic divorce requires compliance with domestic law. Section 253 of the N.Y.Dom.Rel.L. (Consol.1994) now requires the plaintiff in a divorce action to file, prior to final judgment, a verified statement that he or she has taken all steps to remove all barriers to the defendant's remarriage. "Barriers" includes "religious constraints." The purpose of the provision is to require compliance with religious requirements (for instance, the delivery of a *get*) when a *foreign* country (e.g., Israel) would not recognize a New York civil divorce, standing alone, and therefore would not permit remarriage.

NOTES

1. See Comment, United States Recognition of Foreign, Nonjudicial Divorces, 53 Minn.L.Rev. 612 (1969). In England, the matter is now largely regulated by the Family Law Act of 1986 which replaced the Recognition of Divorces and Legal Separations Act of 1971. It has been held that a *get* may constitute a "proceeding" within the meaning of sec. 46(1) of the Act and the resulting divorce entitled to recognition in England. However, the "proceeding" must be a single act and effected outside of Britain. Hence, a *get* written in England and delivered to the wife at a rabbinical court in Israel might serve to divorce the parties under Jewish law, but such a divorce would not be entitled to recognition under the Act in England. Berkovitz v. Grinberg, [1995] Fam. 142, [1995] 1 All E.R. 681, [1995] 2 W.L.R. 553 (Fam.Div.). For a decision involving a *talaq,* see Z. v. Z., [1992] F.L.R. 291 (Australia). For comprehensive review of English law, see Stone, The Recognition in England of Talaq Divorces, 14 Anglo–American L.Rev. 363 (1985). See also Pilkington, Transnational Divorces Under the Family Law Act of 1986, 37 Int'l & Comp.L.Q. 131 (1988); Scoles and Hay, Conflict of Laws 522–526 (2d ed. 1992); Dicey & Morris, Conflict of Laws 740 (12th ed. 1993 by Collins, and 1995 Supp.).

2. For France, see Moatly v. Zagha, [1982] Revue critique de droit int. privé 298 (Ct.App., Aix-en-Provence); for Germany BGH (Supreme Court) in [1982] NJW 517.

3. In Shapiro v. Shapiro, 110 Misc.2d 726, 442 N.Y.S.2d 928 (Kings County 1981), modified as to counsel fees, 88 A.D.2d 592, 449 N.Y.S.2d 806 (2d Dept.1982), the New York court enforced an order of the Rabbinical Court of Israel by entering its own order that the husband perform the ritual acts of the *get* to enable the wife to remarry. In Avitzur v. Avitzur, 58 N.Y.2d 108, 459 N.Y.S.2d 572, 446 N.E.2d 136 (1983), cert. denied, 464 U.S. 817 (1983), the Court of Appeals ordered specific performance of a marriage contract requiring submission of marital disputes to a Jewish tribunal (Beth Din). See also Golding v. Golding, 176 A.D.2d 20, 581 N.Y.S.2d 4 (1992) (separation agreement not enforced because wife signed under duress when husband threatened to withhold the *get*); Tal v. Tal, 158 Misc.2d 703, 601 N.Y.S.2d 530 (N.Y.Sup.Ct.1993) (Israeli rabbinical court divorce not recognized for lack of personal jurisdiction, prior New York rabbinical court divorce not given weight because non-judicial). The change in New York's Domestic Relations Law now also covers cases in which there is no prior decree of another court or tribunal or any marriage contract. For an overview and comment, see Broyde, The New York State Jewish Divorce Law, 30 Tradition: A Journal of Jewish Thought ___ (1995). See also Berger and Lipstadt, Women in Judaism from the Perspective of

Human Rights, in: Witte and Van der Vyver (eds.), Religious Human Rights in Global Perspective 295, 304 et seq. (1995).

4. With respect to divorce in accordance with Indian tribal customs, see Marris v. Sockey, 170 F.2d 599 (10th Cir.1948).

Section 3. Annulment*

Whealton v. Whealton
Supreme Court of California, 1967.
67 Cal.2d 656, 63 Cal.Rptr. 291, 432 P.2d 979.

■ Traynor, Chief Justice. Defendant appeals from a default judgment annulling her marriage to plaintiff on the ground of fraud.

Plaintiff, a petty officer on active duty with the United States Navy, married defendant at Bel Air, Maryland, on June 15, 1964. Thereafter his military duties took him from place to place on the east coast until he was assigned to the U.S.S. *Reposte* at the San Francisco Naval Shipyard. He arrived in California on July 14, 1965. Plaintiff and defendant lived together for only six or seven weeks on the east coast.

On September 3, 1965, plaintiff filed this action for annulment of the marriage. Summons was issued and an order for publication of summons was filed on the same day. Publication of the summons was accomplished as prescribed by law. Defendant received a copy of the summons by mail at her home in Maryland on September 7, 1965.... On October 11, 1965, the court entered her default, heard testimony in support of the complaint, and entered a judgment annulling the marriage. On October 19, 1965, defendant made a motion to set aside the default and the judgment by default and to permit the filing of an answer and a cross-complaint. The motion was denied on November 9, 1965.

[The Court first found that the judgment was void because it had been prematurely entered.]

Even if the default judgment were not premature, it would have to be reversed, for neither the pleadings nor the evidence establish that either party was a domiciliary of California. The court therefore lacked jurisdiction to award an ex parte annulment....

Ex parte divorces are a striking exception to the rule that a court must have personal jurisdiction over a party before it may adjudicate his substantial rights.... The legal fiction that explains the exception by regarding the marital status as a res present at the permanent home of either of the spouses provides doctrinal consistency with other rules governing jurisdiction over things, but the appellation "in rem" is unnecessary to support the conclusion that jurisdiction is properly assumed. (Williams v. State of North Carolina (1945) 325 U.S. 226.) *Williams* does hold, however, that

---
* Restatement, Second, Conflict of Laws §§ 76, 286.

due process requires something more than mere presence of a party within a jurisdiction before that party can invoke the legal process of the forum to force an absent spouse to defend her marital status in an inconvenient forum and to subvert the policies of other interested jurisdictions in preserving marriages. When the forum state is also the domicile of one of the parties, however, its interest and that of its domiciliary justify subordinating the conflicting interests of the absent spouse and of any other interested jurisdiction.

Jurisdiction to grant annulments has followed an analogous, but somewhat divergent course. An annulment differs conceptually from a divorce in that a divorce terminates a legal status, whereas an annulment establishes that a marital status never existed. The absence of a valid marriage precluded reliance on the divorce cases in formulating a theory of ex parte jurisdiction in annulment, for no res or status could be found within the state.... The courts, however, did not let jurisdictional concepts of in personam and in rem dictate results in annulment actions. They recognized a state's interest in providing a forum for some annulment actions even though the court lacked personal jurisdiction over one of the parties.... The crucial question, then, is whether there are sufficient factors to justify the court's exercising ex parte annulment jurisdiction....

... The primary issue under the facts of this case is whether due process concepts of fairness to defendant permit plaintiff to choose a forum inconvenient to her absent personal jurisdiction over her.... We find no factor here that would justify an exception to the general rule requiring personal jurisdiction and thereby shift the burden of inconvenience to defendant. The marriage ceremony took place elsewhere, defendant lives elsewhere, the matrimonial domicil was elsewhere, and witnesses are likely to be located elsewhere. Although domicile of a plaintiff here would afford jurisdiction to award an ex parte annulment, plaintiff in this case did not plead or prove that he was a domiciliary of California when the default judgment was entered. The court was therefore without jurisdiction to enter the default judgment.

Since the entry of the judgment, however, defendant has appeared in the action. We must therefore determine for purposes of proceedings on retrial whether the court may award an annulment when both parties are before it, even though neither is a domiciliary of the state.

The primary basis for jurisdiction to resolve disputes between parties is their presence before the court. Plaintiff initiated this action in the only jurisdiction practically available to him because of his military service. Although defendant was not within the jurisdiction of the court when the default was erroneously entered, she voluntarily appeared while the action was before the court. Her appearance was not limited to challenging the jurisdiction of the court, but included a request for relief on the merits by way of an answer and cross-complaint for separate maintenance....

Since both parties are properly before the court, we confront the questions whether we may treat the action as a transitory cause ... and whether the interest of another state compels us to refuse to hear this cause.

The rule that domicile is a prerequisite to a valid divorce, even when the parties are before the court, may be justified by the superior interests of the domiciliary jurisdiction. Such jurisdiction is primarily concerned with the status of its domiciliaries and the application of its own law in preserving or terminating marriages in accord with its social policies.... When both parties to a divorce action are before the court, however, it is questionable whether domicile is an indispensable prerequisite for jurisdiction. If the moving party's mobility is greatly restricted, for instance, access to a domiciliary forum may be practically unavailable.... Moreover, when parties secure a divorce without the prerequisite domicile in the forum state, it may not be attacked at a later date by either of them.... Hence, the prerequisite of domicile may be easily avoided at the trial by parties wishing to invoke the jurisdiction of a court, with little fear in most instances that the judgment will be any less effective than if a valid domicile in fact existed....

However valid the rationale for the domicile prerequisite may be in divorce actions, it does not apply to annulment actions. In divorce actions, the applicable substantive law changes as parties change their domicile, but in annulment actions courts uniformly apply the law of the state in which the marriage was contracted.... We conclude, therefore, that the interests of the state of celebration of the marriage or the state of domicile of either party do not preclude a court that has personal jurisdiction over both parties from entertaining an annulment action.

It does not follow that because a court may exercise that jurisdiction it must do so in all cases. In the present case plaintiff was under a special disability in terms of access to any forum other than California. Moreover, defendant was not caught inadvertently within California, and personal jurisdiction was not exercised on a territorial power theory but was obtained over defendant through her consent. Hence, we assume that no undue burdens are placed on her by the trial of the action in California. In other annulment actions where personal jurisdiction is the sole jurisdictional basis, however, the doctrine of *forum non conveniens* might well be invoked by one of the parties, or asserted by the court, to cause a discretionary dismissal when fairness and the interests of judicial administration so demand....

The judgment is reversed.

Wilkins v. Zelichowski

Supreme Court of New Jersey, 1958.
26 N.J. 370, 140 A.2d 65.

[The case appears at p. 825, supra.]

NOTES

1. There is uncertainty about the bases of judicial jurisdiction for annulment. It is usually held that, at the least, a court has jurisdiction to decree an annulment if it could render a divorce. Under this view, personal jurisdiction over the defendant spouse is not necessary but suit must ordinarily be brought in the domicile of the plaintiff spouse. A few courts, on the other hand, believe that personal jurisdiction over the defendant spouse is essential. See, e.g., Owen v. Owen, 127 Colo. 359, 257 P.2d 581 (1953). Rarely, however, has this latter view been carried to the extreme of holding that an annulment action can be brought in any state where personal jurisdiction over both spouses can be obtained. A number of cases hold that the state where the marriage was celebrated has jurisdiction to annul it if both spouses are before the court. See, e.g., Feigenbaum v. Feigenbaum, 210 Ark. 186, 194 S.W.2d 1012 (1946); Sawyer v. Slack, 196 N.C. 697, 146 S.E. 864 (1929).

According to Section 76 of the Restatement, Second, a state has jurisdiction to annul a marriage (a) if it would have jurisdiction to dissolve the marriage by divorce or (b) if the respondent spouse is subject to the judicial jurisdiction of the state and either the marriage was contracted there or the validity of the marriage is determined under its law.

2. See generally Storke, Annulment in the Conflict of Laws, 43 Minn.L.Rev. 849 (1959); Vernon, Labyrinthine Ways: Jurisdiction to Annul, 10 J.Pub.L. 47 (1961).

3. Sutton v. Leib, 342 U.S. 402 (1952). Suit in a federal district court in Illinois to recover alimony due under an Illinois divorce decree requiring payment of alimony to plaintiff until remarriage. The plaintiff had remarried in Nevada, but thereafter this marriage was annulled by a New York court for the reason that the man plaintiff married "had another wife living at the time of said marriage." The District Court rendered summary judgment for the defendant, and the Court of Appeals affirmed on the ground that plaintiff's Nevada marriage, since it was good in that state, terminated the liability for alimony under the Illinois divorce decree. On writ of certiorari to the Supreme Court, held reversed. Since plaintiff and her second husband were before the New York court, that court's annulment decree is entitled to full faith and credit and therefore plaintiff's Nevada marriage must be held void. Illinois, however, was held "free to decide for itself the effect of New York's ... annulment on the obligations of respondent, a stranger to the decree." As a result, the case was remanded for a determination whether under Illinois law plaintiff's invalid marriage released respondent from the obligation to pay further alimony.

SECTION 4. JUDICIAL SEPARATION

RESTATEMENT, SECOND, CONFLICT OF LAWS *

§ 75. Judicial Separation.

(1) A state may exercise judicial jurisdiction to grant a judicial separation under the circumstances which would give the state jurisdiction to dissolve the marriage by divorce.

* Quoted with the permission of the copyright owner, The American Law Institute.

(2) A state may exercise judicial jurisdiction to grant a judicial separation when both spouses are personally subject to the jurisdiction of the state.

Comment:

a. Nature of judicial separation. A decree of judicial separation does not affect the existence of the marriage. It does, however, modify the incidents of the marriage relationship by relieving the spouses from the duty of living with each other.

Jurisdiction to render a decree of judicial separation and so to end the duty of the spouses to live together does not necessarily entail the jurisdiction to affect their economic rights and duties, such as by ordering one to provide for the support of the other or of the children of the marriage. For the latter purpose, it is essential that the court have personal jurisdiction over the respondent spouse or over so much of his property as it seeks to affect by its decree . . .

Comment on Subsection (1):

b. A state may exercise judicial jurisdiction to grant a judicial separation whenever it would have jurisdiction to dissolve the marriage by divorce . . . . Hence a state which is the domicil of both spouses, or which is the domicil of one spouse and has personal jurisdiction over the other, may exercise judicial jurisdiction to grant a judicial separation. Under these circumstances the state also may exercise judicial jurisdiction to affect the spouses' economic rights and duties, such as by ordering one to provide for the support of the other. As between States of the United States, such a decree is entitled to full faith and credit . . . .

A state which lacks personal jurisdiction over the respondent spouse, but which nevertheless would have judicial jurisdiction to grant a divorce, either because it is the state of domicil of the plaintiff spouse or because it has some other appropriate relationship to the plaintiff spouse . . . may exercise judicial jurisdiction to grant a judicial separation. As between States of the United States, such a decree is entitled to full faith and credit . . . . Under these circumstances, however, the state lacks judicial jurisdiction to affect the respondent spouse's economic rights and duties . . . except to the extent that it has jurisdiction over the respondent's property . . .

Comment on Subsection (2):

c. A state may exercise judicial jurisdiction to grant a judicial separation even though it would not have jurisdiction to grant a divorce. This is because separation is a less drastic remedy than divorce and because it is essential that a state have power to protect a spouse, who is present within its territory, from the violence or cruelty of the other. Accordingly, a state with personal jurisdiction over both spouses may exercise judicial jurisdiction to grant a judicial separation. It follows that a decree rendered with personal jurisdiction over both spouses is entitled to full faith and credit. . . .

SECTION 5. LEGITIMATION

RESTATEMENT, SECOND, CONFLICT OF LAWS *

Topic 2. Legitimacy

INTRODUCTORY NOTE

At common law only children born in lawful wedlock were legitimate. In most states, this rule has now been modified by statute. It is usually provided that the offspring of certain invalid marriages shall be legitimate. In addition, children, originally born illegitimate, can commonly be legitimated by events occurring after their birth, such as by the marriage of their parents or by some form of recognition on the part of one or both. Differences in the pertinent statutes of the various states give rise to choice-of-law problems. It may be possible for a child to be legitimate as to one parent and illegitimate as to the other.

It is commonly said that a person's status as legitimate or illegitimate does not vary but remains constant from state to state. The incidents which flow from his status, however, may vary, since they depend upon the law which governs the question at hand.

. . .

§ 287. Law Governing Legitimacy

. . .

(2) The child will usually be held legitimate if this would be his status under the local law of the state where either (a) the parent was domiciled when the child's status of legitimacy is claimed to have been created or (b) the child was domiciled when the parent acknowledged the child as his own.

§ 288. Incidents of Legitimacy Created by Foreign Law

A state usually gives the same incidents to a status of legitimacy created by a foreign law under the principles stated in § 287 that it gives to the status when created by its own local law.

NOTES

1. The courts of the state of the parent's domicile at death have usually interpreted the provisions of their law to require that the legitimating act have been done at a time when the parent is domiciled in the state. See, e.g., Meekins v. Meekins, 169

---

* Quoted with the permission of the copyright owner The American Law Institute.

Ark. 265, 275 S.W. 337 (1925); Eddie v. Eddie, 8 N.D. 376, 79 N.W. 856 (1899); In re Presley's Estate, 113 Okl. 160, 240 P. 89 (1925).

A number of cases, however, have not imposed such a requirement. Estate of Bassi, 234 Cal.App.2d 529, 44 Cal.Rptr. 541 (1965); In re Lund's Estate, 26 Cal.2d 472, 159 P.2d 643 (1945); Colpitt v. Cheatham, 267 P.2d 1003 (Okl.1954); Rhode Island Hospital Trust Co. v. Hopkins, 93 R.I. 173, 172 A.2d 345 (1961); In re Engelhardt's Estate, 272 Wis. 275, 75 N.W.2d 631 (1956); In re Estate of Watts, 106 Misc.2d 35, 431 N.Y.S.2d 295 (1980). See also In re Blanco Estate, 117 Mich.App. 281, 323 N.W.2d 671, 675–76 (1982) (summarizing case law and reviewing evolution of Michigan legislation).

2. For an application of Section 288 of the Restatement, Second, see Matter of Estate of Del Valle, 126 Misc.2d 78, 481 N.Y.S.2d 232 (Sur.1984).

3. At common law, illegitimate children inherited from no one; by statute, however, most states granted inheritance rights to such a child with respect to the mother. In Trimble v. Gordon, 430 U.S. 762 (1977), the Supreme Court struck down such a restriction. Equal Protection requires that illegitimate children may also inherit from their father by intestate succession. However, state law may require that the decedent's paternity have been judicially determined during his lifetime. Lalli v. Lalli, 439 U.S. 259 (1978). State statutes and decisions differ widely on how paternity is to be established. See also the Uniform Parentage Act, 9A U.L.A. Matr., Fam. & Health Laws 579 (1979). Section 2–109 of the Uniform Probate Code, in force in a minority of states, provides that if a state has not adopted the Uniform Parentage Act, a person is a "child" for purposes of interstate succession if paternity was adjudicated before the decedent's death "or is established thereafter by clear and convincing proof. . . ."

If paternity must be established by adjudication, the Supreme Court has held in the context of support claims that equal protection requires that the claimant be given an adequate opportunity to do so. In Clark v. Jeter, 486 U.S. 456 (1988), the Court invalidated a six-year statute of limitations as too short. The 1984 federal child support amendments require states wishing to qualify under the federal program to enact 18–year statutes of limitations. 42 U.S.C.A. § 666(a)(5)(ii) (West 1994).

See generally Scoles and Hay, Conflict of Laws, 553–559 (2d ed. 1992).

SECTION 6. ADOPTION *

INTRODUCTORY NOTE

Adoption was unknown to the common law and is purely the creature of statute. In the sense here used, it is the process whereby the adoptive parent is substituted for the natural parents, and whereby in many states the child's legal relationship with the latter is severed entirely. Some statutes, however, employ the term in a sense closely akin to legitimation, such as when provision is made for the so-called adoption by a natural parent of his illegitimate child. On rare occasions, adoption is used in a restricted sense to describe a process whereby the child becomes no more than an heir presumptive of the adopter and his relations with his natural

---

* See Restatement, Second, Conflict of Laws §§ 78, 289–290.

parents remain undisturbed. Adoption, as here defined, exists by virtue of statutory enactment in the great majority of States in this country.

Unlike legitimation (see Section 5), adoption is usually effected by court proceedings. The two main conflicts problems in the field are the judicial jurisdiction of a state to grant an adoption and the effect which will be accorded an adoption in another state. The statutes differ rather widely in their details, particularly as to the circumstances under which a court can decree an adoption and with respect to the rights of inheritance of the adopted child. There is agreement in common law countries that in determining whether to grant the adoption, the forum will apply the local provisions of its own law and not those of some other state.

There is some uncertainty as to what jurisdictional bases must exist to enable a state to grant an adoption through its courts. It is believed that such jurisdiction exists in a state (a) which is the domicile of either the child or the adoptive parent and (b) which has personal jurisdiction over the adoptive parent and over either the adopted child or the person having legal custody of the child. Two principal questions are involved in an adoption proceeding: first, whether the child's situation is such as to make adoption advisable in his own best interests and, if so, whether the would-be adopter is a desirable person from the child's point of view. Courts sitting in either the domicile of the child or in that of the adoptive parent will normally be equally well situated to determine such issues. And the interests of the two states in the matter are of approximately equal weight.

An adoption, decreed in a state with judicial jurisdiction, will usually be given the same legal incidents in another state as the latter gives to a decree of adoption by its own courts.

Incidents arising from an adoption include such matters as the right of the adoptive parent to the custody and control of the child and the right of either the child or the adoptive parent to share in the other's estate and to recover damages for the other's wrongful death. To date, the bulk of the cases involving the effect of a foreign adoption have concerned the inheritance rights of the adopted child. According to most of the decisions, such rights are determined by the law governing succession; that is to say by the law of the situs in the case of immovables and by the law of the decedent's last domicile in the case of movables. So, if the question concerns the right of a child adopted in state X to inherit the movables of an adoptive or of a natural parent or some other relative who died domiciled in state Y, the case will be decided by Y law rather than by that of X. See, e.g., Pazzi v. Taylor, 342 N.W.2d 481 (Iowa 1984); Warren v. Foster, 450 So.2d 786 (Miss.1984); In re Avery, 176 N.J.Super. 469, 423 A.2d 994 (1980), petition for certification denied, 85 N.J. 499, 427 A.2d 587 (1981); In re Dreer's Estate, 404 Pa. 368, 173 A.2d 102 (1961). However, some courts take the position that the inheritance rights of the adopted child pertain to status itself and hence are governed by the law of the state where the adoption was granted. See, e.g., Slattery v. Hartford–Connecticut Trust Co., 115 Conn. 163, 161 A. 79 (1932).

NOTES

1. In Anglo–American countries, the forum will look to its own law in determining whether to grant an adoption. 1 Rabel, Conflict of Laws 681 (2d ed. 1958). The courts of civil law countries, on the other hand, apply what they deem to be the proper law (frequently the state of the adoptive parent's domicile or nationality) to govern the case. Scoles and Hay, Conflict of Laws 559–561 (2d ed. 1992). An adoption decree entered by a court with competent jurisdiction will ordinarily be recognized everywhere. See, e.g., Bonwich v. Bonwich, 699 P.2d 760 (Utah 1985), cert. denied, 474 U.S. 848 (1985); In re Estate of Hart, 165 Cal.App.3d 392, 209 Cal.Rptr. 272 (1984). But see Notes 4 and 5 infra.

In 1993, the Hague Conference on Private International Law proposed the new Convention on Protection of Children and Cooperation in Respect of Intercountry Adoption. The convention sets minimum standards for the intercountry adoption of children, and many of these children come from developing countries. The convention may prove important for the United States where over 6,500 children from abroad were adopted in 1992. For text of the convention and an Introductory Note by Pfund, see 32 Int'l Leg.Mat. 1134 (1993). For comment, see Bisignaro, Intercountry Adoption Today and the Implications of the 1993 Hague Convention on Tomorrow, 13 Dick.J.Int'l L. 123 (1994); Katz, A Modest Proposal? The Convention on Protection of Children and Cooperation in Respect of Intercountry Adoption, 9 Emory Int'l L.Rev. 293 (1995).

2. See generally Baade, Interstate and Foreign Adoptions in North Carolina, 40 N.C.L.Rev. 691 (1962); Cowen, English and Foreign Adoptions, 12 Int'l & Comp. L.Q. 168 (1963); Kennedy, Adoption in the Conflict of Laws, 34 Can.B.Rev. 507 (1956).

3. In Armstrong v. Manzo, 380 U.S. 545 (1965), no notice of the Texas adoption proceedings was given the natural father although those seeking the adoption (the mother and her new husband) "well knew his precise whereabouts in ... Texas." It was held that, as a result of this failure to give notice, the adoption decree was constitutionally invalid. In Quilloin v. Walcott, 434 U.S. 246 (1978), and Lehr v. Robertson, 463 U.S. 248 (1983), the Supreme Court held that an unwed father who had not lived in a home situation with the child nor legitimated his child was not allowed to object to the child's adoption by the husband whom the mother subsequently married. By statute, Oklahoma now requires notice of adoption proceedings also to the unwed father. 10 Okla.St.Ann. § 60.6(3) (1986).

4. In Barry E. (Anonymous) v. Ingraham, 43 N.Y.2d 87, 400 N.Y.S.2d 772, 371 N.E.2d 492 (1977), the court refused on public policy grounds to give effect to a Mexican decree providing for the adoption by a New York couple of a child born in New York to a New York mother.

5. In Doulgeris v. Bambacus, 203 Va. 670, 127 S.E.2d 145 (1962), inheritance rights were denied a child who had been adopted in Greece on the ground that the Greek adoption procedures, which placed primary emphasis upon the welfare of the adoptive father rather than of the adoptive child, were repugnant to Virginia public policy. The effect of the decision was to deny the child's inheritance rights from her adoptive brother. Would Virginia's public policy have been seriously contravened by permitting the child to inherit? For cases recognizing Greek adoption decrees, see Corbett v. Stergios, 257 Iowa 1387, 137 N.W.2d 266 (1965); In re Christoff's Estate, 411 Pa. 419, 192 A.2d 737 (1963).

Section 7. Custody of Children

May v. Anderson

Supreme Court of the United States, 1953.
345 U.S. 528, 73 S.Ct. 840, 97 L.Ed. 1221.

■ Justice Burton delivered the opinion of the Court.

The parties were married in Wisconsin and, until 1947, both were domiciled there. After marital troubles developed, they agreed in December, 1946, that appellant should take their children to Lisbon, Columbiana County, Ohio, and there think over her future course. By New Year's Day, she had decided not to return to Wisconsin and by telephone, she informed her husband of that decision.

Within a few days he filed suit in Wisconsin, seeking both an absolute divorce and custody of the children. The only service of process upon appellant consisted of the delivery to her personally, in Ohio, of a copy of the Wisconsin summons and petition.... Appellant entered no appearance and took no part in this Wisconsin proceeding which produced not only a decree divorcing the parties from the bonds of matrimony but a decree purporting to award the custody of the children to their father, subject to a right of their mother to visit them at reasonable times. Appellant contests only the validity of the decree as to custody....

Armed with a copy of the decree and accompanied by a local police officer, appellee, in Lisbon, Ohio, demanded and obtained the children from their mother. The record does not disclose what took place between 1947 and 1951, except that the children remained with their father in Wisconsin until July 1, 1951. He then brought them back to Lisbon and permitted them to visit their mother. This time, when he demanded their return, she refused to surrender them.

Relying upon the Wisconsin decree, he promptly filed in the Probate Court of Columbiana County, Ohio, the petition for a writ of habeas corpus now before us. Under Ohio procedure that writ tests only the immediate right to possession of the children. It does not open the door for the modification of any prior award of custody on a showing of changed circumstances. Nor is it available as a procedure for settling the future custody of children in the first instance.

. . .

Separated as our issue is from that of the future interests of the children, we have before us the elemental question whether a court of a state, where a mother is neither domiciled, resident nor present, may cut off her immediate right to the care, custody, management and companionship of her minor children without having jurisdiction over her *in personam.*

Rights far more precious to appellant than property rights will be cut off if she is to be bound by the Wisconsin award of custody....

In Estin v. Estin [page 866, supra] ... this Court upheld the validity of a Nevada divorce obtained *ex parte* by a husband, resident in Nevada, insofar as it dissolved the bonds of matrimony. At the same time, we held Nevada powerless to cut off, in that proceeding, a spouse's right to financial support under the prior decree of another state. In the instant case, we recognize that a mother's right to custody of her children is a personal right entitled to at least as much protection as her right to alimony.

In the instant case, the Ohio courts gave weight to appellee's contention that the Wisconsin award of custody binds appellant because, at the time it was issued, her children had a technical domicile in Wisconsin, although they were neither resident nor present there. We find it unnecessary to determine the children's legal domicile because, even if it be with their father, that does not give Wisconsin, certainly as against Ohio, the personal jurisdiction that it must have in order to deprive their mother of her personal right to their immediate possession....

Reversed and remanded.

■ JUSTICE CLARK, not having heard oral argument, took no part in the consideration or decision of this case.

■ JUSTICE FRANKFURTER, concurring.

The views expressed by my brother Jackson make it important that I state, in joining the Court's opinion, what I understand the Court to be deciding and what it is not deciding in this case.

What is decided—the only thing the Court decides—is that the Full Faith and Credit Clause does not require Ohio, in disposing of the custody of children in Ohio, to accept, in the circumstances before us, the disposition made by Wisconsin. The Ohio Supreme Court felt itself so bound. This Court does not decide that Ohio would be precluded from recognizing, as a matter of local law, the disposition made by the Wisconsin court. For Ohio to give respect to the Wisconsin decree would not offend the Due Process Clause. Ohio is no more precluded from doing so than a court of Ontario or Manitoba would be, were the mother to bring the children into one of these provinces.

Property, personal claims, and even the marriage status ... generally give rise to interests different from those relevant to the discharge of a State's continuing responsibility to children within her borders. Children have a very special place in life which law should reflect. Legal theories and their phrasing in other cases readily lead to fallacious reasoning if uncritically transferred to determination of a State's duty towards children.... But the child's welfare in a custody case has such a claim upon the State that its responsibility is obviously not to be foreclosed by a prior adjudication reflecting another State's discharge of its responsibility at another time. Reliance on opinions regarding out-of-State adjudications of property rights, personal claims or the marital status is bound to confuse analysis when a claim to the custody of children before the courts of one

State is based on an award previously made by another State. Whatever light may be had from such opinions, they cannot give conclusive answers.

■ JUSTICE JACKSON, whom JUSTICE REED, joins, dissenting.

The Court apparently is holding that the Federal Constitution prohibits Ohio from recognizing the validity of this Wisconsin divorce decree insofar as it settles custody of the couple's children. In the light of settled and unchallenged precedents of this Court, such a decision can only rest upon the proposition that Wisconsin's courts had no jurisdiction to make such a decree binding upon appellant....

The Ohio courts reasoned that although personal jurisdiction over the wife was lacking, domicile of the children in Wisconsin was a sufficient jurisdictional basis to enable Wisconsin to bind all parties interested in their custody. This determination that the children were domiciled in Wisconsin has not been contested either at our bar or below. Therefore, under our precedents, it is conclusive....

The Court's decision holds that the state in which a child and one parent are domiciled and which is primarily concerned about his welfare cannot constitutionally adjudicate controversies as to his guardianship. The state's power here is defeated by the absence of the other parent for a period of two months. The convenience of a leave-taking parent is placed above the welfare of the child, but neither party is greatly aided in obtaining a decision. The Wisconsin courts cannot bind the mother, and the Ohio courts cannot bind the father. A state of the law such as this, where possession apparently is not merely nine points of the law but all of them and self-help the ultimate authority, has little to commend it in legal logic or as a principle of order in a federal system....

The difference between a proceeding involving the status, custody and support of children and one involving adjudication of property rights is too apparent to require elaboration. In the former, courts are no longer concerned primarily with the proprietary claims of the contestants for the *"res"* before the court, but with the welfare of the *"res"* itself. Custody is viewed not with the idea of adjudicating rights *in* the children, as if they were chattels, but rather with the idea of making the best disposition possible for the welfare of the children. To speak of a court's "cutting off" a mother's right to custody of her children, as if it raised problems similar to those involved in "cutting off" her rights in a plot of ground, is to obliterate these obvious distinctions. Personal jurisdiction of all parties to be affected by a proceeding is highly desirable, to make certain that they have had valid notice and opportunity to be heard. But the assumption that it overrides all other considerations and in its absence a state is constitutionally impotent to resolve questions of custody flies in the face of our own cases....

I fear this decision will author new confusions. The interpretative concurrence, if it be a true interpretation, seems to reduce the law of custody to a rule of seize-and-run. I would affirm the decision of the Ohio courts that they should respect the judgment of the Wisconsin court, until it or some other court with equal or better claims to jurisdiction shall modify it.

■ [A dissenting opinion by JUSTICE MINTON is omitted.]

NOTES

1. Is Justice Burton's notion that personal jurisdiction over the defendant parent is essential to the rendition of a valid custody decree out of line with the realities of the situation? How, under these circumstances, could a custody issue be resolved in a situation where each parent is domiciled in a different state and neither proves willing to appear in the courts of the other's domicile? Does the reference in *Shaffer* to the special case of jurisdiction in "status" matters (supra p. 138, footnote 30) permit the inference that custody may be awarded in an ex parte proceeding? The general consensus has rejected Justice Burton's position in favor of Justice Frankfurter's. Weintraub, Affecting the Parent–Child Relationship Without Jurisdiction Over Both Parents, 36 Sw.L.J. 1167 (1983); Weintraub, Commentary on the Conflict of Laws 265–68 (3d ed. 1986).

Personal jurisdiction over the defendant parent, although not essential to the rendition of a valid custody decree, is essential for the rendition against the parent of a valid judgment for support. Kumar v. Santa Clara County Superior Court, 124 Cal.App.3d 1003, 177 Cal.Rptr. 763 (1981), order vacated, 32 Cal.3d 689, 186 Cal.Rptr. 772 (1982); In re Hudson, 434 N.E.2d 107 (Ind.App.1982). Is this sensible?

2. In People of State of New York ex rel. Halvey v. Halvey, 330 U.S. 610 (1947), the Supreme Court held that under full faith and credit a custody decree is as subject to modification in F–2 as it is in F–1. Almost invariably, custody decrees are subject to modification in the state of their rendition on a showing of changed circumstances. Since these can usually be found, the net effect of the Halvey decision was to attenuate markedly the role of full faith and credit in the custody area. This had the disadvantage of making it possible for a parent who was displeased with a custody decision of one state to seek a fresh determination in another state. Moreover, to give the courts of that other state jurisdiction, one parent might in effect kidnap the child and take it there. The other parent might then retaliate in kind and the custody battle might go on and on unless and until the courts of one state chose of their own volition to respect the other state's decree. The child would, of course, be the principal victim in the tug-of-war.

3. The Supreme Court did nothing to alleviate the situation. In one typically unfortunate battle the Georgia and California courts handed down inconsistent custody decrees within the space of a few months, although, so far as appears, the merits were litigated by both parents in each state and the courts of each state were apprised of the contrary decision that had been reached by the courts of the other. The Supreme Court of the United States denied certiorari in each case. Stout v. Pate, and Pate v. Stout, 347 U.S. 968 (1954).

Today, the situation has drastically changed. Questions involving the recognition, enforcement and modification of sister state and foreign country decrees are now regulated in large part by statute. All states have adopted the Uniform Child Custody Jurisdiction Act and the federal Parental Kidnaping Prevention Act of 1980 (28 U.S.C.A. § 1738A) entitles some custody decrees to full faith and credit. The interplay of these two statutes is illustrated by the next case.

Quenzer v. Quenzer
Supreme Court of Wyoming, 1982.
653 P.2d 295.

■ THOMAS, JUSTICE.

The task confronting our court in this case is that of reconciling, in the context of the power to enter a judgment modifying a child-custody decree, the laws of the State of Texas, the State of Wyoming, and the United States of America....

The appellant, Fred August Quenzer, Jr., and the appellee, Nola Kathleen Quenzer (now Sharrard), were divorced in Texas in 1975. Primary custody of the parties' daughter was awarded to the mother pursuant to the Decree of Divorce which followed the provisions of a Property Settlement Agreement previously entered into by the parties. Not long after the divorce the mother removed herself from Texas with the result that the father could not exercise weekend visitation rights as provided for in the Decree of Divorce....

In August of 1977 the father petitioned the circuit court in Oregon [to which the mother had gone] to enforce the visitation provisions of the Texas decree in accordance with Oregon's adoption of the Uniform Child Custody Jurisdiction Act. A cross-petition by the mother sought modification of the Texas decree and also arrearages in child and spousal support payments, and an increase in the amount of monthly child support.... The father then filed a motion for a change in custody of the daughter.... Essentially the Oregon decree continued custody in the mother; ... Although appealed, that judgment was affirmed by the Oregon Court of Appeals.

... In August of 1979 the mother married her present husband and the mother, daughter and the stepfather moved to ..., Alaska ... In June of 1980 the daughter was sent to visit in Texas. The father was entitled to custody for a six-week period starting on the second Sunday of June of each year. During the period of this visit the mother and her husband moved from Alaska to Teton County, Wyoming, where they intended to establish a permanent residence. On July 8, 1980, which was less than a week before the scheduled visitation in Texas was to end, the father filed a motion in the Texas district court, seeking a modification in custody of the child. Process was served upon the mother in Eugene, Oregon, where she was visiting prior to returning to Wyoming.

Thereafter the mother instituted a separate habeas corpus proceeding in the Texas court, seeking enforcement of the Oregon decree returning the child to her custody. The return to her custody was ordered by the Texas court, and on August 16, 1980, the mother and daughter left Texas, and since that time they have resided in Wyoming.... In the meantime the modification proceeding had been held in abeyance pending a determination of the status of the mother, who had attempted to appear specially. The Texas court, by the same judge who had heard the habeas corpus proceeding, entered an order denying the mother's special appearance and ordering the case to proceed to trial on the merits. Thereafter, in January of 1981, trial was held with respect to the proceeding seeking modification of custody. On January 12, 1981, an Order of Modification in Suit Affecting Parent–Child Relationship was entered in Texas in which the court held that custody should be given to the father with visitation rights to the mother. January 26, 1981, was specified as the date for transferring possession of the child, and the Texas court did enter findings that it had jurisdiction and that the mother had not been a continuous domiciliary or resident of any state for six months preceding the filing of this action. It further found that no other court had or has continuing jurisdiction of the suit or of the daughter and that it had jurisdiction of the child because it was the most convenient forum to determine the best interest of the child.

The proceeding in Wyoming was commenced on February 23, 1981.... The Wyoming court found that it had jurisdiction under the Wyoming version of the Uniform Child Custody Jurisdiction Act; that the mother was the proper person to have custody of the child; and that the circumstances before the court showed that any orders of any court in the past should be modified, because of a change in circumstances, to give the mother custody of the child. While critical of the Texas proceeding, the Wyoming district court premised its authority upon the existence of jurisdiction pursuant to Wyoming statute, and it did proceed to modify the Texas modification order by restoring permanent custody to the mother; denying visitation rights in the father "at the present time unless substantial safeguards are erected in that regard" ... The father has appealed from this order....

The father argues earnestly, that the Parental Kidnaping Prevention Act of 1980, Pub.L. 96–611, 94 Stat. 3569 (1980) ... forecloses the Wyoming court from modifying the modification decree entered by the Texas court....

This legislation, if applicable, must be afforded primary consideration under the Supremacy Clauses of our federal and state constitutions. Constitution of the United States, Art. VI, Cl. 2; Constitution of the State of Wyoming, Art. 1, § 37. By this statute Congress has provided for the effect to be given to the judicial proceedings in the state originally exercising jurisdiction, and thus has defined what full faith and credit requires in such instances.[1]

---

1. It would appear that this legislation was intended to supplement existing state legislation such as the Uniform Child Custody Jurisdiction Act to promote interstate judicial cooperation and communication, facilitate the enforcement of custody and visitation decrees of sister states, discourage interstate controversies over child custody, prevent jurisdictional competition and conflicts between state courts, and to deter parental kidnapping and forum shopping. See § 7(c), Pub.L. 96–611, 94 Stat. 3569 (1980)....

Any child-custody determination made consistently with the provisions of the Parental Kidnaping Prevention Act is required to be enforced according to its terms by the courts of every other state (28 U.S.C.A. § 1738A), and the authorities of another state are not permitted to modify except as provided in subsection (f) of 28 U.S.C.A. § 1738A such a child-custody determination. Subsection (f), which is referred to, provides as follows:

"(f) A court of a State may modify a determination of the custody of the same child made by a court of another state, if—

"(1) it has jurisdiction to make a child custody determination; and

"(2) the court of the other State no longer has jurisdiction, or it has declined to exercise such jurisdiction to modify such determination." ...

There is, however, a threshold test which must be applied.... The modification order in Texas must have been made consistently with the provisions of the Parental Kidnaping Prevention Act. Subsection (c) of the Parental Kidnaping Prevention Act provides as follows:

"(c) A child custody determination made by a court of a State is consistent with the provisions of this section only if—

"(1) such court has jurisdiction under the law of such State; and

"(2) one of the following conditions is met:

"(A) such State (i) is the home State of the child on the date of the commencement of the proceeding, or (ii) had been the child's home State within six months before the date of the commencement of the proceeding and the child is absent from such State because of his removal or retention by a contestant or for other reasons, and a contestant continues to live in such State;

"(B)(i) it appears that no other State would have jurisdiction under subparagraph (A), and (ii) it is in the best interest of the child that a court of such State assume jurisdiction because (I) the child and his parents, or the child and at least one contestant, have a significant connection with such State other than mere physical presence in such State, and (II) there is available in such State substantial evidence concerning the child's present or future care, protection, training, and personal relationships;

"(C) the child is physically present in such State and (i) the child has been abandoned, or (ii) it is necessary in an emergency to protect the child because he has been subjected to or threatened with mistreatment or abuse;

"(D)(i) it appears that no other State would have jurisdiction under subparagraph (A), (B), (C), or (E), or another State has declined to exercise jurisdiction on the ground that the State whose jurisdiction is in issue is the more appropriate forum to determine the custody of the child, and (ii) it is in the best interest of the child that such court assume jurisdiction; or

"(E) The court has continuing jurisdiction pursuant to subsection (d) of this section." ...

The Texas determination ... was not made consistently with the second requirement of the Parental Kidnaping Prevention Act, in that its exercise of jurisdiction did not fit any of the conditions contained in 28

U.S.C.A. § 1738A(c)(2). Obviously Texas was not the home state of the child under subsection (A) of that provision. The father cannot rely upon subsection (B) of that provision because the daughter had been living in Alaska for at least six consecutive months immediately preceding the time she went to visit the father, and [therefore] Alaska would be the home state of the child as defined in 28 U.S.C.A. § 1738A(b)(4). The Texas court therefore could not, and it did not, find that no other state would have jurisdiction under subparagraph (A) of 28 U.S.C.A. § 1738A(c)(2)(A). Subsections (C), (D), and (E) of the title similarly are not applicable, and we must conclude that the jurisdiction of the district court in Wyoming was not foreclosed by the provisions of the Parental Kidnaping Prevention Act because the modification order entered in the State of Texas was not a "custody determination made consistently with the provisions of this section by a court of another State."

Having concluded that neither the Full Faith and Credit Clause nor the provisions of the Parental Kidnaping Prevention Act foreclosed the exercise of jurisdiction by the district court in Wyoming, we still must consider whether the exercise of that jurisdiction was precluded under some provision of Wyoming law. Our conclusion with respect to this proposition will also dispose of the first issue urged by the father in his appeal. Section 20–5–104, W.S.1977 [U.C.C.J.A. § 3] is the provision governing the jurisdiction of Wyoming courts in child-custody proceedings, and it provides as follows:

> "(a) A court of this state competent to decide child custody matters has jurisdiction to make a child custody determination by initial decree or modification decree if:
>
> "(i) This state is the home state of the child at the time of commencement of the proceeding, or was the child's home state within six (6) months before commencement of the proceeding and the child is absent from the state because of his removal or retention by a person claiming his custody or for other reasons, and a parent or person acting as parent continues to live in this state;
>
> "(ii) It is in the best interest of the child that a court of this state assume jurisdiction because the child and his parents, or the child and at least one (1) contestant, have a significant connection with the state and there is available in this state substantial evidence concerning the child's present or future care, protection, training and personal relationships;
>
> "(iii) The child is physically present in this state and has been abandoned or if it is necessary in an emergency to protect the child because he has been subjected to or threatened with mistreatment or abuse or is otherwise neglected or dependent; or
>
> "(iv) It appears that no other state would have jurisdiction under prerequisites substantially in accordance with paragraphs [subdivisions] (i), (ii) or (iii) of this subsection, or another state has declined to exercise jurisdiction on the ground that this state is the more appropriate forum to determine the custody of the child and it is in the best interest of the child that this court assume jurisdiction.

"(b) Except under paragraphs [subdivisions] (a)(iii) and (iv) of this section, physical presence in this state of the child or of the child and one (1) of the contestants is not alone sufficient to confer jurisdiction on a court of this state to make a child custody determination.

"(c) Physical presence of the child, while desirable, is not a prerequisite for jurisdiction to determine his custody."

Both subsections (a)(i) and (a)(ii) in this instance justify the exercise of jurisdiction by the courts of the State of Wyoming. In § 20–5–103(a)(v), W.S.1977, [U.C.C.J.A. § 2] "Home state" is defined as follows:

"... 'Home state' means the state in which the child immediately preceding the time involved has lived with his parents, a parent or a person acting as parent, for at least six (6) consecutive months, and in the case of a child less than six (6) months old the state in which the child has lived since birth with any of the persons mentioned. Periods of temporary absence of any of the names [sic] persons are counted as part of the six (6) month or other period; ..."

The record is clear that the daughter had resided with her mother in Wyoming from the time of the conclusion of the habeas corpus proceeding in Texas until the commencement of the Wyoming proceeding, which was more than six months. It is equally apparent that there did exist in this instance a significant connection with the State of Wyoming, and that there was available in this state substantial evidence concerning the child's present or future care, protection, training and personal relationships. Friends, neighbors, school personnel, and a professional psychologist were all present to assist the court in making determinations with respect to the best interest of the child. We note by contrast that the testimony in the Texas proceeding duplicated some of this testimony, and that the Texas witnesses appeared primarily as character witnesses for the father and his second wife. Any balanced comparison of these factors results in a clear preference for the State of Wyoming as the appropriate forum. The district court [determined] that it was in the best interest of the child that it exercise its jurisdiction. The evidence present in the record sustains this determination, and in the absence of some other inhibiting factor or prohibition the district court had jurisdiction over this matter under Wyoming law.

The father, however, points to the provisions of § 20–5–107(a), W.S. 1977, [U.C.C.J.A. § 6] and urges that this section prohibits the exercise of jurisdiction in Wyoming. Section 20–5–107(a), W.S.1977, provides:

"(a) A court of this state shall not exercise its jurisdiction under this act if at the time of filing the petition a proceeding concerning the custody of the same child was pending in a court of another state exercising jurisdiction substantially in conformity with this act, unless the proceeding is stayed by the court of the other state because this state is a more appropriate forum or for other reasons."

Again the record is clear that when this proceeding was commenced in the Wyoming district court the proceedings in the courts of Texas had been concluded, and become final there according to local law. Since there was no proceeding pending in Texas, § 20–5–107(a) did not interfere with the exercise of jurisdiction by the district court in Wyoming. We note in this regard that the father apparently has abandoned his claim that the district court abused its discretion by failing to decline jurisdiction as an inconvenient forum in favor of Texas under § 20–5–108, W.S.1977 [U.C.C.J.A. § 7].

Relying upon still another contention, the father argues that the district court committed error in asserting and exercising jurisdiction to determine child custody in the light of §§ 20–5–114 [U.C.C.J.A. § 13] and 20–5–115(a) [U.C.C.J.A. § 14] W.S.1977. The provisions of those statutes read as follows:

> "§ 20–5–114. Recognition and enforcement of initial or modification decree made by court of another state.
>
> "The courts of this state shall recognize and enforce an initial or modification decree of a court of another state which had assumed jurisdiction under statutory provisions substantially in accordance with this act, or which was made under factual circumstances meeting the jurisdictional standards of the act, so long as this decree has not been modified in accordance with jurisdictional standards substantially similar to those of this act."
>
> "§ 20–5–115. Modifying custody decree made by court of another state.
>
> "(a) If a court of another state has made a custody decree a court of this state shall not modify that decree unless it appears that the court which rendered the decree does not now have jurisdiction under jurisdictional prerequisites substantially in accordance with this act or has declined to assume jurisdiction to modify the decree, and the court of this state has jurisdiction."

The mother meets these contentions by asserting that the district court correctly refused to recognize and enforce the Texas order because the statutory provisions in Texas are not substantially in accordance with the Uniform Child Custody Jurisdiction Act, and she asserts that the factual circumstances were such that the jurisdictional standards of the Uniform Act were not met in Texas.... She points out that, while tit. 2, § 11.045(1)(2)(A), Tex.Fam.Code Ann. (Vernon 1975), facially is similar to § 20–5–104(a)(ii), W.S.1977, the State of Texas has no provision similar to § 20–5–109(b), W.S.1977. [U.C.C.J.A. § 8] This latter provision provides as follows:

> "(b) Unless required in the interest of the child and subject to W.S. 20–5–115(a), the court shall not exercise its jurisdiction to modify a custody decree of another state if the petitioner without consent of the person entitled to custody has improperly removed the child from the physical custody of the person entitled to custody or has improperly retained the child after a visit or other temporary relinquishment of physical custody. If the petitioner has violated any other provision of a custody decree of another state the court in its discretion and subject to W.S. 20–5–115(a) may decline to exercise jurisdiction."

The record before us discloses that while the father filed his action for modification in Texas during the period that the daughter was visiting him pursuant to the provisions of the Oregon decree, his retention of custody beyond the time provided by the decree was wrongful and in derogation of the mother's rights. We agree with the mother that ... a Wyoming court under these circumstances would not be permitted to exercise its jurisdiction to modify a custody decree.

It would appear from the circumstances that the policy of the State of Texas differs. Consequently, if the issue in this case were confined to the enforcement of the Texas order it well might be that the doctrine of res judicata, combined with the provisions of our Wyoming law and the Parental Kidnaping Prevention Act, would require the recognition and enforcement of the Texas decree.... Still the availability of the jurisdiction of the district court to modify the provisions of the Texas order is not foreclosed. Unless the prohibition contained in § 20–5–115(a), W.S.1977, is applicable, the district court in Wyoming had the power to act and enter its own order modifying the custody provisions upon a sufficient showing of a change in circumstances to warrant a different decree....

We conclude that it is the duty of the Wyoming court to determine the applicability of § 20–5–115(a), W.S.1977, i.e., to determine whether the Texas court at the time the jurisdiction of the Wyoming court was exercised had jurisdiction under jurisdictional prerequisites substantially in accordance with the Uniform Child Custody Jurisdiction Act or had declined to assume jurisdiction to modify the decree.... This determination, which must be made by the Wyoming court, is to be made not at the commencement of the Wyoming action, but rather at the time of the hearing on the matter in light of the evidence presented.... Other courts which have construed this Uniform Child Custody Jurisdiction Act generally have applied a two-stage test in determining whether the local court had jurisdiction to modify a foreign custody determination. First the court must consider whether the court whose decree is sought to be modified no longer has jurisdiction under standards such as those set forth in § 20–5–104, W.S.1977 [U.C.C.J.A. § 4], and secondly it may consider whether the court whose decree is sought to be modified has declined jurisdiction to modify its prior judgment. If either of these tests is met, then the forum state must determine whether it has jurisdiction under its own laws....

On the date that the Wyoming court held its hearing the Texas court no longer had jurisdiction under standards which substantially comply with the Uniform Child Custody Jurisdiction Act. This test having been met, the Wyoming court was not foreclosed from exercising jurisdiction by the provisions of § 20–5–115(a), W.S.1977. We justify this holding first by alluding to one of the general purposes of the Uniform Child Custody Jurisdiction Act set forth in § 20–5–102, W.S.1977 [U.C.C.J.A. § 1] as follows:

"(a) The general purposes of this act are:

. . .

"(iii) To assure that litigation concerning the custody of a child take place ordinarily in the state with which the child and his family have the closest connection and where significant evidence concerning his care, protection, training and personal relationships is most readily available, and that courts of this state decline the exercise of jurisdiction when the child and his family have a closer connection with another state;"

We find in this statement of policy an explicit recognition that the paramount consideration of the best interest of the child mandates that custody determinations be made in the forum having the best access to the relevant evidence....

At the time that Wyoming exercised its jurisdiction in this matter it was the "home state" under the Uniform Child Custody Jurisdiction Act and § 20–5–104(a)(i), W.S.1977.... At the pertinent date the state which had the most significant connections with the child and her mother was Wyoming. In February of 1982 the daughter had been present in Wyoming nearly eighteen months. She was attending local schools and receiving weekly counseling in Jackson, Wyoming, from a professional psychologist. Evidence of the mother's parental fitness and her relationship with the daughter was most accessible in Wyoming. Most importantly, however, the child's presence in this state gave the district court the best opportunity to gather evidence concerning the daughter's emotional and personal development, as well as furnishing to it the opportunity for the child to testify directly with respect to her early allegations in the Texas habeas corpus proceeding of drug use and mistreatment at the hands of her mother. She had earlier recanted that testimony by a letter to the Texas judge, and the Wyoming court had the opportunity to evaluate personally with the daughter the two versions of her prior testimony. The evidence available in Wyoming was relevant and substantial with respect to the issue of the best interest of the child. Under these criteria the Wyoming court properly exercised jurisdiction in the matter and entered its decree modifying the custody provisions of the Texas decree....

[T]he last argument of the father relates to the sufficiency of the evidence to justify the finding by the district court of a substantial change in circumstances.... He also urges the proposition that the brief period between the date of the modification order in Texas and the beginning of the Wyoming proceedings negates the possibility that a change of circumstances occurred in the interim.

Once vested with jurisdiction over the cause, it is the duty of the court to hear evidence to determine whether a substantial material change in circumstances has occurred so that the welfare of the child will be best served by a change in custody.... Although the brief period of time between the entry of the order sought to be modified and the institution of new proceedings may indicate that circumstances have not changed, we cannot as a matter of law hold that the movant, who bears the burden of proof, could not present such sufficient evidence....

... The district court in this instance made detailed and explicit findings concerning the changes in the daughter's circumstances. In addition, the record contains exhibits ... including the depositions of the daughter and the psychologist, both of which support the findings made by the district court. The evidence is sufficient to support a conclusion that the mother has established a stable home with her new husband, and this has greatly aided the daughter's own emotional stability and maturity. The deposition of the psychologist details the advances the daughter has made since treatment was obtained. The daughter is happy and manifesting significant improvement in her school work and social development under the mother's care and supervision. She has established a strong parent-child relationship with her stepfather. Other improvements in the daughter and the mother's circumstances are detailed in the record. The record in this case is adequate to support the action of the district court....

The order of the trial court hereby is affirmed on the basis of the conclusions reached in the foregoing opinion.

NOTES

1. Among other things, the Parental Kidnaping Prevention Act makes available the facilities of the Federal Parent Locator Service in aid of attempts to ascertain the whereabouts of a kidnaped child.

The Parental Kidnaping Prevention Act does not confer custody jurisdiction on the federal courts, nor does it give them jurisdiction to determine which of two or more competing state courts has jurisdiction. Compliance with the Act must therefore be tested by appeal within the state court system and thereafter by petition for certiorari to the Supreme Court. Thompson v. Thompson, 484 U.S. 174 (1988). See also California v. Superior Court of California, 482 U.S. 400 (1987): the Extradition Act required California to extradite a father to Louisiana where he had been charged with parental kidnapping. California could not refuse to do so on the ground that the father had custody under a prior and valid California decree. The effect to be given to the California decree was to be determined by the Louisiana courts. For comment on Thompson, see Weintraub, Commentary on Conflict of Laws, 1991 Supp. to 3d ed. 60–61 (1986).

2. In Greenlaw v. Smith, 123 Wn.2d 593, 869 P.2d 1024 (1994), a father asked the Washington court to modify its custody decree in his favor even though the minor child and his mother, the custodial parent, had not resided in Washington State for six years prior to the request for modification. The Washington Supreme Court held that the lower court's exercise of jurisdiction was proper because the father remained in Washington State and the child continued to have more than slight contact with Washington as a result of visiting his father.

For further discussion of the relationship between the Parental Kidnapping Act and the UCCJA, see Katz, Child Snatching (1981); Foster, Child Custody Jurisdiction: UCCJA and PKPA, 27 N.Y.L.Sch.L.Rev. 297 (1981); Bruch, Interstate Child Custody Law and Eicke, 16 Fam.L.Q. 277 (1982); Coombs, Custody Conflicts in the Courts, 16 Fam.L.Q. 251 (1982); Coombs, Interstate Child Custody: Jurisdiction, Recognition, and Enforcement, 66 Minn.L.Rev. 711 (1982); Note, The Parental Kidnapping Prevention Act, 27 N.Y.L.Rev. 553 (1982); Note, The Effect of the Parental Kidnapping Prevention Act of 1980 on Child Snatching, 17 N.Eng.L.Rev. 499 (1982); Baron, Federal Preemption in the Resolution of Child Custody Jurisdiction Disputes, 45 Ark.L.Rev. 885 (1993); Note, Judicial Wandering Through a Legislative Maze: Application of the Uniform Child Custody Jurisdiction Act and the Parental Kidnapping Prevention Act to Child Custody Determinations, 58 Mo.L.Rev. 427 (1993); Note, Interstate Child Custody and the Parental Kidnapping Prevention Act: The Continuing Search for a National Standard, 45 Hastings L.J. 1329 (1994).

Articles on the Uniform Child Custody Jurisdiction Act by Professor Brigitte Bodenheimer, its principal draftsman, include Bodenheimer, Interstate Custody: Initial Jurisdiction and Continuing Jurisdiction Under the UCCJA, 14 Fam.L.Q. 203 (1981); Bodenheimer, Progress Under the Uniform Child Custody Jurisdiction Act and Remaining Problems: Punitive Decrees, Joint Custody, and Excessive Modifications, 65 Calif.L.Rev. 978 (1977); Bodenheimer, The Rights of Children and The Crisis in Custody Litigation, 46 Colo.L.Rev. 495 (1975); Bodenheimer, The Uniform Child Custody Jurisdiction Act: A Legislative Remedy for Children Caught in the Conflict of Laws, 22 Vand.L.Rev. 1207 (1969).

For a discussion and intensive examination of the Uniform Child Custody Jurisdiction Act, see Ratner, Procedural Due Process and Jurisdiction to Adjudicate, 75 Nw.L.Rev. 363 (1980); Note, The UCCJA Coming of Age, 34 Mercer L.Rev. 811 (1983); Rosen, The Uniform Child Custody Jurisdiction Act, 3–FEB S.C.Law. 36 (1992).

3. The Parental Kidnapping Prevention Act is applicable only to sister-state custody decrees. The International Parental Kidnapping Crime Act of 1993, 107 Stat. 1988, 19 U.S.C.A. § 1204, makes the removal of a child from the United States with intent to obstruct the exercise of parental rights a federal crime. Parental rights include custody based on a court order or derived from a legally binding agreement between the parties.

4. The Uniform Child Custody Jurisdiction Act also applies to custody decrees rendered in foreign countries. See, e.g., Custody of a Minor (No. 3), 392 Mass. 728, 468 N.E.2d 251 (1984) (Massachusetts court would not modify an Australian custody decree): "We see no basis ... for concluding that the Australian custody determination was not made in substantial conformity with [the U.C.C.J.A.] or ... that the Australian court does not have jurisdiction under the jurisdictional prerequisites of [the Act].... If a Massachusetts court had the power to disregard a foreign judgment by considering [its] propriety ... in a substantive, rather than a procedural sense, the very purpose of the law would be undermined...." See, similarly, Vause v. Vause, 140 Wis.2d 157, 409 N.W.2d 412 (App.1987) (the mother had received reasonable notice of the German proceeding and an opportunity to appear, the German proceeding satisfied the standards of the UCCJA, and the resulting decree was entitled to recognition). However, Missouri, New Mexico, Ohio, and South Dakota have omitted § 23 of the UCCJA. In Minton v. McManus, 9 Ohio App.3d 165, 458 N.E.2d 1292 (1983), the trial court therefore was not required to recognize a Scottish decree awarding custody to the former wife.

In the case of In re Stephanie M., 7 Cal.4th 295, 27 Cal.Rptr.2d 595, 867 P.2d 706 (1994), cert. denied, 115 S.Ct. 277 (1994), the Supreme Court of California upheld the jurisdiction of a lower court over a custody action involving the minor child of Mexican nationals despite the assertion of concurrent jurisdiction by Mexico. California asserted jurisdiction over the matter because of the emergency presented by the abuse of the minor. Much of the evidence regarding the abuse and the investigation of the parents' capacity to provide a future home free from abuse was located in California. The state supreme court held that the lower court had not abused its discretion although it had been informed of the child's Mexican grandmother's interest in having the child live with her in Mexico.

When the decree of an American court provides for the child to visit a parent abroad, it becomes important that the continuing jurisdiction of the American court be preserved and that no inconsistent decree be entered abroad. See Tischendorf v. Tischendorf, 321 N.W.2d 405 (Minn.1982), cert. denied, 460 U.S. 1037 (1983) (father, residing in Germany, required to post security in the form of an irrevocable letter of credit and to obtain German court order recognizing the exclusive jurisdiction of the American court). See also Annotation, Court–Authorized Permanent or Temporary Removal of Child by Parent to Foreign Country, 30 A.L.R.4th 548 (1984).

5. The Hague Convention on the Civil Aspects of International Child Abduction came into force for the United States on July 1, 1988, by the International Child Abduction Remedies Act, P.L. 100–300. The Convention does not provide a mechanism for the determination of custody disputes. Instead, it seeks "to restore the factual situation that existed prior to the child's removal or retention.... The international abductor is denied legal advantage from the abduction to or retention in the country where the child is located, as resort to the Convention is to effect the child's swift return to his or her circumstances before the abduction or retention." President Reagan's message to the Senate, 99th Cong., 1st Sess., Sen. Treaty Doc. 99–11 (Nov. 5, 1985). An aggrieved parent may enlist the aid of the "Central Authority" designated by each ratifying country as well as resort to the courts. Under the federal implementing Act, state and federal courts have concurrent original jurisdiction. See Comment, Taking Away the Pawns: International Parental Abduction and the Hague Convention, 20 N.C.J.Int'l L. & Com.Reg. 137 (1994); Note, The Hague Convention on the Civil Aspects of International Child Abduction: Are the Convention's Goals Being Achieved?; 2 Ind.J.Global Legal Stud. 553 (1995).

For application of the Convention in American courts, see Rydder v. Rydder, 49 F.3d 369 (8th Cir.1995) (child returned to Poland); Feder v. Evans–Feder, 63 F.3d 217 (3d Cir.1995) ("habitual residence" was defined as a place where the child was physically present for an amount of time sufficient for acclimatization and that has a degree of "settled purpose" from the child's perspective, taking into account the child's circumstances and the parents' shared intentions regarding the child's presence in such a place); Brooke v. Willis, 907 F.Supp. 57 (S.D.N.Y.1995) (United Kingdom found to be the child's habitual residence because even though child spent only one summer there, he had become "settled" in England). For application of the Convention in the courts of the United Kingdom, see Re: M., [1995] 1 F.L.R. 1021 (C.A.1994); C. v. C., [1989] 1 W.L.R. 654, 1 F.L.R. 403 (C.A.1988).

SECTION 8. SUPPORT

A. ENFORCEMENT OF SUPPORT CLAIMS WITHOUT REGARD TO RECIPROCAL SUPPORT LEGISLATION

INTRODUCTORY NOTE

If a claim for support arises against a husband who has abandoned his wife and children and fled to another state, what are the methods of enforcing the claim in the other state? What are the legal and practical difficulties in the way? How much better off are the wife and children if the claim for support has been reduced to judgment in the first state? These are some of the questions suggested by the cases incorporated below.

Kulko v. California Superior Court

Supreme Court of the United States, 1978.
436 U.S. 84, 98 S.Ct. 1690, 56 L.Ed. 132.

[Sharon Kulko Horn commenced an custody and support action in a California state court against her former husband, Ezra Kulko. Prior to their separation, the former spouses resided in New York with their two minor children. After the couple separated, the mother moved to California. A subsequent Haitian divorce obtained by her incorporated a separation agreement that had been negotiated in New York. The agreement provided that the children were to live with the father during the school year and with the mother during vacations. The father made support payments in the amount of $3,000 per year for the time in which the children were in the mother's care. When the daughter asked to live with her mother in California during the school year, the father acquiesced and bought the daughter a one-way ticket to California. The son also joined his mother in California after she sent him a ticket, unbeknownst to the father. The mother then brought an action in a California state court in order to seek full custody and an increase in child support payments. The father did not object to jurisdiction over the custody claim, but he did object to the court's assertion of personal jurisdiction over the claim for increased child support. The father had visited California only twice during brief military stopovers years earlier. California courts held that California could exercise personal jurisdiction over the father because the father had "purposefully availed himself of the benefits and protections of California." The Supreme Court reversed.]

■ JUSTICE MARSHALL delivered the opinion of the Court.

The issue before us is whether, in this action for child support, the California state courts may exercise in personam jurisdiction over a nonresident, nondomiciliary parent of minor children domiciled in the State. For reasons set forth below, we hold that the exercise of such jurisdiction would violate the Due Process Clause of the Fourteenth Amendment.

. . .

II

The Due Process Clause of the Fourteenth Amendment operates as a limitation on the jurisdiction of state courts to enter judgments affecting rights or interests of nonresidents. See Shaffer v. Heitner, 433 U.S. 186, 198–200, 97 S.Ct. 2569, 2577, 53 L.Ed.2d 683 (1977). It has long been the rule that a valid judgment imposing a personal obligation or duty in favor of the plaintiff may be entered only by a court having jurisdiction over the person of the defendant. Pennoyer v. Neff, 95 U.S. 714, 732–733, 24 L.Ed. 565, 572 (1878); International Shoe Co. v. Washington, 326 U.S., at 316, 66

S.Ct., at 158. The existence of personal jurisdiction, in turn, depends upon the presence of reasonable notice to the defendant that an action has been brought. Mullane v. Central Hanover Trust Co., 339 U.S. 306, 313–314, 70 S.Ct. 652, 656–657, 94 L.Ed. 865 (1950), and a sufficient connection between the defendant and the forum State to make it fair to require defense of the action in the forum. Milliken v. Meyer, 311 U.S. 457, 463–464, 61 S.Ct. 339, 342–343, 85 L.Ed. 278 (1940). In this case, appellant does not dispute the adequacy of the notice given, but contends that his connection with the State of California is too attenuated, under the standards implicit in the Due Process Clause of the Constitution, to justify imposing upon him the burden and inconvenience of defense in California.

The parties are in agreement that the constitutional standard for determining whether the State may enter a binding judgment against appellant here is that set forth in this Court's opinion in International Shoe Co. v. Washington, supra: that a defendant "have certain minimum contacts with [the forum State] such that the maintenance of the suit does not offend 'traditional notions of fair play and substantial justice.'" 326 U.S., at 316, 66 S.Ct., at 158, quoting Milliken v. Meyer, supra, 311 U.S., at 463, 61 S.Ct., at 342.

... But we believe that the California Supreme Court's application of the minimum-contacts test in this case represents an unwarranted extension of International Shoe and would, if sustained, sanction a result that is neither fair, just, nor reasonable.

A

[I]n holding that personal jurisdiction existed, the court below carefully disclaimed reliance on the fact that appellant had agreed at the time of separation to allow his children to live with their mother three months a year and that he had sent them to California each year pursuant to the agreement. As was noted below, 19 Cal.3d, at 523–524, 138 Cal.Rptr., at 590, 564 P.2d, at 357, to find personal jurisdiction in a State on this basis, merely because the mother was residing there, would discourage parents from entering into reasonable visitation agreements. Moreover, it could arbitrarily subject one parent to suit in any State of the Union where the other parent chose to spend time while having custody of their offspring pursuant to the separation agreement.[6] As we have emphasized:

> "The unilateral activity of those who claim some relationship with a nonresident defendant cannot satisfy the requirement of contact with the forum State.... [I]t is essential in each case that there be some act by which the defendant purposefully avails [him]self of the privilege of con-

---

6. Although the separation agreement stated that appellee Horn resided in California and provided that child-support payments would be mailed to her California address, it also specifically contemplated that appellee might move to a different State. The agreement directed appellant to mail the support payments to appellee's San Francisco address or "any other address which the Wife may designate from time to time in writing." App. 10.

ducting activities within the forum State...." Hanson v. Denckla, supra, 357 U.S., at 253, 78 S.Ct., at 1240.

The "purposeful act" that the California Supreme Court believed did warrant the exercise of personal jurisdiction over appellant in California was his "actively and fully consent[ing] to [the daughter] living in California for the school year ... and ... sen[ding] her to California for that purpose." 19 Cal.3d, at 524, 138 Cal.Rptr., at 591, 564 P.2d, at 358. We cannot accept the proposition that appellant's acquiescence in [the daughter's] desire to live with her mother conferred jurisdiction over appellant in the California courts in this action. A father who agrees, in the interests of family harmony and his children's preferences, to allow them to spend more time in California that was required under a separation agreement can hardly be said to have "purposefully availed himself" of the "benefits and protections" of California's laws. See Shaffer v. Heitner, 433 U.S., at 216, 97 S.Ct., at 2586.[7]

Nor can we agree with the assertion of the court below that the exercise of in personam jurisdiction here was warranted by the financial benefit appellant derived from his daughter's presence in California for nine months of the year. 19 Cal.3d at 524–525, 138 Cal.Rptr., at 590–591, 564 P.2d, at 358. This argument rests on the premise that, while appellant's liability for support payments remained unchanged, his yearly expenses for supporting the children in New York decreased. But this circumstance, even if true, does not support California's assertion of jurisdiction here. Any diminution in appellant's household costs resulted, not from the child's presence in California, but rather from her absence from appellant's home. Moreover, an action by appellee Horn to increase support payments could now be brought, and could have been brought when [the daughter] first moved to California, in the State of New York; a New York court would clearly have personal jurisdiction over appellant and, if a judgment were entered by a New York court increasing appellant's child support obligations, it could be properly enforced against him in both New York and California. Any ultimate advantage to appellant thus results not from the child's presence in California, but from appellee's failure earlier to seek an increase in payments under the separation agreement. The argument below to the contrary, in our view, confuses the question of appellant's liability with that of the proper forum in which to determine that liability.

B

In light of our conclusion that appellant did not purposefully derive any benefit from any activities relating to the State of California, it is apparent that the California Supreme Court's reliance on appellant's

---

7. The court below stated that the presence in California of appellant's daughter gave appellant the benefit of California's "police and fire protection, its school system, its hospital services, its recreational facilities, its libraries and museums...." 19 Cal.3d, at 522, 138 Cal.Rptr., at 589, 564 P.2d, at 356. But, in the circumstances presented here, these services provided by the State were essentially benefits to the child, not the father, and in any event were not benefits that appellant purposefully sought for himself.

having caused an "effect" in California was misplaced. See supra., at 1695. This "effects" test is derived from the American Law Institute's Restatement (Second) of Conflict of Laws § 37 (1971), which provides:

> "A state has power to exercise judicial jurisdiction over an individual who causes effects in the state by an act done elsewhere with respect to any cause of action arising from these effects unless the nature of the effects and of the individual's relationship to the state makes exercise of such jurisdiction unreasonable."

While this provision is not binding on this Court, it does not in any event support the decision below. As is apparent from the examples accompanying § 37 in the Restatement, this section was intended to reach wrongful activity outside of the State causing injury inside of the State, see, e.g., Comment a, p. 157 (shooting bullet from one State into another), or commercial activity affecting state residents, ibid. Even in such situations, moreover, the Restatement recognizes that there might be circumstances that would render "unreasonable" the assertion of jurisdiction over the nonresident defendant.

The circumstances in this case clearly render "unreasonable" California's assertion of personal jurisdiction. There is no claim that appellant has visited physical injury on either property or persons within the State of California.... The cause of action herein asserted arises, not from the defendant's commercial transactions in interstate commerce, but rather from his personal, domestic relations.... Furthermore, the controversy between the parties arises from a separation that occurred in the State of New York; appellee Horn seeks modification of a contract that was negotiated in New York and that she flew to New York to sign. As in Hanson v. Denckla, 357 U.S., at 252, 78 S,Ct., at 1239, the instant action involves an agreement that was entered into with virtually no connection with the forum state. See also n. 6, supra.

Finally, basic considerations of fairness point decisively in favor of appellant's State of domicile as the proper forum for adjudication of this case, whatever the merits of appellee's underlying claim. It is appellant who has remained in the State of the marital domicile, whereas it is appellee who has moved across the continent. Cf. May v. Anderson, 345 U.S. 528, 534–535, n. 8, 73 S.Ct. 840, 843–844, 97 L.Ed. 1221 (1953). Appellant has at all times resided in New York State, and, until the separation and appellee's move to California, his entire family resided there as well. As noted above, appellant did no more than acquiesce in the stated preference of one of his children to live with her mother in California. This single act is surely not one that a reasonable parent would expect to result in the substantial financial burden and personal strain of litigating a child-support suit in a forum 3,000 miles away, and we therefore see no basis on which it can be said that appellant could reasonably have anticipated being "haled before a [California] court" Shaffer v. Heitner, 433 U.S., at 216, 97 S.Ct., at 2586. To make jurisdiction in a case such as this turn on whether appellant bought his daughter a ticket or instead unsuccessfully sought to prevent her departure would impose an unreasonable burden on family relations, and one wholly unjustified by the "quality and nature" of appellant's activities in or relating to the State of California. International Shoe Co. v. Washington, 326 U.S., at 319, 66 S.Ct., at 159.

III

In seeking to justify the burden that would be imposed on appellant were the exercise of in personam jurisdiction in California sustained, appellee argues that California has substantial interests in protecting the welfare of its minor residents and in promoting to the fullest extent possible a healthy and supportive family environment in which the children of the State are to be raised. These interests are unquestionably important. But while the presence of the children and one parent in California arguably might favor application of California law in a lawsuit in New York, the fact that California may be the " 'center of gravity' " for choice-of-law purposes does not mean that California has personal jurisdiction over the defendant. Hanson v. Denckla, supra, 357 U.S., at 254, 78 S.Ct., at 1240. And California has not attempted to assert any particularized interest in trying such cases in its courts by, e.g., enacting a special jurisdictional statute. Cf. McGee v. International Life Ins. Co., supra, 355 U.S., at 221, 224, 78 S.Ct., at 200–201.

California's interest in ensuring the support of children resident in California without unduly disrupting the children's live, moreover, is already being served by the State's participation in the Revised Uniform Reciprocal Enforcement of Support Act of 1968....

IV

... But the mere act of sending a child to California to live with her mother is not a commercial act and connotes no intent to obtain or expectancy of receiving a corresponding benefit in the State that would make fair the assertion of that State's judicial jurisdiction.

Accordingly, we conclude that the appellant's motion to quash service, on the ground of lack of personal jurisdiction, was erroneously denied by California courts. The judgment of the California Supreme Court is, therefore,

Reversed.

■ JUSTICE BRENNAN, JUSTICE WHITE and JUSTICE POWELL dissenting.

NOTES

1. The Montana Supreme Court held that the Kulko decision barred assertion of jurisdiction over a father, resident of California, in an action that sought an increase in child support even though the father had helped the children move to Montana. Heinle v. Fourth Judicial Dist. Ct. In & For County of Missoula, 260 Mont. 489, 861 P.2d 171 (1993).

2. In the context of Barber v. Barber, supra, see also the "Child Support Enforcement Amendments of 1984," 42 U.S.C.A. § 666(a)(5)(ii) (West 1994), which provide additional means for enforcement.

3. In connection with Worthley v. Worthley, supra, p. 293, see also Restatement, Second, Conflict of Laws § 109 (1986 Revisions) which calls for the recognition of modifiable sister-state support judgments.

4. In the European Union, the Brussels Convention provides for jurisdiction "in matters relating to maintenance, in the courts for the place where the maintenance creditor is domiciled or habitually resident." Art. 5, No. 2.

Lynde v. Lynde
Supreme Court of the United States, 1901.
181 U.S. 183, 21 S.Ct. 555, 45 L.Ed. 810.

[The case appears p. 229, supra.]

Yarborough v. Yarborough
Supreme Court of the United States, 1933.
290 U.S. 202, 54 S.Ct. 181, 78 L.Ed. 269, 90 A.L.R. 924.

[The case appears p. 259, supra.]

Barber v. Barber
Supreme Court of the United States, 1944.
323 U.S. 77, 65 S.Ct. 137, 89 L.Ed. 82.

[The case appears p. 290, supra.]

Worthley v. Worthley
Supreme Court of California, 1955.
44 Cal.2d 465, 283 P.2d 19.

[The case appears p. 293, supra.]

Estin v. Estin
Supreme Court of the United States, 1948.
334 U.S. 541, 68 S.Ct. 1213, 92 L.Ed. 1561, 1 A.L.R.2d 1412.

[The case appears p. 866, supra.]

THE LAW GOVERNING SUPPORT

Apart from the problem of enforcement of a foreign support order, there is the question of what law governs the duty of one person to support another. This has been said to be "anything but clear." [1] It is hard to understand why the question has not arisen more frequently, since, as stated in the Commissioners' Prefatory Note to the Uniform Reciprocal Enforcement of Support Act (1950),

"[I]t is little realized how different are the duties [of support] existing in our ... states. Some enforce a duty toward illegitimate children, others do not. Forty jurisdictions require children to support their parents, the others do not. A dozen states require support between brothers and sisters, the others do not. Seventeen states require a wife to support a husband under certain circumstances, the others do not. And even in the duty of a parent to support his child the several states require this support up to different ages, varying from 14 to 21 years."

A related problem concerns the question of what law to apply in the case where a third party seeks recovery for goods furnished a member of the family group.

State of California v. Copus
Supreme Court of Texas, 1958.
158 Tex. 196, 309 S.W.2d 227.

[In 1936 Mrs. Copus, the mother of the defendant, Dale Copus was adjudged mentally ill in California and admitted to a California state institution where she had been a patient ever since. A California statute imposed a duty on a son to pay for the support of his incompetent mother in a state hospital. On July 16, 1951, the son changed his domicile from California to Texas. On May 21, 1953, the State of California brought the present action in a Texas court against the son for the amounts accrued under the California statute during the four years preceding.

California had a four year statute of limitations for the enforcement of the obligation. Texas had a general statute of limitations setting a period of two years for such an obligation. The trial court gave a judgment for the plaintiff for the full amount sued for, $3,470, stating: "... the liability of the defendant ... is a continuing one; and the removal of the defendant ... does not discharge him from such continuing liability under the laws of the State of California, the defendant having been a resident of California at the time of the commencement of such continuing liability."]

■ CULVER, JUSTICE. ... The general rule rather universally recognized is that the statutes of a state ex proprio vigore have no extraterritorial effect. It must be concluded, therefore, that the California statute could not create a legal obligation upon a citizen of Texas who was not a citizen of California when the obligation arose, that is, at the time the mother became institutionalized in California or at any time thereafter. We are aware of no rule of law that would make the obligation a continuing one

---

1. Ehrenzweig, Interstate Recognition of Support Duties, 42 Calif.L.Rev. 382, 384–385 (1954).

after removal from California even though it attached to him while a resident of that state. Citizens of a state equally share the burdens and privileges of citizenship regardless of when or how that status is attained. To say that the support statute compelled liability for that period of time after the respondent moved to Texas would seem to deny to him equality with other citizens of the state....

This cause of action in so far as it concerns the accruals after respondent's removal to Texas cannot be said to have arisen while respondent was under the legislative jurisdiction of California.... We hold, therefore, that respondent is not liable for any sums accrued after his removal to this state.

[W]e prefer to follow those decisions that would treat the [time] limitation in the California statute as substantive and not procedural....

It cannot be said that the maintenance of this suit in Texas and the rendition of a judgment in California's favor for the amount accruing before the respondent became a citizen of Texas is against the public policy of this state. It is true that our Legislature has not seen fit to enact a statute to impose legal liability upon a son for the maintenance of a parent inmate in a state institution, although it does by statute obligate the husband or wife and the father or mother, if financially able, to bear the expense of maintaining a patient in a state hospital where the patient has not sufficient estate of his own.... And not only that, but our Probate Code, Sec. 423, requires that an incompetent person, having no estate of his own, shall be maintained by the husband or wife and by the father or mother and even by the children and grandchildren, if able to do so....

This California statutory requirement of support does not run counter to good morals or natural justice or appear prejudicial in any way to the general interest of the citizens of Texas.

We, therefore, hold that the petitioner is entitled to judgment for the sum of money charged by the State of California for the support of his mother while the respondent was a citizen of that state that accrued within four years of the commencement of this suit and will be denied recovery for any sums that accrued after respondent's removal to this state.

■ GREENHILL, JUSTICE. I respectfully dissent....

As I view it, the bare legal point here is: does the fact that Copus moved to Texas, standing alone, relieve him of his legal obligation to contribute thereafter to his mentally-ill mother's support? I think not. Texas should not become a haven for deserting providers who would ignore or repudiate their duty to support.

Viewed the other way, if Copus and his mother had been Texas citizens and he were obligated in Texas to contribute to her support, should he be able to shirk that responsibility by just moving out of the State?

There is no evidence before us that Copus is unable to support his mother, that other relatives should bear or share in the burden, or that she has forfeited any right to support from her son....

The majority opinion correctly states that it is not against the public policy of Texas to enforce such an obligation. Our policy in that regard has been fixed in comparatively recent times by the enactment of our Uniform Support Act and the Texas Probate Code.

Section 423 of the Probate Code provides:

"Where an incompetent has no estate of his own, he shall be maintained: (a) By the husband or wife ... if able to do so; or, if not, (b) By the father or mother ... if able to do so; or, if not, (c) *By the children and grandchildren of such person,* respectively if able to do so; or, if not, (d) By the county...."

The Legislature has thus determined that it is the policy of Texas that under the circumstances above set out, an incompetent person (such as the mother here) shall be supported by her children, if able. The mother here was incompetent....

The Texas trial court found that "the liability of ... Copus is a continuing one; and that the removal of the defendant [Copus] to Texas ... does not discharge him from such continuing liability."

I would affirm the judgment of the trial court.

NOTES

1. Compare Elkind v. Byck, 68 Cal.2d 453, 67 Cal.Rptr. 404, 439 P.2d 316 (1968) (p. 264, note 1, supra). Following a divorce in Georgia, the wife and children moved to New York and the husband moved to California. In New York the wife initiated support proceedings against the husband and the case was then transferred to a court in California for proceedings pursuant to the Uniform Reciprocal Enforcement of Support Act, which is discussed below. Held that pursuant to the Act the husband's duty of support should be determined under California law. See, similarly, Petersen v. Petersen, 24 Cal.App.3d 201, 100 Cal.Rptr. 822 (1972): California, as the current domicil of the obligor and with jurisdiction over both parties, "can best exercise its discretion by utilizing its familiarity with living costs in California, and applying the California standard...."

2. Hardy v. Betz, 105 N.H. 169, 195 A.2d 582 (1963). The case involved an attempt under the Uniform Criminal Extradition Act to extradite to Massachusetts a New Hampshire man for failure to support what was alleged to be his illegitimate child. The mother had come to Massachusetts from New Hampshire shortly before the birth of the child; the man had remained at all times in New Hampshire. Held that extradition should be denied. "Since the [man] was never present in Massachusetts during the period for which support is sought, no obligation could arise under its laws, and he never became subject to its criminal laws." Two judges dissented.

B. RECIPROCAL SUPPORT LEGISLATION

Originally, attempts to recover support from one who has left the state where his dependents live faced almost insuperable difficulties. Where a support judgment had been obtained against the deserter prior to his flight, it was frequently not enforced by the state of his refuge on the ground that it was modifiable in the state of rendition. In this situation two suits, as well as delay, became inevitable. First, it was necessary to wait until installments under the support decree had had time to accrue. Next, the claimant was forced to recover judgment for the accrued installments in the first state and then sue to enforce this judgment in the second state. In the absence of statute, the entire process would have to be repeated after still further installments had become due, unless, as in Worthley v. Worthley, p. 293, supra, the second court were to prove willing to order the defendant to pay future installments of alimony as they accrued.

If no judgment for support had been obtained before the defendant left the state, the plight of the dependent might be hopeless. At least in the absence of a modern long-arm statute (see pp. 64–66, supra), presumably no judgment could be obtained against the defendant in the first state for lack of jurisdiction or competence. An action to recover support brought against the defendant in the state of his refuge, might involve traveling and legal expenses beyond the means of the dependent. Moreover, the action might be dismissed in the latter state on the ground that no duty of support was there recognized except with respect to dependents who were residing within the state at the time the claim arose.

Until the Uniform Interstate Family Support Act was promulgated in 1992 (for its provisions, reach and impact, see infra p. 913, every state in the country, except New York, had some form of the Uniform Reciprocal Enforcement of Support Act. Apart from any provision made for the extradition of the defendant, the Act operates as follows:

The proceeding opens with the filing of a petition in a court of what will usually be the state where petitioner resides. This court, called the "initiating court," examines the petition to decide whether it "sets forth facts from which it may be determined that the defendant owes a duty of support and that a court of the responding state may obtain jurisdiction of the defendant or his property...."[2] If the court answers these two questions in the affirmative, it will send copies of the petition to an appropriate court of the responding state. The latter court then takes the necessary steps to obtain jurisdiction over the defendant or his property. If the defendant appears and presents a defense, further hearings will be held, but the Act does not specify the procedure to be followed. In some states, the denials are transmitted to the initiating court which will hear the evidence of the petitioner. A transcript of this hearing is transmitted to the responding court, which will give the defendant opportunity to introduce proof and to cross-examine the petitioner and the petitioner's witnesses by written interrogatories.[3] In the alternative, it has been suggested that the testimony of the petitioner be taken by deposition or commission in the initiating state and then mailed to the responding state.

2. Uniform Reciprocal Enforcement of Support Act § 13.

3. Duncan v. Smith, 262 S.W.2d 373 (Ky.1953); Allain v. Allain, 24 Ill.App.2d 400, 164 N.E.2d 611 (1960).

The defendant will be permitted, if he so desires, to conduct his cross-examination in the initiating state by attorney.[4]

After all the evidence is in, the responding court, if satisfied of the petitioner's need for support and of defendant's liability, will enter an order requiring the defendant to make support payments, which will be forwarded to the initiating court and by it delivered to petitioner. To enforce compliance with its orders, the responding court may require the defendant to furnish bond or to make periodic payments or, in case of refusal may punish him for contempt. Both the initiating and responding courts may, in a proper case, request a designated legal officer of the state to represent petitioner without fee.

The Uniform Reciprocal Enforcement of Support Act makes provision for the enforcement either of a previously granted support order or of an original claim for support. Suit to enforce an original claim for support raises the problem of what law determines whether the alleged obligor owes any such duty and, if so, what is its extent. The 1952, 1958 and 1968 versions of the Act provide:

"§ 7. Choice of Law. Duties of support applicable under this law [act] are those imposed or imposable under the laws of any state where the obligor was present during the period for which support is sought. The obligor is presumed to have been present in the responding state during the period for which support is sought until otherwise shown." [5]

The 1968 Act and earlier 1958 amendment to the Act [6] provide for the registration and enforcement of modifiable support orders rendered under the Act in sister states.

Once a support obligation has been judicially established, federal law and mechanisms have now become an increasingly important means for enforcement. See Krause, Child Support in America 281 passim (1981). An example is Title IV–D of the Social Security Act, 42 U.S.C.A. § 651 et seq. See also the 1984 Child Support Amendments, 98 Stat. 1305.[7] 42 U.S.C.A. § 666(a)(5)(ii) (West 1994).

---

4. See Brockelbank and Infausto, Interstate Enforcement of Family Support (The Runaway Pappy Act) (2d ed. 1971).

5. The draftsmen of the Act deliberately employed "presence" rather than "domicile" in § 7 to avoid the technicalities and difficulty of proof which they felt would be engendered by use of the latter term. Brockelbank, The Problem of Family Support: A New Uniform Act Offers a Solution, 37 A.B.A.J. 93 (1951).

Section 7 deals with the case where claimant seeks support for a period that has already passed, since it provides that the law to be applied is that of any state where the obligor was present during the period for which support is sought.

6. §§ 34–38.

7. The Uniform Civil Liability for Support Act was approved in 1954 by the National Conference of Commissioners on Uniform State Laws. It is designed to make the substantive law of support uniform among the states and to make readily ascertainable who owes support duties to whom under the law of a particular state and what factors should be considered in determining the level of support owed. The act has been adopted by three states: Maine, New Hampshire, and Utah.

In 1992, the National Conference of Commissioners on Uniform State Laws approved the Uniform Interstate Family Support Act (UIFSA) to supersede the Uniform Reciprocal Enforcement of Support Act (URESA). As of July 1, 1995, UIFSA had already been enacted in twenty states, although Arizona and Oregon enacted UIFSA Act without repealing URESA. Under UIFSA § 205, if a forum court has issued a child support order, that court has continuing, exclusive jurisdiction over the order so long as the obligor, the obligee, or the child resides in the state, or unless each party files a written consent for a court of another state to modify the order and assume jurisdiction. If a forum court has issued a spousal support order, that court has continuing, exclusive jurisdiction over the order throughout the existence of the support obligation. Under § 303, however, when a forum court is responding to a request to enforce the support order of another state, the law of the forum "shall determine the duty of support and the amount payable in accordance with the law and support guidelines of this State." For comment, see Note, The Uniform Interstate Family Support Act: The New URESA, 20 U.Dayton L.Rev. 425 (1994).

This ability, under both URESA and UIFSA, to frustrate full enforcement of a child support order of a sister state, may now have ended. In 1994, the Full Faith and Credit for Child Support Orders Act (PL 103–383, 108 Stat. 4063, 28 USC § 1738B) took effect. In this Act, Congress exercised its powers under the "effect" provision of the Full Faith and Credit Clause (supra p. 39) to require more credit for sister-state child support orders than the constitutional clause itself would require. Under § 1738B, a child support order made consistently with the Act must be "enforced according to its terms" by sister states and sister states may not modify the order unless (1) the court that issued the order no longer is the residence of the child or of any contestants, or (2) each contestant files a written consent to the modification. A support order is made consistently with the Act if the court, under the laws of its state, has subject matter jurisdiction to enter the order and personal jurisdiction over the contestants. In interpreting a child support order, a court must apply the law of the state of the court that issued the order. Time limitations are governed by either the law of the state that issued the order or the law of the forum, whichever provides the longer period of limitation.

NOTES

1. For a case applying the current version of Section 7 of the Act and determining the duty of support in accordance with the law of the state where the obligor was present during the critical time, see Engelson v. Mallea, 180 N.W.2d 127 (Iowa 1970). See also Smith v. Smith, 3 Haw.App. 170, 647 P.2d 722 (1982). State ex rel. California v. Benjamin, 50 Wn.App. 284, 751 P.2d 1189 (1988); Washington ex rel. Gibson v. Gibson, 8 Haw.App. 304, 800 P.2d 1011 (1990); In re marriage Lurie, 33 Cal.App.4th 658, 39 Cal.Rptr.2d 835 (1995).

2. For a general discussion of the Uniform Reciprocal Enforcement of Support Act, see Brockelbank, Interstate Enforcement of Family Support (2d ed. Infausto 1971); Note, Interstate Enforcement of Support Obligations Through Long–Arm Statutes and URESA, 18 J.Fam.L. 537 (1980). The reciprocal support legislation has survived many constitutional attacks. Among the claims of invalidity that have been urged are those asserting that this legislation confers "extraterritorial jurisdiction" on the initiating court, and that it denies defendant the opportunity to confront and cross-examine the petitioner and his witnesses. The former objection has been overruled on the ground that jurisdiction over the respondent is acquired by the responding court by operation of its own statute rather than by that of the initiating state. See Duncan v. Smith, 262 S.W.2d 373 (Ky.1953). With respect to the latter objection, cross-examination by deposition has been held sufficient. The reciprocal support legislation also does not violate the Compact Clause of the Constitution, Fraser v. Fraser, 415 A.2d 1304 (R.I.1980). See Smith v. Smith, 125 Cal.App.2d 154, 270 P.2d 613 (1954). See also Brockelbank, Is the Uniform Reciprocal Enforcement of Support Act Constitutional?, 17 Mo.L.Rev. 1 (1952). Cavers, International Enforcement of Family Support, 81 Colum.L.Rev. 994, 1039 (1981).

3. It has been held that under the Reciprocal Enforcement of Support Act the responding state can modify a decree previously handed down against the defendant in a third state if the decree is also subject to modification in the third state. Moore v. Moore, 252 Iowa 404, 107 N.W.2d 97 (1961). See also Koon v. Boulder Cty., Dept. of Soc. Serv., 494 So.2d 1126 (Fla.1986).

In addition to seeking modification of an existing support decree with the aid of the court and under the law of the state where the obligor now lives, the obligee may also be able to invoke the continuing jurisdiction of the court that originally rendered the decree, especially if the obligee has continued to live there. See Canty v. Canty, 392 Mass. 1004, 465 N.E.2d 770 (1984); Opperman v. Sullivan, 330 N.W.2d 796 (Iowa 1983).

4. The Uniform Support of Dependents Law, in force in New York, does not contain a choice of law provision comparable to § 7 of the Uniform Reciprocal Enforcement of Support Act. On the other hand, it sets forth those relationships which give rise to a duty of support. As a result, the New York courts have construed the New York statute to preclude their acting as either initiating or responding court unless petitioner and respondent are within one of the enumerated relationships. See Robertson v. Collings, 101 Misc.2d 808, 421 N.Y.S.2d 999 (1979); Ross v. Ross, 206 Misc. 1073, 136 N.Y.S.2d 23 (Children's Ct.1954); Vincenza v. Vincenza, 197 Misc. 1027, 98 N.Y.S.2d 470 (N.Y.Dom.Rel.Ct.1950); 30 St. John's L.Rev. 309 (1956).

5. The reciprocal support legislation involves planned and directed cooperation between courts of different states of the Union in hearing and deciding a single controversy and in enforcing the judgment. Are there areas other than support in which such cooperation is needed, and in which it should be established, either through legislation or on the initiative of the courts? What are these areas? How should the cooperation be carried out?

6. Two international conventions, the United Nations Convention on the Recovery Abroad of Maintenance and the Hague Convention on the Recognition and Enforcement of Decisions Relating to Maintenance Obligations, are in force among a number of countries. However, neither convention has been adopted by the United States. Instead, some states of the Union and a number of foreign countries have worked out bilateral arrangements which are based on the "reciprocal" provision of the 1968 version of the Uniform Reciprocal Enforcement of Support Act. For a list of these arrangements see Scoles and Hay, Conflict of Laws 540–542 (2d ed. 1992). See also Dehart, Comity, Conventions and the Constitution: State and Federal

Initiatives in International Support Enforcement. 28 Fam.L.Q. 89 (1994); Cavers, International Enforcement of Family Support, 81 Colum.L.Rev. 994 (1981).

7. See Sanson v. Sanson, 466 N.E.2d 770 (Ind.App.1984) (judgment for alimony payable in installments, entered in German divorce proceeding, was enforceable in Indiana); Herczog v. Herczog, 186 Cal.App.2d 318, 9 Cal.Rptr. 5 (1960) (English decree entitled to recognition in California but, as in Worthley, p. 293, supra, respondent was free to litigate the question of modification since the decree was both prospectively and retroactively modifiable under English law).

SECTION 9. MARITAL PROPERTY*

INTRODUCTORY NOTE

"Marital property" may be defined as the interests which one spouse acquires, solely by reason of the marital relation, in the property, whether movable or immovable, of the other spouse, apart from the bare expectancy of inheriting upon the death of the other intestate. Two marital property systems are in effect in the United States. The common law system prevails in more than forty states and the District of Columbia, while community property is to be found in Arizona, California, Idaho, Louisiana, Nevada, New Mexico, Texas, Washington, and Wisconsin. There have been many drastic statutory modifications, and marked divergencies are to be found between states having the same general system.

There is no need to discuss these two systems in detail or to describe the form they originally took. They protect a spouse's economic interests in different ways. In common law states, a spouse is entitled to a fraction of all the property owned by the other spouse at the time of death. This interest is contingent upon surviving the other, but cannot be affected by any testamentary disposition the other spouse makes. Under community property systems, a spouse has a one-half interest in that part of the other's property which falls into the community. This is a present and vested interest which is not dependent upon surviving the other. Upon the dissolution of the marriage by death or divorce, the community property is divided equally among the spouses or their estates. Some property, however, does not fall into the community. A spouse retains full ownership to (and the other spouse has no marital interest in) property which belonged to him or her at the time of marriage or which he or she acquires thereafter by gift, will or descent. All other acquisitions, except in some states income derived from a spouse's separate property, belong to the community. Originally, the husband had exclusive control over the community property during the existence of the marriage, but this rule has been extensively modified by statute.

Marital property is in this country a fertile field for conflict of laws problems. This is not only because of the differences between common law and community property systems but also on account of the frequent divergencies in the laws of states belonging to the same general system.

* Restatement, Second, Conflict of Laws §§ 233–234, 257–259.

NOTES

1. In no state of the United States at the present time does a spouse acquire a marital property interest in property owned by the other spouse at the time of marriage. Hence the question of what law governs the effect of marriage on existing interests in movables has little practical importance. The majority of cases held, at a time when under the law of some states marriage did affect existing interests in movables, that the governing law is that of the state where the husband was domiciled at the time of marriage. See, e.g., Jaffrey v. McGough, 83 Ala. 202, 3 So. 594 (1888); Mason v. Homer, 105 Mass. 116 (1870). The most recent case, however, held that the governing law is that of the state of the domicile at the time of marriage of the spouse who owned the movables involved. Locke v. McPherson, 163 Mo. 493, 63 S.W. 726 (1901). The rule of this latter case is followed in § 257 of the Restatement, Second.

The question may still arise in cases where the law of a foreign country is involved. An example is Harral v. Harral, 39 N.J.Eq. 279 (1884). There H (an American citizen) and W were married in France where both were domiciled. After H's death, W asserted a community property interest in movables located in New Jersey and owned by H at the time of marriage. The New Jersey courts found for W on the ground that under French law a spouse obtained a community property interest in the movables possessed by the other spouse on the day of marriage.

2. In DeNicols v. Curlier, [1900] A.C. 21, the House of Lords treated a marriage in France between French citizens as creating by tacit contract an agreement that French community property law was to govern acquisition of personal property in England after the parties had become domiciled there. In DeNicols v. Curlier, [1900] 2 Ch. 410, the same rule was applied to real property acquired in England.

The rule of the Curlier cases is not followed in the United States. Saul v. His Creditors, 5 Mart. (N.S.) 569 (La.1827).

3. As to express ante-nuptial contracts, see Harding, Matrimonial Domicil and Marital Rights in Movables, 30 Mich.L.Rev. 859, 873–875 (1932); Henderson, Marital Agreements and the Rights of Creditors, 11 Comm.Prop.J. 105 (1984). For a detailed statutory provision dealing with the recognition and permissible scope of marital property agreements see Wis.Stat.Ann. 766.58 (1985). Americans do not frequently enter ante-nuptial contracts and there appear to be few cases in this country on the subject.

Rozan v. Rozan

Supreme Court of California, 1957.
49 Cal.2d 322, 317 P.2d 11.

■ TRAYNOR, JUSTICE. Plaintiff brought this action against her husband, Maxwell M. Rozan, for divorce, support, custody of their minor child, and division of their community property....

The trial court granted plaintiff an interlocutory judgment of divorce on the ground of extreme cruelty, awarded her the custody of the minor child, ordered defendant to pay $75 per month for child support, $250 per month for plaintiff's support, and $12,500 for attorney's fees. The court adjudged that the parties became domiciled in California ... in any event not later than July 1948 and that the property thereafter acquired was community property....

Although defendant "does not challenge the lower Court for granting the divorce" ... he contends ... that certain oil properties outside of California adjudged to be community property were his separate property....

The first finding essential to the division of the property is that plaintiff and defendant "established their residence and domicile in California ... in any event not later than July, 1948" and "that ever since they have been and still are residents of and domiciled in the State of California." A determination of the domicile is essential, for marital interests in movables acquired during coverture are governed by the law of the domicile at the time of their acquisition.... Moreover, the interests of the spouses in movables do not change even though the movables are taken into another state or are used to purchase land in another state....

... The ... evidence amply supports the trial court's finding of domicile not later than July, 1948....

The last finding on which the division of property depends is that the North Dakota properties "were acquired with community property and community property money." It is undisputed that these properties were acquired after 1949.... It ... appears that the purchase money for the North Dakota properties was acquired by the efforts and skill of defendant as an oil operator subsequent to the establishment of the California domicile and was therefore community property.... Moreover there is a presumption that in the absence of evidence of gift, bequest, devise or descent, all property acquired by the husband after marriage is community property.... There is no evidence that the purchase money was acquired by gift, bequest, devise, or descent. There is, therefore, substantial evidence to sustain the trial court's finding that the North Dakota properties were purchased with community property funds....

After acquiring the real property in North Dakota, defendant divested himself of title thereto by means of various conveyances, and title was eventually put in the name of Eugene Rosen, defendant's nephew, either individually or as trustee of a purported trust for the minor child.... there is abundant evidence to support the trial court's findings that these transactions were fraudulent as to plaintiff.

Defendant contends finally that the judgment directly affects the title to land in another state and therefore exceeded the court's jurisdiction. A court of one state cannot directly affect or determine the title to land in another. Fall v. Eastin, 215 U.S. 1 ... It is well settled, however, that a court, with the parties before it, can compel the execution of a conveyance in the form required by the law of the situs and that such a conveyance will be recognized there.... Currie, Full Faith and Credit to Foreign Land Decrees, 21 U. of Chi.L.Rev. 620, 628–629. If the court has entered a decree of specific performance, but the conveyance has not been executed, the majority of states, including California, will give effect to the decree.... Thus in Redwood Investment Co. of Stithton, Ky. v. Exley, 64 Cal.App. 455, 459, 221 P. 973, 975, the court stated with reference to a Kentucky decree of specific performance to land in California: "It may be pleaded as a basis or cause of action or defense in the courts of the state where the land is situated, and is entitled in such a court to the force and effect of record evidence of the equities therein determined, unless it be impeached for fraud." There is no sound reason for denying a decree of a court of equity the same full faith and credit accorded any other kind of judgment. "Without exception, the courts recognize the validity of a deed executed under the compulsion of a foreign decree. But if the decree did not deal rightfully and constitutionally with the title to the land it would be voidable for duress. Recognition of the deed necessarily involves acceptance of the decree. Whatever intrusion on the state's exclusive control is implied in the recognition of the decree is accomplished through the recognition of the deed. A policy so easily evaded, so dependent on the success of the defendant in eluding the enforcement process of the foreign court, is a formal, lifeless thing, and the truth must be that foreign judicial proceedings of this type pose no real threat to the legitimate interest of the situs state." (Currie, supra, 21 U. of Chi.L.Rev. 620, 628–629.) Thus in the majority of states, such decrees are given effect as a res judicata declaration of the rights and equities of the parties.... Fall v. Eastin, 215 U.S. 1, on which defendant relies did not hold otherwise. In that case the Washington decree directly affected title to land in Nebraska. A commissioner of the Washington court had executed a deed to that land and Mrs. Fall attempted to use this deed as a muniment of title in her action to quiet title against a grantee of the husband.

In the light of the foregoing principles the judgment in the present case is res judicata and entitled to full faith and credit in North Dakota to the extent that it determines the rights and equities of the parties with respect to the land in question. An action on that judgment in North Dakota, however, is necessary to effect any change in the title to the land there. Thus, the judgment must be affirmed to the extent that it declares the rights of the parties before the court and modified to the extent that it purports to affect the title to the land.

Neither Eugene Rosen, who holds record title, nor the minor child, who is the beneficiary of the purported trust, were parties to this action and the judgment is therefore not binding on them....

In several respects the judgment purports to affect title to the land and must therefore be modified. Thus, paragraph ... 21 ... awards 65 per cent of the North Dakota properties and the past, present, and future rents, issues and profits therefrom to plaintiff as her sole and separate property and awards 35 per cent thereof to Rozan subject to a lien for alimony, child support, and attorney's fees. This paragraph ... is therefore modified to read as follows: "21. It Is Further Ordered and Adjudged, that each and every one of the aforementioned North Dakota properties ... were acquired with community property funds of plaintiff and Rozan; ... that plaintiff is entitled to 65% of the aforementioned properties and of the rents, issues and profits thereof as against Rozan; that Rozan is entitled to 35% of the aforementioned properties and of the rents, issues and profits thereof as against plaintiff; and," ...

The judgment is affirmed as modified. Defendant shall bear the costs on appeal.

NOTES

1. Following the decision in the principal case, the wife instituted an action in North Dakota to enforce the California decree. The North Dakota court awarded the wife judgment for the sums accrued under the California decree. It also gave res judicata effect to the California finding that the North Dakota real property had been purchased with community funds and accordingly held that the wife was entitled to a one-half interest in this property. On the other hand, the court held that it would not recognize the California decree insofar as it purported to award the wife a 65% interest in this property. This was because the decree (a) did not order the husband to convey such an interest to his wife and (b) did not have to be recognized under full faith and credit since it directly affected title to North Dakota real property. Rozan v. Rozan, 129 N.W.2d 694 (N.D.1964). See also Fall v. Eastin, pp. 254–259, supra.

2. Estate of Warner, 167 Cal. 686, 140 P. 583 (1914). H and W made their home in Illinois, a common law state. During the marriage, H sent from Illinois certain funds which were used to purchase land in California. After H's death W renounced her rights under H's will and claimed a community property interest in the California land. W's claim was, however, rejected by the California courts on the ground that "it is well settled that separate personal property, enjoyed under the law of the domicile by one of the spouses at the time it was acquired is not lost by its investment in real property in another jurisdiction where a different law is in force." In states which have adopted the quasi-community concept, the result may be otherwise if the spouses had changed their domicile from the common law to the community property state prior to the death of one spouse or to the dissolution of the marriage. See Addison v. Addison, pp. 927–933, infra.

3. For a discussion of the converse situation, where persons move from a community property state to a common law property state, see Lay, Community Property in Common Law States, 41 Temp.L.Q. 1 (1967); Leflar, From Community to Common Law State; Estate Problems of Citizens Moving from One to Other, 99 Trusts & Estates 882 (1960).

4. Depas v. Mayo, 11 Mo. 314 (1848). While domiciled in Louisiana, a community property state, husband and wife accumulated considerable assets. They then moved to Missouri, where the husband used part of the assets accumulated in Louisiana to purchase in his own name a lot in the city of St. Louis. Thereafter the parties resumed their Louisiana domicile and ultimately were divorced. Action was brought by the wife for determination that she was entitled to a one-half interest in the St. Louis property. Held for the wife. Missouri law must decide "all questions" concerning title to the land in St. Louis. "[A]ccording to the law in this state, if A purchases land with the money of B, and takes legal title to himself, a court of equity will regard him as a trustee...." The husband purchased the land with assets in which his wife had a one-half interest. She is therefore entitled to one-half interest in the land. It makes no difference that prior to the purchase the parties had changed their domicile to Missouri.

5. Restatement, Second, Conflict of Laws § 258, Comment c. "... When the spouses have separate domicils at the time of the acquisition of the movable, the local law of the state where the spouse who acquired the movable was domiciled will usually be held to determine the extent of the other spouse's marital interest therein." See also Litner, Marital Property Rights and Conflict of Laws When Spouses Reside in Different States, 11 Comm.Prop.J. 283 (1984).

6. Restatement, Second, Conflict of Laws § 166, Comment b. "[At times] one spouse is injured either through the negligence of the other spouse or through the joint negligence of the other spouse and of a third person. Then, if the injured spouse brings suit against the employer or insurer of the other spouse or against the third person, he may be met with the argument that relief should be denied because the negligent spouse would share in any recovery that might be obtained. It might be thought that the law [selected to determine related issues of tort law] should be applied to determine whether the negligence of one person should be imputed to another if the negligent person would share in any recovery that the other might obtain. On the other hand, it might be thought that the local law of the state of the spouses' domicil should be applied to determine whether any recovery would be community property and thus would be shared by the negligent spouse.... In the majority of the few cases in point, the plaintiff spouse has been permitted to recover...." See also Marsh, Marital Property in Conflict of Laws 193–194 (1952); Oldham, Conflict of Laws and Marital Property Rights, 39 Baylor L.Rev. 1255 (1987).

7. In recent years, community property interests have been recognized in intangible assets such as pension rights and other contractual interests. To what extent should the value of a professional degree earned by a spouse during marriage be considered? See Note, Equitable Interest in Enhanced Earning Capacity: The Treatment of a Professional Degree at Dissolution, 60 Wash.L.Rev. 431 (1985).

8. Choice-of-law problems also occur in the area of community debts. The Sprouls lived in New Mexico, a community property state. The husband signed a loan note with an Ohio bank. Mrs. Sproul was not a party to the transaction between her husband and the Ohio bank. Mr. Sproul defaulted on the note, and the bank sued Mr. Sproul in an Ohio state court and received a default judgment against him. The Ohio bank then asked a New Mexico court to domesticate the Ohio judgment, and the New Mexico court did. The Ohio bank then sought to foreclose its judgment lien against the New Mexico home of the Sprouls. Mrs. Sproul claimed that her husband's loan was not a community debt that would allow the Ohio bank to use her half of the marital residence to satisfy the judgment. The New Mexico ruled in favor of the Ohio bank because the transaction between Mr. Sproul and the bank did not satisfy the statutory requirements necessary to overcome the presumption that a debt created during the marriage is a community debt. Huntington Nat'l Bk. v. Sproul, 116 N.M. 254, 861 P.2d 935 (1993).

9. In a number of states that have traditionally adhered to the common law spousal property system, "equitable distribution" of assets now takes the place of alimony obligations to be paid out of "separate" assets. In some respects, the "equitable distribution" concept resembles the community property system. The conflict-of-laws problems identified above—when spouses move from one state to another, or live in one state while acquiring assets in another, or live and acquire assets separately and in different states—also arise when an "equitable division" state is involved.

10. In some instances, federal law preempts state marital property law, for instance in protecting annuitants under the amendments to the Employee Retire-

ment Income Security Act (ERISA), 29 U.S.C.A. § 1001 et seq. by the Retirement Equity Act of 1984, 29 U.S.C.A. § 1144 (West 1995) (1984) (spouses to be provided for in qualified retirement plans). In other instances, state law controls. See, e.g., Uniformed Services Former Spouses' Protection Act, 10 U.S.C.A. § 1408(c)(1) (states may treat military pensions either as separate or as community property under state law; the act overturned McCarty v. McCarty, 453 U.S. 210 (1981), holding that federal law preempted state law). See Reppy, Conflict of Laws Problems in the Division of Marital Property, 1 Valuation and Distribution of Marital Property § 10.03 (1985). See also Polacheck, The "Un-Worth-y" Decision: The Characterization of a Copyright as Community Property, 17 Hastings Comm./Ent.L.J. 601 (1995).

Wyatt v. Fulrath
Court of Appeals of New York, 1965.
16 N.Y.2d 169, 264 N.Y.S.2d 233, 211 N.E.2d 637.

■ BERGAN, JUDGE. The Duke and Duchess of Arion were nationals and domiciliaries of Spain. Neither of them had ever been in New York, but through a long period of political uncertainty in Spain, from 1919 to the end of the [Spanish] Civil War, they sent cash and securities to New York for safekeeping and investment.

Under the law of Spain this was the community property of the spouses. Substantial parts of it were placed with the New York custodians in joint accounts. In establishing or in continuing these accounts, the husband and wife either expressly agreed in writing that the New York law of survivorship would apply or agreed to a written form of survivorship account conformable to New York law.

The husband died in November, 1957; the wife in March, 1959. After the husband's death the wife took control of the property in New York and undertook to dispose of it by a will executed according to New York law and affecting property in New York.... Some additional property in joint account in England was transferred by the wife to New York after the husband's death which had not been placed by either spouse in New York during the husband's life.

This action is by plaintiff as an ancillary administrator in New York of the husband against defendant as executor of the wife's will to establish a claim of title to one half of the property which at the time of the husband's death was held in custody accounts under sole or joint names of the spouses by banks in New York and London.

The total value of the property in New York is about $2,275,000, of which about $370,000 was transferred by the wife after the husband's death from the London accounts to New York....

The main issue in the case is whether the law of Spain should be applied to the property placed in New York during the lives of the spouses, in which event only half of the property would have gone to the wife at her husband's death, or the law of New York, in which event all of such jointly held property would have gone to her as survivor....

The controversy here is . . . to be governed by the legal capacity of the husband and wife, as citizens and domiciliaries of Spain, to make an agreement as to their community property inconsistent with Spanish law.

The agreements giving full title to the survivor in the joint accounts were executed either in Spain, or if not there at least not in New York, and were, in any event, executed by persons who were domiciliaries and citizens of Spain. Usually rights flowing from this kind of legal act are governed by the law of the domiciliary jurisdiction. . . .

Dispositions of property in violation of this prohibition are shown to be void according to Spanish law. . . .

But New York has the right to say as a matter of public policy whether it will apply its own rules to property in New York of foreigners who choose to place it here for custody or investment, and to honor or not the formal agreements or suggestions of such owners by which New York law would apply to the property they place here. (Cf. Decedent Estate Law, § 47; Personal Property Law, Consol.Laws, c. 41, § 12–a.)

It seems preferable that as to property which foreign owners are able to get here physically, and concerning which they request New York law to apply to their respective rights, when it actually gets here, that we should recognize their physical and legal submission of the property to our laws, even though under the laws of their own country a different method of fixing such rights would be pursued.

Thus we would at once honor their intentional resort to the protection of our laws and their recognition of the general stability of our Government which may well be deemed inter-related things. . . .

The Special Term in the case before us found for the defendant. . . . We agree that this disposition is the correct one as to property placed in New York during the husband's lifetime.

This effect would include, too, those accounts which had formerly been joint accounts but which during the lifetime of the husband were transferred to the wife's sole name. . . .

The assent of the husband to arrangements in respect of joint property transferred to the sole account of the wife with the legal consequence of sole ownership to be anticipated from the effect of New York law would lead us to treat the property as the property of the wife and to be controlled by the same principle applicable to joint accounts. . . .

We would treat the wife's own separate property similarly where, during the lifetime of her husband and apparently with his recognition and assent, she was able to transfer the separate property to New York and keep it here in her own name.

But the property in the value of about $370,000 transferred from London to New York by the wife after the husband's death raises a somewhat different question. Adjudication of its title requires further factual exploration. At the time of the husband's death this property and other property were held in three-name custody accounts by London depositories. The accounts were in the names of the husband, the wife and their daughter Hilda, who had no proprietary interest....

The reasons grounded on New York policy and affected by the physical transfer of the property to New York during the lifetime of the spouses and by their directions relating to it do not necessarily apply to property of Spanish nationals placed in a third country during their lifetime.

If the local law of the third country would deem title to have passed to the wife on the death of the husband, we would treat this property as we now treat that placed in New York during their lives.

But if the third country would have applied the Spanish community property law or, if it is not demonstrated what rule would be applied by the third country and the subject is open or equivocal, we would, under general principles, feel bound to apply the law of Spain to the title of property owned by these Spanish nationals.

. . .

The order should be modified to direct the remission to Special Term to determine the rights of parties in respect of the property transferred by the wife from London to New York after the husband's death in accordance with this opinion and, as modified, affirmed, without costs.

■ DESMOND, CHIEF JUDGE (dissenting). Resolution of the dispute as to this property (or any part of it) by any law other than that of Spain, the matrimonial domicile, is utterly incompatible with historic and settled conflict of laws principles and is not justifiable on any ground. No policy ground exists for upsetting the uniform rules and no precedent commands such a result....

The majority of this court is throwing overboard not one but three of the oldest and strongest conflict rules: first, that with exceptions not pertinent here the law of the domicile of the owner governs as to the devolution of personal property ...; second, that the law of the matrimonial domicile controls as to the property and contract rights of husband and wife *inter sese* ...; and, third, that whether such personalty is separate or community property is determined by the law of the matrimonial domicile....

... The Duke and Duchess of Arion were Spanish nationals, were married in Spain and always had their domicile there as had their ancestors for generations or centuries. Neither was ever in New York. New York State's only contact with this property was that for purposes of convenience or safety the husband and wife left valuable property in the custody of New York banks for safekeeping only. The banks were mere bailees without other title or interest. To say that setting up of joint accounts of personalty in New York subjected that personalty to New York law rather than to the law of the matrimonial domicile is to refuse to follow one of the most basic of Conflict of Laws rules....

... The signing by the Duke and Duchess in Spain of routine joint-account-for-custody agreements on forms supplied by the New York banks is not substantial proof that these people (who had no apparent reason for so doing) were attempting to abrogate as to these items of property the ancient community laws of their country. There is no other proof of such an intent to substitute New York law and a much more reasonable explanation of the documents exacted by the banks is that they operated and were intended merely to release the banks on payment to one spouse or the other....

MATTER OF CRICHTON, 20 N.Y.2d 124, 281 N.Y.S.2d 811, 228 N.E.2d 799 (1967): Crichton died domiciled in New York, where he had moved early in life, owning movables in Louisiana. His will made no provision for his wife, from whom he had been separated for twenty-seven years, and the question was whether she had a community property interest in the Louisiana movables or whether her rights were limited to a forced share under New York law. A Louisiana statute provided that all property acquired in the state by a nonresident should be treated as community property. It was held that the wife's rights in the Louisiana movables were limited to a forced share under New York law. Speaking for the court, Judge Keating said: ...

The choice of law problem here should be resolved by an examination of the contacts which Louisiana and New York have with this controversy for the purpose of determining which of those jurisdictions has the paramount interest in the application of its law....

The issue in this case is whether the community property laws of Louisiana should be applied to govern the property rights of New York domiciliaries in intangible personal property acquired during coverture.... [I]t is clear that the community property system is designed to regulate the property rights of married persons and, in particular, to protect the interest of each spouse in the property accumulated during marriage.... For reasons which become obvious merely in stating the purpose of the rule, Louisiana has no such interest in protecting and regulating the rights of married persons residing and domiciled in New York.

The State of New York which has such an interest has not adopted a community property system. Instead it has sought to protect a *surviving* spouse by giving her a right to take one third of the entire estate of the deceased as against a testamentary disposition by which the deceased has attempted to exclude her from a share of the estate. (Decedent Estate Law, § 18.) And, depending upon the nature of the property in the estate, a surviving spouse under New York law might well be entitled to receive a greater portion of the over-all estate than under the community property system.

By affording the surviving spouse such a right in the estate of the deceased spouse, the Legislature has sought to preserve the right of the testator to distribute his property as he desires, while at the same time to provide protection for the surviving spouse. New York, as the domicile of

Martha and Powell Crichton, has not only the dominant interest in the application of its law and policy but the only interest....

It is urged by the appellant that the Louisiana contacts with this case give it the paramount interest in the application of its law. Among the contacts which are urged as being significant are the facts the deceased was born in Louisiana, that, although he was domiciled in New York, the bulk of his fortune was made in Louisiana, and that the documentary evidences of his intangible property are located in that jurisdiction. Exactly how these contacts are related to the policies sought to be vindicated by Louisiana's community property laws is not made clear. The reason, no doubt, is that they have no relation whatever.[8] ...

[T]his case is distinguishable from Hutchison v. Ross, 262 N.Y. 381, 187 N.E. 65, 89 A.L.R. 1007, supra, and Wyatt v. Fulrath, 16 N.Y.2d 169, 264 N.Y.S.2d 233, 211 N.E.2d 637, supra, relied upon by the appellant in support of her argument for the application of Louisiana law.

In the latter case ... [r]elying upon sections 12–a of the Personal Property Law, Consol.Laws, c. 41, and 47 of the Decedent Estate Law, which are designed to encourage investment of funds in this State by permitting a nondomiciliary to designate New York law as applicable to determine questions of law relating to testamentary dispositions of personal property located here as well as *inter vivos* trusts having a situs in this State, we held that New York law and not the Spanish community property laws would govern. In so doing, we cited the earlier case of Hutchison v. Ross (supra) in which the court, speaking through Judge Lehman, relying upon section 12–a of the Personal Property Law, held that it was the policy of this State to permit out-of-State settlors of trusts to designate that rights in that property be determined by New York law.

In both these cases we were giving effect to New York's policy and governmental interest....

NOTES

1. Subsequent to the New York decision in the principal case, the Louisiana court held in Mrs. Crichton's action against her husband's estate that the New York courts had misinterpreted Louisiana law and that under that law Mrs. Crichton was

---

8. Contacts obtain significance only to the extent that they relate to the policies and purposes sought to be vindicated by the conflicting laws. Once these contacts are discovered and analyzed they will indicate (1) that there exists no true conflict of laws, as in the case at bar and as in most choice of law cases, or (2) that a true conflict exists, i.e., both jurisdictions have an interest in the application of their law. In the former case, of course, the law of the jurisdiction having the only real interest in the litigation will be applied.... (Oltarsh v. Aetna Ins. Co., 15 N.Y.2d 111, 256 N.Y.S.2d 577, 204 N.E.2d 622.) In the case of a true conflict, while our decisions have normally resulted in application of forum law (Wyatt v. Fulrath, 16 N.Y.2d 169, 264 N.Y.S.2d 233, 211 N.E.2d 637, supra), we are not as yet prepared to formulate what may be deemed a rule of general application but prefer rather to give further consideration to the question as the cases arise. (See Currie, The Disinterested Third State, 28 Law & Contemp.Prob., 754, 756–764.)

entitled to a one half interest in the movable property left by Mr. Crichton in Louisiana. The court found for the estate, however, for the reason that it felt required by full faith and credit to give res judicata effect to the New York judgment. Crichton v. Succession of Crichton, 232 So.2d 109 (La.App. 2d Cir.1970), writ refused result correct, 256 La. 274, 236 So.2d 39 (1970).

2. Is Judge Keating's approach in Crichton a sound one? Is marital property an area where there is real need for actual rules of choice of law?

3. Granted that in Wyatt v. Fulrath New York had an interest in applying its law, can it convincingly be urged that New York, rather than Spain, was the state of paramount interest? If not, what is the status of the Wyatt holding in the light of Matter of Crichton? Can the Wyatt decision be justified on other grounds? Does it bear an analogy to the power of the parties to select the law governing their contract? See pp. 536–549, supra.

4. For a fine article comparing the American, French and English approaches to marital property in conflict of laws, see Juenger, Marital Property and the Conflict of Laws: A Tale of Two Countries, 81 Colum.L.Rev. 1061 (1981).

5. See generally Clausnitzen, Property Rights of Surviving Spouse and the Conflict of Laws, 18 J.Fam.L. 471 (1980).

Estate of O'Connor
Supreme Court of California, 1933.
218 Cal. 518, 23 P.2d 1031, 88 A.L.R. 856.

[Plaintiff and defendant were married in Indiana, where both were domiciled at the time. Shortly after the marriage, defendant deserted plaintiff and went to California, where he died leaving a will in which he bequeathed his property to a third person. At the time of the marriage, defendant owned some $200,000 worth of stocks and bonds, and these, or property acquired in exchange therefor, were in his estate at the time of his death. In the California administration proceedings, plaintiff claimed one-third of the estate relying upon the Indiana law which permits a widow to take this amount against the will of her deceased husband. The plaintiff is now appealing from the action of the trial court in sustaining the executor's demurrer to her petition.]

THE COURT. We have re-examined the questions involved in this appeal and find ourselves in entire accord with the conclusion and opinion of the District Court of Appeal, Division One of the First Appellate District, and we hereby adopt that opinion as the opinion of this court in this cause....

. . .

Appellant contends that she is entitled to the portion of decedent's personal estate which she could have claimed under the laws of Indiana notwithstanding his attempted disposal thereof by his will.

. . .

...The community system does not prevail in Indiana, and appellant admits that prior to 1891 there was no statute of that state giving to a surviving widow an interest in her deceased husband's personal estate akin to the common-law right of dower and not subject to be defeated by will.... She claims, however, that the act of March 9, 1891 (Acts 1891, p. 404) (Burns' Annotated Indiana Statutes 1926, sec. 3343 (3025)), gives such right. [The statute, which gives the widow the right to elect, is omitted.] ...

. . .

[N]o statute or decision from that state has been called to our attention which provides or holds that the wife enjoys any ordinary rights of ownership in her husband's personal property during his lifetime, or has a more complete interest therein than that of an expectancy as heir if she survives him.

Appellant concedes that the property in question if governed by the California law would be the separate property of decedent and subject to his testamentary disposition; also that as a general rule the descent of personal property is governed by the laws of the state where decedent was domiciled at the time of his death, but she insists that the contract of marriage in relation to property rights should be governed, as other contracts, by the laws of the jurisdiction where it was to be carried out—in this instance by the laws of Indiana.

This doctrine has been recognized and applied in instances where rights in the property of one spouse were held to have vested at the time of the marriage. The rule is stated in Wharton on Conflict of Laws, section 193a, as follows: 'While ... it is undoubtedly true that the intestacy laws of the last domicile of the deceased govern the distribution of the personal estate of either husband or wife in case of intestacy, a distinction is to be observed between the mere inchoate rights of either spouse to share in the distribution of the other's estate at his death and a vested right which attaches at the time of marriage though its enjoyment may be postponed until the death of the other spouse.' The author says further that the latter right is not divested by a change of domicile, but that a mere statute of distribution of the original matrimonial domicile, or any domicile other than the last, by which either spouse is to share in the other's personal estate upon the latter's death creates no vested right, and therefore offers no obstacle to the application of the statute of distribution of the last domicile....

The mere fact that under the Indiana laws, above cited, the power of the husband to dispose of his personal property by will was subject to the right of his wife at her election to claim a third thereof gave her no more than an expectancy in this portion of his estate. As was held in Spreckels v. Spreckels, 116 Cal. 339 (48 P. 228, 58 Am.St.Rep. 170, 36 L.R.A. 497), such a limitation of the husband's right would give the wife no interest in his property during his lifetime. We are satisfied that appellant had no present fixed right or interest in decedent's personal estate, or more than a mere expectancy, which depended upon survivorship to become a vested right. This being true, and he having established his domicile in California, as he might do (Civ.Code, sec. 129), the property was subject to the law of this state, which governs its disposition and distribution whether he died testate or intestate.

The order appealed from is affirmed.

NOTES

1. It will be noted that in the principal case the plaintiff wife was denied the economic protection accorded a spouse by either the California or Indiana law. Could the court have properly reached a different result? If so, by what reasoning?

2. A pervasive problem is whether a given issue should be characterized as one of marital property or of succession. Questions of marital property are governed by the rules set forth in this Section, while those involving succession are determined by the law of the situs in the case of land and by that of the state where the decedent died domiciled in the case of movables. Whether a spouse has a community property interest in the other's property is considered a problem of marital property. On the other hand, whether a spouse has a nonbarrable interest in the property owned by the other spouse at the time of death is considered a question of succession.

Should application of a given rule of foreign law depend upon the way in which it is characterized by the forum or by the courts of the foreign state? For example, was the court in the principal case correct in refusing to apply the Indiana rule on the ground that it was one of succession rather than of marital property?

Addison v. Addison

Supreme Court of California, 1965.
62 Cal.2d 558, 43 Cal.Rptr. 97, 399 P.2d 897.

■ PETERS, JUSTICE. Plaintiff Leona Addison (hereafter referred to as Leona) was granted an interlocutory decree of divorce from defendant Morton Addison (hereafter referred to as Morton) on the ground of his adultery....

At the time of their marriage in Illinois in 1939, Morton, having previously engaged in the used car business, had a net worth which he estimated as being between $15,000 and $20,000. Leona, however, testified that her husband's net worth was almost nothing at the time of their marriage. In 1949 the Addisons moved to California bringing with them cash and other personal property valued at $143,000 which had been accumulated as a result of Morton's various Illinois business enterprises. Since that time Morton has participated in several California businesses.

On February 20, 1961, Leona filed for divorce and requested an equitable division of the marital property. On trial, Leona ... attempted to apply the recently enacted quasi-community property legislation [3] by

---

3. The key sections of the 1961 legislation which are involved in the instant case are as follows:

Civil Code section 140.5: "As used in Sections 140.7, 141, 142, 143, 146, 148, 149 and 176 of this code, 'quasi-community property' means all personal property wherever situated and all real property situated in this State heretofore or hereafter acquired:

"(a) By either spouse while domiciled elsewhere which would have been community property of the husband and

contending that the property presently held in Morton's name was acquired by the use of property brought from Illinois and that the property would have been community property had it been originally acquired while the parties were domiciled in California.

The trial court ... held the quasi-community property legislation to be unconstitutional.

The trial court ... did find the household furniture and furnishings to be community property and, pursuant to Civil Code section 146, awarded them to Leona. In addition, the court found that the residence of the parties was held in joint tenancy and thus each owned an undivided one-half separate interest therein. Finally, all other property which had been in Morton's name alone was found to be his sole and separate property.

The sociological problem to which the quasi-community property legislation addresses itself has been an area of considerable legislative and judicial activity in this state. One commentator has expressed this thought as follows: "Among the perennial problems in the field of community property in California, the status of marital personal property acquired while domiciled in another State has been particularly troublesome. Attempts of the Legislature to designate such personalty as community property uniformly have been thwarted by court decisions." (Comment (1935) 8 So.Cal.L.Rev. 221, 222).

The problem arises as a result of California's attempts to apply community property concepts to the foreign, and radically different (in hypotheses) common-law theory of matrimonial rights. In fitting the common-law system into our community property scheme the process is of two steps. First, property acquired by a spouse while domiciled in a common-law state is characterized as separate property. (Estate of O'Connor, 218 Cal. 518, 23 P.2d 1031, 88 A.L.R. 856.) Second, the rule of tracing is invoked so that all property later acquired in exchange for the common-law separate property is likewise deemed separate property.... Thus, the wife had the spouse acquiring the property been domiciled in this State at the time of its acquisition; or

"(b) In exchange for real or personal property, wherever situated, acquired other than by gift, devise, bequest or descent by either spouse during the marriage while domiciled elsewhere.

"For the purposes of this section, personal property does not include and real property does include leasehold interests in real property."

Civil Code section 146 provides in part: "In case of the dissolution of the marriage by decree of a court of competent jurisdiction or in the case of judgment or decree for separate maintenance of the husband or the wife without dissolution of the marriage, the court shall make an order for disposition of the community property and the quasi-community property and for the assignment of the homestead as follows:

"(a) If the decree is rendered on the ground of adultery, incurable insanity or extreme cruelty, the community property and quasi-community property shall be assigned to the respective parties in such proportions as the court, from all the fact of the case, and the condition of the parties, may deem just.

"(b) If the decree be rendered on any other ground than that of adultery, incurable insanity or extreme cruelty, the community property and quasi-community property shall be equally divided between the parties."

[margin note: not triggered by crossing of border but by divorce]

original property, and all property subsequently acquired through use of the original property is classified as the separate property of the acquiring spouse.

One attempt to solve the problem was the 1917 amendment to Civil Code section 164 which had the effect of classifying all personal property wherever situated and all real property located in California into California community property if that property would not have been the separate property of one of the spouses had that property been acquired while the parties were domiciled in California. Insofar as the amendment attempted to affect personal property brought to California which was the separate property of one of the spouses while domiciled outside this state Estate of Thornton, 1 Cal.2d 1, 33 P.2d 1, 92 A.L.R. 1343, held the section was unconstitutional. The amendment's effect upon real property located in California was never tested but generally was considered to be a dead letter as the section was never again invoked on the appellate level.

Another major attempt to alter the rights in property acquired prior to California domicile was the passage of Probate Code section 201.5. This section gave to the surviving spouse one half of all the personal property wherever situated and the real property located in California which would not have been the separate property of the acquiring spouse had it been acquired while domiciled in California. As a succession statute, its constitutionality was upheld on the theory that the state of domicile of the decedent at the time of his death has full power to control rights of succession. (In re Miller, 31 Cal.2d 191, 196, 187 P.2d 722). In other words, no one has a vested right to succeed to another's property rights, and no one has a vested right in the distribution of his estate upon his death. Hence succession rights may be constitutionally altered. This theory was a basis of the dissent in Thornton.

In the present case it is contended that Estate of Thornton, supra, 1 Cal.2d 1, 33 P.2d 1, is controlling and that the current legislation, by authority of Thornton, must be held to be unconstitutional. Thornton involved a situation of a husband and wife moving to California and bringing with them property acquired during their former domicile in Montana. Upon the husband's death, his widow sought to establish her community property rights in his estate as provided by the then recent amendment to Civil Code section 164. The majority held the section unconstitutional on the theory that upon acquisition of the property the husband obtained vested rights which could not be altered without violation of his privileges and immunities as a citizen and also that "to take the property of A and transfer it to B because of his citizenship and domicile, is also to take his property without due process of law. This is true regardless of the place of acquisition or the state of his residence." (Estate of Thornton, supra, 1 Cal.2d 1, 5, 33 P.2d 1, 3, 92 A.L.R. 1343.)

The underlying rationale of the majority was the same in Thornton as it had been since Spreckels v. Spreckels, 116 Cal. 339, 48 P. 228, 36 L.R.A. 497, which established, by a concession of counsel, that changes in the community property system which affected "vested interests" could not constitutionally be applied retroactively but must be limited to prospective application.

Langdon, J., in his dissent in Thornton, conceded the correctness of the vested right theory but argued that the statute was merely definitional, giving no rights to anyone except as provided by other legislation. Therefore, the widow would only be acquiring rights pursuant to a right of succession as granted by statute. As to the constitutionality of this application of amended Civil Code section 164 he declared: "It is a rule of almost universal acceptance that the rights of testamentary disposition and of succession are wholly subject to statutory control, and may be enlarged, limited, or abolished without infringing upon the constitutional guaranty of due process of law." (Estate of Thornton, supra, 1 Cal.2d 1, 7, 33 P.2d 1, 3.) The majority refused to construe amended Civil Code section 164 in this limited fashion.

The constitutional doctrine announced in Estate of Thornton, supra, has been questioned. Justice (now Chief Justice) Traynor in his concurring opinion in Boyd v. Oser, 23 Cal.2d 613, at p. 623, 145 P.2d 312, at page 318, had the following to say: "The decisions that existing statutes changing the rights of husbands and wives in community property can have no retroactive application have become a rule of property in this state and should not now be overruled. It is my opinion, however, that the constitutional theory on which they are based is unsound. [Citations.] That theory has not become a rule of property and should not invalidate future legislation in this field intended by the Legislature to operate retroactively." ...

Thus, the correctness of the rule of Thornton is open to challenge. But even if the rule of that case be accepted as sound, it is not here controlling. This is so because former section 164 of the Civil Code has an entirely different impact from the legislation presently before us. The legislation under discussion, unlike old section 164, makes no attempt to alter property rights merely upon crossing the boundary into California. It does not purport to disturb vested rights "of a citizen of another state, who chances to transfer his domicile to this state, bringing his property with him...." (Estate of Thornton, supra, 1 Cal.2d 1, at p. 5, 33 P.2d 1, at p. 3.) Instead, the concept of quasi-community property is applicable only if a divorce or separate maintenance action is filed here after the parties have become domiciled in California. Thus, the concept is applicable only if, after acquisition of domicile in this state, certain acts or events occur which give rise to an action for divorce or separate maintenance. These acts or events are not necessarily connected with a change of domicile at all....

Clearly the interest of the state of the current domicile in the matrimonial property of the parties is substantial upon the dissolution of the marriage relationship....

In recognition of much the same interest as that advanced by the quasi-community property legislation, many common-law jurisdictions have provided for the division of the separate property of the respective spouses in a manner which is "just and reasonable" and none of these statutes have been overturned on a constitutional basis.

In the case at bar it was Leona who was granted a divorce from Morton on the ground of the latter's adultery and hence it is the spouse guilty of the marital infidelity from whom the otherwise separate property is sought by the operation of the quasi-community property legislation. We are of the opinion that where the innocent party would otherwise be left unprotected the state has a very substantial interest and one sufficient to provide for a fair and equitable distribution of the marital property without running afoul of the due process clause of the Fourteenth Amendment....

Morton also asserts that there is an abridgment of the privileges and immunities clause of the Fourteenth Amendment citing Estate of Thornton, supra ... Aside from the due process clause, already held not to be applicable, Thornton may be read as holding that the legislation there in question impinged upon the right of a citizen of the United States to maintain a domicile in any state of his choosing without the loss of valuable property rights. As to this contention, the distinction we have already noted between former Civil Code section 164 and quasi-community property legislation is relevant. Unlike the legislation in Thornton, the quasi-community property legislation does not cause a loss of valuable rights through change of domicile. The concept is applicable only in case of a decree of divorce or separate maintenance....

The judgment is affirmed insofar as it decrees divorce and custody of the minor child. In all other respects the judgment is reversed....

NOTES

1. The facts of In re Thornton's Estate are stated in the principal case. The statute declared unconstitutional in Thornton provided in effect that all movables originally owned by a spouse as separate property, but which would be community property under California rules, would be converted into community property as soon as the spouse acquired a domicile in California. It should be noted that Mrs. Thornton had a nonbarrable interest in her husband's movables under Montana law. The decision in effect held that Mrs. Thornton lost this interest in her husband's movables as soon as she and he acquired a domicile in California. This was the result the California statute sought to avoid.

2. The California Probate Code, as amended in 1957, contains the following sections:

Section 201.5 provides that the surviving spouse of a decedent who dies domiciled in California is entitled to half of his California real estate and to half of all his personal property wherever situated if, (a) "acquired by the decedent while domiciled elsewhere which would have been the community property of the decedent and the surviving spouse had the decedent been domiciled in this State at the time of its acquisition" or (b) "acquired in exchange for real or personal property wherever situated which would have been the community property of the decedent and the surviving spouse if the decedent had been domiciled in this state at the time the property so exchanged was acquired." This Section further provides that the remaining half of the decedent's property shall also go to the surviving spouse if not willed to a third person.

Section 201.7 provides that if the decedent has provided in his will for the surviving spouse, that spouse must elect whether to take under the will or against the will under Section 201.5 unless the will makes clear that the testator intended that the surviving spouse should take both under the will and against it.

Section 201.8 provides that, upon electing to take against the will of a deceased spouse who died domiciled in California, the surviving spouse may require restoration to the estate of one-half of any property transferred by the deceased spouse without substantial consideration if (a) the surviving spouse had an expectancy in this property under § 201.5 and (b) the deceased spouse "had a substantial quantum of ownership or control of the property at death."

3. In 1961 the California statutes were further amended to provide for "quasi community property" interests in the event of a divorce. These provisions are set forth in footnote 3 to the Addison opinion.

4. The California legislation is discussed in Note, Marital Property and the Conflict of Laws, 54 Calif.L.Rev. 252 (1966); Schreter, "Quasi–Community Property" in Conflict of Laws, 50 Calif.L.Rev. 206 (1962); compare Buchschacher, Rights of a Surviving Spouse in Texas in Marital Property Acquired While Domiciled Elsewhere, 45 Tex.L.Rev. 321 (1966).

5. Other community-property states have also adopted the quasi-community property concept. Wisconsin, like California, has adopted the concept for purposes of distribution upon dissolution of the marriage and on the death of a spouse, while Arizona and Texas have done so for divorce and Idaho for distribution on death. The Texas Supreme Court declined to extend the concept beyond dissolution to distribution on death. Estate of Hanau v. Hanau, 730 S.W.2d 663 (Tex.1987).

6. See Cameron v. Cameron, 641 S.W.2d 210 (Tex.1982), noted 14 St. Mary's L.J. 789 (1983), 35 Baylor L.Rev. 168 (1983): common law marital property acquired by one spouse should not be regarded as the "separate" property of that spouse but, if acquired during marriage, should be divided in the same manner as community property upon dissolution, regardless of the spouses' domicile at the time of acquisition. If it were otherwise, the common law property of the particular spouse would be insulated from division even though it would have been subject to claims for alimony or equitable division in the state of acquisition. Estate of Hanau v. Hanau, 721 S.W.2d 515 (Tex.Ct.App.1986), judgment affirmed in part, reversed in part, 730 S.W.2d 663 (Tex.1987). Compare Note (2), p. 919, supra.

7. A basic book in the area is Marsh, Marital Property in Conflict of Laws (1952). For other discussions of marital property, see McClanahan, Community Property Law in the United States (1982, 1984 Supp.); Oldham, Conflict of Laws and Marital Property Rights, 39 Baylor L.Rev. 1255 (1987); and the articles by Professor Lay, Migrants from Community Property States—Filling the Legislative Gap, 53 Corn. L.Rev. 832 (1968); Marital Property Rights of the Non–Native in a Community Property State, 18 Hast.L.J. 295 (1967); The Role of the Matrimonial Domicile in Marital Property Rights, 4 Fam.L.Q. 61 (1970). Note, Community Property and the Problem of Migration, 66 Wash.U.L.Q. 773 (1988); Chappell, A Uniform Resolution to the Problem a Migrating Spouse Encounters at Divorce and Death, 28 Idaho L.Rev. 993 (1991/1992).

CHAPTER 12

ADMINISTRATION OF ESTATES

SECTION 1. DECEDENTS' ESTATES *

INTRODUCTORY NOTE.

The casebook has dealt in earlier chapters with the substantive law applicable to succession to a decedent's property. This section is concerned with the machinery for the transfer of wealth from generation to generation. In the United States the method of transfer is through the personal representative, who is either an executor or administrator and who has been confirmed or appointed by a competent court.

The first stage is the determination in a judicial proceeding that the alleged decedent is dead and that he died either testate or intestate in a certain domicile. These determinations are followed by the appointment or qualification of the personal representative to administer the estate. At this stage there are problems of jurisdiction of courts, the nature of an administration proceeding, whether in rem or in personam, and the effect of foreign judgments.

The second stage is administration of the estate by the personal representative. His functions are essentially three: to collect and protect the property of the decedent, whether by voluntary payment or delivery or by suit; to pay creditors either voluntarily or after suit; and to distribute the net proceeds.

The last stage is the termination of the administration through a report to the court and its discharge of the personal representative.

The second stage presents the greatest difficulties. The central question is whether a personal representative appointed in one state may act and sue or be sued in another state, or whether he is confined to the state of his appointment. In support of wider powers are practical considerations: "An estate is for practical purposes a single thing, whether the items of property which compose it are all within the borders of one State or are scattered among several.... It is difficult to administer an estate as a unit, if that portion of it in each State is to be treated as a completely separate affair." (Restatement, Second, Conflict of Laws, Chap. 14, Topic 1, Introductory Note.) The principal support of the narrower view is the traditional conception of a personal representative as an artificial legal person who by the nature of his being is confined to the territory of the sovereign that created him. There are further complicating elements: the desire to protect local creditors out of local assets and the nature of the

---

* See Restatement, Second, Conflict of Laws §§ 314–366.

property involved, whether it is immovable or movable, tangible or intangible, or represented by a specialty.

Matters of probate and administration, as well as of the substantive validity of wills, are frequently affected by statutes, some of which are designed to simplify the handling of estates with assets in two or more states. An example is the Uniform Probate Code, some provisions of which will be referred to at various places in this chapter. A number of other uniform acts are in effect in some states.

Milmoe v. Toomey

United States Court of Appeals, District of Columbia Circuit, 1966.
123 U.S.App.D.C. 40, 356 F.2d 793.

■ McGowan, Circuit Judge. This appeal challenges the jurisdiction of the District Court ... to appoint an ancillary administrator by reason of an asset in the District of Columbia consisting solely of the protection against liability afforded by an automobile insurance policy....

The decedent was a girl who, for some time prior to June 6, 1964, had been residing in Washington while working for the Peace Corps. On the morning of that day, in company with a fellow employe, she rented a Hertz car and set out for her family home in New York State. In Lebanon County, Pennsylvania, during the early afternoon, the rented car was in a collision, and both of its occupants were killed. Also dying in the crash were a married couple from Illinois who were in the other car; and a minor child with them was seriously injured.

The rental agreement executed by the decedent with Hertz recites her "local address" in Washington to be 3336 P Street. An affidavit submitted in the District Court by her father asserts, however, that before leaving Washington the decedent had resigned from the Peace Corps and given up her P Street apartment; and that her purpose was to return to the family home in New York to live. Execution of the rental agreement with Hertz operated to bring the decedent directly within the coverage of a liability policy issued to Hertz by Royal Indemnity Company. Although not District of Columbia corporations, both Hertz and Royal Indemnity are doing business in the District so as to be subject to suit here.

Appellee O'Keefe is the Illinois administrator of the estate of the deceased Illinois couple. He filed a petition in the District Court reciting the rental agreement and the accompanying insurance coverage, and asked that letters of administration issue to a disinterested attorney in order that suit might be brought against such appointee in the District on behalf of the deceased Illinois couple and their surviving minor child. Appellee Toomey is the ancillary administrator appointed in response to this petition.

Appellant, the decedent's father, appeared in the District Court to oppose the appointment. It was urged by him that the decedent was, at the time of her death, domiciled in New York, and that any relationship of significance between her and the District of Columbia had ended before her death. As the administrator of his daughter's estate duly appointed in New York, appellant represented that he could be sued in New York or in Pennsylvania, as could Hertz and the estate of the decedent's companion on the fatal journey. He further asserted that the insurance policy running to Hertz and its customers was nationwide in character, and that its benefits could be claimed in both New York and Pennsylvania.

At the hearing before the District Court it appeared that a suit had in fact been filed in Pennsylvania; and, promptly after the appointment of the ancillary administrator in the District of Columbia, suit was brought against him in the District Court. So far as we are aware, these actions remain pending before trial.

The immediately relevant statute is Title 20 D.C.Code § 201, which provides as follows:

"On the death of any person leaving real or personal estate in the District, letters of administration on his estate may be granted, on the application of any person interested, on proof satisfactory to the probate court, that the decedent died intestate."

The District Judge conceived that the controversy before him was to be resolved by a scrupulous attention to the terms of this statute; and that, accordingly, the question before him was whether the decedent was an intestate person "leaving ... personal estate in the District" within the contemplation of the statute. He did not find it necessary to choose explicitly and finally between the conflicting contentions as to whether the decedent was a resident of the District at her death. He thought that the decedent's interest in the insurance policy was "personal estate," and that the circumstances surrounding the creation of that interest gave it a *locus* "in the District," within the scope of those phrases as used in the statute. Thus, he considered the conditions of the statute to be met, and that the appointment by him of an ancillary administrator was in order.

We agree with this concept of the issue presented, and see no occasion to disturb the resolution made of it. With respect to the narrow question of whether coverage under an insurance policy constitutes a personal property interest supporting administration, we think the answer is as clear in reason as it is settled in authority.... And, whatever may be the precise outer limits of the relationship of such an interest to the District of Columbia contemplated by Congress as warranting administration here, we agree with the District Judge that they were not exceeded in this case. The decedent was certainly not an ordinary transient in her relationship with the District of Columbia at the time she entered into the Hertz contract which created her insurance rights. Those rights came into being here; and we think that, on this record, they continue to constitute a "personal estate in the District" within the statutory prescription.

Appellant's claim of an absence of jurisdictional power to make the appointment is largely cast ... in terms of the lack of necessity for bringing the tort action here and of the greater appropriateness of other forums for its trial. This argument essentially is that, since the District Court should decline jurisdiction over the tort action from *forum non conveniens* considerations, it must be taken to have lacked jurisdiction to appoint the ancillary administrator. But the logic of this, if such there be, is not to be discovered from the language of the governing statute. Section 201 does not address itself generally to the purposes for which administration is sought, and, in particular, it prescribes nothing with respect to which lawsuits may be appropriately brought in the District of Columbia against the administrator, and which may not. Its concern appears to be mainly, if not exclusively, with the designation of a legal custodian of an asset in the District of an intestate decedent.

The District Judge ... looking only to Section 201, refused to be drawn into the question of whether the tort claim should be tried here or in Pennsylvania. In this he was ... wholly right. He regarded that question as one reserved to the judge before whom the tort suit comes ... There may or may not be persuasive reasons why the issue of liability in negligence should be tried elsewhere than in the District of Columbia ... But that is a matter for exploration and resolution in the tort action itself, and not in [this] proceeding.

The judgment appealed from is Affirmed.

NOTES

1. The circumstances in which a will may be probated, and an executor or administrator appointed, are usually regulated by statute. The District of Columbia statute involved in the principal case is similar to statutes commonly found among the states. The statutes do not usually require that a representative be appointed, but authorize the making of such an appointment in the court's discretion—e.g., if the appointment would be in the best interests of the estate and is required for the protection of local creditors. Restatement, Second, Conflict of Laws §§ 314–315.

2. Local ancillary administrators have frequently been appointed in the circumstances involved in the principal case. See e.g., Gordon v. Shea, 300 Mass. 95, 14 N.E.2d 105 (1938); Estate of Riggle, 11 N.Y.2d 73, 226 N.Y.S.2d 416, 181 N.E.2d 436 (1962). One reason for the appointment of local ancillary administrators in these circumstances is the perceived difficulty involved in bringing suit against a foreign domiciliary administrator. See p. 952, infra.

3. The Shea and Riggle cases were relied upon by the New York Court of Appeals as authority for the proposition that the obligation owed by a liability insurer to the insured is a "debt" subject to garnishment in a state where the insurer does business. Seider v. Roth, p. 150, supra.

4. On the privileges and functions of a consul in dealing with the estate of a national of his country, see Boyd, Consular Functions in Connection with Decedents' Estates, 47 Iowa L.Rev. 823 (1962); Boyd, Constitutional, Treaty, and Statutory Requirement of Probate Notice to Consuls and Aliens, 47 Iowa L.Rev. 29 (1961).

5. On the administration of estates in which aliens have an interest, see Boyd, The Administration in the United States of Alien Connected Decedents' Estates, 2 Int.Law 601 (1968).

In Re Fischer's Estate

Prerogative Court of New Jersey, 1935.
118 N.J.Eq. 599, 180 A. 633.

■ BUCHANAN, VICE ORDINARY. Mrs. Mae Platto Fischer died at Denville (Indian Lake), Morris county, N.J., on August 21, 1933. She left no descendants, but was survived by her husband, Frederick G. Fischer, and by one brother, George Platto, but by no other brother or sister or representative thereof. No will being found, her husband applied to this court for letters of administration, and letters of general administration were issued to him on September 12, 1933.

These letters were issued on Fischer's allegation that decedent was a resident of ("late of") New Jersey, and without notice to the brother, Platto. It is the law of the state of domicile of an intestate decedent, which governs and determines the rights of intestate succession. Under the law of New Jersey, if the decedent had been domiciled here at her death, the husband would have had the sole right to succeed to all the decedent's personal property, and the sole right to letters of administration, and no notice was required to be given to Platto or any one else.

If the decedent, however, were domiciled in New York at the time of her death, the New York law would control, and under that law the brother, Platto, would succeed to a substantial share in the estate.

On October 20, 1933, the brother, Platto, filed petition for administration of Mrs. Fischer's estate, in the Surrogate's Court in New York, alleging her to have been a resident of New York at her death; and process was issued and served on the husband, Fischer.

Fischer had become mentally deranged, and on November 8, 1933, the letters of administration which had been issued to him by this court were revoked on that ground and letters issued in their stead to one Milton Mermelstein....

Mermelstein, as substituted administrator of Mrs. Fischer's estate, appointed by this court, entered appearance and answer in the New York proceeding above mentioned. He also himself filed a petition in the New York court for the issuance of ancillary letters to himself, on the basis of the allegation that Mrs. Fischer had been domiciled in New Jersey and that original letters of administration had been issued to him here. Under the New York law it is a requisite to the grant of ancillary letters that it be shown that original letters have been issued in the state of decedent's domicile. To this petition Platto answered, denying that Mrs. Fischer's residence was in New Jersey, and alleging such residence to have been in New York.

Both proceedings in New York therefore involved the issue as to whether Mrs. Fischer had been domiciled in New York or New Jersey. Both proceedings were consolidated and duly tried in New York, and ... Mr. Fischer also appeared as a party, and contended that the domicile of Mrs. Fischer was not New York but New Jersey. The determination of the issue in and by the New York court was that Mrs. Fischer had been domiciled in New York, and original letters of administration were issued to Platto. In re Fischer's Estate, 151 Misc. 74, 271 N.Y.S. 101....

Following the determination aforesaid in the New York Surrogate's Court, Platto, as general administrator appointed by the New York court, commenced the present proceeding in this court, being a petition for the revocation of the letters issued by this court to Mermelstein and for the issuance of letters to him (Platto), in the place and stead thereof. The basis of this petition is the allegation that Mrs. Fischer was not a resident of New Jersey but of New York; that hence New Jersey had not the right to issue letters of general or original administration on her estate; that although New Jersey had the right to issue letters of administration for the administration of such assets of the estate as were in this state, such letters (on Fischer's becoming incompetent) should have been issued to Platto and not to Mermelstein; that the issuance of the letters to Mermelstein was the result of mistake and misrepresentation, to wit, the mistake of this court in believing that Mrs. Fischer's residence had been in this state, which mistake was caused by the misrepresentation to that effect made to this court by Fischer in his original petition ... that Platto, not having been brought in to the proceedings in this court nor given notice thereof, had had no opportunity to raise or be heard on the issue as to the domicile of Mrs. Fischer, in this court.

. . .

... Fisher ... and the New Jersey substituted administrator, are all bound by the determination in the New York proceeding, because they were all parties to that proceeding, and not only had the opportunity to be heard therein, but therein actively litigated, against Platto, the same issue now sought by them to be relitigated against him herein....

Reopening the action and finding of this court of 1933, and according to Platto, now, the opportunity to be heard on the question of the right to letters of ancillary administration, results in the revocation of Mermelstein's letters and the grant of ancillary letters to Platto....

Riley v. New York Trust Co.
Supreme Court of the United States, 1942.
315 U.S. 343, 62 S.Ct. 608, 86 L.Ed. 885.

[The case appears at p. 242, supra.]

RESTATEMENT, SECOND, CONFLICT OF LAWS: *

§ 317. Effect Given in Other States to Judgments in Administration Proceedings

(1) A judgment in administration proceedings by a competent court in the state where the decedent was domiciled at the time of his death will usually be followed by the forum with respect to local movables insofar as the judgment deals with questions of succession that under the choice-of-law rules of the forum are governed by the law that would be applied by the courts of the state of the decedent's domicil.

(2) A judgment in administration proceedings by a competent court in the state where the decedent was domiciled at the time of his death will not of itself invalidate a prior inconsistent judgment by a court in another state in administering the estate of the same decedent in that state.

(3) A judgment in administration proceedings by a competent court of any state will be held conclusive in other states as to the issues determined upon all persons who were subject to the jurisdiction of the original court if the judgment is conclusive upon such persons in the state of rendition.

(4) If an issue as to the state in which a decedent was domiciled at the time of his death is raised by a person not precluded from raising this issue under Subsection (3), a court will not regard itself as concluded by a prior finding made in another state as to the place of the decedent's domicil.

NOTES

1. In order to facilitate solution of these problems, the Uniform Probate Code provides:

In § 3–202, that when probate or appointment proceedings are pending at the same time in the state of the forum and in one or more other states, "[t]he determination of domicile in the proceeding first commenced must be accepted as determinative in the proceeding in this state." The Comment explains that the "section is designed to reduce the possibility that conflicting findings of domicile in two or more states may result in inconsistent administration and distribution of parts of the same estate," and that "the local suitor always will have a chance to contest the question of domicile in the other state."

In § 3–203, that, in the absence of a contrary provision in the decedent's will, the domiciliary administrator "has priority over all other persons" for appointment as ancillary administrator of local assets.

In § 3–408, that a previous determination by a court of another state of testacy or of the validity or construction of a will must be accepted as conclusive by the local courts provided the previous determination was rendered after proper notice and opportunity to be heard and included "a finding that the decedent was domiciled in the state where the [previous determination] was made." The Com-

* Quoted with the permission of the copyright owner, The American Law Institute.

ment makes clear that the section applies to cases where parties before the local court were not subject to the personal jurisdiction of the foreign court.

Wilkins v. Ellett, Adm'r

Supreme Court of the United States, 1883.
108 U.S. 256, 2 S.Ct. 641, 27 L.Ed. 718.

■ GRAY, J. This is an action of *assumpsit* on the common counts, brought in the circuit court of the United States for the western district of Tennessee. The plaintiff is a citizen of Virginia, and sues as administrator, appointed in Tennessee, of the estate of Thomas N. Quarles. The defendant is a citizen of Tennessee and surviving partner of the firm of F.H. Clark & Co. The answer sets up that Quarles was a citizen of Alabama at the time of his death; that the sum sued for has been paid to William Goodloe, appointed his administrator in that state, and has been inventoried and accounted for by him upon a final settlement of his administration; and that there are no creditors of Quarles in Tennessee. The undisputed facts, appearing by the bill of exceptions, are as follows:

Quarles was born at Richmond, Virginia, in 1835. In 1839 his mother, a widow, removed with him, her only child, to Courtland, Alabama. They lived there together until 1856, and she made her home there until her death, in 1864. In 1856, he went to Memphis, Tennessee, and there entered the employment of F.H. Clark & Co., and continued in their employment as a clerk, making no investments himself, but leaving the surplus earnings on interest in their hands until January, 1866, when he went to the house of a cousin in Courtland, Alabama, and while there died by an accident, leaving personal estate in Alabama. On the twenty-seventh of January, 1866, Goodloe took out letters of administration in Alabama, and in February, 1866, went to Memphis, and there, upon exhibiting his letters of administration, received from defendant the sum of money due to Quarles, amounting to $3,455.22 (which is the same for which this suit is brought,) and included it in his inventory and in his final account, which was allowed by the probate court in Alabama. There were no other debts due from Quarles in Tennessee. All his next of kin resided in Virginia or in Alabama; and no administration was taken out on his estate in Tennessee until June, 1866, when letters of administration were there issued to the plaintiff.

[W]e are of opinion that the court erred in instructing the jury that if the domicile was in Tennessee they must find for the plaintiff; and in refusing to instruct them, as requested by the defendant, that the payment to the Alabama administrator before the appointment of one in Tennessee, and there being no Tennessee creditors, was a valid discharge of the defendant, without reference to the domicile.

There is no doubt that the succession to the personal estate of a deceased person is governed by the law of his domicile at the time of his death; that the proper place for the principal administration of his estate is that domicile; that administration may also be taken out in any place in which he leaves personal property; and that no suit for the recovery of a debt, due to him at the time of his death, can be brought by an administrator as such in any state in which he has not taken out administration. But the reason for this last rule is the protection of the rights of citizens of the state in which the suit is brought; and the objection does not rest upon any defect of the administrator's title in the property, but upon his personal incapacity to sue as administrator beyond the jurisdiction which appointed him.

If a debtor, residing in another state, comes into the state in which the administrator has been appointed, and there pays him, the payment is a valid discharge everywhere. If the debtor, being in that state, is there sued by the administrator, and judgment recovered against him, the administrator may bring suit in his own name upon that judgment in the state where the debtor resides. Talmage v. Chapel, 16 Mass. 71.

The administrator, by virtue of his appointment and authority as such, obtains the title in promissory notes or other written evidences of debt, held by the intestate at the time of his death, and coming to the possession of the administrator; and may sell, transfer, and indorse the same; and the purchasers or indorsees may maintain actions in their own names against the debtors in another state, if the debts are negotiable promissory notes, or if the law of the state in which the action is brought permits the assignee of a chose in action to sue in his own name....

In accordance with these views, it was held by this court, when this case was before it after a former trial, at which the domicile of the intestate appeared to have been in Alabama, that the payment in Tennessee to the Alabama administrator was good as against the administrator afterwards appointed in Tennessee. Wilkins v. Ellett, 9 Wall. 740.

The fact that the domicile of the intestate has now been found by the jury to be in Tennessee does not appear to us to make any difference. There are neither creditors nor next of kin in Tennessee. The Alabama administrator has inventoried and accounted for the amount of this debt in Alabama. The distribution among the next of kin, whether made in Alabama or in Tennessee, must be according to the law of the domicile; and it has not been suggested that there is any difference between the laws of the two states in that regard.

The judgment must, therefore, be reversed, and the case remanded with directions to set aside the verdict and to order a new trial.

NOTES

1. Why should not the state where the decedent died domiciled have power to appoint a universal successor whose title to the decedent's assets in other states would have to be recognized under full faith and credit and who could sue everywhere as of right to collect these assets? Obviously, the existence of such a successor would vastly simplify the handling of a multistate estate. So far as is known, only one court has attempted to appoint such a universal successor, and this appointment was vacated on appeal on the ground that no jurisdiction could be exercised over assets in other states. In re De Lano's Estate, 181 Kan. 729, 315 P.2d 611 (1957); cf. Hanson v. Denckla, p. 56, supra. On the other hand, universal succession has been achieved in the area of debtors' estates through the appointment of a statutory successor. See pp. 963–968, infra and Cheatham, The Statutory Successor, the Receiver and the Executor in Conflict of Laws, 44 Colum.L.Rev. 549 (1944). Why should what is possible in the area of debtors' estates not likewise be possible in decedents' estates? See D. Currie, The Multiple Personality of the Dead: Executors, Administrators, and the Conflict of Laws, 33 U.Chi.L.Rev. 429, 435–438 (1966).

2. The Uniform Probate Code provides in §§ 4–201 to 4–203 that, unless he has been given notice not to do so by a resident creditor, a debtor may without danger of double liability pay a debt owed a nonresident decedent to a foreign domiciliary representative upon the latter's affidavit stating, among other things that "no local administration, or application or petition therefore, is pending in this state." Also under §§ 4–204 to 4–205, that a foreign domiciliary representative, upon filing copies of his appointment and giving bond, "may exercise as to assets in this state all powers of a local personal representative," including the bringing of suit, if no local representative has been appointed and no petition for such an appointment is pending.

3. "Most of the difficulty found in the reported decisions has concerned the effect of a voluntary payment made to an administrator outside the state of his appointment. The results are conflicting and reflect the divergent theoretical conceptions, heretofore discussed, of territorial restriction upon the legal personality of an administrator.... [T]he great majority of decisions have upheld such payments, at least where no local representative has been appointed at the time of payment." Hopkins, Conflict of Laws in Administration of Decedents' Intangibles, 28 Iowa L.Rev. 422, 435, 437 (1943).

4. Most case authority holds that a domiciliary administrator may assign, and the assignee may enforce, a claim which is not represented by a negotiable instrument and which is owed the decedent by a person who is not subject to suit in a state where an ancillary administrator has been appointed. Restatement, Second, Conflict of Laws § 333; Scoles and Hay, Conflict of Laws 850–852 (2d ed. 1992); McDowell, Foreign Personal Representatives 63–66 (1957).

5. For another example of achieving uniformity in the administration of the estate see Matter of Estate of Jones, 858 P.2d 983 (Utah 1993) which gave full faith and credit to the California determination, in an ancillary administration concerning California realty, of the Utah claimant's status as pretermitted child.

ADMINISTRATION OF LAND

Land owned by a decedent is subject to administration as part of his estate only when and to the extent that a statute of the state of the situs so provides. When assets within State X where the land is are insufficient to satisfy claims proved and allowed in X, the land will be ordered sold even though there may be other assets in State Y. The land will also be ordered sold to satisfy claims proved and allowed in State Y when the assets in State Y are insufficient to satisfy creditors. When a will confers upon an executor the power to sell land, he need not receive an appointment from the court of the state where the land is in order to exercise the power to sell. This is because he is said to be acting in an individual and not in a representative capacity. Bacharach v. Spriggs, 173 Ark. 250, 292 S.W. 150 (1927).

Unless authorized by an X statute, an executor or administrator appointed in State Y may not foreclose a mortgage on land in State X. Under certain circumstances, however, his assignee will be permitted to do so. See Restatement, Second, Conflict of Laws §§ 339–340.

Estate of Hanreddy

Supreme Court of Wisconsin, 1922.
176 Wis. 570, 186 N.W. 744.

One Joseph Hanreddy, a resident citizen of Chicago, Illinois, died there testate April 8, 1918. On June 25, 1918, his widow, Margaret Hanreddy, was duly appointed, qualified, and ever since has acted and is still acting as executrix of his estate in the probate court of Cook county, Illinois. Claims were therein filed aggregating more than $50,000. The available assets subject to that jurisdiction do not exceed $4,000.

In August, 1918, in the county court of Milwaukee county, Wisconsin, the will of said Joseph Hanreddy was duly probated and the said Margaret Hanreddy appointed executrix in ancillary proceedings, there being assets aggregating over $50,000 belonging to said estate as well as resident creditors within the state of Wisconsin. Claims have been filed therein by both resident and nonresident creditors in amounts in excess of the assets. Some creditors have filed their respective claims in both jurisdictions.

In August, 1919, the said executrix filed a petition in the county court of Milwaukee county reciting the probate proceedings in Illinois and in this state; the claims filed in the respective proceedings and their respective assets substantially as above set forth; the fact that the assets of the said estate are insufficient to pay all of the debts of the said estate and that the said estate is insolvent; that if all the claims filed were allowed there would be assets in the Wisconsin jurisdiction sufficient to pay the claims filed in that jurisdiction to approximately ninety per cent. thereof, and that as to the claims in the Illinois jurisdiction the assets there would not be sufficient to pay more than a ten per cent. dividend thereon.... She asked that no payment be made upon the claims filed in the Wisconsin jurisdiction until after final adjudication in both states upon all the claims and a determination had of the pro rata percentage that could properly be paid from the entire assets in both jurisdictions upon the respective claims in the several jurisdictions and that after such ascertainment and payment upon such pro rata percentage of the claims filed and allowed in the Wisconsin jurisdiction the surplus should be turned over to her as executrix in the jurisdiction of Illinois, to be there likewise applied.

... After a hearing the court made his findings of fact reciting substantially as above stated and his conclusions of law as follows:

"I. That the assets in said ancillary administration constitute a fund out of which the claims of creditors residing in Wisconsin, and who have duly filed their claims, be paid in full. . . .

"III. That this court has no jurisdiction to consider or allow claims of foreign creditors . . .

"IV. That any residue in the possession of the ancillary administrator after the payment of the claims of Wisconsin creditors duly allowed, and after the payment of the costs and expenses of the ancillary administration, are hereby ordered to be paid and delivered by said ancillary administrator to the executrix of the domiciliary estate."

An appeal was taken from the judgment or order entered in conformity with said conclusions of law. . . .

■ ESCHWEILER, J. . . .

Where the assets of a deceased, though found in several jurisdictions, are sufficient to pay the debts allowed against his estate in the several jurisdictions, ordinarily each of the separate jurisdictions proceeds to adjust claims and provide for their payment out of the assets in their control, each independently of the other; but where, as here, the entire assets of the deceased are insufficient to pay all his just obligations, there is such an interdependence between the various jurisdictions as to require the application of the old maxim that "Equality is equity"; and the several courts administering the affairs of the deceased, each being apprised of that situation, must no longer consider the assets within their respective controls as separate and distinct funds for distribution to the creditors within such jurisdictions, but as one entire fund in which all creditors of the deceased having just claims of equal standing shall share pro rata. It makes no material difference by whom or how the situation is brought to the knowledge of the court. In this case the petition of the executrix alone was sufficient. It is the fact of insolvency that raises the equity. It then becomes the duty of the court itself, administering the assets, to subordinate the demands of the local creditors to be paid in full or to the exhaustion of the assets to the broader rights of the creditors as a whole to share on an equal footing in the assets as a whole. . . .

[This] is but the application in another form of the rule that is applied in the distribution of the assets of an insolvent corporation foreign to the disturbing jurisdiction, where resident and nonresident creditors must share pro rata. Blake v. McClung, 172 U.S. 239, 19 S.Ct. 165, 43 L.Ed. 432; . . .

It is of course proper that sufficient of the assets belonging to the estate and found in Wisconsin should be held here so that when the proper percentage is ultimately determined in the two jurisdictions the creditors whose claims are filed and allowed in this jurisdiction shall be here paid their proper percentage.

[I]t is clear that, there being assets of the deceased and resident creditors within the state of Wisconsin, the county court of Milwaukee county had ... the duty ... to receive, examine, and adjust the claims and demands of all persons against the deceased ...

Under [the Wisconsin] statute as well as under the general principles governing such matters, no distinction can be made between ancillary administration and domiciliary administration as to the rights of nonresident creditors to file, in accordance with the established practice of this state, their claims against such an estate for adjustment and allowance....

■ By the Court. Judgment reversed, and the cause remanded with directions to enter judgment in accordance with this opinion.

NOTES

1. Sister state creditors of an insolvent decedent's estate are undoubtedly entitled to the same constitutional protection that is given to the creditors of an insolvent corporation. See Blake v. McClung, p. 955, infra, which is cited in the principal case.

2. Although the law of the domicile provides that claims not presented against the estate there within the period of limitations shall be forever barred, a claim may be presented in any other state where there is an administration and whose period of limitations has not yet run. Restatement, Second, Conflict of Laws § 345.

3. In support of treating the estate as a unit even though it is composed of assets located in different states or nations, see Scoles and Hay, Conflict of Laws, 859–867 (2d ed. 1992); Scoles, Conflict of Laws and Creditors' Rights in Decedents' Estates, 42 Iowa L.Rev. 341 (1957).

Lenn v. Riche

Supreme Judicial Court of Massachusetts, 1954.
331 Mass. 104, 117 N.E.2d 129.

[During his life, Paul Bonn made a gift to plaintiff of a valuable painting. The gift was made in Germany. Later in France plaintiff loaned the painting to Bonn so that he could exhibit and preserve it. Bonn died in France and by his will duly "allowed" there named his wife as "universal legatee." After she refused to return the painting to plaintiff, plaintiff brought this suit against the ancillary administrator of Bonn's Massachusetts estate. Plaintiff recovered in the court below and defendant excepted.]

■ Qua, Chief Justice. [T]he defendant insists that this action cannot be maintained against the administrator of Bonn's estate in Massachusetts because Bonn left a will duly established in France, in which he made his wife ... his universal legatee, and because under French law, the universal legatee, who takes all the property of the deceased, becomes personally chargeable with his obligations. The argument is that if suit had been brought in France it must have been brought against [his wife] personally. This may be true.... But it is not controlling over the law governing the administration of estates in this Commonwealth. Here the administrator is liable to suit upon obligations of the deceased, and creditors resident here, of whom the plaintiff is one, are entitled to secure payment of their claims out of Massachusetts assets in the manner provided by Massachusetts law. At the moment of Bonn's death he owed to the plaintiff an obligation which had arisen under French law to return her property to her upon request. This obligation was chargeable against his Massachusetts assets. It was like a promissory note owed but not yet due. Even though at Bonn's death there was as yet no breach of his obligation, there was a breach when the plaintiff made her request to the universal legatee for a return of her property. We think the request, if any was necessary, was properly made to the universal legatee in France. She was the general representative of the succession and of the personalty of the deceased at the domicil of the deceased. The defendant had not at that time been appointed administrator here. A request to the defendant after his appointment would have been a barren gesture. There was no reason to suppose that the plaintiff's property was in this Commonwealth or in the control of the administrator appointed here in his capacity as ancillary administrator. The plaintiff can maintain her action here. She was not obliged to see Massachusetts assets swept away and then go to France to assert her rights....

Exceptions overruled.

NOTES

1. The principal case is in line with authority. But was the result reached a desirable one? The administration of a multistate estate would obviously be facilitated by requiring all creditors to file their claims in the court of domiciliary administration. Would the advantages that such a rule would bring to estate administration be outweighed by the hardship that it would visit upon out-of-state creditors? Compare D. Currie, The Multiple Personality of the Dead: Executors, Administrators and the Conflict of Laws, 33 U.Chi.L.Rev. 429, 453–462 (1966).

2. On the different methods in the civil law and the common law for the determination of death and the administration of the property of a decedent and the coordination of the two methods, see Ehrenzweig, Conflict of Laws 180–182 (1962). In Wren, Problems in Probating Foreign Wills and Using Foreign Personal Representatives, 17 Sw.L.J. 55 (1963), special attention is given to differences in the laws of Mexico and Texas.

Ghilain v. Couture

Supreme Court of New Hampshire, 1929.
84 N.H. 48, 146 A. 395, 65 A.L.R. 553.

■ Snow, J. This action was brought by the plaintiff as administratrix by appointment in Massachusetts, the domicile of the deceased, against defendants resident in this state, to recover for death from an injury received here.

In claims for death the nature of the right of action, and the party in whom it is vested, are fixed by the lex loci delicti.... The plaintiff's right of action, if any, is therefore determined by the law of this state. At the time of the accident the sole basis for such a right was P.S., c. 191, ss. 10–13. Poff v. New England Tel. & Teleg. Company, 72 N.H. 164, 55 A. 891. This statute authorized an action to recover damages for death caused by wrongful physical injury to the person, for the benefit of the widow or widower and the children, if any, otherwise for the benefit of the heirs at law of the deceased; said action to be brought at any time within two years after the death of the injured party and not afterwards. Though not expressed in so many words, the statute clearly contemplated that actions to enforce the right should be brought by the "administrator of the deceased party." P.S. c. 191, s. 12; Cogswell v. Concord & M. Railroad, 68 N.H. 192, 194, 44 A. 293. See Laws 1887, c. 71, s. 1. The interpretation of the quoted words is the principal and the controlling issue presented.

The contentions of the defendants are that the plaintiff, domiciliary administratrix, was not an "administrator of the deceased party" within the meaning of the statute, and that she was, therefore, wholly without authority to bring the suit; that her attempted action was a mere nullity; and that, the limitation having run, the plaintiff's writ is incapable of amendment by substitution of herself as the ancillary administratrix so as to relate back and cure her defective suit.*

In support of their contention of the plaintiff's want of authority the defendants cite the general rule that an administrator cannot sue outside of the state of his appointment, . . .

While the rule presupposes that an administrator has no claim to recognition *as a matter of right,* beyond the bounds of the state of his appointment . . . such want of *legal right* is not the reason for the rule. The rule does not arise from any want of inherent authority in the court to accord such recognition. . . . No statute or . . . principle of the common law forbids it. . . .

[I]n a larger sense, the so-called rule that executors and administrators will not ordinarily be granted extra-territorial recognition, and therefore will not generally be permitted to bring actions in the courts of foreign jurisdictions . . . is but an exception to the broader doctrine that the acts of foreign representatives or fiduciaries, as a matter of practice, convenience and expediency, will be given effect through the exercise of a liberal comity. . . . An exception is made whenever such a course would conflict with any principle of public policy. It is in such a conflict with state policy that the denial of the right of action generally to foreign administrators, without first taking out letters here, finds a sufficient, and its only, justification. Upon whatever ground the rule calling for such denial may formerly have been thought to rest it is now generally recognized that it is based solely upon the policy of the courts of each state to protect resident creditors of the decedent against the withdrawal into another state of

---

* The decedent, a resident of Massachusetts, was killed in New Hampshire on May 13, 1924. The present action was brought on May 12, 1926. The plaintiff was appointed administratrix in New Hampshire in 1928. (Editors' note.)

assets on which they may equitably rely for the payment of the debts that may be due them....

The damages recoverable under the statute by its terms (s. 13) "shall belong and be distributed" to the designated beneficiaries. They are not assets of the estate within the ordinary meaning of the word.... As no creditor of the deceased can be either benefited or burdened by any action brought under the statute or have "the slightest ... interest in the recovery sought" ... it is clear that the legislature, in designating the person who shall bring the action, could not have been influenced by a rule which had as its sole justification the protection of local creditors. In interpreting the statute the rule relied upon by the defendants may, therefore, be laid out of the case.

Nor is it perceived that the recognition of a domiciliary administrator as the plaintiff in actions under our death statute offends any state policy so as to require his exclusion under the broader principles of comity.... To assume otherwise would be in effect saying that it would be impolitic to extend the courtesy of our courts to a Massachusetts representative for fear that the courts of that commonwealth would not hold its own appointee accountable for his special trust according to its definitive terms. The acceptance of such a postulate would be to impugn the mutual confidence possessed by the courts of the respective states in each other so essential to the very existence of the doctrine of comity....

We therefore come to the interpretation of the statute unhampered by any rules or questions of state policy peculiar to the ordinary administration of intestate property to which it has no relation, except as it utilizes the personal representative of the decedent, ex officio, as the instrument of enforcement of the right of action which it provides....

While it may fairly be assumed that the legislature had in mind the domestic administrator if there be one, there is nothing in the language showing an intention to restrict the court in the exercise of its powers, under the principles of comity, to recognize the domiciliary administrator in the absence of a local representative. It is our conclusion that the legislature used the words "the administrator of the deceased party" as inclusive of any representative who, by comity or otherwise, may be admitted to sue in this forum without infringing any principle of state policy....

... The suggestion in argument that the defendant would not be protected by a judgment in the suit as instituted is without merit. It seems to be well settled that a judgment for damages for the wrongful death of a person is a bar to an action in another state to recover damages of the same character and for the same death, where the real parties in interest are the same, even though the nominal parties are different....

. . .

... There was no error in the ruling that the plaintiff was not precluded by law on the record from maintaining the suit for her beneficiaries under the statute.

Exceptions overruled.

NOTES

1. See, also, Wiener v. Specific Pharmaceuticals, 298 N.Y. 346, 83 N.E.2d 673 (1949).

2. The common law rule is that a foreign personal representative lacks capacity to maintain an action outside the state of appointment. One way to overcome the ban, where it persists, is for the foreign representative to be appointed ancillary representative in the second state.

3. Courts have created several exceptions to the rule: (a) The defendant waives the defense of incapacity of the representative by failing to plead it promptly. (b) When the representative has "title" in himself personally, he may sue, as when he makes a contract or recovers a judgment after the death of the decedent, or holds negotiable paper. This result may be wise, though the form of expression can scarcely be justified since the personal representative does not hold these assets for himself but must account for them as representative. (c) An action for the death of a decedent may be maintained, at least if the proceeds will go to the members of the family rather than to the general estate, so creditors are not concerned. See Hatas v. Partin, 175 So.2d 759 (1965). (d) An action may be maintained by a foreign personal representative when this would be for the best interests of the estate and would not prejudice the interests of local creditors. The states vary in their recognition of the exceptions mentioned. See Restatement, Second, Conflict of Laws § 354.

Eubank Heights Apartments, Limited v. Lebow

United States Court of Appeals, First Circuit, 1980.
615 F.2d 571.

■ ALDRICH, SENIOR CIRCUIT JUDGE.

On September 28, 1972, Saul L. Lebow executed in Massachusetts a limited partnership agreement and, in connection therewith, six promissory notes.... The payee was the partnership, Eubank Heights Apartments, Ltd. The partnership was created under Texas law, with its general partners and its principal office in Texas. Lebow, a resident of Massachusetts, died on March 12, 1973. His wife, Estelle, was appointed executrix on May 22, 1973. Apparently not until March, 1974, did the partnership, hereinafter plaintiff, learn of Lebow's death and of the probate proceedings. On April 3, 1974, plaintiff exercised its right to make the notes payable in Texas by notifying defendant. On December 13, 1974, plaintiff brought suit on the notes in the state court of Texas, naming as defendant the Estate of Saul L. Lebow. Service was made on the Secretary of State, and notice was sent to, and received by, the executrix. She made no response, and on May 16, 1975, a default judgment for the amounts of the notes, interest, and attorney's fees was entered, naming the Estate as the judgment debtor. There is, of course, no such entity; at least none such is recognized in Massachusetts.... Nor were there any assets, to be denominated an estate, in Texas.

Action was brought on the judgment in the district court for the District of Massachusetts on February 12, 1976, naming as defendant Estelle I. Lebow, Executrix of the Estate of Saul L. Lebow. The above facts having been made to appear by affidavits, plaintiff moved for summary judgment.... The court granted the motion ... and defendant appeals.

The first defense asserted is that decedent did not have sufficient connection with Texas to give that state jurisdiction over him under its longarm statute, Tex.Rev.Civ.Stat.Ann. art. 2031b, §§ 3, 4. This is a conventional statute, whose reach is restricted only by the Constitution.... Although the partnership was created to deal with New Mexico land, it was a Texas-run enterprise, by the terms of the agreement governed by Texas law, and had cumulatively such Texas connections that we see no merit in defendant's attack on the Texas court's in personam jurisdiction so far as the decedent was concerned....

This, however, is only one step. However labeled, this was not an action against the decedent—he no longer existed. The suit was, in effect, against his former assets; obviously defendant would not be liable individually. The fact that Texas would have had in personam jurisdiction over him does not mean that it had jurisdiction in rem, or quasi in rem. Indeed, he died before there even was a claim against his assets. What happens to a person's intangible assets after death is determined by the state of domicile.... We must look, accordingly, to the law of Massachusetts to determine whether plaintiff took adequate steps to secure an interest chargeable against the assets....

... In the district court defendant did not claim that the Estate of Saul L. Lebow was a nonentity, but asserted that it was "a different party ... than the defendant in this action." We think defendant's present claim, that there was no party at all, hypertechnical. Identification was clear, and statutory service was made on the executrix. We would not hold this judgment a worthless piece of paper simply because defendant's name as estate representative was not included thereon. Rather, we take the issue to be whether plaintiff could obtain a judgment in Texas valid against estate assets in Massachusetts by suing the executrix in Texas....

A long held view is that a court-appointed estate representative cannot represent the estate for purposes of suit, whether as plaintiff or defendant, beyond the state borders. It would have advanced consideration of this case substantially if plaintiff had called our attention to Saporita v. Litner, 1976, 371 Mass. 607, 358 N.E.2d 809. It is not our primary obligation to be acquainted with Massachusetts law; counsel owe a duty to the court.[3]

In *Saporita* a Massachusetts creditor succeeded in obtaining a judgment in Massachusetts against an executor of a Connecticut estate. The court, after extensive discussion of the old cases, held that such procedure was in accord with the times. We cannot think that Massachusetts would

---

3. We are also critical of defendant, who either shared plaintiff's negligence in not discovering *Saporita,* or else was disingenuous in arguing that defendant "had no standing to be subject to an action in Texas" without mentioning it.

decline to take the reciprocal view, and refuse to recognize a Texas judgment against a Massachusetts executor. It is true that plaintiff Saporita obtained service in hand on the foreign executor in Massachusetts, whereas defendant here received only substituted service by mail, but we do not think that a significant difference. If the Texas long arm would have reached the decedent, we do not believe it withered on his death.... We hold the judgment valid.

. . .

NOTES

1. Most of the modern long-arm statutes provide that in the event of the defendant's death suit may be brought against his personal representative. For a good discussion of the problem, see D. Currie, The Multiple Personality of the Dead: Executors, Administrators, and the Conflict of Laws, 33 U.Chi.L.Rev. 429 (1966).

2. Section 4–302 of the Uniform Probate Code provides that "a foreign personal representative is subject to the jurisdiction of the courts of this state to the same extent that his decedent was subject to jurisdiction immediately prior to death."

3. Restatement, Second, Conflict of Laws: *

§ 358. Suit Against Foreign Executor or Administrator

An action may be maintained against an executor or administrator outside the state of his appointment upon a claim against the decedent when the local law of the forum authorizes suit against the executor or administrator and

(a) suit could have been maintained within the state against the decedent during his lifetime because of the existence of a basis of jurisdiction, other than mere physical presence . . . , or

(b) the executor or administrator has done an act in the state in his official capacity.

INGERSOLL V. CORAM, 211 U.S. 335 (1908). [An action was brought in a state court of Montana by the Montana ancillary administrator of a New York lawyer against the lawyer's clients for a large fee alleged to have been earned in Montana. On motion of the defendants the complaint was dismissed for failure to state a cause of action. The present action was then brought in the federal court in Massachusetts by the New York domiciliary administratrix, who had also been appointed ancillary administratrix in Massachusetts, of the lawyer to recover the fee. The defense was that the judgment in the Montana proceeding was a bar. The Supreme Court of the United States held, two justices dissenting without opinion, that it was not a bar.]

■ JUSTICE MCKENNA . . . Respondents assert the identity of the action in Montana with the present suit, and upon that identity they urge that such

---

* Quoted with the permission of the copyright owner, The American Law Institute.

action constitutes *res judicata*. Petitioner denies the identity of the actions, and urges besides that there is no such privity between the parties as to make the Montana action *res judicata* of the pending case. In support of the latter contention petitioner urges that an ancillary administrator in one jurisdiction is not in privity with an ancillary administrator in another jurisdiction, and that therefore a judgment against one is not a bar to a suit by the other. . . .

We shall assume that there is identity of subject-matter between the Montana action and that at bar, but the question remains, Was there identity of parties? An extended discussion of the question is made unnecessary by the case of Brown v. Fletcher, 210 U.S. 82 . . . The latter case [Stacy v. Thrasher, 6 How. 42] was quoted from as follows: "Where administrations are granted to different persons in different states, they are so far deemed independent of each other that a judgment obtained against one will furnish no right of action against the other, to affect assets received by the latter in virtue of his own administration; for, in contemplation of law, there is no privity between him and the other administrator." . . . That there is a certain amount of artificiality in the doctrine was pointed out in Stacy v. Thrasher, and that it leads to the inconvenience and burdensome result of retrying controversies and repeating litigations. The doctrine, however, was vindicated as a necessary consequence of the different sources from which the different administrators received their powers, and the absence of privity between them, and that the imputations against it were not greater than could be made against other "logical conclusions upon admitted legal principles." It is not necessary, therefore, to review in detail the argument of respondents.

[The Supreme Court reversing the Circuit Court of Appeals, held the Montana judgment was not binding in the later proceeding in the federal court in Massachusetts and allowed recovery of the fee.]

NOTES

1. It seems likely that if the issue were to arise today the Supreme Court would overrule Ingersoll v. Coram and hold that a judgment involving one administrator is binding on administrators appointed in other states. See Scoles and Hay, Conflict of Laws 884–890 (2d ed. 1992). The Supreme Court of the United States has held that if the same person is executor in two states an adverse judgment in one state will be recognized as binding in the other state.

2. Nash v. Benari, 117 Me. 491, 105 A. 107 (1918). The decedent died domiciled in Massachusetts and Benari was appointed the domiciliary administrator in Massachusetts and the ancillary administrator in Maine. The plaintiff recovered judgment in Massachusetts against Benari, as domiciliary administrator, on an alleged debt owed her by the decedent. This judgment being largely unsatisfied, the plaintiff brought action on the original claim against Benari, as ancillary administrator, in Maine. He claimed by way of defense that this claim had been merged in the Massachusetts judgment. Held for the plaintiff. There is no privity between administrators for the same decedent appointed in different states. ". . . the fact that one and the same person is administrator in both states does not alter the doctrine." Accord: Wisemantle v. Hull Enterprises, Inc., 103 Ill.App.3d 878, 59 Ill.Dec. 827, 432 N.E.2d 613 (1981).

3. According to the majority rule, when a claimant brings suit against an administrator to recover on an alleged debt owed by the decedent and loses, the claimant will thereafter be precluded from bringing an action on the same claim against another administrator in a second state. Restatement, Second, Conflict of Laws § 357.

4. Section 4–401 of the Uniform Probate Code provides that "An adjudication rendered in any jurisdiction in favor of or against any personal representative of the estate is as binding on the local personal representative as if he were a party to the adjudication."

DISTRIBUTION, TAXES, AND PLANNING

Distribution. The domiciliary representative distributes the net estate in his hands after payment of debts and expenses to those entitled to it. The ancillary representative may, subject to the order of the court, transmit the net estate in his hands to the domiciliary representative, or he may turn the net proceeds over to the distributees directly when this is the fair and economical thing to do. The distribution may be made more complex by the assertion of nonbarrable interests or the necessity of election. See, generally, D. Currie, The Multiple Personality of the Dead: Executors, Administrators and the Conflict of Laws, 33 U.Chi.L.Rev. 429 (1966).

Taxes. Problems of disputed domicile in relation to state succession taxes are discussed at pp. 15–16, supra. There are also problems on the apportionment of the burden of the federal estate tax, as the following decision illustrates:

In Gellerstedt v. United Missouri Bank of Kansas City, 865 S.W.2d 707 (Mo.App.1993), the decedent had died domiciled in Missouri. Her will, executed some seventeen years earlier while domiciled in Kansas, was silent as to the allocation of state and federal tax burdens. The defendant bank paid the federal estate tax, thereafter made distribution to specific distributees but did not deduct a prorata portion of the tax liability. Plaintiff seeks a declaratory judgment to the effect that the tax should be prorated among all of the recipients under the will (the Missouri rule) and not be borne solely by the residue (the Kansas rule). The court selected the law of the testator's domicile at death but noted that "such law should not be blindly and mechanically applied. It may be that in some cases the application of the law of domicile at death would produce an absurd and inequitable result, or one that clearly would have been abhorrent to the testator."

Estate Planning. Estate planning with attention to conflict of laws is considered in Casner, Estate Planning ch. 16 (4th ed. 1980); Ester and Scoles, Estate Planning and Conflict of Laws, 24 Ohio S.L.J. 270 (1963); Scoles and Rheinstein, Conflict Avoidance in Succession Planning, 21 Law and Contemp.Prob. 427 (1956).

See generally Scoles and Hay, Conflict of Laws 853–872 (2d ed. 1992).

SECTION 2. DEBTORS' ESTATES *

INTRODUCTION NOTE

The Federal Bankruptcy Act with its national reach has, for the most part, supplanted the old system of administration of insolvent estates through state court receiverships and so has obliterated interstate conflicts problems. The Act does not apply to municipal, insurance or banking corporations and building and loan associations. As to them the old problems of interstate conflicts continue and are similar, in large part, to those arising in decedents' estates. Often the liquidator is elevated from the position of a receiver to that of a "statutory successor" and given the enlarged rights in other states that cases in this section reveal. The section is directed principally to the rights of foreign creditors and of foreign liquidators, especially statutory successors. To the last, the full faith and credit clause gives important protection.

Blake v. McClung

Supreme Court of the United States, 1898.
172 U.S. 239, 19 S.Ct. 165, 43 L.Ed. 432.

[The Embreeville Company, a British corporation, qualified to do business in Tennessee under a statute of the state which contained this provision:

"... creditors who may be residents of this State shall have a priority in the distribution of assets ... over all simple contract creditors, being residents of any other country or countries, ..." The corporation acquired property in Tennessee. In a proceeding in a court of the state it was alleged that the corporation was insolvent and a receiver of its property in the state was appointed. Several classes of creditors filed claims against the corporation in the receivership proceedings. They included British creditors, Ohio individual creditors, a Virginia corporation, and residents of Tennessee. The state court applied the statute quoted above so as to give the Tennessee creditors priority over all the others. The state court judgment was appealed to the Supreme Court of the United States.]

■ JUSTICE HARLAN delivered the opinion of the court....

The plaintiffs in error contend that the judgment of the state court, based upon the statute, denies to them rights secured by the second section of the Fourth Article of the Constitution of the United States providing that "the citizens of each State shall be entitled to all privileges and immunities of citizens in the several States," as well as by the first section of the Fourteenth Amendment, declaring that no State shall "deprive any

---

* See Restatement, Second, Conflict of Laws §§ 367–423.

person of life, liberty or property without due process of law," nor "deny to any person within its jurisdiction the equal protection of the laws." . . .

The suggestion is made that as the statute refers only to "residents," there is no occasion to consider whether it is repugnant to the provision of the National Constitution relating to citizens. We cannot accede to this view. . . . The State did not intend to place creditors, citizens of other States, upon an equality with creditors, citizens of Tennessee, and to give priority only to Tennessee creditors over creditors who resided in, but were not citizens of, other States. The manifest purpose was to give to all Tennessee creditors priority over all creditors residing out of that State, whether the latter were citizens or only residents of some other State or country. . . .

We hold such discrimination against citizens of other States to be repugnant to the second section of the Fourth Article of the Constitution of the United States, although, generally speaking, the State has the power to prescribe the conditions upon which foreign corporations may enter its territory for purposes of business. Such a power cannot be exerted with the effect of defeating or impairing rights secured to citizens of the several States by the supreme law of the land. . . .

It may be appropriate to observe that the objections to the statute of Tennessee do not necessarily embrace enactments that are found in some of the States requiring foreign insurance corporations, as a condition of their coming into the State for purposes of business, to deposit with the state treasurer funds sufficient to secure policy holders in its midst. Legislation of that character does not present any question of discrimination against citizens forbidden by the Constitution. Insurance funds set apart in advance for the benefit of home policy holders of a foreign insurance company doing business in the State are a trust fund of a specific kind to be administered for the exclusive benefit of certain persons. . . .

As to the plaintiff in error, the Hull Coal & Coke Company of Virginia, different considerations must govern our decision. It has long been settled that, for purposes of suit by or against it in the courts of the United States, the members of a corporation are to be conclusively presumed to be citizens of the state creating such corporation . . . ; and therefore it has been said that a corporation is to be deemed, for such purposes, a citizen of the state under whose laws it was organized. But it is equally well settled, and we now hold, that a corporation is not a citizen within the meaning of the constitutional provision that "the citizens of each state shall be entitled to all privileges and immunities of citizens in the several states". . . . The Virginia corporation, therefore, cannot invoke that provision for protection against the decree of the state court denying its right to participate upon terms of equality with Tennessee creditors in the distribution of the assets of the British corporation in the hands of the Tennessee court.

Since, however, a corporation is a "person," within the meaning of the fourteenth amendment . . . may not the Virginia corporation invoke for its protection the clause of the amendment declaring that no state shall deprive any person of property without due process, nor deny to any person within its jurisdiction the equal protection of the laws?

[T]his question must receive a negative answer.... this court has adjudged that the prohibitions of the fourteenth amendment refer to all the instrumentalities of the state, to its legislative, executive, and judicial authorities ... [But the] corporation was not, in any legal sense, deprived of its claim, nor was its right to reach the assets of the British corporation in other states or countries disputed. It was only denied the right to participate upon terms of equality with Tennessee creditors in the distribution of particular assets of another corporation doing business in that state....

It is equally clear that the Virginia corporation cannot rely upon the clause declaring that no state shall "deny to any person within its jurisdiction the equal protection of the laws." That prohibition manifestly relates only to the denial by the state of equal protection to persons "within its jurisdiction." ... Without attempting to state what is the full import of the words, "within its jurisdiction," it is safe to say that a corporation not created by Tennessee, nor doing business there under conditions that subjected it to process issuing from the courts of Tennessee at the instance of suitors, is not, under the above clause of the fourteenth amendment, within the jurisdiction of that state.... Nor do we think it came within the jurisdiction of Tennessee, within the meaning of the amendment, simply by presenting its claim in the state court, and thereby becoming a party to this cause....

What may be the effect of the judgment of this court in the present case upon the rights of creditors not residing in the United States it is not necessary to decide. Those creditors are not before the court on this writ of error. The final judgment of the supreme court of Tennessee must be affirmed as to the Hull Coal & Coke Company ... Rev.St. § 709. As to the other plaintiffs in error, citizens of Ohio, the judgment must be reversed, and the cause remanded for further proceedings not inconsistent with this opinion. It is so ordered.

■ JUSTICE BREWER, with whom CHIEF JUSTICE FULLER concurred, dissenting....

NOTES

1. On the rights of a corporate creditor under the equal protection of the laws clause, see Kentucky Finance Corp. v. Paramount Auto Exchange Corp., 262 U.S. 544 (1923), p. 995 infra.

2. The Federal Bankruptcy Act (11 U.S.C.A. § 508(d)) deals with international aspects and seeks to advance the policy of effectuating equal distribution between foreign and domestic creditors. It prohibits a creditor from receiving any distribution in the bankruptcy case after receiving payment of a portion of his claim in a foreign proceeding, until the other creditors in the bankruptcy case in this country entitled to share equally with that creditor have received as much as the latter has

in the foreign proceeding. On equality in distribution, compare Estate of Hanreddy, p. 944, supra, dealing with an insolvent decedent's estate.

3. "Both in Canada and the United States, the federal legislature has power to pass national bankruptcy legislation .... Internally, creditors are prevented from obtaining more than their equal share in the distribution of the assets of the insolvent debtors. Matters can work out differently on the so-called international level [through a local creditor attaching local assets] ... This need not be so, however. Under the American Bankruptcy Act a nonresident debtor may be adjudged a bankrupt in the United States courts if he has assets in the United States, and this notwithstanding a bankruptcy declared abroad. An attachment or garnishment obtained within the four months preceding the American bankruptcy may be voided ... if the attaching or garnishing creditor does not relinquish his preference, an adjudication in bankruptcy in the United States becomes necessary. The result is concurrent bankruptcies in Canada and the United States ... In such a case, under an amendment to the American Bankruptcy Act, in force since September 25, 1963, the bankruptcy court has power to suspend the exercise of its jurisdiction in view of the bankruptcy pending abroad. A finding that the local creditors will obtain their equal share in the foreign bankruptcy may lead to a suspension of the proceedings after the local assets have been turned over to the foreign trustee in bankruptcy." Nadelmann, Bankruptcy in Canada: Assets in New York, 11 Am.J.Comp.L. 628, 629–630 (1962); see also Booth, Recognition of Foreign Bankruptcies: An analysis and Critique of the Inconsistent Approaches of United States Courts, 66 Am.Bank.L.J. 135 (1992).

Similar questions arise in bankruptcy proceedings in the European Union. Since 1963 European Union member states have made several attempts to negotiate a convention whereby a bankruptcy adjudication in one state would be recognized by all other members. Nadelmann, Bankruptcy Jurisdiction: News from the Common Market and a Reflection for Home Consumption, 56 Am.Bank.L.J. 65 (1982); also, Kim, International Insolvencies: an English–American Comparison with an Analysis of Proposed Solutions, 26 GW J.Int'l L. & Econ. 1 (1992).

Morris v. Jones

Supreme Court of the United States, 1947.
329 U.S. 545, 67 S.Ct. 451, 91 L.Ed. 488, 168 A.L.R. 656.

Certiorari to the Supreme Court of Illinois.

■ JUSTICE DOUGLAS delivered the opinion of the Court.

This case presents a substantial question under the Full Faith and Credit Clause (Art. IV, § 1) of the Constitution.

Chicago Lloyds, an unincorporated association, was authorized by Illinois to transact an insurance business in Illinois and other States. It qualified to do business in Missouri. In 1934 petitioner sued Chicago Lloyds in a Missouri court for malicious prosecution and false arrest. In 1938, before judgment was obtained in Missouri, respondent's predecessor was appointed by an Illinois court as statutory liquidator for Chicago Lloyds. The Illinois court fixed a time for the filing of claims against Chicago Lloyds and issued an order staying suits against it. Petitioner had notice of the stay order but nevertheless continued to prosecute the Missouri suit. At the instance of the liquidator, however, counsel for

Chicago Lloyds withdrew from the suit and did not defend it, stating to the Missouri court that the Illinois liquidation proceedings had vested all the property of Chicago Lloyds in the liquidator. Thereafter petitioner obtained a judgment in the Missouri court and filed an exemplified copy of it as proof of his claim in the Illinois proceedings. An order disallowing the claim was sustained by the Illinois Supreme Court against the contention that its allowance was required by the Full Faith and Credit Clause. People ex rel. Jones v. Chicago Lloyds, 391 Ill. 492, 63 N.E.2d 479....

First. We can put to one side, as irrelevant to the problem at hand, several arguments which have been pressed upon us. We are not dealing here with any question of priority of claims against the property of the debtor. For in this proceeding petitioner is not seeking, nor is respondent denying him, anything other than the right to prove his claim in judgment form. No question of parity of treatment of creditors, or the lack thereof (see Blake v. McClung, 172 U.S. 239), is in issue. Nor is there involved in this case any challenge to the Illinois rule, which follows Relfe v. Rundle, 103 U.S. 222, that title to all the property of Chicago Lloyds, wherever located, vested in the liquidator. Nor do we have here a challenge to the possession of the liquidator either through an attempt to obtain a lien on the property or otherwise. As pointed out in Riehle v. Margolies, 279 U.S. 218, 224, the distribution of assets of a debtor among creditors ordinarily has a "two-fold aspect." It deals "directly with the property" when it fixes the time and manner of distribution. No one can obtain part of the assets or enforce a right to specific property in the possession of the liquidation court except upon application to it. But proof and allowance of claims are matters distinct from distribution. They do not "deal directly with any of the property." "The latter function, which is spoken of as the liquidation of a claim is strictly a proceeding in personam." Id., p. 224. The establishment of the existence and amount of a claim against the debtor in no way disturbs the possession of the liquidation court, in no way affects title to the property, and does not necessarily involve a determination of what priority the claim should have....

Moreover, we do not have here a situation like that involved in Pendleton v. Russell, 144 U.S. 640, where it was sought to prove in a New York receivership of a dissolved corporation a judgment obtained in Tennessee after dissolution. The proof was disallowed, dissolution having operated, like death, as an abatement of the suit. No such infirmity appears to be present in the Missouri judgment; and the Illinois Supreme Court did not hold that the appointment of a liquidator for Chicago Lloyds operated as an abatement of the suit.... The Missouri judgment represents a liability for acts committed by Chicago Lloyds, not for those of the liquidator. The claims for which the Illinois assets are being administered are claims against Chicago Lloyds. The Missouri judgment represents one of them. There is no more reason for discharging a liquidator from the responsibility for defending pending actions than there is for relieving a receiver of that task. Riehle v. Margolies, supra.

Second. "A judgment of a court having jurisdiction of the parties and of the subject matter operates as res judicata, in the absence of fraud or collusion, even if obtained upon a default." Riehle v. Margolies, supra, p. 225 .... The full faith and credit to which a judgment is entitled is the credit which it has in the State from which it is taken, not the credit that under other circumstances and conditions it might have had. Moreover, the question whether a judgment is entitled to full faith and credit does not depend on the presence of reciprocal engagements between the States....

As to respondent's contention that the Illinois decree, of which petitioner had notice, should have been given full faith and credit by the Missouri court, only a word need be said. Roche v. McDonald [p. 305 supra], makes plain that the place to raise that defense was in the Missouri proceedings. And see Treinies v. Sunshine Mining Co., [p. 286 supra]. And whatever might have been the ruling on the question, the rights of the parties could have been preserved by a resort to this Court which is the final arbiter of questions arising under the Full Faith and Credit Clause. Williams v. State of North Carolina, [p. 851, supra]. In any event the Missouri judgment is res judicata as to the nature and amount of petitioner's claim as against all defenses which could have been raised....

It is finally suggested that since the Federal Bankruptcy Act provides for exclusive adjudication of claims by the bankruptcy court and excepts insurance companies from the Act (§ 4, 52 Stat. 840, 845, 11 U.S.C. § 22; ...), the state liquidators of insolvent insurance companies should have the same control over the determination of claims as the bankruptcy court has. This is to argue that by reason of its police power a State may determine the method and manner of proving claims against property which is in its jurisdiction and which is being administered by its courts or administrative agencies. We have no doubt that it may do so except as such procedure collides with the federal Constitution or an Act of Congress.... There is such a collision here. When we look to the general statute which Congress has enacted pursuant to the Full Faith and Credit Clause, we find no exception in case of liquidations of insolvent insurance companies. The command is to give full faith and credit to every judgment of a sister State. And where there is no jurisdictional infirmity, exceptions have rarely, if ever, been read into the constitutional provision or the Act of Congress in cases involving money judgments rendered in civil suits....

The function of the Full Faith and Credit Clause is to resolve controversies where state policies differ. Its need might not be so greatly felt in situations where there was no clash of interests between the States. The argument of convenience in administration is at best only another illustration of how the enforcement of a judgment of one State in another State may run counter to the latter's policies. But the answer given by Fauntleroy v. Lum [p. 302 supra], is conclusive. If full faith and credit is not given in that situation, the Clause and the statute fail where their need is the greatest. The argument of convenience, moreover, proves too much. In the first place, it would often be equally appealing to individuals or corporations engaging in multistate activities which might well prefer to defend law suits at home. In the second place, against the convenience of the administration of assets in Illinois is the hardship on the Missouri creditor if he were forced to drop his Missouri litigation, bring his witnesses to Illinois, and start all over again. But full faith and credit is a more inexorable command; its applicability does not turn on a balance of convenience as between litigants. If this were a situation where Missouri's policy would result in the dismemberment of the Illinois estate so that Illinois creditors would go begging, Illinois would have such a large interest at stake as to prevent it. See Clark v. Williard [p. 964, infra]. But, as we have said, proof and allowance of claims are matters distinct from distribution of assets.

The single point of our decision is that the nature and amount of petitioner's claim has been conclusively determined by the Missouri judgment and may not be relitigated in the Illinois proceedings, it not appearing that the Missouri court lacked jurisdiction over either the parties or the subject matter....

Reversed.

■ JUSTICE FRANKFURTER, with whom concur JUSTICE BLACK and JUSTICE RUTLEDGE, dissenting.

[T]he real issue is this. May Illinois provide that when an insurance concern to which Illinois has given life can, in the judgment of the State courts, no longer be allowed to conduct the insurance business in Illinois, the State may take over the local assets of such an insurance concern for fair distribution among all who have claims against the defunct concern? May the State, pursuant to such a policy, announce in advance, as a rule of fairness, that all claims not previously reduced to valid judgment, no matter how or where they arose, if they are to be paid out of assets thus administered by the State, must be proven on their merits to the satisfaction of Illinois? And may the State specify that this mode of proof apply also to out-of-State creditors so as to require such creditors to prove the merit of their claims against the Illinois assets in liquidation as though they were Illinois creditors, and preclude them from basing their claims merely on a judgment against the insurance concern, obtained after it had legally ceased to be, and after its Illinois assets had by appropriate proceedings passed into ownership of an Illinois liquidator?

... The Full Faith and Credit Clause does not eat up the powers reserved to the States by the Constitution. That clause does not embody an absolutist conception of mechanical applicability. As is so often true of constitutional problems, an accommodation must be struck between different provisions of the Constitution. When rights are asserted in one State on the basis of a judgment procured in another, it frequently becomes necessary, as it does here, to define the duty of the courts of the former State in view of that State's power to regulate its own affairs.... Surely, the Full Faith and Credit Clause does not require a State to give an advantage to persons dwelling without, when State policy may justifiably restrict its own citizens to a particular procedure in proving claims against a State fund....

Precedent and policy sustain the right of Illinois to have each claimant prove his fair share to the assets in Illinois by the same procedure.... Of course Missouri has a right to provide for its methods of administration, in case of default, as to Missouri assets. But we are not here concerned with an attempt to enforce the Missouri judgment against Missouri assets....

... The precise relation of the liquidator's legal position to the Missouri judgment, on the basis of which Morris asserts a claim against the liquidator's assets, reinforces the more general considerations. Morris had no judgment against the company when by Illinois law title to Lloyds' assets passed to the liquidator.... The liquidator, as trustee for the creditors of the extinct Illinois company, represented interests that were not the same as those represented by the extinct company when it conducted its own business. In short, the Illinois liquidator was thus a stranger to the Missouri judgment and it cannot be invoked against him in Illinois.... Indeed, to subject the assets of the Illinois liquidator to the claim of a judgment obtained against Lloyds in Missouri subsequent to the passage of those assets to the liquidator may well raise constitutional questions. Riley v. New York Trust Co. [p. 242 supra].

... Against the claim of out-of-State creditors must be set not merely the interests of Illinois creditors, but also the importance of a unified liquidation administration, the burden to the liquidator of defending suits anywhere in the United States, and the resulting hazards to a fair distribution of the estate.... The resolution of this conflict so that the out-of-State creditor must take his place with the Illinois creditors is another instance of a price to be paid for our federalism ...

This is not to say that the Missouri judgment is invalid. Whether recovery may be based on this judgment in Missouri, or in any other State except Illinois or even in Illinois should the assets go out of the State's hands and return to a reanimated Chicago Lloyds, are questions that do not now call for consideration.

The judgment should be affirmed.

NOTES

1. Can Pendleton v. Russell, discussed by Justice Douglas in his opinion, satisfactorily be distinguished from Morris v. Jones?

2. Restatement, Second, Conflict of Laws: *

§ 299. Termination or Suspension of Corporate Existence

(1) Whether the existence of a corporation has been terminated or suspended is determined by the local law of the state of incorporation.

(2) The termination or suspension of a corporation's existence by the state of incorporation will be recognized for most purposes by other states.

* Quoted with the permission of the copyright owner, The American Law Institute.

Comment ...

e. Statute of state of incorporation extending life of corporation. To facilitate collection by the corporation of its assets, and the assertion of creditors' claims against it, statutes commonly provide that for a period of time after the termination or suspension of the corporate existence, suits may be brought by or against the corporation. Likewise, such statutes usually permit the corporation to settle and discharge claims, to transfer its assets, and to do other acts incidental to the winding-up of its affairs.

A corporation whose existence has been terminated or suspended will usually be permitted to exercise in another state such powers as are accorded it by the state of incorporation even though the other state does not give similar powers to domestic corporations....

f. Statute of other state making corporation subject to suit after termination or suspension of existence. Primarily for the purpose of saving local creditors from the inconvenience of having to present their claims in the state of incorporation, statutes sometimes provide that foreign corporations which own things or do business in the state can sue, and remain subject to suit, in the corporate name for a period after their existence has been terminated or suspended. Even if there is no similar statute in the state of incorporation, such a statute will permit suit to be brought in the state of enactment to wind up the corporation's business in that state or to proceed against corporate property located there....

Reporter's Note: ...

Whether full faith and credit should require extraterritorial enforcement of a judgment rendered against a dissolved foreign corporation under a statute of a State where the corporation did business depends upon which of two considerations is the weightier. The first is the desirability of having a unified winding-up of the corporation's affairs. This can best be achieved by limiting the effect of such statutes to property located within the particular State so as to permit the state of incorporation to insist that, in general, claims against the corporation must be proved before its courts. The second consideration is the convenience of the corporation's creditors who would usually prefer to prove their claims at home and might find it a serious hardship to be compelled to do so in the state of incorporation....

MARTYNE v. AMERICAN UNION FIRE INSURANCE CO., 216 N.Y. 183, 110 N.E. 502 (1915): [The American Union Fire Insurance Company was a Pennsylvania corporation, authorized to carry on business in New York. In 1913, it was ordered dissolved in a court proceeding in Pennsylvania, and its liquidation was directed to be made by the insurance commissioner of that state. There was in force in Pennsylvania a statute which provided that on the dissolution of such a corporation, the insurance commissioner of the state "shall be vested by operation of law with title to all the property, contracts and rights of action of such corporation as of the date of the order so directing him to liquidate." As a result of the dissolution, the policies of fire insurance issued by the corporation became void. After the dissolution, the present action was instituted in New York for the return of unearned premiums under some of the canceled policies, and an alleged indebtedness to the corporation or to the insurance commissioner was attached. A few days later, the New York superintendent of insurance was appointed liquidator of the corporation under the insurance law of New York.

The Pennsylvania insurance commissioner appeared specially in the New York action and moved to have the garnishment and all other proceedings in the action set aside. The trial court granted the motion, and the order was affirmed by the Appellate Division. Appeal, with certain questions of law certified.]

■ CHASE, J. This action is brought against a corporation that has ceased to exist as such....

The insurance commissioner of Pennsylvania is a statutory liquidator and as such took the title to all of the corporate property of the dissolved corporation. The title of foreign statutory assignees is recognized and enforced where it can be without injustice. (Matter of Waite, 99 N.Y. 433, 2 N.E. 440; Relfe v. Rundle, 103 U.S. 222. See 237 U.S. 531.) ...

... The rule in this state seems to be so thoroughly established that the title of an assignee or receiver under involuntary or bankruptcy proceedings in a foreign state will not be upheld as against an attachment obtained and served by a resident of this state, that perhaps it should not be changed except by an act of the legislature.

To hold, however, in this case that the title which vested by the Statutes of Pennsylvania in the insurance superintendent of that state as a statutory liquidator does not extend to property in this state as against an attaching creditor here, would be to extend the rule which permits a local creditor to ignore the laws of a foreign state. We are of the opinion that the plaintiff and those from whom he received assignments of claims against the dissolved corporation have no equity that should prevent enforcing the general rule of comity in this case....

The order should be affirmed, with costs....

CLARK v. WILLIARD, 292 U.S. 112, 54 S.Ct. 615, 78 L.Ed. 1160 (1934): [An Iowa insurance company was adjudged insolvent and ordered dissolved in a state court proceeding in Iowa, and pursuant to a statute of Iowa the state commissioner of insurance was adjudged "the successor to said corporation" and as such to hold "title to all property owned by [the corporation] at the time it so ceased to exist." The Iowa insurance company had been authorized to do business in Montana under a statute providing in effect that the dissolution of a domestic or foreign corporation did not impair any remedy against the corporation for a liability previously incurred. Two creditors had brought an action in a Montana state court against the Iowa corporation prior to its dissolution and recovered a judgment by default after the dissolution.

Another creditor then brought a suit in a Montana state court against the corporation and the Iowa liquidator in which he prayed for an ancillary receivership and a receiver was appointed. The judgment creditors mentioned above then filed a petition for leave to satisfy their judgment out of Montana assets, and the Iowa liquidator filed a cross-petition asserting his title as statutory successor to the dissolved corporation and urging that his title should be recognized under the full faith and credit clause. The Montana Supreme Court held that the Iowa liquidator was only an equity receiver, and that as against such a liquidator the Montana creditors were entitled to satisfy their claims out of Montana assets. On certiorari, the Supreme Court of the United States vacated the state court decree and remanded the cause to the Supreme Court of Montana for further proceedings not inconsistent with its opinion.]

■ JUSTICE CARDOZO.... The question is whether full faith and credit has been given by the courts of Montana to the statutes and judicial proceedings of the state of Iowa....

We assume in accordance with the decision of the Montana court that the respondents' action against the surety company did not abate on dissolution, but was lawfully pursued to judgment.... But this ... is only a partial statement of the problem. To ascertain the procedure by which the [judgment] is to be enforced, whether by the levy of execution or by a ratable division, other considerations must be weighed. In particular, it must be known whether superior interests or titles have developed between the summons and the judgment, and whether the quality or operation of those interests affects the method of distribution. Something did intervene here, the appointment of a liquidator under the statutes of the domicile. That much is undisputed. Did the Supreme Court of Montana misjudge the quality and operation of this intervening interest, and in so doing did it deny to the statutes and decrees of Iowa the faith and credit owing to them under the Constitution of the United States?

In our judgment, the statutes of Iowa have made the official liquidator the successor to the corporation, and not a mere receiver.... His title is not the consequence of a decree of a court whereby a corporation still in being has made a compulsory assignment of its assets with a view to liquidation.... His title is the consequence of a succession established for the corporation by the law of its creation.... So the lawmakers have plainly said. So the Iowa court adjudged in decreeing dissolution.

We think the Supreme Court of Montana denied full faith and credit to the statutes and judicial proceedings of Iowa in holding, as it did, that the petitioner was a receiver deriving title through a judicial proceeding, and not through the charter of its being and the succession there prescribed....

In thus holding we do not say that there is an invariable rule by which the title of a statutory liquidator must prevail over executions and attachments outside of the state of his appointment. The subject is involved in confusion, with decisions pro and con....

Whether there is in Montana a local policy, expressed in statute or decision, whereby judgments and attachments have a preference over the title of a charter liquidator, is a question as to which the Supreme Court of that state will speak with ultimate authority.

NOTES

1. When the cause was remanded to the Supreme Court of Montana, that court by a divided vote again held the judgment creditors had priority over the Iowa statutory liquidator because Montana's law permitted attachments on property in Montana of insolvent corporations, both domestic and foreign, for which a statutory liquidator had been appointed. Mieyr v. Federal Surety Co., 97 Mont. 503, 34 P.2d 982 (1934). The Supreme Court of the United States affirmed this decision. "Iowa may say that one who is a liquidator with title, appointed by her statutes, shall be so recognized in Montana with whatever rights and privileges accompany such recognition according to Montana law ... Iowa may not say ... that a liquidator with title who goes into Montana may set at naught Montana law as to the distribution of Montana assets, and carry over into another state the rule of distribution prescribed by the statutes of the domicile." Clark v. Williard, 294 U.S. 211 (1935).

2. In Relfe v. Rundle, 103 U.S. 222 (1880), a Missouri insurance company had been dissolved under the law of Missouri and its property vested in the Missouri State Superintendent of Insurance. The Missouri Superintendent of Insurance had himself made a party defendant to a suit which had been instituted in Louisiana against this insurance company. Held, this is proper, and the Superintendent can remove the suit to the federal court in Louisiana on the ground of diversity of citizenship. "Relfe is not an officer of the Missouri state court.... He was the statutory successor of the Corporation for the purpose of winding up its affairs.... He is an officer of the State, and as such represents the State in its sovereignty while performing its public duties connected with the winding up of the affairs of one of its insolvent and dissolved corporations."

Converse v. Hamilton

Supreme Court of the United States, 1912.
224 U.S. 243, 32 S.Ct. 415, 56 L.Ed. 749, Am.Ann.Cas.1913D, 1292.

[A creditor of a Minnesota corporation brought a suit in a Minnesota state court against the corporation for the sequestration of its property and the appointment of a receiver. The court found the corporation was insolvent, appointed a receiver, and ascertained it was necessary to resort to the double liability of the stockholders imposed by Minnesota law for the payment of the creditors. The court then levied upon the corporation's stockholders assessments amounting to 100 per cent. of the par value of their shares, and directed the receiver to prosecute such actions within or without the state as were necessary to enforce the assessment.

The present actions were brought by the Minnesota receiver in Wisconsin against Wisconsin stockholders of the corporation to recover the assessments. The Wisconsin stockholders had not been made parties to the Minnesota suit and were not notified, otherwise than by publication or by mail, of the application for the orders levying the assessments. The Wisconsin court refused to enforce the assessments because they were contrary to Wisconsin policy. The receiver sued out writs of error to the Supreme Court of the United States.]

■ JUSTICE VAN DEVANTER delivered the opinion of the court.... This liability is not to the corporation but to the creditors collectively, is not penal but contractual, is not joint but several, and the mode and means of its enforcement are subject to legislative regulation....

The proceedings in the sequestration suit, looking to the enforcement of this liability, were had under chapter 272, Laws of 1899, and sections 3814–3190, Revised Laws of 1905, the latter being a continuation of the former with changes not here material.... It expressly prescribed the mode of enforcement pursued in the present instance; that is to say, it made provision for bringing all the creditors into the sequestration suit, for the presentation and adjudication of their claims, for ascertaining the relation of the corporate debts and the expenses of the receivership to the available assets, and whether and to what extent it was necessary to resort to the stockholders' double liability for levying such assessments upon the stockholders according to their respective holdings as should be necessary to pay the debts, and for investing the receiver with authority to collect the assessments on behalf of the creditors....

Under this statute, as interpreted by the Supreme Court of the State, as also by this court, the receiver is not an ordinary chancery receiver or arm of the court appointing him, but a quasi-assignee and representative of the creditors, and when the order levying the assessment is made he becomes invested with the creditors' rights of action against the stockholders and with full authority to enforce the same in any court of competent jurisdiction in the State or elsewhere.

The constitutional validity of chapter 272 has been sustained by the Supreme Court of the State, as also by this court; and this because (1) the statute is but a reasonable regulation of the mode and means of enforcing the double liability assumed by those who become stockholders in a Minnesota corporation; (2) while the order levying the assessment is made conclusive, as against all stockholders, of all matters relating to the amount and propriety of the assessment and the necessity therefor, one against whom it is sought to be enforced is not precluded from showing that he is not a stockholder, or is not the holder of as many shares as is alleged, or has a claim against the corporation which in law or equity he is entitled to set off against the assessment, or has any other defense personal to himself, and (3) while the order is made conclusive as against a stockholder, even although he may not have been a party to the suit in which it was made and may not have been notified that an assessment was contemplated, this is not a tenable objection, for the order is not in the nature of a personal judgment against the stockholder and as to him is amply sustained by the presence in that suit of the corporation, considering his relation to it and his contractual obligation in respect of its debts....

This statement of the nature of the liability in question, of the laws of Minnesota bearing upon its enforcement, and of the effect which judicial proceedings under those laws have in that State, discloses, as we think, that in the cases now before us the Supreme Court of Wisconsin failed to give full faith and credit to those laws and to the proceedings thereunder, upon which the receiver's right to sue was grounded. It is true that an ordinary chancery receiver is a mere arm of the court appointing him, is invested with no estate in the property committed to his charge, and is clothed with no power to exercise his official duties in other jurisdictions.... But here the receiver was not merely an ordinary chancery receiver, but much more. By the proceedings in the sequestration suit, had conformably to the laws of Minnesota, he became a quasi-assignee and representative of the creditors, was invested with their rights of action against the stockholders, and was charged with the enforcement of those rights in the courts of that State and elsewhere. So when he invoked the aid of the Wisconsin court the case presented was, in substance, that of a trustee, clothed with adequate title for the occasion, seeking to enforce, for the benefit of his cestuis que trustent, a right of action, transitory, in character, against one who was liable contractually and severally, if at all....

In these circumstances we think the conclusion is unavoidable that the laws of Minnesota and the judicial proceedings in that State, upon which the receiver's title, authority and right to relief were grounded, and by which the stockholders were bound, were not accorded that faith and credit to which they were entitled under the Constitution and laws of the United States.

The judgments are accordingly reversed, and the cases are remanded for further proceedings not inconsistent with this opinion.

Reversed.

NOTE

On the law determining whether policyholders of a mutual insurance company are members of the company and hence are liable to pay assessments, see Pink v. A.A.A. Highway Express, Inc., 314 U.S. 201 (1941).

Broderick v. Rosner

Supreme Court of the United States, 1935.
294 U.S. 629, 55 S.Ct. 589, 79 L.Ed. 1100, 100 A.L.R. 1133.

■ JUSTICE BRANDEIS delivered the opinion of the Court.

Pursuant to article 8, section 7, of the Constitution of New York, its Banking Law (Consol.Laws, c. 2) provides, section 120: "The stockholders of every bank will be individually responsible, equally and ratably and not one for another, for all contracts, debts and engagements of the bank, to the extent of the amount of their stock therein, at the par value thereof, in addition to the amount invested in such shares."

The Bank of the United States is a corporation organized under the Banking Law of New York and had its places of business in New York City.

Its outstanding capital stock is $25,250,000 represented by 1,010,000 shares of $25 par value. On November 17, 1933, Joseph A. Broderick, as Superintendent of Banks of the State of New York, brought, in the Supreme Court of New Jersey, this action against 557 of its stockholders who are residents of New Jersey, to recover unpaid assessments levied by him upon them pursuant to law.

The defendant moved to strike out the complaint on the ground, among others, that, by reason of section 94b of the Corporation Act of New Jersey (2 Comp.St.1910, p. 1656), it failed to set out a cause of action enforceable in any court of that State. The section, first enacted March 30, 1897, provides: "No action or proceeding shall be maintained in any court of law in this state against any stockholder, officer or director of any domestic or foreign corporation by or on behalf of any creditor of such corporation to enforce any statutory personal liability of such stockholder, officer or director for or upon any debt, default or obligation of such corporation, whether such statutory personal liability be deemed penal or contractual, if such statutory personal liability be created by or arise from the statutes or laws of any other state or foreign country, and no pending or future action or proceeding to enforce such statutory personal liability shall be maintained in any court of this state other than in the nature of an equitable accounting for the proportionate benefit of all parties interested, to which such corporation and its legal representatives, if any, and all of its creditors and all of its stockholders shall be necessary parties."

Broderick seasonably claimed that to sustain the asserted bar of the statute would violate article 4, section 1, of the Federal Constitution, which provides that, "Full Faith and Credit shall be given in each State to the public Acts, Records and judicial Proceedings of every other State," and the legislation of Congress enacted pursuant thereto. The trial court sustained the motion to strike out the complaint, Broderick v. Abrams, 112 N.J.L. 309, 170 A. 214, on the ground that the statute of the State constituted a bar to the action. Judgment against the plaintiff, with costs, was entered in favor of each of the defendants, and the judgment was affirmed by the Court of Errors and Appeals "for the reasons expressed in the opinion" of the trial court. 113 N.J.L. 305, 174 A. 507. An appeal to this Court was allowed. Broderick v. Rosner, 293 U.S. 613.

First. The conditions imposed by section 94b of the New Jersey statute upon the bringing of suits to enforce such assessments, as here applied, deny to the Superintendent the right to resort to the courts of the State to enforce the assessment of liability upon the stockholders there resident. The requirement that the proceeding be by bill in equity, instead of by an action at law, would, if standing alone, be no obstacle. But by withholding jurisdiction unless the proceeding be a suit for an equitable accounting to which the "corporation and its legal representatives, if any, and all of its creditors and all of its stockholders shall be necessary parties," it imposes a condition which, as here applied, is legally impossible of fulfillment. For it is not denied that according to the decisions of the New Jersey courts "necessary parties" means those whose presence in a suit is essential as a jurisdictional prerequisite to the entry of judgment, so that no decree can be made respecting the subject-matter of litigation until they are before the court ... and that to secure jurisdiction personally over those who are not residents of New Jersey, or engaged in business there, is impossible.... The corporation has no place of business in New Jersey; only a few of the many stockholders and creditors have either residence or place of business there.

Moreover, even if it were legally possible to satisfy the statutory condition by making substituted service by publication upon non-resident stockholders and creditors ..., the cost would be prohibitive. The number of the stockholders is 20,843; the number of depositors and other creditors exceeds 400,000; and the amounts assessed against the individual defendants are relatively small—against some only $50. The aggregate of sheriff's fees alone as to the nonresident defendants, aside from expenses of publication and mailing, would exceed the aggregate amount due from the New Jersey stockholders. The suggestion, in the opinion of the Supreme Court, that leave might be granted to file a bill in equity is, therefore, without legal significance.

Second. But for the statute, the action would have been entertained.... The plaintiff is not, as in Booth v. Clark, 17 How. 322, 15 L.Ed. 164, a foreign receiver. He sues as an independent executive in whom has been vested by statute the cause of action sued on. Converse v. Hamilton, 224 U.S. 243, 257....

Third. The power of a State to determine the limits of the jurisdiction of its courts and the character of the controversies which shall be heard therein is subject to the limitations imposed by the Federal Constitution.... A "State cannot escape its constitutional obligations [under the full faith and credit clause] by the simple device of denying jurisdiction in such cases to courts otherwise competent." Kenney v. Supreme Lodge, [p. 310 supra] [3] ... it may not, under the guise of merely affecting the remedy, deny the enforcement of claims otherwise within the protection of the full faith and credit clause, when its courts have general jurisdiction of the subject-matter and the parties.... For the States of the Union, the constitutional limitation imposed by the full faith and credit clause abolished, in large measure, the general principle of international law by which local policy is permitted to dominate rules of comity.

Here the nature of the cause of action brings it within the scope of the full faith and credit clause. The statutory liability sought to be enforced is contractual in character. The assessment is an incident of the incorporation. Thus the subject-matter is peculiarly within the regulatory power of New York, as the State of incorporation.... In respect to the determination of liability for an assessment, the New Jersey stockholders submitted themselves to the jurisdiction of New York.... Obviously recognition could not be accorded to a local policy of New Jersey, if there really were

---

3. Chambers v. Baltimore & Ohio R. Co., 207 U.S. 142, is not to the contrary; there no claim was made under the full faith and credit clause. [Footnote by the Court.]

one, of enabling all residents of the State to escape from the performance of a voluntarily assumed statutory obligation, consistent with morality, to contribute to the payment of the depositors of a bank of another State of which they were stockholders.

Fourth. The fact that the assessment here in question was made under statutory direction by an administrative officer does not preclude the application of the full faith and credit clause. If the assessment had been made in a liquidation proceeding conducted by a court, New Jersey would have been obliged to enforce it, although the stockholders sued had not been made parties to the proceedings, and, being nonresidents, could not have been personally served with process. Converse v. Hamilton [p. 966 supra]. The reason why in that case the full faith and credit clause was held to require Wisconsin courts to enforce the assessment made in Minnesota was not because the determination was embodied in a judgment. Against the nonresident stockholders there had been no judgment in Minnesota. Wisconsin was required to enforce the Minnesota assessment because statutes are "public acts" within the meaning of the clause, Bradford Electric Light Co. v. Clapper, 286 U.S. 145, 155 [p. 343, supra]; Alaska Packers Association v. Industrial Accident Commission [294 U.S. 532 (1934)]; and because the residents of Wisconsin had, by becoming stockholders of a Minnesota corporation, submitted themselves to that extent, to the jurisdiction and laws of the latter State. Where a State has had jurisdiction of the subject-matter and the parties, obligations validly imposed upon them by statute must, within the limitations above stated, be given full faith and credit by all the other states....

Fifth. The Superintendent contends that his assessment is a "public act" within the meaning of the full faith and credit clause, and is entitled to receive in every other State of the Union, the same recognition accorded to it by the laws of New York. He insists that, while under the law of New York defenses personal to individual stockholders are open to them whenever and wherever sued, Selig v. Hamilton, 234 U.S. 652, 662, 663, his determinations as to the propriety and amount of the assessment, in so far as they involve merely the exercise of judgment, are conclusive; and are not subject to review by any court, except on grounds for which equity commonly affords relief against administrative orders.... Whether this contention is sound, we have no occasion to consider now.... It is sufficient to decide that, since the New Jersey courts possess general jurisdiction of the subject-matter and the parties, and the subject-matter is not one as to which the alleged public policy of New Jersey could be controlling, the full faith and credit clause requires that this suit be entertained.

Reversed.

■ JUSTICE CARDOZO is of the opinion that the judgment should be affirmed.

NOTE

See generally Cheatham, The Statutory Successor, The Receiver and the Executor in Conflict of Laws, 44 Colum.L.Rev. 549 (1944).

CHAPTER 13

AGENCY, PARTNERSHIPS AND CORPORATIONS

SECTION 1. AGENCY

INTRODUCTORY NOTE

A relationship of agency or of partnership may give rise to several choice-of-law problems: what law governs the rights and duties (a) of the principal and agent, or of the partners, as between themselves, (b) of the principal, or of the partnership and partners, on the one hand, and of some third person on the other, on account of one or more acts done on behalf of the principal or partnership by an agent, who in the case of a partnership will frequently be a partner, and (c) as between the agent and the third person on account of an act done by the agent. The second of these questions is the one primarily dealt with in this chapter. The third question is not considered, since the law governing a person's individual liability for an act is the same irrespective of whether he was acting for himself or for another.

YOUNG V. MASCI, 289 U.S. 253 (1933): Action brought by a New Yorker in a New Jersey court to recover for injuries suffered in an automobile accident in New York. The defendant, a New Jersey resident, had loaned his automobile in that state "without restriction upon its use" to one Balbino who drove the automobile into New York and there negligently injured the plaintiff. The New Jersey courts gave judgment to the plaintiff by application of a New York statute which made the "owner of a motor vehicle" liable for injuries caused by the negligence of any person operating the same with the "permission, express or implied, of such owner." The defendant appealed to the Supreme Court of the United States, contending that application of the New York statute under the circumstances violated due process. Affirmed. "When Young [the defendant] gave permission to drive his car to New York, he subjected himself to the legal consequences imposed by that state upon Balbino's negligent driving as fully as if he had stood in the relation of master to servant. A person who sets in motion in one state the means by which injury is inflicted in another may, consistently with the due process clause, be made liable for that injury whether the means employed be a responsible agent or an irresponsible instrument.... The power of the state to protect itself and its inhabitants is not limited by the scope of the doctrine of principal and agent.... No good reason is suggested why, when there is permission to take the automobile into a state for use upon its highways, personal liability should not be imposed upon the owner in case of injury inflicted there by the driver's negligence...."

Agency relationships are usually created by contract but they can arise otherwise. For example, one person may act at another's direction without any express agreement between them but the law may raise the existence of an agency or there may be a ratification by the principal of the alleged agent's acts. The obligations between principal and agent are determined, according to Restatement, Second, Conflict of Laws § 291, "by the local law of the state which, with respect to the particular issue, has the most significant relationship to the parties and the transaction under the principles stated in § 6." The law is selected by applying the rules set forth in Sections 187-188 with regard to contracts. Comment *f* to Section 291 states that "the state where performance by the agent is to take place will usually be given the greatest weight, in the absence of an effective choice of law by the parties (see § 187), in determining what law governs the rights and duties owed by the principal and agent to each other."

Consider again Young v. Masci, supra: may the state of injury impose its vicarious liability statute on a nonresident owner who had entrusted the car to the driver but expressly forbidden the driver from leaving the state? Judge Learned Hand said "no" in Scheer v. Rockne Motors Corp., 68 F.2d 942 (2d Cir.1934). Does this make sense? Also, it is not clear whether Judge Hand would require express or only implied authority. See Cavers, The Two "Local Law" Theories, 63 Harv.L.Rev. 822, 827-28 (1950).

Mercier v. John Hancock Mutual Life Insurance Co.

Supreme Court of Maine, 1945.
141 Me. 376, 44 A.2d 372.

■ MANSER, JUSTICE. [Action to recover on a life insurance policy, the application for which had been written in Maine. From a jury verdict in favor of the plaintiff, the insurance company appealed.]

The defendant Company contested payment upon the ground that [the insured] made false representations to the effect that no albumin or sugar had ever been found in his urine, and that he had never been told that he had symptoms of diabetes, when in truth he had been diabetic for ten years and had used the insulin treatment therefor. Also that he stated his brother was in good health, when he was at the time a patient in a tuberculosis sanitarium, and died soon thereafter....

. . .

The issues presented to the jury were whether there were, in fact, any material misrepresentations or concealments by or on behalf of the [insured]; whether the agent knew or was informed of the diabetes and took the responsibility of assuring the [insured] that it made no difference and need not be mentioned in the application; and again whether the agent failed to ask the question as to the health of the brother of the [insured], and instead assumed the responsibility of inserting a favorable answer.

The testimony was flatly contradictory. The instructions by the presiding Justice were clear and lucid upon the factual issues. It was for the jury to determine as to the credibility of witnesses and the weight of the evidence. The record would not warrant a ruling by this Court that the verdict was manifestly wrong.

This brings us to a consideration of the exceptions. [The defendant complained of the refusal of the trial judge to charge that the Maine statute, which provided that an insurance company could not rely as a defense on misrepresentations known to the agent, was not applicable because the insurance contract was a "Massachusetts contract".]

The question of whether the policy was, technically, a Maine or a Massachusetts contract was not passed upon by the presiding Justice or the jury. It did not need to be.

The situation presented here is simply whether the defendant Company is responsible for the acts of a duly authorized agent, licensed in the State of Maine, in connection with an application for insurance which he procured in Maine from a citizen thereof, when our statute says that such agent stands in the place of the Company with regard to all insurance effected by him.

In the Restatement of the Law upon the title Conflict of Laws, § 345, the rule is succinctly stated as follows:

"The law of the state in which an agent or a partner is authorized or apparently authorized to act for the principal or other partners determines whether an act done on account of the principal or other partners imposes a contractual duty upon the principal or other partners."

Then under the Comment, after discussing the effect of an agent's acts, we find the definite statement:

"But whether or not a particular act of the agent or partner is authorized, the law of the state where the act is done determines whether the principal is bound by a contract with a third person...."

Exceptions overruled.

Restatement, Second, Conflict of Laws: *

§ 292. Contractual Liability of Principal to Third Person

(1) Whether a principal is bound by action taken on his behalf by an agent in dealing with a third person is determined by the local law of the state which, with respect to the particular issue, has the most significant relationship to the parties and the transaction under the principles stated in § 6.

(2) The principal will be held bound by the agent's action if he would so be bound under the local law of the state where the agent dealt with the third person, provided at least that the principal had authorized the agent to act on his behalf in that state or had led the third person reasonably to believe that the agent had such authority.

NOTES

1. See generally Reese and Flesch, Agency and Vicarious Liability in Conflict of Laws, 60 Colum.L.Rev. 764 (1960); Hay and Müller–Freienfels, Agency in the Conflict of Laws and the 1978 Hague Convention, 27 Am.J.Comp.L. 1 (1979).

2. For a case applying the principles of the Restatement, Second, Conflict of Laws, to determine the law governing the liability of an undisclosed principal to the person with whom the agent dealt, see Shasta Livestock Auction Yard, Inc. v. Bill Evans Cattle Management Corp., 375 F.Supp. 1027 (D.Idaho 1974).

3. In state X, P authorizes A to manage P's farm in State X and to use the livestock on it as required. A drives the livestock to state Y and sells them to T, remitting the proceeds to P. By what law will it be determined whether A is liable to P for having exceeded the terms of his authority? By what law will it be determined whether T obtained title to the livestock? See Restatement, Second, Conflict of Laws §§ 291–292.

4. The law governing the agent's contract with the third person will usually be applied to determine whether the principal is bound by the contract and entitled to its benefits.

Maspons Y Hermano v. Mildred, L.R. 9 Q.B.D. 531 (1882). Defendants, a London firm, entered into an agreement with Demestre & Co. whereby defendants were to receive a cargo of tobacco for purposes of resale and were also to insure the cargo for the benefit of all concerned. Defendants realized that Demestre & Co. were acting in the capacity of agents but did not know the names of their principals, who in fact were the present plaintiffs, a Spanish firm carrying on business in Havana. The ship carrying the tobacco sank and plaintiffs brought suit for the proceeds of the insurance which had been paid to the defendants. The defense was that under Spanish law an undisclosed principal was not entitled to sue the person with whom his agent had contracted. Held, for the plaintiffs. Spanish law is material only for the purpose of determining the nature and extent of the authority given by plaintiffs to their agent. "The contract between Demestre & Co. and the defendants is governed by English law, not Spanish, and the persons who can sue

* Quoted with the permission of the copyright owner, The American Law Institute.

and be sued on that contract in England must also be determined by our law, and not by the law of Spain."

5. In the case of land, the law of the situs governs questions relating to the validity and effect of the deed executed by the agent. Clark v. Graham, 19 U.S. (6 Wheat.) 577 (1821); Restatement, Second, Conflict of Laws § 223. On the other hand, since a contract whereby a broker is authorized to buy or sell land does not create an interest in the land, the obligations owed by the principal and broker to each other under the contract are determined by the law governing the contract. This law may or may not be that of the state where the land is. Frankel v. Allied Mills, Inc., 369 Ill. 578, 17 N.E.2d 570 (1938); Johnson v. Allen, 108 Utah 148, 158 P.2d 134 (1945).

Ratification. A ratification by the principal of the agent's act will usually bind the principal if the ratification would be effective under the law of either (a) the state where the agent dealt with the third person or (b) the state whose law governs the principal-agent relationship. Restatement, Second, Conflict of Laws § 293. This is an example of an alternative reference rule to accomplish validation of the contract.

SECTION 2. PARTNERSHIPS AND OTHER ASSOCIATIONS

RESTATEMENT, SECOND, CONFLICT OF LAWS: *

§ 294. Relationship of Partners Inter Se

The rights and duties owed by partners to each other are determined by the local law of the state which, with respect to the particular issue, has the most significant relationship to the partners and the transaction under the principles stated in § 6. This law is selected by application of the rules of §§ 187–188.

NOTES

1. The paucity of conflict-of-laws cases involving the rights and duties owed by partners to each other is perhaps due in part to the nearly universal adoption of the Uniform Partnership Act.

2. Among the legal issues that arise between partners are questions as to the share of each partner in the control and profits of the business, the extent of their liabilities to one another, and the effect of death or withdrawal of a partner on continuation of the firm. Usually, the partnership will conduct its business in the state where it was organized. If so, the law of this state will be applied. If the partnership has little or no contact with the state of its organization, the courts have held that the applicable law is that of another state having a closer relation-

---

* Quoted with the permission of the copyright owner, The American Law Institute.

ship to the partnership. See, e.g., Teas v. Kimball, 257 F.2d 817 (5th Cir.1958); Wright v. Armwood, 107 A.2d 702 (D.D.C.1954).

Restatement, Second, Conflict of Laws: *

§ 295. Contractual Liability of Partnership, Partners and Third Person

(1) Whether a partnership is bound by action taken on its behalf by an agent in dealing with a third person is determined by the local law of the state selected by application of the rule of § 292.

(2) Whether a general partner is bound by action taken on behalf of the partnership by an agent in dealing with a third person is determined by the local law of the state selected by application of the rule of § 292.

(3) The liability of a limited partner for action taken on behalf of the partnership by an agent in dealing with a third person is determined by the local law of the state selected by application of the rule of § 294 [the law governing the relationship of partners inter se], unless the limited partner has taken a significant part in the control of the partnership business or has led the third person reasonably to believe that he was a general partner. In either of these latter events, the liability of the limited partner will be determined by application of the local law of the state selected by application of the rule of § 292.

First National Bank of Waverly v. Hall
Supreme Court of Pennsylvania, 1892.
150 Pa. 466, 24 A. 665, 30 Am.St.Rep. 823.

[Action against Hall and others on promissory notes signed by Crandall. The defendants and Crandall made in Pennsylvania a contract, with the following provisions: Crandall agreed to establish and operate under his sole control a toy factory in New York; the defendants agreed to furnish the necessary working capital, not to exceed three thousand dollars; the defendants were to receive 6 per cent per annum on all sums so furnished, and in addition 40 per cent of the net profits of the business; Crandall was to have the privilege to repay in installments the money so advanced and as the money was repaid the share of the net profits going to the defendants would be correspondingly reduced; the defendants should have a mortgage lien on the machinery and fixtures of the business to secure the repayment of the money advanced; and "nothing in this writing shall be construed to create a partnership between the respective parties except with respect to the net profits as herein provided." The notes sued upon were made by Crandall to a New York bank, apparently in New York, in connection with the operation of the business in that state.]

* Quoted with the permission of the copyright owner, The American Law Institute.

■ Opinion by JUSTICE HEYDRICK . . .

The plaintiff sues upon notes made by C.M. Crandall, one of the defendants, in his own name, and seeks to charge the other defendants as partners of Crandall in a business in which the proceeds of certain other notes, of which these were renewals, were used. . . .

[The court here outlined the agreement between Crandall and the defendants.] These provisions are all consistent with the relation of borrower and lender, and some of them are inconsistent with any other relation. It is therefore manifest that that relation was intended to be established; and the next question is whether, in spite of the intention of the parties, the community of interest in the profits constituted them a partnership as to creditors.

[The court held that this question should be determined by the law which governed the agreement between Crandall and the defendants and that this law was that of New York, the state where the toy factory was to be established. The court found that under the law of New York the agreement did not create a partnership as to third persons, and the judgment for the defendants was affirmed.]

Barrows v. Downs & Co.

Supreme Court of Rhode Island, 1870.
9 R.I. 446, 11 Am.Rep. 283.

These were two actions of assumpsit, one brought by Henry F. Barrows against the defendants, to recover the sum of $8,494.39 alleged to be due on book account for goods sold and delivered, and the other by the Meriden Britannia Company, upon a promissory note for $8,467.82, made by the said J.F. Downs & Co., and also to recover the sum of $1,142.09, alleged to be due on book account for goods sold and delivered.

Service of the writ in each of these cases was made solely upon William C. Downs, described therein as one of the co-partners of the firm of Joseph F. Downs & Co., the said Joseph F. Downs not being found within the state. . . .

■ POTTER, J. . . .

The plaintiffs rely on evidence that said William, while on a visit to this country, held himself out as a partner, and a general partner, in the firm.

The defendant denies these representations, and contends that he was only a special partner in the Havana firm, and under the Spanish law not liable as a general partner.

He testifies to a special partnership existing between him and Joseph for several years previous to 1866, the terms of which were, however, not reduced to writing until April, 1866, a copy of which he produces, and he also offers the evidence of A.F. Bramoso, a Spanish lawyer formerly of

Havana, but now of New York, that said verbal special partnership was valid there....

Being satisfied, ... that the partnership in Havana was a special one and authorized by Spanish law, the next inquiry is, what is the liability of William C. Downs, the special partner in this case.

The orders for these goods were by the general partner, Joseph, by letter or personally. No goods were ever ordered by William except once,— some ear-drops from Mr. Barrows.

Now, if the parties had remained in Havana, and the general partner had made contracts abroad by letter or otherwise, there can be no doubt but that the extent to which he could bind his copartners and make them liable for his acts, would depend upon the law of the place of the partnership; the extent to which they had made him their agent with power to bind them, would be regulated by the law of Cuba. And if the general partner himself went abroad, (the special partners remaining at home,) his authority to bind them would still be regulated by the law of Cuba....

But the plaintiffs offer evidence to show that the defendant, W.C. Downs, was in New York in the summer of 1865, and there represented himself as a partner, and, as they contend, a general partner in the firm. Of course, if he was actually a general partner, he would be liable for the whole amount.

And if he was not a general partner in fact, yet if he made such representations to these parties as to his interest in the concern, his responsibility, and his share in the profits, as to lead them to suppose he was a partner personally liable, and the goods or any portion of them were advanced on the strength of his representations, then he should be liable for all so advanced.

And this is the view we take from all the evidence in the case; that the defendant should be held liable for all the goods advanced after these representations made in the summer of 1865.

Judgment for plaintiffs for $2,054.61 and costs.

NOTES

1. In King v. Sarria, 69 N.Y. 24 (1877), the action was against a special partner of limited liability in a Cuban partnership on a contract made in New York. Cuba was Sarria's domicile and it was found that he had neither participated in managing the business nor held himself out as a general partner. The limitation on his liability was upheld by application of Cuban law. See also Gilman Paint & Varnish Co. v. Legum, 197 Md. 665, 80 A.2d 906 (1951). Cf. Uniform Limited Partnership Act § 303 (1976).

2. Section 901 of the Uniform Limited Partnership Act (1976) provides that "the laws of the state under which a foreign limited partnership is organized governs its organization and internal affairs and the liability of its limited partners."

3. For discussion of the choice-of-law problems relating to limited partnerships, see Note, 52 B.U.L.Rev. 64, 65–69 (1972); Vestal, A Comprehensive Uniform

Limited Partnership Act? The Time Has Come, 28 U.C.Davis L.Rev. 1195, 1233–34 (1995).

Greenspun v. Lindley

New York Court of Appeals, 1975.
36 N.Y.2d 473, 369 N.Y.S.2d 123, 330 N.E.2d 79.

■ JONES, J. In the circumstances of this case we conclude that holders of beneficial shares of interest in this real estate investment trust who desire to challenge investment decisions of the trustees and the payment by them of what are alleged to be excessive management fees must first make a demand on the trustees before commencing what is the equivalent of a shareholders' derivative action against the trustees individually.

Mony Mortgage Investors was organized as a business trust under the laws of the Commonwealth of Massachusetts to carry on business as a "real estate investment trust" as described in the REIT provisions of the Internal Revenue Code (§§ 856–858; US Code, tit 26, §§ 856–858)....

The declaration of trust, initially dated February 25, 1970, provides that there shall be no less than 3 and no more than 15 trustees, to be elected by the shareholders, except that a majority of the trustees shall not be affiliated with the manager to be employed for the transaction of the business of the trust. On April 6, 1970, the trustees approved a management contract with the Mutual Life Insurance Company of New York. At the time of the institution of the present action there were 11 trustees, 5 of whom were officers of the insurance company and 6 of whom were unaffiliated. The 11 trustees, the insurance company and the investment trust were all named as defendants.

The gravamen of the complaint, pleaded in conclusory terms only, is that in consequence of the subservience of the trustees to domination by the insurance company they are paying excessive management fees to the insurance company and make investment decisions only if the interest of the insurance company is thereby served, and that the investments so made are unsuitable for the purposes of the investment trust and inconsistent with its stated investment policy. Plaintiff seeks an accounting by defendants to the investment trust for damages sustained by the trust and for profits realized by defendants, together with counsel fees.

Defendants moved to dismiss the complaint, principally on the ground that plaintiff failed, prior to the commencement of the action, to make a demand on either the trustees or the other shareholders....

We hold, as did the Appellate Division, that the law of the Commonwealth of Massachusetts governs the disposition of the present motions.

The investment trust is a business trust organized and existing under the laws of Massachusetts. The declaration of trust, with which the shareholders became associated only by voluntary choice on the part of each of them, expressly provides that the law of Massachusetts shall be the applicable law as to the rights of all parties. Thus, prima facie Massachusetts law is applicable....

We conclude ... in the circumstances of this case that reference must be made to the authorities in the Commonwealth of Massachusetts to determine the rights of the parties in this litigation. In so holding we incidentally note the pragmatic as well as the theoretical advantages which would appear to flow from a conclusion that the rights of all shareholders of this real estate investment trust in comparable situations should be determined on a trust-wide basis rather than in consequence of the litigants' choice of forum or the assessment by several courts as to which State it is where the investment trust may be said to be present.

In deciding this case as we do, however, we expressly leave open what law we might apply were there proof from which it could properly be found, in consequence of significant contacts with New York State, that this investment trust, although a Massachusetts business trust, was nonetheless so "present" in our State as perhaps to call for the application of New York law. In that sense we reject any automatic application of the so-called "internal affairs" choice-of-law rule, under which the relationship between shareholders and trustees of a business trust by strict analogy to the relationship between shareholders and directors of a business corporation would be governed by the law of the State in which the business entity was formed.

Similarly we do not reach the question of what significance we would accord the explicit agreement of the parties that their rights are to be governed by Massachusetts law, were we disposed, entirely without reference to that provision of the declaration of trust, to apply the law of New York or the law of some State other than Massachusetts.

Turning then to the law of Massachusetts, we conclude ... that the courts of that Commonwealth would treat the shareholders of a Massachusetts business trust the same as they would the shareholders of a Massachusetts business corporation in enforcing conditions precedent to the institution of a shareholders' derivative action. There is no question that the shareholders of a Massachusetts corporation are required to make a demand on the corporate directors prior to bringing a derivative action.... We conclude that a parallel rule would be applied by the Massachusetts courts to a business trust....

Order affirmed ...

NOTES

1. Hemphill v. Orloff, 277 U.S. 537 (1928). Action on a promissory note that had been executed in Michigan and made payable to the Commercial Investment Trust. The Supreme Court upheld the Michigan courts' ruling that the Trust, which had been organized in Massachusetts, was a foreign corporation within the meaning of the Michigan statutes providing that a foreign corporation could not make a valid contract in Michigan unless it had previously obtained a certificate of authority to do business in that state. The Trust had not obtained such a certificate and hence

the judgment was for the defendant. "Clothed with the ordinary functions and attributes of a corporation, [the Trust] is subject to similar treatment...."

2. For discussion of the situations where liability imposed by the state of organization of a business trust will be recognized or rejected in other states, see Comment, Limited Liability of Shareholders in Real Estate Investment Trusts and the Conflict of Laws, 50 Calif.L.Rev. 696 (1962).

3. What law determines the legal power of an unincorporated association to engage in a particular activity? For material dealing with the analogous problem of the powers of a foreign corporation, see pp. 996–1005 infra.

4. Should the same law be used to govern all of the following problems: (a) the capacity of an association to take legal or equitable title to property; (b) the liabilities of the members of an association to third parties; (c) the liabilities of the members of an association inter se; (d) the liabilities of the members of an association to an agent of the association?

5. On the power of a state to impose upon foreign partnerships that wish to do business in its territory essentially the same qualification requirements that are imposed upon foreign corporations, see Note, 52 Corn.L.Q. 157 (1966).

SECTION 3. CORPORATIONS

A. CORPORATE PERSONALITY; BASIC PRINCIPLES

INTRODUCTORY NOTE

With rare exceptions, Anglo–American law holds that the law of the state of incorporation governs such questions as whether the corporation exists at all, what it is authorized to do, and when it ceases to exist. That state's law also determines the rights and liabilities of the corporate officers and of the shareholders with respect to the corporation.

States in which a corporation formed elsewhere (a "foreign corporation") carries on part of its business normally have an interest in regulating or applying their law to its activities. The principles under which a state may subject a foreign corporation to judicial jurisdiction were discussed in Chapter 3 supra. The related question of the state's power to tax a foreign corporation arose in tandem with the issue of judicial jurisdiction in the fountainhead International Shoe case.

A state will also want to regulate conduct and to supervise the activities of foreign corporations, just as it exercises control over its domestic corporations. Qualification statutes and other legislation are designed to make this possible. As in the area of judicial jurisdiction, federal constitutional law may impose limitations.

The materials that follow first explore in historical perspective the concept of corporate personality as it relates to problems of conflict of laws. They then deal with regulation of corporate activity by the state where it takes place, the "internal affairs rule," and issues related to winding-up the corporation.

American legal theory on the subject of foreign corporations was based largely upon four principles embodied in Chief Justice Taney's opinion in Bank of Augusta v. Earle, 38 U.S. 519 (1839), to wit:

(1) A corporation, being a creature of law, cannot exist outside the boundaries of the state of incorporation.

(2) Being a creature of law, a corporation can nowhere exercise powers not granted it either by its charter or by the general laws of the state of incorporation.

(3) A state is under no obligation to adhere to the doctrine of comity and hence has the power not only to refuse recognition to the foreign corporation but also to prevent the corporation from acting within its territory.

This principle was reaffirmed by the Supreme Court in Paul v. Virginia, 75 U.S. 168 (1868), where Justice Field stated: "... Having no absolute right of recognition in other States, but depending for such recognition and the enforcement of its contracts upon their assent, it follows, as a matter of course, that such assent may be granted upon such terms and conditions as those States may think proper to impose. They may exclude the foreign corporation entirely; they may restrict its business to particular localities, or they may exact such security for the performance of its contracts with their citizens as in their judgment will best promote the public interest. The whole matter rests in their discretion."

(4) The fourth principle, largely complementary of the third, is that a state is under no obligation to accord a foreign corporation the privileges which are enjoyed by natural persons who are citizens.

In Paul v. Virginia, the Supreme Court held that a corporation is not a "citizen" within the meaning of the privileges and immunities clause (Art. IV, § 2) and refused to look through the corporation to the stockholders, because "... the privileges and immunities secured to citizens of each State in the several States, by the provision in question, are those privileges and immunities which are common to the citizens in the latter States under their constitution and laws by virtue of their being citizens. Special privileges enjoyed by citizens in their own States are not secured in other States by this provision.... Now a grant of corporate existence is a grant of special privileges to the corporators, enabling them to act for certain designated purposes as a single individual, and exempting them (unless otherwise specially provided) from individual liability...."

Do the conclusions reached by these four principles follow logically from the stated premises and do these principles adequately explain the results reached by the actual decisions? Consider the following:

1. In the course of his opinion in Bank of Augusta v. Earle, Chief Justice Taney stated that "... it has been decided in many of the state courts, we believe in all of them where the question has arisen, that a

corporation of one state may sue in the courts of another." Can these decisions be reconciled with the principle that a corporation has "no existence" outside of the state of incorporation? Is consistency attained by the Chief Justice's suggestion that a corporation can act through agents in other states? How can there be an agent in a state which does not recognize the existence of the principal?

Can this principle of "non-existence" be squared with the present rule that a corporation subjects itself to the judicial jurisdiction of a foreign state by "doing business" within the latter's territory or, as stated by the Supreme Court in International Shoe Co. v. State of Washington, p. 47, supra, when the corporation's contacts with the forum "make it reasonable, in the context of our federal system of government, to require the corporation to defend the particular suit which is brought there"?

Does it follow that because a corporation is "a creature of law," it cannot exist outside the state of incorporation? Does the fact that corporations owe their legal existence to the laws of the incorporating state adequately serve to distinguish them from individuals for the purpose at hand? The problem of legal personality extends throughout the field of conflict laws. An individual's "legal personality"—i.e., one's particular bundle of rights, duties, privileges and powers—is the creation of law. As such, would it not follow that if a New York corporation has no existence in other states, neither would a man and woman who were legally married in New York be considered married elsewhere because their marriage status (like the status of incorporation) is a creation of New York law which is without force in other states?

The problem of legal personality has caused the courts least trouble in the case of individuals, presumably because the need was always apparent of recognizing rights and duties acquired by them under the law of other states. With respect to corporations, a similar need became apparent as soon as significant numbers of them began to spread their activities through two or more states. As a result, the courts have tended more and more to by-pass questions of corporate personality and to concentrate instead upon practical problems. In other areas, particularly in the case of foreign administrators, executors and receivers, difficulties posed by the concept of legal personality have not yet been overcome. See pp. 947–954, supra.

2. The validity of the second principle should be considered in the light of the material contained in Section 2(A), infra. If the first principle is incorrect, must not the same also be true of the second principle?

Since an individual's rights and powers are as much "creations of law" as those of a corporation, it could as logically be contended that an individual can exercise no powers in a foreign state that were not granted by the state of his domicile. That obviously is not the law. See, for example, Milliken v. Pratt, p. 464, supra.

3. The third principle—that a state has the absolute power to prevent foreign corporations from entering its territory—is frequently repeated in

the opinions. See, e.g., Wheeling Steel Corp. v. Glander, 337 U.S. 562, 571 (1949); Asbury Hospital v. Cass County, 326 U.S. 207, 211 (1945).

The development of constitutional law, however, has placed limitations upon premise and conclusion alike. The commerce clause provides one source of limitation. A state cannot forbid corporations from carrying on business in foreign or interstate commerce within its borders (Pensacola Telegraph Co. v. Western Union Telegraph Co., 96 U.S. 1 (1877)) and cannot attach conditions upon their entrance which amount to an undue burden on interstate commerce. Thus, for example, the states do not have unfettered power to tax such corporations or to make them amenable to suit in the local courts (Davis v. Farmers' Co-op Equity Co., p. 215, supra); nor can they place unreasonable conditions upon access by such corporations to the local courts. Eli Lilly & Co. v. Sav-on-Drugs, p. 989, infra; Sioux Remedy Co. v. Cope, p. 215 supra. On the other hand, reasonable taxation and reasonable regulation is permissible. International Shoe Co. v. State of Washington, p. 47, supra; Union Brokerage Co. v. Jensen, p. 993, infra.

Corporations are also "persons" within the due process and equal protection clauses of the Fourteenth Amendment. Thus, a state, once it has permitted a foreign corporation to enter its territory and acquire property therein, cannot subject the corporation to unduly burdensome legislation or discriminate against it unreasonably in favor of domestic corporations. WHYY, Inc. v. Borough of Glassboro, 393 U.S. 117 (1968); Wheeling Steel Corp. v. Glander, 337 U.S. 562 (1949).

The Supreme Court has also developed the doctrine of "unconstitutional conditions" which, in effect, prohibits the states from demanding the surrender of constitutional rights either as the price of admission or to avoid the penalty of expulsion. A state cannot, for example, require foreign corporations to refrain from invoking the jurisdiction of the federal courts. Terral v. Burke Construction Co., 257 U.S. 529 (1922).

4. A state, of course, need not accord to foreign corporations privileges which under its law can be enjoyed only by its citizens in their individual capacity. Situations of this sort, however, are unlikely to arise today. General incorporation laws are now common, and these permit the formation of corporations to engage in a great variety of activities. Incorporation, in other words, is no longer a special privilege as it was at the time of Bank of Augusta v. Earle.

Nevertheless, it is still firmly established that a corporation is not a "citizen" within the meaning of the privileges and immunities clauses of Article IV, Sec. 2 of the Constitution and of the Fourteenth Amendment. Asbury Hospital v. Cass County, 326 U.S. 207 (1945). Apart from the doctrine of Blake v. McClung, p. 955, supra, what is the precise effect of this rule? Is the rule necessary to permit the states to exercise adequate control over foreign corporations within their borders? Note in this regard the control that the states may constitutionally exercise over individuals, partnerships and unincorporated associations which transact business or do certain acts within their borders. Hess v. Pawloski, p. 44, supra; Doherty

& Co. v. Goodman, 294 U.S. 623 (1935). Yet individuals and partnerships, at least, are included within the protection of the privileges and immunities clauses. Flexner v. Farson, 248 U.S. 289 (1918).

Now that the privilege of incorporation is considered no more special or peculiar than that of forming a partnership, is there any reason why corporations should receive less constitutional protection than partnerships?

NOTES

1. What law determines whether a given association is a corporation for the purpose at hand? In Liverpool & L. Life & Fire Insurance Co. v. Massachusetts, 77 U.S. 566 (1870), the Supreme Court affirmed a determination by the Massachusetts courts that a joint-stock association, formed under a British statute which expressly declared an intention not to incorporate, was properly taxed as a corporation under a Massachusetts tax statute. Cf. Greenspun v. Lindley, p. 980, supra.

2. State v. United Royalty Co., 188 Kan. 443, 363 P.2d 397 (1961), involved a "Massachusetts trust," organized in Oklahoma and doing business in Kansas. As a trust, United Royalty was unincorporated, but its organization and powers were very similar to those of a corporation. In a suit in quo warranto the Kansas Supreme Court held that the trust was in effect an unlicensed foreign corporation, and was subject to penalties for doing corporate type business without a permit. The court enjoined United Royalty from doing any business in Kansas until it had complied with the Kansas corporation laws. See Note, Limited Liability of Shareholders in Real Estate and Investment Trusts, and the Conflict of Laws, 50 Calif.L.Rev. 696 (1962).

3. For discussions of the history of the corporation and the development of the theories of corporate personality, see Henn, Law of Corporations 14–35, 144–175 (3 ed. 1983). For a state's power to tax the intrastate activities of a corporation which is also engaged in interstate commerce, see Nowak and Rotunda, Constitutional Law 307 (4th ed. 1991). On the subject of unconstitutional conditions, see Hale, Unconstitutional Conditions and Constitutional Rights, 35 Colum.L.Rev. 321 (1935); Kathleen Sullivan, Unconstitutional Conditions, 102 Harv.L.Rev. 1413 (1989); see also Note, "Doing Business:" Defining State Control of Foreign Corporations, 32 Vand.L.Rev. 1105 (1979).

4. A corporation is often said to have its domicile in the state of incorporation. Bergner & Engel Brewing Co. v. Dreyfus, 172 Mass. 154, 51 N.E. 531 (1898). Dicey & Morris, Conflict of Laws 1103 (12th ed. 1993 by Collins). Can the concept of domicile, developed in the law of individuals and based on the idea of home, appropriately be applied to corporations? Consider what is said in Section 11 of the Restatement, Second, Conflict of Laws:

l. ... No useful purpose is served by assigning a domicil to a corporation. Most of the uses ... which the concept of domicil serves for individuals ... are inapplicable to corporations, which do not, for example, vote, marry, become divorced, beget or bear children and bequeath property. Certain problems, such as judicial jurisdiction and the power to tax and to regulate, are common both to individuals and corporations. But unlike an individual, a corporation has a state of incorporation. This state may tax the corporation, exercise judicial jurisdiction over it and regulate its corporate activities. It is both inaccurate and unnecessary to explain the existence of these powers on the ground that the corporation has its domicil in the state of incorporation....*

5. A corporation is generally said to be a national of the state of incorporation regardless of the nationality of its stockholders. See Sumitomo Shoji America, Inc. v. Avagliano, 457 U.S. 176 (1982): Defendant, incorporated in New York, was a wholly-owned subsidiary of a Japanese corporation. In an employment discrimination suit, defendant sought to invoke a provision of the U.S.–Japanese Treaty of Friendship, Commerce and Navigation which allows companies of each contracting state to do business in the other and to engage employees "of their choice." The Court held that the defendant was a United States company as a result of its New York incorporation and was not entitled to rely on the U.S.–Japanese treaty as if it were Japanese by reason of the nationality of its parent. Practical exigencies, particularly those arising in times of war, may demand a departure from the ordinary rule and on occasion the courts are specifically directed by statute to look through the corporation to the individual stockholder. See Corcoran, The Trading with the Enemy Act and the Controlled Canadian Corporation, 14 McGill L.J. 174 (1968).

6. For legislation providing for the application of local law to corporations incorporated elsewhere but with a high degree of local ownership ("pseudo-foreign corporations") see p. 1003, infra.

7. For purposes of diversity of citizenship, a corporation is deemed a citizen both of the state of incorporation and of the state where it has its principal place of business, 28 U.S.C.A. § 1332(c). In the case of foreign-country corporations, the question has arisen whether diversity jurisdiction exists in the state in the United States where the corporation has a place of business or only if that place of business is its principal place of business worldwide, i.e., is it the principal place of business in the United States or anywhere? Compare Eisenberg v. Commercial Union Assurance Co., 189 F.Supp. 500 (S.D.N.Y.1960); Rubinfeld v. Bahama Cruise Line, Inc., 613 F.Supp. 300 (S.D.N.Y.1985) and Bailey v. Grand Trunk Lines New England, 805 F.2d 1097, 1100 (2d Cir.1986) (worldwide) with Jerguson v. Blue Dot Investment, Inc., 659 F.2d 31 (5th Cir.1981) (dictum: American place of business would suffice). See Note, Diversity Jurisdiction and Alien Corporations: The Application of Section 1332(c), 59 Ind.L.J. 659 (1984).

B. CORPORATE ACTIVITY

"Doing Business" and Qualification Statutes

The term "doing business" is found in three general types of statutes. The first type is directed to the amenability of foreign corporations to service of process in the state, on the basis of their "doing business" in the state.[1] The second type of statute is concerned with the taxing of foreign corporations for the privilege of "doing business" in the state. The third type involves statutes which declare that a foreign corporation which desires to carry on activities constituting "doing business" in the state must "qualify," that is, comply with certain prerequisites such as the payment of a fee, the submission of information on the organization and

---

* Quoted with the permission of the copyright owner, The American Law Institute.

[1] See e.g., IL ST CH 735 § 5/2–209. For discussion of "doing business" generally, see pp. 93–112, supra.

the financial condition of the corporation, and the appointment of an agent for the service of a process. The usual penalty imposed for failure to comply with a qualification statute is to deny the corporation the right to bring suit in the state courts. Another penalty frequently imposed is a fine on the corporation, and sometimes upon its officers, directors and agents as well. A few statutes make the officers and directors individually liable on corporate obligations incurred in the state during the period in which the corporation was doing business there without having qualified or declare void contracts made by the corporation in the state during the period of noncompliance. See Henn, Law of Corporations 231–235 (3d ed. 1983).

Thus, the term "doing business" is used in three distinct situations. But "doing business" for one purpose may not satisfy the requirements of "doing business" for another purpose.

NOTES

1. The Revised Model Business Corporation Act provides in § 15.01 (1984):

... The following activities, among others, do not constitute transacting business [in the qualification sense]:

(1) maintaining, defending, or settling any proceeding;

(2) holding meetings of the board of directors or shareholders or carrying on other activities concerning internal corporate affairs;

(3) maintaining bank accounts;

(4) maintaining offices or agencies for the transfer, exchange, and registration of the corporation's own securities or maintaining trustees or depositories with respect to those securities;

(5) selling through independent contractors;

(6) soliciting or obtaining orders, whether by mail or through employees or agents or otherwise, if the orders require acceptance outside this state before they become contracts;

(7) creating or acquiring indebtedness, mortgages, and security interests in real or personal property;

(8) securing or collecting debts or enforcing mortgages and security interests in property securing the debts;

(9) owning, without more, real or personal property;

(10) conducting an isolated transaction that is completed within 30 days and that is not one in the course of repeated transactions of a like nature;

(11) transacting business in interstate commerce.

See also Restatement, Second, Conflict of Laws § 311.

2. Suppose that on the facts of International Shoe Co. v. State of Washington, p. 47, supra, a Washington retailer had failed to pay for a consignment of shoes. Could the International Shoe Co. have maintained an action in a Washington court to recover the price, assuming that (a) the company had not qualified to do business in that state and (b) the Washington courts were closed by statute to foreign corporations which did business there without having so qualified?

3. See Netherlands Shipmortgage Corp. v. Madias, 717 F.2d 731 (2d Cir.1983), holding "clearly erroneous" the application of New York's qualification statute to a Bermuda company engaged in international and interstate as well as intrastate business.

4. For a detailed discussion of the various statutory penalties for failure to qualify, see Note, Sanctions for Failure to Comply with Corporate Qualification Statutes: An Evaluation, 63 Colum.L.Rev. 117 (1963).

5. See Okilski, Foreign Corporations: What Constitutes "Doing Business" under New York's Qualification Statute?, 44 Ford.L.Rev. 1042 (1976).

Eli Lilly & Co. v. Sav-on-Drugs, Inc.
Supreme Court of the United States, 1961.
366 U.S. 276, 81 S.Ct. 1316, 6 L.Ed.2d 288.

■ JUSTICE BLACK delivered the opinion of the Court.

The appellant Eli Lilly and Company, an Indiana corporation dealing in pharmaceutical products, brought this action in a New Jersey state court to enjoin the appellee Sav–On–Drugs, Inc., a New Jersey corporation, from selling Lilly's products in New Jersey at prices lower than those fixed in minimum retail price contracts into which Lilly had entered with a number of New Jersey drug retailers.... Sav–On moved to dismiss this complaint under a New Jersey statute that denies a foreign corporation transacting business in the State the right to bring any action in New Jersey upon any contract made there unless and until it files with the New Jersey Secretary of State a copy of its charter together with a limited amount of information about its operations[1] and obtains from him a certificate authorizing it to do business in the State.

Lilly opposed the motion to dismiss, urging that its business in New Jersey was entirely in interstate commerce and arguing, upon that ground, that the attempt to require it to file the necessary information and obtain a certificate for its New Jersey business was forbidden by the Commerce Clause of the Federal Constitution.... the trial court ... granted Sav-On's motion to dismiss ... The State Supreme Court ... affirmed ...

The record shows that the New Jersey trade in Lilly's pharmaceutical products is carried on through both interstate and intrastate channels. Lilly manufactures these products and sells them in interstate commerce to certain selected New Jersey wholesalers. These wholesalers then sell the products in intrastate commerce to New Jersey hospitals, physicians and retail drug stores, and these retail stores in turn sell them, again in intrastate commerce, to the general public. It is well established that New Jersey cannot require Lilly to get a certificate of authority to do business in

---

1. The information required is: (1) the amount of the corporation's authorized capital stock; (2) the amount of stock actually issued by the corporation; (3) the character of the business which the corporation intends to transact in New Jersey; (4) the principal office of the corporation in New Jersey; and (5) the name and place of abode of an agent upon whom process against the corporation may be served. N.J.Rev.Stat. 14:15–3. [Footnote by the Court.]

the State if its participation in this trade is limited to its wholly interstate sales to New Jersey wholesalers. Under the authority of the so-called "drummer" cases ... Lilly is free to send salesmen into New Jersey to promote this interstate trade without interference from regulations imposed by the State. On the other hand, it is equally well settled that if Lilly is engaged in intrastate as well as interstate aspects of the New Jersey drug business, the State can require it to get a certificate of authority to do business. In such a situation, Lilly could not escape state regulation merely because it is also engaged in interstate commerce....

We agree with the trial court that "[t]o hold ... that plaintiff [Lilly] is not doing business in New Jersey is to completely ignore reality." Eighteen "detailmen," working out of a big office in Newark, New Jersey, with Lilly's name on the door and in the lobby of the building, and with Lilly's district manager and secretary in charge, have been regularly engaged in work for Lilly which relates directly to the intrastate aspects of the sale of Lilly's products. These eighteen "detailmen" have been traveling throughout the State of New Jersey promoting the sales of Lilly's products, not to the wholesalers, Lilly's interstate customers, but to the physicians, hospitals and retailers who buy those products in intrastate commerce from the wholesalers. To this end, they have provided these hospitals, physicians and retailers with up-to-date knowledge of Lilly's products and with free advertising and promotional material designed to encourage the general public to make more intrastate purchases of Lilly's products. And they sometimes even directly participate in the intrastate sales themselves by transmitting orders from the hospitals, physicians and drugstores they service to the New Jersey wholesalers....

Lilly also contends that even if it is engaged in intrastate commerce in New Jersey and can by virtue of that fact be required to get a license to do business in that State, New Jersey cannot properly deny it access to the courts in this case because the suit is one arising out of the interstate aspects of its business.... We do not think that ... the present suit is ... of that kind. Here, Lilly is suing upon a contract entirely separable from any particular interstate sale ...

Affirmed.

■ JUSTICE HARLAN, concurring....

It is clear that sending "drummers" into New Jersey seeking customers to whom Lilly's goods may be sold and shipped ... and suing in the state courts to enforce contracts for sales from an out-of-state store of goods ... are both so intimately connected with Lilly's right to access to the local market, free of local controls, that they cannot be separated off as "local business" even if they are conducted wholly within New Jersey. However, I do not think that the systematic promotion of Lilly's products among local retailers and consumers who, as Lilly conducts its affairs, can only purchase them from a New Jersey wholesaler bears the same close relationship to the necessities of keeping the channels of interstate commerce state-unburdened. I believe that New Jersey can treat as "local business" such promotional activities, which are pointed at and result initially in local sales by Lilly's customers, and not in direct sales from its own out-of-state store of goods....

... The only aspect of the present case that resembles the "drummer" cases is the fact that Lilly's promotion of local sales ultimately serves to increase its interstate sales. To treat this factor as bringing the present situation within the drummer cases would, in my view, be substantially to extend the reach of those cases....

■ JUSTICE DOUGLAS, with whom JUSTICE FRANKFURTER, JUSTICE WHITTAKER and JUSTICE STEWART concur, dissenting....

(1) If New Jersey sought to collect from appellant a tax apportioned to some local business activity which it carries on in *that State*, I would see no constitutional objection to it....

(2) If appellant were sued in New Jersey, I think its connections with that State have been sufficient to make it subject to the jurisdiction of the state courts ... at least as to suits which reveal a "substantial connection" with the State....

(3) The present case falls in neither of those two categories. New Jersey demands that appellant obtain from it a certificate authorizing it to do business in the State, absent which she denies appellant access to her courts. The case thus presents the strikingly different issue—whether an interstate business can be subjected to a licensing system....

In this case, appellant's employees within the State were engaged solely in the "drumming up" of appellant's interstate trade. They did this, not by direct solicitation of the interstate buyers, but by contacts with the customers of the buyers.... The Court finds these activities to be separable from appellant's interstate business; appellant is "inducing" sales, not "soliciting" them. It is not a distinction I can accept....

ALLENBERG COTTON COMPANY, INC. v. PITTMAN, 419 U.S. 20 (1974): [Action for breach of a contract under which the defendant of Mississippi agreed to sell cotton to the plaintiff, a Tennessee corporation. Plaintiff had no office in Mississippi, did not own or operate a warehouse there and had no employees soliciting business in the state on a regular basis. It did employ an independent broker to identify farmers in the state who would be prepared to sell cotton to the plaintiff. The actual contracts were prepared by the plaintiff in Tennessee and signed by it there; they were then forwarded to the individual farmers in Mississippi for their signatures. The contracts provided that the farmer was to be paid for the cotton upon its delivery to a local warehouse in Mississippi. After delivery to the warehouse, the plaintiff would sort and classify the cotton preliminary to its shipment to mills in other states. The defendant failed to deliver the cotton he had contracted to sell the plaintiff and, when suit was brought against him in a Mississippi state court, claimed that the Mississippi courts were not open to the plaintiff since it was doing business in the state without having obtained the requisite certificate. The defendant was successful in having the suit dismissed by the state courts, but the Supreme Court reversed on the ground that the plaintiff was doing business in interstate commerce.]

■ JUSTICE DOUGLAS delivered the opinion of the Court.

. . .

Appellant's arrangements with Pittman and the broker, Covington, are representative of a course of dealing with many farmers whose cotton, once sold to appellant, enters a long interstate pipeline. That pipeline ultimately terminates at mills across the country or indeed around the world, after a complex sorting and matching process designed to provide each mill with the particular grade of cotton which the mill is equipped to process.

Due to differences in soil, time of planting, harvesting, weather and the like, each bale of cotton, even though produced on the same farm, may have a different quality. Traders or merchants like appellant, with the assistance of the Department of Agriculture, must sample each bale and classify it according to grade, staple length, and color. Similar bales, whether from different farms or even from different collection points, are then grouped in multiples of 100 into "even-running lots" which are uniform as to all measurable characteristics. This grouping process typically takes place in card files in the merchant's office; when enough bales have been pooled to make an even-running lot, the entire lot can be targeted for a mill equipped to handle cotton of that particular quality, and the individual bales in the lot will then be shipped to the mill from their respective collection points. It is true that title often formally passes to the merchant upon delivery of the cotton at the warehouse, and that the cotton may rest at the warehouse pending completion of the classification and grouping processes; but as the description above indicates, these fleeting events are an integral first step in a vast system of distribution of cotton in interstate commerce....

We deal here with a species of control over an intricate interstate marketing mechanism.... Delivery of the cotton to a warehouse, taken in isolation, is an intrastate transaction. But that delivery is also essential for the completion of the interstate transaction, for sorting and classification in the warehouse are essential before the precise interstate destination of the cotton, whether in this country or abroad, is determined. The determination of the precise market cannot indeed be made until the classification is made. The cotton in this Mississippi sale ... though temporarily in a warehouse, was still in the stream in interstate commerce....

Much reliance is placed on Eli Lilly & Co. v. Sav–On–Drugs, Inc. [p. 989, supra], for sustaining Mississippi's action. The case is not in point. There the Court found that the foreign corporation had an office and salesmen in New Jersey selling drugs intrastate. Since it was engaged in an intrastate business it could be required to obtain a license even though it also did an interstate business....

In short, appellant's contacts with Mississippi do not exhibit the sort of localization or intrastate character which we have required in situations where a state seeks to require a foreign corporation to qualify to do business. Whether there were local tax incidents of those contacts which could be reached is a different question on which we express no opinion. Whether the course of dealing would subject appellant to suits in Mississippi is likewise a different question on which we express no view. We hold only that Mississippi's refusal to honor and enforce contracts made for interstate or foreign commerce is repugnant to the Commerce Clause....

■ JUSTICE REHNQUIST, dissenting.

. . .

But even if I were able to agree with the Court that Allenberg's activities in Mississippi were purely "interstate," I do not believe that our cases, properly understood, prevent Mississippi from exacting qualification from a foreign corporation as a condition for use of the Mississippi courts.

. . .

... Mississippi's qualifications statute is concededly not discriminatory. Domestic corporations organized under her laws must submit themselves to her taxing jurisdiction, to service of process within the State, and to a number of other incidents of corporate existence which state law may impose.... [Q]ualifications statutes [aid] in the collection of state taxes by identifying foreign corporations operating within the State and in the protection of citizens within the State through insuring ready susceptibility to service of process of the corporation. The qualification statute also serves an important informational function making available to citizens of the State who may deal with the foreign corporation details of its financing and control. Although the result of Allenberg's failure to comply with the qualification statute is a drastic one, our decisions hold that the burden imposed on interstate commerce by such statutes is to be judged with reference to the measures required to comply with such legislation, and not to the sanctions imposed for violation of it.... The steps necessary in order to comply with this statute are not unreasonably burdensome.

Sioux Remedy Co. v. Cope
Supreme Court of the United States, 1914.
235 U.S. 197, 35 S.Ct. 57, 59 L.Ed. 193.

[The case appears, p. 215, supra.]

Union Brokerage Co. v. Jensen
Supreme Court of the United States, 1944.
322 U.S. 202, 64 S.Ct. 967, 88 L.Ed. 1227, 152 A.L.R. 1072.

[Plaintiff, a North Dakota corporation, which was licensed under federal statute to do business in Minnesota as a custom house broker, brought suit in the Minnesota courts against two former employees for breach of fiduciary obligations. Suit was dismissed by the state courts under a Minnesota statute which denied access to the local courts to all foreign corporations doing business in the state unless they had previously obtained a certificate of authority. The requirements for obtaining such a certificate included (1) the payment of a license fee of $50.00, (2) the filing of a statement containing the name of the corporation, the names and addresses of its directors and officers, the aggregate number of its authorized shares and kindred information and (3) the filing of a consent by the corporation to service of process upon it and appointment of an agent upon whom service of process could be made. Plaintiff appealed to the Supreme Court of the United States contending that, as applied to it, the Minnesota statute was unconstitutional since it placed an undue burden upon a federal instrumentality engaged in foreign commerce.]

■ JUSTICE FRANKFURTER delivered the opinion of the Court.

... In a situation like the present, where an enterprise touches different and not common interests between Nation and State, our task is that of harmonizing these interests without sacrificing either.... The Tariff Act of 1930 ... confers upon licensees certain privileges, and secures to the Federal Government by means of these licensing provisions a measure of control over those engaged in the customhouse brokerage business. But such circumscribed control by the Federal Government does not imply immunity from control by the State within the sphere of its special interests.... The state and federal regulations here applicable have their separate spheres of operation.... Minnesota is legitimately concerned with safeguarding the interests of its own people in business dealings with corporations not of its own chartering but who do business within its borders.... To safeguard responsibility in all such dealings ... Minnesota has made the same exactions of Union as of every other foreign corporation engaged in similar transactions.

[W]e have not here a case of a foreign corporation merely coming into Minnesota to contribute to or to conclude a unitary interstate transaction ... nor of the State's withholding "the right to sue even in a single instance until the corporation renders itself amenable to suit in all the courts of the state by whosoever chooses to sue it there." Sioux Remedy Co. v. Cope, 235 U.S. 197, 205. The business of Union, we have seen, is localized in Minnesota, and Minnesota, in the requirement before us, merely seeks to regularize its conduct.... In the absence of applicable federal regulation, a State may impose non-discriminatory regulations on those engaged in foreign commerce....

The Commerce Clause ... does not imply relief to those engaged in interstate or foreign commerce from the duty of paying an appropriate share for the maintenance of the various state governments. Nor does it preclude a State from giving needful protection to its citizens in the course of their contacts with businesses conducted by outsiders when the legislation by which this is accomplished is general in its scope, is not aimed at interstate or foreign commerce, and involves merely burdens incident to effective administration...."

Judgment affirmed.

NOTES

1. A corporation which has failed to comply with a state qualification statute and is thereby barred from suing in the state courts on a contract made in the state is also precluded from bringing suit on the same claim in a local federal court. Woods v. Interstate Realty Co., 337 U.S. 535 (1949). A foreign corporation that has failed to comply with a state qualification statute may also be precluded from defending itself against a state claim of breach of contract filed in federal court. Farris v. Sambo's Restaurant, Inc., 498 F.Supp. 143 (N.D.Tex.1980) (damage action for breach of a lease). It has been held, however, that the federal courts remain open to the corporation when the issue involves a federal question. Lisle Mills, Inc. v. Arkay Infants Wear, Inc., 90 F.Supp. 676 (E.D.N.Y.1950) (validity of a patent).

2. Fed.R.Civ.P. 17(b) provides in part that "... The capacity of a corporation to sue or be sued shall be determined by the law under which it was organized...." See Sable Corporation v. Dual Office Suppliers, Inc., 1987 WL 14607 (N.D.Ill.1987). For cases applying this rule to a dissolved foreign corporation, see Johnson v. Helicopter & Airplane Services Corp., 404 F.Supp. 726 (D.Md.1975); Stone v. Gibson Refrigerator Sales Corp., 366 F.Supp. 733 (E.D.Pa.1973); Kreindler v. Marx, 85 F.R.D. 612 (N.D.Ill.1979).

KENTUCKY FINANCE CORP. v. PARAMOUNT AUTO EXCHANGE, 262 U.S. 544 (1923): [A Kentucky corporation brought an action of replevin in a Wisconsin State court against a Wisconsin corporation to recover an automobile which the plaintiff alleged had been stolen from it in Kentucky and turned over in Wisconsin to the defendant. Except for the present suit, the plaintiff had engaged in no business activities of any kind in Wisconsin. On the defendant's motion under a Wisconsin statute (applicable only to foreign corporations), the court ordered the plaintiff to send its secretary from Louisville, Kentucky, to Milwaukee, Wisconsin, for an examination before trial. Upon the plaintiff's refusal to comply with the order, the court made a further order that the complaint be dismissed. The plaintiff appealed to the state supreme court, contending that the statute under which both orders were made violated the equal protection clause of the Fourteenth Amendment. The Supreme Court of Wisconsin affirmed the lower court and the plaintiff appealed to the Supreme Court of the United States. Held, reversed.]

■ VAM DEVANTER, J. "The State court whose aid it [the plaintiff] invoked was one whose jurisdiction was general and adequate for the purpose.... [W]hen the plaintiff went into Wisconsin, as it did, for the obviously lawful purpose of repossessing itself, by a permissible action in her courts, of specific personal property unlawfully taken out of its possession elsewhere and fraudulently carried into that state, it was, in our opinion, within her jurisdiction for all the purposes of that undertaking.... And we think there is no tenable ground for regarding it as any less entitled to the equal protection of the laws in that state than an individual would have been in the same circumstances; ... The discrimination was essentially arbitrary."

■ JUSTICE BRANDEIS, with whom JUSTICE HOLMES concurred, dissented. "To sustain the contention that the statute denies to plaintiff equal protection of the laws would seem to require the court to overrule Blake v. McClung [p. 955, supra] ... and many other cases."

C. THE LAW GOVERNING CORPORATE ACTIVITIES *

RESTATEMENT, SECOND, CONFLICT OF LAWS: **

§ 301. Rights Against and Liabilities to Third Person

The rights and liabilities of a corporation with respect to a third person that arise from a corporate act of a sort that can likewise be done by an individual are determined by the same choice-of-law principles as are applicable to noncorporate parties.

NOTES

1. Stone v. Southern Illinois & Mo. Bridge Co., 206 U.S. 267 (1907). Suit by the plaintiff bridge company, an Illinois corporation, to condemn a strip of Missouri land which was to form one of the approaches to a bridge which the plaintiff was about to construct over the Mississippi river. The Missouri courts found for the plaintiff and the defendant landowners appealed to the Supreme Court of the United States on the ground, among others, that the plaintiff did not have the power of eminent domain under the law of Illinois, the state of its incorporation, and that "a corporation of Illinois can only exercise in Missouri such powers as are conferred upon it by the State of its creation." Held for the plaintiff. The question involved "... the powers of corporations under the laws of Missouri ... no federal right was taken from the [defendants] by the action complained of under the state laws as interpreted by the Supreme Court of the State of Missouri...."

2. See generally DeMott, Perspectives on Choice of Law for Corporate Affairs, 48 Law and Contemporary Problems 161 (1985); Kozyris, Corporate Wars and Choice of Law, 85 Duke L.J. 1 (1985); Reese and Kaufman, The Law Governing Corporate Affairs: Choice of Law and the Impact of Full Faith and Credit, 58 Colum.L.Rev. 1118 (1958).

RESTATEMENT, SECOND, CONFLICT OF LAWS: **

§ 302. Other Issues with Respect to Powers and Liabilities of a Corporation

(1) Issues involving the rights and liabilities of a corporation, other than those dealt with in § 301, are determined by the local law of the state

---

* Restatement, Second, Conflict of Laws §§ 301–313.

** Quoted with the permission of the copyright owner, The American Law Institute.

which, with respect to the particular issue, has the most significant relationship to the occurrence and the parties under the principles stated in § 6.

(2) The local law of the state of incorporation will be applied to determine such issues, except in the unusual case where, with respect to the particular issue, some other state has a more significant relationship to the occurrence and the parties, in which event the local law of the other state will be applied.

Comment:

a. Scope of section. The rule of this Section is to be contrasted with that of § 301. The rule of this Section is concerned with issues involving matters that are peculiar to corporations and other associations, whereas the rule of § 301 is concerned with issues arising from corporate acts of a sort that can also be done by individuals. Many of the matters that fall within the scope of the rule of this Section involve the "internal affairs" of a corporation—that is the relations inter se of the corporation, its shareholders, directors, officers or agents.... Other such matters affect the interests of the corporation's creditors.

Matters falling within the scope of the rule of this Section and which involve primarily a corporation's relationship to its shareholders include steps taken in the course of the original incorporation, the election or appointment of directors and officers, the adoption of bylaws, the issuance of corporate shares, preemptive rights, the holding of directors' and shareholders' meetings, methods of voting including any requirement for cumulative voting, shareholders' rights to examine corporate records, charter and by-law amendments, mergers, consolidations and reorganizations and the reclassification of shares. Matters which may also affect the interests of the corporation's creditors include the issuance of bonds, the declaration and payment of dividends, loans by the corporation to directors, officers and shareholders, and the purchase and redemption by the corporation of outstanding shares of its own stock.

The rule of this Section will be applied in the absence of a local statute that is explicitly applicable to the situation at hand. All States of the United States have statutes which regulate in various ways the affairs of foreign corporations within their territory. Blue sky laws and statutes regulating the activities of public utilities are typical examples....

e. *Rationale.* Application of the local law of the state of incorporation will usually be supported by those choice-of-law factors favoring the needs of the interstate and international systems, certainty, predictability and uniformity of result, protection of the justified expectations of the parties and ease in the application of the law to be applied. Usually, application of this law will also be supported by the factor looking toward implementation of the relevant policies of the state with the dominant interest in the decision of the particular issue.

Uniform treatment of directors, officers and shareholders is an important objective which can only be attained by having the rights and liabilities of those persons with respect to the corporation governed by a single law....

In addition, many matters involving a corporation cannot practicably be determined differently in different states. Examples of such matters, most of which have already been mentioned in Comment *a*, include steps taken in the course of the original incorporation, the election or appointment of directors and officers, the adoption of bylaws, the issuance of corporate shares ..., the holding of directors' and shareholders' meetings, methods of voting including any requirement for cumulative voting, the declaration and payment of dividends and other distributions, charter amendments, mergers, consolidations, and reorganizations, the reclassification of shares and the purchase and redemption by the corporation of outstanding shares of its own stock.

Matters such as these must be contrasted with the acts dealt with in § 301, which include, for example, the making of contracts, the commission of torts and the transfer of property. There is no reason why corporate acts of the latter sort should not be governed by the local law of different states. There is no reason, for example, why an issue involving one corporate contract should not be governed by the local law of state X while an issue involving another corporation contract is governed by the local law of state Y. On the other hand, it would be impractical to have matters of the sort mentioned in the previous paragraph, which involve a corporation's organic structure or internal administration, governed by different laws. It would be impractical, for example, if an election of directors, an issuance of shares, a payment of dividends, a charter amendment, or a consolidation or reorganization were to be held valid in one state and invalid in another. Possible alternatives would be either to have matters of this sort governed by the local law of a particular state or else to hold applicable the local law of any state having a reasonable relationship to the corporation which imposed the strictest requirement....

It should be added that certain issues which are peculiar to corporations or to other organizations do not affect matters of organic structure or internal administration and need not, as a practical matter, be governed by a single law. An example is the transfer of individual shares of a share issue. There is no practical reason, for example, why a corporation incorporated in state X should not comply with the requirements of state Y when it seeks to sell its shares in the latter state. Even as to such matters, however, the local law of the state of incorporation has usually been applied in the absence of an explicitly applicable local statute....

The "Internal Affairs" Rule. At one time American courts took the position that they would not entertain actions involving the internal organization, management, capitalization, issuance of dividends, etc., of foreign corporations. This view has given way in more recent times to the thought that this is but one aspect of the forum non conveniens principle. See Chapter 4, p. 197 supra. "A court will exercise jurisdiction over an action involving the internal affairs of a foreign corporation unless it is an inappropriate or an inconvenient forum for the trial of the action." Restatement, Second, Conflict of Laws § 313.*

NOTES

1. Hausman v. Buckley, 299 F.2d 696 (2d Cir.1962), cert. denied, 369 U.S. 885 (1962). This was a derivative action brought by minority stockholders on behalf of the Pantepec Oil Company against its officers and directors to recover damages for what was alleged to be the unlawful sale of the corporation's assets. The Pantepec Company was incorporated in Venezuela, its shareholders' meetings were held there, and it had substantial assets in that country. On the other hand, Pantepec was an American financed and American controlled corporation, and all the parties to the action were American citizens. The defendants moved to dismiss the complaint on the ground that under Venezuelan law actions on behalf of a corporation cannot be brought by minority stockholders but only by persons appointed at a stockholders' meeting. Held for the defendants. The law of the state of incorporation determines the right of a shareholder to object to action taken by the directors and officers in behalf of the corporation. Whether a derivative action can be brought is a substantive, rather than a procedural, question and the Venezuelan law is not contrary to the public policy of New York. Mansfield Hardwood Lumber Co. v. Johnson (Note 2, infra) was distinguished on the ground that Pantepec is not a "paper" corporation of Venezuela.

2. Mansfield Hardwood Lumber Co. v. Johnson, 268 F.2d 317 (5th Cir.1959). Suit in a federal court in Louisiana by minority shareholders against the officers and majority shareholders of a Delaware corporation complaining that the defendants had breached their fiduciary obligations to the plaintiffs in purchasing the plaintiffs' stock. The corporation did all of its business in Louisiana. Held for the plaintiffs. Under Delaware law there was no breach of fiduciary obligation, but the rule calling for application of the law of the state of incorporation should not be applied to determine the internal affairs of a corporation "where the only contact point with the incorporating state is the naked fact of incorporation and where all other contact points ... are found" in the state of the forum.

3. See also McDermott Inc. v. Lewis, 531 A.2d 206 (Del.1987), extending the internal affairs rule to foreign-country corporations.

4. In European and other civil law countries, the basic law governing a corporation's internal affairs and the liability of its officers, directors and shareholders is the law of the corporation's "social seat" which can generally be described as the main office or executive headquarters of the corporation. Latty, Pseudo–Foreign Corporations, 65 Yale L.J. 137, 166–173 (1955); 2 Rabel, Conflict of Laws 33 et seq. (2d ed. 1958); Note, Pseudo–Foreign Corporations and the Internal Affairs Doctrine, 1960 Duke L.J. 477. For a European perspective and comparative treatment, see Kegel, Internationales Privatrecht 408–416 (7th ed. 1995), with numerous

* Quoted with the permission of the copyright owner, The American Law Institute.

references. See also Basedow, Conflicts of Economic Regulation, 42 Am.J.Comp.L. 423 (1994).

German–American Coffee Co. v. Diehl

Court of Appeals of New York, 1915.
216 N.Y. 57, 109 N.E. 875.

[Action brought under a former New York statute by a New Jersey corporation against one of its directors to recover damages for the declaration of a dividend that was illegal under a New York statute. The dividend was also illegal under New Jersey law but under that law an action against the directors could only be brought by the stockholders. The plaintiff corporation has "maintained in New York its main business office; has held in New York the regular and most of the special meetings of its directors; and in New York has 'generally,' to follow the words of the complaint, 'managed, directed and conducted its business.'" Held that the statute was intended to apply to this situation and could constitutionally be so applied.]

■ CARDOZO, J. ... We come, then, to the question of power. On that question the argument has taken a wide range, yet the decision, when confined to the facts of the case at hand, is brought within a narrow compass. As long as a foreign corporation keeps away from this state, it is not for us to say what it may do or not do. But when it comes into this state, and transacts its business here, it must yield obedience to our laws.... This statute makes no attempt to regulate foreign corporations while they keep within their domicile. A prohibition which lasts while business within the state continues, and may be escaped when business within the state is stopped, is, in effect, a condition imposed on the right to do business, and nothing more....

Is the problem of local regulation of the affairs of a foreign corporation as simple as Judge Cardozo apparently conceived it to be in his opinion in the *Diehl* case? Does the fact that a corporation does some business in a state give that state power to regulate all aspects of the corporation's internal affairs? See Edgar v. MITE Corp., p. 1005, infra, and CTS Corp. v. Dynamics Corp. of America, p. 1008, infra.

As seen from the preceding material in this Section, the courts will not hesitate to apply their local law to a corporate act, such as the making of a contract or the commission of a tort, which is of the sort that can likewise be done by an individual. Restatement, Second, Conflict of Laws § 301. On the other hand, the courts will rarely, in the absence of an explicit statute, apply their local law to matters that are peculiar to corporations. Restatement, Second, Conflict of Laws § 302.

Matters that are peculiar to corporations can be grouped into two categories: those that practicably can be regulated differently in different states and those where this cannot be done. Examples of matters falling within the first category are individual sales of a corporation's stock and the power of shareholders to inspect the corporate books. Many states have statutes, such as blue sky laws, that regulate matters falling within this category.

Examples of matters falling within the second category are the declaration and payment of dividends, cumulative voting and the issuance of stock. Other matters falling within this category are set forth in Comment *e* of § 302 of the Restatement, Second, which is set forth above. Relatively few statutes are directed to foreign corporations with regard to matters in this second category. Presumably, a state, which is not that of incorporation, can appropriately apply its law to such matters if the foreign corporation involved does all, or nearly all, of its business within the territory of that state and if all, or nearly all, of the corporation's shareholders reside there. On the other hand, there are undoubtedly constitutional limitations upon the power of a state to apply its law in circumstances where its contacts with the foreign corporation are of lesser extent.

Western Air Lines, Inc. v. Sobieski

California District Court of Appeal, 1961.
191 Cal.App.2d 399, 12 Cal.Rptr. 719.

[Western Airlines, a Delaware corporation, had originally been formed for the purpose of acquiring the assets of a California corporation. Western did substantial business in California and in several other states. It did no business in Delaware. Residents of California held 30% of its stock; 55% of its passenger traffic started or ended in that state; 60% of its wages were paid there; and there were other substantial contacts.

The Board of Directors of Western wished to eliminate cumulative voting on its stock, and, in accordance with Delaware law, started to seek shareholders' approval when the California Commissioner of Corporations intervened. He ruled that this would be a "sale" of stock in California within the meaning of Section 25009(a) of the California Corporations Code which defines "sale" to include "any change in the rights, preferences, privileges, or restrictions on outstanding securities."

The Commissioner granted a permit to proceed with the shareholder vote on condition that the amendment of the articles should not be filed with the Secretary of State of Delaware until a hearing had been held in California on the "fairness" of the proposal, pursuant to the California Corporation Code. At that hearing, the Commissioner found that the plan was "unfair" and disallowed it. The Commissioner noted a strong public policy in favor of cumulative voting which is required for all California corporations. He also treated Western as a "pseudo-foreign corporation," saying that "the fiction of Delaware residence should yield to the totality of California contacts so as to require, in addition to compliance with the Delaware law, the approval of the California Corporations Commissioner as a condition to eliminating the right of cumulative voting by the shareholders."

The ruling of the Commissioner was upheld by the California District Court of Appeal. The court relied, among other things, on the fact that Western had originally been a California corporation and that, when it applied to the California Corporations Commissioner for permission to exchange its shares for those of its California predecessor, it represented to the Commissioner that the shareholders of the California corporation would not be hurt in any way by the exchange.

The Court also said:]

It would appear that the provisions of the Corporate Securities Act here before us are a proper exercise of legislative discretion in requiring that corporate dealings with residents of this state be authorized by the Commissioner of Corporations, particularly where such corporation does a substantial amount of business within the state, and the act is not violative of the constitutional clauses of equal protection, contract, due process and full faith and credit if such legislative enactments operate equally upon such foreign corporations and domestic corporations in this state....

When we consider the complexity of present-day corporate structure and operation, and the far-flung area of corporate activities where transportation or nation-wide distribution of products may be involved, we are persuaded that the commissioner has this discretion. To hold otherwise, and to follow the argument of Western to its conclusion, would be to say that the commissioner might have the power in the first instance to require certain rights to be guaranteed to shareholders before he would permit the sale or issuance of a foreign corporation's stock in this state, but that immediately thereafter, by the device of amending the charter of such corporation in another state, the entire structure of that corporation, even to substantial changes in the rights of shareholders in California, might be legally affected. Such a holding would enable a foreign corporation to destroy the rights which the State of California has deemed worthy of protection by the enactment of the Corporate Securities Act.

This position is not without support in other jurisdictions. The mere fact that the last act here necessary to effectuate the change in the voting rights of the numerous California residents who are shareholders of Western will take place in Delaware does not of itself necessitate a finding that the commissioner for that reason was without jurisdiction in this matter....

NOTES

1. The problem of this case is discussed in Reese and Kaufman, The Law Governing Corporate Affairs: Choice of Law and the Impact of Full Faith and Credit, 58 Colum.L.Rev. 1118 (1958).

2. Section 8–106 of the Uniform Commercial Code provides:

The validity of a security and the rights and duties of the issuer with respect to registration of transfer are governed by the law (including the conflict of laws rules) of the jurisdiction of organization of the issuer.

3. In State ex rel. Weede v. Bechtel, 239 Iowa 1298, 31 N.W.2d 853 (1948), cert. denied, 337 U.S. 918 (1949), Iowa law was held determinative of the validity of a stock issue made by a corporation incorporated in Delaware, but which had nearly all of its assets and transacted nearly all of its business in Iowa. Should the result have been different if the corporation's business had been more equally divided between Delaware and Iowa? What law should govern in a case where an X corporation does substantial business in state X and in several other states as well? See Latty, Pseudo–Foreign Corporations, 65 Yale L.J. 137 (1955); Annotation, 8 A.L.R.2d 1185 (1949). See also p. 1010, infra.

California (in 1976)[1] and New York (in 1962)[2] enacted statutes which provide for application of their law in certain circumstances to foreign corporations with which they have a substantial relationship. Both statutes are expressly made inapplicable to corporations whose shares are listed on a national securities exchange. Hence, in the nature of things, they will rarely affect corporations that do a substantial multistate business. The California statute only becomes operative if two additional tests are met. "[T]he average of the property factor, the payroll factor and the sales factor" (all factors being a proportion of the corporation's California activity to its total activity) must exceed 50 percent during the corporation's "latest full income year." Also, "more than one-half of [the corporation's] outstanding voting securities [must be] held of record by persons having addresses" in California. Once these conditions are met, California law is made applicable to a variety of issues, including the election of directors, the liability and indemnification of directors and the payment of dividends. It seems apparent that California law would not have been applied if this statute had been in effect at the time that Western Airlines, Inc. v. Sobieski was decided.

The New York statute only becomes applicable if the shares of the foreign corporation are not listed on a national securities exchange and if at least half of the corporation's "business income for the preceding three fiscal years ... was allocable to this state for franchise tax purposes under the tax law." In contrast to the California statute, the New York statute does not apply to shareholders' voting rights.

To date, only the California statute appears to have given rise to litigation. Its application to require cumulative voting by the shareholders of a Utah corporation was upheld in Wilson v. Louisiana–Pacific Resources, Inc., 138 Cal.App.2d 216, 187 Cal.Rptr. 852 (1982). The corporation in question "had initially no business connection with Utah and had maintained" its principal place of business in California since at least 1975. In addition, the meetings of its shareholders and directors were held in

---

1. West's Ann.Cal.Corp.Code § 2115. **2.** N.Y.Bus.Corp.Law § 1320.

California and all of its employees and bank accounts were located in that state. Utah law provides for straight voting in an election of directors, but permits cumulative voting if the articles of incorporation so provide. The court held that application of the California statute was not prohibited by any provision of the Constitution, saying:

... California's present law requiring cumulative voting by shareholders continues in effect a policy which has existed in this state since the Constitution of 1879....

Utah, on the other hand, has no interests which are offended by cumulative voting; and, whatever interest it might have in maintaining a *laissez faire* policy on that score would seem to be clearly outweighed by the interests of California, in which a majority of shareholders and the corporation's business activity is located....

There is no suggestion, or evidence, that section 2115 was adopted for the purpose of deterring foreign corporations from doing business in this state; nor is there any direct evidence that it has had or will have such an effect. On the contrary, what evidence there is in the record on this point consists of testimony by appellant's president that he knew of no adverse effect on appellant's business which would be caused by cumulative voting.

Appellant argues that adverse consequences are predictable from "potentially conflicting claims of shareholders as to which state [law] governs" the method of voting by shareholders, and from the "transient nature of the applicability of the California statute." ...

The potential for conflict and resulting uncertainty from California's statute is substantially minimized by the nature of the criteria specified in section 2115. A corporation can do a majority of its business in only one state at a time; and it can have a majority of its shareholders resident in only one state at a time. If a corporation meets those requirements in this state, no other state is in a position to regulate the method of voting by shareholders on the basis of the same or similar criteria. It might also be said that no other state could claim as great an interest in doing so. In any event, it does not appear that any other state has attempted to do so. If California's statute were replicated in all states, no conflict would result. We conclude that the potential for conflict is, on this record, speculative and without substance.

What appellant refers to as the "transient nature" of the statute's applicability, i.e., its application from year to year based upon the prior year's activity, could conceivably be a problem for a corporation whose business activity within the state fluctuated widely, but the "worst-case" scenario—that such a corporation might find it necessary to adopt cumulative voting as a means of assuring compliance on a continuing basis—does not appear to be so burdensome as to result in a significant restraint upon commerce among the states....

NOTES

1. Application of the California statute to require cumulative voting and the annual election of directors of a publicly owned Delaware corporation was held

unconstitutional in Louart Corp. v. Arden–Mayfair, Inc., No. c192091 (Sup.Ct.Cal., Aug. 5, 1977) (an unreported opinion). The court noted that there was an irreconcilable conflict between California and Delaware law and that the corporation might have the requisite contacts with California in some years but not in others. It concluded that application of the California statute would impose an improper burden on interstate commerce because of the uncertainty that would result from the corporation's being subject in different years to different state laws.

2. The choice-of-law problems dealt with here would be mitigated if Congress were to prescribe minimum standards for corporations doing business in interstate commerce. Such a statute, proposed by Professor William L. Cary, would permit corporations to incorporate in the state of their choosing, but would remove many of the present incentives for incorporating in states, such as Delaware, which have lenient corporation laws. See Cary, Federalism and Corporate Law: Reflections upon Delaware, 83 Yale L.J. 663 (1974).

3. Articles on the general subject include Oldham, Regulating the Regulators: Limitations upon a State's Ability to Regulate Corporations with Multi–State Contacts, 57 Denver L.Rev. 345 (1980); Ratner and Schwartz, The Impact of Shaffer v. Heitner on the Substantive Law of Corporations, 45 Brooklyn L.Rev. 641 (1979); Halloran and Hammer, Section 2115 of the New California General Corporation Law, 23 U.C.L.A.L.Rev. 1282 (1976); Kaplan, Foreign Corporations and Local Corporate Policy, 21 Vand.L.Rev. 433 (1968).

Edgar v. MITE Corp.

Supreme Court of the United States, 1982.
457 U.S. 624, 102 S.Ct. 2629, 73 L.Ed.2d 269.

■ JUSTICE WHITE delivered ... the opinion of the Court....

Appellee MITE Corporation and its wholly-owned subsidiary, MITE Holdings, Inc., are corporations organized under the laws of Delaware with their principal executive offices in Connecticut. Appellant James Edgar is the Secretary of State of Illinois and is charged with the administration and enforcement of the Illinois Act. Under the Illinois Act any takeover offer for the shares of a target company must be registered with the Secretary of State. Ill.Rev.Stat., ch. 121½, ¶ 137.54.A (1979). A target company is defined as a corporation or other issuer of securities of which shareholders located in Illinois own 10% of the class of equity securities subject to the offer, or for which any two of the following three conditions are met: the corporation has its principal executive office in Illinois, is organized under the laws of Illinois, or has at least 10% of its stated capital and paid-in surplus represented within the state. Id., at ¶ 137.52–10. An offer becomes registered 20 days after a registration statement is filed with the Secretary unless the Secretary calls a hearing. Id., at ¶ 137.54.E. The Secretary may call a hearing at any time during the 20–day waiting period to adjudicate the substantive fairness of the offer if he believes it is necessary to protect the shareholders of the target company, and a hearing must be held if requested by a majority of a target company's outside directors or by Illinois shareholders who own 10% of the class of securities subject to the offer. Id., at ¶ 137.57.A. If the Secretary does hold a hearing, he is directed by the statute to deny registration to a tender offer if he finds that it "fails to provide full and fair disclosure to the offerees of all material information concerning the take-over offer, or that the take-over offer is inequitable or would work or tend to work a fraud or deceit upon the offerees...." Id., at ¶ 137.57.E.

On January 19, 1979, MITE initiated a cash tender offer for all outstanding shares of Chicago Rivet and Machine Co., a publicly held Illinois corporation, by filing a Schedule 14D–1 with the Securities and Exchange Commission in order to comply with the Williams Act.[2] ... MITE did not comply with the Illinois Act, however, and commenced this litigation on the same day by filing an action in the United States District Court for the Northern District of Illinois. The complaint asked for a declaratory judgment that the Illinois Act was preempted by the Williams Act and violated the Commerce Clause. In addition, MITE sought a temporary restraining order and preliminary and permanent injunctions prohibiting the Illinois Secretary of State from enforcing the Illinois Act....

[In the first part of his opinion, Justice White held that the Illinois Act was preempted by the Williams Act. This part of the opinion did not gain the support of a majority of the Court.]

The Illinois Act is ... unconstitutional under the test of Pike v. Bruce Church, Inc., 397 U.S., at 142, 90 S.Ct., at 847, for even when a state statute regulates interstate commerce indirectly, the burden imposed on that commerce must not be excessive in relation to the local interests served by the statute. The most obvious burden the Illinois Act imposes on interstate commerce arises from the statute's previously-described nationwide reach which purports to give Illinois the power to determine whether a tender offer may proceed anywhere.

The effects of allowing the Illinois Secretary of State to block a nationwide tender offer are substantial. Shareholders are deprived of the opportunity to sell their shares at a premium. The reallocation of economic resources to their highest-valued use, a process which can improve efficiency and competition, is hindered. The incentive the tender offer mechanism provides incumbent management to perform well so that stock prices remain high is reduced....

Appellant claims the Illinois Act furthers two legitimate local interests. He argues that Illinois seeks to protect resident security holders and that

---

2. The Williams Act, 82 Stat. 454, et seq., codified at 15 U.S.C. §§ 78m(d)–(e) and 78n(d)–(f), added new sections 13(d), 13(e) and 14(d)–(f) to the Securities Exchange Act of 1934. Section 14(d)(1) of the Securities Exchange Act requires an offeror seeking to acquire more than five percent of any class of equity security by means of a tender offer to first file a Schedule 14D–1 with the Securities and Exchange Commission. The Schedule requires disclosure of the source of funds used to purchase the target shares, past transactions with the target company, and other material financial information about the offeror. In addition, the offeror must disclose any anti-trust or other legal problems which might result from the success of the offer. 17 CFR § 240.14d–100 (1981). Section 14(d)(1) requires the offeror to publish or send a statement of the relevant facts contained in the Schedule 14D–1 to the shareholders of the target company....

the Act merely regulates the internal affairs of companies incorporated under Illinois law. We agree with the Court of Appeals that these asserted interests are insufficient to outweigh the burdens Illinois imposes on interstate commerce.

While protecting local investors is plainly a legitimate state objective, the state has no legitimate interest in protecting non-resident shareholders. Insofar as the Illinois law burdens out-of-state transactions, there is nothing to be weighed in the balance to sustain the law....

We are also unconvinced that the Illinois Act substantially enhances the shareholders' position. The Illinois Act seeks to protect shareholders of a company subject to a tender offer by requiring disclosures regarding the offer, assuring that shareholders have adequate time to decide whether to tender their shares, and according shareholders withdrawal, proration and equal consideration rights. However, the Williams Act provides these same substantive protections ... [T]he Court of Appeals ... also was of the view that the possible benefits of the potential delays required by the Act may be outweighed by the increased risk that the tender offer will fail due to defensive tactics employed by incumbent management. We are unprepared to disagree with the Court of Appeals in these respects, and conclude that the protections the Illinois Act affords resident security holders are, for the most part, speculative.

Appellant also contends that Illinois has an interest in regulating the internal affairs of a corporation incorporated under its laws. The internal affairs doctrine is a conflict of laws principle which recognizes that only one state should have the authority to regulate a corporation's internal affairs—matters peculiar to the relationships among or between the corporation and its current officers, directors, and shareholders—because otherwise a corporation could be faced with conflicting demands. See Restatement (Second) of Conflict of Laws, § 302, Comment b at 307–308 (1971). That doctrine is of little use to the state in this context. Tender offers contemplate transfers of stock by stockholders to a third party and do not themselves implicate the internal affairs of the target company.... Furthermore, the proposed justification is somewhat incredible since the Illinois Act applies to tender offers for any corporation for which 10% of the outstanding shares are held by Illinois residents, ... The Act thus applies to corporations that are not incorporated in Illinois and have their principal place of business in other states. Illinois has no interest in regulating the internal affairs of foreign corporations.

We conclude with the Court of Appeals that the Illinois Act imposes a substantial burden on interstate commerce which outweighs its putative local benefits. It is accordingly invalid under the Commerce Clause.

The judgment of the Court of Appeals is

Affirmed.

■ [The concurring opinions of JUSTICES POWELL, O'CONNOR and STEVENS are omitted. JUSTICES MARSHALL and REHNQUIST dissented on the ground that the case was moot.]

CTS Corp. v. Dynamics Corp. of America

Supreme Court of the United States, 1987.
481 U.S. 69, 107 S.Ct. 1637, 95 L.Ed.2d 67.

■ JUSTICE POWELL delivered the opinion of the Court.

[The "Control Share Acquisitions Chapter" of the Indiana Business Corporation Law applies to corporations that are incorporated in Indiana and meet several additional tests. They must have at least 100 shareholders, the principal office or substantial assets must be in Indiana; and either 10,000 shareholders or 10% of the shareholders must be Indiana residents or more than 10% of all shares must be owned by Indiana residents. When the acquisition of shares in a company covered by the Act would bring the acquiror's voting power above specified levels, voting rights will not accompany the acquisition unless a majority of the pre-existing shareholders agrees. Dynamics Corporation made a tender offer which would have raised its ownership in CTS above the level specified in the Act. Dynamics sought declaratory relief, which the District Court granted. The Court of Appeals affirmed, holding, on the basis of the plurality opinion in *MITE*, that the Indiana statute was preempted by the Williams Act. It also held that the statute violates the Commerce Clause.

Addressing the first question in the case, Justice Powell concluded that the Williams Act does not preempt the statute because the latter does not frustrate the purposes of the federal law. The Indiana Act protects shareholders against coercive tender offers by permitting them to vote as a group and does not give an advantage to any party in communicating with shareholders. That some tender offers may suffer some delay also does not call for preemption.]

III

As an alternative basis for its decision, the Court of Appeals held that the Act violates the Commerce Clause....

A

The principal objects of dormant Commerce Clause scrutiny are statutes that discriminate against interstate commerce.... The Indiana Act is not such a statute. It has the same effects on tender offers whether or not the offeror is a domiciliary or resident of Indiana. Thus, it "visits its effects equally upon both interstate and local business...."

Dynamics nevertheless contends that the statute is discriminatory because it will apply most often to out-of-state entities. This argument rests on the contention that, as a practical matter, most hostile tender offers are launched by offerors outside Indiana. But this argument avails Dynamics little. "The fact that the burden of a state regulation falls on some interstate companies does not, by itself, establish a claim of discrimination against interstate commerce." Exxon Corp. v. Governor of Maryland, 437 U.S. 117, 126, 98 S.Ct. 2207, 2214, 57 L.Ed.2d 91 (1978).... Because nothing in the Indiana Act imposes a greater burden on out-of-state offerors than it does on similarly situated Indiana offerors, we reject the contention that the Act discriminates against interstate commerce.

B

This Court's recent Commerce Clause cases also have invalidated statutes that adversely may affect interstate commerce by subjecting activities to inconsistent regulations. E.g., Brown–Forman Distillers Corp. v. New York State Liquor Authority, 476 U.S. 583, 584, 106 S.Ct. 2080, 2086–2087, 90 L.Ed.2d 552 (1986); Edgar v. MITE Corp., 457 U.S., at 642, 102 S.Ct., at 2640–2641 (plurality opinion of White, J.).... The Indiana Act poses no such problem. So long as each State regulates voting rights only in the corporations it has created, each corporation will be subject to the law of only one State. No principle of corporation law and practice is more firmly established than a State's authority to regulate domestic corporations, including the authority to define the voting rights of shareholders. See Restatement (Second) of Conflict of Laws § 304 (1971) (concluding that the law of the incorporating State generally should "determine the right of a shareholder to participate in the administration of the affairs of the corporation"). Accordingly, we conclude that the Indiana Act does not create an impermissible risk of inconsistent regulation of different States.

C

The Court of Appeals did not find the Act unconstitutional for either of these threshold reasons. Rather, its decision rested on its view of the Act's potential to hinder tender offers. We think the Court of Appeals failed to appreciate the significance for Commerce Clause analysis of the fact that state regulation of corporate governance is regulation of entities whose very existence and attributes are a product of state law....

... Every State in this country has enacted laws regulating corporate governance. By prohibiting certain transactions, and regulating others, such laws necessarily affect certain aspects of interstate commerce. This necessarily is true with respect to corporations with shareholders in States other than the State of incorporation. Large corporations that are listed on national exchanges, or even regional exchanges, will have shareholders in many States and shares that are traded frequently....

It thus is an accepted part of the business landscape in this country for States to create corporations, to prescribe their powers, and to define the rights that are acquired by purchasing their shares. A State has an interest in promoting stable relationships among parties involved in the corporations it charters, as well as in ensuring that investors in such corporations have an effective voice in corporate affairs.

There can be no doubt that the Act reflects these concerns. The primary purpose of the Act is to protect the shareholders of Indiana corporations. It does this by affording shareholders, when a takeover offer is made, an opportunity to decide collectively whether the resulting change in voting control of the corporation, as they perceive it, would be desirable. A change of management may have important effects on the shareholders' interests; it is well within the State's role as overseer of corporate governance to offer this opportunity....

Dynamics argues in any event that the State has "'no legitimate interest in protecting the nonresident shareholders.'" ... Dynamics relies heavily on the statement by the *MITE* Court that "[i]nsofar as the ... law burdens out-of-state transactions, there is nothing to be weighed in the balance to sustain the law." 457 U.S., at 644, 102 S.Ct., at 2641. But that comment was made in reference to an Illinois law that applied as well to out-of-state corporations as to in-state corporations. We agree that Indiana has no interest in protecting nonresident shareholders *of nonresident corporations*. But this Act applies only to corporations incorporated in Indiana. We reject the contention that Indiana has no interest in providing for the shareholders of its corporations the voting autonomy granted by the Act. Indiana has a substantial interest in preventing the corporate form from becoming a shield for unfair business dealing. Moreover, unlike the Illinois statute invalidated in *MITE,* the Indiana Act applies only to corporations that have a substantial number of shareholders in Indiana.... Thus, every application of the Indiana Act will affect a substantial number of Indiana residents, whom Indiana indisputably has an interest in protecting....

[W]e reverse the judgment of the Court of Appeals.

It is so ordered.

[Justice Scalia concurred in Parts III–A and III–B but would not engage in the interest balancing test, first adopted in *Pike* and invoked in *MITE:* "As long as a State's corporation law governs only its own corporations and does not discriminate against out-of-state interests, it should survive this Court's scrutiny under the Commerce Clause, whether it promotes shareholder welfare or industrial stagnation."

Justice White, joined by Justices Blackmun and Stevens, dissented on the ground that the Indiana statute violates the Williams Act because it will prevent minority shareholders from selling their stock at a premium to a tender offeror. Justice White, by himself, also dissented on the ground that the Indiana statute regulates the purchase and sale of stock in interstate commerce and that the attendant restraint violates the Commerce Clause.]

NOTES

1. The *CTS* case involved the application of forum law to a corporation incorporated under forum law. May the forum state apply its regulatory law to a *foreign* corporation which does a stated amount of business in the state or which is owned to a large extent by local residents? For instance, may it require cumulative voting or specify how directors are to be elected? Does the *CTS* decision limit the applicability of "pseudo-foreign corporation" legislation, pp. 1002–1003, supra?

In a case involving parallel litigation in Delaware and California and concerning a Delaware corporation, the Supreme Court of Delaware forcefully restated and confirmed the internal affairs doctrine (applicability of the law of the state of incorporation) and referred to its "constitutional underpinnings." Draper v. Paul N. Gardner Defined Plan Trust, 625 A.2d 859, 867 (Del.1993).

Art. 10 of the Uniform Limited Liability Company Act also adopts the internal affairs rule: the law applicable to the internal affairs of a foreign limited liability company is that of the state or country where it was organized. The Uniform Act as such has not yet been adopted by any state, but almost all states now have Limited Liability Company Acts with an essential similar provision. See, e.g., Del.Corp.Laws Ann. 1994–95, Title 6, § 18–901(a) (1995).

2. The *CTS* decision probably does not affect a state's ability to regulate the intrastate *conduct* of foreign corporations, so long as the balancing test of *Pike* and *MITE* is satisfied. See, for instance, Haberman v. Public Power Supply System, 109 Wn.2d 107, 744 P.2d 1032 (1987), in which securities fraud claims against out-of-state defendants were adjudicated under Washington law: "... Washington is clearly the state with the most substantial contacts with the subject matter of this case. The bonds ... were issued ... to finance two nuclear power plants in Washington. The [respondent] Supply System, respondent members and directors, one respondent bond counsel, as well as the majority of the respondent Participants are Washington residents.... [O]ur application of the [Washington statute] does not impinge on federal regulation of commerce as did the Illinois statute under scrutiny in [*MITE*].... Unlike the Illinois Statute ..., we do not attempt to apply [the Washington statute] to transactions completely unrelated to Washington. Moreover, in contrast to the corporate takeover regulations at issue in [*MITE*], Congress explicitly provided that federal and state securities regulation may co-exist absent conflict.... Washington's interests in regulating bond issues by municipal corporations, and in providing a forum for claims arising from those issues outweigh the impact that our application of the [Washington statute] will have on interstate commerce, particularly when considering the substantial relationship between this state and the case in controversy...." 744 P.2d at 1053–54.

In *CTS*, the U.S. Supreme Court made express reference to Restatement (Second) § 304. Comment *d* to that section expressly excludes access to stockholder lists from the internal affairs rule. While acknowledging that the Supreme Court did not necessarily "endorse" this exception, the Second Circuit found compelling reason to permit resident stockholders to gain access, under New York law, to an out-of-state corporation's list of non-objecting beneficial owners ("NoBo" list). It held that the Commerce Clause did not preclude such access. Sadler v. NCR Corp., 928 F.2d 48 (2d Cir.1991).

3. Dividends on stock shares often remain unclaimed by shareholders when stock changes hands and the bank or brokerage houses that hold securities do not know the identity of the new owners. In *Delaware v. New York*, 113 S.Ct. 1550 (1993), the question was which of the two states had the right to escheat the unclaimed dividends. A special Master, appointed by the Court, recommended that the right to escheat was in the state where the dividend-paying corporation had its principal place of business. The Supreme Court, dividing 6 to 3, rejected the special master's recommendation and ruled that the right to escheat belonged to the state of incorporation of the brokerage house or bank holding the dividends. Delaware thus became entitled to hundreds of millions of dollars, with New York losing out. Since many brokerage houses are incorporated in Delaware, that state will enjoy a bonanza.

With respect to the application of the law of the state of incorporation, see *CTS* decision. What is the relevance of the broker's state of incorporation to this escheat problem? Are the funds the broker's; if not, does its state of incorporation have regulatory concerns that justify escheat of these funds by it? Are these regulatory concerns greater than those of the state of incorporation of the debtor (the dividend-paying corporation)? Does either of these states have anything to do with the generation of the profits underlying the dividends? Which state does? What is the role of the broker? Is a single rule (state of incorporation—whether that state be that of the broker or of the dividend-paying company) more easily administered than the one proposed by the Special Master? Bankers and brokers argued against the special master's recommendation on the ground it would be an enormous burden for them to search out the headquarters of every dividend-paying corporation.

Section 4. Dissolution and Winding-Up

NOTE

The dissolution of a corporation is also governed by the law of the state of incorporation. Restatement, Second, Conflict of Laws § 299 (1971). However, most state statutes provide for a limited time during which the corporation continues to exist, and is empowered to act, so that it may wind-up its affairs. The time extension provided by the state of incorporation will ordinarily be recognized in other states as well.

Subject to limitations of federal law, especially federal bankruptcy law, a state may also wind-up the local business of a foreign corporation which has not been dissolved in the state of its incorporation. This follows from the state's authority to regulate the intrastate activities of foreign corporations. Restatement, Second, Conflict of Laws § 300 (1971). The rule is the same in England: Dicey & Morris, 2 Conflict of Laws 1117 (12th ed. 1993 by Collins).

What law determines whether a successor corporation is liable for the wrongs of the business it acquired? In Webb v. Rodgers Machinery Mfg. Co., 750 F.2d 368 (5th Cir.1985), the plaintiff was injured in Texas while operating a "Rodgers" wood shaping machine. The defendant enterprise had a long history. Rodgers began business in 1928 as a proprietorship, sold the production equipment of this proprietorship to Olympic Machinery Co., Inc., a California corporation in 1959–60, which ran an operating division called Rodgers from 1960–64, separately incorporating it in 1964 as Rodgers Machinery Manufacturing Co., Inc. The type of machinery that injured plaintiff was discontinued prior to 1959, hence manufactured by the Rodgers proprietorship. The Fifth Circuit noted that Texas, the forum, has adopted the "most significant relationship" test of the Second Restatement. "Although Texas law under that test governs many of the substantive issues of this case such as those dealing with the manufacturer's duty, causation, and damages, the Restatement makes clear that choice of law considerations should be viewed 'with respect to the particular issue'.... Here, the particular issue to be decided is the liability of a succeeding business entity using the trade name of a previously existing proprietorship. All the contacts with respect to that issue occurred in California. The corporations and proprietorships were all Californian. Thus, California clearly has the most significant relationship with respect to the particular issue of whether the defendant Rodgers corporation can be held liable for the torts of the preceding Rodgers proprietorship." 750 F.2d at 374. See also Young v. Fulton Iron Works Co., 709 S.W.2d 927 (Mo.App.1986) (tort, not contract, choice-of-law rule determines tort liability of successor corporation).

INDEX

References are to pages.

ACT OF STATE DOCTRINE
As basis for claim or defense, 390–392, 740–744.

ACTS
As basis of jurisdiction over persons, 41–123.
As basis of jurisdiction over things, 123–156.

ADHESION CONTRACTS, 475–484.

ADMINISTRATION OF ESTATES
See Chapter 12, Administration of Estates, 934–971.

ADMINISTRATIVE ORDERS
Enforcement of, 266–279.

ADMIRALTY
Choice of law, 419–422, 478–484, 648–652.
Insurance, 651–652.
Time limitations, 419–422, 478–484.

ADOPTION, 884–887.
Hague Convention on Intercountry Adoption, 886.

AGENCY
See Chapter 13, Agency, Partnerships and Corporations, 972–1012.

AIRPLANES
Choice of law,
    For injury or death, 503–505, 621–622, 624–625.
    For release, 536–541.
Complex litigation, 624–625.

ALIMONY
See Divorce.

ANNULMENT
See Marriage.

ANTON PILLER ORDER, 147, 280.

APPEARANCE
See Jurisdiction.

ARBITRATION
Choice of law clause in agreement for, 576.
Enforcement of agreement for, 654–656.

ASSIGNMENT
Law governing, 652–654.

ASSOCIATIONS
See Chapter 13, Agency, Partnerships and Corporations, 972–1012.

ATTACHMENT
See also Garnishment.
Choses in action and debts, 130–156.
Obligations insurer or other underwriter, 148.

AUTOMOBILES
See also Insurance.
Conditional sales and chattel mortgages, 793–795.
Guest statutes, 459, 520–532.
Liability of owner, 972–973.
Liability of renter, 499–500.

BANKRUPTCY
See Debtors' Estates.

BEALE, JOSEPH
Theories on choice of law, 450–451.

BETTER LAW
Choice of to resolve conflict, 515, 605–606.

BILLS AND NOTES
See Contracts.

BORROWING STATUTES
As exception to applying forum time limitations, 418–420, 430, 434.

BRUSSELS CONVENTION
See European Union; Judgments; Jurisdiction.

BURDEN OF PROOF
Law governing, 408–411.

BUSINESS TRUSTS, 980–982.

CAPACITY
To contract, 464–467, 502.
To choose domicile, 13–14, 20–25.

CARRIERS
See Interstate Commerce.

1013

CAVERS, DAVID F.
Theories on choice of law, 499–450, 516–517.

CENTER OF GRAVITY APPROACH
To choice of law, 508–511.

CHARACTERIZATION
As escape from established choice-of-law rule:
    Procedure, 493–495, 504.
    Substance, 495–500.
Domicile, 443.
Penal, 375–379, 702–705.
Property as movable or immovable, 487–492, 505–506, 784–786.

CHATTEL MORTGAGES
See Security.

CHATTELS
See Jurisdiction of Courts; Property.

CHEATHAM, ELLIOTT E.
Theories on choice of law, 511–512.

CHILDREN
See Divorce; Marriage.

CHOICE OF LAW
See particular areas of law.

CHOSE IN ACTION
See Intangibles; Property.

CITIZENS
See Nationality.

CIVIL LAW
Choice-of-law under, 19–20, 441, 447, 451, 534–536, 544–548.
Sources of conflicts rules, 4.

CLASSIFICATION
See Characterization.

CODIFICATION ABROAD, 441, 447, 451, 534–536, 544–548.

COGNOVIT NOTE
Appearance and consent in advance, 43–44.

COLLATERAL ESTOPPEL
See Full Faith and Credit; Judgments; Res Judicata.

COMITY
See Full Faith and Credit; Judgments.

COMMERCIAL ARBITRATION
See Arbitration.

COMMUNITY PROPERTY, 915–933.

CONDITIONAL SALES
See Security.

CONFISCATION
See Government Seizure.

CONNECTING FACTORS OR CONTACTS
Characteristic performance, 544–547.

CONNECTING FACTORS OR CONTACTS —Cont'd
Classical choice-of-law rules, 453–506.
Domicile, 7–20.
Grouping of contacts, 508–511.
Place of making, 464–467.
Place of performance, 468–470.
Place of wrong, 453–463.
Situs, 19–20, 485–492, 505–506, 757–789.

CONSENT
Appearance and Consent in Advance, 43–44.

CONSTITUTIONAL LAW
    See also Full Faith and Credit; Judgments; Jurisdiction of Courts.
    See Chapter 6, Impact of the Constitution, 317–374.
Foreign corporations, 982–987, 989–996.
Government Seizure; Interstate Commerce, 371–374.
Influence of Constitution on choice of law, 325–368.
Obligation to Provide or Refuse a Forum, 318–325.
Privileges and immunities clause, 368–371.
Unreasonable Discrimination, 368.

CONSTRUCTION
Of documents, 816–819.

CONTRACTS
Adhesion, 475–484.
Arbitration agreements, 576, 654–656.
Autonomy of the parties, 477–485, 541–544, 547–549, 587–594.
Bills and notes, 660–662.
Capacity, 464–467, 502.
Characteristic performance in European law, 544–547.
Choice-of-court clause, 168–178.
Choice-of-forum clause, 168–178.
Contractual basis of tort liability, 453–455, 497–500.
Discharge, 468–470.
Essential validity, 464–467, 470–472, 587–594.
Formalities, 549–553, 571–573, 638–639.
Grouping of contacts, 508–511.
Intention of the parties, 470–472, 477–485, 541–544, 547–549, 587–594.
Interest, 472–477.
Interpretation and construction of documents, 463, 536–543.
Land, 505–506, 549–553.
Limitations of liability, 468–470.
Negotiable instruments, 660–662.
Place of making, 464–467.
Place of performance, 468–470.
Public policy, 382–389.
Statute of frauds, 467, 549–553, 571–573, 638–639.
Time limitations, 417–426, 434–440, 478–485.
Usury, 472–477.
Validation principle, 470–472, 595–596.

CONTRIBUTORY NEGLIGENCE
Burden of proof, 408–411.

CORPORATIONS
See Chapter 13, Agency, Partnerships and Corporations, 972–1012.
Corporate activity, 987–1012.
Corporate personality, 982–987.
Directors and stockholders, 999.
Dissolution, 1012.
Doing business, 987–996.
Domicile, 982.
Jurisdiction over, 982.
Jurisdiction over internal affairs of, 982.
Law applicable to shares of stock, 999–1005.
Pseudo-foreign corporations, 986–987.
Qualification statutes, 987–996.
Stockholders' liability, 999.

COURTS
See Jurisdiction of Courts.

CRIMINAL LAW, 417, 452–453, 455–456.

CURRENCY, FOREIGN, 733–740, 743, 747–748.

CURRIE, BRAINERD
Theories on choice-of-law, 512–515.

CUSTODY OF CHILDREN, 887–901.
See Chapter 11, Family Law, 820–933.
International Parental Kidnaping Crime Act, 900.
Parental Kidnaping Prevention Act, 890.
Uniform Child Custody Jurisdiction Act, 890.

DAMAGES
See Contracts; Torts.

DEATH TAXES
See Inheritance Taxes.

DEBTORS' ESTATES, 955–972.
See Chapter 12, Administration of Estates, 934–971.
Bankruptcy, 957.
Dissolution of a corporation, 962.
Distribution of assets, 934–954.
Priority to local creditors, 963–966.
Statutory successor, 955–971.
Stockholders' liability, 966–971.
Unincorporated association, 958–962.
Universal successor, 942–943.

DECEDENTS' ESTATES
See Chapter 12, Administration of Estates, 934–971.
Administration of land, 943–954.
Appointment of administrator, place, 934–943.
Claims against estate, 942–947.
Conclusiveness of grant of administration, 934–938.
Debtors' Estates, 955–972.
Distribution, Taxes and Planning, 954.

DECEDENTS' ESTATES—Cont'd
Jurisdiction to appoint administrator, 934–943.
Payment to foreign administrator, 942–943.
Place of administration of property, 934–954.
Suits by and against administrator, 950.

DECLARATORY JUDGMENT
See Jurisdiction of Courts.

DECREE
See Judgments.

DEFAMATION
Choice of law, 441, 631–635.
Single publication rule, 441, 631–635.

DEPECAGE, 635–641.

DIRECT ACTION AGAINST INSURER
No-action clause, 403–407.
Public policy, 407.
Substance or procedure, 403–408.

DISCOVERY
See Procedure.

DISSIMILARITY, 375–386, 497–498, 568.

DIVORCE
See Chapter 11, Family Law, 820–933.
Alimony, 901–915.
Annulment, 878–881.
"Divisible divorce", 866–878.
Durational residence requirement, 836–846.
Extraterritorial effect, 846–856.
Foreign, 874.
Generally, 836–933.
Hague Recognition Convention, 855.
Judicial separation, 881–883.
Jurisdiction, 836–846.
Law applicable, 855.
Limitation of consequences of jurisdictional defects, 856.
Nonjudicial divorces, 876.

DOCUMENTS
Hague Convention on Service of, 105–111, 744–746.

DOING BUSINESS
See Corporations.

DOMICILE
See Chapter 2, Domicile: The Chosen Point of Entry, 7–33.
Characterization, 32–33, 441–445.
Choice of law, 7–20, 441–445, 765–767, 778–781.
Diversity Jurisdiction, 20–26.
Divorce, 836–878.
Domicile of choice, 7–11.
Domicile of origin, 7–12, 16.
Double domicile, 15–17.
English rule, 10–12, 16.
Evidence, 11, 14–16.
Illegal aliens, 28.

DOMICILE—Cont'd
Infants, 13–14, 20–26, 30.
Is domicile unitary?, 31–32.
Jurisdiction of courts, 26–27.
Married persons, 13–14.
Motive, 17.
Persons non compos mentis, 13–14, 20–26, 30.
Refugees, 28.
Renvoi, 441–445.
Residence compared, 16–17.
Soldier, 29–31.
Students, 29–30.

DRAM SHOP ACTS
Choice of law, 506–508.
Judicial jurisdiction to apply, 507–508.
Legislative jurisdiction to apply, 507–508.

DUE PROCESS OF LAW
See Constitutional Law; Jurisdiction of Courts.

EQUAL PROTECTION
Choice of law favoring residents, 525–531, 613–620.

EQUITABLE CONVERSION, 487–492, 505, 764.

EQUITY
Compelling acts outside the state, 198–201.
Decree for conveyance of foreign land, 254–259.
Injunctions against foreign suits, 211–214.

ESCHEAT
See Government Seizure.

ESSENTIAL VALIDITY
Contracts, 464–467, 470–472, 587–594.

ESTATE TAX
See Inheritance Taxes.

EUROPEAN UNION
Choice of law in contract (Rome Convention), 544–549.
Jurisdiction and Judgments (Brussels) Convention, 42–43.

EVIDENCE
See also Burden of Proof; Foreign Law; Judicial Notice; Parol Evidence Rule.
Hague Convention, 744–746.
Privilege, 411–417.
Proof of facts and of law, 392–402, 408–417.

EXEMPTIONS
In attachment or garnishment proceedings, 128.

EXPECTATION OF PARTIES, 470–472, 477–485, 541–544, 547–549, 587–594.

FALSE CONFLICTS, 512–515, 541.

FAMILY LAW
See Chapter 11, Family Law, 820–933.

FEDERAL COMMON LAW, 665–669, 711–726.

FEDERAL COURTS LAW
See Chapter 8, The Problem of Choosing the Rule of Decision, 448–662; Chapter 9, Conflicts Problems in Federal and International Settings, 663–756.
Act of state, 390–392, 740–744.
Complex litigation, 624–628.
Dismissal of federal suit when pending state suit, 686.
Extraterritorial application of public law, 748–756.
Federal common law, 665–669, 711–726.
State interference with foreign relations, 727–730, 740–744.
State or federal law applied,
  After transfer to another federal court, 693–700.
  Arbitration, 655–659.
  Certification to determine state law, 396, 685–686.
  Conflict of laws rules, 687–711.
  Erie doctrine, 663–711.
  Forum-closing rule, 705–711.
  Forum non conveniens, 686–687.
  Judiciary Act, 664.
  Res judicata, 685, 705–711.
  Review of district court determination of state law, 686.
  Rules Enabling Act, 664–665.
  Service of process, 678–684.
  Statutes of limitations, 673, 683–684.
Treaties,
  Generally, 744–746.
  Service abroad, 744.
  Taking evidence abroad, 744–746.

FEDERAL EMPLOYERS' LIABILITY ACT
Suits under, 204–205.

FEDERAL TORT CLAIMS ACT, 446–447.

FISCAL LAWS
See also Taxation.
Enforcement of foreign judgment for taxes, 308–309.

FOREIGN CORPORATIONS
See Corporations.

FOREIGN COUNTRY JUDGMENTS
See Chapter 5, Foreign Country Judgments, 218–316.
In foreign currency, 226–227.
Recognition of, 227–238.

FOREIGN LAW
Absence of proof, 392–401.
Notice and proof, 392–402.

FORUM NON CONVENIENS, 181–198, 686–687.

FORUM SELECTION CLAUSES, 168–178.

FRATERNAL BENEFIT SOCIETIES, 238–240, 333–336.

FRAUD
In procurement of judgment, 178–181.

FULL FAITH AND CREDIT
    See also Judgments; Workers' Compensation.
Adoption, 891–901.
Choice of law, 333–367.
Comity, compared to, 215–217, 333.
Door-closing, 705–711.
Foreign Judgments, limits on, 254–279.
Localizing transitory actions, 208–211.
Policies and purposes, 218–219, 266–279, 349, 362.
Res judicata, 685, 705–711.
Stockholders' liability, 966–971.

GARNISHMENT
Jurisdiction of courts, 128–133, 146–156.
Of chattels, 128–133.

GOVERNING LAW CLAUSES
    Generally, 477–485, 541–544, 547–549, 587–594.
Rome Convention, 547–549.

GOVERNMENT SEIZURE
Escheat, 371–374.

HAGUE CONVENTIONS
Child abduction, 899–901.
Decedents' estates, 19, 758, 786.
Divorce recognition, 855.
Evidence, 744–746.
Law applicable to the international sale of goods, 547–548.
Service of documents, 744–746.
Trusts, 811.

HISTORY OF CONFLICT OF LAWS
    See Chapter 1, Introduction, 1–6.
England, 3.
European civil law countries, 4.
Recent changes, 5.

IMMOVABLES
See Land.

INCEST
See Marriage.

INFANTS
    See also Parent and Child.
Domicile of, 13–14, 20–26, 30.

INHERITANCE TAXES
Double domicile, 15–17.

INJUNCTIONS
Against foreign suits, 192–198.

INJUNCTIONS—Cont'd
Enforcement in another state, 198–200.

INSOLVENCY
See Debtors' Estates.

INSURANCE
    See also Contracts.
Interpleader, jurisdiction of courts, 133–136.

INTANGIBLES
    See also Property.
Jurisdiction of courts, 130–156.

INTENTION
See Contracts.

INTEREST
See Contracts.

INTEREST ANALYSIS, 512–515.

INTERNATIONAL CONFLICT OF LAWS, 746–756.

INTERPLEADER
Jurisdiction of courts, 133–136.

INTERSTATE COMMERCE
Limitation on jurisdiction, 371–374.

JUDGMENTS
    See Chapter 3, Jurisdiction of Courts, 34–167; Chapter 5, Foreign Judgments, 218–316.
Administrative bodies, orders of, 266–279.
Against partnership, 976–982.
Alimony decrees, 286–289.
Basis of enforcement, 218–227.
Custody, 887–901.
Declaratory, 206–208.
Decree for conveyance of foreign land, 254–259.
Decree for support, 259–266, 290–296.
Defenses to enforcement, 279–316.
Enforcement, methods of, 218–316.
Federal court judgments in state courts, 218.
Finality of judgment, 290–296.
Fiscal claims, 307–310.
Foreign administrator, effect, 952–954.
Foreign currency, 226–227.
Foreign nation, 218–316.
Fraud in procurement of, 296–297.
In Personam, 228–235.
Inconsistent judgments, 289.
Issues affected, 251–254.
Judgment not on the merits, 253.
Lack of a competent court, 310–311.
Limitations on Full Faith and Credit, 254–279.
Mutuality of estoppel, 251–253.
Nature of the Original Cause of Action, 297–310.
Nature of the Original Proceedings, 279–297.
Payment or other discharge, 314–315.
Penal claim reduced to judgment, 308–310.
Persons affected, 238–251.

JUDGMENTS—Cont'd
Policies underlying enforcement, 218–227.
Privity, 238–279, 860–862.
Public policy as affecting enforcement of judgment, 302–307.
Reciprocity, 219–223.
Recognition of foreign judgment, 227–238.
Registration of, 231–235.
Representative suits, 238–241.
Res judicata, 685, 705–711,
  As to jurisdictional findings, 291–296.
Reversal of Earlier Judgment, 316.
Splitting of cause of action, 253–254.
State court judgments in federal courts, 246–250.
Statute of limitations, 308–309.
Stockholders' liability, 966–971.
Successive judgments, 315–316.
Suit on judgment for wrongful death, 375–379, 503–505, 566–568, 606–620.
Workmen's compensation awards, 451–452, 644–648.

JUDICIAL NOTICE
Foreign law, 294–296, 392–402, 400–407.

JUDICIAL SEPARATION, 885–886.

JUENGER, FRIEDRICH K.
Theories on choice of law, 518.

JURISDICTION OF COURTS
  See Chapter 3, Jurisdiction of Courts, 34–167; Chapter 4, Limitations on the Exercise of Jurisdiction, 168–217.
Adoption, 884–886.
Anton Piller Order, 147.
Appearance, 43–44.
Chattels, 128–130.
Citizenship, 41–43.
Compelling acts outside the state, 198–200.
Competence of courts, 156–167.
Consent in advance, 43–44.
Continuance of jurisdiction, 122–123.
Corporations, internal affairs, 982.
Custody, 887–901.
Declaratory judgment, 206–208.
Defined, 34–41.
Derivative, over foreign corporation, 103–105.
Divorce, 836–933.
Doing business, 41–123.
Domicile, 26–27.
Exorbitant bases, 41–47.
European practice (Brussels Convention), 38.
Forum non conveniens, 181–198.
Fraud, 178–181.
Garnishment, 128–133, 146–156.
General, 93–111.
General vs. Specific, 38.
Immunity, 178–181.
Influence of the Constitution on taking or refusing jurisdiction, 204–205, 215–217, 307–308, 318–321, 947–950.
Injunctions against foreign suits, 189–192.

JURISDICTION OF COURTS—Cont'd
Intangibles, 130–156.
Interpleader, 133–136.
Interstate commerce, 371–374.
Judgment notes, 43–45.
Land, 125–128.
Limitations on exercise of Jurisdiction,
  Federal Transfer, 194–198.
  First–Filed Rule, 192–194.
  Forum non conveniens, 181–198.
  Fraud, Force or Privilege, 179–181.
  Imposed by contract, 168–178.
  Imposed by forum, 198–206.
  Imposed by state of transaction, 206–214.
  Lis pendens, 192–194.
Local actions or local effects, 44.
Long-arm statutes, 64–66.
Mareva injunctions, 147.
Nationality, 42–43.
Notice, 156–167.
Ownership of property, 41–43, 123–156.
Partnerships, 111.
Power theory, 41–47.
Presence, 47.
Proceedings in rem, 123–156.
Prorogation, 168–172.
Quasi in rem, 123–156.
Race to a judgment, 192–194.
Residence, 42–43.
Right of foreign corporations to sue, 987–996.
Specific jurisdiction, 94–105.
Stream of commerce, 85–89.
Things, jurisdiction over, 123–156.
Transient service, 41–43.
Transfer, 194–198.
Trespass to foreign land, 190–191.
Trusts, 160–167.

JURISDICTION OVER PERSONS
See Jurisdiction of Courts.

JURISDICTION TO TAX
See Taxation.

LAND
  See also Property.
Conveyances and contracts, 505–506, 769–778.
Jurisdiction of courts over, 125–128.
Power of executor or administrator over, 943–954.
Security transactions, 767–769.
Specific performance of contract for sale of, jurisdiction of courts, 141.
Succession on death, 19–20, 759–767.
Trespass to foreign land, jurisdiction of courts, 190–191.

LAW OF THE FORUM
See Dissimilarity; Penal Laws; Procedure; Proof of Laws; Public Policy.

LEFLAR, ROBERT
Theories on choice of law, 515.

LEGISLATIVE JURISDICTION
Extraterritorial application of law, 748–756.

LEGITIMATION, 883–884.

LIMITATION OF ACTIONS
　Generally, 417–441.
　Borrowing and tolling statutes, 418–420, 426–434.
　Constitutional limits, 434–440.
　Contracts for, 417–426, 434–440, 478–485.
　Interest analysis, 422–426.
　Repose statute distinguished, 418.

LIMITATIONS ON THE EXERCISE OF JURISDICTION
See Chapter 4, Limitations on the Exercise of Jurisdiction, 168–217.

LIS PENDENS, 192–194.

LOCALIZING ACTIONS
See Full Faith and Credit.

MAREVA INJUNCTION, 147.

MARITAL PROPERTY
See Marriage.

MARRIAGE
　See Chapter 11, Family Law, 820–933.
　Adoption, 884–887.
　Annulment, 878–881.
　Bigamous, 821–822.
　Community Property, 913–933.
　Custody of children, 887–901.
　Divorce, 836–878,
　　Conditions for decreeing, 836–846.
　　Divisible divorce, 866–878.
　　Extraterritorial recognition, 846–856
　　Extraterritorial recognition: limits on attack for Jurisdictional defects, 856–866.
　　Foreign, 874.
　High seas, 825.
　Incestuous, 821–822.
　Judicial separation, 881–883.
　Polygamous, 835.
　Presumption in favor of, 821–825.
　Prohibition on remarriage, 829–836.
　Property, 915–933.
　Same-sex, 834.
　Status, 820–821.
　Support, 901–915.
　Uniform Marriage Evasion Act, 828.

MASS DISASTERS AND MASS TORTS, 624–628.

MERGER
See Judgments.

MORTGAGES
　See also Security.
　Conflicts, rules applicable to, 767–769, 786–798.

MOST SIGNIFICANT RELATIONSHIP DOCTRINE
　See also Contracts; Torts.
Genesis and development, 518–520.

MOTORISTS
Non-resident, jurisdiction over, 64–66.

MOVABLES
See Property.

NATIONALITY
Compared with domicile, 16.
Jurisdiction of courts, 42–43.

NEGLIGENCE
Comparative or contributory, 408–411, 561–566, 673, 687–688.

NO FAULT, 639–644.

NO–ACTION CLAUSE, 343–346.

NON–RESIDENT
See specific area of law.

NOTICE
See Jurisdiction.

PARENT AND CHILD
See Divorce, Marriage.

PAROL EVIDENCE RULE
See Procedure.

PARTNERSHIPS
See Chapter 13, Agency, Partnerships and Corporations, 972–1012.

PENAL LAWS
　Generally, 376–379, 702–705.
　Cause of action, rejection based upon, 376–379, 702–705.
　Wrongful death statutes, 376–379.

PERFORMANCE
See Contracts.

PHYSICAL INJURY
See Torts.

POLYGAMY
See Marriage.

POWERS OF APPOINTMENT
Choice of law, rules as to, 804–808.

PRESENCE
As basis of jurisdiction of courts, 47—49.

PRESUMPTIONS, 408–411.

PRINCIPAL AND AGENT
See Chapter 13, Agency, Partnerships and Corporations, 972–1012.

PRIVILEGES AND IMMUNITIES
See Constitutional Law.

PROCEDURE
Administration of justice issue, 402–403.

PROCEDURE—Cont'd
Anton Piller Order, 147, 280.
Burden of proof, 408–411.
Characterization, 402–441, 443.
Damages, 503–505, 688–693.
Direct action against insurer, 403–408.
Discovery, 411–417.
Erie v. Tompkins, 663–711.
Evidence, 411–417.
Federal and state law, 663–711.
Federal rules of civil procedure, 664–665, 673, 678–685.
Formalities, 549–553, 571–573, 638–639.
Limitations, statute of, 417–441.
Lis Pendens, 192–194.
Mareva injunction, 147.
Presumptions, 408–411.
Privilege, 411–417.
Reasons for using local law, 402–403.
Statute of Frauds, 572–573.

PROCESS
See Jurisdiction of Courts.

PROOF
Burden of proof, 408–411, 687–688.
Of laws, 392–402.

PROPERTY
 See Chapter 10, Property, 757–819.
Characterization, 487–492, 505–506, 784–786.
Chattel mortgages, 786–789.
Conditional sales, 790–793.
Conveyances and contracts, land, 505–506, 769–778.
Equitable conversion, 487–492, 505, 764.
Future interests and trusts, 799–814.
Inter vivos transactions, movables, 781–786.
Interpretation and construction of documents, 816–819.
Jurisdiction to tax, 15–17.
Security transactions,
 Land, 767–769.
 Movables, 786–798.
Succession on death,
 Land, 19–20, 759–767.
 Movables, 7–20, 778–781.
Trusts, 799–814.

PROROGATION
See Forum Selection Clauses; Jurisdiction of Courts.

PUBLIC POLICY
Basis for choice of law, 375–392, 503–505.
Cause of action, rejection based upon, 375–387.
Defense contrary to, 387–392, 503–505.
Door-closing by forum, 375–387
 Constitutionality, 389, 392.
 Other grounds, 375–387, 705–711.
Federal courts, 705–711.
Illegality, 387–389.
Ordre public, 389.
Suits between husband and wife, 379–382.

QUALIFICATION
See Characterization.

QUASI–COMMUNITY PROPERTY, 915–933.

RACE TO A JUDGMENT, 192–194.

REALTY
See Land

RECEIVERSHIPS
See Debtors' Estates.

RECIPROCITY
See Judgments.

REESE, WILLIS L.M.
Theories on choice of law, 511–512.

REFUGEES
Domicile, 28.

RENVOI
Capacity of married woman to contract, 502.
Capacity to sue spouse, 495–497.
Chattel, 786–790.
Domicile, 32–33, 441–445.
Federal Tort Claims Act, 446–447.
Guest statute, applicability of, 446.
Interest analysis, 446.
Succession on death, 441–445, 757, 765–767.
Tort, interspousal immunity, 495–497.
Use in choice of law, 445–447, 500–502.

RES JUDICATA
See Divorce; Judgments.

RESIDENCE
See Domicile.

REVIVAL OF ACTIONS, 493–495.

ROME CONVENTION (CONTRACTS)
See European Union

SALES, INTERNATIONAL
See Hague Conventions; United Nations.

SEAT OF RELATIONSHIP
Guest-host in automobile accident, 459, 520–532.

SECURITY
Land, 767–769.
Movables, 786–798.

SEIZURE
See Government Seizure.

SEPARATION, JUDICIAL, 881–883.

SERVICE OF PROCESS
See Jurisdiction of Courts.

SHERMAN ACT
Applicability to foreign acts, 748–756.

SMALL LOANS LEGISLATION, 475–477.

SOLDIER
Domicile, 29–31.

STATUS
See Divorce; Legitimation; Marriage; Parent and Child.

STATUTE OF FRAUDS
See Contracts.

STATUTE OF LIMITATIONS
See Limitation of Actions.

STOCK
See Corporations.

STREAM OF COMMERCE JURISDICTION, 85–89.

STUDENTS
Domicile of, 29–30.

SUBSTANTIVE
See Characterization

SUCCESSION ON DEATH
Civil law concepts, 19–20, 758–759, 765–767.
Domicile, 7–20, 441–445, 765–767, 778–781.
Double domicile, 15–17.
Interpretation and construction of wills, 757, 779–781.
Land, 19–20, 759–767.
Movables, 7–20, 778–781.

SUCCESSOR, STATUTORY
See Debtors' Estates.

SUPPORT, 901–915.
Enforcement of support claims, 901–910.
Reciprocal support legislation, 910–915.

SURVIVAL AND REVIVAL
See Torts.

TAXATION
Double domicile, 15–17.
Jurisdiction to tax, 15–17.

THEORIES FOR CHOICE OF LAW
Scholars' views, 511–520.

TORTS
Alienation of affections, 460–463.
Complex litigation, 624–628.
Conduct regulating and loss distributing rules, 524.
Criteria for choice of law,
 Restatement, Second, 518–520.
 Scholars' theories, 511–520.
Damages,
 Applicable law, 503–505.
 Substance or procedure, 503–505, 688–690.
 Wrongful death, 375–379, 503–505, 566–568, 606–620.
Defamation, 631–636.
Federal Tort Claims Act, 446–447.
Guest statutes, 459, 520–532.
Husband and wife, 379–382, 495–497.
Intrafamilial immunity, 379–382, 495–497.
Multiple state torts, 624–628, 631–636.

TORTS—Cont'd
Neumeier Rules, 525–532, 554–566.
No fault, 639–644.
Non-physical injury, 460–483, 631–636.
Survival and revival, 493–495.
Theoretical explanation of use of foreign law, 377–378, 448–449.
Venue-limiting provisions, 403–408.
Vicarious liability, 499–500.

TRAUTMAN, DONALD
Theories on choice of law, 515–516.

TREATIES, 744–746.

TRUE CONFLICTS
See Interest Analysis.

TRUSTS
See Chapter 10, Property, 757–819; Chapter 12, Administration of Estates, 934–971.
Administration of trust estates, 799–814.
Choice of law rules applicable to, 799–814.
Hague Convention, 811.

UNIFORM ACTS
Child custody jurisdiction, 887–901.
Enforcement of foreign judgments, 233–234.
Foreign money claims, 218–316.
Foreign money judgments recognition, 218–316.
International Procedure Act, 401.
Motor vehicles reparations, 641–643.
Reciprocal enforcement of Support Act (URESA), 910–915.
Interstate Family Support Act (UIFSA), 887–901.

UNITED NATIONS
Convention on the international sale of goods, 547.

USURY
Choice of law, 472–477.

VICARIOUS LIABILITY
See Torts.

VIENNA CONVENTION
Convention on Contracts for the International Sale of Goods, 547

VON MEHREN, ARTHUR T.
Theories on choice of law, 515–516

WEINTRAUB, RUSSELL J.
Theories on choice of law, 517–518

WILLS
Interpretation and construction, 816–819

WITNESSES
Jurisdiction to compel appearance of citizen, 42–44

WORKERS' COMPENSATION
Applicable law, 451–452, 644–648

WRONGFUL DEATH
Action on foreign statute, 375–379, 503–505, 566–568, 606–620

WRONGFUL DEATH—Cont'd
Suits for, 375–379, 503–505, 566–568, 606–620

†

1-56662-333-2

9 781566 623339

90000